AF791711

UPSC
Civil Services Examination
GENERAL STUDIES

Main

Solved Papers

Rohit Vadhwana, IFS

(Indian Foreign Service–2010)

HEED PUBLICATIONS
Your partner in success

Printed in India

Corporate Office:
V-6/7, DLF City Phase-III, Gurgaon, Haryana-122002, INDIA.
Phones: 01244257812 , 9811213855 e-mail: contact@heedpublication.com

MRP: ₹570/-

Bulk Sales
Heed Publications Pvt Ltd offers excellent discounts on this book when ordered in quantity for bulk purchases or special sales. Heed Publications books may be purchased for educational, business, or sales promotional use. For general information on our other products and services or to obtain technical support, please contact: 0124-4257812, +91-9811213855 or and you can also buy books from online bookstore at www.heedpublications.com

---

ABOUT THE BOOK

Dear friends,

With this General Studies Mains Solved (Previous Years) Paper Set, I am offering you a book which is aims your glorious success. The requirements of candidates of Civil Services Mains are many in terms of skill, knowledge, material, technique and so on.

What every candidate requires commonly and compulsorily, for writing General Studies Main papers, are included characteristics of this paper set. I have carefully included all relevant aspects to fulfil these needs.

So, this paper-set is with the following qualities :

- **Simplicity of Language:** It is quite necessary to acquire skill of writing in simple and lucid language. It is said by someone "Its quite simple to write tough but quite tough to write simple". Same was the feeling for me while preparing the answers, in simplest possible language. No or rare complex sentences, hard to grasp, are used. Daily routine words' use is maximised to make candidates feel that without having command over or using superfluous language and heavy words or phrases, good answers can be drafted. Candidates will feel more confident having a glance at these answers.
- **Precise Presentation:** To be precise, to go straightly to the point, is sine quanone for writing good answers. You are not expected to write all what you know on the point but only what you are asked in the question. So, without divulging in hitherto discussions or narrations, you must write the answers precisely. As this is the main skill to be acquired and required by all candidates, I should once again bring it to your notice that to be precise doesn't necessitate to go with heavy sentences. Just intelligible, simple and logical structure of questions can pay you a higher dividend.
- **Logical flow of language:** Not just while writing essays but even in questions, an examiner always wants a logical flow of language. Logical flow consists of good connectivity among points, intelligible arrangement and presentation of datas and information. But, of course, they must have perfect relativity with the question. All, what I mean to say is, no word should be missing, no extra word should be added and every word must find place at its proper requirement.
- **Word Limit:** General Studies papers are regarded as decisive in candidate's success or failure. Not because of candidate's lack of knowledge or understanding only, but also and mostly because of not having the skill and discipline of maintaining words limit, he has to lose sometime.

  Though some relaxation and flexibility is permissible in word limit, but not more than ten percent of words. I have tried to maintain word limit, not so strictly, as you can never count in the examination hall, but roughly. You will find much easier to acquire command in writing question answers by following these models.

- **Clarity of thoughts:** What a candidate must command is clarity of thoughts. As the nature of examination is active involvement of candidate and many questions require to present his understanding and views, he must learn to be clear in presentation of his own thoughts and ideas. He is even not required to blindly follow views presented by experts, nor he is expected to think expertly over the matters, but just should have an ability to understand the topic with as much ability as a generally good educated person, without having the topic studied specially and expertly. You will find simple ideas presented in answers and feel that it is so common to think up to that level, and be confident, it is sufficient.
- **Information and data:** Of course, a candidate must have enough information and data regarding the topic. He must include them to sufficient extent but yet, it is to be always, kept in mind that more emphasise over them may prove harmful and create an impression that you have mug-up the question or figures. So, you can have a view that here, though informations and data are included but not emphasised beyond limit. It is used in such a manner that it does not harm the flow of language. Mind of the examiner should not be blocked by attacks of these numbers, figures, names and locations. Yet, you have a space to fill some necessary content and informations in answers.
- **Proper Structure of Answers:** Structure of an answer is decided by the direction of question. If you are asked to examine, you cannot end up just discussing a question. Similarly, when asked to review you are not expected to argue or elucidate the question. So, structure of a question plays an important role in drafting an answer. Using through these model answers, you should try to properly understand them, and to command this phenomena.

Including all these qualities in this paper set, I have endeavoured to take it beyond its limit of just a solved paper-set and to make it a comprehensive guide for your preparation of General Studies for Mains. It will be your companion which can instruct you in acquiring answer writing skill, command over language and boosting your self-confidence, of course, most important amongst all.

I hope this effort on our part will be accepted and appreciated by readers. We have always been active and eager to improve even beyond the best, to provide you with the most ideal of all. In this effort, we invite your valuable suggestions cordially.

We hope and wish to be with you in the path to glorious success in your career and through that the brightest future of our nation.

Wishing You All the Best

– Rohit Vadhwana, IFS
(Indian Foreign Service - 2010)

(**Disclaimer:** All opinions expressed are personal and for educational purpose only. They are in no manner related to my official capacity or views on government policy.)

Contents

How to Score Good Marks in General Studies

A STRATEGY

Candidates of Civil Services Examination have to go through ONE optional subject and Four General Studies papers, all having equal weightage of marks. But then too, candidates have commonly expressed unsatisfactory tone over preparation and results in General Studies papers, even toppers. Even sometimes, toppers cannot score up to their expectations in General Studies. Many reasons can be and are given for this generally accepted problem :

Uncertain Syllabus of the General Studies papers is one of the reason 'Why a strong grasp on and full command cannot be acquired over it.' No candidate, or even classes of high repute can draw a boundary for General Studies, not even a lose boundary can be uttered confidently.

So, to understand these two papers properly and acquire good command, at least, to be relieved of the tension, we must have a perfect strategy to prepare G.S. very methodically. For that let's go through some quite inevitable aspects that we must know and tackle.

Nature of General Studies

As declared earlier, it is quite uncertain and widely unspecified subject matter. Yet UPSC declares it to be acknowledged by every good educated person without having studied the topics specifically. But going through the papers and questions, it comes in mind that even after studying specially in a branch, one cannot answer perfectly some questions. Thus, it is really deep understanding of general topics that is required. For example, Government's policies, bilateral agreements, science and technology, economical issues etc.

Wide Coverage

The Syllabus is undefined. Papers cover a wide area of knowledge and information. It is not only topics from current or national and international issues that are widely scattered, but also in science and technology, economy and geographical spheres, questions cross the limits of tradition. So, a candidate has to be in touch of each and every topics happening around us, having their impact on society, nature or the world.

Deep Understanding

It is not just learning a topic and memorising some facts that pays but a candidate is required to command deep understanding of the incident or phenomena. He should be capable of presenting his views about its impacts.

Active Involvement

A candidate must develop a habit of actively taking interest in important incidents and should read newspapers and magazines for current related topics. He should also be able to think over definitions and explanations of conventional studies, cultivating the habit of 'reading between the lines'.

Command over Every Topic :

In General Studies, a candidate cannot opt any topic as an alternative for another one. A candidate must develop a strong hold and command over every topic of papers i.e. science and technology, statistics, economics, political issues, social issues, geography, current affairs, sports, international relations, institutions, organisations and so on.

Not Only Books :

Only books reading, though many, cannot give a good result. So for the General Studies is concerned, a candidate has to go through newspapers, magazines, and sometimes active discussions or debates also, for at least, over view based topics.

Unlimited

Yes, it is perfectly uncertain, unspecified and therefore unlimited in nature. Its sphere never ends with a boundary. It is like a horizon which shifts for and far as much we approach towards it. So it is also advised to every candidate to be selective in reading and a proper time table must be maintained strictly to follow the schedule. He must decide what he is required to read by suggestions of experienced faculties or at least seniors, friends, or some magazines.

Selective and Intensive

The study of General Studies Mains requires a perfect approach that is selective and intensive. It is quite different from the Preliminary exam. And so some topics, as I mentioned earlier, should be selected for intensive and deep study.

A list of books on every topic, required to be studied, can be prepared and then a time for each of them should be devoted. One can decide number and types of books and extent of time that one can alot to each according to weightage of the topic and one's command over it. For instance, a candidate with Political Science as first or second optional would hardly require to alot much time for the portion of Indian Polity in General Studies. So, this factor varies from candidate to candidate and from stage to stage of preparation.

Moreover, a candidate can decide by the nature of a topic that how much weightage can be given to a topic by considering its importance. We can consider the following points while choosing the self-decided syllabus for the General Studies :

- Previous Years' Papers can be thoroughly studied to understand what topics are frequently emphasised, especially traditional topics like history, polity, economy, geography, statistics etc.
- Current news can guide you to select portions of importance. For example, the topic of bilateral relations can be asked if any agreement or visit of higher authority has taken place during recent period.
- Newly declared policies and its importance should be prepared as it can be expected in papers.
- Any International Conference, organisation or summit in news should be prepared thoroughly.

These are only a few criteria for selection of topics of importance from amongst the unlimited reservoir of issues and incidents.

One more important suggestion, on this topic of selective and intensive study, is that preparation should be based on understanding and information apart from getting knowledge but never should be just a bulk of datas, figures and numbers.

Answer Writing

Its a quite necessary skill for mains examination. No word should be missed and no extra word can be spaced between. Besides shortage of time, words limit is a crucial factor of these papers.

Proper word at proper place' is applied in this exam. If a candidate, reading a lot and knowing a lot, cannot score well, What is justification? No justification, just one fault appears on the surface that is lack of answer writing skill. It can be developed. It can be commanded over impressively.

What a candidate knows is only picturised by words he writes in his answers. He cannot enjoy a smooth flow of ink nor can be create bumpers in logical flow of answer. He has to maintain flow of language on the road. He is directed by the question and that too without bumps, covering the whole distance. He is, in simple words, required to maintain the quality of his answers with the following characteristics:

- Simplicity of language.
- Logical flow of language.
- Clarity of thoughts.
- Proper structure of answers.
- Maintaining word limit.
- Information and data.
- Precise and brief writing.
- Appropriate diagrams, graphs or figures can be drawn.

A candidate cannot just fill up pages without having any relevance to the answer. A story, for instance, explains it. Once there was a person, not much intelligent, rather known as even lacking common-sense as a matter of fact. It was natural from him, not to expect anything that requires intelligent, expertise or skillful knowledge. Yet, being on a high post of reputation, he used to believe and boost of being a scholar, an expert.

And in this illusion, he, among the surprise of all, published a book, "Shivaji—Life and story of a Maratha leader". It was not inspired by interest and curiosity of the story but by curiosity to know what and how he can write, people purchased the book.

Of course, the book was made quite bulky, as if it had to be proved as the level of his intelligence. When the readers were to go through the pages, they found the story something like this :– There was a Maratha leader. His name was Shivaji Maharaj...... He used to ride his horse tik-tak and fight battles with sword sweeping Syuen-shyuen, tik-tak, syuen-syuen (voice of sword, cutting air) and every morning this Maratha leader ride his horse and fight battles, tik-tak, tik-tak, syuen, syuen tik-tak syuen ..... tik-tak syuen.......

(Many pages were just filled up with these two words). Then he concluded the story :

"And this Maratha leader was really great."

How would a reader feel when reading this story of Shivaji with barely three to four sentences or paras but feeled all pages with two words only. tik-tak, tik-tak and syuen shyuen ! Same boredom might be felt by the examiner when a candidate has just filled up pages and completed words.

Morale of this story for us is that we cannot end up with such surprising answers.

A candidate must remember one more thing that he cannot fix in the answer whatever he knows and has learnt. He has to strictly examine relevance of the information he possesses. Only if it is relevant, he can write it in the question. Not only to make it an impression that he knows something extra about the topic – he can be allowed to write whatever he has gained so far.

One more story will explain this bad habit that many candidates have in them.

A student of primary school makes his mind to participate in an Essay competition to be held in near future in his school. He determined his efforts and started to find out a topic which can give him more points or grades. He at last, according to his level, found out and decided to draft a model essay on "A Pig" and he prepared it.

He read it over and over till he could do it by heart ! And not yet satisfied with his efforts and his intense desire to win medal, he also practised to write it, for many a times. When the day of destiny came at last, he entered the competition hall and prepared his arms and ammunition.

The examiner declared topics of essay which did not contain topic "A Pig" that the boy had prepared. He was nervous. He would see his dreams breaking and scattering. But after some time he again collected all his courage. As we are, he was advised so many times by his teachers and parents that even though you don't know anything about the question, you should not left it blank. You should try to think over it and search any knowledge that you might gather from inside and then you should write about it. So, was the case with this "Our dear boy", he again had a glance at the topics and after thinking over them, of course because he was advised, he thought that he knew something about cricket and finally decided to write about cricket. He started in this way :

Cricket is a game. It is played with a bat and a ball and some sticks and many players. Once there was a cricket match. A player threw a ball and another player hit it with bat. The ball went high in the sky and went away from over the wall. The ball fell on road outside. It tumbled and crossed the road. It fell in mud. In that mud, there was a pig........ and not surprisingly, then he wrote the whole essay about a pig which he had prepared.!!

How strange, in an essay about cricket, he could manage to fill up pages, intelligently making his way, with the essay of a Pig.

Sometimes, candidates also, like this boy, direct his answer to accommodate what he knows and then fills up pages with that knowledge only. But it is as foolish act as this boy had done.

I hope, no need to suggest now in clear words that a candidate must not and never unnecessarily try to write whatever he knows unless asked and to pull the answer in the direction, which he has knowledge in.

Time Management

Time Management is required at two stages :

(i) During Preparation

(ii) In the Examination Hall.

(i) During Preparation : While preparing for the mains, especially after result of Preliminary, candidate rests with a little time, hardly three months at hand. In this short span of time, he requires to thoroughly prepare his both optionals and General Studies. Apart from these Six papers, a candidate has to prepare for Essay and two language papers, though not much emphasised by candidates.

In addition to all these, the must required preparation of acquiring writing skill and practice is also there.

Among these needs, one has to manage time for each optional, essay and the G.S.

Some tips can be given on this points :

- Divide total time for all these six papers, sparing an evening a week for essay.
- For each paper, you can again divide the time allocated to it, even for topics separately.
- Confirm a little flexibility in your time division.
- Ensure that you give enough weightage to every topic, providing more time and concern for important one.
- Be confirm that you allocate time for each, based upon two strategies.
  (i) your command, knowledge and background.
  (ii) previous years' questions and marks weightage.
- Do not indulge, in any topic for expert knowledge and just be sure that you are gaining enough knowledge required for General Studies. Even your personal interest should not lead you to this mistake.

(ii) **Time Management in Exam. Hall:**

- Do not read the whole paper in starting, because all questions are compulsory in General Studies.
- Among questions with options, go through each (a), (b), (c) ....., where option is available.
- Think which question you can attempt well.
- After deciding the question to be attempted, jolt down relevant points according to nature of the question. Then start to write answers. No extra words or comments, only straight forward answer on proper direction will surely shorten your time,
- The condition is that before starting to write an answer one must had points and structure of the answers in one's mind.
- Do not waste time in noticing behaviour and impression of others about the papers though this is not to say to a candidate of Civil Services, yet it is necessary.
- Proper managed preparation can give you sweet fruits even in General Studies and allowing you enough time for your optionals also.

Just remember one thing, no one can be perfect in general studies, learn to be satisfied with your preparation, yes, improvement must always be yearned for.

Notes

Many toppers advise to prepare notes and many to follow strategy of underlining important parts. Some combine both. What is the best way for main preparation of General Studies? Should a candidate spare time for notes making?

Answer is again amalgamation of both where to use notes and where underline is an important question. You can follow the stages given below.

- Stage 1 : To be precise, you can underline your references with a pencil and different colours of pens and highlighters.
- Stage 2 : You can underline with pencil, that portion of a book or magazine which you generally find important, as a whole.

- Stage 3 : Now you can, from among these portions underline that sentences which can provide you central idea of the topic with one colour pen, may it be blue.
- Stage 4 : Then again, if you find some words and phrases, numbers, figures and datas of vital importance, underline that part with another colour of pen, as more important for revision and memorising. May it be black or green.
- Stage 5 : Then at last and inevitable task, you can round up or underline or box-up only a few words for the portion which can be used as the stimulation to your grasp of that topic. For example, in History of Modern India, while learning the topic of "Gandhi in Indian National Movement". You can just, for a few, use this last technique and remark words like, 'Champaran', 'Dandi', 'Civil Disobedience', 'Non-Cooperation', 'Swadeshi', 'Round-table', 'Satyagraha', 'Ahimsa' and 'fast'. It is sure that while reading these words only, you can surely recall the whole topic. Am I right?

So, follow these techniques for underlining.

For making notes :

- It must be topic and sub-topic wise,
- It must include only relevant and most important points in brief language.
- Grammar and full sentences are not required to be taken care of.
- It must be handy in size and shape.
- It must be with clean and legible hand-writing.
- It must be attractively drafted and designed.
- It should not be with scattered points but with well arranged topics, indexed based on importance or incidents.
- Even in notes, most important words can be rounded up or highlighted, as in books and references.
- No preface, conclusion, views etc. on a topic, but only relevant explanation in point based language and datas should be there.
- Notes should be prepared subject-wise and if possible topic wise.
- Head points and titles should be given in notes.
- Different colour pens and signs can be used to indicate importance, weightage and probability to be asked in papers for different topics.

Once again, notes must not be like a manuscript of original texts, it must be in your own words and if possible, language and style too.

It must be brief, summarily prepared and portable that can be revised even in a single day before the papers.

Understanding Nature of Topics

When involved in preparation, each topic should be evaluated in contexts of its probability of being asked in examination, its probable weightage and importance.

- How much influence does it create upon the society, politics or nature, is to be taken into account.

- Whether the topic has relevant facts and figures which are important from the examination's point of view.
- If the topic is view based, different types of views, for and against must be acquired with by candidate.
- One cannot be biased to one side of it, one must learn to be natural while understanding the topic, only then candidate can balance answer in examination hall.

Some topics can basked in context of its contribution on particular or various fields, some can be for explaining implication and some for discussion. While learning a topic, according to its nature, a candidate must evaluate its purpose and perspectives. It can be directed to discussion, justification, examination, elucidation, arguments and comments, all or any of these possible manners.

In another way, representing and understanding the same aspects, from the angle of marks and words should also be taken into account.

Topics possible to be asked in two marks only, ten or thirty marks etc., can be decided 0or at least expected by candidatcs and then preparation can be directed to that track.

Model and Practice

Various question papers, as models and practices should be gone through for the exam purpose.

The more one practises papers, the more marks be scores; is hitherto noticed fact. We need to be careful while choosing models which are of good standard and level. Solving such papers can boost a candidate's confidence and can make him aware of some expected topics that can be asked in papers.

It also helps in tackling the problems of time management, exam fear and so on.

Therefore, it is always advisable for every candidate to go through various questions and topics by means of model papers and practice sets.

Reading Material

Having going through all these aspects of strategy, now a candidate, at last, requires to know and decide what material he can use.

For different topics of General Studies, a candidate has to go through various references, guides, magazines and newspapers. One must decide carefully what books can be read for what topics. For this, friends, seniors, faculties or toppers (if not personally than through interviews in magazines) can be taken help of.

Classes materials if found reliable can be used. Guides from various publications can also help understanding very easily.

Dictionaries and Atlas are must

For proper understanding of every topics, points and phenomena, dictionaries and Atlas are must to be used. Otherwise ambiguities of meaning may be created in candidate's mind. No boasting of knowledge or vocabulary should come in way. Neither a candidate should feel boring in using Atlas for Map reading.

Interpreting "Words" Given in the Questions

Candidate should answer the Question in accordance with the terms specified in the question. Some of those terms are mentioned here.

- Elucidate : It means to throw light on or explain. A statement is to be made intelligible by providing relevant facts and figures. You are not going to differ in such questions but just follow the track it provides to you, just giving explanations, if required with examples, to elucidate i.e. convince the statement.
- Explain : It is almost like same as Elucidate. Minor difference that appears in answer writing is that with definition and necessary details, one can just be within the area of statement while explaining it.
- Comment : Requires personal views of a candidate. Remember "to comment" is not "to argue". It is necessary here to be balanced on each aspects, for and against, including every topic of the statement. Though a candidate can conclude either for or against but not necessarily to any one side specifically. Illustrations, incidents, datas, facts can be used to comment your view.
- Examine : This question compulsorily requires result of examination. One cannot be at middle point or remain indecisive to be neutral. The statement requires a close inspection to bring out facts throwing light on various merits and demerits and concluding on any one side.
- Critically Examine : Here too, one must give judgement, most important here. One needs not to justify any fact or point but to be critical to them so that no side – for or against – seems to be favoured. As a critic does not be either for or against but for at some aspects and against at others.
- Discuss : It gives you a chance to narrate various aspects and details of the statement. It is comparatively easy to discuss as you are neither required to explain nor to examine. Just providing necessary detail about various aspects of the question will suffice the answer.
- Analyse : Analysis is something like scientific technique. One by one each aspects of the statement are taken into consideration. While dealing with one aspect, examine it, discuss it and comment upon it and then conclude separately for that aspect without having relevance to others. But remember each aspects, differently analysed must be coordinated and conclusion should be formed as a whole, of the whole analysis.
- Illustrate : To give example to explain the topic in the statement, to make it clear. Here too, relevant datas, quotations and facts can help to point out. But it must be remembered that you are not going to write an opposite to the statement. One needs to follow the direction of the statement and to explain it in that way.

- Simplify : To simplify means to made simple the statement. Give definition, meaning, explanation, details, examples and make the statement easy to grasp.
- Elaborate : It requires to add related details to make it full of meaning. Without necessary details some statements do not bear meaning. You are to provide its back ground, basis and then related detail to clear the whole picture in your words.
- Argue : To argue is to give for and against arguments on different aspects and effects of the statement. Remember, both sides must be covered. Balanced argument is advisable but if the topic is very positive or very negative, that side can be emphasised.
- Review : To review is to have a look on the historical facts of the statement. It is an expertise inspection of any topic. What outcomes and results you get, produce there.
- Justify : A statement regarding any result, decision or fact is given. Candidate has to justify it by explaining its benefits or merits and expressing its effect on minimising the adverse side. To prove propaganda in the statement logically and step by step is the expectation.

Main Examination

(Syllabus and Instructions given by UPSC)

The main Examination is intended to assess the overall intellectual traits and depth of understanding of candidates rather than merely the range of their information and memory.

The nature and standard of questions in the General Studies papers (Paper II to Paper V) will be such that a well-educated person will be able to answer them without any specialized study. The questions will be such as to test a candidate's general awareness of a variety of subjects, which will have relevance for a career in Civil Services. The questions are likely to test the candidate's basic understanding of all relevant issues, and ability to analyze, and take a view on conflicting socio-economic goals, objectives and demands. The candidates must give relevant, meaningful and succinct answers.

The scope of the syllabus for optional subject papers (Paper VI and Paper VII) for the examination is broadly of the honours degree level i.e. a level higher than the bachelors' degree and lower than the masters' degree. In the case of Engineering, Medial Science and law, the level corresponds to the bachelors' degree.

Syllabi of the papers included in the scheme of Civil Services (Main) Examination are given as follows:-

PAPER-I:

Essay: Candidates will be required to write an essay on a specific topic. The choice of subjects will be given.

They will be expected to keep closely to the subject of the essay to arrange their ideas in orderly fashion, and to write concisely. Credit will be given for effective and exact expression.

English Comprehension & English Precis will be to test the English language Comprehension and English Precis writing skills (at 10th standard level).

PAPER-II:

General Studies-I: Indian Heritage and Culture, History and Geography of the World andSociety

- Indian culture will cover the salient aspects of Art Forms, Literature and Architecture from ancient to modern times.
- Modern Indian history from about the middle of the eighteenth century until the presentsignificant events, personalities, issues
- The Freedom Struggle - its various stages and important contributors /contributions from different parts of the country.
- Post-independence consolidation and reorganization within the country.
- History of the world will include events from 18th century such as industrial revolution, worldwars, redrawal of national boundaries, colonization, decolonization, political philosophies like communism, capitalism, socialism etc.- their forms and effect on the society.

- Salient features of Indian Society, Diversity of India.
- Role of women and women's organization, population and associated issues, poverty and developmental issues, urbanization, their problems and their remedies.
- Effects of globalization on Indian society
- Social empowerment, communalism, regionalism & secularism.
- Salient features of world's physical geography,
- Distribution of key natural resources across the world (including South Asia and the Indian subcontinent); factors responsible for the location of primary, secondary, and tertiary sector industries in various parts of the world (including India)
- Important Geophysical phenomena such as earthquakes, Tsunami, Volcanic activity, cyclone etc., geographical features and their location- changes in critical geographical features (including waterbodies and ice-caps) and in flora and fauna and the effects of such changes.

PAPER-III:

General Studies-II: Governance, Constitution,Polity, Social Justice and Internationalrelations

- Indian Constitution- historical underpinnings, evolution, features, amendments, significant provisions and basic structure.
- Functions and responsibilities of the Union and the States, issues and challenges pertaining to the federal structure, devolution of powers and finances up to local levels and challenges therein.
- Separation of powers between various organs dispute redressal mechanisms and institutions.
- Comparison of the Indian constitutional scheme with that of other countries
- Parliament and State Legislatures - structure, functioning, conduct of business, powers & privileges and issues arising out of these.
- Structure, organization and functioning of the Executive and the Judiciary Ministries and Departments of the Government; pressure groups and formal/informal associations and their role in the Polity.
- Salient features of the Representation of People's Act.
- Appointment to various Constitutional posts, powers, functions and responsibilities of various Constitutional Bodies.
- Statutory, regulatory and various quasi-judicial bodies
- Government policies and interventions for development in various sectors and issues arising out of their design and implementation.
- Development processes and the development industry- the role of NGOs, SHGs, various groups and associations, donors, charities, institutional and other stakeholders
- Welfare schemes for vulnerable sections of the population by the Centre and States and the performance of these schemes; mechanisms, laws, institutions and Bodies constituted for the protection and betterment of these vulnerable sections.
- Issues relating to development and management of Social Sector/Services relating to Health, Education, Human Resources.

- Issues relating to poverty and hunger.
- Important aspects of governance, transparency and accountability, e-governance- applications, models, successes, limitations, and potential; citizens charters, transparency & accountability and institutional and other measures.
- Role of civil services in a democracy.
- India and its neighborhood- relations.
- Bilateral, regional and global groupings and agreements involving India and/or affecting India's interests
- Effect of policies and politics of developed and developing countries on India's interests, Indian diaspora.
- Important International institutions, agencies and fora- their structure, mandate.

PAPER-IV:

General Studies-III: Technology, EconomicDevelopment, Bio diversity, Environment,Security and Disaster Management

- Indian Economy and issues relating to planning, mobilisation of resources, growth, development and employment.
- Inclusive growth and issues arising from it
- Government Budgeting
- Major crops cropping patterns in various parts of the country, different types of irrigation and irrigation systems storage, transport and marketing of agricultural produce and issues and related constraints; e-technology in the aid of farmers
- Issues related to direct and indirect farm subsidies and minimum support prices; Public Distribution System- objectives, functioning, limitations, revamping; issues of buffer stocks and food security; Technology missions; economics of animal-rearing.

* Food processing and related industries in India- scope and significance, location, upstream and downstream requirements, supply chain management.
* Land reforms in India.
* Effects of liberalization on the economy, changes in industrial policy and their effects on industrial growth.

- Infrastructure: Energy, Ports, Roads, Airports, Railways etc.
- Investment models.
- Science and Technology- developments and their applications and effects in everyday life
- Achievements of Indians in science & technology; indigenisation of technology and developing new technology.
- Awareness in the fields of IT, Space, Computers, robotics, nano-technology, bio-technology and issues relating to intellectual property rights.
- Conservation, environmental pollution and degradation, environmental impact assessment
- Disaster and disaster management.
- Linkages between development and spread of extremism.
- Role of external state and non-state actors in creating challenges to internal security.

- Challenges to internal security through communication networks, role of media and social networking sites in internal security challenges, basics of cyber security; moneylaundering and its prevention
- Security challenges and their management in border areas; linkages of organized crime with terrorism
- Various Security forces and agencies and their mandate

PAPER-V:
General Studies- IV: Ethics, Integrity, and aptitude

This paper will include questions to test the candidates' attitude and approach to issues relating) integrity, probity in public life and his problem solving approach to various issues and conflicts iced by him in dealing with society. Questions lay utilise the case study approach to determine these aspects. The following broad areas will be covered.

Ethics and Human Interface: Essence, determinants and consequences of Ethics in human actions; dimensions of ethics; ethics in private and public relationships. Human Values - lessons from the lives and teachings of great leaders, reformers and administrators; role of Family, society and educational institutions in inculcating values.

- Attitude: content, structure, function; its] influence and relation with thought and behaviour; moral and political attitudes; social influence and persuasion.
- Aptitude and foundational values for Civil Service, integrity, impartiality and non-partisanship,objectivity, dedication to public service, empathy, tolerance and compassion towards the weakersections.
- Emotional intelligence-concepts and their utilities and application in administration and governance
- Contributions of moral thinkers and philosophers I from India and world
- Public/Civil service values and Ethics in Public administration: Status and problems; ethical concerns and dilemmas in government and private institutions; laws, rules, regulations and conscience as sources of ethical guidance; accountability and ethical governance; strengthening of ethical and moral values in governance; ethical issues in international relations and funding; corporate governance.
- Probity in Governance: Concept of public service; Philosophical basis of governance and probity; Information sharing and transparency in government, Right to Information, Codes of Ethics, Codes of Conduct, Citizen's Charters, Work culture, Quality of service delivery, Utilization of public funds, challenges of corruption.
- Case Studies on above issues.

PAPER-VI & PAPER VII:
Optional Subject Papers I & II

Candidates may choose any optional subject from amongst the list of subjects given in para 2 (Group 1). However, if a candidate has graduated in any of the literatures of languages indicated in Group-2 , with the literature as the main subject, then the candidate can also opt for that particular literature subject as an optional subject.

(MAIN) **Civil Services Exam.**

2003 General Studies

SOLVED PAPERS

PAPER–I

Time Allowed: Three Hours *Maximum Marks: 300*

Candidates should attempt All questions strictly in accordance with the instructions given under each question.

Q. 1 Answer any ONE of the following (about 250 words) : **30**

(a) The reforms of 1909 introduced a cardinal problem and ground of controversy at every revision of the Indian electoral system." Comment.

Important Points for Answer:

- *Reforms of 1909 - provisions*
- *Effects*
- *Electoral –revision*
- *How problems posed?*
- *Conclusion*

Answer: The Indian Council Act, 1909 also known as the 'Morley Minto Reforms' introduced formally electoral system in India.

There was a demand for Self-Government which was not conceded to, even in a part. The electoral system that was introduced contained two divisions of electorates, namely :

(i) General electorates, and (ii) Special electorates.

The General electorate contained non-official members of provincial legislative councils and municipal boards.

The Specialised electorates were of three kinds :

(a) Class based,

(b) Communal-which separates electorates for Muslims and Hindus,

(c) Social Interest based electorates.

No Universal franchise was introduced. Only a class of citizen was qualified for voting which was almost a minority to the total population of each electorate.

Communal Representation introduced here was aimed at dividing Hindu-Muslim to make them weaker. Only an elite class Muslims were interested in such reforms.

Moreover, the elections were not direct elections, but it was by an electoral college which in turn elected from each electorate areas. Special interest was also introduced by providing seats to British capitalists and Zamindars. Communalism was given a fire not only by dividing electorates but also by relaxing conditions for qualifications to be a voter.

All these measures, in name of reforms introduced by the Act of 1909 gave a political and social blow to the national movement.

These policy was made more and more grave at every revision of electoral systems. For example, by Act of 1919 the Communal electorates were introduced for Sikhs, Christians and also for Harijans. These separate communal electorates introduced for Harijans were severely criticised by Gandhiji and were not accepted.

Not only by providing a pseudo majority provisions but especially by introducing a separate communal electorate system, the Act of 1909 put a fire which was given blow at every revision to divide Indians and to make them quarrel among themselves so that the force of unity can be broken and weaken.

(b) Discuss the problems that impeded the integration of the princely states into the Indian Union. How were these problems tackled?

Important Points for Answer:

- *Integration policy*
- *Princely states*
- *Problems*
- *How tackled?*

Answer: Mountbatten Plan made the Princely states free to decide their fate, either to join Indian or Pakistan Dominion. However, they were allowed sovereignty or a separate dominion.

Some states of India wanted to remain free as separate states. Hyderabad, Travancore, Bhopal, etc. were the states which wanted to remain sovereign.

For incorporation and integration of Princely states, a new States Department was constituted in July 1947, under Sardar Vallabhbhai Patel as its incharge.

By tactful handling of the problem, all states except three signed an Instrument of Accession with Indian Government by August 15, 1947.

Junagarh's Nawab wanted to join Pakistan but people wanted to join Indian dominion. People's movement pressurised Nawab and Indian Army help resulted in its merger with Indian dominion.

Hyderabad wanted to remain a separate state but it was included in India by bait and threats by Sardar Patel very tactfully.

Apart from such incorporation of states into Indian dominion, there were problems involved in regard to their integration. Many small states were required to integrate to form a sizeable state.

Many Princely states in Kathiawar were integrated to form Kathiawar Union. Same problems were involved in Vindhya, Madhya Pradesh, Rajasthan, Himachal Pradesh, etc. Issues of boundary redrawing also arose to be tackled by Sardar Patel.

Their titles and positions were required to change for democracy. Privy purses and posts of Governors or Raj Pramukhs were offered to them for their renouncement of titles.

State of Travancore was involved in India by realising them the threats of Communism. Mysore was incorporated by People's movement. Last was the Kashmir to join India after the fear of attack by Pakistan army. Raja Harisingh of Kashmir signed instrument of accession to get help of Indian army against this threat.

By the incorporation of Kashmir, all states had merged with India and their integration was also completed by November, 1948.

Thus, different situational problems arose in integration of Indian Union which were tackled by Sardar Patel very tactfully by use of wisdom, threats, rewards or force according to the needs.

Q. 2 Answer any TWO of the following (about 150 words) : 2 × 15 = 30

(a) The mainstay of Mahatma Gandhi's movements was the rural India. Elucidate.

Important Points for Answer:
- *Gandhi's attitude*
- *Issues–importance & involvement of rural public*

Answer: After returning from South Africa, Gandhiji decided to round all over the country. He first came in struggle with the Government, through Champaran Satyagraha of 1917, that was for the cause of Indigo farmers. He pictured the regional problem at the national level. In the same way, his Satyagraha in Gujarat in 1918 for Kheda district farmers also come from rural India. He changed his life style and adopted simplicity in his living style. He himself lived like a villager.

He adopted programmes like Boycott, Swadeshi, encouragement for Khadi and rural handicraft. His emphasis was always upon the society in rural India. He had even opposed heavy industry because it would have adverse impact on rural economy.

His movement for abolition of castism, untouchability, upliftment of Harijans etc. were basically centered in rural life. Rural mass cooperation was inevitable for achievement of freedom and only educated urban people cannot win freedom, according to Gandhiji, as he regarded rural areas as the soul of India.

After 1920, all movements like Civil Disobedience, Non-Cooperation etc. involved large masses of rural people. This made villages take active part in political actions, making the base of national movement much wider.

(b) Discuss the character of major tribal uprisings in British India in the nineteenth Century.

Important Points for Answer:
- *Tribal uprisings*
- *Reasons*
- *Nature*

Answer: In the nineteenth century, British were establishing themselves in the areas of remote tribes. During this spread, they had to face many regional, tribal revolts for their interference in tribal life and occupation.

Among many main revolts were, Munda Revolt, Khasi Revolt, Santhal Rebellion, Kandh Uprisings, Kol Uprisings, Kukis Revolt, etc.

All these tribal revolts were led by either any Leader or elder person of the tribal group. They were local in their spread and were limited to their regional objectives.

These revolts, sometimes against Land lords, money lenders and British rule acquired violent nature and when suppressed by forces they generally turned to religious character by its leader claiming incarnation of any deity.

However, fragmented in character, they were examples of their true spirit of sacrifice and courage. They set examples for nationalist leaders. Explaining the exploitation and cruelty towards them, they stood to remove them by themselves.

(c) Bring out the ideological basis of the Moderate-Extremist divide in the Indian National Congress.

Important Points for Answer:
- *Ideologies of - moderates, extremists of Congress split*

Answer: Indian National Congress divided in 1907-Surat Session between Moderates and Extremists due to their different ideologies though both groups continued to work for national movement of India.

- The foremost difference was in social base, for moderates zamindars and upper middle class was the base while for the extremists, educated middle and lower middle class formed a wide base.
- Moderates regarded the British rule in India's social, political and cultural interest while extremists thought them as exploiting India.
- Moderates were loyal to the British crown while extremists did not.
- Moderates had no faith in mass movement which the extremists had from starting.
- Moderates meant 'Swaraj' as just Constitutional reforms and increase in share of Indians in services and representation under the crown while the extremists meant it freedom from British rule altogether.
- Moderates followed only constitutional methods of petitions, resolutions, etc. while the later movements boycott, protest, strikes, etc.

These main ideological basis led the Congress to split in its Surat Session.

Q. 3 Write about the following (not exceeding 20 words each): **15 × 2 = 30**

(i) ***Arthasastra***

Answer: A famous work by Kautilya or 'Chanakya' the Prime Minister of Chandragupta Maurya. It deals with Political principles and policies.

(ii) Sarnath Pillar

A pillar erected by Ashoka as a holy mark of Buddha's first sermon. Our national emblem is taken from the top of this pillar.

(iii) The *Jatiya Sarkar* of Tamluk

Answer: It was a parallel Government established by leaders in Tamluk (Midnapur) during December 1942 to September 1944.

(iv) Punnapra-Vayalar

Answer: A localised peason movement by small farmers and artisans against the ambitious Diwan C.P. Ramaswamy in Travancore state in 1946-47.

(v) Sajjad Zahir

Answer: A famous personality of Urdu literature who also belonged to social and religious reformation of Muslims in 19th century.

(vi) *Al-Hilal*

Answer: *A* newspaper started by Abul Kalam Azad in 1912 to spread his socialist thoughts and national spirit among people.

(vii) Har Dayal

Answer: He was the editor and founder of the 'Gadar' newspaper and later on 'Gadar Party'. It was a revolutionary group in San Francisco working for India freedom.

(viii) Khudai Khidmatgar

Answer: Khan Abdul Gafar Khan organised Pathans in Kabul to form a group 'Khudai Khidmatgar' for Indian freedom by following 'Ahinsha' in 1929.

(ix) Mahayana Cult

Answer: This is a cult of Buddhism which regard 'Buddha' as the God. It came into existence from the fourth Buddhist council in first century.

(x) W. W. Hunter

Answer: He was the chairman of Education Commission for India constituted in 1882. His findings and recommendations developed Indian education.

(xi) Indu Lal Yajnik

Answer: He was one of the founder of All India Kishan Sabha in 1936. He was a famous peasant leader of Gujarat.

(xii) Achhut Patwardhan

Answer: He was one of the founders of Congress Socialist Party in 1934. He was a famous socialist thinker and companion of J. P. Narayan.

(xiii) Sir William Jones

Answer: He established Asiatic Society of Bengal in 1784 in Calcutta to bringout prestigeous Indian heritage and culture.

(xiv) James Wilson

Answer: He played a vital role in the revival of Indian ancient education in the time of Lord Bentick. He supported royal grant for development of literature and language.

(xv) *Ghulam-giri.*

Answer: It is a book written by Jyotiba Phule. It condemns castism in India and exposes problems of the depressed classes.

Q. 4 Answer any TWO of the following (about 125 words each) : 2 × 10 = 20

(a) Describe the major characteristics of the rivers of Peninsular India.

Answer: Rivers of Peninsular India radically differ from those of the Northern Indian rivers, called the Himalayan Rivers in vary characteristics. Peninsular Rivers have their origins in Aravallis, Western Ghat, Eastern Ghat and Satpura series of mountains.

- they have little or no water in summer.
- they do not form sedimentary plains because they pass through rocky soil.
- their flow is fast and they are not useful in water transportation due to fast flow and up-down path.
- at some places they form water falls and attract tourists.
- due to fast streams, they can be used to generate hydro-electricity.

(b) Account for the very high concentration of salt extraction industries in the Saurashtra and South Tamil Nadu Coast.

Important Points for Answer:
- *Salt extraction industries, requirements*
- *Locational suitability of Saurashtra and Tamil Nadu*
- *Other reasons*

Answer: For the development of Salt industries, high temperature, dry season, less precipitation and high salinity of water is necessary.

In Gujarat, the coastal districts of Saurashtra, receive less than 50 cm of annual rainfall and hence come under Semi-arid zones. Mean annual temperature is around 25-30° C and the sky is clear and cloudless for a major part of the year. Both these factors lead to less precipitation and more evaporation. Moreover, there are no river delta or estuaries to reduce the salinity of sea water, making the coast ideal for salt industries.

Similarly, in the South coast of Tamil Nadu, away from the Kaveri, annual precipitation remains 60 cm, an average with mean annual temperature of 25 to 30° C. Moreover, salinity in the coastal water is high due to lack of any river drain. So, the ideal and much required condition for salt industries are available here in the South of Tamil Nadu coast also.

These are the reasons for the very high concentration of salt extraction industries in the Saurashtra and South Tamil Nadu coast apart from availability of cheap and experienced labourer activities.

(c) State the four distinctive stages of Indian Demographic history.

> **Important Points for Answer:**
> - *Stages : upto 1921, 1921-1951, 1951-1971 and from 1971*

Answer: The History of Indian Demography can be divided into four distinctive stages as :

Stage-I : Upto 1921. Stage-II : 1921 to 1951

Stage-Ill : 1951 to 1971 Stage-IV : from 1971

- **Stage I** : **upto 1921** - represents the phase of very slow growth rate of population. This was characterised by high birth rate and high death rate. Due to adverse situations, the death rate was very high. Even during 1911 to 1921, there was negative decadal growth rate of - 0 -31%.
- **Stage II** : from **1921 to 1951**—is characterised by medium growth rate. During this period, the medical facilities, food availability etc. contributed in reducing death rate to some extent and continuous high birth rate represented 11 to 14% of decadal growth rate of population.
- **Stage III: from 1951 to 1971** - covering the period from 1951 to 1971 represents very high growth rate. After Independence, availability of medical facilities and food were increased. This impressively reduced death rate and because of no measures to check the growth of population, the birth rate also was higher. So, it resulted in the growth rate of 21 to 24% per decade.
- **Stage IV** : **from 1971** - which is continue from 1971 can be marked with slow reduction in population growth. Due to measures to check the population, education and awareness, the birth rate has slowed down. However, the reduction in decadal growth rate is amongst the higher rate of population.

Q. 5 Write short notes on the following (about 20 words each) : 5 × 2 = 10

(i) Define Terai Region.

Answer: Situated in the south of the Shivalik Range, it is composed of sedimentary deposits. This plains are made by the eroded materials of the main Himalayan ranges.

(ii) Mention the area of Shola forests in India.

Answer: The area of Shola forests in India :

- Western Ghat range
- Eastern Ghat range
- Mountain Hills of Annamalai and Nilgiri in Peninsular region.
- Satpura mountains.

These forests occur between the range of 1000 to 1500 mt. altitude.

(iii) Who are Todas and where do they live?

Answer: Todas are Scheduled Tribes residing in Tamil Nadu's Nilgiri mountain areas. They profess animal husbandry and collection of forest products.

(iv) Name any four principal languages of Andaman and Nicobar Islands.

Four principal languages of Andaman and Nicobar Islands are Nicobari, Tamil, Telugu and Hindi.

(v) What is MRTS? Where it is in operation?

Answer: MRTS is Mass Rapid Transport System. It is in operation in Delhi to improve transport facility in the mega city.

Q. 6 Answer any ONE of the following (about 250 words) : 30

(a) Discuss the question of death sentence and Presidential clemency.

Important Points for Answer:
- *Death sentence*
- *Constitutional powers of President regarding death sentences*

Answer: The President of India is given clemancy powers in respect of death sentence, under Article-72,

- may it be for the violation of any
  - union law, or
  - state law, or
  - martial law.

The President has clemancy powers in the following ways :

- Pardon : completely absolves the offender.
- Commutation : substitution of one form of punishment for another lighter punishment.
- Remission : reduction of sentence without changing character of it, however, it is not possible in case of death sentence.
- Respite : On some special grounds (like pregnancy) awarding lesser punishment.
- Reprive : Temporary suspension of death sentence.

This powers of the President is to be exercised on the advice of the council of ministers. Generally decision of the President in this regard is not questioned in the court of law, but in exceptional cases it can be taken for judicial review, it has been grossly misused out of scope of Article-72.

The presidential clemancy cannot be demanded as a matter of right. It can be rejected even without assigning any ground.

The Supreme Court examined the scope of the President's pardoning power under Article- 72 in the Kehar Singh's case-1989 and held

The President may scrutinise the evidence on the record

- He may decide differently from the court.

- The offender has no right to be heard by the President.
- The manner of consideration is the discretionary decision of the President.
- The court do not guide in exercise of the power under Article-72 to the President.
- The order of the President is not subject to judicial review on its merit.

(b) Explain the discretionary powers of the Governor of a State.

Important Points for Answer:
- *Governor*
- *Discretionary powers*
- *Constitutional provisions*

Answer: The Governor of a State is vested with discretionary powers more than the President of India. In certain circumstances he is not bound to act on the advise of the Council of Ministers, even he need not seek its advise.

Some occassions where the Governor is required to act discretionary are :

(i) Appointment of the Chief Minister

(ii) Advising the President for Proclamation of Emergency.

(iii) Dissolution of Legislative Assembly.

(iv) Dismissal of a Ministry.

(v) Reserving a bill for the President's consideration.

(vi) Schedule 6

- **Appointment of the Chief Minister :** Generally the leader of the party with majority is appointed as the Chief Minister. But in situation where no party gets absolute majority, the Governor exercises his discretionary powers in appointing the Chief Minister.
- **Advising the President for proclamation of Emergency** : Under Article 356, the Governor advises the President to proclaim emergency when he is satisfied that the Government cannot carried on in accordance with the provisions of the Constitution.
- **Dissolution of Legislative Assembly** : Under Article 174, the Governor summons, prorogues and dissolves the Legislative Assembly. When the ministry loses the majority and the Governor is satisfied, he may dissolve the House.
- **Dismissal of a Ministry** : According to Article 164, a minister holds office during the pleasure of the Governor. When the ministry loses support of the House, the Governor will dismiss the ministry. But he cannot dismiss it until it losses majority support.
- **Reservation of a bill for the consideration of the President**: However, situation are mentioned in Article 200, when he will reserve the bill, yet he can use, discretion regarding this matter.
- **Schedule** 6 : It mentions some function expressly to be performed by the Governor at his discretion in the tribal areas of the State of Assam.

In all these situation, the Governor of a state is empowered by the Constitution to use his discretionary powers.

Q. 7 Answer any ONE of the following (about 250 words) : 30

(a) Discuss Parliamentary Control over the Executive.

Important Points for Answer:

- *Control–Financial, Administrative, Legislative, Collective & Individual responsibility, Representative, Control through Information, Control by Suggestions*

Answer: Parliament controls executive in the following ways :

- Financial Control
- Administrative Control
- Legislative Control
- Collective and Individual Responsibility
- Representative Control
- Control through Information
- Control by Suggestions

- **Financial Control :** The Government is required to pass budget and financial bill in both the Houses. Parliament does not allow the Government to expense unnecessarily. The Government cannot withdraw any amount of money from the Consolidated Fund without Parliamentary authority.
- **Administrative Control :** Generally, Parliament does not interfere in Administrative matters but if any policy is formed in wrong way, Parliament may ask for explanations.
- **Legislative Control :** While enacting any law in Parliament, the Government needs to explain its all provisions and answer questions asked by the members of Parliament. Thus, it does not allow the executive to enact any arbitrary acts.
- **Collective and Individual Responsibility :** The whole council of ministers is answerable to Lok Sabha for any step taken by any of the minister of the council of ministers. Even the minister is answerable individually to the Lok Sabha for steps taken by officials of his department. If Lok Sabha does not approve the act of the minister, the whole cabinet has to resign, because of collective responsibility.
- **Representative Control :** Members of Parliament represents different sections of people. They ask questions to the executives as representatives and thus they save the interest of their people through representation.
- **Control through Information :** People, and through them, members of Parliament have unlimited right to seek information.regarding any policy formed or steps taken by the executives. They ask for information and keep control over any irresponsible acts.
- **Control by Suggestions :** Parliament makes some useful suggestions during the discussion of any policy. Members do not allow the executives to make defective policies.

These are various modes how Parliament controls over the executives.

(b) Identify the major obstacles in the smooth functioning of Parliamentary democracy in India.

Important Points for Answer:
- *Parliamentary democracy*
- *Obstacles in India–Hung Parliament, Absence of strong opposition, Regionalism, Criminalisation, Non-secular politics, Lack of (Morality, Literacy, Education), Corruption, Absence of Healthy discussion.*

Answer: India adopted Parliamentary Democracy after independence. After more than half a century of this Parliamentary democracy, the major obstacles noticed so far, in its smooth functioning are :

- **Hung Parliament** : However, this factor has emerged in last decade, nineties, but it has been proved a major obstacle in forming stable governments. It led to frequent elections and ineffective functions of the Governments.
- **Absence of strong opposition party** : Indian Parliament never get a strong and ideal political party to stand as opposition party in Parliament. A strong opposition can effectively play a role in the formation of Government policies. Opposition is not meant to be an obstacle even in effective and necessary decisions just for political reasons.
- **Regionalism** : In last some decades, Indian politics has noticed growth of many regional parties. Problem is not with their being regional, but they sometimes have proved to be hindrances in national interests. These small and regional parties, even effect the stability of the Government.
- **Criminalisation of Politics** : Today, many politicians are with criminal records. Elections are won at the tip of gun. Even in Parliament, criminalisation has affected neutrality.
- **Non-secularism, Castism, etc.** : Nowadays, religion, caste, language and such undesirable factors are used in election propaganda. Such politicians are a threat against the national interest. They disturb Parliamentary proceedings and policy making over their such kind of political issues.
- **Lack of Morality, Literacy, Education** : Many parliamentarians are illiterate or not properly educated to understand and preserve the dignity of Parliament. Even many of the members of Parliament do not have morality enough to maintain the honour of these Houses.
- **Corruption** : Politicians have been started to be identified as corrupt generally. Corruption is so prevalent among political parties that it does not allow the functioning of Parliament on ideological basis. This has effect on the merits of its decisions.
- **Absence of Healthy Discussion** : In Parliament, policies and questions are discussed on their merit and demerit basis, but nowadays only a few politicians bother to get enough knowledge to go into the facts and details of the problem and bring out some effective solutions. The discussions are on the basis of Party politics, mostly.

These are major obstacles in the smooth functioning of Parliamentary democracy in India.

Q. 8 Answer any TWO of the following (about 150 words each) : **2 × 15 = 30**

(a) Highlight the significance of Forty Fourth Amendment to the Constitution of India.

Important Points for Answer:	
• *44th Amendment*	•*Significant changes*

Answer: Forty-fourth (Constitutional) Amendment Act-1978 is a landmark in our constitutional amendments. It has not just restored various provisions of the Constitution which were distorted by the 42nd Amendment Act-1976, but also made some specific provisions providing safeguards against possible misuse.

It has made important changes in the following ways :

- It restored the term of the Lok Sabha and the State Legislative Assembly to five years.
- Question of disqualification of members of Parliament or State Legislature is to be decided, as originally provided by the President or the Governor.
- In Fundamental Rights, it made Articles 20 and 21 non-suspendable even during the Emergency.
- Article 31 is taken out from the Fundamental Rights and now Right to Property, is an ordinary legal right only.
- Now the President can return the advise of the Council of Ministers for its reconsideration.
- For the proclamation'of Emergency, written advise of the Cabinet and not of the Prime Minister only, is required.

Article 352 now requires that the proclamation must be approved within one month and not two months.

- Emergency can be revoked by a simple majority and for this a special session can be summoned by the Speaker or the President on the notice by One-Tenth membership of the Lok Sabha.
- The Presidential rule in the State can be imposed for a limited period of six months and it can be continued only if certain conditions, mentioned therein, prevails.
- Some safeguards against preventive detention are inserted in Article-22.
- It again restored the power of the Supreme Court regarding the elections of the President and the Vice-President.
- Emergency provisions are made justiciable.

Thus, drastic changes in the Constitution, for the safeguards, have been made by this amendment.

(b) Identify the major Fundamental Duties.

Important Points for Answer:
- *Constitutional provisions*
- *Towards nation*
- *Towards society*
- *Towards humanity, environment, etc.*

Answer: Part IV A, containing a single Article-51 A was inserted by the Constitution (forty-second Amendment) Act-1976. It enumerates the 'Fundamental Duties' of every citizen of India. However, no citizen can be punished for its violation, but they are expected to be followed by citizens. After 86th Amendment-2002, there are eleven fundamental duties.

We can classify them as under :

❍ **Towards Nation :**

- To abide by Constitution.
- To respect the National Anthem, the national flag and ideals of our national struggle for freedom.
- To uphold sovereignty and integrity of India.
- To render national service, defend the country.

❍ **Towards Society**

- To promote harmony and spirit of brotherhood.
- To transcend religious, linguistic and regional or sanctional diversities.
- To renounce derogatory practices to the dignity of women.
- To safeguard public property and abjure violence.

❍ **Towards Humanity, Environment, etc.**

- To protect and improve environment.
- To strive towards excellence in all spheres.
- Duty of parents or guardians to provide opportunity to children or wards betweei age of six and fourteen.
- To develop scientific temper.

(c) Explain the relevance of Rajya Sabha as a second chamber in the federal set up of Indian Parliamentary System.

Important Points for Answer:

- *Rajya Sabha - composition*
- *Federal set up*
- *Functions and Powers*
- *Requirement of Rajya Sabha*

Answer: Rajya Sabha is the permanent house of Parliament, representing states and people indirectly. It is not dissolved even in the time of emergency.

It is vested with equal powers to that of the Lok Sabha, except in matters of Money bills. It works as a revising body over the acts passed by Lok Sabha. It re-considers those legislations and brings the defects to the notice of Lok Sabha, which being a busy and much politicised House, could not have noticed it. It returns bills for reconsideration with some amendments to the Lower House and prevents it to take hasty and faulty decisions.

In emergency, it plays an important role, when the Lower House is dissolved, the Government has to pass the acts in Rajya Sabha. Sometimes, when the ruling party has not enough majority in Rajya Sabha, it is prevented from taking decisions with political motives.

Generally, experts, experienced and honourable politicians, social workers and academicians are represented in Rajya Sabha. They are less motivated by politics and so keep a check over the politicians, who may sometimes ignore national interests for their personal political gains.

In India, especially Rajya Sabha is vested with some specific powers, like :

- Article 249 empower Rajya Sabha to pass a resolution to declare that in national interests, some provisions in the state list can be enacted by Parliament.
- Article 312 empowers Rajya Sabha to create new categories of the All India Services, by a resolution.

Because of all these factors, Rajya Sabha helps the federation function smoothly.

Q. 9 Answer the following (about 20 words each) : $5 \times 2 = 10$

(a) What is a point of order? When can it be raised?

Answer: It is a process to suspend the business before the House. It is raised when the process is not in accordance with the rules and regulations of the House, to assist the presiding officer.

(b) What is a Privilege Motion?

Answer: If any member of Legislature does not inform to or keep secret from the House any information or presents it wrongly, other member can pass this motion.

(c) State the difference between Council of Ministers and the Cabinet.

Answer: The Council of Ministers is the body to aid and advise the President, consisting the Cabinet Ministers, Union Ministers of the state level, etc. But the Cabinet is inner body of it which consists only Cabinet Ministers.

(d) How is the Vice President of India elected?

Answer: The Vice-President of India is elected by an electoral college consisting members of both Houses of Parliament. System of proportional representation and means of single transferable vote, by secret ballot is adopted.

(e) What is meant by 'Sine-die' adjournment?

Answer: 'Sine-die' means for an uncertain period. When there are continuous obstacles in the proceedings of the House, Presiding officer adjourns the House 'Sine-die', without any reference to reassembly of the House.

Q. 10 Write on any ONE of the following (about 250 words) : 30

(a) Discuss the steps taken by Government to check child labour and promote child welfare.

Answer: Child labour is a curse upon society. It not only exploits tender age but also prevents growth of potentially intelligent citizens of the future. In India, child labour is prevalent in almost all parts and in every type of works.

Adverse effects of child labour has been accepted by the world and internationally, steps are being taken to check it. Indian Government has also taken some positive steps in this direction.

National policy of 1974 declared that No children below fourteen years of age shall be employed in any hazardous work uncertain labour. Government formed and implemented many policies under the National Policy to progress in this direction. Many children were removed from works in factory.

In 1986, Child Labour Prohibition Act was passed as a launch step to curb the evil. Based on this Act, child labour related National Policy was also prepared.

Indian Government set up a Committee to find out causes leading to child labour and problems arising out of them, under Shri M.S. Gurupadaswamy in 1979. It suggested some measures which were taken into consideration while forming suitable policies.

In case of M. C. Mehta vs. Union of India - 1987, the Supreme Court also directed to remove children from factories and other works which check or reduces their growth. After this case Parliament passed the Constitution (80th Amendment) Act, 2000 which prohibited child labour and made provisions for compulsory education to children of the age of 6 to 14 years as their fundamental right. Also, a fundamental duty was added for parents or guardians to take care of their all over development.

In addition to check of child labour, to give them opportunities to develop in all spheres of life, it is also required to promote child welfare, through positive actions. For child welfare, wholesome food, education, clean and encourageous environment with enough care are also necessary.

Government formed various policies for the development of education. Mid Day Meal programme is one of the steps for this target. Free education, books, etc., are also made available in addition to scholarship.

Vaccination, medical check-up in schools, co-curricular activities for their welfare are under implementation. In field of justice, children below fourteen years of age are treated as minors and are not generally given corporeal punishment but are sent to child-care homes where they are taught various skills of handicrafts, etc. So that they can earn and rehabilitate in society after sentence period.

All these steps for child labour eradication and promotion of child welfare are under implemented through various policies and acts at central and state levels apart from various programme of NGOs.

In 1994, in Sambhalpur, Thane and Gorwa districts, the National Child Labour Projects (NCLP) was launched for suitable programme implementations.

(b) Suggest measures for the eradication of wide spread corruption in Public Life India.

Important Points for Answer:

- *Corruption*
- *Measures suggested*

Answer: Corruption has spread from bottom to top in all branches of public governance system in India. To eradicate corruption, steps can be suggested like :

- Politicians are generally regarded as the main source of corruption. There should be strict laws debaring life-time election and any public post apart from string, punishment for proved corruption.
- Corrupt practices in bureaucracy has spread like an epidemic which can only be controlled through a transport system of work. Records of bureaucracy should be referred at regular interval of time and if found any involvement in corrupt practices, they should be removed from posts.
- Anti-corruption Bureau, Central Branch of Investigation and other organisation should actively investigate into corruption matters and their control should be in judiciary and not in executives.
- Transparency in public dealings is required so that no secret practice can lead to corruption.
- Laws of our country and procedures of public dealings must be made easy so that a general person can understand them and follow without involving any procedural complexities, people should be educated on these matters.
- Help to citizens in curbing corrupt practices must be made very quick and reactive.
- Whistle Blower incidents has provoked a fear among public due to lack of safety and security of the person who tries to expose corruption. Proper investigation, secrecy and security should be there to make the person feel safe who acts to remove corruption.
- Punishment must be made stringent for corruption in public life.

Not only laws and policies but also people's awareness and active support are required to remove corruption from public life.

Q. 11 Write on any TWO of the following (about 125 words each) : 2 × 10 = 20

(a) The issue of gender equality in India.

Answer: This issue has gained a central position in political and social debate. In India, the Constitution provides that there shall be no discriminations on basis of sex, i.e. gender. Laws also regard both men and women equal, yet in practical life, there is a wide gap in matters of development, progress and prosperity.

Women, though are called to be provided with equal opportunities in matters of education and jobs, are clearly not avail of them. Level of education is obviously not equal but even proportionately literacy level has also a wide gap among male and female.

Sex ratio shows a gap of 67 women less than per one thousand men in India. Social practices and policies are yet not so developed to provide females enough chances for their all over development.

Debates are there to provide them more and more reservations in education and jobs apart from facilities for their upliftment. In some fields, a few female persons have achieved glorious success but they are exceptions and not generality of Indian gender issues.

(b) Natural Heritage and Cultural Heritage.

Answer: We are presented with many resources and locations naturally without any effort in their creation. Although they are very useful in the progress of human beings they have been sometimes used thoughtlessly and put into danger of their existence in natural form. Various sanctuaries, National Parks, Biosphere reserves, rivers, mountains, plateaus, valley species of animals, birds and plants are included in natural heritage.

Human culture and development owes much to there heritage. They have contributed and are continue to contribute in our progress. Their use must be in sustainable manner, so that no heritage site is endangered to its existence.

Cultural heritage are those which are made by human beings, dance styles, folk music, art, sculpture, architectural monuments, literature, etc. are, cultural heritage developed by various cultures in the world by their distinct traditions and customs and they expose the evolution and development of human society and culture.

UNESCO prepared a list of Natural Heritage and Cultural Heritage of the World every year. These heritage sites or monuments are conserved with great importance and value to human society.

(c) Identify the types of disabilities.

Answer: Mainly there are two types of disabilities :

(i) Physical disability,

(ii) Mental disability.

But under Physical disabilities, many such types of disabilities are found. The Disabled Persons Act, 1995 enlists and considers disabilities to

Audio-visual disabilities - Deafness or blindness disabilities, related to bones, and some others.

Some mental problems, undeveloped state of mind etc. are considered as mental disabilities under the Act.

Physical Disabilities:

- Blindness : Not necessarily total blind person but it includes lack of vision of one eye, less vision, etc.
- Deafness : Inability to hear or less ability.
- Bone related disabilities include incapacity to work in any muscle on bone or joints resulting in uselessness of that part of body.
- Disability may come by accidents etc., like cutting of hand, leg or loss of eye, etc.

Mental Disabilities :

There are some persons born, idiot, they cannot count twenty or cannot tell name of parents. Such mental uncapacities of various degree, mental disorder and unsoundness of mind are included in mental disabilities.

Q. 12 Write notes on any TWO of the following (about 125 words each) : $2 \times 10 = 20$

(a) What are the distinctive features of the Lokpal Bill introduced in the Parliament this year?

Important Points for Answer:
- *Bill detail*
- *Provisions - Constitution, sphere, independence, procedure and powers*

Answer: The Lokpal Bill introduced in the Lok Sabha on 14th August, 2001 aim at curing corruptions in high offices by following provisions :

- **Constitution:**

  A Committee will appoint the Lokpal and two other members for three years term. The chairman of Lokpal body will be acting or retired Chief Justice of India. Member will be from retired judges or chief justice of the Supreme Court.

- **Sphere:**

  All members of Council of Ministry, Legislators and the Prime Minister will be covered under its sphere.

- **Impartiality of post:**

  It is immunised by political interferences. They can be removed only by the order of the President on proved misbehaviour or infirmity by the Committee of the Chief Justice of India and two other judges of the Supreme Court.

- **Procedure and Powers :**

  It cannot proceed without any report against the Prime Minister, Minister or a Legislator. It is just a recommendatory body to report to the Parliament but cannot punish the corrupt person.

(b) What is the Prime Minister's Five-point agenda for India's development as a Knowledge Society?

Answer: Prime Minister's Five-point agenda is :

- Primary level education by the year 2010, to educate all at primary level, provide access for higher education, increase number of educational institutions like IITs, IIMs, etc.
- In Biotechnology, enlarge the horizons of knowledge, create employment and bio-genetic knowledge for medicine. Develop human resources and potential.
- Protect intellectual property rights, indigenous knowledge and art from electronic media spread.
- To promote IT exports through various provisions for communication and information technology developed and progress, to be aided by information and broadcasting ministers.
- To constitute "Education Development Finance Corporation" in Private sectors.

All these were the main points of the five-point agenda of the Prime Minister, aiming at making India a hub of knowledge and development.

(c) What are the preconditions for the growth of Civil Society? Is Indian democracy conducive to it?

Important Points for Answer:
- *Civil society - meaning*
- *Indian Condition*

Answer: Civil Society means a developed, modern, intellectual, healthy, prosperous and stable society with dignified conditions of life of a citizen in it.

It can be achieved with the fulfillment of some basic requirements. Some pre-conditions for it are:- higher education and literacy level, enough technical and modern knowledge to access the technological inventions and their benefits, intelligent and moral political awareness to govern the society, ideal manner, growth of literature and art to make lives interesting and wholesome, self reliance or at least easy fulfillment of necessities of life, health related services and facilities of modern and efficient technology with skillful professionals, economic prosperity, equality of male-female and religious harmony opportunities to every person to achieve his all over development.

All these ideal pre conditions can construct a civil society. Indian democracy, however, do not fulfill all the pre-conditions. It can provide a base for it and have some characteristics and potential to be developed into a civil society, but not yet, for and only if grown in proper direction.

Q. 13 Write about the following (about 20 words each): 5 × 2 = 10

(a) Anthrax

Answer: It is a disease, quickly spreading through air, caused by bacterias and affecting respiratory system of a person, resulting in death in a short period of time.

(b) Radiation and its effects

Answer: The rays emitted from radioactive matter is called radiation. It damages or destroys cells and so causes skin diseases, cancer, etc. Even they are useful in treatment also.

(c) The Statue of Liberty

Answer: It is in New York, a city of USA, is considered as the symbol of freedom.

(d) George Walker Bush

Answer: He is the President of the USA. He is in controversy due to American attack on Iraq under his government.

(e) Genome

Answer: The whole sequence of genes is DNA, which controls heredity in human being, as Genome. Scientists attempt to map human Genome.

SOLVED PAPERS

PAPER–II

Time Allowed : Three Hours *Maximum Marks: 300*

Candidates should attempt ALL questions strictly in accordance with the instructions given under each question.

Q. 1 Answer any two of the following (in about 150 words each) : 15 × 2 = 30*

(a) Discuss the major issues in Indo-US relations in recent times.

Important Points for Answer:
- *Indo-US relations*
- *Recent Issues*
- *Effects*

Answer: Recently, especially after the attack on the World Trade Centre of America, both countries have agreed to combat terrorism. India supported US actions over Taliban.

Attack on Indian Parliament has attracted support from Bush administration. Over Kashmir issue also, America has pressurised Pakistan and so the process of fight against terrorism has been accelerated. Both countries have frequently made statements to this effect.

India is being considered strategically important by America due to Chinese presence in the Indian ocean. Also, due to China and Pakistan's relations with North Korea makes India more important for America. Due to all these reasons also, American policy has been changed towards India.

Visit of Indian Prime Minister, recently, to New York has turned Indo-US relations towards the direction of strategic cooperation. Bilateral agreement over security and technology training cooperation has been inked. Both decided to prepare Anti-Missile shields jointly. The issues related to security and strategic importance have been floated over the surface in recent times between India and USA, apart from their cooperation in trade and other issues.

(b) Discuss the impact of the collapse of the Soviet Union on Indo-Russian relations.

Important Points for Answer:
- *Collapse of USSR*
- *Indo-US relations*
- *Progress and cooperation*

Answer: The collapse of the Soviet Union has, infact, no effect on Indo-Russian relation, if we consider in the declining terms. But if positive changes are to be considered, Russia has performed the inheritance of the USSR in true sense.

India had to, of course, make some agreements with other separated parts of the USSR according to strategy and foreign policy, depending on individual country.

But Russia and India remained in the same terms. Russian support continue to India. Russia's position in the Security Council was not affected and so India had no fear. Even after the end of cold war, Indo-American relations also get a boost.

Russian President and Indian Prime Ministers or Presidents have frequently visited each other. Recent visit of Russian President Vladimir Putin in December, 2002 and bilateral agreements during it shows solidarity of this relations. Both countries accorded to cooperate in defence, security, trade, scientific research and other fields apart from combating terrorism, in their 'Delhi Declaration' and 8 other agreements.

Russian support to India on Kashmir issue is intact. Though Russia stopped supply of Cryogenic engines due to American pressure but it does not break us from concluding that Indo-Russian relations have been progressive.

(c) Discuss the recent trends in India's relations with China.

Important Points for Answer:
- *IIndo-China relations*
- *Issues involved*
- *Recent progress*

Answer: China visit of the Indian Prime Minister, Mr. Atal Bihari Vajpayee in June, 2003 shows positive turn of Sino-India's relations. During this visit, both countries came to conclusion that leaving the disputes to be solved with time on another route, a new route for cooperation, simultaneuosly can be created.

In this way, both countries agreed to increase trade cooperation via Himachal Pradesh, Uttarakhand and Sikkim. Both countries have a big amount of trade through illegal and two number routes, which can now be prevented and legalised.

After the talk, China removed Sikkim from its website as a separate nation and show it as a part of India. Both have some disagreements about Arunachal, Sikkim and Tibet regions apart from boundry disputes.

For constructive results, both nations have constituted a joint working group of experts. Tai Ping Quo on the part of China and Brijesh Mishra from India will head these groups and will bring out solutions.

Thus, cooperating with each other in the race of development and Asian solidarity, India and China have taken a good policy of two track simultaneously - cooperation on first, solving problem on second.

Q. 2 Answer the following (in about 20 words each) : $2 \times 5 = 10$

(a) Discuss the importance of the Agra Summit on Indo-Pakistan relations.

Answer: It increase co-operation between both countries and the Bus Service between Delhi and Lahore has been started.

(b) What has been the nature of "Track II diplomacy" between India and Pakistan?

Answer: Journalists, Artist, Celebrities and Social workers, individually and in groups, apart from legislators have come and gone on non-official visits to increase interaction under Track- II diplomacy.

(c) Discuss the major irritants to Indo-Bangladesh relations.

Answer: Apart from old problems of illegal infiltration into Indian border and water disputes, new concerns are on the points of Sino-Bangladesh relations and activities of ISI on Bangladesh land.

(d) Discuss India's policy towards international terrorism.

Answer: India supports policy of combating terrorism under the UN and common for all nations. India is in hard-core opposition of terrorism in any form.

(e) In what sense is Indo-Nepal cooperation important for both countries' national security?

Answer: Both countries are part of same geographical region, bordering to each other and commonly with some other nations co-operation in peace would help security of both.

Q. 3 Answer the following (in about 20 words each) : $2 \times 5 = 10$

(a) Under what conditions are NRIs permitted to remit deposits in India in any currency of their choice?

Answer: NRI's are permitted under Non-Resident Foreign Currency accounts to remit deposits in India in any currency apart from some specialised schemes being declared from time to time.

(b) How can NRIs be attracted to invest in India?

Answer: By providing security, facilities, more interests, attractive and liberal term apart from infrastructure, the NRIs can be attracted to invest in India.

(c) What is the significance of the *Pravasi Bhartiya Divas* in modern India?

Answer: Besides soliderating cultural and social bonds, this day is important for economic and political strengthening of India by NRIs cooperation.

(d) In what ways did Idi Amin make life difficult for the people of Indian origin in his country?

Answer: He ordered to evacuate Uganda to Asians without compensating them and migrants had to return home leaving their all properties there. PIOs had to flee India.

(e) What is "Brain Drain"?

Answer: The migration of intellectual people for profession to foreign countries leaving home country is called "Brain drain", as their services can not be availed to home nation.

Q. 4 Answer any one of the following (in about 250 words) : 30

(a) Write a note on the strategy of planning in India since 1951.

Important Points for Answer:
- *Planning*
- *Strategy*
- *Main objectives of all plans*

Answer: The strategy means a decided path to achieve some long term objectives. The main points which have been adopted in and can indicate the strategy are :

- Increase in national income and per capita income.
- Improvement in agricultural production to be self-reliant in food grains production.
- Industrialisation specially in basic and heavy industries.
- More Employment opportunities.
- Equality in income and wealth distribution.
- To achieve self-reliance.
- Eradication of Poverty.
- Economic growth and price stability.

Measures adopted in various Five Years Plan (FYP) can be pointed out as under

- First Five Year Plan (1951-56) : aimed at rehabiliting the economy affected by the Second World War (1939-45), checking inflationary tendencies, saving food crisis with special focus on agriculture, initiating, a new mixed economic pattern.
- Second Five Year Plan (1956-1961) : was a major step towards industrialisation. On Mahalanobis Model it focused on basic and heavy industries on socialistic pattern.
- Third Five Year Plan (1961-1966) : set its principal goal as to secure a marked advance towards self-sustaining growth. It implies savings and investment in the economy to rise sufficiently to secure a high rate of growth of income on a continuing basis.
- Plan Holiday (1966-1969) : During the Periods of 1966 to 1969, there were three annual plans viz. : 1966-67, 1967-68, 1968-69.
- Fourth Five Year Plan (1969-1974) : primarily wanted to achieve growth with stability and to be self-reliant in food-grain.
- Fifth Five Year Plan (1974-1978) : mainly concentrated on poverty eradication and self-reliance. Main focus was to ensure effective public procurement and distribution system, reduction of inequalities in income.
- Rolling Plan (1978-1980) : by the Janata Government, focused at enlarging the employment potential in agriculture and allied activities.
- Sixth Five Year Plan (1980-1985) : included a novel feature of controlling the growth of population through Voluntary adoption of small family norms. Main targets were to accelerate growth in infrastructural sectors, to check inflationary pressures and correction of balance of payment difficulties.
- Seventh Five Year Plan (1985-1990) : It decentralised planning and ensure full participation of people. Apart from target of alleviation of poverty it aimed to generate maximum productive employment opportunities.
- Eighth Five Year Plan (1992-1997) : Only fourth version was really implemented with objectives of containment of population growth, universalisation of elementary education, to generate surplus food for exports, to strengthening infrastructure in order to support growth process on a sustainable basis.

- Ninth Five Year Plan (1997-2002) : focuses at "Growth with Social Justice and Equality" by providing appropriate direction and balance to the socio-economic development of the country.
- Tenth Five Year Plan (2002-2007) : is continue with the objectives of achieving 8% of GDP growth rate, enhancement of human well-being and fulfill the requirements of basic social-services.

(b) What were the major recommendations of the Task Force on direct taxes appointed under the Chairmanship of Shri Vijay L. Kelkar?

Important Points for Answer:
• *Recommendations*

Answer: Two Task Forces were appointed under the Chairmanship of Shri Vijay L. Kelkar,

(i) The Task Force on Indirect Taxes,

(ii) The Task Force on-Direct Taxes.

The Task Force on Direct taxes submitted its final report to the Government in December 2002. Its major recommendations are as below :

A. Personal Income Tax

(i) Increase in exemption limit from Rs. 50,000 to 1,00,000 for general tax payers and Rs. 1,50,000 for widows and senior citizens.

(ii) Two tier tax rate, 20% upto 4 lakhs and 30% above 4 lakh, instead of present three tier.

(iii) Elimination of tax incentives U/S 88, 80 L etc.

(iv) Imposition of tax on Agricultural income above Rs. 1 lakh.

B. Corporate Tax

(i) Reduction in Corporate tax to 30% for domestic companies and 35% for foreign companies.

(ii) Elimination of Minimum Alternative Tax (MAT).

(iii) No tax on dividends to shareholders.

(iv) Exemption of long-term capital gains on listed equity.

(v) Reduction in general rate of depreciation from 25% to 15% for Plan and machinery.

(vi) Elimination of Sections 33 and 35 and no exemptions under them.

(vii) Tax on hotel expenditure to be merged with Service Tax.

(viii) Abolition of Wealth Tax.

C. Tax Administration

(i) To issue PAN (Permanent Account Number) to all citizens.

(ii) Expansion of tax-payer services, easy access through Internet and E-mail.

(iii) Transparency and objectivity.

(iv) Abolition of block assessment of Search and Seizure cases.

The emphasis of these major recommendations was laid down on :

- Raising the Income Tax Limit.
- Exemption to be given on rational basis.
- To concessional treatment of long-term capital gains.
- Abolition of Wealth tax etc.

Q. 5 Answer any two of the following (in about 150 words each) : **15 × 2 = 30**

(a) Outline the important objectives of the Tenth Five Year Plan.

Answer: The Tenth Five Year Plan (2002-2007) is aimed at the following important objectives :

- It aims at the target of 8 per cent GDP growth for 2002-07 period.
- Only GDP growth is not the criteria of development. It defines objectives in broader terms of enhancement of human well-being.
- It aims at providing adequate level of consumption of food and other consumer goods.
- Its one objective is to provide access to basic social services like health, education, basic sanitation facilities and drinking water.
- To fulfill these objectives, it sets some targets like :
  - To increase literacy to 75% by 2007.
  - To provide access to potable drinking water to all villages by 2012.
  - To reduce Infant Mortality Rate (IMR) to 45 per 1000 live births by 2007 and to 28 per 1000 live births by 2012.
  - To reduce Maternal Mortality Ratio (MMR) to 2 per 1000 live births by 2007 and to 1 by 2012.
  - To increase the forest cover to 25% by 2007 and to 33% by 2012.
  - To reduce poverty ratio by 5% by 2007 and by 15% by 2012.

All these are important objectives of the Tenth Five Year Plan.

(b) What is a Finance Commission?

Important Points for Answer:
• *Constitutional provisions*
• *Composition*
• *Function*

Answer: The President of India is required to appoint a Finance Commission under Article-280 of the Constitution of India. It is for the specific purpose of devolution of non-plan revenue resources. Its functions are to make recommendations to the President.

- From the net proceeds of taxes,
  - It distributes the shares of the Union and the States;
  - Also it allocates the share among the States.

- It decides the principles on which the Union will pay the grants-in-aid to the revenues of the states.
- It also recommends in regard to any other matters concerning the financial relations between the Union and the States.

Since the inauguration of the Constitution in 1951, the Finance Commissions are appointed regularly at and for the interval of five years.

Its recommendations are not mandatory to follow, yet it maintains the financial relations between the Union and the States in accordance with the changing needs of time.

(c) Point out the measures undertaken towards flexibility in capital account transaction during the recent past.

Important Points for Answer:
- *Flexibility - requirement*
- *Measures taken*

Answer: Tarapore Committee (1997) was constituted for suggesting measures for flexibility in capital account transactions. The committee suggested various measures for that of which some are implemented by the Government from time to time.

Measures :

– Liberal policies towards other economies.

– To repeal FERA, Foreign Exchange Regulation Act and implement Foreign Exchange Management Act (FEMA).

– For more flexibility, Government allowed more investment in institutional portfolio

– Use of GDR/ ADR to know the conditions of foreign markets.

– Liberal policy and less regulation towards Foreign Direct Investment.

– Bonds which can be exchanged to foreign currency and planting Rate Notes were issued.

– Foreign Currency Accounts were encouraged for the convenience of NRIs and other investors.

– NRI deposits schemes are being promoted.

All these steps are taken apart from making rupee fully convertible, for the encouragement of foreign investment in India.

Q. 6 Answer the following (in about 20 words each) : 2 × 15 = 30

(a) What is Plan Holiday?

Answer: Due to delay in the formation and implementation of the Fourth Plan, there were three annual plans during 1966 to 1969. This period is known as "Plan Holiday" in Indian Economy.

(b) Why did India have a surplus in current account balance in 2001-02 after a gap of 24 years?

Answer: Inflow level reached to 2 9% of GDP and so there was a surplus after 24 years gap in current account balance.

(c) What is Value Added Tax?

Answer: VAT is levied on the net increase of the value of the product at various stages of its production to exclude the possibility of double taxation and tax evasion.

(d) What is the main objective of the Competition Act, 2002?

Answer: To constitute a Regulating Commission to prevent the policy of nationalising or undertaking of companies under the Monopoly Restriction provisions.

(e) Name the two agencies that have helped to promote Foreign Direct Investment (FDI) in India.

Answer: FIPB - Foreign Investment Promotion Board and

FIIA - Foreign Investment Implementation Authority

are the two agencies that have helped to promote FDI in India.

(f) What is the main thrust of the Fiscal Responsibility and Budget Management Bill?

Answer: To legalise financial reforms and give priority to fiscal responsibility and Budget management of the Government.

(g) Highlight the main feature of the policy relating to buy-back of shares.

Answer: Companies buy-back their shares from the market from time to time to derive influential and profitable form to its assets and profits.

(h) Why was Janashree Bima Yojana introduced?

Answer: It was introduced to the people of 18 to 60 years both from rural and urban sectors living below poverty line to cover them under the Insurance policy.

(i) When was the idea of Agriculture Insurance Corporation mooted?

Answer: Under the National Agriculture Policy - the idea of Agricultural Insurance Corporation was mooted to cover all related aspects of Agriculture.

(j) What is the policy of the Government with respect to child labour?

Answer: Government has prohibited employeeing any children under the age of 14 years in any hazardous industry or work, making it illegal.

(k) Explain the objectives of the National Health Policy, 2002.

Answer: With proper planning in next two decades, to raise the Health Services at targeted world level, and provide basic health services to every person.

(l) What was the main objective of the 'Operation Blackboard' scheme?

Answer: To bring qualitative reforms in elementary level education and increase reach of education.

(m) Explain the essential feature of differential rate of interest scheme.

Answer: The public sector banks will lend one percent of its deposit in last year at the minimum interest rate of 4 per cent to the backward classes of society of which 40% will be to SCs and STs.

(n) Which are the three major items of expenditure of the Government of India on revenue account?

Answer: The three major items of expenditure of the GOI on revenue account are :

- Interest payment,
- Plan expenditure,
- Defence.

(o) What was the essential feature of the *Pradhan Mantri Gram Sadak Yojana*?

Answer: It is to construct roads to connect about 1 lakh villages in the next seven years (2007) and also to upgrade about 5 lakh kms of existing roads to provide connectivity through all weather roads.

Q.7 Answer any two of the following (in about 150 words each) : 15 × 2 = 30

(a) What is the 'Veto' in the UN-system?

Important Points for Answer:

- *UN-system*
- *Veto - meaning*
- *Merits*
- *Effectiveness*
- *Demerits*

Answer: The United Nations (UN) aims mainly at maintaining international peace and security, primary responsibility of which is upon the security council, one of its six principal organs of it.

The security council consists of, now fifteen member states of which five are permanent members since the conception of the UN. These five permanent members, known as P--5, have been provided with Veto power.

America, Russia, Britain, France and China are P-5 members, having nuclear capacity. To avoid any confrontation among them, every member is given power to reject any question or vote negatively. This negative vote has the effect to remove that matter from voting and no majority decision is required. This special voting power is given to prevent any clashes among these powerful nations, on any question and thus to make world peace possible in true sense.

In the absence of veto, any confrontation among these nuclear powers would have endangered the world. These veto can be used in any substantive, important question in voting and not in procedural questions.

In procedural questions, simple majority is required. But a procedural question can be turned into a substantive one by using 'veto' and thus giving rise to 'double-veto' system.

(b) Discuss the role of the NATO after the end of the Cold War.

Important Points for Answer:

- *NATO-functions*
- *Role played after cold war*

Answer: North Atlantic Treaty Organisation was established, under the leadership of America, on 4th April, 1949 by signing the North Atlantic Treaty by the member states which established the North Atlantic Alliance.

It is a defence alliance in political and military field, based on the UN Charter.

After the end of the cold war, America emerged as the sole super power in the World. NATO emerged as more important military organisation influencing European countries and removing Soviet influence. Even some of the Communist countries of Europe are now members of NATO, which exemplifies its political importance and influence over strategic concern of the countries.

The NATO has played a role of checking emergence of any strong power group to effect the solidarity of American and European alliance especially after end of the cold war.

Due to its impact on international politics, Russia has once again lead some countries to form a military organisation in Europe.

All these shows that NATO's role has remained strategically of central importance in the world.

(c) Discuss the role of the United Nations in the protection and promotion of Human Rights.

Important Points for Answer:
- *UN*
- *Human Rights*
- *Role of UN*

Answer: The Preamble of the UN charter envisages to conserve peace in the world and that is declared to be possible through economic, political, social development of human. In various provisions of the UN, it is expressly declared to avoid discrimination based only on the grounds of race, sex, language or religion.

The UN adopted 'The Universal Declaration of Human Rights-1948' in December 1948, which most countries of the world have accepted.

Other declaration also, of course apart from the Universal Declaration of Human Rights 1948, declare that every person has right to life, liberty, profess religion of own choice, free expression, right to work, right to dignity, right against bondage 1abour against exploitation, cruelty arid right against derogatory arrest and imprisonment. All these rights are must to be respected by all the nations.

The UN has established The Human Rights Commission and other agencies and organisation to upheld and protect Human Rights in thc world. It is also assisted by and provides various helps to many voluntary organisations in this direction

Q. 8 Answer the following (in about 20 words each) : **2 × 5=10**

(a) What do the following stand for :

(i) IBRD **(ii) UNHCR**

Answer:

(i) IBRD International Bank for Reconstruction and Development

(ii) UNHCR : United Nations High Commission for Refugees.

(b) Who is Hans Blix?

Answer: Hans Blix is the weapons inspector, appointed by the UN, to report about the presence of weapons of Mass Destructions in Iraq.

(c) Why was David Kelly in the news recently?

Answer: David Kelly was British expert appointed in Iraq. He committed suicide ther.

(d) What is the problem in Chechanya?

Answer: Chechanya is a part of Russia. Militants in Chechanya demand for a separate nation to which Russia does not agree. Bloody violence is the result.

(e) What is the significance of the Robin Island?

Answer: The Robin Island is included in the World Heritage List. It is the Island where Mr. Nelson Mandela was imprisoned for 27 years.

Q. 9 Answer the following (in about 20 words each) : 15 × 2 = 30

(a) What is the significance of Enola Gay in world history?

Answer: It was the aircraft which carried and dropped atom bomb on Hiroshima city of Japan on 6th August, 1945.

(b) Why is Guantanamo Bay in the news now?

Answer: A1 Qaida terrorists are kept imprisoned on the Bay of Guantanamo by America where it has Naval base.

(c) What is the theory of "clash of civilisations"?

Answer: Two different types of ideologies, when cannot mix up, produces clash of civilization.

(d) What does the theory of "end of history" mean?

Answer: It shows end of one type of ideology or concepts in the world and gives way to another one. e.g. war with swords has end of its history.

(e) Why was Robert Mugabe in the news recently?

Answer: The President of Zimbabwe, because of malpractices in elections and differences with "whites" is in news recently.

Q. 10 Answer any one of the following (in about 250 words): 30

(a) What do you understand by depletion of ozone layer and why is it considered harmful? Name ozone depleting substances and processes. What international ramifications took place to protect the ozone layer and what was the target agreed upon?

Important Points for Answer:

- *Ozone layer*
- *Depletion*
- *Causes - substances, process*
- *Ramifications*
- *Targets set up*

Answer: Ozone is a gas in the lower level of stratosphere. It is a kind of super-charged oxygen - 0_3. It makes a layer in the atmosphere which acts as a cover to the earth against ultraviolate radiation of the sun. The canopy of ozone layer is with variable extent, less dense near the surface of the earth compared to the height of 30 km.

Some pollutants in the atmosphere like chlorofluoro-carbons (CH_3) cause the depletion of ozone layer. These CFCs and other similar gases when reach to the stratosphere they are broken down by the ultraviolate radiation and as a result they liberate free atoms of chlorine or bromine. These atoms are highly reactive with ozone and disrupts the stratospheric chemistry. The reactions deplete ozone layer.

Due to depletion of ozone layer, the earth is exposed to the ultra-violate radiation. These rays cause harmful effect to living beings on the earth. It affects process of photosynthesis in plants. Raise in the temperature, various skin diseases, decrease of immunity, etc., are the probable results.

For the protection of ozone layer, Vienna Conference in March, 1985 was held. In September 1987, Montreal Protocol was signed. This was followed by the Kyoto Protocol of 1997.

The Montreal Protocol plans to phase out the use of CFCs and other ozone depleting substances. It called for the cessation of CFC production by 1996.

The Kyoto Protocol requires countries to take appropriate steps to reduce green house gases emission level at least 5% below 1990 level by 2008-12.

Apart from these International ramification, yarious conferences and programmes are also held all over the world regularly to protect the ozone layer.

September 16 is declared as the International Day for preservation of ozone by the Montreal Protocol - 1987.

Note : The Kyoto Protocol came into force in January, 2005.

(b) What is interactive television? What special advantages are derived by using. VOD services? What are the components of a typical VOD system? Which feature film was generated first entirely on computers and in which year?

Important Points for Answer:

- *Interactive television*
- *Technology*
- *VOD*
- *Advantage*
- *Film*

Answer: This is generally like a simple television or a personal computer, but it is more advantageous in form that it can be used to derive more informations and entertainment connecting internet. It is connected with the Internet services and so a separate computer is not required to access internet broadcasting. This television can be set up to use both types of services.

VOD services can be helpful in providing internet, telephone and broadcasting of television programmes through Broad Band Tripple Play. This enables a cable operator or user to have such combined services which are made possible by accessing to the Internet Protocol.

The internet protocol based VOD system can provide these facilities the network of the cable operators speedily and efficiently, without interferences, make the entertainment and information available more easily. According to the Internet Protocol, operators will be able to use internet access, voice over services and bro. of television programmes simultaneously in a single service system, VOD. VOD will thus made possible the entry into Internet Protocol for world class facilities.

For education, research and conferences, all the three services, combined can give a new dimension to the information technology. It will also reduce the expenditure of entry and delivery into Internet Protocol, which would be a boon for scientists, technicians, academicians and experts in various fields.

It will require some necessary devices and facilities to enable a user to access VOD services. These requirements are :

- User interface and display
- Network interface
- Local server and database
- Multimedia distributor
- High speed

In 2000, Tway story was the first film generated entirely on computers.

Q. 11 Answer any two of the following (in about 150 words each) : 15 × 2 = 30

(a) What does the solar system consist of? Discuss the motion of the entire solar system as a whole and also the motion of most of the bodies forming the solar system.

Important Points for Answer:

- *Solar system*
- *Components*
- *Motions*

Answer: The solar system consist of a star called the Sun at the centre and all the objects that travel around the sun. The objects travelling around the sun include nine planets and many satellites that travel around them, asteroids, meteoroids, comets and interplanetary dust and plasma.

Nine planets, from the sun are - Mercury, Venus, Earth, Mars, Jupiter, Saturn, Uranus, Neptune, and Pluto.

The solar system is located in a corner of the Milky Way galaxy and it, as a whole, travel around the centre of the galaxy.

The bodies like planets, travel around the sun in their definite orbits and also rotate over their own axis. Planets have two types of motions, concurrently in the solar system:

(1) Revolutionary Motion - they revolve around the sun at their centre, in their definite orbits.

(2) Rotationary Motion - they rotate over their own axis while revolving around the sun. The satellites, that most of the planets consist of, travel around their respective planets and with them around the sun also.

Asteroids, generally found between the orbits of Mars and Jupiter, also travel around the Sun.

Other celestial bodies in the solar system travel constantly in definite or indefinite orbits around the sun.

(b) In which year and by which countries was International Space Station (ISS) launched? How many countries are participating in this program? What are the unique studies being made in the station which could not be made so accurately on the earth?

Important Points for Answer:		
• *ISS*	• *Studies*	• *Features*

Answer: International Space Station (ISS) was launched in 1993 by the USA and Russia. Countries from European Union, Canada and Japan are participating in this program.

There are some situations which help in researches based on the origin and evolution of life on the earth. Special characterized effects of low gravity and vacuum on life can be experimented here very accurately which is not possible on the earth.

Many questions can be, hopefully, answered through research and study in the space station. How did life origin on the earth? Did it transferred to the earth from other planet or matters of space? Did life origin on other planets? What is the effect of space condition on the health of space researches and travellers? How did the solar system come in this condition of present?

All these miseries of universe would be attempted to solve. This space station will also research and provide information for other space missions.

(c) Discuss the elements of 'frozen semen technology'. What are 'embryo transfer' 'transgenic animals', 'DNA recombinant technique'?

Important Points for Answer:
- *Frozen semen technology*
- *Transgenic animals*
- *Embryo transfer*
- *DNA recombinant technique*

Answer: Frozen Semen Technology is used to produce improved quality animal generation. With the help of liquid Nitrogen, semen of a male animal, of species with desired quality, are frozen for a long period in 'Semen Bank' for its use in future to get offsprings by artificial insemination. This is called "frozen semen technology".

Embryo transfer: To produce hybrid offspring, embryo developed in male animal of desired characteristics, are transferred into the uterus of another animal to develop the offspring in its body. By this technique, offsprings with desired qualities can be produced even by less quality animals.

Transgenic animals : In such animals, a transgene is integrated with the genome of the original animal. The gene is entered through DNA by plasmids or DNA vector based on virus. Such transgenic animals possess qualities of both the species.

DNA Recombinant Technique : It is possible to transfer gene from one genome to another through this technique.

Q. 12 Answer the following (in about 20 words each) : $2 \times 5 = 10$

(a) What is 'Sympathetic Haptics'?

Answer: A method of feeling transfer through internet broadcasting. A user's touch and pressure is received by Data Globe, it is sent via internet to another user against him and he can feel them through same divice.

(b) What are special features of 'Linux'?

Answer: 'Linux' is an open source operating system based on UNIX. It is freely down loadable, user supported and being considered as an alternative to windows. It is suitable for certain business applications.

(c) What is an operating system? List the basic services provided by an operating system.

Answer: An Operating System is a programme that runs a computer. It manages files and folders, organizes the internal activities of the computer and its peripheral devices. Moves data to and from devices.

(d) What is an 'Internet Worm'? Explain DDoS.

Answer: Internet Worm is a programme spread through internet and gets activated by itself. DDoS means Distributor's Denial of Service.

(e) What do the following stand for?

(i) **POSIX** - Portable Operating System Interface.

(ii) **EPROM** - Erasable, Programmable Read Only Memory.

(iii) **MODEM** - Modulator demodulator.

(iv) **COBOL** - Common Business Oriented Language.

Q. 13 (a)In the year 2001 there were 18000 workers in a certain factory, of which 13000 were members of a trade union, 12% of workers were women and 60% of them were members of the trade union. In the year 2002 the number of workers increased by 6% of which 480 were women. At the same time the trade union membership of women fell by 304 while the total membership increased by 10%. In the non-members category, the ratio of men and women was 4 :1 in this year. Tabulate this information and supply the missing figures. 8

Answer: Details of workers in a company and trade union membership in 2001-2002.

Year	2001			2002		
Membership / Sex	T-U Member	T-U N-Member	Total	T-U Member	T-U N-Member	Total
Men	11704	4136	15840	13308	3132	16440
Women	1296	864	2160	992	1648	2640
Total	13,000	5,000	18,000	14,300	4,780	19,080

Missing figures are derived from the given data.

e.g. = Total workers = 18,000

Trade-union member = 13,000

Non-member = 18,000 – 13,000 = 5000

And also like,

12% of total workers were women.

So, total women workers $= \frac{12}{100} \times 18,000 = 2,160$

And, of them 60% were trade union members.

Therefore, Total trade-union member women $= \frac{60}{100} \times 2,160 = 2,160$

And so on.

(b) The following table gives the frequency distribution of height for 180 adults males :

Height (in cm)	Frequency
144.5 – 149.5	3
149.5 – 154.5	5
154.5 – 159.5	24
159.5 – 164.5	54
164.5 – 169.5	60
169.5 – 174.5	27
174.5 – 179.5	4
179.5 - 184.5	3

Draw the two ogives ("less than" and "greater than" type cumulative frequency curves). Find the point of their intersection and comment on its significance. **8**

Answer: At first, we have to tabulate the frequency distribution in 'less than' and 'more than' form.

Table of frequency distribution in the forms of 'less than' and 'more than'

Height (cm)	Frequency	'Less than'	Cumulative frequency	'More than'	Cumulative frequency
144 5-149 5	3	144 5	0	144 5	180
149 5-154 5	5	149.5	3	149.5	177

154 5-159 5	24	154.5	8	154.5	172
159 5-164 5	54	159.5	32	159.5	148
164 5-169 5	60	164.5	86	164.5	94
169 5-174 5	27	169.5	146	169.5	34
174 5-179 5	4	174.5	173	174.5	7
179 5-184 5	3	179.5	177	179.5	3
	180	184.5	180	184.5	0

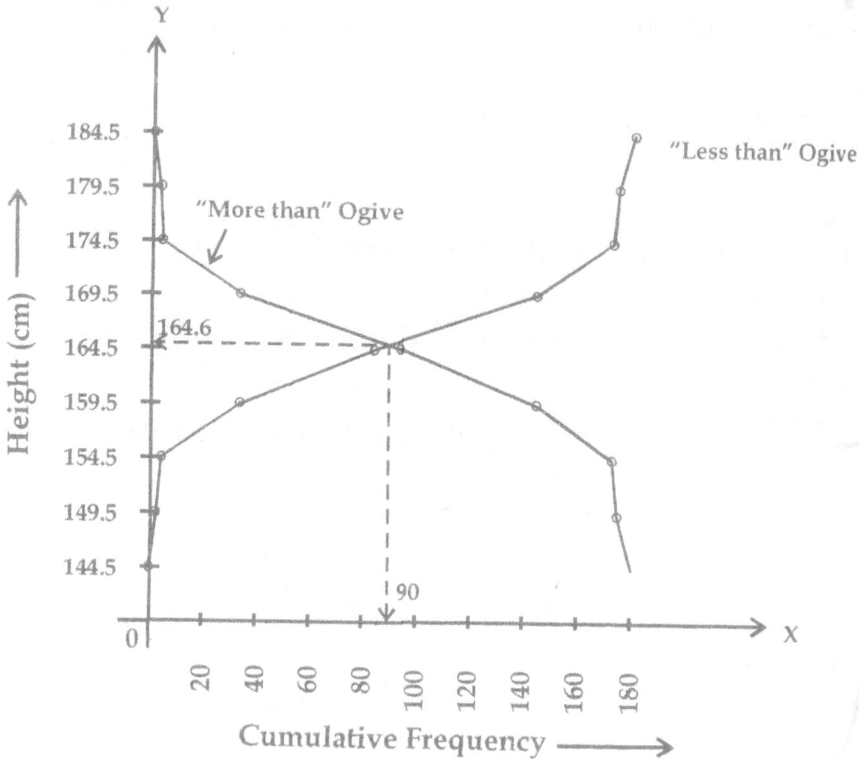

Scale Used : X-axis : 1 unit = 5 cm

164 .6 cm is the intersection point, which also represents 90 students on each side. This point is the medium value of height of adults. Above and below 164.6 cm, there are same number of students, i.e. 90 each.

Q. 14 (a) The mean and variance of a set of 60 observations are 10 and 4 respectively while for a subset of 40 observations these measures are 11 and 2.25 respectively. Find the mean and variance of the other subset. 8

Answer: Mean = 10, Variance = 4, Total observations = 60

Let the mean be in points for our convenience. So, for the 60 observations, the mean is 10 points.

Total points = Mean points × Total observations

= 10 × 60

= 600

While taking its subset of 40 observations, the mean is 11 and variance = 2.25

Total points in the subset of 40 observations = Mean points x Total observations

= 11 × 40 = 440

So, the points in the remaining subset = 600 – 440 = 160

And its mean = Points/Observations = 160/20 = 8

The mean for other subset = 8

Calculation of variance = σ^2

for 60 observations = $\sigma^2 = 4$

for 40 observations = $\sigma_1^2 = 2.25$

for 20 observations = $\sigma_2^2 = ?$

$$\sigma^2 = \frac{N_1\left(\sigma_2^1 + d_2^1\right) + N_2\left(\sigma_2^2 + d_2^2\right)}{N_1 + N_2}$$

here, N = observations, 60

N_1 = observations$_1$, 40

N_2 = observations$_2$, 20

d_1 = Mean of subset – Mean of set

= 11 – 10 = 1

$d_1 = 1$

= Mean of subset – Mean of set

8 – 10 = –2

$d_2 = -2$

$$\text{Now}, \sigma^2 = \frac{N_1\left(\sigma_2^1 + d_1^2\right) + N_2\left(\sigma_2^2 + d_2^2\right)}{N_1 + N_2}$$

Substituting values,

$$4 = \frac{40\left[2.25 + (1)^2\right] + 20\left[\sigma_2^2 + (-2)^2\right]}{40 + 20}$$

$$\therefore 4 = \frac{40\,[2.25 + 1] + 20\left[\sigma_2^2 + 4\right]}{60}$$

$$\therefore 240 = 40\,(3.25) + 20\sigma_2^2 + 80$$

$$\therefore 240 - (130 + 80) = 20\sigma_2^2$$

$$\therefore 30 = 20\sigma_2^2$$

$$\therefore \sigma_2^2 = 1.5 \textbf{ Ans}$$

Variance for the another subset is 1.5 and its mean is 8.

(b) The three outcomes of an experiment; w_r w_2 and w_3 are such that w_3 is twice as likely to occur as w_2 which is twice as likely to occur as w_3. Find the probability of occurrence of each of the three outcomes. **8**

Answer: **w_1** is twice → **w_2**

w_2 is twice → w_3

The possibility of occurrence of w_1 is double than that of w_2.

So, probability of $w_2 = w_1/2$

In the same way, probability of occurrence of w_3 is half than that of w_2.

So, $w_3 = w_2/2$

and now probability of $w_3 = \frac{w_2}{2} \frac{\frac{w_2}{2}}{2} = \frac{w_1}{4}$

Probability of occurrence of $w_1 = \dfrac{w_1}{w_1 + \frac{w_1}{2} + \frac{w_1}{4}}$

$$= \frac{w_1}{\frac{4w_1 + 2w_1 + w_1}{4}} = \frac{4w_1}{7w_1}$$

Probability of occurrence of $w_1 = 4/7$

Probability of occurrence of $w_2 = \dfrac{\frac{w_1}{2}}{w_1 + \frac{w_1}{2} + \frac{w_1}{4}}$

$$= \frac{\frac{w_1}{2}}{\frac{4w_1 + 2w_1 + w_1}{4}} = \frac{\frac{4w_1}{2}}{7w_1} = \frac{2w_1}{7w_1}$$

Probability of occurrence of $w_3 = 1/7$

$$\text{Probability of occurrence of } w_3 = \frac{\frac{w_1}{4}}{w_1 + \frac{w_1}{2} + \frac{w_1}{4}}$$

$$= \frac{\frac{w_1}{4}}{\frac{4w_1 + 2w_1 + w_1}{4}} = \frac{4 \times \frac{w_1}{4}}{7w_1} = \frac{w_1}{7w_1}$$

Probability of occurrence of w_3 =1/7

Thus, the probability of occurrence of each w_1, w_2 and w_3 are 4/7, 2/7 and 1/7 respectively.

Q. 15 (a) What are the problems that a statistician encounters in the process of construction of index number? **2**

Answer: The Statistician has to deal with these problems.

(i) Selection of data : He has to select carefully those datas related to the items of which the index number is to be counted. He needs to be very careful in selection of these items and related datas.

(ii) Selection of base year : He has to select a year which should have moderate values and should not affect the average. There should be minimum fluctuations in the year, which is to be selected as the base year.

(iii) Selection of average, and

(iv) Suitable weights for various items is also to be selected carefully.

No item should be given much more weightage nor should any be given less weightage as to affect the average and the index number value.

(b) Suppose that the regression line of two random variables y and x is given by *y* = 26.38 – 1.35*x* and that of x and y is given by *x* = 16.38 – 0.45*y*. Find the square of the coefficient of correlation between x and y. **2**

Answer: $y = 26 - 38 - 1 - 35$ x

y is variable at x $b_y = -1.35$

and x is variable at y $b_y = -0.45$

b_{yx} = regression coefficient of y on x = –1 .35

b_{xy} = regression coefficient of x on y = – 0 .45

∴ Coefficient correlation between x and y

$$r = \sqrt{b_{yx} \times b_{xy}}$$

$$= \sqrt{1.35 \times -0.45}$$

$$= \sqrt{0.6075}$$

$$\text{Square of } r = 0.6075$$

(c) If the correlation coefficient between two random variables is zero, are the random variables independent? 2

Answer: Yes, if two variables are not connected with each other, than their correlation coefficient will be zero. They will not be related to each other and hence independent.

(d) In a certain factory, a unit of work is completed by A in 10 minutes, by B in 20 minutes. What is the average number of units of work completed per minute? 2

Answer: $\text{A's average of work} = \dfrac{\text{time}}{\text{unit}}$

$$= \frac{1}{10}\frac{\text{unit}}{\text{minute}}$$

$$\text{B's average of work} = \frac{\text{unit}}{\text{time}}$$

$$= \frac{1}{20}\frac{\text{unit}}{\text{minute}}$$

$$\text{Average number of units of work} = \frac{\text{A's average} + \text{B's average}}{2}$$

$$= \frac{\frac{1}{10}+\frac{1}{20}}{2}$$

$$= \frac{2+1}{20\times 2}$$

$$= \frac{3}{40}\frac{\text{unit}}{\text{minute}}$$

(MAIN) **Civil Services Exam.**

2004 General Studies

SOLVED PAPERS

PAPER–I

Time Allowed: Three Hours *Maximum Marks: 300*

INSTRUCTIONS : Answers must be written in the medium specified in the Admission Certificate issued to you, which must be stated clearly on the cover of the answer-book in the space provided for the purpose. No marks will be given for the answers written in a medium other than that specified in the Admission Certificate.

Q. 1 Answer any one of the following (in about 250 words) : **30**

(a) Discuss the major regulations enacted by the British rulers to curb the freedom of Press in India.

Important Points for Answer:	
• *Regulations*	• *Controls*
• *Various Acts*	• *Objectives*

Answer: First newspaper 'The Bengal Gazette' or 'Calcutta General Adviser' was seized in 1812 because of Government's criticism in it. Since then the British rulers has put some curbs and regulations over the newspapers in India through various regulations.

Censorship of Press Act, 1799 was enacted by Lord Wallesley with provisions of Wartime Press restrictions which included pre-censorship. This was relaxed under Lord Hastings and in 1878, pre-censorship was abolished.

John Adams enacted Licencing Regulations, 1823 which made starting or using a press culture without a licence a penal offence, chiefly directed against Indian Language or edited by Indians.

Licencing Act of 1857 imposed licencing restrictions in addition to registration procedure and the Government reserved right to stop publication.

Registration Act 1867 was of a regulatory nature. It required to print the name of the printer and the publisher and the place of publication of every book and/or newspaper. It also required to submit a copy to the local government within one month of its publication.

In addition to all these restrictive and regulative act, the Vernacular Press Act-1878 was enacted to control Vernacular Press and prevent them from seditious writing. It also provided effective punishment apart from repressive measures.

All these acts were aimed to control Indian press and prevent the exposure of criticism against the Government apart from controlling spread of national spirit to secure their rule in India.

(b) Form a critical assessment of the Non-Cooperation Movement.

Important Points for Answer:
• *Movement–Origin, Spread, Objectives, Success, Effect on society*
• *Comment*

Answer: At the time of Khilafat issue, the non-cooperation movement gained a boost. In 1920, the issue of Khilafat non-cooperation movement provided a momentum to masses for raising their voice against the British rule.

September, 1920, special session of the congress at Calcutta, approved the non-cooperation programme till the wrongs done by Punjab and Khilafat issues were remedied. The movement boycotted government schools and colleges, low courts and legislative councils, foreign clothes, renunciated the government titles and honours.

In this movement the congress decided to attain Swaraj as their goal through peaceful and legitimate means. Gandhi promised Swaraj within a year through the non-cooperation movement. Revolutionary groups of Bengal also supported the congress programme.

It was the peak time for the movement when Gandhi withdrew it due to Chauri Chaura incident. With abandonment of the non-cooperation movement, Khilafat movement went critical over Gandhi's decision of withdrawing the movement.

To evaluate the movement, it can be concluded that it could not realise its goal of Swaraj and in fact Swaraj became more far reached goal now. Nor could it solve the Punjab issue

But it resulted in some favourable consequences like arousing a mass spirit in public and their active involvement from every nook and comer of the country first time after the revolt of 1857. People started to wear Khadi and use Swadeshi in place of foreign goods giving a boost to Indian Economy. Nationalist education spread in country and institutes like Jamia Milia and Kashi universities came into existence.

In this way, it created a fertile soil for the national movement involving persons from even religion, caste and sex.

Q. 2 Answer any two of the following (in about 150 words each) : 2 × 15 = 30

(a) What led to the partition of Bengal in 1905?

Important Points for Answer:
• *Partition - reasons*
• *Policy of British*

Answer: The reason which led to partition of Bengal in 1905 were mainly political rather than administrative as was declared by the British Government.

Though to a certain extent, the reason of difficulties in administration of big area and mass of population, forwarded by the Government was justified, real reasons could be pointed out as below:

- **To curb national activities** : Bengal had became a centre of political national activities with Calcutta as its hub. Most of the literate activists were in Bengal, most of nationalist news papers were published from Calcutta. To put a curb on their activities through dividing them, Partition was planned.
- **To divide people** : Bengal was partitioned with a well plan to divide people on the basis of religion and language. Partition was effected in such a manner that areas of religious and linguistic unity were also divided under two different provisions.
- **To weaken spirit and national activities** : To weaken the spirit of nationalism was the main motive apart from propping up muslim communalists to curb nationalist and congress activities. Policy of 'Divide and Rule' was implemented explicitly.

(b) Write a note on the Theosophical Society.

Important Points for Answer:	
• *Establishment*	• *Objectives*
• *Functions*	• *Success*

Answer: The Theosophical Society was founded in the United States in 1875 by Madame H. P. Blavatsky and Colonel M. S. Olcott. They were inspired by Indian thought and culture. In 1882, its headquarter was shifted to Adayar, near Madras. Later on, Annie Besant was elected its President in 1907.

The society believed that relations can be built Op between a soul and God by contemplation, prayer, revelation, etc. It was inspired by the philosophy of Upanishads, Samkhya, Yoga and Vedanta schools of thought. It affirmed its faith in reincarnation and karma. It worked for Universal brotherhood without any distinction of race, caste, sex, creed, colour or so. One of its aims was to investigate the law of nature and latent power of man. It gave a renaissance to Hinduism.

Not only a religious revivalist society, but it also worked as a movement to glorify Indian religion, culture and tradition and gave much required feelings of pride to the Indians in their religion and philosophy. Inspired by the feelings of self respect, they also get encouraged in fighting against the British rule.

(c) Discuss the main findings of the Hartog Committee (1929).

Important Points for Answer:	
• *Committee - formation*	• *Findings*
• *Recommendations*	

Answer: Hartog Committee, under the Chairmanship of Sir Philip Hartog was appointed to find out and recommend measures for progress of education in India. It found out that:

- There is no necessity to make education compulsory or expand it hastily. It also emphasised on the primary education.

- It got some admissions undesirable in High schools and intermediate levels. So, it recommended to admit only deserving students to high schools and intermediate level after standard VIII and other average students should be given vocational education.
- It advocated Vernacular medium of education for rural students and then vocational courses.
- The level of University education was not maintained due to open and unrestricted admissions to every student, so it recommended restricted admissions to university for improvements in its standard.

This committee made some valuable recommendations regarding development of education in India.

Q. 3 Write about the following (not exceeding 20 words each) : **15 × 2 = 30**

(i) Upanishads

Answer: The last part of Vedic Literature, also called "Vedantas". They are 108 in numbers, dealing with philosophical aspects to search "Gyana" (knowledge).

(ii) Vajrayana

Answer: A branch of Buddhism which came into existence in seventh century. It emphasised meat, sex and wine. It also believed in magic and charm. It gave a death knell blow to Buddhism in India.

(iii) Kumarsambhav

Answer: This is a Sanskrit epic by Mahakavi Kalidasa in Gupta period. The epic narrates story of the birth of Kartikeya' son of Lord Shiva and Parvati.

(iv) Razmnama

Answer: It is farsi translation of the epic "Mahabharata". It was translated in time of Akbar by Badayuni, Abul Fazal, Faizi, etc.

(v) Mirza Haidar

Answer: Mirza Haider became ruler of Kashmir in 1540. He was relative of Humayun. Later on, he was removed by a Hindu ruler.

(vi) Muhammad Barkatullah

Answer: Muhammad Barkatullah, a revolutionary leader, was the first Prime Minister of temporary government of India formed in 1915 in Kabul by Mahendra Pratap Singh.

(vii) Sohan Singh Bhakna

Answer: He found 'Hindi Sangh' in America in 1915. He was also related with Gadar Party and Kamagata Maru incident.

(viii) Alluri Sitaramaraju

Answer: He organised an armed force of depressed classes and led the Rumpa revolt. He was killed in 1924. He worked for development of this section of society.

(ix) Canjeevaram Natrajan Annadurai

Answer: He founded Dravida Kangam (federation) in 1944. Later in 1949, he founded Dravida Munetra Kazagam.

(x) Jadong

Answer: He was a naga tribal freedom fighter. He worked for social and religious upliftment of the tribes. Executed in 1931.

(xi) Jadunath Sarkar

Answer: A famous historian. He praised Shivaji in his maratha history. He explained economics and political aspects of marathas.

(xii) Nazir Hasan

Answer: Worked for Muslim development in economic, social and political fields with Sir Syed Ahmad Khan in Aligarh movement.

(xiii) Subhash Gupte

Answer: He died recently. This Indian leg spinner got fame by taking nine wickets against West Indies.

(xiv) Acharya Nirmalya

Answer: A great contributor to Bengal cinema and literature. He wrote an essay "Chalchitra Pratham Sutre" about the starting phase of cinema.

(xv) Jyotirao Phule

Answer: Jyoti Rao Phule founded 'Satya Shodhak Samaj' in 1873. Worked for eradication of untouchability. He wrote "Gulam Giri". He led a movement against Brahamanism.

Q. 4 Answer any two of the following (in about 125 words each) : 2 × 10 = 20

(a) Examine the distribution of oil refineries in India.

Important Points for Answer:
- *Refineries - distribution, reasons*

Answer: India has developed its capacity of refining crude oil, producing petrol, diesel and other products.

India has some refineries distributed over the landmass according to some geographical or economical reasons, like availability of crude oil, as raw materials, from nearest wells and regions, situation of ports where import of oil would become easier and transportation facilities as more important factor.

In Assam, Digboi is a major oil producing region which has availability of oil minerals. In Ankleshwar and Mumbai based refineries, mainly the raw material comes from Bombai High oil region.

Based on the oils of Naharkatia and Huglijan, the refinery is situated in Noonmati.

To Karali from Bombai High and Gujarat oil producing areas, to Jamnagar from Gujarat, Bombay high and imported on the port, oil is available.

Vishakhapattnam, Kochin, Chennai etc. are refineries based on imported oil.

At last, Mathura, Barani and some other refineries are situated due to availability of market and transportation facilities in the region.

Thus, various factors have been decisive in the distribution of oil refineries in India.

(b) Why are the Aravallis called a divide between Mewar and Marwar?

Important Points for Answer:
- *Mewar*
- *Marwar*
- *Aravalli - how divide?*

Answer: Mewar comprises of Udaipur, Chittorgarh, Bhilwada, Dungarpur, etc. districts of Rajasthan Marwar is made of Jodhpur, Jaisalmer, Bikaner, Nagor areas in Rajasthan.

Both areas are divided and separated by a mountain range, spread over south-west to north-east direction, called Aravalli range.

Due to the effects of this mountain range, Mewar experiences an average temperature of 35° C in summer and about 15°C in winter. Rainfall occurs to an average of 75 to 85 cm annually. Given this climatic situation, this region consist of rich resources of natural vegetation.

Quite contrary, Marwar experiences 32 °C to 36 °C average temperature in hot season and 10°C to 15°C in cold seasons. It has only barber vegetation and experiences cyclonic rainfall.

Apart from the geographical differences, the eastern part of Aravalli, Mewar has its dialect known as Mewari different from the western region, Marwar's Marwari dialect.

(c) What is Golden Quadrilateral? How will it help in the economic development of the country?

Important Points for Answer:
- *Golden Quadrilateral*
- *Importance in economic development*

Answer: An ambitious road project joining four mega cities of the country, Delhi, Mumbai, Kolkata and Chennai, with total length of the road amounting to 5,846 km costing about 27 thousand crore rupees, with improved quality, six lane, all weather metallic roads is known as Golden Quadrilateral as it forms a quadrilateral shape.

According to a report, due to improved road network, savings in the fuel cost will be about 8000 crore rupees per year, it will increase inter-state trade, transportation of passengers and goods, reducing time and maintenance cost of vehicle, supplementing Railway and Airlines as a mean of speedy transportation facility, it will surely help Indian trade to grow and develop.

It will help joining important ports with this Road Network in increasing facilities, providing network availability to nearly situated village areas to have the benefit of city markets for their goods.

Q. 5 Write short notes on the following (in about 20 words each) : 5 × 2 = 10

(a) El Nino, La Nina and monsoon rains

Answer: El Nino is a warm ocean current and La Nino is a cold ocean current.

El Nino rises in the Southern Pacific Ocean at Peru coast Effecting the monsoon rain.

Both have effects upon the amount and occurrence of monsoon - that is based upon moisturised winds blowing from over water bodies - rainfall.

(b) The Sambhar lake

Answer: It is situated in Rajasthan, the largest salty water lake. It is a salt producing lake.

(c) The Sundarbans

Answer: Tidal forests, occurring in the deltas and coastal areas with very dense vegetation. Main type of vegetation is Sundri and so named and known as the Sundarbans.

(d) Bombay High

Answer: Situated in Arabian Sea, it is an oil producing region. It is the largest oil producing region of the country in North-east of Mumbai.

(e) Sabarkantha and Banaskantha

Answer: Both are districts of Gujarat. They are mainly dependent on Agriculture, Banaskantha has dairy and animal husbandry while Sabarkantha is arid, in most part.

Q. 6 Answer any one of the following (in about 250 words) : 30

(a) What is the significance of a preamble to a constitution? Bring out the philosophy of the Indian polity as enshrined in the Preamble of the Indian Constitution.

Important Points for Answer:

- *Preamble*
- *Significance*
- *Constitutional philosophy*

Answer: The Preamble is a key to open the mind of makers - it was held so in re Berubary's case-1960 by the Supreme Court of India. It sets out the main objectives that the Constitution sought to be achieved. It is the soul of the Indian Constitution. It has been regarded as a part of our Constitution and it throws light upon the meaning and scopes of a provision if there is any ambiguities.

The Preamble, in short and simple language, enshrines the philosophy of the Indian Politics. In the very start, the words "We the people of India" suggest that the ultimate power lies in the hands of the people. It is a democracy in real sense indicating the rule by the people, for the people and of course, of the people.

Moreover, it is also impregnated with the goals to be achieved. Justice, equality, liberty and fraternity are most sought concepts embodied here. By further narration, it is made clear that justice must be provided in all the spheres of social, economics and political Liberty is given of thought, expression, belief, faith and worship - making it to reach at the very root.

However, the concept of equality in matters of opportunities and of status is not based on Similarity concept but is to be followed with classification. And, the equality among the equals is real motto.

On the other hand, while explaining the nature of political system, it says a "Sovereign, Socialist, Secular, Democratic, Republic" state to India. Socialistic pattern is not meant for nationalisation but for equal distribution of wealth and resources. Secularism has positive meaning which includes respect for all religions.

This is the philosophy of the Indian Policy as enshrined in the Preamble of the Indian Constitution.

(b) Discuss the meaning of "breakdown of constitutional machinery". What are its effects.

Important Points for Answer:	
• *Meaning*	• *Provisions*
• *Measures*	• *Effects*

Answer: The breakdown of Constitutional machinery in a State means that a situation has arisen 1 in which the Government of the State cannot be carried on in accordance with the provisions of the Constitution.

When the Constitutional machinery in a state breaks up, under the provisions of all or any powers of the State Government or other authority. The powers of the State Legislature to make laws remain suspended and these powers are exercised by Parliament. The President may authorise any expenditure from the Consolidated Fund of the State if Lok Sabha is not in session. The sanction for it remains pending for the authorisation of Parliament.

However, the President is not empowered to assume the powers of the High Court of the State. In such a situation, Parliament can confer powers to make laws on the President, for the State. The President can delegate such powers by authorisation of Parliament.

But, the Presidential rule in a State, as this is popularly termed, cannot run beyond the limit of three years in any case it can be extended by the period of 'Six months' at a time by Parliament. But, beyond the period of one year, the certificate from the Election Commission, of the effect that due to difficulties in holding general elections to the Legislative Assembly of the State, it is necessary to extend the Presidential Rule.

It converts the Federal System of our Polity into unitary system for the time being.

Q. 7 Answer any one of the following (in about 250 words) : 30

(a) Discuss how the Constitution of India provides equal rights.

Important Points for Answer:
- *Constitutional provision*
- *Equal Rights*
- *Fundamental Rights*
- *Other provisions*

Answer: The Indian Constitution has made various provisions for the equal rights to all citizens, of which some rights are expressly declared as the Fundamental Rights and some other rights aiming equality are implied in the Constitution.

For example, the declaration, in the Preamble, that India is a socialist state means removal of unequality of wealth and provision of equality, in implied term. In the same way, secularity is to remove partiality of religions and to treat all religions equally.

Article 14 of the Constitution provides equality before law and equal protection of law as a fundamental right. In the same way, no discrimination can be practiced only on the grounds of religion, race, caste, sex or place of birth in matters of education and such grounds are provided for removing discrimination in matters of public services. Untouchability is removed and titles are abolished to make all persons equal.

Even in matters of political participation, the Constitution has, since its conception, provided universal franchise under Article 326.

Provisions relating to freedom of expression and speech are also aimed at giving freedom to every citizen to express and bring out their dissatisfaction, even against the State.

In Part IV, the Directives also contain that men and women are to be treated equally. Same wages are to be provided for same work.

Though, reservation is a provision under the Constitution, it is not unequality but a tool to bring equality in the society. Classification has the same purpose.

All these provisions in our Constitution are aimed to provide equality to all persons in our country, not only to the citizens but to non-citizens also in some matters.

(b) How does the Indian Constitution seek to maintain independence of the Public Service Commission?

Answer: The functions of the Public Service Commission are very important one and hence the independence is necessary to be maintained.

To maintain its independence, the following provisions are made in our Constitution.

1. The member of the Public Service Commission holds office for the term of six years or until he attains the age of 65 years in case of UPSC and 62 years in case of State Public Service Commission.
2. He is ineligible for reappointment.
3. He can be removed by order of the President on the ground of misbehaviour. For such removal, the President is required to refer the matter to the Supreme Court for enquiry. The procedure of enquiry is same as in the case of a Judge of the Supreme Court or the High Court.

4. Other grounds for the removal of a member are :
   - insolvency,
   - any other paid employment during the term of office,
   - being unfit to continue in office by reason of infirmity of mind or body.
5. He is barred from taking interest in any contract or agreement of the Government.
6. They are prohibited to hold office under the government of India or the Government of the State concerned, in accordance with their post in the Public Service Commission, even after they cease to be the member.

   All these provisions make the office of the members of the Public Service Commission free from political interest and influence, making the Public Service Commission an independent body.

Q.8 Answer any two of the following (in about 150 words each) : **2 × 15 = 30**

(a) Define Money-bill. Discuss how it is passed in the Parliament.

Important Points for Answer:	
• *Meaning*	• *Procedure*

Answer: Money Bill is a special kind of financial bill as defined in the Constitution under Article 110. The Money bill contains only those provisions dealing with all or any matters enumerated in Article 110 (1). However, the certificate of the speaker of Lok Sabha is necessary for a bill to be a Money Bill and he is the final authority to decide it.

The Money bill contains any provision regarding tax, borrowings, guarantee, the Consolidated Fund or the Contingency Fund of India or the public account of India and incidental financial transactions.

To pass a Money bill in Parliament :

- it can be introduced only on the recommendations of the President, and in Lok Sabha only.
- The Council of States has to pass it within fourteen days of the receipt. If it does not return the bill within fourteen days, the bill is deemed to be passed by the Council of States.
- The Council of States has power of recommendations but its recommendations are not binding upon the House of the People in matters of the Money bill.

(b) What is a Finance Commission? Discuss the main functions of the State Finance Commission.

Important Points for Answer:	
• *Compositions*	• *Provisions*
• *State Finance Commission*	• *Functions*

Answer: A Finance Commission is a Constitutional body which reviews financial position and makes recommendations. Under Article-280, the President and under Article-2431, the Governor sets up a Finance Commission.

The Governor sets up a State Finance Commission every five years to review the financial position of the Panchayats and to make recommendations to the Governor.

It recommends regarding :

- distribution of net proceeds of the taxes, duties, tolls and fees between the States and the Panchayats.
- What taxes, etc. may be assigned to or appropriated by, the Panchayats.
- The grants-in-aid to the Panchayats from the Consolidated Fund of the State.
- It also recommends the measures to improve the financial position of the Panchayats. Apart from these, the Governor may refer to the Finance Commission any other matter also.

The functions of the Commission are recommendatory in nature and not binding on the Governor or the State Government.

(c) Discuss how state governments can exercise control over panchayats.

Important Points for Answer:
- *Panchayat*
- *Control of State Government*

Answer: Panchayats are formed as the basic units of governance by the 73rd Amendment Act - 1993 which provides many powers to them for their autonomy in governance. Article 40 one of the Directive Principle of the State Policy of our Constitution provides to constitute Panchayats at village level.

However, some controls over their administration is vested in the State governments.

The State Government is empowered to see that all classes are given equal representation, policy of reservations are followed and elections are held from time to time and on free and fair practice. It can also audit the accounts of the Panchayats and it distributes funds to all panchayats from its fund and thus also it can have a control over their financial transactions.

The taxes by Panchayats are imposed to collect revenue for their local administration, the State government. The State government makes the election commission to prepare a list of the voters in the constituencies of panchayats.

Thus, through various constitutional provisions, the state government controls the panchayats in their administration and work.

Q. 9 Answer the following (in about 20 words each) : 5 × 2 = 10

(a) What is Habeas Corpus?

Answer: It means "you have the body". It is a writ issued to effectuate the presentation of the person detained, against the proper authority. It can be issued both under Articles 32 and 226, both by the Supreme Court and the High Courts.

(b) What are the constitutional restrictions imposed upon the power of borrowing of the state governments?

Answer: It can borrow U/ A-293 only within the territory of India. It has to provide security of its Consolidated Fund. It cannot borrow, if there is any outstanding to the Government of India or to which the Government of India has given security, without its consent.

(c) What is the special facility provided to the linguistic minorities under Article 350 A?

Answer: Article 350 A provides facility of primary education in the mother tongue to the children belonging to linguistic minority groups. The State and local authorities shall endeavour to provide it.

(d) How can a judge of the Supreme Court be removed?

Answer: A Judge of the Supreme Court of India is removed by the President by an order, after an address of Parliament following the procedure under Article 124 (4), on the ground of proved misbehaviour or incapacity.

(e) How is the Election Commission of India constituted?

Answer: The President of India appoints the Chief Election Commissioner and other members of the Commission from time to time under Article-324 of the Constitution of India to constitute the Election Commission of India.

Q. 10 Write on any one of the following (in about 250 words):

(a) The Inter-State river water dispute has once again assumed centre-stage after the Punjab Assembly's Bill terminating all previous accords on river waters. Discuss.

Important Points for Answer:	
• *Bill – detail*	• *Dispute*
• *Constitutionality*	• *Position*

Answer: In Indian Constitution, the Inter-State river water is the Central subject under Seventh Schedule's Union List, Entry 56 and under it the Centre Government has establish a Inter-State River Water Dispute Tribunal under Article 262 to solve any dispute in this matter. The Cauvery Water dispute among the peninsular states and Satluj, Yamuna - Water disputes in the North have been at the Central stage from time to time.

Recently the Punjab Assembly passed a Bill terminating all its previous accords on river waters, which got the assent of the Governor and became a law. The question that acquired the ground of debate soon is whether the Act of Punjab Assembly is constitutionally valid.

Earlier an Act of Karnataka invalidating the order of the Cauvery was Tribunal was declared ultra-vires and void, hence unconstitutional.

Punjab contends that Ravi, Beas and Satluj passes through Punjab territory only and the water requirements of Punjab itself are not fulfilled, so it is not bound to distribute waters to Haryana, Rajasthan and Delhi. Recently the Supreme Court has ordered the Central Government to report on the construction of Satluj-Yamuna link Canal Work, by July 13, 2004. So, the Punjab Assembly passed the Punjab Agreement (Abolition) Act, 2004.

This Act has the effect of invalidating provisions, of the India-Pakistan Indus Agreement 1960, in which Rajasthan is declared a riparian state to have benefit of the river water, but the Act of Punjab Assembly provides to exclude Rajasthan, too, from the benefits of water.

The question has emerged that Rajasthan was given benefit of river waters by the Central Agreement since 1960 and Haryana was a part of Punjab, can Rajasthan be excluded by Punjab overriding the Act of the Central Government? Can a state after division exclude the other part, a newly constituted state from water benefits? If it is so, the emerging demands of new small and separate states will have to be aloof from many resources.

It is now upon the Supreme Court to check the Constitutionality of this Act of the Punjab Assembly.

(b) What is PURA? Discuss its major objectives.

Important Points for Answer:
• *PURA - detail, objectives*

Answer: PURA is Providing Urban Amenities in Rural Areas. A suggestion by the President Dr. A. P. J. Abdul Kalam, to develop India by 2020.

In Indian National Science Congress' 90th Conference in Chandigarh, January 2004, Dr. Kalam presented his concept of PURA to succeed in the VISION-2020 goals and objectives, providing India new heights and achievements, developed status and economy.

PURA inlcudes components - Health, Education, Transportation, Electricity, Entertainment, etc. By connecting group of villages with 'Ring Road' around them, joining to the nearest town, many industrial sectors can be established near to them.

Easy access to facilities available in cities is main objective to raise the standard of living in villages having 25 to 50 thousand population in the region.

India has about three fourth component of its population in rural areas, neglecting their development, India cannot become a developed nation by 2020, which is the main goal of PURA—to made India a developed nation by then - cannot be achieved. So, PURA prioritises rural development.

An another benefit to be achieved by PURA, is to develop village-groups or regions as small industrial units so that they can be transformed into producers of basic industrial goods also in addition to agricultural producers.

It is hoped that such development of economy, facilities and education in the region, they will be able to get employment, services of better transportation and health, and availability of better education in their complex will prevent migration of people towards cities from the rural areas.

It is also declared by the NDA government that PURA will be implemented as a national programme for India's all over development and progress towards achieving the goal of becoming a developed country by 2020.

Q. 11 Write on any two of the following (in about 125 words each) : 2 × 10 = 20

(a) Explain UNDP Report on human development in India.

Important Points for Answer:	
• *Report*	• *Indian position*
• *Indicators*	

Answer: United Nations Development Programme (UNDP) prepares 'Human Development Report' annually. In the Report of 2004, based on the theme related to 'Cultural Liberty and Diversity in the World', it provides following facts related to India.

- India is ranked 127th position among total 177 countries.
- In Gender related Development Index, India ranks 103 among 144 total nations.
- The rate of living standard development was 0.595 in 2001.
- Life Expectancy in India is 63.7 years.
- In GDP development, India ranks 117 in the world.
- Poverty Index ranks India 148 among 195 countries of the world.
- The report indicated to Gujarat riots to prove despair among communities. However, the report has positively narrated cultural liberty, linguistic, cultural, economic and regional diversities and the progress achieved by harmonising them.

(b) What is WTO? What are India's objections to its overall functioning?

Important Points for Answer:	
• *WTO - detail*	• *Its functions*
• *Indian contention*	

Answer: The World Trade Organisation WTO - came into existence from the last round of GATT in 1995. It is the main international organisation to promote and regulate international trade. The main objective of WTO is to provide boundaryless and world market for goods and services produced in any market of the world.

India objects to some principles and manners of work in WTO. India contends that it has not taken into consideration the specific conditions of developing and poor countries while allowing free trade access to the developed nations. Many problems of economic growth arises if it is allowed, resulting in exploitation of poor and developing markets.

It has remained an organisation for the promotion of only developed country interest, argues India.

So, India wants some liberal and favourable policies in developed countries for goods of poor and developing countries. So that they can compete with them. Provisions for antidumping should be made so that markets of developing and poor countries do not over flow with goods and services from developed nations breaking away their economy.

(c) Discuss the utility of e-governance in the Indian context.

Important Points for Answer:	
• *e-governance - meaning*	• *Spread*
• *Utility–benefits*	

Answer: Electronic-Governance, means to reach the facilities and services of the Government to citizens through electronic medium. This system will provide all information in electronic form. All documents will be stored and send through information technology making communication and procedure time quick and less expensive. More efficient services can be delivered with this technology and public work will be more accurate and reliable. Direct contacts can be built up and conferences can be held even at far distance places.

At a time, documents can be produced on computers and can be worked upon without delay of time. This leads to easy disposal of work without piling stakes of files in Government offices. Transparency can be maintained regarding the schemes.

But, in India, most of population and even Government officers are not computer literate which will limit its benefit till India becomes hundred percent computer literate. Yet, it offers various possibilities of easy governance and efficient governance through electronic governance.

Q. 12 Write notes on any two of the following (in about 125 words each) : 2 × 10 = 20

(a) Housing for all by 2010 is the goal set by the National Habitat Policy. How far is it achievable?

Important Points for Answer:

- *Policy–details*
- *Provisions*
- *Objectives*
- *Measures*
- *Evaluation*
- *Conclusion*

Answer: Though Housing a state subject, the Union Government is responsible for policy formation. According to the National Housing and Habitat Policy - 1998, the target is to facilitate construction of twenty lakh additional units every year, especially for the economically weaker sections and lower income groups of the society. Of these, twenty lakh units, seven lakhs are to be constructed in urban areas with remaining thirteen lakhs in the rural areas.

The scheme envisages to provides houses with allied basic services to all, based on the "House for All" policy of the Government.

Though the policy aims are very noble and essential for the social development of India, the scheme has no effective distribution of the houses prepared and even implementation is deficient in this field.

One another obstacle is that at the rate of twenty lakh houses per year, the rising population and houseless people's need cannot be fulfilled to achieve the target of House for All by 2010.

However, only if rate of housing is increased, its implementation and distribution is made efficient apart from reforms in the policy, the target can be achieved nearly in 2010.

(b) "Is greater spending on education linked to higher literacy?" Discuss.

Important Points for Answer:

- *Education–requirement*
- *Spending - need to enhance*

Answer: In India, literacy is defined as ability to read and write in any one language in a person above the age of seven.

If a person, above seven years of age can write but cannot read, is not literate according to the definition.

It has been surveyed that many families do not send their children to school cannot afford to the cost of uniform, books etc. If such services are provided along with scholarships, literacy can be raised.

In many remote and village areas, only one teacher handles the school, sometimes, there are no buildings and the school is running in any open compounds, if a money is spent to raise these basic facilities of building, classrooms and availability of teachers, literacy can be raised.

Programmes are required to create awareness among people about need of literacy, programmes for this goal can increase literacy.

Though in these ways, greater spending can raise literacy but some administrative and attitude base changes are also required to really implement various policies and schemes

(c) What is Enterprise Resource Planning?

Answer: For development, of any sector, we require resources as basic needs and then to plan their use for better result. Enterprises, to develop in the economic competition of the market must be established and managed based on proper planning.

This concept of Enterprise Resource Planning has emerged to succeed in developing small scale industries and other units.

Planning of availability of raw material, financial and physical resources, facilities of power supply, transportation and policies would help in growth of enterprises. Information related to market, competition, infrastructure availability, human resources, technological development, latest machinery, etc. and their proper use and management in the enterprise would help to grow economy, through sustainability achieved in the basic units and enterprises.

Q. 13 Write about the following (in about 20 words each) : 5× 2 = 10

(a) ISRO

Answer: Indian Space Research Organisation (ISRO) was established in 1962. It is responsible for all space programmes and research in India with experts on space technology.

(b) Central Vigilance Commission

Answer: Established in 1964, the commission is vested with power and authority of eradication of corruption in central departments and units. It is now a constitutional body.

(c) NDDB

Answer: National Dairy Development Board working under the Department of Animal Husbandry is expert body for the development of Dairy and Dairy products in India.

(d) Hiren Mukherjee

Answer: Ex-member of Parliament, educationist and communist leader of India passed at the age of 97 years. He was honoured with Padma Bhushan and Padma Vibhushan awards.

(e) Pareechu Lake

Answer: It is lake in Tibet, on the northern border of India which cause alarm in Himachal Pradesh of dangerous flood due to accidental and unprecedented rise in its water level recently.

SOLVED PAPERS

PAPER II

Time Allowed: Three Hours *Maximum Marks : 300*

Q. 1 Answer any TWO of the following (Answer to each question should be in about 150 words): **15 × 2 = 30**

(a) Discuss the role played by the United States in promoting /hindering improved relations between India and Pakistan.

Important Points for Answer:
• *Indo-Pakistan relations*
• *US–role, reasons, influence*

Answer: India-Pakistan relations have almost and always down slope graph, with occassional and small period rises. In all the conditions, it has been concluded by experts that American influence exists. Mostly American influence decides the relations between the two nations at a point of time. America wants its supremacy and therefore disturbs the relations.

America gives massive financial support to Pakistan while towards India, it looks as a developed country, considering Pakistan as an under-developed nation.

But due to big market of India and fast developing economy, American shift has changed after 1991. Trade and cooperation in other fields, possible in India is not available in Pakistan which American industries require. On the other hand, Pakistan is its one major arms and weapons purchaser. So, American attempt is to keep both the aims fulfilled by adopting shrewd policy.

After the attack on World Trade Centre, its anti-Iraq and anti-Afghanistan steps, only Pakistan was his ally to use its territory as the base of attack. By this time, a common target of combating terrorism exist with India, but attack was possible only from the land of Pakistan over Taliban.

So, America has infact keep its policy as maintaining both the countries in cordial or al least coordinated relations with it and also with each other.

(b) Explain India s strategic relationship with Russia.

Important Points for Answer:
• *Indo-Russia - relations, progress*
• *Mutual strategic importance*

Answer: From the time of Independence, India had good relations with USSR. After the disolution of USSR, Indo-Russia relation has paved the way of friendship.

Russia had requirement of a world leader which can help in keeping the world multipolar. Same policy was adopted by India. India's agreement with Russia on defence cooperation had provided India a secure position.

Both the countries have come forward with the objectives of multi-polar world, expansion of the security council, etc are the points for which both cooperate.

In 2002-Delhi Declaration, both countries decided to co-operate in various fields. To increase trade relations, science and technology cooperation, security-nuclear energy, defence sector partnership; all were included in it.

Now both the countries have decided to increase bilateral trade, to hold meeting once in every year, between the highest authorities. This summits have produced good result in binding them together. In combating terrorism, both are united to increase awareness and anti-terrorism opinion among the world nations.

(c) Account for India's increasing involvement in the South-East Asian region.

Important Points for Answer:	
• *ASEAN*	• *Cooperation*
• *India's involvement*	• *Benefits*

Answer: Under the South-East Asian Region comes mainly the ASEAN nations . After the Look East policy of India, the trade and political relations with these countries have been increased. Till that time India had negligible trade with them and few political interaction.

After the 1992 'Look East' policy, India was included as Regional Dialogue partner of ASEAN, in 1995 it was accorded Full Dialogue Partner status and in 1996 Indian got membership in the ASEAN Regional Forum (ARF).

Thus, Indian involvement is increasing with the fast emerging economies of the South East Asian countries, and by 2011, India and China will be involved in the Free Trade Agreement of ASEAN.'

Though the nations of the South East Asia like Indonesia, Combodia, Thailand, Singapore, Myanmar, Malaysia, Philippines, etc. have cultural and historical attachment with India, they are now increasingly inclined to develop trade-economic relations with India, as to exploit the benefits of growing economy of India.

Moreover, strategically India acquires a better importance to diffuse the military tension in the block by large Chinese forces, as only India is another major military player in this block.

Q. 2 Answer the following (Answer to each question should be in about 20 words): $2 \times 5 = 10$

(a) The Panchsheel Pact.

Answer: It was endorsed between India and China in 1954, contains five valuable principles of ideal foreign policy.

(b) India-Israel Cooperation.

Answer: Combating terrorism, high technology transfer and cooperation in the field of space research and energy.

(c) European Union's trade restrictions against India.

Answer: Health and quality based, quota and price policy based, anti-dumping and subsidy policy based and also packaging and labelling based restrictions are imposed by EU.

(d) Weak-spots in India-Nepal relations.

Answer: Maoist struggle in Nepal and the hiding in India, ISI agents activities on the land of Nepal, Indo-Sino relations etc. are the weak points of India-Nepal relations.

(e) Hot Line between Islamabad and New Delhi.

Answer: At the level of Director-General of the Coast Guard and Army apart from the decision of starting a hot line at the Foreign Secretary level is under consideration.

Q. 3 Answer the following (Answer to each question should be in about 20 words): 2 × 5 = 10

(a) Categorize the People of Indian Origin (PIO).

Answer: Four categories of the PIO are :

- Those workers taken away from India on contract labour in the Nineteenth century.
- Those who settled in African countries for business.
- Those Indians who are working and residing in Gulf nations.
- The Indians who went to abroad after, 1960s for development of their business.

(b) Point out the difference between the Jewish Diaspora and the Indian Diaspora.

Answer: Some economical and political reasons, time period and cultural interactions are the differences between the Jewish Diaspora and Indian Diaspora.

(c) What are the references made to the NRI in the Union Budget July 2004?

Answer: The Income tax imposed on the interest on deposits of NRIs, in FCNR are reduced from April 1, 2005.

(d) What is known as reverse migration?

Answer: Return of the people who have settled in another countries to their own country is called reverse migration.

(e) Why was January 9 chosen to observe the NRI (Pravasi Bharatiya Diwas) Day?

Answer: Gandhi returned to India on 9th January, 1915 from South Africa after winning Satyagraha for Pravasi Bharatiya there. Based on the recommendation of L. M. Sanghvi Committee, it was chosen to commemorate that day.

Q. 4 Answer any ONE of the following (in about 250 words) : 30

(a) State the comprehensive structural reforms undertaken to improve the Indian economy since 1991.

Important Points for Answer:	
• *Reform of 1991*	• *Structural reforms*
• *Indian economic development*	• *Evaluation*

Answer: After the economic crisis of 1990s, many economic reforms were introduced in our country by the policy of 1991. This policy mainly was based upon the principles of Liberalisation, Privatisation and Globalisation.

The economic policy introduced liberal policies regarding financial management, opening the economy for the world investors. It promoted investment in every field, provided basic facilities and necessary changes in administrative and legal structures to make it convenient for the investors to invest in the fields of their choice. Excluding some sectors of strategic importance, almost all sectors were opened for the Foreign Direct Investment in India.

It ensure easy and efficient availability of raw materials for various industries, removed the Licencing policy, dereserved items from the small scale industries, removed the quantitative restrictions on imports and more importantly introduced automatic routes for foreign investment doing away with the requirements of permission.

It has also made Indian rupee fully convertible in current account and capital account, liberalise tax policies and complexities, reduced duties and taxes on imports and productions.

It established special economic zones to provide an interferenceless area and sector for production for such investors, to promote employment and exports.

To summarise, we can say that the structural changes were directed to target the trade policy, industrial policy, investment policy, disinvestment policy and to develop infrastructure to attract investment.

All the structural reforms introduced, in phases, by the 1991 policy resulted in higher growth rate of GDP, more investment, increased trade, rise of service sector share and decrease in the share of primary sector - a characteristic of developed economy, world level trade market and services availability in India.

Overall, they gave a boost to the Indian economical development.

(b) How is poverty level measured? Evaluate poverty eradication programmes in India.

Important Points for Answer:

- *Poverty line - measure, formula*
- *Programmes - schemes, policies*
- *Result*
- *Evaluation*

Answer: Poverty level, of course, the absolute poverty, is measured in India on the basis of Minimum nutritional level requirement and its availability.

In Rural areas, a person requires 2400 calories a day and in urban areas, the requirements is 2100 calories per person per day, according to the Indian measurement. In terms of money, based on 1993-94 prices, those persons who is not able to spend Rs. 228.90 per month in rural areas and Rs. 264.10 in urban areas, per month are below poverty line. According to the 2000 Census, there is 26 percent people below poverty line in India. To eradicate poverty, employment generation or raising in their earning can be the best way.

From the Fifth Five Year Plan, the Central Government has emphasised the poverty eradication programmes in its plannings, policies and schemes.

Major steps taken towards this direction are :

- During the Fourth Five Year Plan, Small Farmer Development Programme, Marginal Farmer and Agricultural Agency, Crash Scheme for Rural Employment, etc.
- During the Fifth Five Year Plan,
  - Food for Work Programme
  - Minimum Needs Programme
- During the period of Janata Government, Antyodaya Programme was launched in 1977-78.
- In the Sixth Five Year Plan, the Government started the National Rural Employment Programme in 1980 to increase beneficial employment opportunities substituting some earlier programmes.
- TRYSEM, Training to Rural Youth for Self-Employment Plan was started in 1979 to remove poverty among rural youth and to provide self-employment.
- In 1983, Rural Landless Employment Guarantee Programme was started.
- Jawahar Rozgar Yojana in 1989, The Employment Assurance Scheme, Ganga-Kalyan Yojana etc. were also started in this direction.
- Swarna Jayanti Gram Swarojgar Yojana - 1999, Jawahar Gram Samridhi Yojana-1999 etc. are the schemes aimed mainly to eradicate poverty.

All these schemes launched by the Government have aims to provide assistance which can help relief, only some schemes are directed to provide proper employment and only they can give results in this direction, of course, if implemented efficiently.

It can be concluded that till now, though many ambitious programmes are there, only little success has been achieved in this direction. So, awareness among people, effective implementation on the part of administration and absence of corruption are necessary factors for a good result.

Q. 5 Answer any TWO of the following (in about 150 words each): 15 × 2 = 31

(a) Describe the recommendations of Narasimham Committee regarding the banking sector in India.

Answer: Narsimham Committee on Banking Sector Reforms recommendations can be summarised as below:

- To promote banks having capacity and reach to compete in the national and international financial markets.
- To constitute an independent Debt Review System.
- Merger of Public Sector Banks and the merger not to be taken as an instrument to save and protect losing banks.
- In the time of changes, the Development Finance Institutes to convert themselves into Banks in a certain time period so that proper regulations can be m£ financial transactions.
- To bring down the minimum equity share of the Government through the RBI, in Nationalised and State Banks to 33%.
- To remove the liberalised policies in regard to interest over debts to the primary sector.
- All these were the main recommendations of Narsimham Committee to make the Banking Sector's performance more profitable, more efficient and beneficial in growth of the economy.

(b) Examine the effect of economic development on environmental degradation in India

Important Points for Answer:
- *Economical development*
- *Environmental degradation*
- *How does it effect?*
- *Conclusion*

Answer: Since Independence, India has adopted planning, for development. India plans for economic development for social welfare, but in no process, environmental policies were outlined to grow with them, till it was noticed that the development has resulted in the degradation of environment.

The Industrialisation resulted in various types of pollutions. Air pollution due to industries and automobiles has been growing. Wastes of chemicals from industries are being thrown into rivers polluting water. Waste-management has been a problem due to dangerous chemicals in them.

Unconsiderable and thoughtless use of natural resources and minerals have posed a threat against the World including India, of their exhausting.

Even the Green Revolution which is considered to be a boon for India has resulted in degradation of agricultural land due to use of chemical fertilizers and pesticides. Most growing fields of scientific progress, industries or other development have not taken into account the environmental protection and hence, in the absence of sustainable development environment has been continuously degraded.

Now, India and the world have been conscious for the protection and conservation of environment and its various components.

(c) What ails India's road transport economy? Suggest measures of remedy.

Important Points for Answer:
- *Road importance*
- *Improvement – measures*
- *Suggestions*

Answer: India has one of the largest road networks of the world. India's most of I of goods and passengers are through roads. The National Highways (which after the Golden quadrilateral scheme will comprise length of more than 65 thousand km) account for only two percent of total road network but helps transporting 40% of the total transportation of goods and passengers. It is a bitter fact, even after six decades of our freedom, that most of the roads in India are rough-non metallic roads which cannot sustain all weathers.

Though considered to be the life lines of Indian economy, they are not yet treated with priority and so in monsoon conditions, goods cannot be transported from villages to cities due to the rough positions of roads. And even in regular time, such roads cost much higher than the metallic one in terms of fuels and maintenance of vehicles.

The roads are, of course, expensive to build up but cannot be set aside due to their importance in Indian economy and so the following measures can be taken :

- Giving roads to be built up by private sector and then right to operate for some years by collecting tolls.
- Village roads should not be ignored in comparison to the National Highways. ,
- Government-Private partnership and short-cut route development can be proved very useful.

Q. 6 Answer the following (in about 20 words each): **$2 \times 15 = 30$**

(a) What are the major provisions of Agreements on Agriculture in the context of World Trade Organisation?

Answer: The Blue Box contains provisions of 5% subsidy limit, and to reduce in case of higher. To reduce domestic subsidy by 20% to agriculture, according to the WTO agreements.

(b) Elucidate Special Drawing Rights.

Answer: Under the International Monetary Fund Mechanism, SDRs are given as credit to the member nation. These are not paper currency but only reserved in written forms as International currency.

(c) What is Cash Reserve Ratio?

Answer: All Scheduled Banks are required to reserve a part of its total deposits and assets as deposits with the RBI. This is called 'Cash Reserve Ratio'.

(d) What does "priority sector lending" mean?

Answer: Some undeveloped or underdeveloped sectors cannot afford to the market rate in interest and cannot compete with others. To develop them the RBI issues guidelines to all commercial banks for lending. These lendings are called priority sector lendings, i.e. agriculture, small scale industries etc.

(e) What is Minimum Alternative Tax (MAT)?

Answer: Normally a company is liable to pay tax on income computed in accordance with the provisions of the Income Tax Act but the profit and loss account of the company is prepared as par provisions of the Companies Act. It is called MAT.

(f) What is Business Process Outsourcing (BPO)?

Answer: Work completed by workers of and in a country and then send to another country is called BPO. It includes expertise services on contract.

(g) What is 'social justice' in the context of Indian economy?

Answer: Equal distribution of wealth and natural resources to all classes of persons in the society. It requires equal Opportunities to develop.

(h) Explain the objectives of Plant Varieties Right Act, 2002.

Answer: To protect Intellectual Property Rights, related to new varieties of plants, copyrights, seeds and their trade.

(i) How is human development index for life expectancy measured?

Answer: For the life expectancy maximum age is 85 years and minimum age is 25 years. Formula to measure life expectancy index:

$$\text{Index} = \frac{\text{Real age} - \text{Minimum age}}{\text{Index Maximum age} - \text{Minimum age}}$$

(j) What are the objectives of the Twelfth Finance Commission?

Answer: To suggest measures for development, reduction in debt, stability of economy, improvement in state financial condition and balanced budget.

(k) Explain the necessity and role of controls in a mixed economy like India.

Answer: For balanced development in India including welfare of society, the Government requires to control and regulate investment in various sectors, otherwise private sector would invest only for profits.

(l) Distinguish between primary sector, secondary sector and tertiary sector. What is the change in the share of each sector in Gross Domestic Product (GDP) during period of 1950-2000?

Answer: Primary sector include agriculture and other basic economic activities - its share reduced from about 56% to nearly 24%. Secondary sector include industries based on primary' sector - its share increased from about 11% to 22% while the tertiary sector include services of which share has increased to about 54% from nearly 32%.

(m) What is the main objective of Security and Exchange Board of India (SEBI)?

Answer: To safeguard investors' interest, to regulate capital market, to register and control collective investment plans and mutual funds and to eliminate mal-practices of security market.

(n) What has been the policy of agricultural development during last two decades in India?

Answer: To encourage private investment, to introduce modern technology, to use modern techniques of bio-technology, to increase production and quality through application of biotechnology.

(o) What is deficit financing?

Answer: To finance budget deficit of the Government is called deficit financing. Indian Government finances its deficit through loans and debts from the RBI.

Q. 7 Answer any TWO of the following (Answer to each question should be in about 150 words): **15 × 2 = 30**

(a) Discuss the role of 'intelligence' in the making of foreign policy.

Important Points for Answer:
- *Foreign policy - how formulated?*
- *What role can 'intelligence' play?*

Answer: 'Intelligence' means ability to get information which has been concealed by the opposite party. Such information is necessary to direct foreign policy towards any direction.

Foreign policy is the way on which a nation will behave and react. So, the nation's behaviour and reaction depends on the factors that stand against it. So, if intelligence services are active and efficient, hidden factors can be brought to the information of authority.

Sometimes, international relations, largely were dependent on the power of arms and forces of nations. In that time, secret military planning were important to be kept under information to save one's existence. Nowadays, terrorist activities and economic importance have raised need for intelligence.

If a country is ignorant of any terrorist activities being undertaken against it, it can not pose a threat to prevent the same, as was the case of Kargil intrusion with India.

Economic capacities and levels are now deciding factors though not dangerous factors for formation of foreign policy of a nation.

Information through intelligence services are the force which directs foreign policy of a nation.

(b) Describe the role of the Amnesty International in securing human rights.

> **Important Points for Answer:**
> • *Establishment*
> • *Functions*
> • *Contribution in protection of Human Rights*

Answer: Amnesty International was established in 1961 by a British lawyer, Peter Beneson, as one year campaign for the release of the prisoners of conscience.

But it continues as an International organisation and has won the Nobel Peace Prize of 1977. Today, the organisation acts for the protection of Human Rights.

It has adopted the UN Universal Declaration of Human Rights as its mandatory aim. The organisation, therefore, acts to save the people from the Human Rights violation in any manner. It has now over one million members, subscribers and regular donors in more than 100 countries.

The organisation publishes a global report each year to provide details over the violation of human rights in all regions of the world. Thus, it exposes any violation of human rights by any group, government or armed forces. It takes help and provides help for the conservation of human rights to the media and other organisations working in this direction.

Human Rights Index, published by the Amnesty International is circulated and respected in all over the world as a neutral report. Today, the organization has acquired an important place in the human rights conservation field.

(c) Examine the relevance of Pt. Jawaharlal Nehru's ideas in the international relations of today.

> **Important Points for Answer:**
> • *Nehru's ideas*
> • *Importance then*
> • *International scenario*
> • *Their relevance today*

Answer: Pandit Jawaharlal Nehru, the first Prime Minister and Foreign Minister of India was really a world citizen. His ideas about internationalism and world unity are of great importance in todays time. The concept of United Nation's equality of all nations based on their sovereignty are the mirror of Pt. Nehru's ideas which co-exist at that time and even today with emphasis on protection of Human Rights.

Panchsheel Pact of 1954 proposed by Pt. Nehru has been very popular since than and the principles of Sovereignty, Non-aggressive policy, non-intervention and peaceful co-existence have been accepted by all nations either expressly or impliedly.

The Non-Alignment Policy has also acquired and has been proved to be of great importance in the world, at the time of bipolar world and today in unipolar world equally by neutrally expressing and favouring true position in the world.

All these are relevant to the ideas of Nehru in context of economic co-operation and development as it is possible by, as he said, peaceful co-existence and co-operation.

Q. 8 Answer the following (Answer to each question should be in about 20 words): 2 × 5 = 10

(a) ICJ verdict on Israel's erection of barrier on the West Bank.

Answer: In its advisory opinion, the International court of justice gave verdict that the erection of barrier on the west bank by Israel from 2002 was illegal and ordered to remove it earlier.

(b) Beijing-Taiwan Spat.

Answer: Taiwan vested its President with the power of referandum. China is feared that through this power, the President of Taiwan can proclaim the country independent.

(c) Prospects of international water-wars.

Answer: In the Third World Water Forum, the UN Secretary-General, Kofi Annan warned that sovereign countries may go to war in future for control over water resources.

(d) *Al Gharib* Prisoners.

Answer: *Al Gharib* or Abu Gharib is a prison in Baghdad where attrocities and inhuman acts over Iraqi prisoners by American soldiers created world-wide controversies.

(e) Recent developments in India-Myanmar relations.

Answer: Both the countries emphasised the need to develop trade co-operation, road and railway network development and more investment between the two countries through agreements recently.

Q. 9 Answer the following, by expanding and explaining the objectives (Answer to each question should be in about 20 words): 2 × 5 = 10

(a) BIMSTEC

Answer: Bay of Bengal Initiative for Multi-Sector Trade and Economic Co-operation. This is an organisation of 7 bordering nations of the Bay of Bengal. Its main objective is to promote economic co-operation among themselves.

(b) ART

Answer: ASEAN Regional Forum is a platform to join the countries of the South East Asian block on security concern.

(c) Red Cross

Answer: It is an international organisation which helps victims in the time of war and natural disasters.

(d) OPEC

Answer: Organisation of Petroleum Exporting Countries is made of oil producing countries to consolidate petroleum policies so that they can maximise their benefit from oil.

(e) IAEA

Answer: International Atomic Energy Agency is a specialised agency of the UN, working as a watch dog over nuclear programme of nations and to promote peaceful and developmental use of nuclear energy.

Q. 10 Answer any ONE of the following (Answer should be in about 250 words) :

(a) Discuss in detail "Alternative Energy Sources". **30**

Important Points for Answer:

- *Details - various sources*
- *Needs for alternative sources*

Answer: The rapid increase in the demand of energy has caused worry about its supply. The main sources of energy are conventional sources. They are non-renewable and exhaustable sources. The demand of energy has increased all over the world and the condition poses a threat on the sources of energy like Petroleum and Natural gas by the year 2030-35 if any alternative sources do not substitute or supplement them.

The Government of India gives high priority to the use of alternative, non-conventional and renewable energy sources as supplement to the depleting conventional sources of energy. These alternative sources include - Solar energy, Wind energy, Geo-thermal energy, Tidal energy, Biomass energy, etc.

These energy sources have huge potential of energy and they can be useful in various ways.

Solar energy is a wide source. Solar cells, solar cookers, solar ponds etc. are the devices to trap solar energy. It can produce electricity, cook food, heat water and can be converted to other forms of energy.

The solar photovoltaic system which uses solar cells to convert the solar energy into electrical energy is the most promising and progressive sources of alternative energy.

Wind energy is in form of Kinetic Energy. A blade of windmill is moved by blowing winds and could be exploited for doing work. Theoretically about 60% of the wind energy can be converted into other forms of energy. Wind mill farms are being set up in the world to exploit this energy at suitable places.

Geothermal energy can be used to produce electricity. However, the inner heat of the earth not available every where which can be commercially exploited. Such potential has been found in Pegu valley in Jammu and Kashmir in India.

Tidal energy associated with the kinetic energy of tides can be converted into electricity by using turbine. In the coastal areas this possibility is available.

Biomass energy is being used in villages but improvement in method and scientific equipments can increase utilisation. It reduces waste materials and gives cheap energy.

Hydrogen is also proved to be a great advantageous source of energy.

Nowadays, nuclear energy is gaining utmost importance.

Jethropa is a plant that produces diesel and it is pollution free. Besides the railways lines, Jethropa planting is in implementation.

These alternative sources of energy promise a new horizon in sustainable manner.

(b) Global Warming"—Discuss. **30**

Important Points for Answer:
• *Global warming - causes, effects, measures*

Answer: Now not a probability only but Global Warming has started to endanger the environment of the earth. Many reasons may be there for the Global Warming, Primary and main cause is considered to be the Green House Effect. This effect is mainly caused by Carbon Dioxide, Methane, Chlorofluoro Carbon, Nitrous oxides etc. gases. These gases form a cover in the atmosphere around the earth through which hot rays of the sun can enter to the earth but cannot exit. So, the heat of the sun remains in the lower circle of the earth making the temperature rise.

It is feared that the world may experience rise in temperature of about 4° to 5 °C by 2050. The average temperature of the earth has risen by about 1°C in last five centuries and of this half of the warming is caused in Twentieth century alone. The Global Warming is increasing at an alarming rate.

Due to the rise in average temperature of the earth, agricultural crops, forests and life growth is affected adversely. It also changes balanced equations of marine life. Melting of glaciers will result in the rise of sea level posing a threat upon the habitat of coastal areas.

Because of these dangerous effects of 'Global Warming', at the international level, measures are taken in the form of Conferences, agreements and research. The latest and most effective of them is the Kyoto Protocol of 1997 which aims at stopping the emission of three main Green House Gases, $C0_2$, CH_4 and N_zO from 2008 to 2012. It provides to reduce the emission by 5% average of the base of 1990 emission rate. Global Environmental Facilities (GEF) is also working in this direction.

Q. 11 Answer any TWO of the following (Answer to each question should be in about 150 words): **15 × 2 = 30**

(a) What is 'Superconductivity'? Give its uses and applications.

Important Points for Answer:
• *Super-conductivity - meaning, technology, applications*

Answer: Super conductivity is property of losing all electrical resistance. Some materials produce no resistance at the temperature absolute zero (-273°C). Such materials are called superconductors and this property is known as superconductivity.

Some pure metals, alloys and a few other substances display this behaviour. They acquire superconductivity at some specific temperature, known as critical temperature. Below it, they are not superconductors.

Superconductivity, discovered by Heke Kamerlingh of Netherlands in 1911, is useful in the following ways :

- Superconductors can carry a very large electric current and they can be used to make powerful electromagnets.
- They can be used to transmit electricity from one place to another without any loss of electricity. Electric circuits can be closed strictly by using superconductors.
- In treatment of heart diseases, super conductive "quantum interference devices" can be used.
- NMR (Nuclear Magnetic Resonance) machines use super conductive electro-magnet. This machine can produce picture of any internal organ of our body without cutting skin. This property has proved useful in medical and electrical fields.

(b) What is Biotechnology? Discuss the important applications of Biotechnology.

Important Points for Answer:
• *Biotechnology - progress, uses, applications*

Answer: Biotechnology relates to producing useful products from and by the use of various bacterias, plants and other organisms or their parts. Synthesis of various chemical and bio-product are derived for multiple purposes through the use of bio-technology and its branches.

Applications :

- Genetically Modified Varieties of plants and animals are produced. These new breeds are with desired qualities and characteristics and have increased production in agriculture and animal husbandry.
- In fields of medicine and pharmacy, this technology has given new dimensions. New medicines including production of Insulin, Vitamins, Steroids and Anti-biotics are result of progress in this direction.
- As preservatives and for other uses, this technology produces many bio-chemicals.
- To repair genetical disorders, to improve genome, to produce expected quality of breed and to create pest, insect and drough proof plants etc. are boons of genetical engineering.
- Cloning is new research field, with the use of stem cells. It is raising hopes that new organisms, tissues and organs will be created to substitute the damaged one in the body.
- DNA finger-print technology, in investigation and search of criminals is a use of Biotechnology in non-scientific field.

These proves importance of Bio-technology.

(c) Describe the importance of "Laser" in war and peace.

Important Points for Answer:
• *LASER technique*
• *Use - defence related, scientific applications, medical, others*

Answer: LASER stand for Light Amplification by Stimulated Emission of Radiation. It was invented by Theodore Memain in 1960. It is a monochromatic light and very directional and therefore it can be transmitted over great distances without loss or spread. Its intensity is also very high when focussed.

LASERs have find uses in defence equipments. In Radars, they are used to detect the right position of enemy tanks, ships, aircrafts, etc. It has acquired a great strategic importance due to its use as Marked Target Seeker Technology. When fitted into any missile, this MTS directs lasers to the set target and accordingly, when fired, sets its own direction according to the changing situations of the target and hits it. Many uses of laser in war time have made it a technology of security importance.

Even in peace time, the technology is used in some basic sciences like Biology, Chemistry, Spectroscopy, Physical research etc. They induce some chemical reactions. In industrial fields, they find application in survey, welding, cutting, alloying, non-destructive desting, etc. They can be used to drill holes in diamonds.

In Medical field, they can be used for some operations, medicine preparations, diagnostic, etc. Communication, computers, information technology and entertainment are the fields where we find uses of laser in our day to day life.

Q. 12 Answer the following (in about 20 words each): **$2 \times 5 = 10$**

(a) What do you understand by E-governance?

Answer: Electronic Governance is a way to computerised and thus modernise the Governance system of the country to provide easy access, effective implementation and transparency apart from speed and efficiency.

(b) What is a URL?

URL stands for Uniform Resource Locator. It is a system for naming website in the Internet accepted universally.

(c) What do the following stand for?

(i) CD-ROM

Answer: Compact Disc Read-Only Memory.

(ii) USB

Answer: Universal Serial Bus.

(iii) ITES

Answer: Information Technology Enabled Services.

(iv) FORTRAN

Answer: Formula Transmission.

(d) What do you understand by MP3?

Answer: MP3 is nick name for "MPEG-1 Layer-3". It is an encoding format for compressed digital music files. It is a system of music player and visual representation.

(e) What are cyber crimes? How are these protected?

Answer: Various crimes like bank forgery or theft of secret data etc. are conducted through internet connected computers. These are called cyber crimes. True Break and Cyber Check are devices for protection.

Q. 13 (a) The table below shows the average monthly house hold expenditure on different items for the years 2001 to 2004 :

Item	Average monthly expenditure in Rs.			
	2001	2002	2003	2004
Food	4,500	4,800	5,400	5,700
Rent	1,800	1,800	2,200	2,300
Children's education	650	800	1,000	1,200
Others	2,400	2,600	3,000	3,400

Represent the above information by suitable diagram. **8**

Answer:

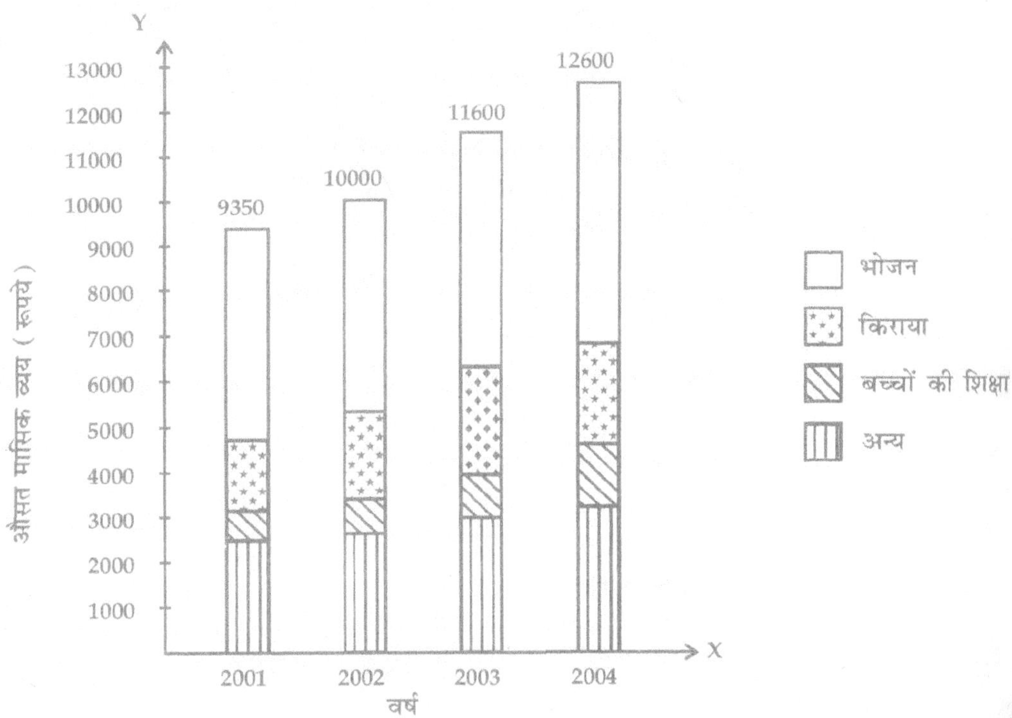

(b) According to the Union Budget 2004-05, the total receipts of Rs. 4,77,829 crore can be approximately broken up as follows :

A.	Direct Taxes	25%
B.	Indirect and other Taxes	32%
C	Non-tax Revenue Receipts	13%
D.	Non-debt Capital Receipts	6%
E.	Borrowings and other liabilities	24%

Represent the above by a Pie-diagram.

Answer:

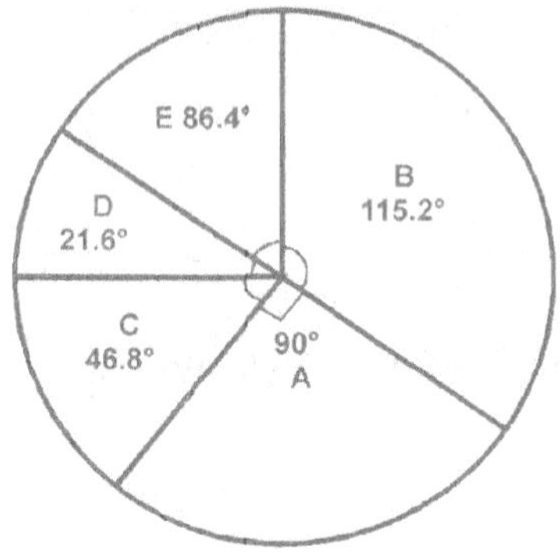

A – Direct tax = 25% = 25 x (18/5) = 90°

B – Indirect and other taxes = 32% = 32 x (18/5) = 115.2°

C – Non-tax Revenue Receipts = 13% = 13 x (18/5) = 46.8°

D – Non-debt Capital Receipts = 6% = 6 x (18/5) = 21.6°

E – Borrowings and other liabilities = 24% = 24 x (18/5) = 86.4°

Q. 14 (a) Read the given data and answer the questions that follow :

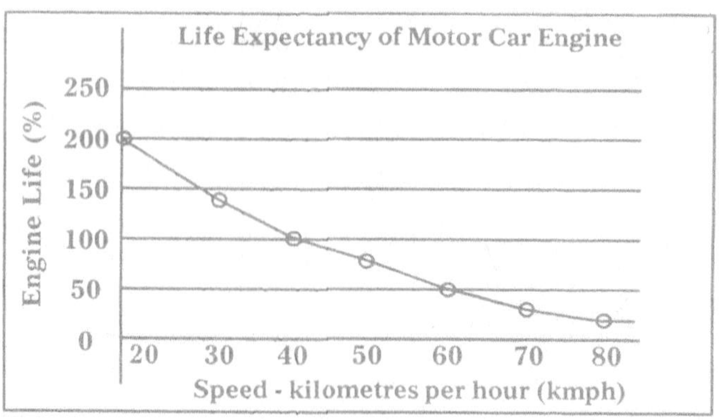

(i) At what speed (kmph) is the engine considered to have its normal length of life?

Answer: 40 kmph, Normal life is 100%. It can be achieved at the speed of 40 kmph.

(ii) The life of an engine driven at 20 kmph is how many times more than the life of an engine driven at 40 km per hour?

Answer: Two times. Driven at 40 kmph, it gives 100% life and at 20 kmph it gives 200%, i.e. double life.

(iii) If an engine, usually driven at speed of 60 km per hour, had a lifespan of 30,000 kilometres, what will be the lifespan of an engine which is usually driven at a speed of 40 km per hour?

Answer: 60,000 kmph. At the speed of 60 kmph life is 50%, 30,000 km. At 40 kmph, it gives 100% = 30000 x 2 = 60,000 kmph.

(iv) Given that the normal lifespan of an engine is 60,000 km, what was the lifespan of an engine, which was driven for 20,000 kilometres at a speed of 60 km per hour and later at a speed of 40 km per hour?

Answer: 40,000 km. While driving at 60 kmph, we get only half life. So, by 20000 we used 40,000 km from 60,000 life span. Now remaining 20,000 is achievable at 40 kmph. If yet driven at 60 kmph, we would get only 10,000 km.

(v) Running an engine between 60 kilometres per hour and 40 km per hour, the lifespan increases by what percent?

Answer: 100%. Life-span driven at 60 kmph = 30,000 km and at 40 kmph, it is 60,000 km. So, we add same number, i.e. 100% by driving at 40 kmph.

(vi) At what speed (kmph) would the engine have the maximum life?

Answer: 20 kmph. At the speed of 20 kmph, the engine gets 200% of life, even double than the normal life.

(b) The Human Development Index (HDI) is a simple average of three indexes :

(A) Life Expectancy Index (to reflect health)

(B) Education Index (to reflect knowledge)

(C) GDP/SDP Index (to reflect standard of living)

The Education Index (B) is a combined index of two indexes : (i) adult literacy rate with *2J3* weight and (ii) combined gross enrolment rate with 1/3 weight.

Compute the HDI for INDIA and KERALA from the following data :

	INDIA	KERALA
(A) Life Expectancy Index	57.2	78.0
(B) Education Index		
(i) Adult Literacy Rate	48.7	86.0
(ii) Combined Gross enrolment rate	59.1	100.6
(C) GDP/SDP Index	19.0	19.5

[*Note:* SDP is State Domestic Product] **8**

Answer: Education Index:- $\frac{2}{3}$ (Adult literacy) + $\frac{1}{3}$ (Combined Gross rate)

$$\text{India} = \frac{2}{3}(48.7) + \frac{1}{3}(59.1)$$

$$= \frac{97.4}{3} + \frac{59.1}{3}$$

$$= 52.17$$

$$\text{Kerala} = \frac{2}{3}(86.0) + \frac{1}{3}(100.6)$$

$$= \frac{172}{3} + \frac{100.6}{3}$$

$$= 90.87$$

$$\text{HDI} = \frac{\text{Life Expectancy Index + Education Index + GDP/SDP Index}}{3}$$

$$\text{India} = \frac{57.2 + 52.17 + 19.0}{3}$$

$$= 42.79$$

$$\text{India} = 42.79$$

$$\text{Kerala} = \frac{78.0 + 90.87 + 19.5}{3}$$

$$= 62.79$$

$$\text{Kerala} = 62.79$$

Q. 15 Attempt all the questions. All questions carry equal marks :

(a) Consider the following data :

Weekly Wages in an Office (Rs.)	
Position in the Office	Weekly Wages
Senior Consultant	700
	600
	550
Position in the Office	Weekly Wages
Junior Consultant	180
	180

	160
	160
Clerical Helpers	100
	100
	100
	100
	100
	100

Which of the three averages—arithmetic mean, median and mode, adequately represents the data?

Answer: Median will be the best average to adequately represent the data. Mode will represent most commonly appearing number.

(b) In a moderately skewed distribution the following values were obtained :

Arithmetic mean = 24.6

Mode = 26.1

Find the value of the median and explain the reason for the method employed.

Answer: Arithmetic mean = 24.6, Mode = 26.1

$Z = 3M - 2\overline{x}$ [where Z = Mode, M = Median, $\overline{x}$ = Mean]

$\therefore$ 261= 3M – 2(24.6)

$\therefore$ 26-1= 3M – 49.2

$\therefore$ 3M = 49 2 + 26.1

M = 75.5/3 = 25.1

(c) Suppose an item is sold at the rates of 18, 20, 22 and 25 rupees per litre in four different months.

Assuming that equal amounts of money are spent on the particular item by a customer in the four months, find the average price in rupees per litre of the item.

Answer: Amount spent = Price × litres

As, the amount spent is equal, we can suppose it Rs. 100/-

At the rates of 18, 100/18 = 5.55 litres

At the rates of 20, 100/20 = 5.00 litres

At the rates of 22, 100/22 = 4.54 litres

At the rates of 25, 100/25 = 4.00 litres

Total money spent = Rs. 400

Total item = 5.55 + 5.00 + 4.54 + 4.00

= 19.09 litres

$$\text{Average Price} = \frac{\text{Total cost}}{\text{Total litres}}$$

$$= \frac{400}{19.09}$$

Average price = 20.95 per litre.

(d) The average of 11 observations is 50. The mean of the first six observations is 49 and **that of the last six observations is 52. Find the value of the sixth observation.**

Answer: Sum of 11 observations = Mean × Observations

= 50 × 11

= 550

Sum of first 6 observations = 49 × 6 = 294

Sum of last 6 observations = 52 × 6 = 312

Sum of 11 observations = 550,

Sum of first six and last six observations = 294 + 312 = 606

Sixth observation is taken twice the difference = 606 – 500

= 56 is the value of the sixth observation

So, the value of sixth observation = 56.

(MAIN)
2005 Civil Services Exam.
General Studies

SOLVED PAPERS

PAPER–I

Time Allowed: Three Hours *Maximum Marks: 300*

Candidates should attempt ALL questions strictly in accordance with the instruction given under each question.

The number of marks carried by each question is indicated at the end of the question.

Q. 1 Answer any one of the following questions (in about 250 words): **30**

(a) What in your opinion were the positive steps taken by the British to modernise India ?

Important Points for Answer:
- *Types of reforms—legal, social, administrative, infrastructure and communications, education*

Answer: Though the British aim was to exploit India as a colony and drain its wealth to Britain to make itself richer. Even then too, in the course of their rule, they introduced some reforms in India for their convenience in ruling it. These reforms which have benefitted India are :

- **Legal** : The concept of rule of law and modernisation of judicial system was introduced by them. They dealt all persons equal before the law irrespective of their caste, sex, etc, exceptions may exist.
- **Social** : Indian traditions and customs were covered with orthodoxy and they were modernised by the British to some extent by law or teachings or influence. Sati system, child marriages, religious customs, etc. were removed from society.
- **Administrative System** : They introduced civil services in India and later on they were made open for Indian candidates also by the Charter Act of 1853 through competitive exams.
- **Infrastructure and Communications** : In 1853, Railways, metalic roads, bridges over rivers were built which gave new pace to Indian transportation and through that trade, etc. For communication they introduced Post, telegram in 1853 as faster means of communications.
- **Education** : Lord MaCaulay modernised education system in 1853 and India was delivered western and english education which in fact led Indians to think of western Philosophies, politics and liberalism. This invited a period of renaissance India.

Apart from these, many charters, council acts etc. introduced some reforms in in India. Indian leaders learnt political lessons from British. Even today we follow the British legislative system in our governance.

(b) Examine the policy of Subordinate Union towards Princely States. Account for the shift from the policy of Subordinate Isolation.

Important Points for Answer:
- *Policy of subordinate union and its result*
- *Policy of subordinate isolation and its result*
- *Their causes and impact*

Answer: The policy of Subordinate Union was adopted by the British Government towards Indian Princely states from 1857 to 1935. They abandoned the policy of annexation and accepted right to adopt heir. The Act of 1858 transferred powers into the hands of the crown. The authority of Princes over their territory were not accepted as their right but as a gift from the paramount power. The Queen adopted the title of 'Kaiser-i-Hind' and later on Lord Curzon cleared that princes exercises their control as agents of the crown. The Government had right to interfere in internal spheres of states as well as external controls over them. Even Lord Curzon's approach was of the view that the princes were required to work side-by-side with the Governor General of India. All these new schemes resulted in a integrated Indian political system. Further, the Chamber of Princes divided the Indian states into three categories.

(i) Directly represented

(ii) Represented through representatives

(iii) Jagirs or feudal holdings

The shift was made to take princes in confidence as under the policy of subordinate isolation. The company annexed states whenever and whichever possible. Six states were annexed by Lord Dalhousie including Satara, Nagpur, etc.

This policy of subordinate union was adopted to use these princely states as break waters in political storms if arise in future. They were given comparatively liberal treatment due to their loyalty to the British Government in the 1857 Revolt.

Q. 2 Answer any tivo of the following questions (in about 150 words each): 15 x 2 = 30

(a) In the Montagu-Chelmsford Report communal representation and reservations were not only retained but considerably extended." Comment.

Important Points for Answer:
- *Report – provisions*
- *Effect on Indian movement*
- *Consequences*
- *Communal differences*
- *Response of leaders*

Answer: The Morley-Minto Reforms of 1909 had accepted the demand of Muslims for separate electorates and representation in excess of their numerical strength. Muslims were given separate electorates and 8 seats reserved for them of total 27 elected non-official seats. This communal representation and reservations were accepted in the Montagu-Chelsford Report also. It introduced bicameral legislature in both the Houses, seats for separate electorates were included. Now the Act provided for reserved seats for Sikhs also. The number of such seats were also increased. Such policy was adopted for Muslims and Sikhs and was for their upliftment according to the reform.

The base of reservation was widened. It was the real position that policy was retained to divide Indian people in more and more groups to make them weak.

(b) Evaluate Subhash Chandra Bose's contribution to India's freedom.

Answer: Subhash Chandra Bose was selected in Indian Civil Services but he joined the Disobedience Movement under the influence of Gandhi. He became an active Congresee. He was also elected the President of Congress in 1938 and 1939. But due to differences with Gandhi, he resigned from Congress Presidentship and formed his Forward Block in 1940.

Due to his activities, British had held him under house arrest in Calcutta. But he secretly left India in March 1941. He approached Russia and Germany for help in India's freedom. He went to Japan in July 1943 and provided leadership to the Indian National Army. He organised soldiers and formed provisional government in October 1943. This provisional Government was recognised by the axis powers. The INA attacked the North Eastern borders and even captured a portion but due to Japanese biased policy and adverse weather conditions, they had to surrender.

Subhash Chandra Bose provided an influential leadership and kept the spirit of nationalism burning during the slack period of national movement in India.

(c) Why and how did the Congress come to accept the partition of the country ?

Important Points for Answer:
- *Partition–necessity, situations*
- *Attitude of Congress*
- *Conclusion*

Answer: Congress failed to integrate Muslims into the nation. The partition of the country was accepted as an inevitable evil. Violent riots of Hindu-Muslims had erupted in the country. The direct action call of Jinnah resulted in bloodshed of masses. To check these communal riots, the congress had to acccpt the partition.

- It was accepted as a price for immediate independence because all other efforts had failed to materialise.
- Gandhi had accepted muslims right to self determination in muslim majority provinces.
- It was argued by some leaders that smaller, unified and strong India would be better and stronger than a bigger but weak India. Jinnah had accepted Pakistan shortened than earlier demands. Princely states had not been given sovereignty rights would have proved dangerous for Indian security and integrity.

All these situations led congress to accept partition of India.

Q. 3 Write about the following (not exceeding *20* words each): 2 × 15 = 30

(a) Yajnavalkya Smriti

Answer: It was written during the Gupta period. It throws light on various aspects of Indian religion and society.

(b) Sutta Pitaka

Answer: This Buddhist text contains all sermons delivered by Buddha throughout his life in the form of an epic.

(c) Bhagawati Sutra

Answer: It is a Jaina religion's holy text. It contains details about Mahavira, the founder of Jainism.

(d) Gangaikonda – Cholapuram

Answer: Founded by Rajendra Chola as his capital city in Tamilnadu to memorise his victory over north India.

(e) Nizamuddin Auliya

Answer: A famous Sufi saint of Sultanate perod. He popularised Sufi doctrines among Hindus and Muslims. Amir Khusro was his desciple.

(f) Raidas

Answer: A famous saint of Medieval Bhakti movement. He belonged to lower caste. He was desciple of Ramananda.

(g) Calcutta Madrasa

Answer: To study teachings of Muslim law and related subjects, Warren Hastings set up it in 1781 in Calcutta.

(h) Jagat Seth

Answer: A banket of Bengal who conspired with British to help them in deposing Siraj-ud-Daula in the battle of Plassey.

(i) Bhawani Mandir

Answer: A journal published by Brindra Kumar Ghosh in 1905. It planned out revolutionary activities in India.

(j) Baba Ram Chandra

Answer: A leader of peasants who organised them to revolt. He led peasant revolts in Uttar Pradesh, during the freedom movement.

(k) Pandita Ramabai

Answer: Founder of Poona Seva Sadan in 1904 to educate women. She dedicated her life to upliftment of women.

(l) Sir Thomas Roe

Answer: A representative of King James I of England. He was sent to India to get permission for trade concession.

(m) Moplah Rebellion

Answer: A violent movement of farmers in Kerala during 19 th century. It was targeted towards Zamindars.

(n) Tavernier

Answer: This French traveller arrived in India during the reign of Shahjahan. He wrote an account of his time.

(o) Darul-Uloom

Answer: An anti-British Islamic Semanary founded by M. Q. Nanawatawi and R. A. Gangohi in 1867.

Q. 4 Answer any two of the following (in about 125 words each): **10 × 2 = 20**

(a) What are the resource bases available for the economic development of the newly created States of Jharkhand and Uttaranchal?

Important Points for Answer:
- *Resources of both States*
- *Prospects of development*

Answer: After the creation of separate states of Jharkhand and Uttaranchal, the Central Government has provided big amounts to them in the name of developmental assistance, for their administration and economy.

Naturally available abundant resources with both the states are also helpful in their economic progress.

Uttaranchal is a hilly state, carved out of Uttar Pradesh, which has many natural and forest resources. Tourism is a developing industry in it. Mineral resources are also available. It has less population and so economic development can be progressed fastly. Jharkhand, on the other hand, cut out from Bihar, is mainly area with rocks and hills, having many minerals under them. Jharkhand is considered with resources of mineral as one of the richest state, potentially, if the growth of economy is well planned and directed.

Both States having various types of resources, have bright pros.pects of economic growth, henceforth not achieved due to political reasons.

(b) Elucidate the factors contributing to the growing need for water harvesting in India, both rural and urban.

Important Points for Answer:
- *Water Harvesting*
- *Conclusion*
- *Usefulness*
- *Indian context–rural, urban*

Answer: In India, the rainfall is generally irregular and uncertain. Moreover, most of the rainfall occurs in two or three months of monsoon while the rest time of the year remains dry or with less rainfall. In such climatic conditions, in India, water harvesting can fulfill the following purposes.

Irrigation : In rural, agricultural lands where water will require for irrigational purposes but no parrenial river exist, the rain water can be stored by check dams in ponds or tanks.

Drinking water : In both the rural and urban areas, potable drinking water shortage is felt in many parts. The rain water, if percolated in the ground, can be availed at such time.

Maintain the level of ground water : By checking, the flow of water, stabilised water can be percolated to recharge the ground water level and make it rise high. Well irrigation can be practiced with this method in dry areas.

Prevention of soil erosion : Flowing water erodes soil cover of the earth and depositing the silt into rivers and sea. Checking water flow at some distances slows the speed and lessens the power of erosion.

All these factors have increased the need for water harvesting in India, both rural and urban.

(c) "Political boundaries and regional boundaries need to be co-terminus." Do you agree!

Important Points for Answer:
- *Meaning*
- *Reasons*
- *Conclusion*

Answer: Boundaries means frontiers of states, between states and countries. Political boundaries may expand to less or more than the regional boundaries.

Political boundary shows the area of administration under one government, demarcated either geographically or politically. While the Regional boundary is a geographical concept of boundaries which divides areas of landmass.

It can be said that while partitioning any country or state, the cultural aspects should be taken into consideration. Unification of cultural integrity is required to maintain political boundary safely.

The political boundary may cover areas very far from the region under administration also. Archaepologers are examples that show that though regional boundaries end on each separate island, the political boundary does not end, and cannot end if the culture and traditional integrity is maintained, though India is an exception with variety of cultures.

So, it is not considered to be necessary to co-terminate political and regional boundaries.

Q. 5 Write notes on the following (in about 20 words each): **$2 \times 5 = 10$**

(a) Regurs

Answer: It is a type of black soil. It is ideal for cotton crop due to its higher moisture retaining capacity.

(b) Karewas

Answer: It is a strip of land on the border of Jammu and Kashmir. It is made of older alluvial soil and disected by many streams into separate blocks.

(c) Negative impacts of shifting cultivation

Answer: Shifting cultivation results in exhaustion of land minerals of a particular type, making it barren and uncultivable for a period. It causes deforestation.

(d) Causes of droughts in India

Answer: Causes of droughts in India are failure of monsoon, uncertain and uneven distribution of rainfall, deforestation, mismanagement of situations.

(e) Significance of Lake Chilka

Answer: It is developed for fishing and prawn culture, under the project of UNDP. It is a coastal lake in Orissa made of brackish water.

Q. 6 Answer any *one* of the following (in about 250 words each): 30

(a) Comment on the financial relations between the Union and the States in India. Has post-1991 liberlization in any way affected it ?

Important Points for Answer:

- *Relations of Union-States - constitutional provisions, financial*
- *Dependency and autonomy of States*
- *Supremacy of Centre*
- *Changes of policy*
- *Conclusion*

Answer: The financial relations between the Centre and the States are controlled by the Constitutional provisions. The Union List mentions the sources of revenue for the Union. The goods and services which the Centre can tax upon are mentioned here. In the same way, the State List mentions items which the States are empowered to tax upon to collect revenue.

Income tax, except agricultural income, custom duty etc. are sources of Union's revenue. Land tax, sales tax, etc., are State's subject.

But apart from these two, there is a provision in the Constitution according to which the Union Government levies some taxes which are collected and appropriated by the State Governments.

These are not the final and substantive provisions in themselves, as Article 280 requires to constitute a Finance Commission for the distribution of revenue between the Union and the States, and after 73rd and 74th Amendment, there is a provision for the Constitution of The Consolidated Fund of the State from which resources are to be provided to the Village, Panchayats and Municipalities.

These are the normally governed financial relations without any special circumstances. But under Article 360, in case of Financial Emergency, these relations can be drastically changed.

Even though not generally as a rule, but customarily, the Union Government supplement the financial resources of the states by :

- Grants-in-aid and
- Advancement of Central loans.

Control of the Centre is maintained under the constitutional provisions by imposing restrictions over the States in raising loans, they are, in some conditions, required to take Central permission.

After the liberalization of 1990s, the Union Government has acquired more importance in developing industries and economic growth. The laws has been liberalised to prevent state interferences to the investors and so a little change has been introduced but it has not affected the financial condition of the states, rather improved.

(b) Is it possible to distinguish between judicial review and judicial activism in India? Does the recent behaviour of the Indian judiciary partake more of judicial activism? Ar with suitable examples.

Important Points for Answer:	
• *Judicial review*	• *Judicial activism*
• *Indian judicial trend*	• *Conclusion*

Answer: Judicial Review means the interpretational and observer role of the judiciary over the Legislature. In India, the judiciary is the final authority for the interpretation of Constitution. If the Legislature transgrasses the powers given to it by the Constitution, the Judiciary can prevent it by declaring the act or action ultra-vires.

This power is called Judicial Review. While Judicial Activism is the concept how actively and quickly the judiciary performs the act of judicial review. The readiness that the courts have achieved in exercising its power to uphold the values of the constitution have been generally come to the extent that judicial review has gradually acquired the form of judicial activism in India.

We can site the following examples, to support the view that Indian judicial behaviour, in recent times, partake more of judicial activism.

Public Interest Litigation (PIL) : The courts have over thrown or at least liberalised the concept of *locust standi* to allow any public spirited person or organisation to bring to the notice of the court any matter of injustice and violation of constitutional rights of any downtrodden and unprivileged classes of society.

The Court has expanded the scope and amplitude of Article 21 to cover many basic rights under it, so that giving them the status of fundamental rights, they can be enforced against the state also, even by PIL.

In many cases, the court has acted *suo moto* to save the constitutional provision of rights.

All these leads to conclude that at least the inclination of the court is towards the judicial activism.

Q. 7 Answer any one of the following (in about 250 words): 30

(a) Would you say that the implementation of the Panchayati System in the last ten years has led to a real restructuring of the Indian polity ?

Important Points for Answer:	
• *Panchayati system*	• *Changes brought*
• *Importance*	• *Evaluation*
• *Conclusion*	

Answer: The Panchayati Raj System came into existence in 1993. It is a Directive Principle of the State Policy enshrined under Article 40 to organise village panchayats as the root level institutions.

The implementation of the Panchayati Raj System has, in many ways, changed a lot, the governance of the country. It has decentralised the governance. It provides to constitute Gram Sabhas at village level. The Panchayati Raj Institutions have started to work as units of democratic set up of our country. They hold elections, do their administration, collect and regulate financial systems of their own, make policies and implement them at the root level and thus train the people for the political system of the nation.

Regular elections, reservation of seats even for women, have really create a great awareness as compared to the first forty three years of our freedom. By no other way, we could have taken the co-operation of villages and grass root level people in the Governance, except by the Panchayati Raj Systems.

No matter, yet there are some rigid problems which lie at the base of this system, too, but these problems have not been able to cover the real-change brought about by the Panchayati Raj.

They really led the country to reconstructuring of the polity. It gave way to a common people participation in real polity rather than being a mere observor of the system after voting in the elections.

(b) Give your views on the right to freedom of religion as enshrined in the Indian Constitution. Do they make India a secular State ?

Important Points for Answer:

- *Right*
- *Constitutional provision*
- *Secularism*
- *Conclusion*

Answer: Our Constitution provides Right to Freedom of religion under Article-25 to 28 as the fundamental rights. Freedom of Conscience and free profession, practice and propagation of religion, freedom to manage religious affairs, freedom as to pay of taxes for promotion of any particular religion, and freedom as to attendance at religious instruction or religious worship in certain educational institutions are provided as the part of this right under Articles 25 to 28.

This right gives all necessary freedoms as from pratice to development of a religion. The religion is a matte' of faith and so a person can develop faith towards any ethics or conducts. He is to respect his faith by the freedom of conscience and is also free to pre' it to others by the freedom of profession, propagation, etc.

However, without freedom as to management of the religious affairs this would have been without great impact.

Q. 8 Answer any two of the following (in about 150 words each): 15 × 2 = 30

(a) What are the constitutional limitations on the free movements of Indians throughout the country?

Important Points for Answer:
• *Free movement - a fundamental right*
• *Limitations - constitutional provision*

Answer: It is to be explained that the freedom of movement is provided as a fundamental right under Article 19(1) of the Constitution. This freedom is only for the citizens of India and not available to other persons.

This right provides right to move freely throughout the territory of India or to reside and settle in any part of the country.

This right to freedom of movement is not absolute right but Article 19(2) - (6) provides that this freedom can be restricted on the grounds of the interest of the general public and for the protection of any Schedule Tribe.

These restrictions can be imposed by law of the State or the Central Government but the ground provided for must be one of the mentioned under clause 2(6) of Article 19. On any other ground, any restriction, if imposed, on free movements of Indians throughout the country will be void. Moreover, these restrictions must be reasonable and related to the public interest.

Q. 8 How has the Indian State tackled the trade-off between environment and development!

Important Points for Answer:	
• *Development*	• *Degradation of environment*
• *Awareness*	• *Measures taken*

Answer: Though we have to accept that in some decades of the starting, we were not much j concerned about the environment protection and conservation but only concentrated on development, economic development, exploiting the natural resources to the extent that imbalance in them was caused. We used the available potential in such a toughtless way that many components of environment witnessed a serious threat.

But, soon India realised and started to grow in sustainable manner, so that environmental degradation can be prevented and remedied.

India participated in the Stockholm Declaration of 1972 and then continuously participate in every international conventions and summit on environment.

It has passed many legal acts to protect environment related to :

– Water Pollution Act - 1972

– Wild Life Act – 1972

– Air Pollution Act – 1981

– Environment Protection Act - 1986

All these laws are aimed at saving environment. India has declared many forest areas as Sanctuaries, National Parks and some Places as Biosphere Reserves.

All industries have to get Environment certificate, to the effect that they do not cause harm to it beyond the permitted level. Environmental measures have been enforced upon all industries and units to balance the development with conservation and protection of environment.

(c) What are the steps that the Election Commission may take if a recalcitrant State Government wants to put off Assembly Elections ?

Important Points for Answer:
• *Election Commission - powers, measures*
• *States' action - effectiveness*

Answer: The Election Commission has power of suprintendence, direction and control of the preparation of the electoral rolls for all elections, including the legislature of every state, and also to conduct elections.

If the State legislature wants to put off Assembly elections, the Election Commission may take required steps to hold the elections according to the Constitutional provisions and laws made by Parliament in this regard.

It is to prepare electoral rolls, the delimitation of Constituencies and other necessary matters for securing the elections.

The Parliament may provide the Election Commission with powers to take corrective measures in such a state.

The Election Commission has power to hold elections from time to time and so, there will be no effect of the state action even if it does not want to hold elections.

Q. 9 Answer the following questions (in about 20 words each): $2 \times 5 = 10$

(a) What is meant by 'double jeopardy' ?

Answer: It means no prosecution or punishment to any person for more than once for the same offence. Indian Constitution, Article 20(2) makes provision of this effect.

(b) What are the protections afforded to Scheduled Tribes in the Fifth Schedule of the Indian Constitution ?

Answer: It contains provisions for the administration and control of Scheduled Areas and Scheduled Tribes, under Article 244 of the Constitution.

(c) In what ways can the President of India ascertain the views of the Supreme Court on a particular bill ?

Answer: Under Article 143, the President can ask for advisory opinion of the Supreme Court, even I on a bill.

(d) What is the common point between Articles 14 and 226 of the Indian Constitution ?

Answer: Both Articles 14 and 226 of the Indian Constitution are available to every person for redressal of arbitariness of the State.

(e) Who and what does the Indian Parliament consist of ?

Answer: The Indian Parliament consist of the President, the Lok Sabha (Lower house) and the Rajya Sabha (Upper house).

Q. 10 Answer any one of the following questions (in about 250 words):

(a) Discuss the impact of globalization on higher education in India.

Important Points for Answer:
• *Globalization*
• *Higher education–benefits, demerits*
• *Final conclusion*

Answer: Globalization has given boost to the higher education in India by opening horizons of progress in every sectors. For example, by Globalization, IT sector has progressed by leaps and bounds and so many software technicians and IITans have got glorious opportunities of prosperous career. This has encouraged students for pertaining higher education and educational institutions for imparting modernised and skillful education which can prepare workers and officers to compete in the world.

BOPs have also given various opportunities in this field.

Foreign Investment has played a great role in modernising and developing education. The funds of Government was limited and not enough to make such world level educational services available to Indian students.

Multi National Companies are also taking interest in providing education and government j has also liberalised policies to allow private colleges and schools.

Not only impact on economic side by Globalization but also on the knowledge part has been impacting educational growth by visits of faculties from foreign countries. Educational institutes invite and send experts for the purpose of more interaction in this direction, making Indian education aware of the world requirements.

Various modern techniques like multi-media and digitization have also improved the educational level in India. Expensive libraries, laboratories and infrastructure with latest instruments and equipments have certainly help education level to grow.

Not only all these positive effects but also some negative aspects have been invited in Indian educational system, like commercialisation of education making it out of reach of poor classes and withering Indian tradition and ethos. But these can be carefully avoided without losing any benefit of global education which has opened interchange of students with many countries.

(b) What is disaster management ? Discuss the steps required to tackle natural disasters.

Important Points for Answer:
• *Disaster management - meaning, requirement*
• *Steps suggested*
• *Natural disasters*

Answer: Disaster management is concept of compensating the loss and rehabilitating public and property affected by any disaster, whether man-made or natural. Disaster management also includes preventive steps in the direction to make such preparations and take such precautions that minimum loss is sustained due to the disaster.

There are, yet many, natural disasters which cannot be prevented by men even after such a progress in science and technology. Such disaster occurring without any control of mankind can be managed by proper planning.

Various natural disasters and steps to tackle them can be enumerated as under :

- **Flood :** Over flow of water causing loss of life and property are both natural and anthropogenic.

  The flood forecasting stations can be established to get prior warning. First such station was established in 1959. Now about 157 stations are there in the country. People can be transferred at safer places.
- **Cyclones :** These are forced winds blowing violently. Weather satellites can forecast cyclonic conditions and then only way would be to evacuate the possible way area.
- **Drought :** Non occurrence or less precipitation which may cause failure of crops and shortage of water. It also can be managed by taking contingency measures. Remote sensing satellites are useful for this purpose.
- **Earthquakes :** The vibration of earth cover due to pressure from beneath or some other reasons, much loss of lives and property can occur.

  Best way is to build up houses and other buildings with quakeproof methods of engineering. It can be forecasted by some scientific instruments.
- **Tsunami :** It is waves from seas and oceans coming violently with huge water mass destroys the whole area. Tsunami warning system can help forecasting its occurrence. That Evacuation of the probable area can be managed quickly as a preventive measure.

Q. 11 Answer any two of the following questions (in about 125 words each): 10 × 2 = 20

(a) Explain the implications of the recent Supreme Court verdict on reservations in private and minority educational institutions.

Important Points for Answer:			
• *Reservation*	• *Issue involved*	• *Verdict*	• *Implications*

Answer: The Supreme Court verdict has ordered to remove the fee regulations and quota, provided by the draft for weaker sections in private, unaided and educational institutions.

The Court has given its verdict to the effect that merit should not be done away with in such private and minority educational institutions by the regulations of the Government. The judgement has presented the Government from interfering into the matters of admissions, in absence of any malpractices, in the unaided educational institutions.

Two types of effects are possible by this order. One and the positive is that merit and intellectual level of the education and thus higher quality will be possible. While on the other hand, management quotas can be misused by such institutions to earn more fees and donations.

And, in absence of fee regulations, poor students will not be able to get admission in such institutions.

(b) What is the energy independence ? Discuss how India can be transformed into an 'Energy-independent Nation.'

Important Points for Answer:
- *Energy independence - requirement, sources*
- *Steps and measures for energy-independence*
- *Indian condition*

Answer: Energy independence is self-reliance in resources of energy for various domestic uses. Many forms of energy available to fulfill the requirements of the nations, at sufficient level, is called energy independence.

India can be transformed to an 'Energy Independent Nation' by following measures:

- exploit domestic conventional energy resources with full efficiency.
- manage them according to demand and availability.
- conserve energy resources with proper policies
- utilize capacity of the fuels to derive maximum energy from them with the use of efficient and latest technology.
- explore oil and natural gas resources available indigenously.
- to use energy saving devices in day to day life for optional use.
- reduce dependency upon less available and conventional energy resources and maximise the use of renewable and easily available technology for sustainable growth.

(c) What is eco-tourism ? How could it be promoted in India ?

Important Points for Answer:
- *Eco-tourism - meaning*
- *Steps towards India*

Answer: Eco-tourism is the concept of developing tourism with due consideration of the environment. The environment should not be disturbed when we develop the tourism industry, neither by wastes nor by preparing tourist place and not by disturbance to the components of environment by the tourists.

It can be promoted in India by :

- Combating environmental problems at the places of tourist interest.
- At the places of tourism, a section should be reserved for maintaining natural environment.
- At various national parks, zoos, mountains, biosphere reserves and such other places, restrictions on tourist activities should be kept to check them disturbing the ecological balance of the place.
- By providing better conservated and promoted natural environment, we can attract more tourists.

Because of its natural beauty and diversity, India has better chances to promote eco-tourism.

Q. 12 Write notes on any two of the following (in about 125 words each): 10 × 2 = 20

(a) Sethusamudram Project

Important Points for Answer:	
• *Project - details*	• *Importance*

Answer: This project is proposed because there is a sandstone reef, called Adam's bridge at Pamban bear Rameshwaram. It is not possible for ships, therefore, to navigate from there. It will link Palk bay and the Gulf of Mannar. It is 300 mt wide and 20 km long channel costing about 2000 crore rupees.

It is a navigational project joining the Bay of Bengal, the Palk Strait and Arabian Sea. It is to reduce the navigable distance of ships avoiding journey circumferencing Sri Lankan Island. It will lessen time taken in journeying, through sea route, from east coast to west coast, by larger ships, conserve fuel resources.

It will also develop ports on both the coasts by increasing frequency of ships.

It is proposed to produce electricity also through this project which would be available to the coastal areas.

In bilateral trade with Sri Lanka, it can help to develop relations, economic, cultural and track II based diplomacy.

The project encarves the whole travelling path through Indian territorial water avoiding confrontation or insecurity in transportation.

Environmentalists however, say that it may damage bio-diversity of the Andaman and Nicobar coast and coral reefs. It may also damage ecological balance of coastal areas.

(b) Causes of soil erosion and its control in India

Important Points for Answer:	
• *Soil erosion*	• *Causes*
• *Indian condition*	• *Steps to control*

Answer: Soil erosion is washing away and removal of the cover of the earth by water, wind, etc. Types of erosions, geographically, are as :

- Run-off erosion : This erosion is caused by rills and gullies, in Chambal, Betwa areas.
- Sheet erosion : due to run-off process of winds and water.

The erosion is caused by water flow and wind blow. These reasons have intense effects now as the deforestation has exposed the earth to them.

Control over them can be maintained by increasing the forest cover of the earth by afforestation programmes, mulching programmes implementation to maintain the moisture in the soil, checking the rumiing of water by building check-dams in their way, social forestry over the governmental and waste lands to hold the soils together by the roots of the trees, building programmes in open fields so that blow of wind can be prevented and flow of water can be reduced.

Tree plantation is considered to be the best way to control the erosion, of any type and by any cause.

(c) Use of Information Technology in health management in India

Important Points for Answer:	
• *IT - use*	• *Health sector*

Answer: Information Technology can be helpful in many ways, ranging from getting latest and recent knowledge and technological know how via conferences, distribution of tele medicine for performance of operations by robots.

Tele-medicine, that is consulting doctors via information technology, diagnosing the patient and prescribing medicine, has made it possible to deliver expertise services even to rural areas.

Robots have been prepared using latest technology, controlled by computers to perform operations under the instructions of the doctor. This technique can help to simultaneously perform more than one operations by a single doctor.

For medical science experts, it is quite necessary to update their knowledge. World level conferences can be held to train and guide doctors by foreign experts without journeying and attending classrooms.

Indirectly, the Information Technology has been helpful in creating awareness via media about health maintenance apart from some of the direct uses and utilities mentioned above.

Q. 13 Write short notes on the following (in about 20 words each): $2 \times 5 = 10$

(a) Equal rights for women in parental property

Answer: By amendment to The Hindu Succession Act 1956, women are made entitled to parental property, however this is not applicable to a joint family.

(b) National knowledge Commission

Answer: The commission is set up under the chairmanship of Mr. Sam Pitroda to make India knowledge producing, sharing and consuming nation.

(c) Genetically modified seeds

Answer: These are hybrid seeds produced by combining good qualities of two different genotypes to make the crop more nutritious.

(d) Ban on bar dancing

Answer: Maharashtra government banned bar dancing to curb vulgarity and alcoholism and to check anti-social activities.

(e) Rehabilitation of street children in India

Answer: They are required to be handled with great care by the Government policies and schemes and with the help of NGOs to provide them opportunities to develop and grow.

SOLVED PAPERS

PAPER - II - 2005

Time Allowed : Three Hours *Maximum Marks : 300*

Candidates should attempt All questions strictly in accordance with the instructions given under each question.

The number of marks carried by each question is indicated at the end of the question.

Q. 1 Answer any two of the following (answer to each question should be in about 150 words): $2 \times 15 = 30$

(a) Present a complete picture of India's efforts for a permanent seat in the UN Security Council.

Important Points for Answer:

- *UN Security Council - permanent seat*
- *India's efforts*
- *Progress*
- *Present position*

Answer: India wants and deserves a permanent seat in the UN Security Council. A formula to expand the Security Council is being prepared.

India has started efforts in this direction by adopting various policies to secure its permanent candidature.

India has formed a group with Japan, Germany and Brazil, collectively known as G-4, who want permanent seats for themselves. This G-4 has prepared a draft resolution in this regard.

India has also campaigned this cause at various meetings, summits, conferences and forums to win support from nations of the world and has succeeded in this attempt to a greater extent.

In bilateral talks and relations also India discusses this point and gets support from friend countries.

A collective talk of G-4 with the African Union is going on, however with a very slow motion to secure affirmative votes of the countries of the Union. African Union has also prepared a resolution for a permanent seat, collective, in the Security Council.

All these efforts of India have yield better fruits in form of affirmative support of the UN member countries to back-up the candidature of India for permanent seat in the UN, Security Council.

(b) Explain the political and economic implications of the Indo-Iran gas pipeline.

Important Points for Answer:

- *Indo-Iran gas pipeline*
- *Importance*
- *Implications - political, economical*
- *Prospects*

Answer: Indo-Iran gas pipeline is proposed having great impact on the eco-political equation in Indian sub-continent and also over the world.

The pipeline project will effect India by providing gas-energy security and good relations in neighbourhood with Iran. It also profits Iran by a beneficial deal and opening more scopes for its trade relations with India, one of the fastest growing economy of the world. By securing energy source, India can hope for a sustained economic growth.

Pakistan is also getting benefit of this project as the pipeline is passing through Pakistan and it will get transit fees and maintenance charges worth billions of dollars. It will also prove one, more important Confidence Building Measure.

Politically, this agreement has forwarded India towards a strategic office. As the nuclear tension between Western countries and Iran is increasing day by day, India is proposed to work as a mediator between the two. Iran is to be persuaded by India, though impliedly and informally, to come to the table for talks while the western powers are to be convinced to think for the cause of Iran and defuse the tension by solving the problem with peaceful manners.

(c) Examine the developments in Afghanistan in the post-Taliban period.

Important Points for Answer:
- *Afghanistan-Taliban issue, development*
- *Conclusion*

Answer: The fall of Taliban in 2001 has yield a path for the development of Afghanistan, It was chosen to lead the country towards democracy. The UN sponsored "Bonn Conference" which created a council of 30 members for internal administration. For internal security, an International peace force was deployed under the UN mandate. As the head of the interim administration, Hamid Karzai was choosen.

For a formal governance set up Loya Jirga - the grand assembly, assembled to prepare a constitution in December 2003. In January 2004, the Constitution was ready and was adopted as a law.

According to the Constitution, Afghanistan is a democratic country with Presidential system of government, having two-house Parliament. In the lower house of parliament, 25% seats are reserved for women. Men and women are given equal rights under the Constitution.

During the phase of this political development in the country, it was also developing in the field of international relations, internal administration, economy and infrastructure. India has helped by financial aid to the country and has provided technical assistance also. The country held its first direct elections in October, 2004 and Mr. Hamid Karzai won it.

Q. 2 Write about the following (answer to each question should be in about 20 words):

5 × 2 = 10

(a) Indians in China

Answer: With liberalisation of both economies and increased trade, Indians have turned to China increasing number of Indian businessmen and workers in China.

(b) Cyber-terrorism

Answer: Hacking, stalking and entering viruses are forms of Cyber-terrorism to create economic strategic loss and political propaganda. This is spread through internet and computers.

(c) Military rule in Myanmar

Answer: Military Generals are ruling Myanmar with Than Shwe as the Chairman of State Peace and Development Council. Movement for democracy under Aung San Sun Kyi is continue against the Military rule.

(d) Camp David Accord of 1978

Answer: The USA mediated Peace agreement between Egyptian President, Sadat and Israel's Prime Minister Mechanem Begin to maintain peace in the middle-east.

(e) Future of Indian expatriates in the Gulf

Answer: Restrictions placed on migrant communities resulted in return of many expatriates to India from Gulf nations but the demand is rising in the field of IT and knowledge sectors for Indians.

Q. 3 Write about the following (answer to each question should be in about 20 words):

5 × 2 = 10

(a) Full convertibility

Answer: Domestic currency convertibility into foreign currency and vice-versa without any restriction is called full convertibility.

(b) Physical Quality Life Index

Answer: It is given by Jim Grant. It uses indices :

(i) adult literacy,

(ii) Infant Mortality Rate,

(iii) Life Expectancy.

It is a social development index of nations.

(c) Differences between absolute poverty and relative poverty

Answer: According to UN parameters, a person earning less than one dollar per day is absolute poor. If persons cannot get even minimum requirements of the life, they are under absolute poverty. Relative poverty is in comparison to other classes of society. Even a person may not be absolutely poor, he may yet be relatively poor in his society.

(d) India - US nuclear pact

Answer: India has agreed to put its all civilian nuclear facilities under the IAEA Inspections and Safeguards while the USA agreed to supply India with fuel for them under Civilian Nuclear Cooperation Pact.

(e) Medical tourism

Answer: By providing modern and skilled solutions and facilities with cheap rate and higher care for health problems, India is trying to attract patients to India for treatment. It is termed as medical tourism.

Q. 4 Answer any one of the following (in about 250 words) : 30

(a) Discuss the causes and ramifications of hunger in Africa.

Important Points for Answer:
• *Africa - hunger, reasons, ramifications*
• *Present scenario*

Answer: Many reasons prevail for the hunger and other curses in Africa. Many countries freed from Colonial bondages in the second half of the Twentieth century are under political evils. They are fighting against the problems that prevail in the social, economical, political and administration fields.

We can divide the causes of African hunger under the following heads :

- Political unstability : After the independence, many dictatorship and military rule have floated in African countries. There are many civil wars to disturb the peace of the continent. Non-stable governments are also reasons why they have not been able to provide food security.
- Social reasons : Due to lack of literacy, awareness and employment, there is overwhelming poverty in these countries.
- Various causes which can be enumerated as undemocratic rule, corruption, failure of administration to effectively exploit and distribute the resources available, underdeveloped agriculture, waste of power and resources in tribal wars and civil upsurges, etc. as the main hurdles in their progress and development.

Ramifications

- migration of people on mass bases.
- clashes to occupy food generating agricultural areas.
- aggrevated problems of epidemics, AIDS, etc.
- International Organisations aid of food and other basic requirements by UNICEF, WHO and others.
- Developed countries coming to assist them and getting benefit of mineral rich areas by exploiting them.
- G-8, developed nations' group helped by waiving loans and debts apart from increasing aid to the poorer countries.

It has been the opinion of the world that democratic rules should be established in the African countries so that stability in governance can be achieved and proper utilisation of International aid and domestic resources apart from exploiting the potentials, can be made possible.

(b) What are the reasons for industrial sickness in India ? Suggest suitable remedies.

Important Points for Answer:
- *Industrial sickness - reasons, measures, remedies*

Answer: Industrial sickness is explained as the situation of an industry in which its entire net worth is eroded; it has suffered cash losses for current and preceding financial year equal to or exceeding its net worth, is the total of its losses.

The Sick Industries Companies (Special Provisions) Act 1985 deals with the sick industries. In India, the reasons for Industrial sickness are found mainly as : External and Internal causes.

The external causes like non-availability of energy resources, raw-materials, changes in government policies, increased competition, reduced demand or increased supply making the industry market losses.

Among internal causes we can include faulty planning, mis-management, financial constraints, unskilled labour to work with the modern technology, non-efficient machinery, process, labour force or management.

As remedies for the sick industries, the government provides with liberal policies, financial assistance from banks and other institutes, exemption from taxes, etc.

Apart from the steps being taken by the Government, we can suggest the following remedies for the sick industries :

- The units should be provided with financial and management assistance, by expert groups.
- Management should be taken over by the group of experts for a certain period of time to remove faults.
- Mal-practices must be punished strictly.
- Technological upgradation should be introduced and required assistance should be provided.
- Market zones for them can be created, export promotion can be provided by policy measures.
- Subsidies and raw material availability can be improved.
- Supply of power, transportation, infrastructures, management can be made more efficient.

Q. 5 Answer any two of the following (answer to each question should be in about 150 words): **2 × 15 = 30**

(a) What is the role of external financial assistance in Indian economy ?

Important Points for Answer:
- *EFA–importance, merits and demerits*
- *Indian position–contribution*

Answer: Since Economic Reforms, post-1991, India has experienced large flow of external investment in form of finance. The growing investment has reduced the requirements of External Financial Assistance (EFA) after the 1990s crisis.

In pre-1991 era, India had to depend upon the EFA even for importing food-grains, and other requirements of the nation. But fast growth of the economy and billions of dollars in form of foreign investment has stop India taking such EFA, except from a few countries like Japan, Russia and some of the European countries.

External Financial Assistance has been given by the World Bank, Asian Development Bank and some other international organisations to India.

However, India's dependancy over EFA has been reduced but its role in India's development has been very important. In developing infrastructure, raising basic facilities to create an environment to attract the investors, providing social-services like electricity, drinking water, irrigation, development of science and technology and many other areas, India has emerged out as developing fast on the basis of these External Financial Assistances, to a larger extent.

(b) Enumerate the objectives of Latin American Reserve Fund. Do you favour such a fund for Asian countries ?

Important Points for Answer:
- *Fund - details*
- *Objectives*
- *Suitability for Asia*
- *Suggestions*

Answer: The Latin American Reserve Fund was formed in 1991. It is successor of the Andean Reserve Fund. This fund is established to correct payment imbalance of the member countries and for that it provides loans upto four year. This fund co-ordinates the monetary, exchange and finance policies. This fund has, also objectives of developing growth of trade between the member countries and for that it promotes liberalisation of trades and payments.

This fund has, Bolivia, Colombia, Equador, Peru and Venezuela as its member countries.

Such a fund can be proposed for Asian countries also as, post 1997 economic crisis has affected many countries in this region. The fund is to provide loans in time of crisis and also to encourage trade relations between the member countries. Development of this region can be boosted by such fund and in time of crisis, which is quite frequent phenomena now a days because of world trade integration and competition. Though SAARC and ASEAN are organisations for trade growth and ASEAN Regional Fund has been established, more staunch can be done by establishing Asian Reserve Fund on the terms of the Latin American Reserve Fund.

(c) Examine the functions of the European Free Trade Association.

Answer: The European Free Trade Association (EFTA) was established on 3rd May, 1960. It signed the Vaduz Convention in June 2001 to liberalise the trade relations amongst the EFTA countries. It is the responsibility of the EFTA to oversee the operation of Free trade area among the member nations.

It performs the following functions namely :

- to achieve free trade in industrial goods among EFTA countries; to cooperate with EU.
- it formed European Economic Area (EEA) by the Agreement with EU.

- to ensure free movement of goods, services, capital and labour throughout the EFTA and EU member countries.
- to ensure the implementation of agreements among the EE A - EFT A member countries it has established a Surveillance Authority and Court.
- the EEA agreement recognises EU rules on company law, consumer protection, education environment, research, etc.

The EFTA was founded by Australia, Denmark, Norway, Portugal, Sweden, Switzerland and U.K. but after the formation of EU, now it has four members, Iceland, Lichestein, Norway and Switzerland. The main aim and objective of the EFTA is to eliminate internal barriers in non-agricultural goods.

Q. 6 Answer or write about the following (in about 20 words each): 15 × 2 = 30

(a) What is Mekong - Ganga Co-operation ?

Answer: In 2000, in Laos six nations of the Mekong-Ganga rivers region formed a group. India, Laos, Cambodia, Myanmar, Thailand and Vietnam - countries grouped for economic cooperation.

(b) What is IFC ?

Answer: International Finance Corporation, an organ of the World Bank group aimed at growth of private government enterprises.

(c) Crude oil price and Indian economy

Answer: Rising crude oil prices increases burden of import bills upon India affecting its balance of trade account.

(d) What is Gandhian economy ?

Answer: Gandhi concepted for village and agriculture based economy, village industries and allied activities to grow, making villages a self-sufficient units with full employment.

(e) Second Green Revolution

Answer: This aims at increasing productivity of various crop in sustainable and balanced manner so that regional growth and environmental balance can be maintained.

(f) Kasturba Gandhi Balika Vidyalaya Yojana

Answer: For SC, ST, OBC and minorities girls, this scheme was launched to set up residential schools for elementary level education in 2004-05.

(g) What is Euro-control ?

Answer: This is norm for emission from vehicles pollution. It measures level in stages like Euro I, II and III. In India, Bharat I, II, and III are used.

(h) Dow Jones

Answer: New York based stock exchange. Shares listed in New York are traded and this index is sensitive to their ups and downs.

(i) 'Bluetooth'

Answer: It is a wireless technology for data transfer from one device to another, connecting computers, mobiles etc. Working in short distance.

(j) MFN status to India by Pakistan

Answer: Most Favoured Nation status is yet not accorded by Pakistan to India, which would end discrimination in trade.

(k) The notion of development of under-development

Answer: It shows down world development i.e. negative growth of GDP. Social standards, etc. when a nation is pushed towards under development.

(l) Cost-push inflation

Answer: It is rise in prices due to increase in the cost of production. It may result because of :

- rise in wages.
- rise in profit margin.
- rise in prices of raw material.
- imposition of heavy taxes.

Some or all of these factors.

(m) What is Green GDP ?

Answer: Green GDP concentrates not only on economic growth but also on environmental issues. It is for the development of economy in sustainable manner maintaining environment balanced. When we deduct environmental depreciation from GDP, we get Green GDP.

(n) What were the terms of reference of the Abid Hussain Committee ?

Answer: The Committee was related to Small Scale Industries and Village Industries, to suggest measures for their growth and remove weaknesses.

(o) What is structural unemployment ?

Answer: Due to change in production methods, like introduction of new technology, demand of labour fall short to the supply. It causes unemployment, called Structural unemployment.

Q. 7 Answer any two of the following (answer to each question should be in about 150 words): **2 × 15 = 30**

(a) Detail the salient features of project 'Anthareeksha.'

Important Points for Answer:
- *Anthareeksha - details, features*

Answer: "Anthareeksha" is space. Every person now can travel into the space due to this commercial project "Anthareeksha". This project is launched by "Scaled Composist" company of the USA. It has prepared a space-shuttle named "Spaceship One". It is a shuttle which can travel a person around in the space and return on the earth. Michael Melvine was the pilote who travelled successfully in this shuttle in the space. Founders of the company, Paul Allen and Burt Rutan are hopeful to increase this facility and make it avail commercially with reduced cost in near future.

(b) Will a grand axis of India, China and Russia challenge the unipolar supremacy of the US? Elaborate your views.

Important Points for Answer:

- *Unipolarism*
- *Axis-formation*
- *Possibilities*
- *Political scenario*
- *Influence*

Answer: After the end of the cold war, America has been the sole military, economically and politically influential super power in the world, changing the international political equations to unipolarism. This supremacy of the US has, in fact, disturbed the democratic structure of the world politics, in UN, WTO and other international institutions and affairs.

If India, China and Russia come together, as the possibilities are there and the progress is in this direction, they can form, together, an axis with having almost half of the world population, majority of the countries under their leadership and fastly growing economies. These factors, apart from having great political influence, technological development and other positive factors, can lead them to form a second super-power axis, to really democratize the world again.

However, Non-Align India cannot come into groupism with these communist friends, but only in matters of leadership, to give and raise voice of poor, developing and under developed nations, India can have co-operation in the form of this unbounded axis. And this axis just needs to be democratic and not Anti-US.

The need of time is to reduce centralisation of international power by lessening US influence. This can be performed by this grand axis.

(c) Explain the China - US textile war.

Important Points for Answer:

- *US-China relations*
- *Textile trade*
- *Issues*

Answer: China is a major exporter of textile to the US. Both countries have their bilateral trade agreements in force for some years, even before China's entry into the WTO.

From May 2005, the question arose on the quantitative restrictions put by the USA on imports of such textile, especially cotton goods from China. China claims that these restrictions are against the quota-system provision of the World Trade Organisation's multi lateral trade agreement. While the Bush Administration claims that it is to protect the interests of domestic industrialists and in accordance with the bilateral agreements that exist between the two.

The US Committee on Implementation of Textile Agreement has taken this decision and the Government does not seem to be willing to remove these protectionist measures.

China contends that, through the WTO, these restrictions should be removed and Chinese trade interest should not be restricted. Even it has expressed dissatisfaction by declaring that such measures by the US may affect the Sino-American Trade relations if the arbitrariness is not removed.

This textile war between two major market players of the world has posed a question against the utility and effectiveness of the WTO.

Q. 8 Answer or write about the following (answer to each question should be in about *20* words): **5 × 2 = 10**

(a) What is Gender Empowerment Measure (GEM) ?

Answer: It is a concept based on a Composite Index. It includes three areas :

(i) Economic participation and decision making.

(ii) political participation.

(iii) Economic resources.

(b) What is the concept of copyleft ?

Answer: Copyleft is a group of licenses. It enable every person to use, modify or redistribute any copy of works. It is applied to software, art and other copyright works.

(c) What is a rogue state ?

Answer: This word is used by the USA and allies for those states who violates democratic principles or uses or develops hidden projects of biological nuclear or chemical weapons.

(d) Repo market

Answer: Re purchasing options are traded in this market for a short time period. Repo is Re Purchasing offer by the RBI.

(e) What is banana war ?

Answer: It is a matter of dispute between the US and EU, arose due to biased trade policies to banana growers of former colonies in comparison to the Latin American growers.

Q. 9 Answer the following, by expanding or explaining (answer to each question should be in about 20 words) : **5 × 2 = 10**

(a) OAPEC

Answer: Organisation of Arab Petroleum Exporting Countries. Arab countries with petroleum asset organised to save their economical and trade interests.

(b) IFAD

Answer: International Fund for Agricultural Development

The fund assists nations to develop and modernise agriculture to increase food production towards food security.

(c) UPU

Answer: Universal Postal Union

To develop and combine services of communication of the world, now under the UN.

(d) SAVE

Answer: The SAARC Audio Visual Exchange (SAVE) Committee is one of the original areas agreed at the inception of the SAARC. It aimed at increasing the awareness of each other among the peoples of the region and disseminating information about Member Countries was established by the Council of Ministers at its Third Session (New Delhi, June 1987). The Committee has been entrusted with the task of producing and implementing the SAVE Programmes

(e) ODA

Answer: Official Development Assistance (ODA) is a category of development aid. It is administered with the promotion of the economic development and welfare of developing countries as its main objective, and it is concessional in character and contains a grant element of at least 25% (calculated at a rate of discount of 10%).

Q. 10 Answer any one of the following in about 250 words : 30

(a) Describe the sources of ionizing and non-ionizing radiations and their effects on the biotic components of the atmosphere.

Important Points for Answer:	
• *Sources*	• *Effects*

Answer: Ionizing radiation are of two types, caused either by (1) Particles or by (2) electromagnetic rays. However, in both types, atoms carry enough energy to ionize an atom or molecule in atmosphere by completely removing an electron from its orbit.

Ultra-violate rays, X-ray of high energy, Gamma-rays are some of the sources of ionizing radiation.

In cases of nuclear weapons, gamma rays of atom bombs and explosions etc. emit such energy. Cobalt-60, Caesium-137, Americium-241, Iodin-131 etc. are some particle sources of ionizing radiation.

Non-ionizing radiation is any type of electromagnetic radiation that does not carry enough energy to ionize atoms or molecules by completely removing electron from their orbit.

Visible light, Infrared, micro-wave, radio wave etc. are sources of non-iodizing radiations. They are less dangerous for human health and so used in medical field for surgical and diagnostical approach.

These radiation have proved very dangerous for the stability in atmospheric balance. They cause atoms or molecules of atmospheric components ionized and so they react with other ions creasing many a types of dangerous chemicals in atmosphere.

It also harm genetic composition of biotic organisms in atmosphere and then they may be transferred to dangerous form to other lives on the earth.

Recently, some conventions and protocols have been signed and are being implemented to prevent such type of radiations which could pose a great threat to the existence of life on the earth.

(b) What is digital convergence? Examine its implications for modern society.

Important Points for Answer:
- *Meaning*
- *Implications*
- *Benefits*

Answer: Digital convergence is transformation of analog data to digital representation. Various types of chemical or physical datas can be transformed to digital data. Such digital data are, then available on computer and other mediums. These data are now accessible and can be stored, manipulated, or edited according to the requirements. This digitization of information of various forms is called convergence. It provides accuracy, accessibility and efficiency in work.

It brings benefits of the growth of IT sector to use of common men. Satellites, mobiles, etc., are also used.

Main and foremost feature of digital convergence are that digital images or sounds from various sources can easily be combined, filtered, edited or otherwise, altered for variety of purposes, so that easy communication, reproduction of information, use of the same information simultaneously at various places, easy, quick and efficient access to everybody effective representation and wide networking can be achieved.

This technology may prove helpful not only in e-governance of the country making the system transparent and to the reach of common people but also in weather forecasting for coastal areas and fisherman and farmers about rainfall and conditions of humidity, very much required to them. Connected with satellites, equipment can provide services like expertise satellite education and medical services to remote areas also.

This technology, useful in scientific research, industry, governance, entertainment, education, medicine and astronomy, has widened the scope of human knowledge and reach.

Q. 11 Answer any two of the following (answer to each question should be in about 150 words each): 2 × 15 = 30

(a) Why do environmentalists regard asbestos and polythene as pollutants?

Answer: Pollutants are those matter which make any component of our environment dangerous for life. Asbestos and polythene are two non-biodegradable matters. They do not decay by biological actions and remain as wastes.

Asbestos is a mineral fibre which is hard and so used as a construction and covering material. It is also used as an insulation and fire retardant. Small particles of asbestos float in the air invisibly. They get inhaled by us and accumulate in our lungs causing lung or chest cancer. They cause a disease called Asbestosis.

Polythene is also a commonly used non-biodegradable material. They are used as hand bags, covers and packets. They are made up of Polyvinyl Chloride (PVC) which dangerously affect our health. It can cause various diseases like Raynand's syndrome, angiosarcoma, brain cancer or arcostrloloysis.

Due to these reasons, environmentalists regard them as pollutants and advice to reduce their use.

(b) What is the therapeutic cloning ? Describe briefly the method and its potential applications.

Important Points for Answer:
- *Therapeutic cloning - meaning, technique*
- *Applications - possibilities*

Answer: Therapeutic cloning is to clone human tissues or organs using stem cells but not for the purpose of creating a baby. Thus, therapeutic cloning, in other words, is a limited use of the human cloning technology.

It can be achieved by getting an egg from a woman and then entering DNA from any other person, this stem cell will grow into desired type of tissue. Stem cells are necessary for cloning. Stem cells can be provided by the person himself, they are reproductive. The Parkinson's disease, diabetes and other diseases can be cured with the use of this technique.

The heart patient can be cured by therapeutic cloning. It would be possible, in future, to replace the whole organ of the patient on failure of any. For example, a patient of Leukaemia can be cured by cloning the stem cell, may be taken from his own body, into the bone marrow. And thus, the need of any donor of bone-marrow can be done away with.

In short, the therapeutic cloning process can prove helpful in curing any disease by replacing the degenerative ill cells of the tissue or organ by newly cloned cells.

(c) Why is hydrogen being acclaimed as the fuel of the future ?

Important Points for Answer:
- *Hydrogen–source of energy*
- *Future prospects*

Answer: Hydrogen (H) is the main concern as an alternative future source of energy for scientists in the world. Hydrogen is present in abundant amount in water (H_20). Hydrogen from the sea water can be used as a source of energy. It gives three times more energy than petrol.

Other important property is that Hydrogen when combust with Oxygen, gets converted to water and so no question of pollution arises.

When other conventional sources of energy are at danger of being exhausted hydrogen gives no such doubt. As the availability of sea water is reliably sufficient it is an inexhaustive source of energy.

Various uses of hydrogen are possible as a fuel. It can run a motor, can produce electricity and can be used as a domestic fuel also. Hydrogen is being used in space programme. It is available in every part of the world in one or another form. It is also, used in nuclear energy and spin-off in defence.

Because of all these qualities hydrogen is acclaimed as the fuel of the future and technological research for its uses are being conducted by scientists.

Q. 12 Answer the following (in about 20 words each): 5 × 2 = 10

(a) What is an exabyte ?

Answer. It is a unit of a large storing capacity of a computer. It can store data of a billion gigabytes size.

(b) What is VIRUS ?

Answer: VIRUS stands for Vital Information Resources Under Siege. It is a set of instruction which can be used to operate the data of another user. It is an illegal act.

(c) What do the following stand for ?

(i) XML

(ii) MASER

(iii) SECAM

(iv) TIPS

Answer:	(i) XML	:	Extensible Mark-up Language
	(ii) SECAM	:	Microwave Amolification by Stimulated Emission of Radiation
	(iii) SECAM	:	Sequential Couleur a Memoire (Sequential Colour with Memory)
	(iv) TIPS	:	Technology Information Pilot System

(d) What is avatar ?

Answer: 'Avatar' is a project to design and develop a hyperplane which is half rocket and half aircraft in India. It will take off like a plane, fly into low orbit of the Earth and return to the base station executing its mission.

(e) What is Wikipedia ?

Answer: It is an encyclopedia on internet available in multi-lungual form, biggest till the date.

Q. 13 (a) Put the following information into a frequency distribution table, assuming the range of monthly wage is from Rs. 300 to Rs. 4500, and draw a histogram on a graph paper: **8**

"10%, 30%, 60%, 80% and 90% of a group of monthly wage earners receive less than Rs. 600, Rs. 1000, Rs. 1800, Rs. 2800 and Rs. 3300 respectively and 5% receive Rs. 3600 and above."

Answer:

Monthly wage (Rs.)	Earner's Frequency (%)	Earner's Frequency (%) on Rs. 300
300–600	10	$\frac{10}{300} \times 300 = 10$
600–1000	30 – 10 = 20	$\frac{20}{400} \times 300 = 15$
1000–1800	60 – 30 = 30	$\frac{30}{800} \times 300 = 11.25$
1800–2800	80 – 60 = 20	$\frac{20}{1000} \times 300 = 6$
2800–3300	90 – 80 = 10	$\frac{10}{500} \times 300 = 6$
3300–3600	5	$\frac{5}{300} \times 300 = 5$

3600–4500	5	$\frac{5}{900} \times 300 = 1.66$

The upper limit for monthly wage is Rs. 4500.

The basic class size is 300 (basic size is the lowest class size).

Histogram representing distribution of wage earners according to monthly wage

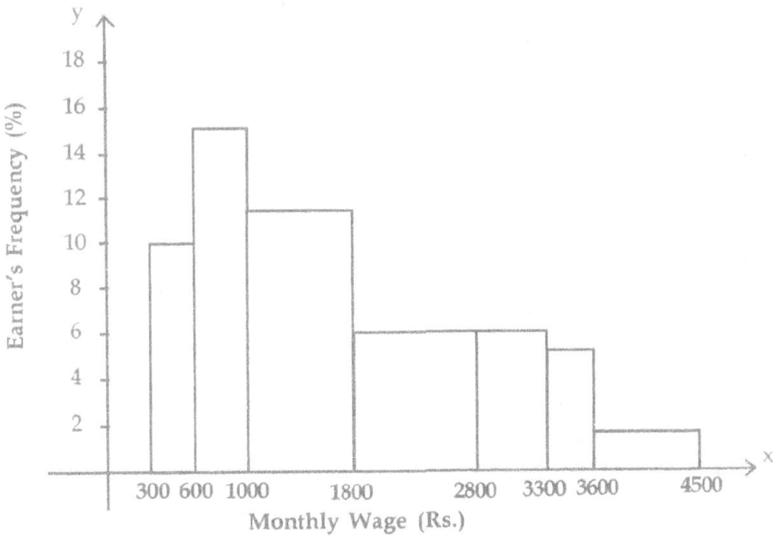

Scale used:
y-axis : 1 unit = 2
x-axis : 1 unit = Rs. 300

(b) The marks obtained by 32 students of 12th class of a Government school are:

628, 665, 560, 328, 421, 525, 480, 470, 405, 424, 664, 668, 620, 300, 305, 520, 420, 370, 326, 440, 328, 480, 565, 650, 480, 360, 325, 450, 360, 426, 440, 306

Form a Cumulative Frequency Table with class interval of 50. **8**

Answer: Cumulative Frequency Table

Marks	Frequency	Cumulative frequency
300–349	卌 = 7	7
350–399	III = 3	10
400–449	卌 II = 7	17
450–499	卌 = 5	22
500–549	II = 2	24

550–599	II = 2	26
600–649	II = 2	28
650–699	IIII = 4	32
	Total = 32	

Q. 14 (a) Represent the following data by a histogram : 8

Daily Earnings (Rs.)	No. of Stores
0–50	3
50–100	7
100–150	4
150–200	5
200–250	4
250–300	3
300–350	2
350–400	2

Answer:

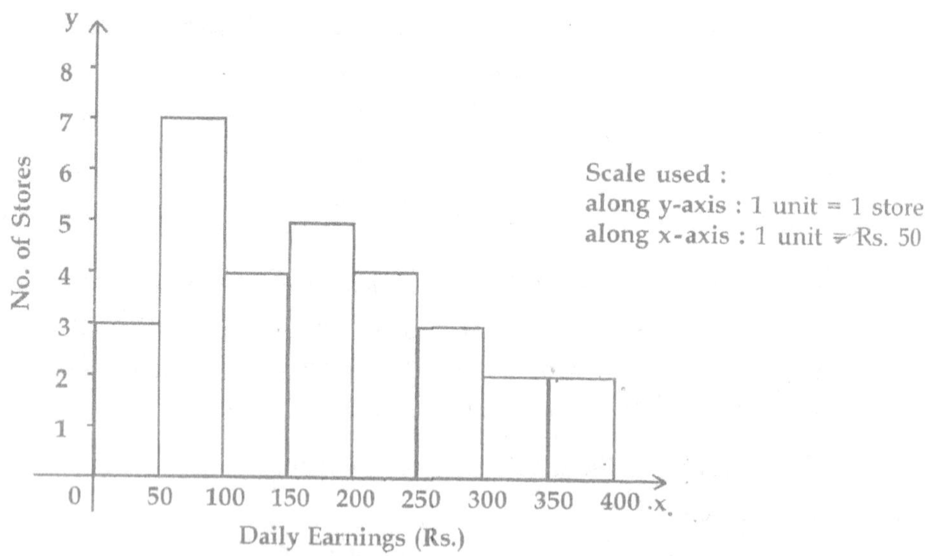

(b) Construct a cumulative distribution table from the following frequency distribution and find the number of students obtaining below 15 marks : 8

Marks	Frequency
0–5	4

5–10	12
10–15	10
15–20	8
20–25	3
25–30	2

Answer:

Marks	Frequency	Cumulative frequency
0-5	4	4
5-10	12	16
10-15	10	26
15-20	8	34
20-25	3	37
25-30	2	39
	$n = 39$	

The number of students obtaining below 15 marks is 26.

Q. 15(a) A train travels first 300 kilometres at an average speed of 30 kmph and further travels the same distance at an average speed of 40 kmph. What is the average speed over the whole distance ? 2

Answer: Average speed $= \frac{\text{Times of Distance covered}}{\Sigma(f)}$

$$= \frac{2}{\frac{1}{30}+\frac{1}{40}}$$

$$= \frac{2\times 120}{7}$$

$$= 34.28 \text{ kmph.}$$

(b) The arithmetic mean of 12 observations was computed to be 6. Afterwards, it was found that one of the figures was wrong. Instead of 7 (seven, which is the correct figure) it was read as 1 (one, the wrong figure). Find the correct value of the arithmetic mean after incorporating this information. 2

Answer: Sum value = mean × observations

$$= 6 \times 12$$

$\therefore$ Sum value = 72

(i) Wrongly taken value removing = 72 – 1

= 71

(ii) True value adding = 71 + 7

= 78

Again getting the arithmetic mean = 78/12 = 65

Hence, True mean = 6.5

(c) A firm of readymade garments makes both men's and women's shirts. Its average profit is 6% of sales. Its profit in men's shirts average 8% of sales and women's shirts comprise 60% of output. What is the average profit per sales rupee in women's shirts ? 2

Answer: Suppose there is total output of 100 items,

out of these 60%, i.e. 60 are women's shirts.

Holding that items 100 is total output,

of which → 40 are men's shirts

→ 60 are women's shirts

(d) The mean and variance of two seta of data are given below with the data size:

	Data Size	Mean	Variance
I	12	64	23
II	9	72	18

What can you say about the mean and variance of the combined set of observations as compared to the individual means and variances without performing any calculation ? 2

Answer: It can be concluded that :

- Value of observations are higher in data II
- Less variances (difference among them) is seen in data II.
- Value of observations are smaller in data I.
- Larger differences exist in data I.

Thus Data I : More observations, small in value, with larger differences.

Data II : Less observations, large value, less differences (variances).

(MAIN) **Civil Services Exam.**

2006 General Studies

SOLVED PAPERS

PAPER–I

Time Allowed: *Three Hours Maximum Marks: 300*

Candidates should attempt ALL questions strictly in accordance with the instruction given under each question.

Q. 1 Answer any *one* of the following (in about 250 words) : 30

(a) Regardless of distance in time, there were lots of similarities between Lord Curzon and Jawahar Lal Nehru. Discuss.

Important Points for Answer:
- *Time*
- *Similarities in: • administration, • reforms, • development, • industries, • foreign policy, • partition*

Answer: Lord Curzon's time is 1899 to 1905 A.D., while Nehru worked for India both in pre and post independence era.

Conditions against them were, of course, different. Then too, their attitude show us many similarities in their nature and method of work.

Administration : Both were firm administrators. Curzon worked for the interest of British India and Nehru for the interest of India and both of them worked efficiently. They were able to work in spite of having differences with system. For example, Curzon did not fully agree with Parliamentary and Viceroy-in-Council matters. Nehru, on the other hand, had differences with Congress over the issues like socialism, international stand, policy objectives, constitutional reforms, etc.

Reforms : Curzon reformed the police administration and judicial system. Nehru, during his interim government also tried to do it. Both Curzon and Nehru make some structural changes in army by dividing it into commands.

Development : Curzon constructed canals on rivers Jhelum, Chenab and Bari. Nehru constructed Bhakhra dam. Curzon recommended to set up the Railway Board.

Industries : To develop industry or commerce, Curzon set up a department. Nehru followed the policy of public sector industries to boost industrial development.

Foreign policy : Curzon was expert in this area and so was about Nehru. To make India interferenceless territory, he had some attempts against possible infiltration of Russia, France or Germany. While Nehru gave Panchsheel providing principle of non-interference.

Partition : Lord Curzon ruled the controversial partition of Bengal in the interest of British India's peaceful rule. Same had been done by Nehru regarding the partition of India-Pakistan for peace and development of India.

Thus, we can find out many similarities among them in their nature, method of work, rule, administration etc., at least, from a single point of view.

(b) How did the Government of India Act, 1935 mark a point of no return in the history of constitutional development in India ?

Important Points for Answer:

- *Constitutional Development*
- *Provisions of Act - 1935*
- *How a point of no return ?*

Answer: In India, constitutional development can be traced back to about 1861 Act or if we go back, yet, to the Regulating Act of 1773.

But the Act of 1935 made some important provisions which were directly adopted in the Constitution of India with or without some modifications.

The Act provided to establish an All India Federation including all provinces at that time under the paramountcy of the British Crown. Same was there in our Constitution.

The Governor-General was to administer federal subjects with the assistance and advice of a Council of Ministers. These ministers were to be chosen from and were responsible to the federal legislature. Now the Constitution provides for the same mechanism under the President of India and Centre's Council of Ministers.

This Act introduced responsible government both at the Centre and the Province which is intact now in our Constitution.

Bicameral Legislatures were introduced in some provinces. Provinces were made autonomous in their respective subjects. Now too, our States are autonomous by the authority under Constitution.

The Act made provision for a Federal Court at Delhi. Now the Constitution makes provision for the Supreme Court of India, which is vested with all the functions of the federal court.

Lists were introduced in this Act. This provision made separation of power between the Centre and Provinces. Now our Constitution provides for three lists, dividing power between Centre and State Governments.

All these provisions were so important that there was no return from them but the Constitution adopted them, though not in toto. So, it can be said that the Act marked a point of no return in the history of Constitutional development in India.

Q. 2 Answer any two of the following (in about 150 words) : **2 × 15 = 30**

(a) What was the attitude of Indian Industrialists towards the Indian National Congress in the pre-independent era ?

Important Points for Answer:	
• *Industrialist*	• *Congress-industrialis2ation*
• *Attitude*	

Answer:

In the pre-independence era, industry in India grew at slow rate. Some industrialists cum- patriots established industries. Jamnalal Bajaj, G. D. Birla, Ambalal Sarabhai were some of them.

It is evident from the National Movement that Congress widely boycotted foreign goods. This led as an alternative to grow Indian industries. Therefore, Indian industrialists, who flourished under patriotic feelings, helped Congress.

They even joined and financed Congress. Jamnalal Bajaj remained exchequer of Congress for his life time.

Congress supported Swadeshi goods and by turn, Swadeshi industries. Indian industrialists influence, to some extent, power of Congress by providing it with finance and the society with Swadeshi goods.

To support the program of Congress, they had their free industrial policy without interference of the British rule. FICCI was established by them in 1927 and supported Congress directly.

Though, later Congress turned Socialist, to some extent, but this does not show more diversion from patriotism - pro-congress attitude of Indian Industrialists.

(b) Critically assess Sir Tej Bahadur Sapru's views on Indian Nationalism.

Important Points for Answer:	
• *Sir T. B. Sapru's views*	• *Assessment*

Answer: Sapru, under the influence of Gokhale believed in Constitutional means of agitation. But they were not in concurrance with the extra-constitutional methods of agitation that were adopted by Congress later on.

Sapru wanted to accept Jinnah's proposals and concede some more seats to him, if peace and agreement could be procured through it. But here he failed to understand Jinnah's attitude.

He wanted India as a federation of the whole territorial units, under the British rule, by Indian Constitution. It shows appreciable feelings of unity in him.

As a liberal leader he favoured formation of interim government and he opposed creation of "Pakistan" as a separate state. He was with national feelings of undivided India. He always tried to make Indian National Movement more participatory in nature. He educated people for public opinion. His national spirit was filled up with deep patriotism.

(c) Characterise the main features of Indian Renaissance.

Answer: Indian Renaissance was started under the influence of the British or Western thinkers. It was characterised by the following features :

- It was influenced by Western thinkers.
- It gave rise to study of English literature, thoughts, philosophies and books of history.
- Indian past was studied in a new way.
- Reinterpretation of Indian religious texts and rituals was made. This exposed irregularities and mal-practices in our religion prevailing at that time.
- Under Raja Ram Mohan Roy and others, it started new movements for socio-religious reforms. Sati abolition, prevention of child marriages etc. were preached and movements gained force.
- Different classes of Indian society looked at such reforms with varied perspectives.
- It has some influence over political movements in India and later on it was perfectly adopted by political movements gained force.
- Different classes of Indian society looked at such reforms with varied perspectives.
- It has some influence over political movements in India and later on it was perfectly adopted by political movements.

Q. 3 Write about the following (not exceeding 20 words each) : 15 × 2 = 30

(a) Kalhana

Answer: Kalhana was a 12th century Kashmiri poet and historian. He was the celebrated author of 'Rajatarangini'. He wrote this book during 1147-1149. He was in Harsha's court, of Lohar dynasty. He received help in writing the book from his father Champak who was the minister in the kings court.

(b) Panini

Answer: He was a Sanskrit grammarian from Gandhara, near modern day Peshawar. His grammar of Sanskrit consists of four parts : (i) Shiva Sutras (phonology), (ii) Ashtadhyayi (means eight chapters) (morphology), (iii) Dhatupatha, (iv) Ganapatha.

(c) Yakshagana

Ans. It is a typical folk form of drama. It is a true people's theatre. It is an amalgam of the sky with the earth. It is an ancient form of art. It includes song, dance and drama and is popular in Uttara, Malenadu and Dakshina Kannada districts of Karnataka.

(d) Natyasastra

Ans. It was written by Bharat Muni. It covers aspects of dance-drama. It is a book on principles of art, in Sanskrit.

(e) Tabaqat-i-Nasiri

Ans. It was written by Minhaj-us-Siraj in 1260, during the early medieval period of Delhi Sultanate. In Tabaqat-i-Nasiri, he starts with the account of earlier prophets and ancestors of Muhammad, leading to birth of Islam.

(f) Madhura Vijayam

Answer: Madhura Vijayam (of 1350s) is related to Kampana's expedition. This was against Madhura Sultanate in the time of Bukka-I.

(g) Pandurang Mahatmya

Answer: It is a holy literary work by Sridhar. It is divided into 10 Adhyayas and celebrating the virtues of Pandharpur, probably the greatest centre of pilgrimage in Maharashtra.

(h) Prithviraj Raso

Answer: Composed by Chand Baradai, Prithviraj's court poet. It narrates life of Prithviraj - III, of Chauhan Vansa who ruled Ajmer and Delhi. It is an epic. It is a source of information of the Kshattriya community of northern India.

(i) "The Insider"

Answer: It is a novel published by former Indian Prime Minister, Mr. P.V.Narsimha Rao in 1998. It is controversial book which follows a man's rise through the ranks of Indian politics. It throws light on political conditions during his period.

(j) Ali Sardar Jafri

Answer: He was an Urdu poet and received famous Jnanpith Award. He took part in freedom struggle and was a famous person of literature. He contributed to highlight the cause of the oppressed class and realities of life through his works.

(k) Aruna Roy

Answer: Her name is related to the Right to Information Act. She received the Magsaysay Award. Her contribution in public life is notable in RTI development.

(l) Dr. J.C. Daniel

Answer: Father of Malayalam cinema. He brought cinema to Kerala. He had produced "Vigathakumaran", first film in Kerala. He himself scripted and directed it.

(m) Balwant Gargi

Answer: For his play "Rang Manch", he received the highest literary award of the Sahitya Akademi. He is a Punjabi dramatist and short story writer.

(n) Dr. Jayant Narlikar

Answer: He is a distinguished astrophysicist and cosmologist of India. He is conferred with the Padma Vibhushan Award. He set up IUCAA in Pune in 1988.

(o) Shashi Tharoor

Answer: India nominated him as a candidate for UN Secretary - General election. Later he withdrew his candidature. He was the first Indian to be nominated for this post.

Q. 4 Answer any two of the following (in about 125 words) : $2 \times 10 = 20$

(a) Bring out the prospects of development of alternative energy sources of India.

Important Points for Answer:	
• *Alternative energy resources*	• *Prospects of development in India*

Answer: For a vast country, like India, energy crisis is a big hurdle in its development.

Some alternative energy sources like solar, hydel, biogas, geo-thermal, wind, etc., are available here. These sources have great potential of development in India.

Its total capacity is assumed as about 8000 MW in 2006. It is also expected that by 2012, total capacity of alternative sources will be about 20,000 MW.

At present, part of alternative energy sources is about 6% of the total energy requirement. India has second position in the world[1] in Biogas plants. It has also wide potential of solar energy due to its vast sunny territory.

Many rivers provide facilities for development of hydel-energy. Sea shore and open fields can be utilized to produce wind energy by installing wind-firms.

CNG, Bio-diesel etc. are new fields in this area but are widely popular.

India is technologically developing on this front to utilize its optimal resources of alternative, unexhaustive, renewable energy sources, which are environment friendly.

(b) Blue Revolution has definite advantages in India but it is not free from environmental impacts. Discuss.

Important Points for Answer:	
• *Meaning*	• *Scope*
• *Environmental impact*	

Answer: Blue Revolution relates to the production of fish. India is the third largest producer of fish (2nd largest in Inland fish) in the world.

Blue Revolution is proposed to increase fish production on scientific line. This can be

Blue Revolution is proposed to increase fish production on scientific line. This can be made possible due to its 7517 km long sea shore and big rivers like Ganga, Brahmaputra, etc.

Environmental impact over Blue Revolution can fade away India's hope for progress.

- Oil trade, that is mostly carried out through the Indian ocean threatens survival of fish in times of oil spills.
- Chemicals flown in the ocean and rivers have also produced a threat for the growth of fish.
- In India, climate is generally hot and so, fish can not be kept fresh without facilities of refrigeration.
- Kerala and Tamil Nadu practice sand mining. Its dust causes adverse effects on fisheries.

(c) Why do the rivers of west coast not form a delta ?

Important Points for Answer:
- *Nature of rivers of West Coast*
- *Why do not form delta ?*
- *Requirements to form a delta*

Answer: Generally west coast rivers are fast flowing. They do not have perennial flow of water. Their path is generally rough. They do not pass through plains. They have steep side flow, sometimes causing water-falls.

To form a delta, the flow of river must contain a slow flow of water. Water quantity is required to be large and must bring a big amount of alluvial. These rivers should be perennial in nature, generally.

So, it is not possible for West Coast rivers to form delta because they generally do not allow its silt and alluvial to be deposited on its coasts. But it drifts away them in the sea. Therefore, the rivers of West Coast do not form a delta.

Q. 5 Write notes on the following (in about 20 words each) : $5 \times 2 = 10$

(a) Mixed economy

Answer: Here both private and public sectors play their role. This is a combination of capitalism and socialism. Also called as a mix market or command economy.

(b) Winter rains in India

Answer: In coasts of Tamilnadu and Andhra Pradesh, rainfall is received in winter. Cause for it is western disturbances in North India. It benefits some crops.

(c) New Moore Island

Answer: India has possession of this island since 1970, the time of its birth. It is a controversial island between India and Bangladesh. It is an uninhabited Island.

(d) National Water Grid

Answer: The idea is connected with interlinking of rivers. To provide water, to water deficit areas and to reduce devastating effects of floods in surplus areas, it is proposed to prepare a National Water Grid.

(e) Hussain Sagar

Answer: Hazrat Hussain Shah Wali constructed this lake. It is situated in Hyderabad. It was constructed during the rule of Ibrahim Kuli Kutub Shah.

Q. 6 Answer any *one* of the following (in about 250 words) : 30

(a) What is right to life and personal liberty ? How have the courts expanded its meaning in recent years ?

Important Points for Answer:
- *Right to life and Personal Liberty*
- *Cases expanding its meaning*

Answer: Article -21 of the Constitution of India provides to every person 'Right to life and personal liberty' as a fundamental right.

According to this article, no person can be deprived of his life or personal liberty except in accordance with the procedure established by law.

Starting from the case of Menaka Gandhi - 1978, the Supreme Court has constantly expanded meaning and scope of Article-21. In this case natural justice was included under the scope of Article-21. It also included here a right to live with human dignity. M. C. Mehta's case opened a new horizon by including pollution free environment as a component of the right to life.

Similar importance was given again when it was interpreted to cover the right to education in case of Unnikrishnan v. Union of India - 1993.

Also by various cases, the Supreme Court has covered many other rights under it.

Right to free legal aid and speedy trial is a part of right to life.

Even a prisoner has right to speedy trial and legal aid. Fair procedure cannot be denied to him.

Even the court has awarded compensation to the victim whose right under Article-21 has been violated here important is Rahul Shah's case.

Combining Article 21 with various other rights under Part III and Part IV of the Constitution, a new dimension has been started by the court to protect a person's right to life and personal liberty.

As, without education, pollution free environment, air and water, shelter, health care, food and such basic requirements, the Article would be dead words of a book, all these provisions are rightly covered under it along with others.

(b) On what grounds can a member be disqualified from either House of Parliament ?

Ans.

Important Points for Answer:	
• *Provisions of the Constitution*	• *Amendments*

Answer: Article - 102 makes provisions for such disqualification. The grounds are as follows :

- If he holds any office of profit, he shall be disqualified. Such office may be under Central or State Government.
- If a competent court declares him of unsound mind.
- If he becomes an undischarged insolvent.
- If he is not a citizen of India or if he later voluntarily accepts citizenship of any other state.
- If any law of parliament disqualifies him.

Apart from these grounds, he also may be disqualified under the Tenth Schedule, for the following grounds :

- If he voluntarily gives up membership of any political party.

– If he votes against the political party or abstains from voting in favour of the party, whose member he is.

– If he joins any political party after his election without being elected as a member of that party.

– If a nominated member joins any political party after six months.

The schedule was amended by 85 th Amendment Act of 1985 which made provision that if a group of members accounting one-third of the existing party splits from the party and forms a new party or joins any other party, then this will not be a ground for disqualification of such members.

But again by 91st Amendment Act - 2003, the provision has been omitted and so split is a ground for disqualification.

All these are grounds provided in our Constitution for disqualification of a member of either House of Parliament.

Q. 7 Answer any *one* of the following questions (in about 250 words) : 30

(a) What is the 'strategic partnership' between India and United States of America ? What are its implications for both the partners ?

Important Points for Answer:

- *NSSP - nature, scope*
- *Implications - on India, on USA*
- *Benefits*

Answer: NSSP–Next Step in Strategic Partnership is announced between India and USA as a major initiative in bilateral relationship. This strategic partnership does not limit itself only to defence and political matters but also covers economy, technology and cultural matters.

This started when in Jan. 2004, both nations agreed for co-operation. This agreement focussed mainly on

– Civil nuclear activities - Civil space programme – Trade in high-technology This makes provisions for cooperation through specific agreements and steps on bilateral basis from time to time.

The NSSP has, at first, mainly concentrated on non-proliferation and trade issues, especially export control.

Its implication for both countries will surely result into benefits.

In terms of nuclear programme,

– Strategic partnership will have effect to legitimate Indian nuclear programme and after a period of time, recognising India as a nuclear power.

– India's requirement of technology and nuclear materials can be fulfilled via NSSPs.

– India will get a strong position in Asian political-strategic equations and its relations with countries of European Union will get positive support by this agreement.

– Russia, France, Australia, etc. will get green signals to deal with India in nuclear technology and material trade.

– India's requirement of energy will be met by development of nuclear energy programme. US support will play a critical role in such development.

On the other hand, USA will get an access to Indian economy and would be able to exploit its vast potential.

USA's interest in creating balance in the regional block will also be fulfilled.

USA will be able to reduce Indian contact with Iran for energy by helping India to create alternative nuclear energy resources.

Thus, the strategic partnership will benefit both countries in strengthening political ties, building economic ties and trade relations, mutual cooperations, fighting terrorism by a joint mechanism and other fields.

(b) Discuss economic backwardness as a major challenge of Indian democracy. Can democracy and development go together smoothly ?

Important Points for Answer:

- *Indian economic backwardness*
- *Democracy and development–how related ?*
- *Its impact of democracy*
- *Conclusion*

Answer: India is not having equal economic development for its all classes and in its all parts. It is the main reason why Indian democracy cripples slowly.

Economic backwardness in many parts of India have resulted in poverty, under-nutrition, lack of proper education, health awareness and facilities of development. In such circumstances, a citizen is not and cannot be expected to be able to participate in the process of democratic governance of the country.

Therefore, due to economic backwardness, a large part of Indian public remain out of democratic process and so nation is not running as a true democracy.

If every citizen can take part in process of democracy without any influence or compulsion, without any threat and with well aware information and knowledge, only then a democracy can succeed.

Here, economic backwardness has become a real challenge to our democracy. Democracy and development are inter-related phenomena. Only if full democratic governance is implemented, requirements of people can be known.

Democratic country pays equal attention to every requirements of all classes of citizens, irrespective of their level and number.

Development can be achieved only after satisfying all basic requirements. Development is all over upliftment of social, political, cultural, educational and economical levels of public life.

To achieve development, democratisation of a nation can help and boost the process.

It can be said that it is the basic requirement and result that democracy and development can go together smoothly, only together and not otherwise.

Q. 8 Answer any two of the following questions (in about 150 words) : 2 x 15 = 30

(a) How would you differentiate between the passage of a Constitution Amendment Bill and of an Ordinary Legislative Bill ?

Important Points for Answer:
- *Constitution Amendment Bill – procedure*
- *Ordinary Legislative Bill - procedure*

Answer: Article - 368 provides procedure for the passage of a Constitutional Amendment Bill. According to it, such bill can be introduced in either House of Parliament. It must be passed by

– a majority of the total membership of that House and also by

–` a majority of not less than two thirds of members present and voting.

There is no provision for a joint sitting for such Amendment Bill.

While the procedure to pass an Ordinary Bill is as following :

– It can, also, be introduced in either House and it can be introduced by a Private Member also.

– No prior recommendation of the President is required for an Ordinary Bill while such recommendation is pre-requisite for a Constitutional Amendment Bill.

– In case of failure of the bill due to lack of majority, a joint sitting under Article - 108 can be called upon.

– Rajya Sabha can amend it or reject it.

An Ordinary Bill can be rejected, approved or returned for reconsideration of Parliament by the President, but he is not empowered to do so in case of a Constitutional Amendment Bill.

(b) How does the Inter-State Council establish co-ordination between States ?

Important Points for Answer:
- *Inter-State Council*
- *Role*
- *Co-ordination : a function*

Answer: Our Constitution makes provision vide Article - 263 for establishment of an Inter-state council. This was established by the President in 1990.

This council is to perform the following role :

– The President may confer upon its function to discuss any Inter-State dispute and find out solution.

– It may investigate and discuss subjects involving interest of states and/or union.

– As the Chief Ministers are members of this council, they may express and save public opinion of each state in solution of any dispute.

– This council may recommend for formation of such policies that would serve common interest of states.

The President can establish such council and define nature of role and functions to be performed by it.

In times of growing inter-state trade and other relations, coordination is must between them. This council can perform this role. Each state can express its interest and involving them, a common policy and understanding for them can be made possible here. Such coordination is possible when representatives of every state come in contact on a common platform. This Inter-State Council provides a platform for such co-ordination.

(c) Is the High Courts' power to issue 'writs' wider than that of the Supreme Court of India ?

Important Points for Answer:	
• *Provisions*	• *Comparison*

Answer: Article-226 provides that High Courts have powers to issue writs. This powers can be used to enforce any fundamental rights or any other right.

Article-32 declares that it is the duty of the Supreme Court to issue an appropriate writ to enforce any of the fundamental rights.

It can be compared that the High Courts can issue writs even to enforce any other legal rights also, whereas the Supreme Court can enforce only fundamental rights.

Both can issue writs of the nature of *Habeas Corpus,* Mandamus, Prohibition, *Certiorari,* or *quo warranto.*

However, it must be noticed that a person can avail of the right under Article-32 as of a right because it is a fundamental right whereas Article-226 do not confer any duty upon the High Courts to issue a writ. It is simply dependent upon discretionary power of high courts.

However, in matter of areawise jurisdiction, the Supreme Court has wide power whereas the High Courts' jurisdiction is limited to any particular area.

Q. 9 Answer the following questions (in about 20 words each) : 5 × 2 = 10

(a) Explain the following terms :

(i) Dissolution of the House

Answer: President can end the business of the House of People, by dissolving it.

(ii) Prorogation of the House

Answer: Termination of the session of the House.

(iii) Adjournment of the business of the House

Answer: Postponement of the business of the House for a specified time by the Speaker or the Chairman of the House.

(b) What is Consolidated Fund of India ?

Answer: Under Article - 266, Consolidated Fund of India is created by Parliament. All revenues, loans, repayment and interests of loans are deposited in it. Authorisation of Parliament is required to withdraw any amount out of it.

(c) To what extent can the President withhold his assent to a Bill already passed by the Parliament ?

Answer: At first he can return a bill once for reconsideration. If it is passed again, he must assent it. Otherwise he may choose to withhold his assent.

(d) What is India's 'Look East' Policy ?

Answer: To boost economic, trade, technology and other area of cooperation with neighbouring countries of South East Asia, *Look East* policy was formed by the Prime Minister of India.

(e) What is meant by 'empowerment of women' in India ?

Answer: To uplift economical, social, political and educational status of women. To create possibilities for their progress by provisions and policies of government.

Q. 10 Answer any one of the following questions (in about 250 words) : 30

(a) What are the social and economic consequences of abolishing child labour in India ?

Ans.

Important Points for Answer:	
• *Child labour*	• *Abolition of child labour - result*
• *Social consequences*	• *Economic consequences*

Answer: India is facing the curse of child-labour. A large number of children have to work as child labourer in industries or other places of works like hotels, stalls, shops, etc.

Laws have been made to abolish child labour from India. Various schemes and programmes have been formulated to meet this end. But yet it is a far goal to be achieved.

If the child labour is abolished, India will have to face some consequences in socioeconomic fields.

In social field, they are required to be educated. If they have no work to do, their poor families will not be able to meet requirements of life. Even to some families starvation will be a result.

Apart from this, children will require enough nutrition. Activities for their upliftment will be a first priority. But the position does not appear that government will be able to provide food, clothes, shelter and education on its own if children do not earn.

Adult members will have to replace the children. Children are always low-paid. An adult cannot afford to work for such low payment.

On economic front, there are some protests from USA and European countries regarding child labour in India. After abolishing it, Indian export will grow.

But earning amount of a family will be reduced. As children support their families, income deficiency will result in poverty.

Employers of children will not be able to employ an adult person because of their inability to pay higher wages.

Even after working, some children afford their own food and education, this burden is then to be handled by their poor parents. Economic conditions of Government is not so sound to afford all these costs.

This will result in higher cost of wages to small scale industries and small employers. All these seem to lead that perhaps it is also not possible for India to abolish child labour immediately.

(b) Explain the implications of the implementation of Intellectual Property Clauses in our patent law regime after joining the WTO.

Important Points for Answer:	
• *Intellectual Property clauses*	• *Implications*

Answer: The Patents Act of 1970 has been amended and implemented with effect from 1st January, 2005. The Indian Patents (Amendment) Act - 2005 makes provisions to fulfill the obligations of the WTO.

After joining the WTO, we were under obligation to respect the TRIPs (Trade Related Patent Rights) Agreement of WTO. Therefore, India amended the Patent Act to protect Intellectual Property Rights of other nations' companies.

It now covers all fields of technological intellectual property rights related to drugs, food and chemicals.

Indian Pharmaceutical Companies will have to suffer a lot. Many companies will not be able to export their drugs. However, to save them, it is provided that they will not be liable retrospectively. They are free to export even patented drugs to least developed countries (LDCs).

Other chemical and food industries will now require to submit to other big farms who have patented for a product.

It is possible to contract with the companies who have patented for any drug or chemical or food item and then to produce that item. It means contract based work as an agency can be taken by them.

Of course, research in drugs and chemicals are expensive and long term process. Only big firms are able to do it and so it is not possible for India's small companies to have patent rights registered in their work field. This alteration creates difficulties for Indian economy.

Q. 11 Answer any two of the following questions (in about 125 words each) : 2 × 10 = 20

(a) Explain full convertibility of Indian Rupee.

Important Points for Answer:	
• *Convertibility - meaning*	• *Current Account*
• *Capital Account*	

Answer: Convertibility means a system of transaction where a country's currency becomes a convertible in foreign exchange and vice-versa.

Full convertibility of Indian Rupee was proposed to promote foreign trade and investment in India, especially in post-reform era.

Current Account Convertibility is a system by which Indian Rupee has been made fully convertible in current account transaction related to goods and services, since 19 th August, 1994.

Capital Account Convertibility implies convertibility of currency of a nation into bonds, shares as assets of another country. In India, RBI had appointed a committee in 1997, under Mr. S. S. Tarapore to give suggestions on full convertibility of Indian Rupee in Capital Account. It recommended some phases for it. But the Finance Ministry has ruled out any possibility of in capital account convertibility in near future.

However, it must be noted here that full convertibility helps every exchange of one currency into another. That facilitates trade and transaction among nations.

(b) What are the linkages to be developed under the Knowledge Revolution for Rural India Plan ?

Important Points for Answer:
- *Plan*
- *Linkages*
- *Prospectives*

Answer: The Knowledge Revolution for Rural India Plan is a part of larger Plan to make India a developed nation. "Every Village a Knowledge Centre" plan was born out of policies at M. S. Swaminathan Research Centre.

The plan, to succeed, at primary stage requires linkages among private sectors, NGOs, Cooperative Societies, various R & D institutions and government agencies. The launching of the National Virtual Academy for Food and Security and Rural Prosperity is an initiative in this direction.

To bring knowledge, livelihood and prosperity, Information and Communication Technologies are to be used.

Various linkages in the form of Schools, Colleges, Research Centres, Special Training Centres are parts of this plan.

Apart from these, centres and hubs of technologies, information and knowledge via radio and televisions will also play their parts to link Rural India with main sources of information and knowledge.

(c) What do we understand by 'Doha Round' of talks ?

Important Points for Answer:
- *Explanation*
- *Importance*
- *India's stand*

Answer: 'Doha Round' of talks is related to the World Trade Organisation. In this special round of talks at Doha, various matters related to agricultural subsidies and trade barriers were discussed.

To implement free and fair competition in world trade, it is necessary to reduce the level of agricultural subsidies provided by the developed countries to their farmers. This does not allow a free competition and so agricultural products of developing and poor nations cannot compete with them.

Moreover, export subsidies were also proposed to be phased out, in agricultural products. Quota-free access to commodities exported from developing countries and reduction in trade barriers were proposed in Doha Round of talks. But most of these proposals are yet to be agreed upon and accepted by the developed countries. Only then boundary-less trade can be made possible among the nations of the world.

Q. 12 Answer any *two* of the following questions (in about 125 words each) : $2 \times 10 = 20$

(a) Explain the social constraints in bringing about gender equality in Indian society.

Important Points for Answer:	
• *Gender equality*	• *Social constraints*

Answer: Gender equality is a great challenge for Indian society. Apart from various traditional customary problems various social constraints are also there. They are :

- In patrimonial, male-dominated society of India, female have always been subjected to domestic expressions. They are psychologically dominated by male. This creates lack of confidence among them to face social challenge.
- They are not well aware of economical and political systems. So they cannot participate in such fields without proper training. It requires a long time.
- They are not aware of legal provisions favouring and protecting them.
- They, if come out of houses to participate in the mainstream of society, male would unable to handle children and other household works on their part.
- Female are regarded as machines to produce children and satisfy sexual instincts of male at night. This attitude is yet to be changed.
- Proper upliftment of women is much required in Indian society.

Note: India ranks 108 among 174 countries in the UNDP's Gender Development Index.

(b) What are the problems related to the rehabilitation of the mentally challenged persons in India?

Important Points for Answer:	
• • *Mentally challenged persons*	• *Rehabilitation programmes*
• *Problems*	

Answer: Mentally challenged persons are suffering from some deficiency of brain or nervous system.

They are to be protected and rehabilitation is required through government programmes.

Various schemes and policies are required to be implemented through efficient machineries.

Challenges:

- Traditionally they are looked at derogatorily.

- India lacks facilities for their cure and rehabilitation.
- As medical practices, there is not well developed system of cure for mentally challenged persons. Well trained psychiatrists are not available in India in required number.
- Government fund is not allocated in proper amount.
- Proper family care and attitude is not available to them. They are not attended with due care.
- According to Psychiatrists, if proper treatment is delivered, they can be well cured, but people are not aware of such treatments.

(c) Bring out the issues involved in implementing compulsory primary education in India.

Important Points for Answer:	
• *Compulsory Primary Education*	• *Issues*

Answer: Even the Constitution makes provision for compulsory primary education to all children between the age of 6 to 14 years.

But no success can be predicted in near future. Because, there is higher drop-out ratio. Children are not aware of education benefits and so is the case with parents. So they are not willing for education.

Poverty and compulsion of work makes it impossible for some children to have education. Even proper facility of schools, buildings, teachers and funds are not available in our country.

Psychologically trained teachers to encourage children for education are not available. Though many policies and schemes are there for compulsory primary education, proper implementation machinery and willingness on bureaucracy is not available.

Q. 13 Write about the following (in about 20 words each) :

(a) Business Process Outsourcing

Answer: BPO - It is method where a company based in Country A, purchases services from another Country B by establishing its base there or otherwise.

(a) Female foeticide

Answer: By sex determination, sometimes if the foetus is found of a female child then it is destroyed in the womb, called femal foeticide.

(b) RCI

Answer: Rehabilitation Council of India. It is a council to supervise the rehabilitation process after various development project makes displacement of people.

(c) UNIDO

Answer: United Nations Industrial Develbpment Organisation. This provides technical and financial assistance to developing and undeveloped nations for their Industrial development.

(d) S. Chandrashekhar

Answer: Subramanyam Chandrashekhar, an India astro-physicist who gave Shekhar limits theory regarding development of stars. He is a recepient of 1983 Physics Nobel prize.

SOLVED PAPERS

PAPER–II

Time Allowed : 3 hours *Maximum Marks : 300*

Candidates should attempt ALL questions strictly in accordance with the instructions given under each question.

Q. 1 Write about any *two* of the following (in about 150 words each) : 15 x 2 = 30

(a) US policy on Iran's nuclear programme

Important Points for Answer:		
• *Issue*	• *US attitude*	• *Policy*

Answer: Iran claims its right to peaceful research in nuclear power, but US alleges that in the guise of peaceful energy research Iran wants to prepare nuclear weapons.

US is at hard-core opposition to Iran. US wants to drag Iran to the Security Council from the IAEA.

It scolds Iran for its alleged violation of NPT and some UN principles.

It took tough stand when Iran expelled IAEA inspectors from its territory. Means, it is totally anti-Iran. Some interest of US in Iran, regarding energy resources is there behind such attitude.

But China and Russia do not favour the policy and want IAEA to handle the problem of Iran. Even Russia proposed a dialogue with Iran on the issue.

They do not want US to interfere in Iran's domestic matters particularly and generally Middle East.

(b) Terrorism : Sources in Pakistan and Afghanistan Points :

Important Points for Answer:	
• *Terrorism - spread*	• *Sources in Pakistan*
• *Sources in Afghanistan*	

Answer: Terrorism has widely affected almost all parts of the world. Though it may be of local, regional or world origin, now a days, some parts are being regarded as its main sources. Pakistan and Afghanistan have been pointed out as such areas by USA.

In Pakistan, Quetta is considered as a strong support-base for Taliban. Taliban's activities are being organised and planned from here, according to some sources of information. In Afghanistan, main areas are Kabul, Khost, Jalalabad, Gardez, etc. in southern part. In the areas, making borders of Pakistan and Afghanistan, we can mention Waziristan mountain region. This area mainly comprises tribal parts in Pakistan. It is known as FATA i.e., Federally Administered Tribal Area. Terrorist activities have grown here.

To curtail such terrorism sources, US-NATO has taken some actions in identified areas of Pakistan and Afghanistan.

Suicide bombers, soldiers, civil terrorists and group of armies are being trained in these areas.

(c) Crippling the King in Nepal

Important Points for Answer:		
• *Incidents*	• *Provisions*	• *Effects*

Answer: At the end, the King has to transfer power to democratically elected government in Nepal, pending election and Constitution formation. Agreement between Government and Maoist is also a step in this direction.

- Now the King in Nepal will be merely a nominal head. Title of His Majesty's Government has been replaced by Nepal Government,
- Nepal's forces were known as Royal Nepali Army (RNA). Now it will be called Nepali Army. Cabinet will appoint the chief of Army. King will be no longer the head of Army.
- Even King will come under perview of laws made by Parliament.
- King will have to pay taxes as an ordinary citizen.
- As now there is no requirement, The Raj Parishad (King's advisory council) will be dissolved.

All these will make Nepal a fully Democratic State with all powers in the hands of, ultimately, citizens. Nepal has made agreement with Maoists also to include them in the main stream of politics.

Q. 2 Write about the following (in about 20 words each) : 2 × 5 = 10

(a) Simla Agreement

Answer: This agreement was entered into by India and Pakistan to end the war of 1971, in December, 1971. Indira Gandhi signed it.

(b) India-Israel cooperation in the field of agriculture

Answer: Indian - Israely companies enter into agreements for such cooperation. Biotechnology and drip-irrigation technology are main areas.

(c) Pakistan's role in Sri Lanka

Answer: As Sri Lanka is emerging as a growing economy, and there is a political unrest due to LTTE, Pakistan is taking chances to get Sri Lanka's favour as it can influence India in the subcontinent.

(d) Indo-US military cooperation

Answer: India consented to the Kick lighter proposals of USA. Both had some joint military and naval exercises to increase cooperation.

(e) Nuclear Non-proliferation Treaty

Answer: The NPT aims to prevent spread of Nuclear Weapons and related technology. It was entered into in 1968. India and Pakistan have not signed it.

Q. 3 Write about the following (in about 20 words each) : 2 × 5 = 10

(a) Contribution of the NRIs to GCC countries

Answer: Indians employed there gave their support and services to the development of Gulf countries. Indian labour, technicians, doctors and software engineers are at great demand there.

(b) Future of Indians in Fiji

Answer: After the removal of Mahendra Chaudhari's Government, the recent development show a trend for possibilities of peaceful existence of Indians in Fiji.

(c) Indians in the House of Lords, UK

Answer: Recently Lord Paul Swaraj gained a seat in the House of Lords, UK. This will help boost interest of Indian Community residing in UK.

(d) Contribution of Indians in Silicon Valley

Answer: Indian software and technology experts have help Silicon Valley's growth. Vinod Khosla is one of such Indians.

(e) Exodus of persons of Indian origin from Uganda

Answer: Dictator Idi Amin had expelled many Indian from Uganda. It had caused problems for Indians. Yet there are about fifteen thousand Indians in Uganda.

Q. 4 Answer any one of the following (in about 250 words) : 30

(a) Discuss the importance of World Trade Organisation (WTO) to Indian economy in the light of various opportunities and challenges at the global level.

Important Points for Answer:
- *Opportunities : World Market, Clothes and Textiles, Investment,*
- *Agriculture, Trade-share*
- *Challenges : Competitiveness, Agriculture, Patent*
- *Conclusion*

Answer:

- **Opportunities:**

– ***World Market*** **:** WTO aims at boundaryless trade-market. Its provision when effectuated in letter and spirit will open for Indian products and services markets of all member countries. This will help utilise India's wide labour potentials.

– ***Clothes and Textiles*** **:** In textile industries, India can expect much growth after Multi Fibre Agreement. India's export is being increased in this sector. This sector earns India a big amount of foreign currencies.

– ***Investment*** **:** While accepting the WTO norms, free competition is allowed in India for foreign investors. Due to liberalization of laws and regulations, due to WTO, huge inflow of foreign investment is coming in the country.

– ***Agriculture*** **:** Though India is technologically yet unable to squeeze all potential it possesses in this sector, but when the research and development in Biotechnology, irrigation and modern techniques will start to give fruits in near future, it will help India to unexpected high extent.

– ***Trade Share :*** Having the benefits of WTO membership, Indian foreign trade has grown year by year. India's share in total world trade has increased from 0 5% to about 1 percent.

❍ Challenges:

– ***Competitiveness :*** The country needs to remove all protective measures. It will require Indian industries to be very much competitive to the world level.

– ***Agriculture :*** Our agricultural production have to face unnecessary troubles from the developed countries. They provide subsidies to agriculture and we are required to phase out agricultural subsidies. Terms are being discussed.

– ***Patent*** **:** Our industries, especially pharmaceuticals will have to face some challenges due to patent regimes of WTO.

❍ **Conclusion :**

WTO - World Trade Organisation can help Indian economy grow to its peak by providing enough opportunities to utilize its potentials. Even challenges, in long term will improve condition of our economy.

(a) Describe the main sources of Industrial finance in India. How could India be benefitted from recent developments in International finance ?

Important Points for Answer:
• *Sources : IDBI, SIDBI, SFCs, IRBI*
• *Benefits from international finance*

Answer:

❍ **Sources :**

– ***IDBI :*** Industrial Development Bank of India was established in 1964. Its main objective is to provide financial credit for development of big and small industries.

– ***SIDBI*** **:** Small Industrial Development Bank of India was established to help SSIs. It helps them by promoting and financing.

SIDBI also provides assistance to modernise small scale industries in/technological field, to make them competitive.

– ***SFCs :*** State Financial Corporations working in states provide loans to needy industries. They also promote shares and debentures, If required', they would provide guarantee for loans of third parties.

– ***IRBI :*** Industrial Reconstruction Bank of India has main aim to revive sick industries and make them able to exist and compete in market, by assistance.

Some other sources may also help industrial finance. But these are main sources.

On the International front, recent developments have make the horizons of such financial assistance very wide. They helped in easying rules and regulations for such assistance. Foreign technological assistance can help Indian industrial modernization.

Emense opportunities of investment have been created by foreign Direct and Institutional investments.

When domestic capital cannot suffice the demand of industrial requirements, capital flow from international flora is now possible in India to supplement domestic savings and capital sources.

Such liberalization has lead to develop infrastructural and technological base for Indian economy. Development of financing facilities in international area is obviously large and that makes India's world trade grow.

Q. 5 Answer any *two of* **the following (in about** *150* **words each) : 15 x 2 = 30**

(a) Discuss the role of public sector during the post-reform period of Indian economy.

Important Points for Answer:	
• *Changes in post-reform period*	• *PSUs role*

Answer: Post-reform period shows much development in Public Sector Units. Liberalization, Privatisation and Globalisation has changed attitude and structure of PSUs.

Government policies have been directed to make them much more autonomous and this autonomy is utilised by them for growth.

PSUs grow in open market. Post-reform period removed their monopoly. They make themselves more competitive to survive, in the market led economy.

Even in this period, when abundant in India, they have fulfilled the requirement of people. They do not only concentrate on profit but have efficiently serve the goal of socialism.

Removing corruptions, improving efficiency and overcoming deficiency, they won trust of people in stock market also.

Profitability and foreign partnership of PSUs have provided Indian economy good amount of capital and service.

Their public issues, profitable contract, areas of focus, commercial attitude and competitive ability are praiseworthy in post-reform period.

(b) Examine the effects of globalisation on poverty removal in India.

Important Points for Answer:	
• *Focus of Globalisation*	• *Disparities*
• *Release of public money*	

Answer: We can discuss various aspects of Globalisation on poverty removal in India.

The areas of focus for investment have been almost those which do not help create job opportunities for poor-illiterate labour forces. Yet, technologically advanced industries have attracted educated youth to employment. Capital is mostly directed to production of those goods and services which are not labour intensive and so less chances for employment, ruling out possibilities of poverty removal.

Investment has even created disparities among classes of people and among regions of India. For example, Maharashtra, Delhi, etc. receive great part of FDI while BIMARU states have less on their part. These disparities also widen gap and create poverty.

On the other hand, Globalisation has made government free to invest on many fields and so that fund, now, can be utilise for poverty alleviation programmes and schemes. Government could privatise PSUs and the released funds were allocated to social programmes.

(c) What are the implications of gender disparities in India ?

Important Points for Answer:	
• *Gender inequality*	• *Implications*

Answer: Gender inequality is seen, in India, as less number of female than male.

Average sex-ratio is 933 female per 1000 male. Less education rate among female as compared to male.

Apart from these, and due to these, the following implications are resulted :

- Women do not participate in the main stream economic activities. This make India's almost half population directly dependent, apart from children and old persons.
- In social field, female are domestically supressed and they do not enjoy respectable position. They are not regarded as intelligent and powerful as male.
- Politically they do not participate and even where they participate as a voter or representative, mostly they are used as rubber-stamps in the hands of their male relatives.
- They are generally devoted to household work in India's patrimonial society. They are not properly educated and so cannot deliver proper training to children.
- Such under-privileged condition of female lead them to face domestic violence, sexual abuse at working place and improper opportunities for progress in every areas of life.

Q. 6 Answer the following (in about 20 words each) : $2 \times 15 = 30$

(a) What is Phillips curve ?

Answer: It is proposed by prof. A. W. H. Phillips. It shows relationship between the percentage of money wages versus the level of unemployment. It shows that the lower unemployment, the high the rate of change of wages.

(b) What is Hundi ?

Answer: It is a bill of exchange. Person A gives an order to pay to another person C; the amount written in the Hundi, to the bearer, i.e. person who holds the Hundi.

(c) What is twin deficit ?

Answer: Twin deficit is fiscal deficit and current account deficits. For India, it is about 11% of GDP. When both deficits occur together, that is called twin deficit.

(d) What is the main difference between free trade area and common market ?

Answer: Free Trade Area is a policy among a group of countries, limited to the members, e.g., SAARC.

Common market implies uniform tariff policy by members with outsiders. Among members; free trade is practised e.g., EU.

(d) What is forward currency market ?

Answer: It is a mechanism in the city of London. It can help enhance profit and reduce risk of fluctuations in international trade.

(f) What is offshore currency market ?

Answer: It is a situation where currency is sold when external demand for a currency exceeds liberation of that currency. It depends on the growth of an economy.

(g) What is Laffer curve ?

Answer: This curve shows that there is one optional tax rate. This rate can give maximum tax revenue and boost production. Change from this rate may have negative impact.

(h) What are Eurobonds ?

Answer: The bonds that can be issued in one country but can also be traded in other countries in Euro currency are called Eurobonds.

(i) What is disguised unemployment ?

Answer: When people seem to be employed but they are infact not have added any production on their part, e.g. Indian agriculture where more persons than requirement are employed.

(j) What are nifty and the nifty junior ?

Answer: Both are Stock Market Indexes. Nifty has 50 companies on its list. Nifty Junior also has 50 but smaller companies.

(k) What is Agri-Trade ?

Answer: Trade of agriculture and related products to promote export of fruits, vegetables, flowers, etc. This helps growth and commercialisation of Agriculture.

(l) What is CEMA bloc ?

Answer: The Council for Mutual Economic Assitance (CEMA) - 1949 was formed by the Soviet Union against NATO. Balkan states joined it.

(m) What is rolling settlement ?

Answer: In rolling settlement system, trade is allowed to set off next day or after a period of days.

"Straight through" process is used. This practice is followed in stock markets also.

(n) What is the difference between Green Box subsidies and Blue Box subsidies ?

Answer: Both are under the WTO. Green box do not related to any particular product, while Blue Box requires the farmers to accept some conditions and limitations.

(o) What are non-factor services in India's balance of payments ?

Answer: Non-factor services have been emerged as a key factor in India's invisible trade, in the period of 1991 to 2001. They have proved a base for India's economic growth.

Q. 7 Write about any two of the following (in about 150 words each) : 15 × 2 = 30

(a) G-8 Summit in Russia

> **Important Points for Answer:**
> • *Summit* • *Points discussed*
> • *Result*

Answer: The G-8 Summit , representing world's most industrialised eight countries was held in Russia recently. This proves the rising influence of Russia in the world.

- Summit voiced in favour of Indo - US nuclear deal, supporting it in principle.
- Leaders condemned vehemently activities of terrorism. They affirmed their joint cooperation to fight against it.
- They proposed to increase cooperation in overcoming threat of AIDS and other diseases.
- Iran issue towerred the agenda of meeting. Iran rejected offers of western powers to suspend its enrichment programme. They discussed the issue in detail.
- To create knowledge-based economy, they expressed their concern for educational development by modern systems.
- They discussed modalities to help poor countries of Africa and other parts of the world.

(b) Expanding role of Amnesty International

> **Important Points for Answer:**
> • *Amnesty* • *Objectives* • *Role*

Answer: Amnesty International is an organisation that fights for the protection of human rights, improving conditions of prisoners and war criminals. Fair procedure of justice and no abuse of soldiers and freedom of all prisoners of conscience are also goals of Amnesty. It does not only concentrate on publication of information and materials but also concentrates campaigning for public opinion by individual, regional or thematic campaigns. Due to its significant role played in these fields it was awarded the Nobel Prize.

In times of natural or other crisis Amnesty has played praiseworthy role in recent years. International Legal aspects and their proper implementation for improving conditions of refugees, non-citizen labourers and workers, it works against governments and nongovernmental organisations.

It publishes annual report regarding condition of human rights in every countries of the world. This report is given great concern all over the world.

(c) Role of European Parliament

> **Important Points for Answer:**
> • *Parliament structure* • *Functions & Powers*

Answer: European Parliament consists of all member countries of European Union. Therefore, it has total 732 members. This Parliament represents about 450 million European Citizens. So, it is a large democratic body of Europe.

Then too, it has to play a limited role. It has no power to legislate for the member countries.

Council has also significant role to play in the EU.

European Parliament approves the budget of the Union. It also legislates on the matters of common policy decision matters, not falling within purely domestic jurisdiction.

Parliament approves the appointment of the President of EU. It also approves the remaining members of the Commission.

Parliament has power to supervise the EU's activities.

Parliament, being a democratic body can be entrusted with making policy of common benefit to all members, like trade, agriculture, technology, etc.

However, the European Parliament has not unfettered powers in entrusted matters, but by discussion members can bring to surface their concerns to the notice of others.

This makes possible the coordination among member countries.

Q. 8 Write about the following (in about 20 words each) : 2 × 5 = 10

(a) Trade through Nathu La Pass

Answer: This is a new route opened for trade after a long period between India and China. To promote trade some exemptions have been allowed.

(b) Outer Space Treaty

Answer: It contains main legal aspects of outer space in International field. The Treaty of 1967 makes provision for free and peaceful use of Outer Space.

(c) Withdrawal of Japanese Troops from Iraq

Answer: Due to home pressure and its international policy, Japan withdrew its troops from Iraq. It had sent its troops along with the USA and UK.

(d) Maastricht Treaty

Answer: The Treaty of 1992 created the European Union and the currency of euro. This is the treaty which bring together all countries to form a common market.

(d) Cuba and Castro

Answer: Cuba, is a small country. Castro is its President. He opposes American policies and Cuba is banned on many issues by USA for many years.

Q. 9 Write about the following, by expanding and explaining the objectives (in about 20 words each) : 2 × 5 = 10

(a) ICJ

Answer: International Court of Justice : It aims to solve legal problems arising among states in their interaction. It helps interpretation of International law and settles legal disputes between states and gives advisory opinion to UN and its specialised agencies.

(b) INTELSAT

Answer: International Telecommunications Satellite Organisation : Its objective is to provide telecommunication facilities to states and to solve problems related to it.

(c) IBRD

Answer: International Bank for Reconstruction and Development (set up in July, 1944) : It helps developing and under developed countries to reconstruct economy by providing them with financial support.

(d) WMO

Answer: World Meteorological Organisation (entered into force in 1950) : It provides services related to meteorology to member states. Its main purpose is to facilitate exchange of weather data to establish a world-wide network of meteorological stations.

(e) WHO

Answer: World Health Organisation : This organisation was set up in 1948 with the aim to provide services to maintain health of poor and under nourished people of the world. Its chief organs are the World Health Assembly, the Executive Board and a Secretariat.

Q. 10 Answer any *one* of the following (in about 250 words) : 30

(a) Justify with necessary logic "Biological clean-up methods can be cheaper than the conventional physical and chemical pollution treatments".

Important Points for Answer:

- *What are Biological clean-up methods*
- *What are physical and chemical methods*
- *Advantage*

Answer: Pollution causes many hazardous compounds in air, water and soil. To convert these hazardous compounds into non-hazardous chemicals, various clean-up methods are employed.

Such conventional methods use physical and chemical treatments of these compounds.

Biological clean-up methods have proved effective in converting toxic compounds into biodegradable substances and in phases, into water and carbon dioxide.

Bioil-FC is one of such Biological agent. Bioremediation is also employed as a secondary treatment.

Bioremediaton is a technique for environmental detoxification. Micro organisms are used to break down toxic organic compounds. They convert them into less toxic ones.

Such biological treatment systems are permanent in nature and require little maintenance. Physical and chemical methods use various techniques of boiling, pressure, reactions, etc. Various chemicals and systems used are expensive and requires technical know-how. In comparison to these, biological clean up are less expensive and simple. Though research requires deep study for such methods, but they are less complex in their application.

Moreover, Biological methods have .shown effective results in many countries. But some limitations are there. They can be most effective between a range of temperature.

Yet, these methods are ecofriendly in themselves. They use natural mechanisms like use of anoxic drains, limestone rock channels, alkaline recharge of ground water, etc.

So, it can be said that in a long term calculation, these can be cheaper than conventional physical and chemical methods.

(b) Explain how Nanoscience and Nanotechnology have revolutionized modern technology.

Important Points for Answer:
- *Nano-science or Nanotechnology*
- *Advantage*
- *Their application*

Answer: Nanoscience is a branch of science related to small particles and their actions. Size of particles are in range of nano metre—i.e. 10^{-9} m.

Nanotechnology develops various technological uses of such smaller particles.

Nowadays, these have gained wide applications in various fields ranging from electronics to medicines.

Such small particles can offer multiple functions in smaller sizes. Due to this technology, now we are able to have a match box size Television sets and smaller cellular phone sets. On military front, this technology has helped to create small but more powerful weapons and tools of surveillance.

Even quality and efficiency of instruments will increase at much lower price.

On medical field, Nanotube Injection can be used to heal bones.

Carbon nano tubes are also useful in medical field.

Now a capsule-size computer robot is able to perform operation inside the body of patient, monitored by doctor through computer.

Small size CDs and floppies can be availed using this technology.

Nano-medicines, nano-chemicals are emerging fields.

Application of Nano technology in agriculture field would boost production and quality of crops.

Q. 11 Answer any *two* of the following (in about 150 words each) : 15 × 2 = 30

(a) What do you understand by optical computing ? Why is optical computing envisaged to have much better performance than that of electronic computing?

Important Points for Answer:
- *Optical Computing*
- *Advantages of Optical Computing*
- *Electronic Computing*

Answer: Optical computer uses isolating crystals with bound electrons. It does not use either modulator or demodulator.

While electronic computer uses transistors with free electrons.

It provides smaller equipments with more speed and efficiency.

In place of integrated electronics circuit chip, optical fibres are much thinner and efficient.

Photons are used to perform computing functions. Electron based computation is conventional system approach.

Optical principles are used in this technology. Data interference and waste of energy through electrons is not present in optical computers.

By small equipments, more functions with more efficiency can be performed.

Polymers of optical computers have 1000 times faster function ability than silicon transistors.

Optical pathways in them can carry many different frequencies of light over each pathway.

(b) Write a note on 'Bio-refinery versus Fossil fuels'.

Important Points for Answer:	
• *Bio-refinery*	• *Fossil-fuels*

Answer: Bio-refinery refers to system which converts biomass into valuable chemicals and emits energy. This can be useful to minimise waste, produce useful chemicals and energy.

Fossil fuels or mineral fuels include coal, petroleum, other hydrocarbons etc. They are formed of decayed plants and animal fossils. Such fossils when subjected to heavy pressure under the earth and heat of the sun, they get converted into coal, crude oil and natural gas.

Biorefinery have the following advantages :

- production of pure chemicals.
- no use of polluting agents.
- there takes place controlled decomposition and other processes.

Bio-refineries are largely eco friendly while fossil fuels produce a large amount of carbon dioxide, carbon monoxide and other hazardous gases, causing pollution and global warming.

(c) What are normal osmosis and reverse osmosis ? Why has reverse osmosis become popular in India today ?

Important Points for Answer:	
• *Normal Osmosis*	• *Reverse Osmosis*
• *Advantages of RO*	

Answer: In Osmosis, the movement of particles are directed from high concentration to low concentration through a membrane.

While in Reverse Osmosis, the reverse process takes place. Here water leaves salty side of membrane under pressure created mechanically or electronically. Required pressure, for disalination of sea water through RO, is about 50-60 bars.

Water of sea is generally very saline and contain many chemicals dissolved in it. River water is also of same condition after flowing its path. To make this water potable, desalination through osmosis process is necessary.

When such water is subjected to normal osmosis, it is not so cleaned to make it hygienic. Arsenic, Iron, etc. are chemicals that are dissolved in water. They can be removed only by heavy pressurised conditions of Reverse Osmosis process.

So, due to the quality of water that can be achieved by RO, that process has been more popular than normal osmosis process.

Q. 12 Answer all the *five* (in about 20 words each) : **2 × 5 = 10**

(a) What do you understand by a 'search engine' in computing ?

Answer: It helps to find out required information by providirig matching indexes of datas or sites.

(b) Expand the following:

(i) CAD

(ii) CAM

(iii) CIM

Answer: (i) CAD : Computer Aided Design

(ii) CAM : Computer Aided Manufacturing

(iii) CIM : Computer Integrated Manufacturing

(c) Explain what is Thin Film Memory in computers.

Answer: Sperry Rand in his research project developed this high-speed memory. It is a type of memory which adds to efficiency of a computer.

(d) Write a short note on 'Artificial Intelligence'.

Answer: Computers are being developed to response on their logic. Robots are examples of it. Centre for Artificial Intelligence and Robotics (CAIR), Bangalore, researches on the point.

(e) Who are called 'Hackers' in computer world ?

Answer: They are invadors of computer datas, programmes, etc. They are criminals under Cyber laws. Their action is unauthorised interference.

Q. 13 (a) In an opinion survey regarding a proposed civil measure to be introduced, altogether 2878 persons took part of which 1652 were males. 1226 persons voted against the proposal

of which 796 were males. 1425 persons voted for the proposed measure. 156 females were undecided in their opinion.

(i) Put the above information in a neat statistical table.

Answer:

Statistical Table : Opinion Survey

Voted	Male	Female	Total
For	785	640	1425
Against	796	430	1226
Undecided	71	156	227
Total	**1652**	**1226**	**2878**

From the table, calculate:

(ii) the percentage of males among those voting for the proposal;

Answer: Percentage of males ; $= \dfrac{\text{Total number of males voting for}}{\text{Total number of person voter for}} \times 100$

$$= \frac{785}{1425} \times 100$$

$$= \mathbf{55\ 08\ \%}$$

(iii) the percentage of those voting for the proposal among the males.

Answer: Percentage of those voting for the proposal among the males

$$= \frac{\text{Voting for the proposal among males}}{\text{Total number of males}} \times 100$$

$$= \frac{785}{1652} \times 100 = \mathbf{47.51\%}$$

(b) Present the following information using a suitable diagram :

State	Percentage of Literates (2001 Census)		
	Male	**Female**	**Overall**
Kerala	94.20	87.86	90.72
Maharashtra	86.27	67.51	77.27
Tamil Nadu	82.33	64.55	73.47
West Bengal	77.58	60.22	69.22

Answer: Diagram representing Percentage of Literates (2001 Census)

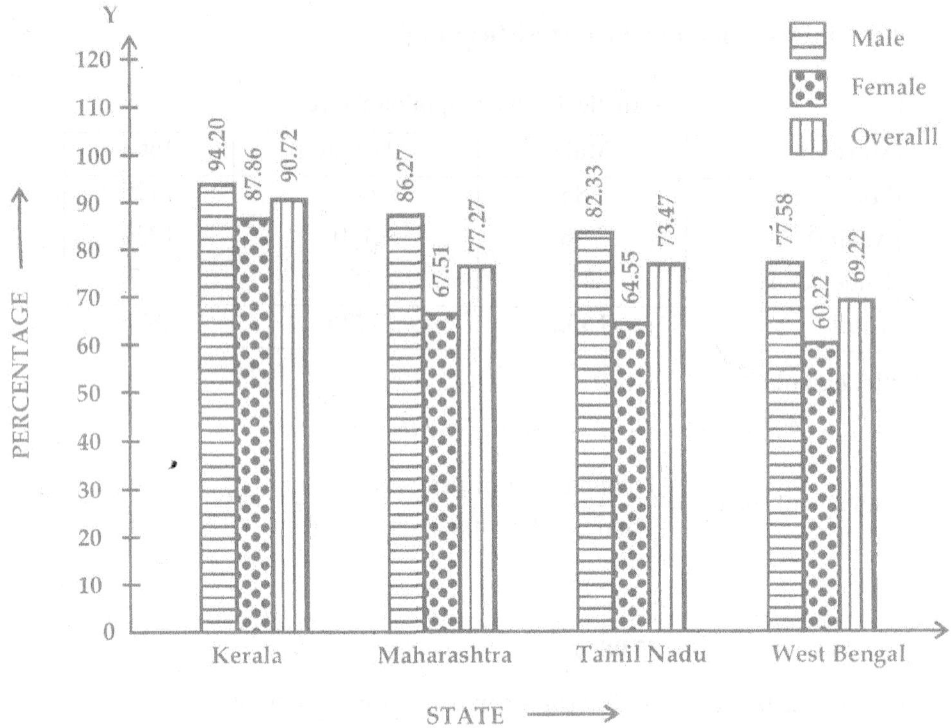

Q. 14 (a) From the following frequency distribution of 260 housewives of a locality according to their TV-watching habit:

(i) draw the graph of cumulative frequencies of less than type :

Hours per week watching TV	Number of housewives
5-9	13
10-14	39
15-19	60
20-24	75
25-29	42
30-34	27
35-39	4
Total	260

Answer:

Interval	Frequency	Less than type Cumulative Frequency	More than type Cumulative Frequency
4.5–9.5	13	13	260
9.5–14.5	39	52	247
14.5–19.5	60	112	208

19.5–24.5	75	187	148
24.5–29.5	42	229	73
29.5–34.5	27	256	31
34.5–39.5	04	260	04
Total	**260**		

Graph:

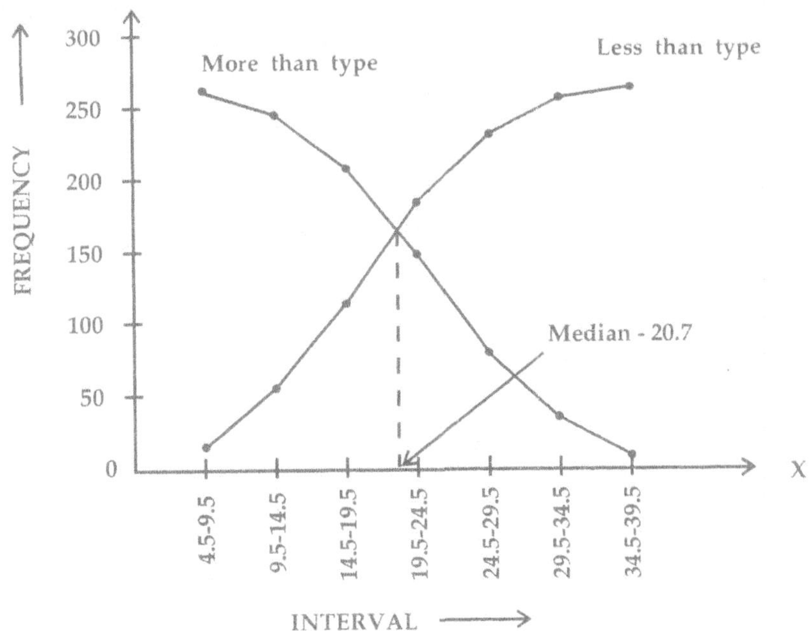

Estimate using the above graph :

(ii) The median of the distribution;

Answer: Median class $= \left(\dfrac{\text{Size N}}{2}\right)^{\text{th}}$ item class

$= \left(\dfrac{260}{2}\right)^{\text{th}}$ item class

$= 130^{\text{th}}$ item class

Median class $= 19.5 - 24.5$

$$\text{Median} = L_1 + \frac{\frac{N}{2} - c}{f} \times i$$

$$= 19.5 + \frac{\frac{260}{2} - 112}{75} \times 5$$

$= 20.7$

(iii) Number of housewives spending at most 18 hours per week watching TV. 8

Answer: Total number of House-wives spending at most 18 hours per week watching T.V. is 112.

(b) The following table shows the average percentage of family expenditure, as also percentage increase in price in 2005 compared to 2000, for the major heads of expenditure for the urban middle class families in a State in India. Calculate the percentage increase in cost of living for this segment of population in 2005 compared to 2000 : 8

Head of expenditure	% of family expenditure	% increase in price in 2005 compared to 2000
Food	25	32
Clothing	18	25
Fuel & Electricity	16	30
House Rent	15	20
Miscellaneous	26	45
Total	100	—

Answer: In this table, quantity remains unchanged

Suppose that : p_0 is price, q_0 is quantity, p_1 is current price

$$\text{Cost of living index} = \frac{\Sigma q_0 p_1}{\Sigma q_0 p_0}$$

$$= \frac{132}{100} \times 100 \text{ (see table below)}$$

$$= 132\%$$

The percentage of increase in cost of living is 132%.

Calculation :

Head of expenditure	% of family expenditure q_0P_0	% increase in price in 2005 compared to 2000 q_0P_1
Food	$\frac{25}{100} \times 100$	$\frac{25}{100} \times 100$
Clothing	$\frac{18}{100} \times 100$	$\frac{18}{100} \times 100$
Fuel & Electricity	$\frac{16}{100} \times 100$	$\frac{16}{100} \times 100$
Home-Rent	$\frac{15}{100} \times 100$	$\frac{15}{100} \times 100$
Miscellaneous	$\frac{26}{100} \times 100$	$\frac{26}{100} \times 100$
Total	**100**	**132**

Q. 15 Answer *all* the questions : **$2 \times 4 = 8$**

(a) A union leader complained : that the owners of this factory have adopted a policy of gradually decreasing the wages of its workers is amply evident from the fact that the average monthly wage of the workers has dropped down to Rs. 2,530 in January, 2006 from Rs 2,570 in January, 2005. Comment on the validity of the argument.

Answer: The argument cannot be accepted only based on the provided data. The data is inadequate.

Because extreme values can affect the average.

- If the retiring persons are with very high wage, it would reduce average,
- If the newly employed labours are with low wages, it would also reduce wages.

(b) As high as 45% of the under-5 children, brought to the outdoor clinics of 4 major State-run hospitals in Kolkata last year, were found to be victims of malnutrition. Incidence of malnutrition among the under-5 children in the city must, therefore, be alarmingly high. Explain why you support the argument, or disagree with it.

Answer: The data is inadequate and the argument is not acceptable.

- The children when brought to clinic, are ill and so malnutrition is there.
- Total number of children in the town is not compared here.
- All children are not always brought to state run clinics.
- The survey is not exhaustive of all under-five children.

(c) In a community support project, the average grants (in Rs) received by the male and the female beneficiaries were 5,200 and 5,800 respectively, while the average grant received by all the beneficiaries was 5,560. What percentage of beneficiaries were females ?

Answer: Ratio-Proportion Method

Ratio of male to female = 2:3

Percentage of women $= \frac{3}{5} \times 100 = 60\%$

So, Male = 40% and Female = 60%

This can be calculated as following :

Average = 5560, Male = 5200, Female = 5800

Difference : Male = 5560 – 5200 = + 360

Female = 5560 – 5800 = –240

Suppose, male = (x) percent

female = 100 – (x) percent

Again suppose, total number of beneficiaries = 100

So, total grant = Average grant received by all × total beneficiaries

= 5560 × 100

= 556000 Rs. .... (i)

Total grants to male = Average grant received by the males × total male beneficiaries

$= 5200 \times (x)$

$=$ Rs. $5200\ (x)$ ....(ii)

Total grants to female = Average grant received by the females × total female beneficiaries

$= 5800\ x\ (100 - x)$

$=$ Rs. $580000 - 5800\ x$ ....(iii)

Combining equations (i), (ii) and (iii), we get

Total grant = Male + Female

$556000 = 5200\ x + 580000 - 5800 \times 24000 = 600\ x$

$\therefore$ $x = 40$

Thus, x = male = 40 and female = 60.

(d) The amounts of rainfall (in mm) in a town on 10 consecutive days are as follows : 8.5, 0, 6.8, 3.2, 4.8, 10.5, 76.2, 9.4, 0, 1.2

Use a suitable measure to throw light on the central tendency of the data.

Answer: Suitable tendency is arithmetical mean of rainfall.

$$\text{Average rainfall } \overline{X} = \frac{\Sigma x_i}{n}$$

$$= \frac{120.6}{10} \text{ mm}$$

$\therefore$ Average rainfall = 12.06 mm/day

(MAIN) **2007**

Civil Services Exam.
General Studies

SOLVED PAPERS

PAPER - I

Time Allowed : Three Hours *Maximum Marks : 300*

Candidates should attempt ALL questions strictly in accordance with the instructions given under each question.

Q. 1 Answer any one of the following (in about 250 words) : **30**

(a) What was the character of socio-religious reforms in the 19th Century and how did they contribute to the national awakening in India ?

Important Points for Answer:
- *Reforms in the 19th century*
- *Character*
- *Contribution in national awakening*
  - *Positive*
  - *Negative*

Answer: In the 19th century various factors led to socio-religious reforms in Indian society. Western influence and education played a vital role in this awakening.

These reforms aimed at abolition of social evils like Purdah system, child marriage, polygamy, polytheism, female infanticide, restriction on widow remarriage, sati etc. It also reformed religious rigidities, dogmas, superstition, idolatory, caste hierarchy, obscurantism, etc.

These reforms came through various movements and acts. Movements like Brahmo Samaj by Raja Rammohan Roy, Prarthna Samaj, Young Bengal Movement by Derozio, Women empowerment by Ishwarchandra Vidhyasagar and others played important role in reforming social and religious spheres of India in 19th century.

Character:

- They aimed at removing the superstition in religion,
- helped in reducing caste rigidities,
- spread education,
- some were revivalist in nature which awakened past glory of India, like Arya Samaj by Dayanand Saraswati,

- some movements aimed at religious upliftment and consciousness,
- social practices were aimed to be purge of ill-habits and effects,
- movements like Wahabi Movement, Aligarh Movement, Deoband Movement were concerned with Muslim socio-religious reforms, which sometimes became critical to national interest, same was the case with some Hindu religious movements like Bharat Dharma Mahamandal, which preached Orthodoxy.
- some legislations like Hindu Widows' Remarriage Act-1856, Age of Consent Act-1891, Bengal Regulation of 1829 banning Sati etc. were also influenced by social reforms.

Contribution:

These movements were not directly aimed at national awakening. Many of them were limited in their sphere except some all India movements like Ramakrishna Movement, i Arya Samaj and Theosophical Movement. But yet they positively contributed

- in liberating individual
- in making worship and religion more personal affairs
- in reducing caste-based and religion based differences
- in strengthening secularism
- in providing a base for social modernisation

And, ultimately increasing, as summing up all these effects, national consciousness.

Some negative contributions, like

- having narrow social base, increasing differences as side effects,
- indirectly contributing to increase mystic vision,
- leading communal differences among Hindus and Muslims etc.

They also limited the scope of their contribution in national awakening.

Concluding as a whole, it is true that these reforms helped in national awakening in the time where no other means were available for that purpose.

(b) The crisis of the colonial order during 1919 and 1939 was directly linked to the constitutional reforms, disillusionment and militant anti-colonial struggles. Elucidate.

Important Points for Answer:
- *Crisis in Colonial order*
- *Constitutional Reforms*
- *Disillusionment*
- *Militant anti-colonial struggles*

Answer: During 1919 and 1939, the colonial order faced a threatening crisis in India as all over the world. Even before the end of the first world war, some revolutionary activities had created a trouble in colonial order.

At the end of the first world war in 1919, the Government gave India the Government of India Act-1919. This was wholly unsatisfactory and was protested commonly by all groups and leaders.

Though the protest of Rowlatt Act and Jallianwala Bagh incident was of much importance in this crisis, yet another major protest after the Khilafat and Non-Cooperation Movement was the Anti-Simon agitation which became violent.

Again, the Civil Disobedience and Dandi March were the major crisis creating actions for the colonial order.

To get rid of these crisis and as a response to them, some constitutional reforms were awarded by the British Government.

Like, the Act of 1919 enlarged the Indian membership in legislative council and also introduced dual government system. Again, Simon Commission was introduced to recommend measures to amend the Act of 1919 but it was severely protested. But the Government of India Act-1935 gave a popular election and federal structure to the Indian polity. Election was participated by Indian parties and they formed government in the Centre and provinces.

On the other hand, these crisis break away the illusionments of Indians towards the British rule. The Act of 1919 disappointed freedom fighters. British style of reforming Indian Constitution without respecting Indian opinion e.g. Constitution of the Simon Commission was also a shock. Now Congress adopted 'freedom' as its goal in 1929. Also the illusion that the League represented the Muslims and Congress to the Hindus was also done away with by the result of the 1937 elections.

As response to these crisis, encouraged by them, some activists choose a violent path of struggle to get rid of colonial rule. They killed unpopular British officers, looted government treasures and committed robberies like Kakori-1925, etc. Bhagat Singh, Rajguru anti Sukhdev threw a bomb in Central Assembly and let themselves hanged in 1931.

Thus, we can sum up that colonial crisis during 1919 to 1939 was responsible for awakening Indians for more constitutional reforms - even to the extent that Indians themselves tried their Constitution in the form of the Nehru Report-1928. These crisis also encouraged militant struggles. All these happened because this period helped in disillusioning the old beliefs regarding Indian conditions and British supremacy.

Q. 2 Answer any two of the following questions (in about 150 words each) : 15 × 2 = 30

(a) What are the salient features of the Government of India Acts of 1858 and 1909 ?

Important Points for Answer:
- *Salient features of:*
- *Government of India Act 1858*
- *Government of India Act 1909*

Answer: Salient features of the Government of India Act - 1858 :

- It transferred to the British Crown the powers of Company to govern India.
- The administration was to be run by Her Majesty, through the Secretary of State for India, assisted by the Council of India.

- Council of India had 15 members, 8 appointed by the Crown and 7 elected by the Court of Directors.
- The Court of Directors and Board of Control were abolished.
- The Council of India-was an advisory body, with the Secretary of State as its Chairman.
- This act made India a direct colony of the British Crown.

Salient features of the Government of India Act-1909 :

- It is also known as the Morley-Minto Reforms.
- It increased the number of elected members in the Imperial Legislative Council and the Provincial Legislative Councils. However, overall majority of non-elected members remained intact.
- Even elected members were to be elected indirectly by electoral college, elected by local bodies.
- Separate electorate was introduced. Muslims were allocated 8 seats, British capitalists 6 seats, landlords 2 seats and general electorate were allocated 13 seats out of total 27 non-official seats of total 68 seats in Imperial Legislative Council.
- Muslims were also provided representation in excess to their strength.
- Powers of legislatures were enlarged to enable it to pass resolution and ask questions and supplementaries, but yet not able to vote upon the budget as a whole.
- One Indian was to be appointed to the Viceroy's executive council.

This was criticised by Indian freedom fighters.

(b) Do you think Mahatma Gandhi's support to Khilafat Movement had diluted his secular credentials? Give your argument based on the assessment of events.

Important Points for Answer:

- *Khilafat Movement*
- *Anti-secular element*
- *Justification*
- *Conclusion*

Answer: The Khilafat Movement had nothing to do with the Indian politics. It was a purely Islamic movement supporting the cause of Khalifa of Turkey on religious bases, against the British Government. It rose out of the defeat of Turkey and allies in the first world war against the British and allies.

Gandhi had always advocated for secular politics. He was against the use of religion as an agenda. But supporting the Khilafat issue was severely criticized by many leaders as diluting his secular credentials.

But Gandhi was justified. Because the League had started to advocate itself as a Muslim representative organisation and branding the Congress as a Hindu body. This issue gave a chance to wash away these branding blames. Again, here the nation saw an unprecedented Hindu-Muslim unity during

1919 to 1922. Both community spiritedly opposed the British. And after it, Gandhi never supported religion based politics. He even opposed the partition on religious bases.

So, it can be concluded that it was not an anti-secular act by Gandhi but only an opportunity to cement the Hindu-Muslim unity to make Indian politics more participatory and really secular, i.e. supported by all religions equally.

(c) Evaluate the contribution of revolutionary terrorism represented by Bhagat Singh to the cause of India's struggle for independence.

Important Points for Answer:
- *Revolutionary Activities*
- *Contribution*

Answer: Bhagat Singh was one of the youth who opted for a violent way to get rid of the British rulers and to end exploitation. He provided a good leadership to such youth. He was one of the founder of the Hindustan Republican Association. They undertook revolutionary activities like robberies, killing of unpopular officials, e.g. murder of Saunders', bombing in Central Assembly as the main influencing act. They believed in sacrifice for the cause of nation.

Their way, especially that of the group led by Bhagat Singh, created a new wave of national spirit among people when there was an environment of soothing struggle. Youthas well as other ages were inspired by his heroic acts. He did not only created an unvisioned violence but he was really a visionary of exploitationless world order. His ideas and act inspired people as well as leaders. On the eve of his execution, even British officials like Lord Irwin was afraid that nation may rose in a huge protest. Even Gandhi was given an insulting welcome on his way to Karachi by showing black flags.

This was a person who not only created violence but also violated the belief of British rule that they will be able to rule India easily.

Q.3 Write about the following (not exceeding 20 words each): **2 × 15 = 10**

(a) Age of Sangam Literature

Answer: During the time of third century B.C. to first century B.C. Tamil literature flourished to give a classic age of literature in South India. It was during and among the ruling of the dynasties, namely, Cholas and Pandyas.

(b) Bhakti

Answer: It is a form of worship in Hinduism. Along with Gy ana (Knowledge), Karma (Action), Bhakti (Devotion and Prayer) is one of the way to Moksha. It is to devote oneself to the deity and to worship god. 15th century A.D. is the time when Bhakti was at its peak.

(c) *Ashtadhyayi of Panini*

Answer: It is a book of grammar written by Panini. This book contains eight (Asta) chapters (Adhyaya) of Sanskrit Grammar. Panini was from Gandhara. The book also narrates contemporary social, political, economic and cultural account.

(d) Charvakas

Answer: A totally materialistic/philosophy. It does not accept even the existence of God. It believes neither in Karma nor in Dharma. It was established by Charvaka Rishi, it is also known as Lokayata Philosophy.

(e) Ajivikas

Answer: Established in nearly 6th century B.C. by Maskari Gosal, it was a community that believed in determination and did not believe in existence of God.

(f) Gandhara Art

Answer: Gandhara art developed in 1st and 2nd century B.C. in Gandhara region due to confluence of Indian and Greek art. It is mainly related to idol making. This architectural art is one of the most beautiful in India.

(g) ***Mlechchhas***

Answer: Mlechchhas were tribes not believing in brahmanical religion. They also not followed Vedic religion. They were living out of towns.

(h) Lingayats

Ans Lingayats worship Lord Shiva in the form of 'Linga'. This Veerashiva community was founded by Vasava, a brahman. This is a form of Shaivism.

(i) Megasthenes

Answer: Ambassador of Seleucus Niketar in the court of Chandra Gupta Maurya. He wrote 'Indica', which gives a vivid account of Indian society of that time. But he could not understand Indian social system perfectly, so it is defective.

(j) R. C. Dutt

Ans.The author of "the history of economics" in British India. He was an economist. He also played a role in explaining how British exploited India economically.

(k) Nagarjunakonda

Answer: Situated in Andhra Pradesh at present, it derives its name from the great Buddhist philosopher Nagarjuna. Here is also an ancient Buddha stupa of Maurya age.

(l) Pastoralism

Answer: Pastoralism is a form of nomadic life, where people depend on cattle as their main source of livelihood. They wonder from one place to another in search of fodder. Initial vedic period belongs to pastoralism.

(m) Rudramadevi

Answer: A Kakatiya dynasty lady ruler of Warrangal. She ruled for more than three decades. She was the first lady ruler of India.

(n) ***Sati***

Answer: Sati was a socio-religious evil practised among various Hindu communities. Here a widow burns herself along with the dead body of her husband on the funeral pyre.

(o) Ramanuja

Answer: A religious preacher of Bhakti movement. He gave slogan of 'Brahma Satya, Jagat Satya'. He preached 'Visista-advaitavada'.

Q.4 Answer any *two* of the following questions (in about 125 words each) : 10 × 2 = 20

(a) Explain how the Himalayan and the Tibetan highlands play an important role in the development of the South - West monsoon.

Important Points for Answer:
- *Development of S-W Monsoon*
- *Role of Himalayan and Tibetan Highlands*

Answer: In hot season of April-May, the landmass of Indian sub-continent gets heated by the sun rays. This decreases pressure and increases temperature of the land in comparison to the water bodies of the Indian ocean and Arab Sagar. As a result, air on Indian landmass goes up developing jet stream and moisturised air from Arabian sea approaches India on the starting of June from South-west direction causing rain.

The Himalayan and the Tibetan plateau are highlands. They help in getting much heat and so decreasing pressure. Then they prevent the moisturised winds blowing from water bodies. So, they give rainfall in India. They are important for maximum rainfall in north Indian states and north-west land rainfall. These highlands not only help in getting rain but also help in getting for a longer period. Otherwise, the winds would have crossed India and duration and amount of rainfall would not be as high as it is.

(b) Technological changes have brought in a major shift in the use of roads as transport corridors in India. How far do you agree with this view?

Important Points for Answer:
- *Use of roads*
- *Technological changes*
- *Shift*

Answer: Roads are considered the "Life line" of transportation system in India. Indian roads are increasing in length due to their rising importance and use. Today, there is about 33 lacs km of roads. Of which only 2% of National Highways carries nearly 40% of transportation. This is due to good quality of these NHs.

Technological changes have given a boost to transportation facilities. Even air-travelling is now much easier and cheaper. Railway has also assumed more importance. These have effects on road transport. But improving quality of all weather metallic roads, Golden quadrilateral and East-West, North-South national corridor, Express highways etc. have sustained importance of roads. Moreover, modern technologies in road vehicles also help in it. Subways and flyovers are also technological changes that lead roads to claim for more importance.

The shift is due to demand of good quality road that is hurdle free and cost and fuel saving. Therefore, there is a shift in road use as transport corridors.

(c) Explain the nature and causes of growing slum problems in the metropolitan cities of India.

Important Points for Answer:
• *Slums in metropolitan cities*
• *Nature*
• *Causes*

Answer: In India, number of metropolitan cities are increasing and with that increases slums attached to them. Accordingly, about 1440 lacs of people today, live in slums. The nature and causes of slums are as below

Nature :

- They develop at the outer edges of cities, on sides of roads and other cheap places;
- They lack pure drinking water facilities;
- There are no sanitation system maintained properly;
- They are dirty places without hygienic air, space or light;
- Dwelling facilities are also not properly liveable;
- Disease and mortality rates are high;
- Law and order is also not properly maintained.

Causes :

- Unemployment in rural area drift people to cities in search of job and without property they became slum dwellers.
- Development of industries and services are mainly concentrated in cities.
- Cities have no space to accomodate immigrates in proper facilitated space so this result in increase of slums.
- Lack of proper management and implementation of law on the part of town authorities.

Q.5 Write notes on the following (in about 20 words each): 2 × 5 =10

(a) Special Economic Zone (SEZ)

Answer: SEZs are territories which are excluded from normal rules and regulations of the sovereign land for the purpose of economic development. There is also some tax benefit. It is implemented from April 2000.

(b) Inceptisol

Answer: It is a kind of brown soil. It contains less aluminium and iron, so it is brown. New land classification includes it.

(c) Jarawas

Answer: Jarawas is a Andaman-Nicobari tribal community since ancient times. This community is at the risk of extinction now. So government is worried for their conservation.

(d) Indira Point

Answer: Indira Point is the southern most land point of India. It is an island. It is the part of Andaman and Nicobar situated in the Indian Ocean.

(e) Causes of Chambal Ravines

Answer: The flowing river current towards lowlands from the hills of Chambal causes soil erosion in its way, creating ravines. This is the cause of Chambal Ravines.

Q.6 Answer any one of the following questions (in about 250 words) : 30

(a) What is a Constitution ? What are the main sources of the Indian Constitution ?

> **Important Points for Answer:**
> • *What is a Constitution ?*
> • *Sources of Indian Constitution.*

Answer: Wade and Philips defined a Constitution as : A Constitution means a document having a special legal sanctity which sets out the framework and the principal functions of the organs of the Government of a State and declares the principles governing the operation of those organs.

It is also said that the Constitution is the supreme law of the land which cannot be violated even by the Government. It is an Umbrella Legislation.

Sources of Indian Constitution

- Parliamentary System : India adopted the Parliamentary system of government. One of the main reasons was that this system was familiar to India. This was adopted from the United Kingdom.
- Again, related to this, the Legislative procedure and the Parliamentary privileges were directly adopted from the United Kingdom.
- Republican model was chosen from the Constitution of France.
- The procedure of amending the Constitution is adopted from South African Constitution.
- Federal structure of Government is directly inherited from the Government of India Act-1935.
- Some features related to judiciary, like the Supreme Court—its organisation and powers, judicial review and the provisions of the fundamental rights are inspired from the U.S.A. Constitution.
- Legal processes like "Rule of Law" and the "due process of law" are accepted from U.K. and U.S.A. respectively.

  Similarly, procedure established by law is taken from Japan.
- The post of Vice-President of India is similar to provisions of the Constitution of USA.
- The Directive Principles of State Policy are ensourced from Ireland and the Emergency provisions are from the Constitution of Germany.
- Again, federal aspects like the Concurrent list is derived from Australian system.
- Federation with a strong centre is mainly Canadian tendency.
- Fundamental duties are taken from the Russian Constitution.

Thus, Indian Constitution has taken many features borrowed from other systems of the world to make it more comprehensive and effective.

(b) Bring out the differences between the Fundamental Rights and the Directive Principles of State Policy. Discuss some of the measures taken by the Union and State Governments for the implementation of the Directive Principles of State Policy.

Important Points for Answer:
- *Difference between the Fundamental Rights & Directive Principles of State Policy*
- *Measures*

Answer: These are the following differences between the Fundamental Rights (FRs) and the Directive Principles of State Policy (DPSPs).

First and the foremost difference is that the FRs are justiciable in a court of law and DPSPs are no so.

The fundamental rights are negative instructions to the state that it shall not taken away on abridge any of the rights provided in Part III except following the procedure of the Constitution, while the DPSPs are positive in the form and are directions to the State to enact legislations to give effect to them.

DPSPs in Part IV are essential in the governance of the country for achieving the goals enshrined in the Preamble of the Constitution of India.

Fundamental Rights are very basic for all over development of a person as a human being.

Article 12 to 35 provides the FRs, Article 36 to 51 deals with DPSPs.

Implementation measures : Zamindari, Jagirdaris etc. old institutions of hereditary proprietory have been abolished by the Government under Article-39 (b) which provides for distribution of ownership and control of the material resources of the community to the common good.

Untouchability is now a punishable offence under the Constitution aiming at equality.

The Government has fixed minimum wages for workers and has also modernised the labour laws, to improve the conditions of labourers, this is to implement Article-42 providing for just and human conditions of work.

Panchayats have been established by the 73rd and 74th Amendments in 1992 under Article-40.

For promotion of cottage industries, the government has established All India Khadi and Village Industries Board, Small Scale Industries Boards, Silk Board, All India Handicrafts Board, All India Handloom Board etc. and other boards.

Compulsory education to children between the age of 6 to 14 has been made a fundamental right under Article 21-A. Many states have enacted laws to prohibit slaughters of cows and calves (Article 48).

Separation of judiciary from the executive under Article-50 is also implemented in some states like Punjab, Gujarat, Haryana, Kerala, Andhra Pradesh, etc.

To protect monuments and places and objects of national importance (Article 49), Ancient and Historical Monuments and Archaeological sites and remains (Declaration of National Importance) Act, 1951 has been enacted.

By adding a new Article 31C to the Part III Article 39(b) and (c) have been given supremacy over the Fundamental Rights.

Nationalisation of Banks in 1971 and Land Reforms are also similar measures.

Even the judiciary has adopted a trend to evolve some of the DPSPs to the status of the FRs to made them justiciable.

Thus, the Centre and the State Governments have implemented various DPSPs through suitable measures.

Q.7 Answer any *one* of the following questions (in about 250 words) : 30

(a) What is Regionalism ? In which way regionalism has affected the Indian polity ?

> **Important Points for Answer:**
> • *Regionalism*
> • *Effect on Indian Polity.*

Answer: Regionalism is a tendency of people to feel more affinity to their territory, language, culture and social habits. They give more importance to their own territorial region in comparison to other parts of the nation.

This tendency creates feelings of doing more and getting more for the interest and development of own region. Though it helps in development and growth of a region by its people but on the other hand, it also creates feelings of ignorance or neglecting towards other regions. This hurts the all over development of a country like India.

India is a country with various diversity. In geographical, historical, social, cultural and linguistic fields such differences can be seen among various regions of India. These differences lead to politically different ideologies and give rise to regional political parties to protect and preserve specific interest of a region. Since 1990s, India notices tremendously increasing role of regional political parties.

Even we can find its genesis in the protest of Hindi as a national language by the South Indian states, in the era of coalition government, we can see that allied parties in the government pressurises the main ruling party to tilt its policies in the interest of any specific regions. It many times, subsides national interest.

Moreover, such regionalism has became a big hurdle in two party politics and stable government. Today, regional parties are growing importance. They mostly stuck to their region specific demands.

Inter-state water disputes, emerging demands of new states and sometimes region specific violent struggle are evils of regionalism.

Vidarbha, Telangana etc. are demanding their own separate states. North-eastern groups are even demanding for freedom - or at least autonomy in the forms of 'Nagalim" and 'The Great Assam'.

It is admitted that nationalism must be respected over regionalism and so national spirit should be spread.

(b) What are the main determinants of voting behaviour in India ?

Important Points for Answer:
- *Voting behaviour*
- *Indian determinants*

Answer: Voting is essential process in a democratic set up. Parties try to capture maximum number of votes to come in power to govern the state. To this end, they have to develop and determine the voting behaviour of the voters. In India, the study of last 57 years of democracy show the following factors as determining the voting behaviour :

- Castism : Various castes are represented by a person as the main agenda of election. This is the most ancient and most widely used factor. Rajputs, Harijans, Brahmins etc. are some of the mostly used castes as agenda in electoral process.
- Religion : Secondly comes religion Hinduism, Islam, etc. are mostly used. The league had started representing Islamic community. Though in a secular state like India, it must not be used. Yet it is a fact that religion plays a vital role especially where both followers are situated in a constituency.
- Regionalism : It is getting more and more importance since 1990s. Demanding separate region, promoting region specific interest, claiming representation to end exploitation etc. are the emerging causes from regionalism that determines voting behaviour.
- Language : At state level politics, language does not play a big role but at national level, it is a deciding factor. For example, Anti-Hindi agitation in South India was one such method.
- Race : Sometimes and in some regions, yet race plays a role like in North Eastern states, it will be very tough to get elected by any South Indian and so is the case with South India also.
- Charismatic personality : Some political leaders magnetise a huge mass to attract votes. Like Jawahar Lai Nehru, Indira Gandhi etc. They due to their personal influence of behaviour, look, style and ideology attract a number of voters.
- Incidences : Some important and sudden events and incidences can change the equations in politics. Like, proclaiming emergency was such an incident that drove Indira Gandhi out of power and so Janta Government could come to power.
- Ideology : Some political ideologies play a deciding role like Communism, Socialism, democrats etc. in Kerala and West Bengal, its tough to ride out Leftists because people have communist ideology in their tendency but it is limited to those states only.
- Development : It is an agenda that is practised in developed democracy. When development is used as a factor, it is a sign of old and smooth running democratic system. It is admitted that this is the main and desirable factor that should play a big role in determining the voting behaviour.

These are the determining factors of voting behaviour in India.

Q.8 Answer any *two* of the following questions (in about 150 words each) : 15 × 2 =30

(a) What are the exceptions when the President of India is not bound by the aid and advice of the Council of Ministers ?

> **Important Points for Answer:**
> • *Position of the President of India*
> • *When can President exercise discretionary powers ?*

Answer: In India, the President is nominal head of the state while real executive powers are vested in the Prime Minister, who is the head of the Council of Ministers.

The President of India is bound to follow the advice of the Council of Ministers. But in the following exceptional situations, he can exercise his discretionary powers.

- The President can require the Council of Ministers to reconsider the bill sent to him under Article 111.
- He can ask for information from the Prime Minister regarding functioning of the Government (Article 78).
- The President generally appoints the head of the party that wins majority of the seats as the Prime Minister but in situations where no party can claim absolute majority to form a government, he can use his discretion to appoint a person as the Prime Minister but he has to give a time to prove that person his majority.
- The Council of Ministers is answerable to the Lok Sabha, if any government loses the support of the Lower House, the President is not bound to follow the advice of such Council of Ministers.

Except these situations, the President has to follow the advice of the Cabinet Ministers and he has no authority to exercise his powers personally.

(b) What is pro tem speaker?

> **Important Points for Answer:**
> • *Pro-tem Speaker*
> • *Constitutional provisions*
> • *Importance or functions*

Answer: The Pro tern Speaker is a temporary and operative person on the chair of the Speaker of the Lok Sabha on State Legislative Assemblies. He is to work for a limited period.

Till the new speaker and deputy speakers are elected after the election, a Pro tern speaker is chosen. Newly elected house is yet to elect its speaker. So to run activities till he is elected, the house chooses one of them with an agreement to work as a Pro tern speaker. Even on other situations, where the posts of the speaker and deputy speaker lie vacant e.g. death, resignation etc. In such situations, a Pro tern speaker is to handle the activities of the House.

Except in routine work, the Pro tern speaker has not as much a power with himself as the speaker. He is to run the activities for a limited period and so he cannot or at least does not exercise the serious powers of the speaker like defection, etc.

But in regular routine, he enjoys same powers, position, privilege and immunities as that of a speaker.

(c) Under what circumstances, Parliament may legislate on State subjects ?

> **Important Points for Answer:**
> • *Parliament's powers*
> • *When it can legislate upon the State subjects ?*

Answer: In normal circumstances, the Centre and the State cannot interfere into the fields of each other. But in exceptional circumstances, as provided herein, Parliament can legislate upon the state subjects :

- Article-249, when the Rajya Sabha by a two third majority passes a resolution giving Parliament such power in national interest.
- During proclamation of emergency under Article 250. Such law remains in effect for six months after the emergency ceases to operate.
- When two or more states passes a resolution that it is desirable to have a law passed by Parliament on any specified matter in State list. This is power given by consent.
- Even to give effect to treaties and international agreements, Parliament can enact a law under Article 253. Here, normal distribution of power does not stand in the way.
- In case of failure of the constitutional machinery in a State, under Article 256. When the Parliament declares that the Government of the State cannot be carried on in accordance with the provisions of the Constitution.

In these situations, the Parliament gets power to enact a law upon the State subject.

Q.9 answer the following question (in about 20 words each): $2 \times 5 = 10$

(a) What is criminalization in politics?

Answer: Criminalization of politics means to use criminal force for political purpose by the politicians either in winning elections or other political works. It also suggests increasing number of criminals in politics.

(b) How is the President of India elected ?

Answer: The President of India is elected by an electoral college, consisting of the elected members of both Houses of Parliament and MLAs, through a transferable vote in the form of secret ballot under Article 55.

(c) What is casting vote ?

Answer: When any bill or motion is being voted in a legislature, and both sides gets equal votes than the Presiding Officer has a right to cast a vote on either side, it is called Casting Vote.

(d) What is the difference between Council of Ministers and Cabinet?

Answer: The Cabinet is the inner circle of the highest rank of Ministers of any government while the Council of Ministers is a larger circle that includes more ministers.

(e) What is the importance of Right to Constitutional Remedies ?

Answer: To give effect to any of the fundamental rights, the right to remedy is essential. Without right to remedy (under Article 32 and 226), the fundamental rights would be of no use. It is considered as the soul of the Constitution.

Q. 10 Answer any *one* of the following questions (in about 250 words) : 30

(a) What were the main recommendations of the Platform for Action (PFA) adopted at the Beijing Women Conference, 1995 ?

Important Points for Answer:
- *Main Points*
- *Main Recommendations*

PLATFORM FOR ACTION (PFA)

Answer: The 1995 Conference will adopt a "Platform for Action", analyzing obstacles to women's advancement and recommending steps for overcoming them.

– they are intended to mobilize society to meet the challenges and demands of the next century.

– much of the Conference was dedicated to planning for the future,

In 1985, when goals to the year 2000 were established at the Nairobi Conference, known as the Nairobi Forward-looking Strategies for the Advancement of Women to the Year 2000, those goals were an appeal for government strategies to address the impact on women of government policies in areas such as employment, education, industrial investment, housing, transportation and the environment.

The Platform is intended to speed up the process of making the Forward-looking Strategies a reality, by proposing actions to be taken by policy makers and by women and men at the grass roots.

The proposed actions have realistic and quantifiable targets; the average woman could ither undertake them herself or ask her political leaders to do so.

They focus on ten critical areas of concern: poverty; education and health; violence against women; the effects of arpred or other kinds of conflict; economic participation; powersharing; insufficient mechanisms to promote women's advancement; human rights; mass media; and environment and development.

The goals of the Forward-looking Strategies, which were intended to be implemented by the year 2000, are deliberately ambitious. In the legal domain, they include equal rights for women, the abolition of slavery and prostitution, establishing a legal minimum age for marriage and punishing female infanticide.

At the social policy level, the Strategies call for access by all women to maternity leave, maternal health care, family planning, nutrition and education, as well as for increased national health budgets.

Governments are asked to develop incentives for the provision of child care and to start campaigns for equal sharing of domestic responsibilities.

The percentage of women in politics and management is to be increased, and there is a call for legislation to prevent violence against women and eliminate female circumcision.

(b) Discuss the steps to get rid of child labour in India.

Important Points for Answer:
- *Child labour*
- *Steps recommended*

Answer: Child labour is a blame upon the Indian democracy. It is a curse upon the society that children in the age of 'study and play' have to work to earn money.

Indian poverty has made it compulsory to employ children in payable work as self-employment to meet the ends of the family. Many a times, children have to work due to compulsion by their drunkered parent.

Steps must be taken to prevent the child labour, as the children are the future of our country. They must be provided with opportunities of education, skill-building and their development. Crores of children work today and policies and plannings have failed to achieve their goals.

So, following steps must be taken :

- Implementation of legislations properly.
- Stringent punishment to employers.
- Social awareness regarding evill effects of the child labour upon the future of the society and that of the child and family itself.
- Alternatives to the abolition of the child labour in the form of Funds for their rehabilitation and compensation for the loss of income to the vulnerably poor families.
- Welfare funds by the government can be established to take care of such children.
- Proper facilities of free education to such children.
- They should be provided free meal and scholarship apart from free books and literature of their study.
- They can be given vocational education so that at the age of earning, they should not have to search for a job which is tough to find.
- Child labour policy should be re-examined to make it more effective.
- A Commission should be set up in each district to monitor the implementation of related laws and to create awareness in the society'.
- Where possible and necessary, alternate employment should be provided to an adult from the family of the child so removed from labour.
- The employers violating the laws should be forced to deposit an amount in a fund which can be utilised to remove this curse from India.
- Hazardous industries are already banned from child employment and now domestic work is also banned.
- Related bills and acts can be drafted or amended in such a way as to make them more operative rather than more oppressive.
- At the base, social awareness is must to remove child labour, so education in such vulnerable localities can help to improve their conditions.
- A Commission can be set up to recommend on this aspect and the directions of the Supreme Court given in the case of the M.C. Mehta case can be followed.

Q. 11 Answer any two of the following questions (in about 125 words each) : 10 × 2 = 20

(a) What is stealth technology ?

Important Points for Answer:
- *Stealth technology*
- *Purpose & Use*

Answer: Stealth technology is a sub-discipline of electronic countermeasures which covers a range of techniques used with aircraft, ships and missiles, in order to make them less visible (ideally invisible) to radar, infrared and other detection methods.

It is a defence technology used in preparing fighter planes, sub-marines and other vehicles for the purpose of war through land, water or air medium.

The instruments using stealth technology cannot be traced by the enemy radars or other detective systems, so they can safely attack their target.

Enemy cannot destroy such weapons because of failure in locating them as wrongful location given to them.

At present, America, Russia have such stealth technology. Some other nations are also developing it. If this technology is developed and used widely, they can change the nature of war. It can result in only destruction and no prevention.

So, stealth missiles, planes, tankers or ships are being developed to attack from any front. Anti-stealth radars or other tracing instruments have yet not been developed by any country.

(b) Differentiate between Natural and Cultural heritage.

Important Points for Answer:
- *Natural heritage*
- *Cultural heritage*

Answer: Natural heritage are those which are gifted naturally to mankind. Like rivers, mountains, desert, vegetation etc. are natural gits. Streams, lakes, vegetations, animals, fields may also be natural heritage. Everything that is natural is not heritage. Only those natural things which have specific importance to the area or nation as a whole. In India, some biosphere reserves like Sunderbans, Nilgiri etc. are recognised as natural heritage.

On the other hand, those sites which are developed by mankind during the course of evolution of cultural civilisation can be included in cultural heritage. Some form of art, music, painting, dance, architecture etc. In India, Lai Killa, Kathak dance, Bhagwad Gita are included in Cultural heritage.

UNESCO prepares a list of Cultural and Natural heritage every year.

Thus, certainly, natural heritage is gifted to mankind without any human efforts while the cultural heritage are man-made.

(c) What is value-based politics ?

Important Points for Answer:
- *Value based politics*
- *Importance*

Answer: Value-based politics means political ideology and practice that is based on certain values like secularism, national benefit, truth, welfare state, democratic preservation, etc. Such value-based politics is necessary to create an ideal democracy. Idealistic ideology can lead a corruption free politics.

So, value-based practice can help in national development. It is aimed at national, social and human interests. It does not use corruption, criminal force, men or money power, regionalism, religion or caste, language or race as the agenda of politics.

It is also seen that value-based politics is a sign of developed democratic and social order. It is sadly confirmed that India at present is much far from value-based politics. Today, no party in India is strictly following an ideology. They can give up any ideals and that too, to any extent for power or position.

Therefore, value-based politics is required to be developed in India.

Q. 12 Write notes on any txvo of the following (in about 125 words each) : 10 × 2 = 20

(a) Integrated Child Development Services (ICDS)

Important Points for Answer:
• *The Scheme*
• *Main Objectives*
• *Main Provisions*

Answer: The Integrated Child Development Sevices Programme aims at providing services to preschool children in an integrated manner so as to ensure proper growth and development of children in rural, tribal and slum areas. ICDS is a centrally sponsored scheme.

Objectives:

- To improve the nutritional and health status of children in the age group of 0 to 6 years.
- To lay the foundations for proper psychological, physical and social development of the child.
- To reduce the incidence of mortality, morbidity, malnutrition and school drop-out.
- To achieve effective coordination of policy and implementation amongst the various departments to promote child development.
- To enhance the capability of the mother to look after the normal health and nutritional needs of the child through proper nutrition and health education.

The delivery of sevices to the different beneficiary groups is as follows:

Beneficiaries Services

1. Children below 6 months of age i. Immunization, ii. Health Check-up, iii. Referral Services
2. Children between 6 months to 3 years of age i. Supplementary Nutrition ii. Immunization, iii. Health Check-up, iv. Referral Services

3. Children between 3 to 6 years of age i. Supplementary Nutrition, ii. Immunization, iii. Health Check-up, iv. Referral Services, v. Non-formal pre-school education
4. Expectant and nursing mothers i. Health Check-up, ii. Immunization of expectant mothers against tetanus, iii. Referral Services, iv. Supplementary Nutrition, v. Education on Nutrition & Health
5. Other women 15 to 45 years i. Education on Nutrition & Health
6. Adolescent girls between 11 to 18 years of age (Under Kishori Shakti Yojana) i. Education on Nutrition & Health, ii. Supplementary Nutrition, iii. Awareness generation on women and children rights

(b) Prime Minister's 5-point agenda for India's development as a knowledge society

Important Points for Answer:
- *5-points agenda*
- *India as a Knowledge society*

Answer: To develop India as a knowledge society, the Prime Minister has given 5-point agenda.

These are related to :

- Information Technology : to develop and get benefit of the IT sector in telecommunication, medical, engineering, economic services and other fields of science and technology.
- Education expansion : to aim at expanding educational services and access to all to the education to create education oriented society.
- Networking : to expand a world wide network of telecommunication and broadcasting services to interact with the world community.
- Interconnection : interconnection among the power based technologies, economic flora and information related topics.
- Law and implementation : to educate people and to create such an environment where there is close contact between people and government and a law and order situation is maintained.

These were the themes of the PM's 5-point agenda aimed at making India a knowledge society.

(c) The Lokpal Bill

Important Points for Answer:
- *Lokpal Bill*
- *Main points*

Answer: The Lokpal Bill is aimed at getting rid of the corruption in the political system. This is based on the system of Ombudsman. The bill is yet not passed and it is most sought bill by educated people.

Main points and features are :

- It creates a quasi-judicial authority, namely the Lokpal, who shall be selected by a committee under the chairmanship of the Vice-President.

- A person who is or has been the Chief Justice of the Supreme Court of India can be appointed as the Lokpal. He shall be co-operated with other members.
- The Lokpal shall have authority to hear an application of complaint against any of the Member of Parliament and also a Member of the Council of Ministers.
- The President and the Vice-President are kept out of the authority of Lokpal's jurisdiction.
- Even the Prime Minister is brought in the scope of his jurisdiction except regarding his working in the fields of National Security or National Systems.
- If the Chairman of the Lokpal is blamed and charges against him are proved, then he may be removed from his office.

This system, if established would help in improving administration and governance of the nation.

Q. 13 Write short notes on the following (in about 20 words each) : 2 × 5 = 10

(a) Yakshagana

Answer: Started by Vijayanagar artists in the 14th and 15th century, this form of dance is a local art of South India.

(b) PACE

Answer: PACE is a super computer. It is developed by the Department of Research and Development Organisation to develop and design missiles, fighter aircrafts and other strategic services.

(c) Footloose Industries

Answer: These industries are those which are movable to some extent. Not attached to any particular place or religion, they have an advantage of greater mobility.

(d) The Statue of Liberty

Answer: Situated in New York, U.S.A., it is a symbol of liberty of mankind. It depicts a lady with a torch in her rised hand. It was established on the American Independence.

(e) Genome

Answer: A collection of genes in an organism. This is responsible for the hereditary qualities of it. It is situated within DNA.

SOLVED PAPERS

PAPER–II

Candidates should attempt ALL questions strictly in accordance with the instructions given under each question.

Q. 1 Answer any two of the following (answer to each question should be in about 150 words): 15 × 2 = 30

(a) Indo-Russian Defence Co-operation

Important Points for Answer:
- *Areas*
- *Co-operation*
- *Importance*

Answer:

- India entered into treaty of peace, friendship and co-operation in August 1971 with the Soviet Union as a concrete step in defence co-operation with it.
- This twenty years treaty helped in expanding scope in defence co-operation. It continues even after USSR's disintegration with Russia.
- Both nations have worked jointly in R & D, manufacturing & marketing in defence field.
- Both are jointly engaged in producing fifth generation of state-of-the-art fighter jet.
- Brahmos missile is another milestone in this field. It is supersonic anti-ship cruise missile.
- India has agreed to join Russian programme of developing a next generation fighter, by Sukhoi-planned to make its maiden flight by 2009.
- Recently during President Putin's visit to New Delhi on 26th January, 2007 both expressed need to expand India-Russia-China trilateral co-operation.
- Both expressed strong support to the UN Security Council Resolution 1737 on Iran's nuclear issue on international defence field.
- Russia will transfer technologies and licences for the production of sophisticated military equipments, namely T-90 main battle tank, 50-30 MK-I fighters, etc.
- Russia also co-operates in Navy, Air Force and Army fields of India.

Thus, Russia has helped strengthening India's defence power and India has proved a big customer to Russia.

(b) India's response to political crisis in Bangladesh

Important Points for Answer:
- *Political crisis in Bangladesh*
- *Indian Response*

Answer:

- When the term of Begum Khaleeda Zia led Government of Bangladesh National Party (BNP) ended in 2006, political crisis started.

- The President declared emergency in January, 2007 and also he appointed Dr. Fakhruddin Ahmed as the Chief Advisor to the caretaker government. He also formed a new interim government.
- To this political crisis, India responded very positively in the interest of Bangladesh. After this emergency Indian External Affairs Minister Mr. Pranab Mukherjee visited Dhaka in February 2007 and held talks with top leadership.
- In June, 2007 Foreign Secretary level talks were held at Dhaka where India's Foreign Secretary Shiv Shankar Menon addressed on "Creating A South Asian Identity : India- Bangladesh Relations".
- He said that the people of Bangladesh and their political parties should resolve outstanding issues through discussions and dialogue among themselves, rather than through external intervention or pressure.
- India also believes that people should be able to exercise their franchise in free and fair elections. On this point, India supports ongoing electoral reforms.
- India also favours Bangladeshi President's attempt to make parties free of corruption.
- India is ready to develop relations with Bangladesh and it wants the crisis must be solved with better result immediately.

(c) Elaborate on India's Nuclear Doctrine.

Important Points for Answer: • *Nuclear Doctrine* • *Main points*

Answer: India declared its nuclear doctrine in 1999 after its second nuclear explosion. This doctrine is the policy that India follows regarding its nuclear programme.

The doctrine has following main points :

- India shall not use first its nuclear weapons.
- No use against any non-nuclear state.
- Use only in case where Indian territory or armed forces are attacked by nuclear weapons or biological or chemical weapons.
- Nuclear weapons shall be maintained under a Nuclear Command Authority under Political representatives.
- India shall have always maintain a stock required for minimum deterrence.
- India voluntarily declared ban on further nuclear test or explosion but it can revive the programme if national security so demands.
- India shall always dialogue with other nations to make the world free of nuclear weapons and disarmament on equal basis.
- India will also continue dialogue on treaty for reduction of weapons of mass destruction (WMD).

It is admitted that the Indian nuclear doctrine is perfectly in accordance with requirement of world peace.

It shall not surrender its right even under 123 Agreement to conduct nuclear tests, if situation demands so.

Q. 2 Write about the following (answer to each question should be in about 20 words) : 10

(a) SAFTA

Answer: SAFTA - South Asian Free Trade Agreement. It is an agreement among SAARC members to develop free trade among them and to co-operate in economic development of each other and the region as a whole.

(b) India and East Asia Summit (EAS)

Answer: East Asia Summit was held in Cebu in 2007 which comprises ASEAN + 6 countries. India is one of these six nations. It is a platform for India to cultivate trade and economic relations with ASEAN members.

(c) Shanghai Co-operation Organisation (S.C.O.)

Answer: S.C.O. is established in 2001 by six nations - Russia, China, Kazakhstan, Kyrgystan, Tajikistan and Uzbekistan. It is for mutual co-operation in the fields of economic, defence and cultural sector.

(d) Panchsheel in India's Foreign Policy

Answer: Panchsheel, five principles were enunciated by Jawahar Lai Nehru and Chou-en-lai, leaders of India and China, have became cornerstones of India's foreign policy of peaceful co-existence in international relations.

(e) Relevance of NAM

Answer: Relevance of NAM : NAM - Non-align Movement has now assumed a multi-dimensional role in all over development of a state in various areas, with the passage of time, and has maintained its importance.

Q. 3 Write about the following (answer to each question should be in about 20 words): 2 × 5 = 10

(a) Pravasi Bhartiya Bima Yoiana, 2006

Answer: This scheme guarantees insurance for death, accident, disability etc. to new Indians and others living abroad. It is for the welfare of those people who migrate abroad.

(b) Indian All-Women Contingent to Liberia

Answer: Indian women mission is praised by the General Assembly. The mission was related to the mission of rapid action forces in Liberia-2006. The Trained Women Battalions had performed their work well.

(c) Madheshis in Nepal

Answer: Madheshis in Nepal are a hindi speaking community having descent of Uttar Pradesh and Bihar community of India. They are mainly cultivators having land ownership. They are being attacked by Maoists.

(d) Know India Programme (KIP)

Answer: KIP is a programme to introduce Indian culture, social and religious practices, architectural and geographical beauties to the foreigners and thus to attract tourists to India.

(e) Ministry of Overseas Indian Affairs

Answer: MOIA is a Union Ministry. It is responsible for the issues related to overseas Indians, their tour to India, their investment and developments related to these issues.

Q.4 Answer any one of the following (in about 250 words): 30

(a) What is Dumping ? Evaluate the remedial measures taken by Government of India *vis-a-vis* WTO provisions regarding dumping.

Important Points for Answer:
- *What is Dumping ?*
- *WTO provisions*
- *Measures by India*

Answer: Dumping is a process to sell goods to foreign market at very lower prices. When production of a specified goods increases to a level where a threat is posed to the domestic market of falling prices even to the level below than the stipulated prices, the country opts to sell those goods in abroad even at a thrown away prices to save loss to its producers. But such dumping causes loss to the country where the goods are exported to. So it also takes some remedial measures to protect its domestic producers.

Generally every country opted to put some quantitative restrictions upon the dumping and also charged high income tax. But according to changed guidelines of the WTO, such restrictions are prohibited now and so no country can impose quantitative restrictions upon imports.

Due to these prohibitions, now India adopts some preventive measures which are allowed under the WTO rules. So, India gives subsidy to its farmers so that their production costs can be brought down and they can compete with imported goods. Also as second remedial measure, India imposes countervailing duties and additional charges on the goods thus imported. These charges brings the prices of the goods up and so to make them dearer.

These measures help in making the domestic industries more competitive and due to competition and enhanced technological upgradation, consumers also get cheaper goods and with good qualities.

Indian Commerce Ministry has established an organisation called 'Directorate of Anti- Dumping' to tackle with the issues of dumping. Main threats of dumping to India is in the spheres of agricultural produces and manufactures that are alloted to the small sector industries.

(b) Comment on the relationship between credit availability and agricultural growth in India.

Important Points for Answer:
- *Agriculture in India*
- *Requirement of Credit*
- *Relationship between credit and growth.*

Answer: In India, more than 60% of population still depends upon agriculture, directly or indirectly. Most of the cultivators are landless farmers or marginal farmers. They are not able to invest enough to get more production and use technological developments for their cultivation. This is one of the main reasons why Indian agriculture has less production per hectare and why facilities of technology and irrigation cannot be utilised properly.

Credit would transform the labour intensive agriculture into capital intensive venture. It will also lead to land reforms and increase management process. Credit will also prevent post-harvest loss, it is a known fact that the Green Revolution could give result due to investment in agriculture and related technologies. The states like Punjab, Haryana, Andhra Pradesh, Maharashtra which emphasize on agriculture credit are showing growth in agriculture. They have made available credit to their farmers. On the other hand, Orissa, Uttarakhand, Jharkhand etc. have not taken proper steps to avail credit to farmers and so cannot achieve success.

In India, many sources of credits like personal credits and non-governmental credits by money lenders have clutched farmers in the net of interest that has negative impacts of agricultural growth and proper steps are required to be taken. Suicide by farmers are consequences of it.

Kisan Credit Card scheme is one of the best government scheme in this direction. Commercial and scheduled banks can be given guidelines to credit loans to farmers on softer terms, lower rate of interest and no requirements of securities etc. Proportion of credit to farmers should be increased to the total loans.

Q.5 Answer any tivo of the following (answer to each question should be in about 150 words): $15 \times 2 = 30$

(a) What is the meaning and aim of Social Forestry ? What are the main weaknesses noticed in Social Forestry Programme ?

Important Points for Answer:
- *Meaning*
- *Aims / Objectives*
- *Weaknesses*

Answer: The term 'Social Forestry' first used in 1976 by The National Commission on Agriculture, Government of India. It was then that India embarked upon a social forestry project with the aim of taking the pressure off the forests and making use of all unused and fallow land.

Government forest areas that are close to human settlement and have been degraded over the years due to human activities needed to be afforested. Trees were to be planted in and around agricultural fields. Plantation of trees along railway lines and roadsides, and river and canal banks were carried out. They were planted in village common land, Government wasteland and Panchayat land

Objectives of Social Forestry & Environment Wing :

Social forestry, schemes that have been started all over the country have made a considerable difference in overall forest cover in a short time. Afforestation outside the conventional forest area for the benefit of rural and urban communities. The main objective is to:

1. Improve the environment for protecting agriculture from adverse climatic factors,
2. Increase the supply of fuel wood for domestic use, small timber for rural housing, fodder for livestock, and minor forest produce for local industries,
3. Increase the natural beauty of the landscape; create recreational forests for the benefit of rural and urban population,
4. Provide jobs for unskilled workers and
5. Reclaim wastelands.
6. Finally, its object is to raise the standard of living and quality of life of the rural and urban people

4 Social forestry scheme can be categorized into groups :

- 4.1 Farm forestry
- 4.2 Community forestry
- 4.3 Extension forestry
- 4.4 Agro- forestry

Weakness :

- Lack of awareness about the programme among people.
- Illegal use and cutting of forest trees and products.
- Unsatisfactory implementation by state administration.
- Corruption and misuse of funds.
- Ignorance and avoidance of responsibility by people.

(b) Bring out the main objectives of Rashtriya Krishi Bima Yojana. The scheme is being implemented by which agency ?

Important Points for Answer:
- *Rashtriya Krishi Bima Yojana*
- *Objectives*
- *Implementing agency*

Answer: On June 22, 1999 The Prime Minister Shri Atal Bihari Vajpayee dedicated to the nation a new Agriculture Insurance Scheme known as *Bashtriya Krishi Bima Yojana.* Rashtriya Krishi Bima Yojana is a national level insurance scheme for agriculture. It provides insurance cover protection to farmers against crop failing and reimburse loss to them.

Main objectives :

- To provide insurance protection to farmers against natural calamities like drought, flood, fire or attack by pest which may result in crop failing or harm to crop.
- The insurance is also aimed to encourage and motivate farmers to invest in agriculture without undue fear of such failure or harm to crop.
- It is the main aim to cover even landless and marginal farmers under this scheme even though they may be indebted.
- To guarantee good standard of living to farmers and prevent incidents of suicides in case of loss in agriculture.
- To encourage farmers to cultivate food and cash crops apart from regularly cultivated crops.

This scheme is implemented by the agencies like New India Insurance, Oriental Insurance, NABARD and the United India Insurance Company Limited according to Indian Insurance Act-1956.

(c) Explain Mega Food Park Scheme of Government of India.

Important Points for Answer:
• *Mega Food Park Scheme - What is it ?*
• *Explanation*

Answer: Mega Food Park Scheme is a government scheme to develop retail market in food. To solve problems of food conservation and distribution, storage and transportation, this scheme is being promoted from April, 2007.

The Government has decided to establish 30 Mega Food Parks. These MFPs are places where farmers can sell their produce to retailers or to big companies or to customers directly. This is a consolidated form of mandis in villages.

This will help farmers to save their efforts of storing and conserving food after harvest. So, it will also help in preventing post-harvest loss. Because the food shall directly go either to consumers or to such sellers who have enough facilities to store them.

This will in turn, encourage retail marketing in food sector. Many big companies are showing interest in opening retail stores. Transportation and delivery system will be easier due to a specified location for a whole region for buying and selling of food products at Mega Food Parks.

The Commerce and Industry Ministry and the Ministry of Food and Agriculture are implementing this MFP scheme.

Q. 6 Write about the following (answer to each question should be in about 20 words) :

2 × 15 = 30

(a) Explain the term Merit Goods.

Answer: Merit goods are products generally not distributed by means of the price system, but based on merit or need, because people although having perfect knowledge would buy the wrong amount of them. Merit goods are, for example, education and to some extent the health-care. They are provided by state as "good for you".

(b) What is Cheap Money ?

Answer: Cheap Money is that money that is available at lower interest rates and easy conditions and also on softer terms.

(c) What is Countervailing Duty ?

Answer: It is a duty against dumping. This is aimed to raise the prices of the goods dumped and that is imposed to protect producers and farmers against evil effects of dumping.

(d) Wat is Hot Money ?

Answer: Funds which flow into a country to take advantage of favourable rates of interest in that country. These funds are highly volatile and subject to frequent shifts.

(e) Explain the Concept Trickle Down Theory.

Answer: It is a policy where emphasise is on the heavy industries and it is expected that it will trickle its benefits to the basic level, i.e. consumer goods industries.

(f) What is Stagflation ?

Answer: It is a state of the economy in which economic activity is slowing down, but wages and prices continue to rise. The term is a blend of the words stagnation and inflation. Stagflation occurs when inflation rises while output is either falling or at least not rising.

(g) What is Engel's Law ?

Answer: This law signifies that groups with lower income spends a larger part of their income on food and other similar items and with increase in income proportion of expenditure over such items decreases.

(h) Meaning of CCIL.

Answer: CCIL is Clearing Corporation of India Limited. It is an organisation related to trade and commerce.

(i) What is Administered Price ?

Answer: Administered Price are fixed by government to keep control on rise or fall of prices of particular commodities so that vulnerable groups have not to suffer

(j) What is Venture Capital ?

Answer: It is a capital invested in such business, company or project where risk of loss is high. Therefore such capital carries higher rate of interest.

(k) Explain the term Balance on Current Account.

Answer: It is net balance of export and import of goods and services - both visible and invisible during the period of a year. It may be positive or negative, i.e. surplus or deficit.

(l) What is Consolidated Fund ?

Answer: The funds where all receipts of the government is deposited except those deposited in Contingency Fund and the Public Accounts. This fund is put under the head of the state i.e. the President or the Governor, as the case may be.

(m) What is Budget Deficit ?

Answer: Budget Deficit indicates surplus of total expenditure over total income of an economy during a financial year.

(n) Explain the term Most Favoured Nations.

Answer: It is a status in International commercial relations. Where one state confers on another MFN status. It means henceforth that state shall be treated specially and exclusively in rules and policies related to trade and commerce.

(o) Meaning of Capital-Output Ratio.

Answer: Capital Output Ratio indicates how much capital shall be required to increase one unit of output of the product.

Q.7 Write about any two of the following (in about 150 words each) : 15 × 2 = 30

(a) Impact of globalization on state system and its institutions.

Important Points for Answer:	
• *Globalization*	• *Its impact on*
• *State System*	• *its institutions*

Answer: Globalization is a process of removing boundaries among states for the purpose of economic and cultural interaction. Countries are coming closer to each other due to globalization and new concept of global human and global governance are emerging due to globalization process.

State system is being greatly influenced by globalization. States have to open their economies for this process. To develop the country, to get benefit of barrierless trade co-operative government systems are adopted. Number of trade groups and blocks are increasing. Bilateral and multilateral agreements are entered into to enhance trade. Multinational companies are coming into existence and they are getting larger and larger. WHO and IMF are organizations which are helping in the process of globalization. Even states have to limit their sovereign decisions to such multi-lateral forums.

Also state institutions have to change their structures and organisation to get themselves accomodate with the process. Insurance, education, banks and finance, agriculture and PSUs have to make themselves more competitive, more qualitative to sustain competition given by the globalization process.

(b) SAARC Summit 2007.

Answer: SAARC Summit - 2007

- 14th SAARC - South Asian Association for Regional Co-operation, was held in New Delhi, India on 3rd and 4th April-07.
- It approved jointly the Delhi Declaration.
- Summit decided in favour of establishment of a regional food bank, South Asian University and tele-medicine mechanism and early operationalisation of SAARC Development Fund (SDF).
- Afghanistan was formally accepted as its eighth member.
- A Mutual Legal Assistance Treaty at regional level was agreed upon with all members' committing not to allow even fund raising by terror groups.
- They emphasised need for connectivity among member nations, particularly physical, economic and people-to-people.
- Also they agreed to harmonise customs procedures.

- India allowed zero duty access to Least Developed Countries (LDC) of South Asia by the end of the year.
- It was also decided to increase co-operation on national and regional telecom infrastructure and to utilize the potential of the IT and Communications sector.
- Members welcomed decision of Bangladesh to host first SAARC Youth Camp in 2007.
- Further, SAARC nations decided to earmark one rural community as SAARC village in each member state as innovative models of development.
- India described this summit as "smoothest and least contentious." The summit thus covered security, terrorism, trade, energy, connectivity and food security related themes for co-operation.

(c) The UN conference on Environment and Development (The Earth Summit)

Answer:

Important Points for Answer:
• *The Earth Summit*
• *Issues*
• *Main achievements*

The United Nations Conference on Environment and Development, also known as the Earth Summit (or, in Portuguese, Eco '92) was a major conference held in Rio de Janeiro from June 3 to June 14, 1992.

178 governments participated, with 118 sending their heads of state or government. Some 2,400 representatives of non-governmental organizations (NGOs) attended, with 17,000 people at the parallel NGO Forum, who had so-called Consultative Status.

The issues addressed included :

- systematic scrutiny of patterns of production—particularly the production of toxic components, such as lead in gasoline, or poisonous waste
- alternative sources of energy to replace the use of fossil fuels which are linked to global climate change
- new reliance on public transportation systems in order to reduce vehicle emissions, congestion in cities and the health problems caused by polluted air and smog
- the growing scarcity of water

An important achievement was an agreement on the Climate Change Convention which in turn led to the Kyoto Protocol.

Another was agreement to "not carry out any activities on the lands of indigenous peoples that would cause environmental degradation or that would be culturally inappropriate".

The Convention on Biological Diversity was opened for signature at the Earth Summit, and made a start towards redefinition of money supply measures that did not inherently encourage destruction of natural ecoregions and so-called uneconomic growth.

The Earth Summit resulted in the following documents:

- Rio Declaration on Environment and Development
- Agenda 21
- Convention on Biological Diversity
- Forest Principles
- Framework Convention on Climate Change

Q. 8 Write about the following (in about 20 words each) : $2 \times 5 = 10$

(a) G-8 Summit 2007

Answer: 33rd G-8 Summit was held in June, 2007 in Germany. This Summit had main themes on its agenda like : poverty in Africa, Climate change, environmental conservation, regional security etc.

(b) Hyde Act of 2006

Answer: Hyde Act is an enabling act that will be passed by the US Congress to allow co-operation between the USA and India on nuclear deal of July-2005.

(c) Global Governance

Answer: It is a concept of administering global issues like social, economic, environment and legal, political at international level through global governance.

(d) Operation Silence

Answer: To vacate Lai Masjid, Pakistani army implemented Operation Silence. It was targeted against fundamentalist terrorists.

(e) SAARC Human Rights Report 2006

Answer: India has topped the list in SAARC Human Rights Report-2007 regarding Least violating nation of HRs. Due to its huge population, it could top even after having Godhra incident. All over HR conditions are not good in the region according to the report.

Q. 9 Write about the following by expanding and explaining the objectives (in about 20 words each): $2 \times 5 = 10$

(a) ICT4D

Answer: Information and Communication Technologies for Development. It is a technology that is to be used for socio-economical development. It is a novel use of communication and information technolog)'.

(b) BEMs

Answer: The purpose of a Building Energy Management System is to automate and take control of these operations in the most efficient way possible. It is therefore a vital tool in the University's drive to improve energy efficiency and reduce fuel use and costs.

(c) IAEA

Answer: International Atomic Energy Agency. It is situated in Vienna. It is a watchdog institute of the UN over nuclear weapons and non-proliferation apart from assisting in peaceful civil use of atomic energy.

(d) BIMSTEC

Answer: Bay of Bengal Initiative for Multi Sector Technical and Economical Co-operation. It is an organization of seven member nations situated on the Bay of Bengal for economical and technical co-operation.

(e) ECJ

Answer: European Court of Justice. It is the apex court in European Union to take care of human rights and legal issues in member states that are of regional importance.

Q. 10 Answer any one of the following in about 250 words : 30

(a) Explain the phenomenon of ozone depletion, its causes and effects. What effects are needed to reduce it ?

Important Points for Answer:	
• *Ozone depletion*	• *Causes*
• *Effects*	• *Efforts to reduce*

Answer: Ozone Depletion : Atmosphere of the earth consists of a layer of Ozone (0_3) gas at the height of 30 to 60 km above the earth. This ozone layer is essential for living beings. As this layer prevents the ultraviolet (OV) rays of the sunlight coming to the earth, it protects animals and vegetation from the dangerous effect of UV rays. But due to some causes, the depletion of 0_3 is noticed which pose a danger to mankind as well as other forms of life.

Causes : Human activities like industrialisation and others have polluted the environment. These pollutant contains chlorofluorocarbons (CFCs) as an ingredient. These CFCs are the main elements causing depletion of Ozone layer. Chlorine, Bromine, Florine etc. halone gases are the main destroyers of 0_3. Due to refrigerator, plastic, paints and aerosol industries such compounds are produced. Electronics and optical industries also produce ozone destroying chemicals. UV rays separate chlorine from the CFC and this chlorine reacts with Ozone (0_3) and turns it into simple oxygen (0_2). At present USA, Europe, Chile, Australia etc. are at danger due to 0_3 depletion.

Effects : The Ozone depletion has various consequences dangerous to lives on the earth.

The UV can cause skin cancer and other diseases of skin. It increases temperature of the earth and therefore ice melts. This in turn raises level of the sea and may submerge the islands and the coastal areas causing damage to lives and property.

Efforts : To cope with this phenomena, international community has started efforts of reducing ozone depleting chemicals. For this, many agreements and conventions are signed. Vienna Conference of 1983, and the Montreal Protocol of 1987 are among these efforts. They prohibit production of CFCs. London Conference is also one of the important landmark in this direction. Kyoto Protocol 1997 is also related to that.

But for this, international consensus is required on technological measures. They require to develop ozone friendly technologies and to share it with other nations also.

(b) What do you understand by the term 'biodiversity' ? Examine the causes and consequences of degeneration of biodiversity.

Important Points for Answer:	
• *Biodiversity*	• *Causes*
• *Consequences*	

Answer: Biodiversity means existence of various types of species of animals, vegetation and micro-organisms in a habitat. These diversity of living creatures make the habit, biologically diverse in resources. It contains various species, sub-species, and types. Different species and sub-species have different types of nature and qualities. These nature and qualities are exploited by mankind for his benefit and progress. For example, we use some types of vegetation for food purpose and some types of animals for transport at others for food also.

But this bio-diversity gets degenerating due to some or the other reason as narrated below :

- Over exploitation of a particular type of specie gets them reduced to such a lower number to sustain.
- Some species of birds are in danger due to hunting and/or loss of their natural habitats
- Some animals are also on the verge of extinction because of hunting, loss of their natural home in forests, etc.
- Some species of animals and birds are used for medicinal and experimental purposes.
- Some vegetations have lost their existence due to clearing of forests for mining, setting up of industries, agricultural or human dwelling purposes.
- Some forests are being destroyed for urbanisation and with them gets destroyed habitation of many species of living beings.
- Climate change also destroys species because some species cannot changes adapt to such changes.
- Sometimes some natural calamity or sudden change in geographical set up may destroy species.

Consequences:

Such degeneration of biodiversity creates imbalance in the food-chain. This does not only affect the nature but also human being and their daily activities. Such changes also destroys other species dependant upon the diversity. For example, oceanic activities change chemistry of oceanic climate that destroy corals and some other organisms dependant upon them. India is one of the 12 countries with most bio-diverse area. So, naturally its economical, cultural and social activities are closely related to them. Extinction of any of them can destroy such practice. For example, the Royal Bengal Tiger, our national animal itself is at the verge of its extinction. Similarly destroying forests causes flood, reduction in precipitation and other consequences.

So, to sum up, we can say that biodiversity is a natural gift. That is getting degenerated due to mostly human activities. Such destruction must be stopped or evil consequences will follow.

Q. 11 Answer any two of the following (answer for each question should be in about 150 words): **15 × 2 = 30**

(a) What are the alternative fuels available for the transport sector ? Discuss their characteristics, advantages and disadvantages in their utilization.

Important Points for Answer:	
• *Alternative fuels*	• *Characteristics*
• *Advantages*	• *Disadvantages*

Answer: Due to limited quantity of petroleum fuels, and its pollutant effects, it is necessary to find out alternative fuels for transportation.

- CNG-Compressed Natural Gas
- Bio-diesel
- Gasohal
- Solar batteries
- Hydrogen

Characteristics :

- These fuels are not available ready-made, some process is required to derive them.
- They are generally modern in their use.
- They have yet not gained much importance in use.
- They require technological upgradation.

Advantages :

- They produce less pollutant effects.
- They are generally renewable and non-exhaustible.
- They are comparatively less expensive.
- They are available domestically and we will not have to depend on imports.
- Solar energy is much available in India.
- Hydrogen has the largest calory value.
- Bio-diesel will give economical activity to farmers.

Disadvantages :

In name of disadvantages, we can sum up some limitations in their use.

- Hydrogen is explosive and problem of storage is also there.
- Sunlight is available in less degree in monsoon and winter seasons.
- More cultivation of Jethropa and other species of bio-diesel may occupy land necessary for food cultivation.
- Technological upgradation is required.
- Huge investment is required to change today's petrol and diesel running vehicles to adopt such technologies.

(b) Explain the objectives and the current achievements of human genome project.

Important Points for Answer:
- *Human Genome Project*
- *Objectives*
- *Achievements*

Answer: It is a project to get information about gene-sequence and structure in human beings. This was adopted by America in 1988.

The human genome project has following objectives :

- To decode the sequence of genes arrangement.
- To trace genome structure in human cells.
- To get information about proteins made and developed by human genes.
- To keep watch on process taking place of generating and degenerating of proteins in genes and to find out functions and importance of various proteins in human genes.
- To know how some diseases are caused and how some disorders are developed due to genes defects.

Current development in human genome project is :

- That scientists are able to find out gene structure and some codes. Using some techniques in tracing out and repairing ailing genes will be made possible due to this project. It is now possible to treat some hereditary diseases. By using DNA interference, now many incurable diseases can be cured. This project has also achieved success in finding out roots and cures of many diseases.

(c) Discuss the missile technology initiatives undertaken by India.

Answer: For defence purposes, India started a missile development programme in 1983. DRDO (Defence Research and Development Organisation) is main responsible agency for it. India has developed various types of missiles through this initiative. Main among India's missiles are Prithvi. It is a short range ballistic missile. It is a surface to surface missile with a range up to 250 km. Dhanus is ship launched version of Prithvi. It is also surface to surface missile. This naval missile has striking range up to 150 km.

Agni is a re-entry technology demonstrator missile. Agni-I, Agni-II and Agni-III are part of Agni project. It has capacity to beat 500 to 3500 km far targets.

Akash ia medium range surface to air missile while Trishul is also a short range surface to air missile.

Nag is anti-tank missile which has fire and forget technology.

Ashtra is air to air targeting missile. Brahmos is the latest anti-ship cruise missile developed in collaboration with Russia. It has a target range of about 290 km with 200- 300 kg of payload capacity. Surya is being developed as inter-continental ballistic missile by India.

Q. 12 Answer all the five (in about 20 words each) : **2 × 5 = 10**

(a) What is firewall ?

Answer: Firewall is a technique for the security of computers. It prevents unwanted programmes and commands and allows only permitted ones.

(b) What is malware ?

Answer: It is a short form of malicious software. It is prepared to damage any computer system. Sometimes, it is considered as a virus but it is different from it in the sense that it does not spread like a virus.

(c) What do the following stand for ?

(i) MPEG (ii) ISP (iii) HTML (iv) ASCII

Answer:

MPEG : Moving Picture Expert Group

ISP : Internet Service Provider

HTML : Hyper Text Mark Up Language

ASCII : American Standard Code for Information Interchange

(d) What is Root kit?

Answer: It is a key to operate a programme, able to destroy whole system and steal information from it.

(e) What is computer architecture?

Answer: It is a technique that can be used to make designs for various purposes. It is a software that helps using computer system in architectural areas.

Q. 13 (a) In the year 2000 out of a total 1750 workers of a factory 1200 workers were members of a union. The number of women employed was 200 of which 175 did not belong to the union. In 2005, the number of union workers increased to 1510 of which 1290 were men. On the other hand the number of non union workers fell down to 208 of which 180 were men. **8**

(i) Put the above information in a proper table with title.

(ii) Calculate the increase in the percentage of the female workers belonging to the union in that five year period.

Answer: (i) Table showing Male-Female membership of Union in years 2000 and 2005

Year	**2000**			**2005**		
Membership of Union	**Male**	**Female**	**Total**	**Male**	**Female**	**Total**
Member	1175	25	1200	1290	220	1510
Non-members	375	175	550	180	28	208
Total	1550	200	1750	1470	248	1718

Hint: To count the missing datas easily, fill up the available data in the table and then find out missing datas from relevant figures.

Example: from statement, we get in 2000, total workers are 1750, of them members are 1200. Putting it in table, we easily find number of non-members are 550.

Similarly, when we find non-member males are 180 in 2005 and total number of non-members are 208, we can count non-member female must be 28 in number.

Then putting these derivative datas, we can calculate other figures also easily.

Note - Derivative numbers are bold.

(ii) Increase in number of the female workers belonging to the union

= Number of such females in 2005 - Number of such females in 2000

$= 220 - 25 = 195$

Increase in percentage of such female $= \frac{\text{उनकी संख्या में वृद्धि}}{\text{उनकी वर्तमान संख्या}} = 100\%$

$= \frac{195}{25} \times 100 = 780\%$

(b) The marks obtained by 20 students in a subject are given : **8**

32, 62, 72, 46, 52, 74, 53, 42, 58, 61, 59, 46, 36, 76, 58, 77, 62, 48, 36, 39

Form a frequency distribution table with class interval 10. Also draw the histogram.

Answer: Frequency Distribution Table

Marks	No. of students
31-40	4
41-50	4
51-60	5
61-70	3
71-80	4
	Total = 20

Histogram showing marks of 20 students

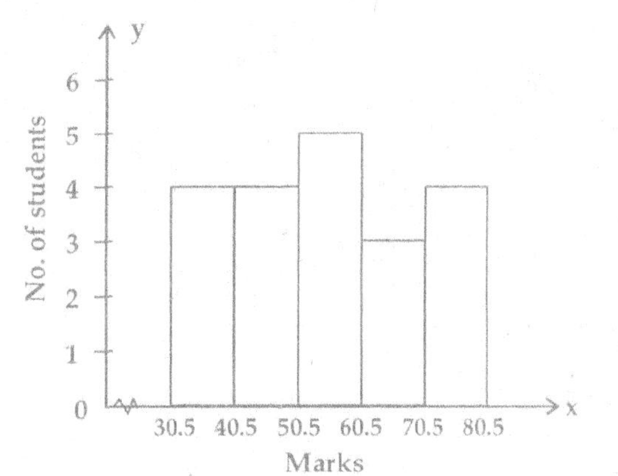

Q. 14 (a) For the following distribution of statistics test grades, construct a frequency polygon and answer the following : **8**

(i) How many test grades are greater than 87 ?

(ii) That percentage of test grades are greater than 83 ?

(iii) What percentage of test grades are lower than 72 ?

(iv) What percentage of test grades are between 72 and 79 (inclusive) ?

Test Grades :

73, 92, 57, 89, 70, 95, 75, 80, 47, 88, 47, 48, 64, 86, 79, 72, 71, 77, 93, 55, 75, 50, 53, 75, 85, 50, 82, 45, 40, 82, 60, 55, 60, 89, 79, 65, 54, 93, 60, 83, 59.

Answer: To prepare frequency polygon, we should first classify the data in a frequency table

Marks	No. of students	
1-10		0
11-20		0
21-30		0
31-40	I	1
41-50	IIII I	6
51-60	IIII II II	9
61-70	III	3
71-80	IIII IIII	10
81-90	IIII III	8
91-100	IIII	4
Total		41

* To prepare frequency polygon, we have to represent number of students on the point of mid-value of each class.

Frequency polygon

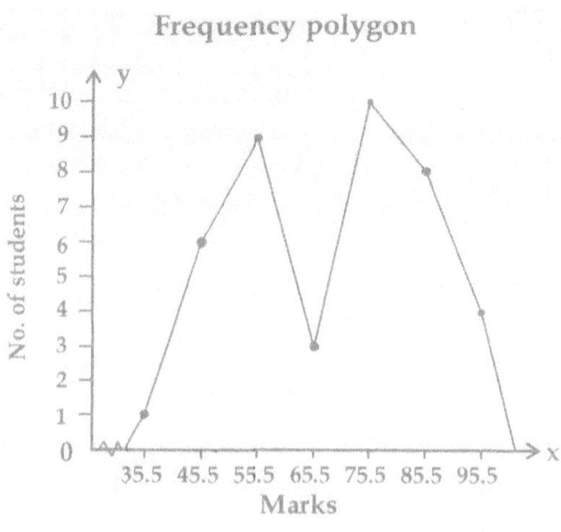

Marks

(i) No. of test grades greater than 87 = 6

(ii) Percentage of test grades greater than 83,

$$= \frac{\text{No. of grades } > 83}{\text{Total grades}} \times 100$$

$$= \frac{9}{41} \times 100 = 21.95$$

(iii) Percentage of test grades lower than 72,

$$= \frac{\text{No. of grades } < 72}{\text{Total no. of grades}} \times 100$$

$$= \frac{20}{41} \times 100 = 48.78\%$$

(iv) Percentage of test grades between 72 and 79 inclusive

$$\frac{\text{No. of grades between 72 and 79}}{\text{Total no. of grades}} \times 100$$

$$= \frac{8}{41} \times 100 = \mathbf{19.51\%}$$

(b) Construct an appropriate diagram to show the following data of a University

Course	No. of students
Engineering	440
Arts	220
Agriculture	120
Home Science	80
Economic	60
Total	920

Answer: We can use Pie-diagram to represent the given data.

Total degree = 360

Total students = 920

We can calculate number of students in degree as following.

920 students = 360°

$$\therefore \text{Engineering 440 students} = \frac{440}{920} \times 360^\circ$$

$$= 17.172^\circ \propto 172^\circ$$

$$\therefore \text{Arts 220 students} = \frac{220}{920} \times 360°$$
$$= 86.09° \propto 86°$$

$$\therefore \text{Agriculture 120 students} = \frac{120}{920} \times 360°$$
$$= 46.96° \propto 47°$$

$$\therefore \text{Home Science 80 students} = \frac{80}{920} \times 360°$$
$$= 31.30° \propto 31°$$

$$\therefore \text{Economics 60 students} = \frac{60}{920} \times 360°$$
$$= 23.48° \propto 24°$$

Pie-diagram

H. Sc. = Home Science

Eco. = Economics

Agri = Agriculture

Q. 15 (a) What do you understand by :

(i) Primary and Secondary Data

(ii) Data classification

(iii) Measures of central tendency

(iv) Characteristics of good average

Answer: (i) Primary data indicates the information collected on the first hand. They are basic in nature. They can be used to calculate and derive secondary data.

(ii) Data classification is a process of grouping of any data using tables, diagrams or curves or any other methods.

(iii) It is represented by mean, mode and median.

(iv) It should be nearest to the highest and the lowest item with possible least variation and should not include extreme values.

(b) The mean wage of 100 labourers working in a factory running two shifts of 60 and 40 workers respectively is Rs. 38. The mean wage of 60 labourers working in the morning shift is Rs. 40. Find the mean wage of 40 labourers working in the evening shift. **2**

Answer: Mean wage of 100 workers = 100

So, total wage paid = 38 × 100

= Rs. 3800

Morning shift of 60 workers,

Mean wage = Rs. 40

Total = 60 × 40 = Rs. 2400

So, wage paid to evening shift of 40 workers = Rs. 3800 – 2400

= Rs. 1400

$$\text{Mean wage} = \frac{\text{Total wage}}{\text{Workers}}$$

$$= \frac{1400}{40} = \text{Rs. } 35$$

(c) The mean age of the group 5 boys is 16 years. Another boy joins the group and then the mean age of the group becomes 18 years. How old is the newcomer?

Answer: Mean age of 5 boys = 16 years

Total years = 16 × 5 = 80 years

6th boy joins, now mean age = 18 years

Now, total years = 18 × 6

= 108 years

So, age of 6th boy = Total age of six boys – Total age of five boys

= 108 – 80

Hence, age of new comer = 28 years

(d) Arithmetic means of two completely different sets of values may be the same.
When extreme values are taken into consideration, the arithmetic mean is largely affected. Is it merit or demerit of arithmetic mean and give reasons for your statement. **2**

Answer: Yes, it is possible that arithmetic means of different sets of values may be same because mean represents only average value of the given data, e.g.

e.g. Set-1 = 6, 8, 7, 5, 4

Set-2 = 12, 1, 5, 4, 8, 9, 3

Both Set-1 and Set-2 have same arithmetic mean = 6.

(MAIN) 2008 Civil Services Exam. General Studies

SOLVED PAPERS

PAPER–I

Time Allowed : Three Hours — *Maximum Marks : 300*

Candidates should attempt ALL questions strictly in accordance with the instructions given under each question.

Q. 1 Answer any two of the following (in about 150 words each) : 15 × 2 = 30

(a) "The emergence of new social classes in British India was the direct consequence of the establishment of new social economy, new state system, administrative machinery and Western education." Discuss.

Important Points for Answer:
- *New social classes*
- *How emerged*

Answer: After coming of British, India witnessed a new social order.

A new, middle class, english educated social group came into existence. They were not loyal to British. They used the English education to create awareness among Indians. They prepared a platform for national movement.

A high-class, english educated group, which was loyal to British, was a small number of people. They joined either British services or were directly related to the ruling system. Similarly, Zamindars and Princes were loyal to British.

And the remained Indians were illiterate farmers and other small entrepreneurs. They get exploited either by the British or by Indians.

These classes were dominating the old caste-based division of Indian Society.

Reasons behind these new classes were : British social policies like abolition of Sati, widow remarriage act etc. Economical changes also dragged people from their old-traditional village professions to urban industrial labouring.

Equality before law of the new judicial system wiped out earlier differences of Indian Society. Concepts of western education not only awakened Indians but also prepared them to research in their ancient history.

Concluding, it can be said that all new classes were direct result of British policies.

(b) "British vision of India had no single coherent set of ideas. On the contrary, the ideas were shot through with contradictions and inconsistencies." Discuss.

Important Points for Answer:	
• *British Policy*	• *Indian situational reflection*
• *Opportunistic*	• *Different ideologies*

Answer: British crown assumed all responsibility of ruling India in its own hand after 1857 revolt. Uptil now, the Britishers interfere in social and religious matters of India but after 1857 revolt, they stopped such interference and assumed the policy of non-interference.

Various Governor-Generals also had their different sets of ideas regarding India, e.g. Lord Dalhousie's Doctrine of Lapse, Lord Wellesley's Subsidiary Alliance System etc.

Sometimes Britishers supported Hindus and another time Muslims. Towards Princely States, they first assumed suspicious policies but after revolt, they started to take interest in them.

During the time of national movement, their reactions were more opportunistic than based on policy. The Round Table Conferences were examples of it.

They reacted according to the Indian situations. Their soft or hard attitude towards Congress or Muslim League was just based on incidents that took place.

Various ideologies of British rulers have effected Indian administration and government. Partition of India was also passed from mutually controversial stages and policies of the Britishers.

(c) Non-Cooperation Movement gave new direction and energy to the National Movement." Explain.

Important Points for Answer:
- *Non-Cooperation Movement*
- *More people join national movement*
- *Wide area covered*

Answer: Non-Cooperation Movement was launched by the Indian National Congress which brought Gandhi as the most influential leader of Indian politics.

This movement expanded goal of Congress to 'Swaraj' from 'dominion status'. This movement brought out rural-common people in the national movement.

Henceforth, all classes of Indian Society started to take part in national movement. Its united goals with the Khilafat Movement gave a hopeful scene of Hindu-Muslim unity in Indian politics.

New national symbols like Flag, Slogan, Dress and Language were accepted. Now the working method of Congress changed.

Vastness of objectives and simplicity of movement gave chance to all classes to participate. Even rural illiterate and farmers started to participate in National movement.

This was stopped by Gandhi after Chauri-Chaura incident. But this incident itself is an evident that people were fired by the national spirit.

Thus, a new energy and direction was given to the Indian freedom struggle by this Non- Cooperation Movement.

Q. 2 Write about the following (not exceeding 20 words each): 2 × 15 = 30

(a) Lakshmi Bai, Rani of Jhansi

Answer: Her kingdom Jhansi was captured by Lord Dalhousie by 'Doctrine of Lapse'. She assumed leadership at Jhansi and fought in the revolt of 1857.

(b) Ilbert Bill

Answer: It was passed to give the Indian District and Sessions Judges, the same jurisdiction as the European judges. But due to British opposition, it was changed.

(c) Lala Hara Dayal

Answer: He set up the Ghadar Party at San Francisco in November 1913. He was also allegedly involved in bombing of Lord Hardinge II in 1906 in Delhi.

(d) Vaikom Satyagraha

Answer: Vaikom Satyagraha (1924-25) was a satyagraha in Travancore, Kerala against untouchability in Hindu society. The movement was centered at the Shiva temple at Vaikom, near Kottayam.The Satyagraha aimed at securing freedom of movement for all sections of society through the public roads leading to the Sri Mahadeva Temple at Vaikom.

(e) Indian States Commission

Answer: It was also known as State Reorganisation Commission. It was set up under the chairmanship of Fazal Ali after independence. It recommended formation of states on the basis of language.

(f) Bodhisattva

Answer: A person who attains nirvana by working for the welfare of the world and voluntarily postpones release from rebirth; also regarded as an incarnation of the Buddha, prior to his own birth in the world.

(g) Megasthenes

Answer: Megasthenes was the Greek Ambassador in the Court of Chandragupta Maurya from the Court of Selecus. He wrote "Indica", an account of contemporary India.

(h) Brihadeshwara Temple, Tanjore

Answer: The Brihadishwara Temple, also known as Rajarajeswaram, at Thanjavur is a brilliant example of the major heights achieved by Cholas in temple architecture. The temple is part of the UNESCO World Heritage Site "Great Living Chola Temples".

(i) Perini Shivatandavam

Answer: The Perini dance tradition was widely prevalent in die courts of the kings belonging to the Kakatiya dynasty. Perini Sivatandavam, a dynamic male-oriented dance was presented by the Vijayawada Cultural Academy at Sri Sivaramakrishna Kshetram.

(j) Allasani Peddana

Answer: Allasani Peddana (15th and 16th centuries CE) was a famous Telugu' poet and was ranked as the foremost of the Astadiggajalu the title for the group of eight poets in the court of King Krishnadevaraya, a ruler of the Vijayanagara Empire.

(k) Golkonda Fort

Answer: Golkonda a ruined city of south-central India and capital of ancient Kingdom of Golkonda (1364-1512), is situated west of Hyderabad. Golkonda consists of four distinct forts with a 10 km long outer wall.

(l) Chishti Silsila

Answer: The Chishti Silsila was of Khawaja Gharib Nawaz Ajmeri. He was a Sufi of Great Stature and is revered by both Hindus and Muslims. In sufi terminology, silsila means one's spiritual genealogy from one's spiritual guide (sheikh/murshid) to the Holy Prophet Muhammad (sallalahu alaihi wasallam).

(m) Chauth and Sardeshmukhi

Answer: Chauth means claim to one-fourth of the government's share of revenue.

Sardeshmukhi means claim to one-tenth of the government's share of revenue, based on status.

(n) Poona Sarvajanik Sabha

Answer: It was established by Mahadev Govind Rande in 1870, with the object of promoting the political welfare and advancing the interest of the people of this and other parts of the country.

(o) 'Rama Sethu'

Answer: Rama's Bridge or Ram Setu also known as Adam's Bridge, is a chain of limestone shoals, between the islands of Mannar, near northwestern Sri Lanka, and Rameswaram, off the southeastern coast of Tamil Nadu, India. Geological evidence indicates that this bridge is a former land connection between India and Sri Lanka.

Q. 3 Answer any two of the following (in about 150 words each): 15 × 2 = 30

(a) The winter rains in North India are largely related to Jet Streams and Western Disturbances. Bring out the relationship.

Important Points for Answer:

- *Winter Rains*
- *Westerly Disturbances*
- *Jet Streams*
- *Relationship*

Answer: North India receives rainfall during the winter season. The rainfall is due to modification created by the Jet Stream.

Jet Stream is the high-speed winds which blow from the west in the upper atmosphere over mid-latitude areas. They are three dimensional movement of air mass.

Sub-tropical Easterly Jet Stream blows to the Indian sub-continent from the Mediterranean region.

The disturbances caused by the Mediterranean region in the North India is called Western Disturbance in the Northern part of India.

This disturbance is a short term condition of North India and is caused by the sub tropical easterly jet stream.

During winter, landmass experience high pressure in North-Western Part and low

pressure is maintained in the regions occupied by Tropical Easterly Jet Stream.

This is the main reason why North India receive rainfall in winter.

(b) Agricultural Productivity in India remain low. Explain the reasons for this situation.

Important Points for Answer:

- *Low Productivity*
- *Reasons*

Answer: Productivity in Indian agriculture remain low in comparison to other developed countries. We may cite following reasons :

- Dependency upon rainfall.
- Irregular rainfall (in time).
- Irregular distribution of rain (in amount of water).
- Less availability of fertilizer.
- No use of modern scientific techniques.
- No improved seeds, pesticides, tools, etc.
- Lack of basic infrastructure.
- Per head smaller pieces of farm.
- Less investment.
- No availability of easy and cheap credit.
- No proper irrigation facility.
- Lack of proper food processing and storage facility.
- Natural calamities like droughts, floods, etc.

All these are factors responsible for low productivity in Indian agriculture. Today India produces nearly 210 million tonnes of food grains. This must increase with requirement of Indian Population.

Therefore, Green Revolution was launched in 1969. Presently, Second Green Revolution is being planned to increase agricultural productivity.

(c) Bring out the pros and cons of Special Economic Zones.

Answer: Pros :

- SEZs are termed as growth engines. Because, they can help to grow other industries also.
- They bring investment.
- They help in developing infrastructural capacity of the region.
- SEZs enrich FOREX reserve of the country.
- They bring latest technologies to the area.
- Export increases.
- More employments are generated in the country.

Cons :

- SEZs are given tax holidays. So, government revenue suffers losses.
- Agricultural land is also allocated, sometimes, for industrial purposes. It reduces availability of land for agriculture. So, food security is endangered.
- Relocation of domestic industries from other areas to SEZs is a big issue. It does not involve any new investment.
- Mostly employment is generated for educated youth. Farmers and labourers unemployed, by sale of land, are hardly getting new employment.
- Disputes related to allocation and acquisition of land have arisen.

Q. 4 Write about the following (not exceeding 20 words each): $2 \times 5 = 10$

(a) Buckingham Canal

Answer: The Buckingham Canal is a 420 km long salt water navigation canal, running parallel to the Coromandel Coast of South India from the Vijayawada in Andhra Pradesh to Villupuram District in Tamil Nadu.

The canal connects most of the natural backwaters along the coast to the port of Chennai. It was constructed by the British Raj, and was an important waterway during the late nineteenth and the twentieth century.

(b) Terai Region

Answer: The Terai ("moist land") is a belt of marshy grasslands, savannas, and forests at the base of the Himalaya range in India, Nepal, and Bhutan, from the Yamuna River in the west to tite Brahmaputra River in the east.

(c) Organic Farming

Answer: Organic farming is a form of agriculture that relies on crop rotation, green manure, compost, biological pest control, and mechanical cultivation to maintain soil productivity and control pests, excluding or strictly limiting the use of synthetic fertilizers and synthetic pesticides, plant growth regulators, livestock feed additives, and genetically modified organisms.

(d) Demographic Dividend

Answer: A rising share of working age people in a population resulting in the rate of economic growth. This usually occurs late in the demographic transition when the fertility rate falls and the youth dependency rate declines.

(e) Nor'westers

Answer: They originated over the Chotanagpur Plateaus and blow in the north-east direction. They bring rainfall in Assam, West Bengal, Orissa and nearby regions. Useful for tea crops. Also known as Kalbaisakhis of West Bengal.

Q. 5 Answer any one of the following (in about 250 words): 30

(a) What is meant by 'Judicial Activism' ? Evaluate its role in the context of the functioning of Indian polity.

> **Important Points for Answer:**
> - *El Meaning*
> - *Role of Judicial Activism*
> - *Indian Political System*

Answer: Judicial Activism means active role of judiciary in upholding rights of citizens and preserving the constitutional and legal system of the country.

In the case of Keshavanda Bharti or known as the fundamental rights case, judicial activism was given, due consideration. It is a water-mark case.

For the first time a court held that a constitutional amendment duly passed by the legislature was invalid as damaging or destroying its basic structure. This was a gigantic innovative judicial leap unknown to any legal system.

Judicial activism earned a human face in India by liberalising access to justice and giving relief to disadvantaged groups and the have-nots under the leadership of justices V.R. Krishna Iyyer and P.N. Bhagwati.

The Supreme Court gained in stature and legitimacy. Later, when the independence of the judiciary was threatened by punitive transfers, the court entered the arena of judicial appointments and transfers.

With the increasing criminalisation and mis-govemance and the complete apathy of the executive, the court took up the case of terrorist funding linked to political corruption through the 'Hawala' root in the Vineet Narain case (Jain Hawala case).

The Courts on several occasions have issued directions in public interest litigation (PIL) covering a wide spectrum such as road safety, pollution, illegal structures in VIP zones, monkey menace, dog menace, unpaid dues by former and serving legislators, nursery admissions and admissions in institutions of higher learning.

There is no doubt that sometimes these orders are triggered by righteous indignation and emotional responses.

The common citizens have discovered that the administration has become so apathetic and non-performing and corruption and criminality so wide spread that they have no recourse except to move the courts through PIL, enlarging the field for judicial intervention. The great contribution of judicial activism in India has been to provide a safety valve in a democracy and a hope that justice is not beyond reach.

(b) Discuss the major extra-constitutional factors influencing the federal polity in India.

Important Points for Answer:

- *Federalism in India*
- *Extra-constitutional factors*
- *Planning Commission*
- *Regional Parties*
- *Population*
- *Resources*

Answer: India has opted for Federal Structure in Indian Political System. Division of powers between the Centre and States is fundamental to the federalism.

The Constitution has made some provisions for maintaining federal policy. Some constitutional and extra-constitutional factors are affecting the working of Indian polity. Major extra-constitutional (not mentioned in the Constitution) factors may be mentioned as below :

Planning Commission is an extra-constitutional body. Formation of Five Year Plan is a work of the Planning Commission. Allocation of Financial Resources to states for their development is influenced by the decisions of the Planning Commission.

Principle of State Autonomy is somehow violated in this way.

Regional political parties have gained importance in the phase of coalition governments at Centre. Their bargaining powers have increased. The Centre inclines towards the region which supports the Central Government. It affects fair decisions of Centre. Principle of equality and autonomy is thus violated.

Regions having more population, have more seats in Parliament. Their voice at the Centre is more clear than any State having less number of MPs.

Decisions are taken according to the interest of more powerful states, (numerically strong) in Parliament.

Demographic division of states is one of the factors which affect Indian Polity.

Resources of any state are important source for the development of the State itself and the country as a whole. Many a times, the Centre acquires resources from region of a State and allocates financial grants in that proportion to it. Distribution of natural resources should not be the criteria for distributing grants. But, somehow it impacts financial strength of a State.

All these extra constitutional factors have affected Indian federal system.

Q. 6 Answer any two of the following (in about 150 words each): 15 × 2 = 30

(a) Enumerate the Fundamental Duties incorporated in the Constitution after the 42nd Amendment.

Answer: Fundamental duties were inserted by the 42nd amendment.

Article 51 A. It shall be the duty of every citizen of India—

(a) to abide by the Constitution and respect its ideals and institutions, the National Flag and the National Anthem;

(b) to cherish and follow the noble ideals which inspired our national struggle for freedom;

(c) to uphold and protect the sovereignty, unity and integrity of India;

(d) to defend the country and render national service when called upon to do so;

(e) to promote harmony and the spirit of common brotherhood amongst all the people of India transcending religious, linguistic and regional or sectional diversities; to renounce practices derogatory to the dignity of women;

(f) to value and preserve the rich heritage of our composite culture;

(g) to protect and improve the natural environment including forests, lakes, rivers and wild life, and to have compassion for living creatures;

(h) to develop the scientific temper, humanism and the spirit of inquiry and reform;

(i) to safeguard public property and to abjure violence;

(j) to strive towards excellence in all spheres of individual and collective activity so that the nation constantly rises to higher levels of endeavour and achievement;

*[(k) who is a parent or guardian to provide opportunities for education to his child or, as the case may be, ward between the age of six and fourteen years.]

*Ins. by the Constitution (Eighty-sixth Amendment) Act, 2002

(b) Examine the demand for greater state autonomy and its impact on the smooth functioning of Indian polity.

Important Points for Answer:

- *Centre-State relations*
- *Central control over States*
- *Centralisation*
- *Regional parties & Politics*
- *Sarkaria Commission*
- *M.M. Punchhi Commission*

Answer: The Constitution of India has framed the Centre-State relations primarily on federal pattern. However due to some historical and political reasons and regional diversities among states, the Centre is given some control over states.

Some areas where the Centre can control States are :

- appointment of Governors
- power to make laws with respect to state lists

- residuary power with Centre
- dependence of the States on the Centre for financial assistance apart from these direct constitutional controls.

The Centre has constituted the Planning Commission which makes five year plans, both for the Centre and the States, and thus the pace of development is decided by the Centre. All these factors have resulted into centralisation of the federal system adding a point to the unitary character of our Constitution.

But with the rise of regional political parties in different states the situation has changed. They have demanded more and more autonomy for States. Some provisions like a separate list for State subjects and hard procedure to amend federal character of the Constitution are in their favour. But the demands of more and more autonomy has resulted into conflicts and frictions between the Centre and States. Sarkaria Commission has suggested some measures to normalise Centre-State relations. Recently appointed M.M. Punchi Commission is also to report on this question.

It is concluded that genuine autonomy to States with necessary centralisation factor is the way for political progress.

(c) Discuss the composition and functions of the Union Public Service Commission.

Important Points for Answer:
- *Composition*
- *Functions*

Answer: The Union Public Service Commission (UPSC) is a constitutional body in India authorized to conduct examinations for appointment to the various civil services of the Union. The Indian Constitution (Part XIV - Services Under the Union and the states - article no. 315 to 323) provides for a Public Service Commission for the Union and a Public Service Commission for each state.

The President appoints its chairman and members.

Functions

Functions of the UPSC are to conduct examinations for appointment to the services of the Union.

- Recruitment to services & posts under the Union through conduct of competitive examinations;
- Recruitment to services & posts under the Central Government by selection through Interviews;
- Advising on the suitability of officers for appointment on promotion as well as transfer-on-deputation;
- Advising the Government on all matters relating to methods of Recruitment to various services and posts;
- Disciplinary cases relating to different civil services; and
- Miscellaneous matters relating to grant of extra ordinary pensions, reimbursement of legal expenses, etc.

Q. 7 Answer the following (in about 20 words each): **2 × 5 = 10**

(a) What is a Censure Motion ?

Answer: It is passed to ensure a policy of the government or a minister. It means showing lack of confidence in the government. If it is passed successfully, the government will fall.

(b) Distinguish between the auditing and accounting functions of the CAG of India. *

Answer: The CAG audits accounts at both the Union and State level but his accounting function is related only to states.

(c) Distinguish between a starred question and an unstarred one asked in the Parliament.

Answer: Starred questions are to be answered orally and supplementary questions can be asked, but unstarred questions are tq be answered in written and no supplementary question is allowed.

(d) What is contempt of Parliament ?

Answer: Parliament is a court and any violation of its order results in its contempt. For that Parliament can inflict punishment.

(e) What were the two major considerations to have the Governor appointed and not elected?

Answer: 1) Governor to be the agent of Centre to maintain federal structure.

2) There cannot be two elected heads in a State, i.e. Chief Minister and Governor.

Q. 8 Answer any one of the following (in about 250 words): **30**

(a) What, in your opinion, are the causes of terrorism ? Suggest suitable measures to deal with the threat of terrorism in India.

Important Points for Answer:

- *Causes of Terrorism : Political, Social, Economical, Religious*
- *Indian scenario*
- *How to curb it ?*

Answer: Terrorism has increased to alert a responsible person about the safety and security of person and property.

Main causes of terrorism may vary among : Political, Social, Economical, Religious etc.

Among main political causes, we may cite lack of equality, freedom etc. as the most important. Suppressing a community, political exploitation, rule without representation etc. may give rise to armed struggle, resulting into terrorist movements.

But terrorists do not have always genuine demands.

Social differences, racial unrest or ethnical divisions have sometimes lead to violent movements. A group may turn to arms for their social justice and causes terror in an area.

Economic disadvantage, exploitation or suppression can be a reason for terrorism.

Religious fundamentalism has been found to be the most important reason for terrorism. Some groups of terrorists are being trained and prepared for religious causes.

In India, terrorism is spread due to economical and religious causes. To tackle with such violent activities India needs to restructure its political and economical structure.

Terrorists have a wide spread network throughout the world. The latest developed technologies have helped them to be more dangerous.

Use of latest vigilance techniques is necessary. Government has to win confidence of all people for their security. Religious tolerance should be spread among people. Education can play a role in this regard.

Laws must be stringent and enforcement machinery should be effective.

(b) Do you think there is a need for a review of the Indian Constitution ? Justify your view.

Important Points for Answer:	
• *Constitutional Review*	• *Amendments*
• *Indian Constitution*	• *Conclusion*

Answer: Constitutional Review means reconsideration of the provisions of Constitution, in the light of new demands and requirements of the time.

Indian Constitution was framed in 1946-47 when condition of India was different one. Today, after 60 years of its working, Indian political system has changed much far. Influence of outer world, changes ushered by globalisation and other influences have made it necessary to review our Constitution.

The Constitution forms the base of whole system. So, it must be with the pace of time. Situations that may come in time, must be handled by the provisions of Constitution.

Some major changes that may demand constitutional review are :

- More than one hundred amendments have been done so far. It suggests requirement of changes.
- The Constitution was framed at the time of British rule. Some British influences have crepted in the Constitution.
- Some provisions related to federal structure of India are very tough to amend. So, review will help to rethink them.
- Provisions regarding the post of Governor and imposition of the Presidential rule in State have been very controversial.
- Changes made by globalisation have also bring new situations which may be tough to handle by the present constitution.
- Demand for greater autonomy to states is an issue demanding early attention.
- Special status to Jammu and Kashmir and other States like Sikkim etc. are some provision which should be changed.

Not on these, but some recent political issues like coalition government, hung parliament, emergence of many regional parties etc. are requiring review of Indian Constitution.

Also, the Supreme Court has pronounced that Constitutional Review is inherent in the provisions of our Constitution.

Q. 9 Answer any two of the following (in about 150 words each): 15 × 2 = 30

(a) Examine the role of caste in Indian politics.

Important Points for Answer:
- *Castes - Devisive, Cohesive*
- *Role*
- *Theories*

Answer: Caste is a social section of Indian Society. It has gained influential position in Indian Politics.

It plays on both sides - Devisive and Cohesive roles. It becomes devisive when question comes of national unity. But regarding a localitepr group matter, it gives a cohesive force by uniting people of a caste.

Even politicians attach their slogans and manifestoes to particular castes. Caste groups utilise their numerical strength to bargain political cause. Lower castes7 upliftment has remained a central issue.

Leaders are choosen from a dominant caste of the region. Many politicians use caste theories, e.g. Jinabhai in Gujarat gave KHAM (Kshatriya, Harijan, Aahir, Muslim) theory.

Policy of reservation emanate from caste factor of Indian society. Government's policies are also inspired by casteism.

Indian Political System is largely dependent upon factors like caste, religion, etc., which can be termed as unhappy situation.

(b) Discuss the problems in achieving National Integration in India.

Important Points for Answer:
- *National Integration*
- *Various factors as obstacles*

Answer: National Integration is a basic need to make a nation strong and developed. India has faced many problems on this front.

India is a country of diversity. Many factors such as : Geographical, Historical, Political, Social, Religious and Economical, influence integration of India.

Geographically all parts of India have not similar evolution. Also, structurally India is divided in many parts.

Historically, people have different inspiration from history. Diverse groups remain in Indian Society.

Politically, multi-party loyalty has divided nation. Emergence of small parties have preached different ideologies.

Socially, Indian society is divided into many castes and ethnicities. People are attached to social stratas more cohesively.

Religions like Hinduism, Islam, Buddhism, Jainism, Christianity etc. co-exist in India. They also, though sometimes, play a devisive role. Religious riots have played destructive role.

Economical gap is seen in the society from time of ancient history. Kings and Zamindars had exploited their subjects. Even today, wealth distribution is not equal in India.

All these are main factors that impede national integration in India.

(c) Examine the impact of Regional Political Parties in Indian politics.

Important Points for Answer:

- *Single party politics-till 1967*
- *Emergence of Regional Parties*
- *Coalition Government*
- *Impact*

Answer: Till 1967, India had a single party political system, dominated by Congress. Even States were ruled by Congress Governments.

After 1967, regional parties came into picture. They gain some powers in their regions.

But it was only 1980s when regional parties participated in the Centre's coalition government also.

Sometimes central government and state governments have different parties. This impact development due to political causes.

Similarly coalition governments have many a times proved short-lived. Elections before five-year terms have resulted in instability.

But on the contrary, regional parties have raised causes of particular regions at national level and demanded for more share in developmental grants. Parties like TDP, AIADMK,, DMK, Akali Dal, BSP, SP, CPI (M), etc. have played influential role in Indian Politics.

To sum up, regional parties have increased importance of their regions on the one hand and have increased instability on the other. But overall, Indian politics has become more democratic.

Q. 10 Answer any one of the following (in about 250 words): 30

(a) Globalization has brought about a distinct class divide in India instead of ushering in a classless society/' Critically examine this argument.

Important Points for Answer:

- *Earlier Classes*
- *New employed/Unemployed class*
- *Globalization - Impact*
- *Entrepreneurs, Industrialists etc.*
- *LPG in 1991*
- *Widening gap and result*

Answer: Indian Society was divided in many classes since time immemorial. Based on religions, castes, Kula, Gotra etc. many groups dissected Indian society.

Globalization has many fold impacts on Indian society. Since 1991 LPG Policy, India started to witness them.

Liberalization and Privatisation came as necessary requirements of globalization.

More foreign companies and investment came in India. Private players got bigger role in Indian economy. Globalised market opened many horizons in India.

Educated youth get many opportunities, English speaking and skilled class started to earn attractive salaries. Unexpected hike in earning capacity of this class gave way to consumerism in India.

Small and medium size entrepreneurial and industrialist class come into existence. Their expenditure capacity increased.

But on the other hand, uneducated and unskilled class, got no benefit of the globalization. They remained in their low wages earning society.

Gap between two classes widened. Now, old classes based on caste, religion, etc. started to dilute. But economical gap divided the society into classes.

The class of educated youth who get opportunities in BPOs and MNCs came among high' earning employed class.

While, educated but employed in traditional work remained middle class youth. To contrast with both of them, unemployed youth is yet a dark reality of Indian booming economy.

New rich industrialists and entrepreneurs is a small but wealthy class in India.

Thus, globalization just reshaped Indian classes of society but not wiped them off at all.

(b) The conditions of the urban poor are more deplorable than that of their rural counterparts." Give your views.

Important Points for Answer:

- *Comparison*
- *Sanitation*
- *Habitation*
- *Environment*
- *Health, mental health*
- *Social matters*

Answer: More and more people are migrating to urban areas either for employment or for education. Number of poor in urban areas are increasing fast.

But only skilled persons in urban areas are having good living standard.

Unskilled labourers are in worst condition. They may not have regular job or work. Casually employed persons have to change work or find new work after sometime.

In urban areas, poor have to live in outskirts or slum areas. They are not having good houses to live in. The areas in which they live are not having well sanitation facilities.' In rural areas, the sanitation is not well-maintained but then too, vast space help to dispose waste properly.

In matters of houses - habitation, the rural poor have large space to live in, while the urban poors have to live only in small houses. In urban areas, no proper light and air is available in houses. Density is more in urban areas in comparison to rural areas. So, urban poor have to face problems of unhealthy house-facilities.

Rural poors are having access to clean atmosphere in their natural environment. But their urban counterparts have to face pollution problems. Air, water and soil are polluted in urban areas. The noise pollution is another problem for urban poor.

Health of urban poor are always at risk. While rural poor, though not having more money to spend, but they are not facing much health problems. Urban poors are more prone to epidemics like dangue, malaria, cholera etc.

Social problems in rural poor are less grave than their urban counterpart. Urban poors are not having as good social cohesion as that of the rural poors.

They are more exposed to ill-habits like drinking, drugs, gambling, etc. Other social evils also easily crept in the lives of urban poors.

Mental health is always at risk for urban poors as their life is more tense than that of the rural poors. More work and less rest, no social atmosphere, feeling of being backward etc. can make them mentally disturbed, in most cases.

Thus, it seems that rural poors are having better life than urban poors.

Q. 11 Answer any two of the following (in about 150 words each): 15 × 2 = 30

(a) Examine whether rural women in India have been empowered by their active participation in Panchayat Raj System.

Important Points for Answer:

- *Panchayati Raj System*
- *Empowerment*
- *Rural Women*

Answer: By 73rd and 74th Amendment Acts of 1992, Panchayati Raj System was established in India. This system gave grass-root level democracy.

Rural women were not getting their due share in development process. Social and political backwardness prevented them from taking part in decision making. But these amendments made provision for one-third, reservation for women.

Hence, women get due share in policy making.

Illiteracy among women could be reduced. Their leadership skill developed. They came out of four walls of houses. Played decisive role in development. Gender bias is reduced. They became more aware about their rights. They have started to demand reservation in Parliament also.

All these are ideally expected results. They have materialised to some extent. But in somer cases, women have been used as rubber-stamps. Actual decisions are being taken by male partners.

But, signs are there to show that Panchayati Raj System has empowered rural women.

(b) Decline in the sex ratio in India is an alarming sign for India's future social development." Discuss.

Important Points for Answer:

- *Sex Ratio - Indian situation*
- *Decline - Impact on social Development*

Answer: Sex ratio indicates number of female per thousand male. It is indicator of social status of women. Generally lower sex ratio represents suppressed level of women.

India has 933 female per 1000 males according to the 2001 Census. Comparing to 1991 Census, it has increased from 927.

But juvenile sex ratio (0-6 years) has been dropped from 945 of 1991 Census to 896 in 2001 Census. This will show future decline.

It causes imbalance in social structure. Declining number of female means less number of marriages. It will also be responsible for crimes like rape, etc.

Many reasons play role for declining sex ratio. Prominent of them are : Class and caste traditions, dowry, economic and social burden, etc.

Government is taking measures to reduce the gender-gap of population. Education to girl child and prevention of female foeticide is necessary.

Declining sex ratio has socio-cultural effects of long consequences. To prevent them, awareness is required to be spread among people.

(c) What should be the role of the media to project 'mass reality' in place of 'illusion of reality?

Important Points for Answer:
- *Role of Media*
- *Exposure of Reality*

Answer: Media is a tool to bring out reality to surface. It is media's duty to expose truth and wipe out dust over it. It can help people in creating awareness. In the time of national movement, Indian media played a praiseworthy role.

But today, instead of bringing out mass reality, media is just involved in spreading illusion. Media has made it a business to weave stories on a point and increase their viewership or readership. The news are off the reality.

More importantly, the problems of people like poverty, hunger, suicide by farmers, migration of people etc. are not given due consideration. On the other hand, today media is more concentrated on the issues like personalities in news, politicians in their personal life, film and other related stories.

Some issues of corruption have been exposed by media but sometimes it tends to stretch a small issue for a long time, more than necessity.

More than 70% mass who are either rural people or lower middle class, have no place in media. Their problems or reality is never exposed.

To sum up, it is bitter truth that media has diverted its path from its duty towards people, nation and democracy.

Q. 12 Write about the following (in about 20 words each): 2 × 5 = 10

(a) MTP Act

Answer: It is an Act to provide for the termination of certain pregnancies by registered Medical Practitioners and for matters connected therewith or incidental thereto. It came into existence in 1971 and was amended in 2002.

(b) Supreme Court on Ragging

Answer: The supreme court warned senior students that if they harass freshers physically or mentally, they would be booked by the police, expelled from college and denied future admissions. It declared ragging as an illegal act.

(c) New Seven Wonders of the World

Answer:

Wonder	Location
Chichen Itza	Yucatan, Mexico
Christ the Redeemer	Rio de Janeiro, Brazil
Colosseum	Rome, Italy
Great Wall of China	China
Machu Picchu	Aguas Calientes, Peru
Petra	Jordan
Taj Mahal	Agra, India

And one listing has honorary status: Giza Pyramid Complex (The last remaining ancient wonder of the world), Cairo, Egypt.

(d) M. M. Punchi Commission

Answer: The Commission on Centre-State relations is headed by the former Chief Justice of India, M. M. Punchi. The commission will review the working of the existing arrangements between the Union and the States as per the Constitution.

(e) Lakshmi Mittal

Answer: Lakshmi Narayan Mittal is a British Indian industrialist. He was born in Sadulpur village, in the Churu district of Rajasthan, India, and he resides in Kensington, London. He is the chairman and CEO of ArcelorMittal (founder of Mittal before merger with Arcelor) and also serves as a non-executive director of Goldman Sachs, EADS and ICICI Bank.

SOLVED PAPERS

PAPER–II

Time Allowed : Three Hours *Maximum Marks : 300*

Candidates should attempt All questions strictly in accordance with the instructions given under each question.

Q. 1 Write notes on any two of the following (answer to each question should be in about 150 words): 2 × 30 = 60

(a) India and the New World Order

Important Points for Answer:
- *New World : Political and Economical*
- *India*

Answer: After the end of the Second World War, two blocs - Capitalist led by the USA and Socialist led by the USSR emerged.

But India wisely opted to remain neutral and joined Non-Alignment Movement.

Later on, the world became unipolar after the break up of the USSR. The USA remained sole super power.

Globalisation captured the world economic condition. Almost all nations, even including Russia and China opened their economies.

India too adopted new economic policies to match steps with the new trend.

Today, India, Russia, China, Japan and European Union have emerged as blocs of Balance of Power.

India has restructured its foreign policy by Look East Policy, Confidence Building Measures with Pakistan, etc.

New bilateral and regional agreements are increasing.

Though India not aligned militarily with any bloc, but it co-operates on the economical fronts.

India has expressed full faith in the UN System. WTO has not succeeded up to expectations.

In such situations, India has also bargained political decisions on the basis of market and economic sides.

Recent Indo-US nuclear deal indicates increasing importance of India.

India has always co-operated, even taken lead, in solving problems of the new world, order, like Global Warming, Poverty, Human Rights, Terrorism, etc.

(b) Indo-Bhutan Relations

Important Points for Answer:
- *Indo-Bhutan relations from British rule period*
- *Buffer State*
- *Friendship Treaty*
- *Transportation, Power, Security*

Answer: India and Bhutan are neighbouring countries. Bhutan remains a buffer state between India and China. India has relations with Bhutan from time of British rule.

Both countries had a friendship treaty in 1949. Recently it was reviewed and Bhutan was allowed to adopt an independent foreign policy, to acquire defensive arms. Both have also new extradition provisions.

Recently Bhutan was transformed to democracy from Monarchy. India welcomed the decision.

On transportation sector, Indian Border Road Organisation assists Bhutan to construct roads, especially on border.

India started first railway link between Hastimara (in North Bengal, India) and P I hunt Shoeling (in Bhutan) in memory of former Prime Minister Jawahar Lai Nehru's first visit to Bhutan.

India has acquired rights to use hydro-power capacities of Bhutan and constructed power project like Chulka, Tata Power Project and others.

On the front of terrorism and security, army of Bhutan conducted 'Operation All Clear' to demolish insergent camps of ULFA, KLO, NDFB, etc. .

India has accepted geo-political importance of Bhutan and given due consideration to this neighbouring state in its foreign policy.

(c) India and China : Strategy to Boost Ties

Important Points for Answer:

- *Indo-China relations*
- *Disputes*
- *Strategy to solve*
- *Attempts*

Answer: India apd China are neighbouring countries but have hostile relations for almost past sixty years.

Nehru and Mao Zedong tie up was a happy phase but Chinese attack on India wiped out the effect.

Other issues like border disputes, Dalai Lama of Tibet issue etc. are other hurdles in Indo-China relations.

Indian Prime Ministers Rajiv Gandhi and A. B. Vajpayee visited China in 1988 and 2003 respectively. In 2005, during the visit of Chinese Premier Jiang Zemin, a strategic agreement was signed. It included guiding principles on border settlement.

In 2008, Dr. Manmohan Singh, Indian Prime Minister, visited Beijing Both countries have fixed target of $ 60 Billion of bilateral trade to be achieved by the year 2010. China also got observer status in SAARC. Importance of geo-economics has increased than geo-politics.

People to people contact, cultural exchange programmes, student exchange programme etc. are other strategies to boost up ties.

In various regional and world forums, both countries have attempted to come closer. Leaving the disputes and problems to be solved in their process, both countries have started to find out areas of co-operation. Thus, conflicts should not come in the way of co-operation, is the main strategy to boost up ties.

Q. 2 Write about the following (answer to each question should be in about 20 words):
5 × 2 = 10

(a) India's Ocean Development Policy

Answer: India's Ocean Development Policy's aim is to utilise living resources, exploit non-living resources and to harness renewable ocean energy resources.

(b) Major hurdles in Indo-Pak ties

Answer: Main hurdles include - Spread of terrorism, issue of Jammu and Kashmir, Siachin and Sir Creek disputes.

(c) India-Nigeria: Abuja Declaration

Answer: India signed "Abuja Declaration" with Nigeria, setting the stage for a strategic partnership with the world's fifth largest producer of oil on October 15, 2007 in Abuja, the declaration was signed by PM Manmohan Singh & President of Nigeria, Umaru musa yar'adua.

(d) India-Bangladesh Border Road cum fencing

Answer: India has problem of Chakma Refugees infiltering into Indian boundary. Problems of crimes like terrorism, drug traffick, insurgency etc. are the reasons for Border Road cum Fencing.

(e) India's L.C.A. (Tejas)

Answer: Third Generation Light Combat Aircraft, Wing Fly-by-wire system Tejas will be loaded with 'Astra', air-to-air missile. It will use indigenously built 'Karer' engine.

Q. 3 Write about the following (answer to each question should be in about 20 words):
5 × 2 = 10

(a) Pravasi Bharatiya Diwas

Answer: The Government of India recognizes the 9th of January as the Pravasi Bharatiya Divas. The occasion is marked by special programs to recognize the contributions of NRI/PIO individuals of exceptional merit, felicitate NRI/PIO individuals who have made exceptional contribution in their chosen field/profession Pravasi Bharatiya Samman and provide a forum to discuss issues and concerns that people of the diaspora.

(b) Council for Promotion of Overseas Employment (CPOE)

Answer: The Union Cabinet gave approval for constitution of CPOE.

Functions:

(i) Study, monitor, research and analyze employment potential in the world manpower market

(ii) Initiate, Institute and monitor skill development programmes and standardize skill certification, by coordinating with concerned agencies/ organizations in Government & Private Sector.

(c) Overseas Citizenship of India (OCI) Scheme

Answer: The Citizenship (Amendment) Bill, 2003 provides for overseas citizenship of India to the PIOs in 16 countries who have acquired citizenship in those countries under the Overseas Citizenship of India Scheme.

(d) Indian Diaspora in Singapore

Answer: Indians constitute second largest diaspora, next to Chinese. They are mainly Tamils, so Tamil is one of the official language of Singapore.

(e) Indian Diaspora and Bollywood

Answer: Bollywood films are released outside India also. Many films are funded by NRIs. This shows connection between Indian Diaspora and Bollywood.

Q. 4 Answer any one of the following (in about 250 words): 30

(a) Discuss India's stand on agricultural issues in WTO's Ministerial Conferences since Doha Round.

Important Points for Answer:	
• *WTO Ministerial Conferences*	• *Doha Round*
• *Next Rounds*	• *India's Stand*

Answer: Ministerial Conference is the highest decision making 6ody of the WTO. It meets at least every two years.

First Ministerial Conference was held in Singapore from 9-13 December, 1996.

Doha Round of Ministerial Conference was held from 9 to 14 November, 2001 in Doha, Qatar. It was fourth Conference.

Fifth Ministerial Conference was held in Cancun (Mexico) in 2003.

Sixth Round was held in December 2005 at Hong Kong.

Geneva Round on 21st July to 25th July 2008 was the latest Ministerial Conference held on the issue.

On the matters of agriculture, India has taken leadership of the poor and developing countries.

Main issues raised on the agricultural matter were to remove export subsidies to farmers given by the developed nations. India argued that export is only a trade for developed countries but agriculture is a matter of livelihood for fanners of developing and poor natiohs.

The lives of crores of people can not be put at stake for free trade.

Food Security for the third world countries is a bigger issue.

Reduction of domestic support and elimination of export subsidies to farmers, provided by the US and EU is main demand of third world countries under the leadership of India.

However, repeatedly the talk has failed to achieve consensus on the issue. Even recently in Geneva, the talk could not result into final draft. This was due to stand of EU and US on their demands regarding agriculture. Their demand is that developing and poor countries should allow free market access to agricultural products of the developed nations. But on the other hand, the later argue that such import will destruct lives of their farmers.

Because, agricultural products of the developed nations are supported by domestic subsidies and export subsidies, they are very cheap. If they enter into markets of developing nation, their farmers will not be able to compete with them. So their livelihood will be at stake.

India, a leading member of G-20 (formed in WTO especially to fight for such issues) is always at raising the issue of lives against trade.

(b) Assess the performance of India in attracting Foreign Direct Investment (FDI).

Important Points for Answer:
• *FDI in India*
• *Performance of various sectors*
• *All over performance*

Answer: India opened its market in 1991 by accepting the policy of LPG. Big market in India gives a bright opportunity to Global companies.

So, many companies come in India and started their business. MNCs started their subsidiaries or centres in Indian economy. We have been performing well in attracting Foreign Direct Investment (FDI) from across the world.

According to the report of UN agency, India performed well in inward FDI Performance Index and reached to 113 position in 2006 among 141 countries. In outward FDI also, India reached to 56 position in 2006 from its earlier position of 65 in 2005.

Thus, India is performing well in overall FDI attraction terms.

Various sectors in India have been opened for FDI. Except in a few, FDI is allowed in almost all sectors of economy.

According to latest data, electrical equipments including computer softwares and electronics are performing best in attracting FDI, amounting to 17.4% of total. Next comes Telecommunications, transport sector and services sector.

In 1990-91, net FDI was only US $ 96 million which increased to US $ 3240 million in 2004-05.

Taking region wise, New Delhi has attracted largest amount of FDI so far. Next come Mumbai, Bangalore, Chennai and Ahmedabad. While in terms of FDI approvals by states, Maharashtra tops in the list followed by Delhi, Tamil Nadu, Karnataka and Gujarat.

The list of countries from which FDI comes into India is topped by Mauritius amounting for nearly 37% of total inflow. USA is next to it with about 15% share.

Q. 5 Discuss any two of the following topics (answer each question in about 150 words):
2 × 15 = 30

(a) Assistance to the States for Development of Export Infrastructure and other Activities (ASIDE).

Important Points for Answer:	
• *Scheme*	• *Purposes*

Answer: The scheme is to provide an outlay for development of export infrastructure which will be distributed to the States according to a pre-defined criteria. The existing EPIP, EPZ and CIB schemes are merged with the new scheme.

The specific purposes for which the funds allocated under the Scheme can be sanctioned and utilised are as follows :

- Creation of new Export Promotion Industrial Parks/Zones (including Special Economic Zones (SEZs)/Agri-Business Zones) and augmenting facilities in the existing ones. Setting up of electronic and other related infrastructure in export conclave.
- Equity participation in infrastructure projects including the setting up of SEZs.
- Development of complementary infrastructure such as roads connecting the production centres with the ports, setting up of Inland Container Depots and Container Freight Stations,
- Stabilising power supply through additional transformers and islanding of export production centres etc.
- Development of minor ports and jetties of a particular specification to serve export purpose.
- Assistance for setting up common effluent treatment facilities for which guidelines are placed.
- Projects of national and regional importance.

Please Note

The Export Promotion Industrial Parks Scheme (EPIP), Export Promotion Zones scheme (EPZ), and the Critical Infrastructure Balancing Scheme (CIB) are also implemented to help create infrastructure for exports in specific locations and to meet specific objectives.

(b) Convertibility of Indian Rupee.

Important Points for Answer:
- *Meaning of Convertibility*
- *Convertibility of Indian Rupee : Capital Account, Current Account*

After opening Indian market in 1991 by the LPG policy, it was necessary to made Indian rupee convertible.

Convertibility of a currency implies free exchange of a currency into any foreign currency and vice-versa.

Tarapore Committee was appointed in 1997 on Capital Account Convertibility, by the Reserve Bank of India. Lastly, in 2006, for Current Account Convertibility, Tarapore Committee was appointed by the Reserve Bank of India.

Since, August, 19,1994, Indian rupee has been made fully convertible in current account transactions related to goods and services.

The Committee also had suggested full convertibility but yet Indian rupee has not been made fully convertible in capital account.

Today, the final position is that Indian rupee is partially convertible. The Finance Ministry has relaxed norms but ruled out full convertibility on Capital Account in near future.

Though full convertibility may help India attract more FDI but it will also expose the economy to more risk.

(c) India on Global Competitiveness Index - 2007.

Important Points for Answer:
- *Global Competitive Index*
- *Indian Position*

Answer: The Global Competitive Index is released by the World Economic Forum. In its 2007 report, it covers 131 economies. They are measured on twelve parameters.

India is placed at 48th rank, five notches down than previous index position (43rd place).

India is ranked second among emerging markets after China. The Index parameters include :

• Institution	• Infrastructure
• Macro-economic stability	• Health and Primary Education
• Higher Education and Training	• Goods Market Efficiency
• Labour Market Efficiency	• Financial Market Sophistication
• Tcchnological Readiness	• Market size
• Business Sophistication	• Innovation

There are three sub-indices :

1. Efficiency Enhancers
2. Basic requirements
3. Innovation factors

India ranks 31, 74 and 26 respectively on the above three indices.

This index is designed to capture a range of factors affecting an economy's business climate. The report says "The quality of the business environment in India has improved tangibly in recent years".

Q. 6 Write about the following (answer to each question in about 20 words): $5 \times 2 = 10$

(a) Special Drawing Rights (SDRs)

Answer: The term is related to IMF. They are used to manage liquidity. They are not real money but just credit entries in the account of a nation.

(b) NAMA

Answer: Non-Agricultural Market Access. This term is related to WTO. NAMA is used to enhance trade in Non-Agricultural Sector, i.e. Manufacturing and Service Sector.

(c) Non-tariff trade barriers

Answer: Additional trade barriers to restrict imports. They are :

- Phytosanitary measures,
- Prohibition of Child Labour in manufacturing etc.

(b) Current Account Balance

Answer: Difference between a country's savings and investment. It shows position of a country in international trade. Positive CAB means more export and negative CAB means more import.

(c) Free Trade Area

Answer: Free Trade Area refers to economic arrangement between two or more countries, removing all import tariffs among themselves. There is also no quota or export subsidies.

Q. 7 Write on any one of the following (answer in about 150 words): 15

(a) South-South Cooperation

Important Points for Answer:
- *Meaning*
- *Aims*
- *Necessity*

Answer: South-South Cooperation suggests economic co-operation among developing countries of the world. They bring third world economies together for their common development.

The all over aim of South-South Co-operation is to jointly promote development. The collective strength can be utilised to bring faster growth in their economies. Their voice can be heard because of their numerical strength.

There are many common challenges like poverty, hunger, disease, unemployment, pollution, global warming, corruption, terrorism etc. which need to fight together. Therefore, south- south cooperation has brought the members together. As the result, many organisations like SAARC, IBSA, NAM, G-77, Mercosur, etc. have come into existence. Common grievances have been raised by them in WTO, UN and other world forums.

It was necessary to revoke the myth that co-operation can be only among developed and developing countries. It was a demand of the hour, because developed countries had only concentrated on their personal interest and not taken into consideration demands of the developing and poor economies. So, to increase bargaining power, collaboration was necessary.

(b) Universal Declaration of Human Rights

Important Points for Answer:
- *Why came into existence ?*
- *Important Provisions*
- *Main objectives*

Answer: The Second World War opened eyes of the whole world that any violative action will result only in destruction of human being. So, world leaders expressed importance of Human Rights. As a result, International Bill of Human Rights was prepared.

First expression of Human Rights came into existence by the Universal Declaration of Human Rights on December 10, 1948. Its main objective is to recognise the inherent dignity and the equal and inalienable rights of all members of human family. It also aims to protect human rights by rule of law. Granting to women the same political rights as to men is an important objective enshrined in its preamble.

The declaration contains 30 Articles. They are universal in nature. They have been elaborated in subsequent conventions, Protocols etc. Article-1 says all human beings are born free and equal in dignity. Article-7 provides for equality before the law and equal protection of the law. Article-9 is a right against arbitrary arrest, detention or exile. Article-20 provides for right to freedom of peaceful assembly and association. Article-17 enumerates the right to own property. Freedom of thought, conscience and religion is provided in Article-18.

Q. 8 Briefly write about the following (answer to each question should be in about 20 words):
5 × 2 = 10

(a) Look East Policy and North-East India

Answer: Look East Policy was launched in 1992. It helped to connect North-Eastern States with other countries and to improve their economic condition.

(b) India at the Beijing Olympics

Answer: In Beijing Olympics 2008, India won one gold for 10 m Air Rifle Men's Event by Abhinav Bindra, two Bronze, one in Free Style Wrestling by Sushil Kumar and the second in Boxing by Vijendra Kumar.

(c) India's role in Afganisthan Today

Answer: India has taken a leading role in Afghanistan's development by undertaking partnership in hydro-electricity, road, agriculture, industrial development and telecommunications related projects.

(b) IPCC Report on Global Warming

Answer: The Intergovernmental Panel on Climate Change (IPCC) concludes that most of the temperature increase since the mid-twentieth century is "very likely" due to the increase in anthropogenic greenhouse gas concentrations. Climate model projections indicate that global surface temperature will likely rise a further 1.1 to 6.4 °C (2.0 to 11.5 °F) during the twenty-first century.

(c) Indo-EU Economic Ties

Answer: India's bilateral trade with the European Union (EU) is of the order of approximately US $ 20 billion annually. Nearly 26 per cent of India's exports are to die EU, while India's imports from the EU constitute 28 per cent of her total imports.

Q. 9 Briefly write about the following (answer to each question should be in about 20 words):
5 × 2 = 10

(a) G.CC

Answer: It stands for Gulf Co-operation Council, created in May, 1981. It consists of Bahrain, Kuwait, Oman, Qatar, Saudi Arabia and the United Arab Emirates. It works as a trade bloc.

(b) G-77

Answer: Constituted under the UN banner in 1964, now consists of 130 member countries of the Third World. Aims at protecting economic interest of the member countries.

(c) I.CR.C

Answer: It stands for International Committee on Red Cross. It is a neutral organisation. It works for humanitarian protection and assistance for victims of war and armed violence.

(d) MERCOSUR

Answer: A common market among four South American countries - Brazil, Argentina, Paraguay and Uruguay. It was started in January, 1995.

(e) INTERPOL

Answer: Stands for International (Criminal) Police Organization. Facilitates co-operation among international police. Its headquarters is in Lyon, France.

Q. 10 Answer any one of the following (in about 250 words): 30

(a) In what way 'Medical Biotechnology' and 'Bioengineering' are useful for technological development of India ?

Important Points for Answer:

- *Biotechnology*
- *Bio-engineering*
- *Medical Biotechnology*
- *Useful to India*

Answer: Biotechnology is a science that uses living plants or animals as their products and technically develops useful products from them.

Simply, it is a technology related to bio-life. It has emerged as a developing science branch.

Bio-engineering and Medical bio-technology are specialised branches of bio-technology. Medical bio-technology is use of techniques in medical field. Diagnostic system, clinical research, drug production, delivery and discovery are important areas. Medical biotechnology can be useful to India in .the following ways :

- India can become a medical tourism place.
- India can earn foreign revenue.
- Pharmaceutical companies can grow.
- Improved technology will help promote health standard.

Bio-engineering is a branch which applies engineering principles to living system. Various branches of life science like - molecular biology, bio-chemistry, pharmacology, micro-biology, cytology, etc. are used in bio-engineering. They help to develop and design devices and components, useful in various fields.

Genetic science is also related to it. New discoveries in human genome have expanded horizons of bio-engineering and medical biotechnology. These can be useful in India for development of medical facilities.

Export of services and BPOs have also started to use these knowledge. This gives more employment opportunities to Indians.

The efficiency and efficacy of molecular medicines can be enhanced. Quick and effective result can be obtained by using them. New researches can remove pain of mankind by discovering medicines.

GDP growth can be boost up by the scientific development and their commercialisation. The Department of Bio-technology has emphasised genomes and bioinformatics as the areas of special focus.

Thus, India can get advantages from the Medical Bio-technology and Bio-engineering.

(b) What do you know about Indian National Satellite Systems ? Describe its important features.

Important Points for Answer:
• *Indian National Satellite Systems*
• *Satellites in Service*

Indian National Satellite System

Answer: INSAT or the Indian National Satellite System is a series of multipurpose Geo-Stationary satellites launched by ISRO to satisfy the telecommunications, broadcasting, meteorology, and "search and rescue" needs of India. Commissioned in 1983, INSAT is the largest domestic communication system in the Asia-Pacific Region.

Satellites in Service

There are currently 11 satellites in service out of 21 which have ever been part of INSAT system.

INSAT-2E : It is the last of the five satellites in INSAT-2 series.

INSAT-3 Series

INSAT-3A : The multipurpose satellite, INSAT-3A, was launched by Ariane in April 2003. It is located at 93.5 degree East longitude.

INSAT-3B : Launched in March 2000, INSAT-3B is collocated with INSAT-2E at 83 degree East longitude.

INSAT-3C : Launched in January 2002, INSAT-3C is positioned at 74 degree East longitude.

INSAT-3E : Launched in September 2003, INSAT-3E is positioned at 55 degree East longitude.

KALPANA-1: KALPANA-1 is an exclusive meteorological satellite launched by PSLV in September 2002.

GSAT-2 : Launched by the second flight of GSLV in May 2003.

EDUSAT: EDUSAT was launched by GSLV in September 2004. Its transponders and their ground coverage are specially configured to cater to the educational requirements

INSAT-4 Series

INSAT-4A : Launched in December 2005 by the European Ariane launch vehicle.

INSAT-4B : It was launched in March 2007 by the European Ariane launch vehicle. INSAT-4C was to be India's most advanced communications satellite, and was the second satellite in the INSAT 4 series.

INSAT-4CR was launched on 2 September 2007 by GSLV-F04. It is a replacement satellite of INSAT-4C which was lost when GSLV-F02 failed and had to be destroyed on its course.

Q. 11 Explain any three of the following (in about 150 words each): 3 × 15 = 45

(a) Internet Protocol Television (IPTV)

Important Points for Answer:
- *Advantages*
- *Interactivity*
- *VoD*
- *IPTV based conversed services*
- *Limitations*

Answer: IPTV (Internet Protocol Television) is a system where a digital television service is delivered using Internet Protocol over a network infrastructure, which may include delivery by a broadband connection.

IPTV is typically supplied by a service provider using a closed network infrastructure. This closed network approach is in competition with the delivery of TV content over the public Internet, called Internet Television. In businesses, IPTV may be used to deliver television content over corporate LANs.

Advantages

The IP-based platform offers significant advantages, including the ability to integrate television with other IP-based services like high speed Internet access and VoIP.

Interactivity

An IP-based platform also allows significant opportunities to make the TV viewing experience more interactive and personalised.

VoD

VoD stands for Video on Demand. VoD permits a customer to browse an online programme or film catalogue, to watch trailers and to then select a selected recording for playback. IPTV based Converged Services

Another advantage of an IP-based network is the opportunity for integration and convergence. This opportunity is amplified when using IMS-based solutions. Converged services implies interaction of existing services in a seamless manner to create new value added services.

Limitations

Because IPTV requires real-time data transmission and uses the Internet Protocol, it is sensitive to packet loss and delays if the streamed data is unreliable. If the IPTV connection is not fast enough, picture break-up or loss may occur.

(b) Spintronics

Important Points for Answer:
- *What is Spintronics ?*
- *Metals based spintronic devices*
- *Semiconductor based spintronic devices*

Answer: Spintronics is an emerging technology which exploits the intrinsic spin of electrons and its associated magnetic moment in addition to its fundamental electronic charge, in solid-state devices.lt is also known as magnetoelectronics.

Metals based spintronics devices

The simplest method of generating a spin-polarised current in a metal is to pass the current through a ferromagnetic material. The most common application of this effect is a giant magnetoresistance (GMR) device.

Spintronics-enabled devices like GMR and TMR sensors have increased the sensitivity of the read head which measures the magnetic state of small magnetic domains (bits) on the spinning platter.

Semiconductor-based spintronic devices

In early efforts, spin-polarized electrons are generated via optical orientation using circularly-polarized photons at the bandgap energy incident on semiconductors with appreciable spin-orbit interaction (like GaAs and ZnSe).

Advantages of semiconductor-based spintronics applications are potentially lower power use and a smaller footprint than electrical devices used for information processing.

(c) Wifi

Important Points for Answer:

- *What is WiFi?*
- *Purpose*
- *Advantages*
- *Limitations*

Answer: Wi-Fi is the trademark for the popular wireless technology used in home networks, mobile phones, video games and other electronic devices that require some form of wireless networking capability.

Purpose

The purpose of Wi-Fi is to provide wireless access to digital content. This content may include applications, audio and visual media, Internet connectivity, or other data.

A Wi-Fi enabled device such as a PC, game console, mobile phone, MP3 player or PDA can connect to the Internet when within range of a wireless network connected to the Internet.

The coverage of one or more interconnected access points—called a hotspot—can comprise an area as small as a single room with wireless-opaque walls or as large as many square miles covered by overlapping access points.

Wi-Fi also allows connectivity in peer-to-peer mode, which enables devices to connect directly with each other.

Advantages

Wi-Fi allows LANs to be deployed without cabling for client devices, typically reducing the costs of network deployment and expansion.

Spaces where cables cannot be run, such as outdoor areas and historical buildings, can host wireless LANs

Answer: Limitations

Spectrum assignments and operational limitations are not consistent worldwide.

(d) Components of Robots

> **Important Points for Answer:**
> - *Components for various functions :*
>   - *Actuation*
>   - *Manipulation*
>   - *Locomotion*

Components of robots

Actuation : Actuators are the "muscles" of a robot, the parts which convert stored energy into movement. Actuators include-

- Motors: Robots use electric motors, including, brushed and brushless DC motors.
- Stepper motors: They do not spin freely like DC motors; they rotate in discrete steps, under the command of a controller.
- Piezo motors: The advantages of these motors are nanometer resolution, speed and available force for their size.
- Air muscles: A simple yet powerful device for providing a pulling force. When inflated with compressed air, it contracts by up to 40% of its original length.
- Electroactive polymers: A class of plastics which change shape in response to electrical stimulation.
- Elastic nanotubes: These are a promising, early-stage experimental technology.

Manipulation

The 'hands' of a robot are often referred to as end effectors, while the arm is referred to as a manipulator.

- Mechanical Grippers
- Vacuum Grippers
- General purpose effectors

Locomotion

Rolling Robots

- Two-wheeled balancing
- Ballbot
- Track Robot

Walking Robots

- ZMP Technique
- Hopping
- Dynamic Balancing
- Passive Dynamics

Other methods of locomotion

- Flying
- Skating
- Snaking
- Swimming

Q. 12 Write brief notes on all the five (in about 20 words each) below : 5 × 2 = 10

(a) Copyright and Trade-mark

Answer: Copyright is a form of intellectual property which gives the creator of an original work of authorship exclusive rights to control its distribution for a certain time period.

A trademark is a type of intellectual property, and typically a name, word, phrase, logo, symbol, design, image, or a combination of these elements.

(b) TIFAC

Answer: TIFAC, an autonomous organisation under Department of Science and Technology chaired by Dr. R. Chidambaram, aims to keep a technology watch on global trends arid formulating preferred technology options for India.

(c) Aspartame

Answer: Aspartame or APM is the name for an artificial, non-saccharide sweetener, *aspartyl-phenylalanine-l-methyl ester,* that is, a methyl ester of the dipeptide of the amino acids aspartic acid and phenylalanine.

(d) Gene doping

Answer: Gene doping is defined by the World Anti-Doping Agency as "the non-therapeutic use of cells, genes, genetic elements, or of the modulation of gene expression, having the capacity to improve athletic performance".

(d) Sappan

Answer: SAPPAN WOOD or East Indian red wood is a multipurpose tree. It is botanically known as *Caesalpitiia Sappan L.*

It is a natural dye yielding medicinal plant. In India it is cultivated in parts of Tamil Nadu, Kerala, Karnataka, Andhra Pradesh and West Bengal.

Q. 13 (a) The principal exports of India for the financial year 2001-2002 are given in the following table :

Sl. No.	Category	Export (Rs. Crores)
1	Agriculture and allied products	29312
2	Ores and minerals	4736
3	Manufactured goods	161161
4	Fuels and lubricants	10411
5	Others	3398
	Total	209018

Represent the above date by a suitable diagram and comment on the export performance of the country. **6**

Answer: Suitable diagram will be a pie-chart.

To represent the data by a pie-chart, first we need to convert the data into degrees.

SI. No.	Category	Export (Rs. Crore)	Rs. to Degree	Degree
1	Agriculture	29312	$\frac{29312}{209018} \times 360°$	50.5°
2	Ores and Minerals	4736	$\frac{4736}{209018} \times 360°$	8.2°
3	Manufactured goods	161161	$\frac{161161}{209018} \times 360°$	277.6‘
4	Fuels and lubricants	10411	$\frac{10411}{209018} \times 360°$	17.9°
5	Others	3398	$\frac{3398}{209018} \times 360°$	5.8°
	Total	209018		

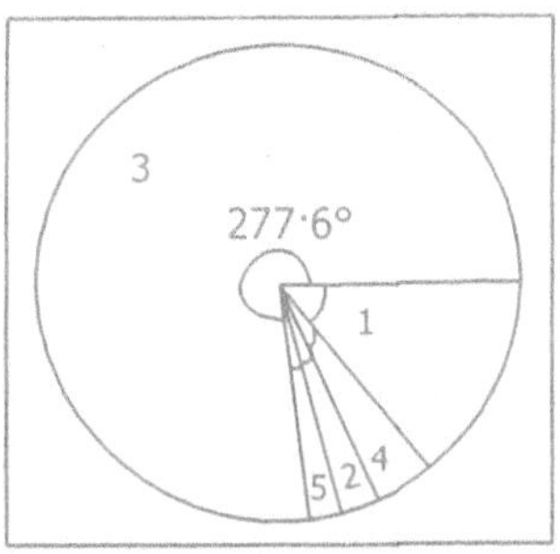

Comment: Manufactured goods is the largest contributor to Indian export.

It constitutes about 77.11% of total export.

Agriculture and allied products constitute nearly 14% of total export. Fuels and lubricants contents about 4.9%.

Ores and minerals contribute 2.3% of total export,

While all other exports constitute 1.6%.

(b) Prior to constructing a dam on a river the engineers performed a series of tests to measure the water flow at the proposed location of the dam. The results of the testing were used to construct the following frequency distribution.

Water flow (Thousands of gallons per minute)	Frequency
1001 - 1050	7
1051 - 1100	21
1101 - 1150	32
1151 - 1200	49
1201 - 1250	58
1251 - 1300	41
1301 - 1350	27
1351 - 1400	11

Construct an appropriate diagram to estimate what proportion of the flow occurs at less than 1300 thousands of gallons per minute. Give the estimate. **6**

Answer:

Less than table

Water flow	Frequency
Less than 1050	7
Less than 1100	28
Less than 1150	60
Less than 1200	109
Less than 1250	167
Less than 1300	208
Less than 1350	235
Less than 1400	246

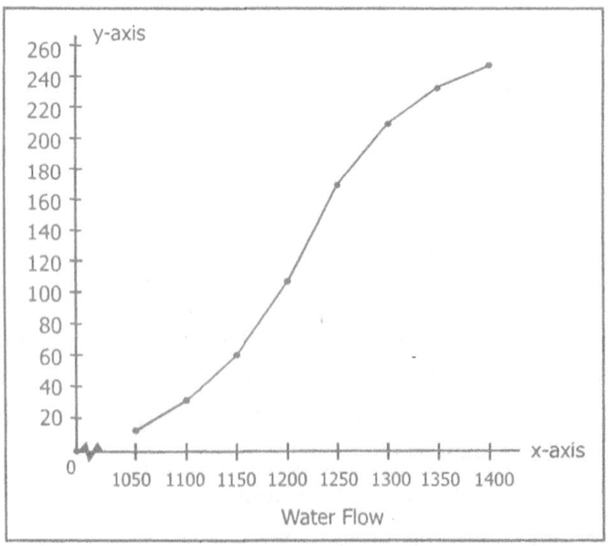

Q. 14 (a) A company files its sales vouchers according to their sales value so that they falls in four strata. Two hundred vouchers are received on a business day. The information is listed in the following table :

Stratum	Number of Vouchers	Mean value (Rs.)
Above Rs. 1000	50	1800
Rs. 800 but under Rs. 1000	60	890
Rs. 400 but under Rs. 800	50	560
Less than Rs. 400	40	180

Calculate the mean value and the total value of the vouchers received by the company on the day in question. Use the histogram to estimate the modal value of the vouchers.

Answer: Mean Value = $\frac{n\overline{X}}{n}$

where n = number of vouchers, $\overline{X}$ = mean value (because it is already given)

$$\text{Mean Value} = \frac{n_1\overline{X}_1 + n_2\overline{X}_2 + n_3\overline{X}_3 + n_4\overline{X}_4}{n_1 + n_2 + n_3 + n_4}$$

$$= \frac{50\times1800 + 60\times890 + 50\times560 + 40\times180}{50 + 60 + 50 + 40}$$

$$= \frac{9000 + 53400 + 28000 + 7200}{200}$$

$$= \frac{178600}{200} = \text{Rs. } 893$$

So, mean value of the voucher is Rs. 893, and total value of the vouchers received by the company is 1,78,600.

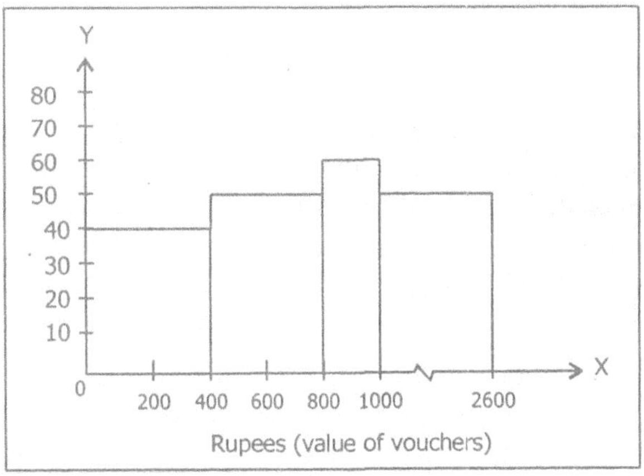

Note: Because mean value of vouchers above 1000 is 1800, so it can be assumed that the upper limit of the class may be nearly 2600. The modal value of voucher is in the class of 800-1000 i.e., 900.

(b) A trip to a destination is made in the following way:

900 kms by train at an average speed of 60 kms/hr
3000 kms by plane at an average speed of 500 kms/hr

400 kms by boat at an average speed of 25 kms/hr

15 kms by taxi at an average speed of 45 kms/hr

What is the average speed for the entire journey ? 6

Answer: A trip to a destination

$$\text{Average speed} = \frac{\text{Total journey}}{\text{Total time taken}}$$

Here, for 900 kms, by train, average speed is 60 kms/hr.

$$\text{Time taken} = \frac{\text{Total journey}}{\text{Average speed}}$$

$$= \frac{900}{60}$$

Similarly, using other datas,

$$\text{Average speed} = \frac{900 + 3000 + 400 + 15}{\frac{900}{60} + \frac{3000}{500} + \frac{400}{25} + \frac{15}{45}}$$

$$= \frac{4315}{15 + 6 + 16 + 0.33}$$

$$= \frac{4315}{37.33}$$

Average speed = 115.6 kms/hr.

Q. 15(a) A hotel owner has nine refreshment stalls located at various points in a large compound. He wants to make one of the stalls as a supply place such that amount of travel between the stalls and the source of supply is minimized. He has to visit all stalls almost equal number of times with a view to supplying the refreshment stuff everyday. The distances of stalls from the first stall are 250, 500, 650, 800, 850, 910,940 and 1000 yards respectively. Which stall should he choose to use as the supply place ? Give reason in favour of your answer. 2

Answer:

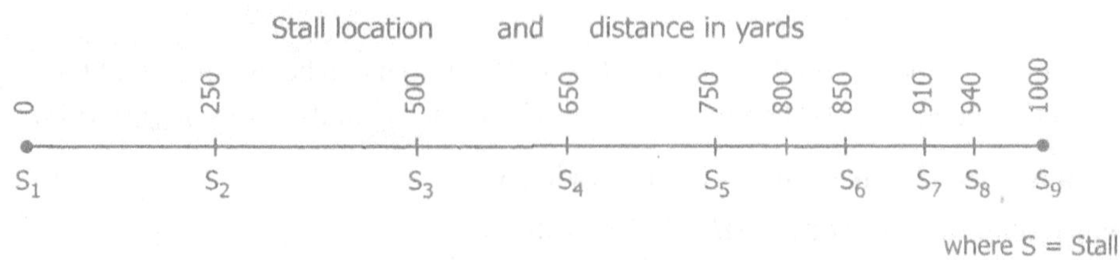

The median stall should be chosen as supply stall because sum of absolute distance from the median.

$$\text{Median} = \left(\frac{n}{2}+1\right)^{th} = \left(\frac{9+1}{2}\right)^{th} = 5^{th} \text{ stall}$$

(b) In a statistical investigation of 1003 families of a city, it was found that 63 families had neither a radio nor a TV, 794 families had a radio and 187 had a TV. How many families of the city selected in the sample had both ? 2

Answer: Total Families = 1003

Families with No Radio, No TV = 63

Families with TV = 187

Families with Radio = 794

Here, total families are 1003 of which 63 families had neither radio nor TV. So, 1003 - 63 = 940 families had either radio or TV or both.

794	+	187	=	981
(Families with Radio)		(Families with TV)		(Total)

But, total number of families having access either to Radio or TV is 940.

So, 981 – 940 = 41 families had access to both Radio and TV.

In, mathematical formula,

$$R \cup T = U - W = 1003 - 63 = 940$$

where, R = Radio; T = T.V.; W = No Radio, No TV

U = Total families

$$R \cap T = R + T - (R \cup T) = 794 + 187 - 940 = 41$$

$R \cup T$ = Radio or TV

$R \cap T$ = Radio + TV

(c) The mean monthly income of a person is Rs. 18190/- and his mean monthly expenditure comes out to be Rs. 17930/-. What is his average monthly saving ? 2

Answer: Mean monthly income = 18190

Mean monthly expenditure = 17930

Average monthly saving = Income – Expenditure

= 8190 – 17930

= Rs. 260

(MAIN)

2009 Civil Services Exam. General Studies

SOLVED PAPERS

PAPER–I

Time Allowed : Three Hours *Maximum Marks : 300*

Candidates should attempt ALL questions strictly in accordance with the instructions given under each question.

Q. 1 Critically analyse any two of the following statements with reference to the contexts in which they were made (in about 150 words each): 15 × 2 = 30

(a) "Many Englishmen honestly consider themselves the trustees for India and yet to what a condition they have reduced our country."

(b) "The foreign power will be withdrawn but for me real freedom will come only when we free ourselves of the dominance of western education, western culture and the western way of living which have been ingrained in us."

(c) "Satan cannot enter till he finds a flaw A great ocean separates us educated few from the millions in our country."

Important Points for Answer:

- *British rule*
- *Trusteeship theory*
- *Economic exploitation*
- *Effect on India*

Answer: This statement shows that the Britishers have exploited India economically for the benefit of Britain. The rule of British has reduced Indian economic condition to a worse situation.

This statement is similar to 'Drain of Wealth' theory of Dada Bhai Naoroji. Earlier Dada Bhai Naoroji and R. C. Dutt had exposed that British imperialism has phases of economic exploitation of India.

Gandhi believed in trusteeship theory. According to that theory, British government was trustee of people of India and so it should govern India in such a way as may result in most beneficial to India.

But this theory was proved wrong as it could clearly be seen that Britishers have not acted in good faith for India's benefit.

They at the time of British East India Company, used the monopoly status to get trade benefits. During 1765 to 1857, it used its position to dictate terms to rulers to maximise its income from revenue. Later-on, after 1857, industrialist and capitalist phase exploited India.

(b)

Important Points for Answer:	• *India's position*
• *British rule*	• *Dominance of British*
• *British Impact*	• *Freedom*

Answer: This statement is similar to Gandhian thoughts expressed in various works of Gandhi and especially in 'Hind Swaraj'.

Gandhi said that freedom or Swaraj does not mean just release from foreign rule. He said that dependency on britishers is real symbol of rule. Western influence and dominance in the spheres of education, culture and way of living was condemned by him.

He said that freedom or swaraj is to be achieved by every individual for himself. Unless such freedom from western dominance is achieved, India will not become free in real sense, even though britishers would leave the country.

Therefore, promoting our cultural values, respecting them and using them was essential. Education system followed in ancient India was better and that should be adopted according to him.

He opposed the british way of living followed by many IndiAns.

So, not only political authority that rules India but in other spheres also, where India could have been free, India is ruled by British.

(c)

Important Points for Answer:	
• *Divide between educated and uneducated*	• *Differences*
• *Political ideology*	• *Impact*

Answer: During the time of movement for freedom against british government, there arose differences among two groups of politicians. One group was of the view that only educated people are able to lead and participate in political process.

But other group believed that the movement should spread to even rural uneducated people. They had faith in ability of mass to participate in the freedom struggle.

The difference of attitude led to the partition in Congress also in 1907 Surat session. The same reason is the basis of this statement which identifies some reasons and evils that separated educated few from the millions in the country.

But it was really the support of villagers - uneducated people which made the movement successful and in a real sense a national movement.

Later on, Gandhi used the power of villagers and women in spreading the movement to every corner of India.

Q. 2 Write about the following (not exceeding 20 words each) : 2 × 10 = 20

(a) Kiang Nongbah **(b) Maski**

(c) Govind Guru **(d) 'Brahmadeya'**

(e) 'Egmore Faction' **(f) Haileybury College**
(g) Ijara System **(h) Taji Mideren**
(i) Gurudwara Reform Movement **(j) 'Marumakkathayam'**

Answer: (a) Kiang Nongbah : He was the leader of the Jaintiya Rebellion of 1862. He was betrayed, captured and hanged by Britishers. He was also known as U Kiang Nongbah. Cause of rebellion was income tax and house tax.

(b) Maski : A minor rock-edict by King Ashoka was found at Maski in Karnataka. This discovery of 1919 clearly established that "Ashoka" and "Devanaampriyadass" was same king.

(c) Govind Guru : He was the founder of Samp Sabha. Under his leadership, in 1908, Bhil tribals, dalits and other people revolted against British rule and feudal Indian princes.

(d) 'Brahmadeya' : It was a land grant given to Brahmanas. It was non-taxable land. Village settlements in such land was dedicated for Brahmana's upkeep so as to enable them for their usual works.

(e) 'Egmore Faction' : It was a mixed group of Brahmins and non-Brahmin professionals, including T. M. Nair. This group came into existence as an opposition to Brahmin dominated Mylapore Clique of justice party of moderates.

(f) Haileybury College : A college based in Hertford, UK was imparting education and learning to English youths for civil services in East India Company. It selected Indian Civil Servants by competitive examination for East India Company till 1958.

(g) Ijara System : It roughly means lease system. During Mughal period, Ijara or lease of land was given to contractors for administrative purposes. Ijaredars had right of revenue collection.

(h) Taji Mideren : He led the people in revolt against expansion of British rule in Arunachal Pradesh area. He organised his Mishmi followers to establish Mishmi Confederacy. He was finally imprisoned and died in prison.

(i) Gurudwara Reform Movement : Gurudwara Reform or Akali movement started in 1920s. It was a movement against corrupt Mahants of gurudwaras. Finally Shiromani Gurudwara Prabandhak Committee was established to administer Gurudwaras.

(j) 'Marumakkathayam' : It is a non-conjugal relation practiced in Kerala. It is mainly prevalent in Nair community. Aim was progeny. Women enjoyed respect and prestige.

Q. 3 Answer any four of the following (in about 150 words each) : 15 × 4 = 60

(a) Assess the significance of coastal regions in the economic development in India.

Important Points for Answer:
- *Area of coastal region*
- *Foreign trade*
- *Habitation*
- *Industries and Handicrafts*
- *Petroleum*
- *A mid-way destination*
- *EEZ*

Answer: (a) India has about 7516 km long coastline, including two island groups. Nine states have sea coast. There are many ports - minor as well as major.

About 90% of our foreign trade by volume and nearly 70% by value is carried out through sea route.

The coastal zone supports about one-fourth of our total population. It also provides economic activities like fishing, salt-farming, handicrafts based on coastal materials likes and, rocks, etc.

The sea-coast also helps India in security. Three boundaries are covered by sea. India's strategic location in sea is helpful. India is one mid-journey destination for ships travelling in Indian Ocean. India gets earning from such visiting ships.

India's Exclusive Economic Zone area constitutes about 2 million sq. km. This area gives economical benefits in terms of marine resources like minerals, vegetation and aqua-life, Fishing and oil - exploration are very beneficial activities supported by coastal area. Bombay High Oil fields account for more than 15% of nation's total petroleum output.

Global warming and rising sea-level is a threat to coastal benefits.

(b) Discuss the wetlands and their role in ecological conservation in India.

Important Points for Answer:	• *Importance*
• *Meaning of Wetland*	• *Steps taken for conservation*
• *Area*	• *Conclusion*

Answer: Wetland is an area with high water content in the soil. It may be covered with shallow water. Water may be fresh, brackish or salt water.

Wetland accounts for about 18% of India's total geographical area. Wetland helps in ecological conservation in following ways :

- Provides habitation to a large number of species of flora and fauna.
- Helps in conservation of endangered species.
- Provides nesting home to marine animals and fishes.
- Prevents spread of salty water and thus helps in conservation of fertile soil.
- Trees in such area are of hard-wood, so can be useful in making of furniture etc.
- Woods of the trees in wetland are prone to saline water, so can be used in boat-making.
- Residues of ecosystem are useful manure for increasing soil productivity.

India has identified some wetlands for conservation under the National Wetlands Conservation Programme. India is a signatory to Ramsar Convention on Wetlands. It is an inter-governmental convention on wetland conservation adopted in 1972.

The wetlands are productive ecosystem, helpful in biodiversity conservation, providing shelter to rare and endangered species, act as a carbon sink and a source of water.

(c) Elaborate the steps taken by the Government for regionally differentiated approach to increase crop production and diversification in the country.

Important Points for Answer:	
• *Agriculture*	• *Regionally differentiated approach*
• *Importance in Economy*	• *Policies and Schemes*

Answer: Agriculture is an important area for India's economic growth. To achieve double-digit growth rate, agriculture must grow at 4% per annum. So, eleventh plan set the target of 4% agricultural growth.

It is accepted by the authority that to achieve a sustainable growth in agriculture, spread of technology and benefits to all parts of India is necessary.

The Green Revolution was concentrated only in a part of India and on cereal crops only. But now it is identified that other regions are to be covered under some area specific schemes.

National Food Security Mission targets to increase production of rice, wheat and pulses by 10, 8 and 2 million tons respectively.

There are micro-irrigation schemes for dry areas. There are area specific approach in all insurance and credit schemes.

Soil health management is also concerned on testing of soil and providing required categories and quantities of fertilizers.

Crops are also promoted on the basis of climate and soil conditions.

(d) Bring out the significance of the various activities of the Indian Meteorological Department.

Important Points for Answer:	
• *Established*	• *Activities*
• *Objectives*	• *Importance*

Answer: Indian Meteorological Department (IMD) was established in 1875. It is the principal organisation to study meteorology, seismology and allied subjects.

It provides information regarding weather conditions. It issues warning against severe weather conditions like cyclone, dust storm, heavy rainfall, cold and heat waves. The department records earthquakes and conducts research.

Information provided by IMD is useful for general public to know about the weather forecast. It is vital for fishermen, civil aviation activities and farmers. IMD has high power radars and uses satellite system also.

IMD participates in various international research which studies monsoon mechanism. Various forecasting helps farmers to plan their agricultural activities. IMD has installed many digital receivers on east and west coast to disseminate information on cyclone and other oceanic phenomena.

It helps in creating awareness about importance of climate and weather in life and economy of India. IMD has certainly played vital role in India.

(e) Examine the status of urbanization among the states in India and bring out spatial inequalities.

Important Points for Answer:	• *State wise difference*
• *Urbanisation*	• *Reasons*
• *Indian Status*	• *Effect*

Answer: Urbanisation has grown in India in last some years. Yet India is not one of the most urbanized countries in the world. According to 2001 Census, only about 28% of Indians live in urban areas.

Some states like Kerala, Maharashtra, Tamil Nadu, Gujarat and West Bengal have more urbanization, averaging more than 38%. But on the contrary states like Uttar Pradesh, Bihar, Orissa, Jharkhand, Himachal Pradesh, etc. have hardly 17% of population living in urban areas. National Capital Territory of Delhi has 93% urbanization while Chandigarh has 84% urbanization.

There are some mega cities, metrocities and other small cities and towns in $tates. Even in a single state, density and population in various regions are not equally distributed. People in various parts of India get uneven urban facilities. Sex ratio, literacy and other demographic parameters among urban areas is also unevenly developed.

Industrialisation, agricultural development, education, health and other social amenities are some of the reasons behind spatial inequalities in urbanization among states.

Q. 4 Write about the following (not exceeding 30 words each): **3 × 10 = 30**

(a)	**'bhuvan' website**	**(b)**	**National Waterways**
(c)	**Ultra Mega Power Projects**	**(d)**	**NNRMS**
(e)	**BSUP Scheme**	**(f)**	**GAGAN Project**
(g)	**Fruit Production in India**	**(h)**	**Section 377 of IPC**
(i)	**'Whereabouts' clause of WADA**	**(j)**	**Barren Island**

Answer:

(a) **'bhuvan' website :** It is a geo-portal of ISRO. It can take images of the earth with upto 10 mt. resolution. It can provide images of earlier date also. It will compete with Google Earth. It was launched in August, 2009.

(b) **National Waterways :** National Waterways are in big rivers like Ganga, Brahmaputra and others. Total length is 2716 kms. The longest is Allahabad-Haldia, National Waterway-I. It will be operational from March 2010.

(c) **Ultra Mega Power Projects :** It is a project with 4000 MW capacity. The centre has taken initiative to generate low cost, clean electricity. Some UMPPs are started in Public Private Partnership. Reliance, Tata, etc., are constructing UMPPs. Some sites are Tilaiya in Jharkhand, Mundra in Gujarat, etc.

(d) **NNRMS :** It is National Natural Resource Management System, established in 1983. Its headquarter is at ISRO, Bangalore. Department of Space is nodal agency for implementation of NNRMS. Aim is to utilize expertise in space science and technology in management and development of natural resources.

(e) **BSUP Scheme :** It is a Basic Scheme for Urban Poor. It is a sub-mission under Jawaharlal Nehru National Urban Renewal Mission (JNNRM). It includes housing, water, sanitation, drainage and other basic facilities in urban areas. Urban infrastructure and social amenities are covered under BSUP.

(f) **GAGAN Project :** It is a GPS Aided Geo Augmented Navigation. It is an indigenous GPS based satellite navigation system. It helps in locating an object. It can be useful in air, sea and land exploration. It can be used by civil or military purposes. GLONASS, GALILEO are such projects at international level.

(g) **Fruit Production in India :** India produces about 10% of world's total fruit production. In mango, banana, sapota and acid lime fruits, India leads the world. Tropical, subtropical and deciduous fruits are produced in India. Himachal Pradesh leads all states in apple production.

(h) **Section 377 of IPC :** The Delhi High Court decriminalised consensual sexual acts of adults in private even though being against the course of nature. Section 377 penalises unnatural sexual intercourse. It is just decriminalised and not legalised. There was an appeal to the Supreme Court of India.

(i) **'Whereabouts' clause of WADA :** It requires players to inform WADA of their where abouts even during off-season of sports. Indian cricketers raised opposition citing privacy and security concerns. It is mainly aimed at random checking of sports persons to tackle the problem of doping.

(j) **Barren Island :** It is situated 135 km. east of Port Blair. It is only active volcano in the Indian sub-continent. There is no habitation. Only some species of flora and fauna are found on this barren island. Rats, flying foxes, bats, crabs, birds etc. live on this island.

Q. 5 Answer any two of the following (in about 100 words each) : 10 × 2 = 20

(a) Analyse India's achievement in the sports sector during 2008-09.

(b) List the salient features of the important folk dances of either Central India or North Eastern India.

(c) What are the important similarities and differences between the Hindustani and the Carnatic styles of classical music ?

(a)

Important Points for Answer:

- *Sports 2008*
- *Olympics*
- *Tennis, Cricket, Badminton, Others*

Answer: In Olympic 2008 : India won total three medals, one gold and two bronze. Abhinav Bindra became the first Indian to win gold in 10-metre air rifle event. Boxer Vijender Singh and wrestler Sushil Kumar won bronze medals.

In cricket: IPL was inaugurated with eight teams in April, 2008. India won Commonwealth Bank tri-series in Australia after 41 years.

In tennis : Sania Mirza and Mahesh Bhupathi became first Indian pair to win a mixed doubles grand slam in Australian Open. Yuki Bhambri became first junior to win Australian junior title.

In Badminton : Saina Nehwal became first Indian to win the super series in Indonesian Open. She also became first Indian to enter into top-ten ranking in the world.

Others : Pankaj Advani in Snooker, M. C. Mary Kom in Women's boxing, Vishwanathan Anand in Chess and football team in Nehru cup won titles.

(b)

> **Important Points for Answer:**
> - *Dances - Naga, Bihu, Thang-Ja, Nangkrem, Hajgiri*
> - *Features*

Answer: Salient features of North-Eastern Indian folk dances :

- Naga dances :
  - They are performed during harvest seasons.
  - There are many movements of legs but comparatively there is little use of upper body parts like shoulders and torso.
- Bihu dance :
  - That is performed in Assam in mid-April, i.e. during harvesting seasons.
  - It is a group dance of young men and women on the tunes of drums and pipes.
  - Dance is accompanied with love songs.
- Thang - ta and Dhol - Cholom Dance :
  - It is evolved from martial arts exercises. This is a folk dance of Manipur.
  - This dance uses swords and shields. Drum is extensively used as musical instrument.
- Nangkrem Dance :
  - It is performed in Meghalaya during autumn. It uses gestures of animals and birds.
- Hajgiri Dance :
  - This dance is performed to appease goddess Lakshmi in Tripura.

(c)

> **Important Points for Answer:**
> - *Carnatic Music*
> - *Hindustani Music*
> - *Similarities*
> - *Differences*

Answer: Carnatic music is associated with the southern part of India. Hindustani music is associated with North India and is deeply influenced by Persian and Islamic music systems.

- **Similarities:**
  - Basic elements of swara, raga and tala as foundation of both are same.
  - Both musics have great association with religion. Samaveda and Rigveda are basic books for both of these forms of music.
  - Both have evolved from Sanskrit language scripts.
- **Differences :**

– Main emphasis in carnatic music is on vocal music and most compositions are to be sung, involving gayaki style. In Hindustani music vocal - centric music group is required. Many instruments are designed to accompany the singer.

– Origin of Hindustani is earlier than Carnatic. It synthesis with vedic chants, islamic traditions and persian Musiqu - e - Assil style. Carnatic is comparatively pure and was developed in 15th-16th century during Bhakti movement and also get boost in 19th- 20th century.

Q. 6 Answer any two of the following (in about 150 words each) : 15 × 2 = 30

(a) What are your views on the features and impact of the Domestic Violence Act, 2005 ?

(b) Are the traditional determinants of voting behaviour in India changing ? Examine in the context of the last General Elections.

(c) Examine corruption as a serious development challenge in Indian Polity.

Important Points for Answer:	
• *Act*	• *Effect*
• *Main Provisions*	• *Requirements*

Answer: Domestic Violence Act-2005 has enlarged the sphere of protection given to women in their domestic relationship. The Act covers even verbal abuse and threat under the definition of violence. So, physical and actual violence is not required to be proved by women complaint. Relationship required by this act can be of marital or other nature. Even live-in partners, brother-sister and paternal relationships are covered under this act.

The act shifts the onus to prove innocence on the part of the perpetrator of violence. The person who is convicted under this act may be imprisoned. Even during imprisonment, he may be obliged to provide shelter and food to the dependent woman.

Persons may be prevented from entering into certain limits of area where the victim resides so that the safety of victim can be effectively ensured.

Special investigation officers are appointed under this act. There will be women-cell in police station.

All these provisions will actually reduce and gradually eliminate domestic violence. But remedy lies in creating proper awareness and social cohesion apart from ensuring strict implementation of provisions of the act.

(b)

Important Points for Answer:	• *Voting Behaviour*
• *Election 2009*	• *Result*
• *Political Condition*	• *Analysis*

Answer: The last general election was held in April 2009. This election has somewhat broken traditional beliefs in India's voting behaviour.

Uneducated people are voting more in number rather than educated one. Also one thing that is seen as constant is that rural India is coming out for voting but urban, people are less enthusiastic for election.

But the change that is drastic and most important is high percentage of voting in naxal affected areas. This somehow proves that people are to find out solution of their grievances in political methods and not through naxalism.

Caste based and religion based politics has got worse result. People have defeated such parties badly. Same is the fate of regional parties.

Leaders' one - time visit for votes in their constituencies are not accepted by people in many areas and they have even not voted for long term ruling candidates.

Anti-incumbency factor of election is termed to be wrong and Indians have voted for consistency in ruling. Factor of multi-party government is reduced as single party Congress (I) getting many seats, so as to reduce its dependency upon other small parties.

(c)

Important Points for Answer:	• *Bureaucracy*
• *Corruption*	• *Politics*
• *Indian Position*	• *Judiciary*
• *Acts*	• *Prevention*

Answer: India is showing downward movement in Corruption Perception Index of Transparency International.

Corruption has increased in India in last years and all efforts to tackle this curse have failed badly. Recently even Dr. Manmohan Singh has to accept Corruption as a major challenge in Indian polity.

In a Conference, Law Minister Mr. Veerappa Moily has emphasised for amendment of the Prevention of Corruption Act -1988 and to widen its coverage. Some provisions of IPC - 1860 are also identified for amendment. To effectively deal with corruption, Article 310 and Article 311 of the Constitution need to be amended, as remarked by Indian Home Minister P. Chidambaram.

Not only in bureaucracy but mainly in political establishments, the corruption has strong roots. Helped and promoted by individuals and groups interests, corporate field has also shown rampant corruption. Scam in Satyam Computers is an example of it.

Criminalisation of politics and politicisation of crimes are due to maximisation of corruption in systems of Indian polity and governance.

Q. 7 Answer any two of the following (in about 150 words): **15 × 2 = 30**

(a) Mushrooming of Higher Educational Institutions was a matter of grave concern for Yashpal Committee. With reference to the relevant portion of that report give your views how to harmonise private investment and quality of education.

(b) In the changing context of governance in the country, what should be the role of the UPSC?

(c) In the context of recent incidents, suggest measures on how security of passengers and property can be improved over Indian Railways.

(a)

Important Points for Answer:	
• *Committee*	• *Highlights*
• *Objective*	• *Private Management*
• *Recommendations*	• *Conclusion*

Answer: Yashpal Committee was constituted to give its report on conditions of higher education in country. It concerned with the "mushrooming of higher educational institutions" in India.

It observed that deemed university status has been given without concerning quality and necessity. It expressed great worry about monetization on education.

The Committee recommended the creation of a National Commission for higher education and research. It also advocated creation of a Higher Education Council.

It posed private management running educational institutes as profit making enterprises. It accepted need for private investment educating India. But it favoured public-private partnership.

On entry of foreign universities, the Committee gave warning signal. While allowing private investment, government should undertake the mentor-cum-trustee's role.

Thus, the Committee report on the one hand does not reject need for private investment in education but on the other hand, recommended great care and circumspection in this area.

(b)

Important Points for Answer:	• *Role & Functions*
• *UPSC*	• *Suggestions*
• *Provisions*	• *Importance*

Answer: UPSC is the highest Public Service Commission for recruitment to services under the Union.

Provisions for UPSC are given from Article 313 to 323 of the Constitution. UPSC makes recommendations for appointment to services and it is also consulted on all disciplinary matters regarding higher services.

Today the governance demands more active role from UPSC. It is a body which has proven its capabilities. Its role should not be limited to appointment related recommendation. It should be given supervisory authority over performance of services under union.

It should be an active suggestion making body for other state PCS. UPSC should also be a transparent body which can be relied upon by people.

UPSC should be consulted on recruitment to other Central Organisations like ISRO, CSIR, etc.

Recommendations of UPSC should be made compulsory for Government. Only in an exceptional case, which should be informed in writing, its recommendations could be ignored.

(c)

Important Points for Answer:	
• *Indian Railway*	• *Incidents*
• *Safety and Security*	• *Suggestions*

Answer: Indian Railway is one of the largest railway network of the world. There are many instances of railway accidents, insecurity of passengers and property in recent times.

Many criminal elements are nurtured in railway premises. Effective Railway Police System can make railway premises crime free. There should be no incidences of pick-pocketing, looting or theft in that areas.

Recently naxalites blown up railway track in Jharkhand. This should be prevented. Railway signals should be installed with CCTV Camera on them with a long distance visual capabilities. Nearest railway stations can be equipped with monitors.

Railway guards should be provided with effective communication system. Work of RPF should be effective to deal with all threats to railway security.

Recommendations of Khanna Committee on minimization of human errors in accidents can be taken seriously. ACDs (Anti - Collision Devices) installed on Konkan Railway can be expanded on whole Indian Railway track to avoid accidents.

Q. 8 Answer any one of the following (in about 250 words) : 30

(a) Comment on the salient features of the Integrated Energy Policy recently approved by the Government and its implications on the energy security needs of the country.

(b) How far has the impact of the global meltdown been reflected in the Economic Survey 2008 - 09 ? Identify some of the core areas given priority to neutralise the adverse effects of the global downturn.

(a)

Important Points for Answer:	• *Energy requirements*
• *Policy*	• *Energy Security*
• *Features*	• *Importance*

Answer: India recently adopted the Integrated Energy Policy. This is a comprehensive policy on energy for India.

The policy envisages a competitive energy market and market-determined energy pricing. Today the price is decided by the government and which increases burden on public sector oil companies. To reduce this burden a policy is formed.

Allocation of energy resources shall be based on competition. This policy of pricing and allocation will reduce amount of POL subsidies and thus bring down fiscal deficit.

Though there will be subsidies, but they will be based on transparent and target oriented system. Policy seeks to reduce black-marketing of subsidised petroleum products.

The policy seeks optimal exploitation of domestic energy resources and also vigorous exploration and acquisition of energy assets abroad, so that energy security can be attained effectively.

The policy aims to meet energy demands of all sectors. Therefore, not only production of energy will be increased but also its transfer will be made cost-effective. Consideration of environment is also taken into account.

The Integrated Energy Policy is formed under the expert panel of Planning Commission. The IEP was need of the hour because if India wants to continue its economic growth trajectory at high rate, it must have sufficient energy sources to meet demands of economic as well as non-economic activities.

Again, according to the IEP, energy should be sustainable and reasonably cost-effective.

(b)

Important Points for Answer:

- *Global Meltdown*
- *Impact on India Economy*
- *Points from Economic Survey*

Answer: The Economic Survey 2008-09 clearly reflects the effect of global meltdown. The GDP growth of India decelerated in 2008-09 to 6.7 %. It is a 2.1 percent decline from the average growth rate of 8.8 % in the previous 5 years (2003-04 to 2007 -08).

There was a sharp rise in Wholesale Price Index (WPI) inflation followed by an equally sharp fall.

Per capita GDP growth in 2008-09 was estimated at 4.6%. The Ratio of fixed investment to GDP increased to 32.2% of GDP in 2008-09.

According to Economic Survey, performance of six core industries comprising :

1. Crude oil, 2. Petroleum - refinery products, 3. Coal, 4. Electricity, 5. Cement, and

6. Finished steel grew only at 2.7% as compared to 5.9% in 2007 -08.

The Economic Survey identifies adverse effect on export due to (1) drying up of international financial and trade credit and (2) fall in global demand.

There was growth in export which was robust till August 2008, which was dip in September 2008 and that went negative in October 2008 and remained negative till end of financial year.

For 2008-09, overall import growth was subdued at 14.4% in dollar terms and import growth began to decline in October 2008 which remained negative during January 2009 to March 2009.

The Economic Survey also indicates that the impact of global melt-down was less witnessed by India in Gross Capital Formation which increased to 39.1% of the GDP in 2007-08.

Thus, the global meltdown has impacted Indian Economy at the end of financial year but its resilient ability is also proved by maintained growth rate and attraction of FDI in India.

The government took some steps to reduce effect of financial crunch. In India, investment was better in the first and second quarter of 2008-09 as India witnessed 'positive shock' and 'decoupling effect' during the period.

Q. 9 Answer any two of the following (in about 150 words each) : 15 × 2 = 30

(a) Trace the significant steps in the evolution of Television in the country.

(b) The last National Family Health Survey (NFHS) displayed a very dismal picture of nutrition as regards several indicators for average Indians. Highlight the salient aspects of this problem.

(c) 'As we live in a plural society we need the greatest freedom to express our opinions even if others find it offensive' - Do you agree? Discuss with reference to some recent incidents in the Indian context.

Important Points for Answer:
- *Doordarshan*
- *Starting*
- *Development*
- *Importance*
- *Role*

Answer: In 2009, Doordarshan celebrated 50th anniversary of Television of India. It was started in 1959 with USA assistance. It was a black and white telecasting.

With 1982 ASIAD Games, the television broadcasting became colourful. It has transformed the world of entertainment and information in India. Now television has reached to even remote areas.

The INSAT satellite system is being used for TV broadcasting. Earlier it was covering only Indian sub-continent. Then it covered South - Asian region. But with Ku - band, there is a great television revolution.

Direct to Home (DTH) is the latest mode of digitally compressed signals bringing television to us. IPTV is internet protocol based TV. This new technology is yet to be launched in India.

It is not only state-run Doordarshan but there are more than 500 local channels in India. Gyandarshan is a channel run by IGNOU for educational purpose. Siminarly, Eklavya is another channel dedicated to technical education only.

This is a high growth trajectory of Indian television.

(b)

Important Points for Answer:
- *NFHS*
- *Highlights*
- *Condition of India*
- *Conclusion*

Answer: Third National Family Health Survey was published recently. This report presents a comprehensive picture of India's health indicators. It reveals problems of mal – nourishment and under nourishment in India.

It reveals the following aspects

- India is home of largest number of children suffering from mal - nourishment, which constitutes about 115 million.
- It shows that calorie intake criteria of BPL family in India does not properly reveal the real picture.
- More than three-fourth of Indian females are severely anemic.
- Of every five children born in India, two have less than 10 % chances to live.
- There is severe lack of micro - nutrient in Indian food habits.
- There is no proper awareness about food - intake even among urban educated class of people.
- Proper calorie planning in food is lacking in India.

(c)

Important Points for Answer:	
• *Freedom of Speech*	• *Incidents*
• *Right to Reputation*	• *Balance*

Answer: Recently, there are several incidents in India which has raised the issue of balance between freedom of speech and expression on the one hand and right to reputation on the other.

Recently published book on Jinnah and Indian Partition by Jaswant Singh has raised the issue. Little before that there were some problems by a speech of Varun Gandhi which raised some communal issues. Even before that, media crossed its limit by helding Dr. Talwar guilty of his daughter even before any judgement of courts.

All these incidents are based on freedom of speech and expression given as a Fundamental Right in Indian Constitution Article 19(1)(a). But there are certain limitations on this right mentioned in Art. 19(2) itself.

The right to express opinion cannot run a riot. It cannot go so as to violet the feelings of others without reasonable grounds.

Though in a plural society like India, this right is required and a person should be allowed to express his opinion but certain limit is also necessary to maintain balance between private and public interest.

Q. 10 Write on the following (in about 20 words each) : 2 × 10 = 20

(a) Significance of 26 th November in the country's polity

(b) Desert National Park **(c) Rajiv Gandhi Seva Kendra**

(d) Deep Joshi's recent achievement **(e) Girni Kamgar Union**

(f) Ayush-64 **(g) Rashtriya Gramin Vikas Nidhi (RGVN)**

(h) Satya Vrat Shastri's recent achievement

(i) Pocket Veto **(j) PES A, 1996**

Answer: (a) On the 26th November, 1949 our constituent assembly adopted the Constitution of India. On this day the Supreme Law of the land came into existence which was enforced on 26th January, 1950.

(b) It is situated in Jaiselmer, Rajasthan. It is home to the great Indian Bustard. It is rich in fauna. Desert ecosystem can be studied in this park. In Thar Desert National Park Blackburn, Chinkara, Wolf, Indian fox and some other animals are also found.

(c) It is proposed mini - secretariat for NREG A, at Panchayat level. It will keep records of NREGA implementation. Each Kendra will be a forum for discussion on the scheme and will be built as NREGA project.

(d) He is the co-founder of PRADAN, an NGO. He won the Magsaysay award - 2009. He advises government on poverty alleviation. He is a social worker.

(e) It was established in 1928 by S. A. Dange and others. It was a labour union which striked in 1928 and 1929. Kranti was a marathi journal, mouth piece of the Union. S.A. Dange and others were arrested for their role in strike.

(f) It is an anti-malarial drug developed by NRDC. It is prepared from four indigenously available herbs. Clinical trials have been completed for the drug.

(g) It was floated by IFCI and later on joined by NABARD, IDBI and Tata Social Welfare Trust. It is to focus on North Eastern India. Its headquarter is in Guwahati. Its activities are extended to Eastern India also.

(h) He became the first Sanskrit poet to win the Jnanpith award. He has been visiting Professor in Six Universities on three continents.

(i) This type of veto can be used by the President of India. In it, the President withholds the bill and does neither assent it nor return it. There is no express provision of veto power in India.

(j) It is Panchayats (Extension to the Scheduled Areas) Act - 1996. This act was related to expansion and regulation of Panchayati Raj System in Scheduled Areas also, as mentioned in clause (1) of Article 244.

SOLVED PAPERS

PAPER II

Time Allowed : Three Hours *Maximum Marks : 300*

Instructions

Candidates should attempt all questions strictly accordance with the instructions given under each question. The number of marks carried by each question is indicated at the end of the question.

Q. 1 Write notes on any three of the following in about 150 words each: **3 × 15 = 45**

(a) India's strategic interests in South Asia

(b) China's 'peaceful rise' doctrine

(c) India - Russia Defence Ties

(d) India's 'soft' and 'hard' power strategy in Foreign Policy.

Important Points for Answer:
- *South Asia*
- *Indian position*
- *Strategic interest*

Answer: South Asia comprises of nations coming around India and India is the biggest of them.

India has been an accepted leader of South Asia. Now India is rising at a stature of becoming global leader. In this desire, India requires to maintain its stand in South Asia.

India has trade and economic interest in this region. Most of the countries are having traditional economic trade relations with India. India launched "Look East Policy" in this direction.

India is sharing river water with Pakistan, Bangladesh etc. This requires co-operation among them. India has constructed hydro-power projects in neighbouring countries to expand strategic relations.

To maintain internal security and stability, India requires not only good relations with them but also their internal stability.

Economic prosperity of South Asia is also vital for progress of the region as a whole due to inter-dependency among nations.

In defence, India has to maintain peace and security in the region.

(b)

Important Points for Answer:
- *China's rise*
- *Peaceful rise doctrine*
- *Meaning*
- *Strategy*

Answer: China is rising in economic, political and diplomatic fronts, peacefully, smoothly without annoying other powers.

This time, China has grown on economic front unprecedentedly. It is achieving growth rate even during global melt - down. It has flooded world market with Chinese goods.

China has growing relations with USA. It has also maintained good harmony with Russia and India by BRIC and troika of RIC.

Indo-Chinese partnership is growing even though China has been continuously helping Pakistan. It is diplomatic skill of China that has proven itself in international front.

It became a mediator in North Korea and Myanmar issues. It also got entry in South Asian Organisation.

It managed Olympics. Problems of Tibbet were surfacing but it managed to suppress them. China is filling the gap of Asian power vacuumed by Japan.

This is called 'peaceful rise' doctrine of China. The world expresses that the dragon is rising but this time it is not exhaling fire.

(c)

Important Points for Answer:
- *India - Russia*
- *Defence ties*
- *Conclusion*

Answer: Russia is an old friend which has provided defence technology and equipments to India in times of need.

Both are presently developing a Supersonic cruise missile - called as Brahmos jointly. It will have 3 Mach speed.

MIG series of fighter planes have been procurred from Russia. There were issues of defective parts which questioned the genuiness of the deal.

Recently India has purchased a fighter carrier submarine called Akula. It met with some defect in its first test itself.

There are issues of delaying delivery of armed equipments and technology transfer by Russia.

Even issues of price escalation has been a hamper sometimes. Admiral Gorshkows are being sold to India.

India wanted to enter into an agreement with Russia that required timely delivery. But Russia refused to do so.

Now India has options to enter into defence deals with USA and other countries. Russia has lost one biggest deal to USA in 2008 from India. This creates irritant in Indo - Russia defence ties.

(d)

Important Points for Answer:	
• *Indian foreign policy*	• *Soft power strategy*
• *Hard power strategy*	• *Conclusion*

Answer: In diplomatic area, there may be "soft" or "hard" power strategy in foreign policy. India is presently using both of them simultaneously.

On the front of economic issues, energy resources and co-operation politics India is soft. India adopts method of slow but steady progress and achievement. India has started to play "market diplomacy" and "population diplomacy".

India becomes hard on boundry-issues and terrorism incidents. India stationed fighter aircrafts on Aksai-Chin border to realise China that India is ready for any consequences for protection of its territories. It also spoke in clear and strong words that Arunachal is an integral part of India. India stopped dialogue with Pakistan for sometime after 26/11 terror attack.

Similarly, India also has been strategically soft when it entered into 123 agreement with USA and put 14 reactors under IAEA inspection. But on the front of right to conduct nuclear test and not signing of CTBT and NPT. India follows hard strategy.

Q. 2 Write brief notes on any four of the following in about 50 words each: 4 × 5 = 20

(a) Nuclear Supply Group (NSG) and India

(b) Your views on the recent 'Gilgit-Baltistan Empowerment and Self-Governance Order 2009'

(c) Wakhan Corridor

(d) Nuclear Submarine 'Arihant'

(e) National Security Advisory Board (NSAB).

Answer:

(a) NSG is a multi - national body of uranium suppliers. It has 45 members. Its guidelines prohibit a member from exporting uranium fuel to a country which has not signed NPT.

For Indo-US nuclear deal to come into effect, waiver of this guidelines for India was effected by US pressure.

Now, members of NSG can enter into nuclear trade with India.

(b) This is an ordinance in Pakistan. It granted political autonomy to Pakistan's Northern Areas. It assigned the region a new identity of Gilgit-Balistan. This order will actually strengthen the terrorist foothold in the region. It will have adverse impact on India's internal security.

(c) It is about 210 kilometres long land corridor that forms the north-eastern extremity of Afghanistan, in Pamir Mountains. It separates Gorno-Badakhshan region of Tajikistan from the North West Frontier Province and Gilgit - Balistan of Pakistan.

Afghanistan is asking China to open this corridor as a route to fight Talibans, which China is refusing.

(d) INS Arihant is country's first indigenously built nuclear submarine. It can carry torpedoes and missiles including 12 ballistic missiles. It is powered by an 85 megawatt capacity nuclear reactor. It can acquire speed of 22 to 28 kmph on surface and about 44 kmph when submerged.

It put India in selected group of US, Russia, China, France and UK.

(e) It is a part of National Security Council. The NSAB has been reconstituted recently. Now it will consist of 19 members and will advise the PM on new challenges for the internal and external security of India. Mr. M. K. Rastoga, former Foreign Secretary has been appointed as the Convenor for second consecutive term. Experts in external security, strategic analysis, foreign affairs, defence, internal security etc. will be the members of NSAB.

Q. 3 Comment on any two of the following in about 100 words each : 2 × 10 = 20

(a) India-USA as strategic partners

(b) Ethnic conflicts in South Asia

(c) 'NEPAD' and its objectives.

> **Important Points for Answer:**
> - *India-USA relations.*
> - *Recent developments*
> - *Strategic partnership*

Answer: India and USA have entered into third and transformative phase of strategic partnership. The area of co - operation has increased from bi-lateral trade to security and climate change.

Recent visit of Mrs. Hillary Clinton, Secretary of State for USA to India identified five pillars of strategic partnership. They are :

- Energy
- Climate Change
- Education and Development
- Trade and Agriculture
- Science and Technology

There is also military to military link between India and US in the form of joint-exercises and high level visits.

USA wants India to shoulder greater responsibilites and play greater role in world issues.

(b)

> **Important Points for Answer:**
> - *South Asean countries*
> - *Ethnic problems*
> - *Current Status*

Answer: Ethnic conflicts in South Asia is an increasing problem. Recently Sri Lanka, Pakistan and India is facing greater ethnic problems.

Sri Lankan army defeated LTTE. The issue of resettlement of Tamils became an important one. The demand for separate Eelam will now be changed into autonomy and power sharing between minority tamils and majority sinhalas.

In India Gurkha tribes of North-Eastern India is demanding autonomy and non-interference in usual life by the Government. There is also problems in Kashmir and issues of naxalism.

In Pakistan, Mohazir, Biloch and Sindhi groups started anti-state violence and demanded separation or autonomy and equality. Struggle is going on. Pakistan army took strong actions in SWAT valley.

(c)

Important Points for Answer:
- *NEPAD*
- *Objectives*
- *Strategy*

Answer: NEPAD stands for New Partnership for Africa's Development. It is a vision and strategic framework for Africa's renewal. Main objectives of NEPAD :

- To eradicate poverty
- To attain sustainable growth and development
- To stop marginalisation of Africa in the on going process of globalisation
- To enhance Africa's full and beneficial integration into the global economy
- To accelerate the empowerment of women.

NEPAD is an attempt for holistic development of Africa.

Q. 4 Write on any Two of the following in about 50 words each : 2 × 5 = 10

(a) Indo - Bhutan trade relations

(b) Sino - Myanmar relations

(c) Geopolitics and Geostrategy.

Answer: (a) India is the largest trade partner of Bhutan. Free Trade Regime exists between them. There is a framework, "India Bhutan Trade and Commerce Agreement" which regulates trade between the two. It was renewed for ten years in 2005. In 2008, India's export to Bhutan constituted more than 73% of Bhutan's total import. 99% of Bhutan's total export is to India. Both are members of SAARC.

(b) Myanmar is a military ruled country. China has strong relations with it. It supplies defence equipments and provides economic aid, diplomatic assistance, strategic and military cooperation to Myanmar. China has access to Myanmar's ports. Bilateral trade between them exceeds US $ 1.4 billion. Recently refugee problems strained relations between them.

(c) Geopolitics is using political power over a given territory. It suggests impact of geography in shaping up political conditions.

Geo-strategy is using foreign policy to use geographical position as a guiding principle in international affairs. It is a strategy to utilise geo-status in international political strategy.

Q. 5 Comment critically on any One of the following statements in not more than 200 words: 20

(a) "Foreign investment is far from being critical to India's economic growth."

(b) "The lesson of the current global financial crisis is that India should halt and may be even reverse financial liberalisation."

(a)

Important Points for Answer:	
• *Indian Economy*	• *Impact*
• *Investment Policy*	• *Conclusion*

Answer: Indian economic growth is witnessing a high growth trajectory for last some years. India is also one of the most prefered destination for world investors. Even during recent global crisis India emerged as a reliable destination in the world with somehow "positive shock" as well as "de-coupling" effects.

India received 85.1% growth in FDI inflows which was the highest globally, in 2008. India has received 46.5 billion dollars in 2008 as against US $ 25.1 billion in 2007. This was even despite a 14.5% decline in global FDI inflows world over.

India holds 9th position in world's total FDI inflows in 2008. The UNCTAD Survey 2008-10 says China is the most preferred investment destination, followed by India.

Recently, following the same policy of investment liberalisation and attracting foreign investment, the RBI and Government of India announced many steps as most important among others.

Recently, initiatives are taken to liberalise flow of External Commercial Borrowings. ECB limit is enhanced up to US $ 500 mi. per year under approval route for borrowers in infrastructure. Similarly, ECB up to US $ 500 mi. per borrower per financial year is allowed for rupee and or foreign currency expenditure for permissible end-use under automatic route.

Government allowed 49% FDI in credit information companies in 2008-09. FDI up to 100% under automatic route is allowed both in setting up and in establishing industrial parks. All these policy measures have actually helped India to grow and so are far from being critical.

(b)

Important Points for Answer:	
• *Financial Crisis*	• *Financial liberalisation in India*
• *Impact on India*	• *Decision*

Answer: Current financial crisis started from the USA and later on it spread to the whole world including India.

In the starting phase of this crisis, India and other developing countries witnessed positive effects. There was a theory of "decoupling" Indian econmy.

However, in the last quarter of 2008-09, India also suffered. The investment that arrived in India in first two quarter due to stability and chances of good return faced reversal because of financial crunch at home countries. So, India also witnessed financial growth on negative in last quarter.

Indian rupee fall in exchange rate against dollar. RBI has to take steps to stabilize exchange rate. RBI released foreign currency for that purpose. To increase flow of money liquidity in market, RBI changed SLR, CRR, repo rate and reverse repo rate.

The Government had to announce bailout packages for industries. Tax exemptions and duty waivers resulted in increased fiscal deficit. All these steps were required due to financial meltdown at global level.

India witnessed the effect to this global meltdown but resiliance of Indian economy proved stronger. Even after-effects of crisis, India achieved a growth rate of 6.7% of GDP.

This shows that India does not require to halt financial liberalisation. Although some regulations can be there on behalf of the government. As this crisis emerged in USA in absence of any regulatory authority, so it is well accepted fact that regulation and monitoring is required.

Q. 6 Answer any One of the following in about 200 words : 20

(a) "In the WTO negotiations over the years of the DOHA Round, India appears to be diluting its stand on agriculture issues to pursue perceived gains in services."

Critically examine this statement.

(b) Discuss the Indo-US knowledge initiative in Agriculture.

Important Points for Answer:

- *Doha Round*
- *India's stand*
- *Agriculture*
- *Conclusion*

Answer: (a) Doha Round of negotiation was held in 2001. It mainly stuck on the issues related to agriculture. This round is yet going on. It is yet not complete. In this round of talks, members adopted Agreement on Agriculture (AoA). The all over issue is known as Doha Development Agenda (DDA).

Developed countries have argued in favour of opening market for agricultural products. They argue that free trade should involve agriculture also.

India and other developing countries are arguing that agriculture is not only an area of trade and commerce but also basic source of earning livelihood for a large number of people. More than 70% of Indians are dependent upon agriculture.

So, India has always been reluctant to open its market for agricultural goods. But the DDA progressed to some extent and it was agreed upon that developing countries can take special safeguard measures (SSMs) to protect poor farmers in case of either import surge or price fall in domestic product.

SSMs empower developing and poor countries to restrict import of agricultural produce in the given two situations.

Again the problem is that how to settle the issues of "import surge" on "price fall" is not agreed upon in recent Round of Talks in Geneva - 2008, these issues could not be agreed upon and so the talks were halted.

Another issue raised by India is various types of subsidies provided by developed nations to agriculture. These have indirect effect of export promotion.

India has, since starting of the talks, been the mouth piece of all developing and poor countries on AoA. Many a times India has been criticised as a "tough market to open" but it is necessary in the interest of large section of population.

It seems that India has not diluted its stand even though it has tried to be cooperative in the round of talks.

Important Points for Answer:	• *Importance*
• *India - USA*	• *Features*
• *KIA*	• *Objectives*

Answer: (b) In November 2005, India and USA formalised a joint declaration of Knowledge Initiative in Agriculture (KIA). Main objective of KIA is to promote teaching, research, service and commercial linkages to address contemporary challenges against agriculture.

KIA will be carried out through Public Private Partnership. KIA will facilitate technology transfer, bolster agricultural research and education and also expand and strengthen trade and regulatory capacity building.

The following fields shall be covered by KIA :

- Education : Under it, both countries will focus on curriculum development and training, the proposals on building human and institutional capacity. For this purpose, Indo-US joint working group is established.
- Food Processing and Marketing : Work plan is made to target training, capacity building and joint research. This plan includes quality assurance and food safety, reduction in post harvest losses etc.
- Biotechnology : Both countries have envisaged a strateg'c alliance for training and research on development of transgenic crops with resistance to economically important viruses, tolerance to heat, drought and salinity.
- Water Management: Sustainable use of water resources, water quality management, use of modern tools and imparting training and education for these purposes are included under it.

Q. 7 Answer any Two of the following (Each answer must not exceed 150 words): 2 × 13 = 30

(a) Evaluate the prospects for greater economic co - operation between India and China.

(b) Does India need the World Bank ?

(c) Critically assess the recent Free Trade Agreement entered into by India with ASEAN.

Important Points for Answer:	• *Co-operation*
• *India - China relations*	• *Strategy*
• *Trade*	• *Suggestions*

Answer: (a) India and China are bordering countries. They are the fastest growing economies of the World.

Recently Indo-China bilateral trade has crossed US \$ 50 bi border in 2008, despite economic slowdown. In 2007, it was US \$ 38 bi and in 2015 it is expected to reach US \$ 100 billion. Both countries can expect more co-operation on economic front, because they are complementary economies and not competitive one. India is mainly service sector hub while China is considered manufacturing hub.

China and India have large pool of manpower and mineral resources. Co-operation on long term is possible for joint sectors operating in automobiles, cement, steel and other machinery- based industries.

India has become a knowledge-hub. This can be helpful to China. Chinese manufacturing technology can be helpful to India.

But there are issues of concern also. They include dumping by China, balance of trade in favour of China and India exporting mainly raw materials to Chinese industries, etc.

Important Points for Answer:

- *World*
- *Bank*
- *Role & Function*
- *India's need*
- *World*
- *Bank's role in*
- *Indian development*
- *Conclusion*

Answer: (b) The World Bank is an international banking-financial institute. It includes multilateral funding agencies like IDA, IFC etc.

The World Bank provides loans for developmental projects to developing and poor countries. These projects include infrastructure, health, education etc.

India is one of the oldest member of the bank since 1944. India is the single largest borrower of the Bank with cumulative lending of more than US 47 billion dollars.

India is also the top annual borrower of the Bank. Bank has lent India for rural development, education and health, infrastructure and energy projects.

Various states of India have also been receiver of loans and aids from the Bank. Andhra Pradesh became the first state to get benefit of state - focused lending.

Currently Bank's lending portfolio to India comprises about 80 ongoing projects.

It is clear that India has got much benefit from the Bank and developmental projects of India are financed by the Bank. This also helped India in improving on social indicators. So, India surely needs the World Bank.

Important Points for Answer:

- *India - ASEAN*
- *Trade Relations*
- *FTA*
- *Impact*

Answer: (c) India and ASEAN signed Free Trade Agreement (FTA) in August, 2009. This FT A will come into force on January 1, 2010.

There are 4185 items included in the FTA. There will be a sensitive list of 489 articles, on which concessional tariff will not apply. There are 590 articles including plantation on which tariffs elimination will not apply.

In the first year itself, the trade between India and ASEAN is expected to reach at US $ 60 bi from present US $ 38 billion. ASEAN is India's fourth largest trading partner.

There are certain areas of concern in India that may get affected, by this FTA. They are mainly—Rubber, Coffee, Crude and Refined Palm oil. India will not reduce tariff on such items with immediate effect.

On other areas also, it is near zero duty provision and not complete elimination of duty.

Indian auto-mobiles, steel, chemical, cement and some other heavy industries will be benefitted by this FTA. But India has an advantage in service secor which is not included in this FTA.

Q. 8 Answer any Three of the following (in about 150 words each) : 3 × 15 = 45

(a) What do you understand by 'Biosignatures' ? Discuss briefly.

(b) Write about Green Fluorescence Protein (GFP) and its applications.

(c) Define 'Bioinformatics'. How does it work ? What are its major branches and applications?

(d) What is the 'Hubble Space Telescope' ? How many Servicing (SMs) have been Missions conducted for it?

Important Points for Answer:	
• *Bio-Signature*	• *Meaning*
• *Technology*	• *Applications*

Answer: Bio indicates life and signature means any mark that can prove identity. Thus, simply biosignature means using biological traits as identification and authentication mark of an individual.

Individuals have different traits in various aspects. This can be characterised to produce biosignature. Hairs, ratina, finger print, glucose level, blood group and other phenomenas can be used in this field.

Biosignatures can be helpful for authenticity of identity and records. They can be stored on a micro-chip and information can be decoded by machines.

These may help in implementation of government programmes, diagnosis, diseases, defence purposes, etc.

In astrobiology, a biosignature can represent the fact of existence of life on extra-terrestrial surface.

Similarly, fossils and other textures found from the earth can be used to study biology of ancient time.

In geochemistry, geobiochemistry and geomicrobiology also this is often used to find out what type of organisms are present in which place, from samples of their residues.

Important Points for Answer:	
• *GFP*	• *Technology*
• *Meaning*	• *Application*

Answer: (b) GFP is a protein comprising 238 amino acids. They exhibit bright green fluorescene when exposed to blue light.

It was first isolated from the jellyfish Aequorea Victoria.

GFP gene can be used as a reporter of expression in cell biology. When modified, they are used as biosensors to indicate status of body of the organism.

To use a Green Fluorescent Protein as a biosensor in a organism, it can be injected in the body. It can also be introduced by breeding or transformation of cells.

In 2008, Martin Chalfie, Osamu Shimomura and Roger Y. Tsein were awarded 2008 Nobel for Chemistry for their discovery of GFP.

Scientists have study the usefulness of GFP by introducing GFP gene into many bacteria, yeast and other species of fungi, plants, fly, fish and mammalian cells. Even research is conducted on human being also.

This branch will help in treating, diagnosing and regulating diseases apart from its uses in biotechnology.

Important Points for Answer:	
• *Bioinformatics*	• *Application*
• *Technology*	• *Importance*

Answer: (c) Bioinformatics is an interdisciplinary approach in which application of computer science and information technology is to the field of molecular biology.

Mathematical and computing approaches are used to understand biological processes. Development in the field of genomics and other molecular research technologies and development in information technologies have combinely produce large amount of information related to molecular biology giving way to this new branch of science.

Bioinformatics is useful in mapping and analysis of DNA and protein sequence. It also compares different DNA and protein sequences to compare them. It helps in creating 3-D view models of protein structures.

The Human Genome project has increased importance of bioinformatics. The research will help development and success in sequence alignment, protein structure prediction, prediction of gene expression and protein-protein interactions, genome-wise association studies and many other areas.

Important Points for Answer:
- *Hubble Space Telescope*
- *Features*
- *Missions*

Answer: (d) It is a space telescope. It was canied into orbit by the space shuttle in April, 1990. The name is given after American astronomer Edwin Hubble.

It is one of the largest telescope for research in astronomy. It was developed in collaboration between NASA and European Space Agency (ESA). It is one of NASA's Great Observatories.

The Hubble Space Telescope is only one telescope designed by astronauts to service in space. There are total five service missions. The fifth mission was in May 2009. Service Mission is sent to repair any defect in the telescope.

First service mission was sent in December, 1993 to correct imaging flow.

Second, 3 A and 3B servicing missions were sent to repair various sub-systems and replaced many observing instruments with more modern and capable version.

Last service mission STS - 125 was sent to install two new instruments and make some repairs.

Q. 9 Explain any Four of the following (in about 100 words each) : $4 \times 10 = 40$

(a) DN A Finger Printing and its utility.

(b) What is 'Nanotech' ? Give a brief account of its basic concepts, materials used and applications.

(c) What is "Graphene" ? Mention at least three of its applications.

(d) Define 'optical frequency comb'. Suggest at least three applications.

(e) Why is tele-medicine important for country like India ?

Important Points for Answer:
- *DNA Finger Print*
- *Meaning*
- *Technology*
- *Applications*

Answer: (a) It is a technique which help in identifying an individual at molecular level. This technique was developed by British Scientist Alec Jeffrey in 1984.

Each organism has a unique pattern of genes in their chromosomes and only exception to this is twins.

This technique can be used in identification of criminals by checking saliva, hair, drop of blood, semen or any other mark of body. This technique can also be used for sure identification of maternity/paternity, missing child, twins etc.

DNA finger printing technology is used in forensic science widely.

Important Points for Answer:
- *Nano – Technology*
- *Applications*
- *Importance*
- *Development*

Answer: (b) It is short form of Nano-technology. It is study of matter which is atleast in one dimension smaller than 100 nanometres. One nanometre is one-billionth of a metre.

The technology involves controlling and developing material at this size. Matters will change their property.

Materials used - microprocessor, giant magneto-resistance - based hard drives, NEMS and microscope tips with Atomic force.

This technology can create new materials. It can be used in defence, medicine, electronics, technology, space programme and environment and ecology related devices.

Using nano-robots, operations can be performed in body with greater accuracy and without bigger cuts on body. Similarly, nanotech can reduce weight of equipments of a soldier and can reduce size of electronic and communication devices.

Important Points for Answer:
- *Graphene*
- *Meaning*
- *Usefulness*

Answer: (c) Graphene is a one - atom thick planar sheet of sp2- bonded carbon atoms. They are densely packed in honeycomb crystal lattice.

Length of carbon-carbon bond in graphene is about 0.142 nm. It is a basic structural element of some carbon allotropes including graphite, carbon nanotubes and fullerenes.

Application of Graphene : -

- Integrated circuits
- Biodevices : It is helpful for detection and diagnosis in mammalian and microbial by graphene - sheets which is functional with antibodies.
- Transparent conducting electrodes Graphene has high electrical conductivity and high optical transparency. Such properties make it useful as transparent conducting electrodes. It is used in touch screens, liquid crystal displays, organic photovoltaic cells, organic light-emitting diodes and other devices.

Important Points for Answer:
- *Meaning*
- *Techology*
- *Applications*

Answer: (d) An 'Optical Frequency Comb' is a precise tool for measuring different colours and frequencies. This technology can measure very high frequency with greater accuracy.

They are in use in meteorology laboratory and reasearch in physics. Now they are available in commercial market also.

These Optical Frequency Comb can be used in making of optical atomic docks, detection of toxic biochemical agents in body, studies of ultrafast dynamics and quantum computing.

This technology can be applied in medical tests, telecommunication systems in defence operations and equipments. Use of Optical Frequency Comb will be possible for remote detection and range measurements.

Main benefit of this technology is accuracy.

Important Points for Answer:	
• *Meaning*	• *Indian Context*
• *Importance*	• *Conclusion*

Answer: (e) Tele means remote. Tele-medicine means providing medicine from remote place.

Tele-medicine may include diagnosis, treatment, monitoring or prescribing medicines.

Tele-medicine may also cover performing surgery and operations using remote controlled and computer operated devices in near future on wide scale. At present, guiding in operations and surgery is used.

Combined used of medical and telecommunication as well as information technology refers to tele-medicine.

In a country like India this will prove a boon because it will provide services of experts even in remote areas without travelling there.

Less-Number of doctors, hospitals and facilities of equipments will not become a reason for improper treatment of a patient. Patient will not require to travel to Delhi, Mumbai or Chennai for treatment but will be able to get treatment from AIIMS, Delhi even sitting at a far village of Sikkim. It will also impart training and education via tele-conferences.

Q. 10 Write brief notes on any Five of the following (in about 30 words each) : 5 × 3 = 15

(a) Artificial Sun **(b) 'Vegetable Gold'**

(c) PFCs and'liquid breathing' **(d) The'P-8A Poseidon'**

(e) Biometric ATMs **(f) Extra Vehicular Activity (EVA)**

Answer: (a) It refers to replicating the ongoing nuclear fusion process of the core of the sun in the Earth to produce energy. International Thermo-Nuclear Experiment Project (ITER) is based on this concept.

Plasma can be heated to produce large quantity of nuclear energy.

(b) Saffron is also called vegetable gold. It is useful to colour and flavour foods. It is also a stimulant in medicine. Saffron of J&K is very famous. It has been the world's most expensive spice for decades.

(c) PFCs are Perfluoro Carbons. They are derived from hydrocarbons. They can dissolve high concentration of gases like oxygen. Leland C. Clark experimented in 1966 with liquid breathing using this quality of PFCs. This liquid breathing can be used in treating of some diseases also.

(d) It is a military aircraft. It is being developed for US Navy. It will be able to conduct antisubmarine warfare, shipping interdiction and engagement in an electronic intelligence (ELINT) operations. It is developed by Boeing's Integrated Defence Systems division from the 737-800.

(e) Biometrics is used in such ATMs for identity of operator instead of password. Using biological traits like face, voice, retina, iris or fingerprint, the ATMs can be accessed. These methods are for uniquely recognising humans based on their physical traits.

(f) It is an activity performed by an astronaut outside the spacecraft. It may be space walking or activity on extra-terrestrial surface like Moon or Mars. Recently Chinese astronaut performed EVA for a record longest time.

Q. 11 (a) The total areas of cultivation of high, medium and low sugar-content sugarcanes in four regions of a state are given below :

Sugar Content	Region			
	North	South	East	West
High	100	100	200	50
Medium	300	300	400	250
Low	800	400	1000	700
Total	1200	800	1600	1000

Draw suitable diagram that facilitates the comparison of areas of cultivation of different sugar-content varieties among the four regions. **6**

(b) The following table gives the production of soda ash (in tons) by three companies (A, B and C) over seven years period :

Company	1996	1997	1998	1999	2000	2001	2002
A	20	25	28	31	34	36	41
B	15	18	23	35	40	46	50
C	45	43	40	37	30	26	20

Draw a suitable diagram so as to compare the performance of these companies.

(a) **Sub-divided bar diagram**

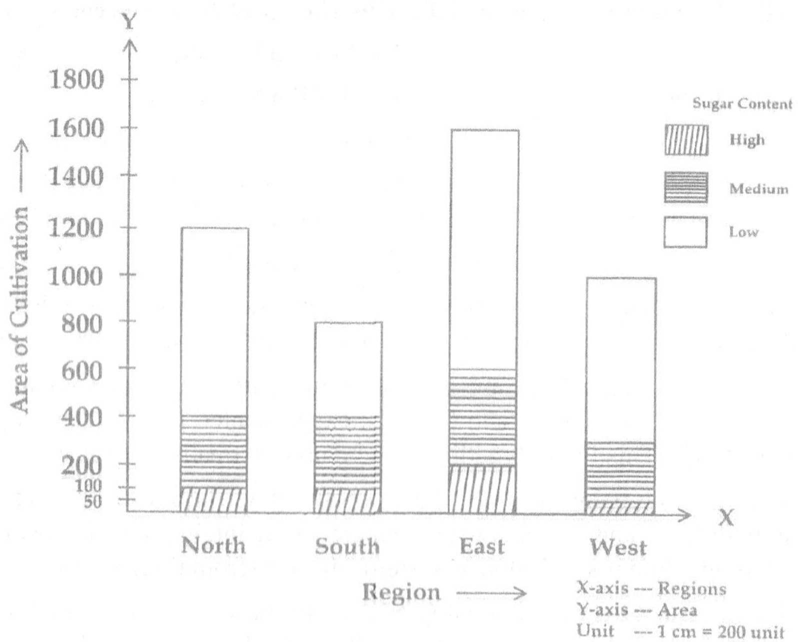

Region → X-axis — Regions

Y-axis — Area

Unit — 1 cm = 200 unit

(b) **Multi-bar diagram**

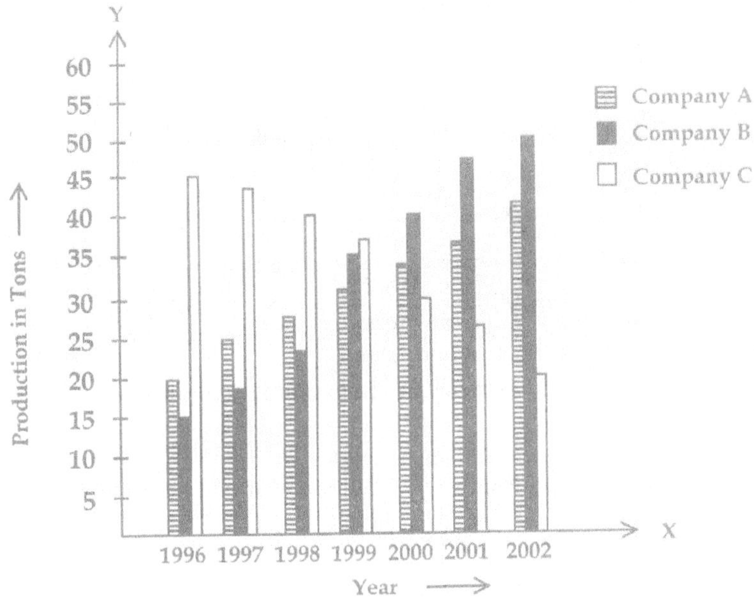

(c) The following data relate to the sales and net profit (in Rupees Crores) of a company :

Years	1994-95	1995-96	1996-97	1997-98	1998-99
Sales	100	250	300	290	680
Net Profit	2.5	4.5	6	8.5	12

(i) In which year the percentage of growth in sales, relative to the previous year is higher?

(ii) In which year the percentage of growth in net profit, relative to the previous year, is higher ?

(iii) Let the profitability be defined as the ratio of Net Profit to Sales. In which year the profitability is higher ? **4**

Answer: (i) % of growth in sales, relative to the previous year

It can be obtained by following steps :

(1) Find out growth in sales over previous year

(2) Find out percentage of growth

So, for comparison of 1995-96 over 1994-95,

Growth = Sale of 1995-96 - Sale of 1994-95 = 250 - 100 = 150

1995-96's Growth = 150

$$\text{Percentage of growth} = \frac{\text{Growth of sale}}{\text{Previsous Year sale}} \times 100 = \frac{150}{100} \times 100 = 150$$

Similarly, for all years

$$\text{For } 1995 - 96 = \frac{250-100}{100} \times 100 = 150\% \text{ ;}$$

$$\text{For } 1996\text{-} 97 = \frac{300-250}{250} \times 100 = 20\%$$

$$\text{For } 1997\text{-}98 = \frac{290-300}{100} \times 100 = -3.3\%$$

$$\text{For } 1998\text{-}99 = \frac{680 - 290}{290} \times 100 = 134\%$$

So, percentage of growth in sale relative to the previous year was higher in 1995-96 which represents growth of 150% in sale.

(ii) Percetage of growth in net profit, relative to previous year can be obtained by following steps :

(1) Obtain growth in profit relative to previous year

(2) Find out percentage of growth in profit

So,

$$\text{For } 1995\text{-}96 = \frac{\text{Growth in Profit over Previous Year}}{\text{Profit of Previous Year}} \times 100$$

$$= \frac{4.5 - 2.5}{2.5} \times 100 = 80\%$$

$$\text{For } 1996\text{-}97 = \frac{6-4.5}{4.5} \times 100 = 33.3\%$$

$$\text{For } 1997\text{-}98 = \frac{8.5-6}{6} \times 100 = 41.67\%$$

$$\text{For } 1998\text{-}99 = \frac{12-8.5}{8.5} \times 100 = 41.12\%$$

Thus, answer is 1995-96 = 80%

(iii) Profitability = Net Profit / Sales

Profitability for 1994-95 = 2.5/100 = 0.025

Profitability for 1995-96 = 4.5/250 = 0.018

Profitability for 1996-97 = 6/300 = 0.020

Profitability for 1997-98 = 8.5/290 = 0.029

Profitability for 1998-99 = 12/680 = 0.018

Thus, Profitability is higher in the year 1997-98.

(d) The total sales (in '000 rupees) of a particular item in a shop, on 10 consecutive days, is reported by a clerk as follows :

35 · 00, 29 · 60, 38 · 00, 30 00, 40 · 00, 41 · 00, 42 · 00, 45 · 00, 3 · 60, 3 · 80

Later, it was found that reports of the 4th and 8th days were 10 00 more than the true values and that in the last two days the clerk put a decimal wrongly one place to the left (for example, 3 · 60 was really 36 · 0). Calculate the true mean value of sale. **5**

Answer: Given value of total sales (in '000 rupees) =

35 · 00, 29 · 60, 38 · 00, 30 · 00, 40 · 00, 41 · 00, 42 · 00, 45 · 00, 3 · 60, 3 · 80

- On 4th Day → given value = 30·00
  On 8th Day → given value = 45·00
  Now it is found that reports on these days were 10·00 more than the true values.
  So true values on 4th Day = 20·00 and on 8th Day = 35·00.
- On last two days decimal was wrongly put one place to the left i.e. given value is 3·60 and 3·80, so true values will be 36·0 and 38·0.
  Now after correction, sale value is 35·00, 29·60, 38·00, 20·00, 40·00, 41·00, 42·00, 35·00, 36·00, 38·00.

Mean = Total Sales / Days

$$= \frac{35.00 + 29.60 + 38 + 20 + 40 + 41 + 42 + 35 + 36 + 38}{10} = \frac{354.6}{10} = 35.46$$

Mean Value = 35.46

Q. 12 (a) In a factory, 1500 women are working. Eight hundred of them come from rural areas and 450 of the married women are skilled labourers. The number of skilled, rural and married labourers is 300. Of the 400 unmarried and skilled women labourers, 250 are from urban area. The number of married, semi-skilled women labourers from urban areas is 200. One hundred married rural women are semi-skilled labourers.

Tabulate the above information. **4**

(b) The mean score of a class in an examination is 70. If the mean score of boys is 60 and that of girls is 75, obtain the percentage of girls in the class. **4**

(c) In a city 20% people read newspaper A, 25% people read B and 10% read both A and B. What is the percentage of people who read at least one of the two newspapers ? **2**

(d) In order to study the effect of inoculation on TB, it was found that the number of inoculated and unaffected from TB is 28, and not inoculated and affected from TB is 13. If inoculation was performed over 40 persons out of 60 persons, complete the table and obtain the missing numbers. **2**

(e) The percentage of literates in six villages of an area are noted as follows:

52, 46, 21, 30, 17, 24.

Can you compute the percentage of literates in the entire area from this information ? If yes, compute the percentage. If no, state what additional information you would need for the computation. **2**

(a)

Area	Skilled		Semi-skilled		
	Married	Unmarried	Married	Unmarried	Total
Urban	150	250	200	100	700
Rural	300	150	100	250	800
Total	450	400	300	350	1500

(b) **Mean score of class = 70** **Mean score of boys = 60**

Mean score of girls = 75

Let total number of boys in class = B

Let total number of girls in class = G

Mean score of Boys = Total score of boys / Total number of boys

60 = Total score of boys / B

60 B = Total score of boys

Similarly, 75 G = Total score of girls

Mean score of class = Total score of boys and girls / Total number of boys and girls

70 = (60B + 75G)/ (B + G)

70 (B + G) = 60 B + 75 G

2 B = G

Thus Girls are twice than boys in the class.

Total students in class = 100 %

Of them, Girls are double than boys.

So, (2/3) × 100 = 66.67% Girls and 33.33 % Boys.

(c) Using rules of sets,

$A \cup B = A + B - (A \cap B)$

$A \cup B$ = Total percentage of people reading newspapers

A = % of people reading newspaper A = 20 %

B = % of persons reading newspaper B = 25 %

$\therefore$ $A \cap B$ = % of persons reading both A and B newspapers = 10 %

$A \cup B = 20 + 25 - 10 = 35$ %

So, 35% of people read at least one of the newspaper.

(d) Inoculated and unaffected = 28

Inoculation = 40

Not inoculated and affected = 13

Total = 60

TB	Affected	Unaffected	Total
Inoculated	12	28	40
Not inoculated	13	7	20
Total	25	35	60

(e) No, percentage of literates in entire area cannot be computed from this information. For computation, population of each of six villages will be needed, additionally.

(MAIN) Civil Services Exam.

2010 General Studies

SOLVED PAPERS

PAPER–I

Time Allowed: Three Hours *Maximum Marks: 300*

Candidates should attempt ALL questions strictly in accordance with the instructions given under each question. The number of marks carried by each question is indicated at the end of the question.

Q. 1 Answer the following (in about 250 words for each answer): 20 × 2 = 40

(a) "Disputes between the- riparian states on sharing of river waters in post- Independence India are becoming increasingly complex." Objectively analyse the major disputes in this connection, with special reference to the Southern States.

(b) Critically examine the differing estimates for (i) poverty figures, and (ii) GDP growth data for April - June 2010, that have been in the news recently. In your view, what estimates are more reflective of the ground reality, and why?

Important Points for Answer:

- *Reason for Disputes*
- *Main Disputes*
- *Analyses*
- *Complexity*

Answer: India is divided into 28 states and 7 union territories for administrative purpose. This divisions do not resemble geographical boundaries. Therefore, it happens that a river originates in one state, flows through one or more other states and then its mouth is in yet another state. So, disputes arise regarding water sharing of such inter - state rivers. In northern India, there are 16 river basins and in Southern India, there are 14 river basins.

We can take cases of Krishna - Godavari river basin and Cauveri Dispute for our analysis.

One reason for such disputes is that sharing agreements are based on old datas and parameters. With time, water quantity and requirements have undergone a drastic change. So, it gives rise to dispute.

Again, in South India, main cultivation is paddy. So, every state requires more water, being the need of crop.

Cauvery dispute has its own Tribunal but no proper conclusion has yet arrived at. Dispute remains between Karnataka and Tamil Nadu.

Between Kerala and Tamilnadu, there is a dispute over Mullaperiyar dam height. It is a historic earthern dam built by British government in agreement with Tranvancore state.

On river Krishna, dispute remains between Andhra Pradesh and Karnataka states. Godavari gives rise to a dispute between Maharashtra and Andhra Pradesh.

All these disputes, now have not remained only water - based. They have their socio - economic effects. Political movements have taken their pace on the basis of these disputes.

Earlier society was mainly rural and agricultural, now urbanisation and industrialisation have also increased demand of water, blowing air to the fire.

(b)

Important Points for Answer:

- *Poverty Measurement*
- *Different figures*
- *GDP Data*
- *Analysis*

In India (and also in the world) there are different criterias for measuring poverty.

We have four different figures for poverty in India, based on different criterias. According to Planning Commission, poverty is 28 per cent. N. C. Saxena Committee reported poverty at about 50 per cent. Recently Suresh Tendulkar Committee reported poverty at 37.2 per cent but in the estimates of the National Commission for Enterprises in the Unorganised Sector (NCEUS), poverty may be around 80 per cent in India.

These differences occurred due to different measures used by them. Again figure also represent how strict or Liberal parameters were used in figuring out poverty.

Recently, estimation of GDP growth rate of India for the first quarter of 2010-11 i.e. April - June 2010 was published. According to the data, real GDP growth at factor cost is estimated at 8.8% while it was indicated at 3.65% at market price. However within a day government has raised the economic growth at market price to 10.02% from 3.65% stated earlier.

Many statistical institutions provide their data of GDP growth and they are varying to some extent. But we can say that for the purpose of GDP growth RBI data shows more ground reality because it has to come out with liquidity and monetary measures. Similarly, Planning Commission's data on poverty can be relied upon.

Q. 2 Answer any TWO of the following in about 150 words each : $12 \times 2 = 24$

(a) Dalhousie's predecessors had acted on the general principles of avoiding annexations, if these could be avoided. Dalhousie acted on the principles of annexation, if he could do so legitimately. His annexations were both of war and peace." Analyse.

(b) With respect to Cooperative Societies what are the salient features of the 106th and 111th Constitutional Amendment Bills as at present?

(c) " Small - holder farms need to be strengthened to achieve national food security." Do you agree with this assessment? Substantiate.

Important Points for Answer:
- *Predecessors Policies*
- *Dalhousie - his policy*
- *Annexations by Dalhousie*

Before the policy of "Subsidiary Alliance" by the Wellesley, the British was concentrated mainly on the gains and resources in India. Cornwallis, the predecessor of Wellesley, wanted to gain the anger of Indian major powers.

The "Subsidiary alliance" system was used by Wellesley to bring the Indian states within the orbit of the British political power. The system played a very important role in the expansion of the company's dominions.

This policy was accepted by Nizam of Hyderabad, the ruler of Mysore, Raja of Tanjore, the Nawab of Awadh, the Peshwa, Scindia, etc.

During Dalhousie's period, the annexation policy was more aggressive. He acted very firmly from the beginning to extend the British rule as much as possible in India. He implemented the policy named "Doctrine of Lapse".

According to the doctrine, any princely state or territory under the direct influence of the British East India Company, as a vassal state under the British Subsidiary System would automatically be annexed if the ruler was either "manifestly incompetent or died without in a direct - heir".

By using this policy they look over the princely states of Satara (1848), Jaipur and Sambalpur (1849), Nagpur and Jhansi (1854). Dalhousie also annexed Punjab, Burma and Sikkim by direct wars.

Thus, predecessors of Dalhousie were more peaceful in their policy while Dalhousie became more aggressive in expansion of British Raj in India.

(b)

Important Points for Answer:
- *106th Amendment*
- *111th Amendment*
- *Their main provisions*

The Constitution (106th Amendment) Bill proposed to insert a new part IX B in the Constitution and adding Articles 243ZH through 243ZT providing for incorporation, regulation and winding up of co-operative societies.

1. The bill specified maximum number of Board members and the tenure of the members.
2. The bill also specified for elections to be held before the expiry of the term of the Board.
3. The bill specified that the Board of a co-operative society that has government shareholding or loans can be superseded for the maximum period of six months.

The Constitution (One Hundred and Eleventh Amendment) Bill, 2009 was introduced in the Lok Sabha on November 30, 2009.

Background:

- The Bill adds a new Directive Principles of State Policy stating that the "State shall endeavour to promote voluntary formation, autonomous functioning, democratic control and professional management of co-operative societies."
- It further inserts a new part IX B in the Constitution (adding Articles 243ZH through 243ZT), which outlines certain guidelines for running co - operative societies.

Important Points for Answer:
- *Small Holdings*
- *Importance in agriculture*
- *Measures needed*

The National Food Security Bill - 2010 has been passed in the parliament with the object to ensure the food security to every citizen in the country. For this purpose, we have to strengthen every aspect in the field of agriculture. Small holder farmers are those who own or cultivate less than 2.0 hectares of land in the marginal and submarginal farm households.

According to agricultural census of 1990 - 91, 33 % of the total cultivated land in India is small farms and it contributes 41 % of the National grain production. Besides these, the families of the small holder's constitutes more than half of the national population.

Strengthening of small holder farms is important for two reasons :

(i) For their high contribution in agricultural output due to high levels of productivity as compared to large farms.

(ii) For its role in alleviating poverty across the nation, as majority of the poor still depend on it for their life.

The Government should be committed to implement various schemes and provide and educate the agricultural people about new technologies, encourage them to use various hybrid and high yielding immune seeds to increase the production and to facilitate for the effective market management to sell their products.

Q. 3 Answer any TWO of the following in about 150 words each: 12 × 2 = 24

(a) Comment on the spatial components in urban solid waste management in the country.

(b) Assess the contributions made by the Indian Council of Agricultural Research (ICAR) in agricultural development.

(c) List the significant local storms of the hot-weather season in the country and bring out their socio-economic impact.

Important Points for Answer:
- *Rules*
- *Applicability*
- *Responsibility & Authority*

Answer: (a) The Municipal Solid Wastes (Management and Handling) Rules, 2000.

Applicability:- Apply to all municipal authorities responsible for collection, segregation, storage, transportation processing and disposal of municipal solid wastes.

Responsibility of Municipal Authority:

1. Every municipal authority shall, within the territorial area of the municipality, be responsible for the implementation of the provisions of these rules, and for any infrastructure development for collection, storage, segregation, transportation, processing and disposal of municipal solid wastes.
2. The municipal authority or an operator of a facility shall make an application for grant of authorisation for setting up waste processing and disposal facility including landfills from the State Board or the Committee in order to comply with the implementation programme.
3. The municipal authority shall furnish its annual report.
   (a) to the Secretary-in-charge of the Department of Urban Development of the concerned State or as the case may be of the Union Territory, in case of a metropolitan city; or
   (b) to the District Magistrate or the Deputy Commissioner concerned in case of all other town and cities, with a copy to the State Board or the Committee on or before the 30th day of June every year.

Important Points for Answer:
- *ICAR*
- *Its Contribution*

(b) The Indian Council of Agricultural Research (ICAR) is the apex body for co-ordinating, guiding and managing research and education in agriculture including horticulture, fisheries and animal sciences in the entire country. With 97 ICAR institutes and 45 agricultural universities spread across the country this is one of the largest national agricultural systems in the world.

The ICAR has played a pioneering role in ushering Green Revolution and subsequent developments in agriculture in India through its research and technology development that has enabled the country to increase the production of foodgrains by 4 times, horticultural crops by 6 times, fish by 9 times (marine 5 times and inland 17 times), milk 6 times and eggs 27 times since 1950-51, thus making a visible impact on the national food and nutritional security.

It has played a major role in promoting excellence in higher education in agriculture. It is engaged in cutting edge areas of science and technology development and its scientists are internationally acknowledged in their fields.

Important Points for Answer:
- *Conditions*
- *Their impact*
- *Local storms*
- *Complexity*

(c) From March to May the 'belt of great heat' changes from south to north, due to the seeming northward motion of the sun. Deccan Plateau records the highest day temperatures in March.

They arb approximately around 38 °C. In April, the heat belt travels further north towards Gujarat and Madhya Pradesh, where they roughly record around 42 °C to 43 °C. In May, the heat belt moves further north. In the north-western part of the country temperatures close to 48 °C are not exceptional.

In the centre of the low pressure trough in the north-west, dry and hot winds blow during the afternoon and frequently they remain even up till midnight. These hot and dry day winds are locally known as 'loo'.

At times, the moisture - laden winds are drawn towards the fringe of the trough. An abrupt contact between dry and moist air-masses gives rise to local storms of immense strength. These local storms are connected with brutal winds, uncontrolled downpour and even hail storms.

Towards the closing of summer, pre - monsoon showers are a frequent occurrence in Kerala and coastal areas of Karnataka. Locally they are known as '**mango**' showers, because they aid in the early ripening of mangoes. Entry of pre-monsoon showers and early advancement of monsoons further north, is arrested by a belt of comparatively high air pressure, lying over the Deccan plateau.

The horrendous north-westerly and northerly winds in Bengal and Assam also cause very precipitate downpours. They are fundamentally evening thunder storms. Their unfavoured nature can be understood from the local terminology of '**Kalbaisakhi**'-'calamity of the month of Baisakh'.

Q. 4 Answer any TWO of the following in about 150 words each: 2 × 2 = 24

(a) What are the grounds of disqualification of a Member of Parliament from either House? Quote relevant provisions in your answer.

(b) Distinguish between the objectives, structure and functioning of the 'Kendriya Vidyalaya Sangathan' and the 'Navodaya Vidyalaya Samiti'

(c) Bring out the salient features of the evolution and the current status of the 'Bharat Stage' vehicle emission norms in the country.

Important Points for Answer:

- *Grounds provided in :*
- *Article -102,*
- *Anti-Defection Law,*
- *Representation of Peoples Act*

Answer: Article 102: Disqualifications for membership

(1) A person shall be disqualified for being chosen as, and for being, a member of either House of Parliament

(a) if he holds any office of profit under the Government of India or the Government of any State, other than an office declared by Parliament by law not to disqualify its holder;

(b) if he is of unsound mind and stands so declared by a competent court;

(c) if he is an undischarged insolvent;

(d) if he is not a citizen of India, or has voluntarily acquired the citizenship of a foreign State, or is under any acknowledgement of allegiance or adherence to a foreign State;

(e) if he is so disqualified by or under any law made by Parliament Explanation; for the purposes of this clause a person shall not be deemed to hold an office of profit under the Government of India or the Government of any State by reason only that he is a Minister either for the Union or for such State.

(2) A person shall be disqualified for being a member of either House of Parliament if he is so disqualified under the Tenth Schedule

The grounds for disqualification under the Anti-Defection Law (Tenth Schedule)

(a) If an elected member voluntarily gives up his membership of a political party;

(b) If he votes or abstains from voting in such House contrary to any direction issued by his political party or anyone authorised to do so, without obtaining prior permission.

Disqualifications for membership of Parliament under provisions of The Representation of People Act 1951:

- Disqualification on conviction for certain offences.
- Disqualification on ground of corrupt practices.
- Disqualification for dismissal for corruption or disloyalty.
- Disqualification for Government contracts, etc.
- Disqualification for office under Government company.
- Disqualification for failure to lodge account of election expenses.

Important Points for Answer:

- *Objectives*
- *Distinctions*

(b) Kendriya Vidyalaya is a system of central government schools under the Ministry of Human Resource Development.

The system came into being in 1965 under the name "Central Schools" and has been affiliated with CBSE since then. Later, the name was changed to Kendriya Vidyalaya.

Objectives of Kendriya Vidyalaya Sangathan:

1. To cater to the educational needs of children of transferable Central Government including Defence and' Para-military personnel by providing a common programme of education;
2. To pursue excellence and set the pace in the field of school education;
3. To initiate and promote experimentation and innovations in education in collaboration with other bodies like the Central Board of Secondary Education (CBSE) and the National Council of Educational Research and Training (NCERT) etc. and
4. To develop the spirit of national integration and create a sense of "Indianness" among children.

Navodaya Vidyalaya Samiti is an autonomous organisation under the Ministry of Human Resource Development, Department of Secondary & Higher Education, Govt. of India. The Chairman of the Samiti is the Hon'ble Minister of Human Resource Development.

First established in 1985 at Amravati, Maharashtra. They started with the name Navodaya Vidyalayas and renamed later as Jawahar Navodaya Vidyalayas in the birth-centenary year of Pandit Jawahar Lal Nehru.

Navodaya Vidyalayas are affiliated to Central Board of Secondary Education (CBSE).

Objectives of Navodaya Vidyalaya Samiti

- to provide good quality modern education to the talented children predominantly from the rural areas, without regard to their family's socio-economic condition.
- to ensure that all students of Jawahar Navodaya Vidyalayas attain a reasonable level of competence in three languages as envisaged in the Three Language Formula.
- to serve, in each district, as focal points for improvements in quality of school education in general through sharing of experiences and facilities.

Important Points for Answer:

- *Emission Regulations*
- *Evolution in India*
- *Fuel Policy*

(c) The first Indian emission regulations were idle emission limits which became effective in 1989.

Since the year 2000, India started adopting European emission and fuel regulations for four - wheeled light - duty and for heavy - duty. Indian own emission regulations still apply to two - and three - wheeled vehicles.

On October 6, 2003, the National Auto Fuel Policy has been announced, which envisages a phased program for introducing Euro 2-4 emission and fuel regulations by 2010.

These standards apply to all new 4 - wheel vehicles sold and registered in the respective regions. In addition, the National Auto Fuel Policy introduces certain emission requirements for interstate buses with routes originating or terminating in Delhi or the other 10 cities.

For 2 - and 3 - wheelers, Bharat Stage II (Euro 2) will be applicable from April 1, 2005 and Stage III (Euro 3) standards would come in force preferably from April 1, 2008, but not later than April 1, 2010.

Q. 5 Write brief but precise notes on any SIX of the following. Your answer should not exceed 50 words in each case. **5 × 6 = 30**

(a) Transhumance in India

(b) Frontogenesis and Frontolysis

(c) Golden Revolution

(d) Sea-floor spreading

(e) Legislative powers assigned to the Rajya Sabha under Art. 249 and Art. 312 of the Constitution

(f) Causes for dominant dendritic pattern of drainage in the Cangetic plains

(g) " Break-of-bulk" towns

Answer: (a) Transhumance means seasonal movement of people along with their livestock. They move for livelihood purpose, generally over a short distance.

Siwalik, Ladakh and Nilgiris still follow the practice. It supports pasture needs.

They may also undertake Zhoom cultivation as an occupation. They collect forest products and sell them. Now transhumance is declining.

(b) Both terms refer to atmospheric conditions created by front.

Frontogenesis, in meteorology, refers to the formation or strengthening of an atmospheric front. During frontogenesis, the temperature gradient tightens and as a result the thermal wind becomes imbalanced.

Frontolysis - in meteorology, is the dissipation or weakening of an atmospheric front.

(c) Golden Revolution is related to increased production of fruits and vegetables. Share of horticulture in GDP of agriculture is now more than 30 % in India.

Research and promotion of this sectot has increased income of farmers. It promises a potential to increase per-capita income of farmers in rural areas. It can also be promoted in environmental friendly manner.

(d) Seafloor spreading is a process that occurs at mid-ocean ridges, where new oceanic crust is formed through volcanic activity and then gradually moves away from the ridge.

Seafloor spreading helps explain continental drift in the theory of plate tectonics.

Sea floor spreading, if it continues to the point that the continent is completely severed, then a new ocean basin is created.

(e) Under Article 249 Rajya Sabha can empower Parliament to enact a law on any matter of state list. It has to pass a resolution that such enactment is necessary in national interest.

Under Article 312 Rajya Sabha has power to create a new category of All India Service by a resolution.

(f) Almost all river channel of Gangetic plain follow the slope of terrain i.e. west to east. This is one reason for dendritic pattern of drainage.

Monotonons character of the vast alluvial plain help river to easily make its course in the direction of the slope. This is another reason for the same.

(g) Break of bulk town is a place where goods are unloaded, i.e. ports. Town situated in middle of hills may also act as a break of bulk town due to their location, i.e. Dehradun.

Similarly, cargo ports are break of bulk towns. The port may handle any particular type of cargo or various cargo - types. Bharuch in Gujarat was a break of bulk town in ancient India.

Q. 6 Answer any THREE of the following in about 150 words each: 12 × 3 = 36

(a) While bringing out their salient features, distinguish between either 'Madhubani' Art and 'Manjusha' Art or 'Rajasthani' schools of painting and the 'Pahari' school of Painting.

(b) Bring out the powers and responsibilities attached to the office of the Speaker of the Lok Sabha.

(c) Distinguish between the following four literary awards:

(i) Jnanpith Award **(ii) Sahitya Akademi Award**

(iii) Vyas Samman **(iv) Saraswati Summan**

(d) After the September I[st] changes, do you think that Unit Linked Insurance Plans (ULIPs) and Mutual Funds (MFs) are on a level playing field? Substantiate your answer from the perspective of an ordinary investor.

> **Important Points for Answer:**
> - *Salient Features of all forms of schools*

Answer: Madhubai Art: The art of painting initially practised in Mithila region of Bihar state. It is antique art of painting. It is said that this art originated at the time of king Janak.

Traditionally done by women of villages around present town of Madhubani. Initially it was done on plastered mud wall of huts. But now also done on clothes and handmade papers and canvass. Colours are derived from plants, themes generally revolves around hindu deities, natural object and Tulsi.

Manjusha Art or **Angika Art**: Traditional and indegenous art form of Bihar, used in Bihar Vishnavi Puja, usually referred as a snake printings only left part of the painting is painted.

Pink, yellow and green colours are used. Human being depicted in the form of english letter X.

Rajasthani Schools of Painting: It developed in 15th century. Also called as Rajput or Hindu school of painting.

In the beginning, the style was inspired by religion, mostly Hindu Vaishnav religion. In later stage, paintings were done on romance and great folk themes. Bright colours were used. Faminian beauty like lotus eyes, waving hairs, thin waist rounded and long fingers and graced is portrayed.

Main schools of this art: Mewar school, Kishangarh school, Bikaner school, Bundi school, Jaipur school.

Pahari School of Painting: It developed and flourished during 17th to 19th century in the foothill of Punjab, Himachal Pradesh, Jammu and Garhwal.

Painters are great lover of nature and depicts nature with care. Its main centeres are Basholi, Kangra and Gular.

In Basholi portration of simplified forms of trees and faces is used with bold lines and brilliant colors.

In Gular, women in the absence of their love is depicted.

Kangra rather advanced includes towns, cluster of houses in the distance.

This art dwelt largely on the themes and symbols from literature and mythology.

Main schools are Kangra and Dagra.

> **Important Points for Answer:**
> - *Position*
> - *Power / Function*

(b) The Speaker is the presiding officer of the lower house of Parliament of India.

His/her role is similar to that of Speakers elsewhere in other countries that use the Westminster system of government.

The Speaker presides over the sessions of the Lok Sabha and conducts the business in the house.

He/she decides whether a bill is a money bill or a non money bill.

He/she maintains discipline and decorum in the house and can punish a member for their unruly behaviour by suspending them.

He/she permits the moving of various kinds of motions and resolutions like the motion of no confidence, motion of adjournment, motion of censure and calling attention notice as per the rules.

The Speaker decides on the agenda to be taken up for discussion during the meeting. The date of election of speaker is fixed by the President.

> **Important Points for Answer:**
> - *Four Awards*
> - *Foundation and other criteria*

(c) The Jnanpith Award is the highest literary award in India. It is presented by the Bharatiya Jnanpith, a trust founded by the Sahu Jain family, the publishers of The Times of India newspaper.

Sahitya Akademi Award is a literary honor in India which Sahitya Akademi, India's National Academy of Letters, annually confers on writers of outstanding works in one of the twenty - four major Indian languages.

The Vyas Samman is a literary award in India, first awarded in 1991. It is awarded annually by the K.K. Birla Foundation and includes a cash payout of Rs 2.5 lakh (as of 2005).

To be eligible for the award, the literary work must be in the Hindi language and have been published in the past 10 years.

The Saraswati Samman is an annual award for outstanding prose or poetry literary works in any Indian language. It is named after an Indian goddess of learning and is considered to be among the highest literary awa,ds in India. It includes a monetary award of Rs five lakh (as of 2006). The Saraswati Samman was instituted in 1991 by the K. K. Birla Foundation.

> **Important Points for Answer:**
> - *ULIP*
> - *MF*
> - *Difference*
> - *Problem*
> - *Recent decision*

(d) Investment in ULIPS or MFs result to the. turf war between IRDA and SEBI. ULIPs are Unit Linked Insurance Plans and MFs are Mutual Funds or purely invested in equity.

ULIPs are combination of insurance and investment.

In ULIPs, less than 5% of the premium for insurance and other used for buying equity, making it more or less a conventional MF. Since MF money is equity investment, so lot of regulatory structures were built into it. This provided for a natural inclination of financial regulatory arbitrage to favour ULIPs over MFs.

Preference to ULIPs affected MFs market. Ordinary investors in the name of insurance cover was getting into uninformed investment territory of equity market.

So there was a lot of chorining in the MF domain. And this was being missold to a symmetrically interested investor on the pretext of handsome return as this lead to a regulatory dispute between IRDA and SEBI. Post to the 1st September decision, the scenario was become clear.

Now lock - in period for all ULIPs has been increased from 3 yrs to 5 yrs making them long term financial instrument which basically provide risk protection.

Now IRDA has been restored with the regulatory position of ULIPs, thus clarifying to the market that it is insurance product where maximum portion of the premium should be allocated to the insurance coverage, this has reduced the regulatory arbitrage between both these products thus giving them level playing field.

Q. 7 Answer any FIVE of the following in about 150 words each: 12 × 5 = 60

(a) What do you understand by 'repo rate' and 'reverse repo rate'? What are the implications in raising these rates?

(b) "Cost - benefit analysis should not be the sole consideration, while deciding to host events like the Commonwealth Games." Critically comment on this perspective.

(c) List any eight 'Ramsar' wetland sites located in India. What is the 'Montreux Record' and what Indian sites are included in this Record?

(d) Are the 'Dedicated Freight Corridor' railway project and the 'Golden Quadrilateral' road project mutually complementary or competitive? Assess.

(e) " Upliftment of the neglected sections of society will be best served with many more centers of the Indira Gandhi National Tribal University." Expand on the assertion made.

(f) Comment on the salient features of the recent draft Model Real Estate (Regulation of Development) Act of the Ministry of Housing and Urban Poverty Alleviation of the Central Government.

Important Points for Answer:

- *Repo rate*
- *Reverse repo rate*
- *Effect of raise*
- *Use by RBI*

(a) When banks have any shortage of funds, they can borrow it from Reserve Bank of India or from other banks. The rate at which the RBI lends money to commercial banks is called repo rate, a short term for repurchase agreement. A reduction in the repo rate will help banks to get money at a cheaper rate. When the repo rate increases borrowing from RBI becomes more expensive.

Reverse Repo rate is the rate at which Reserve Bank of India (RBI) borrows money from banks. Banks are always happy to lend money to RBI since their money is in safe hands with a good interest. An increase in Reverse repo rate can cause the banks to transfer more funds to RBI due to these attractive interest rates. It can cause the money to be drawn out of the banking system.

Due to this fine tuning of RBI using its tools of CRR, Bank Rate, Repo Rate and Reverse Repo rate our banks adjust their lending or investment rates for common man.

Important Points for Answer:
- *Important of Games*
- *Its measurements - Monetary, others*
- *Measures of analysis*

(b) Hosting games like Commonwealth, Olympics or Asian games leads to invest lot of money in infrastructure. States run facilities which will provide great base to the states. It is one of imperative to analyse cost benefits but here cost benefit analysis is not just a monetary turn. Cost in a same includes investment in state run facility and in infrastructure, sports infrastructure which includes stadiums, training camps that also of international standards.

Consequently hosting big games leads to short term as well as long term benefits. In short term benefits it helps to inspect transport system, security measures and to fulfill loopholes if any.

Firstly sports helps in National Integration and spreads enthusiasm among citizens in different region and encouragement to the sportsman leading to great performance which promotes sports spirit in the country and securing respectable place among different countries of the world.

Hosting country is on a stage to show to the world, its economic and social developments which will lead to better relationship with other countries which helps to enforce to economic policy as well.

Government gets a chance to communicate its public diplomacy through tourist and foreign players which also leads to promote the tourism and cultural integration among different parts of the world.

When we analyse in this way we find hosting big games like commonwealth is very necessary to every country especially country like India which is emerging on international stage seeking a place in Security Council of UN. However this investment in country is necessarily needed to regulate through proper channel, otherwise it will lead to big scams and maladministration.

Important Points for Answer:
- *Ramsar sites*
- *Montreux record*
- *Montreux sites*

(c) The list of Ramsar Sites in India comprises Indian wetlands deemed to be of "international importance" under the Ramsar Convention. 8 Ramsar wetland sites located in India are:

Ashtamudi Wetland, Kerala; Bhitarkanika Mangroves, Orissa; Bhoj Wetland, Madhya Pradesh; Chandertal Wetland, Himachal Pradesh; Chilika Lake, Orissa; Deepor Beel, Assam; East Calcutta Wetlands, West Bengal; Harike Lake, Punjab

The Montreux Record is a register of wetland sites on the List of Wetlands of International Importance where changes in ecological character have occurred, are occurring, or are likely to occur as a result of technological developments, pollution or other human interference. It is maintained as part of the Ramsar List.

Indian sites in the Montreux Record are Keoladeo National Park, Rajasthan; Loktak Lake, Manipur.

Important Points for Answer:
- *Dedicated Freight Corridor*
- *Golden Quadrilateral*
- *Analysis*
- *Conclusion*

(d) Dedicated Freight Corridor is planned under 11th Five Year Plan. It will cover 2762 km route in two parts. One is the Eastern Corridor from Ludhiana to Dankuni and another is Western Corridor from Mumbai to Dadri. Both will interlink at Khurja.

Golden Quadrilateral is the largest highway project in India of 5846 km consisting of four or six lane express highways. The project is to join four mega cities on all four directions of India - Delhi, Mumbai, Kolkata and Chennai.

Both Road and Railway networks in India are already over - burdened by traffic. Recently Indian economic growth is poised to be around 8 to 10 percent for coming years. This will demand better infrastructure and transportation facility. Therefore, these projects will be helpful.

Again, the Dedicated Freight Corridor covers only east and west part, in North India. There is no such corridor in South India.

Important Points for Answer:
- *University*
- *Benefits of more centres*

(e) The **Indira Gandhi National Tribal University** envisages to provide higher education to tribals all over India. It has been established by an act of Parliament of India at Amarkantak, Madhya Pradesh. It is fully funded by the Central Government through University Grant Commission.

Tribals in India require special focus for their upliftment. Eventhough they are culturally very rich, they lack proper and higher education. Any effort to expose them to urban culture will be surely a failure for their development, tribal - based programmes have to be developed.

Recently the Tribal University has opened its first regional campus at Manipur in September 2009. Such more centres can provide them an opportunity to opt for higher education in their own area. They will contribute to higher studies and research. Tribal art, traditions, culture, language, medicinal system, forest based economical activities, advancement in technology etc. can be main focus apart from other curriculum.

Important Points for Answer:
- *Draft model*
- *Key points*

(f) The Model Real Estate Act was announced by Ministry of Housing and Urban Poverty Alleviation.

Now it is arduous task for builders and developers to mislead the buyers using misleading details of the property or confusing them with Jargom terms.

This Act seeks to balance to disorganise the sector and transparency needed.

Key highlight of the Act:

- No advertisement before registration with authority. Registration will ensure that project has obtained all sanctions.
- Advertisement should be specific and clear, no misleading images.
- Proper technology used, detailed specification of materials.
- Clear information of extra charges.
- Any individual can inspect any time any document related to the project.
- Sale and purchase will be lodged in to an AIR thereby making income tax an obligation to ensure no illegitimate property or black money involved.
- Certification to the agent.
- The regulatory body make it sure that end product is same as the investor invested into initially.

The above mentioned improvements in the real estate sector are for sure going to give the segment a boost. It will add much to the relief of the buyers. It will ensure transparency and accountability.

Q. 8 Answer each of the following, briefly but precisely. Each answer should be less than 50 words. 5 × 6 = 30

(a) How is disagreement between the Legislative Council and the Legislative Assembly of a State in passing of an ordinary Bill, resolved?

(b) Comment on the recent HFC - 23 emissions controversy that includes in its ambit some Indian companies.

(c) Comment on the recommendations of the Wadhwa Commission on the Public Distribution System.

(d) What are the salient features of The National Oil Spill Disaster Contingency Plan?

(e) You arrive first at, the scene where a bus accident has just occurred. What emergency measures should you immediately and safely adopt?

(f) Bring out the sectoral and state - wise distribution patterns of Foreign Direct Investment (FDI) inflows into the country.

Answer: (a) Where any controversy arises between the houses of Parliament on passing a bill, the President, according to Article 108 of the Constitution, can Summon both the houses to meet in a joint sitting to resolve the controversy. Like that, there is no any constitutional provision to summon the joint sitting in the state legislature over any ordinary bill.

So, in case of disagreement between Legislative Council and Legislative Assembly over an ordinary bill, according to art. 197, the will of the Assembly prevails over that of the Council. The Council can only delay the bill. The power of the Legislative Council has been restricted under Art. 197 in case of bills other than money bills.

(b) Controversy is brewing over HFC 23 destruction in CDM. Many viewed HFC 23 destruction as a cheap money maker. HFC is a potentially dangerous greenhouse gas. It is used in diverse niche applications and it produced as a byproduct of HCFC 22. It is used in refrigerator, air conditioner and foam industries.

UNFCCC try to mitigate its emission as clean development mechanism project by which its emission reduced substantially because sale of CERs generating significant revenue streams. Member of UN panel decided to analyse the scheme as companies from countries like India and China are getting huge credits (around half of carbon credits only by using 1% CDM project methodology).

Indian companies are also reducing emission of HFC 23 by CDM to get carbon credit.

(c) To check maladies affecting the proper functioning of PDS, Supreme Court constituted the Wadhwa Committee by an order passed in a writ petition and also to suggest the remedial measures.

Committee submitted its report on 21 August 2007. The recommendations are as follows:

(i) Computerization of PDS operations.

(ii) Identify the exact quantity of poor families living below poverty line to effect the profit to the real beneficiary. So that they can get their due entitlements at fixed price and quantity in a fixed period.

(iii) Distribution on minimum rate.

(iv) Food Security to increase nutrition especially in malnutrition areas.

(v) There should be zero tolerance approach as there are more leakages and maladministration.

(vi) System lacks transparency and accountability, also it needs enforcing strict monitory measures.

(d) A draft National Oil Spill Disaster Contingency Plan (NOS-DCP) was prepared on 14 Apr 1988 and forwarded to all concerned agencies for comments. Final draft was approved by the Committee of Secretaries on 04 Nov 1993.

Objectives: The objectives of the plan are

(a) To develop appropriate and-effective systems for the detection and reporting of spillage of oil.

(b) To ensure prompt response to prevent, control, and combat oil pollution.

(c) To ensure that adequate protection is provided to the public health and welfare, and the marine environment.

(d) To ensure that appropriate response techniques are employed to prevent, control, and combat oil pollution, and dispose off recovered material in an environmentally accepted manner.

(e) To ensure that complete and accurate records are maintained of all expenditure to facilitate cost of recovery.

(e) The measures to be taken immediately after the bus accident are:

(i) We should start the rescue work immediately and get the help of all those who are available there.

(ii) We should give the first aid to those who are in dangerous condition.

(iii) Inform the nearest ambulance or emergency care or hospital.

iv) Inform the police.

(v) We should take timing actions according to the situation and also coordinate the available resources to save the lives as early as possible.

(f) According to RBI, 35% of Mumbai region in 2000 - 2009, which comprising Maharashtra, Dadar Nagar Haveli and Daman & Diu. The Delhi region comprising UP, Haryana getting 15% cumulatively during the same period. Share of Gujarat, Karnataka, Tamilnadu and Andhra Pradesh is 7%, 7%, 6%, 4% respectively.

Thus, more than 65% of total FDI inflow has been received by these states constituting 41% of the total population. BIMARU states having 40% of the population received as low as 0.67 % of total FDI. North east states received 0.1%. It is very low. Government is taking measures to project the North east states in the upcoming years.

Q. 9 Write brief notes on each of the following, in about 20 words each: 2 × 8 = 16

(a) Contributions of Latika Ghosh to the freedom struggle

(b) Bhai Maharaj Singh as a freedom fighter

(c) Chandrayaan - II

(d) Agni-V

(e) Babli Project

(f) ' Swavajamban' Scheme

(g) National Investment Fund

(h) 'Aerostat'balloon

Answer: (a) She was an Oxford scholar. She set up Mahila Rashtriya Sangha in 1928. She got 300 women in national movement.

(b) Bhai Maharaj Singh, the spiritual leader and Sikh nationalist, took up weapons against the British rule in 1847, he was imprisoned in Outram Jail Singapore where he died.

(c) Chandrayaan-2 is a joint lunar exploration mission proposed by the ISRO and the Russian Federal Space Agency (RKA) and has a projected cost Rs 425 crore, to be launched in 2013 by a GSLV.

(d) The Agni-V is a three stage solid fueled missile with range of about 6000 km. Agni-V will be able to carry multiple warheads and will have counter - measures against Anti- ballistic missile systems.

(e) The Babli project is a barrage being built by Maharashtra across the Godavari River in the Pochampad dam area. It created dispute between Maharashtra and Andhra Pradesh.

(f) Swawlamban (NORAD) Scheme is being implemented by the Department of Women and Child Development, Government of India with partial assistance from Norway since 1982.

(g) It was set up for ploughing of 75 per cent of its income—derived through the disinvestment proceeds of Central Public Sector Enterprises (CPSEs)—for funding social sector projects. The balance 25 per cent is to be utilised for the revival of the ailing PSEs.

(h) Aerostat helium gas Balloon was the star attraction in the Commonwealth Games, Delhi. It is a 70 Crore Rupees Balloon and largest in any games ever used.

Q. 10. Who are the following and why have been in the news recently? (Each answer should not exceed 20 words) **$2 \times 8 = 16$**

(a) Divya Ajithkumar

(b) N.C. Saxena

(c) Islam A. Siddiqui

(d) Swarnalatha Cherukutty

(e) Nitin Nohria

(f) Deepak Mondal

(g) Gaurav Singh Saini

(h) Upendra Limaye

Answer: (a) A 21-year-old youngster from Chennai has written her name in a fresh page of Indian history by becoming the first woman to be conferred by the Army with the coveted 'Sword of Honour'.

(b) In August 2010, a committee headed by him warned that plans by Vedanta Resources to mine on Dongria Kondh land in eastern India threaten the survival of the tribe. This lead to the Indian government refusing clearance to the project.

(c) An Indian American has been appointed as the chief agriculture negotiator of the United States, who would carry out all critical negotiations for the country in the crucial Doha round and other bilateral discussions.

(d) South Indian film playback singer Swarnalatha passed away. She was 37. She won the National Film Award for Best Female Playback Singer.

(e) Nitin Nohria became the tenth dean of Harvard Business School on 1 July 2010. He previously served as co-chair of the Leadership Initiative, Senior Associate Dean of Faculty Development, and Head of the Organizational Behavior unit.

(f) Deepak Mondal received the Arjuna Award in 2010. He became the first footballer in eight years to receive the award.

(g) Thirteen-year-old Gaurav Singh Saini of Haryana has been given the Bharat award for saving more than 60 lives in a stampede at the Naina Devi temple.

(h) Upendra Limaye bagged the best male actor award at the 56th National Film Awards for 2008.

Limaye bagged the top honour for the Marathi feature film Jogva.

SOLVED PAPERS

PAPER–II

Candidates should attempt ALL questions strictly in accordance with the instructions given under each question.

Q. 1 Answer the following in not more than 250 words each: 20 × 2 = 40

(a) Critically examine the implications of the disintegration of the Soviet Union on India's security and strategic perspectives. What further responses would you suggest in India's foreign policy to accommodate these implications?

(b) Evaluate India's approach towards meeting the country's growing energy demands. Compare the success of this approach with that of another Asian giant which has perhaps the fastest growing energy demands.

Important Points for Answer:
- *Impact of USSR disintegration*
- *Changes in Indian foreign policy*
- *Suggestions*

Answer: (a) Soviet Union was one of the two super powers. It disintegrated in 1991 making the world unipolar. India had very good friendship with USSR.

Although India was following non - alignment policy, USSR was a major source of grant and trade. India was almost dependent on USSR for its defence procurement. USSR provided a big amount of financial aid to India.

With USSR's disintegration, India faced a situation where it had to adjust its foreign policy in a new way so as to further its interests.

After 1991, Russia itself tried to improve relations with western powers. It was consolidating its economy. India had to find out new sources after 1991 economic crisis.

Russia had supported Pakistan baked resolution in UN for Nuclear free South Asia. Russia was also of the view that India should sign NPT. It cancelled many defence deals with India under US pressure.

So these changing defence, economic and diplomatic conditions came against India after disintegration of USSR.

Suggestions for India's foreign policy:

- India must not rely on any one country for its defence requirements. We should try to find out new suppliers.
- For balance of power situation in South Asia and Indian Ocean region, we have to improve relations with US and other western powers, rather than relying on Russia.
- On economic front, we have to foster out trade links with major economic powers and blocks.

Important Points for Answer:	
• *Demand*	• *Approach*
• *Compare*	

(b) India is the 2nd largest populated country in the world. It needs huge amount of energy to fulfill the various needs including cooking gas and fuels for the Aeroplanes. Energy plays a vital role in the economic growth. It has a direct influence or impact over the fields of industry, health, education, agriculture, transport, etc.

India's energy policy can be summarised as follows:

(i) Till market matures, regulation across the energy streams is necessity.

(ii) Fixing the price and source allocation to be determined by market forces under an effective and credible regulatory oversight.

(iii) Transparent and targeted subsidies.

iv) Improved efficiencies across the energy chain.

(v) Policies that reflect externalities of energy consumption.

(vi) Giving incentives / disincentives to regulate market and consumer behaviour.

(vii) Management reforms to foster accountability and incentives for efficiency.

The policy shows the view of the Government to meet the demand for energy services of all sectors at competitive prices. And to provide subsidies to the energy needs of the households.

India's per capita electricity consumption is only 615 KWh per year as compared to world average of 2516 KWh and 1585 KWh in China. Despite the fact that India is the sixth largest electricity market in terms of power generation.

India's per capita oil consumption is 530 kg of oil, whereas the world average is 1770 kg of oil. And China's per capita oil is 1240 kg of oil.

These facts shows that we are very much far behind even to the average level of International Standard. We are making civil nuclear agreement with world countries which are rich in this field to establish the Nuclear powered reactors to produce the electricity to meet the demands and also reduce the thermal power plants in order to control the pollution and also considering the availability of Coal.

We have got an exception from the NSG to import the nuclear power technology as well as resources to develop the nuclear power sector, at present it has only 4% in our total production of 1,50,574 mn. As per 31 July 2009, India's power generation is as follows:

1. Thermal - 96,295 MW
2. Hydro - 36,917 MW
3. Renewable energy resources - 13,242 MW
4. Nuclear - 4,120 MW

However, China is presently engaged in a strong effort to control its rising energy use while promoting its rapid growth of its economy.

Both the Asian giants are progressively marching towards their goal of achieving self - sufficiency in energy sector. But China is marching fast on the track. China follows state controlled pricing formula, whereas India follows market controlled pricing formula.

Q. 2 Answer any FOUR of the following in not more than 150 words each: 12 × 4 = 48

(a) How far have Japan's principles of Hikaku San Gensoku impacted bilateral ties with India?

(b) Assess the contributions of Indian Diaspora in the Caribbean.

(c) Do you agree with the view that Israel is a 'natural ally' of India?

(d) Bring out the FDI and employment implications of China being a manufacturing hub and India a services hub?

(e) Have the Uruguay Round negotiations and the resultant Trade Related Intellectual Property Rights (TRIPS) agreement helped in resolving trade conflicts arising out of variations in different nations' IPR regimes? Also list the steps taken by India to conform to TRIPS.

(f) Examine the recent developments towards the solution of the Bangladesh - Myanmar maritime boundary dispute. What implications do these have for India?

Important Points for Answer:
Principles
Impact for India

Answer: (a) In late 1960, Parliament of Japan made a resolution called "Hikaku San Gensoku" also called "Three non-nuclear principles". This is considered as a guiding principle of the Japan's nuclear policy.

The former Prime Minister of Japan Mr Eisaku Sato has outlined the principles as follows:

(i) Japan shall neither possess nor manufacture the nuclear weapons.

(ii) Japan shall not permit their introduction into Japanese territory.

India is one of the major country which needs to fulfill their energy demands. We are making nuclear cooperation agreement with all major nuclear powered countries like USA, France, Russia etc. On this track, Japan also increasing the export of infrastructure technology including nuclear technology. For that they have established International Atomic Energy Development Company with an aim to form a centralised platform to increase Japan's competitiveness to win the nuclear power project contracts in the overseas.

In 2006, Prime Minister Manmohan Singh and then Japan Prime Minister Shinzo Abe signed a joint statement under which Japan made a commitment to India to enhance Civil Nuclear Energy Cooperation under safeguard of IAEA. Due fo India's status in the NPT, Japan acted in a snail speed towards its commitment. Finally, Japan came to negotiation in 2010.

Because of the India's stand on nuclear issue with regard to NPT and IAEA, Japan's anti-nuclear lobbies and the media expressed their concern about the deal and criticized the government for promoting the agreement.

Important Points for Answer:
- *Indians in Caribbean*
- *Their contribution*

(b) The Indian Diaspora in Caribbean countries are mainly descendants of our Indian migrated people. More than 20 lakh Indian Diaspora are living in various Caribbean countries.

They have contributed their performance in all fields including politics, arts and culture, sports, economic and industry.

Indian origins are holding many key post in the Government of various countries such as Former President of Guyana, Bharat Jagdeo, and the current Prime Minister of Trinidad and Tobago Mrs. Kamla Parsad Bissessar. Another Indian origin Mr. Basdeo Pandey had held that post from 1995 to 2001. Mr. Siddharth Ramphal was the Secretary General of the commonwealth twice.

The booker price winner Sir. V. S. Naipal and Samuel Selvon contributed much in the field of literature. Women writers such as Mahadai Das, Rambhai Erpinet and Niala Maharaj have played a vital role in this field.

In terms of sports, some good cricketers of West Indies are of Indian origin such as Ram iVaresh Sarwan, Sfu've iVarme Chancfrapau/, *Dinesh Ramdin and Alvin Kalicharan.* They made good contribution in their field.

Medicine is one of the important sector in which Indian doctors are playing crucial role all over the world especially a noted Cardiologist Dr. Anne Dipchand and Dr. Budhendra Doobey are prominent.

Important Points for Answer:
- *India - Israel Relations*
- *Natural Ally or Not*

(c) India and Israel established their diplomatic relations only in 1992. Earlier India had voted against creation of Israel in UNSCOP in 1947. India also voted against the admission of Israel into UN in May 1949.

But changed circumstances in forty years prompt India to establish diplomatic relations with Israel in 1992. Oslo Accord of 1993 helped more in changing India's attitude towards Israel.

India and Israel have many common things to bring them closer. Both are neighboured by Islamic enemy-like countries. Both suffered by Islamic terrorism. Both are democracies.

India and Israel developed co-operation in science and technology. India turned towards Israel for procurement of arms and military equipments of sophesticated nature specially after collapse of USSR. In satellite technology also both co - operated. All these factors can make India and Israel good friends but not natural ally. Because India has its Non-Alignment Policy and being natural ally requires to abandon the same. Again there is no defence agreement between two countries.

Important Points for Answer:
- *Chinese economy*
- *Indian economy*
- *Impact of FDI in employment*

(d) China and India are the fastest growing economies of the world. Even during the recession time, both countries poised an attractive growth rate. This attracted more FDI in both of them.

Due to reasons of vast resources and huge population in rural area, China has emerged as a manufacturing hub. Labour laws and human rights, salary structure and union activities are at minimal in China supporting manufacturing industries. In India, there is a large mass of educated middle class youth. This developed India as a service sector including BPOs, KPOs, LPOs, and all types of call centres apart from medical and financial services.

According to a hypothesis, per **US $ 100** investment, manufacturing industry generates 8 jobs while service sector generates 43 jobs. High level of mechanization has reduced jobs in manufacturing industries.

This scenario helps India generating more jobs being a service sector with per unit of FDI in comparison to manufacturing hub of China.

Important Points for Answer:

- *IPR*
- *TRIPS*
- *Uruguay Round*
- *India's measures*

(e) IPR Regime covers Intellectual Property Rights protection for original invention. They provide economical protection to original inventor. Different countries have their own laws for IPRs. Developing and poor countries have not developed a strong mechanism in IPR. IPR violations are maximum there.

Developed countries demanded a strong IPR regime to protect their interest. Big MNCs and corporate houses can register an invention and will get exclusive right of marketing.

During Uruguay Round of GATTS, negotiations were held on TRIPS. TRIPS protected Intellectual Property Rights and demanded strengthening of IPR laws in developing countries. During the negotiations developing countries were put under pressure to accept a very liberal definition of IPR resulting into their disadvantage.

India, a member of WTO has amended its IPR related laws so as to conform to TRIPS. India had "process patent" and now it started moving towards "product patent". India is registering own patents on traditional knowledge and inventions.

Important Points for Answer:

- *Dispute*
- *Solution*
- *Reason*
- *Impact on India*

(f) Dispute between Bangladesh and Myanmar started in 2008 when Myanmar started lifting of mineral resources from a disputed block in Bay of Bengal. The block is disputed because there is no proper demarcation of maritime boundary between the two nations. Forces faced each other in Bay of Bengal but tension was solved by diplomatic efforts.

Both countries tried to demarcate border in 2008, after a gap of 22 years, but failed. Bangladesh raised the issue at Arbitration Tribunal of the UN in October 2009.

Now in 2010 both countries agreed to settle their maritime boundary according the principle of equi-distance. The area is rich in minerals and so tension occurred. The dispute has obvious impact on Indian security and peace. The solution is a boost to India's concern for energy security. Once both countries settle their differences and start exploring oil and gas, India can look forward for cheap oil and gas from in neighbours.

Q. 3 Answer any EIGHT of the following in not more than 50 words each: 5 × 8 = 40|

(a) Compare and contrast the role of the IMF with that of the World Bank.

(b) What are the major capacity-building and reconstruction projects being undertaken by India in Afghanistan?

(c) Bring out the significance of GDI and GEM as components of the UN's Human! Development Report (HDR). Comment on India's relative rankings with regard to HDI and GDI.

(d) What is 'Round Tripping' in the context of FDI inflow, and why has it been in the! news recently in the case of India?

(e) Comment on the reason for the recent hike in visa processing fees for certain categories of US visas. What is the likely impact of this hike on India?

(f) In the context of the United Nations Framework Convention on Climate Change (UNFCCC), distinguish between 'Annex I' and 'Annex II' countries.

(g) Highlight the role of the Indian peacekeeping contingent as part of MONUSCO.

(h) List the salient features of the Riyadh declaration and the bilateral agreements between India and Saudi Arabia signed earlier this year.

(i) Comment on the reasons for the recent economic crisis in the so-called 'PIGS' countries of Europe.

Answer: (a) IMF is a European based institution that is primarily engaged in regulating the International movement of currencies depending upon the exchange value of nation's currency. It is also engaged in export and import facilitation among nations.

The US based World Bank (IBRD) is more developmental financial institution that is engaged in creating more infrastructures among the nations particularly the emerging and least developed nations. It gives more grants or money on easy terms and conditions for the developmental and reconstruction works.

(b) In Afghanistan, India is helping in rebuilding the air link, providing humanitarian assistance which includes sending doctors, medicine, and investing in health and education, setting up of child care hospital in capital Kabul.

It also provides foodgrains including 2,50,000 mts of wheat and other grains and constructing the Zaranj-Delaram highway which will help immensely in promoting the transport and economic activities. India constructed the Salma dam project and 220 KV transmission line from Pul-e-khumri to Kabul. Also India providing training to Afghan police and military in India. It gives training to Afghan civil servants also.

(c) The Human Development Report 1995 has introduced two new measures of human development that especially highlighted the status of women

(i) Gender related Development Index (GDI)

(ii) Gender Empowerment Measure (GEM)

The GDI measures achievement in the same basic capabilities as the HDI does but it considers the inequality in achievement between women and men.

The GEM is a measure of agency. It evaluates progress in advancing women's standing in political and economic forums. It examines the equality of men and women in economic, political and decision making activities.

India's ranking is 139 as compared to general HDI which is 134 for the year that ended. India is thus relatively more of political empowerment due to legislative provision that makes India farely well placed in GEM ranking.

(d) Round - tripping is a money laundering technique. It is also known as round-trip transactions or "Lazy susans". The method, involves a company selling an unused asset to another company while at the same time agreeing to buy back the same or similar assets at about a same price. Simply we can say this as a money laundering technique.

Indian Government and RBI have introduced the PN (Participatory Note) mechanism of FII regime which has given a fillip to this practice of round tripping. In fact, Government and RBI support this PN and do not want to disclose the information about the investors. It results in such a way to this practice of round - tripping.

(e) India is the third largest immigration labour provider to US after Mexico and China is badly hit by these measures taken by the US including hike the H1B visa processing fees from 25% to 200%.

Since more than two-third of India's GDP comes from service sector majority of which comes from the software companies and the employees remittances bulges the nations forex reserves, all these are adversly affected. Now the situation is returning to normal condition but it will take sometime to back on track.

(f) In the UNFCC, the world countries has been classified as:

(i) Industrialised countries and countries in transition as Annex 1 countries. (There are 40 countries in Annex I)

(ii) Developed countries, which pay for costs of developing countries as Annex II countries. (There are 23 countries in Annex II)

The UNFCCC's prime object was to establish National greenhouse gas inventories of greenhouse gas (GHG) emissions and removals, which were used to create 1990 bench mark levels for accession of Annex I countries to the Kyoto Protocol and for the commitment of those countries to GHG reduction. The updated inventories must be submitted to Annex I countries regularly.

(g) In May 2010, the UNSC, adopting Resolution and announced that MONUC would renamed from July 1, 2010 to the United Nations Organisation Stabilisation Mission in the Democratic Republic of the Congo (MONUSCO).

India also has sent its troops as a part of the UN peace-keeping force in Congo (MONUSCO). Over 3,500 soldiers from various countries have been deployed in Congo to monitor the peace process of second Congo war, though much of its focus subsequently turned to the Ituri conflict, the Kivu conflict and the Dongo conflict.

(h) After Delhi Declaration in 2006, India and Saudi Arabia has moved to the next stage in their friendly relationship.

Our Prime Minister's visit to Saudi Arabia has brought some fruitful results in the relationship with the oil rich nation in the Gulf.

The Riyadh Declaration—a new era of strategic partnership was signed by Prime Minister Manmohan Singh and Saudi Arabia's king Abdulla Bin Abdul Aziz on March 1, 2010 in Riyadh.

We can summarise the declaration as follows:

(i) Both the countries reiterated their mutual desire to develop as knowledge - based economies based on advances in the areas of IT, space science and other technologies.

(ii) As per the New Declaration, the two leaders decided to raise their co-operation to a strategic partnership covering security, economic defence and political areas.

(iii) The two countries agreed to enhance cooperation in exchange of information relating to terrorist activities, money laundering, narcotics, arms and human trafficking and develop joint strategies to combat these threats.

(i) The crisis in Portugal, Italy, Greece and Spain collectively called PIGS threatened the Eurozone.

The root cause of this crisis was the sudden rise of the scale of deficit finance of each government triggered by increased government spending in order to settle down global financial crisis. Greece, one of the member of PIGS, was the economic centre of this crisis.

The ratio of deficit finance VGDP increased.

Increase in national debt over 11% versus GDP simultaneously this triggered the drastic surge of Credit Default Swap (CDS), which leads to sovereign risk.

Q. 4 Answer any TWO of the following in not more than 150 words each: $12 \times 2 = 24$

(a) Examine the opportunities for a lasting West Asia peace solution in the context of the 'historic' talks started in September 2010.

(b) Has the February agreement between the Sudanese government and the Justice and Equality Movement (JEM) been more successful in ending the strife in Darfur than the Abuja peace agreement of 2006? Evaluate.

(c) Comment on the present status of the Biological Weapons Convention (BWC). What important issues, do you think, need to be taken up at the seventh review conference of the BWC scheduled for 2011?

Important Points for Answer:

- *West Asia*
- *Effect*
- *September talk*

Answer: (a) In September 2010, leaders from Israel and Palestine started direct talk in Washington, hosted by US. This was after a 20 months halt in dialogue. The talk aimed at resolving all final status issues between the parties.

US President Obama noted objective of the talk at Palestine and Israel living side by side in peace and security. This talk has surely increase chances of a durable peace in this region.

The talk involved issues of Palestinian refugees, guaranteeing Israel security, sharing of Jerusalem and adjusting the border.

However, there cannot be a long lasting peace in West Asia till some issues are solved successfully. One among them is solution of ongoing hostility between Israel and Palestine, which claims lives of hundreds of civilians frequently. Second issue is that Israel must extend the partial moratorium on construction of settlements in the occupied West Bank. Thirdly, Hamas should restraint from aggressive policies. Fourth important point is that Hamas should be involved in peace process.

Important Points for Answer:
- *Problems in Sudan*
- *Abuja Peace Agreement*
- *February Agreement*
- *Conclusion*

(b) Sudan is facing problems of civil war, especially in Darfur region. War is between Government backed Janjaweeds and four tribal rebel groups. Main tribal group is Justice and Equality Movement (JEM).

Abuja Peace Agreement was signed on 5th May between Government of Sudan and Sudanese Liberation Movement. Two rebel groups refused to sign the agreement. It was agreed that UN Peacekeeping Forces would replace AU forces. It also required disarming of Janjaweeds.

However, this agreement is not followed. AU Forces continue in Sudan and UN Forces are yet not allowed. Neither Janjaweeds have been disarmed.

Recently, Doha agreement was signed in February, 2006. This agreement continues discussion. It involves power-sharing, prisoner amnesty and integration of rebel groups in the Sudanese army.

However, success depends on consensus among rebel groups. It has better chances to succeed as all rebel groups are involved.

Important Points for Answer:
- *BWC*
- *Important issues*
- *Review Conference*

(a) Biological Weapon Convention was opened for signature on April 10, 1972 but it was entered into force on March 26, 1975. It is a Biological Weapon Disarmament Convention. It currently commits 163 states signatory and non-signatories that are partly to it, to prohibit the development, production and stock piling of Biological and toxin weapons.

It is fostering collaboration between bio security stake holders.

To strengthen this convention, subsequent review conferences have reaffirmed that general purpose of future collaboration, scientific and technological developments have been done.

- To enhance the confidence and promote co-operation among states, not to use and store pathogenic organism and toxins.
- Submitting annually confidence building measures to UN (2nd review conference).
- To establish a group of government expert known as VEREX.

Allowing state parties to lodge a complaint with UN Security Council, if they suspect other member states are violating the convention. Although there are some violative countries as Russia, Iraq, Syria, China, North Korea.

Although absence of any formal verification regime to monitor compliance has limited, the effectiveness of convention and rejection of ad hoc group protocol by US concerning national security leads to some loosening of the convention.

Important issues to be taken up at Seventh Review Conference:

- Co-operation on verification system.
- Enhancing international responding capability investigating and mitigating the fact.
- National mechanism to establish and maintain the security and oversight of pathogenic organism and toxins.
- Co - operation on exchange information and data.
- Member states should add measures to declare legislation, regulation and other measures.

Q. 5 Answer any FOUR of the following in not more than 150 words each: 12 × 4 = 48

(a) Bring out the applications of computer models in studying climate changes, with special reference to the Community Earth System Model (CESM).

(b) What is phytoremediation? Discuss its applications.

(c) Explain and differentiate among 'Plasma', 'LCD' and 'LED' television technologies.

(d) What is 'cloud computing'? Bring out its essential features and list its advantages and limitations.

(e) Discuss the applications of nanotechnology in the health care sector.

Important Points for Answer:
- *CESM*
- *Applications*

Answer: (a) To study the dynamics of climate system CESM (Community Earth System Model) is a fully coupled, global climate model that provides state of the art computer simulations of earth's past, present and future climate states. Its process is used by IPCC. It is made by National Centre for Atomic Research.

It represents the pinnacle of complexity in climate models and internalise as many process as possible with detailed regional predictions.

CESM will help to find with great precision to some specific questions like:

1. What impact warming temperatures have on the massive ice sheets of green land and Antarctica?
2. How might climate change influence the severity and frequency of tropical cyclones, including hurricanes?
3. Effects of aerosols on clouds and temperatures.
4. How might platform in the ocean and atmosphere affect regional climate in coming decades?

Important Points for Answer:
- *Phytoremediation*
- *Applications*

(b) Phytoremediation describes the treatment of environmental problems (bioremediation) through the use of plants that mitigate the environmental problem without the need to excavate the contaminant material and dispose it elsewhere.

Applications: Phytoremediation may be applied wherever the soil or static water environment has become polluted or is suffering ongoing chronic pollution. Examples where phytoremediation has been used successfully include the restoration of abandoned metal-mine workings, reducing the impact of sites where polychlorinated biphenyl have been dumped during manufacture and mitigation of on-going coal mine discharges.

Phytoremediation refers to the natural ability of certain plants called hyperaccumulators to bioaccumulate, degrade,or render harmless contaminants in soils, water or air. Contaminants such as metals, pesticides, solvents, explosives, and crude oil and its derivatives, have been mitigated in phytoremediation projects worldwide.

Phytoremediation is considered a clean, cost-effective and non-environmentally disruptive technology, as opposed to mechanical cleanup methods such as soil excavation or pumping polluted groundwater. Over the past 20 years, this technology has become increasingly popular and has been employed at sites with soils contaminated with lead, uranium, and arsenic.

Important Points for Answer:
- *Plasma TV*
- *LCD*
- *LED TV*

(c) Plasma TV: These are called Plasma TV because pixels rely on plasma cells or fluorescence chambers. Plasma cells get activated when electricity is passed to TV.

Plasma TV's display is bright. These have low luminance "dark room" black level compared to the light grey of the unluminised parts of LCD display.

Although power consumption varies with picture content with bright scenes drawing significant more power than darker one.

Plasma TV is having wider viewing angle.

Less susceptible to reflection glare in bright room with superior performance.

Plasma TVs are heavy in weight and big in size comparatively these are very susceptible to screen burn in.

LCD: It means Liquid Crystal Display. It produces a black and coloured image by selectively filtering white light.

Light is typically provided by a series of cold cathode flourescent lamps (CCFL) at back screen.

LCD are inefficient relatively in terms of power use per display size.

The accuracy and quality of the resulting colours depends on the back light sources.

LED: These are LED TVs that use LED BACKLIGHT rather than the CCFL.

LED BACKLIGHT leads to dramatic impact resulting in thinner panel, less power consumption and heat dissipation.

It is having bright display with better contrast level.

It is having wide colour capacity. It is less environmental pollutant on disposal.

Important Points for Answer:

- *Cloud - computing - what is it?*
- *Its applications*
- *Advantages*
- *Limitations*

(d) Cloud computing is Internet-based computing, whereby shared servers provide resources, software, and data to computers and other devices on demand, as with the electricity grid. Cloud computing is a natural evolution of the widespread adoption of virtualization, service-oriented architecture and utility computing. Details are abstracted from consumers, who no longer have need for expertise in, or control over, the technology infrastructure "in the cloud" that supports them.

Advantages: Reduced Cost—It is paid incrementally, saving organization's money.

- Increased storage—can store more data on private computer.
- Highly automated—No need to keep software updated manually.
- Flexibility
- Mobility - Information can be accessed anywhere.

Limitations:

- Security—It uses the power of online connectivity to handle processing request. Data can be used by unwanted persons.

- End-user connectivity - Strong internet connection is required, may not work with weak connection.
- Infrastructure is again a challenge when a company opts for its own server.

Important Points for Answer:
- *Nanotechnology in health sector*

(e) Nanotechnology has the potential to completely change the health care sector for next generation. As a matter of fact, nanotechnology may bring an ongoing revolution in health care.

Nanotechnology will help medical professionals in today's most excruciating medical issues, such as repairation of damaged organs, diagnosis and treatment of cancer cells, removal of obstruction in brain and it can help in better drug delivery system.

Nanotechnology can be used for both in vivo and in vitro biomedical research and applications. Nano particles can be used in targeting tumour cells at initial stage. Particles like dentrine, quantandofs and fallevene.

- Antimicrobial coating to stop microbial infection.
- Use of "signature protein" to treat cancer.
- Nanotechnology can help in design certain drugs that are difficult to make because of their structural constraints by controlled manufacturing system at the molecular level.

Q. 6 Comment on any THREE of the following in not more than 50 words each: 5 × 3 = 15

(a) Rotterdam Convention

(b) The Mavi Marmara incident

(c) Significance of the Kampala declaration of the International Criminal Court (ICC)

(d) Trial chamber of the Extraordinary Chambers in the Courts of Cambodia (ECCC) and its recent verdict.

Answer: (a) Rotterdam Convention, is a multilateral treaty to promote shared responsibilities in relation to importation of hazardous chemicals.

The convention promotes open exchange of information and calls on exporters of hazardous chemicals to use proper labeling, include directions on safe handling, and inform purchasers of any known restrictions or bans.

Parties can decide whether to allow or ban the importation of chemicals listed in the treaty, and exporting countries are obliged to make sure that producers within their jurisdiction comply.

(b) On the MV Mavi Marmara, clashes broke out after activists violently resisted the Israeli forces. Nine activists were killed (Eight Turkish nationals and one Turkish - American), and dozens of activists and seven Israeli commandos were wounded. Widespread international condemnation followed, Israel-Turkey relations were strained, and Israel subsequently eased its blockade.

The Gaza flotilla raid was a military interception by Israel against six ships of the "Gaza Freedom Flotilla" on May 31, 2010.

(c) Significance of the Kampala declaration of the International Criminal Court (ICC): The Review Conference of ICC concluded its general debate on 1 June, 2010. The Conference adopted the Kampala Declaration which deals mainly with the reaffirmation of the commitment of States to the Rome Statute and its full implementation, as well as its universality and integrity. States also decided to henceforth celebrate 17 July, the day of the adoption of the Rome Statute in 1998, as the Day of International Criminal Justice.

(d) The Trial Chamber of the Extraordinary Chambers in the Courts of Cambodia (ECCC) recently found KAING Guek Eav alias Duch guilty of crimes against humanity and grave breaches of the Geneva Conventions of 1949 and sentenced him to 35 (thirty-five) years of imprisonment.

The substantive part of the trial against KAING Guek Eav commenced on 30 March 2009. Closing arguments ended on 27 November 2009 after a total of 72 trial days, during which 24 witnesses, 22 Civil Parties and nine experts were heard.

Q. 7 Comment on any SIX of the following in not more than 50 words each: 5 × 6 = 30

- **(a) MRSA infection**
- **(b) HRP-2M Choromet**
- **(c) Maglev vehicles**
- **(d) Super absorbent polymers (SAP)**
- **(e) Ginkgo biloba**
- **(f) CARTOSAT-2B**
- **(g) Various generations of mobile phone technology**

Answer: **(a)** Methicillin-resistant Staphylococcus aureus (MRSA) is a bacterium responsible for several difficult-to-treat infections in humans. It may also be called multi drug- resistant Staphylococcus aureus or oxacillin - resistant Staphylococcus aureus (ORSA).

MRSA is, by definition, any strain of Staphylococcus aureus bacteria that has developed resistance to beta-lactam antibiotics which include thepenicillins (methicillin, dicloxacillin, nafcillin, oxacillin, etc.) and the cephalosporins.

(b) HRP - 2M Choromet is a 35 cm tall, $1\frac{1}{2}$ pound humanoid robot which is, in a sense, the younger brother of HRP-2. It runs on ART - Linux which is a hard real time linux developed at the National Institute of Advanced Industrial Science and Technology in Japan. Choromet's CPU is an SH - 4 which runs at 240 MHz and has 32 MB of Random access memory and 32 MB of Flash ROM.

Choromet was developed in partnership between General Robotix, Inc. and Moving Eye, Inc., Pirkus Robotics and Dai Nippon Technical Research Institute.

(c) Maglev (derived from magnetic levitation), is a system of transportation that suspends, guides and propels vehicles, predominantly trains, using magnetic levitation from a very large number of magnets for lift and propulsion. The highest recorded speed of a Maglev train is 581 kilometres per hour (361 mph), achieved in Japan in 2003, only 6 kilometres per hour (3.7 mph) faster than the conventional TGV wheel-rail speed record.

(d) Superabsorbent polymers (SAP) (also called slush powder) are polymers that can absorb and retain extremely large amounts of a liquid relative to their own mass.

A SAP's ability to absorb water is a factor of the ionic concentration of the aqueous solution. In deionized and distilled water, a SAP may absorb 500 times its weight (from 30-60 times its own volume), but when put into a 0.9% saline solution, the absorbency drops to maybe 50 times its weight.

(e) Ginkgo (Ginkgo bilcba; in Chinese and Japanese) known as the Maidenhair Tree, is a unique species of tree with no close living relatives. The tree is widely cultivated and introduced, since an early period in human history, and has various uses as a food and traditional medicine.

(f) CARTOSAT - 2B: CARTOSAT 2B is an Earth observation satellite in a sun-synchronous orbit. The satellite is the seventeenth satellite in the Indian Remote Sensing (IRS) satellite series to be built by the Indian Space Research Organisation.

The satellite carries a panchromatic (PAN) camera capable of taking black-and- white pictures in the visible region of electromagnetic spectrum.

(g) Various generations of mobile phone technology:

OG - Pre - cellular mobile telephony technology in 1970s.

OSG - Improved features of 0G.

1G - First Generation of Wireless Telephone Technology of 1980s.

2G - Provided SMS facilities.

3G - Includes broad band services and multi - media communication.

4G - High speed communication including TV services.

Q. 8 Who / What are the following and why have they been in the news recently? (Your answers should be in a sentence or two only): $3 \times 8 = 24$

(a) Craig Venter

(b) Shahran Amiri

(c) Wolfram Alpha

(d) 'Dreamliner' aircraft

(e) Blue gene project

(f) 'Predator' drones

(g) 'Deepwater Horizon' incident

(h) ACTN 3 gene

Answer: (a) John Craig Venter is an American biologist and entrepreneur, most famous for his role in being one of the first to sequence the human genome and for his role in creating the first cell with a synthetic genome in 2010.

(b) Shahram Amiri is an Iranian nuclear scientist who disappeared during an apparent umrah pilgrimage to Mecca, Saudi Arabia in either May or June 2009. The Iranian government accused the US government of kidnapping him.

(c) Wolfram Alpha is an answer engine developed by Wolfram Research. It was released to the public on May 15, 2009. It was voted the greatest computer innovation of 2009 by Popular Science.

(d) The Boeing 787 Dreamliner is a long range, mid - sized, wide - body, twin - engine jet airliner developed by Boeing Commercial Airplanes. It seats 210 to 330 passengers.

(e) Blue Gene is a computer architecture project to produce several supercomputers, designed to reach operating speeds in the PFLOPS (peta FLOPS) range, and currently reaching sustained speeds of nearly 500 TFLOPS (tera FLOPS).

(f) The General Atomics MQ-1 Predator is an unmanned aerial vehicle (UAV) used primarily by the United States Air Force (USAF) and Central Intelligence Agency (CIA). It carries cameras and other sensors.

(g) The Deepwater Horizon oil spill is an oil spill in the Gulf of Mexico which flowed for three months in 2010. It is the largest accidental marine oil spill in the history of the petroleum industry.

(h) Alpha - actinin - 3, also known as alpha-actinin skeletal muscle isoform 3 or F-actin cross-linking protein, is a protein that in humans is encoded by the ACTN3 gene. This gene expression is limited to skeletal muscle.

Q. 9 (a) The distribution of rent of 150 residential houses surveyed in a locality is as follows:

Rent in Rs.	Number of Houses
101-150	10
151-200	18
201-250	27
251-300	35
301-350	30
351-400	16
401-450	8
451-500	6

Find %

(i) The percentage of houses having rent higher than ₹ 300.

(ii) The percentage of houses having rent more than ₹ 250 but less than ₹ 401. 5

(b) Work out the trend values by any suitable method from the following data showing the number of murders (in thousand) in a country for the years 1985-1995. 5

Year	**1985**	**1986**	**1987**	**1988**	**1989**	**1990**
Murders	19.0	20.6	20.1	20.7	21.5	24.7
Year	1991	1992	1993	1994	1995	
Murders	24.7	23.8	24.5	23.3	21.6	

(c) The data on the total investment on different heads under the eighth five year plan are shown below:

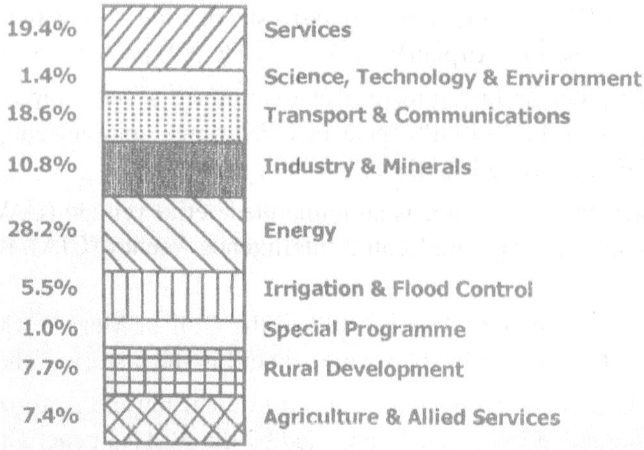

If the total proposed outlay on different heads is ₹ 4,34,100 crores at 1991-92 prices, obtain separately the proposed outlay on each of the heads and make an overall comment. 4

(d) Represent the following data through a suitable diagram:

Region	'A'	'B'	C'	D'
Married Criminals	95	80	63	32
Unmarried Criminals	72	25	41	26

Answer: (a)

(i) Percentage of houses having rent higher than Rs. 300

$$= \frac{\text{Number of houses having rent higher than Rs. 300}}{\text{Total number of houses}} \times 100$$

$$= \frac{30+16+8+6}{150} \times 100 = \frac{60}{150} \times 100 = 40\%$$

(ii) Percentage of houses having rent higher than Rs. 250 but less than Rs. 401

$$= \frac{\text{Number of houses having rent more than Rs. 250 but less than Rs. 401}}{\text{Total number of houses}} \times 100$$

$$= \frac{35+30+16}{150} \times 100 = \frac{81}{150} \times 100 = 54\%$$

(b) Various methods of trend-line:

1. Free hand method
2. Semi - Average method
3. Moving Average method
4. Method of Least Squares

We will use semi - average method for trend - line.

Here, total years given are: 1985 to 1995

We can divide them into two groups: 1) 1985 to 1990, 2) 1990 to 1995

$$\text{Average murders during 1985 to 1990} = \frac{19.0 + 20.6 + 20.1 + 20.7 + 21.5 + 24.7}{6} = 21.1$$

$$\text{Average murders during 1990 to 1995} = \frac{24.7 + 24.7 + 23.8 + 24.5 + 23.3 + 21.6}{6} = 23.8$$

Trend Line

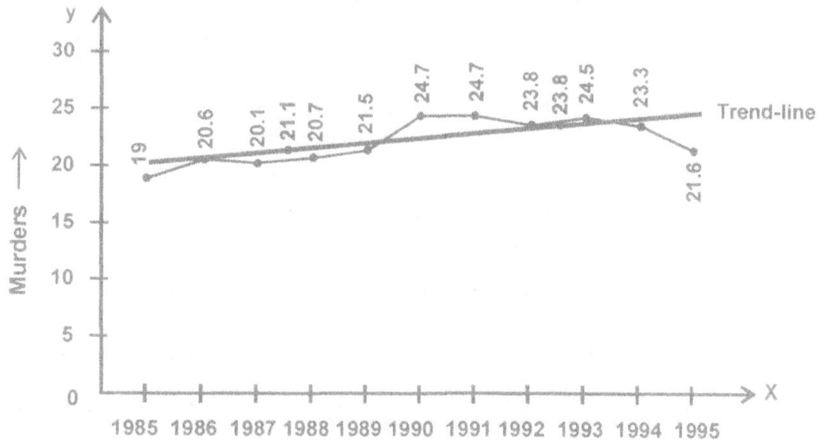

Years →

Mid point of year group 1985 – 1990 is 1987 – 1988

Average = 21.1

Mid point of year 1990-95 is 1992 – 93

Average = 23.8

(c) Total outlay = 4, 34, 100 cr.

Agri. & allied services = 4341 × 7.7 = 32132.4 cr.

Rural Development = 4341 × 1.0 = 4341.0 cr.

Irrigation and Flood control = 4341 × 5.5 = 23875.5 cr.

Energy = 4341 × 28.2 = 122416.2 cr.

Industry and minerals = 4341 × 10.8 = 46882.8 cr.

Transport and communication = 4341 × 18.6 = 80742.6 cr.

Science, Tech and Environment = 4341 × 1.4 = 6077.4 cr.

Services = 4341 × 19.4 = 84215.4 cr.

(d) Number of Married and Unmarried Criminals

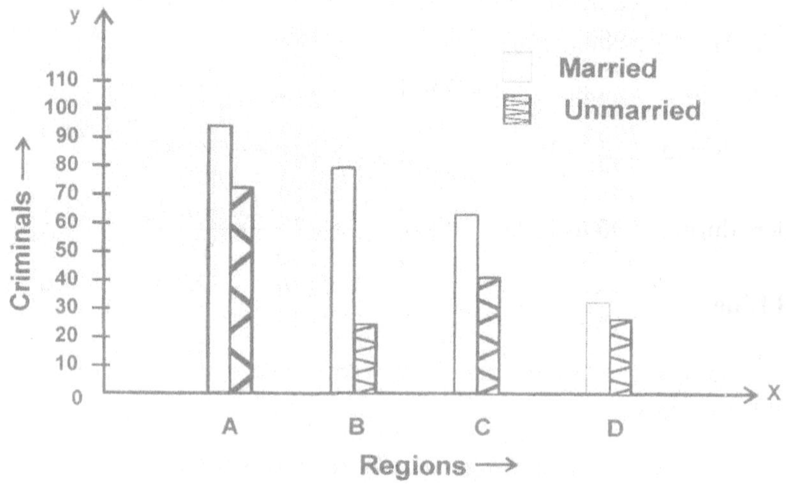

Q. 10 (a) Data on flight arrivals from several cities for two airlines are shown below for the last six months. **5**

Table: Citywise "ontime and delayed flights" for airlines A and B

Airline A

	Ontime	Delayed
City I	497	62
City II	221	12
City III	212	20
City IV	503	102
City V	1841	305

Airline B

	Ontime	Delayed
City I	694	117
City II	4840	415
City III	383	65
City IV	320	129
City V	201	61

It is known that City II was mostly sunny and City V was mostly foggy during the six month period of data collection. Compare the performance of the two airlines A and B over the cities in terms of percentage of delayed flights. What is your conclusion when the data on all the cities are combined.

(b) The arithmetic mean of two observations is 127.5 and their geometric mean is 60. Find (i) the two observations and (ii) their harmonic mean. **3**

(c) The following table shows the number of bushels of wheat and corn produced in a farm during the years 1950-1960.

Express the yearly number of bushels of wheat and corn as percentages of total annual production. Graph the percentages by suitable bar charts and comment. **4**

Year	No. of bushels of wheat	No. of bushels of corn
1950	200	75
1951	185	90
1952	225	100
1953	250	85
1954	240-	80
1955	195	100
1956	210	110
1957	225	105
1958	250	95
1959	230	110
1960	235	100

(d) Following are the maximum daily temperature (°C) recorded in a week in a particular city:

38, 40, 36, 35, 30, 32, 34

During that week the average maximum daily temperature in another city was 92°F. Determine which city on the average, has higher maximum daily temperature during that week. 2

Answer: (a) Citywise "ontime and delayed flights" in % age

City	Airline A		Airline B	
	Ontime	Delayed	Ontime	Delayed
I	88.91	11.01	85.57	14.43
n	94.85	5.15	92.10	7.90
HI	91.38	8.62	85.49	14.51
IV	83.14	16.86	71.27	28.73
V	85.79	14.21	76.72	23.28

Conclusions:

- City II witnessed maximum Ontime flights of both airlines.
- City IV witnessed maximum Delayed flights of both airlines.
- Airline A performed better than Airline B in all cities.
- Performance of both airlines is better in City I, not being sunny city.

(b) Guess that two observations are × and y.

Arithmetic mean = (x + y) / 2

127.5 = (x + y)/2

x + y = 255......................(1)

Geometric mean = $\sqrt{x \times y}$

$$60 = \sqrt{x \times y}$$

$$x \times y = 3600 \ldots\ldots\ldots\ldots\ldots(2)$$

Now, we have value of (x + y) and (x × y), we can put them in

$$(x - y)^2 = x^2 - 2xy + y^2$$
$$= (x + y)^2 - 4xy$$
$$= (255)^2 - 4(3600)$$
$$= 65025 - 14400 = 50625$$
$$(x - y) = \sqrt{50625} - 225 \quad \ldots\ldots\ldots\ldots(3)$$

Adding (1) and (2), we get

$$(x + y) + (x - y) = 255 + 225$$
$$2x = 480$$
$$x = 240 \text{ and } y = 15$$

(i) Both observations: x = 240, y = 15

(ii) Harmonic mean $= \dfrac{2xy}{x+y} = \dfrac{2 \times 240 \times 15}{240 + 15} = \dfrac{7200}{255} = 28.23$ (approx.)

(c) Yearly Number of bushels in %

Year	**Bushels of Wheat**		**Bushels of Corn**	
	Number	**%**	**Number**	**%**
1950	200	72.73	75	27.27
1951	185	67.27	90	32.73
1952	225	69.23	100	30.77
1953	250	74.63	83	25.37
1954	240	75.00	80	25.00
1955	195	66.10	100	33.90
1956	210	65.63	110	34.37
1957	225	68.18	105	31.82
1958	250	72.46	95	27.54
1959	230	67.65	110	32.35
1960	235	70.15	100	29.85

Multiple Bar Diagram

Yearly Production of Wheat and Corn as %age of Total Production

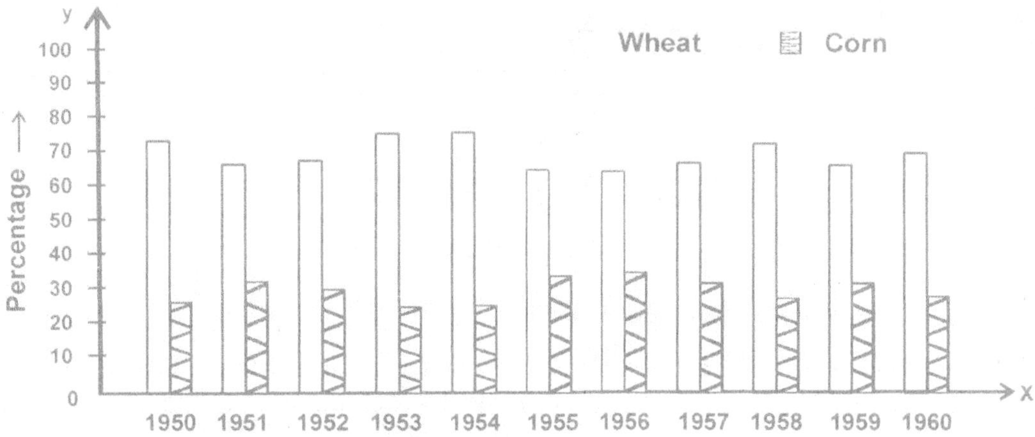

Years →

(d) Average daily maximum temperature for the week

$$= \frac{38 + 40 + 36 + 35 + 30 + 32 + 34}{7} = 35°C$$

Another city average daily max. temperature of the week = 92° F

$$= (92 - 32) / 1.8 = 33.33°C$$

So, first city has higher maximum daily temperature during that week.

(MAIN) **Civil Services Exam.**

2011 General Studies

SOLVED PAPERS

PAPER–I

Time Allowed: Three Hours *Maximum Marks: 300*

Candidates should attempt ALL questions strictly in accordance with the instructions given under each question. The number of marks carried by each question is indicated at the end of the question.

Q. 1 Answer any three of the following in about 250 words each: 20 × 3 = 60

(a) 'Essentially all that is contained in Part IV - A of the Constitution is just a codification of tasks integral to the Indian way of life.' Critically examine this statement.

(b) 'The exercise of executive clemency is not a privilege but is based on several principles, and discretion has to be exercised in public considerations.' Analyse this statement in the context of the judicial powers of the President of India.

(c) Discuss the extent, causes, and implications of the 'nutrition transition' said to be underway in India.

(e) Bring out the salient features of the PCPNDT Act, 1994, and the implications of its amendment in 2003.

Important Points for Answer:
- *Part IV A of the constitution*
- *Legal effect*
- *Repository of Indian social values*

Answer: (a) The fundamental duties of citizens were added by the 42nd Amendment Act in 1976 on the recommendation of Swaran Singh Committee. The ten fundamental duties which were given in Article 51A of the Constitution can be classified as either duties towards Self, duties concerning the Environment, duties towards the State and duties towards the Nation.

This was inserted into the Constitution to make the fundamental rights more meaningful. In fact, there can be no rights in a society where there are no duties. Almost every religion emphasized the concept of duties and all the religion has imposed several moral duties on its followers. Failure to perform such duties resulted in sin for which there was punishment in another world.

The Hindu jurisprudence has emphasized the concept of duty in the form of command of the god. Everyone has to perform the religious duties in his life time as per the law of the religion.

The Fundamental Duties are not enforceable in court of law. But now this trend has been changing by various judicial decisions of the Supreme Court. Though they are not enforceable but they can be used while interpreting the fundamental rights and directive principles of state policy for the welfare of the state and people.

They lack judicial effect but their constitutional and moral impact is effective in inspiring some legislative actions. Therefore, they are truly codification integral to the Indian way of life, but effective and inspiring codification.

Important Points for Answer:

- *Power to Pardon (Clemency)*
- *Discretionary ?*
- *Judicial cases*
- *How to use the Power*
- *Guiding Principles*

(b) In the popular Government as well as monarchies it is considered prudent to vest in the executive authority the power to ameliorate or avoid particular criminal judgements. Article 72 of the Constitution gives the President the power to grant *pardons, reprieves, respite or remission of punishment and to suspend, remit or commute, the sentence of any person convicted of any offence.* The power is available where:

The punishment is by a court Martial;

The punishment is for an offence against any law relating to a matter to which the executive power of the Union extends; and in all cases where a person is sentences to death.

This power like all other powers is exercised by the President on the advice of the Council of Ministers.

The object of conferring such power on the Constitutional Head is to keep the door open to correct judicial errors and to provide relief from undue harshness or evident mistake in the operation of law.

Judges are after all human beings and are likely to commit mistakes. In *Kehar Singh* case *(Kehar Singh v. Union of India,* A.I.R. 1989. S.C. 653), the Supreme Court examined the Presidential power to grant pardon and laid down following principles:

The petitioner who seeks pardon from the President has no right to an oral hearing by the President. There is no need for the Court to lay down specific guidelines for the exercise of power under Art. 72.

The power is to be exercised on the advice of the Central Government.

It is open to President to scrutinize the evidence on record and take a view different from the view taken by the court.

The exercise of the power by the President is not subject to judicial review.

The President is not bound to give reasons for his order.

Judicial Review of the Pardon

Judicial review of the order of the President or Governor under Art. 12 or Art. 161 is available on the following grounds:

(a) that the order has been passed without application of mind.

(b) that the order is *mala fide.*

(c) that the order is based on extraneous or wholly irrelevant considerations.

(d) that relevant material has been kept out of consideration.

(e) that the order suffers from arbitrariness.

A person was granted pardon on the ground that he was a "good congress worker" and implicated and false witnesses were produced. The court held that irrelevant and extraneous materials entered into the decision. The decision was vitiated. The order granting pardon was set aside (*Epuru Sudhankar v. Govt, of A.P., 2006 (10) SCALE 98).*

Important Points for Answer:	
• *What is Nutrition Transition*	• *Extent*
• *Causes*	• *Impact*

(c) Increased consumption of unhealthy foods compounded with increased prevalence of overweight in middle-to-low-income countries is typically referred to as the "**Nutrition Transition**." It occurs in conjunction to the Epidemiological Transition and has serious implications in terms of public health outcomes, risk factors, economic growth and international nutrition policy.

According to the World Health Organization's global database, India has a preschool childhood obesity prevalence of about 1%. Repeated episodes of malnutrition, followed by nutritional rehabilitation, are known to alter body composition and increase the risk of obesity.

Rapid quantitative changes in dietary intake in developing countries indicate an increase in per capita availability of food and are also accompanied by qualitative changes in the diet. Food balance data from the Food and Agriculture Organization (FAO) of India show that higher - income groups consumed a diet with 32% of the energy from fat while the lower - income groups consumed only 17% energy from fat. More recent dietary surveys in Delhi also confirm that the upper income groups in urban India currently consume higher levels of energy from fat as compared with the urban poor or rural populations.

Dietary deficits and excesses—and the lifestyle changes that accompany industrialisation and urbanisation with economic development - make a significant contribution to this epidemic. In this brief overview some of the crucial contributors to the nutrition transition in India, are important determinants of the burgeoning problem in this country.

Important Points for Answer:	
• *PCPNDT Act, 1994*	• *Salient Features*
• *Amendment in 2003*	• *Implications*

(d) The "Pre-conception and Pre - natal Diagnostic Techniques (prohibition of sex selection) Act 1994" is enacted with the object to increase the child sex ratio.

Since 1992, the child sex ratio has shown a considerable downward trend. In 2001, though the sex ratio showed an increase, but the child sex ratio declined to 927 (Census 2001). This decline was despite the enactment of PCPNDT Act, 1994 indicating the ineffectiveness and improper implementation.

The salient features of the PCPNDT Act, 1994 are :

(i) Regulation of parental diagnostic techniques (eg., amniocentesis and ultrasonography) for detection of genetic abnormalities, by restricting their use to registered institutions.

(ii) Prohibition of sex selection, before and after conception.

(iii) The Act allows the use of these techniques only at registered places for a specified purpose and by a qualified person, registered for this purpose.

(iv) Prevention of misuse of such techniques for sex selection before or after conception.

(v) Prohibition on sale of ultrasound machines to persons not registered under this Act.

(vi) Prohibition of advertisement of any technique for sex selection as well as sex determination.

(vii) Provides punishments for the violation of provisions of this Act.

In order to the ineffectiveness of the PCPNDT Act, the Government wanted to give more teeth to that Act and amended the Act with effect from 14th February, 2003. And renamed as "Pre-conception and Pre-natal Diagnostics Techniques (Prohibition of sex selection), Act, 1994".

The 2003 Amendment made the Act more comprehensive and strong to fulfill the purpose of the Act, and to increase the child sex ratio and bring the gender equality in the society.

Q. 2 Answer ONE of the following in about 250 words : 20

(a) Trace the salient sequence of events in the popular revolt that took place in February 1946 in the then 'Royal Indian Navy' and bring out its significance in the freedom struggle. Do you agree with the view that the sailors who took part in this revolt were some of the unsung heroes of the freedom struggle ?

(b) Evaluate the influence of the three important women's organizations of the early twentieth century in India on the country's society and politics. To what extent do you think were the social objectives of these organizations constrained by their political objectives ?

Important Points for Answer:	
• *RIN Revolt*	• *Reasons*
• *Effect - Significance*	• *Unsung heroes*

Answer: (a) After the Second World War, three officers of the Indian National Army (I.N.A.), General Shah Nawaz Khan, Colonel Prem Sahgal and Colonel Gurbaksh Singh Dhillon were put on trial at the Red Fort in Delhi for "waging war against the King Emperor", i.e. the British sovereign personifying British rule. The three defendants were defended at the trial by Jawaharlal Nehru, Bhulabhai Desai and others. Outside that, the trials inspired protests and discontent among the

Indian population, who came to view the defendants as revolutionaries who had fought for their country. In January 1946 British airmen stationed in India took part in the Royal Air Force Mutiny of 1946 largely over the speed of their demobilisation, but also in some cases issuing demands against being used to continue British Imperialism. The Viceroy at the time, Lord Wavell, noted that the actions of the British airmen inspired both the RIAF and RIN mutinies.

The mutiny was initiated by the ratings of the Royal Indian Navy on 18 February 1946. It was a reaction to the treatment meted out to ratings in general and the lack of service facilities in particular. On 16 January 1946, a contingent of 67 ratings of various branches arrived at Castle Barracks, Mint Road, in Fort Mumbai. This contingent had arrived from the basic training establishment, F1MIS *Akbar,* located at Thane, a suburb of Bombay, at 1600 in the evening. One of them Syed Maqsood Bokhari went to the officer on duty informed him about the galley (kitchen) staff of this arrival.

The sailors were that evening alleged to have been served sub-standard food. Only 17 ratings took the meal, the rest of the contingent went ashore to eat in an open act of defiance. It has since been said that such acts of neglect were fairly regular, and when reported to senior officers present practically evoked no response, which certainly was a factor in the buildup of discontent. The ratings of the communication branch in the shore establishment, HMIS *Talwar,* drawn from higher strata of society, harboured a high level of revulsion towards the authorities, hawing complained of neglect of their facilities fruitlessly.

It was the Royal Indian Navy revolt that sparked the great fire which led to freedom of India, therefore the contribution of soldiers is undoubtedly unique. It is disappointing that the heroes who took part in that revolt are forgotten in the pages of history and remain unsung.

Important Points for Answer:
- *Women's organizations*
- *Objectives*
- *Constrains*

(b) Women-only organizations like All India Women's Conference (AIWC) and the National Federation of Indian Women (NFIW) emerged. Women were grappling with issues relating to the scope of women's political participation, women's franchise, communal awards, and leadership roles in political parties.

The **All India Women's Conference (AIWC)** was founded in 1927 "as an organization dedicated to upliftment and betterment of women and children". As well as continuing its original mission, the AIWC has since diversified into various social and economic activities involving women. Today there are more than 100,000 members in over 500 branches. AIWC is recognized worldwide as a premier organization working for women's development and empowerment.

AIWC was registered in 1930 under the Societies Registration Act, XXI of 1860. (No. 558 of 1930) with the following main objectives :

- To work for a society based on the principle of social justice, personal integrity and equal rights and opportunities for all.

- To secure recognition of the inherent right of every human being to work and to achieve the essentials of life, which should not be determined by accident of birth or sex but by planned social distribution.
- To support the claim of every citizen to the right to enjoy basic civil liberties.
- To stand against all separatist tendencies and to promote greater national integration and unity.
- To work actively for the general progress and welfare of women and children and to help women utilize to the fullest, one of the fundamental rights conferred on them by the Constitution of India.
- To work for permanent international amity and world peace.

National Federation of Indian Women is the women's wing of Communist Party of India. It was established in 1954 by several leaders including Aruna Asaf Ali.

The first women's university, SNDT Women's University, was founded on June 2,1916 by the social reformer Dhondo Keshav Karve with just five students.

Of these organizations, Naional Federation of Indian Women was purely or mostly a political organization and had to achieve welfare of women through political progress. But SNDT University was founded with social objectives and concentrated on educational development of women and their rightful place in the society. But of course, AIWC was largely a political cum social women's organization whose social objectives were constrained by political ones.

Q. 3 Answer one of the following in about 250 words: **20**

(a) Critically examine the design of the National Rural Livelihoods Mission (NRLM) scheme. Do you think it has a better chance of success than the Swarnajayanti Gram Swarojgar Yojana (SGSY) in achieving its objectives ?

(b) Highlight the structure, objectives and role of the Advertising Standards Council of India. In what way has the August 2006 government notification made it more effective ?

Important Points for Answer:
- *NRLM*
- *Comparison with SGSY*
- *Conclusion*

Answer: (a) The National Rural Livelihood Mission (NRLM) was announced in the Budget 2009-10 to replace the Swarna Jayanti Gram Swarojgar Yojana (SGSY). It is targeted to reduce the rural poverty by 2015 by redesigning the SGSY.

Though the NRLM promises a lot with regard to creation and strengthening of rural livelihoods, it does suffer some serious shortcomings, which if not addressed are likely to see it more in the same path as the IRDP, SGSY and other rural welfare programs. The criticisms are as follows :

(i) Its emphasis on SHG for providing livelihood. Over emphasis of NRLM on SHGs could lead exclusion (rather than inclusion) of rural low income people, who are not able to participate through SHGs. Hence, the NRLM focuses on the household as the primary target of the program.

(ii) The NRLM has been designed to treat the rural economy as one. But in reality, there are many segments exist in the low income peoples.

(iii) The NRLM also has another defect, it lacks serious attention to value added agriculture and rural MSMEs - which, as the experiences of many countries suggest, can play a major role in enabling and sustaining inclusive growth in rural areas.

(iv) The strategy of the NRLM is too broad and sweeping. The design is also too academic and top down with the minimal involvement of "next target group". This was the reason for the failures of IRDP and SGSY—in fact, if these had not failed, we would not need an NRLM today.

On account of the above deficiencies in NRLM design, it is feared that it may also meet the same fate similar to SHSY.

Suggestions for effective implementation and design are :

(i) NRLM may focus on covering all the willing households under SHGs, irrespective of BPL/ APL status.

(ii) NRLM may have two - fold strategy for poverty alleviation and rural prosperity.

(iii) There should be a permanent implementation mechanism at the district and block level.

(iv) To get the desirable employment transformation and to take full advantage of booming secondary and tertiary sectors, under livelihood promotion, NRLM may promote small and medium enterprises in 'services' and 'manufacturing' sectors with SHG federations.

Generally, the social welfare schemes must be implemented with the people's participation and in transparent manner. The implementing aiuthority should reach the people.

Important Points for Answer:

- *ASCI*
- *Objectives*
- *2006 Notification*
- *Structure*
- *Role*

(b) ASCI is a self-regulatory voluntary organization of the advertising industry. It was established in 1985 and is committed to the cause of self-regulation in advertising, ensuring the protection of the interest of consumers.

The ASCI was formed with the support of all four sectors connected with Advertising viz., Advertisers, Ad agencies, Media (including Broadcasters and the Press) and others like PR Agencies, Market research companies, etc.

Its main objective is to promote responsible advertising and thus enhancing the public's confidence in advertising. The ASCI's membership of the European Advertising Standards Alliance (EASA) ensures that it gets valuable advice, learning and even influence at the international level.

The ASCI seeks to regulate the content of advertising with the primary purpose of protecting consumer interest and also to ensure fairness in competition. It deals with complaints received from consumers and industry against advertisements which are considered as false, misleading, indecent, illegal, leading to unsafe practices or unfair competition, and is in contravention of the ASCI codes for self-regulation in advertising.

ASCI's role has been acclaimed by various agencies including the Government. However, it lacked the forces of legal recognition. The Government of India taking note of this and in August 2006 vide a notification amended the caste. Television Networks Rules, 1994 to ensure that at least as far as TV commercials go, they abide by the ASCI Code. Hence, violation of ASCI's codes is now violation of Government rules. ASCI thus aims to achieve the own over-reaching goal; to maintain and enhance the public's confidence in advertising.

Q. 4 Comment on any FIVE of the following in about 150 words each: 12 × 5 = 60

(a) Salient recommendations of the RBI-appointed Damodaran committee on customer service in Banks.

(b) Deendayal Disabled Rehabilitation Scheme (DDRS).

(c) Evolution of "Green Benches' in our higher judiciary.

(d) Distinction between "Department Related Parliamentary Standing Committees' and 'Parliamentary Forums'.

(e) Benefits and potential drawbacks of 'cash-transfers' to 'Below Poverty Line' (BPL) households.

(f) New initiatives during the 11th Five Year Plan in the National Programme for Control Blindness (NCPB).

Important Points for Answer:	
• *Damodaran Committee*	• *Recommendations*

Answer: (a) The Damodaran Committee on customer service constituted by the RBI submitted its report in August 2011. The recommendations are :

(i) To include the customer service and grievance redressal as a mandatory parameter in the performance appraisal report of every employee.

(ii) It has recommended active involvement of the boards of banks to guarantee customer satisfaction.

(iii) It has suggested an agenda on the level of implementation of the Bank's Code of Commitments to customers and an overview on the grievance redressal mechanism in the bank should be placed before the bank every quarter before the customer service committee.

(iv) Every bank should ensure that they have comprehensive policies for customer acceptance, cane and severance.

(v) Emphasising on 'customer centricity', it has recommended that bank boards should evolve human resources policies which will "recruit for attitude and train for skills".

(vi) The Bench level customer committee meetings should be replaced with a meeting of customers of all banks of that area and is hold in the presence of representatives of banks at periodic interest.

Important Points for Answer:	
• *DDRS*	• *Structure*
• *Objectives*	

(b) The Umbrella Central Sector scheme of the Ministry of Social Justice is called the "Scheme to promote voluntary action for persons with disabilities". It was revised on 2003 and renamed as "Deendayal Disabled Rehabilitation Scheme (DDRS)".

Under the Scheme, funds for the welfare of persons with disabilities are provided to the non-governmental organizations for projects like special schools for disabled, vocational training centres, half way homes, community based rehabilitation centres, early intervention centres for disabled and rehabilitation of leprosy cured persons, etc.

NGOs are being given assistance under DDRS for providing a wide range of services to children/ persons with disability, e.g.,

(i) programmes for pre-school and early intervention
(ii) special education
(iii) vocational training and placement
(iv) community based rehabilitation
(v) manpower development
(vi) psycho - social rehabilitation of persons with mental illness
(vii) rehabilitation of leprosy-cured persons, etc.

The DDRS guidelines include model projects covering various services provided by voluntary agencies which can be supported through grant-in-aid. Model projects give the following details :

(i) objective, needs to be addressed, target group in terms of type of disability and age and minimum permissible number of beneficiaries
(ii) teacher-beneficiary ratio (for pre - schools and special schools)
(iii) number of trades and an illustrative list of trades (for vocational training)
(iv) maximum amount of recurring and non - recurring assistance admissible for a specified number of beneficiaries in the form of cost norms.

Important Points for Answer:	
• *Green Benches*	• *Cases of concern*
• *Benefits*	

(b) In several cases, the Supreme Court of India, has upheld that "The Right to Life" under Article 21 includes the "right to clean environment" also, and derived various doctrines to uphold the right to environment, such as, polluter's pays principle, precautionary principles, sustainable development, etc.

The Supreme Court exercising its power under Article 142 of the Constitution created the Compensatory Afforestation Management and Planning Authority. Further, the Constitution of the Forest Commission by the Supreme Court, establishment of 'Green Courts' in various states and the pro-active role of the higher judiciary in environmental matters culminated in the enactment of National Green Tribunal Act of 2010, that proposes to efficiently and expeditiously dispose of cases relating to environmental protection.

For environmental governance in India, the Constitution of a "Green bench" of judiciary to adjudicate environmental matters will be further significant step towards improving the quality of environment when the India has been caught in tussle between developmental and sustainability issues.

Law Commission of India also recommended in its 186th report for the specialised Environmental Courts to strengthen and revitalise environmental governance in the country.

Important Points for Answer:
- *Standing Committees*
- *Distinctions*
- *Parliamentary Forums*

(d) To make the parliamentary activity more effective and to make the executive more accountable to the legislature, the beginning had been made in the Eighth Lok Sabha in 1989 by setting up 3 departmental related subject committees.

There are at present, 24 departmental related parliamentary standing committees. Each of these standing committees consists of not more than 45 members - 30 from Lok Sabha and 15 from Rajya Sabha. A minister is not eligible to be nominated to these committees. The term of member of these committees is one years. The functions of these committees include consideration of Demand for Grants, consideration of Annual Reports.

There are, at present, five parliamentary forums. The first one on water conservation was constituted in 2005. The parliamentary forums do not interfere with or encroach upon the jurisdiction of the concerned departmentally related standing committees.

Members are appointed by speaker of Lok Sabha and Chairman of Rajya Sabha, each forum consists of not more than 31 members out of which 21 from Lok Sabha and 10 from Rajya Sabha.

The new committee system was inaugurated by the then Vice - President and Chairman of Rajya Sabha Shri K. R. Narayanan in 1993. It is considered as historical landmark in the evolution of committee system in our Parliament.

Important Points for Answer:
- *Cash-transfer scheme*
- *Benefits*
- *Drawbacks*

(e) The Government has announced the replacing of public distribution system through which subsidised food-grain is made available to people, with "direct cash subsidies", where fixed amount will be transferred into the people's bank accounts each month.

The Government made the first move towards this by announcing in the recent budget that fertilizer and kerosene will be replaced by cash transfers.

On the other hand, the Right to Food Campaign strongly feels that the PDS must not be dismantled, as it plays an important role in not only improving people's access to food but also revitalising agriculture and promoting food production.

As per Arjun Sengupta Committee report:

(i) Nearly 77% of countries' population live on less than 23.20 per day.

(ii) Almost half of the children are malnourished.

(iii) 70% of women are anemic.

(iv) One third of adult have low body mass index.

Advantages: Cost efficient, choice, multiplier effect, avoids disincentive effect, power costs for recipients.

Disadvantages: Consumption/nutrition, less available from donors, disadvantages to women, more prone to diversion, anti social use.

Important Points for Answer:

- *NPCB*
- *New Initiatives in 11th FYP*

(f) The National Programme for Control of Blindness (NPCB) was launched in 1976 as a 100% centrally sponsored scheme with, the goal of reducing the prevalence of blindness from 1.4% to 0.3%. According to the Survey of 2001-02, prevalence of blindness was estimated at 1.1%.

The NPCB has planned to develop the eye care facilities in every district level and to develop human resources for providing eye care services to reduce the backlog of blindness through identification and treatment of blind.

The vision 2020- The Right to sight initiative programme also planned to reduce the blindness from 1.49% to 0.3%.

In the Eleventh Five Year Plan, the funding to this programme has been enhanced. It was pegged at Rs. 1200 million. Further, capacity building programmes has been launched under the plan. To streamline the efforts the programme has been subsumed under the NRHM in the Eleventh Five Year Plan.

Currently, nearly 20,000 donated eyes are collected each year in India. The lack of awareness is the main cause for this low performance. The NPCB is also working to increase the numbers by implementing various awareness programmes.

Q. 5 Examine any THREE of the following in about 150 words each: **12 × 3 = 36**

(a) The impact of climate change on water resources in India.

(b) Measures taken by the Indian government to combat piracy in the Indian Ocean.

(c) The significance of counter-urbanisation in the improvement of metropolitan cities in India.

(d) Problems specific to the denotified and nomadic tribes in India.

> **Important Points for Answer:**
> - *Climate change*
> - *Impact on water resources in India*

Answer: (a) The impact of climate change on water resources in India is evident through erratic monsoon, more frequent floods and droughts, stronger cyclones and rivers changing their course frequently. The severity is also due to the prevailing more than 7000 km. of coastline.

The changing rainfall pattern has adversely affected ground water recharge, wetlands both coastal and terrestrial. Climate change has resulted in melting of Himalayan glaciers. It has the potential of making the Himalayan Rivers swell first and then turning them into seasonal rivers, threatening the source of freshwater. It can also lead to salt water intrusion and threatening aquaculture and coastal agriculture.

The impact has been severe also because India is still an agricultural country with its large population being dependant on weather related livelihood through agriculture, forestry, etc.

> **Important Points for Answer:**
> - *Piracy in Indian Ocean*
> - *Indian Govt's. Measures*

(b) Indian government has used INS Talwar to foil several bide by pirates near the Gulf of Aden. Indian government is coordinating the anti-piracy measures at the international level with China, European countries and with the Gulf countries.

Indian government has placed surveillance radars in countries like Maldives and Sri Lanka to secure the sea lanes in the Indian Ocean. It has signed agreements with Madagascar, Seychelles and Mauritius for anti-piracy measures. Government has also taken measures in strengthening the coastal security by equipping and reforming the coast guards. However, incidents like unmanned vessel drifting in the ocean and reaching the coast of Mumbai have highlighted the holes in our coastal security which needs to be plugged.

Supreme Court has recently asked the Central Government to formulate separate piracy law for trying the pirates and to take care of the compensation to the victim's family. Currently, piracy is being dealt under the provision of Indian Penal Code.

> **Important Points for Answer:**
> - *Counter-urbanisation*
> - *Metropolitan cities*
> - *Effect in improvement*

(c) Counter-urbanisation is a demographic and social process where people move from large urban areas into rural areas, thereby leapfrogging the rural urban fringe. It might mean daily commuting but could also require lifestyle changes and the increased use of ICT (home working or teleworking). It is the process of migration of people from major urban areas to smaller urban settlements and rural areas. Counter-urbanisation affects the layout of rural settlements. Modern housing estates locate of the edge of small settlements. Industrial units are sited on main roads leading into the settlement. Counter-urbanisation will reduce pressure on the metropolitan cities and its basic amenities like drinking water supply, sewage facilities, continuous supply of electricity, education facilities, etc. as people move out due to following :

(i) Increase in car ownership enabling their movement, growth in information technology (E-mail, faxes and video conferencing) meaning more people can work from home.

(ii) Urban areas are becoming increasing unpleasant place to live. This is the result of pollution, crime and traffic congestion.

(iii) More people tend to move when they retire.

(iv) Now business parks being developed on the edge of cities (on Greenfield sites) meaning people no longer have to travel to the city centre. People now prefer to live on the outskirts of the city where they work.

Important Points for Answer:
- *Denotified and nomadic tribes*
- *Reasons and status*
- *Their problems*

(d) Post-independence the Criminal Tribe Act 1871 was replaced; and criminal tribe nomenclature was replaced with Denotified Tribe (DNTs) which is still considered derogatory. They have been discriminated; British government included some of the tribes like Gonds, Ho and Santhals under this categorisation as they had rebelled against the British Raj.

A major challenge in the intervention comes due to dispersed nature of the tribes and having a nomadic culture surviving on shifting cultivation. This results in health and educational services a challenging task to deliver. It also makes the implementation of nutritional initiative like addressing iodine deficiency a challenging task.

Preservation of their culture, script, practices also gets hampered due to the same reason.

Two different opinions arise with regard to the reservation for the DNTs to raise their social and economic conditions. One view supports providing reservation within existing group of SCs, STs and OBCs while the other view supports creation a new group for the reservation of DNTs.

Q 6 In the context of the freedom struggle, write short notes (not exceeding 50 words each) on the following: 5 × 3 = 15

(a) 'Benoy-Badal-Dinesh' martyrdom.

(b) Bharat Naujawan Sabha

(c) Babbar Akali' movement.

Answer: (a) On December 1930, Benoy along with Dinesh Chandra Gupta and Badal Gupta, dressed in European costume, entered the Writers' Building and shot dead Simpson, the Inspector

General of Prisons, who was infamous for the brutal oppression on the prisoners. This inspired further revolutionary activities in Bengal. After Independence, Dalhousie square was named B.B.D. Bagh—after Benoy-Badal-Dinesh.

(b) Bharat Naujawan Sabha was an association of Indian youths which was established at a convention held in April 1928 at the Jallianwala Bagh in Amritsar. The aims of the Sabha were to create a youth wing of peasants and workers with a view to usher in revolution in the country and overthrow the British rule. Bhagat Singh was its secretary and principle organiser.

(c) Babbar Akali Movement was a radical outgrowth of the Akali movement for the reform of Sikh places of worship during the early 1920's. The latter, aiming to have the shrines released from the control of priests who had become lax and effete over the generations, was peaceful in its character and strategy. In the course of the prolonged campaign, Akalis true to their vows patiently suffered physical injury and violence at the hands of the priests as well as of government authority.

Q. 7 Comment on the following in NOT more than 50 words each: 5 × 6 = 30

(a) Phase - IV of the tiger monitoring programme in India.

(b) Why the Central Statistics Office has notified a new series of Consumer Price Index from this year?

(c) Composition and functions of the National Executive Committee of the National Disaster Management Authority.

(d) The Bihar Special Courts Act, 2009 and why it has been in the news recently?

(e) The Telecommunications Ministry's proposed Spectrum Management Commission.

(f) The Community-Led Total Sanitation (CLTS) approach to sanitation.

Answer: (a) The Ministry of Environment and Forests initiated the phase - IV of the tiger monitoring programme. This will initiate intensive, annual monitoring of tigers at the tiger reserve level, across 41 protected areas in the country. According to Ministry, this marks an important milestone in the comprehensive tiger conservation strategy. Annual monitoring at the tiger reserve level will allow getting regular updates on the number and health of tiger populations across the country, and will strengthen the conservation efforts. Until now monitoring was done once in four years.

(b) The Central Statistical Office has notified a new series of consumer price index with 2010 as its base year, for rural and urban areas and for the nation as a whole. It will give a comprehensive picture of inflation at the national level for retail prices. Government also proposes to use it for giving dearness allowance for government employees in the Seventh Pay Commission.

(c) The National Executive Committee of the National Disaster Management Authority comprises the union home secretary as the chairperson, and the secretaries to the government of India in the Ministries/Departments of Agriculture, Atomic Energy, Defence, Drinking Water Supply, Environment and Forests, Finance (Expenditure), Health, Power, Rural Development, Science and Technology, Space, Telecommunication, Urban Development, Water Resources and the Chief of the Integrated Defence Staff of the Chiefs of Staff Committee as members.

(d) Bihar Special Court Act, 2009 provides that the property of corrupt persons can be attached even when the probe is under way, if the authorised officer concludes that the acquisition of the property was the result of the offence committed by the accused. Bihar implemented it and some officials came under this Act. Its constitutional validity was questioned in Supreme Court which refused to stay this Act.

(e) Spectrum Management Commission is a new entity to manage and regulate spectrum allocation. The commission will subsume wireless planning coordination wing of the department of telecom and will get wider powers including dispute settlement, pricing and regulation related to spectrum. While the DoT will continue to be the licensor, all issues pertaining to spectrum allocation will be brought under Spectrum Management Commission.

(f) Community Led Total Sanitation (CLTS) : CLTS is an innovative methodology for mobilising communities to completely eliminate open defection (OD). Communities facilities are to conduct their own appraisal and analysis of open defecation and take their own action to become ODF (open defecation free). CLTS focuses on the behavioural change needed to ensure real and sustainable improvement. It invests in community mobilisation instead of hardware, and shifting the focus from toilet construction for individual households to the creation of open defecation free villages.

Q. 8 Attempt the following in not more than 50 words each: $5 \times 4 = 20$

(a) Distinguish either between the 'Moatsu' and 'Yemshe' festivals of Nagaland or the 'Losar' and 'Khan' festivals of Arunachal Pradesh.

(b) Write a sentence each on any five of the following traditional theatre forms :

(i) Bhand Pather (ii) Swang (iii) Maach

(iv) Bhaona (v) Mudiyettu (vi) Dashavatar

(c) What are the major different styles of unglazed pottery making in India?

(d) List the classical dance forms of India as per the Sangeet Natak Akademi.

Answer: (a) Moatsu festival : It's an annual event celebrated in the month of May, by the Ao tribes of Nagaland. The festival is a time of gaiety and recreation after the hectic work of cleaning fields, burning jungles and sowing seeds. This work also includes cleaning up the wells and repair and construction of houses by elders. Major attractions of this festival is Sangpangtu; a fire is lit and men and women sit around it and the women serve meat and wine.

Yemshe festival : Festival celebrated in the month of October by Pochury tribe in Nagaland to commemorate the arrival of the new harvest season. It is a festival that strengthens relationships. The newly wedded couples share their food and eat together, during the festival the unmarried boys and girls look for a match for themselves.

OR

Losar festival: Losar is the new year festival celebrated by Monpas (who forms the major portion) in Tawang, Arunachal Pradesh. They enjoy the festival with friends and family. Festival falls in the end of February or early March, for about 8 to 15 days.

Khan festival : Khan is a festival celebrated by the Mill tribe of Arunachal Pradesh. It brings together people from every background irrespective of their caste and creed. The priest ties a piece of wool in the neck of all the participants. This thread is considered to be sacred because they are prepared specially by the priest for the welfare of the whole community.

(b) (i) Bhand Pather is a social drama incorporating mythological legends and contemporary social satire of Kashmir.

(ii) Swang is a popular folk dance drama or folk theatre form in Rajasthan, Haryana, Uttar Pradesh and Malwa region of Madhya Pradesh.

(iii) Maach is originally a Rajasthan folk theatre that survives in the villages of Madhya Pradesh. The Maach of M.P. is a folk theatre form presented largely through song and dances. Men portray all the characters and the themes are generally historical. There is not much of acting.

(iv) Bhaona is a dance drama popular in the state of Assam, Sankardeva who was scholar and social reformer, was the father of Bhaona.

(v) Mudiyettu is ritualistic dance drama performed after the harvest of summer crops in Kerala, in 2010, Mudiyattu was included in UNESCO Intangible Cultural Heritage List.

(vi) Dashavatar refers to the ten most famous incarnations of Vishnu or sometimes Krishna.

(c) Different styles of unglazed pottery making in India : It is the oldest form of pottery practiced in India, which has developed with time, there are basically three types of unglazed pottery :

(i) Paper thin pottery, wherein biscuit coloured pottery is decorated with incised patterns.

(ii) Scrafito technique, wherein the pot is polished and painted with red and white slips along with intricate patterns, while the outline is incised.

(iii) Highly polished pottery, which is given strong, deeply incised, stylized patterns of arabesques.

Unglazed pottery is practiced throughout the country, with each region having its own speciality. Black pottery is yet another form of unglazed pottery, which resembles the Harappan pottery style.

(d) The Sangeet Natak Akademi currently confers classical status to eight Indian dance forms. They are as follows :

1. Bharatnatyam - Tamil classical dance.
2. Odissi - Odisha classical dance.
3. Kuchipudi - Andhra Pradesh (Telugu) classical dance.
4. Mohiniattam - Kerala classical dance.
5. Sattriya - Assamese classical dance.
6. Kathkali - Malayalam classical dance.
7. Kathak - Northern Indian classical dance (Rajasthan, Punjab, Delhi, Uttar Pradesh).
8. Manipuri - Manipur classical dance.

Q. 9 Comment on the following in not more than 50 words each: **$5 \times 5 = 25$**

(a) Nisarga - Runa technology of BARC.

(b) The first - aid that you can safely administer to a person standing next to you at the bus - stop who suddenly faints.

(c) The Kaveri K -10 aero - engine

(d) Molecular Breast Imaging (MBI) technology.

(e) E-governance initiatives by the Union Public Service Commission (UPSC).

Answer: (a) Nisarga - Runa technology of BARC : It is a Kitchen Waste (Biodegradable) based Bio-Gas Plant. This plant can process biodegradable waste such as kitchen waste, paper, grass, gobar and dry leaves. It offers zero garbage and zero effluent and provides high quality, manure and methane gas. Weed free manure obtained from such waste has high nitrogen contents and acts as an excellent soil conditioner. This plant could be set up for ecofriendly disposal of wet waste generated in kitchens, canteens of big hospitals, hotels, factories, residential complexes and can avoid health hazards due to dump sites. The technology of biphasic biomethanation has high potential of solving the solid waste management problems of the urban areas and provides organic manure and biogas as a fuel.

(b) Fainting occurs when the blood supply to the brain is momentarily inadequate, causing the person to lose consciousness. First check the person is breathing ? If he is breathing, restore blood flow to the brain by raising the person's legs above heart level if possible. Loosen belts, collate or other constrictive clothing. To reduce the chance of fainting again, don't get the person up too quickly. If the person doesn't regain consciousness within one minute call to the local emergency number. Check the person's airways to be sure it's clear. Watch for vomiting. Check for signs of circulation (breathing, coughing or movement). If a person was injured in a fall associate with a faint, treat any bumps, bruises or cuts appropriately. Control bleeding with direct pressure.

(c) The Kaveri K -10 aero - engine : Kaveri K-10 engine is being developed to be used in the Light Combat Aircraft, Tejas. It is being developed in collaboration of French firm, Snecma. It will have less weight and more replicate thrust to meet the requirements of the Indian Army.

(d) Molecular Breast Imaging (MBI) technology : Breast cancer is a foremost health problem for women worldwide and it is growing in numbers, early detection is critical for improving breast cancer and survival rates. This technology is intended to improve early detection in women who are at high risk for developing breast cancer, or in women with dense breasts who are less likely to benefit from conventional mammography. This technology is a gamma camera dedicated for breast imaging based on accumulation of a radioactive tracer in hyper metabolic cancer cells. The innovation of the MBI technology is the use of imaging detectors, cadmium zinc telluride (CZT) to replace the standard Nal detectors routinely used for gamma cameras, in a dedicated breast device.

(e) E-governance initiatives by the Union Public Service Commission (UPSC)**:** E-governance defined as, the employment of the internet and the world-wide-web for delivering governments information and services to the citizens. UPSC has introduced the system of online submission of applications for the competitive examinations it conducts. Good lead taken by the UPSC as it reduces the paper use, risk of postal delays, low risk of rejection since online applications built in self-scrutinising features not allowing an applicant to leave any column blank, one can view and take a printout of one's application for future reference, one can apply hassle 'free manner at the convenience of sitting at home or cyber cafe, any time even during night, overall its a user friendly initiative taken by the UPSC.

Q. 10 Who are the following and why have they been in the news recently? (Each answer should not exceed 20 words). **2 × 7 = 14**

- **(a) Lieutenant Navdeep Singh**
- **(b) Rahim Fahimuddin Dagar**
- **(c) Lobsang Sangay**
- **(d) P. R. Sreejesh**
- **(e) Nileema Mishra**
- **(f) V. Tejeswini Bai**
- **(g) Aishwarya Narkar**

Answer: (a) Lieutenant Navdeep Singh lost his life in gun battle in J&K, while fighting terrorists during an anti-infiltration operation along LOC in Gurez section of Bandipora district of north-Kashmir in Kashmir valley. 26 year old officer, after doing his MBA, was commissioned in March into the Army Ordinance corps and was serving in the 15th Battalion of the Maratha Light Infantry. (

(b) Rahim Fahimuddin Dagar, the 19th generation khalifa of the musical lineage known as the Dagar Gharana, that kept alive the tradition of Dhrupad, died with illness. He was honoured with the Padma Bhushan in 2008 and Sangeet Natak Akademi Ratna Puraskar also.

(c) Lobsang Sangay, political successor to the Dalai Lama, was sworn in as Prime Minister of the Tibetan government in exile at a public ceremony in Dharamsltala.

(d) P. R. Sreejesh played a stellar role in India's victory at the inaugural Asian Champions Trophy of Hockey. Sreejesh's two saves in the tie—breaker led to India's 4–2 win over Pakistan in the championship in Ordos in China. Sreejesh was given an official reception by Hockey Kerala at Thiruvananthapuram.

(e) Nileema Mishra, a woman leader to the poorest in Maharashtra, has been awarded Asia's prestigious Ramon Magsaysay award for 2011. She along with US-trained Indian engineer Harish Hande (who revolutionized use of solar lights, one among the six people who have been awarded the same) had helped to harness technologies to empower their countrymen and created waves of progressive change across Asia.

(f) V. Tejeswini Bai, the first Karnataka women to be conferred with the Arjun Award in Kabaddi. She received the same from President Pratibha Patil on August 29th 2011. She also had been given the state's Eklavya award in 2006. She represented India from 2006 to 2010 and captained Indian team for four years.

(g) Aishwarya Narkar, is a Marathi film actress and also performs in Hindi TV serials. She has received the National Film Award from the President of India.

SOLVED PAPERS

PAPER-II

Time Allowed : Three Hours *Maximum Marks : 300*

Answers must be in the medium specified in the Admission Certificate issued to you, which must be stated clearly on the cover of the answer-book in the space provided for the purpose. No marks will be given for the answers written in a medium other than that specified in the Admission Certificate.

Candidates should attempt ALL questions strictly in accordance with the instructions given under each question.

Two (2) graph sheets are attached to this question paper for attempting questions 9(b) and 10 (c). The graph sheets are to be carefully detached from the question paper and surely attached to the answer-book by the candidate.

Q. 1 Answer any TWO of the following in about 250 words each: 20 × 2 = 40

(a) List the Central Asian Republics and identify those of particular strategic and economic importance to India. Examine the opportunities and bottlenecks in enhancing relations with these countries.

(b) Critically examine the security and strategic implications of the so-called 'string of pearls' theory for India.

(c) "Compared to the South Asian Free Trade Area (SAFTA), the Bay of Bengal Initiative for Multisectoral Technical and Economic Cooperation Free Trade Area (BIMSTEC FTA) seems to be more promising." Critically evaluate.

Important Points for Answer:
- *Central Asian Republics*
- *Strategic and economic importance*
- *Opportunities in relations*
- *Bottlenecks in relations*

Answer: (a) The Central Asian Republics are Uzbekistan, Kazakhstan, Kyrgyzstan and Tajikistan.

The Central Asian Region, as a whole, not only connects Asia to Europe, but is also rich in natural resources. It provides the shortest transit route to Europe from Asia, and has a 55-million strong consumer market. It therefore occupies a special place in India's foreign policy priorities.

Unlike the past, the importance to India today is not merely civilisational, but also geopolitical and economic. India has joined in the "New great game" in the Central Asian region for the area's vast energy resources. India considers Turkmenistan an extended neighbour, a natural ally and a key partner in Central Asia.

India's Vice-President Hameed Ansari visited Kazakhstan and signed MoU, expressing readiness to work on a project specific made of hydrocarbon sector, food production, information technology and education.

Bottlenecks : One of the major issues standing in the way of greater relation between India and Central Asian States is a lack of efficient transportation capabilities, road, railways, etc. However, the Indian press has reported that an International North-South transport Corridor linking Central Asia with India will soon be developed by the recent steps taken by Kazakhstan, Turkmenistan and Russia to increase road and rail connectivity, may help in the development of the corridor.

India is surrounded by Unstable or Authoritative states, so direct access to the Central Asia is difficult as the route passes through the Pak-Afghanistan region. China's growing influence in the region is also a hurdle for India's growth in that region.

Important Points for Answer:
- *String of pulse theory*
- *Implications for India*

(b) China's 'String of Pearls' policy started in the 1980 and its basic aim was to give China increased energy security with requesting stations through the world.

'String of pearl' describes the manifestation of China's rising geo-political influence through efforts to increase access to ports and airfields, develop special diplomatic relationships and modernize military forces that extend from the South China Sea through the Strait of Malacca, across the Indian ocean and on to the Arabian Gulf.

As a part of that, China has helped Sri Lanka in developing its Hambantota port in Southern Sri Lanka, though China says its commercial, China's naval presence in Hambantota would add to the concerns of the Indian Navy.

Similarly, China had helped Pakistan with a similar project in Gwadar on the Mekran Coast in Baluchistan, the first phase already completed.

Though India is trying to make a strong hold in South Asia, China seems to have been making consistently over the last four decades to strengthen its South Asian presence and fulfill its string of pearl policy, and that has made India worried.

Recently China has announced its decision to set up a naval base of Sychelles Island on the Indian Ocean, which caused grave concern to India.

The 'String of Pearl' policy includes the following steps taken by China in India's neighbouring countries.

(i) building road in PoK.

(ii) building road from China-Gilgit-Neelam valley also planned number of tunnels and bridges.

(iii) The Karakoram Highway which connects China's Xinjian region with North- Pakistan (The highway called the 9th wonder of the world by some because of its altitude). Naval port at Gwadar on the Makran Coast in Baluchistan, Pakistan.

(iv) Naval base at Sychelles island, in Indian Ocean.

Which makes India to worry about its security and sovereignty in.the region and also in the Indian Ocean and Southern hemisphere.

Important Points for Answer:	
•*SAAFTA*	• *BIMSTEC FTA*
• *Comparison*	• *Evaluation*

(c) The present situation retreats that there are enormous opportunities for forging closer economic relations among SAARC countries. These opportunities could be fully utilized through twin process of trade liberalization and industrial restructuring which are complementary to each other.

SAFTA which came into effect in January 2006, has been below the potential PTA. The intra-trade between the SAARC countries stands at US $ 4 million as compared to its potential of US $ 80 billion.

The main reasons being the self-interest of the member countries, viewing India as possessing the "big-brother" attitude despite India's attempt to dispel fears of the smaller countries of SAARC.

SAARC is a geo-political region rather than an economic block as evidenced by the increased participation of China and the most important factor being the rivalry of India and Pakistan which has led Pakistan not to grant MFN status to India. Now, Pakistan has announced MFN status to India after a long delay since India has given MFN status to Pakistan long before.

On the other hand, BIMSTEC member countries agreed to establish the BIMSTEC Free Trade Area frame work agreement in order to stimulate trade and investment in the partners. It holds greater promises to India. BIMSTEC along with the Mekong Ganga Cooperation can act as a gateway to greater access to the large ASEAN Services market of 565 million service buyers.

Therefore, India has been actively signing many PTAs bilaterally with the ASEAN members like Singapore, Malaysia and Thailand.

India occupies 70% of the SAARC region, both geographically and economically, and the remaining 6 nations of the SAARC borders only with India and not with each other. As the biggest and the most industrialized trading partner among the SAARC countries, India has to recognise that a special responsibility devolves on her and take a lead in making a regional economic co-operation or reality in South Asia.

Q. 2 Answer any THREE of the following in about 150 words each : 12 × 3 = 36

(a) Subsequent to the Nuclear Suppliers' Group (NSG) waiver in 2008, what are the agreements on nuclear energy that India has signed with different countries ?

(b) Trace the progress of India's efforts for a joint counter-terrorism strategy with China. What are the likely implications of the recent Xinjiang violence on these efforts ?

(c) Bring out the importance of the 'Small and Medium Enterprises Expo and Conference' held in Dubai last year for Indian business.

(d) What are the salient features of the political and economic relationship between India and South Africa ?

Important Points for Answer:	
• *NSG*	• *Waiver for India*
• *Nuclear energy agreements*	

Answer: (a) India has a flourishing and largely indigenous nuclear power program and expects to have 20,000 MWe nuclear capacity on line by 2020 and 63,000 MWe by 2032. It aims to supply 25% of electricity from nuclear power by 2050.

After the 34 years exclusion, India was given the waiver of the NSG and has been recognized as the de facto nuclear power. It paved the way for major international companies to have a share in the vast nuclear market of India. France was the first country to sign the civil nuclear deal in 2008 followed by eight other countries.

These are Russia, Mongolia, Namibia, Argentina, UK, Canada, Kazakhastan and South Korea.

Recently, Australia, the largest uranium exporter of the world, has removed the ban on India and consented to export Uranium to India.

Important Points for Answer:	
• *Joint counter-terrorism strategy*	• *India - China efforts*
• *Xinjiang violence*	

(b) The two Asian giants clearly know that the 'terrorism anywhere is a threat everywhere'. That was the main theme of the joint counter terrorism mechanism signed by India and China in 2002. After 9/11 attacks, India has signed many bilateral mechanism with several countries.

A significant addition was made to this mechanism in 2005, the joint counter terrorism was extended to include "Separatism and extremism", so as to suit Chinese problem of Uighur extremism and Dalai Lama's separatism movement despite the working of this bilateral mechanism since 2002.

The First India-China Joint anti-terror Military Exercise ("Fland-in-Hand, 2007") held at Kunming in the Yunnan province of China from December 19 to 25, 2007, which involves 103 troops each from the two armies.

Beijing's policy, like that of the US, shows a marked disinclination to hold Pakistan accountable for the Jihadi terrorism in the Indian Territory. The recent incidents in Xinjiang and its probable links with ISI has not led to any change in China's policy except supporting Pakistan efforts in dismantling terrorism, and it is this aspect which has strategic implication for India.

Important Points for Answer:	
• *SME Expo and Conference*	• *Importance*

(c) The SMEs Expo, will offer a great platform to small units to promote their brands, products and services, as well as explore business opportunities in the Middle-East and North African markets.

Besides giving a major impetus to networking activities with other visiting countries such as Pakistan, Mauritius, Nigeria and Vietnam, the event will offer Indian SMEs the opportunity to acquaint themselves with the latest technologies in their industries and from alliances with international clients. Indian SMEs from sectors such as plastic, petrochemicals, garments and textiles, and art and handicrafts, among others, are likely to gain from participation at the expo.

Indian SMEs attending the event could also seek to scout for partnership possibilities with Dubai and Gulf Cooperation Council (GCC) based countries such as Kuwait, Saudi Arabia, the UAE, Oman, Bahrain and Qatar.

Significantly according to the Dubai Customs Department, with bilateral trade between India and Dubai shooting above US $ 23.14 billion, India was Dubai's biggest direct trade partner during the initial seven months of 2010.

There is also a vast opportunity for India to boost India's banking presence in the UAE to enhance two-way trade and investment.

Important Points for Answer:	
• *India - South Africa*	• *Political Relations*
• *Economic Relations*	• *Importance*

(d) India's relationship with South Africa starts since Mahatma Gandhi started his Satyagraha Movement in South Africa more than a century ago.

Following a commencement of talks between the then South African Government and the African National Congress (ANC), India's relations with South Africa were restored after four decades with the opening of a cultural centre in Johannesburg in May 1993. Thus against the background of India's consistent support to the anti-apartheid struggle, close and friendly relations - strategic, political, economic and cultural between the two countries have subsequently been consolidated.

Various bilateral agreements have also been concluded between India and South Africa in diverse areas ranging from economic and commercial cooperation, defence, culture, health, human settlements, public administration, science and technology and education.

On the other hand, the economic relationship also reached the new age, the bilateral trade has trebled from US $ 2.5 billion in 2003-04 to US $ 7.5 billion in 2008-09. The trade target to be achieved has been US $ 15 billiion by 2014.

An important initiative under negotiation is the India-SACU preferential Trade Agreement. Commercial interaction has been aided by an Indo-South Africa CEO's Forum. An India Business Forum (IBF) was launched in March 2007 in South Africa.

Q. 3 Answer either of the following in about 250 words : 20

(a) "The causes and implications of the Jasmine Revolution and its spread are as much economic in nature as they are political." Critically evaluate.

(b) In the context of the 'Euro-zone' debt crisis, examine the proposed 'six-pack' solution. Do you think that this has a better chance of success than the earlier Stability and Growth Pact ?

Important Points for Answer:	
• *Jasmine Revolution*	• *Causes*
• *Implications*	

Answer: (a) The Arab uprising started when an unemployed youth "Mohammed po Agasi" committed suicide by self-immolation due to police torture for bribe to run a road side fruit shop in Tunisia. This incident ignited a fire in the minds of the people. They were already looking for an opportunity to raise their voice against the Autocratic Government.

Arab spring is the name given to the pro-democracy movement in the western and northern African nations.

- **Economic causes** : Youth unemployment, high level of poverty, impact of global financial crisis, widening gulf between rich and poor and likewise.
- **Political causes** : Autocratic regime and tribocracy, increasing intervention of major powers to acquire the strategic resources, the civil unrests, high level of corruption and likewise.
- **Hindrances** : Lack of effective central leadership and the problem between the Shia and Sunni Peoples, tribal conflicts, active role of revolutionary groups with the help of NATO and US Forces and weapon supplies.

Important Points for Answer:	
• *Euro - zone debt crisis*	• *Six pack solution*
• *Stability and Growth Pact*	• *Comparison*

(b) The European Parliament has voted for the adoption of six legislative proposals on EU economic governance, popularly known as the "Six Pack", effectively giving unprecedented power to European commission on member state's fiscal and budgetary affairs.

(i) It hands the European Commission greater powers to sanction countries that do not keep down their debts and deficits.

(ii) The European Commission can also impose fines of 0.2 percent of GDP which can only be overturned by a majority vote of member states in the council.

(iii) The EU Parliament has been given the right to call finance ministers from countries that have been warned.

(iv) It also provides for European Semester so as to annually assess national budgets.

Generally, the six pack is about more than a sanctions. It is about prevention. It also emphasize the "prevention is better than cure" principle. It is also about more than fiscal discipline, it is about keeping European economics, competitive to create jobs and archive sustainable growth.

The stability and growth pact (SGP) is a rule based frame work for the co-ordination of national fiscal policies in the economic and monetary union (EMU).

Also, it was established to safeguard sound public finances, an important requirement for EMU to function properly.

Q. 4 Answer any four of the following in about 150 words each: 12 × 4 = 48

(a) "As regard the increasing rates of melting of Arctic Sea ice, the interests of the Arctic Council Nations may not coincide with those of the wider world." Explain.

(b) Is there still a role for the concept of balance of power in contemporary international politics ? Discuss.

(c) "Strategic interests seem to be replacing commercial interests for the host country with regard to Cam Ranh Bay." Amplify.

(d) To what extent has the withdrawal of al-Shabab from Mogadishu given peace a real chance in Somalia? Assess.

(e) On a Formula-one (F-l) racing car track, information to drivers is generally signalled through the standardized use of flags of different colours. Describe the meanings associated with any six of the flags listed below :

(i) White flag **(ii) Black flag**

(iii) Yellow flag **(iv) Blue flag**

(v) Black and white flag divided diagonally

(vi) Chequered flag **(vii) Yellow and red striped flag**

Important Points for Answer:

- *Melting of Arctic Sea ice*
- *Arctic Council Nations*
- *Interest of the World*

Answer: (a) Global warming has changed the Arctic and the region is now facing a very different future that many nations and companies want to be a part of it. The Arctic countries are set to make a big short term earnings, at the cost of climate change.

The disappearing of Arctic Sea ice has been known for decades. The underlying cause is believed by all but handful of climatologists to be a global warming brought about by greenhouse gas emissions. Yet the rate at which the ice melting differs in every models.

It is predicted that there will be no ice meltings in the Arctics at the end of this century, if the level of CO_2 and Methane continues to rise at the present level. Some scientists predicts that it may happen in 2050 itself.

Interest of Arctic Council Nations :

The Arctic Nations are showing very much interest to tap the untapped reserves of oils and gas. It is believed that 25% of the world's untapped reserves of oil and gas are in the North of the Polar Circle.

The Eight member Arctic Council nations are looking for the way to tap the resources rather than take stern actions to curb the menace of the climate change.

The fast growing commercial interests, brings challenges to the Nordic nations and they are competing themself for the economical benefits without considering its consequences.

Important Points for Answer:
- *Balance of Power*
- *Role and Concept*

(b) The concept of Balance of Power (BoP) exists when there is a parity or stability between competing forces. The concept describes a state of affairs in the international system and explains the behaviour of states in that system.

As a concept in international law, it is considered as "just equilibrium" between the members of the family of nations. It expresses the doctrine intended to prevent any one nation from becoming sufficiently strong so as to enable it to enforce its will upon the rest.

Even now, the nations are forming regional and economic co-operations, councils and Security Councils among themselves to make a balance of power in the various region of the world, such as NATO, EU, SAARC, SCO, ASEAN, AU, etc.

US led NATO groups wanted to make a strong hold in all regions of the world, but to counter this NATO, Russia plans to make more strong SCO and post-several union nations groups in the Asian region.

So, still all the countries in the world are some way or other trying to make a power strong hold to survive in the globalised era.

Important Points for Answer:
- *Cam Ranh Bay*
- *Interests - Strategic vs. Commercial*

(c) In the South-East Asian region, the rowing deterent attitude of China, is considered as a threat to all south-east Asian nations, including Vietnam. The Vietnam's military modernisation programme has also escalated tension with Beijing over disputes islands in the South-China Sea. Once operational, the submarines will provide Vietnam with a potent deterrent aimed at China's increasingly powerful navy.

The Cam Ranh Bay is one of the finest deep water anchorages in the south-east Asia and provides access to the commercially and strategically vital sea lanes which pass through the South-China Sea.

The base established by the trench in the late 19th century, occupied by Japan in the Second World War, become major base of operations for the US military in 1978, then lased to Russia for 25 years, and again come back to Vietnam in 2002.

Now, Vietnam has announced the lease proposal to the foreign navies. But it is viewed as a part of larger strategy by Vietnam to strengthen defence ties with US and facilitate the US military presence in South-east Asia as a counter to China's rising power in this region. The regular presence of the US warships at Cam Ranh Bay might make China think twice about using coercive military diplomacy against Vietnam.

Important Points for Answer:	
• *Conditions of Somalia*	• *Al-Shabab Withdrawal*
• *Chances of peace*	

(d) Somalia is one of the worst famine affected country in the world. The living condition of the people is very-very low. There is no proper food, sanitation and basic amenities.

Due to a long civil war, the international agencies could not do any humanitarian aid to the affected people properly. The al-Shabab guerilla is one of the militant outfits which imposed the blockade in the region.

This had been one of the causes of worsening famine in the country as al-Shabab didn't allow international body to work there.

Now, with the withdrawal of al-Shabab, the humanitarian crisis can be properly handled and the chances of lasting peace will increase in the region.

(i) **White flag :** a slow - moving vehicle such as a retiring car, an ambulance or tow truck ahead on the track, and instructs drivers to slow down.

(ii) **Black flag** : orders a particular driver to return to his pit within the next lap and report immediately to the Clerk of the Course, usually because they have been disqualified from the race.

(iii) **Yellow flag** : A single yellow indicates danger ahead, such as debris from a crash. Drivers must slow down as they pass; no overtaking is permitted, unless it is unavoidable such as a driver retiring in the section, or a driver is lapped.

(iv) **Blue flag** : During a race, a light blue flag waved on the track warns the driver that they are about to be lapped by a faster car and must let it pass. A driver may incur penalties if they ignore three successive blue flags.

(v) **Black and white flag divided diagonally** : informs a driver that their behaviour has been deemed unsporting and if they do not begin acting in a sporting manner immediately they will be disqualified. A sign with the car number accompanies the flag.

(vi) **Chequered flag** : signals the end of the race, practice session, or qualifying session. During the race it is shown first to the winner and then to the rest of the field as they finish; otherwise it is shown at a predetermined time.

(vii) **Yellow and red striped flag** : warns drivers that the track surface ahead is slippery, or there is debris present.

Q. 5 Comment on any THIRTEEN of the following in about 50 words each : 5 × 13 = 65

(a) International Year of Chemistry

(b) The scourge of e-waste

(c) 'Designer' poultry eggs

(d) INSPIRE programme of the department of Science and Technology

(e) The 'Kessler syndrome' with reference to space debris

(f) Omega-3 fatty acids in our food

(g) Difference between 'spin-drying' and 'tumble-drying' technology with reference to drying of washed clothes.

(h) The diminishing population of vultures

(i) 'Arsenic-bug' and the significance of its discovery

(j) F-22 'Raptor' aircraft

(k) 'Concentrated' solar energy and 'photovoltaic' solar energy

(l) Analog, hybrid and IP systems in CCTV technology

(m) Various applications for Kevlar

(n) Differences between Compact Disc (CD), Digital Versatile Disc (DVD) and Blu- ray Disc

Answer: (a) International Year of Chemistry : The International Year of Chemistry 2011 (IYC, 2011) is a world-wide celebration of the achievements of Chemistry and its contribution to the well-being of the whole human kind.

The goals of IYC-2011 are to increase the public appreciation of Chemistry, to encourage interest in Chemistry among young people, and to generate positive approach for the creative future of Chemistry.

(b) The scourge of e-waste : Due to technology development, the world is facing another major problem in the name of e-waste. It leads to various environment and health problems. The amount of various chemical compounds, and other toxic materials present in the electronic compounds can cause cancer and other skin diseases. Also they pollute the environment in various ways.

(c) 'Designer' poultry eggs : Designer eggs are those eggs produced by flocks of chickens that have been fed special diets to modify the nutrition of the eggs they produce.

The composition of the feed leads to the desired composition of the eggs, adding the nutritive profile in the eggs through enrichment in the diet and not by use of any drugs or hormones.

(d) INSPIRE programme of the department of Science and Technology : INSPIRE means Innovation in Science Pursuit for Inspired Research. It is an innovative programme to commemorate to the youth of the country the excitements of creative pursuit of science at an early age and thus build the required critical human resources pool for strengthening and expanding the science and technology system and research and development in the field of science.

(e) The 'Kessler syndrome' with reference to space debris : It is a scenario in which the density of objects in low earth orbit (LEO) is high enough that collisions between objects could cause a cascade, each collision generating debris which increases the likelihood of further collisions.

It was first proposed by the NASA Scientist Donald J. Kessler in the year 1978. Hence, it is called Kessler Syndrome.

(f) Omega-3 fatty acids in our food : Omega - 3 fatty acids are very essential and helpful in alleviating cardiovascular disease. And also the diseases like diabetes, inflammatory ailments and autoimmune disorders.

The source of Omega - 3 are fish oil, marine foods, cod liver oil, and also found in bread, milk and dairy products, fruit juices, salads, and mayonnaise, etc.

(g) Difference between 'spin-drying' and 'tumble-drying' technology with reference to drying of washed clothes : The two technology has been used in drying the clothes. The spin drying spins the drums faster than a typical washer could in order to extract additional water from the load whereas tumbler dryer uses the heated rotating drum for clothes dryer.

Spin dryer on the other hand may remove more water in two minutes than a heated tumbler dryer can in twenty minutes, thus saving significant amount of time and energy.

(h) The diminishing population of vultures : This is mainly due to use of diclofinac in animals has led to the sharp decline in the vulture population in the Indian subcontinent.

Vultures eat the carcasses of livestock that have been administered veterinary diclofinac, and are poisoned by the accumulated chemical which causes renal failure, a known side effect of diclofinac.

The vulture population has declined 95% in 2003 and 99.9% in 2008.

(i) 'Arsenic-bug' and the significance of its discovery : NASA-supported researchers have discovered the first known micro-organism on earth able to thrive and reproduce using the toxic chemical arsenic. The microorganism which lives in California's Mono Lake, substitutes arsenic for phosphorus in the backbone of its DNA and other cellular components.

(j) F-22 'Raptor' aircraft : It is a single seat, twin engine fifth generation maneuverable fighter aircraft that uses stealth technology. The F-22 Raptor is made up of 39% titanium, 24% composite, 16% aluminium and 1% tormoplastic by weight. Titanium is used for its high strength-to-weight ratio in critical stress areas, including some of the bulkheads, and also for the head-resistant qualities in the hot sections of the aircraft. Carbon fibre composites have been used for the fuselage frame, the doors, intermediate spars on the wings, and for the honeycomb sandwich construction skin panels. A BAE systems head-updisplay (HUD) shows target status, weapon status, weapon envelopes and shoot cues. A video camera records data on the HVD for post mission analysis.

(k) 'Concentrated' solar energy and 'photovoltaic' solar energy : Concentrated solar power (CSP) systems use mirrors or lenses to concentrate a large area of sunlight, or solar thermal energy, onto a small area. Electrical power is produced when the concentrated light is converted to heat, which drives a heat engine, usually a (steam turbine) connected to an electrical power generator.

Photovoltaics (PV) is a method of generating electrical power by converting solar radiation into direct current electricity using semi-conductors that exhibit the photovoltaic effect. The solar panels composed of a number of solar cells contain photovoltaic materials, such as monocrystalline silicon, polycrystalline silicon, amorphous silicon, cadmium felluride and copper indium and gallium setanide/ sulfide.

(l) Analog, hybrid and IP systems in CCTV technology : The closed circuit television (CCTV) system has different technologies in which, analog cameras cost less than IP Network cameras. Widespread compatibility. Analog CCTV systems capture video in its purest electric form.

IP CCTV can send video, audio and data from the city to another up to 30 kilometers away. A Hybrid CCTV system can record and display IP cameras and analog cameras into the same security recorder.

(m) Various applications for Kevlar : Kevlar is a brand fiber which is used for various purposes:

(i) It is used as heat resistant during rocket and satellite launches.

(ii) It is used to make protection vests, military helmets and resistant gloves, bullet proof jackets, etc.

(iii) It is used to vehicle armor and helps to protect the law enforcement personnel who face multiple threats from fire arms, knives and puncture-producing weapons.

(iv) It is also used to improve the performance and durability of power train and body components used in passenger vehicles, trucks and race cars.

(v) The fibers and filaments also help to strengthen countless miles of castes containing glass fibers that transmit voice, data and video signals.

(n) Differences between Compact Disc (CD), Digital Versatile Disc (DVD) and Blu-ray Disc :

Compact Disc (CD) is a small portable round medium made up of molded polymer for electronically recording storing and has storage capacity of 700 MB of data uses semiconductor laser;

Digital Versatile Disc (DVD) is an optical disc technology with 4.7 GB storage capacity on a single-sided, one-layered disc. DVD can be single-or-double sided, and can have a layer on each side. Two-layered DVD will hold up to 17 GB of video, audio or other information, uses 650 nm wavelength laser diode light;

Blue-Ray Disc (BD) is designed to supersede the DVD format. The plastic disc is 120 mm in diameter and 1.2 mm thick, same as DVD. It contain 25 GB per layer uses blue laser.

Q. 6 Comment on the following in about 50 words each: 5 × 5 = 25

(a) Functions of the World Customs Organisation (WCO)

(b) Success of international intervention in Cote d'Ivoire (Ivory Coast)

(c) Strategies adopted by Colombia to eliminate its drug cartels

(d) World Food Programme (WFP) of the United Nations (UN)

(e) Sculpture of the broken chair in front of the UN building at Geneva

Answer: (a) Functions of the World Customs Organisation (WCO) : The WCO is situated in Brussels, it is considered as a sister organisation of WTO. Its primary function is to enhance the efficiency and effectiveness of member customs administrations, thereby assisting them to contribute successfully to national development goals. Especially in the areas of revenue collection, national security, trade facilitation with other nation community protection and collection of trade statistics which enables the member states in all fronts to improve their trade with international community.

(b) Success of international intervention in Cote d'Ivoire (Ivory Coast) : The Conflict in Ivory Coast had entered a decisive phase as Laurent Ghagbo, who has hung on to power despite losing in the general election, fights an end game against the rightful President. Unlike what happened in Libya, Iraq and Afghanistan, the intervention in Coast de'Ivorie worked within a week, former President Laurent Ghagbo, accepted the defeat in an election and plunged his country into a steadily escalating spiral of violence and repression, was in custody. With in a week, the majority of his forces had surrendered or rallied to the new President's side. Moreover, **it** did not lead to civil war, which often occurs in the African countries.

(c) Strategies adopted by Colombia to eliminate its drug cartels : As of 2011 Colombia remains the world's largest cocaine producer. Since the establishment of the war on drugs, the US and European countries have provided financial, logistical, tactical and military aid to Colombia to curb the drug cartels.

The most notable of this step is "**Plan Colombia**", a program to combat drug cartels and leftist organisations, and deployed police and military forces to retake the territory controlled by the cartels. A second part of the strategy is to bring down the top bosses. Colombia managed with the help of the USA and the UNODC to rid itself of the drug cartels. As a signatory to the 1988 Vienna Convention against drug trafficking, Colombia has been taking stern actions to curb the menace of drugs.

(d) World Food Programme (WFP) of the United Nations (UN): WFP is the United Nations frontline agency in the fight against global hunger. Since its launch, WFP staff around the world have worked timelessly towards reducing hunger. In 2010, WFP aims to provide food assistance to more than 90 million people in 72 countries.

WFP of the UN is the world's largest humanitarian agency fighting hunger worldwide. It was formed in 1961 with the vision of alleviating hunger from the globe in cooperation with FAO and IFAD.

(e) Sculpture of the broken chair in front of the **UN building at Geneva** : In order to show the opposition and to remain to the world leaders, the Broken chair is a monumental sculpture in wood by the Swiss artist Daniel Berset, constructed by the carpenter Louis Geneve. It symbolises the opposition to land mines and cluster bombs, and acts as a remainder by politicians and others visiting Geneva. It's one of the peaceful way to show our angry and disappointment with the world leaders, and to remain their failures to take actions against the injustice.

Q. 7 Why have each of the following been in the news recently? (Each answer in a sentence or two only) **2 × 10 = 20**

(a) Tiangong-1	**(b) K-computer**
(c) Gliese 581 g	**(d) MABEL robot**
(e) 'Operation Shady Rat'	**(f) SAGA - 220**
(s) 'Billion Acts of Green'	**(h) L'Aquila earthquake**
(i) OPERA detector at Gran Sasso	**(j) Saturn's Titan**

Answer: (a) Tiangong-1 : It is the first space laboratory module of China.

(b) K-computer : It is the fastest super computer produced by Fujitsu Japan. It can operate over 2 petaflops.

(c) Gliese 581 g : It is an earth-sized planet orbiting a nearby star. Liquid water could exist on the surface of the planet.

(d) MABEL robot: It is the fastest bipedal robot with knees running at a speed of 6.8 miles per hour.

(e) 'Operation Shady Rat' : It is a cyber attack which have hit at least 72 organizations including defence, business, UNO, IOC, etc.

(f) SAGA-220 : It is ISRO made super-computer.

(g) 'Billion Acts of Green' : An environment campaign, with a goal to reach a billion act of environmental service.

(h) L'Aquila earthquake : The deadliest earthquake that hit Italy recently.

(i) OPERA detector at Gran Sasso : It observed neutrinos travelling faster than the speed of light.

(j) Saturn's Titan : This is the largest moon of Saturn and only known to have devise atmosphere.

Q. 8 Why have the following been in the news recently ? (Each answer in a sentence or two only) **2 × 5 = 10**

(a) 'News International' newspaper
(b) Mustafa Abdul - Jalil
(c) Abel Kirui
(d) Natalie Portman
(e) Nawaf Salam

Answer: (a) 'News International' newspaper : Employees of the newspaper were accused of engaging in phone hacking, police bribery and various illegal ways to collect the news. News International announced the closure of the newspaper on 7 July 2011. The final issue reads in big title : "THANK YOU AND GOODBYE".

(b) Mustafa Abdul - Jalil : He is the Chairman of National Transitional Council of Libya's care taker government.

(c) Abel Kirui : He won gold medal for Kenya in men's marathon at world athletes championship.

(d) Natalie Portman : The actress has won the Academy, Golden Globe, and BAFTA Awards, for her role in Black Swan in 2011.

(e) Nawaf Salam : He is the Lebanon's representative of the Security Council. He held the rotating presidency of the Security Council in September 2011.

Q. 9 (a) List the requisites of a good table. **5**

Present the following in a suitable tabular form :

In 1980 out of a total of 1750 workers of a factory, 1200 were members of a union. The number of women employed was 200 of which 175 did not belong to the union.

In 1985 the number of union workers increased to 1580 of which 1290 were men. On the other hand the number of non-union workers fell down to 208 of which 180 were men. In

1990 there were 1800 employees who belonged to the union and 50 who did not belong to the union. Of all the employees in 1990, 300 were women of which only 8 did not belong to the union.

Answer: Requisites of a good table :

- **Title** : Title is generally given at the top of the table. It should relate to **what, where, when** and **how** about the given information. It should be clear and concise.
- Table number : The purpose is to identify a particular table, it is to be used when in a given discussion we have more than one tabular presentation.
- Stub : The title given to the rows is called a stub.
- Caption : The title for the columns is referred to as a caption. It is also called a Box Head. There may be various sub-captions under one caption.
- **Field/Body** : The numerical information presentation in the set of rows and columns is called the Field or Body of the table.
- **Footnote** : This is an explanatory note which is to be written beneath the table and hence the name. The objective is to classify or explain omission(s), ambiguity (ambiguities), if any.
- **Totals / Sub-totals** : Wherever required, totals and sub-totals for columns and rows can be given for enhancing the utility of the presentation for the reader.

Tabular Presentation of the data :

Year →	**1980**			**1985**			**1990**		
Union ↓	Men	Women	Total	Men	Women	Total	Men	Women	Total
Member	1175	25	1200	1290	290	1580	1508	292	1800
Non-Member	375	175	550	180	28	208	42	8	50
Total	1550	200	1750	1470	318	1788	1550	300	1850

(b) Draw an ogive for the following distribution. Read the median from the graph. How many students get between 60 and 72 ? **5**

Marks	**No. of students**
50-55	6
55-60	10
60-65	22
65-70	30
70-75	16
75-80	12
80-100	15

Answer: Less than Commulative Frequency Table :

Marks	No. of Students in c.f.
Less than 50	0
Less than 55	6
Less than 60	16
Less than 65	38
Less than 70	68
Less than 75	84
Less than 80	96
Less than 100	111

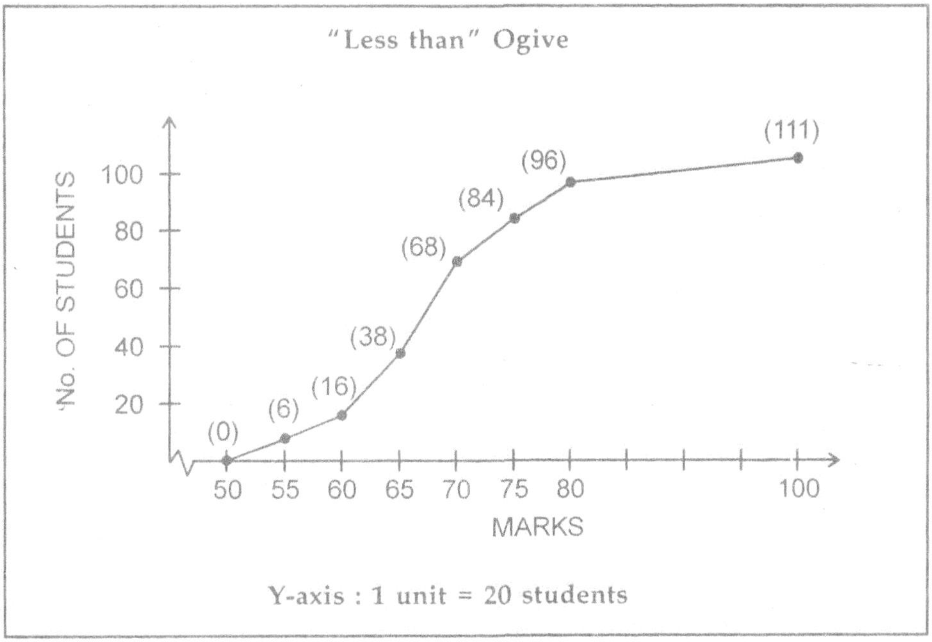

(c) From the following data calculate the missing frequency : 4

No. of tablets	No. of persons cured
4–8	11
8–12	13
12–16	16
16–20	14
20–24	?
24–28	9
28–32	17
32–36	6
36–40	4

The average no. of tablets to cure fever was 19.9.

Answer:

No. of Tablets	No. of Persons (f)	m	d = m – A	$d' = \frac{m - A}{c}$	fd′
4–8	11	6	–16	–4	–44
8–12	13	10	–12	–3	–39
12–16	16	14	–8	–2	–32
16–20	14	18	–4	–1	–14
20–24	x	22	0	0	0
24–28	9	26	4	1	9
28–32	17	30	8	2	34
32–36	6	34	12	3	18
36–40	4	38	16	4	16
	Σf = 90 + x				Σfd′ = –52

$$\bar{x} = A + \frac{\Sigma fd'}{\Sigma f} \times c = 22 + \frac{-52}{90 \times x} \times 4$$

$$19.9 - 22 + \frac{-208}{90 + x} = \frac{22(90 + x) - 208}{90 + x}$$

$$19.9\,(90 + x) = 1980 + 22x - 208$$

$$1791 + 19.9x = 1772 + 22x$$

$$x = 9.05$$

(d) Life-time of 400 tubes tested in a company is distributed as follows :

Life-time (Hours)	No. of tubes
400–499	14
600–699	46
800–899	58
1000–1099	76
300–399	68
500–599	62
700–799	48
900–999	22
1100–1199	6

Determine

(i) Relative frequency of sixth class

(ii) Percentage of tubes whose life-time does not exceed 600 hours.

(iii) Percentage of tubes whose life-time is greater than or equal to 900 hours

(iv) Percentage of tubes whose life-time is at least 500 but less than 1000 hours.

Answer:

(i) Sixth class is 800 - 899

Frequency of sixth class is 62.

Relative Frequency = Frequency of class / Total Observations

= 62 / 400 = 0.155

(ii) No. of tubes with less than 600 hrs life = 14 + 46 + 58 = 118

$$\text{Required Percentage} = \frac{118}{400} \times 100 = 29.5$$

(iii) Tubes in classes from 900-999, 1000-1099 and 1100-1199 are having life of greater than or equal to 900 hours.

Such total tubes = 48 + 22 + 6 = 76

$$\text{Required percentage} = \frac{76}{400} \times 100 = 19$$

(iv) Total no. of tubes with life between 500 and 100 hours = 58 + 76 + 68 + 62 + 48 = 312

$$\text{Required percentage} = \frac{312}{400} \times 100 = 78$$

Q. 10(a) A car travels 25 km at 25 kph, 25 km at 50 kph, and 25 km at 75 kph. Find the average speed of the car for the entire journey. **4**

Answer:

$D_1 = 25$ km $S_1 = 25$ kph $t_1 = ?$

$t_1 = D_1/S_1 = 25/25 = 1$ hr

$D_2 = 25$ km S2 = 50 kph $t_2 = ?$

$t_2 = D_2/S_2 = 25/50 = 1/2$ hr

$D_3 = 25$ km $S_2 = 75$ kph t3 = ?

$t_3 = D_3/S_3 = 25/75 = 1/3$ hr

Average Speed = Total Distance / Total Time

= (25 + 25 + 25) / {1 + (1/2) + (1/3)}

= 75 / (11/6)

= 40.9 kph

(b) The mean of 200 items was 50. Later on it was found that two items were wrongly read as 92 and 8 instead of 192 and 88. Find the correct mean. **4**

Answer: Mean = Sum of All Frequencies/ Total Frequency

50 = X/200

X = 10000

But sum total 10000 includes two wrong items. We can subtract them and add two correct items.

So, 10000 – (92 + 8) = 9900

And then add two correct items : 9900 + (192 + 88) = 10100

New mean = 10100/200 = 50.5

(c) Students were asked how long it took them to walk to school on a particular morning. A cumulative frequency distribution was formed. **6**

Time taken (minutes)	c.f.
<5	28
<10	45
<15	81
<20	143
<25	280
<30	349
<35	374
<40	395
<45	400

(i) Draw a cumulative frequency curve

(ii) Estimate how many students took less than 18 minutes

(iii) 6% of students took x minutes or longer. Find x.

Answer:

(i) Cummulative Frequency Curve

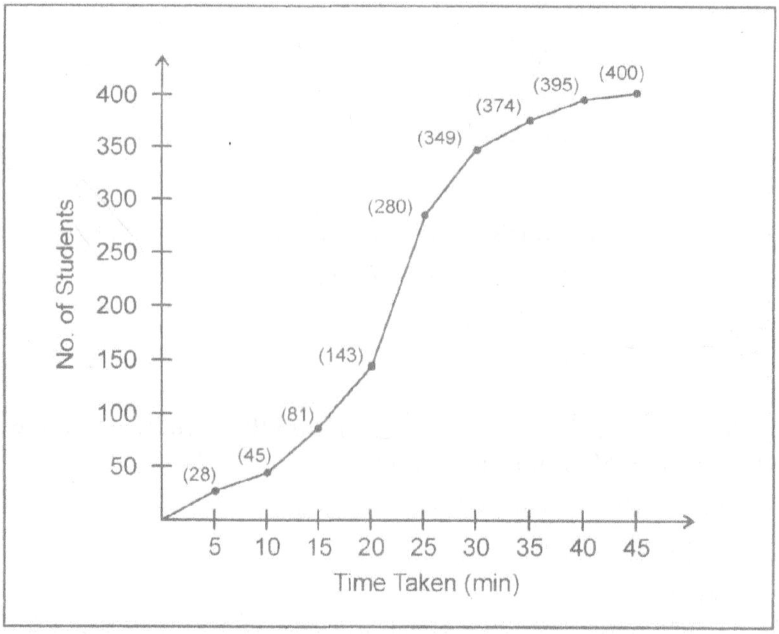

(ii) Students took less than 15 min. = 81

Between 15 and 19 number of students = 143 - 81 = 62

(Between 15 and 19 can be divided into 5 equal parts considering equal distribution of frequency) = 62/5 = 12.4

Students took less than 18 min (15 to 17 min = 3 min) = 81 + (12.4 x 3)

= 81 + 37.2 = 118.2 ≈ **118**

(iii) 6% of 400 = 400 x 6 / 100 = 24 students

These 24 students took x min or longer. It means they are the last six students. So, students after cumulative rank of (400 - 24 = 376) took X min or longer. In less than 35 min category total number of students are 374. And in less than 40 min category total number of students are 395.

So, on the scale of 35, 36, 37, 38 and 39 total students are 395-374= 21.

So, 21/5 = 4.2 students per minute.

If we consider that 4 students took 35 minutes, then 22 students took more than 35 minutes'.

So, 6% of students, i.e. 24 students took 35 min or longer. Therefore, x is 3 minutes.

(d) An investor buys ₹1200 worth of shares in a company each month. During the first five months he bought the shares at a price of ₹10, ₹12, ₹15, ₹20 and ₹24 per share. After 5 months, what is the average price paid for the shares by him ? 4

Answer:

Month	**?**	**Price**	**No. of shares**
1st Month	1200	10	120
2 nd Month	1200	12	100
3 rd Month	1200	15	80
4th Month	1200	20	60
5th Month	1200	24	50
Total	6000	–	410

Average Price = Total Amount / Total number of shares = 6000 / 410 = **14.63**

(MAIN) **2012**

Civil Services Exam. General Studies

SOLVED PAPERS

PAPER–I

Time Allowed: Three Hours *Maximum Marks: 300*

Instructions: Candidates should attempt all questions strictly in accordance with the instructions given under each question. The number of marks carried by each question is indicated at the end of the question.

Important: Whenever a question is being attempted, all its parts/sub-parts must be attempted contiguously. This means that before moving on to the next question to be attempted, candidates must finish attempting all parts / sub-parts of the previous question attempted. This is to be strictly followed. Pages left blank in the answer-book are to be clearly struck out in ink. Any answers that follow pages left blank may not be given credit.

Q. 1 Answer any five of the following in about 250 words each: **$25 \times 5 = 125$**

(a) What do you understand by the term "Innovation" ? Discuss the need for launching a national innovation policy in India.

Answer: Innovation is the development of new values through solutions that meet new requirements, inarticulate needs, or old customer and market needs in value adding new ways.. This is accomplished through more effective products, processes, services, technologies, or ideas that are readily available to markets, governments, and society.

India has a long tradition of innovation and a significant pool of qualified people, both within country as well as the diaspora, presently engaged in innovative activities. This talent pool has to be leveraged to drive the innovation agenda. Further, there is also a need to capture the multiple innovations happening in various domains such as government, R&D labs, universities, and across sectors, to give an impetus to the innovation process in the country. NIC (National Innovation Council) will act as a platform to facilitate this engagement and collaboration with domain experts, stakeholders and key participants to create an innovation movement in India. The aim is to herald a mindset change and create a push at the grassroots level so that more and more people in education, business, government, NGOs, urban and rural development engaged in innovative activities are co-opted and are part of shaping the national level innovation strategy.

Realising that innovation is the engine for the growth of prosperity and national competitiveness in the 21st century, the President of India has declared 2010 as the 'Decade of Innovation'.

Towards this end, the Prime Minister has approved the setting up of a National Innovation Council (NInC) under the Chairmanship of Mr. Sam Pitroda, Adviser to the PM on PIII to discuss analyse and help implement strategies for inclusive innovation in India and prepare a Roadmap for Innovation 2010-2020. NIC would be the first step in creating a crosscutting system which will provide mutually reinforcing policies, recommendations and methodologies to implement and boost innovation performance in the country.

(b) Keeping in view the informal sector's share in the total workforce of the country, critically examine the relevant inclusive measures initiated by the Government of India and their effectiveness.

Important Points for Answer:
- *Informal sector in India*
- *Various schemes*

Answer: Informal sector in India consist of unorganized labour workers in rural and urban area. They constitute nearly 85% of total work force and contribute to more than 50% of total production. For their welfare, the Government has, from time to time, implemented various inclusive measures.

Some of them are:

- **Aam Admi Bima Yojana**, a Social Security Scheme for rural landless household was launched on 2nd October, 2007. The head of the family or one earning member in the family of such a household is covered under the scheme. The premium of Rs.200/- per person per annum is shared equally by the Central Government and the State Government. The member to be covered should be aged between 18 and 59 years.
- **The Mahatma Gandhi National Rural Employment Guarantee Act** aims at enhancing the livelihood security of people in rural areas by guaranteeing hundred days of wage-employment in a financial year to a rural household whose adult members volunteer to do unskilled manual work.
- **Rashtriya Swasthya Bima Yojana** (RSBY) has been launched by Ministry of Labor and Employment, Government of India to provide health insurance coverage for Below Poverty Line (BPL) families. The objective of RSBY is to provide protection to BPL households from financial liabilities arising out of health shocks that involve hospitalization. Beneficiaries under RSBY are entitled to hospitalization coverage up to Rs. 30,000/- for most of the diseases that require hospitalization

These welfare schemes have certainly uplifted living standard of unorgani labour and unskilled workers.

(c) Examine the causes and the extent of 'desertification' in India and suggest remedial measures.

Important Points for Answer:
- *What is Desertification ?*
- *Causes*
- *Legislative Framework*
- *Schemes/Programmes*

Answer: Desertification is the degradation of land in any dryland. It is caused by a variety factors, such as climate change and human activities. Desertification is a significant global ecological and environmental problem.

Nearly 25% of the country's geographical area is affected by desertification. The Space Application Centre in 2007 brought out the Desertification and Land Degradation Atlas which shows 81.45 million hectare land in the country has turned into arid, semi-arid or dry sub humid region.

Desertification is caused by a number of factors including climatic variations and human activities. Some of the human activities that can cause desertification are:

- Expansion of agriculture- over-cultivation of soils, or exposure to erosion by wind or water;
- Reduction in the fallow period of soil, and lack of organic or mineral fertilizers;
- Overgrazing - often selectively - of shrubs, herbs and grasses;
- Over-exploitation of forest resources; deforestation;
- Uncontrolled use of fire for regenerating pasture, for hunting, agricultural clearing, or for settling;
- Poor irrigation practices-irrigation of soils prone to salinisation, alkalinisation or even water logging.

Policy and legislative frameworks that contribute to combating desertification in India:

- National Water Policy, 1987;
- National Forest Policy, 1988;
- National Agricultural Policy, 2000;
- Forest (Conservation) Act, 1980;
- Environment (Protection) Act, 1986;
- National Environmental Policy, 2006;
- National Policy for Farmers, 2007;
- National Rain-fed Area Authority (NRAA)- 2007 .

Some major schemes/programmes that have contributed to desertification control are:

- Drought Prone Areas Programme (DPAP), 1973-74;
- Watershed Development Project in Shifting Cultivation Areas (WDPSCA), 1974-75;
- Desert Development Programme (DDP), 1977-78;
- Reclamation & Development of Alkali Soil (RAS), 1985-86;
- Watershed Development Fund (WDF), Integrated Wasteland Development Programme (IWDP), 1989;
- National Watershed Development Project for Rain fed Areas (NWDPRA) - 1990-91;
- Soil Conservation in the Catchment of River Valley Projects (RVP) 1992;
- Sustainable Land and Ecosystem Management (SLEM Programmatic Approach) 2007;
- Common Guidelines for Watershed Development Programme, 2008;

- Integrated Watershed Management Programme (IWMP);
- Guidelines for Convergence between NREGA and NAP 2009.

National Afforestation Programme (NAP) 2002-03 is also one of the major programmes in which Association of Scheduled Tribes and Rural Poor in Regeneration of Degraded Forests (ASTRP), launched in 1992-93 and Integrated Afforestation and Eco-Development Projects Scheme (LAEPS) 1989-90 were merged into the National Afforestation Programme.

(d) In the context of the growing demands for the ban of Endosulfan in the country, critically examine the issues involved. What, in your view, should be done in the matter ?

Important Points for Answer:
- *What is Endosulfan ?*
- *Its effects*
- *Banning of Endosulfan*

Answer: Endosulfan is an off-patent organochlorine insecticide and acaricide that is being phased out globally. The two isomers, endo and exo, are known popularly as I and II.

Endosulfan became a highly controversial agrichemical due to its acute toxicity, potential for bioaccumulation, and role as an endocrine disruptor. Because of its threats to human health and the environment, a global ban on the manufacture and use of endosulfan was negotiated under the Stockholm Convention in April 2011. The ban was to take effect in mid-2012, with certain uses exempted for five additional years.

The Supreme Court banned the production and sale of endosulfan in the country. In April 2012, it asked the Centre to ascertain the quantity of raw material lying with three companies (producers of the banned pesticide endosulfan) and the manner in which the raw material could be disposed of.

The international conventions and global practices also suggest phasing out. The FAO also recommends disposal of live stock of pesticides through phasing out by its judicious use as per good agricultural practices for crop protection purposes.

Of the 19 States which participated in the meeting convened by the expert committee, except Kerala and Karnataka, other States were in favour of the continued use of endosulfan for the reasons being broad spectrum, cheaper, most popular among farmers, safe to pollinations, no reports of resistance/resurgence or ill effects on human beings, animals and environment. Thus, States other than Kerala and Karnataka are ready to use endosulfan for agricultural pest control.

(e) "The Indian independence movement was a mass - based movement that encompassed various sections of society. It also underwent the process of constant ideological evolution." Critically examine.

Answer: Indian independence movement started from the 1857 uprising of sepoys. The uprising led to nationwide protest against British. Everywhere local people joined with the rebels and rose up against British. This is the first indication that Indian freedom movement was a mass-based movement.

Many peasants uprisings and revolts occur till the independence in 1947. Establishment of Indian National Congress and its political movement, Home Rule League and its support by people, Gandhi's Satyagrahas and Civil Disobedience Movement encompassed almost all sections of the society. Muslim League also enjoyed a mass support of muslims which acted to overthrow British. People of all religion, status and creed joined against the British rule.

In 1857 it was predominantly a revolt against foreign rule, to establish local rulers. Peasant uprisings were to overthrow insensitive rulers. INC movement was to gain political advantage and establish a political order, initially dominion status and later complete independence. Gandhi's movement also underwent ideological changes ranging from support to British rule with demand of more freedom and political right to complete independence.

The independence movement passed through small uprisings, organized political struggle under congress, mass movement under congress, Gandhi's non-violent movement along with revolutionary struggle.

Thus, the independence movement encompassed various sections of society and underwent different ideological phases.

(f) The issue of tourism in core areas of tiger reserve forests in the country is a subject matter of debate. Critically examine various aspects of this issue, keeping in view relevant recent judicial pronouncements.

Answer: The Supreme Court lifted the ban on tourist activities in core areas of tiger reserve forests.

After the ban, several States and other stake holders urged the Centre to revisit the guidelines and sought the lifting of the ban. Accordingly, the Centre filed an application seeking modification of the order. Subsequently, the court asked the Centre to hold consultations with the States and others and come out with fresh guidelines. Accordingly, the NTCA formulated fresh guidelines.

The Comprehensive Guidelines on Strategy, Tiger Conservation and Tourism in and around Tiger Reserves envisaged that 20 per cent of the core reserve area should be permitted for tourism. Shifting the focus from wildlife tourism to eco-tourism, the NTCA had recommended that a maximum of 20 per cent of the core/critical tiger habitat usage (not exceeding the present usage) for regulated, low-impact tourist visitation might be permitted by the court. It said, "In case the current usage exceeds 20 per cent, the Local Area Committee may decide on a time frame for bringing down the usage to 20 per cent. Such area may be demarcated as tourism zone and there should be strict adherence to site-specific carrying capacity."

Some suggestions in this regard are:

The States should enact law to regulate tiger tourism—tourist facilities; tour operators should not cause disturbance to animals; tourism infrastructure must be environment-friendly like usage of solar energy, waste recycling and rainwater harvesting, etc; permanent tourist facilities located inside the core areas should be phased out in a time frame and 10 per cent of the revenue generated from pilgrim centres located in tiger reserves must be used for development of local communities.

Q. 2 Answer any seven of the following in about 150 words each: 15 × 7 = 105

(a) "There is an urgent need for the Planning Commission to revise the chapter on health in the 12th Plan document." Comment.

Answer: The 12th Plan document recommends, in its chapter on Health, increase in public expenditure on health from the present 1 per cent to 1.58 per cent of GDP, in sharp contrast to the High Level Expert Group recommendation of raising this expenditure to at least 2.5 per cent of GDP.

This will ensure that India remains among the bottom 10 nations in terms of public spending on health. Health activists feel the focus of the document has shifted to a 'managed care' approach, paving the way for greater private role in public healthcare. It is feared that this would lead to the Government abandoning its role in providing healthcare and becoming just a 'manager' of a largely corporatised system. This would also decisively halt and eventually reverse the moderate achievements of the National Rural Health Mission, in expanding public health infrastructure and services in parts of the country.

Union Health Minister Ghulam Nabi Azad has written a letter to the Planning Commission and added that the Minister was personally looking into the matter. The Minister's letter hits out at the Plan panel's suggested pilot models that "heavily promote corporatisation of health", and reiterates that the Ministry's stance of developing a strong public health system be supplemented by private sector participation, not vice-versa.

(b) The Union Cabinet recently cleared the proposal to rename and amend the Child Labour (Prohibition and Regulation) Act, 1986. What are the salient features of the proposed amendments ?

Answer: The amendments included renaming of Child Labour (Prohibition & Regulation) Act as Child and Adolescent Labour (Prohibition) Act and provided that there will be no bar on children helping their families after school hours and in vacations, in fields, home-based work (except commercial purpose).

The proposal is also for prohibiting employment of persons below 18 years (instead of present age 14 years) in hazardous occupations and processes in line with an International Labour Organisation Convention.

Their conditions of work are regulated in non-hazardous occupations and processes under the Act.

The amendments would ensure that all children would be compulsorily admitted in schools as per Right to Education Act, 2009 instead of working in workplaces.

Parents and guardians of children would be punishable under this Act only when they permit engagement of their children for commercial purposes in contravention to this Act.

The punishment to the offender under the Act would be stricter and the offences would be cognizable. The maximum punishment under the Act has been increased from one year of imprisonment)co two years, and fine from Rs 20,000 Rs 50,000 or both. For repeated offences, it ha s been raised to three years of imprisonment.

The overall responsibility for implementation of the Act will be vested with the district magistrate/ deputy commissioner and monitoring and inspection will be done by the labour department.

(c) "Domestic resource mobilization, though central to the process of Indian economic growth, is characterized by several constraints." Explain.

Answer: Domestic Resource Mobilization (DRM) refers to the savings and investments generated by households, domestic firms, and governments.

A greater emphasis on DRM can help developing countries to enhance their growth and economic performance, contribute toward increasing their policy space and ownership of development strategies, and reduce aid dependence. Although ultimately the private sector plays the more significant role in the process of mobilizing and investing domestic resources, the key policy and institutional drivers are in the hands of governments, particularly in low-income countries.

Constraints:

- What national strategies are currently in place with regards DRM?
- What are the main reasons behind lack of implementation?
- What is (or should be) the role of the state and its development partners in financial market infrastructure development?
- What role could private sector participants (in particular, foreign banks and nonbanking financial institutions) play in financial sector infrastructure development?
- Given the constraints of financial markets, what are the kinds of investment instruments that would be relevant, both in terms of mobilizing and pooling savings, and risk diversification?
- What is the realistic potential of alternatives and innovations, such as micro credit in consolidating the otherwise highly fragmented financial markets in the region?
- Are there structural limits to what can be achieved (e.g. market density, income levels, financial education levels, urbanization levels, real returns and risk perceptions)? How can these be overcome ?

(d) The 'flute - playing Krishna' theme is very popular in Indian art. Discuss.

Answer: In Indian art, Krishna is often described and portrayed as an infant or young boy playing a flute as in the Bhagavata Purana, or as a youthful prince giving direction and guidance as in the Bhagavad Gita.

Common depictions show him as a little boy, or as a young man in a characteristic relaxed pose, playing the flute. In this form, he usually stands with one leg bent in front of the other and raises a flute to his lips, known as Tribhangi Mudra, accompanied by cows, emphasizing his position as the divine herdsman, Govinda, or with the gopis (milkmaids) i.e. Gopikrishna, stealing butter from neighbouring houses i.e. Navneet Chora or Gokulakrishna, defeating the vicious serpent i.e. Kaliya Damana Krishna, lifting the hill i.e. Giridhara Krishna ..so on and so forth from his childhood / youth events.

Krishna is also called Murli Dhar. The flute of Krishna means the flute of revelation and not the physical flute. Krishna lived like humans and he was a prophet.

Depiction of Krishna playing flute in the temple constructed in AD 752 on the order of Emperor Shomu; Todai-ji Temple, Great Buddha Hall in Nara, Japan is also noteworthy.

(e) What are the salient features of the Consumer Protection (Amendment) Bill, 2011 introduced in the Lok Sabha in December 2011 ?

Important Points for Answer:
- *Consumer Protection (Amendment) Bill*
- *Various Key features*

Answer: The Consumer Protection (Amendment) Bill, 2011 was introduced in the Lok Sabha on December 16, 2011 by Mr. K.V. Thomas. It has been referred to the Standing Committee on Food, Consumer Affairs and Public Distribution.

The Bill defines unfair contract to include a contract which has one or more of the following clauses (a) excessive security deposit; (b) imposition of disproportionate penalty; (c) refusal to accept early repayment of debt and; (d) termination of contract without reasonable cause.

Under the Bill unfair trade practice includes a (i) a failure to take back the goods or withdraw the services within a period of 30 days after the receipt of the goods by the consumer; and (ii) disclosure of confidential personal information.

Under the Act, a maximum of two members are to be appointed to the District Forum. The Bill proposes that a minimum of two members should be appointed and the maximum number of members should be prescribed by the state government.

Under the Act, the state government appoints the members of the District Forum on the recommendation of the Selection Committee. The Bill proposes that the state government may refer back the recommendation to the Selection Committee if in its opinion the nominee is not fit to be appointed.

The Bill permits online filing of complaints. Under the Act, the admissibility of a complaint has to be decided within 21 days from date on which the complaint was received. The Bill proposes to increase it to 28 days.

(f) What do you understand by the term "Multi - Drug Resistant Tuberculosis" (MDR- TB) ? What measures would you advocate for its containment and what are the implications of its spread in the community ?

Important Points for Answer:
- *Definition of MDR-TB*
- *Measures adopted for its containment*

Answer: Multi-drug-resistant tuberculosis (MDR-TB) is defined as tuberculosis that is resistant to at least isoniazid (INH) and rifampicin (RMP), the two most powerful first-line treatment anti-TB drugs. Isolates that are multiply resistant to any other combination of anti-TB drugs but not to INH and RMP are not classed as MDR-TB.

MDR-TB develops during treatment of fully sensitive TB when the course of antibiotics is interrupted and the levels of drug in the body are insufficient to kill 100% of bacteria.

In addition to the obvious risks (i.e., known exposure to a patient with MDR-TB), risk factors for MDR-TB include HIV infection, previous incarceration, failed TB treatment, failure to respond to standard TB treatment, and relapse following standard TB treatment.

Patients with MDR-TB should be isolated in negative-pressure rooms, if possible. Patients with MDR-TB should not be accommodated on the same ward as immune-suppressed patients (HIV-infected patients, or patients on immunosuppressive drugs). Careful monitoring of compliance with treatment is crucial to the management of MDR-TB (and some physicians insist on hospitalization if only for this reason).

(g) Given the accelerated pace of development and demand for energy, would you consider renewable energy as a viable option for India's future ?

Answer: The energy policy of India is largely defined by the country's burgeonmg energy deficit and increased focus on developing alternative sources of energy, particularly nuclear, solar and wind energy.

About 70% of India's energy generation capacity is from fossil fuels, with coal accounting for 40% of India's total energy consumption followed by crude oil and natural gas at 24% and 6% respectively.

Due to rapid economic expansion, India has one of the world's fastest growing energy markets and is expected to be the second-largest contributor to the increase in global energy demand by 2035, accounting for 18% of the rise in global energy consumption. Given India's growing energy demands and limited domestic fossil fuel reserves, the country has ambitious plans to expand its renewable and nuclear power industries. India has the world's fifth largest wind power market and plans to add about 20GW of solar power capacity by 2022. India also envisages to increase the contribution of nuclear power to overall electricity generation capacity from 4.2% to 9% within 25 years. The country has five nuclear reactors under construction (third highest in the world) and plans to construct 18 additional nuclear reactors (second highest in the world) by 2025.

Given the situation, it is recommended that renewable energy should supplement other sources of energy, to maintain pace of development and fulfill the demand for energy.

(h) Many food items contain "trans fats". What do you understand by this term ? Which Indian food items contain trans fats ? What are the implications of trans fats on human health?

Answer: Trans fat is the common name for unsaturated fat with trans-isomer (E-isomer) fatty acid(s). Because the term refers to the configuration of a double carbon-carbon bond, trans fats are sometimes monounsaturated or polyunsaturated, but never saturated.

Trans fats do exist in nature but also occur during the processing of polyunsaturated fatty acids in food production.

The consumption of trans fats increases the risk of coronary heart disease by raising levels of LDL cholesterol and lowering levels of "good" HDL cholesterol.

A type of trans fat occurs naturally in the milk and body fat of ruminants (such as cattle and sheep) at a level of 2-5% of total fat. Natural trans fats, which include conjugated linoleic acid (CLA) and vaccenic acid, originate in the rumen of these animals. CLA has two double bonds, one in the configuration and one in trans, which makes it simultaneously a cis- and a trans-fatty acid.

Animal-based fats were once the only trans fats consumed, but by far the largest amount of trans fat consumed today is created by the processed food industry as a side effect of partially hydrogenating unsaturated plant fats (generally vegetable oils).

Q. 3 Answer the following in about 50 words each: **5 × 11 = 55**

(a) What is the 'Parivarik Mahila Lok Adalat' ?

Answer: The National Commission for Women has evolved an innovative concept of PMLA for redressal and speedy disposal of cases under Legal Service Authority Act, 1987, which has its roots in the traditional Nyaya Panchayats. The essential features of PMLA are amicable mutual settlement and flexibility in functioning. The NGOs in association with District Legal Aid and Advisory Board, activists, advocates and others, organize Parivarik Mahila Lok Adalats with the Commission's financial assistance.

(b) List the main objectives of the National Manufacturing Policy (NMP), 2011.

Answer: The major objectives of the National Manufacturing Policy, 2011 are to increase the sectoral share of manufacturing in GOP to at least 25% by 2022; to increase the rate of job creation so as to create 100 million additional jobs by 2022; and to enhance global competitiveness, domestic value addition, technological depth and environmental sustainability of growth.

(c) Comment on the significance of *Rasamava* in studying the history of Indian Chemistry.

Answer: *Rasamava* was written in Sanskrit in the period of 12th century AD by an unknown author. It is a "Treatise on Metallic Preparations", and describes Trantric, Mecial and Chemical practice of the time. It deals with Rasas - i.e. Mercury and other important minerals, Uparasas and metals.

(d) What are the Rights within the ambit of Article 21 of the Indian Constitution ?

Answer: Article 21 provides for Protection of life and personal liberty. It says, "No person shall be deprived of his life or personal liberty except according to procedure established by law." The Supreme Court has by various judgements included right to pollution free environment, right to shelter, right to food, right of locomotion and travel abroad, right to speedy and fair trial etc. under the ambit of Article 21.

(e) Comment on the significance of the Preamble contained in the Right to Information Act.

Answer: As per Preamble to RTI Act, it is to provide for setting out the practical regime of right to information for citizens to secure access to information under the control of public authorities, in order to promote transparency and accountability in the working of every public authority, the constitution of a Central Information Commission and State Information Commissions and other matters connected with them.

(f) To implement one key recommendation of the Mohini Giri Committee, the Government has recently announced the constitution of a National Council. Highlight the composition and the mandate of this National Council.

Answer: Composition of the National Council:

Chairman: Minister of Social Justice & Empowerment; Minister of State, Social Justice & Empowerment; Oldest Members of Lok Sabha and Rajya Sabha; Representatives of 5 State Governments + 1 Union Territory (by rotation.); 5 representatives each from Senior Citizens' Associations, Pensioners' Association, NGOs working for Senior Citizens and Experts.

Mandate of the National Council:

This council will advise the Central and State Governments on issues related to:

- policies, programmes and legislative measures for the welfare of senior citizens.
- promotion of physical and financial security, health and independent and productive living
- awareness generation and community mobilization.

(g) Comment on the recent launching of the National Mission on Libraries (NML).

Answer: The National Knowledge Commission (NKC) in its Report to the Nation (2006-2009) made ten major recommendations on libraries. In pursuance of this, a High Level Committee to be called as National Mission on Libraries (NML) has been set up by the Government of India. Raja Rammohun Roy Library Foundation (RRRLF), an autonomous body under the Ministry of Culture will be the nodal agency for the National Mission on Libraries for administrative, logistics, planning and budgeting purposes.

(h) What are the groups into which musical instruments in India have traditionally been classified?

Answer: Indian musical instruments can be broadly classified into four categories:

- **Chordophobut (String Instruments):**
  - Plucked
  - Bowed
- **Aerophones:**
  - Flutes
  - Single reed
  - Double reed
  - Bagpipes
  - Free reed
  - Free reed and bellow
  - Brass
  - Other wind instruments
- Percussion instruments:
  - **Membranophones**
    - Hand drums
    - Hand frame drums
    - Stick and hand drums
    - Stick drums
- **Idiophones:**
  - Melodic

(i) Comment on the significance of fire in Zoroastrianism.

Answer: Fire is a symbol of Ahura Mazda (The Aryans, who originated in the area near Persia, used fire in their ritual activities. For them fire - ["ignite"] - was a god). The most important sacred places for Zoroastrians are the Fire Temples where priests chant prayers, hymns and blessings around the clock.

(j) Why is Laurie Baker called 'the conscience keeper of Indian architecture' ?

Answer: Laurie Baker is known for building affordable, elegant and energy efficient homes in Kerala. People called his designs 'Baker-model houses'. Received Padam Sri for his works. In Thiruvananthapuram he designed and built Centre for Development Studies (CDS) which continues to be a pilgrim centre for budding architects from across the country.

(k) You are stationed in a small district town in the plains of Northern India. The summer has been severe. Suddenly, a colleague, who had been out since morning, returns to the office complaining of headache, restlessness and confusion. Shortly, he becomes unconscious. His body temperature is 40°C. What first aid steps would you take to revive him ?

Answer: These are the symptoms of "heatstroke". Hence the Treatment should be:

Move the victim to a cooler environment immediately. Cover him with a towel/blanket soaked with water to cool the victim's body. Loosen clothing and ensure that the person gets plenty of ventilation. When he gains consciousness, immediately give him water containing salt or lemon juice.

Q. 4 Comment on each of the following in about 20 words each: 2 × 5 = 10

(a) The significance of Patharughat in the Indian freedom struggle

Answer: Patharughat, is a place in Assam, known as Assam's Jallianwala Bagh, famous for 1894 Patharughat Ran, where on January 28, 1894 some 140 persons were killed in an unprovoked police firing while protesting against enhanced revenue.

(b) Bagurumba folk dance

Answer: Bagurumba, also called "butterfly dance", is a folk dance of Assam, performed by the Bodos during Bwisagu, a festival of the Bodos in the Bishuba Sankranti or Mid-April.

(c) Determining the 'value' assigned to the vote of a Member of a State Legislative Assembly and of a Member of Parliament in the Indian Presidential elections.

Answer: Article 55 (2) (a) says: every elected member of the Legislative Assembly of a State shall have as many votes as there are multiples of one thousand in the quotient obtained by dividing the population of the State by the total number of the elected members of the Assembly.

(d) Significance of the SPOT - 6 rocket launch for ISRO

Answer: The 100th Indian space mission of ISRO has launched a PSLV, carrying the French SPOT-6 Earth observation satellite with a mass of 712 kilograms.

(e) Issues highlighted through the work of Palagummi Sainath

Answer: Palagummi Sainath, a 'rural reporter', is an Indian journalist and photojournalist focusing on social problems, rural affairs, poverty and the aftermaths of globalization in India. He is the Rural Affairs Editor for The Hindu.

Q. 5 Why have the following been in the news recently ? (Answer to be in one sentence only). 1 × 5 = 5

(a) P.V. Sindhu

Answer: P.V. Sindhu, the 17-year-old Indian female badminton player, who beat London Olympics gold medalist Li Xuerui in the quarterfinals of the China Masters, achieved the 20th place in the BWF ranking.

(b) Aditya Kumar Mandi

Answer: Aditya Kumar Mandi, who is a constable in CISF, won the Sahitya Akadami Prize for his poetry in Santhali language.

(c) Cyrus Mistry

Answer: Cyrus Mistry, a leading businessman, is going to take over as Chairman of Tata Group, from Ratan Tata, from December 2012.

(d) Ashoke Sen

Answer: Ashoke Sen is an Indian theoretical physicist who won the Fundamental Physics Prize, 2012, for his work on string theory.

(e) Mario de Miranda

Answer: Mario Miranda was an Indian cartoonist of Goa who died in 2011 and was awarded a posthumous Padma Vibhushan in 2012.

SOLVED PAPERS

PAPER–II

Time Allowed: Three Hours *Maximum Marks: 300*

Candidates should attempt ALL questions strictly in accordance with the instructions given under each question.

Q. 1 Answer any four of the following in about 250 words each: 25 × 4 = 100

(a) Do you think that China's emergence as one of the largest trading partners of India had adversely affected the settlement of the outstanding border problem ?

Important Points for Answer:
- *El Indo-China Trade*
- *Bilateral Boundary Problems*

Answer: Trade between India and China is likely to achieve the $100-billion mark by 2013, two years ahead of the target set in 2009 by governments of the two countries.

China has become India's largest country trading partner, while the latter is attaining the position of the former's 10th largest trade partner.

Trade volumes reached $61.7 billion in 2010. India's exports to China jumped 68.8 per cent to $19.6 bn last financial year from 11.6 bn in 2009-10. Overall imports also increased 41 per cent to $43.5 bn from $30.8 bn in the same period.

Bilateral trade is booming, while China and India are equally concerned over unsettled boundary issues.

However, the 15th round of Sino-Indian Special Representatives (SR) Talks was held in New Delhi in January 2012. These talks were the latest in a process of bilateral boundary negotiations that have been taking place for the last three decades. Later, in early January, the Chinese denied a visa to an Indian Air Force officer from Arunachal Pradesh who was part of an official Indian military delegation to China. This kind of interaction would have previously resulted in prolonged acrimony between the two sides. But in a sign of growing maturity in bilateral ties, the fourth India-China Annual Defence Dialogue took place as scheduled in New Delhi in December 2011. The SR talks were also rescheduled without further ado, amid efforts to set a positive tone for the talks. The boundary talks are now officially in the second stage of a three-step process involving agreements on principles, a framework and, finally, a boundary line. The latest SR talks resulted in a new Working Mechanism for Consultation and Coordination on India- China Border Affairs. This mechanism aims to ensure real-time contact between the two foreign ministries should either side trespass the Line of Actual Control (LAC).

China and India also perhaps realise they cannot afford mutual hostility at a time of global economic uncertainty. Therefore, it seems that increasing bilateral trade has pacified the grudge over border issue.

(b) Discuss the globalization of R&D and its impact on India's development. Provide an illustration from at least one sector such as Information Technology or Health.

Answer: More and more companies are conducting R&D outside their home countries. Lower costs, access to talent, and proximity to markets drive the geogfaphical mobility of R&D and innovation.

Reflecting a broader trend towards the offshoring of services, a number of developing countries are attracting foreign direct investment in research and development.

Transnational corporations, including the ones headquartered in developing countries, are selecting developing countries as locations for such activities. With the offshoring of research and development, firms aim to access the skills of new locations, adapting products to local markets and reducing their costs, in response to competitive pressures, technological changes and a more liberal trade and investment environment.

In particular, information and communication technologies have had a profound effect on the way economic activities, including research and development, are organized, enabling firms to allocate tasks on a global scale through intra-firm information networks.

At the same time, keeping up with new developments in information and communication technologies is a major challenge for developing countries wishing to accelerate their economic development.

Whereas the rise was relatively modest in developed host countries, it was quite significant in developing countries: the share of foreign affiliates in business R&D in the developing world increased from 2% to 18% between 1996 and 2002. The share of R&D by foreign affiliates in different countries varies considerably. Conversely, it remained under 10% in Chile, Greece, India, Japan and the Republic of Korea. The top 10 destinations included China (in first position), India (third) and Brazil (sixth).

In some cases TNCs may contribute indirectly to upgrading technologies as innovations emerge and consumption patterns change.

The encouragement of commercial culture among scientists and engineers.

The implantation of an R&D and innovation culture among local companies.

The inflow of manufacturing-related FDI to commercialize R&D results at the same location if other conducive parameters are in place.

Employee spin-offs of R&D companies.

(c) Discuss the contentious issues that have caused the prolonged constitutional logjam in Nepal.

Answer: Nepal President Ram Baran Yadav and Prime Minister (PM) Baburam Bhattarai are locked in a stand-off in Nepal, on November 22, the government had originally proposed to hold fresh Constituent Assembly (CA) polls.

However, the Nepal Army (NA) has conveyed that the "political process" should be allowed to take its own course.

Nepal President said that the government will cease to have any legitimacy after its failure to hold polls on the declared date. He feel strongly that Dr. Bhattarai plunged the country into a crisis by declaring elections, "without making appropriate arrangements". And the President feels he has a responsibility to break "the constitutional and political deadlock".

Nepal President has refused to endorse any ordinances forwarded by the government, and only allowed a one-third budget on the grounds dfjat there was no political consensus for a full budget.

The PM wants the President to use his constitutional power to remove obstacles under Article 158, but how it would be approved by the Parliament given there is no legislature. This is the root of the problem. The one-third budget runs out in mid-November.

The government saved the country from a political vacuum by declaring elections on May 27, when the CA's term ended without a Constitution. The President, a former Nepali Congress (NC) leader has made the PM's resignation a precondition for consensus. Nepal PMO point out that the government is legitimate by virtue of being elected on the floor of the House and there is no way to constitutionally dismiss or replace the Prime Minister.

Dr. Bhattarai's aides allege Nepal President is over-stepping his constitutional brief. They cite his refusal to promulgate ordinances forwarded by the government and endorse a full budget; his regular meetings with political leaders; and public interventions on political issues, as proof.

Nepal President believes he would command wide political support if he chose to replace the government. Since the CA ended, the NC, Communist Party of Nepal (Unified Marxist Leninist), the Upendra Yadav-led Madhesi Janaadhikar Forum, and the ultra-nationalist Maoist splinter outfit led by Mohan Vaidya 'Kiran', have all urged the President to dismiss Dr. Bhattarai. Dr. Yadav's aides have been in touch with the judiciary to solicit support. And since he is of Madhesi background, the President believes that there will be no resistance in the Tarai.

The new chief, General Gaurav Shumsher Rana, has publicly pledged to abide by the constitution and the Army Act, which clearly stipulates specific conditions under which forces can be mobilised.

India has largely adopted a hands-off approach in Nepal at the moment, despite some intensive lobbying from all sides to intervene on their behalf.

(d) The human population is slated to grow to 9 billion by 2050. In this context, many scientists predict that plant genomics would play a critical role in keeping out hunger and preserving the environment. Explain.

Important Points for Answer:
- *Problems related to increase in population*
- *Plant Genomics and its importance*

Answer: In 2009, the human population increased by 74.6 million, which is projected to fall steadily to about 41 million per annum in 2050, at which time the population will have increased to about 9.2 billion. With such a huge growth of population, obviously the, requirement of food and other recourses will also increase. To feed the increasing population, more food production will be required.

Plant Genomics is a discipline in genetics that applies recombinant DNA, DNA sequencing methods, and bioinformatics to sequence, assemble, and analyze the function and structure of genomes (the complete set of DNA within a single cell of an organism). Such genetically engineered plants are generated in a laboratory by altering their genetic makeup and are tested in the laboratory for desired qualities. This is usually done by adding one or more genes to a plant's genome using genetic engineering techniques.

The plant genomics will help to preserve existing species of plants and improve their productivity, apart from deriving new variants of food producing plants with desired nutrients. The science can help into producing more food for feeding the population.

Plant genomics can also help in preserving environment by maintaining bio diversity and preventing deforestation. Environmental issues can be easily dealt with by genetic engineering.

However, presently there is no consensus about use of genetically engineered food due to health and economic issues but looking at the future; it seems that plant genomics is going to be a science for keeping out hunger and preserving the environment.

(e) "The situation today is far different to that prevalent fifty years back when the Indus Water Treaty was signed." Highlight the complexity of the current challenges on both sides of the border in this regard. Do you think that a review of the Treaty is in India's best interests ?

Answer: The Indus Water Treaty is a water-sharing treaty between the Republic of India and Islamic Republic of Pakistan, brokered by the World Bank (then the International Bank for Reconstruction and Development). The treaty was signed in Karachi on September 19, 1960 by Indian Prime Minister Jawaharlal Nehru and President of Pakistan Mohammad Ayub Khan. The treaty was a result of Pakistani fear that since the source rivers of the Indus basin were in India, it could potentially create droughts and famines in Pakistan, especially at times of war. However, India did not revoke the treaty during any of three later Indo-Pakistani Wars.

Where once there was only a narrow strip of irrigated land along these rivers, developments over the last century have created a large network of canals and storage facilities that provide water for more than 26 million acres (110,000 km^2) - the largest irrigated area of any one river system in the world.

Pakistani experts have calculated that if the flow of water from J&K to Pakistan is reduced by a level of one percent, the economic loss to its farmers will be catastrophic. Experts consider the question of Indus water more important than the J&K issue.

India has operated within the framework of this Treaty for over four decades. During this time a host of problem areas have been encountered which were not visualised earlier.

In 1960, the Treaty did not consider the exponential growth of population and the consequent rise in demand for water for drinking and irrigation. Today, over 2,00,000 hectares of fertile land in drought-prone J&K remain un-irrigated resulting in a great loss of agricultural and horticultural potential. This is particularly acute in Kashmir Valley. This can only be alleviated by greater access to waters of the Jhelum and Chenab.

Therefore, it can be argued that revision of Indus Water Treaty can result into benefit to India.

Q. 2. Answer any five of the following in about 150 words each: 15 × 5 =75

(a) Write a short analytical note on Indian Diaspora. How is the "New Diaspora" different from the "Old Diaspora"?

Important Points for Answer:
- *Meaning of Indian Diaspora*
- *Emergence of New Diaspora*

Answer: The Indian Diaspora is a generic term to describe the people who migrated from territories that are currently within the borders of the Republic of India. It also refers to their descendants. The Diaspora is currently estimated to number over twenty million. Composed of "NRIs" (Indian citizens not residing in India) and "PIOs" (Persons of Indian Origin who have acquired the citizenship of some other country). The Diaspora covers practically every part of the world. It numbers more than a million each in eleven countries, while as many as twenty-two countries have concentrations of at least a hundred thousand ethnic Indins.

A new diaspora is the displacement, migration, and dispersion of individuals away from their homelands by forces such as globalization, neo-liberalism, and imperialism. Such forces create economic, social, political, and cultural difficulties for individuals in their homeland that forces them to displace and migrate.

New Diaspora is a revival or a build upon the standard meaning of Diaspora in the sense that it is focused on the cultural, economic, political, and social causes driving it, as well as analyzing the multi-locality and self-consciousness developed by the social group. This concept also analyzes the ties within diaspora communities to their native lands, which are expressed through strong political and cultural participation in their ancestral lands. Other significant qualities of new/neo Diasporas are the thoughts of return to their native land, relationships with other communities in the Diaspora, and lack of full assimilation to the host country.

(b) Why have the resource rich African and South Asian countries remained poor for decades? Explain.

Answer: The countries of Africa and South Asia have been exploited under colonization by western countries. The countries have not been able to utilize their natural resources. Their technological development has not at par with the developed world. People have been living under stark poverty, lake of education, unemployment, unhealthy living conditions and customary practices.

Resources of these countries have been taken away by the industrialized countries in the form of raw material and finished products have been supplied to them for decades, thus exploiting their resources and economic condition.

Due to unavailability of technical know-how, they are not able to utilize resources available to them. As a result, industrialized countries are still taking away their resources without giving them proper reward for the same.

Educated and expert people of these countries have not used their skill to develop own countries. Rather they have migrated to western countries for better facilities and thus helped them to continue their exploitation.

These are the reasons why resource rich African and South Asian countries have remained poor for decades.

(c) Does Putin's return as President of Russia mark a shift to a confrontationist stance in international diplomacy towards the West ?

Answer: Putin, an old president was elected in through new elections.

The West should not expect a serious transformation in the coming phase of relations with Russia. There are certain tangible signs of this. Putin has announced that he will invest EUR 580 billion in defence. Accordingly, Russia will augment its defence system with 400 intercontinental ballistic missiles, 600 warplanes, 20 submarines and 2,300 tanks. Putin has also announced the target of this armament programme. Russia is undertaking this move due to NATO. The missile defence system or shield the USA is establishing under the NATO in Europe could paralyse Russia's national security. Putin has announced that Russia is to develop new weapons against the missile shield.

Putin stands between the West and Syria and Iran. Vladimir Putin's energy policy and his perspective on the Middle East and North Africa are seriously incompatible with the assessments and preferences of the Western alliance. Putin's outlook on Tunisia, Libya and Egypt, just like previously on Iraq, has not been in synch with the priorities of the Western alliance. Indeed, the attitude and stance of Putin on Syria and Irat has caused concern in many important western capitals.

There is no doubt that Putin's return as President of Russia marks a shift towards a staunch, if not confrontationist stance in international diplomacy towards the West.

(d) Analyse critically the interlinkages between the Convention on Biological Diversity and FAO Treaty on Plant Genetic Resources for Food and Agriculture.

Answer: The Convention on Biological Diversity (CBD) entered into force on 29 December 1993. It has 3 main objectives:

1. The conservation of biological diversity
2. The sustainable use of the components of biological diversity
3. The fair and equitable sharing of the benefits arising out of the utilization of genetic resources.

CBD also notes in preamble that conservation and sustainable use of biological diversity is of critical importance for meeting the food, health and other needs of the growing world population, for which purpose access to and sharing of both genetic resources and technologies are essential.

The FAO Conference adopted the International Treaty on Plant Genetic Resources for Food and Agriculture, in November 2001. This legally-binding Treaty covers all plant genetic resources relevant for food and agriculture. It is in harmony with the Convention on Biological Diversity.

The Treaty is vital in ensuring the continued availability of the plant genetic resources that countries will need to feed their people. We must conserve for future generations the genetic diversity that is essential for food and agriculture. Its objectives are the conservation and sustainable use of plant genetic resources for food and agriculture and the fair and equitable sharing of benefits derived from their use, in harmony with the Convention on Biological Diversity, for sustainable agriculture and food security.

(e) Critically review the international concern in achieving the targets set for the Millennium Development Goals.

Important Points for Answer:
- *MDGs*
- *International concerns and debates*

Answer: The Millennium Development Goals (MDGs) are eight international development goals that were officially established following the Millennium Summit of the United Nations in 2000, following the adoption of the United Nations Millennium Declaration. All 193 United Nations member states and at least 23 international organizations have agreed to achieve these goals by the year 2015. The goals are:

1. Eradicating extreme poverty and hunger,
2. Achieving universal primary education,
3. Promoting gender equality and empowering women,
4. Reducing child mortality rates,
5. Improving maternal health,
6. Combating HIV/AIDS, malaria, and other diseases,
7. Ensuring environmental sustainability, and
8. Developing a global partnership for development.

Each of the goals has specific stated targets and dates for achieving those targets.

Debate has surrounded adoption of the MDGs, focusing on lack of analysis and justification behind the chosen objectives, the difficulty or lack of measurements for some of the goals, and uneven progress towards reaching the goals, among other criticisms.

Progress towards reaching the goals has been uneven. Some countries have achieved many of the goals, while others are not on track to realize any.

Although developed countries' aid for the achievement of the MDGs have been rising over recent years, it has shown that more than half is towards debt relief owed by poor countries.

Many development experts question the MDGs model of transferring billions of dollars directly from the wealthy nation governments to the often bureaucratic or corrupt governments in developing countries.

(f) Discuss the likely negative impact of the protectionist measures proposed by the US on India's software industry.

Answer: The government has raised issues relating to American policies that are hurting the Indian IT industry with the US government.

The last couple of months have seen some measures in the US that have caused concern in the Indian IT industry. These include a controversial bill that proposed to strengthen security along its border with Mexico by increasing H-1B and LI visa fees and state of Ohio recently banning outsourcing by government departments to offshore locations. The IT companies, which receive more than half of their revenue from the US, are also facing challenges of a double-dip recession in the US.

However, India's information technology industry does not expect any immediate impact from protectionist steps being considered in the U.S. against outsourcing information technology services.

Q. 3. Answer any six of the following in not more than 100 words each: 10 × 6 = 60

(a) In the context of Assisted Reproductive Technologies, India has emerged as a hub of commercial surrogacy. What key biological, legal and ethical issues merit consideration while framing the regulation to govern surrogacy in India ?

Important Points for Answer:
- *Meaning of Surrogacy*
- *Issues relating to surrogacy*

Answer: Surrogacy is defined as a woman who agrees to carry a pregnancy using her own oocytes but the sperm of another couple and relinquish the child to this couple upon delivery.

As with donor gametes, surrogates and gestational carriers are subject to significant medical and emotional risks from carrying a pregnancy and undergoing a delivery. As such, extensive counseling and meticulous informed consent are required. Some also are concerned that the use of surrogates and gestational carriers is a form of "child selling" or the "sale of parental rights". Additionally, the rights of the surrogate or gestational carrier to not relinquish the infant following deliver are not well described.

Due to financial and legal considerations, international surrogacy has emerged as an emerging industry, especially in developing nations like India. At the present time, issues surrounding issues of individual rights, exploitation, citizenship of the offspring of international gestational carriers, and even fair trade are largely unresolved internationally.

(b) Why is international trade perceived to have failed to act as an "engine of growth" in many developing countries including India ?

Answer: International Trade is not the sole base of growth story of developing countries, including India. Many developing countries have experienced growth mostly based on domestic economic factors than on international trade.

Moreover, for developing countries, international trade has remained unbalanced and favourable to developed country. This situation has resulted into more import - less export situation, creating huge debt of foreign currency.

Sometimes, international trade has been patterned in a way that developing economies have to export raw material and import finished good, which finally has not resulted into growth of economy.

Given these reasons, the international trade has failed to act as an engine of growth for them.

(c) Despite strict prohibitory regulations, "doping" has become increasingly common amongst athletes. Name five commonly used performance - enhancing drugs. What are the risks associated with their use?

Answer: The use of banned performance-enhancing drugs in sports is commonly referred to as doping, particularly by those organizations that regulate competitions.

Some of the drugs commonly taken by athletes are:

- amphetamines,
- fencamfamine,
- beta-2 agonists,
- cocaine,
- ephedrine,
- methamphetamines,
- pseudoephedrine,
- mesocarb

Side effects in men

- acne
- increase in estrogen
- impaired liver function
- erectile dysfunction
- impotency
- increased sex drive
- breast formation (gynecomastia)
- male pattern baldness

Side effects in women

- hair loss
- male pattern baldness
- hypertrophy of the clitoris
- increased sex drive
- irregularities of the menstrual cycle
- development of masculine facial traits
- increased coarseness of the skin
- premature closure of the epiphysis

(d) Compare the significance of IBSA and BRICS in the context of India's multilateral diplomacy.

Answer: IBSA is a dialogue forum of India, Brazil and South Africa for promoting international cooperation among them. IBSA represents three important poles for galvanizing South-South Cooperation and helps greater understanding between three important continents of the developing world namely, Asia, South America and Africa. IBSA is an important platform for Indian foreign policy to discuss issues in the field of agriculture, trade, culture and defence. IBSA emerged after the failure of Cancun Conference of WTO to strengthen cooperation in trade, investment and economic diplomacy.

BRICS is the title of an association of emerging national economies: Brazil, Russia, India, China and South Africa. BRICS is considered as defender and promoter of developing countries and a force for world peace. However, the group can also help resolving issues among members - like border issue between India and China - by increasing interdependence among them. BRICS is a group based on economic interests of members.

For Indian diplomats, both IBSA and BRICS are platforms for promoting India's interest.

(e) The safe landing of the "Curiosity" Rover under NASA's space programme has sparked many possibilities. What are those and how could humankind benefit from them ?

Answer: Curiosity is a car-sized robotic rover exploring Gale Crater on Mars as part of NASA's Mars Science Laboratory mission (MSL). Curiosity was launched on November 26, 2011 and successfully landed on Aeolis Palus in Gale Crater on Mars on August 6, 2012.

The rover's goals include: investigation of the Martian climate and geology; assessment of whether the selected field site inside Gale Crater has ever offered environmental conditions favorable for microbial life, including investigation of the role of water; and planetary habitability studies in preparation for future human exploration.

Curiosity's design will serve as the basis for a planned unnamed 2020 Mars rover mission. In December 2012, Curiosity's two-year mission was extended indefinitely.

(f) How have the US sanctions against Iran affected India's bilateral relations with Iran?

Important Points for Answer:
- *US sanctions on Iran*
- *Effects on India-Iran relations*

Iran is under US Sanctions for its controversial nuclear programme. The US sanctions impose restrictions on trade with Iran.

The sanctions require other countries, including India, to drastically cut oil imports from Iran. This results into a great hurdle to India in its energy security.

Banks cannot have financial transaction with Iran. A few banks which have no exposure to US are exempted from impact of sanctions. India's UCO Bank is the only bank in India presently to act as a channel for trade with Iran.

Even though India and Iran are keen to trade with each other, there hurdles like effective payment mechanism, banking channel, shipping facility and insurance cover for trade and transportation to facilitate bilateral trade.

On the issue of nuclear programme, India believes that every country has a right to have access to nuclear technology for peaceful purposes, including Iran but at the same time India believes that development of nuclear weapons by Iran is not in the interest of international peace and security.

Thus, US Sanctions have affected India's relations with Iran in both political and commercial fields.

(g) What is Permaculture? Give at least three common examples where permaculture concepts are being put to use.

Answer: Permaculture is a branch of ecological design, ecological engineering, and environmental design which develops sustainable architecture and self-maintained horticultural systems modeled from natural ecosystems.

The core tenets of permaculture are:

- Take care of the earth
- Take care of the people
- Share the surplus

Common Examples of Permaculture

Agroforestry: Agroforestry is an integrated approach of using the interactive benefits from combining trees and shrubs with crops and/or livestock.

Hugelkultur: Hiigelkultur is the practice of burying large volumes of wood to increase soil water retention.

Natural building: A natural building involves a range of building systems and materials that place major emphasis on sustainability.

Rainwater harvesting: Rainwater harvesting is the accumulating and storing of rainwater for reuse before it reaches the aquifer.

Q. 4 Answer the following in not more than 50 words each: **5 × 6 = 30**

(a) The Sequoia supercomputer was launched this year. What are its specific features and what is its purpose?

Answer: IBM Sequoia is a petascale Blue Gene/Q supercomputer constructed by IBM for the National Nuclear Security Administration as part of the Advanced Simulation and Computing Program (ASC). It was fully deployed in June 2012. The Sequoia uses 7.9 MW power, requires 280 sq m space, has 1.6 PB memory and works at 16.32 PFLOPS speed.

(b) What is meant by the G8+5 group?

Answer: The Group of Eight + Five (G8+5) is an international group that consists of the leaders of the heads of government from the G8 nations (Canada, France, Germany, Italy, Japan, Russia, the United Kingdom, and the United States), plus the heads of government of the five leading emerging economies (Brazil, China, India, Mexico, and South Africa).

(c) The Human Papilloma Virus vaccine has been making the headlines in the recent months. Who make the ideal candidates for receiving this vaccine and what are its benefits?

Answer: The human papilloma virus (HPV) vaccine prevents infection with certain species of human papillomavirus associated with the development of cervical cancer, genital warts, and some less common cancers. Two HPV vaccines are currently on the market: Gardasil and Cervarix. Both vaccines protect against the two HPV types (HPV- 16 and HPV-18) that cause 70% of cervical cancers, 80% of anal cancers, 60% of vaginal cancers, and 40% of vulvar cancers.

(d) What are India's stakes in the South China Sea?

Answer: India has a strong interest in keeping sea lanes open in the South China Sea. The SCS is not only a strategic maritime link between the Pacific and the Indian Oceans, but also a vital gateway for shipping in East Asia. Almost, 55% of India's trade with the Asia Pacific transits through the

SCS. India was taken aback after Beijing denounced plans by an Indian Company to develop oil fields in the region. The Chinese objection was to ONGC Videsh's (OVL) venture for off-shore oil exploration in water's belonging to Vietnam (not recognized by China), Beijing urged India to refrain from entering into deals with Vietnamese firms exploring oil and gas in the disputed SCS over which China enjoys 'indisputable' sovereignty.

(e) Explain the concepts "Environmental Sustainability" and "Sustainable Development of People".

Answer: Environmental sustainability involves making decisions and taking action that are in the interests of protecting the natural world, with particular emphasis on preserving the capability of the environment to support human life.

Sustainable Development of People refers to a mode of human development in which aims use resource to meet human needs while ensuring the sustainability of natural systems and the environment so that these needs can be met not only in the present, but also for generations to come.

(f) Explain briefly the "Clean Development Mechanism" as provided under the United Nations Framework Convention on Climate Change (UNFCCC).

Answer: The Clean Development Mechanism (CDM), defined in Article 12 of the Protocol, allows a country with an emission-reduction or emission-limitation commitment under the Kyoto Protocol (Annex B Party) to implement an emission-reduction project in developing countries. Such projects can earn saleable certified emission reduction (CER) credits, each equivalent to one tonne of C02, which can be counted towaids meeting Kyoto targets.

Q. 5. (a) The following table gives the number of mistakes made by 16 data entry clerks who enter medical data from case report forms. The column Entered indicates the number of values entered, and the column Errors gives the number of coding errors that were detected among these.

Entered	Errors	Entered	Errors
4,434	35	5,706	34
4,841	42	3,770	40
6,280	15	3,363	36
1,958	28	1,740	23
7,749	36	3,404	27
2,829	42	1,640	26
4,239	18	3,803	56
3,303	54	1,529	20

(i) Make a scatter - plot of these data. Which do you choose for the response and which for the explanatory variables? Describe any patterns.

(ii) Does the scatter - plot indicate any relation between the two variables?

(iii) One analyst concluded, "The clerks who enter more values make more mistakes. Evidently they become tired as they enter more values." Is this an appropriate conclusion? 9

Answer:

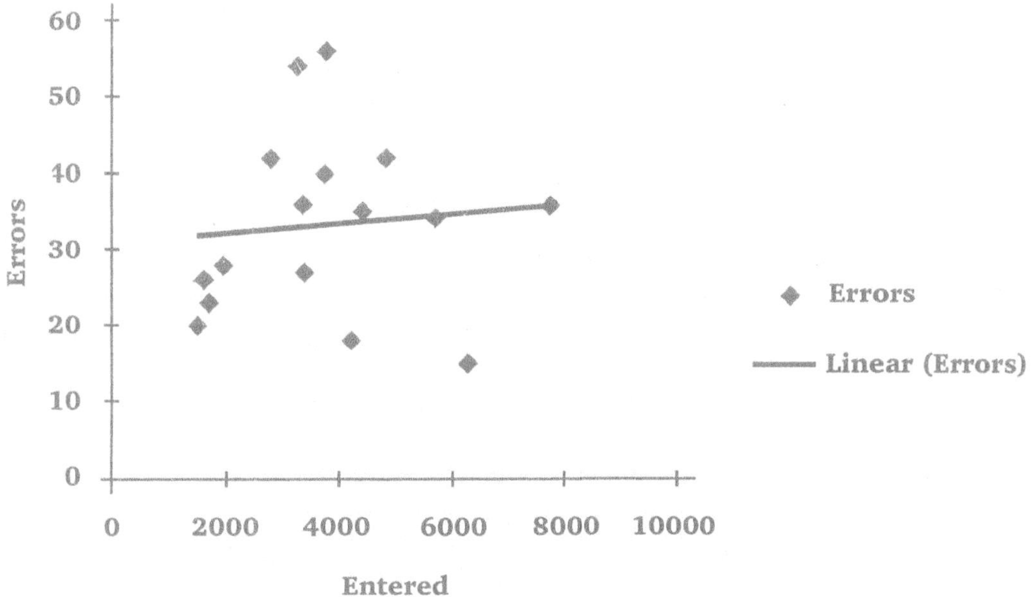

(i) In the scatter plot shown above, the errors are shown at y-axis and number of values entered are shown at x-axis.

Explanatory variable is the number of values entered and response variable is the number of coding variables.

(ii) The scatter plot indicates that the more values are entered, the more errors are committed. The pattern of errors is linear.

(iii) The conclusion of analyst is appropriate because pattern of errors is linear and it resembles upward trend on scatter-plot, indicating higher number of errors with increasing number of values entered.

(b) The following table provides the Rural and Urban population of West Bengal according to the Censuses of 1921-1951.

Census - year	Population (in lakhs)	
	Rural	Urban
1921	139.94	24.32
1931	147.92	28.97
1941	171.97	46.79
1951	200.25	62.82

(i) Construct a suitable diagram to compare the population figures.

(ii) Comment on the changes in populations. 6

Answer: (i)

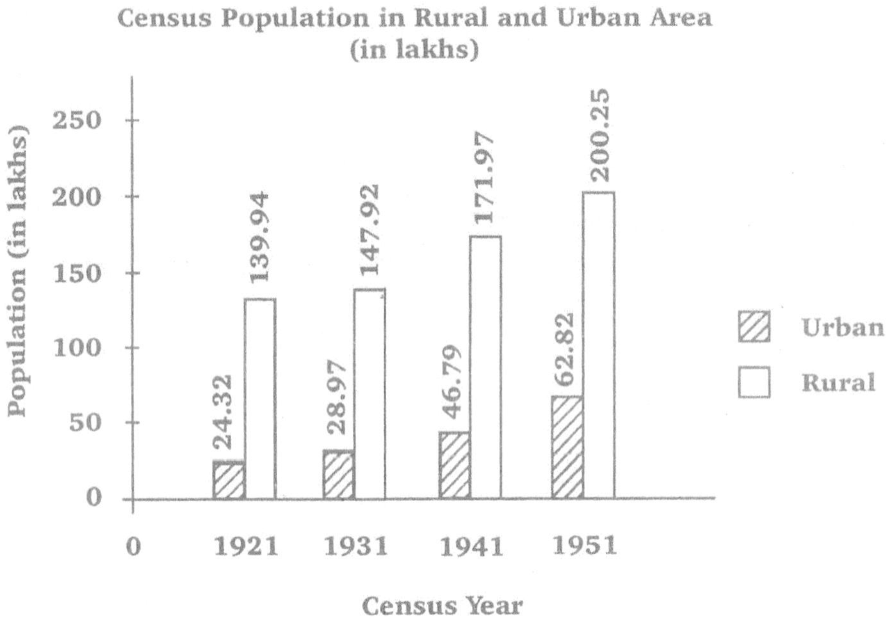

A suitable bar diagram is constructed above.

(ii) The Population changed consecutively every Census. Percentage of Urban population decreased with increase in total population.

(c) Suppose milk is being sold at the rates of 18, 20, 22 and 25 rupees per litre in four different months. Assuming that equal amounts of money are spent on milk by a family in the four months, using a suitable measure, determine the average price in rupees per litre. 2

Answer: L.C.M. of 18, 20, 22 and 25 is 9900. Suppose every month family has spent Rs. 9900 in four months at the given price of milk. So, total amount of money spent is Rs. 9900 × 4 = Rs. 39600. Total quantity of Milk is 1891 litres and total amount spent is Rs. 39600. So, average price of milk = 39600/1891 = Rs. 20.94

Month	Price of Milk	Quantity	Total
A	18	550	9900
B	20	495	9900
C	22	450	9900
D	25	396	9900
		1891	39600
Average Price of Milk			**20.9413**

Q. 6 (a) (i) Determine the median and mode for the following distribution of monthly income for 580 middle-class people of a country: **8**

Monthly income (in ₹ thousands)	Frequency
25-30	53
30-35	81
35-40	114
40-45	195
45-50	63
50-55	32
55-60	20
60-65	11
65-70	8
70-75	3

(ii) Also obtain an approximate value of the mean income from the values of median and mode.

(iii) Comment on the nature of the income distribution. **8**

Answer:

Monthly Income (in 7 thousands)	Frequency	Cumulative frequency
25–30	53	53
30–35	81	134
35–40	114	248
40–45	195	443
45–50	63	506
50–55	32	538
55–60	20	558
60–65	11	569
65–70	8	577
70–75	3	580

$\frac{N}{2} = 290$ c = 248

f = 195 I = 40

i = 5

$$\text{Median} = \frac{\text{I} + \left(\frac{N}{2} - c\right)}{f \times i}$$

$$\frac{40 + (290 - 248)}{195 \times 5} = 41.076$$

Median = 41.076 (in ₹ thousands)

$$\text{Mode} = \frac{I + D_1}{(D_1 + D_2)} \times i$$

Where, 1 = lower limit of the modal class = 40

i = class interval = 5

D_1 = absolute (i.e. neglecting sign) difference between the frequency of the modal class and pre-modal class = (195 –114 = 81)

D_2 = absolute difference of frequency of modal class and post-modal class = 195-63 = 132

$$\text{Mode} = \frac{40 + 81}{(81 + 132)} \times 5 = 41.901 \text{ (in ₹ thousands)}$$

(ii) Approximate value of the mean from the values of median and mode is:

Mode = 3 Median – 2 Mean

41.901= 3(41.706) – 2 Mean

41.901= 123.228 – 2 Mean

$$\text{Mean} = \frac{123.228 - 41.901}{2}$$

Mean = 40.668 (in ₹ thousands)

(iii) Nature of the income distribution shows that average income of people is nearly 42 thousand while more people are having income nearly the same amount. Therefore, distribution of income seems more even.

(b) From the frequency distribution of height for 177 Indian adults given below, draw the 'more than type' ogive.

Height (cm) Class Interval	Frequency
144.55–149.55	1
149.55–154.55	3
154.55–159.55	24
159.55–164.55	58
164.55–169.55	60
169.55–174.55	27
174.55–179.55	2
179.55–184.55	2

Also locate the position of the median.

Answer:

Height (cm)	Frequency	More than type Cum. Frequency
144.55 - 149.55	1	177
149.55 - 154.55	3	176
154.55 - 159.55	24	173
159.55 - 164.55	58	149
164.55 - 169.55	60	91
169.55 - 174.55	27	31
174.55 - 179.55	2	4
179.55 - 184.55	2	2

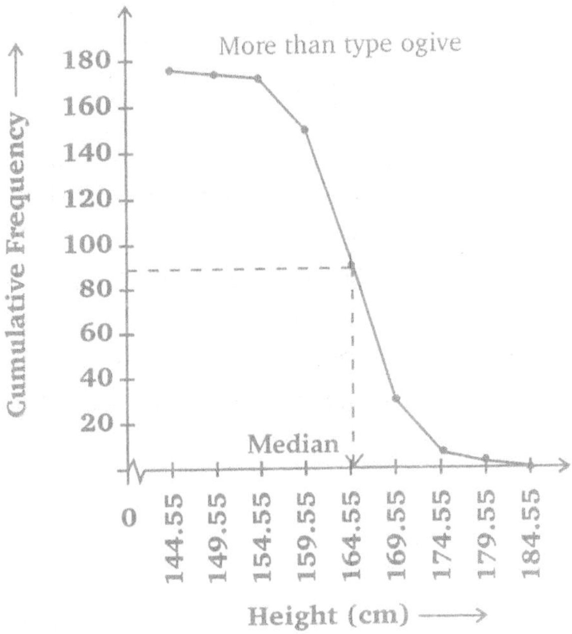

(c) A survey of 1000 large U.S. companies conducted by a Research Organisation asked their plans for outsourcing high-level white-collar jobs to countries outside the U.S. The following table shows the percentage that indicated a certain action. The data for 2003 are real, the data for 2008 are speculative.

Plan to	2003(%)	2008(%)	
Do virtually no white-collar	63	46	offshoring
Offshore white-collar work to	33	44	some extent
Offshore any white - collar	4	10	work possible

The following Bar chart with side-by-side columns summarizes the data :

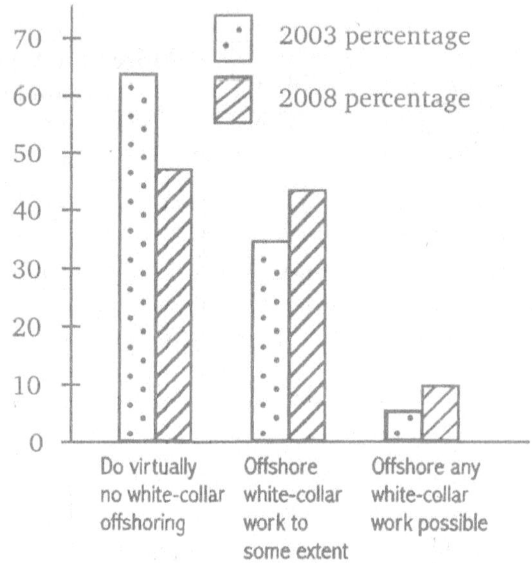

(i) Does the Bar chart compare the impression of any anticipated trend in outsourcing of the white - collar jobs?

(ii) Does the mode differ from the median for the distribution of percentages in 2003 and 2008?

7

Answer: (i) The Bar chart indicates anticipated trend in outsourcing of the white collared jobs.

(ii) No. The mode does not differ from the median for the distribution of percentages in 2003 and 2008.

(MAIN) **Civil Services Exam.**

2013 General Studies

SOLVED PAPERS

PAPER–I

Time Allowed : Three Hours *Maximum Marks : 250*

Instructions: There are TWENTY FIVE questions printed both in English and Hindi. All questions are compulsory. The number of marks carried by a question/part is indicated against it. Answers must be written in the medium authorized in the Admission Certificate which must be stated clearly on the cover of this Question-cum-Answer (QCA) Booklet in the space provided. No marks will be given for answers written in medium other than the authorized one.

Word limit in questions, if specified, should be adhered to.

Any page or portion of the page left blank in the Question-cum-Answer Booklet must be clearly struck off.

Answer questions in NOT MORE THAN the word limit specified for each in the parenthesis. Content of the answer is more important than length.

1. Though not very useful from the point of view of a connected political history of South India, the Sangam literature portrays the social and economic conditions of its time with remarkable vividness. Comment. (200 words) 10

Important Points for Answer:
- *Sangam Literature*
- *Description of Social & Economic conditions*

Answer: Sangam literature is a body of classical Tamil literature which was composed in the period between the years c. 600 BCE to 300 CE, which is also known as the Sangam Period. This collection of Sangam Literature contains 2381 poems which are composed by 473 poets. However, about 102 of these poems are anonymous.

The poems belonging to the Sangam literature were composed by Tamil poets, both men and women, from various professions and classes of society. Sangam literature is primarily secular dealing with everyday themes in a Tamilakam context.

The literature does not depict political scenario of the time to noticeable extent but mainly deals with emotional and material topics such as love, war, governance, trade and bereavement of the contemporary society of the time.

Sangam Literature consists of 'inner field' and 'outer field'. The 'inner field' topics refer to personal or human aspects, such as love and sexual relationships, and are dealt with in a metaphorical and abstract manner. It also serves as educational literature for human nature.

The 'outer field' topics discuss all other aspects of human experience such as heroism, valour, ethics, benevolence, philanthropy, social life, and customs. It is in outer field that it covers social customs and traditions, giving remarkable vividness of social and economic condition of the time.

(Total 215 words)

2. (a) Discuss the 'Tandava' dance as recorded in early Indian inscriptions. (100 words) 5

Answer: Tandava is a divine dance performed by the Hindu God Shiva, considered to be the source of the cycle of creation, preservation and dissolution.

The Rudra Tandava depicts his violent nature, first as the creator and later as the destroyer of the universe, even of death itself.

In Shaiva Siddhanta tradition, Shiva as Nataraja, „Lord of dance", is considered the supreme lord of dance.The Ananda Tandava depicts Shiva as enjoying.

The Tandava name is derived from Tandu, the attendant of Shiva, who instructed Bharata, author of the Natya Shastra, in the use of Angaharas and Karanas, modes of the Tandava at Shiva's order.

(Total 104 words)

(b) Chola architecture represents a high watermark in the evolution of temple architecture. Discuss (100 words) 5

Answer: The period of Cholas (850 - 1250 CE) was an age of continuous improvement and refinement of the Dravidian art and architecture. They built stone temples and exquisite bronze sculptures.

Airavatesvara Temple was built by Rajaraja Chola II in the 12th century CE which is a magnificent Hindu temple of Dravidian architecture in Tamil Nadu.

The Great Living Chola Temples include the Brihadisvara temple at Thanjavur, the Temple of Gangaikondacholisvaram and the Airavatesvara Temple at Darasuram. The Brihadisvara Temple was declared by UNESCO as a World Heritage Site in 1987. The other two were added as extensions to the site in 2004, now known as the „Great Living Chola Temples". (Total 109 words)

3. Defying the barriers of age, gender and religion, the Indian women became the torch-bearer during the struggle for freedom in India. Discuss. (200 words) 10

Important Points for Answer:

- *Indian Women in Freedom Struggle*
- *Princely States*
- *Constitutional Movements*
- *Young Women*
- *Foreign Women*

Answer: In the Indian Freedom Struggle, contribution of Indian women is remarkable. In the fights against British conquest of Indian princely states Indian women fought bravely against British army. Rani Laxmibai of Jhansi and Begum Hazrat Mahal were prominent among them.

Later in the period of Satyagraha, Civil Disobedience and other types of constitutional movements Indian women joined enthusiastically and contributed immensely. Kasturba Gandhi, Swarup Rani Nehru, Kamala Nehru, Sarojini Naidu, Vijaya Laxmi Pandit and Sucheta Kripalani participated in Gandhi's various programmes for freedom.

Madam Bhikhaji Cama was an active member of Congress who led various movements against the British rule.

Sister Nivedita, an Irish lady played very important role in religious and educational upliftment of Indian women who in turn became active in the freedom struggle.

Padmaja Naidu, a young lady participated in freedom struggle while Indira Gandhi raised a children's army called Vanar Sena to fight against British.

These women had diverse social and educational background and hailed from different parts of India and world.

The programme of self-imposed poverty and periodical jail going was possible only because of the willing co-operation of the worker's family.

Illiterate women from rural areas also played role by participating in boycott and picketing movement.

Home Rule Movement by Annie Besant was very successful. (Total 213 words)

4. Several foreigners made India their homeland and participated in various movements. Analyse their role in the Indian struggle for freedom. (200 words) 10

Important Points for Answer:
- *Foreigners in Indian Freedom Struggle*
- *Their contribution*

Answer: During the National Movement, many foreigners also participated for the freedom of India. They included Annie Besant, Charles Freer Andrews, Sister Nivedita, Madeleine Slade, Samuel Evans Stokes Jr. etc.

Annie Besant was a theosophist, socialist, orator, activist and writer who came to India as a part of the Theosophical Societyand afterwards became a patron of Indian self-rule. She demanded a self rule for India and set up the Home Rule League.

Charles Freer «Dinabandhu» Andrews came to India as a Missionary Philanthropist but soon became a part of the social and political movements and worked for the causes of the laborers, railway workers, untouchables and other such downtrodden people.

Madeleine Slade, influenced by Gandhi, began a simple life at the Sabarmati Ashram and even took part in all the Gandhi's socio-political struggles in India and promoted Khadi and Satyagraha.

Samuel Evans Stokes Jr., known as Satyananda Stokes, was a wealthy American who championed the cases of the laborers in areas adjoining Shimla and fought relentlessly for their welfare. He was the sole foreigner and the sole American to sign the Congress Manifesto in 1921 and was also jailed on the charge of sedition.

There were many other foreigners who, directly or indirectly, contributed to the Indian freedom movement. (Total 211 words)

5. "In many ways, Lord Dalhousie was the founder of modern India". Elaborate (200 words) 10

Important Points for Answer:
- *Dalhousie*
- *His main policies*
- *Contribution in modern India*

Answer: Lord Dalhousie's served as the Governor-General of India from 1848 to 1856. His work in the fields of communication, railways, roads, postal and telegraph services contributed to the modernization and unity of India. His notable achievement included creation of modern and centralized states.

Bengal, long ruled by the Governor-General or his delegate, was placed under its own Lieutenant-Governor in May 1854.

A department of public works was established in each presidency, and engineering colleges were established. An imperial system of telegraphs followed in the same period. The first link of railway communication was also completed in 1855.

The construction of massive irrigation works such as the 350-mile Gangas Canalcontaining thousands of miles of distributaries was a project, beneficial for the largely agricultural India, carried out during his time.

Lord Dalhousie also created an imperial system of post-offices, reducing the rates of carrying letters and introducing postage stamps. He created the department of public instruction; he improved the system of inspection of goals, and enlarged the Legislative Council of India.

He gave improved leave and pension rules for the Civil Servants and purified its moral by forbidding all share in trading corporations. Another consequential set of reforms, were those aimed at modernizing the land tenure and revenue system. (Total 213 words)

6. Critically discuss the objectives of Bhoodan and Gramdan movements initiated by Acharya Vinoba Bhave and their success. (200 words)10

Important Points for Answer:
- *Bhoodan Movement*
- *Gramdan Movement*
- *Assessment*

Answer: The initial objective of the Gramdan movement, started by Acharya Vinoba Bhave, was to secure voluntary donations of land and distribute it to the landless, but the movement soon came out with a demand of 1/6 share of land from all land owners.

In 1952, the movement had widened the concept of gramdan (village in gift) and had started advocating commercial ownership of land. The first village to come under gramdan was Mangroth in Hamirpur district of U.P.

The mission of the movement was to persuade wealthy landowners to voluntarily give a percentage of their land to the landless people. This land could not be sold.

The Government of various Provinces, passed Bhoodan Acts which generally stipulated that the beneficiary had no right to sell the land or use it for a non-agricultural purpose including forestry.

Initially genuine donors were coming forward. However, because the Bhoodan movement did no follow-up, the land thus gifted often wasresumed by the heirs of the donor.

Vinoba Bhave walked across India on foot, to persuade landowners to give up a piece of their land. He also wanted peasants to give up using bullocks or tractors or other machines for agricultural purposes, known as 'rishikheti'. Bhave said that rural rich must participate in voluntary distribution of land. (Total 217 words)

7. Write a critical note on evolution and significance of the slogan 'Jai Jawan Jai Kisan'. (200 words) **10**

Important Points for Answer:

- *Jai Jawan - Defence*
- *Jai Kisan - Agriculture*
- *Jai Vigyan - Science*

Answer: Jai Jawan Jai Kisan was a slogan given to India by the Prime Minister of India LalBahadurShastri in 1965. It means *'Hail the Soldier, Hail the Farmer'*.

Soon after Lal Bahadur Shastri took over the prime ministership of India after Nehru's death, India was attacked by Pakistan. At the same time there was scarcity of food grains in the country. Shastri gave the slogan *'Jai Jawan Jai Kisan'* to enthuse the soldiers to defend India and simultaneously cheering farmers to do their best to increase the production of food grains to reduce dependence on import.

India began its own Green Revolution program of plant breeding, irrigation development, and financing of agrochemicals. Similarly, Indian defence forces have also achieved commendable success in war and peace time.

It became a very popular slogan.After Pokaran tests in 1998 AtalBihari Vajpayee added *'Jai Vigyan' (Hail knowledge)* to the slogan to underline the importance of knowledge in India's progress.

Scientifically India has achieved success in various fields including space, IT, medical, engineering and other fields of technology.

Shri Lal Bahadur Shastri's slogan Jai Jawan Jai Kisan reverberates even today through the length and breadth of the country. Underlying this is the inner-most sentiments 'Jai Hindustan'.

(Total 205 words)

8. Discuss the contributions of Maulana Abul Kalam Azad to pre and post independent India. (200 words) 10

Important Points for Answer:
- *Maulana Azad in Congress*
- *Freedom Fighter*
- *Independent India*
- *Education Minister*
- *Bharat Ratna*

Answer: Maulana Azad joined the Indian National Congress in January 1920 and extended support to Gandhi's non-cooperation movement. He presided over the Special Session of Congress in September 1923 and was the youngest man elected as the President of the Congress.He was again elected as Congress President in 1940.

In 1928, Maulana Azad endorsed the Nehru Report, formulated by Motilal Nehru. Interestingly, the Motilal Nehru Report was severely criticized by number of Muslim personalities involved with the freedom movement.

Azad also advocated for the ending of separate electorates based on religion and called for a single nation committed to secularism. In 1930, Maulana Azad was arrested for violation of the salt laws as part of Gandhiji's Salt Satyagraha. He was put in Meerut jail for a year and a half.

After partition, he helped in establishing the refugee camps and ensured uninterrupted supply of food and other basic materials.

He was appointed as India's first Minister for Education and inducted in the Constituent Assembly to draft India's constitution.

Under Maulana Azad's tenure, a number of measures were undertaken to promote primary and secondary education, scientific education, establishment of universities and promotion of avenues of research and higher studies.

In February1958, MaulanaAbul Kalam Azad passed away. He was posthumously awarded, Bharat Ratnain 1992. (Total 216 words)

9. Analyze the circumstances that led to the Tashkent Agreement in 1966. Discuss the highlights of the Agreement. (200 words) 10

Important Points for Answer:
- *Circumstances for the Agreement*
- *Main provisions of the Agreement*
- *Reaction in India*

Answer: The Tashkent Declaration of 10 January 1966 was a peace agreement between India and Pakistan after the Indo-Pakistani War of 1965.Peace had been achieved on 23 September by the intervention of the other big powers that pushed the two nations to a ceasefire for the fear that the conflict could escalate.

A meeting was held in Tashkent, Capital of the Uzbekistan, USSR beginning on 4 January 1966 to try to create a more permanent settlement.The Soviets moderated between Indian Prime Minister LalBahadurShastri and Pakistani President Muhammad Ayub Khan.

The declaration provided that Indian and Pakistani forces would pull back to their pre-conflict positions; both the nations would not interfere in each other's internal affairs; economic and diplomatic relations would be restored; there would be an orderly transfer of prisoners of war; the two leaders would work towards improving bilateral relations.

The Tashkent conference, under United Nations, American and Soviet pressure, compelled India to give away the conquered region in Pakistan occupied national boundary ofIndia and the 1949 ceasefire line in Kashmir.

The agreement was criticized in India because it did not contain a no-war pact or any renunciation of guerrilla warfare in Kashmir. After signing the agreement, LalBahadurShastri died mysteriously at Tashkent. (Total 212 words)

10. Critically examine the compulsions which prompted India to play a decisive role in the emergence of Bangladesh. (200 words) **10**

Important Points for Answer:

- *Atrocities on East Pakistan*
- *Refugees in India*
- *Mukti Bahini*
- *Support to Bangladesh*

Answer: The Pakistan army conducted widespread genocide against the Bengali population of East Pakistan. The atrocities were aimed at the minority Hindu population, leading to approximately 10 million people fleeing East Pakistan and taking refuge in the neighbouring Indian states.

The East Pakistan-India border was opened to allow refugees safe shelter in India. The governments of West Bengal, Bihar, Assam, Meghalaya and Tripura established refugee camps along the border. The resulting flood of impoverished East Pakistani refugees placed an intolerable strain on India's already overburdened economy.

General Tikka Khan earned the nickname 'Butcher of Bengal' due to the widespread atrocities he committed.

The Indian government repeatedly appealed to the international community, but failing to elicit any response, Prime Minister Indira Gandhi on 27 March 1971 expressed full support of her government for the independence struggle of the people of East Pakistan.

The Indian leadership under Prime Minister Gandhi quickly decided that it was more effective to end the genocide by taking armed action against Pakistan than to simply give refuge to those who made it across to refugee camps.

Exiled East Pakistan army officers and members of the Indian Intelligence immediately started using these camps for recruitment and training of Mukti Bahini guerrillas. The Mukti Bahini Sena played important role in creation of Bangladesh. (Total 214 words)

11. "'Latecomer' Industrial Revolution in Japan involved certain factors that were markedlydifferent from what West had experienced." Analyze. (200 words) 10

Important Points for Answer:
- *Industrialisation of Japan*
- *Reforms*
- *Comparison with West*
- *Effects on Society*

Answer: Japan avoided falling under Western economic control during the nineteenth century. Unlike western countries where industrialisation was led by capitalists, Japan heavily dependent on the government to assume much of the burden of the needed capital. Japan faced heavy pressure in the nineteenth century.Japan did industrialise without sacrificing the distinctive character of its society, unlike the social changes faced by Western countries.

The Meiji emperor initiated a series of reforms that abolished feudalism. He established a centralised government. The reforms also promoted industrialisation. The government played a key role in industrial development, building the railroad network and operating mines, shipyards, and heavy industry, while private initiatives dominated in the textile industry.

Industrialisation changed the social structure as the new business elite was drawn from all classes, ranging from former samurais to wealthy peasants, but did not divide the society into labourers and industrialists like Western countries.Despite industrialisation, Japan retained many of its traditional characteristics, including the Shinto religion and the inferior position of women.

By 1900, Japan was an industrial power and the success of Japanese industrialisation surprised the world. But produced great stress in Japanese society, which threatened revolution. Japanese leaders turned to nationalism, devotion to the emperor, and police repression as an antidote to insecurity and dissent. (Total 211 words)

12. "Africa was chopped into States artificially created by accidents of European competition ". Analyze. (200 words) 10

Important Points for Answer:
- *Advent of Africa*
- *European colonisation*
- *Conference of competitors*
- *Division*

Answer: From the 1800s, European countries began to take control of coastal areas in Africa, like French Algeria, the British Cape Colony in modern-day South Africa. Yet 1880, only small areas of the African continent were under European rule.

In European power politics, Britain, France, Germany, Belgium, Italy, Portugal, and Spain were competing among themselves. One way to demonstrate national preeminence was through the acquisition of territories around the world, including Africa.

From 1880, in the space of just 30 years, the whole of Africa was carved up by the main European powers. By 1913, the Europeans had drawn boundaries for their 40 new states or 'colonies'. These boundaries form the basis of the African nations.

The European imperialist designs and pressures of the late nineteenth century provoked African political and diplomatic responses and eventually military resistance. This situation was compounded by commercial conflicts between Europeans and Africans.

During and after the Berlin Conference various European countries sent out agents to sign so-called treaties of protection with the leaders of African societies, states, kingdoms, decentralised societies, and empires. But African leaders did not welcome the Berlin Conference.

The chopping off of Africa was done among the Europeans, without consulting or having consensus of Africa. (Total 205 words)

13. "American Revolution was an economic revolt against mercantilism. Substantiate. (200words) 10

Important Points for Answer:

- *Economic policy of Britain*
- *Economic burden on Americans*
- *Dissatisfaction*
- *Revolt*

Answer: After the Seven Years' War with heavy war debts, Britain's new policies attempted to exert more control over the colonies and taxing the colonists so that they would help pay for the imperial defence by which they were protected.

Old laws designed to benefit British mercantilists were enforced with more severity. A series of new laws, designed to shape American economic activities to benefit Britain, were passed.

The Stamp Act was more powerful in arousing widespread anger among the colonists than any of the previous laws. Outraged colonists protested the tax.Two other new laws that caused dissent among the American colonists were the Proclamation of 1763 and the Quartering Act of 1765.

American merchants were angry about the hampering of trade and industry by English mercantilist laws. Plantation owners and frontiersmen resented the limitations on Western expansion. Professionals disliked the Stamp Act because it made paper, and thus, newspapers, pamphlets, and legal documents expensive. Consumers hated the high cost of living, due to import duties. Few people cared for the British soldiers packed into the cities and accomplishing little beyond asserting Britain's supremacy.

American opposition to these acts was expressed initially in a variety of peaceful forms. Later it led to the war of independence. (Total 206 words)

14. What policy instruments were deployed to contain the Great Economic Depression? (200 words) 10

Important Points for Answer:
- *Hover's response*
- *Agencies for assistance*
- *Assessment*
- *Roosevelt's response*
- *3Rs*
- *Assessment*

Answer: Herbert Hoover was president when the Great Depression began with the stock market crash in 1929.

The two presidents during the Great Depression, Herbert Hoover (1929-1933) and Franklin D. Roosevelt (1933-1945) had varying attitudes about the economy and response.

Hoover called for a series of conferences to talk about the problem. He increased public works programs, including government financed building projects. But the public works provided by Hoover were not on a large enough scale to really help.

He created agencies to provide assistance, which included:

(a) National Credit Corporation–money for banks to continue to operate.

(b) Reconstruction Finance Corporation – loans to railroads, agriculture and banks,were given out.

(c) Relief– money that went directly to impoverished families.

Hoover did not respond immediately so his actions can be summarized as "too little, too late."

Roosevelt's response included the New Deal. Roosevelt's plan (1933) for ending the Great Depression was to create many agencies and programs to address specific needs in the economy. In 1935, Roosevelt created the Second New Deal to make the economy grow faster which focused on the three R's:

1. Relief– ease the suffering of the needy
2. Recovery – lay the foundation for economic growth
3. Reform – prevent a future economic crisis

They helped to some extent in providing relief during the great depression. (Total 220 words)

15.Discuss the various social problems which originated out of the speedy process of urbanization in India. (200 words) 10

Important Points for Answer:
- *Urbanisation*
- *Reasons*
- *Problems*

Answer: Population residing in urban areas in India, according to 1901 census, was 11.4%. It increased to 28.53% according to 2001 census, and crossing 30% as per 2011 census.

Better government services, developed infrastructure, more employment opportunities, educational and healthcare facilities attracted more and more people to migrate towards urban areas.

Urbanisation is taking place at a faster rate in India.Rapid rise in urban population, in India, is leading to many problems like increasing slums, decrease in standard of living in urban areas, also causing environmental damage.

India has around 300 million people living in metropolitan areas. This has greatly caused slum problems, with so many people over-crowding cities and forcing people to live in unsafe conditions which also includes illegal buildings.

Water lines, roads and electricity are lacking which is causing fall of living standards. It is adding to the problem of all types of pollution. Urbanisation results in a disparity in the market, owing to the large demands of the growing population and the primary sector struggling to cope with them.

The unemployment rate is increasing. Due to unemployment, crime rate is increasing which creates social and legal problems for administration of urban areas. Lack of fund also results into insufficiency of infrastructure. (Total 206 words)

16. "Male membership needs to be encouraged in order to make women's organization freefrom gender bias". Comment. (200 words) 10

Important Points for Answer:
- *Gender bias*
- *Reasons*
- *Male perspective*
- *Complementary role*

Answer: Sometimes in the zeal of protecting women, feminism grows to the extent of chauvinistic approach. This leads to complete bias picture of the society and organisation. The women's organisation, focused on the rights and upliftment of women, should be made more inclusive to have better understanding of the society.

Gender bias occurs due to personal values, educational and social upbringing of a person.

Gender bias can easily crept in women's organisation due to higher sensitivity towards the women specific issues. Intervention and opinion of men can bring a new perspective.

Having men in women's organisation will also make them sensitive towards crimes and mis-happening against women.

Men member can suggest measures for upliftment of women and protection of their rights in the society.

False allegations of crimes and harassment raised against men, taking advantages of existing women friendly law, should be examined not only by women but also by a men member.

Male member can provide moral support to the organisation of women and thus encourage them by assuring that in fight against injustice women are not alone.

Therefore, to bring counter and complementary view of the societal values, men members in women's organisation can be useful to make it unbiased. (Total 202 words)

17. Critically examine the effect of globalization on the aged population in India. (200 words)10

> **Important Points for Answer:**
> - *Globalisation*
> - *Aged population in India*
> - *Positive impacts*
> - *Negative impacts*

Answer: Globalisation has made trade and commerce easy among nations. It also resulted into increased socio-cultural interactions among different communities of the world. It certainly has impacted all class and category of people, including ageing population.

India is a country of youth but still being the second largest populated country in the world, it has sizeable aged people number of which is expected to reach 135 million by 2021.

India has become medical hub, due to globalisation, of which first impact on aged population is availability of better medical facilities. However, prices of medical services have gone up but government hospitals are a boon. Age related health issues are no more incurable in India.

Internet connected society has developed due to globalisation which has engaged all generations, including aged. Good impact on aged people is that they have connectivity but demerit is less attention by youth on elderly people. Many facilities are now available through internet which helps elderly people.

Travelling has become faster, smoother and easier for elderly people due to benefits of globalisation.

Pension schemes and insurance schemes are available to elders from many private sector companies which have improved financial status of aged population of India.

However, globalisation has increased migration which has left more and more elderly people alone.

Thus, globalisation has mixed impact on aged population of India. (Total 223 words)

18. Growing feeling of regionalism is an important factor in generation of demand for aseparate State. Discuss. (200 words) 10

> **Important Points for Answer:**
> - *Regionalism*
> - *Demands for separate States*
> - *Reasons for such demands*
> - *Assessment*

Answer: Regionalism is attachment and respectful feeling of people who are living in a geographical area towards the region. It also results into political chauvinistic attitude, sometimes. In india, diversity has melted into unity. But regional groups have grown stronger politically. Their region specific demands and interests have strengthened regionalism.

Such regionalism has generated demands for separate states. Demand for Harit Pradesh in the Western Uttar Pradesh, Purvanchal in Eastern Uttar Pradesh, Bodoland in Northern Assam, Saurashtra in Southern Gujarat, Ladakh in Eastern Jammu and Kashmir, Gorkhaland in Northern West Bengal, Kongu Nadu in South Tamil Nadu, Vidarbha in Eastern Maharashtra, Telangana in Andhra Pradesh, Tulu Nadu in Karnataka, Kukiland in Manipur are the main demands being raised by various regions in India.

Regionalism is main factors for such demands for a separate state which arises when the people of particular area feel their regional identity is distinct and separate from the rest of the people of the State. Sometimes this regional identity is also accompanied by feeling of being marginalised or alienated.

In 2000, Chhattisgarh from Madhya Pradesh, Uttaranchal from Uttar Pradesh and Jharkhand from Bihar were created due to such demands. As per one report, if all demands for creation of separate states are conceded to, there would be almost 50 states in India. (Total 215 words)

19. (a) What do you understand by the theory of 'continental drift'? Discuss the prominentevidences in its support. (100 words) 5

Answer: (a) Continental drift is the movement of the Earth's continents relative to each other by appearing to drift across the ocean bed. The speculation that continents might have 'drifted' was first given by Abraham Ortelius in 1596.

Evidence:

Similar plant and animal fossils are found around different continent shores, suggesting that they were once joined.

The fossils of Mesosaurus, a freshwater reptile rather like a small crocodile, found both in Brazil and South Africa.

Widespread distribution of Permo-Carboniferous glacial sediments in South America, Africa, Madagascar, Arabia, India, Antarctica and Australia was one of the major evidence for the theory of continental drift. (Total 102 words)

(b) The recent cyclone on east coast of India was called 'Phailin'. How are the tropical cyclones named across the world ? Elaborate. (100 words) 5

Answer: (b) Tropical cyclones have officially been named since 1945. More than one can occur in the same region at the same time, therefore names are given for identification.

Names are drawn in order from predetermined lists and are usually assigned to tropical cyclones with one-, three-, or ten-minute sustained wind speeds of more than 65 km/h (40 mph) depending on which area it originates.

'Phailin', a Thai word meaning sapphire, was a cyclone along the Bay of Bengal. It was named by Thailand in the list of assigned names. The next cyclone in the region will be Helen, a name by Bangladesh. (Total 103 words)

20. (a) Bring out the causes for the formation of heat islands in the urban habitat of theworld. (100 words) 5

Answer: (a) An urban heat island (UHI) is a metropolitan area that is significantly warmer.

The main cause of the urban heat island effect is from the modification of land surfaces, which use materials that effectively store short-wave radiation.

Waste heat generated by energy usage is a secondary contributor.

Population centre tends to expand its area and increase its average temperature.

Nighttime warming is due to the short-wave radiation which is still within the concrete, asphalt, and buildings.

Other reasons are decreased amount of vegetation, geometric effects, changes in the thermal properties of surface materials and lack of evapotranspiration in urban areas. (Total 102 words)

(b) What do you understand by the phenomenon of 'temperature inversion' in meteorology? How does it affect weather and the habitants of the place? (100 words) 5

Answer: (b) In meteorology,"temperature inversion", is an increase in temperature with height, or to the layer within which an increase of temperature occurs.

An inversion can lead to pollution such as smog being trapped close to the ground, with possible adverse effects on health. An inversion can also suppress convection by acting as a «cap». Temperature inversion can notoriously result in freezing rain in cold climates.

Temperature inversion stops atmospheric convectionfrom happening in the affected area. It can lead to the air becoming stiller and murky from the collection of dust and pollutants. This can become a problem in cities where many pollutants exist. (Total 104 words)

21. Major hot deserts in northern hemisphere are located between 20-30 deg N latitudes and on the western side of the continents. Why? (200 words) 10

Important Points for Answer:
- *Hot Deserts*
- *Ocean currents*
- *Distance from ocean*
- *Rain shadow*
- *High pressure*

Answer: The hot deserts are located between 20-30° latitude and on the western side of the continents are because these climatic deserts are produced due to cold ocean currents, distance from oceanic moisture sources, mountain produced rain shadow which are the main factors for desert in these latitudes.

Earth rotates from west to east, so first the sun rays will fall on the eastern side of earth. As a result of high temperature, low pressure is created which will result in rainfall. There will be many obstructs on the way of these moisture laden clouds. So the western part will remain dry, creating deserts.

In the horse latitudes where constant high pressure and low temperature caused cold current, such deserts are created.

Complex air circulation patterns caused by the rotation of earth, Coriolis effect, is also a reason.

Areas within a continent may become desert because air currently reaching them already lost the moisture.20-30 degree latitude appears directly overhead at the noon.

- Major desert land appears in these two discontinuous belts because more land surface occur in these latitudes.
- The Great Basin of USA and deserts Australia are caused by "rain shadow effect" through which coastal mountains milk rain from the air before it passes inland. (Total 208 words)

22. (a) Bring out the causes for more frequent occurrence of landslides in the Himalayasthan in the Western Ghats. (100 words) **5**

Answer: (a) Landslide includes a wide range of ground movements, such as rockfalls, deep failure of slopes and shallow debris flows.

The Himalayas and the Western Ghats are the two regions most vulnerable to landslides.

The Himalayas Mountain belt comprise of tectonically unstable younger geological formations. They are subjected to severe seismic activity. The slides in the Himalayas region are huge and massive.

The Western Ghats and nilgiris are geologically stable. However, they have uplifted plateau margins influenced by neo-tectonic activity.

Some natural activities such as heavy rainfall, large temperature variation, occurrence of large magnitude of earthquakes etc cause frequent landslides in Himalaya region. (Total 103 words)

(b) There is no formation of deltas by rivers of the Western Ghats. Why? (100 words) **5**

Answer: (b) There are many rivers flowing from Western Ghats such as Narmada, Tapti, Godawari, Krishna, Kaveri, Tunga, Many of which originate from the western Ghat Mountains and fall in to the Arabian Sea. As they pass through the hard rocks, these rivers contain very little amount of slits. Due to the high gradient and steep slope of Western Ghat, these rivers flow at a high speed and so they are unable to deposits slits. There is lack of plain land to slow down the velocity of rivers and bifurcate in to tributaries. Rock terrain of western ghats does not allow the rivers to spread out much. Therefore, they do not make delta, but estuaries. (Total 113 words)

23. (a) Do you agree that there is a growing trend of opening new sugar mills in southernstates of India? Discuss with justification. (100 words) **5**

Answer: (a) Main centre for sugar mills of India had been North India, especially UP. New sugar mills opening in South India is a new trend. Recently plantation of sugarcane has started in south India which has attracted more sugar mills. Uniform temperature, better irrigation facilities, moisture effects of ocean has better effect on sugar contents which yields high productivity of sugar. Transportation of sugarcane from south India to north India is expensive but establishment of a sugar mill is not heavy capital intensive industry. Sugar is also an export oriented commodity which are better facilitated by vicinity of South Indian ports. Due to all these reasons, south India has more sugar mills now. (Total 112 words)

(b) Analyze the factors for the highly decentralized cotton textile industry in India. (100 words) 5

Answer:(b) India is the second largest producer of cotton in the world. Its cotton textile industry was primarily located in Gujarat and Maharashtra. But with widespread cultivation of cotton seeds throughout India, cotton textile industry are also becoming decentralised. Local weavers, artisans, market, less transport cost, local fashion and traditions and entrepreneurship has been responsible for such widespread of industry. Irrigation facilities, better return in cotton, non-perishable commodity and less capital required in growing cotton seeds has encouraged farmers to grow cotton instead of other crops. This has resulted into establishment of less capital intensive mills at clusters. Availability of labour and technology has also played role. (Total 107 words)

24. With growing scarcity of fossil fuels, the atomic energy is gaining more and more significance in India. Discuss the availability of raw material required for the generation of atomic energy in India and in the world. (200 words) 10

Important Points for Answer:
- *Scarcity of fossil fuel*
- *India's atomic energy programme*
- *Availability of raw material*

Answer: Fossil fuels are formed after a lengthy process of millions of years. Due to limited reserve, they are going to be exhausted in 50-80 years of period. They are environmental hazard. India is mostly dependent of imported fossil fuels which costs on FOREX reserve. In such situation, the atomic energy programme is very the best alternative.

Atomic energy is the source of Nuclear power, which uses sustained nuclear fission to generate heat and electricity.Among all the radioactive elements - Uranium and Thorium are the most critical for generation of Nuclear Energy. Thorium is much more abundant in nature than uranium. India has around 1-2% of the global uranium reserves and about 21% of the world's known thorium reserves.

India has three-stage nuclear power programme which was initiated by Dr. Homi Bhabha.

Uranium and thorium reserves are found in the monazite sands of coastal regions of South India. Kazakhstan, Canada, Australia, Niger, Namiba and Russia are largest Uranium reserves of the world.

Largest deposits of thorium is found in Malabar coast of Kerala which is sufficient to generate 3.5 lakh MW energy for 300 years. India is the largest reserve of thorium, followed by Australia, USA and Turkey. (Total 200 words)

25. It is said that India has substantial reserves of shale oil and gas, which can feed the needsof the country for quarter century. However, tapping of the resource does not appear to be high on the agenda. Discuss critically the availability and issues involved. (200 words) 10

Important Points for Answer:

- *Shale oil and gas*
- *India's reserve*
- *Policy in India*
- *Difficulties*
- *Assessment*

Answer: Shale gas & oil is defined as natural gas & oil from shale formations. Shale gas is natural gas which is found trapped within shale formations. The shale acts as both the source and the reservoir for these unconventional hydrocarbons.

India has an estimated 96 trillion cubic feet of recoverable shale gas reserves. In India, shale oil and gas reserves are found mainly in Tamil Nadu, Andhra Pradesh and Rajasthan. Sedimentary basins like Cambay Basin, Gondwana Basin, KG Basin, Cauvery Basin, Indo-Gangetic Basin, Assam & Assam-Arakan Basin etc are considered prospective from Shale oil and gas point of view.

Shale gas requires complex extraction process and its drilling requires more land than natural gas or coal bed methane. Minimum 80-160 acres necessary for each well. Technology and investment are also major issues. Only shale formations with certain characteristics will produce gas and oil.

To exploit shale gas and oil in the country, the government on October 14, 2013 announced the policy guidelines for exploration and exploitation of shale gas and oil by ONGC and OIL in their on-land Petroleum Exploration Licence and petroleum mining lease areas awarded under the nomination regimes.

However, the policy is yet to be tested on the anvil of time. (Total 205 words)

SOLVED PAPERS

PAPER–II

Time Allowed : Three Hours *Maximum Marks : 250*

Instructions : There are TWENTY FIVE questions printed both in English and in Hindi. All questions are compulsory. The number of marks carried by a question/part is indicated against it. Answers must be written in the medium authorized in the Admission Certificate which must be stated clearly on the cover of this Question-cum-Answer (QCA) Booklet in the space provided. No marks will be given for answers written in medium other than the authorized one.

Word limit in questions, wherever specified, should be adhered to.

Any page or portion of the page left blank in the answer book must be clearly struck off.

1. The role of individual MPs (Member of Parliament) has diminished over the years and as a result healthy constructive debates on policy issues are not usually witnessed. How far can this be attributed to the anti-defection law which was legislated but with a different intention? (200 words) 10

Important Points for Answer:
- *Individual MPs role*
- *Anti-Defection Law*
- *Whip*
- *Assessment*

Answer: Parliament can be effective only if individual MPs have a significant role as law makers, and if they can be held accountable for their actions by their electorate. In the last few years, the role of individual Members of Parliament diminish on account of the Anti-Defection Law.

The 10th Schedule to the Constitution, popularly referred to as the 'Anti-Defection Law,' was inserted by the 52nd Amendment in 1985. It specifies grounds of disqualification. A member would incur a disqualificationwhen he "voluntarily gives up his membership of a party" and when he/she votes or abstains from voting contrary to the directive issued by the party.

The ruling party can ensure the support of each of its MP by issuing a whip. If it needs to build further support to get a majority, it only needs to convince the leaders of other parties, and not individual MPs. In a sense, the role of an MP is diminished to just a person who has to follow orders from the party bosses.

It was believed that Anti-Defection Law would ensure stability of the government in an environment where money power can be used to persuade individual MPs to bring down elected governments. The other argument is that MPs are elected on the party ticket. (Total 215 words)

2. Discuss Section 66A of IT Act, with reference to the alleged violation of Article 19 of the Constitution. (200 words) 10

Important Points for Answer:
- *PILs against Section 66A*
- *Restriction on speech*
- *Violation of Article 19*

Answer: Recently several PILs have been filed challenging the constitutionality of Section 66A of the IT Act. It is submitted to the Supreme Court that Section 66A curbs freedom of speech and expression and violates Articles 14, 19 and 21 of the Constitution.

The petition further contends that the expressions used in the Section are "vague" and "ambiguous" and that 66A is subject to "wanton abuse" in view of the subjective powers conferred on the police to interpret the law.

The Union government has defended the constitutionality of Section 66A relying first on the "Advisory on Implementation of Section 66A of the Information Technology Act 2000" issued by the Department of Electronics and Information Technology on January 9, 2013.

The drafters of Section 66A(b) have equated known criminal offences in the real world with acts such as causing annoyance and inconvenience that can never constitute an offence in the real world and should not be offences in the virtual world.

Therefore, the legislative restrictions on freedom of speech in Section 66A(b) cannot be considered as being necessary to achieve a legitimate objective. Section 66A should not be considered a 'reasonable restriction' within the meaning of Article 19 of the Constitution and must be struck down as an unconstitutional restriction on freedom of speech. (Total 214 words)

3. Recent directives from Ministry of Petroleum and Natural Gas are perceived by the 'Nagas' as a threat to override the exceptional status enjoyed by the State. Discuss in light of Article 371A of the Indian Constitution. (200 words) 10

Important Points for Answer:
- *Nagaland and Article 371A*
- *Resources in Nagaland*
- *Order of MoPNG*
- *Legal status*
- *Solution*

Answer: The 1960 Agreement was the basis for the creation of Nagaland in December 1963. Article 371A facilitated negotiated sovereignty of the Nagas on matters pertaining to their religious and social practices, customary laws and procedure, administration of civil and criminal justice, ownership and transfer of land and resources.

Legal luminaries have concurred that "land and its resources" as used in Article 371 A(1)(a)(iv) includes mines and minerals.

The Nagaland Legislative Assembly passed a resolution on July 26, 2010 to the effect that laws made by Parliament on petroleum and natural gas would be inapplicable in Nagaland with retrospective effect. Then after Ministry suspended all oil operations in the State.

Recently Nagas have objected to the June 2013 request of Union Minister Mr. Moily to withdraw the Nagaland Petroleum and Natural Gas Resolution, 2012. The Nagaland government held a consultative meeting with various sections of civil society and rejected Mr. Moily's request and also demanded that the GoI implement the unfulfilled clauses of the Sixteen Point Agreement, 1960, and place Nagaland under the Ministry of External Affairs. This may set up a new confrontation with the Central government.

The issue needs to be resolved, given the constitutional status of Nagaland under Article 371A, Centre government has to take into confidence the Nagas on the issue at hand. (Total 219 words)

4. 'The Supreme Court of India keeps a check on arbitrary power of the Parliament in amending the Constitution". Discuss critically. (200 words)10

Important Points for Answer:
- *Article 368 and amending power*
- *Judicial decisions*
- *Amendments*
- *Severability*

Answer: The Constitution can be amended only by Parliament and only in the manner provided in Article 368. Although Parliament must preserve the basic framework of the Constitution, there is no other limitation placed upon the amending power, meaning that there is no provision of the Constitution that cannot be amended.

The current limitation on amending power of Parliament comes from the decision of Keshavananda Bharati v. The State of Kerala, 1973 where the Supreme Court ruled that amendments of the constitution must not violate the "basic structure" of the constitution, and certain fundamental features of the constitution cannot be altered by amendment.

Parliament attempted to remove this limitation of 'basic structure' by enacting the Forty-second Amendment, 1976 which declared, inter alia, that "there shall be no limitation whatever on the constituent power of Parliament to amend". However, this change was itself later declared invalid by the Supreme Court in Minerva Mills v. Union of India, 1980.

The entire constitutional amendment is not void for being violative of the limitations provided by the constitution and judicial decisions on the parliament. As declared by the Supreme Court in Kihota Hollohonv.Zachilhu 1993, that if part of amendment which is violating the basic structure of constitution is severable, only part will be void and rest of the amendment will be valid.

(Total 220 words)

5. Many State Governments further bifurcate geographical administrative areas like Districts and Talukas for better governance. In light of the above, can it also be justified that more number of smaller States would bring in effective governance at State level ? Discuss. (200 words) 10

Important Points for Answer:

- *Administrative divisions*
- *Small states benefits*
- *Small states disadvantages*
- *Assessment*

Answer: Country is divided into states, states into districts, districts into talukas, talukas into villages, villages into wards for administrative purposes. Smaller divisions can be administered and managed efficiently.

On the same argument, though for different reasons, there are demands for smaller states in India. The premise of creating smaller States in India shifted from the formation of linguistic states to one of, since the 1990s, rearranging them on the basis of backwardness and a lack of development.

Smaller states mean key decisions will be taken closer to the ground. Administering large and diverse states is more complex and probably inefficient as well, though there can be economies of scale in some ways.

The average Indian state is 4.2 crores people, where actual sizes vary from the 20 crores of Uttar Pradesh to states such as Arunachal, with just a few thousand people scattered all over.The 50-state USA has an average state population of just 62 lakh.

A smaller state is vulnerable politically and on local, racial, cultural or religious issues. Ananalysis of Uttarakhand, Chhattisgarh and Jharkhand proves that mere formation of a smaller State is no guarantee for better lives.

Therefore, all options need to be weighed but we do not need to be completely averse to the idea. (Total 212 words)

6. Constitutional mechanism to resolve the inter-state water disputes have failed to address and solve the problems. Is the failure due to structural or process inadequacy or both? Discuss. (200 words) 10

Important Points for Answer:

- *Act of 1956*
- *Creation of tribunals*
- *Awards of tribunals*
- *Inadequacy*
- *Assessment*

Answer: The Interstate River Water Disputes Act, 1956 (IRWD Act) is an Act of the Parliament of India enacted under Article 262 of Constitution of India. It aims to resolve the water disputes that would arise in the use, control and distribution of an interstate river or river valley.

All these tribunal awards were issued before the year 2002 which cannot be altered by the new tribunals. The tribunals formed on sharing water of Ravi & Beas rivers, Cauvery/Kaveri river,

Vamsadhara River, Mahadayi/Mandovi River and Krishna River (tribunal 2) are either yet to pronounce the verdicts or the issued verdicts are to be accepted by the Government of India.

Recently, Cauvery water disputes tribunal order was notified by the GoI in February 2013.In the case of Cauvery River basin, SC directed the GoI to set up a temporary Supervisory Committee to implement the tribunal order till the constitution of Cauvery Management Board by GoI. GoI established the said temporary Supervisory Committee in May 2013. The issue has yet not been resolved.

In the case of Babli barrage dispute, SC itself constituted the Supervisory Committee to implement the water sharing agreement between Maharashtra and Andhra Pradesh in middle Godavari sub basin. The issue remains unresolved.

Thus, the mechanism has not proved to be adequate and no dispute has been solved satisfactorily.

(Total 221 words)

7. Discuss the recommendations of the Thirteenth Finance Commission which have been a departure from the previous commissions for strengthening the local government finances. (200 words) 10

Important Points for Answer:
- *13th FC*
- *Two types of grants*
- *Nine conditions*

Answer: The 13th FC has given some recommendations departing from the previous Finance Commissions. It has divided the grants to be distributed to the states for local bodies into two parts - general basic grant and general performance grant.The performance grant can be accessed only if the state complies with nine conditions, which in other words can be called reforms. States are given one year 2010-2011 to comply with these conditions before they can access the performance grant from 2011-2012.

These nine conditions are:

- The State Government must put in place a supplement to the budget documents for local bodies.
- The State Government must put in place Audit System.
- The State Government must put in place a system of independent local body Ombudsmen.
- The State Government put in place a system to electronically transfer local body grants provided by the Commission.
- The State Government must prescribe through an Act the qualifications of persons eligible for appointment as a member of the SFC.
- All local bodies should be fully enabled to Levy Property Tax without hindrance.
- The State Government must put in place a State Property Tax Board.
- The State government must gradually put in place standards for delivery of essential services.

- All municipal corporations with a population of more than one million (2001 census) must put in place a Fire -hazard Response and Mitigation plan for their respective jurisdictions. (Total 230 words)

8. The product diversification of financial institutions and insurance companies, resulting in overlapping of products and services strengthens the case for the merger of the two regulatory agencies, namely SEBI and IRDA. Justify (200 words) 10

Important Points for Answer:
- *Insurance Products*
- *Financial Products*
- *IRDA function*
- *SEBI function*
- *Proposed merger*

Answer: Insurance companies are offering equity linked plans, mutual fund type of policies and various other products which are mainly dependent on market performance. This is no more a insurance product but more on share, debenture and equity based policies.

Similarly financial institutions like banks have started offering insurance policies and mutual funds. Financial institutions have also embarked in the fields of equity, shares and insurance

IRDA has the duty to regulate, promote and ensure orderly growth of the insurance business and re-insurance business.

SEBI's primary function is described to protect the interests of investors in securities and to promote the development of, and to regulate the securities market and for matters connected therewith or incidental thereto. A multiplicity of regulatory agencies has created scope for regulatory arbitrage and are facing difficult to protect consumer interest.

But as the products have divulged the boundaries and submerged into each other's domain, these institutions cannot control them in isolation. Therefore, the Financial Sector Legislative Reforms Commission (FSLRC) has recently recommended for a single or super regulator to replace those in equity, commodities, pensions and insurance sectors.

The 2010 spat between SEBI and IRDA on the jurisdiction over ULIP is a case in point.The idea is to move from sectoral regulation to a broader framework of rules and principles. (Total 217 words)

9. The concept of Mid Day Meal (MDM) scheme is almost a century old in India with early beginning in Madras Presidency in pre-independent India. The scheme has again been given impetus in most states in the last two decades. Critically examine its twin objectives, latest mandates and success. (200 words) 10

Important Points for Answer:
- *Mid Day Meal in Madras*
- *Aims/Objectives of MDM*
- *Right to Food a Fundamental Right*

Answer: The Mid Day Meal scheme was first introduced in Madras Corporation by the British administration in 1925 which was followed in Puducherry by French administration in 1930.

The Mid-day Meal Scheme involves provision of lunch free of cost to school-children on all working days which aims at addressing malnutrition by ensuring that every child is provided at least one nutritious meal every day.

It also aims at enhancing school enrollment and attendance, since kids are encouraged by the meal to attend school.

Other benefits of the scheme, such as helping kids to concentrate on classroom activities, improving socialization among children belonging to different castes, and providing employment to women to cook the midday meal are also ancillary.

Cooked midday meals are provided to all children attending Classes I-VIII in government, local body, government aided, and National Child Labour Project (NCLP) schools.

The cooked meal provides an energy content of 450 calories and protein content of 12 grams at primary stage and an energy content of 700 calories and protein content of 20 grams at upper primary stage.

The Supreme Court delivered a judgement that under the People's Union for Civil Liberties(PUCL) v Union of India, providing that Article 21 read with Articles 39(a) and 47 makes the right to food a fundamental right. (Total 218 words)

10. Pressure group politics is sometimes seen as the informal face of politics. With regard to the above, assess the structure and functioning of pressure groups in India. (200 words) 10

Important Points for Answer:

- *Pressure groups*
- *Their importance*
- *Types and examples*
- *Their importance in India*

Answer: Pressure groups play a vital role in democracy by seeking to promote, discuss, debate and mobilize public opinion on major public issues. They educate people and widen their vision, enhance their democratic participation and raise and articulate various issues. In India, there are many pressure groups.

There are pressure groups based on traditional social structure.There are groups like Arya Pratinidhi Sabha, Sanathan Dharma Sabha, Parsee Anjuman, and Anglo-Indian Christian Association.

There are the caste groups such as the Brahmin Sabha, the Nair society, and the language groups such as the Tamil Sangh, the Anjuman-e-Terraqi-e-Urdu.

Bodies such as the Federation of the Indian Chambers of Commerce and Industry (FICCI) or those related to workers and peasants like All India Trade Union Congress, Bharatiya Mazdoor Sangh, the Kisan Sabha, etc. also play important role in Indian politics.

The Self-Employed Women's Association (SEWA) has influenced the government to improve its policies on the rights of women workers.

Mazdoor Kisan Shakti Sangathan led the people's movement which got the government to bring about the law on ,Right to Information'.

Pressure groups also use politicalmethods of holdingdemonstrations, sitting on dharnas, going on strikes, organizing public meetings, presenting memorandums to legislative committees, promoting their causes through use of media and creation of public opinion. (Total 217 words)

11. The legitimacy and accountability of Self Help Groups (SHGs) and their patrons, the micro-finance outfits, need systematic assessment and scrutiny for the sustained success of the concept. Discuss. (200 words) 10

Important Points for Answer:
- *SHG*
- *Problems*
- *Recommendations*

Answer: Self-Help Group (SHG), a smallassociation of people, more or less from the same socio-economic background, are formed to protect and promote interest of the group. The purpose of solving their common problems through self-help and mutual help is served through SHG. They promote small savings among its members which is kept in a bank. Usually, the number of members in one SHG does not exceed twenty.

However, legitimacy and accountability of Self Help Groups are facing a lot of problems, including multiple lending, over borrowing, ghost borrowers and coercive method of recovery. For this purpose, a Sub-Committee of the Central Board of the RBI under the Chairmanship of Y. H. Malegam was constituted. It suggested, inter alia, to have a sufficient moratorium period between the start of repayment and the disbursement of loan, to restrict borrower membership of only one SHG to tackle multiple-lending, to allow MFI to give loans to people as members of SHGs, and not as mere individuals, to avoid multiple lending and over-borrowing, to ensure that one borrower is not taking a loan from two MFIs at a time and no further loan until prior loans are not paid fully. (Total 201 words)

12. The Central Government frequently complains on the poor performance of the State Governments in eradicating suffering of the vulnerable sections of the society. Restructuring of Centrally sponsored schemes across the sectors for ameliorating the cause of vulnerable sections of population aims at providing flexibility to the States in better implementation. Critically evaluate. (200 words) 10

Important Points for Answer:
- *Centrally Sponsored Schemes*
- *Implementation*
- *Problems*
- *Restructuring*
- *Solutions*

Answer: Centrally Sponsored Schemes (CSSs) are those for which finance is provided by Centre Government but their implementation rests on the states.

Centre complains poor performance on the parts of States in implementation of these schemes. States lay emphasis on release of funds by the Centre rather than ensuring the quality of expenditure and attainment of the objectives. Misuse of the funds provided for vulnerable sectors and sections of the society is also a problem. It happens some time due to political reasons, corruption, infrastructural and other issues. Union government, due to lack of machinery, is not able to controltvhe execution of such schemes. It results into poor result, overrun of cost, maladministration etc.

Therefore, to get better result, central schemes need restructuring so that the vulnerable sections of the society get intended advantage. Number of central government schemes are reduced and instead of fully funded schemes of centre, now partially funded schemes are implemented which encourages states to perform better in execution. Direct transfer of funds to the beneficiaries, involvement of Panchayats, Social audit and other checks are useful for better result. It is also considered that more financial autonomy to states may result into better implementation of central schemes. (Total 200 words)

13. Electronic cash transfer system for the welfare schemes is an ambitious project to minimize corruption, eliminate wastage and facilitate reforms. Comment. (200 words) 10

Important Points for Answer:
- *Electronic Cash Transfer*
- *Project*
- *Benefits in Welfare Schemes*
- *Reforms*

Answer: Government launched cash transfer by electronic mode in 51 districts in 2013 for 29 schemes. Subsidies in kerosene, fertilisers and LPG will be transferred as cash to the beneficiaries in their bank accounts. Benefits such as scholarships, pensions, and MGNREGA (Mahatma Gandhi National Rural Employment Guarantee Act) wages will be directly credited to the bank or post office accounts of identified beneficiaries.

This is linked to the Aadhaar number of Individuals to prevent cash leak, duplication, fake subsidy and other problems related to the benefit transfers of welfare schemes of the government. It will reduce paper work and ensure that only intended beneficiaries get the cash. Fast, efficient and automated system will be set up. It will minimise inclusion and exclusion errors as well as corruption that are associated with manual processes.

However, there are challenges like non availability of bank accounts with all beneficiaries, bank or post offices do not have branches in small rural areas, illiteracy and lack of infrastructure and logistics. Time frame for bringing all schemes and beneficiaries under direct electronic transfer of cash is longer and will require a robust IT infrastructure.

Given the size of population and geographical extent of country, it will be a robust task but will ensure efficient, non-corrupt and targeted cash benefits. (Total 213 words)

14. The basis of providing urban amenities in rural areas (PURA) is rooted in establishing connectivity. Comment (200 words) 10

> **Important Points for Answer:**
> - *Concept*
> - *Main objectives*
> - *Strategy*
> - *Benefits*

Answer: Provision of Urban Amenities to Rural Areas (PURA) was given by former president Dr. A.P.J. Abdul Kalam and discussed in his book Target 3 Billion which he co-authored with Srijan Pal Singh.

This concept PURA proposes that urban infrastructure and services be provided in rural hubs to create economic opportunities outside of cities.

Main aspect of PURA is dependent on physical connectivity by providing roads, electronic connectivity by providing communication network, and knowledge connectivity byestablishing professional and Technical institutions. It will have to be done in an integrated way so that economic connectivity will emanate. Such a model of establishing a circular connectivity among the rural village complexes will accelerate rural development process.

The Indian central government has been running pilot PURA programs since 2004.The Mission & Vision of PURA is to bring together the experience & expertise of both public & private players to achieve the objectives.

To make the basic amenities like good roads and drinking water accessible to people even in remote villages, The Ministry of Rural Development (MoRD), re-launched the scheme PURA as a Central Sector scheme during the remaining period of the eleventh five-year plan.

The vision of the scheme in particular is providing dual benefits like rural infrastructure development along with economic re-generation activities. (Total 215 words)

15. Identify the Millennium Development Goals (MDGs) that are related to health. Discuss the success of the actions taken by the Government for achieving the same. (200 words) 10

> **Important Points for Answer:**
> - *MDG*
> - *Health related MDG*
> - *Indian programmes*

Answer: Eight Millennium Development Goals (MDGs) for 2015 were set by UN in 2000. All 191 countries and 22 international organisations committed to them.

The goal to combat HIV/AIDS, malaria and other diseases included target to halt and begin to reverse the spread of HIV/AIDS, to halt and begin to reverse the incidence of malaria and other major diseases. Government of India launched a comprehensive National Rural Health Mission (NRHM) (2005) to improve and strengthen the existing rural health care.National AIDS Control Programme aims at prevention for those whole infected and care, support and treatment for those who have been infected. Launched in July 2007, National AIDS Control Programme Phase-III (2007 - 2012) has the goal to halt and reverse the epidemic.

The goal to reduce child mortality included target to reduce under five mortality rate by two-thirds. Government of India has launched various programmes in this direction which include Integrated Management of Neonatal and Childhood Illnesses (IMNCI), Home-Based Newborn Care (HBNC), New Born Care Scheme (NBCS), and Immunization facilities.

The goal to improve maternal health included target to reduce maternal mortality ratioby three quarters. The Janani Suraksha Yojana launched in 2005 by government aims to bring down the MMR by promoting institutional deliveries conducted by skilled birth attendants. (Total 214 words)

16. Though Citizens' charters have been formulated by many public service delivery organizations, there is no corresponding improvement in the level of citizens' satisfaction and quality of services being provided. Analyse. (200 words) 10

Important Points for Answer:

- *Citizens' Charter*
- *Purpose*
- *Non-binding*
- *Limitations*

Answer: Citizen's Charter is a document which represents a systematic effort to focus on the commitment of the Organisation towards its Citizens in respects of Standard of Services, Information, Choice and Consultation, Non-discrimination and Accessibility, Grievance Redress, Courtesy and Value for Money.This also includes expectations of the Organisation from the Citizen for fulfilling the commitment of the Organisation.

However, the Citizen's Charter is not legally enforceable and, therefore, is non-justiciable. But it is a tool for facilitating the delivery of services to citizens with specified standards, quality and time frame etc. with commitments from the Organisation and its clients.

Sometimes though Citizens' Charter is prepared but Citizens' are not satisfied due to various reasons like not being transparent, not being self-explanatory, being too complex, or for not being followed. Sometimes important functions are delegated to non-responsive and less efficient officers which results into failure to deliver service in time bound manner.

The charter is prepared, sometimes, without consultation, without realising limits of resources in the organisation, which results into failure to implement it properly. Charter is not updated and revised properly, resulting into outdated information. Lack of awareness among general public may also result into dissatisfaction of the beneficiaries. (Total 203 words)

17. 'A national Lokpal however strong it may be, cannot resolve the problems of immorality in public affairs.' Discuss. (200 words) 10

Important Points for Answer:

- *Lokpal bill*
- *Objectives*
- *Public morality*
- *Limitations*
- *Awareness*

Answer: Lokpal bill, which aims to prevent corruption but to punish the corrupt, targets executive, bureaucratic and judicial authorities. By absorbing all existing anti-corruption agencies, the Lokpal will have complete powers of independent investigation and prosecution. There is lack of an approach which is qualitatively different from that of existing institutions of the state.

But if public morality is touching lows, this will not help. A transparent system will prevent corruption. In order to ensure transparency, the process of decisionmaking has tobe fundamentally altered.

There are cases where people encourage officers to take bribe and do illegal work, not the other way round. Lokpal can tackle corruption only if a complaint is brought forward by people. In case public is conniving to bypass the system and get advantage by avoiding procedures, Lokpal will not be able to detect such corruption with agreement.

If people are not aware of Lokpal and its power, function of Lokpal will be limited and curtailed. Therefore, there is requirement of education and awareness of people to not encourage or promote corruption by getting involved in these practices. Apart from enacting Lokpal bill, there is need to start an active campaign to improve public morality. (Total 201 words)

18. The proposed withdrawal of International Security Assistance Force (ISAF) from Afghanistan in 2014 is fraught with major security implications for the countries of the region. Examine in light of the fact that India is faced with a plethora of challenges and needs to safeguard its own strategic interests. (200 words) 10

Important Points for Answer:

- *Withdrawal of ISAF*
- *Inability of ANSF*
- *Political instability*
- *Taliban*
- *Drug trade*
- *India's interest*
- *India's options*

Answer: Withdrawal of ISAF from Afghanistan would be a proven security threat to the region. Militants might be restructured and could threaten the peace of south and central Asia.

Afghan forces are not ready and able to discharge their responsibility effectively. NATO's withdrawal from Afghanistan can provide a chance to Taliban to challenge the Afghan National Security Force(ANSF).

As political process and nation building is not very effective, Jihadi groups can affect the process.

Islamabad has assisted the Taliban and is accused of supporting the Taliban groups fighting ISAF forces in Afghanistan.

Afghanistan remains a leading cultivator and producer of opium in the world, threatening the health and well-being of people and fuel crime and corruption, and can be used to finance terrorist activity.

India has vital strategic interests in Afghanistan and has invested in various projects. It provides strategic depth to India and peace and stability of Afghanistan is of utmost importance to India.

Options for India include active engagement with government and people of Afghanistan as also providing economic aid, technical assistance and training to armed forces and police.

Afghanistan is vital for the revival of the silk route, a gateway for India to Central Asia for trade and energy resources. (Total 204 words)

19. What do you understand by "The String of Pearls"? How does it impact India ? Briefly outline the steps taken by India to counter this. (200 words) 10

Important Points for Answer:
- *String of Pearls*
- *Ports with China*
- *Indian strategy*

Answer: China has established a number of port relationships in the Indian Ocean that make it possible for them to support increased navy operations.All these ports are commercial operations, where Chinese firms have upgraded or built commercial ports and run them.

This makes it easy for the Chinese Navy to visit (for repairs, supplies, or shore leave for the crews). Till now"string of pearls" includes Bangladesh (Chittagong), Burma (Sittwe and Coco Island), Sri Lanka (Hambantota), Pakistan (Gwadar), and Tanzania (Bagamoyo).

In 2007, the Indian Navy published the "Indian Maritime Doctrine", a document outlining prospective Indian naval strategies. It describes ambitions for an active Indian naval presence from the Strait of Hormuz to the Strait of Malacca.

The doctrine makes explicit mention of the need to police international shipping lanes and control choke points of Indian Ocean trade in particular. In 2011, the Indian government further announced that the government-financed deepwater port in Sittwe, Burma is to be functional by June 2013, with an additional highway connecting the port to India to be completed by 2014.

In the last two decades, India has stealthily straddled its interests in the Indian Ocean Rim.

This is the classical strategy of gaining influence by conjoining economic perks and power, with military diplomacy called 'Showing the Flag'. (Total 214 words)

20. Economic ties between India and Japan while growing in the recent years are still far below their potential. Elucidate the policy constraints which are inhibiting this growth. (200 words) 10

Important Points for Answer:
- *Bilateral trade & investment*
- *Cooperation in projects*
- *Policy constraints*

Answer: Japan is currently India's third largest source of foreign direct investment with Japanese companies have made cumulative investments of around US$2.6 billion in India since 1991.

Japan has assisted India in infrastructure development projects such as the Delhi Metro Rail Project. Both sides are discussing the Delhi-Mumbai Industrial Corridor Project and Dedicated Freight Corridor Projects on the Mumbai- Delhi and the Delhi-Howrah routes.

The Japanese government has expressed interest to help establish a Chennai- Bangalore Industrial corridor and a Dedicated Freight project in the South, connecting the cities of Bangalore and Chennai.

During Prime Minister Manmohan Singh'svisit to Japan in 2010, both countries agreed expand cooperation.

After signing the Comprehensive Economic Partnership Agreement between India and Japan, it is expected that trade might double in the coming years.

Despite all this, economic ties between India and Japan are far below from their potential. Some of the policy constraints which are inhibiting this growth are:

- Japan is reluctant to provide free movement of professionals between the two countries.
- The mutual complementarities among the two countries has been remained underexploited.
- The lack of a civil nuclear agreement is stopping Japanese big companies like Hitachi, Toshiba and Mitsubishi from exporting nuclear reactors and technology to India who wants to its nuclear capacity. (Total 213 words)

21. The protests in Shahbag Square in Dhaka in Bangladesh reveal a fundamental split in society between the nationalists and Islamic forces. What is its significance for India? (200 words) 10

Important Points for Answer:

- *The protest*
- *Reasons*
- *Reactions*
- *India's concerns*

Answer: The 2013 Shahbag protests began on 5 February 2013 and later spread to other parts of Bangladesh.

The International Crimes Tribunal had sentenced Abdul Quader Mollah to life in prison after he was convicted on five of six counts of war crimes. People demanded capital punishment for Abdul Quader Mollah who had been sentenced to life imprisonment, and for others convicted of war crimes by the International Crimes Tribunal.

Later demands included banning the Bangladesh Jamaat-e-Islami party from politics and a boycott of institutions supportingthe party.

Protesters considered sentence too lenient, given his crimes. Tens of thousands of people joined the demonstration, which gave rise to protests across the country.

The Bangladesh Nationalist Party (BNP) welcomed the Shahbag protest, while warning the government not to make political mileage from a movement demanding capital punishment for war criminals.

India cannot intervene or step in but can demand the Bangladeshi State to look after its minorities and prevent further attacks on Hindus.

The protests were a sign of the open-mindedness of the Bangladeshi youth, who were battling extremism and upholding fundamental values of democracy.They show their concern, their involvement, and their aspiration. India is affected by any turbulence in Bangladesh which may result into instability and influx of refugees in India. (Total 214 words)

22. Discuss the political developments in Maldives in the last two years. Should they be of any cause of concern to India? (200 words) **10**

Important Points for Answer:
- *Protest in Maldives*
- *Demonstration*
- *India's concern*
- *Resignation of Nasheed*
- *New elections*

Answer: A series of peaceful protests broke out in the Maldives on 1 May 2011. The protests occurred during the Arab Spring.

They continued, eventually escalating into the resignation ofPresident Mohamed Nasheed in disputed circumstances inFebruary 2012.

Demonstrators were protesting government's mismanagement of the economy and were calling for the ouster of President Mohamed Nasheed.

The main political opposition, Maldivian People's Party, led by the former president of the country Maumoon Abdul Gayoom accused President Nasheed of talking about democracy but not putting it into practice. The primary cause for the protests was rising of commodity prices and a poor economic situation in the country.

The protests led to a resignation of President Mohamed Nasheed on 7 February 2012, and the Vice President Mohammed Waheed Hassan Manik was sworn as the new president of Maldives.

In April 2012, new elections were announced to be held in July 2013. Maldives police joined the protesters after refusing to use force on them.

Stability in Maldives is of concern for India from strategic, political and economic perspective. India has provided extensive economic aid. Approximately 29,000 Indians live and work in the Maldives and almost 22,000 of them live in the capital city. The Indian government has expressed concern over continuing political instability in the Maldives. (Total 213 words)

23. In respect of India-Sri Lanka relations, discuss how domestic factors influence foreign policy. (200 words) **10**

Important Points for Answer:
- *Tamil community*
- *Pressure from Tamilnadu*
- *International issues*
- *Effects on bilateral relations*

Answer: India and Sri Lanka relations are greatly influenced by domestic politics because of fate of sizeable Tamil community living in Sri Lanka.

In 2012 Washington sponsored a resolution intended to press for accountability for the events that took place at the end of Sri Lanka's civil war. India's "yes" vote reflected pressure from Tamil Nadu. This was a departure from normal practice of not voting for country-specific resolutions.

The second act took place at the March 2013 UNHRC meeting. The release of film footage reportedly showing the killing of the Tamil rebel leader's twelve-year-old son, created widespread revulsion in India.

The Sri Lanka conflict is deeply embedded in Tamil parties and they use alliances and disputes with the party in power in Delhi to further their quest for state primacy.

The DMKmounted a demand that India not just vote for the resolution but amend it to accuse the Sri Lankan government of "genocide and war crimes."

The DMK took its campaign on the road. The Government of India cancelled the upcoming India-Sri Lanka defence dialogue. The DMK pulled out of the government coalition, citing the U.N. resolution.

India and Sri Lanka were left with some difficult fences to mend. (Total 205 words)

24. What is meant by Gujral doctrine? Doesithave any relevance today? Discuss. (200 words) 10

Important Points for Answer:

- *Doctrine*
- *Five principles*
- *Relevance*

Answer: The Gujral Doctrine is a set of five principles to guide the conduct of foreign relations with India's immediate neighbours as spelt out by IK Gujral, first as India's foreign minister and later as the prime minister.

These five principles arise from the belief that India's stature and strength cannot be divorced from the quality of its relations with its neighbours. The doctrine recognises the supreme importance of friendly, cordial relations with neighbours.

These five principles are:

1. With neighbours like Bangladesh, Bhutan, Maldives, Nepal and Sri Lanka, India does not ask for reciprocity, but gives and accommodates what it can in good faith and trust;
2. No South Asian country should allow its territory to be used against the interest of another country of the region;
3. No country should interfere in the internal affairs of another;
4. All South Asian countries must respect each other's territorial integrity and sovereignty;
5. They should settle all their disputes through peaceful bilateral negotiations.

The Gujaral doctrine remains of relevance even today because if these five principles, adhered to, would achieve a fundamental recasting of South Asia's regional relationships. The implementation of these principles would create mutual cooperation in the region. (Total 200 words)

25. The World Bank and the IMF, collectively known as the Bretton Woods Institutions, are the two inter-governmental pillars supporting the structure of the world's economic and financial order. Superficially, the World Bank and the IMF exhibit many common characteristics, yet their role, functions and mandate are distinctly different. Elucidate. (200 words)10

Important Points for Answer:
- *Bretton Woods Institution*
- *World Bank Functions*
- *IMF Functions*

Answer: Known collectively as the Bretton Woods Institutions after a place where they were founded in July 1944, the Bank and the IMF are twin intergovernmental pillars.

The World Bank is to deal with issues more related to structure within a country. There is a major difference that world bank provide a long term loan for distressed economy and member countries. Three priorities guide World Bank with countries to end poverty and boost prosperity for the poorest people. To create sustainable economic growth, as the surest path out of poverty. To invest in people, through access to health care, education, water and sanitation, and energy. To build resilience to shocks and threats that can roll back decades of progress.

The IMF concerns itself with macroeconomics issues, such as balance of payment issues, international trade policy, and exchange rates. The IMF grants the short term loans to develop the cyclical disturbance in economy.The IMF's fundamental mission is to ensure the stability of the international monetary system. It does so in three ways: keeping track of the global economy and the economies of member countries; lending to countries with balance of payments difficulties; and giving practical help to members.

Thus, having many common characteristics, the Bretton Woods Institutions have distinct functions.

(Total 209 words)

SOLVED PAPERS

PAPER–III

Time Allowed : Three Hours *Maximum Marks : 250*

Instructions : There are TWENTY FIVE questions printed both in English and in Hindi. All the questions are compulsory. The number of marks carried by a question/part is indicated against it. Answers must be written in the medium authorized in the Admission Certificate which must be stated clearly on the cover of this Question-cum-Answer (QCA) Booklet in the space provided. No marks will be given for answers written in medium other than the authorized one.

Word limit in questions, wherever specified, should be adhered to.

Any page or portion of the page left blank in the Question-cum-Answer Booklet must be clearly struck off.

1. With a consideration towards the strategy of inclusive growth, the new Companies Bill, 2013 has indirectly made CSR a mandatory obligation. Discuss the challenges expected in its implementation in right earnest. Also discuss other provisions in the Bill and their implications. (200 words) 10

Important Points for Answer:
- *Companies Act 2013*
- *Provisions of the bill*
- *CSR Mandatory*
- *Challenges in implementation*

Answer: The Companies Act 2013 received assent of the President in August 2013 and replaced the earlier Act of 1956 in partial manner.

The act requires companies to set up a CSR board committee consisting of at least three directors, one of whom must be independent. The company requires to spend at least 2 percent of the average net profits made during the three immediately preceding financial years on CSR activities. If the company fails to spend this amount on CSR, the board must disclose reasons in its annual report.

The act defines CSR as activities that promote poverty reduction, education, health, environmental sustainability, gender equality, and vocational skills development. Companies can choose which area to invest in, or contribute the amount to central or state government funds earmarked for socio-economic development.

New provisions of the Act may be hailed as a positive step forward in ensuring that profit making corporates contribute to equitable and sustainable development of the society. However, it may not greatly improve CSR. Indian companies still equate CSR with corporate philanthropy.

Among others, it makes provision requiring one-third of a company's board comprise independent directors, and that at least one board member be a woman. (Total 201 words)

2. What were the reasons for the introduction of Fiscal Responsibility and Budget Management (FRBM) Act, 2003? Discuss critically its salient features and their effectiveness. (200 words) 10

Important Points for Answer:
- *FRBM 2003*
- *Salient Features*
- *Effectiveness*

Answer: The Fiscal Responsibility and Budget Management (FRBMA) Act, 2003 is an Act which was enacted with objective to institutionalise financial discipline, reduce India's fiscal deficit, improve macroeconomic management and the overall management of the public funds by moving towards a balanced budget.

The main purpose of FRBM was to eliminate revenue deficit of the country and bring down the fiscal deficit to a manageable 3% of the GDP by March 2008. It was expected that the act would benefit the country by maintaining stable inflation rates which in turn would promote social progress.

However, due to the 2007 international financial crisis, the deadlines for the implementation of the targets in the act was initially postponed and subsequently suspended in 2009. In 2011, given the process of ongoing recovery, Economic Advisory Council advised the Government to reconsider the FRBMA.

The Act is criticised as it might require the government to cut back on social expenditure and general upliftment of rural poor of India.

There were some critical failure points of the Act which were not taken into account while fixing targets that including the vagaries of monsoon in India, the social dependence on agriculture and over-optimistic projections of the task force in-charge of developing the targets. (Total 207 words)

3. What is the meaning of the term 'Tax expenditure'? Taking housing sector as an example, discuss how it influences the budgetary policies of the government. (200 words) 10

Important Points for Answer:
- *Tax Expenditure*
- *Housing Sector*
- *Budgetary Policy*

Answer: A tax expenditure is government spending through the tax code. Tax expenditures alter equity of the basic tax system by allowing exemptions, deductions, or credits to select groups or specific activities. Tax expenditures have the same effect on the budget deficit as appropriations spending.

Tax expenditure function like government's social programmes which means that it may be considered harmful or gainful depending on perspective. As subsidy on fertiliser harms exchequer but at the same time is very useful for agriculture.

Exemptions allowed for deduction of HRA from Income tax and various other income tax deductions and exemptions; Exemptions allowed for interest payment and principal repayment for housing loans, etc are some examples of tax expenditure of housing sector.

Due to various policies of government, the number of persons who own houses have increased. People can afford to spend on infrastructure as they don't have to give taxes.

Impact of tax expenditure on budgetary policy can be seen from Union Budget of 2013 where first home loan from a bank of housing finance corporation upto INR 25 lakh is entitled to additional deduction of interest up to INR 1 lakh. As per an estimate, revenue forgone by tax expenditure is around 6.5% of GDP which amounts to 80% of the realised revenue. (Total 211 words)

4. Food Security Bill is expected to eliminate hunger and malnutrition in India. Critically discuss various apprehensions in its effective implementation along with the concerns it has generated in WTO. (200 words) 10

Important Points for Answer:

- *Food Security Bill*
- *Provisions*
- *Effectiveness*

Answer: The National Food Security Act, 2013 aims to provide subsidized food grains to approximately two-thirds of India's 1.2 billion people. Under the provisions of the bill, beneficiaries will be able to purchase 5 kilograms per eligible person per month of cereals at the following prices of Rs. 3 per kg for rice, Rs. 2 per kg for wheat and Re.1 prt kg for coarse grains (millet). Pregnant women, lactating mothers, and certain categories of children are eligible for daily free meals.

The bill has been highly controversial and its effectiveness has been argued politically and economically. The enactment of the Bill could be expected to induce severe imbalance in the production of oilseeds and pulses. It may result into demand pressures which will spillover to market prices of food grains.

The higher food subsidy burden on the budget will also raise the fiscal deficit, resulting into exacerbating macro level inflationary pressures. There are also concerns over the procurement and distribution of highly subsidised food grains.

It will shift money from investments in agriculture to subsidies, and continue focus on cereals production when shifts in consumer demand patterns indicate a need to focus more on protein, fruits and vegetables.

The Bill would restrict private initiative in agriculture, reduce competition in the market. (Total 213 words)

5. What are the different types of agriculture subsidies given to farmers at the national and at state levels? Critically analyse the agricultural subsidy regime with reference to the distortions created by it. (200 words) 10

Important Points for Answer:

- *Types of Subsidies at:*
- *National Level*
- *State Level*
- *Distortion*

Answer: Subsidies have been central to the development of the agricultural sector, especially since the Green Revolution. The major subsidies are as follows-

Central level

- Fertilizers: Urea is sold at statutory notified uniform sale price as it is the only controlled fertilizer. Other nutrients (P and K) are under nutrient based subsidy regime.
- Minimum Support Price (MSP) regime: This enables the state to cushion farmers in case crop prices fall below MSP.
- Fuel subsidy-agricultural sector is provided subsidized diesel
- Agricultural credit
  - Loans are disbursed through Regional Rural Banks, Cooperatives etc
  - Interest subvention scheme (2006-07) to enable banks to provide short term credit upto Rs.3 lakh at 7% interest to farmers.
  - Agricultural Debt Waiver and Debit Reliever Scheme, 2008
  - Kisan Credit Card Scheme (1998-99) to enable farmers to purchase agricultural inputs

State level

- Electricity is provided at low prices, or free of cost.
- Irrigation subsidy, such as in the form of subsidy for electrical pumps.

The distortions arising from the subsidy regime are as follows-

- The urea subsidy has led to unbalanced use of (NPK) nutrients and soil degradation.
- MSP incentivized rice and wheat cultivation only.
- Debt waivers erode the credit culture.
- Electricity and irrigation subsidies have led to ground water depletion and poor financial condition of Discoms mainly benefiting rich farmers. (Total 214 words)

6. India needs to strengthen measures to promote the pink revolution in food industry for ensuring better nutrition and health. Critically elucidate the statement. (200 words)

Important Points for Answer:	
• *Pink Revolution*	• *Impact*
• *Measures*	

Answer: Pink Revolution refers to the meat and poultry sector. There is vast scope for development of the sector in light of India's huge population of cattle and poultry and average annual sectoral growth rate of 10-15%.

India is one of the largest exporter of meat and now in India 100% FDI is permitted in this sector. Comprehensive scheme for the modernization of slaughter houses to address quality standards and meat wastage have been launched.

More than 50% of the Indian population is under-nourished. In fact, India ranks number one in terms of low birth weight infants at an estimated 7.4 million undernourished kids.

Due to food habits of Indians, current per capita meat consumption is 6 grams/day which is expected to increase to 50 grams/day in a decade. India accounts for only 2% of the global market despite its large livestock population.

This shows poor nutrition choices in our food habit which results into nutrition deficiency related health issues.

The Pink Revolution has to result into better nutrition and health of Indians by increasing consumption of nutrition rich meat and poultry products. For this, food industry, including packaging and processing, needs to be developed by modernisation, investment and upgradation of technology. (Total 205 words)

7. Examine the impact of liberalization on companies owned by Indians. Are they competing with the MNCs satisfactorily? Discuss. (200 words) 10

Important Points for Answer:
- *LPG of 1991*
- *Impact on Indian companies*
- *Disadvantages viz a viz MNCs*
- *Current situation*

Answer: The 1991 LPG reforms were aimed at opening up the Indian economy and reducing bureaucratic controls so as to facilitate faster economic growth. They succeeded in making India globally competitive, especially in the services sector, software sector etc.

The impact on Indian companies includes:

- Ease in setting up and expanding businesses. This had faced restrictions in the License Raj era, especially in light of the Monopolies and Restrictive Trade Practices Act. Firms can now benefit from economies of scale.
- Greater operational autonomy, such as through abolition of the phased manufacturing programme
- Access to investors due to increased financial inflows in the form of FDI and FII.
- R&D growth and technological advancement, leading to rise in innovation
- Improvement in delivery of services
- Better corporate governance
- Fewer industries are reserved solely for the public sector.

However, introduction of global MNCs has created an unequal situation and many Indian companies often find themselves unable to compete. This is because of their limited financial capacity and inability to incur losses. Higher cost of capital for Indian companies and rigid labour laws have given better status to MNCs who had access to better R&D facilities and technical personnel.

This initially led to displacement of many Indian companies by their foreign counterparts. However, with time, Indian companies have growth strong by mergers, acquisitions and expansion to compete with MNCs. (Total 225 words)

8. Establish relationship between land reforms, agriculture productivity and elimination of poverty in the Indian economy. Discuss the difficulties in designing and implementation of agriculture-friendly land reforms in India. (200 words) 10

Important Points for Answer:
• *Relationships*
• *Land reforms*
• *Implementation*

Answer: In light of inequalities in Indian agriculture, land reforms have been a top priority for the India since1947. The First Five-Year Plan termed it as a fundamental issue of national importance.

Land reforms refer to re-distribution of land from large holders to poor tenants and tillers. The objective relationship that was expected by land reforms programme was to eliminate poverty by giving land to landless farmer. However, it has resulted into smaller land holdings and productivity has been affected due to lack of modernisation and capital.

In light of its anti-inequality goals, poverty alleviation has always been a central thread. There is a strong link between tenancy reform and poverty reduction. Further, they establish that land reforms primarily benefit the landless.

Productivity enhancement, which leads to improvement in economic conditions of farmers and tenants and thus enables them to invest in agriculture, has also been a crucial goal of land reforms.

However, there are some difficulties in design and implementation:

- Lack of political and administrative will, as a result of laws were kept pending for decades and were full of loopholes.
- High ceiling limits by states
- Lack of uniformity in laws due to land being a state subject
- Small size of landholdings creates structural problems
- Patriarchal mindset still prevalent in the society.
- Absence of land ownership records led to decades-long litigations. (Total 225 words)

9.(a) Discuss the impact of FDI entry into Multi-trade retail sector on supply chain management in commodity trade pattern of the economy. (100 words) 5

Answer: (a) Retailing in India accounts for 14 to 15 percent of its GDP and is estimated to be US$ 500 billion and one of the top five retail markets in the world by economic value. With 1.2 billion people, India is one of the fastest growing retail markets in the world.

India's government announced retail reforms, in November 2011, for both multi-brand stores and single-brand stores. These market reforms paved the way for multi-brand retailers such as Walmart, Carrefour and Tesco.

It is envisaged that FDI investment into retailing may change trade pattern from small shops to big super markets. (Total 102 words)

(b) Though India allowed Foreign Direct Investment (FDI) in what is called multi-brand retail through the joint venture route in September 2012, the FDI, even after a year, has not picked up. Discuss the reasons. (100 words) 5

Answer: (b) In September 2012, the Government notified the FDI reforms for single and multi brand retail. In December 2012, the Government allowed 51% FDI in multi-brand retail in India.

PWC estimates the multi-brand retail market to grow to $220 billion by 2020. A number of merger and acquisitions have begun in Indian retail market. Over 90% of trade in India is conducted through independent local stores. However, there are significant challenges against FDI attraction in India's retail sector such as geographically dispersed population, small ticket sizes, complex distribution network, and little use of IT systems, limitations of mass media and existence of counterfeit goods. (Total 105)

10. Discuss the rationale for introducing Goods and Services Tax (GST) in India. Bring out critically the reasons for the delay in roll out for its regime. (200 words) 10

Important Points for Answer:
- *GST*
- *Provisions*
- *Benefits*
- *Criticism*
- *Reasons for delay*

Answer: The Goods and Services Tax (GST) is a Value Added Tax (VAT) to be implemented in India which will replace all indirect taxes levied on goods and services by the Indian Central and State governments. The GST is aimed at being comprehensive for most goods and services.

Exports will be zero-rated and imports will be levied the same taxes as domestic goods and services adhering to the destination principle.

It is claimed that CGST, SGST and IGST are nothing but new names for Central Excise/Service Tax, VAT and CST and hence GST brings nothing new to the table.

Roll out of GST is being delayed as GST will be implemented concurrently by the central and state governments as the Central GST and the State GST respectively. As there is heterogeneous State laws on VAT, the debate on the necessity for a GST has taken place. The best GST systems across the world use a single GST while India has opted for a dual-GST model. This change in the tax structure is going to have a huge impact in the supply chain of India. It is currently in sub-optimal and has been structured in such a fashion to avoid taxes. (Total 203 words)

11. Write a note on India's green energy corridor to alleviate the problem of conventional energy. (200 words) 10

Important Points for Answer:
- *Green Energy Corridor*
- *Problems of conventional energy*
- *Solution*

Answer: The Ministry of New and Renewable Energy (MNRE) has firmed up international cooperation agreements with Germany and United States to establish "Green Energy Corridors" in the country.

The conventional energy has various problems like it is non-renewable, causes pollution, creates burden on India's forex, makes India dependable on energy supply from oil and gas reach countries which creates perpetual risk on energy security.

India's wind and solar capacity has more than doubled in the last five years. As of 2013, India has 19,564 MW of wind energy while solar has 1,208 MW of installed capacity. India could break the 2 GW solar power barrier by 2020 due to plummeting costs, extensive roof space and the rising demand for electricity.

Therefore, the green energy corridor aims to facilitate the flow of renewable energy into its grid electricity. The corridor will be built across seven states over the next five to six years. The project will be implemented with the assistance of Germany. The grid will also receive support from the World Bank and India's National Electricity Fund. It aims to connect the southern grid to the national grid by 2014 to create the single largest transmission grid in the world. (Total 200 words)

12. Adoption of PPP model for infrastructure development of the country has not been free from criticism. Critically discuss pros and cons of the model. (200 words) 10

Important Points for Answer:
- *PPP Model*
- *Criticism*
- *Pros & Cons*

Answer: PPP model involves government and private sector partnership in execution and operation of projects. The PPP model can be highly beneficial if projects are designed intelligently and innovative models such as the Swiss Challenge Method are incorporated.

Pros of PPP model:

- Speedy, efficient and cost effective project delivery
- optimal risk management
- Efficiencies from integrating design and construction of public infrastructure with financing, operation and maintenance/upgrading
- value addition through synergies through the integration and cross transfer of public and private sector skills, knowledge and expertise
- Alleviation of capacity constraints and bottlenecks in the economy through higher labour productivity and capital resources availability
- Competition and greater construction capacity
- Accountability in public service delivery through performance incentive management/ regulatory regime.
- Innovation and diversity in the provision of public services
- Effective utilisation of state assets to the benefit of all users of public services

Cons of PPP model:

- PPP contracts are typically much more complicated than conventional procurement contracts.
- Development, bidding and ongoing costs are likely to be greater.

- Given the long-term nature and complexity of these projects, it is not possible to account for all contingencies.
- Profits of the projects can vary depending on the assumed risk, complexity etc
- Government representative must be highly specialized personnel and contracting experts so as to be able to protect public interest. (Total 217 words)

13. Bringing out the circumstances in 2005 which forced amendment to the section 3(d) in Indian Patent Law, 1970, discuss how it has been utilized by the Supreme Court in its judgment in rejecting Novratis' patent application for 'Glivec'. Discuss briefly the pros and cons of the decision. (200 words) 10

Important Points for Answer:
- *Amendment of Patent Act in 2005*
- *Decision in Novartis case*
- *Section 3(d)*
- *Pros of decision*
- *Cons of decision*

Answer: In March 2005, Indian Parliament approved patent regulations to stop local drug makers from copying new drugs developed by Western companies. The new law amends India's 1970 Patent Act.

Novartis v. Union of India & Others is a landmark decision by the Supreme Court on the issue of whether Novartis could patent Gleevec in India. The Supreme Court upheld the Indian patent office's rejection of the patent application. In applying 3(d) of the Act, the Court decided to interpret "efficacy" as "therapeutic efficacy" because the subject matter of the patent is a compound of medicinal value.

Pros of the decision:

Exclusions under section 3(d) present the hard cases that lie at the margins of the patent system.

There will be huge price difference between patented Glivec of Novartis and the generic versions of other companies.

Strict patent requirement would actually enhance innovation as the pharmaceutical companies would have to invest more in R&D to come up with new cures rather than repackage known compounds.

Cons of the decision:

Companies like Novartis would invest less money in research in India as a result of the ruling.

It is another example of a deteriorating innovation environment in India.

This decision is a setback for patients that will hinder medical progress for diseases without effective treatment options. (Total 216 words)

14. What do you understand by Fixed Dose Drug Combination and demerits. (200 words) 10

Important Points for Answer:
- *FDCs*
- *Reasons for FDCs*
- *Demerits*

Answer: Combination products, also known as fixed dose drug combinations (FDCs), are combinations of two or more active drugs in a single dosage form.

It is accepted that most drugs should be formulated as single compounds. Fixed ratio combination products are acceptable only when the combination has a proven advantage over single compounds administered separately.

FDCs are highly popular in the Indian pharmaceutical market. The rationality of FDCs should be based on certain aspects such as:

- The drugs in the combination should act by different mechanisms.
- The combination should not have supra-additive toxicity of the ingredients.

Most FDCs have the following demerits:

Dosage alteration of one drug is not possible without alteration of the other drug. There are increased chances of adverse drug effects and drug interactions compared with both drugs given individually. FDCs expose patients to unnecessary risk of adverse drug reactions.

In India, a variety of NSAID combinations are available, often as over the counter products. These combinations are an easy way to sell two drugs when one may be needed for the patient.

There is no synergism when two drugs acting on the same enzyme are combined. Combinations of NSAIDS/analgesics with antispasmodic agents are also available in India. They are not only irrational but also could be dangerous. Irrational FDCs also impose unnecessary financial burden on consumers. (Total 221 words)

15. What do you understand by Umpire Decision Review System in Cricket? Discuss its various components. Explain how silicone tape on the edge of a bat may fool the system ? (200 words) **10**

Important Points for Answer:

- *Umpire Decision Review System*
- *Components*
- *Silicone tape*

Answer: The Umpire Decision Review System is a technology-based system first introduced in Test cricket, for the sole purpose of reviewing controversial decisions made by the on-field umpires in the case of a batsman being dismissed or not.

A fielding team may use the system to dispute a "not out" call and a batting team may do so to dispute an "out" call.

The challenge can be invoked by signalling a "T" with the arms. Once the challenge is invoked, acknowledged, and agreed, the Third Umpire reviews the play. Field umpires may also request the Third Umpire for certain close calls such as line calls, boundary calls, or for close catch calls.

Hot Spot technology is used as part of a decision review system in professional cricket. It uses thermal imaging (infra-red) technology to look for the heat left behind when the ball makes contact with a surface. As the cricket ball just skims the edge of the bat, friction between the two will generate a small amount of heat at the point of contact. The thermal imagers can detect this heat and therefore prove whether the ball hit the bat or not.

If a batsman put silicon tape on the outside edge of the bat it will reduce or eliminate the 'hot spot' left by a ball grazing the edge. (Total 223 words)

16. (a) What is a digital signature? What does its authentication mean? Give various salient built-in features of a digital signature. (100 words) 5

Answer: (a) A digital signature is a mathematical scheme for demonstrating the authenticity of a digital message or document. It is commonly used for software distribution, financial transactions, etc.

Authentication:

Digital signatures can be used to authenticate the source of messages. When ownership of a digital signature secret key is bound to a specific user, a valid signature shows that the message was sent by that user.

Feature:

All public key/private key cryptosystems depend entirely on keeping the private key secret.

A private key can be stored on a user's computer, and protected by a local password, but this has two disadvantages:

The user can only sign documents on that particular computer. (Total 111 words)

(b) How does the 3D printing technology work? List out the advantages and disadvantages of the technology. (100 words) 5

Answer: (b) 3D printing is the fully automated manufacturing process of building three dimensional objects from a digital blueprint or model.

Advantages:

The manufacturing speed for a large number of final products is equally fast.

Even though the initial setup costs are higher, 3D printing has become cheaper.

Possibility of manufacturing of customizable human body parts or organs.

Disadvantages:

Manufacturing jobs will decrease.

As of now it manufactures products out of plastic, resin, certain metals, and ceramics.

The printing of copyrighted products to create counterfeit items will become common and nearly impossible to determine.

It can create dangerous items, such as guns and knives, with very little or no oversight.

It will be used to create more useless stuff. (Total 117 words)

17. (a) What is an FRP composite material? How are they manufactured? Discuss their applications in aviation and automobile industries. (100 words) 5

Answer: (a) Fibre-reinforced plastic/polymer (FRP) is a composite material made of a polymer matrix reinforced with fibres. The fibres are usually glass, carbon, basalt or aramid, although other fibres such as paper or wood or asbestos have been sometimes used.

Manufacturing FRP involves two processes. The first is the process whereby the fibrous material is manufactured and formed, the second is the process whereby fibrous materials are bonded with the matrix during moulding. They are often manufactured in sheets, continuous mats, or as continuous filaments for spray applications.

Applications in Aviation and Automobile industry:

They provide structural strength comparable to metallic alloys, but at a lighter weight. This leads to improved fuel efficiency and performance. (Total 115 words)

(b) What do you understand by Run-of-river hydroelectricity project? How is it different from any other hydroelectricity project? (100 words) 5

(b) Run-of-river hydroelectricity (ROR) is a type of hydroelectric generation whereby little or no water storage is provided. ROR power plants may either have no storage at all, or a limited amount of storage, in which case the storage reservoir is referred to as pondage.

ROR projects are dramatically different in design and appearance from conventional hydroelectric projects. Traditional hydro dams store enormous quantities of water in reservoirs, necessitating the flooding of large tracts of land. Most run-of-river projects do not require a large impoundment of water, which is a key reason why such projects are often referred to as environmentally friendly, or "green power". (Total 108 words)

18. How important are vulnerability and risk assessment for pre-disaster management ? As an administrator, what are key areas that you would focus on in a Disaster Management System. (200 words) 10

Important Points for Answer:
- *Risk Assessment*
- *Key Areas to focus*

Answer: Understanding the interaction of hazards, exposure and vulnerability is crucial to effective disaster prevention. Risk assessment determines the nature and extent of such risk, by analysing hazards and evaluating existing conditions of vulnerability.

Key areas that an administrator should focus on in a Disaster Management System, consists of the following steps:

Step 1: Understanding of current situation, needs and gaps to assess what already exists, avoids duplication of efforts, and builds on existing information and capacities.

Step 2: Hazard assessment to identify the nature, location, intensity and likelihood of major hazards prevailing in a community or society.

Step 3: Exposure assessment to identify population and assets at risk and delineate disaster prone areas.

Step 4: Vulnerability analysis to determine the capacity (or lack of it) of elements at risk to withstand the given hazard scenarios.

Step 5: Loss/impact analysis to estimate potential losses of exposed population, property, services, livelihoods and environment, and assess their potential impacts on society.

Step 6: Risk profiling and evaluation to identify cost-effective risk reduction options in terms of the socio-economic concerns of a society and its capacity for risk reduction

Step 7: Formulation or revision of DRR (Disaster Risk Reduction) strategies and action plans that include setting priorities, allocating resources (financial or human) and initiating DRR programmes. (Total 215 words)

19. What are the consequences of illegal mining ? Discuss the Ministry of Environment and Forests' concept of GO AND NO GO zones for coal mining sector. (200 words) 10

Important Points for Answer:
- *Illegal Mining*
- *Coal Mining*
- *GO and NO GO zones*

Answer: Illegal mining in India has raised many concerns among government as well as public level as it does not raise any revenue for government. Natural resources obtained through such practice deprives public of facilities that can be created by government revenue.

Illegal mining is not controlled or regulated by authorities and therefore it encroaches upon forest areas and damages environment irreparably.

The environment ministry had carried out a joint exercise with the coal ministry studying nine major coal mining areas fields (Singrauli, IB valley, Mand Raigarh, Sohagpur, Talcher, Vardha valley, Hasdeo-Arand, North karanpura and West bokaro). The ministry classified blocks into categories of 'A' or 'NO GO areas' and 'B' or 'GO areas'.

The concept of 'go and no go' areas is a new strategy formulated by the Environment Ministry to categorise coal-bearing areas in the country for miners.

Under the Forest Conservation Act, 1980, all diversion of forest cover for non-forest uses requires the approval of FAC.

There is an overlap of the regulations by the Coal Ministry and Environment Ministry over the coal mine rights. The Ministry of Coals had earlier (2010) considered keeping 10% of thickly forested areas in the "no go" zone and open others for mining after following the due clearance process. (Total 210 words)

20. Enumerate the National Water Policy of India. Taking River Ganges as an example, discuss the strategies which may be adopted for river water pollution control and management. What are the legal provisions of management and handling of hazardous wastes in India. (200 words) 10

Important Points for Answer:
- *National Water Policy*
- *Pollution Control*
- *Hazardous wastes*
- *Strategies - Ganges*

Answer: National Water Policy governs the planning and development of water resources and their optimum utilisation.

It envisages that each State shall formulate its own State Water Policy and an operational Action Plan in a time-bound manner so as to promote sustainability and availability of water resources.

It seeks to establish a Water Regulatory Authority and support a National Water Framework Law.

River pollution is a major problem in India, as demonstrated by the Ganga's status as the sixth most polluted river in the world. While a number of river-clean up initiatives have been undertaken, they have failed to deliver desired results.

Ganga Action Plan (1986) was launched to reduce the pollution load. Supreme Court has ordered relocation of various industrial plants along the Ganges and declared the Gaumukh-Uttarkashi stretch as an "eco-sensitive zone".

In order to control pollution, strategies to be adopted are :

- Inclusion of civil society in pollution management and spread of best practices.
- Stringent penalties for polluting industries. The fine amount should be used for pollution management.
- Utilize traditional and social media for awareness generation.

Legal provision for hazardous waste:

- Water (Prevention and Control of Pollution) Act, 1974
- Hazardous Wastes (Management, Handling and Transboundary Movement) Rules, 2008 under Environment (Protection) Act, 1986
- India is a signatory to the Rotterdam Convention (Total 216 words)

21. Money Laundering poses a serious security threat to a country's economic sovereignty. What is its significance for India and what steps are required to be taken to control this menace? (200 words) **10**

Important Points for Answer:

- *Money laundering*
- *Significance*
- *Steps required*

Answer: Money laundering seriously damages economy by creating a parallel economy. Illegally accumulated wealth impedes with decision making by using financial means. Money laundering has been used to finance terrorist and criminal activities.

In India, to control money laundering, it should be ensured that businesses are required to establish appropriate risk-sensitive policies and procedures in order to prevent activities related to money laundering and terrorist financing.

The procedure should provide for identification and scrutiny of complex or unusually large transactions.

Any unusual patterns of transactions with no apparent economic or lawful purpose and other activities should be immediately reported.

Internal control, risk assessment and management, compliance monitoring, management and communication should be part of the policy.

It should also prevent of use of products favouring anonymity.

Procedure should involve customer due diligence involving procedures designed to acquire knowledge about the firm's clients and prospective clients and to verify their identity as well as monitor business relationships and transactions.

Businesses should ensure sufficient senior management oversight, appropriate analysis and assessment of the risks of clients.

Record keeping, including details of customer due diligence and supporting evidence for business relationships, records of transactions, should be made compulsory.

Businesses are required to take measures to make relevant employees aware of the law relating to money laundering and terrorist finance and also to train those employees. (Total 227 words)

22. What are social networking sites and what security implications do these sites present ? (200 words) 10

Important Points for Answer:
• *Social Networking*
• *Security implication*

Answer: Social networking sites are websites which enable users to share content, original or otherwise, and network with other users. In recent times, they have become one of the primary sources of news dissemination. They are also a key avenue for targeted advertisements and this has solidified their economic importance.

These sites present some major security implications-

- They provide an easy avenue for criminal activities due to negligent regulation of activities on the sites.
- The anonymity available on these sites enables hate speech and radicalisation of youth. Some terrorist organisations misuse social media for brainwashing young adults.
- Such sites have access to our personal data. Since they are private bodies, they are not accountable in the same manner that governments with access to such data are.
- The proliferation of fake accounts and troll bots has led to harassment of individuals and groups. Such accounts are sometimes weaponised by sovereign nations as a tool for cyber attack.
- Porn activities attacks mainly children and vulnerable ladies.
- They have been medium to commit white collar crimes including banking scams.

The state must facilitate effective regulation of such sites, while taking care that such regulation does not stifle positive aspects of social media such as free speech. (Total 202 words)

23. Cyber warfare is considered by some defense analysts to be a larger threat than even A1 Qaeda or terrorism. What do you understand by Cyber warfare ? Outline the cyber threats

which India is vulnerable to and bring out the state of the country's preparedness to deal with the same. (200 words) 10

Important Points for Answer:
- *Cyber warfare*
- *Threat*
- *India's vulnerability*
- *Preparedness*

Answer: Cyber warfare is motivated hacking to conduct sabotage and espionage. It is a form of information warfare.

There were 23 reported cyber security breaches in 2004. The Department of Information Technology created the Indian Computer Emergency Response Team (CERT-In) in 2004 to thwart cyber-attacks in India. Yet the breaches increased to 13000 in 2011. So, the government created a new subdivision, the National Critical Information Infrastructure Protection Centre (NCIIPC) to thwart attacks against energy, transport, banking, telecom, defence, space and other sensitive areas.

Nuclear Power Corporation of India (NPCIL) reported to block up to ten targeted attacks a day. CERT-In was left to protect less critical sectors.

A high profile cyber attack in July 2012 breached the email accounts of about 12,000 people, including those of officials from critical organisations of government. A government-private sector plan began in October 2012 and is overseen by National Security Advisor (NSA). It intends to strengthen India's cyber security capabilities.

The NCIIPC finalized policies related to national cyber security that would focus on domestic security solutions, reducing exposure through foreign technology.

Other steps include the isolation of various security agencies to ensure that a synchronised attack could not succeed on all fronts and the planned appointment of a National Cyber Security Coordinator. (Total 212 words)

24. Article 244 of the Indian Constitution relates to administration of scheduled areas and tribal areas. Analyse the impact of non-implementation of the provisions of the Fifth schedule on the growth of Left Wing extremism. (200 words) 10

Important Points for Answer:
- *Article 244*
- *Fifth Schedule*
- *Left Wing Extremism*

Answer: Article 244 requires that the provisions of the Fifth Schedule shall apply to the administration and control of the Scheduled Areas and Scheduled Tribes in States.

The Fifth Schedule of the Constitution [Art 244(1)] appoints Governors as the custodians of tribal rights. It appoints tribal advisory councils to assist Governors in their mandate to development and maintenance of peace.

Customary law has been given primacy in such areas so as to facilitate protection of indigenous cultures.

Governors must make annual reports to the President, and the President is further empowered to issue such directives to the State as might be necessary.

Tribal people are given rights over minor forest produce and minor minerals, and their lands cannot be alienated to non-tribals or otherwise acquired without the Governor's approval. This is in recognition of the historical harm rendered by outsiders such as 'Dikus'.

No legislation is applicable to Fifth Schedule Areas unless approved by the Governor with or without modifications.

Despite these extensive provisions, the Schedule is largely ignored in routine governance. This approach towards tribal rights has led tribal peoples to the bosom of Maoists-Naxalists as they have promised preservation of their 'Jal-Jangal-Jameen' rights, an approach that tribals find lacking in the governmental machinery. (Total 209 words)

25. How far are India's internal security challenges linked with border management particularly in view of the long porous borders with most countries of South Asia and Myanmar ? (200 words) 10

Important Points for Answer:
- *Internal Security*
- *Border issues*
- *Impact*

Answer: India's internal security, act of keeping peace within the borders of a sovereign state, problems are influenced by a host of factors including its colonial legacy and socio-economic disparities. India's internal security is also inextricably linked with the border management too, as India shares international borders with 7 countries.

The Indo-Pak border has given rise to internal security challenges stemming from cross-border terrorism, such as in Kashmir.

Illegal immigration, trafficking, smuggling etc along the Indo-Bangladesh border makes it an area of concern, with illegal immigrants in particular presenting a security threat.

India's open border with Nepal is used for easy entry and exit by terrorists. Further, since Nepal is a surrender route for transformed militants, terrorists can enter in the guise of such militants.

Ethnic clashes in Myanmar impact India's internal security, as seen in the Bodh Gaya blasts. The Free Movement Regime also aids illegal activities.

China's assertive posturing towards the Indian state of Arunachal Pradesh and its potential plans to enter India through Myanmar establish it as a threat to Indian borders.

India's 7500 km maritime border is also vulnerable to infiltration as demonstrated by the 2008 Mumbai terror attacks.

These are some of the challenges faced by India at its borders, which need to be effectively tackled to secure peace within the country. (Total 220 words)

SOLVED PAPERS

PAPER–IV

Time Allowed : Three Hours *Maximum Marks : 250*

Instructions : There are FOURTEEN questions divided in two Sections and printed both in Hindi and in English. All questions are compulsory. The number of marks carried by a question/part is indicated against it. Word limit in questions, wherever specified, should be adhered to. Any page of portion of the page left blank in the Question-cum-Answer Booklet must be clearly struck off.

Answer questions in NOT MORE than the word limit specified for each in the parenthesis. Content of the answer is more important than its length.

Section–A

1. What do you understand by 'values' and 'ethics'? In what way is it important to be ethical along with being professionally competent? (150 words) 10

Answer: Values principles or standards of behaviour and it is one's judgement of what is important in life.

Ethics are moral principles that govern a person's behaviour or the conducting of an activity.

Being professionally competent is required for progress in career. Without competency, there will be no growth.

Being ethical is equally important in profession. Otherwise a person may use his professional competency to the disadvantage of the organisation and other colleagues.

A person who professionally competent in an accounting firm but holds very low ethical standards can embezzle money. A bank employee who is aware of banking and book keeping principles can cheat the bank and customers if he is unethical.

If a civil servant is corrupt, he may create havoc in the system, even though he is very competent. He may not be caught due to competency but impact of corruption will destroy value of the organisation.

Therefore, being professionally competent as well as high in ethical standards is important for an individual. (Total 165 words)

2. (a) What do you understand by the following terms in the context of public service? (250 words) 3 x 5 = 15

(i) Integrity

(ii) Perseverance

(iii) Spirit of Service

(iv) Commitment

(v) **Courage of Conviction**

Answer: (i) Integrity: It is the quality of being honest and having strong moral principles. It implies maintaining absolute standard of behaviour and certain moral code. It means the state of being whole and undivided. It is non-corrupt and ethical practice.

(ii) Perseverance: It is persistence in doing something despite difficulty or delay in achieving success. In spite of problems being faced in any act, one must continue to do work in the direction. A public servant working constantly despite non-cooperative attitude of politician, local public and subordinates towards implementation of government policy is perseverance.

(iii) Spirit of Service: Devotion for public duty is the spirit of service. This is relevant for civil servant as they have to keep public interest above private interest. Many people devote their lives to the service of people, in the spirit of service.

(iv) Commitment: Commitment is an engagement or obligation that restricts freedom of action. It is firm decision to perform one's duty with full dedication without being diverted. It is the attitude of someone who works very hard to do or support something.

(v) Courage of Conviction: Courage means taking decision fearlessly, strength in the face of pain or grief. While conviction is a firmly held belief or opinion. A civil servant should be able to courageously uphold his conviction which is based on rules and integrity.

(b) Indicate two more attributes which you consider important for public service. Justify your answer. (100 words) **5**

(b) Two more attributes important for public services are:

(i) Accountability: It means answerability of civil servant for his decision to public for his acts or omission. Accountability helps in curtailing corruption and increases public confidence. It will increase trust and faith of people on the system and provide a strong interface between public servant and public.

(ii) Fairness and justice: Fairness means impartial and just treatment or behaviour without favouritism or discrimination. Justice is the legal or philosophical theory by which fairness is administered. It means a civil servant should be fair and just in performing own duties. It is absolute necessity for maintaining unbiased system and people's confidence in governance. (Total 105 words)

3. Some people feel that values keep changing with time and situation, while others strongly believe that there are certain universal and eternal human values. Give your perception in this regard with due justification. (150 words) 10

Answer: Values, certain standards of moral and ethical behaviour, are important to direct one's behaviour. A person is guided by his value system that he imbibes from family, society and personal experiences.

Some people believe that values are absolute and therefore no compromise can be accepted at anytime or any place. Speaking truth is absolute value and it cannot be compromised. Not stealing is absolute value and cannot be compromised.

But on the contrary, others believe that such values are dependent on time and situation. Speaking lie if it helps someone is allowed or stealing for larger gain is justified.

People sometimes believe that the value keep changing with time and place. For instance, as per modern standards, living in nuclear family does not harm family respect and value. But in old times, living separate from brothers and parents were absolute wrong.

Therefore, it can be said that some values are absolute and do not change with time but many other values are adjustable. (Total 163 words)

4. What is 'emotional intelligence' and how can it be developed in people? How does it help an individual in taking ethical decisions? (150 words) 10

Answer: Emotional intelligence (EI) is the ability to identify and manage your own emotions and the emotions of others.

EI is generally said to include three skills:

1 - emotional awareness;

2 - the ability to harness emotions and apply them to tasks like thinking and problem solving; and

3 - the ability to manage emotions, which includes regulating your own emotions and cheering up or calming down other people.

EI is a skill which can be learnt through training, contrary to the general belief that EI is an inborn characteristic.

Ethical decisions are taken based on the moral values of an individual. He would always balance emotions on ethical and unethical side and take decision based on good values and ethics.

EI creates self awareness in a person which is ability to control one's emotions while taking decision.

Similarly, self management developed by EI is also helps in making ethical decisions.

Ability to apply emotions to thinking process leads to ethical consideration.

Therefore, EI helps an individual in taking ethical decisions. (Total 168 words)

5. (a) What do you understand by the term 'voice of conscience'? How do you prepare yourself to heed to the voice of conscience? (150 words) 10

(b) What is meant by 'crisis of conscience'? Narrate one incident in your life when you were faced with such a crisis and how you resolved the same. (150 words) 10

Answer: (a) Conscience is a person's moral sense of right and wrong, viewed as acting as a guide to one's behaviour.

Voice of conscience refers to a process of alertness and alarm reminding an individual to stick. To the moral sense, conscience.

It happens in the time of crisis when a person faces dilemma. In such situations, his conscience does not allow him to go on wrong path. He maintains his values and directs ones behaviour based on own conscience. It is a complex process that takes place at time of emotional conflicts.

It requires to hear once inner-self, by meditation, self-actualisation and adherence to honesty of belief to heed to one's voice of conscience. Reflective system of mind prevents from taking negative action or entering into immoral activity by heeding to voice of conscience. Constant reading, training and affirmation can help to prepare oneself to heed to one's voice of conscience. (Total 152 words)

Answer: (b) 'Crisis of conscience' is conflict of emotions of what we consider good and bad. Choice is difficult. Though we know what is right according to our conscience but the other option seems to be more endearing.

In a situation, I had Rs. 5000 saved for buying nice clothes on my birthday. When I went to a shopping mall to buy clothes, my friend called me to inform that his mother was sick and they were rushing to hospital. I knew he was poor and would need some spare money. I had crisis of conscience whether to spend the money on my clothes or keep them spare lest my friend would need it. The choice was difficult. If I spend the money and he faces problem, I would feel guilty. Strong crisis of conscience happened between my personal choice and my duty towards a friend.

Finally, with a lot of conviction, I decided to keep the money in spare and not buy clothes on that birthday. (Total 165 words)

6. Given below are three quotations of great moral thinkers/philosophers. For each of these quotations, bring out what it means to you in the present context:

(a) "There is enough on this earth for every one's need but for no one's greed." - Mahatma Gandhi (150 words) 10

Answer: (a) Mahatma Gandhi was a man who lived on minimalist need. He believed in non collection of material aspects and believed that the earth has enough resources to satisfy need of humankind but it is because of greed of man that the earth has become place for bloodshed and exploitation. He referred to colonial powers and greedy capitalists who exploited poor people for amassing wealth.

Today the situation has not changed. Bureaucrats, politicians and industrialists employ corrupt practices for personal gain at the cost of others. This results into disadvantage to the society. Greed of such people results into poverty and pain of masses. Policies of government are not executed and the benefits do not reach to targeted beneficiaries due to such greed.

If those who are instrumental in policy making, implementation and administration understand the deep meaning of this statement and do not demand more than their need, the earth would be a better place. (Total 155 words)

(b) "Nearly all men can withstand adversity, but if you want to test a man's character, give him power." - Abraham Lincoln (150 words) 10

Answer: In adversity people become humble, seek help and surrender to god. But when men of weak character get power, opportunity and position of control, they forget all duties, morality, ethics and politeness.

As is famously said, power corrupts and absolute power corrupts absolutely, men cannot control power.

It is therefore seen in bureaucrats and politician do not fulfil their duty as public servant when they become powerful due to their position. Judges, Generals or Journalists are also susceptible to power and posts. Their absolute dedication to the duty and ethics is required for the society to function well. Reminding this statement of Abraham Lincoln, we should look for men of great character who are true to their values and moral standards.

The power is nothing but ability to perform, which should be used for the welfare of people, and not for personal gain, by avoiding adverse influence of the available power. (Total 151 words)

(c) "I count him braver who overcomes his desires than him who overcomes his enemies." - Aristotle (150 words) 10

Answer: A person can overcome enemies by gaining more strength but not himself. Conquering oneself is the biggest challenge. As the person has unlimited desires, he falls pray to them.

Every time he acts on own desire, without thinking of consequences, he loses control over himself. Therefore, the more desires he fulfils, weaker he becomes. Wining over enemies requires strength while falling for desires require weakness. Anyone who cannot overcome this weakness does not reach to greatness.

The people who have become great in own fields have controlled and conquered their own desires. They did not have enemies in external world but inside their own selves.

Temptation to go for satisfying desire is a common human folly. It is very difficult to resist them. Always there is a chance to fall victim of such desires which may lead towards dishonesty, unethical behaviour, immorality or illegal acts. Therefore, overcoming desires should be the final aim of an individual. (Total 156 words)

7. " The good of an individual is contained in the good of all". What do you understand by this statement? How can this principle be implemented in public life? (150 words) 10

Answer: The good of an individual results from the good of his family, friends and society of which he is a part. As man is merely a social animal, he does not grow alone. There has to be a collective progress.

Therefore, all economic, social, scientific or political progress has to be done in a manner which benefits all. Promoting selfish interest at the cost of others does not result into progress.

Inclusive growth, welfare schemes, social progress and upliftment of weaker sections of society are required for individuals growth, progress and happiness.

Increase in income of one person does not make the society rich. Skewed distribution of benefits of economic progress has resulted into gap in Indian society which is a cause of concern.

A person may be rich and build a beautiful house but if there is slum around his house, he cannot enjoy it. Collective progress is very much necessary for Individuals's good. (Total 155 words)

8. It is often said that 'politics' and 'ethics' do not go together. What is your opinion in this regard? Justify your answer with illustrations. (150 words) 10

Answer: Ethics are certain code of conduct applicable to standard of behaviour. Politics works for social progress and welfare. Therefore, using ethics in politics can actually result into better society.

In the current situation, where there are many political parties representing different sections of society and fighting for promotion of narrow purposes, it seems difficult if any political party can be able to succeed in politics with ethical ideology. However, there is no need for complete absence of ethics from politics.

For example, Gandhi managed to drive the britishers out of India through political means but he maintained ethics in his political strategy. There was no need to completely divorce ethics and politics. He did not hate Britishers, he just wanted to bring freedom. He behaved with British in friendly yet firm manner without being submissive to their tyranny.

Therefore, it can be concluded that ethics and politics are not opponents but complementaries. Politics without ethics results into chaos, corruption, nepotism and lack of governance. (Total 164 words)

Section–B

In the following questions, carefully study the cases presented and then answer the questions that follow.

9. A Public Information Officer has received an application under RTI Act. Having gathered the information, the PIO discovers that the information pertains to some of the decisions taken by him, which were found to be not altogether right. There were other employees also who were party to these decisions. Disclosure of the information is likely to lead to disciplinary action with possibility of punishment against him as well as some of his colleagues. Non-disclosure or part disclosure or camouflaged disclosure of information will result into lesser punishment or no punishment.

The PIO is otherwise an honest and conscientious person but this particular decision, on which the RTI application has been filed, turned out to be wrong. He comes to you for advice.

The following are some suggested options. Please evaluate the merits and demerits of each of the options :

(i) The PIO could refer the matter to his superior officer and seek his advice and act strictly in accordance with the advice, even though he is not completely in agreement with the advice of the superior.

(ii) The PIO could proceed on leave and leave the matter to be dealt by his successor in office or request for transfer of the application to another PIO.

(iii) The PIO could weigh the consequences of disclosing the information truthfully, including the effect on his career, and reply in a manner that would not place him or his career in jeopardy, but at the same time a little compromise can be made on the contents of the information.

(iv) The PIO could consult his other colleagues who are party to the decision and take action as per their advice.

Also please indicate (without necessarily restricting to the above options) what you would like to advise, giving proper reasons. (250 words) 20

Answer: (i) Merits: The senior will taken into account his honesty and diligence so will advise appropriately. The advice will have merit and following him may save the PIO him from any wrongdoing.

Demerit: The concerned authorities might suspend PIO for his wrong decisions and inquiry might be initiated.

(ii) Merit: It may relieve him from mental stress that he is facing and someone may dealt with it according to own judgement. Impartiality will also be maintained in disclosure of information.

Demerit: PIO is running away from his responsibility and thereby showing his inability to take ethical decisions.

(iii) Merit: He will protect himself and his colleagues. May be the matter will be buried under ground with time.

Demerit: Since tampering of official documents is a crime, PIO's honesty, integrity and accountability to his work shall be questioned. Applicant may understand that half information is given.

(iv) Merit: Other colleagues were also privy to the decision. Their consultation may bring out some ways.

Demerit: The colleagues might also influence him to take decision in their favour.

My advice to PIO :

First he should try to find out if the information pertains to some of the non-disclosable areas as provided by RTI Act. If yes, he can deny the information. Otherwise, according to RTI Act, PIO is responsible to disclose the information, so he should perform his duty with integrity. If required, PIO should take the moral responsibility of the wrong decision.

10. You are working as an Executive Engineer in the construction cell of a Municipal Corporation and are presently in-charge of the construction of a flyover. There are two Junior Engineers under you who have the responsibility of day-to-day inspection of the site and are reporting to you, while you are finally reporting to the Chief Engineer who heads the cell. While the construction is heading towards completion, the Junior Engineers have been regularly reporting that all construction is taking place as per design specifications. However, in one of your surprise inspections, you have noticed some serious deviations and lacunae which, in your opinion, are likely to affect the safety of the flyover. Rectification of these lacunae at this stage would require a substantial amount of demolition and rework which will cause a tangible loss to the contractor and will also delay completion. There is a lot of public pressure on the Corporation to get this construction completed because of heavy traffic congestion in the area. When you brought this matter to the notice of the Chief Engineer, he advised you that in his opinion it is not a very serious lapse and may be ignored. He advised for further expediting the project for completion in time. However, you are convinced that this was a serious matter which might affect public safety and should not be left unaddressed.

What will you do in such a situation? Some of the options are given below. Evaluate the merits and demerits of each of these options and finally suggest what course of action you would like to take, giving reasons. (250 words) 20

(i) Follow the advice of the Chief Engineer and go ahead.

(ii) Make an exhaustive report of the situation bringing out all facts and analysis along with your own viewpoints stated clearly and seek for written orders from the Chief Engineer.

(iii) Call for explanation from the Junior Engineers and issue orders to the contractor for necessary correction within targeted time.

(iv) Highlight the issue so that it reaches superiors above the Chief Engineer.

(v) Considering the rigid attitude of the Chief Engineer, seek transfer from the project or report sick.

Answer: (i) Merits: The project would be completed on time. Contractor will be saved from probable loss.

Demerits: As there is safety lapse, the flyover might collapse in the future. It would endanger public safety and reputation of organisation.

(ii) Merit: A written report and analysis would enable the Chief Engineer to understand seriousness of lapse. It will also save me if any inquiry is conducted in future.

Demerit: It would be considered as insubordination. Chief Engineer and contractor would not like it. It will also take more time and may delay the project.

(iii) Merit: Since it was the duty of junior engineers, they should be asked explanation for their lapse or oversight. They may be held responsible in the future. Contractor will have to deal with the problem so he should also be held accountable.

Demerit: This course of action would delay the completion of the project, endanger jobs of junior engineer and cause loss to contractor.

(iv) Merit: Highlighting the matter to higher authorities will ensure disciplinary action against the wrongdoers.

Demerit: Project might be delayed. It will show my inability to do job efficiently. I might not be heard and insubordination may be punished.

(v) Merit: It may save me from accountability if anything takes place in the future.

Demerit: It will indicate that I am escaping my responsibility. It would project me as irresponsible officer of the organisation and in case of inquiry, my absence might be proved as my connivance.

My Decision: I would firmly report the incident to higher authorities and seek their guidance. If the matter is not solved satisfactorily, I might take it to Municipal Commissioner. There should be no compromise with public safety as the collapse of bridge may result into loss of many lives. The contractor must be held responsible for correcting the lapse.

11. Sivakasi in Tamil Nadu is known for its manufacturing clusters on firecrackers and matches. The local economy of the area is largely dependent on firecrackers industry. It has led to tangible economic development and improved standard of living in the area.

So far as child labour norms for hazardous industries like firecrackers industry are concerned, International Labour Organization (ILO) has set the minimum age as 18 years. In India, however, this age is 14 years.

The units in industrial clusters of firecrackers can be classified into registered and non-registered entities. One typical unit is household-based work. Though the law is clear on the use of child labour employment norms in registered/non-registered units, it does not include household-based works. Household-based work means children working under the supervision of their parents/relatives. To evade child labour norms, several units project themselves as household-based works but employ children from outside. Needless to say that employing children saves the costs for these units leading to higher profits to the owners.

On your visit to one of the units at Sivakasi, the owner takes you around the unit which has about 10-15 children below 14 years of age. The owner tells you that in his household- based unit, the children are all his relatives. You notice that several children smirk, when the owner tells you this. On deeper enquiry, you figure out that neither the owner nor the children are able to satisfactorily establish their relationship with each other.

(a) Bring out and discuss the ethical issues involved in the above case.

(b) What would be your reaction after your above visit? (300 words) **25**

Answer: (a) Child labour deprives children of their right to education and enjoyment of childhood. Their growth is hampered due to such work. Child employment in India has still been rampant under one pretext or other. Employing children in small household based units manufacturing firecrackers is a legal escape. But it is unethical as subverting law is not permitted, though it would be difficult to hold them legally liable.

Other ethical issue involved in exposing and punishing these industry is that some children might be actual relative to the manufacturer. Therefore, taking action against such units involve a delicate balance.

Poverty of children and their family is heart shaking issue. There should be more employment opportunities for parents which generates enough income to send the children to school.

(b) Reaction after the visit:

Suspicion of violation of the labour laws in the unit should be brought to the notice of the concerned authorities immediately.

NGOs working for prevention of child labour should be involved. They can take up the issue in media and court.

If the employer is found guilty of violating the law, he should be punished and licences should be cancelled.

Alternative employment should be provided to the adult members of the family under state and centre sponsored schemes like MNREGA.

Guidelines of the supreme court in M C Mehta Case should be strictly adhered to.

Implementation of Sarva Siksha Abhiyan should be strengthened in the villages so that enrolment to schools can be increased.

A detailed report should be prepared and sent to the Chief Secretary of the State, Ministry of Women and Child Development as well as relevant commissions to consider banning employment of children below 14 years even in the household units.

12. You are heading a leading technical institute of the country. The institute is planning to convene an interview panel shortly under your chairmanship for selection of the post of professors. A few days before the interview, you get a call from the Personal Secretary (PS) of a senior government functionary seeking your intervention in favour of the selection of a close relative of the functionary for this post. The PS also informs you that he is aware of the long pending and urgent proposals of your institute for grant of funds for modernization, which are awaiting the functionary's approval. He assures you that he would get these proposals cleared.

(a) What are the options available to you ?

(b) Evaluate each of these options and choose the option which you would adopt, giving reasons. (250 words) 20

Answer: (a) Possible available:

I can accept the proposal of Personal Secretary of the senior government functionary and hire the proposed candidate.

I do reject the proposal of Personal Secretary of the senior government functionary and hire a candidate who is suitable to the job.

I do not reject the proposal of Personal Secretary of the senior government functionary and interview the candidate proposed by him. If he is found suitable, I hire him otherwise I hire a candidate who is suitable to the job.

(b) Evaluation of the options:

In the first option, I may end up with hiring a candidate proposed by the personal secretary of government officer who may not be suitable for the job. But my institute receives fund for modernisation. This will help in modernising the institute. But it will keep other suitable candidate devoid of job.

Second option will lose me the approval of fund for modernisation of institute. But I will follow my conscience and hire only a candidate who is most suitable for the job on the basis of his qualification and other qualities.

In the third option, as I have not rejected the proposal, I will have a chance to evaluate the candidate proposed by the personal secretary. If the candidate turns out to be the suitable one, I would be able to claim that the candidate proposed by his stands hired. It will help me in getting approval for the fund. However, if the candidate is not suitable, I may not hire him. This will be the most pragmatic option and not be an unethical practice.

Option I would choose:

I would choose the third option for the reasons mentioned above.

13. As a senior officer in the Finance Ministry, you have access to some confidential and crucial information about policy decisions that the Government is about to announce. These decisions are likely to have far-reaching impact on the housing and construction industry. If the builders have access to this information beforehand, they can make huge profits. One of the builders has done a lot of quality work for the Government and is known to be close to your immediate superior who asks you to disclose this information to the same builder.

(a) What are the options available to you ?

(b) Evaluate each of these options and choose the option which you would adopt, giving reasons (250 words) 20

Answer: **(a)** Options available to me are:

(i) Listen to senior's instruction and disclose the information to the builder.

(ii) Not listen to the senior's instruction and refuse to disclose the information to the builder.

Any other option would just emanate out of these two.

(iii) In case of insistence by my senior, I could ask him to give me instruction in writing which he would not dare to do so. If my senior gives me order in writing, I can take it to senior most in organisation for instruction.

(b) If I to listen to and follow the instruction of the senior and disclose information to the builder, it will certainly be against the rules.

If I decide to remain ethical, I have to refuse to follow the instructions of senior who happens to be close to the builder.

The builder having done some good work is not a valid justification to allow him get confidential information. It would result into unjust enrichment of him at the cost of other builders. There should be a level playing field for all.

However, if my senior insists, I would ask him to give me a written order. He would not do so. And if he does it, I can take that order to the senior most in the organisation and ask for his advise.

This would certainly create a hurdle in such malpractice.

Rather than submitting to the oral instruction of senior officer, a junior should explore further options to remain ethical and follow the rules to its letter and spirit.

14. You are the Executive Director of an upcoming Infotech Company which is making a name for itself in the market.

Mr. A, who is a star performer, is heading the marketing team. In a short period of one year, he has helped in doubling the revenues as well as creating a high brand equity for the Company so much so that you are thinking of promoting him. However, you have been receiving information from many corners about his attitude towards the female colleagues, particularly his habit of making loose comments on women. In addition, he regularly sends indecent SMS's to all the team members including his female colleagues.

One day, late in the evening, Mrs. X, who is one of Mr. A's team members, comes to you visibly disturbed. She complains against the continued misconduct of Mr. A, who has been making

undesirable advances towards her and has even tried to touch her inappropriately in his cabin.

She tenders her resignation and leaves your office.

(a) What are the options available to you ?

(b) Evaluate each of these options and choose the option you would adopt, giving reasons. (250 words) **20**

Answer: (a) I have the following options in this situation:

(i) I can accept her resignation and not lose Mr. A's performance which is beneficial to the company.

(ii) Not accept her resignation and take strict action against Mr. A. So no other employee harasses women in the company.

(iii) Find out a compromising solution.

(b) (i) If I accept resignation of Mrs. X, it would send a wrong signal to other employees about our policy on protection of female employees. It would also allow persons like Mr. A to behave in such wrong manner unhindered.

(ii) if I do not accept her resignation and take strict action against Mr. A, I may lose a good employee who could have been given a chance to improve.

(iii) Therefore, I would prefer a series of actions, as a third option to find out compromising solution.

I would allow Mrs. X to calm down in that situation and talk to her to take a view of the situation. I will not accept her resignation but will assure her of taking necessary action against Mr. A.

Once I have understood the incident, I will call Mr. A to my office and reprimand him for his indecent behaviour. I would inform him about strict policy of the company with regard to female harassment.

I will organise a meeting with both Mr. A and Mrs. X in my office to resolve the issue. Mr. A has to apologise to Mrs. X in front of me and give us an assurance that he would not repeat the behaviour with anyone else.

(MAIN) **2014**

Civil Services Exam. General Studies

SOLVED PAPERS

PAPER–I

TimeAllowed:ThreeHours *Maximum Marks : 250*

Instructions : There are TWENTY FIVE questions printed both in English and Hindi. All questions are compulsory. The number of marks carried by a question/part is indicated against it. Answers must be written in the medium authorized in the Admission Certificate which must be stated clearly on the cover of this Question-cum-Answer (QCA) Booklet in the space provided. No marks will be given for answers written in medium other than the authorized one.

Word limit in questions, if specified, should be adhered to.

Any page or portion of the page left blank in the Question-cum-Answer Booklet must be clearly struck off.

Answer questions in NOT MORE THAN the word limit specified for each in the parenthesis. Content of the answer is more important than length.

Q. 1. To what extent has the urban planning and culture of the Indus Valley Civilization provided inputs to the present day urbanization? Discuss. 10

Important Points for Answer:
- *Towns of Indus Valley*
- *Features of Towns*

Answer: The people of Indus Valley were primarily urban people. The Indus cities like Harappa, Mahenjo-daro, Kalibangan, Lothal and Sarkotada show Town planning of the time. The cities were built on a uniform plan.They had the following features which can be useful for modern town planners:

Fine drainage system, well arranged water supply system were carefully adopted.

The street lights system, watch and ward arrangement at night, specific places to throw waste materials, public wells in every street, well in every house etc. revealengineering and town planning of the people.

The streets intersected in right angles.

Drains were made of gypsum, lime and cement, covered with portable stabs. House drains connected in the main drains running under the main streets and below many lanes.

Double storied dwelling houses were widely prevalent.

Almost every house had a bathroom at the ground floor and some even on the first floor.

All these aspects of Indus Valley towns are useful and inspiring for present town planning system.

(Total 166 words)

Q. 2. Gandhara Sculpture owed as much to the Romans as to the Greeks. Explain. 10

Important Points for Answer:

- *Gandhara Sculpture*
- *Roman Sculpture*
- *Greek Sculpture*
- *Relations*

Answer: Gandhara style of Buddhist art has developed from merger of Greek, Syrian, Persian, and Indian artistic influence which began mainly during the Parthian Period but the Gandhara style flourished and achieved its pinnacle during the Kushan period, from the 1st to the 5th centuries.

Gandhararegion was crossroads for cultural influence and therefore this school of art had maintained contacts with Rome and Greece. Motifs and techniques from classical Roman art were incorporated in Gandhara School which included vine scrolls, cherubs bearing garlands, tritons and centaurs.

The materials used for Gandhara sculpture were green phyllite and gray-blue mica schist and stucco. The sculptures were originally painted and gilded.

Gandhara School started representing Buddha with a youthful Apollo like face, dressed in garments resembling to Roman imperial statues.

The Gandhara school incorporated many motifs and techniques from Classical Roman art, including vine scrolls, cherubs bearing garlands, tritons, and centaurs. The basic iconography, however, remained Indian.

Both Roman and Greek traditions were used to enrich Gandhara art. (Total 166 words)

Q. 3. Taxila University was one of the oldest universities of the world with which were associated a number of renowned learned personalities of different disciplines. Its strategic location caused its fame to flourish, but unlike Nalanda, it is not considered as a university in modern sense. Discuss. 10

Important Points for Answer:

- *Taxila University - its importance*
- *Nalanda University - its importance*
- *Taxila not a University*

Answer: Taxila, also known as Taxshila university is considered one of the oldest universities in the world. Located in modern day northwest Pakistan was situated at the pivotal junction of South Asia and Central Asia. It taught ancient scriptures, arts of eighteen types including skills like archery, elephant lore, hunting, law, medicine, military science etc. Chanakya, Chandragupta Maurya, Charaka, Panini, Jivaka, Prasenajit are some of the famous personalities associated with Taxila university.

Nalanda, located in the ancient kingdom of Magadha was a centre for learning from 5th to 12th century which flourished under the patronage of Gupta empire and Hardhavardhana of Kanauj. It attracted students from various Janapadas of India, and also Tibet, China, Korea and Central Asia. Buddha, Mahavira, Aryabhatta, Aryadeva, Atisha, Dharmakirti, Dharmapala, Nagarjuna Yijing and Naropa studied in Nalanda. The university taught Buddhism, Vedas, logic, grammar, philosophy, medicine, magic, law, astronomy and city planning.

Taxila had no lecture halls and residences, but Nalanda had all these facilities to consider it a modern university. (Total 165 words)

Q. 4. The third battle of Panipat was fought in 1761. Why were so many empire–shaking battles fought at Panipat? 10

Important Points for Answer:
- *Battles of Panipat*
- *Location of Panipat*
- *Reasons for Panipat wars*

Answer: The third battle of Panipat fought in 1761 between Afghans and the Marathas resulted in defeat and subsequent decline of Marathas. The first battle of Panipat was between Babur and Ibrahim Lodi, resulting into Babur establishing Mughal dynasty in India. The second battle was between Akbar and Hemu for supremacy in India.

Because of Panipat's vicinity to Delhi which has remained the capital of India since medieval times. Therefore capturing Delhi used to give control over India.

Additionally, Panipat was located in the middle of two of the most agriculturally productive regions i.e. the plains of the Indus and the plains of Ganges.

All forces took route of Kandhar and Panipat fell on the G.T. Road as a battleground for such invaders and the Indian rulers because Indian rulers wanted to fight outside Delhi to no disturb the life of people.

Panipat terrain consisted of large plains making it suitable for battles tactics.

Therefore, so many empire-shaking wars were fought in Panipat. (Total 165 words)

Q. 5. Sufis and medieval mystic saints failed to modify either the religious ideas and practices or the outward structure of Hindu/Muslim societies to any appreciable extent. Comment. 10

Important Points for Answer:
- *Sufi & Mystic Saints*
- *Impact on Hindu/Muslim Society*
- *Assessment*

Answer: During the Medieval period, two most influential movements, Sufism and Bhakti Movement started in India. Both were either to increase Islamic influence or to save Hindu traditions.

Khwaja Muinuddin Chisti, Farid-ud-din Ganj-i-Shakar, Nizam-ud-din Auliya, etc were main sufi saints of the period. Medieval saints opposed the orthodoxy and superstition in the Hindu religion, and condemned the prevailing social order.

The Sufi movement was the result of the Hindu influence on Islam.

The chief exponents of Bhakti movement were Ramanuja, Nimbarka, Ramananda, Vallabhacharya, Kabir, Nanak and Sri Chaityana. They preached to local people at village gatherings. They moved from one place to another place to propagate and such nomadic nature of saints did not leave long lasting impact. No institutional structure was created and so the message was forgotten by audience.

They could not modify either religious ideas and practices or the outward structure of Hindu/ Muslim societies as their influence remained confined to small pockets and ideas remained mostly abstract. (Total 166 words)

Q. 6. Examine critically the various facets of economic policies of the British in India from mid-eighteenth century till independence. 10

Important Points for Answer:
- *BEconomic Policies of British*
- *From 1750s to 1947*
- *Analysis*

Answer: Mid eighteenth century is marked by an important even in British India. The Battle of Plassey (1757) and Battle of Buxar (1764) opened way for the East India Company to assume the Diwani rights of large part of East India.

Britishers implemented various reforms in the Indian land revenue system like- Zamindari (Permanent Settlement), Ryotwari and Mahalwari systems during the second half of the 18th century. Discouraging industrialisation in India, British made it a supplier of raw material and market for their finished products. English transformed Indian exports to cheap Indio, Tobacco and opium.

During the British period, irrigation systems were built to provide impetus for growing cash crops for export and raw materials for industry, especially jute, cotton, sugarcane, coffee and tea.

The British also built a modern railway, postal services, telegraph system in late 19h century. British dictated the terms of international trade for India and often restricted the Indian traders to transact with nations, that were hostile to Britain. (Total 162 words)

Q. 7. In what ways did the naval mutiny prove to be the last nail in the coffin of British colonial aspirations in India? 10

Important Points for Answer:
- *Naval Mutiny*
- *Reasons*
- *Result*

Answer: Royal Indian Navy (RIN) revolt started as a strike by ratings in one of the battleships at Bombay in February, 1946. It was a protest against conditions of service, discrimination, etc. The revolt spread and found support throughout India.

It found immense support among the Indian population which supported the soldiers by demonstration which included a one-day general strike in Bombay. The strike also spread to other cities and was joined by Royal Indian Air Force and local police forces. Widespread rioting took place across the nation.

The point that Sardar Patel could pacify soldiers and not the Britishers made them understand that the control of the Indian politics had finally shifted from the English to the Indian hands.

At the same time, Britishers were weakened in the World War-II which resulted in emergence of US and USSR as super-powers who were against imperialism and colonialism. This Naval mutiny and its repercussions shattered the argument of moral authority of British to rule India. (Total 166 words)

Q.8. What were the major political, economic and social developments in the world which motivated the anti-colonialstruggleinIndia? 10

Important Points for Answer:
- *Political Developments*
- *Economic Developments*
- *Social Developments*
- *Impact on Indian freedom struggle*

Answer: The Anti-Colonial struggle in India was inspired by various events and ideologies. Some major International events also played catalyst role in India's freedom struggle.

Politically the unification of Germany and successful Irish struggle against British inspired the minds of millions of Indian people to unite as a nation.

World War I was the reason for first mass movement of Non-Cooperation Movement and Khilafat Movement. It also sowed seeds of Ghadar movements.

World War-II resulted in the weakening of British as the colonial power and gave rise to US and USSR as new super-powers who were against Colonialism and Imperialism which inspired the process of Decolonisation.

The establishment of United Nations was a moral pressure against colonial powers like Britain.

Economically, Great Economic Recession exposed the vulnerable nature of the colonial powers.

French revolution, Communist movements, Home-Rule Movement of Ireland, etc. were also responsible for creating national movement in India. (Total 154 words)

Q. 9. What were the events that led to Suez Crisis in 1956? How did it deal a final blow to Britain's self-image as a world power? 10

Important Points for Answer:
- *Suez Canal Crisis*
- *Reasons*
- *Reactions*
- *Result*

Answer: The Suez Canal opened in 1869, connecting the Mediterranean and Red Seas, initially as a private corporation owned by French investors and the Egyptian government. But Egypt sold its shares to Britain in 1875. Suez Canal was primarily a commercial venture. Britain had secured permission from Egypt to maintain a military presence in the Canal Zone to reinforce its status as the world's supreme naval power.

In 1956, Egyptian President Gamal Nasser seized the Suez Canal from its French and British owners, leading to an invasion by those Western nations and their ally, Israel.

Britain and France invaded Egypt to regain control of the Suez Canal and to remove Egyptian President Nasser from power. There was also an invasion of Egypt's Sinai Peninsula by Israel which was later joined by UK and France. This unilateral action of Britain and France was condemned internationally as a result of which they were forced to withdraw. It was considered undiplomatic and lowered Britain's esteem as a super power in the world. (Total 168 words)

Q. 10. The New Economic Policy-1921 of Lenin had influenced the policies adopted by India soon after Independence. Evaluate. 10

Important Points for Answer:
- *New Economic Policy 1921*
- *Indian Policy*
- *Planning*
- *PSUs*

Answer: The New Economic Policy of 1922 was described by Lenin as an economic system that would include "a free market and capitalism, both subject to state control" while socialised state enterprises were to operate on "a profit basis". A system of mixed economy was introduced which allowed private individuals to own small enterpriseswhile the state continued to control banks, foreign trade, and large industries. It was also called "State Capitalism".

Indian economic policy after independence was strongly influenced by success of planned Soviet economy. Nehru and Mahalanobis formulated the economic policy that focused on development of heavy industry by public sector which will percolate to small industries in private sector. Public Sector Undertakings led the economic growth for many years.India also adopted protectionist policy with characteristics like public sector enterprises run by government, central planning, restriction on foreign trade, import substitution and licensing regime for various industries. May industries like telecommunication, steel, mining, machinery, insurance, etc.were under state control.

(Total 162 words)

Q.11. How does patriarchy impact the position of a middle class working woman in India? 10

Answer: Patriarchy is male centred social system. Male members play dominating role in politics, society and other spheres. Fathers or father-figures hold authority over women.

The patriarchal set up of the Indian society affect middle class working women in following ways:

1. Contribution of women is under-valued and under-paid therefore they are given only low paying jobs.
2. Women perform dual responsibility of work as well as home. The middle class women are allowed to work professionally, but they are expected to manage household tasks as well. It creates an additional burden on working women. They are not able to pursue professional career.
3. The concept of women as the bread-winner is not accepted. Whatever she earns is counted as additional income.
4. Woman is required to sacrifice her career for child birth and devote herself to the family.
5. They are vulnerable to eve teasing and other crimes.
6. There are also instances of sexual harassment by superiors. (Total 162 words)

Q. 12. Why do some of the most prosperous regions of India havean adverse sex ratio for women? Give your arguments. 10

Important Points for Answer:
- *Sex Ratio in India*
- *Situation in Prosperous regions*
- *Reasons*

Answer: In the Population Census of 2011 it was revealed that the population ratio of India 2011 is 943 females per 1000 of males.

Pondicherry (1037) and Kerala (1084) houses the maximum number of female while the regions of Daman and Diu (618) and Haryana (879) have the lowest density of female population. Even Delhi (868), Chandigarh (818), Dadra and Nagar Haveli (774), Jammu and Kashmir (890), Sikkim (890) and Punjab (895), Gujarat (918), Rajasthan (928), Maharashtra (929) are rich and well doing regions of India but their sex ratio is lower than national average.

Decline of the sex ration in India is due to the biased attitude which is meted out to the women. The main cause of this gender bias is inadequate education. The deep-rooted bias against women and economic growth not translating into gender parity are also reasons why female face social and cultural discrimination. Demographic reasons, like migration by working male in the economically prosperous regions is also responsible for adverse sex ratio. (Total 167 words)

Q. 13. The life cycle of a joint family depends on economic factors rather than social values. Discuss. 10

Important Points for Answer:
- *Joint family tradition*
- *Economic Reasons*
- *Nuclear family trend*
- *Economic Reasons*

Answer: India has social tradition of joint and large families. It was mainly due to economic factors. Majority of population in India were living in villages and were dependent on agriculture and related activities which required physical labour. More family members were involved in the activities of earning, so the family can sustain in poverty. Labourer and tenants were dependent on cumulative income and efforts to run family.

However, in modern time, situation has changed. After industrialisation, companies and urban areas have become attractive source of employment. Individual has to migrate to cities to earn better income and provide better education to children. Attractiveness of service over agriculture has also led to migration. It has resulted into split, nuclear family. A male member of family, along with wife and children, would shift to urban areas for employment purpose.

Such economic factors were reasons for the traditional joint family system and now new economic situations have created a social trend of nuclear families. (Total 161 words)

Q.14. Discuss the various economic and socio - cultural forces that are driving increasing feminization of agriculture in India. 10

Important Points for Answer:
- *Feminization of agriculture*
- *Economic reasons*
- *Socio-cultural reasons*

Answer: Feminization of agriculture means increase of women's participation in agricultural activities.

Economic Reasons:

1. Most of the agricultural fields have low productivity, serving only as subsistence agriculture. Women work on field while male look for other jobs.
2. Male members of family committed suicide due to debts. Responsibilities of earning livelihood for the family remain on female.
3. Less educated and untrained for skilled work women have less opportunities for work. It resulted into lack of option for women so they are forced to work in unskilled jobs, like agriculture and manual labour.

Socio-cultural Reasons:

1. Loosening of patriarchal attitude has led to greater participation of female on farm fields.
2. State-sponsored welfare programmes have prompted male members to enroll for state-aided activities. So the task of farming fell upon the female members of the family.
3. The high rate of migration of male from rural to urban areas for better jobs has resulted in women coming to the front and taking charge of family as well as farm. (Total 166 words)

Q.15. How do the Indian debates on Secularism differ from the debates in the west? 10

Important Points for Answer:
- *Secularism*
- *Westen Secularism*
- *Reasons*
- *Indian Secularism*

Answer: Secularism means non partiality based on religion. In political and social aspects, no one should be deprived of any opportunity due to his religious faith. It is a negative and prohibitive concept.

In the West, secularism has been considered as a wall between politics and religion. There is complete absence of religious influence in western concept of secularism. No religious influence in governance is permitted.

This has happened due to historical influence of Church affecting politics and lives of people in western countries in the middle ages. Later, it was decided to keep Church at a hand's distance from politics.

However, in India, secularism has a positive concept. Politics is not allowed to discriminate anyone on the basis of religious affiliation. India, rather believes in promoting all religions equally. Therefore, in India, we have personal laws based on religious beliefs. This is an example of positive and protective secularism. This has happened due to historical reasons where since ancient time, we have concept of *Sarva Dharma Samabhava*. (Total 167 words)

Q.16. Most of the unusual climatic happenings are explained as an outcome of the El-Nino effect. Do you agree? 10

Important Points for Answer:
- *El Nino*
- *Effects*
- *Disagreement*

Answer: El Niño is the warm phase of the El Niño-Southern Oscillation cycle. El Niño is a naturally occurring phenomenon that is linked to a periodic warming in sea surface temperatures across the central and east-central Equatorial Pacific. El Niño occurs every 2-7 years, and can last anywhere between nine months and two years.

Main effects of El Niño include, a drastic increase in the risk of flooding on the western coast of South America. In eastern countries, like India and Indonesia, there is an increase in droughts.El Niño causes vast amounts of rainfall in the eastern parts of the Pacific and very dry weather on the western parts (India, Indonesia).With all the extra heat at the surface of the Pacific Ocean, energy is released into the atmosphere, causing an overall warming of the global climate temporarily.

However, it has limited effects that arises out warm ocean currents therefore it cannot be attributed with other geographical or climatic effects. (Total 163 words)

Q.17. Why are the world's fold mountain systems located along the margins of continents? Bring out the association between the global distribution of fold mountains and the earthquakes and volcanoes. 10

> **Important Points for Answer:**
> - *FoldMountains*
> - *Formation*
> - *Reasons for earthquake and volcanoes*
> - *Examples*

Answer: Fold mountains form when two tectonic plates move towards each other at a convergent plate boundary. Fold mountains are associated with continental crust. Convergent plate boundaries are sites of collisions, where tectonic plates crash into each other.

At a compression zone, tectonic activity forces crustal compression at the leading edge of the crust formation. For this reason, most fold mountains are found on the edge or former edge of continental plate boundaries.

Rocks on the edge of continental crust are often weaker and less stable than rocks found in the continental interior. This makes them more susceptible to folding and warping. It results into volcanic activities and earthquakes. Therefore, in the regions of folded mountains like the Jura Mountains in the Alps, the 'Simply Folded Belt' of the Zagros Mountains, The Himalayas, The Akwapim-Togo ranges in Ghana as well as the Ridge-and-Valley Appalachians in the eastern part of United States, such activities are frequent. (Total 157 words)

Q.18. Explain the formation of thousands of islands in Indonesian and Philippines archipelagos. 10

> **Important Points for Answer:**
> - *Archipelago*
> - *Indonesia & Philippines Archipelagos*
> - *Formation of Islands*

Answer: Archipelago, a cluster of islands, is the result of an underwater volcanic activity in the ocean. Countries such as Indonesia, New Zealand, Philippines, United Kingdom and Japan are archipelagos.

Indonesian and Philippines Archipelagos fall between the Pacific and the Indian Ocean which were originally part of the Asian landmass.

Indonesian Archipelago is made up of approximately 17,500 islands out of which more than 6,000 are populated. Out of 400, about 150 are active volcanoes. Not all Indonesian Islands are volcanic. When the glaciers melted, these islands emerged. The Philippine archipelago has 7100 islands.

Beneath the earth's surface is a 'hot spot' that releases magma or semi molten rock. This forms rock-like structures underwater. As magma continues to flow, over a period of time these structures rise up out of water. This forms an island. While the single hot spot remains, the persistent plate movements on the earth's surface shift the magma, and a series of islands is formed in one area. (Total 162 words)

Q.19. Tropical cyclones are largely confined to South China Sea, Bay of Bengal and Gulf of Mexico. Why? 10

Important Points for Answer:
• *Tropical Cyclones*
• *Formation*
• *Reasons for location*

Answer: Tropical cyclone is an intense circular storm that originates over warm tropical oceans and is characterised by low atmospheric pressure, high winds, and heavy rain. They are also known as typhoon or hurricane.

Every year during the late summer months (July–September in the Northern Hemisphere and January–March in the Southern Hemisphere), cyclones strike regions as far apart as the Gulf Coast of North America, northwestern Australia, and eastern India and Bangladesh.

Almost 90 percent of these storms form within 20° north or south of the Equator. Poleward of those latitudes, sea surface temperatures are too cool to allow tropical cyclones to form.

The Pacific Ocean generates the greatest number of tropical storms and cyclones. The most powerful storms, sometimes called super typhoons, occur in the western Pacific. The Indian Ocean is second in the total number of storms. The Atlantic Ocean ranks third.

Therefore, tropical cyclones are largely confined to South China Sea, Bay of Bengal and Gulf of Mexico. (Total 162 words)

Q.20. Bring out the relationship between the shrinking Himalayan glaciers and the symptoms of climate change in the Indian sub-continent. 10

Important Points for Answer:
• *Shrinking Himalayan Glacier*
• *Symptoms of Climate Change*
• *Relations*

Answer: Himalayan glaciers are shrinking at an alarming rate due to climate change. It is leading to significant impact on the water resources of population living in downstream basins.

Climate change decreases snowfall which means less snow in glaciers.

The shorter duration of snowfall prevents the snow from turning into hard ice-crystals which will melt when the summer comes.

Climate change brings rain, rather than snow, thus melting glacier faster. Heavy rainfall in high altitudes cause flash floods and washes away homes and fields, trees and livestock.

Widespread flooding of the melting glacier is initial phenomena but as the snow disappears, there will be drought in the summer season.

The biodiversity in Himalayan drainage and Himalayan region has become vulnerable.

Because of the melting ice, the sea level is rising at an average of 3.5 mm per year.

Tropical cyclones are expected to increase in future as a result of ice-melting. (Total 152 words)

Q.21. Whereas the British planters had developed tea gardens all along the Shivaliks and Lesser Himalayas from Assam to Himachal Pradesh, in effect they did not succeed beyond the Darjeeling area. Explain. 10

Important Points for Answer:
- *British Planters*
- *Tea Gardens in N-E India*
- *Why not beyond Darjeeling?*

Answer: India is one of the largest tea producers in the world. Britishers introduced Tea in India. They brought it from China and offered perks for developing Tea gardens in India. Due to climatic conditions, it was started in the North Eastern parts of India including Assam. Tea shrubs require fertile mountain soil mixed with lime and iron.

Tea grows best in regions with a warm, humid climate and a rainfall measuring at least 100 centimetres a year. Ideally, it likes deep, light, acidic and well-drained soil. Given these conditions, tea grows in areas away from sea level up to altitudes as high as 2,100 metres above sea level. Therefore, Assam region was very favourable to tea plantation. Presence of cheap labour from the adjoining regions of Bihar and Bengal also made Darjeeling more suitable for tea cultivation.

But due to cold climate and low gradient in Shivaliks and lesser Himalayas, absence of deep clay soil, steep slops in Shivaliks, year round rains, etc., doesn't allow the tea plantation to succeed in these areas. These factors were not favourable to tea gardens to succeed.

Thus, the location inhibited the growth of tea cultivation as dominant agricultural practices in these areas. (Total 200 words)

Q.22. Why did the Green Revolution in India virtually bypass the eastern region despite fertile soil and good availability of water? 10

Important Points for Answer:
- *Green Revolution*
- *Factors required*
- *Eastern India bypassed*

Answer: The Green Revolution was implemented only in areas which had assured supplies of water and the means to control it, large inputs of fertilisers, and adequate farm credit. Introduction of high-yielding varieties of seeds after1965 and the increased use of fertilisers and irrigation are known collectively as the Green Revolution.

These inputs were easily available in at least parts of the states of Punjab, Haryana, and western Uttar Pradesh. But in other states, such as Andhra Pradesh and Tamil Nadu, in areas where these inputs were not assured, the results were limited or negligible, leading to considerable variation in crop yields within these states.

Large land holdings were required, which was available in Western India. East India has fragmented land holdings due to population pressure. Supporting infrastructure like cold storage, availability of electricity and transport was relatively poor in Eastern India. Irrigation facilities, mechanisation and investment facilities were also other hurdles. Due to this, the eastern India was not involved in the Green Revolution. (Total 166 words)

Q.23. Account for the change in the spatial pattern of the Iron and Steel industry in the world. 10

Important Points for Answer:

- *Steel Industry*
- *Factors*
- *Shift*
- *Reasons*

Answer: With Industrial Revolution, the growth and development of iron and steel industry started. The spatial pattern of the this industry depends upon various factors such as availability of raw materialslike iron ore, coking coal, limestone and water as well as availability of power resources. Demand of steel, transportation cost, etc., also play a role.

Traditionally this industry was located in Western Europe, North America, Japan and USSR. However there has been change in spatial pattern of the industry.

Now they are shifting towards coastal areas so that the produced steel can be exported and the raw materials can be imported easily.The industry is shifting to countries like China, India and South Korea.The traditional industrial regions are either abandoned, like Michigan region in USA, or have been transformed into developing cutting edge technology.The industry is shifting towards industrial hub so that the finished products can be consumed by automobile, heavy engineering and other industries which will reduced the cost of transportation. (Total 164 words)

Q.24. Critically evaluate the various resources of the oceans which can be harnessed to meet the resource crisis in the world. 10

Important Points for Answer:

- *Resources of Ocean*
- *Usefulness*

Answer: The ocean is one of Earth's most valuable natural resources. It provides food in the form of fish and shellfish—about 200 billion pounds are caught each year. It's used for transportation—both travel and shipping. It provides a treasured source of recreation for humans. It is mined for minerals (salt, sand, gravel, and some manganese, copper, nickel, iron, and cobalt can be found in the deep sea) and drilled for crude oil. Production of energy through ocean waves is also a viable option.

The ocean plays a critical role in removing carbon from the atmosphere and providing oxygen. The ocean is an increasingly important source of biomedical organisms with enormous potential for fighting disease. These are just a few examples of the importance of the ocean to life on land. Explore them in greater detail to understand why we must keep the ocean healthy for future generations.

These all resources of ocean can be very useful to meet recourse crunch in the world. (Total 164 words)

Q.25. How does India see its place in the economic space of rising natural resource rich Africa? 10

Important Points for Answer:
- *India-Africa Relations*
- *Economic Cooperation*

Answer: Africa–India relations are deep in the historical, political, economic, military and cultural spheres.

Indian firms are conducting numerous takeovers abroad and are venturing into Africa. Indo-African trade volume reached US$ 53.3 billion in 2010-11 & US$ 62 billion in 2011-12.

Indian companies have already invested more than US$ 34 billion in the resource-rich continent as of 2011 & further investments worth US$ 59.7 billion are in the pipeline.

The Indian government has promised to extend loans worth US$ 5.4 billion (during 2011-14) to several African nations in order to nurture growth in those nations.

The India–Africa Forum Summit (IAFS) is the official platform for African-Indian relations. The IAFS is held once in every three years. It was first held from April 2008 in New Delhi. The Prime Minister also announced $5 billion in lines of credit for African nations. India made further commitments to Africa at the third India-Africa Forum Summit in 2014. (Total 160 words)

SOLVED PAPERS

PAPER–II

Time Allowed : Three Hours *Maximum Marks : 250*

Instructions: There are TWENTY questions printed both in English and in Hindi. All questions are compulsory. The number of marks carried by a question/part is indicated against it. Answers must be written in the medium authorized in the Admission Certificate which must be stated clearly on the cover of this Question-cum-Answer (QCA) Booklet in the space provided. No marks will be given for answers written in medium other than the authorized one.

Word limit in questions, wherever specified, should be adhered to.

Answer the questions in not more than 200 words each. Contents of the answer is more important than its length. All questions carry equal marks.

Q.1. Starting from inventing the 'basic structure' doctrine, the judiciary has played a highly proactive role in ensuring that India develops into a thriving democracy. In light of the statement, evaluate the role played by judicial activism in achieving the ideals of democracy. **12**

Important Points for Answer:
- *Basic Structure doctrine*
- *Judicial Activism*
- *Contribution to democracy*

Answer: To keep prevent the government from destroying the fundamental structure and philosophy of the Constitutuion, the Supreme Court adopted the doctrine of Basic Structure in Keshavanand Bharati Case 1973.

Till now judiciary have been successful in fulfilling its role by inventing basic structure doctrine to bring constitutional amendment within purview of judicial review along with extending right to life and liberty by linking it to DPSPs to promote compulsory education as well as right to safe and fresh environment.

Judicial activism is a mechanism through which judiciary puts check on legislative adventurism as well as executive tyranny by enforcing constitutional limits. Judicial activism is necessary to ensure that our constitutional offices and institutions does not become tools for extending any authoritarian agenda of government in power.

However, it is important to note that in a democracy, where judiciary is one of the three pillars of the system. Therefore, in the zeal of judicial activism, judges of Supreme Court and High Courts should not assume the role of an independent policy makers but should act only as interpreter of the constitution to maintain spirit and sanctity of the constitution.

Thus, judicial activism is imperative for Indian democracy but judiciary should maintain confidence and support of public by taking rational and cautious approach. (Total 211 words)

Q.2. Though the federal principle is dominant in our Constitution and that principle is one of its basic features, but it is equally true that federalism under the Indian Constitution leans in favour of a strong Centre, a feature that militates against the concept of strong federalism. 12

Important Points for Answer:
- *Federalism in India*
- *Strong Centre*
- *Weak federalism*

Answer: Popularly Federalism is known as a set-up of government where the powers to govern is equally and clearly distributed between federal government and its state units.

Indian constitution defines India as a Union. As the Seventh Schedule distributes powers between the centre and states with help of three lists, each State has own government and right to enact laws on the subjects assigned, Indian polity is a kind of federalism.

But within constitution there are several features which provide prominence to the centre over states, some of these features are:

(a) Centre appoints Governor.

(b) In case of conflict between centre and state laws, the centre's law will prevail.

(c) In case of constitutional machinery or law and order breakdown along with threat to national security, the centre can takeover states administration through emergency provisions.

(d) The control of Constitutional Bodies like Election commission, CAG, etc., lies in the hands of centre.

(e) Unified judiciary is also going against federal spirit. Judges of Supreme Court and High Courts are appointed by Union.

(f) States do not have own constitution.

However, Indian federalism is often described as quasi-judicial federal system because it can be converted into unitary in case of emergency. (Total 202 words)

Q.3. The 'Powers, Privileges and Immunities of Parliament and its Members' as envisaged in Article 105 of the Constitution leave room for a large number of uncodified and un-enumerated privileges to continue. Assess the reasons for the absence of legal codification of the 'parliamentary privileges'. How can this problem be addressed? 12

Important Points for Answer:
- *Article 105*
- *Parliamentary Privileges*
- *Problems and Codification*

Answer: Article 105 of constitution provides certain privileges to Members of Parliament by granting immunity from any action or speech by them while performing their duties within Parliament. Similar provisions are made for MLAs under Article 194.

As the privileges are not codified, they continue to be same as what were enjoyed by British Parliamentarians at the time of Constitution.

The parliament has not passed any law to regulate parliamentary privileges which is mandated by Article 105(3).Thus MPs and MLAs continue to enjoy unhindered immunity for serving political vendetta.

But within article 105 there is huge space which is occupied by a large number of uncodified and unenumerated privileges, which fails the purpose of parliamentary privileges.

Such as, legislative members indulge in hate speech, pass on derogatory remarks on each other while shielding under immunity granted by article 105.

These privileges have created tussle with the fundamental right to freedom of speech and also with judiciary's right to decide scope of privileges. In cases, Parliament has summoned journalists for reporting debate of Parliament/State legislature.

Thus, it is high time now to pass such a law to regulate privileges and immunities of legislative members so that integrity of parliament can maintained. (Total 202 words)

Q. 4. What do you understand by the concept "freedom of speech and expression"? Does it cover hate speech also? Why do the films in India stand on a slightly different plane from other forms of expression? Discuss. 12

Important Points for Answer:

- *Freedom of speech and expression*
- *Hate speech*
- *Films in India*

Answer: Freedom of speech and expression is a fundamental concept of freedom and liberty which is also endorsed by Indian constitution. It provides Freedom of speech and expression as fundamental right to every citizen of India under Article 19. It covers right to express one's opinion in any form such as by speech writing or even by staying silent.

However, Freedom of speech and expression does not cover hate speech as it violates right of others and disturbs harmony in society, affects law and order which is counterproductive to both nation and its citizen. Thus, hate speech is crime under Indian Penal code and prohibited by constitution.

On the same issue film industry has slightly different position:

- As the industry claims film is virtual and fictional rather than real unlike hate speeches.
- Films are means to entertain as well as to provide learning, thus they need freedom to show reality.
- Apart from that, there is film certification board to rate the film for appropriate audience, thus full freedom is necessary in making of film.

Hence, films are product of creativity and expression and need freedom of speech and expression. Even then if movie offends someone, filmmaker will be responsible. Until then film makers should be granted full freedom of speech and expression. (Total 211 words)

Q.5. Instances of President's delay in commuting death sentences has come under public debate as denial of justice. Should there be a time limit specified for the President to accept/ reject such petitions? Analyse. 12

Important Points for Answer:

- *Commutation of Death Sentence*
- *Constitutional provisions*
- *Delay*
- *Judgements*

Answer: Article 72 of constitution of grants power to the President to reprive, respite, pardon or commute punishment of a convicted personeven in the case of capital punishment. The same is exercised by the President on the advice of Council of Ministers.

There has been cases where the President has not disposed off the petition for pardon for more than a decade. It delays execution of punishment. The basic principle of administration of justice is that justice delayed is justice denied. This undue delay accounts for denial of justice. Resultantly, Supreme court held prolonged delay in commuting death sentence have "dehumanising effect" and it is tortuous for condemned convict. Such a delay violates this right of an individual and therefore the clemency petition must be disposed off in a reasonable time by the President or Governor.

Though the Constitution does not provide for any time limit within which the President or the Governor should dispose off the matter. The Supreme Court has also said in various cases that any time limit cannot be prescribed for the President to deal with mercy petitions.

However, such system should be put in place in informal manner as any regulation and law mandating such time limit will breach independence of office of president of India. (Total 211 words)

Q.6. The size of the cabinet should be as big as governmental work justifies and as big as the Prime Minister can manage as a team. How far is the efficacy of a government then inversely related to the size of the cabinet? Discuss. 12

Important Points for Answer:

- *Cabinet*
- *91st Amendment*
- *Efficiency of Government*

Answer: Cabinet is a close group of Ministers, headed by Prime Minister, which is responsible for the government. This cabinet works as a team based on principle of collective responsibility to Parliament, to ensure that country remains up and running.

In India, the size of cabinet is fixed as 15% of Parliament or State Legislature strength by the 91st Constitutional Amendment Act. This provision was introduced to put check on large and cumbersome size of cabinets, which are made to fulfil political commitments to coalition parties.

If the cabinet is very large, it is difficult to manage by Prime Minister as a team. There would be too much division of work among the Ministers which will make it difficult to coordinate.

However, even small size of cabinet is not free from issues. Since it tends to centralise powerin few hands and goes against the principle of collective responsibility. Moreover, it puts extra burden on few person which may delay decision making, such as single minister handling more than on portfolio.

Therefore, size of cabinet should be optimum based on the requirement of workload and responsibility as well as which prime minister effectively control and lead the ship of nation.(Total 199 words)

Q.7. Though 100 percent FDI is already allowed in non-news media like a trade publication and general entertainment channel, the government is mulling over the proposal for increased FDI in news media for quite some time. What difference would an increase in FDI make? Critically evaluate the pros and cons. 12

Important Points for Answer:

- *FDI*
- *FDI in News Media*
- *Pros and Cons*

Answer: Foreign Direct Investment brings with itself much needed capital, technology, management and knowledge. Non-News Media is one of the sector where 100% FDI is permitted.

Government is considering proposal for 100% FDI in New Media also. However, News media is the fourth pillar or estate of democracy. It has to play an immense role in democracy in India.Therefore, news media is not comparable to ordinary entertainment channels.Given to this, currently only 26% FDI is allowed in news media.

The proposal to raise it 100% have both pros and cons:

PROS:

- FDI will provide the much needed financial support to news channel.
- Better technology will help them to raise their quality of broadcasting.
- Competition induced by FDI will compel channels to raise their standard of reporting and mitigate yellow journalism.

CONS:

- There is a threat that Indian media can be painted in western colours.
- If the control of a media house pass on to foreign hands, it directly risks security of India.
- Any misreporting will impact wide range of public as well as bureaucrats, politician and officials.

Therefore, government should take a cautious approach and extend the limit to 49% rather than 100%, so that control remains in Indian hands and media can have access to better financial resources, without compromising with freedom of Media. (Total 217 words)

Q.8. The setting up of a Rail Tariff Authority to regulate fares will subject the cash strapped Indian Railways to demand subsidy for obligation to operate non-profitable routes and services. Taking into account the experience in the power sector, discuss if the proposed reform is expected to benefit the consumers, the Indian Railways or the private container operators. 12

Important Points for Answer:
- *Rail Tariff Authority*
- *Function*
- *Implications*
- *Power Sector*

Answer: Indian railways is running in huge losses, thanks to its cross subsidisation model, in which freight trains cross subsidise losses for passengers. This model is adopted by railways fulfil a social obligation to provide cheap source of transportation.

Similar situation was prevalent in electricity sector also which is now reformed by enactment of Electricity Act, 2003. The act brings in private players in electricity distribution companies,which made certain improvement in this sector.

On the same line, government intends to set up an independent Rail Tariff Authority (RTA), which will rationalise the passenger fair to stop cross subsidisation. The idea to establish an Indian Railways Regulatory Authority (IRRA) was first mooted in the Rakesh Mohan Committee Report (2001), which had other innovative recommendations.

RTA will not only reduce the losses of Railways but also make railways competitive for freight and passenger transport. Moreover, by better pricing policy, railways will enable to provide better quality services.

By introducing system like dynamic pricing, railways can provide high quality service to premium passengers, and with better finances required infrastructure can be created to serve its social obligation.

Thus, setting up of RTA is a step in right direction but cautiousness is required so that railway can turn into a commercially viable unit without losing its social face. (Total 214 words)

Q.9. National Human Rights Commission (NHRC) in India can be most effective when its tasks are adequately supported by other mechanisms that ensure the accountability of a government. In light of above observation assess the role of NHRC as an effective complement to the judiciary and other institutions in promoting and protecting rights standards. 12

Important Points for Answer:
- *National Human Rights Commission*
- *Support required*
- *Assessment*

Answer: National Human Rights Commission (NHRC) was constituted as a statutory body in 1993 by an act of Parliament to protect and promote human rights such as right to life, liberty, equality and dignity.

NHRC is vested with powers equal to a civil court but due to some shortcomings it could not fully achieve its intended goal.

These limitations are:

Lack of financial autonomy keeps NHRC completelydependent on government even for day to day finances.

Functional Autonomy is missing for NHRC as there several restrictions on it's functioning.

Further, they do not have power to enforce their decision, however it they can recommend corrective action.

Members of NHRC tend to remain soft and biased towards government as there is no officer cadre for NHRC. Appointment based members do not have job security.

Statutory restrictions such as bar on NHRC to investigate Human Rights violation by armed forces put further limitation.

Undoubtedly, there is huge scope and need to reform and empower NHRC, which can be done by legislature by granting more autonomy and authority to NHRC. It can be turned into a specialised agency which can support court and civil society to stop human rights Violation. NHRC has played complementary role of judiciary by being a whistleblower and giving recommendations to Parliament. (Total 212 words)

Q.10. The penetration of Self Help Groups (SHGs) in rural areas in promoting participation in development programmes is facing socio-cultural hurdles. Examine. 12

Important Points for Answer:
- *Self Help Groups*
- *Importance*
- *Hurdles*

Answer: Self Help Groups (SHG) are voluntary groups consisting of 10-20 individual, mostly coming from similar background. People in these groups helps each other by financial as well as technical support to create livelihood. Worldwide SHGs are quite popular and successful among women. In india, after initial success, the SHGs are facing various socio-cultural hurdles. Some of them are:

(a) Lack of social support to women as their capabilities are always doubted.

(b) Family support is also missing, as women is burdened with other family chorus and face restriction.

(c) Lack of knowledge because of high illiteracy level of women and low exposure to outside world keep their practical knowledge very limited.

(d) Resultantly, women remain disadvantaged in marketing and dealing with middleman.

(e) Prevalence of caste system in India put barrier in formation of SHGs in rural India.

Although limited by various factors, SHGs model has immense potential in India. Realising the same, government has come up with various skill and financial support programmes to help NGOs, micro finance institute, NABARD and RRB. However, the pace of implementation of these structured skill training package remains low. SHGs can be useful tool for empowerment of women and betterment of society. (Total 201words)

Q.11. Do government's schemes for uplifting vulnerable and backward communities by protecting required social resources for them, lead to their exclusion in establishing businesses in urban economies? 12

Important Points for Answer:

- *Schemes*
- *Protection*
- *Exclusion*

Answer: Communities which are not able to meet their basic needs by using the available resources are termed as vulnerable and backward communities. Government is consistently working for their welfare and upliftment by implementing various schemes in social and economic sectors. The welfare schemes like MNREGA,Atal Bima yojna,NRHM, Food security Act, Sarva Shiksha Abhiyan etc. are some of them. Most of the schemes intend to provide reservation, opportunities or resources without upgrading their skills to compete in urban and business environment.

It is difficult for these communities to come up with resources and expertise needed to start a business in urban communities. Further, they are not qualified enough to take up good jobs in urban centres.

Moreover, even government is trying to keep them in villages to check migration to overcrowded urban centres. It has also been noticed that SC/STs are more comfortable in doing work in their or close to their native places.

In this scenario, government should push for a revamped PURA i.e. Providing Urban Amenities in Rural Areas. This will create employment is RURBAN areas and help in eliminating need to migrate to urban centres. By following this approach, with Shyama Prasad Mukherjee Programme, government has taken a step in direction for holistic development of rural India.(Total 213 words).

Q.12. An athlete participates in Olympics for personal triumph and nation's glory; victors are showered with cash incentives by various agencies, on their return. Discuss the merit of state sponsored talent hunt and its cultivation as against the rationale of a reward mechanism as encouragement. 12

Important Points for Answer:
- *Athlete and sportsmen*
- *Cash rewards*
- *Suggestions*

Answer: In a developing country like India, due to socio-economic condition of a common household, adopting sports as a profession remains low in priority. However,there some exceptional athletes who raise the flag of India in important events namely commonwealth games and Olympic games.

On their victory in national and international events, many states and agencies offer them cash rewards. This is certainly useful for the athletes coming from poor and middle-class background to keep their interest in sport. It also encourages other sports persons.

However, these rewards benefits only particular athlete rather than helping entire generation of athlete. Moreover, it promotes winner takes it all approach, which is counterproductive for creating a good sports environment.

Accordingly, state should engage in talent hunt programme and train capable athlete to participate in sports events. It would create necessary infrastructure helping both future as well present sportsperson and promote and encourage youth to take up sports as a carrier.

It is required to create a transparent system where talented athlete will get fair chance to represent the country. Talent hunts will give a chance to athletes from rural and backward regions to come forward. More importantly, it will create a healthy sports environment, which will also help keeping youth away from drugs and other vices. (Total 214 words)

Q.13. Should the premier institutes like IITs/IIMs be allowed to retain premier status, allowed more academic independence in designing courses and also decide mode/criteria of selection of students. Discuss in light of the growing challenges. 12

Important Points for Answer:
- *Importance of IIT/IIMs*
- *Status and shortcoming*
- *Need for independence*
- *Balanced conclusion*

Answer: IIT/IIMs are regarded as symbol excellence when it comes to higher education in India. As only best young minds are able to get admission in these premiere institutions.

However, even these premiere institutions stand average when compared to worlds best institutions of higher learning.

One of the reasons for this average ranking in world is unnecessary political interference in their functioning. As these institutions do not enjoy the needed independence in setting up and changing their curriculum as per changing needs of industry and society.

Moreover, India is a country having demographic dividend and needs better quality institutions. For this ample space should be provided to these premiere institutions for revising and updating their courses, recruitment, research, granting scholarship etc.

Further, better resource allocation should be provided by government so that best facilities could be provided to students.

However, some positive government control could be there as these institutions are financed by tax payer's money, and government have to ensure these institutions are working in public welfare rather than pure commercial consideration.

Overall, in this era of globalisation and competition government should extend every possible support to these premiere institution, so that they can contribute in harnessing India's massive demographic dividend and maintain their premier status. (206 words)

Q. 14. Has the Cadre based Civil Services Organization been the cause of slow change in India? Critically examine. 12

Important Points for Answer:

- *Rationale behind cadre based civil service*
- *Debate over its existence*
- *Need for change*
- *Possible reforms*

Answer: Civil servants in India are seen as symbol excellence in field of administration. These cadre based civil servants are working on the top positions, all over country and across departments.

However, with changing times it has been noticed that generalist civil servants are not suitable for technical positions like accounting and economic planning etc. It has been noticed that they are making government functioning slow, and they are not adapting changes as per changing nature of society.

Moreover, lack of competition and promotions based on seniority do not encourage them to work on their toes. Apart from that, discrimination between all India services and other services have been creating a demoralising effect on officers of other services.

Further, in present times a large number of important expertise and knowledge generates in private sector which can be productive for bringing excellence in government administration.

To make this outside knowledge available for public use, and increase competition in civil services the concept of lateral entry is gaining currency in government policymakers. More importantly, it can be a good idea bring best practice, professionalism and discipline of private sector in public servants.

Ultimately, the goal of government must be to achieve excellence in delivering good governance and every necessary change for this purpose is welcome. (210 words)

Q.15. Two parallel run schemes of the Government, viz. the Aadhar Card and NPR, one of voluntary and the other as compulsory, have led to debates at national levels and also

litigations. On merits, discuss whether or not both schemes need run concurrently. Analyse the potential of the schemes to achieve developmental benefits and equitable growth. 12

Important Points for Answer:
- *Schemes*
- *Functioning*
- *Overlap*
- *Analysis*

Answer: Both NPR and UIDAI intends to create a register of residents by creating demographic data, biometric data and AADHAR number. Both the schemes collect similar kind of biometric data.

However, while NPR is concerned to achieve better national security and UIDAI is concerned with assigning unique ID to every AADHAR holder to stop leakages financial transitions like wages and subsidies disbursing.

But still there is a huge overlap between two systems resulting into duplication of efforts, and making the whole process slow cumbersome. That's why, continuation of both schemes together is not advisable.

While government should try to use available data in creating a mechanism by which digital infrastructure could be created and using which leakages in social security benefits and subsidies could be eliminated. Moreover, such system is in line with government's effort in providing better governance.

This new data system will also save lots of money and time, thus making India financially stronger.

All this can be done by sending data collected by NPR after authentication of identity, place of residence, to UIDAI for creating AADHAR number.

Following which both the schemes should be linked up to different departmental project for their better functioning and ensuring transparency in their functioning. (200 words)

Q.16. With respect to the South China sea, maritime territorial disputes and rising tension affirm the need for safeguarding maritime security to ensure freedom of navigation and over flight throughout the region. In this context, discuss the bilateral issues between India and China. 12

Important Points for Answer:
- *South China sea*
- *Dispute*
- *India's concerns*
- *Steps taken by India*
- *China's response*

Answer: South China sea has become a theatre of territorial dispute between several countries including China, Brunei, Vietnam, Malaysia and Philippines. All these countries have put forward their claims over some or other portion of south china sea, which is currently occupied by China across Nine Dash line.

Though India is not party to this dispute but it concerns India because:

- Over 2 trillion-dollar trade passes through this route, China's control over these lanes is direct threat to India's interest.
- Moreover, it is a part of Chinese strategy, namely "String of Pearls" to contain India in South Asia by building ports around her.
- Apart from this, India is also exploring oil in Vietnam and recently offered two more oil fields by Vietnam in disputed Territory, this does not go down well with China.
- The dispute of South China sea also affects India's look east policy, as it involves India South East Asian neighbours.

In response to this dispute, and china's plan to encircle India, now we are combing with

"Necklace of diamond strategy" which also prompted sharp reaction from China.

However, in any case India must put her weight for freedom of navigation and trade in all international waters, but in doing so, India should try to not raise much eyebrows and should maintain her image as a peace-loving nation. (215 words)

Q.17. The aim of Information Technology Agreements (ITAs) is to lower all taxes and tariffs on information technology products by signatories to zero. What impact would such agreements have on India's interests? 12

Important Points for Answer:

- *Information Technology Agreement*
- *Impact on India*

Answer: India joined Information Technology Agreement 1 in 1997. This WTO agreement intends to eliminate duties and tariffs on IT products. But these agreements could go both sides and for India it went south, making India stay away from ITA2 talks.

The main Impacts of Information Technology Agreement are listed below:

Positive effects:

(a) Such agreements can provide boost to IT manufacturing thus creating more jobs in this sector, which will help India in harnessing her Demographic Dividend.

(b) Cheap IT imports will help the digitisation initiative i.e. "Digital India" of government and give boost to E governance in country.

(c) Information Technology Agreement could give boost to country's IT exports as lower tariffs can open up new markets for Indian IT products especially in the emerging economies of Asia and Africa.

Negative impact of Information Technology Agreement:

(a) It will be counterproductive for India's MAKE IN INDIA initiative as markets can be flooded by cheap imports.

(b) Such agreements benefit countries which have developed enough capacity to compete in international markets rather than countries like India which is a service giant and whose manufacturing sector is still in nascent stage.

(c) Information Technology Agreement makes India vulnerable to dumping by countries like China as similar situation witnessed in Steel sector. (209 words).

Q.18. Some of the International funding agencies have special terms for economic participation stipulating a substantial component of the aid to be used for sourcing equipment from the leading countries. Discuss on merits of such terms and if, there exists a strong case not to accept such conditions in the Indian context. 12

Important Points for Answer:
- *Foreign aid and its purpose*
- *Conditions with such aid*
- *Impact on India*

Answer: Transfer of goods, services or capital from one country to another country or from an international organization to a country can be termed as foreign aid.

Though on its face these aids appear to be for the benefit of receiving country but often they also further interest of the donor country.

Since at times, these aids come with strings attached to procure things from certain countries or companies only. Such conditions with aids, in long term can even threatenfinancial sovereignty of receiving country.

For India, such aids have both positive and negative impacts:

Positive:

- Such aids provide much needed capital support to India's capital starved infrastructure sector.
- Moreover, it helps in creation of employment and helps society by creating public assets, for e.g. Japanese Aid in Bharatmala Project.
- It also brings new technology and administrative experience to nation.

Negatives:

- Restriction put by aid, reduce options for India to find value for money in other countries.
- There can be a situation when India have to buy products which are not suitable for Indian conditions.
- In present polarised world, aid receiving country without any intention can be seen as enemy nation by the other block.
- In longer term, such condition can create unhealthy dependencies on a single country, especially in case of critical technologies like nuclear reactors.

Thus, India should go for trade diversification and avoid situations like putting all eggs in same bucket. (230 words)

Q.19. India has recently signed to become founding member of New Development Bank (NDB) and also the Asian Infrastructure Investment Bank (AIIB). How will the role of the two Banks be different? Discuss the strategic significance of these two Banks for India. 12

> **Important Points for Answer:**
> - *NDB and AIIB*
> - *Differentiate*
> - *Strategic significance for India*

Answer: In effort to increase her role in developing world, and shift economic power from west to east, India recently joined two new International Financial institution which are discussed below.

New development bank: also known as BRICS bank by taking first letter of name of its five members. It will be headquartered in Shanghai. The unique nature of this bank is its provision of equal voting power, which is major shift from west dominated institutions like world bank and IMF. Moreover, the bank has global focus.

Asian Infrastructure Investment bank: it is a project led by china. The Voting power in this bank is according to contribution of member countries, resultantly, China enjoys veto power here. As the name suggest its main purpose is to finance infrastructure projects in developing countries.

These banks are strategically up against Bretton woods twins to break their dominance, however, for India these banks are even more significant because:

a) These banks provide chance to India in taking up leadership role among developing countries.

b) India needs massive investment in infrastructure which can be funded by these banks and more options will also increase India's bargaining power to get favourable loans from ADB and world bank.

Overall, these new entrants are expected to join hands and help poor and developing countries to achieve their full potential. (210 words)

Q.20. WTO is an important international institution where decisions taken affect countries in a profound manner. What is the mandate of WTO and how binding are their decisions? Critically analyse India's stand on the latest round of talks on Food security. 12

> **Important Points for Answer:**
> - *WTO*
> - *Role and Function*
> - *Decisions*
> - *India's stand*

Answer: World Trade organisation (WTO) is an international organisation which aims to reduce tariff barriers in international trade. The WTO is run by its members and all decisions are taken by negotiation and consensus, which makes all decision acceptable to member countries. The decision is imposed by use of trade sanction against members who violates terms agreed in WTO.

The trade facilitation agreement is one such agenda of WTO which it took up in 2001 ministerial conference. It intends to create comprehensivedevelopment agenda for trade with minimum barriers. However, decision to include agriculture support mechanism such as MSP with in TFA does not go well down with developing countries.

As WTO rules cap MSP at 10% of total value which is not viable developing countries as they do not have deep pockets like advanced nations. Moreover, such cap also threatens food security of developing countries because they need to procure food grains to redistribute in their poor population.

On this issue India by taking lead for developing countries and successfully negotiated a peace clause for continuation of food subsidy. But India also made a statement in general assembly that all such talks of TFA must be stopped until we do not reach to a permanent solution over public stockholding issue. (210 words)

SOLVED PAPERS

PAPER–III

Time Allowed : Three Hours *Maximum Marks : 250*

Instructions : There are TWENTY questions printed both in English and in Hindi. All tire questions are compulsory. The number of marks carried by a question/part is indicated against it. Answers must be written in the medium authorized in the Admission Certificate which must be stated clearly on the cover of this Question-cum-Answer (QCA) Booklet in the space provided. No marks will be given for answers written in medium other than the authorized one.

Word limit in questions, wherever specified, should be adhered to.

Answer the questions in not more than 200 words each. Contents of the answer is more important than its length. All questions carry equal marks.

Q.1. Normally countries shift from agriculture to industry and then later to services, but India shifted directly from agriculture to services. What are the reasons for the huge growth of services vis-A-vis industry in the country? Can India become a developed country without a strong industrial base?

Important Points for Answer:

- *Agriculture to industry*
- *Agriculture to services*
- *Lack of growth of industry*
- *Growth of services*
- *Assessment*

Answer: In all societies, initial economic activities are related to agriculture which slowly shifts towards mechanization, modernization and industrialization as the economy develops. The next stage is service sector.

However, India has more than 50% of workforce engaged in agriculture sector which produces only 14 percent of the GDP. Currently, service sector contributes about 60% of GDP while manufacturing sector accounts for 26%.

In India, industry sector did not grow due to various factors like lack of infrastructure, transportation, energy and capital investment. Government policies, like stringent labour laws, were also hindrance for industrial growth till 1991. Foreign Investment has also not been attracted to industry sector.

However, due to huge demographic dividend, educated young population shifted towards less capital intensive sectors like IT and related industry, tourism, banking, insurance, medical and other sectors.

As Indian economy is already growth riding at the back of service sector, Governement has taken measures like Make in India, Skill India, Start Up India, to promote manufacturing and industry sector. (Total 165 words)

Q.2. "While we flaunt India's demographic dividend, we ignore the dropping rates of Employability." What are we missing while doing so? Where will the job that India desperately needs come from? Explain.

Important Points for Answer:
- *Demographic dividend*
- *Unemployability*
- *Reasons & Loss*
- *Sources of employment*

Answer: India is a young country with 50 percent of population below age of 25 but productiveness of this available workforce is questionable.

As per a study, only 10% of MBA graduates in India and 17% of engineering graduates are employable. Thus, by 2020, we could have a skill gap of 75-80% across industrial sectors.

The main reason for this low employability is India's education system which does not focus on training students in employable skills. Moreover, link between industries requirement and education curriculum is largely missing. Resultantly, most industries are currently struggling with scarcity of skilled workforce.

National Policy on Skill Development and has set a target for providing skills to 500 million people by 2022. The policy emphasises on providing vocational education and training to the workforce.

Another issue for decreasing employability is direct shift of Indian economy from agriculture to service sector. But, the services sector employs only highly educated people, whereas most of the Indian labour force is comparatively illiterate. Apart from this, agriculture sector is also lagging behind because of limited land and poor technological base.

To revive the manufacturing, government needs to push labor and tax reforms. The recent roll out of GST and labor reforms along with the Make in India initiative are steps in the right direction to reap India's demographic dividend. (220 words)

Q.3. There is also a point of view that Agricultural Produce Market Committees (APMCs) set up under the State Acts have not only impeded the development of agriculture but also have been the cause of food inflation in India. Critically examine.

Important Points for Answer:
- *Problems with APMC*
- *Mention Link between mandis and inflation*
- *Needed Reforms*

Answer: The APMC (Agriculture Produce Marketing Committee) is a mandi set up by the state acts to provide an organized market for farmers to sell their produce in fair and transparent manner.

However, over the years APMC mandis have become counterproductive to their cause and created problems for farmers due to restrictions imposed by APMC Acts.

The farmer fail to realize fair price for their produce because of collusion of middleman and traders in the mandi. Moreover, due to lack of cold storage and transportation facility farmers is in no position to take back their produce or to store it.

Farmers have to bear the cost of transportation and multiple mandi taxes which jack up cost.Apart from that hoarding by traders of commodities like onion creates artificial inflation of food prices. The barriers created by APMC act of states prove hinder in free flow of farm produce compelling farmers to sell their produce on low prices.

Thus, APMC reforms are required including de-listing vegetables and fruits from APMC Act and creating network of E-Mandis as it will give the farmers freedom to sell their products directly to retailers/consumers without the agricultural produce being routed through mandi or middlemen.It will help in bring down food inflation and increase farm income.(213 words)

Q.4. "In the villages itself no form of credit organization will be suitable except the cooperative society." ***—All India Rural Credit Survey***

Discuss this statement in the background of agricultural finance in India. What constraints and challenges do financial institutions supplying agricultural finance face? How can technology be used to better reach and serve rural clients?

Important Points for Answer:
- *Agricultural Finance*
- *Challenges to Agricultural financing*
- *Use of Technology*

Answer: Cooperatives are best financing institutions for small farmers in rural areas. They provide access to competitive credit and inputs sources, manage risks and assess technical assistance and other services. It is the best model for rural finance in India because it saves the farmer from the cost of high interest rates and risk of losing mortgage. Borrowing from non-institutional sources like money lenders and middleman increases risk.

Agricultural financing faces various challenges as even after government efforts like priority sector lending, farm subsidies and expansion of rural bank branches, only five percent of the credit offtake reserved for primary sector is taken by small and marginal farmers. It is due to strict guidelines and norms, such as KYC issued by the banks. And, due to lack of awareness, small farmers are not able to get the loans from the financial institutions such as banks, RRBs or NABARD.

Use of technology in agricultural financing may open up the ways to reach to the poor and rural farmers. Simple mobile enabled technology which can be linked with rural banks can be useful. Multi-lingual apps can facilitate the process. All these efforts will result in making agriculture sector productive to harness India's demographic dividend. (204 words)

Q.5. The Right to Fair Compensation and Transparency in Land Acquisition, Rehabilitation and Resettlement Act, 2013 has come into effect from 1st January, 2014. What are the key issues which would get addressed with the Act in place? What implications would it have on industrialization and agriculture in India?

> **Important Points for Answer:**
> - *Main Features of the Act*
> - *Main issues address*
> - *Implications on agriculture and industrialisation*

Answer: The acquisition of land in India is governed by LARR Act, 2013. Lack of transparency and allegation of corruption reduces confidence of people to give their land.

The new act has the following features:

- Higher compensation of four times the market value in rural areas and two times of the market value in urban areas.
- Consent of 70 percent affected people in for PPP projects and 80 percent in private project.
- Mandatory Social Impact Assessment for affected population with remedial measures for rehabilitation and resettlement.

Implications of the act on agriculture and industrialization in India:

(a) It will provide an efficient mechanism in resolving the conflicts between the community and industries on lower compensation.

(b) The large scale agricultural land acquisitions will have a negative effect on the agricultural development because of the absence of the clause, that only non-agricultural land can be acquired for projects.

(c) Absence of clear cut policy for returning the unused land would seriously harm the land resources and also affects the food security negatively.

(d) Private industries fear delay in projects because of mandatory Social Impact Assessment and 80% consent requirements.

(e) The act might affect the manufacturing industries in a significant manner as these units require large land and acquiring such large amount of might be a problem. (216 words)

Q.6. Capitalism has guided the world economy to unprecedented prosperity. However, it often encourages short-sightedness and contributes to wide disparities between the rich and the poor? In this light, would it be correct to believe and adopt capitalism for bringing inclusive growth in India? Discuss.

> **Important Points for Answer:**
> - *Capitalism*
> - *Benefits of capitalism*
> - *Limitations of capitalism*
> - *Relevance in bringing inclusive growth in India*

Answer: Capitalism is an economic system in which means of production are largely or entirely in private hands. Historically, capitalism has been one of the most successful economic system, but at times it also breeds inequality, repression of workers and concentration of wealth in few hands. Labour revolutions are result of such capitalism which has neglected social and moral aspects of society and concentrated only on profit making.

As India strives to become an economic giant in the world wherecapitalism and globalization remain the two important drivers.India need to create a free market to shoot up its growth but it must be the inclusive growth.The business environment in India is changing, allowing entrepreneurial spirit to flourish. This trend is reflected in corporate profit and wages relative to GDP.

With effective and rational regulations and fair competition, capitalism can bring fast and inclusive growth in India. Measures like corporate social responsibilitygive a welfare face to capitalism in India.

Overall, in India the meaning of capitalism should not be absence of regulations over industries but to provide mechanism to facilitate industries to function for benefits of workers as well as to ensure environmental sustainability.(195 word)

Q.7. Explain how Private Public Partnership arrangements, in long gestation infrastructure projects, can transfer unsustainable liabilities to the future. What arrangements need to be put in place to ensure that successive generations' capacities are not compromised?

Important Points for Answer:
- *What is PPP?*
- *Burden on future*
- *Needed reforms*

Answer: Private Public Partnership arrangements (PPP) as defined by government of India is an agreement where public sector entity (sponsored authority) and a private sector entity collaborate to manage or create a public infrastructure project.

These projects often have long gestation with limited scope of renegotiation along with other issues like project becoming unviable for private firm, issues in land acquisition, delay in environmental clearance, etc.

Moreover, in majority of cases the project is financed by a public sector bank and failure of project creates problem of non performing assets.

Accordingly, urgent PPP reforms are suggested:

- Timing and cost of the project should be assessed and fixed in more transparent manner with well defined penalties in case of delay of project.
- The model should be prepared with assessment of future conditions in mind.
- Risk-sharing model should be more comprehensive and critical issues should be addressed with future reference in mind.
- PPP policy should focus on creating investor friendly atmosphere so that finance is available to finish project on time.

- New investment options like sovereign bonds must be introduced.

India needs infrastructure to boost her economic growth and rolling out PPP project is the best option to reduce infrastructure crunch, thus prompt reforms must be taken. (205 words)

Q.8. National Urban Transport Policy emphasises on 'moving people' instead of 'moving vehicles'. Discuss critically the success of the various strategies of the Government in this regard.

Important Points for Answer:
- *National Urban Transport Policy*
- *Measures*
- *Strategies*
- *Success*

Answer: With a vision to create sustainable cities, government has come up with the National Urban Transport Policy(NUTP) in 2014.The policy aims to move people rather than vehicles by taking the following steps:

- To allocate more road space for public vehicles
- Introduction of Bus Rapid Transit (BRT) system
- Integration of land use and transportation planning

Moreover, the government has, under the NUTP, required that cities must comply with the new NUTP to have access to JNNURM funds for city development. Now, each city must come up with a City Mobility Plan to guide future growth of transportation in cities.In addition to that, the Government has also initiated the Sustainable Urban Transport Project in partnership with Global Environment Facility, World Bank and UNDP.

Government has initiated Sustainable Urban Transport Project (SUTP) with the support of Global Environment Facility (GEF) and the World Bank.

However, even while government is trying to encourage people to use public transport but, with exception of a few cities, people still prefer private vehicles. As people find issues with availability, condition of public vehicles and dissatisfactory safety arrangements in public transport.

Thus public transportation needs more improvement but cooperation and support of city dwellers is also required to turn cities into engine of growth.(Total 209 words)

Q.9. Foreign Direct Investment (FDI) in the defence sector is now set to be liberalized. What influence this is expected to have on Indian defence and economy in the short and long run?

Important Points for Answer:
- *FDI in defence manufacturing*
- *Influence of liberalised FDI in defence*

Answer: India, the largest importer of defence equipment, has recently liberalised FDI norms in defence sector with 49% investment allowed under direct route and 100% investment allowed in special cases where sensitive technology would be brought in.

This is a very critical step to boost up India's defence manufacturing sector, which till now remains untapped due to the strict regulations. Easing up FDI would positively affect the defence sector and Indian economy in various ways.

In the short term, the defence sector will attract much needed capital from both foreign as well as Indian investors. Now with liberalised FDI India, defence sector will have access to state of the art technology through transfer of technology arrangement. It will keep Indian defence forces up to date and reduce cost of import of military equipment.

In long term, the liberalised FDI policy will save precious FOREX of India and will help in strengthening Indian rupee. Over the time India could turn from defence equipment importer to exporter. Additional employment opportunities will be created at defence manufacturing units. With arrival of private defence manufacturers, DRDO will be able to increase its capability and performance to remain in competition.

If explored carefully and utilised properly, the FDI measures can bring India enormous benefits for her economy as well as defence.(Total 215 words)

Q.10. Scientific research in Indian universities is declining, because a career in science is not as attractive as are business professions, engineering or administration, and the universities are becoming consumer-oriented. Critically comment.

Important Points for Answer:
- *Situation of research in India*
- *Reasons for the dismal picture*
- *Importance of research and way forward*

Answer: One of the important task of universities is to perform research over the important needs of society with changing times. However, India spends less than 1% of its GDP in R&D, while China as well as some other nations spend around 5% of their GDP on research. The primary issue for this peculiar position is the flawed policy framework which do not provide enough opportunities for students to pursue research.

Research in science requires huge supporting facilities such as laboratories, equipment and finances. But due to lack of government encouragement and funding, universities are not able to provide the same. Therefore, students do not get opportunities to conduct and carry on science research. Therefore, universities provide demand based education.

Similarly, as mostly Indian students come from middle class, without adequate government support, they tend to go in field which provides adequate and immediate financial benefits.

Further, Government and big universities has failed to make young populace aware about the importance of research which makes them to go for engineering, management, banking, etc. rather than towards research.

Other avenues are giving profitable careers than science research. Poor IPR regime also leads to patent violation of scientific research. It discourages students to invest valuable time in invention and R&D in science. (Total 211 words)

Q.11. Can overuse and free availability of antibiotics without Doctor's prescription, be contributors to the emergence of drug-resistant diseases in India? What are the available mechanisms for monitoring and control? Critically discuss the various issues involved.

Important Points for Answer:
- *Antibiotics-overuse*
- *Problems*
- *Drug Resistance*
- *Monitoring and Control*

Answer: An antibiotic is a bio-chemical agent that kills or inhibits the growth of microbes. However, its frequent and inappropriate use can develop resistance in microbes such as NDM1, XDR-TB, MDR-TB and I TDR-TB.

In India, the problem is very serious because of popular use of self medication, over the counter sale of antibiotics and presence of quacks.In addition that antibiotics fed to poultry and mulched animals also contribute in creating drug resistant bacteria strain.

Available mechanism to control this menace are:

Over the counter sale of antibiotics should be restricted and sale of drugs without doctors prescription must be banned by enforcing available regulations.

Awareness campaign for reduced use of antibiotics must be started in an aggressive mode.

People must be made aware of importance of keeping hygiene around themselves. It would reduce bacterial spread.Swacth Baharat mission is a good step in this direction.

Various livestock farms and hospital units should be monitored carefully so that overuse of antibiotics can be controlled.

Advance antibiotics must be used on line with the directions of WHO.

India has already started her fight against anti-microbial infection with Chennai Declaration and „RED LINE CAMPAIGN". (Total 197 words)

Q.12. In a globalized world, Intellectual Property Rights assume significance and are a source of litigation. Broadly distinguish between the terms—Copyrights, Patents and Trade Secrets.

Important Points for Answer:
- *Intellectual Property Right*
- *Significance and Litigations*
- *Distinguish—Copyrights, Patents and Trade Secrets.*

Answer: Intellectual Property Right is a legal right granted to protect a form of intellectual property for example, a patent right, design right, trademark right or a copyright. The right is accorded to a creative work, invention or design, if it is an original work of a person. The same being intangible property is susceptible to theft and commercial misuse to the disadvantage of the owner. Therefore, it has become a source of litigation in the globalised work.

These terms - Copyrights, Patents and Trade Secrets can be differentiated on the basis of type, requirement, period and need of registration.

Patent: Patent grants exclusive rights for the production, sale and profit from the invention. It is usually granted for 15-20 years. And needs compulsory registration in original country.

Copyright: Legal right granted to an author, composer, playwright, publisher or distributor to exclusive publication, production, sale or distribution of literary, musical, dramatic or artistic work. It is based on originality and wide utility and granted for different period in different type of works. Its infringement is very common.

Trade Secret: It is a form of industrial property which refers to a non-patented process, mechanism or formula, known only to its owner that is used in producing something of commercial value. It involves something confidential. It also does not grant any legal rights.(Total 221 words)

Q.13. Should the pursuit of carbon credits and clean development mechanisms set up under UNFCCC be maintained even though there has been a massive slide in the value of a carbon credit? Discuss with respect to India's energy needs for economic growth.

Important Points for Answer:
- *Carbon credit*
- *Reason for decline in prices*
- *India's Position*
- *Way Forward*

Answer: A carbon credit is a generic term for any tradable certificate or permit representing the right to emit one tonne of carbon dioxide or the mass of another greenhouse gas equivalentto one tonne of carbon dioxide.

In recent times, because of the following reasons, carbon credit prices took a slump:

- Over supply of carbon credits.
- Speculation about ban of carbon credits in European Union system.
- Recession resulted reduced production, hence, reduced demand of carbon credits.
- Non-materialisation of KYOTO protocol also discouraged businesses to adopt clean energy.

India along with other developing countries is a major seller of carbon credits and reduced prices are hurting India. Moreover, energy needs of India is increasing given to her expanding urbanisation and rising living standards. In this scenario continued pursuit of carbon credit may have long term investments in power plants, which would be very negative in the context of Indian energy needs.

However, the concept of carbon credit is for reducing green house gases, pollutants and having replaceable clean environment to compensate the industrial growth. Any shift from cleaner practice, only because of reduced prices and non following of carbon credit, would harm environment. India being a developing and energy hungry economy, addition in pollutant would harm in long term as expenditure in health sector would be costlier. (Total 217 words).

Q.14.Drought has been recognized as a disaster in view of its spatial expanse, temporal duration, slow onset and lasting effects on vulnerable sections. With a focus on the September 2010 guidelines from the National Disaster Management Authority (NDMA), discuss the mechanisms for preparedness to deal with likely El Nino and La Nina fallouts in India.

Important Points for Answer:
- *Droughts*
- *El Nino, La Nina, Indian monsoon*
- *Guidelines and their implemention*

Answer: Droughts is a condition of water stress. It can be caused due non-availability of water or mismanagement of water. India with over 40 percent rain fed agriculture area is very much prone to droughts almost every year.

Since El Nino and Indian Monsoon are inversely related, so during the El Nino years, monsoon have generally been poor in India. While La Nina usually results in better than normal monsoon in India.

In response to this condition, National Disaster Management Authority(NDMA) issued guidelines in 2010 on the management of drought, so that the consequences of drought can be minimized. The guidelines include establishment of India Drought Management Centre as well as Separate Drought Monitoring Cells at the State level, who will work under the control of the respective State Governments.

The other important guidelines suggest that when the monsoon is good, i.e. during the La Nina period, promoting conservation of water with rainwater harvesting, promoting watershed approach, and use of remote sensing to determine crop water needs can be practiced.

Establishment and maintenance of transportation links to ensure regular supply of food and other essentials. Increased insurance coverage for crops as well as livestock. Implementation of works under MNREGA should also be priortised. Delineation of drought prone areas is also necessary for effective mitigation and targeted response.(219 words)

Q.15. Environmental Impact Assessment studies are increasingly undertaken before a project is cleared by the Government. Discuss the environmental impacts of coal-fired thermal plants located at coal pitheads.

Important Points for Answer:
- *Environment Impact Assessment (EIA)*
- *EIA of coal fired thermal plants*

Environmental Impact Assessment (EIA) is a process of evaluating the likely environmental impacts of a proposed project or development, taking into account inter-related socio-economic, cultural and human-health impacts.

However, in case of coal mining and coal based power plants, EIA is recently started and still a rare phenomenon. Resultantly, coal based thermal power plants continues to create problems. Moreover, it becomes local problem for coal bearing areas as maximum coal based power plants are located at coal pitheads to avoid transportation costs.

Coal based thermal power plants create heavy air pollution in surrounding areas. It contributes to 20 per cent of greenhouse gas emissions.

- Most of the coal bearing areas in India are situated in the place with thick forests, hence its exploitation would have adverse impact of deforestation combined with pollution.
- The dumping of coal slurry pollutes local land and water resources by heavy metals like boron.
- Further, the natural soil near coal pitheads becomes more alkaline due to fly-ash, thereby damaging the agriculture in the surrounding region.
- Thus, EIA should be made compulsory for both existing and newly planned thermal power plants.Effective ash usage policy and strengthened monitoring by regulators will go in a long way to reduce this localised pollution with global effect. (Total 211 words)

Q.16. "The diverse nature of India as a multi-religious and multi-ethnic society is not immune tothe impact of radicalism which is seen in her neighbourhood." Discuss along with strategies to be adopted to counter this environment.

Important Points for Answer:
- *Radicalism*
- *Radicalisation in neighbouring countries*
- *India's vulnerability*
- *Measures needs*

Answer: Radicalisation is the process by which individuals, usually young people, are introduced to an overtly ideological message and belief system that encourages movement from moderate, mainstream beliefs towards extreme views.

Radicalism has become a primary threat in neighbouring areas of Pakistan, Iran, Iraq, etc.,due to rise of Islamic groups like ISIS and Al Qaeda.

India is also not completely immune from radicalisation due to various reasons including diverse population and different religions. There are poverty and illiteracy to add to the vulnerabilities. Possible religious extremism and dissatisfaction towards the governance system may also result into radicalism in India. Multi religious society has many fractured lines on religious grounds which can be exploited by domestic and external factors. Similarly, ethnicity has, on occasions, created tension among various parts of india, thus, creating a risk of radicalism.

Therefore, India needs to adopt effective strategy to counter radicalization. It includes various steps like:

Firstly, terrorism must be controlled and uprooted from India.

Secondly, intelligence network need to be strengthened and law and order situation must be closely monitored in critical areas.

Thirdly, India needs to remain vigilant against cyber indoctrination which is a preferred method for spreading terrors by the extremists.(Total 199 words)

Q.17. International civil aviation laws provide all countries complete and exclusive sovereignty over the airspace above their territory. What do you understand by 'airspace'? What are the implications of these laws on the space above this airspace? Discuss the challenges which this poses and suggest ways to contain the threat.

Important Points for Answer:
- *Airspace*
- *Laws which guides air space*
- *Challenges and ways*

Answers: Airspace, in international law, is the space above a particular national territory, treated as belonging to the government controlling the territory. Sovereignty of a nation includes territorial waters but excludes outer space.

It may be categorised as :

(a) Controlled airspace: it exists where it is deemed necessary, that air traffic control has some form of positive executive control over aircraft flying in that airspace.

(b) Uncontrolled airspace: is airspace in which air traffic control does not exert any executive authority, although it may act in an advisory manner

This exclusion of outer space remains a very serious issue. As there is no single definition of vertical extent of air space. And in every country, there is a different limitation,eg USA considers 100 km limitation of outer space.

In present technological advanced era, this loophole provides space for militarisation of outer space. Technically advanced countries can place weapons vertically over another country by claiming it as free zone outside airspace of target country. This uncontrolled outer space may create existential threat to a nation.

Thus now its high time for countries and international organizations to take up this issue and declare outer space as no weapon zone on the line of Antarctica for sake of whole humanity.(Total 207 words)

Q.18. How does illegal transborder migration pose a threat to India's security? Discuss the strategies to curb this, bringing out the factors which give impetus to such migration.

Important Points for Answer:
- *Transborder migration*
- *Impact on India's security*
- *Strategy*

Answer: Open, porous and non demarcation of eastern borders of India creates a conducive environment for illegal immigrants to sneak in towards India. This has become a major issue in states of North-East especially Assam.

Lack of job oppurtunities in home countries and better opportunities in India, threat of persecution, etc., drive people out of their country. Recent Rohingya crisis is result of such exodus.

This illegal immigration poses numerous threats to country's security:

It creates pressure over scarce resources which leads to conflict and violence.

Illegal border crossing is disturbing regional demographics,resulting into mass clashes with the local residents.

Migrants have also promoted anti-national extremism in border states.

Terrorist also use Trans-border illegal migration to get into Indian borders.

Fake currency and drugs smuggled into the Indian territory with help of illegal migrants.

Even flesh trading is being reported.

Some of the suggested strategies to curb illegal migration are:

Use of unique identification methods like UIDAI to weed out illegal migrants.

Better border management practices like fencing, introduction of floating barriers etc will help in reducing flow of illegal migrants.

Use of diplomacy to pursue neighbouring countries to stop illegal migration and take back those which are illegally living in India.

Moreover, it should be communicated that any threat to Indian security will be dealt stringently. (220 words)

Q.19. In 2012, the longitudinal marking for high-risk areas for piracy was 65 degrees east to 78 degrees east in the Arabian Sea by the Int Maritime Organization. What impact does this have on India's security concerns?

Important Points for Answer:
- *Explain reasons of change*
- *Highlight impacts it have on India's maritime security.*

Answer: Indian ocean remained vulnerable to piracy especially on Somalia coast but sometimes piracy incidents extend upto Lakshdweep. International Maritime Organization and the Contact Group on Piracy Off the Coast o (CGPCS) decided to move the longitudinal marking of the high risk area in Arabian Sea from 65° to 78° east.

This decision of IMO is having following implication on India:

Now merchant vessels can have armed guards while sailing close to Indian shores. Thus it can create situation like enrica lexica where two Italian marines shot Indian fisherman.

Moreover, insurance has become 300 times more expensive for Indian ships because they have to sail into high risk zones.This makes shipping costly which makes imports expensive and exports uncompetitive for Indian traders.

Along with that, navigation of international ships creates hindrance in Indian coastal traffic.

This action creates a serious issue for India's maritime trade as well as its national security.

It will also deviate ships to other routes, which may create loss to Indian industry as availability of ships will be reduced.

Due these issues along with the fact that piracy is coming down,India has been demanding rollback of this international regulation.(194 words)

Q.20. China and Pakistan have entered into an agreement for development of an economic corridor. What threat does this pose for India's security? Critically examine.

Important Points for Answer:
- *China Pakistan Economic Corridor (CPEC)*
- *Strategic importance*
- *Threats to India*

Answer: China-Pakistan Economic Corridor (CPEC) is a network of railways, roads and pipeline which connects Xinjiang province of China to Gwadar port of Pakistan located in Persian gulf of Indian ocean.

Though China sells the project as an economic project but its strategic importance is much more than its economic importance. The project has direct security and strategic implications for India.

Firstly, the projects runs through POK and Aksai Chin areas which are de jure Indian territories, thus, infringes India's territorial integrity.

Secondly, the presence of Chinese troops near construction site have military implications for India.

Thirdly, this multi model project provides improved connectivity to Indian borders which could be used by Pakistan based terrorist groups to harm India.

Strategically, presence of Chinese in Persian Gulf undermines India's security in that area. Resultantly, India's energy security becomes vulnerable, since India's oil imports pass through Persian Gulf.

However, on a positive note, the corridor can bring stability and jobs for Pakistani youth which is good news for India as it will make harder for terrorist group to hire youth.

Overall India must take a cautious approach while dealing with issue of this China Pakistan Economic Corridor on the ground of violation of its sovereignty as it passes through Indian territory. (Total 209 words)

SOLVED PAPERS

PAPER–IV

Time Allowed : Three Hours *Maximum Marks : 250*

Instructions : There are FOURTEEN questions divided in two Sections and printed both in Hindi and in English. All questions are compulsory. The number of marks carried by a question/part is indicated against it. Word limit in questions, wherever specified, should be adhered to. Any page of portion of the page left blank in the Question-cum-Answer Booklet must be clearly struck off.

Answer questions in NOT MORE than the word limit specified for each in the parenthesis. Content of the answer is more important than its length.

Section–A

Q.1. (a) All human beings aspire for happiness. Do you agree? What does happiness mean to you? Explain with examples. (150 words) 10

Answer: Pursuit of Happiness has been enlisted as the most important goal of human life. It has been established for millennia that happiness brings all good to a person. Therefore, without doubt, all human being aspire for happiness.

However, happiness means different to different people. For a person who loves to paint, he may derive happiness by painting. A sport lover may be happy when he watches or plays sport. Person becomes happy at success and sad at failure.

To me, happiness is a feeling of success and satisfaction in a field. It may be due to my volition or on its own. For example, if I am preparing for an exam, success and satisfactory grade in that exam is a matter of happiness. When I would be reading a book that I like, I would derive happiness from reading. Similarly, when my family and friends are happy, healthy, successful and satisfied, it becomes a cause of happiness for me. (Total 159 words)

(b) What does ethics seek to promote in human life? Why is it all the more important in public administration? (150 words) 10

Answer: Ethics is a system of moral principles. They affect how people make decisions and lead their lives and help them to do what is good for society and other individuals.

Honesty, uprightness, empathy, impartiality, accountability, etc., are some qualities of an ethical person.

Ethics is more important in public administration because a public servant has to deal with power, and as rightly said by Gandhiji that power can corrupt a human being and only an honest and upright person can use his power for public welfare.

Moreover, at times a public servant finds himself in dilemmas between his personal and public duties, e.g. accepting a transfer which can negatively affect his family.

Apart from that, a public servant has to remain unbiased and courageous at times when he is being pressured from outside forces.

Therefore, a public servant cannot serve his purpose without being ethical and this makes ethics indispensable in public administration. Thus, a public servant must always strive to remain ethical. (Total 164 words)

Q.2. (a) In the context of defence services, 'patriotism' demands readiness to even lay down one's life in protecting the nation. According to you, what does patriotism imply in everyday civil life? Explain with illustrations and justify your answer. (150 words) 10

Answer: (a) Patriotism is natural love and attachment a person has for one's country, it reflects a cultural connect and sense of duty for working towards betterment of one's country.

The patriotism of a soldier reflects from the fact that he/she always ready for supreme sacrifice and spend their youthful years in hostile terrain so that country remains safe.

But in civil life also a person can be patriotic by doing right things and by avoidingindulgence in selfish and evil things. A person should do all his civil duties by being aware ofthe constitutional spirit, casting vote in elections, taking pledge to not to litter in public places, paying taxes on time and by protecting our natural as well as cultural heritage.

Moreover, a person should never indulge in black marketing, hoarding, tax evasion,etc. But on the contrary, a patriotic person should always be ready to take up fight against people indulging in such activities. (Total 157 words)

(b) What do you understand by 'probity' in public life? What are the difficulties in practicing it in the present times? How can these difficulties be overcome? (150 words) 10

Answer: (b) Probity is the quality of having strong moral principles; honesty and decency. It involves practising values like integrity, uprightness, honesty and remain transparent and accountable.

Public servants are expected to maintain probity while performing their duties. Where probity is missing, corruption breeds.Public servants are beholders of public trust and public funds, they shall remain incorruptible.

However, practicing probity is becoming harder every day because of the following reasons:

(a) High headedness of public servants as noticed by second ARC.

(b) Decreasing moral values among politicians.

(c) Low awareness among public about their rights giving chance to public servants and representatives to remain apathetic about public needs.

(d) General decline in morality in public life makes it harder even for honest people to practice probity.

To overcome this difficulty, a person should always strive for probity on own end. Moral education and awareness can also increase probity in public life. When whole world is silent even one voice can make difference. (Total 157 words)

Q.3.(a) "Integrity without knowledge is weak and useless, but knowledge without integrity is dangerous and dreadful." What do you understand by this statement? Explain your stand with illustrations from the modern context (150 words) 10

Answer: (a) The above quote is stated by Samuel Johnson. It presents a very true relation between integrity and knowledge and how they are almost worthless without one another.

As a person with integrity and without knowledge cannot produce and contribute to society even if he intends. Similarly, a person who has knowledge without integrity will end up producing undesirable results for himself and society.

Moreover, integrity requires accuracy in one's action and behaviour, but without knowledge desired accuracy is impossible to achieve.

Similarly, a person with knowledge and no integrity becomes dangerous for society as they can hit bulls eye while making harm to society. For example, a terrorist uses his knowledge of chemicals to produce a bomb, in this case the more he is accurate the more dangerous he becomes.

Thus, knowledge and integrity are balancing wheels of the same cart. One shows the right path and other provides willingness to take that path. (Total 154 words)

(b) "Human beings should always be treated as 'ends' in themselves and never as merely 'means'." Explain the meaning and significance of this statement, giving its implications in the modern techno-economic society. (150 words)

Answer: (b) The above statement highlights the philosophy given by Kant, where he highlights the fact that every person is independent being with own goals, respect, integrity and he must be treated in this way by others also. That is, no person shall be used by another person like a tool to serve a purpose. But every person must be respected for one's intrinsic value as a human.

However, in present society where materialism is at its peak, people now value a person based on what he has and how other person can serve my purpose. This kind of behaviour is breeding greed and selfishness in society, which in turn is weakening our social fabric.

In this situation, the mentioned statement can serve as torchlight to guide our path towards harmonious society, where we value and respect every living being including nature. Moreover, by adhering to this principle, every person will get chance to show their talent and grow as a person, which will make world altogether a better place. (Total 168 words)

4. (a) Which eminent personality has inspired you the most in the context of ethical conduct in life? Give the gist of his/her teachings. Giving specific examples, describe how you have been able to apply these teachings for your own ethical development. (150 words) 10

Answer: (a) Swami Vivekananda, is a great personality who has inspired and guided me to behave in ethical manner. His teachings about service, love, humanity and religion have deeply inspired me.

As through his teaching that "service to man is service to god" I came to know about true meaning of service. Moreover, Swamiji has inspired me, by making me aware of my weaknesses and guided me to get rid of them because swamiji believed one should not be weak as weakness is a sin.

Swamiji was a rationalist, thus rather than presenting supernatural image of god, he introduced world to true meaning of Vedanta and its philosophy which guides the humanity towards love and unity.

Most importantly, as a civil service aspirant, Vivekananda helped me in understanding my duty towards downtrodden, making me realise that we all are one i.e Parmatan and until we all are not happy everyone remains miserable.

Lastly, Swamiji was true patriot which reflects in Rabindranath Tagore's comment "If you want to know India, Study Vivekananda". (Total 170 words)

(b) There is a heavy ethical responsibility on the public servants because they occupy positions of power, handle huge amounts of public funds, and their decisions have wide-ranging impact on society and environment. What steps have you taken to improve your ethical competence to handle such responsibility? (150 words) 10

Answer: (b) Public servants in India enjoy wide discretionary power, they have been granted to use it for public welfare. In this process, they not only have to take care of public funds but also have responsibility to preserve the faith public bestowed on them to take decisions which affect their lives.

Thus, a public servant has to remain ethical in his/her conduct, for this, I have taken following steps to improve my ethical competence:

(a) I maintain integrity in my conduct.

(b) I am always ready to be held accountable for my actions.

(c) I try to remain honest in my public as well as private life.

(d) I try to remain conscious and empathetic about problems of others.

(e) I try to avoid conflict of interest.

(f) I do not use public resources for personal gains.

(g) I respect my colleagues and try to be aware about public needs. (Total 150 words)

Q.5. (a) The current society is plagued with widespread trust-deficit. What are the consequences of this situation for personal well-being and for societal well - being? What can you do at the personal level to make yourself trustworthy? (150 words) 10

Answer: (a) Trustworthiness, is one of the most essential and novel quality of human being. As trust makes a society work by making people believe on each other. However, sadly in present materialistic world, people lack belief on one another.

This is the result of decreasing moral values like brotherhood, selflessness, love and replacement of these values vices like enmity, jealousy, selfishness and lust. Resultantly, the social fabric is being torn apart, which does not only affect our personal sphere but also our professional sphere. As trust is the most basic need of doing business, trust deficit is also harming our economy.

Reducing trust propel fear in minds of people which is not good for an individual, as a fearful person can never achieve full potential. Trust deficit between government and citizens results into corruption. This is weakening our democracy.

To make myself trustworthy, I will always remain truthful and honest so that we can create a harmonious society based on trust. (Total 160 words)

(b) It is often said that poverty leads to corruption. However, there is no dearth of instances where affluent and powerful people indulge in corruption in a big way. What are the basic causes of corruption among people? Support your answer with examples. (150 words) 10

Answer: (b) The notion that poverty breeds corruption is entirely wrong because it is the greed and absence of morality which propels corruption.

Corruption in public sphere means using public resources and position for private gains. Moreover, the scope of corruption increases with increase of power and position. Thus, poverty has no connection with corruption.

Further, some specific breeders for corruption are:

(a) Lack of transparency in system which acts as shield for corrupt people. i.e. if there is no information about government scheme, babus can demand bribe.

(b) Lack of punitive measures provide confidence to people indulging in corruption.

(c) Instability in government also provides chance for corruption by floor changing.

(d) Personal desire for unfair advantage push individuals in indulging in embezzlement, bribery and nepotism.

(e) Unfair incentive structure and lack of job security encourage people to make money by corrupt means.

But such acts are inexcusable, because corruption makes country hollow,they should be condemned at every level and in every situation. (Total 164 words)

Q.6. What factors affect the formation of a person's attitude towards social problems? In our society, contrasting attitudes are prevalent about many social problems. What contrasting attitudes do you notice about the caste system in our society? How do you explain the existence of these contrasting attitudes? (150 words) 10

Answer: The pre-determined behaviour or reaction of a person toward another person, thing or situation is known as attitude. The attitude of a person is shaped by various factors like upbringing, prevailing condition in society and personal experience throughout the life.

Caste system divides our society in different strata (jatis).

However, we can notice contrasting attitude in our society for caste system because of the following factors:

(a) People who belongs to forward castes in urban areas are educated because of the opportunities they got by virtue of their caste. People from these castes now support merit based system and caste boundaries in these people are now starting to blur.

(b) Whereas forward castes of villages want the strict stratification as this will allow them to maintain their hegemony.

(c) On the contrary, now people from backward class want to maintain caste system as it provides benefits through affirmative actions.

With increasing education level the caste system is waning but still there is long way to go to make India a casteless society. (Total 170 words)

Q.7. What does 'accountability' mean in the context of public service? What measures can be adopted to ensure individual and collective accountability of public servants? (150 words)

Answer: Accountability in public service means taking responsibility of one's action and decision and being responsive to the needs of entity from which public servant derives authority.

A public official has to remain transparent and answerable to maintain accountability. One of the most important aspect of accountability is to make information assessable to public so that public can remain aware and public trust could be created.

Moreover, following mechanisms can be followed to ensure accountability of public servants:

(a) In every department, internal accountability mechanism should be placed.

(b) RTI act must be strengthened, public disclosure should be encouraged.

(c) Good work culture should be created by making every member of organization aware about goals of organization.

(d) Role of every person in hierarchy must be clearly defined.

(e) Lokpal should be made functional.

(f) Fast track courts must be set up for speedy disposal of the cases related to corruption.

(g) System of check and balance must be established in every department, so that corruption can be stopped. (Total 168 words)

Q.8. We are witnessing increasing instances of sexual violence against women in the country. Despite existing legal provisions against it, the number of incidences is on the rise. Suggest some innovative measures to tackle menace. (150 words)

Answer: It is disheartening that even after 70 years of independence females remain unsafe in our society. The main problem is deep rooted patriarchal mind set which is impending our country in achieving her full potential.

Some suggestions for creating a safer environment for woman are mentioned below:

(a) India must ratify all global and regional treaties which concerns safety women. It will increase pressure on government to take this matter at utmost priority.

(b) Women helplines should be made operational round the clock. New mechanisms like Himmat app of Delhi police is a welcome step.

(c) Women must be financially empowered by providing necessary education, skills as well as financial support for starting business.

(d) Specialized fast track courts should be set up to punish perpetuators and provide sense of closure to violence survivor women.

(e) Police stations must be made gender sensitive.

Finally, awareness about equal rights of women in society is must. It is not only responsibility of government and police but is everyone's responsibility to create a safe environment for women. (Total 174 words)

Section–B

In the following questions, carefully study the cases presented and then answer the questions that follow.

Q.9. Now-a-days, there is an increasing thrust on economic development all around the globe. At the same time, there is also an increasing concern about environmental degradation caused by development. Many a time, we face a direct conflict between developmental activity and environmental quality. It is neither feasible to stop or curtail the developmental process, nor it is advisable to keep degrading the environment, as it threatens our very survival.

Discuss some feasible strategies which could be adopted to eliminate this conflict and which could lead to sustainable development. (250 words) 20

Answer: Development and environmental protection should go hand in hand. There are countries which have maintained this balance. Scandinavian countries have promoted technology and industry but at the sometime not damaged their environment.

We need to take a proper estimation of the proposed project for development. Environmental Impact Assessment should be taken very seriously and pros and cons of a project should be weighed in appropriate balance. Only if the resulting benefits are much greater than environmental degradation, the project should be implemented.

Every project should remedied the nature more than it harms. Therefore an environmental fund should be created by each company and that should be used to create green cover, promote efficient and green technology as well as protect other aspects of environment.

Government can make provisions for tax benefits for taking care of environment and penalty for violating rules related to protection of it.

As far as possible, we should use alternative sources of energy for new industries. Alternatives to a proposed project should always be explored and only that option which is most suitable to conservation of environment should be permitted for implementation.

Green Fund should be created, promoted and used for giving funding and subsidies to environment friendly technology, innovations and projects.

Environmental should not be taken for granted by any government or corporate bodies if we want to maintain proper balance in our economic growth and sustainable development.

We have already damaged environment beyond repair. Any further damage will make us vulnerable. Therefore, we need to implement our environmental laws very strictly. (Total 257 words)

Q.10. Suppose one of your close friends, who is also aspiring for civil services, comes to you for discussing some of the issues related to ethical conduct in public service.

He raises the following points:

(i) In the present times, when unethical environment is quite prevalent, individual attempts to stick to ethical principles may cause a lot of problems in one's career. It may also cause hardship to the family members as well as risk to one's life. Why should we not be pragmatic and follow the path of least resistance, and be happy with doing whatever good we can?

(ii) When so many people are adopting wrong means and are grossly harming the system, what difference would it make if only a small minority tries to be ethical? They are going to be rather ineffective and are bound to get frustrated.

(iii) If we become fussy about ethical considerations, will it not hamper the economic progress of our country? After all, in the present age of high competition, we cannot afford to be left behind in the race of development.

(iv) It is understandable that we should not get involved in grossly unethical practices, but giving and accepting small gratifications and doing small favours increases everybody's motivation. It also makes the system more efficient. What is wrong in adopting such practices?

Critically analyse the above viewpoints. On the basis of this analysis, what will be your advice to your friend?20

Answer: (i) The person who follows the path of least resistance will remain ethical but whenever situation comes, he would also take advantage or bend for the progress of career and personal interest. Such person has no personal moral, ethical code or virtue. He is no different from others. I would not follow this advise and would not advise my friend to follow this option.

(ii) People who are adopting unethical path cannot be compared with minority who follows ethics. Numbers do not matter but conduct matters. This minority is an example for new entrant in civil services. They should continue to follow their standards. There is no frustration as they know their path is correct. Their career and personal satisfaction are completely independent of each other.

(iii) There is no reason that a country cannot achieve economic progress by following ethical means. For example, if a tender is floated, it can be passed with full ethical way, without compromising with requirements. It will just not benefit some corrupt officers and contractors. But the system will certainly be benefited by it. Therefore, adopting to ethical ways does not mean remaining behind in economic growth.

(iv) Any officer who compromises his integrity once, is susceptible to frequent compromising. It would lead to unethical behaviour and there will be no reason for him to differentiate between small gratification and large scale corruption. Secondly, there is no reason to believe that such practice will improve the system.

Therefore, my advice to the friend would be to remain upright ethical and never compromise with Code of conduct and integrity for whatever reason. (Total 266 words)

Q.11. You are a no-nonsense, honest officer. You have been transferred to a remote district to head a department that is notorious for its inefficiency and callousness. You find that the main cause of the poor state of affairs is the indiscipline of a section of employees. They do

not work themselves and also disrupt the work of others. You first warned the troublemakers to mend their ways or else face disciplinary action. When the warning had little effect, you issued a show cause notice to the ringleaders. As a retaliatory measure, these troublemakers instigate a woman employee amongst them to file a complaint of sexual harassment against you with the Women's Commission. The Commission promptly seeks your explanation. The matter is also publicised in the media to embarrass you further. Some of the options to handle this situation could be as follows:

(i) Give your explanation to the Commission and go soft on the disciplinary action.

(ii) Ignore the Commission and proceed firmly with the disciplinary action.

(iii) Brief your higher-ups, seek directions from them and act accordingly.

Suggest any other possible option(s). Evaluate all of them and suggest the best course of action, giving your reasons for it. (250 words) 20

Answer: Evaluation of the options given in the question:

(i) Give your explanation to the Commission and go soft on the disciplinary action.

I have to give explanation to the Commission but going soft is an option which can be taken for the time being. But it will certainly encourage the trouble maker gang. If I surrender in this manner, they will continue with their nasty behaviour and stall the office work. Therefore, I would not go with this option.

(ii) Ignore the Commission and proceed firmly with the disciplinary action.

As the commission has statutory status, I cannot ignore the commission and have to file a reply. However, proceeding firmly against the trouble maker gang is at my option. The Commission can be explained in detail and be informed about the reasons for such false complaint. It will make them understand the real issue.

(iii) Brief your higher-ups, seek directions from them and act accordingly.

This option seems to be the most appropriate. If I take my seniors into confidence, they will cooperate with me to tackle with the problem. They can guide me as how to deal with the current situation. I can prepare a draft according to their suggestions to send my reply to the Women's Commission. This can be endorsed by my senior officers. They can vouch about my behaviour with opposite sex. Seniors can also help me to transfer the trouble makers.

Other Options:

First I can brief seniors and take them into confidence to deal with the problem.

Then I can draft a reply and send it to the Commission.

Then I can call media and give my explanation and make them aware of the reality. I am sure when they will know the actual problem, they will cooperate with me in the interest of good governance and administration. (Total 267 words)

Q.12. Suppose you are the CEO of a company that manufactures specialised electronic equipment used by a government department. You have submitted your bid for the supply

of this equipment to the department. Both the quality and cost of your offer are better than those of the competitors. Yet the concerned officer is demanding a hefty bribe for approving the tender. Getting the order is important both for you and for your company. Not getting the order would mean closing a production line. It may also affect your own career. However, as a value-conscious person, you do not want to give bribe.

Valid arguments can be advanced both for giving the bribe and getting the order, and for refusing to pay the bribe and risking the loss of the order. What those arguments could be? Could there be any better way to get out of this dilemma? If so, outline the main elements of this third way, pointing out its merits. (250 words) 20

Answer: (1) *Arguments in favour of giving the bribe for getting the order:*

As the order is important for my company, I should pay the demanded bribe and get the order.

If I do not pay, someone else may pay and get the order.

To keep my conscience, I can supply better quality goods.

Other bribe giver may even not supply good quality of goods.

Ethics can be managed practically in terms of performing my duties well, but I cannot teach the bribe demanding officer to be ethical.

(2) *Arguments in favour of not giving the bribe for getting the order:*

If I give bribe, I will compromise with my conscience and business ethics.

I can get some other good order than giving bribe.

Temporary loss in business should not discourage me from maintaining my ethos.

(3) *Arguments in favour of third option:*

I can inform the vigilance department about demand of bribe and ask them to advise me for cooperating to catch the officer red handed.

If they give me numbered currency note to give to the officer as bribe, I would do so.

Otherwise I can complain against the bribe demanding officer to his senior.

I can produce all relevant document and under right to information get relevant document of others as well. This can be used to show that my tender was the most eligible.

I can appeal to higher authorities for giving me order.

If it works out, I will get the order and will also do the duty of a whistleblower. (Total 255 words)

Q.13. Rameshwar successfully cleared the prestigious civil services examination and was excited about the opportunity that he would get through the civil services to serve the country. However, soon after joining the services, he realized that things are not as rosy as he had imagined.

He found a number of malpractices prevailing in the department assigned to him. For example, funds under various schemes and grants were being misappropriated. The official facilities were frequently being used for personal needs by the officers and staff. After some time, he noticed that the process of recruiting the staff was also not up to the mark. Prospective candidates were required to write an examination in which a lot of cheating was going on. Some candidates were provided external help in the examination. Rameshwar brought these incidents to the notice of his seniors. However, he was advised to keephis eyes, ears and mouth shut and ignore all these things which were taking place with the connivance of the higher-ups. Rameshwar felt highly disillusioned and uncomfortable. He comes to you seeking your advice.

Indicate various options that you think are available in this situation. How would you help him to evaluate these options and choose the most appropriate path to be adopted? (250 words)20

Answer: Rameshwar has seen the actual vices and malpractices in services and system. He is facing the situation that he never expected in civil services.

I think the following rational and reasonable options are available to Rameshwar.

Option 1: Prepare a report of the situation and send it to senior hierarchy up to the Chief Secretary and mark copies to concerned Minister's office.

Options 2: He may not write it directly, but can encourage the affected parties to write a complaint to higher authorities.

Options 3: He can look for any other officer who is ethical and wants to raise voice against current practice. Both or all such officers can write a joint application to the higher authorities.

Options 4: Listen to his senior's advise and ignore all the malpractices and happenings.

All other options would finally lead to either raising voice against the current system or keeping quiet.

If Rameshwar decides to oppose the practice, he has first three options in which he can either directly or through others affected parties or with other officers can bring the matter to the notice of higher authorities and if required, can bring the matter to political or judicial authorities.

However, this may endanger his career and in some situation even his physical safety and life may be in danger. Therefore, Rameshwar must be careful while raising voice against the system.

But if he decides to keep shut, he will have guilt throughout his life and he cannot forgive himself for it. So I would suggest that best option for Rameshwar is mixture of Option 2 and 3. (Total 265 words)

Q.14. In our country, the migration of rural people to towns and cities is increasing drastically. This is causing serious problems both in the rural as well as in the urban areas. In fact, things are becoming really unmanageable. Can you analyse this problem in detail and indicate not only the socio-economic but also the emotional and attitudinal factors responsible for this problem? Also, distinctly bring out why?

(a) educated rural youths are trying to shift to urban areas;

(b) landless poor people are migrating to urban slums;

(c) even some farmers are selling off their land and trying to settle in urban areas taking up petty jobs.

What feasible steps can you suggest which will be effective in controlling this serious problem of our country? (250 words) 20

Answer: Urbanisation in India has increased at faster pace in this century. Rural youth are attracted to urban areas for white collar and blue collar jobs. Non remunerative jobs in rural areas, including that of agriculture is a reason for migration from rural to urban areas.

As the attitude of a person who has come from rural area is much different from that of the person who was born and brought up in urban areas. Similar is the matter of emotional mismatch between them.

(1) Reasons for educated rural youth trying to shift to urban areas are better job opportunities, better educational facilities for their children, better avenues and scope for progress. They find all lifestyle enhancing amenities in urban areas.

(2) Landless poor people are shifting to urban slums because in rural areas there are less opportunities of employment while in urban areas even unskilled people can get manual jobs. They hope that at least their children will make better future in urban world. Industrialisation has increased in urban places which opens up more avenues for job.

(3) Even some farmers are selling their land and trying to settle in urban areas because due to lack of irrigation, credit, and better pricing mechanism, agriculture has become non-remunerative job and has indebted many farmers. Rather than continuing in loss making agricultural practice, they find it better option to engage in non-risky employments in urban areas where they can get enough to sustain their families.

To counter these problems, we need to provide better job opportunities, facilities in the field of education, health care, services and entertainment, in rural areas. (Total 270 words)

(MAIN) **Civil Service Exam.**

2015 General Studies

SOLVED PAPERS

PAPER–I

Time Allowed: Three Hours *Maximum Marks: 250*

Instructions: There are TWENTY FIVE questions printed both in English and Hindi. All questions are compulsory. The number of marks carried by a question/part is indicated against it. Answers must be written in the medium authorized in the Admission Certificate which must be stated clearly on the cover of this Question-cum-Answer (QCA) Booklet in the space provided. No marks will be given for answers written in medium other than the authorized one. Word limit in questions, if specified, should be adhered to. Answer questions in NOT MORE THAN the word limit specified for each in the parenthesis. Content of the answer is more important than length.

Q. 1 The ancient civilization in Indian sub continent differed from those of Egypt, Mesopotamia and Greece in that its culture and traditions have been preserved without breakdown to the present day. Comment. **12½**

Answer: It may not completely be correct to say that cultures and traditions of Egypt, Mesopotamia and Greece have waded away. Amongst all the civilizations, Indian cultural system has evolved based on principles of acceptance and tolerance, while, also maintaining its own integrity and grit. The influences have been subsumed to make the culture strong. The evolution of the culture rests on sound foundations given by ancient Indian scriptures like Vedas and Puranas. Drawing from such scriptures are religions that have influenced a wider set of populations residing in foreign lands, viz., Buddhism in China and Japan; Sikhism in Pakistan and Canada. Hinduism itself is a religion also practiced in lands other than its own land of origin.

However, other such civilizations succumbed to the powers of more strong ones. In India, Rashtrakutas and Shakas were from different origin, yet were able to assimilate Indian culture well. Even the Moghuls could accept the Indian culture and traditions in their art and lifestyle, so much so that they entered into marital alliance with Indian Hindus.

This was not evident with the Egyptians, who succumbed under the pressure of the Roman Empire and never tried to assimilate the two cultures together. The cultural influences of Mesopotamian civilization could not last far and wide because of the climatic conditions. Such acceptance of cultures and traditions to far and wide areas is not present amongst other such civilizations other than Indians.

Availability of water, agricultural practice, evolution of foreign trade, ability to mix with other civilizations and adaptability to climatic changes were the reasons Indian civilization survived while lack of many of these factors caused Egyptian and Mesopotamian civilization extinct.

Q. 2. Mesolithic rock cut architecture of India not only reflects the cultural life of the times but also a fine aesthetic sense comparable to modern painting. Critically evaluate this comment. **12½**

Answer: The rock-cut art is more similar to sculpture than architecture as structures were produced by cutting out solid rocks. The Rock-cut structures present the most spectacular piece of ancient Indian art specimen. Most of the rock-cut structures were related to various religious communities. In the beginning, remarkable Buddhist and Jain monuments were produced in areas such as Bihar in the east and Maharashtra in the west.

The paintings of the Mesolithic period were used to express the mental thoughts and as a medium of communication. They also exhibited the socio-economic life of that time, thereby indicating the sense of observation these people possess.

The best examples of this are Chaityas and monasteries. Inside these rock-cut structures monks carved windows and balconies and gates in the shape of huge arch shaped openings. Some of the prominent places having Chaityas and Viharas are Karle, Nashik, Bhaja and Kanheri. The rugged hills of the Western Ghats were naturally suited to the creation of living space in the hillside. The Rathas at Mahabalipuram, constructed during the reign of Pallava rulers, are yet another great specimen of rock-cut architecture in ancient India. The Pallavas were founders of the Dravidian Style of temple architecture. The rock cut architecture amply reflected life of that period. Buddhist and Jain Chaityas and Viharas reflect lift of monks and people of the time. Kailashnath temple, Ajanta and Elora caves reflect life of people. Most of the themes were drawn from daily cultural and religious life. Flora and fauna are also given proper place in this art form.

In modern painting emphasis is on reality and details. Aspects of human life and society are depicted vividly in modern paintings. Similarly in rock cut architecture of ancient India, we notice efforts made to depict smallest details in appropriately.

Q. 3 How different would have been the achievement of Indian independence without Mahatma Gandhi? Discuss. **12½**

Answer: When Mahatma Gandhi returned to India in 1915, he carried with him a reputation of successful Satyagraha in South Africa. The image gave him an immediate leadership status.

It was because of Mahatma Gandhi that India started non-violent non-cooperation movement, which was more than political protests and less than armed struggle. Boycott of educational institutions, foreign goods and seats in government institutes gave a strong message to British government and developed mass following for Gandhi. Gandhi started Civil Disobedience Movement which was next stage to non-cooperation.

People started withdrawing support to British administration. Gandhi organized agitation against land revenue, abolition of salt tax, cutting down military expenditure, levying duty on foreign cloth etc. Dandi March proved to be a bigger stroke to British rule. The Quit India Movement was launched under Gandhi in 1942 when the time had ripen. Gandhi went 21 days fast demanding release of leaders, despite his failing health. His slogan of "Do or Die" was adopted by mass.

Gandhi played actively pivotal role from 1915 till freedom by leading the Indian people for freedom from British rule. His saint like personality and ability to bring together people from all class, religion and area of India made him one and the best leader responsible for freedom of India.

There was no single influential leader who had not followed Gandhi and left deep impact on freedom struggle. So, it will not be exaggeration to say that without Gandhi freedom struggle of India would have been different, much disorganized and multipronged.

Q. 4 Mahatma Gandhi and Dr. B R Ambedkar, despite having divergent approaches and strategies, had a common goal of amelioration of the downtrodden. Elucidate 12½

Answer: Mahatma Gandhi and Dr B R Ambedkar were committed to the goal of amelioration^ the downtrodden but their approach were different. Since Gandhiji was born in a merchant class Hindu family, he approached the problem of untouchability from humanitarian perspective and wanted to erode it out from the fabric of the society. Whereas Ambedkar identified himself as the victim of that corrupt practice and stood to protect other dalits from the fallout of this inhuman practice.

Gandhi's approach was more on reformative side where he believed in educating.the society to accept all castes on equal footings. He believed and preached that varna system of society was based on work distribution and it not necessarily mean division of society. In his ideas caste system itself was not discriminatory and therefore it was not required to abolish varna or castes per se. rather he believed in creating respect for human being without discrimination of caste or status in society. He opposed to separate electorate for Dalits on the line of Muslims.

On the other hand, Dr. Ambedkar had more revolutionary approach who completely opposed caste and varna system as basis of discrimination in the society. In his book 'Annhilation of Caste' he adyocated this view. For him, as was the practice, varna and castes were branding people in particular section of the society and not giving them chances of upliftment. Therefore, abolition of caste system was necessary to eliminate discrimination. Dr. Ambedkar demanded separate electorate for Dalits. He ensured provisions of reservation in the constitution.

Thus, both the leaders had completely different approach towards one goal.

Q. 5 It would have been difficult for the Constituent Assembly to complete its historic taskof drafting the Constitution for Independent India in just three years but for the experience gained with the Government of India Act, 1935. Discuss. 12½

Answer: A large part of Indian Constitution is an exact replica of Govt, of India Act, 1935, that's why Indian Constitution is often portrayed as the extension of Government of India Act, 1935. Below mentioned important provisions of Government of India Act of 1935 can be sighted as important provisions that have helped sped up with draft of the Indian Constitution:

- The Act provided for the establishment of an All-India Federation consisting of the Provinces and the Princely States as units, though the envisaged federation never came into being-instead a Union of States on the same lines was formed that planned to do away with the Princely states and created states which stood as subsidiary to union.

- Three Lists: The Act divided the powers between the Centre and the units in items of three lists, namely the Federal List, the Provincial List and the Concurrent List, The forms of lists were renamed to include Union List, State List and Concurrent List. The Union of India is now governed by these lists.
- The residuary powers as envisaged were vested with the Governor-General and according to the Constitution the residuary powers are vested in the Centre.
- Introduced bicameralism in 6 out of 11 Provinces, similarly many states in India today have bicameral legislation.
- Provided for the establishment of Federal Court which is the Supreme Court at the Apex in India.

Thus, the Act of 1935 as a whole, not only acted as an interim constitution, but alsoprovided a basis for the Constitution of Free India. The Act alongwith earlier constitutionalreforms gave direction to the process of change as well as influenced its contents.

Q. 6 Why did the industrial revolution first occur in England? Discuss the quality of life of the people there during the industrialization. How does it compare with that in India at present? 12½

Answer: A number of factors contributed to the England's role as the birth place of Industrial Revolution.

England had coal and iron ores required for any industry to develop. They had means i of transportation and colonies for getting raw material as well as selling products of factories. England had enough capital to invest in technology and factories. Comparatively j isolated by sea, England was protected from issues with neighboring countries like other European countries. Having stable and well established political and social j system helped England to progress on industrial front.

During the industrial revolution England was divided into two classes of society - j capitalists and labors. The Industrial Revolution brought about a greater volume and variety of factory produced goods and raised the standard of living for many people, particularly for the middle and upper classes. However, life for the poor and working classes continued to be filled with challenges. Wages for those who laboured in factories were low and working conditions could be dangerous and monotonous. Children were part of the labour force and often worked long hours and were used for such highly hazardous tasks as cleaning the machinery. Industrialization also meant that some crafts people were replaced machinery. Additionally, urban, industrialized areas were unable to keep pace with the flow of arriving workers from the countryside, resulting in inadequate, overcrowded housing and polluted, unsanitary living conditions in which diseases were rampant. The capitalists were having all facilities and living very comfortable life. Profiteering was very high and so accumulation of wealth with capitalists was out of proportion. Difference in standard of living of two classes was not at all comparable.

Today India has labors working hard and living with lesser means but their lives are not as bad. Working class people in India of present times have protection of law which controls working hours, provides pension benefits, safety standards, minimum wages, leaves and medical benefits. Even in unorganized sectors, many of these legal provisions are applicable to protect labor class people in India.

Q. 7 To what extent can Germany be held responsible for causing the two World Wars?Discuss critically. 12½

Answer: Germany was forced to sign the Versailles Treaty and admit its "guilt" for causing the First World War. Germany may have been partly to blame but others were also at fault to varying degrees. This was partly a reflection of the anger felt by the Entente Powers ("Allies") at how long and hard Germany had fought, and partly due to some things Germany did during the war which seemed barbaric.

Germany had violated international laws based on unrestricted submarine warfare, sinking ships without warning. Germany also introduced the use of poison gas to the battlefield. Probably the worst thing Germany did was to invade Belgium.

Germany did cause the Second World War owing to its International Super Power ambitions. Extreme and narrow nationalism of Germany, Italy and Japan was one of the chief causes of the Second World War. The humiliating terms of the Treaty of Versailles made the German love for nationalism stronger. The problems faced by Germany made the people more conscious of the need for unity and strength. For this purpose, they willingly accepted the dictatorship of Hitler and his policy of restoring the prestige of Germans by taking revenge upon those responsible for humiliating Germany at the Paris Peace Conference.

Q. 8 Describe any four cultural elements of diversity in India and rate their relativesignificance in building a national identity. 12½

Answer:

- Linguistic diversity : Language is the first and foremost diversity of India which has historically played an important role. Language was the issue on which states were created after independence. India has twenty two constitutionally recognized languages with their own script, grammar and literature. There are hundreds of dialects spoken all over India. Although Hindi was recognized as official language by constitution, English has remained effectively first official language till date. Language is a driving force behind unity of a nation's people and make them distinct from other nations.
- Ethnicity is another factor which gives different color to India. Ethnically northern people are different from south, western are different from eastern and north eastern. Their festivals, clothes, food and other aspects of life differ from one another.
- Religious diversity has evolved because of emergence and arrival of different religious groups in India from time to time. India is home to Hinduism, Buddhism, Jainism, Sikhism, Christianity, Islam, Zoroastrians etc. apart from these religions, there are many sects and sub-sects of various religions co-living. The stronger the relation between the nation and the religion, the more is religious homogeneity and the stronger is the national identity.
- Racial diversity : In India, there are a large number of ancient culture prevailing oi still practicing today. Though there are several numbers of diverse cultures in India, still it has unity in diversity.

The modern Indian civilization has been nourished and developed by multiracial contributions. From times immemorial, diverse races migrated into India by via land anil sea routes and get themselves settled here. In course of time they are absolutely absorbed® India's social life.

The ancient ethno-linguistic groups, such as, the Aryans, the Austrics, the Negritos the Dravidians, the Alpines and the Mongoloids, had combined to constitute the modem Indian race.

In the historical period, diverse branches of the aforementioned unique ethnic groups-the Persians, thePallavas, theKushanas, the Greeks, theSakas, the Huns, the Portuguese, the Arabs, the Turks, the English and the European races came to India, and enriched Indian ethnicity and culture by their contribution to the same.

Apart from these four, there are diversities of caste, political affinity, historical and social customs. Each of these diversities has their own role in nation building. Indian democracy and national identify were built on the notion of unity in diversity, guided by the principles of tolerance and mutual respect.

Q. 9 Critically examine whether growing population is the cause of poverty OR poverty is the main cause of population increase in India. 12½

Answer: Population trends and dynamics can have an enormous effect on prospects for poverty reduction and sustainable development. Poverty is influenced by - and influences- population dynamics, including population growth, age structure, and rural-urban distribution. All of this has a critical impact on a country's development prospects and prospects for raising living standards for the poor.

India currently faces a vicious cycle of population explosion and poverty. One of the most important reasons for this population increase in India is poverty. The people, who have to struggle to make two ends meet produce more children because more children mean more earning hands. Also, due to poverty, the infant mortality rate among such families is higher due to the lack of facilities like food and medical resources. Thus, they produce more children assuming that not all of them would be able to survive. The end result is a mounting increase in the population size of India. Due to the increase in population, the problems of scarce resources, jobs, and poverty increases. Thus the cycle continues leading to an ever-increasing population that we see today. This cycle in fact might be considered as a positive feedback, in that the increase in one results in the increase of the other factor. As the poverty and the population both increase, the development of the country and the society seems even more far-fetched.

On the contrary, when there is more population which cannot afford good education and good employment, economic condition is adversely affected. Therefore, increased population which is not converted into valuable human resource and not utilized for economic development has led to big number of poor living in India. In 2012, government of India stated about 22% of its population below official poverty line. Health care, education, civil facilities are not adequately available to such a big population and that had led to improper living conditions for them.

Thus, in India, in turn, both the phenomena have played their role.

Q. 10 How do you explain the statistics that show that the sex ratio in Tribes in India is more favourable to women than the sex ratio among Scheduled Castes? 12½

Answer: Census of 2011 shows that sex ratio among Scheduled Caste population was 945 while the number was as high as 990 among Scheduled Tribes population at India level. This phenomena can be attributed to many social factors prevalent in scheduled castes and scheduled tribes.

Scheduled tribes are predominantly living in rural areas where agriculture remains primary activity in which women play an important role. Many tribes do not have dowry system while in some tribes reverse dowry is practiced. Tribal people follow their customs and traditions and live in their groups and societies and accept minimal influence of outside. These factors are responsible that girl child is welcomed and women have their own roles to play among tribal societies. Mostly women enjoy equal status with men.

Scheduled castes are not living in major groups away from mainstream society. They have faced suppression of customary social system and women are worst victims. Social evils like dowry system and preference of male child over female is well prevalent among scheduled castes. As scheduled castes are not mainly agrarian economy, their employment is dependent on industries and labour opportunities which are not easily available for women. Women do not have equal status vis a vis men. These issues have resulted into lower sex ratio among them.

Q. 11 Discuss the changes in the trends of labour migration within and outside India in the last four decades. 12½

Answer: Many factors have contributed to migration of labour within and outside of India and the trends have been changing from time to time.

Internal migration happens within India which may be either within a state or interstate. Major factor for such migration has been employment opportunities. Some states like Uttar Pradesh, Bihar, Orissa and Rajasthan have seen many migrants moving to other states and cities like Delhi, Gujarat, Maharashtra and Punjab.

Internal migration may be seasonal, depending on employment opportunities. Punjab employs labours in agriculture sector during harvest season. It may be non-permanent, for some projects like Reliance or ESSAR refineries in Gujarat. Educated people migrating for employment are also witnessed in last decades, e.g. Nurses from Kerala and software experts towards Hyderabad and Bengaluru. Migration for better education towards centers of excellence like Delhi, Mumbai, Hyderabad, Bengaluru etc. is a new trend. All these migrations are mainly from rural to urban areas.

International migration earlier was mainly to eastern African countries like Kenya, Uganda for business purposes. Which was followed by labour migration to Middle Eastern countries. Educated and skilled migrants have targeted mainly developed countries like USA, UK, Australia and Canada. Recent trend shows a big number of students going for higher studies in USA, UK, Australia and Canada. Strikingly, migration towards developed and industrialized countries is a type of brain drain. Major reason for internal migration is lack of employment while external migration is not because of unemployment but for better income level and opportunities.

12.Discuss the positive and negative effects of globalization on women in India? 12½

Answer: Globalization has impacted India especially after 1991 when Indian economy was opened up for Liberalization, Privatization and Globalization. English speaking educated young India has emerged as knowledge hub in the world. Similarly, attraction of 1.2 billion people's market in India has drawn all major multinationals to India. In the globalized India, women are greatly impacted, both positively and negatively.

On positive side, young and educated women have gained opportunities to work in equal terms with men. Better education and networking has given wider platform to women. Better mobility has helped them expand horizon of their work. They are playing prominent role in the society and standing up for their rights. Patriarchal social system is being challenged and women are demanding equal rights. Women in India are looking for career oriented life in the globalized world and taking decisions independently. Organizations for empowerment of women are more actively promoting welfare and independence for them.

On the negative side, women who were working in unorganized sector have lost jobs due to entry of big companies. Mechanization of labor and handwork has impacted women more than men. Handicraft and cottage industries of women are giving way to machine-based mass production run by big corporations. Women are also vulnerable to new kinds of crimes. Women are suffering two fold. As women in India move into the work force, their domestic responsibilities are not alleviated. Women work two full time jobs. One in a factory, where they are paid next to nothing, the second is in the home where they are paid nothing.

Q. 13. Debate the issue whether and how contemporary movements for assertion of Dalit identity work towards annihilation of caste. **12½**

Answer: Contemporary movements for assertion of Dalit identity have been focusing on certain issues specific to Dalit identity by securing their interest in every aspect of life.. Creating political vote bank of Dalit groups which support Dalit or Dalit favoring politicians at local and state levels. They mobilize Dalit vote bank and promote their interests like reservation, government jobs, political position etc.

However, most of the times, these movements are not spreader at national level and do not take into account wider interest of even Dalit community at pan India level. Their assertion is against untouchability and discrimination as main agenda. However, the movements have been successful in highlighting issues related to Dalit and give them voice at national level. They have increased awareness among the policy makers. These movements have buildup pressures through various political and pressure groups at local and national level.

However, movements for assertion of Dalit identity are far away from the goal of Dr B R Ambedkar who had desired annihilation of caste system as the final solution of Dalit empowerment. However, they have been able to improvement of position and status of Dalit by challenging the oppression and exploitation of the community. But these movements are in fact* strengthening caste based system in the society.

Q. 14. Explain the factors responsible for the origin of ocean currents. How do they influenceregional climates, fishing and navigation? **12½**

Answer: Ocean currents originate due to many factors, which can be divided mainly into Primary and Secondary.

- Primary factors include planetary winds and Difference of density & salinity. Planetary winds drive surface water along with them. Difference in density causes dense water to sink and push the bottom water to surface, causing undercurrents. Density difference arises mainly due to temperature and salinity.

- Secondary factors include rotation of the earth and shape of the coastlines. Rotation of earth affects direction of movement and deflects pole ward current eastwards, equator wards currents westwards. Shape of coastlines also deflects currents from their direction.

Ocean currents impact climate, fishing and navigation in positive or negative ways. Ocean currents help replacement of cold pole water with hot equatorial water, thus maintaining temperature moderation. In absence, pole would have been frozen and equator boiling.

Mixing of cold and hot currents creates condition for grow of planktons which is food for fishes. At this place we found abundance of fishing potential.

Navigation is affected by direction of currents. Ships move faster and need less fuel while sailing in the direction of currents and vice versa. Cold and warm currents give rise to thick fog, which reduces visibility for ships and area becomes difficult to navigate. Warm currents keep arctic region free from icebergs and help navigation of ships.

Q. 15. Mumbai, Delhi and Kolkata are the three Mega cities of the country but the airpollution is much more serious problem in Delhi as compared to the other two. Why is this so? 12½

Answer: Delhi, Mumbai and Kolkata are all Mega cities but there are important geographical, climatic and cultural differences, as a result of which Delhi's air pollution is worse compared to the other two. The main reasons for more population in Delhi are as under:

- High population density and densely packed architecture of Delhi compared to other two cities.
- Air pollution in Delhi's National Capital Region (NCR) is comprised of a complex mix of pollution from human activities (vehicle emissions, industry, construction and residential fuel burning) as well as natural sources like dust and sea salt.
- The heavy concentration of particulate matter is greatly affected by meteorological conditions -in the winter, cool air causes "inversions" that stagnant the air and trap pollution close to the ground.
- Air flow patterns from Afghanistan and Pakistan pick up emissions as they move over the densely urbanized regions of Punjab and Haryana where farmers burn the straw in their fields and pull this pollution into Delhi.
- Pre-monsoon dust storms also contribute to air pollution in the region.
- The NCR generates 10,000 tons per day of municipal solid waste, much of which is eventually burned, adding particulate pollution to the air and galloping urbanization brings massive construction projects to the area.
- Delhi has more than 7.4 million vehicles on it's roads, with an additional 1,201added each day and the result is a pollution ''hotspot."
- Delhi doesn't get the benefit of sea breeze like Mumbai and Kolkata get. The breea can drive away some of the pollution.
- While Mumbai, and Kolkata [being at the ends] are often terminal points when it comes to vehicular traffic, Delhi gets not just terminal traffic, but also transit traffic,

There is a need to consider reducing the pollution of Delhi in a broader framework of socio-economic development, and rising public awareness about the health risks of such rising pollution. A change in attitudes and regulation towards poor quality fuels is the need of the hour.

Q. 16 India is well endowed with fresh water resources. Critically examine why it stillsuffers from water scarcity. 12½

Answer: India receives about 4,000 cubic kms of fresh water as precipitation every year. About 700 cubic kms of water thus received evaporate immediately and are lost to the atmosphere. About 2,150 cubic kms go to the soil whereas about 1,650 cubic kms are retained as soil moisture while about 500 cubic kms permeate through the soil surface to underground water deposits. Only 1,150 cubic kms of fresh water received annually are retained on land surface.

India's water crisis is predominantly a manmade problem. India's climate is not particularly dry, nor is it lacking in rivers and groundwater. Extremely poor management, unclear laws, government corruption, and industrial and human waste have caused this water supply crunch and rendered what water is available practically useless due to the huge quantity of pollution.

Due to population growth, economic development, rapid urbanization, large-scale industrialization and environmental concerns water stress has emerged as a real threat. [1] Many areas in the country are already under severe water stress.

Another reason for the problem of water scarcity has been poor water quality resulting I from insufficient and delayed investment in urban water treatment facilities. Namami I Gange is a welcome step forward in addressing this issue.

In managing water resources, the Indian government must balance competing demands between urban and rural, rich and poor, the economy and the environment. Some measures like interconnecting rivers of north and south, preservation of flowing river water for dry season, use of better irrigation technology, regulation on industrial use of fresh water, prevention of pollution of fresh water resources and preservation of fresh water resources are essential.

Q. 17 The states of Jammu and Kashmir, Himachal Pradesh and Uttarakhand are reaching the limits of their ecological carrying capacity due to tourism. Critically evaluate. 12½

Answer: Ecological carrying capacity is maximum limit that an ecosystem can sustainably accept, given limitation of resources and habitation. Ecology of mountainous states like Jammu and Kashmir, Himachal Pradesh and Uttarakhand are fragile and vulnerable to various factors. Large number of tourists visiting these states brings change in the natural ecosystem of the area by their presence and consequences. Not only biospherical or natural environmental but cultural, infrastructural and socioeconomic balance is endangered in these states.

These states have natural as well as religious centers which attract a large number of tourists. Recent flood and loss of life and property is clear evidence that resources to protect and mitigate disasters are not enough to protect such a big number of tourists in these states. Recent increase in tourism has not been matched with by infrastructural development in the area. Therefore problems like deforestation, shortage of water, crowded roads, traffic, garbage, illegal construction, improper sanitation facilities are challenging the ecological capacities of these states.

To protect ecology of these three vulnerable Himalayan states without affecting tourism industry, proper planning has to be done. Government has to regulate illegal construction. Water storage, hygienic sanitation, health care, road and railway networks need to be created. Developing system of garbage disposal, waste management, promotion of biodegradable items and spreading awareness among tourists are other vital requirements.

Q. 18 How far do you agree that the behaviour of the Indian monsoon has been changing due to humanizing landscape? Discuss. 12½

Answer: Indian monsoon pattern has been changing recently erratically. Unseasonal rain and below average rainfall during monsoon is becoming frequent phenomena. In 2015, India witnessed hailstorm in March-April which caused loss in crop while monsoon season was deficient in the same year. For last two years continuously India has weak monsoon.

Apart from other factors, changes brought in landscape by human activities are important factor for this change. Expansion of urban areas beyond boundaries has reduced green surroundings. Industrial activities have led to deforestation and reduced jungle cover of the land. Forests are not maintained. Illegal destruction of forests, wide spread construction, expansion of human settlement has penetrated the green cover of earth. Lakes are drying due to lack of supply of water and expansion of cities. River courses are interrupted and flow is decreasing. Not enough water flow is maintained over landscape. Existing water bodies are not conserved. Ground water level is going deep. This results into lack of water available for evaporation and formation of clouds. Pollution and increasing temperature affects heat and pressure balance which in turn affects rainfall. Lack of tree cover and water bodies result into insufficient cloud formation and rainfall. Without water clouds cannot be formed. Without tree cover existing moist in the atmosphere cannot be converted into rainfall.

Q. 19 Smart cities in India cannot sustain without smart vilages. Discuss this statement in the backdrop of rural-urban integration. 12½

Answer: Smart cities concept is facing with many difficulties originating from population burden and migration. Cities are becoming slum and resources are not enough to support inhabitants. On the contrary, rural people are constantly migrating to urban areas for employment, education and healthcare facilities.

Concept of Providing Urban Amenities to Rural Areas (PURA) was incorporated in ShyamaPrashadMukherjiRurban Mission (SPMRM) scheme of Union Government. Village and cities can play complimentary role and smart cities concept can be implemented in villages to make cities more productive.

Villages with good education and healthcare facilities, connection to cities by good road and rail networks and development of small industrial clusters will stop migration to cities. Villages will become supportive and complimentary to urban areas. Smart cities will be benefited from agricultural and auxiliary industrial products of villages. Many online services can be handled from out of cities if we can develop smart villages with good internet connectivity and educated, skilled manpower. Call centers and BPOs can be established in villages, on smaller scale.

Problems related to pollution, slum, drinking water and traffic will be properly addressed in cities by providing good facilities in villages. To sustain smart cities, villages have to be provided better facilities and concept of Smart Villages has to be implemented on priority.

Q. 20 What are the economic significances of discovery of oil in Arctic Sea and its possible environementalconsequences? 12½

Answer: The US Geological Survey estimates that around 13% of the world's undiscovered oil could lie under the area north of the Arctic Circle. In terms of economic significance, at our current oil consumption rate, that's actually only three to five years' worth of resources. The Arctic's extreme weather and freezing temperatures, its remote location and the presence of moving sea ice severely increase the risks of oil drilling, complicate logistics and present unparalleled difficulties for any clean-up operation.

The Arctic is home to four million people, many of whom are descendants of Indigenous communities who have lived in the Far North for thousands of years. It is also home to a diverse range of unique wildlife: hundreds of species of seabirds, millions of migrating birds; 17 different species of whale live there. Mammals including Polar Bears, Arctic Foxes and various species of seal inhabit the Arctic at different points throughout the year.

The impact of a spill on these communities and already vulnerable animal species would be devastating and long-lasting. Its fragile ecosystem is particularly vulnerable to an oil spill and the consequences of an accident would have a profound effect on the environment and local fisheries. Due to climate change, the Arctic sea ice is melting atan alarming rate each summer.

Arctic oil drilling is a dangerous, high-risk enterprise and an oil spill under these icy waters would have a catastrophic impact on one of the most pristine, unique and beautiful landscapes on earth. The Arctic drilling season is limited to a narrow window of a few months during the summer. The oil industry cannot guarantee the safety of Arctic drilling and is recklessly putting profit before the environment.

SOLVED PAPERS

PAPER–II

Time Allowed: Three Hours *Maximum Marks: 250*

Instructions: There are TWENTY questions printed both in English and in Hindi. All questions are compulsory. The number of marks carried by a question/part is indicated against it. Answers must be written in the medium authorized in the Admission Certificate which must be stated clearly on the cover of this Question-cum-Answer (QCA) Booklet in the space provided. No marks will be given for answers written in medium other than the authorized one.

Word limit in questions, wherever specified, should be adhered to.

Answer the questions in not more than 200 words each. Contents of the answers are more important than their length.

Q. 1 Discuss the possible factors that inhibit India from enacting for its citizen a uniform civil code as provided for in the Directive Principles of State Policy. 12½

Answer: Article 44 of the Directive Principles of State Policy describes a duty for the Government to enact a Uniform Civil Code in India. The article does not make it mandatory as it is only a directive but nonetheless it is vital for secularism and equality before law in India.

Currently personal laws of various religious communities are governing marriage, divorce, inheritance, adoption and maintenance related legal questions. British first framed personal laws for Hindus and Muslims to avoid religious opposition and the laws still continue without many reforms. In ShahBano Case of 1985, the topic was raised by the Supreme Court. Demand has since been raised by various groups, more importantly women activists, but All India Muslim Personal Law Board and Congress Party has opposed it.

Personal laws allow polygamy, unilateral divorce, religious practices, and customary traditions to various religious groups. Uniform Civil Code was enacted and applied in Goa during Portuguese occupation which is still in practice.

It is feared that some religious sections of society would consider Uniform Civil Code as encroachment on freedom of religion and attack on identity. Such attempts have, in past, raised severe objections and criticisms and therefore government has not been able to enact Uniform Civil Code in India.

Q. 2 The concept of cooperative federalism has been increasingly emphasised in recentyears. Highlight the drawbacks in the existing structure and extent to which cooperative federalism would answer the shortcomings. 12½

Answer: Recently in India, due to different political parties ruling at center, state and local government levels, differences in policies and implementations have come to surface. In such scenario, experts have raised need for cooperative federalism in India, rather than existing federal structure where center is more powerful.

Cooperative federalism is a concept in which center, state and local governments share responsibility in the governance of the people. It means that national and stategovernments are partners in the exercise of governmental authority.

Currently center is powerful in imposition and collection of tax and revenue where states have to depend on grants by center. States have control over land resources and center cannot implement important infrastructural projects without cooperation of states. Law and order comes under states while armed forces are under center.

For effective governance, both center and states have to cooperate in legislation and policy making. Current structure of Indian constitution divides power into three areas, namely Union List giving supreme power to Center, State List giving exclusive power to States and Concurrent List giving power to both center and states. Though Indian constitution distributes powers among Center and States, but does not provide for consultation and cooperation in terms of policy making and governance, which is a shortcoming in view of cooperative federalism.

To promote the spirit of cooperative federalism, NITI Aayog was established by replacing the Planning Commission and the recommendations of the fourteenth Finance Commission was accepted that provided more fiscal autonomy to the states by the incumbent government.

Q. 3 In the absence of well - educated and organised local level government system, Panchayats and Samitis have remained mainly political institutions and not effective instrument of governance. Critically Discuss. 12½

Answer: In India, local government comprises Panchayat and Municipal system. The constitution of India added feature of local government by 73rd and 74th Constitutional Amendment Acts.

The 73rd and 74th amendments have created uniformity in the structures of Panchayati Raj and Nagarpalika institutions across the country.

Rural Local Governments or Panchayati Raj Institutions comprises of Gram Panchayats, Mandal/ TalukaPanchayats and ZillaPanchayat. Urban Local Governments or Nagarpalikas are made up of Nagar Panchayats, Municipal Councils (Samitis) and Municipal Corporations.

This local governance have come into effect since 1993 but still there is lack of educated government system which gives them mainly political color. The local bodies are working on the basis of caste and religious groups electing their leaders. There are provisions for reservation for women also but most of the time women leaders are used as rubber stamps.

Lack of reasoning and open mindedness made the performance of these PRIs vitiated by political cum caste factionalism, rendering developmental projects into chimeras. Negation of democratic principles in the functioning of these institutions also can be correlated to that illiteracy levels as representatives do not values the importance of democratic ideals.

Effectively implementing policies of state and central government is still out of their purview. Influence of national and state parties are also strong at local governance level. It would have been better if these local bodies have acted as powerful organizations demanding their interest and serving as catalyst of policy making. India is still a country of villages and local governance need to be stronger and effective to manage micro-level policies while center and state can concentrate on bigger picture.

Q. 4 Khappanchayats have been in the news for functioning as extra - constitutional authorities, often delivering pronouncements amounting to human right violations. Discuss critically the actions taken by the legislative, executive and judiciary to set the things right in this regard. **12½**

Answer: Khap is an organization representing a clan in northern India. Khaps are found mainly among the Jats of Western Uttar Pradesh and Haryana. A khappanchayat is an assembly of Khap elders. KhapPanchayat enforces its summons through social prohibitions and sanctions, imposes heavy fines or even kills the victims or makes them commit suicide. Thus, the KhapPanchayats do not have legal authority to give verdict or implement its judgement and therefore they are extra-constitutional in nature. Khapdecisions to prevent marriages in same Gotra and honour killing or forced suicide are clearly violation of human rights.

On April 19 2011, Supreme Court wants a strict criminal action against people forming and ruling in khaps, emphasizing that the khappanchayats are illegal. The Khaps decided to file a review petition in the apex courts after hearing the statement of the Supreme Court.

The law commission has drafted The Prohibition of Unlawful Assembly (Interference with the Freedom of Matrimonial Alliances) Bill, 2011 that proposes no person or any group of persons shall gather with an "intention to deliberate on, or condemn any marriage, not prohibited by law, on the basis that such marriage has dishonoured the caste or community tradition or brought disrepute to all or any of the persons forming part of the assembly or the family or the people of the locality concerned.

Executives have taken steps to prevent honour killings by KhapPanchayats but some political authorities have favored Khap system.

Q. 5 Resorting to ordinances has always raised concern on violation of the spirit of separation of power doctrine. While noting the rationales justifying the power to promulgate, analyse whether the decision of the Supreme Court on the issue have further facilitated resorting to this power. Should the power to promulgate the ordinances be repealed? **12½**

Answer: Article 123 of the Indian Constitution empowers the President to promulgate ordinances during the recess of the Parliament. The ordinances are temporary laws having the effect of an act.

Frequently governments have used ordinance to bring a law which it cannot otherwise enact due to lack of majority in one house of parliament. Though ordinance is supposed to be a temporary in nature, it has been re-promulgated over and over again without bothering to get it passed through both houses of parliament. Ordinance has been misused to bypass legislative system, in many cases.

The Supreme Court in T Venkata Reddy vs. State of Andhra Pradesh (1985), held that the motives behind the exercise of this power cannot be questioned, just as is the case with legislation by the Parliament and state legislatures. The Court has upheld validity of ordinance. There are no restrictions on the ordinance making power of the President, as it is similar to a legislation of the Parliament.

In situations where governments avoid facing legislature and implement laws through ordinance of President, it is advisable that certain rules and procedures are fixed to regulate misuse of Article 123. However, taking into consideration emergency situations and other eventualities, repealing provision of ordinance would not be advisable.

In words of B.R. Ambedkar, "ordinance making powers were necessary since existing laws might be deficient to deal with a situation which may suddenly and immediately arise." So, instead of repealing it, adequate provisions should be made to prevent its misuse.

Q. 6 What are the major changes brought in the Arbitration and Conciliation Act, 1966 through the recent ordinance promulgated by the President? How far will it improve India's dispute resolution mechanism? Discuss. 12½

Answer: The Government of India had promulgated the Arbitration and Conciliation Ordinance 2015 bringing about large scale changes to the Arbitration and Conciliation Act, 1996 with the intention expediting the process and reducing court interference.

- The changes include conferring original jurisdiction exclusively on High Courts to deal with the enforcement of and challenge to international arbitration awards as well as prescribing timelines to streamline arbitration and related court proceedings.
- Under the proposed amendments to the Arbitration and Conciliation Act, 1996, an arbitrator will have to settle a case within 18 months. However, after the completion of 12 months, certain restrictions will be put in place to ensure that the arbitration case does not linger on.
- Another amendment to the law puts a cap on the fee of an arbitrator. The arbitrator will now also have to spell out if there is a conflict of interest in a case he or she is taking up.
- Appointment of arbitrators shall be made by the Supreme Court or High Courts, as the case may be, instead of the Chief Justice of India or Chief Justice of High Court.
- In case of international arbitration, the relevant court would only be the High Court having original ordinary jurisdiction.
- To ensure neutrality of arbitrators, when a person is approached in connection with possible appointment as arbitrator, he is required to disclose in writing, the existence of any relationship or interest of any kind.
- Now, the arbitration tribunal shall have power to grant all kinds of interim measures which the court is empowered to grant.

The amendments to the law will reduce personal favoritism/bias and reduce timeline in settling disputes. It will help to attract the greater foreign investment. Foreign companies will not be hesitant to do business in India because of the long-drawn litigations.

Q. 7 Does the right to clean environment entail legal regulation on burning crackers during Diwali? Discus in the light of Article 21 of Indian Constitution and judgements of the apex court in this regard. 12½

Answer: The right to life has been used in a diversified manner in India. It includes, inter alia, the right to survive as a species, quality of life, the right to live with dignity and the right to livelihood.

The Supreme Court expanded Article 21 in two ways. Firstly, any law affecting personal liberty should be reasonable, fair and just. Secondly, the Court recognised several unarticulated liberties that were implied by article 21. It is by this second method that the Supreme Court interpreted the right to life and personal liberty to include the right to a clean environment.

The real panic in India came to be felt only after the Bhopal gas tragedy in 1984. Indian parliament passed many statutes to protect and improve the environment. Further the constitutional (forty-second Amendment) Act, 1976 incorporated two significant articles viz. Article 48-A and 51A (g) thereby making the Indian Constitution the first in the world conferring constitutional status to the environment protection.

The Supreme Court of India has given various judgements to involving various facets of environment. In Prevention of Environment & Sound Pollution v. Union of India, the apex court laid down a few essential guidelines relating to firecrackers and addressing other problems of sound pollution. The Supreme Court directed the Department of Explosives to divide the firecrackers into two categories- (i) Sound emitting firecrackers, and (ii) Colour/light emitting firecrackers. It was ordered that there shall be a complete ban on bursting sound emitting firecrackers between 10 p.m. and 6 a.m. It is not necessary to impose restrictions as to time on bursting of colour/light emitting firecrackers. In the case of M. C Mehta v. Kamal Nath, the Supreme Court made it clear that any disturbance of basic environmental elements namely air, water and soil which are necessary for life would be hazardous to life and can't be polluted. In the case of Vellore citizens welfare forum v. Union of India, Precautionary principle and polluter pays principle was evolved.

In the case of P.A. Jacob v. Suprintendent of police, Kottayam, the Kerela high Court held that the freedom of speech does not include freedom to use loudspeakers or sound amplifiers to cause noise pollution and risk to human health. Again in M.C Mehta v. Union of India, the apex court directed the closure of certain industries that were not showing any progress towards setting up of air- pollution control system in compliance with their earlier order. Subhash Kumar v. State of Bihar case held that the right to enjoyment of pollution free water and air for full enjoyment of life was held as a part of right to life under Article 21.

In a recent case, 3 toddlers moved to the Supreme Court with a petition to take action against the rising levels of air pollution, which has led to lethal levels of toxic in the air, which is directly affecting the youngest of the population. The Supreme Court dismissed this petition which was aimed at putting a blanket ban on bursting of crackers on Diwali or designating a particular place for bursting crackers. The Supreme Court exclaimed that such a blanket ban would be lethal and would cause an unnecessary uproar in the society. The court, however, has directed the government to spread awareness about the hazardous effects of crackers.

Q. 8 Examine critically the recent changes in the rule governing foreign funding of NGOs under the Foreign Contribution (Regulation) Act (FCRA), 1976. 12½

Answer: In the most important change, government plans to equate "economic security" for NGOs under FCRA with the definition provided in Section 2 of the Unlawful Activities Prevention Act (UAPA).

Banks will have to provide online access to the Home Ministry and Intelligence Bureau (IB) for monitoring the utilization of accounts of all FCRA-registered associations.

NGOs and organizations that receive foreign donations will now have to share personal details, bank account details and bio-data of their trustees with the government. According to the amended rules, any foreigner associated with an NGO, who is visiting India, will have to furnish his/her details with the Foreigners Regional Registration Office (FRRO), spelling out the purpose as well as the dates of the visits.

The NGOs will have to list all their activities and declarations on a website, and register themselves under one of the nine Indian Acts: Societies Registration Act, 1860, Indian Trust Act, 1882, Section 25 of the Companies Act, 1956, Religion Endowments Act, 1863, Charitable and Religious Trust Act, 1920, MussalmanWakf Act, 1973, Wakf Act, 1954, Public Wakfs Act, 1959 and Section 12 A of IT Act.

Further, the NGOs need to display the audited statement of accounts including income and expenditure statements and balance sheet of previous financial year on its website. Banks that receives foreign funds on behalf of NGOs have to report the transactions within 48 hours.

These regulations are aimed at monitoring activities of NGOs and prevent foreign agencies from using NGOs as extended arms to promote political and terrorism related activities.

Q. 9 The Self Help Group (SHG) Bank Linkage Program (SBLP), which is India's own innovation, has proved to be one of the most effective poverty alleviation and women empowerment programme. Elucidate. 12½

Answer: In order to achieve the mission of reaching those families who did not access to credit by any formal financial institution and, therefore, were dependent on informal sources and moneylenders, the NABARD introduced the "SHG - Bank Linkage Programme" as a pilot project in 1992.

These programmes have become a very effective tool of uplifting the socio economic status of poor women. There are adequate facts across the globe to show, how the SHG and bank linkage programme through its functioning can provide productive employment opportunities, safe credit facilities, saving opportunities and thereby can eradicate poverty.

Apart from myriad programs relating to poverty alleviation has been started, it was observed that micro credit system through SHGs bank linkage programme plays a very significant role for the woman empowerment in rural areas so as to the poor families could be benefited. Rapid progress in SHG formation has now turned into an empowerment movement among women across the country. Economic empowerment results in women's ability to influence or make decision independently, increased self confidence, better status and role in household etc.

The SHGs have been linked with Banks for micro financing. Under the programme, the Banks would provide a loan of Rs. 2 to 3 lakhs on seven per cent interest to each SHG for initially starting its venture which would be repeated up to Rs. 10 lakh depending on the performance of the SHG. These SHGs will also get additional interest subvention of 3 per cent on regular repayment of loan, reducing the effective rate of interest to 4 per cent. This interest subvention is being provided by the Government of India. For coordinating and smoothening of the SHG Bank linkages and delivery of interest subvention, a sub-committee of State Level Bankers Committee (3LBC) has been constituted.6345 SHGs have been linked with the Banks providing them the credit of Rs. 59.09 crore against target of Rs. 148 crore. Revolving fund of Rs. 2.97 crore has also been distributed amongst the groups by the Department. During the current fiscal, the focus will be on capacity building and institutionalization of SHGs.

This program has helped in social mobilization, institution building, creating human resources and alleviating poverty by direct financial benefits through bank linkages.

Q. 10 How can be the role of NGOs be strengthened in India for development worksrelating to protection of the Environment? Discuss throwing light on the major constraints. 12½

Answer: The NGOs network is interacting with Governments in shaping environmental policies, and can be helpful in creating awareness among the public on current environmental issues and solutions. They can facilitate the participation of various categories of stakeholders in the discussion on environmental issues. Conducting participatory rural appraisal, being involved in the protection of human rights to have a clean environment, protecting the natural resources and entrusting the equitable use of resources can be additional role of NGOs in protection of environment. There are large number of NGOs in India and other countries that are exclusively working for environmental, protection, conservation, and awareness.

Role of NGOs can be strengthened by involving them directly in governmental and industrial projects and policies. They should be allowed to express free opinion and act for protection of environment. Funding and activities should be allowed freely.

Major constraints on strengthening NGOs roles in environmental protection come from governmental restrictions which restrict activities and regulate strongly. Industries also look at these NGOs as acting against economic growth of India. Theories of conspiracy and international funding are also floated against such NGOs. Choice between environment and economic growth has to be made and without restricting NGOs, a pragmatic view should be taken on case to case basis.

Q. 11 The quality of higher education in India requires major improvement to make it internationally competitive. Do you think that the entry of foreign educational institutions would help improve the quality of technical and higher education in the country. Discuss. 12½

Answer: The QS World University Rankings had no Indian institutes in the top 200 of its recently released global list for 2013. India has one of the poorest Gross Enrolment Ratios (GER) for higher education in the world. According to 2010 data, India's GER was a meager 13.8 percent, compared with the global average of around 26 percent.

Low employability of graduates, driven by several factors including outdated curricula, shortage of quality faculty, high student-teacher ratios, lack of institutional and industry linkages, and lack of autonomy to introduce new and innovative courses are factors need to be improved in higher education of India. Low impact research output and patents filed given relatively low government and corporate spending on research, insufficient doctoral students, missing research focus and culture in most institutions

and lack of international research collaborations contribute to the reason why Indian higher and technical education is not internationally competitive. Complex regulatory requirements and hurdles, poor institutional governance standards, and lack of professional management also need to be taken into consideration.

Institutions would need to adopt a transformative and innovative approach across all levels of higher and technical education: from curricula and pedagogy to the use of technology to partnerships, governance and funding, to become globally relevant and competitive.

Foreign Universities coming to India in higher and technical education sector would bring funds, expertise and better curriculum for students. They will give better exposure and methods of learning. Concern of being costly and profiteering may not be ignored but scholarships and loans can take care of deserving poor students. Foreign universities have so far kept away from India because of the high level of regulations. In a major reform push in higher and technical education, the Centre may not only allow foreign universities to set up campuses in India but also permit them to repatriate profits from operations.

Q. 12 Public health system has limitation in providing universal health coverage. Do you think that private sector can help in bridging the gap? What other viable alternatives do you suggest? 12½

Answer: The public health system in India comprises a set of state-owned health care facilities funded and controlled by the government of India. Governmental spending on health care in India is exclusively through this system; hence most of the treatments in these institutions are either fully or partially subsidized.

This includes Primary Health Centers at village level, Community Health Centers in Urban areas, Taluk Level Hospitals, General Hospitals in Districts, Medical colleges and Speciality Hospitals in big cities and All India Institutes of Medical Science. However, Public health system is not able to provide service to all villages due to lack of infrastructure and shortage of staff.

In this regard, government can direct corporations to spend CSR fund on creating health facilities. Government can also tie up with private hospitals and cover beneficiaries through medical insurance. The insurance can be provided by government at subsidized rate. Private hospitals can be directed to provide treatment to insured beneficiaries. Private practitioner doctors can also be bridged under the insurance scheme. Government can start public - private partnership in health care system whereby companies can build hospitals and government can provide tax benefits for providing medical services to poor and underprivileged group of people.

To sustain its economic growth, India will need to have a healthy population and address health inequities. In this context, UHC can be the driver and benefit the entire population. Accelerating UHC is the key to successfully addressing the new public health challenges and inequities in health outcomes.

Q. 13 Though there have been several different estimates of poverty in India, all indicatereduction in poverty levels over time. Do you agree. Critically examine with reference to urban and rural poverty indicators. 12½

Answer: In India, we have a long history of studies on the measurement of poverty. The methodology for the estimation of poverty used by the erstwhile Planning Commission was based on recommendations made by various expert groups.

The official measure of Indian government, before 2005, was based on food security and it was defined from per capita expenditure for a person to consume enough calories and be able to pay for associated essentials to survive. Since 2005, Indian government adopted the Tendulkar methodology which moved away from calorie anchor to a basket of goods and used rural, urban and regional minimum expenditure per capita necessary to survive.

Dandekar and Rath, on the behalf of Indian government, estimated that the poverty rate in 1960s remained generally constant at 41%.

Ojha, in contrast, estimated that there were 190 million people (44%) in India below official poverty limit in 1961, and that this below-poverty line number increased to 289 million people (70%) in 1967. Bardhan also concluded that Indian poverty rates increased through the 1960s, reaching a high of 54%.

Another Expert Group was instituted in 1993, chaired by Lakdawala, to examine poverty line for India.

In June 2012, the government of India appointed an expert group (with C. Rangarajan as chairman) to take a fresh look at the methodology for the measurement of poverty .The Rangarajan expert group has gone back to the idea of separate poverty line baskets for rural and urban areas. Based on the analysis presented in the expert group report, monthly per capita consumption expenditure of Rs 972 in rural areas and Rs 1,407 in urban areas is treated as the poverty line at the all-India level. The expert group estimates that 30.9 per cent of the rural population and 26.4 per cent of the urban population were below the poverty line in 2011-12. The all-India ratio was 29.5 per cent.

All these poverty estimates have indicated decline in poverty in India. Separate reference is useful because requirement and cost of living in urban and rural areas differ dramatically.

The poverty indicators, both rural and urbam, measures deprivations like food, education, health, shelter, sanitation, safe drinking water etc., among the poor. A large proportion of India's urban and rural population lacks the income or assets to meet basic needs. But most of these living in poverty are not considered poor by official definitions. Poverty in India is just defined and measured by specifying a poverty line based on a particular level of per capita consumption or income and assessing what proportionof the population falls below this line.

Q. 14 In the light of Satyam Scandal (2009), discuss the changes brought in the corporate governance to ensure transparency and accountability. 12½

Answer: B RamalingaRaju, the founder of Satyam Computer Services, confessed to aRs 7,000-crore fraud on its balance sheet, which he had hidden from the IT company's board, employees and auditors for several years. The Satyam scandal was the largest accounting fraud in the history of corporate India. Satyam revealed many alarming truths about the inadequacies of the country's corporate governance standards. The government reacted to the fraud by overhauling the regulatory framework, with the new Companies Act 2013, which fixed liabilities of auditor and independent directors. In 2014, market regulator SEBI amended Clause 49 of listing guidelines to improve corporate governance. The market watchdog have also set up a monitoring committee to ensure company's compliance with clause 49, ascertain adequacy and accuracy of disclosures in the quarterly compliance reports received from the companies and submit a consolidated compliance report to it within 60 days from the end of each quarter.

There is much more vigilance to ensure that companies and auditors have put in greater checks to prevent fraud. Most organizations have digitized their business processes and strengthened internal controls to prevent and detect frauds. Boards must have at least one woman director.

Audit firms now have to be rotated every 10 years beginning April 2017. Auditors have come under intense scrutiny - they have to see to it that every internal financial control (IFC) prescribed under the Companies Act is followed by a company. However, the main obstacle is that most Indian companies are controlled by promoters. Independent directors are only independent on paper.

Q. 15 "If amendment bill to the Whistleblowers Protection Act 2011 tabled in the Parliament is passed, there may be no one left to protect." Critically Evaluate. 12½

Answer: Whistleblowers - public servants, non-profit organizations or individuals - will not be allowed to reveal any documents classified under the Official Secrets Act of 1923, even if the purpose is to disclose acts of corruption, misuse of power or criminal activities. This is in addition to any information that could "prejudicially affect the interest of the sovereignty and integrity of India, the security of the State, friendly relations with foreign State" - information that is already off-limits in the existing Whistleblowers Protection Act.

The proposed amendments allow whistleblowers to disclose some kinds of information only if it has been obtained through a Right to Information query. This includes intellectual property, trade secrets and even information that can be considered the "unwanted invasion of privacy" of an individual.

Whistleblowers would be entitled to official protection only if all of these conditions are met, could face action if they are not, and the central and state governments would be the final authorities with the power to judge each case.

Whistleblowers in any society take on the severest of personal risks and often make unprecedented sacrifices in order to safeguard the rights of their fellow citizens from corruption and other forms of maladministration in public institutions. Providing a whistleblower with a safe alternative to silence is the foundational principle of everywhistleblower protection law.

The introduced bill is likely to dissuade anyone from blowing the lid off corruption in the government or bureaucracy.

Q. 16 "For achieving the desired objectives, it is necessary to ensure that the regulatory institution remain independent and autonomous." Discuss in the light of experiences in recent past. 12½

Answer: Any regulatory institution must remain independent and autonomous for taking unbiased decisions and giving impartial judgements. Any control or influence on such authority may affect its ability to regulate and administer its area of authority. Regulators should be appointed in a manner that conflict of interest does not arise and their integrity remains beyond doubt. Rules should be made to keep the position holders insulated from outside influences that may affect their judgement. Regulatory bodies should be given enough power and authority so not to be subordinate to any other authority which in turn can again control independent decisions.

For example, if environmental clearance authority is not independent and autonomous, we cannot maintain balance between industrialization and environmental protection. Similarly, if an audit institution does not act independently and impartially, investors cannot know the real financial situation of a company.

Courts of law should also be independent to administer justice to parties without bias or partiality.

Recently some of the actions taken by the government appeared to be encroaching upon the autonomy of the institutions. Some such actions were the controversy associated with the appointment of the post of director to the Film and Television Institute of India, proposed IIM Bill, attempt to bring NJAC to appoint members to higher judiciary thereby government accused of interfering in the court's appointment process (however the provision got struck down by the Supreme Court), and above all, a draft version of the Indian finance code proposes to limit the RBI's veto in the monetary policy committee, which would severely dent the central bank's competency. If anyhow, the institutional autonomy gets impacted then these institutions, which are entrusted with the responsibility of creating knowledge, regulating different sector of the Indian economy, ensuring justice, etc. may not work well.

Q. 17 Increasing interest of India in Africa has its pro and cons. Critically Examine. 12½

Answer: India is focusing on trade and commerce with Africa, with specific reference to increasing sharing of technical knowledge. India is currently the fourth-largest trading partner of Africa, after China, the United States and the European Union. India-Africa trade figures of $72 billion and investment in the continent is around $32 billion. India can look to surpass China during its slowdown and also aim at creating a resource base for its own 'Make in India' campaign on the other.

India, in order to diversify its sources of supply, has to concentrate on Africancontinent, as it has emerged as a crucial region for oil supply diversification due to fragile nature of hydrocarbon supply in West Asia, India's traditional oil supplier. While oil and gas dominates the India's resource interests in Africa, India also imports coal, copper, iron as well as agricultural raw materials. Certain regions of the African continent serve as the hotbed for the spread of the fundamentalist Islamic terrorism movements and another issue is concerned with the security of sea lines of communication (SLOC) and the threat of maritime piracy. Both these issues makes it imperative and advantageous for India to enter into positive engage with Africa to garner her support and cooperation.

Africa can also give allies in India's bid for a permanent seat on the United Nations Security Council and stronger support in other international forums such as World Trade Organization.

On the other hand, India needs to focus more on domestic issues like poverty, healthcare, education and other infrastructure facilities. India is growing as a knowledge economy and western countries can be better trade partners for India. On international front also, neighboring countries should be priority, followed by big powers. Focusing more on Africa is not the demand of time. Resources have to be allocated appropriately and India is not in position to give too much aid or development assistance to African countries.

Q. 18 Discuss the impediments India is facing in its pursuit of a permanent seat in UN Security Council. 12½

Answer: India has been actively pursuing its quest for permanent membership of the UN Security Council. It has pushed for text based negotiations in the UN General Assembly as a step to move forward the agenda of UNSC reform and expansion stuck fruitlessly in the Open-Ended Working Group all these years. Many would rightly say that the start of text based negotiations does not mean that India is anywhere near obtaining permanent membership.

India must gain the approval of the five nations (China, Russia, France and Great Britain) that currently have permanent seats on the Council, any of whom can cast a veto against status changes on the Council. USA has already voiced support. It is well-known that China has reservations about its neighboring Asian states gaining a presence on the Council and would likely at this time block the entries of both India and Japan.

Even the US said that it first wanted a "reformed" Security Council that includes India. Probably it means that, before India's request should be acted upon, the Council's membership must be expanded to at least 21 or 22 countries.

In addition, there is the question of whether India, if it does get voted onto the Security Council, gets the seat with a veto or without one. The five permanent members will have a say in that decision — and the issue will be whether India would accept a spot sans the veto.

India has problems with bordering countries that may not support India's permanent membership to UN. Internal law and order situation of India is grappling withinsurgencies and left-wing extremism. This showcases India's inability to tackle internal issues and therefore, a bigger role in international arena gets undermined. The economic strength of India is yet to show its muscles to the world, as it is still smaller in terms of GDP with respect to other three in the group of G4. Also, India is struggling with weak currency making her economy vulnerable to external as well as internal economic shocks.

All African countries may also not support India as their votes will be divided. India has to still grow economically to support international organizations financially. Still having world's largest number of poor, India cannot afford to shoulder more financial responsibilities of international organizations.

Q. 19 Project 'Mausam' is considered a unique foreign policy initiative of Indian government to improve relationship with its neighbours. Does the project have a strategic dimension? Discuss. 12½

Answer: Project Mausam is essentially a Ministry of Culture project concerning the creation of cultural links with India's maritime neighbours. The project's objective is two-fold: at the macro level to re-connect with the countries of the IOR with the aim of enhancing the understanding of cultural values and concerns; and, at a more localized level, to enable an understanding of national cultures in a regional maritime milieu.

Mausam, for instance, aims to explore maritime routes that link India to different parts of the Indian Ocean littoral. One of its sub-themes is the sharing of knowledge systems and ideas between the many coastal canters along the maritime routes connecting India with the Indian Ocean's sub-systems. This could in the long-term imply an aspiration for greater Indian influence in the IOR.

One of the main deliverables of this project is nomination of maritime cultural landscapes across the Indian Ocean as a trans-national property on the World Heritage List of UNESCO.

The endeavour of Project Mausam is to position itself at two levels : at the macro level, it aims to re-connect and re-establish communications between countries of the Indian Ocean world, while at the micro level, the focus is on understanding national cultures in their regional maritime mileu.

Project 'Mausam' is an exciting, multi-disciplinary project that rekindles long-lost ties across nations of the Indian Ocean 'world' and forges new avenues of cooperation and exchange. The project, launched by India in partnership with member states, will enable a significant step in recording and celebrating this important phase of world history from the African, Arab and Asian-world perspectives.

It does have strategic dimensions in a way that India will have more soft power in these nations and will generate goodwill towards India. It will increase people to people and cultural contacts.

Q. 20 Terrorist activities and mutual distrust have clouded India - Pakistan relations. To what extent the use of soft power like sports and cultural exchange could help generate goodwill between the two countries. Discuss with suitable examples. 12½

Answer: India-Pakistan relations are subject to various conflicting issues since partition like water dispute, border dispute, Kashmir dispute and terrorism etc., which resulted in three wars between the two neighbouring countries.

There have been numerous attempts to improve the relationship —notably, theShimla summit, the Agra summit and the Lahore summit but efforts are eclipsed by terrorist activities carried out by outfits based in Pakistan.

But, despite all the political differences, the citizens of both the nations remains strongly inter-connected and inter-related through same culture, language, sartorial way, geographical conditions, socio-cultural traditions etc. These are some of the threads that are still bonding the people of these not so friendly nations. In addition to these, arts, music and sports too form certain amount of mutual linkages between India and Pakistan.

Civil Society in both the countries want peaceful resolution to all the conflicts and it can be forged through utilizing soft power such as sports and cultural exchanges. Both countries have tried for cultural and sports exchange and people to people contact to improve relations which have been successful to some extent. Indian TV serials and movies are popular in Pakistan. Many Pakistani artists have become famous in India. Sports, especially Cricket and Hockey between two countries are played with great zeal and enthusiasm, drawing a big crowd of viewers. These efforts need to be streamlined and increased.

Sports as a tool of soft power can bridge many differences and find peoplea common ground to unite. In Indo-Pak relations, cricket is the main sport, which helps enhance dialogue. Cricket could be used to create congenial atmosphere between people of two nations.

In the modern world, culture, media and technology play as crucial a role as weapons and diplomacy. So, lets not talk to Pakistan, invade them not with guns, but with culture.

SOLVED PAPERS

PAPER–III

Time Allowed: Three Hours *Maximum Marks: 250*

Instructions: There are TWENTY questions printed both in English and in Hindi. All the questions are compulsory. The number of marks carried by a question is indicated against it. Answers must be written in the medium authorized in the Admission Certificate which must be stated clearly on the cover of this Question-cum-Answer (QCA) Booklet in the space provided. No marks will be given for answers written in medium other than the authorized one.

Word limit in questions, wherever specified, should be adhered to.

Answer the questions in not more than 200 words each. Contents of the answer is more important than its length.

Q. 1 The nature of economic growth in India in recent times is often described as a jobless growth. Do you agree with this view? Give arguments in favour of your answer. 12½

Answer: Historically, from 2000 until 2011, India's average quarterly GDP growth was 7.45 per cent. The economy has posted an average growth rate of more than 7 per cent in the decade since 1997. In 2014 GDP growth was more than 7%.

The growth in labor force in India is much higher than the growth of jobs. The unemployment rate in India was last reported at 9.4 per cent in fiscal year 2009-10. From 1983 until 2000, the unemployment rate averaged 7.20 per cent reaching the historical high of 8.30 per cent in December 1983 and a record low of 5.99 per cent in December 1994. But since 2011 unemployment rate has slowed down to 7.3% in 2014. However, the unorganized sector in India accounts for 90% of the employment. Self- employment accounts for more than 60% of the employed population of India. Casual workers, who get jobs only at times and remain unpaid when they don't have work, constitute 30% of the workforce, while only 10% are regular employees. At this rate, India is expected to have a 30% unemployment rate by 2020. This would mean that there would be 21 crore jobless people in India.

The World Bank's country strategy advocates greater investments in infrastructure as a priority to attract investment and generate employment. Even though the country tried to keep its pace of growth at higher levels with more economic reforms, it failed to generate more employment. This means the growth rate is not able to reduce the unemployment rate.

Q. 2 Livestock rearing has a big potential for providing non- farm employment and income in rural areas. Discuss suggesting suitable measures to promote this sector in India. 12½

Answer: Livestock rearing is a key livelihood and risk mitigation strategy for small and marginal farmers, particularly across the rain-fed regions of India. Livestock products comprised 32 per cent of the total value of agriculture and allied activities in 2006-07 which was a noticeable increase from 27 per cent of the agricultural gross domestic product in 1999-2000. The livestock sector has therefore been growing faster than many othersectors of agriculture and if this trend continues then the sector will be the engine growth for Indian agriculture that many have predicted.

Most often we see livestock as providers of essential food products, draught power, manure, employment, household income and export earnings. However, it is a very important fact that livestock wealth is much more equitably distributed than wealth associated with land. The goal of inclusive growth, from equity and livelihood perspectives, can be achieved through livestock rearing and it must be at the centre of the stage in poverty alleviation programmes.

Livestock rearing at the household level is largely a women-led activity, and therefore 1 income from livestock rearing and decisions related to management of livestock within the household are primarily taken by women. Livestock rearing has contributed significantly to the empowerment of women and an increasing role in decision making at both the household and village level. Livestock rearing, particularly in the rain-fed regions of the country, is also emerging as a key risk mitigation strategy for the poorest. They face increasingly uncertain and erratic weather conditions which negatively impact crop productivity and wage labour in the agriculture sector.

To promote livestock rearing in India, government has to work to increase awareness on aspects of farm management to ensure full productivity of dairy animals. There is high mortality rate in calves and poor growth. Remedial measure has to be taken in this regard. Another problem among milking animals is low milk performance and mineral deficiencies. Proper nutrition and research can improve milk productivity. Loans and financial support can be provided by government to purchase more livestock. Veterinary services should be improved. Farmers should follow good milking management practices, especially cleanliness and hygiene at the milking place.

In an attempt to promote innovations in livestock farming and increase milk production, the National Bank for Agriculture and Rural Development has launched an initiative ⊠ to facilitate adoption of new technologies by farmers with the help of research institutions. RashtriyaGokul Mission and National Livestock Mission are a welcome step taken by Government for the development of this sector with the objectives of sustainable development of livestock sector.

Q. 3 In the view of the declining average size of land holdings in India which has made agriculture non - viable for a majority of farmers should contract farming and land leasing be promoted in agriculture? Critically evaluate the pros and cons. 12½

Answer: At 157.35 million hectares, India holds the second largest agricultural land globally, only after the United States. 60.3 percent of India's land area is agricultural land. But, as per Agriculture Census 2010-11, small and marginal holdings of less than 2 hectare account for 85 percent of the total operational holdings and 44 percent of the total operated area. The average size of holdings has declined and has come down to 1.16 hectare in 2010-11 from 2.82 hectare in 1970-71. The biggest challenge for Indian agriculture is the decreasing size of land holdings, which can potentially make the profession unfeasible.

Contract farming involves a pre-agreed price between the company and the farmer. The agreement is defined by the commitment of the farmer to provide an agricultural commodity of a certain type at a time and a price and in the quantity required by acommitted buyer, mostly a large company.

The contract farming model being implemented in India ensures that land is permanently owned and cultivated only by farmers. The model which is most popular in the country today is the one in which the contractor supplies all the inputs required for cultivation, while the farmer supplies land and labour. A model of leasing land and allowing the private sector to acquire it for cultivation is not encouraged.

Business houses seek to integrate the supply chain to ensure timely availability of quality and quantity of raw material. Significantly, it also reduces the procurement cost for them by doing away with the middlemen. It leads to significant gains for them, as not only do they get the raw material as per their specific demands, the cost is also much less. It is also believed that the participation of the corporate sector in the farming segment will play a crucial role in technology transfer, capital inflow as well as lead to assured markets for crop production.

The main concern is that the land, which is currently used to grow staple crops like wheat and rice, will be used to grow crops required by the food-processing industry, which also has a significant overseas market. The switch to contract farming, therefore, leads to a rise in exports. In fact, many corporates enter contract farming to fulfil their export obligations.

Q. 4 How can thc 'Digital India' program help farmers to improve farm productivity and income? What step has the government taken in this regard? 12½

Answer: Digital India project launched on 1st July 2015, envisions empowering citizens with e-access to government services and livelihood related services, among others.

The project has three core components, viz. digital infrastructure, digital services and digital literacy. The mAgriculture and mGramBazar, out of the seven components covered under mServices (Mobile Service), directly impact agricultural extension and marketing services.

The project will benefit small farmers as it seeks to

i. transform rural India into a digitally-empowered knowledge economy

ii. provide universal phone connectivity and access to broadband in 250,000 villages

iii. extend timely services to farmers through information technology and its tools

iv. enhance efficiency in agricultural governance through digital literacy and electronic delivery of services. This article briefly highlights government's initiatives and suggests the need for harnessing potential of digital India for agricultural development.

v. Communicate the news about weather phenomena or hazardous events so that preventive measures can be taken early.

Information and Communication Technology (ICT) has the potential to revolutionize Indian agriculture in terms of raising crop productivity and profitability per unit area and resources. For India, at a time when national, regional and international research institutes have already developed technologies, farmers need motivation and encouragement to adopt these proven yield-enhancing, cost-efficient and environment- friendly technologies.

Digital India will enable farmers to gain access to information regarding various stages of agriculture, pre harvest to post harvest. Farmers will get scientific and expert guidance regarding cultivation of crops, harvest and management. Farmers will also have direct and digital access to markets, including online market which will improve their ability of decision making. This will finally lead to better productivity and better income.

Various steps taken by Govt, in this regard are :

a. Launch of Soil Health Card Scheme and a Kisan TV Channel for the development of agriculture sector.

b. An online National Agricultural Market has been approved that will provide more options to farmers for selling their produce.

c. Govt/ has also approved the setting up of Agri-tech Infrastructure Funds for making farming competitive and profitable.

d. Govt, has put in operation three portals viz., farmer portal, Kisan Call Centre and mKisan portal to help farmers take informed decisions for efficient farming under varying agro-climatic conditions.

Q. 5 In what way could replacement of price subsidy with direct benefit Transfer (DBT) change the scenario of subsidies in India? Discuss. 12½

Answer: Direct Benefit Transfer or DBT is an attempt to change the mechanism of transferring subsidies launched by Government of India on 1 January 2013. This program aims to transfer subsidies directly to the people through their bank accounts. It is hoped that crediting subsidies into bank accounts will reduce leakages, delays, etc.

The primary aim of this Direct Benefit Transfer program is to bring transparency and terminate pilferage from distribution of funds sponsored by Central Government of India. In DBT, benefit or subsidy will be directly transferred to citizens living below poverty line. Central Plan Scheme Monitoring System (CPSMS), being implemented by the Office of Controller General of Accounts, will act as the common platform for routing DBT. CPSMS can be used for the preparation of beneficiary list, digitally signing the same and processing of payments in the bank accounts of the beneficiary using the Aadhaar Payment Bridge of NPCI.

The subsidy on LPG cylinders will be credited directly to consumers' Aadhaar-linked bank accounts. The centre saved around Rs 14,000 crore last fiscal due to weeding out of the fake and, duplicate LPG connections through DBTL. The government announced the launch of Direct Benefit Transfer (DBT) for kerosene subsidy in a bid to cut down the diversion and black marketing of the fuel. Government has also linked Students Scholarship and Fertilizer subsidy to Direct Benefit Transfer scheme.

Apart from reducing divergence of subsidy amount, additional benefit is to create direct link to beneficiary through their account which will provide useful database. Good information will be available by fertilizer subsidy transfer as those farmers who had no bank accounts and adhar cards till now will also be joining the stream.

Q. 6 What are the impediment in marketing and supply chain management in developing the food processing industry in India? Can e-commerce help in overcoming this bottleneck? 12

Answer: Food processing industry requires supply of raw material, processing units and market for sale. In India, food processing industry is yet to develop to its true potential. Various impediments are reasons why food processing industry in India is still in bad shape. On the side of marketing and supply chain management, Indian food processing industries are facing challenges of infrastructure and connectivity. Till now, food processing is not localized. Big companies are supplying to remote areas through its processing units located regionally. Infrastructure of road and rail, supply management and professional delivery systems are bottlenecks. Storage capacity has to be created for food processing companies. Local management team and offices have to be opened. Small city centers can be established for better supply and marketing. Localized, small industries can be established with small investment in the area of supply, storage and marketing management which can provide services to the companies engaged in food processing.

Other major impediments in FPI includes traditional technological methods, less investment on R&D. no efficient market survey, large number of middlemen, unsupportive APMC Acts and lack of organised retail.

E-commerce can help to some extent by utilizing local warehouses and delivery system. By e-commerce data, companies can understand demand in any particular area and start storing and delivering from local warehouses.

However, localization and spread out units can best help the food processing industries.

Q. 7 Craze for gold in Indians has led to surge in import of gold in recent years and put pressure on balance of payments and external value of rupee. In view of this, examine the merits of Gold Monetization scheme. 12½

Answer: In India people consider gold as safe investment for future apart from having importance in social customs. As economic condition is improving, people have more money to save. This leads Indians to buy gold and as a result there is surge in import of gold in recent years.

Import of foreign commodity requires payment in foreign currency. Import affects balance of payments adversely and high demand of foreign currency reduces value of rupee.

Government of India launched Gold Monetization scheme which would replace both the present Gold Deposit and Gold Metal Loan Schemes. The new scheme would allow the depositors of gold to earn interest in their metal accounts and the jewellers to obtain loans in their metal account. Banks/ other dealers would also be able to monetise this gold. Once the gold is deposited in metal account, it will start earning interest on the same.

Under the scheme, Government expected to bring in market the unutilized gold to reduce import of gold.

Benefits of the scheme to Customers

- The gold grows itself in this scheme. The weight of gold remain same forever if you keep is in the house. But the GMS increases the weight of the gold according to the given interest rate.
- You will get the true value of your gold. Getting cash in place of gold is very easy. Tax Benefit

There is no tax at all. The investment, interest and maturity is tax-free. There is no capital gains tax on the gold interest. There is wealth tax as well.

Benefit To Government

- It will reduce the country's reliance on the import of gold to meet domestic demand.
- Gold Monetization Scheme would benefit the Indian gems and jewelry sector which is a major contributor to India's exports.

- The mobilized gold will also supplement RBI's gold reserves and will help in reducing the government's borrowing cost.

Q. 8 "Success of 'Make in India' program depends on the success of 'Skill India' programme and radical labour reforms." Discuss with logical arguments. 12½

Answer: Make in India is an initiative launched by the Government of India to encourage multinational, as well as national companies to manufacture their products in India. But to attract investment in manufacturing and industrial sector, India needs to create skilled and manual labour force. Although, in 2014, India's labour force was estimated to be about 490 million, or 40 per cent of the population, 93 per cent of this force was in the unorganised sector.

The Economic Survey for 2014-15 has suggested that transformational sectors could be in registered manufacturing or services. Raising economy wide skills must compliment efforts to improve the conditions for manufacturing. Prime Minister NarendraModi has made the revival of Indian manufacturing a top priority reflected in the Make in India campaign. It has clearly stated that the Prime Minister's Skill India objective should be accorded high priority in order to realise the Make in India objective.

Indian growth should balance the nation's comparative advantage in availability of low skilled labour with skill development required by future generations to take advantage of lost opportunities. The registered manufacturing must be expanded to take leverage of India's abundant unskilled labour. While "Make in India" occupies prominence as an important goal, the future trajectory of Indian development depends on both "Make in India" and "Skilling India".

Efforts to improve the conditions of labour-intensive manufacturing need to be complemented with rapid skill upgrade because skill-intensive sectors are dynamic sectors in India and sustaining their dynamism will require that the supply of skills keeps pace with the rising demand of these skills, otherwise even these sectors might become uncompetitive.

Investors also faces difficulty by labour law regime of India as it has always been at loggerheads with industrial development and the ease of doing business. India need to focus on cutting down red tape, by amending nearly 40 Central and 150 State labour laws, has been launched, with significant consequences on hiring and firing. Labour reforms must be linked to the ease of doing business, creating a habitat where jobs can be fostered. Reforms must be linked to worker benefits, while simultaneously easing the compliance burden on small and medium enterprises. The labour law must be rationalized by defining minimum wages and linking them to inflation. Minimum wages ought tobe revised annually, with penalties for their violation dramatically raised.

Skilled manpower and industry friendly labour laws will help India attract more investment and bring success to Make in India program.

Q. 9 To what factors can be the recent dramatic fall in equipment cost and tariff of solarenergy be attributed? What implications does the trend have for thermal power producers and related industry? 12½

Answer: Recently there has been drastic reduction in equipment cost and tariff of solar energy. Total module costs of Chinese solar companies have decreased from $76 a watt in 1977 to 1.31 a watt in 2011 to around S0.50/W in 2014. This was primarily due to the reduction in processing costs, the fall in polysilicon costs and improvement in conversion efficiencies. Total costs could fall another 30-40 per cent over the next several years, with the greatest cost reductions are likely to come from the residential segments as scale and operating efficiencies improve.

Solar, and other technologies such as wind power, are no longer more expensive than traditional fossil fuels in many parts of the world. With this competitive price, solar energy could extend its reach of "grid parity" to 80 per cent of global markets within the next two years, assuming a 40 per cent cut in solar costs by the end of 2017. At least half of the 140,000GW of power capacity to be installed in the Middle East and north Africa in the coming decade to be solar.

This will affect installation of new thermal power projects and even currently installed thermal power projects will have to be more competitive in price. However, simultaneous drastic reduction in oil price will not make thermal power uncompetitive in near future. Availability of solar radiation varies from region to region and from season to season, so there is no immediate threat to thermal power producers and related industries, but future will belong to renewable energy sources like solar.

Q. 10 There is a clear acknowledgement that Special Economic Zones (SEZs) are a tool of industrial development, manufacturing and exports. Recognising this potential, the whole instrumentality of SEZs require augmentation. Discuss the issue plaguing the success of SEZs with respect to taxation, governing laws and administration. 12½

Answer: The Special Economic Zones were established to promote industrial development leading to generation of employment for local people. However, of late, the SEZ policy has suffered on following counts:

1. The introduction of Minimum alternate tax and Dividend distribution tax have neutralized income tax benefits which was originally available in SEZs
2. The absence of complementary infrastructure to support the SEZ has stalled progress of industrialization.
3 The lack of proactive assistance from development officials have created red-tapism type of atmosphere in SEZ as well.
4. The export incentives granted to industries outside the zones have not been extended to the SEZ thus making them less attractive to invest in.
5. The free trade agreements signed with other countries have garnered an edge over the SEZs due to advantage available to other industries outside SEZ.

To overcome these issues, it is suggested that:

1. Rather than withdrawing MAT and DDT, discussions must be made on the level at which they can be levied.
2. A more predictable taxation policy for making the environment conducive for investment.
3 The creation of complementary infrastructure, power, roads and ports should be promoted promptly.
4. The procedures should be made simple for new and existing industries.

Q. 11 What do you understand by "Standard Positioning System" and "Precision positioningsystem" in the GPS era? Discuss the advantage India perceives from its ambitious IRNSS programme employing just seven satellites. 12½

Answer: GPS provides two different positioning services: the Precise Positioning Service (PPS) and the Standard Positioning Service (SPS).

The GPS Standard Positioning Service (SPS) is a positioning and timing service provided by way of ranging signals broadcast at the GPS LI frequency which contains signal with a navigation data message that is available for peaceful civil, commercial, and scientific use.

The GPS Precise Positioning Service (PPS) is a positioning and timing service provided by way of authorized access to ranging signals broadcast at the GPS LI and L2 frequencies. The LI frequency contains signal that is available for peaceful civil, commercial, and scientific use; and a precision (P) code ranging signal with a navigation data message, that is reserved for authorized use.

The Indian Regional Navigation Satellite System or IRNSS is an indigenously developed Navigation Satellite System that is used to provide accurate real-time positioning and timing services over India and region extending to 1500 km around India. IRNSS would have seven satellites, out of which six are already placed in orbit. The constellation of seven satellites is expected to operate from June 2016 onwards. The IRNSS would provide two services, with the Standard Positioning Service open for civilian use, and the Restricted Service (an encrypted one) for authorized users (including the military).

Q. 12 What are the areas of prohibitive labour that can be sustainably managed by robots? Discuss the initiatives that can propel the research in premier research institutes for substantive and gainful innovation. 12½

Answer: There has been a long debate about replacing human labour with robot and arguments against mechanization and human being losing jobs. But there are certain dangerous areas where using robots can save human lives.

Robots can be used for work in dangerous mines where loss of lives is very high. In dark and deep mines where level of oxygen is low, poisonous gases and chances of landslides create danger for human life, robot can be used.

In agricultural areas where pesticides, rain and other circumstances make it difficult for hum^n being to carry out the job, robots can be employed.

Robdts can also be used in heavy industries and heavy labour works to save human efforts. Heavy industries create working environment where electricity, water, oil, otherdangerous substances and heavy machinery are dangerous for human presence, robots can be useful for carrying out work.

To propel research institutes, government and big corporations need to fund the programs. Policy initiative can be taken by government. Legal and economic debates have to be directed towards right direction to create a positive mindset among people. Use of Robot need not be perceived as encroachment upon human labour area but supplement to human efforts. Scientific collaboration can be institutionalized at international level for cooperation in advanced research. Conferences, exhibitions, awards and seminars can be organized to give due recognition to the research being carried out in robotics.

Q. 13 Discuss the advantage and security implication of cloud hosting of servers vis-a-vis in house machine based hosting for government business. 12½

Answer: Cloud hosting services are the hosting services that are provided to customers via multiple connected servers that comprise a cloud, as opposed to being provided by a single server or virtual server.

Advantages of Cloud Computing

Cost Savings : Perhaps, the most significant cloud computing benefit is in terms of IT cost savings. Businesses, no matter what their type or size, exist to earn money while keeping capital and operational expenses to a minimum.

Reliability : With a managed service platform, cloud computing is much more reliable and consistent than in-house IT infrastructure. An organization can benefit from a massive pool of redundant IT resources, as well as quick failover mechanism - if a server fails, hosted applications and services can easily be transited to any of the available servers.

Manageability : Cloud computing provides enhanced and simplified IT management and maintenance capabilities through central administration of resources, vendor managed infrastructure and SLA backed agreements.

Strategic Edge : Ever-increasing computing resources give you a competitive edge over competitors, as the time you require for IT procurement is virtually nil. Your company can deploy mission critical applications that deliver significant business benefits, without any upfront costs and minimal provisioning time.

Moving towards a cloud-based environment, however, requires careful planning and analysis. It also has significant security implications that your organization needs to ensure it fully understands and manages:

- Identity management. Manage personal identity information so access to computer resources, applications, data, and services are properly controlled.
- Detection and forensics. Businesses must separate legitimate and illegitimate activities, since there is a greater chance of unauthorized access in the cloud.
- Encryption. Code to protect your information assets since cloud-based systems are shared by a variety of users.
- Manageability. You need a consistent view across your on-premises and cloud-based environments. After all, your organization is one entity, and therefore your systems also must be integrated as one.
- Standards. A standard is an agreed-upon approach for doing something. Cloud standardsensure interoperability, so you can use tools, applications, virtual images, and more in another cloud environment without having to do any rework.
- Governance and compliance. Governance defines roles and responsibilities, as well as policies and procedures that your personnel or groups need to follow. Cloud governance should include your own infrastructure as well as infrastructure you do not completely control.
- Storing data in the cloud. Managing data stored in the cloud requires data security and privacy, including controls for moving data from point A to point B. It also includes managing data storage and the resources for data processing.

Q. 14 India's Traditional Knowledge Digital Library (TKDL) which has a database containing formatted information on more than 2 million medicinal formulations is proving a powerful weapon in the country's fight against erroneous patents. Discuss the pros and cons of making the database publicly available under open source licensing. 12½

Answer: The Traditional Knowledge Digital Library (TKDL) is an Indian digital knowledge repository of the traditional knowledge, especially about medicinal plants and formulations used in Indian systems of medicine. Set up in 2001, the objective of the library is to protect the ancient and traditional knowledge of the country from exploitation through biopiracy and unethical patents, by documenting it electronically and classifying it as per international patent classification systems. Apart from that, the non-patent database serves to foster modern research based on traditional knowledge, as it simplifies access to this vast knowledge of remedies or practices.As the database project reached its completion, in 2006 the government allowed access to the library to international patent offices, including European Patent Office (EPO), Japan and the UK, subject to a non-disclosure clause. This allows patent examiners to evaluate patent applications and stop attempts to patent traditional knowledge as "new" inventions. If the database is made publicly available, millions of people all over the world would be able to use medicinal formulations for better health. These are already freely available to the people who know Indian language or at least with some research can be availed. Open source licensing will prevent claims of invention but will allow access and utilization of the medical system that has developed over thousands of years.

One problem can be profiteering by multinational companies using the medical formulations developed by ancient Indian knowledge system.

Q. 15 Discuss the NamamiGange and National Mission for Clean Ganga (NMCG) programmes and causes of mixed results from the previous schemes. What quantum leaps can help preserve the river Ganga better than incremental inputs? 12½

Answer: The Ganga is the largest river in India with an extraordinary religious importance for Hindus, providing water to about 40% of India's population across 11 states. A number of initiatives have been undertaken to clean the river but failed to deliver desired results.

The Ganga Action Plan or GAP was a program launched in January 1985 to reduce the pollution load on the river. The plan was withdrawn on 31 March 2000.

National River Ganga Basin Authority (NRGBA) was established by the Central Government of India in February 2009 which declared the Ganga as the "National River" of India.

In 2010 the government declared the stretch of river between Gaumukh and Uttarkashi an "eco-sensitive zone". In 2010, the Indian government embarked on a $4 billion campaign to ensure that by 2020 no untreated municipal sewage or industrial runoff enters the 1,560-mile river.

Namami Ganga project was announced by the Government in July 2014 budget. As a part of the program, government of India ordered shutdown of 48 industrial units around Ganga.

Ganga Manthan, a national conference was held by the National Mission for Clean Ganga on 7 July 2014 at Vigyan Bhawan in New Delhi to discuss issues and possible solutions for cleaning the river.

National Ganga River Basin Authority (NGRBA) has started the Mission Clean Ganga with a changed and comprehensive approach to champion the challenges posed to Ganga through four different sectors, namely, of wastewater management, solid waste management, industrial pollution and river front development.

Piecemeal approach has failed to address problem of Ganga water pollution, it is expected that National Mission Clear Ganga will deliver a result as it envisages various aspects related to pollution of the river.

The frequency of earthquakes appears to have increased in the Indian subcontinent. However, India's preparedness for mitigating their impact has significant gaps. Discuss various aspects.

Answer: India is a part of continental plate that is convergig with the Eurasian plate along the Himalayas. This zone of convergence is prone to earthquakes, so, there are frequent incedence of Earthquakes in the Indian sub-continent. As per the current seismic zone map of the country over 59 per cent of India's land area is under threat of moderate to severe earthquakes.

There were six earthquakes in 2015 in Indian subcontinent, one in 2014, two in 2012 and one in 2011 totaling ten earthquakes in last five years. Between 2006-2010 there was only one earthquake; between 2001-2005 there were three. This shows that frequency of earthquakes appears to have increased in Indian subcontinent in recent years. Disasters and their management generally get discussed in their aftermath but practically it should result in planning and preparing the strategy to tackle and mitigate disasters in a responsible and effective manner.

The Government of India adopted mitigation and prevention as essential components of their development strategy. The Tenth Five Year Plan document has a detailed chapter on Disaster Management. Each State is supposed to prepare a plan scheme for disaster mitigation in accordance with the approach outlined in the plan. In brief, mitigation is being institutionalized into developmental planning. However, this disaster management is lacking in many ways in preparedness for mitigating impact of earthquakes. Disaster management has no trained force sufficient to take immediate actions. They have to rely on support of military or paramilitary forces for disaster management which is more incidental than permanent.

Q. 17 Human right activists constantly highlight the fact that the Armed forces (Special Powers) Act, 1958 (AFSPA) is a draconian act leading to cases of human right abuses by security forces. What sections of AFSPA are opposed by the activists. Critically evaluate the requirement with reference to the view held by Apex Court. 12½

Answer: The Armed Forces (Special Powers) Act (AFSPA), a controversial piece of legislation confers vast powers on the armed forces deployed in "disturbed areas" of the country Indian Parliament enacted AFSPA in September 1958 in the context of the nascent Naga insurgency.

AFSPA's lack of clarity as to what constitutes a "disturbed area" and the rather arbitrary manner in which AFSPA can be imposed is opposed severely.

AFSPA grants the army, central police forces, and state police personnel in "disturbed areas" "certain special powers," including the right to shoot to kill, to raid houses, and destroy any property that is "likely" to be used by insurgents, and "to arrest without warrant" even on "reasonable suspicion" a person who has committed or even "about to commit a cognizable offence." Besides conferring extensive powers on the armed forces, AFSPA provides them immunity from prosecution.

It is alleged that the sweeping powers vested in the hands of the armed forces and especially the protection it gives them from prosecution encourages soldiers to kill, raid and rape. In an insurgency situation it is difficult for soldiers to differentiate between sympathizer and insurgent.

Referring to AFPSA in Manipur, the Supreme Court of India recently observed that AFSPA was supposed to be a temporary measure, but it has been there for the last 35 years. The use of AFPSA as a permanent mechanism is being criticized by Supreme Court however in an earlier judgment the apex court had upheld validity of the act per se.

Q. 18 Religious indoctrination via social media has resulted in Indian youth joining the ISIS. What is ISIS and its mission? How can ISIS be dangerous to the internal security of our country. **12½**

Answer: ISIS has used social media to spread its propaganda and terror across the globe. It has posted videos of beheading on youtube. ISIS has been successful to indoctrinate Indian youth via social media to join ISIS.

The Islamic State of Iraq and the Levant, alternatively translated as Islamic State of Iraq and Syria or Islamic State of Iraq and al-Sham is a Salafi jihadist militant group that follows an Islamic fundamentalist, Wahhabi doctrine of Sunni Islam. The group is also known as Daesh. The group has referred to itself as the Islamic State or IS ever since it proclaimed a worldwide caliphate in June 2014 and named Abu Bakr al-Baghdadi as its caliph. As a caliphate, it claims religious, political and military authority over all Muslims worldwide.

In June 2014, ISIL published a document in which it claimed to have traced the lineage of its leader al-Baghdadi back to Muhammad and upon proclaiming a new caliphate on 29 June, the group appointed al-Baghdadi as its caliph. As caliph, he demands the

allegiance of all devout Muslims worldwide, according to Islamic jurisprudence. ISIL has detailed its goals in its Dabiq magazine, saying it will continue to seize land and take over the entire Earth until it covers all eastern and western extents of the Earth, filling the world with the truth and justice of Islam and putting an end to the falsehood and tyranny of jahiliyyah [state of ignorance],

Islamic State propaganda includes India among its list of enemies — which also includes Pakistan and Bangladesh. The numbers of Indians who have responded to the Islamic State's call, are however very few - less than two dozen. Islamic State sympathisers have also tried to set up cells inside India. It can be dangerous for internal security of India. In the periphery, people have to be made aware of the foolishness of the ideological beliefs that ISIS espouses. There have been worrisome reports of Indians joining the fundamentalist groups. This has to prevented at all costs - a stitch in time saves nine.

Q. 19 The persisting drives of the government for development of large industries in backward areas have resulted in isolating the tribal population and the farmers who face multiple displacements. With Malkangiri and Naxalbari foci, discuss the corrective strategies needed to win the Left Wing Extremism (LWE) doctrine affected citizens back into mainstream of social and economic growth. **12½**

Answer: When a large scale industry is established in an area, lot of land is required which causes displacement of local population. Added to displacement is depriving of agricultural land and making the people jobless. Considering technical nature of work, majority of the local people are not able to get any job in the industry being set up. One time payment is not invested properly and therefore in short period, the displaced people become unemployed poor. Apart from losing land, home and job, is feeling of encroachment in their culture and resources which causes bitterness among the locals for newly entrant industrialists and employees.

This causes Left Wing Extremism (LWE) to prevent such industrialization. Collector was kidnapped in Malkangiri area of Orissa by LWEs which shows a violent method to raise their concern against industrialisation and development process implemented by government. In West Bengal Naxalbari area is also affected by the same issue. Government has to take into mainstream the section of population affected by this type of ideology by giving them benefits of development, removing poverty and ensuring fair share in social infrastructural and economical development. Better communication and connectivity to modern education and employment will pave a way in this direction. A National Strategy—involving governance, development, empowerment and security—is the basic prerequisite for resolving the challenge posed by Naxalism/Left Wing Extremism in the country. Some of the major challenges include achieving national consensus on the Naxal issue, achieving inclusive growth, perception management, prevention of the further spatial spread of Naxalism, empowerment of youth, implementation of development initiatives, isolation from external support, capacity building of the Security Forces and proper implementation of the already existing legislations dealing with tribal rights.

Q. 20 Considering the threats cyberspace poses for the country, India needs a "Digital Armed Forces" to prevent crimes. Critically evaluate the National Cyber Security Policy, 2013 outlining the challenges perceived in its effective implementation. 12½

Answer: Cyber-attacks are defined as "deliberate actions to alter, disrupt, deceive, degrade, or destroy computer systems or networks or the information and/or programs resident in or transiting these systems or networks."

As threat to cyberspace is increasing, Indian government published its first ever National Cyber Security Policy (NCSP), in early July, 2013. The NCSP essentially speaks of a framework for the protection of information in cyberspace by eliminating vulnerabilities. Major clauses include greater emphasis on research and development of indigenous security technology, and their effective testing and deployment. The policy also calls for enhanced public and private partnership vis-a-vis technical and operational cooperation, aimed at encouraging organizations to adopt individually tailored IT regulations and infrastructure, in conformity with international best practices.

The policy envisions creating a workforce of 500,000 cyber specialists in the next five years. In fact India needs a Digital Armed Force type mechanism which can carry out secret operations in India and abroad.

Despite being a positive step towards securing India's cyber assets, the NCSP is far from answering all nuances of the cyber threat, as they exist today. The most critical factor is the lack of details, along with a feasible nationwide strategy to achieve the objectives set out in the policy. Policy is neither binding nor enforceable, but merely provides guidelines for a standard operating procedure. In this regard, the NCSP does not maximize its potential for optimum benefit. A crucial point missing entirely from the NCSP is the security concerns in the telecom industry.

SOLVED PAPERS

PAPER–IV

Time Allowed: Three Hours *Maximum Marks: 250*

Instructions: There are FOURTEEN questions divided in two Sections and printed both in Hindi and in English. All questions are compulsory. The number of marks carried by a question/part is indicated against it. Word limit in questions, wherever specified, should be adhered to. Any page or portion of the page left blank in the Question-cum-Answer Booklet must be clearly struck off.

Answer questions in NOT MORE than the word limit specified for each in the parenthesis. Content of the answer is more important than its length.

Section-A

Q. 1 (a) What is meant by 'environmental ethics'? Why is it important to study? Discuss any one environmental issue from the viewpoint of environmental ethics. (150 words.) 10

Answer: Environmental ethics indicates relation between the moral relationship of human beings to, and also the value and moral status of, the environment and its non-human contents. It is important to study environmental ethics because it forces people to consider how their actions affect others and the environment. When people realize their effect, they are more likely to take steps to change uncomfortable behaviors; for instance, they may decide to recycle, to be compassionate towards animals, or to be an advocate for wilderness preservation.

One major environmental issue in India is water pollution, which can be considered from environmental ethical view point.

Discharge of untreated sewage is the single most important cause for pollution of surface and ground water in India. Should we continue continue to release untreated sewage on surface of ground?

India lacks sufficient treatment capacity and sewage treatment plants that exist do not operate and are not maintained.The majority of the government-owned sewage treatment plants remain closed most of the time due to improper design or poor maintenance or lack of reliable electricity supply to operate the plants, together with absentee employees and poor management. Government should inve;t more and maintain strict control to make sure that installed treatment capacity is properly utilized.

The uncollected wastes accumulate in the urban areas cause unhygienic conditions and release pollutants that leach to surface and groundwater. It should be make mandatory by government to keep surrounding clean and collection of waste should be properly facilitated.

Out of India's 3,119 towns and cities, just 209 have partial sewage treatment facilities, and only 8 have full wastewater treatment facilities. Over 100 Indian cities dump untreated sewage directly into the Ganges River. Investment is needed to bridge the gap between 29000 million litre per day of sewage India generates, and a treatment capacity of mere 6000 million litre per day.

(b) Differentiate between the following (200 Words)

(i) Law and ethics

(ii) Ethical management and management of ethics

(iii) Discrimination and preferential treatment

(iv) Personal Ethics and Professional Ethics. 10

Answer: (i) Laws are values and principles backed by authorized legislatures while Ethics are those rules or customs which are supported by moral and social backups. Although laws are mostly ethical but ethics are not always having lawful authority. Ethical obligations typically exceed legal duties.

(ii) Ethical management refers to corporate management that not only fulfills economic goals and legal responsibilities, but also meets the ethical expectations imposed by social norms in conducting business.

Management of ethics is the ethical treatment of employees, stockholders, owners and the public by a company. A company, while needing to make a profit, should have good ethics. Employees should be treated well, whether they are employed here or overseas.

(iii) Discrimination is treatment or consideration of, or making a distinction in favor of or against, a person or thing based on the group, class, or category to which that person or thing is perceived to belong to rather than on individual merit. Preferential Treatment literally refers to "job or employment preference given to someone who is of the right race, ethnicity, or gender" as defined in the government's approved list of historically disadvantaged. Since preferential treatment is based on race and gender it is quite discriminatory.

(iv) Personal ethics is a category of philosophy that determines what an individual believes about morality and right and wrong. This is usually distinguished from business ethics or legal ethics. These branches of ethics come from outside organizations or governments, not the individual's conscience. Professional ethics encompass the personal, organizational and corporate standards of behavior expected of professionals. How the use of knowledge should be governed when providing a service to the public can be considered a moral issue and is termed professional ethics.

Q. 2 Given are two quotations of moral thinkers/philosophers. For each of these bring out what it means to you in the present context.

(a) "The weak can never forgive; forgiveness is the attribute of strong." (150 words) 10

Answer: Mahatma Gandhi wrote, "The weak can never forgive; forgiveness is the attribute of strong." In freedom struggle against British Raj, Gandhi started and led non-vilest movement, only one of its kinds in the world. Gandhi preached to love enemy and forgive them for their sins.

Forgiveness is a way of declaring one's integrity. A weak can never forgive as weakness is a mental and intellectual deficiency. It is the result of lack of judgement. It is a mental state of inability to withstand temptation, whereas strong refers to 'determination of spirit'.

Gandhi believed that by forgiving the sinner you give him a chance to repent and improve. Strong people can have this attribute to trust the sinner again by giving a

chance to reform. Those who do not forgive, they cannot move away from enmity. Animosity is poisonous and creates destruction.

Gandhi had virtuous ideas and he believed that if a person slaps on your one cheek, you should forward another cheek. By doing this, you create feeling of regret and wrongfulness in the wrongdoer. In the same manner, when anyone does something wrong, rather than punishing him, give him a chance to reform and regret his act by forgiving him.

(b) "We can easily forgive a child who is afraid of the dark; the real tragedy of life is when men are afraid of the light" (150 words) 10

Answer: Plato wrote, "We can easily forgive a child who is afraid of the dark; the real tragedy of life is when men are afraid of the light." A great philosopher and seeker of truth, Plato warned mankind of wrong attitude of moving face away from truth, the light.

It is but natural that a child would be afraid of the dark but most of the time grown up people is living in darkness of ignorance and lies. They are afraid of seeking wisdom, knowledge and truth. They keep following wrong practices set up by traditions and are afraid to see new light of truth and raise their voice against the dark and wrong customs. Plato says that such people live in world of myth and do not dare to change. This is particularly dangerous because new inventions are not accepted and anyone revealing truth is suppressed by the majority of this kind of people. As per Plato, this is the tragedy of life.

The given quote states about general tendency of an adult who many a times runs away or call-off from his duty due to fear of getting caught of the wrong act done intentionally or unintentionally by him. It is at this point of time that men loses their integrity and accountability, and run away from the light which falls upon them.

Q. 3 (a) "A mere compliance with law is not enough, the public servant also has to havea well developed sensibility to ethical issues for effective discharge of duties". Do you agree? Explain with the help of two examples, where (i) an act is ethically right, but not legally and (ii) an act is legally right, but not ethically. (150 words) 10

Answer: A person living in a village and not having necessary documents for availing benefit of government scheme, even though he deserves it the most, cannot be legally extended benefit of the scheme. It would be ethically right to make him beneficiary of the scheme because he would fulfill all required conditions but due to lack of certain documents if an officer covers him under the scheme, it will be legally wrong.

On the contrary there may be a situation where a resourceful person can produces all required document to be eligible for benefit of certain government scheme while in no circumstances he deserves it. It would be legally wrong to deny him benefit of the scheme but ethically right.

If a public servant follows only rule book and extends or denies benefits of certain governmental scheme, without using his discretion, for the best implementation of governmental policy, it would defeat the purpose. Therefore, a public servant has to have well developed sensibility to ethical issues for effective discharge of duties and should not merely comply with the laws.

(b) How do the virtues of trustworthiness and fortitude get manifested in publicservice? Explain with examples. (150 words) 10

Answer: Trustworthiness is a position of deserving of trust or confidence of a class of people including feeling of dependability and reliability. Such outward perception of trustworthiness gets manifested in public service by providing impartial service and maintaining full integrity towards duty. A public servant who extends benefits of various government schemes to deserving people or prevents corrupt practices or diversion of funds for unauthorized activities commands such trustworthiness. Fortitude is mental and emotional strength in facing difficulty, adversity, danger, or temptation courageously. A public servant has to withstand all opposition, vested interests and dangers coming in the way to implementation of his duties and obligation. His strict adherence to laws and rules manifests fortitude in his public service through his conducts.

If a public servant is in charge of identifying a piece of land for implementing a government project, and he averts influence of local groups and businessmen who intend to promote personal interest in such project, and considers public interest at large and implements the project strictly according to the spirit of law, manifests fortitude and trustworthiness.

Q. 4 (a) "Social values are more important than economic values." Discuss the abovestatement with examples in the context of inclusive growth of a nation. (150 words. 10

Answer: Social values form an important part of the culture of the society, account for the stability of social order and provide the general guidelines for social conduct. While economic value is represented by the maximum amount a consumer is willing to pay for an item in a free market economy, or the amount of time an individual will sacrifice waiting to obtain a government-rationed good in a socialist economy.

To realize inclusive growth of a nation, economic resources have to be utilized in a manner that Creates benefits for those who deserve more, rather than for those who can pay more. Investment has to be made in social infrastructure where return is less but benefit is spreader to everyone.

Construction of a luxury hotel will certainly generate more economic benefit in comparison to construction of a charity hospital - but social value derived from the latter is much more to achieve inclusive growth.

Similarly, construction of infrastructure and providing basic facilities in rural areas where return on investment is less creates social value.

If we think only in terms of economic value, inclusive growth would not be possible for a nation. Everyone cannot compete in a free market and therefore only economic value cannot be a parameter for giving benefit of growth to everyone. Therefore, social values are more important than economic values for inclusive growth.

(b) Some recent developments such as introduction of RTI Act, media and judicial activism, etc. are proving helpful in bringing about greater transparency and accountability in the

functioning of the government. However, it is also being observed that at times the mechanisms are misused. Another negative effect is that the officers are now afraid to take prompt decisions. Analyse the situation in detail and suggest how the dichotomy can be resolved. Suggest how thesenegative impacts can be minimised. (150 words) 10

Answer: On the one side developments like implementation of RTI Act, active journalism by media and proactive role of judiciary by judicial activism are helping to bring greater transparency and accountability government functioning but sometimes unnecessary harassment is affecting independent and efficient function of government officers. Many incidents have come to light where these machineries have been misused for personal or vested interests.

Officers are also afraid to take prompt decision based on their analysis of situation unless they have all supporting evidence to prove their decision because such mechanisms may put them in trouble.

To avoid this dichotomy, it is suggested that officers who have good track record should be given protection against any harassment.

To minimize negative impact of such mechanism, strict control has to be maintained against use of them against any individual. Certain guidelines should be given for use of these mechanisms. If required, action should be taken against those who misuse the mechanism against any officer for vindictive purpose. Officers should be given protection for the decisions taken in good faith and for discharge of duties.

Q. 5 Two different kinds of attitudes exhibited by public servants towards their work have been identified as bureaucratic attitude and the democratic attitude. (150 words. 10

(a) Distinguish between these two terms and write their merits and demerits.

Answer: Bureaucratic attitude refers to over adherence to procedures which delays functioning of the office. It creates hurdle in prompt discharge of duties and over secure approach of the public servant without using discretionary power vested in him results into ineffective functioning.

Democratic attitude is an approach where public servant tries to keep everyone happy irrespective of rules and procedures. In this attitude public servant tries to satisfy demands of all groups without looking into due procedure and requirements.

While democratic attitude is necessary for representing public interests, peace and harmony in the society; it may lead to delay in decision making awaiting consensus and hinder its implementation with expediency and required pragmatism.

(b) Is it possible to balance the two to create a bette- administration for the faster development of our country?

Answer: It is possible to balance the two attitudes so that bureaucratic attitude helps in following due procedures and fulfilling paper works requires in office formalities, but at the same time showing democratic and sympathetic attitude to keep people happy delivers beneficial results of schemes to applicants. Similarly over democratic attitude combined with bureaucratic attitude will not waste public money for keeping undeserving people happy and requirement of due process will be followed.

A judicious combination of these two attitudes will result into lawful administration with humanitarian approach.

Q. 6 Today we find that in-spite of various measures like prescribing codes of conduct, setting up vigilance cells/commissions, RTI, active media and strengthening of legal mechanism, corrupt practices are not coming under control.

(a) Evaluate the effectiveness of these measures with justifications

Answer: Legislation stipulates the obligation to publish all information relating to specific tenders on the internet.

Sometimes punishments for corruption are not so severe. Sanctions will increase for bribery, scheming to defraud in public tenders or vote buying. Officials will face up to ten years in prison for corrupt behaviour.

If an employee draws attention to corrupt behaviour at his place of work, he will be provided with more legal protection than has been the case so far.

The conditions for the use of wiretapping and agent provocateur have not bfeen defined. A range of corruption-type crimes for which investigators will be able to use these practices will be defined in the Criminal Procedure Code.

Sometimes undesirable ties between investigators and public functionaries will be limited.

RTI has empowered the ordinary citizen to get respect as an individual from the government and its officials. Citizens are becoming the monitors of their government. In the past few years, it appears that the decisions of the information commissions and judiciary are expanding the grounds on which information can be denied, be it on obstructing the national development and integration, or destroying the peace, tranquility and harmony among its citizens.

(b) Suggest more effective strategies to tackle this menace (150 words) **10**

1. **Value education:** Parents and teachers should inculcate moral values in children. Practice is more persuasive than preaching.
2. **Effective and regular vigilance:** Strict action should be taken against lazy and corrupt officials. Number of agencies and officials should be increased.
3. **Responsible citizen:** If an individual is corrupt, he cannot expect those in power to be free from corruption. Hence, it is essential for every citizen to perform his duties faithfully and to the best of their abilities.
4. **Strong and Effective leadership and administration:** All those who are granted powers and authority by people should fulfil their promises and pledge. They should strive their utmost to eradicate corruption from systems and administrations.
5. **Media:** Media should frequently expose the cases of corruption. It should educate people against corruption on regular basis.

Q. 7 At the international level, bilateral relations between most nations are governed on the policy of promoting one's own national interest without any regard for the interest of other

nations. This lead to conflicts and tension between the nations. How can ethical consideration help resolve such tensions? Discuss with specific examples. (150 words) 10

Answer: Bilateral relations are generally fueled by mutual interests, where both nations try to promote own interest in a way that the other party accepts it. In cases where one party is dominant, even one sided agreements and deals are signed. A stronger party provides protection, military support, economic assistance or technical support to weaker one and in return tries to get votes in international forums, better contracts for its companies, rights over natural resources and cultural or economic dominance. Sovereign nation has right to decide own policy but other factors influence such decisions.

As is always, each party tries to forward its own interest which, if not mutually agreed, leads to conflict of interest and tension. Border issues between India and Pakistan are unsolved for more than six decades because of these reasons. At multilateral level, like WTO or in environmental issues, each country would try to take less responsibility on its part which will create stall back in decision making.

In case a country, ethically and unilaterally takes some decision to reduce tension, it helps in resolving situation of conflict and tension. For example, India unilaterally allows free trade on the border of Kashmir for POK residents, to help economic growth in the region. Similarly, India unilaterally announced no-first use policy of nuclear weapons, to give message of peace and security in the region.

Q. 8 Public servants are likely to confront with the issues of "Conflict of Interest". What do you understand by the term "Conflict of Interest" and how does it manifest in the decision making by public servants? If faced with the conflict of interest situation how would you resolve it? Explain with the help of examples. (150 words) 10

Answer: A conflict of interest is a set of circumstances that creates a risk that professional judgement or actions regarding a primary interest will be unduly influenced by a secondary interest

Conflict of interest include pecuniary interests i.e. financial interests or other material benefits or costs, or non-pecuniary interests i.e. favouritism, cronyism, nepotism, political, religious, family or other interests. Conflict of interest may manifest itself in the decision making by public servants when their private interests conflict with the impartial fulfillment of their official duties and the public interest.

Public servants has to have primary interest in due discharge of his duties while secondary interest may be in financial gain or extending favour to relatives etc conflict in these two interests may deviate the public servant from discharge of duties neutrally. In case, such conflict of interest created situations for corrupt practice or deviation from due procedure arises, Public servant should avoid such situations or handover the task to another officer.

Example of such conflict of interest may be appointment of a subordinate where rules provide for due qualification and procedure but one of the applicant being relative of the decision making authority. In such cases conflict of interest is between following due procedure or giving favour to relative.

Q. 9 A private company is known for its efficiency, transparency and employee welfare. The company though owned by a private individual has a cooperative character where employees feel a sense of ownership. The company employs nearly 700 personnel and they have voluntarily decided not to form union.

One day suddenly in the morning, about 40 men belonging to political party gate crashed into the factory demanding jobs in the factory. They threatened the management and employees, and also used foul language. The employees feel demoralized. It was clear that those people who gate crashed wanted to be on the payroll of the company as well as continue as the volunteers/members of the party.

The company maintains high standards in integrity and does not extend favoursto civil administration that also includes law enforcement agency. Such incident occur in public sector also.

(a) Assume you are the CEO of the company. What would you do to diffuse the volatile situation on the date of gate crashing with the violent mob sitting inside the company premises?

Answer: I will initiate a dialogue with them on table and try to explain company policies of hiring. It would primarily to buy time and make them calm. Meanwhile I will order my office to call police to take charge of the situation. Further, the security of the company premises will be strengthened so that this type of situation would not arise in future.

(b) What can be the long term solution to the issue discussed in the case?

Answer: A long term solution will be to talk to the party leader and convince him to stop such agitations. Media can be informed and the incident may be given due publicity to stop recurrence of such incidents. It may be made clear to the agitators that company hires on the basis of a procedure and they can follow the same. I will take the issue to the board of directors for long-term solution. With approval of Board of Director I can initiate dialogue with the agitators or party leadership that company would try to accommodate a small number of workers as employee in case they can qualify in the procedure and accept to give away party membership.

(c) Every solution/ action that you suggest will have a positive and a negative impact **on you as (CEO), the employees and the performance of the employees. Analyse the consequences of each of your suggested actions. (250 words)**

Answer: Impact on me will be that I would be held responsible for the result of immediate actions taken while board of director will decide long term solution. My impression will also be created in the organization as a man of principle and long-term vision. Employees will not be discouraged and will have high enthusiasm for having a job in prestigious company which does not surrender to illegal pressures.

By taking actions against those men, I will get more recognition and establish myself in the organisation. By these actions, a clear message will be sent to the employees as well as outsiders, that our organisation is strong enough to safeguard the ethical principles as well as interests of our organisation. However, the fallout of this action would inflict violence on you as well as your employees, making your life at risk.

Q. 10 You are the Sarpanch of a Panchayat. There is a primary school run by the government in your area. Midday meals are provided to children attending the school. The headmaster has now appointed a new cook in the school to prepare the meals. However, when it is found that cook is from Dalit community, almost half of the children belonging to higher castes are not allowed to take meals by their parents. Consequently the attendance in the schools falls sharply. This could result in the possibility of discontinuation of midday meal scheme, thereafter of teaching staff and subsequent closing down the school.

(a) Discuss some feasible strategies to overcome the conflict and to create right ambiance.

Answer: The situation given in the case portrays the practice of untouchability, an age old cultural practice prevalent mainly in rural India. Some feasible strategies to overcome the conflict and to create right ambience includes :

(i) Being the Sarpanch of the village, it is my duty to take this matter to the notice of Gram Sabha wherein all the elder members will be explained about the consequences of such an evil practice.

(ii) We should start right from the beginning, by informing children that we all are equal. Much can be achieved by creating feelings of brotherhood and removing caste biases from the minds of our future generation.

(iii) Public awareness is necessary to abolish this problem. For the eradication of this problem, propaganda should be relentlessly directed by the Govt, and other social organisations against this evil practice through use of mass media and social media.

(iv) I would also persuade the people to adhere to the fundamental duty of sending their children to school and make them understand the available legal mechanism- - Prevention of Atrocities Act - defying which can result in a legal action against them.

(v) Promote inter-community events and seek public participation in eliminating the social bias by collective efforts.

(vi) Various NGOs, Civil Society organisations and district administration should be informed and seek their assistance in serving the people cutting across the case barriers for the development of society as a whole.

(vii) By citing specific examples from our cultural epic like Ramayana (about the incident of Shabri) and Mahatma Gandhi who proclaimed untouchabes as Harijans may also attract social change.

(b) What should be the responsibilities of different social segments and agencies to create positive social ambiance for accepting such changes?(250 words. 20

Answer: Different social segments and agencies should participate in SamuhBhojan organized by Panchayat and eat food cooked by Dalit ladies. This will give a message to each segment of the society about breaking barrier of caste discrimination.

Students should be given positive message of equality. Teachers can organize small groups of students with membership of Dalit students in each of them, and Parent Teacher meetings can be called for each group of students. This is give chance to parents to mix with each other. Such groups can be given tasks and projects to be accomplished in cooperation of each other and involvement of parents.

Different agencies should promote participation of each caste in social functions to promote harmony.

Cultural programs should be organized where Dalit members should be given prominent roles to play so that they can show their skills and an atmosphere of respect is created in the society.

NGOs and SHGs may also act as an asset to cure the problem. They should promote awareness about the role of dalit community in rural as well as national development. Police and district administration must be sensitized to address the issue of the community.

Q. 11 One of the scientists working in the R&D laboratory of a major pharmaceutical company discovers that one of the company's bestselling veterinary drugs has the potential to cure a currently incurable liver disease which is prevalent in tribal areas. However, developing a variant of thc drug suitable for human being entailed a lot of research and development having a huge expenditure to the extent of Rs. 50 crores. It was unlikely that company would recover the cost as the disease was rampant only in poverty stricken areas having very little market otherwise.

If you were the CEO, then

(a) Identify the various actions that you could take

Answer: As CEO of the company, first **I** will bring the property of medicine to cure an otherwise incurable disease to the notice of Board of Directors and ask for their permission to start Research on the variant required for particular medicine.

Considering possible financial lose that company may incur, I would suggest for tie up with government health care program for financial support. It can be linked to government scheme which can fund a part of research.

I will request the Board of Director to use a part of CSR fund for this purpose which can be used for developing the variant of proposed drug.

I can propose the government to subsidize the medicine cost so company does not incur much loss and medicine is made available at affordable price to the poor tribal population.

(b) Evaluate the pros and cons of each of your actions(250 words. 20

Answer: When I propose the plan to start research to Board of Directors, it is likely to meet with resistance given possibility of financial loss to the company.

But suggestion and possibility to connect with government health care scheme will probably take them on board positively. This action will also earn goodwill for the company and it will help in expanding its network through government schemes. Use of CSR may again be resisted due to ongoing schemes of utilization of the fund; however some of the board members would accept the proposal. I would strongly propose to do the project partly in charity and party in commercial manner.

Subsidy by government may be possible if the threat of disease is properly explained over the life of tribal population who has no mean to fight against the incurable disease.

Q. 12 There is a disaster prone state having frequent landslides, forest fires, cloudbursts, flash floods and earthquakes, etc. Some of these are seasonal and often unpredictable. The magnitude of the disaster is always unanticipated. During one of the seasons a cloudburst caused a devastating floods and landslides leading to high casualties. There was major damage to infrastructure like roads, bridges and power generating units. This led to more than 100000 pilgrims, tourist and other locals trapped across different routes and locations. The people trapped in your area of responsibility includes senior citizens, patients in hospitals, women and children, hiker, tourist, ruling party's regional president along with his family, additional chief secretary of the neighboring state and prisoners in jail.

As a civil services officer of the state, what would be the order in which you would rescue these people and why? Give Justifications. (200 Words) 20

Answer: As more than 100000 people are trapped across different routes and locations, I would start with the location of hospital where patients are trapped because their need for immediate health care service is urgent and cannot be delayed without risk to their lives. Secondly I will focus on senior citizens and women and children who are delicate in physical temperament and would not have tolerance to sustain the adverse climate created by the causalities.

Simultaneously I will ensure that agencies start work on road, infrastructure, power and communication.

Food and necessary items would be supplied across all areas of causalities through helicopters and units of army and doctors will be sent to rescue other people as well. Prisoners in jail: Since the prisoners are kept in a jail which is surrounded by very high walls, so in the case of disaster, they might stuck inside the jail and eventually die. Further, criminals should not be allowed to escape taking the advantage of the adverse situation.

Ruling Party's President with his family : Since he has a family with him which might include children and women, so they should be given next preference in the order of rescue. Moreover, being the leader of the area, he might have some relations with the local government authorities, which will ultimately help in the evacuation process as he can help in providing temporary arrangements for the affected people.

Tourists : Since they are unaware of the topography of the area, so they might suffer the most during the time of disaster. Moreover, it is most likely that at the time of cloudburst, tourists might be the one very close to the water bodies without any means to tackle the disaster, so rescuing them will require more state efforts.

Chief Secretary of the other state : Being an experienced officer, he can help us in rescue operation, and moreover he is well-trained to tackle the adverse situations, so he can be rescued at last.

Hikers : Being more physically fit and trained to tackle these situations, hikers can be rescued at last. Moreover, they can also help us in the rescue operation and can wait till others are rescued.

Natural disasters are not man-made but we can reduce its adverse impacts by a proper pre-disaster management planning.

Q. 13 You are heading a district administration in a particular department. Your senior officer calls you from the State Headquarters and tells you that a plot in Rampur village is to have a building constructed on it for a school. A visit is scheduled during which he will visit the site along with the chief engineer and the senior architect. He wants you to check out all the papers relating to it and ensure that the visit is properly arranged. You examine the file which relates to the period before you joined the department. The land was acquired for the local panchayat at a nominal cost and the papers showed that clearance certificates are available for the two of the three authorities who have to certify the site's suitability. There is no certification by the architect available on file. You decide to visit Rampur to ensure that all is in the order as stated on file. When you visit Rampur, you find that the plot under reference is a part of Thakurgarh fort and that the walls, ramparts, etc., are running across it. The fort is well away from the main village, therefore a school here will be a serious inconvenience for the children. However, the area near the village has potential to expand into a larger residential area. The development charges on the existing plot, at the fort, will be very high and question of heritage site has not been addressed. Moreover, the Sarpanch, at the time of acquisition of the land, was a relative of your predecessor. The whole transaction appears to have been done with some vested interest.

(a) List the likely vested interest of the concerned parties.

Answer: Sarpanch

(i) Deliberately chosen the land away from village so that he could have a larger share of land that falls near the village and can have the maximum advantage at the time of development of residential area near the school.

(ii) Helps in image building in the village that he is providing space for development of school in the village.

(iii) Maintaining the personal relationship with my predecessor so that in future in case of any government scheme, both of them will mutually have the maximum benefit.

My Predecessor

(i) Maintaining personal relationship with the Sarpanch so that in case of any checking in future, his government job will not be adversely affected.

(ii) Illegally earn money by approving the transaction of acquisition of land by the Sarpanch.

Certifying authorities

(i) Possibility of earning illegal money or other gratifications for approving easy clearances.

(b) Some of the options for action available to you are listed below. Discuss the merits and demerits of each of the options:

(i) You can await the visit of the superior officer and let him take a decision.

(ii) You can seek his advice in writing or on phone.

(iii) You can consult your predecessor/colleagues, etc, and then decide what to do.

(iv) You can find out if any alternate plot can be got in exchange and then send a comprehensive written report.

Can you suggest any other option with proper justification? (250 Words) **25**

Answer: (i) You can await the visit of the superior officer and let him take a decision. Merits

a. Being more experienced, the seniors will take the most appropriate decision, after considering all the best available evidences.

b. It will help in ensuring the line of hierarchy during the decision-making process.

c. I will be free from any investigations since the issue of heritage site can be looked upon by the competent authority.

Demerits

a. I will be guilty of running away from my duties/responsibilities.

b. It might delay the project as a lot of time of the seniors will be wasted in carrying out investigations.

(ii) You can seek his advice in writing or on phone.

Merits

a. It will be a more time saving and expeditious way to tackle the situation.

b. It will help in appraising the seniors quickly about the problem and will help in quicker decision-making.

c. Experience of the seniors and the cooperation of the juniors will be utilised properly.

Demerits

a. Not a good option taking into account, the seriousness of the problem.

b. Getting written orders from the seniors will delay the process of solving the issue.

c. Seniors will not have the clear picture regarding the problem and will depend upon your advice.

(iii) You can consult your predecessor/colleagues, etc, and then decide what to do. Merits

a. It will help me in knowing the exact reason behind the decision of my predecessor which will ultimately help in taking the appropriate action.

b. By incorporating the views of others, a better decision can be taken to tackle the problem.

c. A more democratic approach towards problem resolution as it will help in proving the wrong done by my predecessor.

Demerits

a. The predecessor, in case of having ill-vested interests, might hide the true picture thus crucial time will be lost without gaining much.

b. The colleagues might also have some biased opinions in order to refrain themselves from the issue.

(iv) You can find out if any alternate plot can be got in exchange and then send a comprehensive written report.

Merits

a. Village would get the much needed school without harming the heritage site.

b. Charges against those involved in the fraud would be mentioned in the comprehensive written report for any possible enquiries in the future.

c. Seniors will be aware of the every aspect of the issue through the detailed report and might take the best possible decision.

Demerits

a. Finding an alternative site for school construction will be a time consuming as well as very costly process as all the formalities regarding land acquisition, and clearances will have to be done right from the start.

b. The wrong-doings of the previous authorities will not come to light and they might use the acquired land for some other unlawful purpose.

It would be better to inform the superior officer about file and absence of clearance from architect. Views of the engineer can be taken on cost of developing land. Superior officer may be briefed about distance and inconvenience to students. Hinting at the possible vested interest, a suggestion may be given to the superior officer to reopen the file and form a committee to locate a proper location for the proposed school.

Q. 14 You are recently posted as district development officer of a district. Shortly thereafter you found that there is considerable tension in the rural areas of your district on the issue of sending girls to schools.

The elders of the village feel that many problems have come up because girls are being educated and they are stepping out of the safe environment of the household. They are of the view that the girls should be quickly married off with minimum education. The girls are also competing for jobs after education, which have traditionally remained in boys' exclusive domain, adding to unemployment amongst male population.

The younger generation feels that in the present era, girls should have equal opportunities for education and employment, and other means of livelihood. Theentire locality is divided between the elders and the younger lot and further subdivided between sexes in both generations. You come to know that in Panchayat or in other local bodies or even in busy crosswords, the issue is being acrimoniously debated.

One day you are informed that an unpleasant incident has taken place. Some girls were molested, when they were en route to schools. The incident led to clashes between several groups and a law and order problem has arisen. The elder after heated discussion have taken a joint decision not to allow girls to go to school and to socially boycott all such families, which do not follow their dictate.

(a) What steps would you take to ensure girls' safety without disrupting their education?

Answer: Girls education is both an intrinsic right and critical lever to reaching development objectives. Providing girls with an education helps break the circle of poverty. However, girls all over the world face violence and intimidation in, around and on their way to and from school. Some steps should be taken strictly to ensure girls safety, which are

(i) Educating moral values in people, and have to make them understand consequences of committing crime, a fear in the system, fear of law should be implanted in people's mind for committing a crime.

(ii) Society should be advised to react sharp other than being a spectator to crimes against women or just giving knee jerk reactions.

(iii) The self-defense training should be made mandatory at all levels of schooling.

(iv) It would be advisable to establish a safe and violence free environment by improving infrastructure such as transportation, separate and adequate sanitation facilities, improved street lighting, and enforcing penalties for violence against girls.

(v) Since civil society has a bigger role to play in the gender equality so they should keep pressurising the governments to ensure safety for girls.

(vi) Schools should be encouraged to establish reflection sessions for girls to share experiences and build solidarity and confidence.

(vii) Parents and elder people should be sensitized to value girls and recognizing the value of their education.

(viii) Families should be linked to government programs that provides incentives for educating girls.

The current government has also made a positive move to ensure girls safety by announcing a Beti Bachao Beti Padhao Campaign which aims to generate awareness and improving the efficiency of welfare services meant for women.

(b) How would you manage and mould patriarchic attitude of the village elders to ensure harmony in the inter- generational relations? (250 words) 25

Answer: I will call leaders of two generations separately and advise them to maintain peace and moderate their attitude.

To the leaders of old generation who are against girls' education, I will show benefits of educating girls and making them able to get employment. I will take lady officers with me to show example. The myth that girls' competing for employment is detrimental formale employment will be debunked. I will convince that having working women in family has its own benefits.

To young generation I will encourage to continue with their attitude of women empowerment, girls' education and equal opportunity for girls and boys in the society. I will promise them adequate security.

I will call gathering of both generations and hold programs giving message of women upliftment and gender equality. I will invite famous personality to speak on the issues. Intervention by respected people of the society will help in building a bridge between the two generations and their attitude towards girl education.

(MAIN) **Civil Service Exam.**

2016 General Studies

SOLVED PAPERS

PAPER–I

Time Allowed: Three Hours *Maximum Marks: 250*

Instructions: There are TWENTY questions printed both in English and Hindi. All questions are compulsory. The number of marks carried by a question is indicated against it. Answers must be written in the medium authorized in the Admission Certificate which must be stated clearly on the cover of this Question-cum-Answer (QCA) Booklet in the space provided. No marks will be given for answers written in medium other than the authorized one. Word limit in questions, wherever specified, should be adhered to. Any page or portion of the page left blank in the Question-cum-Answer Booklet must be clearly struck off.
Answer all the questions in NOT MORE THAN 200 words each. Contents of the answer are more important than its length. All questions carry equal marks.

Q. 1 Early Buddhist Stupa-art, while depicting folk motifs and narratives, successfully expounds Buddhist ideals. Elucidate. **12½**

Answer: Stupas were raised in various kingdoms in honour of Buddha after his death over relics. The Buddhist stupas depict Jataka stories and main incidents of Buddha's life in pictorial format.

The Jataka stories are depicted on torans of Stupas, teaching Buddhist lessons of karma, samsara and dharma. It also narrates the cycle of samsara that the Buddha had experienced before reaching to enlightenment.

Main structure of the stupa consists of a flattened hemispherical dome, known as Anda. This Anda or Egg represents the latent creative power. It also replicates the infinite dome of heaven representing cycle of birth and death.

The harmika, located at the summit of the anda, symbolizes the zenith beyond life and death and resembles a sacrificial altar of particular significance for the attainment of nirvana.

The parasol is a distinguishing feature of stupa implying royalty and dignity, as well as symbolizing the sacred Tree of Life or enlightenment.

The three elements of the chattra at Sanchi stupa represent the Three Jewels of Buddhism: The Buddha, The Dharma and The Sangha.

Vedikas are repeated around stupa and on the terrace demarcating the boundries of the sacred precinct with the secular world.

Thus, stupas are successful depiction of folk motifs and narratives expounding Buddhist ideals.

Q. 2 Krishnadeva Raya, the king of Vijayanagar, was not only an accomplished scholar himself but was also a great patron of learning and literature. Discuss 12½

Answer: Krishnadeva Raya ruled the kingdom of Vijayanagar from 1509 to 1529 as the third ruler of the Tuluva Dynasty. He is regarded as an icon, earning titles like Kannada Rajya Rama Ramana, Andhra Bhoja and Mooru Rayara Ganda.

The rule of Krishna Deva Raya is known as the golden age of Telugu literature. His time also witnessed prolific growth of literature in many languages. Many Telugu, Sanskrit, Kannada and Tamil poets enjoyed patronage of the emperor.

Eight poets known as Astadiggajalu (eight elephants in the eight cardinal points such as North, South etc.) were part of his court (known as Bhuvana-vijayamu).

He patronised Kannada poets Mallanarya who wrote Veera-saivamruta, Bhava-chinta- ratna and Satyendra Chola-kathe, Chatu Vittal-anatha who wrote Bhagavata, Timmanna Kavi who wrote a eulogy of his king in Krishna Raya Bharata.

Allasani Peddana is considered to be the greatest and is given the title of Andhra Kavita Pitamaha.

Dhurjati wrote Kalahasti Mahatyamu and Ayyal-raju Rama-bhadrudu wrote Rama- abhyuday-amu.

Nandi Timmana wrote Paari-jaata-apaharan-amu.

Bhattumurty alias Rama-raja-bhushanudu wrote Kavyalankara-sangrahamu, Vasu- charitramu, and Harischandra-nalopakhyanamu.

Madayya-gari Mallana wrote Raja-sekhara Charitramu.

Pingali Surana wrote the still remarkable Raghava-pandaveeyamu, a dual work with double meaning built into the text, describing both the Ramayana and the Mahabharata.

Thus, Krishnadeva Raya not only was himself a scholar but also a great patron of learning and literature. Emperor Krishna Deva Raya was fluent in many languages.

Q. 3 Explain how the uprising of 1857 constitutes an important watershed in the evolution of British policies towards colonial India. 12½

Answer: The uprising of 1857 was an important event in the history of India giving a big jolt to the British administration. The Government of India's policies and structure changed significantly after it.

By the Act of Parliament of 1858, the British Crown took over power to govern India from the East India Company. Henceforth, the Secretary of State for India aided by his Council would exercise authority over India.

The Indian Council Act of 1861 again enlarged the Governor General's Council for the purpose of making laws, which was known as the Imperial Legislative Council.

The Presidencies, Bombay, Madras and Bengal, were administered by a Governor and his Executive Council of three, appointed by the Crown.

European branch domination over the army started. Proportion of Europeans to Indians in the army was raised. Crucial branches were in the hands of Europeans only. Indians were excluded from higher posts.

After the revolt, Muslims were suppressed; their lands and property were confiscated on large scale and the Hindus were declared to be favorite. After 1870s the policy was reversed to turn Muslims against the nationalist movement carried out by Hindus. Thus policy of divide and rule was followed after Revolt of 1857.

Princely states had remained loyal to the Crown and their loyalty was rewarded.

Thus, 1857 revolt marks an important phase in change of British government's attitude and policy towards India.

Q. 4 Discuss the role of women in the freedom struggle especially during the Gandhian phase. 12½

Answer: Annie Besant an Irish lady became the leader of the Theosophical Society. In 1902 while in London she criticized England for the conditions prevalent in India. In 1914 she joined the Indian National Congress and gave it a new direction.

Kasturba Gandhi, Mahatma Gandhi's wife, was a leader of Women's Satyagraha for which she was imprisoned. She helped her husband in the cause of Indigo workers in Champaran, Bihar and the No Tax Campaign in Kheda, Gujarat. She was arrested twice for picketing liquor and foreign cloth shops, and in 1939 for participating in the Rajkot Satyagraha.

The remarkable woman elected to the presidentship of the Indian National Congress was Sarojini Naidu. She contributed to the freedom struggle actively.

Aruna Asaf Ali became an active member of Congress Party after marriage and participated in public processions during the Salt Satyagraha. Aruna was dubbed the Heroine of the 1942 movement for her bravery in the face of danger and was called Grand Old Lady of the Independence movement in her later years.

Indira Gandhi from her early years was active in the national liberation struggle. During the 1930 movement, she formed the 'Vanar Sena'. She became a member of the Indian National Congress in 1938. Soon after her return to India in March 1941, she plunged into political activity.

Apart from them, Sister Nivedita, Mridula Sarabhai, Kamla Nehru Gandhi, Vijya Laxmi Pandit, Madam Kama, Kamlaben, Sarlaben etc. played important roles in freedom struggle of India. Some ladies who participated in revolutionary movement were Kalpanadutta, Bina Das, Durga Bhabhi and Usha Mehta.

Q. 5 Highlight the differences in the approach of Subhash Chandra Bose and Mahatma Gandhi in the struggle for freedom. 12½

Answer: Subhash Chandra Bose and Mahatma Gandhi, two legendary leaders of Indian freedom struggle, were completely different in their approach towards the movement.

Bose had revolutionary mindset and intended to launch all out struggle for freedom against British. Gandhi, on the other hand, believed in peaceful resistance method which involved non-cooperation struggle-truce-struggle method.

Gandhi and other senior leaders demanded dominion status as first step while Bose and other young leaders of Indian National Congress were for Self-Rule and Purna Swaraj.

Bose had revolutionary urge while Gandhi was propagator of ahimsa, non-violence in freedom struggle.

While Gandhi was completely against involving foreign powers in freedom struggle, Bose was keen to take help of any powerful country to secure freedom from British Rule. Bose formed Indian National Army with help of Japan and attacked British Indian frontiers.

Bose was impressed with fascism and communism and intended to have strong political system in India while Gandhi did not believe in any extreme political system. Gandhian views of economic and political system were very liberal while Bose had ideas of strong governance based on planning and control.

Even after having different views, both leaders contributed tremendously in the success of Indian freedom struggle by leading people in their own ways.

Q. 6 Has the formation of linguistic states strengthened the cause of Indian unity? 12½

Answer: The post-independence period saw the ascent of political movements for the creation of new states developed on linguistic lines. The demand for states on linguistic basis was developed even before India achieved independence from British rule.

In 1948, the government appointed commission under S K Dhar, a judge of the Allahabad High Court, to examine the case for the reorganization of states on the linguistic basis. It favoured reorganization on the basis of administrative convenience rather than linguistic considerations.

In December 1948, Congress appointed a committee under Jawaharlal Nehru, Vallabhbhai Patel and Pattabhi Sitaramayya (known as the JVP Committee) to examine the issue afresh. The committee, in a report submitted in April 1949, dismissed the idea of reorganization of states on a linguistic basis.

In 1953, the government was forced to create a separate state of Andhra Pradesh for Telugu-speaking people following the long-drawn agitation and death of Potti Sriramulu after a hunger strike for 56 days.

In December 1953, Jawaharlal Nehru announced the appointment of a commission under Fazl Ali to consider this demand.

The States Reorganisation Act, 1956 was a major reform of the boundaries of Indian states and territories, organising them along linguistic lines.

Creation of states on linguistic basis is due to public demand than politically considered decision for national unity. However, creation of states on linguistic basis has not proved to be disastrous for India and it has rather created unity among people on the basis of language.

But, there is no additional advantage arising out of interaction among different linguistic groups that could have resulted into removing linguistic, cultural and ethnic differences among people. The diversity of India has not intermixed to create a pan- India culture due to linguistic states.

Q. 7 The anti-colonial struggles in West Africa were led by the new elite of Western - educated Africans. Examine. 12½

Answer: Europeans had colonized western Africa in the later 19th and early 20th centuries.

The political changes over the time turned out to be inadequate to accommodate African aspirations—which had been derived from social changes occasioned during the classical period of colonial rule and further whetted by the policies of active economic development.

By the late 1940s both the French and the British territories possessed an educated, politicized class, which felt frustrated in its legitimate expectations; it had made no appreciable progress in securing any real participation in the system of political control.

There was enough education to make European-style political activity possible in all the coastal colonies. In 1946 politicians in French West Africa organized a federationwide political association, the African Democratic Rally (RDA).

Anti-colonial activity started in the 1890s in Gold Coast where professionals and some chiefs founded the Aborigines' Rights Protection Society (ARPS) to prevent the wholesale expropriation of African lands by European entrepreneurs or officials. In 1947 the established politicians of the Gold Coast brought in Kwame Nkrumah, who had studied in the United States and Britain and had been active in the Pan-African movement, to organize a nationalist party with mass support.

Similar examples can be traced in other Western African countries where anti-colonial struggles were led by the new elite of Western educated Afric**ans.**

Q. 8 To what extent globalisation has influenced the core of cultural diversity in India? Explain. 12½

Answer: India is a country of cultural diversity where language, food, clothing and way of life differ from region to region. This diversity is interwoven in Indian culture.

Globalization has merged traditional borders and reduced distances. Close contacts and frequent interaction among people have led to exchange of ideas, culture and values. This has impacted Indian cultural diversities in various methods and degrees.

Caste system, a strong phenomenon of Indian society has been dying slow death due to globalization and resultant mixing of people from different caste groups for economic and social purposes.

Similarly, impact of globalization is evident on family system. Joint family tradition of India is slowly and partially giving way to nuclear families. Rural people are migrating to urban areas for education and employment with immediate family members, leaving parents and siblings back home in villages.

Role of women had been traditionally of a home maker and helping hand in agriculture and animal rearing activities. Due to impact of globalization, women have found new perspective of contributing to the society in direct and more meaningful manner. Education and employment opportunities have increased for women in India due to globalization.

Lifestyle of people has changed across the diversity of culture, bringing them to follow or adopt international clothing style and lifestyle.

Moreover, the most evident cultural factor of different languages are bridging gap through a common language of the world - English in day to day Indian life.

Q. 9 "An essential condition to eradicate poverty is to liberate the poor from the process of deprivation." Substantiate this statement with suitable examples. **7 + 5½ = 12½**

Answer: Poverty arises out of lack of opportunity and ability to participate in the main stream of economic activities.

Poverty leads to lack of education and vocational training which results into unskilled manpower. Unskilled people do not earn enough to come out of poverty. They are also not able to make beneficial use of available natural, social and economic resources. These situations of deprivation lead to poverty on a mass scale.

To eradicate poverty, people should have access and utilization of resources available in the country. Their deprivation has to be ended.

Mahatma Gandhi National Rural Employment Guarantee Act of 2005 provides employment guarantee to an able bodied person on demand for minimum of 100 days. This ensures livelihood for poor.

Similarly Right to Education makes provision for free and compulsory education for children in the age group of 6-14 years.

Skill India Program will scale up skill development efforts in rural and urban areas which would generate more employment opportunities for skilled people.

These programs are aimed at bringing an end to deprivation from society so that people come out of poverty.

Make in India program will increase manufacturing activities in India, including in rural areas, and will provide more employment opportunities for people.

Q. 10 Why are the tribals in India referred to as 'the Scheduled Tribes'? Indicate the major provisions enshrined in the Constitution of India for their upliftment. 4½ + 8 = 12½

Answer: Tribal people in India are recognized by the Constitution as Scheduled Tribes which constitutes 8.6 percent of total population of India. The Constitution (Scheduled Tribes) Order, 1950 lists 744 tribes across 22 states in its First Schedule. A number of laws were enacted to implement the provisions in the Constitution like Scheduled Caste and Scheduled Tribe (Prevention of Atrocities) Act, 1989.

Several provisions have been incorporated in the Constitution for safeguarding and promoting the interests and rights of the Scheduled Tribes in various spheres so as to enable them to join the national mainstream.

Article 46 of the Constitution provides that the State shall promote with special care the educational and economic interests of the weaker sections of the society.

Reservation in educational institution has been provided in Article 15(4) while reservation in posts and services has been provided in Article 16(4), 16(4A) and 16(4B) of the Constitution.

Article 23 which prohibits traffic in human beings and beggar and other similar forms of forced labour has a special significance for Scheduled Tribes. In pursuance of this Article, Parliament has enacted the Bonded Labour System (Abolition) Act, 1976.

Article 24 which prohibits employment of Children below the age of 14 years in any factory or mine or in any other hazards activity is also significant for Scheduled Tribes as a substantial portion of child labour engaged in these jobs belong to Scheduled Tribes.

Article 243D provides reservation of Seats for Scheduled Tribes in Panchayats.

Article 330 provides reservation of seats for Scheduled Tribes in the House of the People.

Article 332 provides reservation of seats for Scheduled Tribes in Legislative Assemblies of the States.

Article 334 provides that reservation of seats for Scheduled Castes and Scheduled Tribes in the Lok Sabha and the State Vidhan Sabhas (and the representation of the Anglo-Indian Community in the Lok Sabha and the State Vidhan Sabhas by nomination) would continue up to January, 2020.

Other specific safeguards have been provided in Article 244 read with the provisions contained in Fifth and Sixth Schedule to the Constitution.

Article 371A has special provisions with respect to the State of Nagaland.

Article 371B has special provisions with respect to the State of Assam.

Article 371C has special provisions with respect to the State of Manipur.

Article 371F has special provisions with respect to Sikkim.

Q. 11 With a brief background of quality of urban life in India, introduce the objectives and strategy of the "Smart City Programme." **4 + 8½ = 12½**

Answer: Some of the major problems of urbanization in India are Urban Sprawl, Overcrowding, Housing, Unemployment, Slums and Squatter Settlements, Transport, Water, Sewerage Problems, Trash Disposal, Urban Crimes and Problem of Urban Pollution.

The Smart Cities Mission is an innovative and new initiative by the Government of India to drive economic growth and improve the quality of life of people by enabling local development and harnessing technology as a means to create smart outcomes for citizens.

Smart Cities focus on their most pressing needs and on the greatest opportunities to improve lives. They tap a range of approaches - digital and information technologies, urban planning best practices, public-private partnerships, and policy change - to make a difference.

The Union Ministry of Urban Development is responsible for implementing the mission in collaboration with the state governments of the respective cities. The Government has a vision of developing 100 smart cities as satellite towns of larger cities by modernizing the existing mid-sized cities. It will cover aspects like:

- Adequate water supply,
- Assured electricity supply,
- Sanitation, including solid waste management,
- Efficient urban mobility and public transport,
- Affordable housing, especially for the poor,
- Robust IT connectivity and digitalization,

- Good governance, especially e-Governance and citizen participation,
- Sustainable environment,
- Safety and security of citizens, particularly women, children and the elderly, and
- Health and education.

Q. 12 What is the basis of regionalism? Is it that unequal distribution of benefits of development on regional basis eventually promotes regionalism? Substantiate your answer. 3½ + 9 = 12½

Answer: Regionalism is a feeling of attachment to one particular region which results into preferences to region over national interest. Loyalty of people is focused on the region.

Various factors can be responsible for regionalism.

Geographical factor can lead population to identify itself with particular region.

Historical and cultural factors which have played important role in growth and development of human society also results into regionalism.

Caste and religion have played important role in India to grow regionalism.

Economic factors like development or underdevelopment creates sense of being privileged or deprived in the people living in particular region.

Political and administrative factors have been cultivated strongly resulting into polarization and regionalism.

One important and strong factor responsible for promotion of regionalism is unequal distribution of economic benefits of development. Jharkhand and Chhattisgarh have abundance of natural resources which are being used for development of industries. Actual benefit of development has not resulted into better life standards for the people in these areas. This led to creation of new states.

Telangana is recent example where people felt deprived of the benefit of economic development of Andhra Pradesh.

All these factors, leading to strong feeling of regionalism, have to be tackled in national perspective. Without hurting regional identities and pride, national interest and 'India First' attitude should be developed among people.

Q. 13 Discuss the concept of air mass and explain its role in macro-climatic changes. 12½

Answer: An air mass is a large uniform volume of air that has consistent properties of density, temperature, and humidity, compared to the air surrounding this air mass which may have different properties.

The type of air mass at a location will determine the type of weather conditions the site experiences.

The climates of most regions worldwide are affected by air masses. For example, maritime-tropical air sourced over warm waters of the Atlantic Ocean, Caribbean Sea and Gulf of Mexico, primarily between 10 and 30 degrees north of latitude, is the main contributor of precipitation for much of North America and east of the Rocky Mountains.

Air mass also is the cause of the persistent humidity typical of that big region's summer season. In the Pacific Northwest, maritime-polar air tracking inland from the Aleutian Low in the winter supplies the heavy mountain rain and snowfall that nourish vast temperate rainforests and extensive alpine glaciers.

Such maritime air masses also contribute to a moderating climatic influence on coastal temperatures, as oceans heat up and cool down more slowly and less dramatically than landmasses.

An air mass that forms over the Arctic in winter would be cold and dry, while an air mass that formed over a tropical ocean would be warm and moist.

Air masses are pushed around the globe by wind and follow the pattern of the troughs and ridges in the flow of air around the earth.

Q. 14 "The Himalayas are highly prone to landslides."Discuss the causes and suggest suitable measures of mitigation. 12½

Answer: Landslides are very common in the Himalayas especially during monsoon season.

Himalayan landslides can be attributed to the fact that Himalayas lies at the convergence zone of two lithospheric plates, i.e., Indian plate in the south and Eurasian plate in the north.

Mostly Himalayan landslides are of very shallow depth and minor.

Recurring landslides are significantly more in Himalayas. These are noticed particularly in highly fractured and sheared rock-mass and also in soft-hard rock alterations.

Though, monsoon rains begin in the month of June in the Himalaya, devastating landslides mostly take place in later part of the monsoon, i.e., August and September. Perhaps, this is because of the fact that initially the sub-soil accommodates lot of percolation, when the sub-soil becomes saturated after a few months; it cannot absorb abundant water.

Many failures are known to occur due to slip along fractures during construction. Generally, these fractures are hidden under overburden or undergrowth.

Landslide mitigation refers to construction and other man-made activities on slopes with the goal of lessening the effect of landslides.

Landslide mitigation is difficult task but some techniques can be used to prevent or reduce occurrence of landslides.

Treating vulnerable slopes in existing hazardous landslides are important. Restricting development in landslide-prone areas can be useful.

Preparing codes for excavation, construction and grading should be included in the standard operating procedure of disaster management program.

During the time of monsoon, disaster management team should be stationed in the landslide prone areas to respond urgently to any occurrence of landslide.

Q. 15 The effective management of land and water resources will drastically reduce the human miseries. Explain. 12½

Answer: Human settlement depends on availability of land and water. Fertile land and potable water supply is essential for survival of human life in any area.

Non-availability of land in urban areas, underutilization of land in village areas, inability to convert barren land into arable and industrial area is mostly a result of mismanagement than actual shortage.

Similarly, availability of water, its usage and conservation is also subject to effective management of water resources which is lacking.

Both of these factors add to human miseries which can be solved by effectively managing these resources.

Land use should be planned in a manner that allocation to agriculture, industry and human settlement are balanced according to requirement. Barren land should be converted into industrial zones rather than using arable and fertile area. Industrial areas can trigger development and growth of urbanization which can be planned in advance in the barren land stretches.

Water resources should be conserved and protected. Flowing rain water can be conserved through watersheds and other techniques. In agriculture, most effective micro-irrigation systems should be used. Water pollution is a big hazard which must be controlled by making effective policy. Industrial waste should not be allowed to pollute water and land.

Managed properly, limited resources of water and land can result into abundance and efficient utilization, bringing welfare to human society.

Q. 16 South China Sea has assumed great geopolitical significance in the present context. Comment. 12½

Answer: The South China Sea is a marginal sea that is part of the Pacific Ocean, encompassing an area of around 3,500,000 square kilometres. The area's importance largely results from one-third of the world's shipping sailing through its waters and that it is believed to hold huge oil and gas reserves beneath its seabed.

The sea and its mostly uninhabited islands are subject to competing claims of sovereignty by several countries including Philippines, Vietnam, Malaysia, Combodia and other regional countries. These claims are also reflected in the variety of names used for the islands and the sea to varying degrees.

The South China Sea has become an important area for the implementation of China's naval strategy, including blockading Taiwan, and power projection into the Indian and Pacific Oce**ans.**

America's concern with the South China Sea is a result of China's effort to secure control over the maritime territory and the resources it contains.

In January 2013, the Philippines formally initiated arbitration proceedings against China. On July 12, 2016, the arbitral tribunal backed the Philippines, saying that there was no evidence that China had historically exercised exclusive control over the waters or resources, hence there was "no legal basis for China to claim historic rights" over the nine-dash line.

India supports freedom of navigation in international waters, including in the South China Sea, and the right of passage in accordance with accepted principles of international law.

Q. 17 Major cities of India are becoming more vulnerable to flood conditions. Discuss. 12½

Answer: Floods in urban area have become recurring phenomenon. In 2015 in Chennai; in 2014 in Srinagar; and in 2013 in Mumbai and Kolkata floods have resulted into devastation.

Urban flooding has acquired extraordinary dimensions. Earlier, when cities received excessive rainfall, it would usually result in waterlogging in low-lying areas.

Growing cities are creating excessive pressure on natural systems such as marshlands, wetlands, lakes and rivers and resultantly a high rainfall event leads to massive urban flooding, crippling urban life and the economy.

Urban floods begin with an unanticipated high rainfall event which seriously disrupts public transport, electricity and communications and also plays havoc with the urban economy.

Complex administrative set-up of cities, where multiple authorities and agencies function with competing jurisdiction, results into lack of coordination. Steering disaster management in urban areas through various stages - from early warning and response to relief and recovery - remains a huge challenge.

The time has come to become proactive for urban floods are a certainty now, occurring on an annual basis. Starting from July 2011, Bangkok remained flooded for more than five months, indicating major warning.

As more and more cities get affected by floods at regular intervals in India and elsewhere, climatic impacts attributed to the urban environment demand a closer scrutiny.

Q. 18 Present an account of the Indus Water Treaty and examine its ecological, economic and political implications in the context of changing bilateral relations. 12½

Answer: The Indus Waters Treaty is a water-distribution treaty between India and Pakistan. It was brokered by the World Bank in 1960.

According to the treaty, India is given control over the three "eastern" rivers - the Beas, the Ravi and the Sutlej, while control over the three "western" rivets- the Indus, the Chenab and the Jhelum belongs to Pakistan.

Currently India-Pakistan relations are marred by cross border terrorism issues. It makes the river sharing agreement critical.

Pakistan's rivers first flow through India. The treaty allowed India to use them for irrigation, transport and power generation, while laying down precise regulations for Indian building projects along the way. More controversial are the provisions on how the waters were to be shared.

Ecological disturbance in the flow of water by India can create problem in Pakistan. As a result, Pakistani farmers and industry may lose source of water, causing a great loss. The Treaty can be a potential tool with India to use against Pakistan if India decides so.

It is sometimes argued that since the rivers originate in the Indus basin in India, there is possibility of India creating droughts and famines in Pakistan, especially at times of war. But since the ratification of the treaty in 1960, India and Pakistan have not engaged in any water wars.

However, disagreements and disputes have been settled via legal procedures, provided for within the framework of the treaty.

Q. 19 Enumerate the problems and prospects of inland water transport in India. 12½

Answer: India has numerous small and large rivers which can be used for inland waterway transportation. But due to various reasons, this possibility has not been utilized to its fullest extent.

Peninsular Indian rivers receive mostly seasonal water level which can handle transportation and during summer season they become dry.

North Indian Rivers have water throughout the year but other geographical conditions make their use for inland waterway transport system difficult.

Many rivers like Bhagirathi-Hooghli face problem of silting. Some of the rivers like Narmada, Tapti are passing through difficult terrain and have waterfalls and cataracts which is not supportive for transportation.

Salinity in coastal stretches also affects transport system.

In India inland water transport has not been developed to more than 3% of its capacity and therefore it has bright prospects. Although India has 14,500 km of navigable inland waterways but due to silting problem they are not used for transportation except in monsoon season when draft is sufficient.

Asian Development Bank figures show that India is trying to create waterways to handle 1500 tons vessels while EU and China can handle 40,000 tons of vessels in their inland waterways. Bangladesh is using inland waterways for more than 35% of its cargo movement.

Q. 20 In what way micro-watershed development projects help in water conservation in drought-prone and semi - arid regions of India? 12½

Answer: A watershed is an area of land that drains all the streams and rainfall to a common outlet such as the outflow of a reservoir, mouth of a bay, or any point along a stream channel.

These water bodies supply our drinking water, water for agriculture and manufacturing, offer opportunities for recreation and provide habitat to numerous plants and animals.

Watershed can be useful in scientific soil and water conservation in order to increase the biomass production. The aim is to develop primary resources of land and water to produce secondary resources of plants and animals for use in a manner which will not cause ecological imbalance. The process of creating and implementing plans, programs, and projects to sustain and enhance watershed functions that affect the plant, animal, and human communities within a watershed boundary.

Micro-watershed development projects can be useful in prevention and accumulation of seasonally flowing rain water. The stored water can be useful for a period of time to mitigate impact of drought and provide water for the semi-arid region for drinking and agricultural purposes.

Water conservation through micro-watershed can also increase ground water level which would be useful to the people in semi-arid and drought prone areas.

SOLVED PAPERS

PAPER–II

Time Allowed: Three Hours *Maximum Marks: 250*

Instructions: There are TWENTY questions printed both in English and in Hindi. All questions are compulsory. The number of marks carried by a question/part is indicated against it. Answers must be written in the medium authorized in the Admission Certificate which must be stated clearly on the cover of this Question-cum-Answer (QCA) Booklet in the space provided. No marks will be given for answers written in medium other than the authorized one.

Word limit in questions, where ver specified, should be adhered to.

Answer the questions in not more than 200 words each. Contents of the answers are more important than their length.

Q. 1 Discuss the essentials of the 69[lh] Constitutional Amendment Act and anomalies, if any, that have led to recent reported conflicts between the elected representatives and the institution of the Lieutenant Governor in the administration of Delhi. Do you think that this will give rise to a new trend in the functioning of the Indian federal politics? 12½

Answer: The 69th Constitutional Amendment Act of 1991 came into effect on T[1] February 1992. It inserted Articles 238AA and 239AB, making provisions for a Legislative Assembly and Council of Ministers and designating Delhi as National Capital Territory. Earlier, as a Union Territory, Delhi was governed only by Lt Governor under Article 239. The Amendment has created special administrative structure in Delhi where Lt Governor is advised by Council of Ministers on all matters except those which are purely at his discretion. This has created ambiguity resulting into conflicts between Lt Governor and elected Government of Delhi.

Recently conflicts have taken place regarding power of Lt Governor and role of Council of Ministers. Whether Lt Governor has discretionary power or he should abide by advice of Council of Minister.

The question was alsc raised before High Court who ruled that even after 69th Amendment, Delhi does not acquire the status of a State but remains a Union Territory with Lt Governor as its administrative head. The special ccnstitutional provision of Article 239AA dealing with Delhi does not dilute the effect of Article 239 which relates to the Union territory and hence, concurrence of the LG in administrative issues is mandatory.

Distribution of Power between Centre and States is clearly demarcated in the Constitution. Though such conflicts have kept arising time and again, they may not threaten or deviate the overall Federal Structure of India but may require more clarity with respect to administration of Delhi.

Q. 2 To what extent is Article 370 of the Indian Constitution, bearing marginal note "temporary provision with respect to the State of Jammu and Kashmir", temporary? Discuss the future prospects of this provision in the context of Indian polity. 12½

Answer: According to the Constitution of India, Article 370 provides temporary and transitional provisions to the state of Jammu and Kashmir, granting it special autonomy. Under Article 370 the

Indian Parliament cannot increase or reduce the borders of the state. Except on external affairs, defence, communication and ancillary matters, Parliament has no power to make laws for the State of Jammu and Kashmir. On other matters listed in the Union and Concurrent List, Parliament can make laws only with the consent of the State.

Clause 3 of Article 370 is clear. Article 370 can be revoked only if a new Constituent Assembly of Jammu and Kashmir is convened and is willing to recommend its revocation. The State Constituent Assembly was empowered to recommend abrogation of Article 370, but it was dissolved in 1957 without making such recommendation. Now, the State Legislative Assembly has to agree to convene a new Constituent Assembly. It seems the article has become permanent feature of Indian Constitution.

Parliament has the power to amend the Constitution to change this provision. But this could be subject to a judicial review which may possibly find that the clause is a basic feature of the relationship between the State and the Centre and cannot, therefore, be amended.

Q. 3 "The Indian party system is passing through a phase of transition which looks to be full of contradictions and paradoxes." Discuss. 12½

Answer: India follows multi-party system of polity where Election Commission grants recognition to political parties at National, State and District level. Currently India has 7 National parties, 48 State parties and a number of other unrecognized parties.

Indian party system, which started with Congress dominance, has progressively followed a trend of more and more localization and coalition based changing from election to election. The Congress, which strongly followed personality cult and family influence, has seen ups and downs in Indian polity, winning and losing Centre and States from time to time. It is mainly due to rise or fall of Congress that other regional and national political parties have filled the gap, except sometimes on the basis of strong electoral agenda.

Regional parties have grown stronger and indispensable in Indian governance, not only at states but also at national level. Since 1980s they have been in coalition with one or more national political party in the Centre government. It is only in 2014 that a party has again managed strong majority at Centre. Regional parties have also been changing partners, compromising ideological stands frequently, to be part of ruling government.

An analysis of Indian party system reveals that political parties have taken paradoxical stand which is many times contradictory to its own promises and ideology. Unlike other developed democracies, Indian parties have not followed issue based politics and have rarely fulfilled election promises.

Q. 4 Exercise of CAG's powers in relation to the accounts of the Union and the States is derived from Article 149 of the Indian Constitution. Discuss whether audit of the Government's policy implementation could amount to overstepping its own (CAG) jurisdiction. 12½

Answer: Article 149 of the Constitution makes provision for the office of Comptroller and Auditor General (CAG) of India. The Comptroller and Auditor General's (Duties, Powers and Conditions of Service) Act, 1971 provides for his powers and duties. To keep his office impartial and independent, Constitution makes provisions under Articles 148-151.

CAG is guardian of public purse, traditionally an auditor for the Government of Union and States, keeping watch on expenses made from the Consolidated Fund of India under legislative approval. However, recently the CAG has widened its spectrum by starting performance audit of governmental schemes and expenditures related to them.

A CAG report on issue of Licenses and Allocation of 2G Spectrum resulted in a huge controversy. The report estimated that there was a presumptive loss of Rs. 1,76,600 crores by the UPA government.

A 2012 CAG report on Coal Mine Allocation received massive media and political reaction as well as public outrage.

The scandal was first exposed due to the CAG report in the matter in December 1995. The report alleged of fraudulent withdrawal of government funds worth Rs. 9,500 crores in the Bihar animal husbandry department.

The oil ministry imposed a fine of INR 7,000 crores on Mukesh Ambani's company for the sharp drop in production of gas and violations mentioned in CAG's 2011 report.

In November 2009, the CAG requested the government to amend the 1971 Audit Act to bring all private-public partnerships (PPPs), Panchayti Raj Institutions and societies getting government funds within the ambit of the CAG.The amendment further proposes to enhance CAG's powers to access information under the Audit Act. The claim of government regarding acting beyond authority by CAG has been rejected by the Supreme Court of India.

Q. 5 Discuss each adjective attached to the word 'Republic' in the 'Preamble'. Are they defendable in the present circumstances? **12½**

Answer: The Preamble to the Constitution of India describes India as a Sovereign, Socialist, Secular, Democratic, Republic. Words Socialist and Secular were inserted by the 42nd Amendment Act of 1976.

Sovereignty of India lies in the fact that country conducts its affairs without interference of any other country or power. Even though India has accepted membership of Commonwealth but it is only ceremonial in nature and therefore sovereignty is not affected. Requirements arising out of membership of International Organizations also cannot be termed as limitation on sovereignty.

India is a secular country which gives equal importance to all religions. Special protections and provisions in favour of minorities are not against the spirit of Secularism that India follows.

Socialism is a philosophy of governance where resources are owned and shared commonly. But economic pattern of India has changed more towards a mixture of capitalism-socialism, with heavier tilt to capitalist economy, after LPG policy in 1991. Term Socialist, though true to the spirit of our constitutional system of governance, does not actually describe our economic pattern. Many supporting provisions in the constitution including Directive Principles of State Policy are in favour of socialism.

Democracy is in the root of Indian polity. With universal adult franchise, India is the largest democracy in the world. Democratic institutions in India are maturing with time and experience.

Q. 6 What was held in the Coelho case? In this context, can you say that judicial review is of key importance amongst the basic features of the Constitution? **12½**

Answer: The case of I R Coelho (dead) v State of Tamil Nadu was decided by a nine judges batch of the Supreme Court of India which delivered a unanimous verdict upholding the basic structure doctrine and authority of the judiciary to review any law that destroys or abrogates basic structure of the Constitution. A law, if violates basic structure, cannot be protected from Judicial Review even by putting in 9th Schedule after 24th April, 1973.

The 42nd Amendment Act of 1976 tried to do away with limitation on its amending power and exclude Judicial Review of any amendment on the ground that it violates basic structure of the constitution. The Supreme Court decided that though Parliament has power to amend any provision of the Constitution but it cannot violate the Basic Structure of the Constitution. It also held that Court has power to review any legislation or amendment in case it violates the basic structure.

Therefore, it was held, the Judicial Review is Basic Structure of the Constitution which cannot be excluded.

It may be noted that Judicial Review safeguards important provisions of the Constitution from amending or legislative power of Parliament.

Q. 7 Did the Government of India Act, 1935 lay down a federal constitution? Discuss. 12½

Answer: The Government of India Act 1935 provided for Diarchy at the Centre. The British Government, through the Governor-General of India - Viceroy of India, would continue to control India's financial obligations, defense, foreign affairs and the British Indian Army.

As per the Act, the British Government would make the key appointments to the Reserve Bank of India (exchange rates) and Railway Board.

The Act stipulated that no finance bill could be placed in the Central Legislature without the consent of the Governor General.

The funding for the British responsibilities and foreign obligations (e.g. loan repayments, pensions), at least 80 percent of the federal expenditures, would be non-votable and be taken off the top before any claims could be considered for social or economic development programs.

The Viceroy, under the supervision of the Secretary of State for India, was provided with overriding and certifying powers that could, theoretically, have allowed him to rule autocratically.

Federation would consist of Provinces and Princely States as units. The Act divided subjects between the Centre and Units into Federal List, Provincial List and Concurrent List.

Unlike the provincial portion of the Act, the Federal portion was to go into effect only when half the States by weight agreed to federate. This never happened and the establishment of the Federation was indefinitely postponed after the outbreak of the Second World War.

Q. 8 What is quasi-judicial body? Explain with the help of concrete examples. 12½

Answer: A quasi-judicial body is an entity such as an arbitrator or tribunal board which has powers and procedures resembling those of a court of law or judge. It is obliged to objectively determine facts and draw conclusions from them so as to provide the basis of an official action.

Their powers are usually limited to a very specific area of expertise and authority, such as land use and zoning, financial markets, employment law, public standards, and/or a specific set of regulations of an agency.

In India, National Human Rights Commission, National Commission for Women, National Commission for Minorities, National Commission for Backward Classes, National Law Commission, National Green Tribunal, National Consumer Disputes Redressal Commission, Armed Forces Tribunal etc. are examples of quasi-judicial bodies.

For example, the basic functions of the Securities and Exchange Board of India is to protect the interests of investors in securities and to promote the development of, and to regulate the securities market and for matters connected there with or incidental there to. SEBI has to be responsive to the needs of three groups, which constitute the market:the issuers of securities, the investors, the market intermediaries. SEBI has three functions rolled into one body: quasi-legislative, quasi-judicial and quasi-executive. It drafts regulations in its legislative capacity, it conducts investigation and enforcement action in its executive function and it passes rulings and orders in its judicial capacity.

Q. 9 Professor Amartya Sen has advocated important reforms in the realms of primary education and primary health care. What are your suggestions to improve their status and performance? 12½

Answer: Professor Amartya Sen said that India is the only country trying to get universally educated and universal healthcare through the private sector. Japan, US, Europe, China, Cuba, Vietnam, Singapore, Hong Kong, all types of economies have felt importance of the state in making education and healthcare widely spread and universal.

India spends less than 4% of GDP on education sector and less than 2% on healthcare sector. Both of these figures are less than world average and much below than even many Asian and African counties. Government needs to increase budgetary allocation in both the sectors of primary importance.

In both the sectors, availability, affordability and quality, should be improved.

More schools at village and hamlet levels with basic facilities and availability of good teachers have to be ensured. Education system, according to Prof Amartya Sen requires drastic change in curriculum and teaching method. Government can revisit the existing system of primary education and increase use of technology to make it better.

In primary healthcare system, government has to take responsibility of providing Primary Health Centers at grass root level ivith availability of trained medical and paramedical staff. Availability and affordability of medicine and other medical services is also part of efficient healthcare system.

India cannot dream of becoming a developed country only by economic growth, it has to ensure quality education, healthcare and other basic social facilities for everyone.

Q. 10 "In the Indian governance system, the role of non-state actors has been only marginal." Critically examine this statement. 12½

Answer: Indian governance system is procedurally very complicated and skeptical of outsides' interference. Elected governments and established bureaucracy has been reluctant to deviate from complex rules and accept participatory approach. This has kept role of non-state actors limited in governance system.

However, non-state actors like Non-Governmental Organizations (NGOs), Media, Caste- based organizations, Religious institutions, Professional Societies, Women's groups, Trade Unions and Universities have been able to influence governance of the country by demanding reforms.

Right to Information Act, National Food Security Act, Right to Education, MNREGA and some other social provisions are result of non-state actors persistence. Demand for more transparency in governance has also resulted in Citizens Charter in public offices.

Industry Organizations have been influencing Economic policies and Foreign Trade policy of India for better economic growth of the country.

Environmental NGOs have been creating awareness about poor standards in pollution and non-implementation of environmental laws.

Health related groups have been able to keep Genetically Modified Crops out from Indian market by raising issues related to health and sustenance of poor farmers in competition of MNCs.

Thus, even though political and bureaucratic system has not been welcoming to suggestions and participation, non-state actors have been persistently trying to make governance better by creating awareness in their fields.

Q. 11 "Effectiveness of the government system at various levels and people's participation in the governance system are inter-dependent." Discuss their relationship in the context of India. 12½

Answer: In governance, especially in democracies, participation of people in the system improves effectiveness of government system. Participation of stakeholders and beneficiaries can guide implementation of governmental programs.

In India, citizens' participation in governance is very less for various reasons, including complex bureaucratic procedures, corruption and lack of transparency. To make governmental programs and services more effective, beneficiaries should be taken on the board. Wherever people have participation in policy making, result would be better.

Right to Information Act, Citizens Charter, Panchayati Raj System, Gram Sabha, Lok Adalat etc. are some of the platforms where participation by citizens is possible. These platforms have actually helped in effective governance and efficient policy implementations.

But unfortunately, in India, many times the beneficiaries are not aware of new schemes launched by government. Expecting people to take part in and support governmental policies is futile unless they are informed in appropriate manner. As it has been happening in India, people do not come to know about benefits available to them. This is because of lack of transparency in our system. Resultantly, most of the governmental policies are not able to achieve expected results.

It may be noted that recently launched schemes like Swachch Bharat Abhiyan and Campaign to provide Toilets to every home need more participation to get effective result.

Q. 12 In the integrity index of Transparency International, India stands very low. Discuss briefly the legal, political, economic/social and cultural factors that have caused the decline of public morality in India. 12½

Answer: India ranks 76 among 168 countries with very low score of 38 out of 100 in the Transparency International's Corruption Perception Index of 2015.

Public morality in India has declined in every sphere for various reasons.

Legal factors like lack of strict implementation of anti-corruption laws, complex procedures, lack of enthusiasm on parts of executives and judiciary to act strictly against corruption has finally resulted into disinterest in public to fight against corruption.

Starting from opaque funding system of political parties to excessive use of muscle and money power during elections, buying of votes to buying of tickets, non-implementation of election promises, changing of parties and no ideology on the parts of politicians have affected trust of people over political system in India.

Society has accepted corruption as a part of system even for smaller public services. There is no shunning against corrupt office holders. Public has rather, in absence of effective remedy, taken bribing as a measure for getting the work done urgently.

Culturally there has been no strengthening of moral and value system in society in recent time. Society has accepted success and riches of people valid even if amassed through unethical means. Lack of moral education, systematization of corrupt practices, strengthening of corruption chain and social hierarchy has resulted into corruption in the society.

Widening of economic gap amongst different classes of society is also a reason for increasing of corruption in Indian society.

Q. 13 Has the Indian governmental system responded adequately to the demands of Liberalization, Privatization and Globalization started in 1991? What can the government do to be responsive to this important change? 12½

Answer: Due to FOREX crisis, India had to change its economic policy and adopt Liberalisation, Privatisation, Globalisation (LPG) in 1991.

As the name suggests, economic and commercial policies were made liberal to allow businesses to grow. Henceforth, the attitude of government was to curtain private sector by keeping majority of areas under license. The procedures were liberalized and made open for private sectors.

Privatization of governmental PSUs started in phased manner to reduce direct stake in market. Government had shaken off the responsibility of fulfilling market demand by allowing private sectors to play major role. Except few important sectors, government decided to disinvest its stake from PSUs.

Globalisation was demand of time that India had missed due to inward looking, import substitution policies. Now, by LPG, India allowed foreign companies and investors by opening its market. Initially the move was slow, so domestic industries can learn from experience, to compete with international players. It also helped in avoiding knee-jerk to Indian industries.

Indian LPG has been slow, steady and constant movement that is still ongoing process. Not all PSUs have been privatized, not all required services are left on private sectors, not all licenses are done away with, and not all sectors are fully opened to investment by private and foreign companies. Government can expedite this process.

Q. 14 "Traditional bureaucratic structure and culture have hampered the process of socioeconomic development in India." Comment. 12½

Answer: Traditional bureaucratic structure and culture, synonymous with inefficiency, corruption, red tappism and complex procedures, is widely considered unable to deliver on socioeconomic development agenda.

Role of bureaucracy is to maintain law and order, collect revenues, and implement governmental projects and schemes. Identify problems at ground level and suggest policy inputs. However, due to delay in decision making, insensitivities towards problems of people and prevailing corruption bureaucracy has not been able to deliver.

Given the lack of participatory approach, centralized decision making, strong hierarchy, complex rules and regulations, bureaucratic approach has been complete failure, in socio-economic development of India.

Healthcare issues, primary education, poverty alleviation, women and minority empowerment, employment generation, infrastructure building and many other areas of relevance to common men have been lacking in progress. Political-Bureaucratic nexus, Mafia raj, inability of honest and efficient officers to deliver, inefficient administration are some more reasons in this regard.

Initiatives like time bound service to people under Citizens Charter, transparency through Right to Information Act, participation through Panchayati Raj and overall attempt to make system accountable and answerable to the beneficiary has been useful and results are self-evident. Role of media, education and awareness in people is also helpful in changing the system.

Socio - economic development requires bottoms-up approach and therefore sensitization of bureaucrats towards problems faced by people is very important.

Q. 15 Examine the main provisions of the National Child Policy and throw light on the status of its implementation. 12½

Answer: The Government has adopted a new National Policy for Children, 2013 on 26th April, 2013. The Ministry also developed a Draft National Plan of Action for Children (NPAC).

The Policy recognizes every person below the age of eighteen years as a child and covers all children within the territory and jurisdiction of the country.

The Policy has identified four key priority areas: survival, health and nutrition; education and development; protection and participation, for focused attention.

As per the Policy, government is required to take all necessary measures to:

(i) Provide universal and equitable access to quality Early Childhood Care and Education (ECCE) of all children below six years of age

(ii) Ensure that every child in the age group of 6-14 years is in school

(iii) Promote affordable and accessible quality education up to the secondary level for all children

(iv) Foster and support inter sectoral networks and linkages to provide vocational training options and enable career counseling and vocational guidance

(v) Ensure that all out of school children are tracked, rescued, rehabilitated and have access to their right to education

(vi) Address discrimination of all forms in schools and foster equal opportunity, treatment and participation

(vii) Prioritise education for disadvantaged groups by creating enabling environment

(viii) Ensure physical safety of the child and provide safe and secure learning environment

(ix) Ensure that all processes of teaching and learning are child friendly

(x) Ensure formulation and practice of pedagogy that engages and delights children

In terms of implementation of the policy, still universal education, quality of education, physical safety, continuing child labour in the society, coordination in various government schemes related to children, amendment to various laws and establishment of implementing agency are major issues to be tackled by government.

Q. 16 "Demographic Dividend in India will remain only theoretical unless our manpower becomes more educated, aware, skilled and creative." What measures have been taken by the government to enhance the capacity of our population to be more productive and employable? 12½

Answer: Demographic Dividend refers to the economic growth potential that can result from shifts in a population's age structure, mainly when the share of the working-age population is larger than the non-working-age share of the population. Demographic dividend gives benefits like, increased labor supply, increase in national savings due to less number of dependents, human capital and increasing domestic demand brought about by the increasing GDP per capita and the decreasing dependency ratio.

However, availability of labour supply in India cannot be absorbed productively unless they are educated, skilled and creative. Rather than saving in governmental and personal expenditure due to less dependency ratio, will be useless if the working age population is not able to contribute in national production. Human capital and increase in domestic demand also depend on employment and increase in PPP.

Government has launched National Skill Development Corporation under the Pradhan Mantri Kaushal Vikas Yojana to impart vocational and skill based education.

Make in India, Digital India and Skill India programs are also relevant in utilization of working age population of india.

Programs related to increase of National Literacy, Right to Education, National Policy of Education and National Policy on Children are other important measures taken which can contribute in making the Demographic Dividend more meaningful.

Increasing skill, productivity and employability of Indian youth is more important.

Q. 17 "The broader aims and objectives of WTO are to manage and promote international trade in the era of globalization. But the Doha round of negotiations seem doomed due to

differences between the developed and the developing countries." Discuss in the Indian perspective. **12½**

Answer: WTO aims to manage and promote international trade and make political boundaries irrelevant for the purpose of trade.

After adopting globalization in 1991, India has played important role in WTO. India providing a market of 1.2 billion people has also remained a great attraction for all global players.

The Doha Development Round commenced in November 2001 with objectives to lower trade barriers around the world and facilitates increased global trade. Progress in negotiations stalled after the breakdown of the July 2008 negotiations over disagreements concerning agriculture, industrial tariffs and non-tariff barriers, services, and trade remedies. The most significant differences are between developed nations led by the European Union (EU), the United States (US), and Japan and the major developing countries led and represented mainly by India, Brazil, China, and South Africa. Since the breakdown of negotiations in 2008, there have been repeated attempts to revive the talks, so far without success.

On agricultural front, Special Safeguard Mechanism for protecting the interests of poor farmers in developing countries is yet to be resolved. India and other developing countries do not want discussions on labour and environment related issues to be part of Doha Round. They can be discussed under ILO and UNFCCC. Terming them as Non- Trade Issues, India wants them to be negotiated separately.

Q. 18 Evaluate the economic and strategic dimensions of India's Look East Policy in the context of the post Cold War international scenario. **12½**

Answer: India's Look East policy, initiated in 1991 marked a strategic shift in India's perspective of the world after end of Cold War. It is an effort to cultivate extensive economic and strategic relations with the nations of Southeast Asia in order to strengthen its standing as a regional power and a counterweight to the strategic influence of China.

Sensing the shift of global economic trend toward South East Asian countries, India has entered into numerous free trade agreements with East Asian economies, including a Comprehensive Economic Cooperation Agreement with Singapore and an Early Harvest Scheme with Thailand, while it is negotiating agreements with Japan, South Korea, and Association of Southeast Asian Nations (ASEAN) member states.

India signed trade agreements and increased its investments in Burma; although private sector activity remains low, India's state corporations have landed lucrative contracts for industrial projects and the construction of major roads and highways, pipelines and upgrading of ports.

Ties have been strengthened with Taiwan, Japan and South Korea over common emphasis on democracy, human rights and strategic interests. South Korea and Japan remain amongst the major sources of foreign investment in India.

India signed free trade agreements with Sri Lanka and Thailand and stepped up its military cooperation with them as well.

By engaging with South East Asian countries in frequent security and strategic dialogues, joint exercises, consultation and exchange of views on areas of global security, counter terrorism and security of the region, India has established strong commercial, cultural and military ties with them.

Q. 19 "Increasing cross-border terrorist attacks in India and growing interference in the internal affairs of several member-states by Pakistan are not conducive for the future of SAARC (South Asian Association for Regional Cooperation)." Explain with suitable examples. 12½

Answer: SAARC **was** founded in Dhaka on 8th December, 1985. The organization promotes development of economic and regional integration. It launched the South Asian Free Trade Area in 2006.

Peace and prosperity in the Indian subcontinent is affected by various ongoing conflicts in the region. Political dialogue is often conducted on the margins of SAARC meetings which have refrained from interfering in the internal matters of its member states.

Afghanistan has frequently alleged Pakistani interference in its internal affairs and active support to Taliban and causing deadly attacks. Afghanistan even warned to take Pakistan to UN. Pakistani meddling in Afghanistan dated before the 1979 Soviet invasion.

Bangladesh strongly protested against the statement issued by Pakistan following the execution of Mir Quasem Ali, terming Islamabad's remarks an interference in its internal affairs.

On trade liberalization and cross-border trade in energy during the last years, Pakistan pulled back when the agreements were ready for signature. Pakistan's policy towards India has been making difficult for effective implementation of SAARC policy.

The SAARC process has been in limbo since India-Pakistan tensions spiked after a terror attack on an Indian Army camp at Uri. September 2008 attack in Mumbai had also affected smooth functioning of SAARC.

The 19th SAARC summit scheduled to be held in Pakistan was called off as India, Bangladesh, Bhutan and Afghanistan decided to boycott it. It was for the first time that four countries boycotted a SAARC summit.

Q. 20 What are the aims and objectives of the McBride Commission of the UNESCO? What is India's position on these? 12½

Answer: The MacBride report also known as Many Voices One World was a 1981 UNESCO publication written by the International Commission for the Study of Communication Problems. It was named after its chairman Sedn MacBride, an Irish Nobel laureate.

Aim of the commission was to analyze communication problems in modern societies, particularly relating to mass media and news, consider the emergence of new technologies.

It was also mandated to suggest a kind of communication order to diminish these problems to further peace and human development. It is called as New World Information and Communication Order.

The report identified problems like concentration of the media, commercialization of the media, and unequal access to information and communication.

The commission proposed democratization of communication and strengthening of national media to avoid dependence on external sources. Internet-based technologies considered in the work of the Commission, served as a means for furthering MacBride's visions.

While the report had strong international support, it was condemned by the United States and the United Kingdom as an attack on the freedom of the press, and both countries withdrew from UNESCO in protest in 1984 and 1985, respectively and later rejoined in 2003 and 1997, respectively.

The Commission's seminal session on new technologies to address the identified problems, was hosted by India at New Delhi in March 1979. Indian member of the Commission was Boobli George Verghese. India supported and accepted the reports finding.

SOLVED PAPERS

PAPER–III

Time Allowed: Three Hours *Maximum Marks: 250*

Instructions: There are TWENTY questions printed both in English and in Hindi. All the questions are compulsory. The number of marks carried by a question is indicated against it. Answers must be written in the medium authorized in the Admission Certificate which must be stated clearly on the cover of this Question-cum-Answer (QCA) Booklet in the space provided. No marks will be given for answers written in medium other than the authorized one.

Word limit in questions, wherever specified, should be adhered to.

Answer the questions in not more than 200 words each. Contents of the answer is more important than its length.

Q. 1 How globalization has led to the reduction of employment in the formal sector of the Indian economy? Is increased informalization detrimental to the development of the country? 12½

Answer: Formal sector of employment in India has mainly been in industrial and governmental sector.

Globalisation opened Indian economy to foreign companies who brought technology and investment in India. With latest technology and heavy investment production pattern shifted from manual to mechanical. Labour intensive industries have shifted towards capital and technology intensive pattern of production.

This required skill, which is lacking in Indian labour. In India skill development in labour force has been seriously neglected due to various reasons.

Globalization also encouraged government and private companies to outsource their work to contracting firms which reduced their operative cost and increased efficiency. This further reduced employment in formal sector.

To match the competition of other countries, Indian industries had to adapt to the new trend of economic development. Some industries which could not compete to the demand of open economy have vanished.

Given the trend of more informalised economy, government cannot plan its policies effectively and sometimes loses revenue generation. In India tax to GDP ratio remains low due to very small formal sector economic activities. Many industries have shifted to service sector which are not regulated and do not come under tax net. Small industries have stopped production and turned to cheap import. Resultantly, government programs of social security and other benefits which are available to formal sectors are not implemented widely. This becomes detrimental to the development of the country.

Q. 2 Women empowerment in India needs gender budgeting. What are the requirements and status of gender budgeting in the Indian context? 12½

Answer: Gender Budgeting is a practice that accounts budgetary measures to support gender commitments as a powerful tool for achieving gender mainstreaming so as to ensure that benefit of development reach women as much as men.

Women form 48% of our population but their presence in mainstream economy is very less. In men dominated society, gender budgeting ensures that allocation of women are made properly. This will help in empowerment of women and help them contribute to the economy in more effective manner.

Gender budgeting in India follows the following measures in accounting gender specific programmes:

(i) Specifically targeted expenditure to women and girls;

(ii) Pro-women allocations, which are the composite expenditure schemes with a significant women's component; and

(iii) Residual public expenditures that have gender-differential impacts.

Indian government introduced gender budgeting in 2005-06 as a budgetary practice and institutionalized it by introduction of a Gender Budget Statement since 2005-06. The Statement captures the total quantum of resources earmarked for women in a financial year. Budgetary resource allocation and the specific expenditure amount for women specific programs are separately mentioned as part of gender budgeting.

In 2016-17 budget, Rs. 17,412 crores were allocated to 100% women specific programmes (Part A) while for 30% women specific programmes (Part B) total allocation was INR 73,212 crores. Thus total of Rs. 90,302 crores were reported as allocation in gender budget statement of 2016-17 budget.

Q. 3 Pradhan Mantri Jan Dhan Yojana (PMJDY) is necessary for bringing unbanked to the institutional finance fold. Do you agree with this for financial inclusion of the poor section of the Indian society? Give arguments to justify your opinion. 12½

Answer: Pradhan Mantri Jan-Dhan Yojana (PMJDY) aims at ensuring access to various financial services like availability of basic savings bank account, access to need based credit, remittances facility, insurance and pension to the excluded sections i.e. weaker sections & low income groups.

As a National Mission on Financial Inclusion PMJDY encompass an integrated approach to bring about comprehensive financial inclusion of all the households in the country.

The beneficiaries would get RuPay Debit card having inbuilt accident insurance cover of one lakh rupees.

PMJDY also envisages channeling all Government benefits (from Centre/State/Local Body) to the beneficiaries' accounts and pushing the Direct Benefits Transfer (DBT) scheme of the Union Government.

With the proactive approach of opening zero balance account with minimum requirement of documentation, the scheme will be able to bring larger section of population under banking mechanism.

Financial Inclusion of poor class people will allow government to increase their participation in governmental projects by ensuring benefits of governmental schemes.

It will not only create direct link between government and people but will also remove bureaucratic hurdles, bring transparency in dealings, reduce corruption and delay in delivery mechanism. PMJDY has been implemented successfully in rural areas, especially given the compulsion of demonetization scheme of government.

Q. 4 What are 'Smart Cities'? Examine their relevance for urban development in India. Will it increase rural-urban differences? Give arguments for 'Smart Villages' in the light of PURA and RURBAN Mission. 12½

Answer: Smart Cities are not defined in Indian context by the Smart Cities Mission of government but it describes them as cities with better amenities as per requirement of dwellers. Ideally, any smart city should have basic facilities like availability of water and electricity, schools and colleges to provide quality education, hospitals to provide good healthcare, transportation facilities like bus, train, airport, metro etc. and other amenities like telephone and internet connectivity, governmental offices, courts, e-governance, industries to provide employment and better sanitation.

These smart cities are required in India but actually 68% of Indian population is living in rural areas which also require better facilities which can be modeled as Smart Villages. Earlier concepts of Providing Urban Amenities to Rural Areas (PURA) and newly launched Rurban Mission are good steps in the direction of Smart Villages.

Big numbers of city dwellers are also temporary migrants for employment and education purposes. If these facilities are created in rural areas, there will be no requirement for migration towards urban areas.

If government does not think in terms of improving facilities in rural areas, burden will increase on cities. Due to lack of space and infrastructure, cities are becoming uninhabitable. This also increases gap in living standards of people in urban and rural areas.

Q. 5 Justify the need for FDI for the development of the Indian economy. Why there is gap between MOUs signed and actual FDIs? Suggest remedial steps to be taken for increasing actual FDIs in India. 12½

Answer: Foreign Direct Investment is required for any economy, especially in developing stage, to meet its requirement of infrastructure, industrialization, increasing economic activities, creating employement and sometimes also to provide social sector infrastructure to the population.

India, as a developing economy, does not have enough funds to finance all its requirement of the economy. This makes India looking for FDI. FDI also brings with itself expertise and technological know-how from developed countries.

In India, there has been cases where MoUs are signed for intention to invest but actual realization of FDI is much less than projected in MoUs. Many factors are responsible for this, including, complex bureaucratic system, delay in decision making, corruption as a hurdle in project implementation, environmental issues, local politics, allotment of land, lack of infrastructure, electricity and energy deficiency and skilled man power. Many projects have not taken off due to some of the above mentioned reasons.

India also ranks very poorly, 130^{lh} in the Ease of Doing Business Index of the World Bank. This shows why projects intended to attract FDI are not moving ahead and actual realization of FDI remains low.

To improve inflow of FDI, India needs to improve upon all the problems creating hurdles in business environment. Easing out the procedure for FDI, opening up of the economy for foreign investors, reducing complexity of procedures, streamlining policies and facilitating investors on fast track basis can help in increasing actual FDI in India.

Q. 6 Comment on the challenges for inclusive growth which include careless and useless manpower in the Indian context. Suggest measures to be taken for facing these challenges. 12½

Answer: Inclusive growth requires spreading out benefit of economic growth to everyone in the society, including those who are not able to contribute to the growth meaningfully. These classes of unskilled people who have become useless in the growth story are also to be taken care of to maintain inclusive growth. There is also a class of society which is careless towards own progress and growth of the nation as a whole. This section also cannot be neglected while distributing benefits of nation's achievement.

This requires a holistic approach on the side of the government to make and implement policies which covers the unskilled and unemployable persons by providing them with suitable jobs and activity. This is also essential to prevent them from entering into antisocial activities.

As per a survey, only 2% of Indian labour force is certified skilled labour. This compares very poorly to 96% of the South Korea. Government can plan to impart skill training to the labour force.

While making primary education universal, government can start providing technical and vocational training to the poor and weaker section of students who do not show interest or are not capable of studying further.

Financial inclusion scheme of PMJDY can be utilized to provide them certain monetary and other incentives.

Industries can be encouraged by giving them incentives to employ some of this class of manpower.

Q. 7 What is water - use efficiency? Describe the role of micro-irrigation in increasing the water - use efficiency. 12½

Answer: Water - use efficiency refers to the ratio of water used in plant metabolism to water lost by the plant through transpiration. Increase in water-use efficiency is required in areas facing soil water deficit and drought problems.

Micro - irrigation techniques like Sprinkle irrigation and Drip irrigation are very useful in increasing water-use efficiency. Rather than canal or open irrigation system as widely used in India, adapting to micro-irrigation will result into better yield in less water and less area.

Pipeline network in the field sprinkles or drops water through nozzles at required interval in necessary quantity to reduce waste of water through evaporation and consumption by weed. This water is used by plants efficiency.

As per reports, Drip Irrigation provides 90% water use efficiency in comparison to less than 40% resulting from surface method of irrigation. Reduction in amount of water also reduces consumption of electricity that is used to supply water. Countries like Israel have made excellent use of micro irrigation techniques.

'More Crop Per Drop' scheme of government also focuses on improving water use efficiency. Pradhan Mantri Krishi Sinchayee Yojana is also a step forward in this direction. Vision of providing 'Har Khet ko Pani' can be successfully implemented by saving water through use of micro irrigation techniques. Areas with shortage of water and high sunlight must use micro irrigation system to increase water use efficiency.

Q. 8 What is allelopathy? Discuss its role in major cropping systems of irrigated agriculture. 12½

Answer: Allelopathy is a biological phenomenon referring to capability of an organism to produce one or more bio-chemicals to influence the germination, growth, survival and reproduction of other organisms. These biochemicals are known as allelochemicals and have beneficial or detrimental effects on target organisms.

Allelopathy is a chemical mechanism that provides plants with an advantage for competing for limited resources. The ability of plants to suppress weeds is thus determined by crop allelopathy and competitiveness.

Allelopathic applications, such as straw mulching, provide sustainable weed management, further reducing the negative impact of agriculture on the environment.

To ensure sustainable agricultural development, it is important to exploit cultivation systems that take advantage of the stimulatory/inhibitory influence of allelopathic plants to regulate plant growth and development and to avoid allelopathicautotoxicity.

Allelopathy has been known and used in agriculture since ancient times but its recognition and use in modern agriculture are very limited.

Allelopathy plays an important role in investigations of appropriate farming systems as well as in the control of weeds, diseases and insects, the alleviation of continuous cropping obstacles, and allelopathic cultivar breeding.

Allelochemicals can act as environmentally friendly herbicides, fungicides, insecticides and plant growth regulators, and can have great value in sustainable agriculture.

With increasing emphasis on organic agriculture and environmental protection, increasing attention has been paid to allelopathy research, and the physiological and ecological mechanisms of allelopathy are gradually being elucidated.

Q. 9 Discuss the role of land reforms in agricultural development. Identify the factors that were responsible for the success of land reforms in India. 12½

Answer: Land reforms in India started immediately after independence with dual objectives of effective utilization of land and social justice. The system of Zamindari and Fuedal System had left farmers landless. To end tyrannies of farmers, land reforms were advocated by many activists including Acharya Vinoba Bhave through his Bhoodan Movement.

The most notable and successful example of land reforms are in the states of West Bengal and Kerala. After promising land reforms and elected to power in West Bengal in 1977, the Communist Party of India (Marxist) (CPI(M)) kept their word and initiated gradual land reforms, such as Operation Barga. The result was a more equitable distribution of land among the landless farmers, and enumeration of landless farmers. In land reform in Kerala, state administrations have actually carried out the most extensive land, tenancy and agrarian labor wage reforms in the non-socialist late- industrializing world. Another successful land reform program was launched in Jammu and Kashmir after 1947.

Land reforms involved re-distribution of land ownership rights, re-sizing of agricultural land, reforms in wages and possessory rights, reforms in tenancy rights of arable land.

Main reasons for success of land reforms were political will and desire of farmers to have ownership of land. Independence had created high mood in political sphere to implement land reforms in favour of poor farmers. However, actual and effective implementation happened much later and only in some areas.

Q. 10 Given the vulnerability of Indian agriculture to vagaries of nature, discuss the need for crop insurance and bring out the salient features of the Pradhan Mantri Fasal Bima Yojana (PMFBY). **12½**

Answer: In india, crop failure due to lack or excess rainfall or other natural reason is very common and recurring problem in such condition, farmers require protection uf insurance for their crop. Pradhan Mantri Fasal Bima Yojana (PMFBY) was launched with the objectives of providing insurance coverage and financial support to the farmers in the event of failure of any of the notified crop as a result of natural calamities, pests & disease. It also aims to stabilise the income of farmers to ensure their continuance in farming. PMFBY will encourage farmers to adopt innovative and modern agricultural practices. It will ensure flow of credit to the agriculture sector.

Under the PMFBY, the following risks will be covered:

- Yield Losses (standing crops, on notified area basis). Comprehensive risk insurance is provided to cover yield losses due to non-preventable risks, such as Natural Fire and Lightning, Storm, Hailstorm, Cyclone, Typhoon, Tempest, Hurricane, Tornado. Risks due to Flood, Inundation and Landslide, Drought, Dry spells, Pests/ Diseases also will be covered.
- In cases where majority of the insured farmers of a notified area, having intent to sow/ plant and incurred expenditure for the purpose, are prevented from sowing/planting the insured crop due to adverse weather conditions, shall be eligible for indemnity claims upto a maximum of 25 per cent of the sum-insured.
- In post-harvest losses, coverage will be available up to a maximum period of 14 days from harvesting for those crops which are kept in "cut & spread" condition to dry in the field.
- For certain localized problems, Loss/damage resulting from occurrence of identified localized risks like hailstorm, landslide, and Inundation affecting isolated farms in the notified area would also be covered.

Thus, PMFBM will be useful in de-risking farmers from vagaries of nature.

Q. 11 Give an account of the current status and the targets to be achieved pertaining to renewable energy sources in the country. Discuss in briefthe importance of National Programme on Light Emitting Diodes (LEDs). 12½

Answer: The Ministry of New and Renewable Energy revised its target of renewable energy to have grid connected installed capacity of 1,75,000 MW by 2022 which will comprise of 1,00,000 MW solar energy, 60,000 MW wind energy, 10,000 MW biomass and 5,000 MW small hydro power projects.

Currently the grid connected installed capacity of renewable energy stands at 50,000 MW of which wind energy is 28,700 MW, solar energy makes around 9,000 MW, Biomass less than 8,000 MW while small hydro power is approx. 4,400 MW.

To increase renewable energy, government has decided to set up a trading platform for clean energy to help states to buy, sell and trade renewable energy. Government will also provide 10 years tax exemption for solar energy projects. Unproductive and nonarable agricultural land may be used for solar power generation.

Prime Minister launched the Prakash Path, a National Programme for LED based Home and Street Lighting on 5 January 2015. Government will replace 77 crore conventional bulbs and 3.5 crore conventional streetlights with LED bulbs. The change will save INR 45,500 crore and reduce electricity consumption by 21,500 MW. LED bulbs consume 90% less energy in comparison to incandescent bulbs, emits less $C0_2$, emits more light, they may last up to 20 years.

The program will work towards the conservation of energy.

Q. 12 Discuss India's achievements in the field of Space Science and Technology. How the application of this technology has helped India in its socio-economic development? 12½

Answer: Indian space technology journey started with The Aryabhata. Aryabhata spacecraft was country's first satellite, which marked a milestone in India's space programme because it was completely designed in the country and launched from a Russian facility in 1975.

Indian National Satellite system is a network of satellites that facilitates communications and broadcasting across the south Asian region. The first satellite in the series was placed into orbit in 1983.

Polar Satellite Launch Vehicle was developed in the 1990s and has become the Indian space mission's most reliable workhorse. The PSLV carried out its first mission in 1993 but its first successful outing was the next year.

ISRO successfully tested Reusable Launch Vehicle — Technology Demonstrator (RLV- TD) in May 2016.

Launching 104 satellites on a single mission, India has created history by successfully overtaking the previous record of 37 satellites launched by Russia in 2014.

The Mars Orbiter Mission, Mangalyaan successfully entered the martian orbit in September 2014 in its maiden attempt. India became the first country to successfully complete maiden Mars mission and also the fourth country to successfully venture into Mars.

Chandrayaan is Indian Lunar Exploration Programme. The first mission Chandrayaan- 1 was launched on October 2008 on board PSLV XL rocket. The Chandrayaan-1 mission carried Moon

Impact Prob payload that made contact with the Moon and made the stunning discovery of water on Moon. India's second lunar mission, Chandrayaan 2, is expected to be launched in 2017.

Indian Regional Navigation Satellite System IRNSS is an indegeniously built constellation of seven satellites which has been now given an operational name of NAVIC (Navigation with Indian Constellation). The satellites can provide accurate real-time positioning and timing services and extend its service to regions 1500 km. around India.

Q. 13 Why is nanotechnology one of the key technologies of the 21st century? Describe the salient features of Indian Government's Mission on Nanoscience and Technology and the scope of its application in the development process of the country. 12½

Answer: Nanotechnology is the manipulation of matter with at least one dimension sized from 1 to 100 nanometers. As applications of nano-technology various nano materials are being used to create nano products.

Titanium dioxide is used in sunscreen, cosmetics, surface coatings and some food products.

Silver is used in food packaging, clothing, disinfectants and household appliances.

Zinc oxide is used in sunscreens and cosmetics, surface coatings, paints and outdoor furniture varnishes.

Cars are being manufactured with nano materials so they may need fewer metals and less fuel to operate in the future.

Scientists are now turning to nanotechnology in an attempt to develop diesel engines with cleaner exhaust fumes.

Government of India launched a Mission on Nano Science and Technology (Nano Mission) in May 2007. The Nano Mission is an umbrella programme for capacity building which envisages the overall development of this field of research in the country and to tap some of its applied potential for nation's development. The mission will help development of infrastructure for nano science and technology research. For optimal use of expensive and sophisticated facilities, it is proposed to establish a chain of shared facilities across the country. The Mission will also promote application-oriented R&D Projects, establish Nano Applications and Technology Development Centres, Nano-Technology Business Incubators etc. The Mission shall focus on providing effective education and training to researchers and professionals in diversified fields so that a genuine interdisciplinary culture for nanoscale science, engineering and technology can emerge.

Q. 14 Rehabilitation of human settlements is one of the important environmental impacts which always attracts controversy while planning major projects. Discuss the measures suggested for mitigation of this impact while proposing major developmental projects. 12½

Answer: To implement major projects, vast land is necessary, sometimes demanding rehabilitation of human settlement. Rehabilitation, especially in country like India where people develop emotional attachment with the land, is very difficult task.

Cabinet has approved the National Policy on Rehabilitation and Resettlement, 2007, to replace the National Policy on Resettlement and Rehabilitation for Project Affected Families, 2003.

Government has promoted policy of non-displacement or least displacing alternatives of human settlement. It also aims at ensuring adequate rehabilitation package and expeditious implementation of the rehabilitation process.

The policy aims at striking a balance between the need for land for developmental activities and, at the same time, protecting the interests of the land owners, and others, such as the tenants, the landless, the agricultural and non-agricultural labourers, artisans, and others whose livelihood depends on the land involved.

The benefits under the new Policy shall be available to all affected persons and families whose land, property or livelihood is adversely affected by land acquisition or by involuntary displacement of a permanent nature due to any other reason, such as natural calamities, etc. The Policy will be applicable to all these cases irrespective of the number of people involved.

Right to fair compensation and Transparency in Land Acquisition, Rehabilitation and Resettlement Bill 2015 provides if private company acquires or purchases more than 50 acres of land in urban areas or 100 acres of land in rural areas, it will be required to rehabilitate and resettle affected families.

Q. 15 The frequency of urban floods due to high intensity rainfall is increasing over the years. Discussing the reasons for urban floods, highlight the mechanisms for preparedness to reduce the risk during such events. 12½

Answer: Recently India has witnessed frequently occurring urban floods e.g. in Gurugram, Mumbai and Srinagar. This is a new phenomenon which has alarmed city planners and administrators. Loss of life and property can be more in urban areas given the density of population.

Reasons for Urban floods:

Monsoon brings heavy rainfall in India, apart from some other seasonal rain. Storms at coastal areas can also cause floods.

Urban areas have developed as islands of heat which has resulted in increased rainfall. This is changing weather pattern due to global climate change.

Poor maintenance and lack of capacity increase in drainage system results into inability of absorbing higher volume of water.

Encroachments on the banks of water flowing natural drains have reduced space for passing off water which results into flood.

Improper disposal of solid waste and dumping of debris into drains also creates clogging of water.

Mechanism for preparedness to reduce the risk:

To reduce risk of flood, widening and de-silting of natural drains, de-clogging of water drainage system can help in smooth flow of water.

Increasing water flow capacity in proportion to the increased population will be required.

Protection and conservation of wetlands can help in reducing impact of coastal storms. Rain water harvesting will be useful in reducing load of excess rain water.

Proper disposal of waste and regular maintenance of urban drainage system can be useful in absorbing water flow.

Q. 16 With reference to National Disaster Management Authority (NDMA) guidelines, discuss the measures to be adopted to mitigate the impact of recent incidents of cloudbursts in many places of Uttarakhand. **12½**

Answer: Cloudburst refers to a short-term extreme precipitation of 10 cm or more in an hour occurring over a small area. It causes heavy rain,flash floods and landslides resulting into loss of lives and property. It is difficult to detect or forecast cloudburst and therefore taking preventive measures will be difficult.

National Disaster Management guidelines suggest taking holistic and integrated approach in case of disaster management events. It emphasizes on building strategic partnerships at various levels. Community based disaster management, including last mile integration of policy, plans and execution will be required. Capacity development in all spheres has to be ensured in the impacted areas. Past initiatives taken as preparatory measures or responsive actions can be consolidated and best practices can be adopted to reduce calamities. National and international level agencies have to coordinate in such cases to bring out multi-sector synergy in response to such event.

These guidelines can be adopted in response to the cloudbursts incidents that have happened in many places of Uttarakhand. In addition, Uttarakhan being hilly area, specific measures have to be taken to reduce impact of any disaster. This may include ban on haphazard and hazardous construction in hilly areas, prevention of encroachment in riverbeds, afforestation programs on the hill slops to prevent landslides, solidification of hill side rocks, alert-relay and early warning systems to warn evacuation. Alert medical and disaster rescue teams can be deployed in areas of frequent occasions of disasters to reduce delay in response.

Q. 17 The terms 'Hot Pursuit' and 'Surgical Strikes' are often used in connection with armed action against terrorist attacks. Discuss the strategic impact of such actions. **12½**

Answer: Recent Surgical Strike across the Line of Control has created debate on strategy to curtail terrorism.

Hot Pursuit refers to the urgent and direct pursuit of a criminal suspect by law enforcement officers, or by belligerents under international rules of engagement for military forces. It grants more power to the officers in command than they ordinarily have.

A surgical strike is a military attack which results in or is intended to result in damage to the intended legitimate military target only. It aims at no or minimal collateral damage to surrounding structures, vehicles, buildings, or the general public infrastructure and utilities.

Hot Pursuit and Surgical Strike are armed actions which result mostly out of territory of the state. When a criminal or pirate or terrorist group or armed group is not located in the territory of the state carrying out such operation, it sends a team of officers/ soldiers to conduct hot pursuit or surgical strike to eliminate the threat.

Hot pursuit is also used against ships and pirates in the sea, mainly carried out by Navy or Cost Guard officers.

Such operations are strategically useful to end threat by having targeted attack. In case the target is situated in another country, surgical strike is a measure to avoid full scale war. However, this violates sovereignty and the state can decide to challenge it.

Q. 18 'Terrorism is emerging as a competitive industry over the last few decades." Analyse the above statement. 12½

Answer: Number of terrorist groups has increased and their ideologies, followers' base, area of operation, modus operandi and purpose are different from each other. While A1 Qaeda under Osama bin Laden had been the terrorist group most infamous for its attack on Twin Towers, recently ISIS is in news for various deadly attacks.

Earlier, terrorist groups had been operating as small organizations, recruiting fighters mainly from local base and depending on funding or some minor trade activities. But ISIS and some other terrorist groups now own their resources by controlling territory in Iraq and Syria.

ISIS has started using social media for increasing followings and recruiting youth from all over the world. ISIS has promoted Lonc Wolf attack strategy where a terrorist can carry out an attack at the local area where he is based. This does not require joining the camp to fight with the group. Such strategy has been effective in spreading terror in the territories which had remained secure till now.

Terrorist groups are now competing with each other in attempt to establish themselves in the mindset of followers, gain more funding, spread its ideology. By making themselves different from others, they can create a space for themselves. Other groups like Taliban, Boko Haram, JeM are also following the path.

It poses a challenge to the international security because terrorism becoming a competitive industry and their attempt to expand -influence can only lead to more and more bloodshed.

Q. 19 Border manawmpnf is a romnlex task due to difficult terrain and hostile relations with some countries. Elucidate the challenges and strategies for effective border management. 12½

Answer: India shares border with Bangladesh, China, Pakistan, Nepal, Myanmar, and small portion with Afghanistan, totaling around 15,106 km.

To manage such a long border creates many challenges, especially due to hostile relations with some countries.

Terrain is very difficult on the border between India and China, making supply and maintenance very costly and challenging affair.

Climatic conditions in Himalayan area is harsh which poses challenge for soldiers posted at border.

Hostile population and lack of trust on some of the border areas with Pakistan is another challenge in border management.

Porous border with some countries makes it difficult to prevent illegal human trafficking, arms and drug smuggling.

Some strategies, to manage the border can be suggested as following:

Effective use of technology to monitor areas where access of human being is difficult. Coordination among various agencies at border can make the task easier.

To improve border security, smart border management system can be implemented with facilities of internet, communication and identification process.

Use of drone, night vision cameras, sensors and lasers to check illegal migration, terrorist movement can also help in effective border management.

If possible, physical fencing of the border can also be done along the hostile neighbours to avoid risks to security.

Effective coordination among security and border management agencies of neighboring countries can help in joint efforts of border management.

Q. 20 Use of internet and social media by non-state actors for subversive activities is a major security concern. How have these been misused in the recent past? Suggest effective guidelines to curb the above threat. **12½**

Answer: Internet and social media are powerful tools which are being used by non-state organisations, terrorist groups for spread of their propaganda and recruitment of youth. ISIS used Facebook and other social media to post videos of atrocities committed and also for recruiting youth from all over the world. Radicalization is being spread through social media.

Cyber warfare is also a dangerous phenomenon which can affect damage system of countries. Stuxnet virus affected computers in many countries.

Compromising of ATM cards data in India was recent example of misuse of internet by non-state actors.

To curb threat arising out of use of social media by non-state actors and terrorist organisations, some guidelines can be as follow:

Appointment of First Chief Information Security Officer (CISO) by India is a welcome step in the direction to protect cyber space.

A comprehensive policy can be developed to fight cyber-crime and manage cyber security.

A National Cyber Security Agency can help in improving India's resilience and defense system.

India's National Cyber Security Policy of 2013 aims at protection of information infrastructure in cyber space, and reducing vulnerabilities.

National Critical Information Infrastructure Protection Centre (NCIIPC) will deal with cyber threats.

A Computer Emergency Response Team (CERT-In) has been designated to act as Nodal agency for coordination of crisis management efforts.

SOLVED PAPERS

PAPER–IV

Time Allowed: Three Hours *Maximum Marks: 250*

Instructions: There are FOURTEEN questions divided in two Sections and printed both in Hindi and in English. All questions are compulsory. The number of marks carried by a question/part is indicated against it. Word limit in questions, wherever specified, should be adhered to. Any page or portion of the page left blank in the Question-cum-Answer Booklet must be clearly struck off.

Answer questions in NOT MORE than the word limit specified for each in the parenthesis. Content of the answer is more important than its length.

Section–A

Q. 1 (a) Explain how ethics contributes to social and human well-being. (150 words) 10

Answer: Ethics are principles of value that guide human being in making decisions and choosing a way of life and behavior among many. It is set of standards and beliefs influencing decisions of people.

Anyone guided by ethics will not do anything harmful to the society and thus will remain away from anti-social activities. Ethics also prevents person from taking path of crime or violence in case of dissatisfaction.

Ethics lead society towards more welfare activities resulting into larger good than personal gains or selfish motives. Individual preferences may be different from the societal ones, ethics encourage us to make decision and act on the path, which contributes better to social and human wellbeing.

In business, science or politics, ethics contribute for the larger betterment over individual and narrow gains. Personal welfare should be sacrificed if in contravention of public good on the basis of ethical principles.

Happiness, health, freedom, safety, security and other aspects of human wellbeing and society as a whole should be promoted by ethical thinking and way of life.

Q. 1 (b) Why should impartiality and non-partisanship be considered as foundational values in public services, especially in the present day socio-political context? Illustrate your answer with examples. (150 words) 10

Answer: Current socio-political context has reduced to favoritism or bias on the basis of personal relations, castes, religion, region, race or colour.

In such situation, especially in India, public service has to remain impartial and non- partitioned to perform public duties. Partiality may favour one particular class of persons but will create atmosphere of hatred in the society. Partitionship will result into polarization and patronage.

An example can be a public servant favouring personal relative for a vacancy in job ignoring other meritorious candidates. Another example can be giving priority to members of certain political group over others in public offices. It can be in terms of limiting access of public resources to one class of society. Partiality can be in maintaining law and order and not securing lives and liberties of one class of society by remaining bias.

These incidents will result into feeling of hatred and people will lose faith from system.

Q. 2 (a) What do you understand by the terms 'Governance', 'Good governance' and 'Ethical governance'. (150 words) 10

Answer: Governance is manner or action of governing a state or organization. It may refer to government, company, civil society, NGO, trusts or any other organization. It is based on set of rules, incorporating standard operating procedures and guiding principles.

Good governance means taking actions or using manner which results into better governance of the state or organization. Making the system more efficient, making it transparent and accountable, more responsive to requirement of people, based on rule of law, providing effective and efficient system based aiming at inclusion and equity.

Ethical governance can include all aspects of good governance in addition to focusing more on ethical values aiming at public welfare, integrity, honesty and selflessness. It may be guided by ethical values rather than standard operating procedure and rule based system. When welfare demands, dead letter printed in the rule books should be interpreted in most possible positive manners, guided by ethical values of the governance.

Q. 2 (b) Discuss Mahatma Gandhi's concept of seven sins. (150 words) 10

Answer: Mahatma Gandhi published Seven Social Sins in his weekly newspaper Young India in 1925. These are:

1. **Wealth without Work:** Gandhi gave importance to parishram, hard work and considered w'ealth earned without parishram as a sin. He objected to the system of Zamindari, profiteering and capitalism.
2. **Pleasure without Conscience:** Gandhi suggested enjoying the life with conscience. Any way of pleasure should not be against value system of society and conscience of the person. In this way he suggested celibacy and avoiding vyabhichar.
3. **Knowledge without Character:** Knowledge, Gyan must be accompanied by Character, Charitra. In absence of strength and integrity of character, knowledge may lead to disaster. Intellectual development should commensurate with internal development.
4. **Commerce without Morality:** Commercial activities must be guided by moral principles of restrain and welfare. Kalabazar and profiteering are considered sin. While earning profit and doing business, requirement of consumer should be kept in mind.
5. **Science without Humanity:** Science can make progress but its final aim should be wellbeing of humanity. Every scientific development has to be for the ultimate purpose of human welfare. Green Revolution may be considered good scientific development but invention and use of atom bomb may not be.
6. **Religion without Sacrifice:** Gandhi was a strict vegetarian and therefore by religious sacrifice he suggested personal sacrifice, not bali, animal sacrifice. Fasting, restraint on personal desires, sacrifice of personal comfort etc are important in religion.

7. **Politics without Principle:** Politics should be for promotion of certain beliefs and ideology, based on strict principles, guided by ethics and morality. Unprincipled, violent, corrupt politics is considered a sin.

Q. 3 (a) Analyse John Rawls's concept of social justice in the Indian Context. (150 word) 10

Answer: John Rawls in his book "A Theory of Justice" attempts to solve problem of distributive justice - socially just distribution of goods in society. His theory, a variant of social contract, is known as Justice as Fairness.

He gives two principles: Liberty principle and Difference principle.

Principle of Liberty explains that each person has equal right to the most extensive basic liberty compatible with a similar liberty for others.

The Difference principle talks of social and economic inequalities to be arranged so that:

1. They are to be of the greatest benefit to the last advantaged members of society, consistent with the just saving principle.
2. Offices and positions must be open to everyone under conditions to fair equality of opportunity.

   In Indian context, John Rawls theory can be interpreted as providing equal right to everyone which respects rights of others as well, and equal distribution of wealth among all members of the society.

   Indian constitution also aims at providing liberties enshrined in provisions of freedoms under article 19, limited by certain factors, respecting freedoms of the society at large.

   Inclusive growth and directive principles of state are other provisions incorporating the second principle of Rawls for fair distribution of economic benefits.

Q. 3 (b) Discuss the Public Services Code as recommended by the 2 Administrative Reforms Commission. (150 words) 10

Answer: The Second Administrative Reforms Commission recommends preparation of Public Service Code for guiding public service employees and manages their conduct. It aims at promoting public service values and ethics in public servants. It requires public servants to discharge their duties with:

1. Competence and Loyalty
2. Care and diligence
3. Responsibility
4. Integrity
5. Honesty
6. Objectivity and Impartiality
7. Without discrimination
8. In accordance with the law

ARC envisages a Public Service Authority to oversee the implementation of the code, incorporating punishment and penalties for violation. In absence of code of ethics for civil servants in India, this Public Service Code will serve as a set of guiding principles for public servants. The code aims to prevent misuse of official position or information.

Q. 4 (a) "Corruption causes misuse of government treasury, administrative inefficiency and obstruction in the path of national development." Discuss Kautilya's views. (150 words) 10

Answer: Kautilya in his book Arthashastra mentions 40 kinds of embezzlements. It mentions that corruption can be in various manners by public servants and functionaries. Corrupt practices results in less revenue collection which costs loss to the government treasure. This type of corruption involves functionary and public both getting benefit but loss to government revenue.

Corruption creates flaws in system resulting into inefficiency of administration. When the functionary does not follow rules and procedures but misuses them for personal or professional gains, it brings inefficiency.

National development requires dedication and diligence by all who are part of nation building. Public functionaries play pivotal role in development. Corrupt practices divert them from performing their duties towards nation and finally hampering development of the nation.

To reduce practices of corruption he favoured strict vigilance over functionaries and periodic transfer of government servants. Continuity in a place and function may allow the functionaries to pick holes in system and manipulate it to own advantage.

Q. 4 (b) How could social influence and persuasion contribute to the success of Swachh Bharat Abhiyan? (150 words) 10

Answer: Launched on 2nd October 2014, Swachh Bharat Abhiyan (SBA) is a campaign to clean streets, roads and infrastructure of the country. Government also aims to achieve an Open-Defecation Free India by 2nd October 2019, the 150th anniversary of birth of Mahatma Gandhi.

Influence is a cognitive factor having an effect on person's decisions without direct or apparent efforts. Social influence works on people to imitate action of others when they see it as becoming a trend or common habit. It can also be followed as fashion or new normal. Cleanliness drive can be used as a social influence on majority of people by making the affluent class follow it. Once the class which is taken as high regard starts following the trend of cleanliness, remaining people will be socially influenced.

Persuasion means to create an opinion, sentiment, view or thought which can be an active process of explanation and discussion. Government can hold discussions; create opinions by media and social events to persuade people to adapt to cleanliness.

This will result into success of Swachh Bharat Abhiyan.

Q. 5 Law and ethics are considered to be the two tools for controlling human conduct so as to make it conducive to civilized social existence.

(a) Discuss how they achieve this objective.

Answer: Law and Ethics are tools which shape human behavior in a manner to make them conducive to civilized existence by setting up guidelines to follow. Law sets up rules and regulations which cannot be violated without attracting penalty or punishment. Ethics prescribe standards of behavior which are followed by a set of individuals out of morality, social norm, professional customs or other persuasions.

Both of them help in modifying behavior of people to certain extent. Law has back up of legislation and legal machinery which creates compulsion to adhere to. Ethics gain strength from sources other than legislation or government. Organizations, society and personal belief create ethics.

Law achieves the objective through prohibitive instructions like, doing this is prohibited, or this action is not allowed. While ethics guide by saying one should do this, or one should take such actions. Thus, negative and affirmative actions are attached with laws and ethics respectively.

(b) Giving examples, show how the two differ in their approaches. (150 words) 10

Answer: Approach of Law and Ethics is completely different in achieving objective of shaping human behavior. In law, everyone is subject to the same machinery and it has wider application. It also has a force to compel obedience. Violation of law may result into judicial actions.

Ethics are more of guiding nature and there is mostly no governmental punitive action. It may have organizational or societal prohibitive value. People not following certain standards of ethics may not be accepted in some organization but legally they cannot be punished for failure to adhere to those ethics.

Ethics have wider scope than law. Ethics guide daiiy life and wider range of actions. Law does not cover such a wide spectrum but limits itself to manage social interaction smoothly. For example, Law forbids causing harm to others, while ethics suggests doing good to others. Law says what is wrong to do; ethics say what is right to do.

Q. 6 Our attitudes towards life, work, other people and society are generally shaped unconsciously by the family and the social surroundings in which we grow up. Some of these unconsciously acquired attitudes and values are often undesirable in the citizens of a modern democratic and egalitarian society.

(a) Discuss such undesirable values prevalent in Today's educated Indians.

Answer: Unconsciously we develop some values and attitude from society, family, work and other people which is undesirable in the citizens of a modern democratic and egalitarian society.

Patriarchal mindset we acquire from family and society which is completely undesirable in modern time. This results into keeping difference between girl and boy in family, attitude of considering women inferior to men.

Caste differences are still prevalent in our social system which must be avoided.

Corruption has become a new norm accepted by our society and our mindset develops in a manner that bribing is acceptable if work can be expedited.

Dowry, though legally banned, is still prevailing in milder and subtle form.

Accepting sub-standard quality of services and goods is also one undesirable attitude that we have acquired due to social and historical circumstances of India.

Uncleanliness has also become part of our social and cultural life.

Use of offensive language and abusive words, discrimination on the basis of economic and social status of person etc. are the factors crippling in our unconscious mind from our social interaction.

Attitude of demeaning others for their shortcomings or limitations, not accepting physically or mentally challenged people as equals are also most undemocratic and inhuman attitudes acquired unconsciously.

(b) How can such undesirable attitudes be changed and socio-ethical values considered necessary in public services be cultivated in the aspiring and serving civil servants? (150 words) 10

Answer: The undesirable attitudes developed and prevalent in the society has deep roots in history and cultural behavior. To change them and cultivating desirable socio-ethical values is not only a task of utmost importance but ,also a challenge.

Serving civil servants will be easy to train. They are subject to conduct rules which can be modified or new set of rules dealing with social and behavioural aspects can be implemented. They can be given trainings prior to or in middle of their career. Seminars, conferences , communications and other means can be utilized. Sensitization will also play a big role. As they are already following certain service rules and are subject to scrutiny, their obedience will be possible through legal and ethical code.

For aspiring civil servants, who are just like any other students in society, are subject to social pressure and influence of surroundings.

It can be through ethical teaching, moral lessons and social change that such students can learn about faults in our social behavior and habits.

As educatedyoung people, they will be open to change but conscious efforts and constant feedback will be required to make them realize problem and adopt solution.

School and college curriculum can be modified to include lessons of ethical and social change.

Evils like corruption, dowry, patriarchy, substandard of life or other undesirable social norms must be criticized strongly.

Syllabus, Exams, Camps, Quizzes and other formats of education can be utilized to train students who would be aspiring civil servants.

Q. 7 Anger is a harmful negative emotion. It is injurious to both personal life and work life.

(a) Discuss how it leads to negative emotions and undesirable behaviors.

Answer: Anger is a strong feeling of annoyance, displeasure or hostility. It is uncomfortable and. emotional response to a perceived provocation, hurt or threat.

Uncontrolled anger can lead to arguments, physical fights, physical abuse, assault and self-harm.

Anger triggers the body's 'fight or flight' response, including fear, excitement and anxiety.

Heart rate, blood pressure and respiration increase, the body temperature rises and the skin perspires.

Anger causes headache, digestion problems, abdominal pain, insomnia, increased anxiety, depression, high blood pressure, skin problems, eczema, heart attack and stroke.

The external expression of anger can be found in facial expressions, body language, physiological responses, and at times public acts of aggression.

In such situation, person cannot think logically, cannot stay calm and composed, behaves in unacceptable way. Responses that come from anger are haste which are lacking in proper application of mind and thoughtfulness.

This creates negative emotions and undesirable behavior.

(b) How can it be managed and controlled? (150 words) **10**

Answer: Anger management and control is very important for social interaction, personal comfort and professional success. As anger is a feeling and response it can be managed by controlling response towards particular feeling. Attitude to respond to a set of situation is mostly individual specific. One situation may make a person angry but no other. Therefore, one can analyze situations which make him uncomfortable, generate anger and affect his behavior. Once identified, person can start taking control of his response in such situations.

The way you typically express anger may take some time to modify. Suggestions to manage and control anger include:

- Keeping a diary of personal anger outbursts, to try and understand how and why one gets angry.
- Considering assertiveness training, or learning about techniques of conflict resolution.
- Learning relaxation techniques, such as meditation or yoga.
- Seeing a counsellor or psychologist if one still feels angry about events that occurred in the past.
- Exercising regularly is also important.

Q. 8 "Max Weber said that it is not wise to apply to public administration the sort of moral and ethical norms we apply to matters of personal conscience. It is important to realize that the state bureaucracy might possess its own independent bureaucratic morality." Critically analyse this statement. (150 words) **10**

Answer: Max Weber was a German sociologist who propounded that bureaucracy constitutes the most efficient and rational way in which one can organize human activity. He believed that state bureaucracy required systematic processes and organized hierarchies to maintain order, maximize efficiency, and eliminate favoritism.

As per him, most efficient and rational way of maintaining effective public administration as key part of the rational-legal authority was bureaucratization. He recognized bureaucracy as the most efficient form of organization and indispensable in the modern state.

Weber considered that to keep the public administration and bureaucracy effective in its functioning, human elements like personal ethics and conscience should be removed and strict procedure and rule based system should be established. As per him, bureaucracy has its own standards to flow to achieve order and efficiency. Ideal-typical bureaucracy is characterized by hierarchical organization, delineated lines of authority in a fixed area of activity.

Weber believed that both the public and private bureaucracy is based on specific competencies of various offices. These competencies are specified in various rules, laws, and administrative regulations. These rules and laws can be considered as independent bureaucratic morality.

Therefore, bureaucracy does not need to be burdened with social, moral or ethical norms applicable to individual. However, Weber himself did not believe the bureaucracy to be the perfect organization.

Section–B

Q. 9 A fresh engineering graduate gets a job in a prestigious chemical industry. She likes the work. The salary is also good. However, after a few months she accidentally discovers that a highly toxic waste is being secretly discharged into a river nearby. This is causing health problems to the villagers downstream who depend on the river for their water needs. She is perturbed and mentions her concern to her colleagues who have been with the company for longer periods. They advise her to keep quite as anyone who mentions the topic is summarily dismissed. She cannot risk losing her job as she is the sole bread-winner for her family and has to support her ailing parents and siblings. At first, she thinks that if her seniors are keeping quiet, why should she stick out her neck. But her conscience pricks her to do something to save the river and the people who depend upon it. At heart she feels that the advice of silence given by her friends is not correct though she cannot give reasons for it. She thinks you are a wise person and seeks your advice.

(a) What arguments can you advance to show her that keeping quiet is not morally right?

Answer: Arguments in favour of not keeping quiet:

Morality in business is essential and therefore she should made public the secretive discharge of toxic waste by company.

As a fellow human being it is her duty to disclose the health hazard being caused by company so actions can be taken by authorities to stop it.

Considering impact on health of poor villagers, she should think of some possible way to preventing company from releasing toxic waste in river.

She may have to face consequences in the company which may even result into loss of job. But loss of self-respect and conscience is worse than loss of job.

She may hope for another opportunity or alternative career if she loses the job but health problems to many villagers cannot be ignored.

Her personal loss is not more than collective loss of the villagers.

Company works for making profit. If the hazard can be proved, villagers will get reparation which will be useful in medical treatment.

(b) What course of action would you advise her to adopt and why? (250 words) **20**

Answer: Course of action suggested:

Considering the moral responsibility to resolve the problem, she should once again meet her colleagues and try to convince them to collectively bring the matter to Managerial Board.

She may make the villagers aware of possible health hazard and create public opinion against the company. Villagers may be convinced to organize a protest march against the company.

She should collect samples of toxic wastes, manage to test the water in laboratory and assess health risks.

She has to be ready for possibility of losing the job and therefore start looking for another job.

She may consult some NGO for taking up the matter.

District Authority may be reported of the problem being caused by release of toxic waste by the company.

A Public Interest Litigation may be filed by her in High Court or Supreme Court. The court may be requested to set up an enquiry commission and set the machinery in motion.

Q. 10 Land needed for mining, dams and other large-scale projects is acquired mostly from Adivasis, hill dwellers and rural communities. The displaced persons are paid monetary compensation as per the legal provisions. However, the payment is often tardy. In any case, hit cannot sustain the displaced families for long. These people do not possess marketable skills to engage in some other accusation. They end up as low paid migrant laborers. Moreover, their traditional ways of community living are destroyed. Thus, the benefits of development go to industries, industrialists and urban communities whereas the costs are passed on to these poor helpless people. This unjust distribution of costs and benefits is unethical.

Suppose you have been entrusted with the task of drafting a better compensation- cum-rehabilitation policy for such displaced persons, how would you approach the problem and what would be the main elements of your suggested policy? (250 words. 20

Answer: Mining, dams and other large scale projects need land which is acquired by displacing local habitants which mostly comprises of Adivasis, hill dwellers and rural communities settled in interior areas.

My approach would include

- To ensure that least possible migration and rehabilitation is required for the project in question
- To ensure that rehabilitation of all families is done in timely and effective manner To make the compensation according to market price of the land To include cost of resettlement in compensation
- To calculate and include cost of displacement of the family and its impact in earning livelihood

With this approach in mind, main elements in the bill would be:

The project developer shall ensure minimum possible displacement of the local population.

It shall be duty of the developer to provide employment to atleast one member of each family displaced at appropriate level in the project.

Amount payable to each family for acquisition of land shall be at the market rate prevailing in similar areas.

A rehabilitation fund specific to the project shall be constituted by the developer to meet unforeseen expenditure resulting out of rehabilitation and replacement.

The developer shall also pay, as compensation, a lump sum amount to each family in proportion to the area of land acquired, for the future loss and inconvenience in rehabilitation and resettlement.

The developer shall also make provisions for housing, schooling, hospital and other aspects related to rehabilitation. This can be done from a fund allocated for rehabilitation.

A committee shall be set up, consisting of representatives of community, local administrative authorities, NGO and project developer to assess the compensation amount, ensure timely payment, employment to displaced people, resettlement provisions and related aspects.

Q. 11 Suppose you are an officer in-charge of implementing a social service scheme to provide support to old and destitute women. An old and illiterate woman comes to you to avail the benefits of the scheme. However, she has no documents to show that she fulfills the eligibility criteria. But after meeting her and listening to her you feel that she certainly needs support. Your enquirers also show that she is really destitute and living in a pitiable condition. You are in a dilemma as to what to do. Putting her under the scheme without necessary documents would clearly be violation of rules. But denying her the support would be cruel and inhuman.

(a) Can you think of a rational way to resolve this dilemma?

Answer: Having been satisfied with the fact that visiting old and illiterate woman deserves benefit of the scheme, I would see if there is any discretionary power vested in competent authority to relax criteria of documents.

I would ask an official colleague to help the old woman in arranging documentation formalities, if possible.

Simultaneously I would bring the case to notice of my senior with positive recommendation to providing benefit of the scheme to her.

I would also take help of some NGO working for old and destitute women in the locality to support her in fulfilling requirement of documentation.

Considering this as a typical case, I would request competent authority to look into problems of documentation procedure and relax the same so deserving candidates may avail benefit of the scheme.

In this manner, to avoid violation of rules set up for the scheme, I will explore possibility to providing her necessary benefits.

(b) Give your reasons for it. (250 words) **20**

Answer: This effort to make sure that deserving woman avails benefit of the scheme is necessary to fulfill purpose of the policy made by government. As the scheme is for old and destitute women, on being satisfied with the fact that visiting women comes under the category, I should help her in completing document. In case she cannot provide necessary documents, I should use discretionary power or ask for relaxation from superior officers to provide benefit to the woman.

All schemes are launched with specific objective in mind. Each and every person who comes under the criteria must be given benefit to make the scheme successful. Only paper work does not bring result. Administration has to be sensitive to the fact that India has many illiterate people who are not aware of procedural requirements of government.

Ethical and considerate administration can bring change in the society and create welfare for people. Bureaucratic inertia in the name of procedure would fail governmental policies.

Q. 12 You are a young, aspiring and sincere employee in a Government office working as an assistant to the director of your department. Since you have joined recently, you need to learn and progress. Luckily your superior is very kind and ready to train you for your job. He is a very intelligent and well-informed person having knowledge of various departments. In short, you respect your boss and are looking forward to lean a lot from him.

Since you have good tuning with the boss, he started depending on you. One day due to ill health he invited you at his place for finishing some urgent work.

You reached his house and before you could ring the bell you heard shouting noises. You waited for a while. After entering the house the boss greeted you and explained the work. But you were constantly disturbed by the crying of a woman. At last, you inquired with the boss but his answer did not satisfy you.

Next day, you were compelled to inquire further in the office and found out that his behavior is very bad at home with his wife. He also beats up his wife. His wife is not well educated and is a simple woman in comparison to her husband. You see that though your boss is a nice person in the office, he is engaged in domestic violence at home.

In such a situation, you are left with the following options. Analyse each option with its consequences.

(a)Just ignore thinking about it because it is their personal matter.

(b)Report the case to the appropriate authority.

(c) Your own innovative approach towards the situation. (250 words) 20

Answer: In this situation, an educated senior government officer is involved in domestic violence against a woman, which is legally wrong.

(a) Just ignoring to think about the incident because it js their personal matter may keep my conscience hurting continuously. Inner voice would keep reminding me of the wrong path I am following.

This may prevent the course of uneasiness and probable problems that would arise in my new job in case I take some action against my boss.

But keeping quiet is legally, morally and ethically wrong. This will also result into persistent violation of a woman's rights and she will suffer the problem continually.

(b) Reposting the case to the appropriate authorities will result into harassment of my boss, but it will bring his sense into correct line. He would stop committing violence against his wife. The uneducated lady will be saved of daily torture and will live in peace.

However, it may go against me in office as my boss would start creating problems and may also report negatively about me. He may also put adverse remarks in my annual report.

But I can certainly inform higher authority in the company about the reasons for such reporting by my boss.

(c) My innovative approach would be to arrange a lady NGO representative to visit wife of my senior officer in private and explain her about legal rights available to her. The NGO can also offer to help in counseling my boss as a first measure.

The NGO may, in presence of his wife, explain to my boss, at his house, that beating and torturing a woman is a crime and he may end up facing legal consequences.

This may prevail over the bad temper of my boss and he may rectify his behavior appropriately. This can save him from embarrassment, disrespect and public disapproval. The NGO may also take legal action, if required. It will also not bring me in confrontation with my boss.

Q. 13 ABC Ltd. Is a large transnational company having diversified business activities with a huge shareholder base. The company is continuously expanding the generating employment. The company, in its expansion and diversification programme, decides to establish a new plant at Vikaspuri, an area which is underdeveloped. The new plant is designed to use energy efficient technology that will help the company to save production cost by 20%. The company's decision goes well with the Government policy of attracting investment to develop such underdeveloped regions. The government has also announced tax holiday for five years for the companies that invest in underdeveloped areas. However, the new plant may bring chaos for the inhabitants of Vikaspuri region, which is otherwise tranquil. The new plant may result in increased cost of living, aliens migrating to the region, disturbing the social and economic order. The company sensing the possible protest tried to educate the people of Vikaspuri region and public in general that how its Corporate Social Responsibility (CSR) policy would help overcome the likely difficulties of the residents of Vikaspuri region. In spite of this the protests begin and some of the residents decided to approach the judiciary as their plea before the Government did not yield any result.

(a) Identify the issues involved in the case

(b) What can be suggested to satisfy the company's goal and to address the residents' concerns? (300 words) 25

Answer: (a) In this case ABC Ltd is a large transnational company while residents are poor and less resourceful people. Trust deficit will be the first issue coming to the front.

People would think of the company as a profit making entity which would ditch development of community.

Increased cost of living would make life of villagers difficult due to less income and limited resources available to them.

Entry of big project would bring large number of migrants creating pressure on ecology and infrastructure capability of the region.

Tranquil place would be converted into a humming industrial area due to the project and ancillary facilities. It will result into a small township. The villagers who have lived a confined and less exposed life, preserving own culture and custom would not like it.

(b) The company's goal is to diversify and expand its business. Vikaspuri is identified because of tax benefits provided by Government and other advantages attached with the area.

The company has shown readiness to address concerns of local people through its Corporate Social Responsibilities policy.

Residents of the area are concerned about actual implementation of CSR to their advantage. They would also not like migration of big number of people in their village where resources are limited. Any migration would bring outsider influence on their culture and custom.

Environmental and ecological issues would be very serious and loss of land and possible displacement would disrupt order of life for villagers.

These issues can be concerned by creating Environmental Impact Assessment through independent authorities. Bringing reputed local leaders, NGOs and local authorities will help in convincing people of benefits that would result from implementation of the new project. Company can also ensure fair compensation and more employment opportunities for the people.

A monitoring committee and development fund can be established in advance to win trust of villagers.

Q. 14 Saraswati was a successful IT professional in USA. Moved by the patriotic sense of doing something for the country she returned to India. Together with some other like minded friends, she formed an NGO to build a school for a poor rural community.

The objective of the school was to provide the best quality modern education at a nominal cost. She soon discovered that she has to seek permission from a number of Government agencies. The rules and procedures were quite confusing and cumbersome. What frustrated her most was the delays, callous attitude of officials and constant demand for bribes. Her experience and the experience of many others like her has deterred people from taking up social service projects.

A measure of Government control over voluntary social work is necessary. But it should not be exercised in a coercive a corrupt manner. What measures can you suggest to ensure that due control is exercised but well meaning, honest NGO efforts are not thwarted? (300 words) 25

Answer: Procedures in India are discouragingly complex. It may result into disappointing honest social efforts by good intending individuals and NGOs.

There is requirement of regulation and control in every country. But over emphasise on procedure and corrupt system may actually prevent growth and development of nation and society.

Here, Saraswati and her friends intended to bring positive change by their efforts which involved dedication and sacrifice. But due to corruption and cumbersome procedures resulting into delays discouraged them. In this case, even if government has provided for temporary license, subject to renewal, Saraswati and her friends could have happily started their noble activity. This would have resulted into great social change. On being satisfied of meeting all standards prescribed in rules, permanent license could have been granted to Saraswati and her friends.

Government requires to ease out procedure and formalities in each sector, including governance. License and control system has to be relaxed to allow people to function well and contribute to the society. NGOs can be regulated by monitoring their activities but preventing them from starting activities is not fruitful.

Corruption in social sector activities should be removed and only officers with strong ethical record should be posted in such departments. Sense of responsibility should be cultivated in such officers who feel responsible towards requirement of society.

NGOs fund and their procedures can be monitored in manner which does not prevent them from working. Only those NGOs whose records are tainted should be subjected to strict control. NGOs performing functions as per government policies and promoting social development should be encouraged.

Simplification of paper work, easy entry to social entrepreneurs, reduction in red- tapism and fast clearances from various departments should be progressively achieved in social sector of India.

Of course, to discourage malpractices, fouling NGOs may be imposed with heavier fines, their license may be cancelled and people responsible may be punished severely.

(MAIN) **2017**

Civil Services Exam. General Studies

SOLVED PAPERS

PAPER–I

Time Allowed : Three Hours *Maximum Marks : 300*

Candidates should attempt ALL questions strictly in accordance with the instructions given under each question.

Q.1. How do you justify the view that the level of excellence of the Gupta numismatic art is not at all noticeable in later times? (150 words)

Important Points for Answer:

- *Gupta period achievements*
- *Coins of Gupta period*
- *Coins of later period*

Answer: Gupta age is considered to be the golden age of ancient Indian civilisation. India made remarkableprogress in the fields of science, technology, art and architecture. This also includes "Numismatic Art."

During the Gupta period, coins of various shape, size and materials were minted. A silver coin "RUPAK" was introduced. Similarly gold coins called "DINARA" was introduced that was inspired from Roman coins. Another coinmade up of gold, "SUVARNA" was introduced.

Gupta coins were aesthetically very strong and depicted images of Gods and Goddesses along with Gupta Kings playing musical instrument. The variety and creativity that can be seen in coins of this period was never replicated later.

In Sultanate period, coins wore simpler, less artistic and not made of gold. Similarly coins introduced by Tughlaq dynasty and later by Sher Shah were also not made of precious metals. Nor were such coins available in Mughal or British period.

Thus it can be seen that Gupta numismatic art is not noticeable in later times. (Total 165 words)

Q.2. Clarify how mid-eighteenth century India was beset with the spectre of a fragmented polity. (150 words)

Important Points for Answer:

- *Mid 18th Century India*
- *Political Situations*
- *Fragmentations*

Answer: Since Akbar reign, Indian was ruled by a strong central authority under Mughal monarchy. It was a period of economic growth and political stability. However, after the death of Aurangzeb in 1707, Mughal empire started crumbling during mid-18th century and ultimately lead to end of Mughal empire giving way to various regional powers.

By mid 18th century following powers emerged:

Sikh carved out their kingdom in North west by defeating Mughals and Rajputs kings.

Rajputhad accepted Mughal sovereignty but after Aurangzeb they started asserting their independence.

Marathas emerged as the most powerful political force in Deccan and Central India. They pursued own expansionist policy and formed Maratha Confederacy.

Mysore emerged as a powerful Deccan kingdom under Hyder Ali and Tipu and constantly engaged in wars with Marathas, Hyderabad and Britishers.

Hyderabad under Nizam disassociated himself from Mughal crown and engaged in bitter war with Marathas.

By mid 18th century, Indian polity was completely fragmented which also had European powers like British, French and Portuguese as players. (Total 168 words)

Q.3. Why did the 'Moderates' fail to carry conviction with the nation about their proclaimed ideology and political goals by the end of the nineteenth century? (150 words)

Important Points for Answer:
- *Moderates*
- *Their methods*
- *Weaknesses*
- *Split*

Answer: Moderates were primarily western educated lawyers, economists, or Civil servants. Their goals was to increase Indian participation in administration and push for certain constitutional reforms.They organised themselves politically formed Indian National Congress in 1885. The method adopted by them to achieve their goals werePetition, Persuasion, Criticism through press and Organising meeting, etc.

All these worked well for them till partition of Bengal in 1905. Partition led to "Swadeshi and Boycott" movement in which Indian masses openly challenged British authorities and Boycotted their goods.

This proved to be a watershed movement in Indian freedom struggle as:

Moderates failed to lead masses into a mass movement.

Masses related more to methods like boycott, picketing, hartals, etc

Moderate leaders, though intellectual, lacked charisma to lead masses.

Their outlook was more elitist which failed to appeal to masses.

Also, dispute arose between moderates and extremists.

This eventually led to "Surat split" and also beginning of "Revolutionary phase" of freedom struggle and end of moderate era. (Total 163 words)

Q.4. What problems are germane to the decolonization process in the Malay Peninsula? (150 words)

Important Points for Answer:
- *Malay colony*
- *Reasons for independence*
- *Decolonisation*
- *Partition*

Answer: The history of British involvement in Malaya goes back to 1786, when the East India Company established a trading post on Penang Island.

During the second World War 2, the Japanese overran Malaya and took Singapore in 1942. After the war, in 1948, a Federation of Malaya was created under British protection.

A Communist insurrectionlasted into the early 1950s which was put down by British and Commonwealth troops. British agreed to give independence to Malayan Peninsula to counter the Communist influence.

An election was held in 1955. The United Malay National Organisation (UMNO) won the election and Rahman became prime minister of the independent Federation of Malaya in 1957.

The federation was renamed Malaysia in 1963. It included all the Malay states, Singapore,and two areas in North Borneo – Sarawak and Sabah. Singapore opted out and went its own way in 1965.

Thus, decolonisation of Malaysia was mostly a peaceful process but involved communist and British rivalry. (Total 158 words)

Q 5. How does the Juno Mission of NASA help to understand the origin and evolution of Earth? (150 Words)

Important Points for Answer:
- *Juno*
- *Objectives*
- *Understanding Earth*

Answer: Juno was selected in 2005 as the next in "New Frontiers Mission". According to number of theories that describe evaluation and formation of earth, there is a common premise that most of the planets have common origin.

It is believed that most planets of our solar system, except "kuiper belt" bodies, are made up of similar material and are in different phase of evaluation.

The scientific objectives of Juno are :

Determine ratio of oxygen and hydrogen.

Analyzing Jupiter's core.

Map Jupiters gravitational field.

Map Jupiters magnetic field etc.

Juno will improve our understanding of the solar system's beginnings by revealing the origin and evolution of Jupiter.Once conclusive evidence is obtained about Jupiter by JUNO, it will enable scientist to extrapolate it for study about earths past and it evaluation.It will help to substantiate the theories with scientific data and uncover origin & evaluation of our planet. (Total 147 words)

Q.6. "Inspite of adverse environmental impact, coal mining is still inevitable for development". Discuss (150 words)

Important Points for Answer:
- *Coal Mining*
- *Environmental Impact*
- *Requirement*

Answer: Coal mining became an integral part of economic activities since industrial revolution. It served as principle source of power generation.

In todays time, it is an established fact that coal mining has an adverse impact on environment in following ways.

1. Impact on humans.
   (a) Cardio-vascular diseases
   (b) Cerebral diseases
   (c) Breathing/Lung cancer
   (d) Death during mining activities due to flooding of mines and accidental fires.
2. Impact on Environment
   (a) Release of SO_2 in air.
   (b) Acid Rain
   (c) Contamination of ground water and streams.
   (d) Release of G H G gases in Environment.

However, inspite of all these impacts, it is still inevitable because :-

1. Cost of power generation through coal is economical in terms of production and per unit consumption.
2. Technology : Emerging economies do not have advantage of latest R &D, therefore they rely on traditional means.
3. Ubiquitous in Nature : Coal is largely found in all continents if not all countries.

4. Legal frame work : Internationally there is no bar on coal production on import unlike the fissile material. (Total 162 words)

Q.7. Mention the advantages of the cultivation of pulses because of which the year 2016 was declared as the International Year of Pulses by United Nations. (150 words)

Important Points for Answer:
• *Pulse*
• *Advantage of cultivation*
• *International Year of Pulses*

Answer: Pulses is leguminous crop. It is known to have different varieties which are called with different names around the world like tur, chick pea, etc.

The advantages of cultivation of pulses are.

It is an affordable source of protein for poor.

Pulses help to reduce diabetes and heart problem.

Pulses can be sown in rain fed areas which can help poor farmers.

Pulses fix nitrogen, thus require less fertiliser.

It can help to reduce release of GHG that happens in paddy cultivation and animal husbandry.

Pulses, despite instant advantages, have traditionally been neglected as compared to wheat and paddy.

This is largely due to the fact that most research happened in agriculture section to address problem of food security. This research was largely confined to few crops which excluded pulses.

To push pulse cultivation, it is being promoted by UN by declaring the Year 2016 as International Year of Pulses. Even domestically government has appointed a committee under Arvind Subramanyam to promote its production. (Total 164 words)

Q.8. How does the cryosphere affect global climate? (150 words)

Important Points for Answer:
• *Cryosphere*
• *Effect on Climate*

Answer: Cryosphere refers to frozen water part of surface which include polar ice caps on both earth surface and water. For example, Artic, Antartic region.

Cryosphere affects global climate in following ways:

Oceanic influence: Cryosphere is a natural desalination of our oceans. It mixes fresh water by melting ice to maintain adequate salinity of water.

Climate significance: Cryosphere is a region of high pressure and low temperature. It therefore helps to maintain balance of planetary winds.

Precipitation: The winds that originate from poles lead to precipitation when they come in contact with moist winds of sub polar region. This helps in farming.

Upper air circulation: The westerlies and the Jet streams are influenced by Cryosphere on its polar region. This helps in maintaining equilibrium in global air circulation.

Vegetation and wildlife: Though not very diverse but it does support, lichens, masses and wild life that depends on it. Polar bears, penguins and Eskimos live on it. (Total 155 words)

Q.9. In the context of the diversity of India, can it be said that the regions form cultural units rather than the States? Give reasons with examples for your view point. (150 words)

Important Points for Answer:
- *Creation of States*
- *Cultural units*
- *Reasons*

Answer: States were created on linguistic basis after independence. Language was identified as uniting factor for people to live in one administrative unit, called State. Linguistic similarity generally results into cultural unity. Later on, smaller states were created for administrative and political reasons.

In the North-East, the entire region have almost common climate, common food habits, similar type of settlement and housing. They have similar dressing sense and have a matrilineal society. Thus they form one cultural unit, rather than seven states.

Similarly, in South India, dravidian culture is unity among Karnataka, Andhra, Tamil Nadu and Kerala. Their food, clothes and rituals are similar. In the western India, Maharashtra, Gujarat and Rajasthan have common food habit. UP, Bihar, MP and Haryana have similar culture, patriarchal society, similar temple and architecture style. In the Jammu and Kashmir, Uttarakhand and Himachal Pradesh people are united by their culture, though not by language.

Therefore, it can be said that in India, regions form cultural unity. (Total 162 words)

Q.10. What are the two major legal initiatives by the State since Independence addressing discrimination against Scheduled Tribes(STs)? (150 words)

Important Points for Answer:
- *Tribal Panchsheel*
- *Reservation for Tribals*
- *Community rights*
- *Ministry of Tribal Affairs*

Answer: Nehruadopted a policy which is reflected in document "TRIBAL PANCHSHEEL" which guided our tribal policy.

After Independence in 1947, Government of India passed various resolutions and a ministry was made to safeguard the rights of tribal people. Even in the Constitution special rights are guaranteed to the people belonging to the Scheduled Castes and Scheduled Tribes.

Government has made reservation for the tribes in educational institutes under Article 15 (4) and employment under Article 16(4) of the Constitution of India.

With regard to the protection of the tribal rights over community forests and other lands, following the central legislation introduced in 1996, the Gram Sabha (Village Assemblies) in the tribal areas has been entrusted to protect the community rights over community land and forest.

Ministry of Tribal Affairs was set up in 1999 after the bifurcation of Ministry of Social Justice and Empowerment with the objective of providing more focused approach on the integrated socio-economic development of the Scheduled Tribes (STs). (Total 164 words)

Q 11. The spirit of tolerance and love is not only an interesting feature of Indian society from very early times, but it is also playing an important part at the present. Elaborate. (250 words)

Important Points for Answer:
- *Ancient Values of India*
- *Mixture of religions, cultures, languages*
- *Constitutional and social traditions*

Answer: The spirit of love and tolerance has been a unique feature of Indian society. Our philosophy since ancient time has been based on "Vasundhaiv Kutumbakam" which means World Family and "Sarva Dharma Sambhava" which means equality of all religions.

India is a civilisation that has preached global peace, harmony and co-existence. And it is for this reason that four preeminent religions of the world,Hinduism, Buddhism, Jainism and Sikhism were born and coexisted in India. India even embraced Islam when it reached its soil.Most of the sects of Islam–Ahmediyas, Sunnis, Shias, etc are found here.

India gave refuge to Parsis and it is the place where anti-Semitism was never allowed to grow. India is a land where hundred of languages exist and some of which even have constitutional recognition under the eighth schedule.

When most westerners had predicted our disintegration right after independence but we grew stronger as a nation. The reason is this spirit of tolerance.

In the contemporary times when the world is plagued with linguistic struggles, religions persecution, terrorism and chauvinism, India could remain peaceful despite so much diversity and fault lines.

In term of culture, we celebrate festivals of all faith. In terms of religion, we have adopted secularism as its basic structure of constitution. Politically, Centre shares power with states and for some parts there are special provision in constitution like fifth and sixth schedules.

Thus when most countries that get independence from colonialism are crumbling and transforming, India is peaceful and democratic. (Total 252 words)

Q.12.Examine how the decline of traditional artisanal industry in colonial India crippled the rural economy. (250 words)

Important Points for Answer:
• *Artisan industry of India*
• *Decline in colonial era*
• *Effect on Rural economy*

Answer: When East India Company arrived in India, it had a running economy. It had a large share in world GDP.This economic prosperity largely depends on two pillars, agriculture and traditional artisanal industry.

British through their land revenue policies completely shattered our agricultural backbone which had its repercussions on artisan al industry as well.

After occupation of Bengal, Bihar, Orissa Madras and Bombay, the land revenue policies transformed our agriculture into raw material provider to British industries. They made farmers grow tobacco, indigo, opium which were of no use to Indian artisans.

Indian artisan industry includedworks of handicrafts, gems and jewellers, precious metals and stones. Demands for Indian Ivory goods, miniature artefacts were huge in European and Arab markets.

But as the colonisation happened, the new material required for this industry vanished from market. This was the burial death blow to Indian economy. Rather than net exporter,India become importer of foreign goods. It led to drain of our capital and resources and made Indian economy a debtor.

This was discontentment along with agrarian crisis that eventually led to revolt of 1857 and other subsequent movements. It led to destruction of artisanal rural industries, increase in unemployment and conversion of Indian economy into a cheap labour supplier economy.

The policy of British India continued to be of using colonies as supplier of raw material for the industries in Britain and sale the British goods to Indian market. Development or encouragement to artisan and cottage industry of India was not in their agenda. (Total 253 words)

Q 13 : Highlight the importance of the new objectives that got added to the vision of Indian Independence since the twenties of the last century. (250 words)

Important Points for Answer:
• *New Objectives*
• *Vision of Indian Independence*

Answer: Revolt of 1857 was our first struggle for independence. However, it had limited objections to free princely states from the company raj and assert feeling of non interference in religious affairs of Indian society.

After this, struggle for independence evolved in a more organised manner which incorporated new objectives from time to time. Establishment of Congress in 1885 was one landmark even in organised freedom struggle of India. Some of the new objectives added in the twenties of last century were:

Democracy and constitutions: Congress under moderates emphasized on demands for constitutional reforms. This led to various acts like Government of India Act 1909, 1919 and 1935. This process led to drafting of Constitution at the time of independence.

A Socialist Economy: Our freedom movement was inspired from socialist revolution that happened in USSR. Since that time our economic policy had been based on socialist principal of "self reliance".

Secularism: It was clear to our leaders that country like India cannot survive without religious freedom and equality. Secularism was incorporated in our constitution.

Welfare of depressed classes: Poona Pact was watershed moment which led to political acknowledgement of welfare of scheduled class in India.

Socio-ReligiousReforms: With the progress of freedom movement, Socio-religious reform become integrated part of vision for Indian Independence. Legislations like Hindu Marriage Act, Untouchability Laws, etc., were passed.

Welfare and Equality of women: Women played important role in our freedom struggle. Upliftment of women also became an objective of independence.

These new objectives emerged in 1920s of our freedom struggle. (Total 256 words)

Q.14. Account for variations in oceanic salinity and discuss its multi-dimensional effects. (250 words)

Important Points for Answer:

- *Oceanic Salinity*
- *Variation*
- *Effects*

Answer: Salinity is the amount of dissolved minerals like sodium chloride (NaCl),potassium chloride, calcium, etc., in water. Oceanic salinity is an extremely impartial geographic phenomena, but which has its variation in terms of its distribution,latitudinally and in depth.

Variations in term of latitude:

Highest salinity is formed near tropics due to high evaporation.

Equators account for law salinity due to torrential rainfall.

Poles are areas of long salinity due to constant mixing of fresh water due to melting of ice.

Inland seas water account for highest salinity as compared to coastal water body, examples areDead sea, Red sea.

Variation with depth:

Salinity at surface is high due to evaporation.

It decreases to depth of 1000 m.

It again increases till ocean bed as a salt settled at lower levels.

Effects of Oceanic salinity are:

Climatic/Rainfall: Very high salinity hinders proper rainfallon evaporation.

Suitability of Food: Fish,crabs, lobsters, etc., do not survive in highly saline water.

Human settlement: High salinity water body is unsuitable for human survival and it does not provide more of sustenance like sea food, etc.

Adverse effect on coral formation: Coral polyps do not grow is highly saline water.

Coastal Ecosystem: High salinity hampers growth of plants like weeds sea grass on sea floor as its ecosystem is acutely affected.

Thus, a proper equilibrium of salinity is essential for overall evolution of marine ecosystem. High salinity reduces utility of ocean for human and other living beings. (Total 244 words)

Q 15 Petroleum refineries are not necessarily located nearer to crude oil producing areas, particularly in many of the developing countries. Explain its implications. (250 words)

Important Points for Answer:
- *Refineries*
- *Locations*
- *Reasons*
- *Implications*

Answer: Refining of crude oil is the most essential process after the excavation of crude oil. It is the process of refining that separates crude oil into various products like natural gas, petrol, diesel, kerosene, was, bitumen, etc. Thus a refinery has a great industrial significance. It is only after refining that petroleum products are sent to the consumers.

Locational distribution of oil refineries across the world few observation can be made:

Refineries are largely located in developed countries.

Most refineries are located at sea coast.

Most refineries are located away from oil producing areas

This third locational trend is common to most of OPEC countries.

It has following implications:

Loss of revenue to oil producing regions since refinery leads to value additionthat generates more revenue.

Technological backwardness to oil producing region: refinery require, state of art technology whereas oil producing region has a relatively simple technology.

Ease of Export: if refineries are located near ports, it helps to export products to other countries and also reduce cost of transportation.e.g. Visakhapatnam, Jamnagar and Kochi in India.

More avenues for Research &Development: Since oil producing areas are generally arid deserts or oil rigs are in ocean, establishment of a lab for R &D is different matter.

Strategic significance: Establishing refineries away from oil wells also help to locate petroleum depots and sources in strategically safe and secure places. However, Jamnagar refinery has a strategic disadvantage for Indian as it is very close to the Pakistan Air force base located in Sindh province. (Total 253 words)

Q.16. In what way can floods be converted into a sustainable source of irrigation and all-weather inland navigation in India? (250 words)

Important Points for Answer:
- *Flood in India*
- *Prevention and Storage*
- *Irrigation & Navigation*

Answer: Flood is a hydrological phenomena in which water overflows from a water channel and submerges the areas adjoining it. India has been majorly affected by floods. In some of the regions it is an annual phenomena that causes large scale destruction of lives and properties.

There has been arguments about using flood to our advantages. This can be done by:

Flood water as a source of irrigation:

The problem with India's water utilisation is that a huge quantity of our surface water gets washed away un-utilised. This surface runoff along with additional water during floods can be utilised for irrigation.

If we successfully store or divert flood water to rain deficit areas, we can solve the problem of draught.

It will help us to increase our net sown area.

It will bring additional land under green cover.

Also it will reduce loss of life and property in flood prone areas. Thus save huge revenues.

All weather Inland Navigation:

Inland water navigation has been a neglected area in evolution of India's transportation sector. Inspite of many number of rivers, tributaries and distributaries, we have failed to exploit inland navigation. A big factor for it has been seasonal water fluctuation. If we can divert additional flood water into streams it will create an alternative mode of transport. But this will require interlinking of rivers, creating dams at strategic places, use of modern navigation technology.

However, there are challenges against this concept. Major among them include difficult terrain, huge investment, technology and displacement of local population. (Total 254 words)

Q.17. What characteristics can be assigned to monsoon climate that succeeds in feeding more than 50 percent of the world population residing in Monsoon Asia? (250 words)

Answer: The word monsoon has been derived from Arabic word "Mausim", it means seasonal reversal of winds.

Monsoon climate is endemic to South Asia, Malay peninsula, East China and few part of Japan, collectively called—Monsoon Asia.

Characteristic features are:

Erratic in nature:Therainfall received during monsoon is not uniform. Sometimes it is below average and other time it may cause floods.

Seasonal fluctuation: It has no precise fixed time of occurrence. Sometimes it may break early, other time it gets delayed.

Spatial variation: Amount ofrainfall received is not uniform, it differs from region to region. Ex: N-E region in India get heavy rainfall, but Rajasthan gets very low rainfall.

Temporal Variation: There is no uniform time when entire region gets rainfall. It usually starts from coasts and inland areas are last to receive rains.

Floods and draughts: When rainfall in monsoon exceeds the average it causes flooding while when it is below average it leads to draughts.

Monsoon Climate Characteristicsare:

In months usually of July to September this region receives heavy rainfall. Precipitation is confined to these months only and an average is 250-300 cm of rainfall.

The coastal regions have moderate climate whereas extremes of both heat and cold are observed in Inland areas in non-monsoon months. Average temperature in inland India is: 25-30°C in summers and 10-20°C in winters.

Associated seasonal phenomenon like dust storms, thunder storms and other local phenomena are part of monsoon climate.

These factors playa significant role in cultivation and have local significance and support around half of the world population. (Total 268 words)

Q.18. The women's questions arose in modern India as a part of the 19th century social reform movement. What are the major issues and debates concerning women in that period?

(250 words)

Important Points for Answer:
• *19th Century social reforms*
• *Women in Modern India*
• *Issues and debates*

Answer: The 19thcentury social reform movement can be said to be renaissance in evolution of our society.

These movements happened in all parts of the country and at a different scale. The most prominent aspects of these movements were the question of "Emancipation of Women".

The major issues and debates concerning it were:

Education for girls: Education was denied to women in our society. Reformers like Jyotibha Phule and Ishwarchandra Vidya Sagar were pioneers in this field. They opened many girls schools and initiated movements for it.

Widow Remarriage: A prestige ofwomenin Indian society was associated to her husband. After death of husband, women were looked down in society. Rajaram Mohan Roy worked hard for window remarriage acceptance in society.

Banning of Sati and Female Infanticide: These were most regressive practices of our society. Reformers like Rajaram Mohan Roy and Kashab Chandra Sain pressurised government to ban *Sati* by law. Finally William Bantik passed prohibition of Sati law.

Corporeal Rights to girls in property: As usual practice, only male heirs were recognised as successor of property. However, reformers fought hard for equal rights of girls to inherit property.

Admission of Muslim girls in schools and right to inheritance: Sir Syed Ahmed played important role for reforms amongst Muslims. He fought against Purdah and encouraged girls to study.

These reforms were not confined to any part of society or region. It is because of these movements that finally led to participation of woman in freedom struggle and eventual participation of women in economy and governance of country after independence. (Total 260 words)

Q.19. Distinguish between religiousness/religiosity and communalism giving one example of how the former has got transformed into the latter in independent India. (250 words)

Important Points for Answer:
- *Religiousness*
- *Communalism*
- *Examples*
- *Transformation in India*

Answer: Religiousness is a phenomena of devotion towards ones religion, deity or God. It is a matter of personal faith and belief without any interference in faith of others. Religiousness does not includes any competition, or a sense of superiority in comparison to other faiths.

Communalism, on the other hand, is a feeling that interests of a community having common faith are congruent. Whereas, the interest of other community which practice different faith are always at logger heads. This leads to a sense of competition, hostility and superiority to be asserted on other faith.

Unfortunately, in India, this feeling of religiousness is gradually transforming into communalism. Each passing decade after independence had its own events showing ugly face of communalism. One most prominent example of this is displacement of Kashmiri Pandits from Kashmir Valley. For hundreds of years Pandits and Muslims had coexisted in valley. They shared common neighbourhood and cultural heritage. Even the surname of number of families are common, indicating a common ancestry.

However, with emergence of militancy and radicalisation after 1990's this religiousness transformed into communalism. The radical elements started looking at Pandits as enemies who were responsible for all problems.

A systematic program started in valley which also included destructions of religious shrines and cultural cleansing. As a result, worse form of human displacement happened in independent India.

This transformation is extremely harmful for our country and its future. The so called fringe elements of all religion must be dealt with strongly by the government to preserve our country and its unity in diversity. (Total 258 words)

Q.20. "The growth of cities as I.T. hubs has opened up new avenues of employment, but has also created new problems". Substantiate this statement with examples (250 words)

Important Points for Answer:

- *IT Hubs*
- *Employment avenues*
- *Problems*
- *Examples*

Answer: IT industry in India has completely transformed its economy and its urban landscape. IT industry had led to emergence of big cities as IT hubs which attract technocrats from all parts of the country. To support this industry and resultant urbanisation other types of employment such as cab service, restaurants, blue collar labour, etc., have come up which has further added to urbanisation.

This growth has led to numerous problems as well. Some of thee are:

As the blue collar working class cannot afford proper housing and cost of living in big cities, they resort to illegal colonies.

Since the growth of IT cities has been rapid as compared to urban planning, the sewage is dumped in rivers without treatment.

The municipal corporations in cities are understaffed, lack expertise and lack funds to recycle this waste.

Thesecentres of prosperities lead youth to various addictions and other organised crimes.

Every big city has a red light district in which girls are brought through trafficking.

Most of our IT cities like Bengaluru, Hyderabad, do not have adequate "Mass Rapid Transit System" like metros, monorail, etc.

The vehicles, generators discharge affluent in air which pollute the environment.

Most cities have poor doctor to patient ratio and medical treatment is expensive.

Police lack technology and expertise to check crime in IT cities, like Cyber crimes, Bitcoins etc.

IT cities require planning to meet demands.

To curb these problems, government come up with scheme like RURBAN, JNNURM, Metro, Smart City, etc., for development.

However, the pace at which these schemes needs to be increased. (Total 260 words)

SOLVED PAPERS

PAPER–II

Q.1. "The local self government system in India has not proved to be effective instrument of governance". Critically examine the statement and give your views to improve the situation.

(150 words)

Important Points for Answer:
- *Constitutional Provisions*
- *Objectives*
- *Performance*
- *Limitations*
- *Suggestions*

Answer: Local Self Government started at village and district level after 73rd and 74th Constitutional Amendments in 1993. It comprises of Gram Panchayats, Mandal or Taluka Panchayats and Zilla Panchayats in Panchayati Raj Institution. At Urban level there are Nagar Panchayats, Municipal Councils and Municipal Corporations.

The main aim of local government was to involve grassroots level population in decision making. Local bodies were also to serve the purpose of participation of people and training in politics.

These institutions have worked well in many parts of India where local people have actively participated and contributed in decision making and governance.

However, due to various reasons, these institutions of governance have not proved to be effective. Illiteracy, use of money and muscle power, caste dominance, etc are evident problems. On reserved seats, mostly rubber-stamps are working.

Therefore, better education, training, awareness, actual devolution of power, participation of larger section of society, adherence to constitutional provisions, stringent action against violators are suggested for better functioning of local governance. (Total 166 words)

Q.2. Critically examine the Supreme Court's judgement on ⊠National Judicial Appointments Commission Act, 2014' with reference to appointment of judges of higher judiciary in India.

(150 words)

Important Points for Answer:
- *Appointment of Judges*
- *NJAC*
- *Amendent*
- *Judgement*
- *Result*

Answer: Judges of the Supreme Court and High Courts are appointed by the President under Articles 124(2) and 217 of the Constitution.

After receiving Presidential assent on Dec. 31, 2014, the collegium system of appointing judges to the SC and high courts was replaced by a new body called the National Judicial Appointments Commission.

The Supreme Court Bench in a majority of 4:1 rejected the 'National Judicial Appointments Commission Act, 2014' and and the 99th Constitutional Amendment as "unconstitutional and void." It held that the collegium system, as it existed before the NJAC, would again become "operative."

With this verdict, the Collegium system as it existed before the NJAC Act was passed, will become operative again. The collegium system is the system of appointment and transfer of judges that has evolved through judgments of the Supreme Court, and not by an Act of Parliament or by a provision of the Constitution. (Total 152 words)

Q.3. 'Simultaneous election to the Lok Sabha and the State Assemblies will limit the amount of time and money spent in electioneering but it will reduce the government's accountability to the people' Discuss. (150 words)

Important Points for Answer:
- *Electorate in India*
- *Simultaneous elections*
- *Advantages*
- *Disadvantage*
- *Possibile Experiment*

Answer: India has a direct electoral system for Lok Sabha and State Assemblies, held every five years. With 29 States, two union territories with Legislative Assemblies and Lok Sabha elections, the election commission is overburdened and the expenses of such elections are huge.

Holding of simultaneous elections for Lok Sabha and State Assemblies can be helpful in reducing frequency of elections and expenditure involved in them. It will also systematise the process as it is required to be held only once every five years. Stability of government will allow them to implement their policies.

But there are fears that people will have no chance to judge a government and its performance at state and national level for a period of five years. Having separate elections gives political message to parties. It also keeps the parties on toe to perform for retaining or gaining states and centre government.

Having both pros and cons of such simultaneous election, an experiment in this direction, with a limited number of state legislative assemblies. (Total 168 words)

Q.4. How do pressure groups influence Indian political process? Do you agree with this view that informal pressure groups have emerged as powerful than formal pressure groups in recent years? (150 words)

Important Points for Answer:
- *Pressure Groups*
- *Influence on Politics*
- *Formal Pressure Groups*
- *Informal Pressure Groups*

Pressure Groups are groups of people whose interest coincide. They try to influence the decision making and policy formation of government by various political methods.

Their influence depends on the size and status of people as their membership or affiliation. It may also depend on the method of expression. Some groups use strike or dharna as their method while others use judiciary and PIL. Some groups may directly try to influence political parties.

Formal pressure groups are those who are organized, may be in areas of trade and commerce like FICCI, CII, etc. or student unions like ABVP, NSUI, etc.

Informal pressure groups come into existence on certain issues and create pressure on the government to change or formulate policy. Like candle march organised in support of the rape victim of Delhi or gathering in support of Anna Hazare.

Of late, it has been noticed that informal groups have exerted pressure on governments.

(Total 153 words)

Q.5. Discuss the role of Public Accounts Committee in establishing accountability of the government to the people. (150 words)

Important Points for Answer:
- *PAC*
- *Role of PAC*
- *Achievements*

Answer: The Public Accounts Committee (PAC) is a Parliamentary Committee, sometimes referred to as a post-mortem committee.

The PAC's role is to examine the audited consolidated financial statements of the country, known as the Public Accounts, as well as those of ministries, departments and regions. The PAC's examination seeks to ascertain to what extent expenditure has been incurred in the way Parliament intended.

The committee has kept the executive accountable to Parliament, thereby lending an additional dimension to the nation's fiscal policies and programmes.

The committee has been able to bring to light certain cases where parliamentary authority on the administration of tax laws had been diluted by the executive fiat, and other cases of the government not carrying out the intentions of Parliament as expressed in laws. The PAC's scrutiny of the national accounts along with the reports of the Auditor General is an integral part of public accountability.

(Total 150 words)

Q.6. 'To ensure effective implementation of policies addressing water, sanitation and hygiene needs, the identification of beneficiary segments is to be synchronized with the anticipated outcomes'. Examine the statement in the context of the WASH scheme. (150 words)

> **Important Points for Answer:**
> - *WASH Scheme*
> - *Policy formation*
> - *Anticipated outcome*

Answer: WASH is the collective term for Water, Sanitation and Hygiene. Due to their interdependent nature, these three core issues are grouped together to represent a growing sector. For example, without toilets, water sources become contaminated; without clean water, basic hygiene practices are not possible. Various schemes are being implemented in WASH, including that by UNICEF.

While forming policy in WASH, it is essential that the targeted beneficiary has to be considered before deciding modalities. Anticipated outcomes can be achieved only when the delivery and implementation is in synchronisation with the beneficiary status. For example, for poor and uneducated rural people, facilities of toilet and related schemes can be formed and implemented but the same may not be required for urban rich educated class. In such areas, government may have to focus on garbage collection, pure drinking water, sewage treatment plants, etc. Requirement of different classes of people with regard to Water, Sanitation and Hygiene are different. (Total 156 words)

Q.7. Does the Rights of Persons with Disabilities Act, 2016 ensure effective mechanism for empowerment and inclusion of the intended beneficiaries in the society? Discuss (150 words)

> **Important Points for Answer:**
> - *The Bill 2016*
> - *Main provisions*
> - *Inclusion*
> - *Implementation*
> - *Assessment*

Answer: The Rights of Persons with Disabilities Bill - 2016 has replaced the existing PwD Act, 1995, which was enacted 21 years back. Disability has been defined based on an evolving and dynamic concept. The types of disabilities have been increased from existing 7 to 21 and the Central Government will have the power to add more types of disabilities.

Speech and Language Disability and Specific Learning Disability have been added for the first time. Acid Attack Victims have been included. Dwarfism, muscular dystrophy has been indicated as separate class of specified disability. This makes the act more inclusive and will cover intended beneficiaries.

Similarly, for better implementation mechanism, responsibility has been cast upon the appropriate governments to take effective measures to ensure that the persons with disabilities enjoy their rights equally with others. Special Courts will be designated in each district to handle cases concerning violation of rights of PwDs.

The Bill intends to be inclusive and ensure better implementation. (Total 159 words)

Q.8. Hunger and Poverty are the biggest challenges for good governance in India still today. Evaluate how far successive governments have progressed in dealing with these humongous problems. Suggest measures for improvement. (150 words)

Important Points for Answer:
- *Hunger & Poverty*
- *Programmes*
- *Results*
- *Suggestions*

Answer: Poverty and Hunger have remained the biggest challenges for India. Due to large population and lack of economic resources, government has not been able to completely eradicate them.

Main poverty elevation programmes include Jawahar Gram Samridhi Yojana (JGSY), National Family Benefit Scheme (NFBS), National Maternity Benefit Scheme, Annapurna, Integrated Rural Development Program(IRDP), Pradhan Mantri Gramin Awaas Yojana and Mahatma Gandhi National Rural Employment Guarantee Act (MGNREGA). Due to these programmes, poverty rate has been reduced from 65% in. 1950s to 12% in 2015.

It is suggested that implementation of the programmes should be increasingly based on approaches and methods which involve the poor themselves in the process of poverty eradication and economic growth. This is possible through a process of social mobilisation, encouraging participatory approaches and institutions and empowerment of the poor. In this the PRIs, the voluntary organisations and community based Self-Help Groups will be more closely involved. (Total 151 words)

Q.9. 'China is using its economic relations and positive trade surplus as tools to develop potential military power status in Asia', In the light of this statement, discuss its impact on India as her neighbor. (150 words)

Important Points for Answer:
- *China's economic status*
- *Use in foreign policy*
- *China's Military Power*
- *India's Concern*

Answer: China has emerged as world's largest manufacturing hub and has gained status of largest or second largest trading partner status with most of the countries in the world. This has also resulted into huge trade surplus with most of the countries.

China has used the economic gain to develop its military power status as well. As a very large territory, having big army, air force and large naval forces, now China is a dominant player in the world. It has modern defence equipments and technology which it sometimes uses as a tool of diplomacy in its relations with others.

During its rise as a potential global super power, China has used trade and commerce as a tool of foreign policy to have influence on partner countries. It has also implemented String of Pearls strategy in maritime defence.

India believes in independent foreign policy and not a reactionary one but China's interference in immediate neighbourhood may certainly cause discomfort to India. (Total 160 words)

Q.10. What are the main functions of the United Nations Economic and Social Council (ECOSOC)? Explain different functional commissions attached to it. (150 words)

Important Points for Answer:
- *ECOSOC*
- *Functions of ECOSOC*
- *Commissions*

Answer: The UN Charter established Economic and Social Council (ECOSOC) in 1945 as one of the six main organs of the United Nations. Its main function include:

- Promoting sustainable development
- Managing the transition from MDGs to SDGs
- Advandcing policy integration
- Development cooperation forum
- Financing for sustainable development
- Coordinating humanitarian action
- Guiding operational activities for development
- Providing coordination and oversight
- Building partnerships
- Engaging youth
- Raising awayness on emerging issues
- Advising on Haiti's long term development
- Working with civil society

ECOSOC Functional Commissions:

- Statistical Commission
- Commission on Population and Development
- Commission for Social Development
- Commission on the Status of Women
- Commission on Narcotic Drugs
- Commission on Crime Prevention and Criminal Justice
- Commission on Science and Technology for Development
- United Nations Forum on Forests

ECOSOC Regional Commissions:

- Economic Commission for Africa (ECA)
- Economic and Social Commission for Asia and the Pacific (ESCAP)
- Economic Commission for Europe (ECE)
- Economic Commission for Latin America and the Caribbean (ECLAC)
- Economic and Social Commission for Western Asia (ESCWA) (Total 160 words)

Q.11. Explain the salient features of the constitution(One Hundred and First Amendment) Act, 2016. Do you think it is efficacious enough 'to remove cascading effect of taxes and provide for common national market for goods and services'? (250 words)

Important Points for Answer:

- *101 Amendment Act, 2016*
- *GST - Purpose*
- *Provisions*
- *Proposed Benefits*

Answer: The Constitution (One Hundred and First Amendment) Act, 2016, introduced a national Goods and Service Tax (GST) in India from 1st April, 2017. The amendment Act contains 20 amendments.

The present amendments would subsume a number of indirect taxes presently being levied by Central and State Governments into GST. It will do away the cascading of taxes and provide a common national market for Goods and Services.

The GST is a Value added Tax (VAT) and is proposed to be a comprehensive indirect tax levied on manufacture, sale and consumption of goods as well as services at the national level which will replace all indirect taxes levied on goods and services by a single tax on the supply, right from the manufacturer to the consumer.

The aim to bring about these amendments in the Constitution is to confer simultaneous power on Parliament and State legislatures to make laws for levying GST simultaneously on every transaction of supply and Goods and Services.

GST will make India a common market with common tax rates & procedures and remove economic barriers. While framing GST Acts and Rules, enhanced 'Ease of doing business' for the taxpayers was a key consideration therefore GST is made largely technology driven and will reduce the human interface to a great extent. Resultantly, GST is expected to improve ease of doing business in India.

The biggest tax reform since independence - GST—will pave the way for realization of the goal of One Nation - One Tax—One Market. GST will benefit all the stakeholders namely industry, government and consumer. (Total 258 words)

Q.12. Examine the scope of Fundamental Rights in the light of the latest judgement of the Supreme Court on Right to Privacy. (250 words)

Important Points for Answer:
- *Judgement of the SC*
- *Privacy as FR*
- *Relations with FR*
- *Aspects of Privacy*

Answer: A nine-judge bench of the Supreme Court ruled that Indians enjoy a fundamental right to privacy. It was held that right to privacy is intrinsic to life and liberty and thus comes under Article 21 of the Indian constitution.

The bench, led by Chief Justice J.S. Khehar, pronounced an unanimous judgement even if the judges had slightly different arguments as to how privacy is intrinsic to right to life and liberty. Elements of privacy arise in varying contexts from the other facets of freedom and dignity recognised and guaranteed in Fundamental Rights.

As per the Supreme Court, Privacy is the constitutional core of human dignity. Privacy protects heterogeneity and recognises the plurality and diversity of our culture. Privacy includes at its core the preservation of personal intimacies, the sanctity of family life, marriage, procreation, the home and sexual orientation.

Privacy has both a normative and descriptive function. At a normative level privacy sub-serves those eternal values upon which the guarantees of life, liberty and freedom are founded. At a descriptive level, privacy postulates a bundle of entitlements and interests which lie at the foundation of ordered liberty.

Privacy also connotes a right to be left alone. Privacy safeguards individual autonomy and recognises the ability of the individual to control vital aspects of his or her life. Personal choices governing a way of life are intrinsic to privacy.

The Supreme Court has overruled verdicts given in the M.P. Sharma case in 1958 and the Kharak Singh case in 1961, both of which said that the right to privacy is not protected under the Indian constitution. (Total 274 words)

Q.13. The Indian Constitution has provisions for holding joint session of the two houses of the Parliament. Enumerate the occasions when this would normally happen and also the occasions when it cannot, with reasons thereof. (250 words)

Important Points for Answer:
- *Joint Session*
- *Provisions*
- *Occasions*
- *When cannot be held*

Answer: Article 108 of Constitution makes provision for a Joint session of Parliament which can be summoned in certain situations.

The President of India has power to summon joint sitting of both the houses of parliament in three conditions. If the bill has been passed by one House and transmitted to the other House then:

1. the other House rejects the Bill; or

2. the Houses have finally disagreed as to the amendments to be made in the Bill; or

3. more than six months elapse from the date of the reception of the Bill by the other House without the Bill being passed by it.

In these three conditions, the President may summon both the Houses to meet in a joint sitting.

However, joint sitting cannot be summoned if the Bill has elapsed by reason of a dissolution of the House of the People.

Not all bills can be refereed to a joint sitting of Parliament. There are two exception: Money Bill and Constitutional Amendment Bill.

On money bill, Rajya Sabha's approval is not required. Rajya Sabha has recommending power only.

On Money Bill, Rajya Sabha can make recommendations which are not binding. If Rajya Sabha fails to pass a money bill within 14 days, it is deemed to have been passed by both the Houses.

As per Article 368 of Indian constitution, there is no provision to summon joint session of parliament for amendment of the constitution.

Joint sessions of Indian parliament have been called on three occasions: Dowry Prohibition Act, 1960, Banking Service Commission Act, 1977 and POTA, 2002. (Total 261 words)

Q.14. To enhance the quality of democracy in India the Election Commission of India has proposed electoral reforms in 2016. What are the suggested reforms and how far are they significant to make democracy successful? (250 words)

Important Points for Answer:
- *Reforms suggested by EC*
- *Main Recommendations*
- *Effects*

Answer: The Election Commission (EC) is working towards a comprehensive review of the election lawsto cleanse the political funding and decriminalize politics. The recommendations were made in a document, "Proposed Electoral Reforms", published on the EC's website. Total 47 proposals of Electoral reforms sent by the EC from time to time for law making have been examined by the Law Commission and many proposals have been endorsed for legislation.

The EC's proposals could broadly be divided into three categories:

1. Reforms to cleanse the electoral system (debarring criminally-tainted politicians from contesting, checking money power, empowering the EC to deregister defunct and dubious parties);

2. Reforms to make the EC stronger and more independent (appointment of election commissioners through a collegium, their elevation to CEC on the criterion of seniority and their protection from removal only through impeachment as available to the CEC and;

3. Reforms to make the electoral system more efficient (like the introduction of totaliser machines to prevent disclosure of polling patterns in a polling booth).

As per the EC recommendation, there should be well defined electoral laws rather than using residuary powers under Art 324 frequently. The EC can be give power to countermand elections in cases of money power abuse.

These reforms will go a long way to make the elections free and fair, reduce criminalisation of politics and use of money and muscle powers to win elections. Democracy can be healthy only if it is born out of fair elections. (Total 246 words)

Q.15. Is the National Commission for Women able to strategise and tackle the problems that women face at both public and private spheres? Give reasons in support of your answer. (250 words)

Important Points for Answer:
- *NCW*
- *Problems of women*
- *NCW's role*
- *Limitations of NCW*

Answer: The National Commission for Women was set up as a statutory body in January 1992. It reviews the Constitutional and Legal safeguards for women, recommends remedial legislative measures, facilitates redressal of grievances and advises the Government on all policy matters affecting women.

It has been giving recommendations to the government in the areas of its mandate for improving situation of women in India. Problems concerned with women in public and private spheres are studied by the NCW and measures to tackle them are suggested.

Women still face various issues like sexual harassment at workplace, problem of disparity with male workers, lower status in family and public life, partiality in organisations, lack of understanding of women specific problems by society, etc. Still India faces problem of human trafficking, child marriage, domestic violence and prenatal diagnosis for preference to male child.

The NCW has, from time to time, suggested strategies and measures to deal with such issues. It gives advise to various ministries on devising guidelines to deal with women specific problems. Welfare of pregnant women and lactating mothers are also important for NCW. NCW can be helpful in dealing with women's emotional and psychological issues as well.

Many aspects can be dealt with strongly only by strict implementation of law. In areas where legal and government machineries have to function, NCW is not able to resolve them. Though given power to summon and enforce attendance of any person from any part of India and examine him on oath, NCW has its own limitations. (Total 252 words)

Q.16. 'The emergence of Self Help Groups(SHGs) in contemporary times points to the slow but steady withdrawal of the state from developmental activities'. Examine the role of the

SHGs in developmental activities and the measures taken by the Government of India to promote the SHGs. (250 words)

Important Points for Answer:
- *SHGs*
- *Their role*
- *Promotion by Government*
- *Limitations of SHGs*

Answer: Self Help Groups (SHGs) are small group of like minded people whose interest coincide. They come together for development through promotion of self interest for which they liaise with government.

Today, number of SHGs has increased manyfold. It is mainly due to the encouragement given by government. They try to function as mediatory between government bodies and beneficiary of government schemes. Their role has increased due to the approach of Public Private Partnership adopted by government. In this approach, government has left many services to private sector. While many facilities are stopped from government side, some are given but in participatory method. Various schemes require the beneficiary to function on their own while the government only supports financially and by giving training.

The Self-Help Group (SHG)-Bank Linkage Programme has emerged as the major micro-finance programme in the country. They are made intermediary agency to promote welfare programmes. SHGs are used for various other programmes of government and therefore NABARD is given target to promote micro financing through SHGs. Benefits of SHGs are evident as households with membership of SHGs are likely to get loans and credit facilities easier. Training as well as entrepreneurship gets of SHGs get formal support from government.

However, it is required that Self-help groups should be regularly monitored, and their promoters must reinforce structures that ensure the members have the requisite help for at least the first five years.Resources should go toward periodic capacity-building of all members, to make the group the collective, democratic effort of all members instead of a few who are better informed. (Total 266 words)

Q.17. 'Poverty Alleviation Programmes in India remain mere show pieces until and unless they are backed by political will'. Discuss with reference to the performance of the major poverty alleviation programmes in India. (250 words)

Important Points for Answer:
- *Poverty alleviation*
- *Various programmes*
- *Hurdles*
- *Solution - Political will*

Answer: Poverty and Hunger have remained the biggest challenges for India. Due to large population and lack of economic resources, government has not been able to completely eradicate them. A number of programmes have been initiated to tackle the problem of poverty. They are sometimes election and political agenda without intention to implement them. Lack of supporting infrastructure, corruption and bureaucratic hurdles make their performance drastic failure. Unless accompanied by political all to strictly implement them, they are not pursued to desired end.

The five year plans immediately after independence tried to focus on poverty alleviation through sectoral programmes.Integrated Rural Development Programme, a poverty alleviation programme, was initiated on October 2, 1980. The programme has been designed in a manner that the benefits flow to the poorest as the first priority. Other main poverty elevation programmes include Jawahar Gram Samridhi Yojana (JGSY), National Old Age Pension Scheme (NOAPS), National Family Benefit Scheme (NFBS), National Maternity Benefit Scheme, Annapurna, Integrated Rural Development Program(IRDP), Pradhan Mantri Gramin Awaas Yojana and Mahatma Gandhi National Rural Employment Guarantee Act (MGNREGA). Due to these programmes, poverty rate has been reduced from 65% in. 1950s to 12% in 2015.

It is suggested that implementation of the programmes should be increasingly based on approaches and methods which involve the poor themselves in the process of poverty eradication and economic growth. This is possible through a process of social mobilisation, encouraging participatory approaches and institutions and empowerment of the poor. In this the PRIs, the voluntary organisations and community based Self-Help Groups will be more closely involved. (Total 261 words)

Q.18. Initially Civil Services in India were designed to achieve the goals of neutrality and effectiveness, which seems to be lacking in the present context. Do you agree with the view that drastic reforms are required in Civil Services. Comment (250 words)

Important Points for Answer:
- *Civil Service*
- *Quality*
- *Deterioration*
- *Reforms*

Answer: Civil Services in India are inherited from the British administration, which was considered still frame of India due to its efficient, ethical, unbiased and neutral performance of the functions assigned to it.

After independence, we decided to continue with civil service. It is a system where talented youth join from various parts and backgrounds of India for contributing to the development of nation.

However, various factors including political pressure, regionalism, corruption, use of money and muscle powers have affected the civil services, resulting into a decaying system of bureaucracy where power, money and position have taken over service, dedication and efficiency. Integrity, objectivity and non-partisanship are some of the general qualities which are necessary to be present in a civil servant and it should be ensured that all civil servants adhere to them.

Civil service requires drastic reforms in terms of accountability of officers, non-interference by political class, fixed tenure for posting, check on undue favours or biases. There should be time to time evaluation of performance of civil servants which should be neutral. Sidelining of honest civil servants is deterrent and affects morale of an officer, which should be stopped. Performance based evaluation system can also help in motivating honest and hardworking officers. New skills and use of modern technology should be encouraged among them. Officers should be encouraged to have leaves from time to time as they are overburdened with work which results into poor work-life balance. Mid career training and skill upgradation programmes will also be useful. (Total 253 words)

Q.19. The question of India's Energy Security constitutes the most important part of India's economic progress. Analyze India's energy policy cooperation with West Asian Countries. (250 words)

Important Points for Answer:

- *Energy Security*
- *Energy Policy*
- *West Asian Countries*
- *Initiatives*

Answer: India's energy Security is under pressure from dependence on imported oil, regulatory uncertainty and unclear natural gas pricing policies. Coal, oil and natural gas are the most important sources of primary energy in India. Inadequate domestic supplies of these hydrocarbons are forcing the country to increase its import bill.

The supply of natural gas as well, which was expected to alleviate our energy security from the new domestic fields, remains well below projections. Of late, driven by accelerated capacity addition in power generation and decline in domestic coal production, India's imports of coal have risen. For industrial growth, India needs assured supply of energy.

Countries of West Asia includes Iran, Iraq, Saudi Arabia, UAE, Oman, Kuwait, Qatar, Syria, Turkey, etc. who are important for India's energy security as more than 70% of India's energy needs, including oil and gas, is met by West Asia.

In this direction, India has entered into long term gas purchase contract with Qatar which ensures supply of gas. India is also considering a gas pipeline from Iran to reduce transportation cost of gas. Import of oil is also based on friendly relations with West Asian countries. To reduce dependence on a region or country, India has also adopted diversification policy for its oil and gas import.

Towards achieving the energy security, India has to also develop a source of renewable energy. In this direction, Prime Minister announced launching of International Solar Alliance which will enhance solar energy towards clean fuel initiative in the world. West Asian countries, with ample sunlight, are important partners in this initiative. (Total 261 words)

Q.20. Indian Diaspora has an important role to play in South-East Asian countries' economy and society. Appraise the role of Indian Diaspora in South- East Asia in this context (250 words)

Important Points for Answer:
- *Indians in South East Asia*
- *Interaction*
- *Population*
- *Role of Indians*

Answer: Historically South East Asia has been influenced by India in the realms of art, culture, architecture, court etiquettes, religion and many other things. The region was intertwined with Indian culture. Indian civilisation was naturally extended to the territories of present day South East Asia.

Indian migration started towards South East Asia in ancient time. Old Sanskrit inscriptions in many of these countries and ancient temples are witness of Indian presence there. During the colonial period, Britishers took Indian labours for working in these countries.

Indian diaspora in south east asian countries vary. Indians roughly constitute 8% in Malaysia, 9% in Singapore and 4% in Myanmar. Brunei has 2.3% Indians while in Cambodia, Indonesia, Laos, Philippines and Vietnam number of Indians is negligible.

Indian professionals hold senior positions in local and multinational companies, in these countries, in the fields of IT, education, technology, etc. Indians are well represented in judiciary, civil service and armed forces of Singapore. In Indonesia, traditionally the Sikhs, Sindhis and Tamils are engaged in various small businesses. Thailand also has sizeable Indian community.

Given the status of India and Indians in the world, especially after 1991 economic reforms and IT boom, Indians have gained important position in industry, business, society and politics of various countries. Rich Indians influence business and economy of these countries. Socially, Indian traditions have left deep imprint on the culture of these south east asian countries.

At the same time, India has also benefited economically, socially and culturally from contacts with south east Asia. (Total 251 words)

SOLVED PAPERS

PAPER–III

Q.1. Among several factors for India's potential growth, savings rate is the most effective one. Do you agree? What are the other factors available for growth potential? (Answer in 150 words)

Important Points for Answer:
- *Importance of Saving Rate*
- *Other factors for growth*
- *Factors for slow growth*

Answer: As per one estimate, India's savings rate needs to go up to 35 per cent if the country wants to boost GDP growth to 7-8 per cent. Saving provides the much needed capital for the economic growth.

Various factors are responsible for economic growth in India which include, high domestic savings rate (above 30%), higher rate of gross capital formation, low current account deficit (CAD), high agricultural growth, better annual manufacturing growth rate, large capital flows, increase in the accretion to reserves, moderate rate of inflation, etc.

Abundance of skilled and unskilled manpower, vast natural resources including land, minerals and jungles, availability of long sea cost and ports, progress towards knowledge based economy, etc are other factors which can be responsible for the potential growth of India.

However, deterioration in external economic environment, fall in agricultural production due to natural calamities, reduction in coal and iron ore production due to court orders, failure to realise more investment, etc. can result into slow growth. (Total 164 words)

Q.2. Account for the failure of manufacturing sector in achieving the goal of labour-intensive exports rather than capital-intensive exports. Suggest measures for more labour-intensive rather than capital-intensive exports.(Answer in 150 words)

Important Points for Answer:
- *Labour Intensive Export*
- *Capital Intensive Export*
- *Benefits*
- *Measures suggested*

Answer: Labour intensive export means any export which involves manufacturing through labour intensive method rather than capital intensive methods. Export of software, heavy engineering, petroleum products, high technology items etc are capital intensive products while textile, garments, jewellery, police diamonds, handicrafts, etc. are labour intensive products. Agro products can also be in such list.

Foreign trade in labour intensive export can lead to more employment generation. As we are facing problem of unemployment, more export in the sector will be also useful in generating more economic activities.

To increase export of labour intensive products, we need to create identity and a niche market for Indian products. Hand made products or small scale industry products can have their own place in the world. Some products can be identified and training can be organised for the sector. Necessary assistance from government can be helpful to promote their export. Loans and export credit may also help. (Total 152 words)

Q.3. Examine the developments of Airports in India through Joint Ventures under Public-Private Partnership(PPP) model. What are the challenges faced by the authorities in this regard.(Answer in 150 words)

Important Points for Answer:
- *Airports & PPP Model*
- *Progress*
- *Challenges*
- *Solution*

Answer: India's decision to invite private capital to participate in the modernisation of its metro airports has delivered significant benefits for passengers, airlines and the government.

The two leading private promoters involved in the sector, GMR and GVK, have implemented dramatic improvements in airport infrastructure at Delhi, Mumbai, Bengaluru and Hyderabad. These airports have transformed the passenger experience, improved efficiency and capacity for airline operators, and delivered a massive dividend to the state-owned Airports Authority of India.

Despite the successes, there are areas for improvement, particularly in terms of economic regulation, land monetisation, management of project costs and at a broader level creating a more predictable operating environment on issues such as bilateral policy, airspace efficiency and airline viability.

A clear process has not been established for determining the appropriate level of capital expenditure in airports.

Monitoring project costs is required to prevent budget over-runs which have resulted into higher charges on airlines and passengers. (Total 156 words)

Q.4. Explain various types of revolutions, took place in Agriculture after Independence in India. How these revolutions have helped in poverty alleviation and food security in India?(Answer in 150 words)

Important Points for Answer:
- *Agriculture in India*
- *Revolutions*
- *Poverty and Food Security*

Answer: In India, agriculture is major employment provider. Food security of the nation depends on agricultural progress. As majority of population is dependent on agriculture for their livelihood, improvement in agricultural productivity and income is sine qua none for bringing them out of poverty.

After independence, India faced shortage of food. To cope up with that problem, Green Revolution was launched in 1961 in Punjab for wheat production. It led to historic success which was followed by Second Green Revolution. Yellow Revolution led to increase in oil seed production, especially in mustard and sunflower. Blue revolution was aimed at increasing fish production, Golden fibre revolution was related to jute production, Golden revolution was related to fruits, honey and horticultural development. Pink revolution is for minion and prawn production while evergreen revolution is for overall agricultural production in the country.

These revolutions have brought India from net importer of food to one of the largest exporter of food in the world resulting into decline in poverty rate among farmers. (Total 167 words)

Q.5. What arc the reasons for poor acceptance of cost effective small processing unit? How the food processing unit will be helpful to uplift the socio-economic status of poor farmers?(Answer in 150 words)

Important Points for Answer:
- *Small food processing units*
- *Reasons for poor acceptance*
- *Uplifting status of farmers*

Answer: Small Food Processing Units are established with less investment and without using heavy machinery or technology. They may be involved in manufacturing of pickle, ice cream, petha, onion paste, potato chips, beverage, besan, papad, namakin masala, etc.

These units have received poor acceptance in society and market due to non availability of brand name, limitations of transportation and marketing facilities, lack of credit and other aspects to compete with major brands.

However, if small food processing units at village and cluster levels can be developed and accepted in market, they would result into benefit to farmers. These units will depend on local products and market. As both will be available in locality, transportation and other costs will be reduced. Problems of storage facility due to lack of which farmers are incurring loss will not be hurdle. Farmers will be able to sell their products at good price and improving economic conditions and poverty elevation of farmers. (Total 156 words)

Q.6. Stem cell therapy is gaining popularity in India to treat a wide variety of medical conditions including leukaemia, Thallessemia, damaged sornea and several burns. Describe briefly what stem cell therapy is and what advantages it has over other treatments?(Answer in 150 words)

Important Points for Answer:
- *Stem Cell Therapy*
- *Useful in diseases*
- *Advantages*

Answer: Stem Cell Therapy (SCT) is the treatment of various disorders, non-serious to life threatening, by using stem cells. These stem cells can be procured from a lot of different sources and used to treat more than 80 disorders, like Leukaemia, Thalassemia, Aplastic anaemia, Sickle cell anaemia and MDS, with potential to treat neuromuscular disorders, degenerative disorders and genetic disorders, for example Autism, Cerebral Palsy, Muscular Dystrophy, etc.

At present, there aren't any effective conventional treatments for many of these disorders, but stem cell therapy has been showing a lot of promising results in India and all over the world. This is possible due to the amazing and unique features of stem cells. The treatment is safe, speedy and often completed within a day or two. Yet, the results are far better than the long and ineffective conventional therapies.

Therapy using stem cells from various sources, including those from bone marrow and umbilical cord, has been successfully used to treat diseases since 1988. (Total 163 words)

Q.7. India has achieved remarkable successes in unmanned space missions including the Chandrayaan and Mars Orbiter Mission, but has not ventured into manned space mission, both in terms of technology and logistics? Explain critically. (Answer in 150 words)

Important Points for Answer:
- *India's unmanned space missions*
- *Current focus*
- *Manned Space Mission*

Answer: Chandrayaan-1 was India's first space mission launched by ISRO in October 2008 which gave a major boost to India's space programme.

It was followed by Mars Mission (MOM) also called Mangalyaan in September 2014.

The 11th FYP gave some importance to manned missions by 2020, including a space station. However, the 12th FYP focused instead on a number of satellite related technologies, including commercial launches, an Indian GPS system, increasing the number of transponders for communication, and deploying more earth observation satellites.

It was informed in Lok Sabha that ISRO's immediate priority is to meet the basic needs of communication, navigation and remote sensing.ISRO has plans for a mission carrying a crew of two to three members, but the mission is pending approval from the Government as the expected cost of the mission is between 3 and 4 billion US dollars.

Due to huge financial costs and pending the technological developments, currently India has focused on various satellite technologies. (Total 161 words)

Q.8. Not many years ago, river linking was a concept but it is becoming reality in the country. Discuss the advantages of river linking and its possible impact on the environment.

(Answer in 150 words)

> **Important Points for Answer:**
> - *River Linking project*
> - *Advantages*
> - *Concerns*

Answer: The river-linking projects was first proposed in 2002 which was stalled due to political hurdles. India has again began work on an $87 billion scheme.

The plan entails linking nearly 60 rivers, including the Ganges, which will cut farmers' dependence on monsoon rains by bringing millions of hectares of cultivatable land under irrigation. It would also generate thousands of megawatts of electricity.

Around half clearances for environmental and forest protection have been obtained for the scheme to link the Ken and Betwa. The projects in western India linking the Par-Tapi with the Narmada and the Daman Ganga with the Pinjal will follow.

Environmentalists and wildlife enthusiasts have warned of ecological damage.The 425-km (265-mile) Ken flows through a tiger reserve nestled in a verdant valley. The government plans to clear out 6.5 percent of the forest reserve to build the dam, relocating nearly 2,000 families from 10 remote villages. (Total 153 words)

Q.9. Discuss the potential threats of Cyber attack and the security framework to prevent it.(Answer in 150 words)

> **Important Points for Answer:**
> - *Threat of Cyber Attack*
> - *Security Framework*

Answer: With internet pervading in all aspects of individual and national life, the threat of cyber attacks are increasing. Cyber warfare is considered dangerous than conventional one.

In India, there were 23 reported cyber security breaches in 2004. The Department of Information Technology created the Indian Computer Emergency Response Team (CERT-In) in 2004 to thwart cyber-attacks in India.

The government created a new subdivision, the National Critical Information Infrastructure Protection Centre (NCIIPC) to thwart attacks against energy, transport, banking, telecom, defence, space and other sensitive areas in 2011.

A high profile cyber attack in July 2012 breached the email accounts of about 12,000 people, including those of officials from critical organisations of government. A government-private sector plan began in October 2012 and is overseen by National Security Advisor (NSA). It intends to strengthen India's cyber security capabilities.

The NCIIPC finalized policies related to national cyber security that would focus on domestic security solutions, reducing exposure through foreign technology. (Total 160 words)

Q.10. The north-eastern region of India has been infested with insurgency for a very long time. Analyze the major reasons for the survival of armed insurgency in this region.(Answer in 150 words)

Important Points for Answer:
- *Insurgency in NE region*
- *Insurgent groups*
- *Reasons for survival*

Answer: Multiple armed factions are operating in north eastern states of India. Some of them are asking for separate state, some demand regional autonomy while others ask for complete independence.

The United Liberation Front of Assam (ULFA), The National Democratic Front of Bodoland (NDFB), The Karbi Longri NC Hills Liberation Front (KLNLF), NSCN(IM), UNLF, KLO, etc are some of the groups operating in north east.

The armed insurgency has survived in north eastern part of India due to various reason, including porous borders and geographical situations. Due to porous borders, insurgents are able to easily make cross border movement with neighbouring countries and make their bases near border areas. They also get funding and arms from across the border. Due to difficult terrain, Indian security forces are not able to curb the insurgents. Insurgents are mostly from the local tribal people who understand the topography well and have experience of operating there. Therefore, insurgency has survived in north east area. (Total 160 words)

Q.11. One of the intended objectives of Union Budget 2017-18 is to 'transform, energize and clean India'. Analyse the measures proposed in the Budget 2017-18 to achieve the objective. (Answer in 250 words)

Important Points for Answer:
- *TEC India*
- *Major schemes for TEC*
- *Ten themes of budget*

Answer: Finance Minister Shri Arun Jaitley proposed 2016-17 Union Budget with the agenda to Transform, Energise and Clean India, i.e. TEC India.

TEC India seeks to 'transform' the quality of governance and quality of life of people; 'energise' various sections of society, especially the youth and the vulnerable, and enable them to unleash their true potential; and 'clean' the country from the evils of corruption, black money and non-transparent political funding.

Schemes like the National Health Scheme, Sarva Shiksha Abhiyan and Skill India, government is increasing its focus on improving the health facilities.

Promotion of digital economy is an integral part of the government's strategy as it has a transformational impact in terms of greater formalisation of the economy.

Digital India and other technology initiatives after the government's demonetisation exercise are aimed at curbing illegal transactions and ending black money menace.

The ten themes outlined by the finance minister include the following:

- Farmers: providing employment and basic infrastructure
- Rural Population: providing employment and basic infrastructure
- Youth: energising them through education, skills and jobs
- Poor and Underprivileged: ·strengthening the systems of social security, healtcare and affordable housing
- Infrastructure: for efficiency, productivity and quality of life
- Financial Sector: growth and stability through stronger institutions
- Digital Economy: for speed, accountability and transparency
- Public Service: effective governance and efficient service delivery through people's participation
- Prudent Fiscal Management: to ensure optimal deployment of resources and preserve fiscal stability
- Tax Administration: honouring the honest.

Thus, the budget has, under ten themes, attempted to achieve the stated objective of TEC India.

(Total 256 words)

Q.12. "Industrial growth rate has lagged behind in the overall growth of Gross-Domestic-Product (GDP) in the post-reform period" Give reasons. How far the recent changes in Industrial Policy are capable of increasing the industrial growth rate?(Answer in 250 words)

Important Points for Answer:

- *1991 Reforms*
- *Industrial growth*
- *Reasons*
- *New Industrial Policy*

Answer: In 1991, Industrial Reforms were announced which included the abolition of industrial licensing, inviting foreign investment, allowing private investment in a wider array of industries and the scrapping of the MRTP (Monopolies and Restrictive Trade Practices) Act.

The lack of labour reforms continue to be one constraint on industrial growth in the economy, which is essential if India wants to aspire from growth rates between 8-10 percent.Average industrial growth in the 25 years since 1991 has been around 7 percent, higher than any previous 25-year period, but not spectacular in comparison with the fast-growing East Asian countries.Both public and private investment need to pick up and investment in infrastructure needs to be close to 8 percent of GDP. Service sector has led the growth in India.

With the changing manufacturing scenario through the introduction of new technologies, innovation, R&D, artificial intelligence and automation, there is a need to completely revamp the Industrial Policy of 1991. Therefore, the Department of Industrial Policy and Promotion (DIPP) has proposed new industrial policy which will focus on encouraging Indian branded products with higher value addition and will review the existing foreign direct investment (FDI) policy regime to facilitate greater technology transfer.It would also be aligned with the government's flagship programmes such as Make in India, Skill India, Startup India and the Foreign Direct Investment policy. The new policy would focus on several areas to encourage innovation, simplify taxation system and address new challenges of the manufacturing sector.

Therefore, the new industrial policy would be hopefully able to enhance growth of industry in India. (Total 266 words)

Q.13. What are the salient features of 'inclusive growth'? Has India been experiencing such a growth process? Analyze and suggest measures for inclusive growth.(Answer in 250 words)

Important Points for Answer:
- *Inclusive Growth*
- *India and Inclusive Growth*
- *Suggested Measures*

Answer: Inclusive growth is economic growth that advances equitable opportunities for economic participants and benefits all sections of society. It includes providing equality of opportunity, empowering people through education and skill development.

India's economy continues to grow at an impressive rate of average more than 7% in last decade. India is projected to remain the fastest-growing G20 economy. Unprecedented growth in exports in services since the 1990s has made India a global leader in this sector.

Indian growth has remained more or less inclusive. India's economic successes are being translated into increased well-being for its population. As GDP per capita has more than doubled in ten years, extreme poverty has declined substantially. Access to education has steadily improved, and life expectancy has risen. Multiple opportunities present themselves for India, and the right mix of policies is needed to take advantage of them. India has made advances in integrating in global value chains and developing a competitive advantage in fields such as information and communication technology.

To make the growth continue and make it more inclusive, it can be suggested that now is the time to secure continued progress by boosting competition and further lowering barriers to trade and investment. It will be vital to tap into the potential offered by young population. This requires investing in the large numbers of young people entering the labour market. Likewise, the rapid pace of development must be matched with the upgrades to infrastructure necessary to support it. Social sectors like education, health, insurance, technology and infrastructure requires focused attention. (Total 257 words)

Q.14. What are the major reasons for declining rice and wheat yield in the cropping system? How crop diversification is helpful to stabilize the yield of the crop in the system?
(Answer in 250 words)

Important Points for Answer:
- *Reasons for Decline in rice and wheat yield*
- *Crop Diversification*
- *Impact on the Yield*

Answer: Rice and wheat cropping system is the largest agricultural production system in India. But there is significant decline in the rice and wheat cropping system for various reasons.

Rice and Wheat are the intensive crops so they use most of the nutrient in the soil thus result in the reduced nutrient result in more declining yield.

The regular cultivation of these crops causes the degradation of the soil quality result in the low yield as the cropping become difficult.

Soil health is also suffering from micro-nutrients deficiencies which is also effecting the cropping system.

Excessive use of pesticides and fertilizers has affected the quality of soil.

Excessive weed pressure is also one of the major issue in the way of sustainable agriculture.

New breeds of insects and pests have appeared from the last few decades.

Breeders must develop some more tolerant crop cultivators so that new insects and pests do not effect the yield.

The low use of the quality seeds or the lack of disease resistance varieties can also be the cause.

However, crop diversification provides a solution to the farmers with a wider choice in the production of a variety of crops in an area so as to expand production related activities on various crops and also to bring down the possible risk. Crop diversification can be used as a strategy for low yield in area. With crop diversification, soil nutritional balance is maintained and there is no excessive pressure on water resources. It also changes use of fertilisers and pesticides so the weed, insects and pests do not become tolerant. (Total 264 words)

Q.15. How do subsidies affect the cropping pattern, crop diversity and economy of farmers? What is the significance of crop insurance, minimum support price and food processing for small and marginal farmers?(Answer in 250 words)

Important Points for Answer:
- *Subsidies & its effects*
- *Crop insurance*
- *MSP*
- *Food processing*

Answer: India has provided various types of subsidies to agricultural sector which includes cash subsidy, fertiliser subsidy, minimum support price, subsidy in-kind, etc.

These subsidies have encouraged farmers to use the subsidised fertilisers instead of the actual requirement. This also leads to distorted crop decisions which is mainly based on the government announced supports. This has led the country to produce more wheat and rice but less oil seeds and pulses.

The Government of India experimented with a comprehensive crop insurance scheme which failed. The Government formulated the Farm Income Insurance Scheme (FIIS) during 2003-04. The two critical components of a farmer's income are yield and price. The scheme provided income protection to the farmers by insuring production and market risks. The Pradhan Mantri Fasal Bima Yojana was launched in February 2016. Insurance is necessary to protect the farmers from natural calamities and ensure their credit eligibility for the next season.

Minimum Support Price is the price at which government purchases crops from the farmers, whatever may be the price for the crops. The MSP helps to incentivise the framers and thus ensures adequate food grains production in the country.

Food processing combines raw food ingredients to produce marketable food products that can be easily prepared and served by the consumer. It provides better prices of products to farmers and reduces wastage of crops.

Small and marginal farmers are highly susceptible to crop failure, price drop and waste after production. Crop insurance protects them against failure of crops, MSP protects against price drop and food processing ensured marketing of crop. (Total 261 words)

Q.16. Give an account of the growth and development of nuclear science and technology in India. What is the advantage of fast breeder reactor programme in India?

(Answer in 250 words)

Important Points for Answer:
- *Nuclear programme in India*
- *Three Stages*
- *FBR technology*
- *Advantage of FBR*

Answer: India's three-stage nuclear power programme was formulated by Homi Bhabha in 1950's to secure the country's long term energy independence. It was aimed at use of uranium and thorium reserves found in the monazite sands of coastal regions of South India.

The three stages are as follows:

1. Pressurized heavy water reactor (PHWR)
2. Fast breeder reactor (FBR)
3. Advanced Heavy Water Reactor(AHWR)

The Fast Breeder Reactor, the second stage, would use plutonium-239, recovered by reprocessing spent fuel from the first stage, and natural uranium.In FBRs, plutonium-239 undergoes fission to produce energy, while the uranium-238 present in the fuel transmutes to additional plutonium-239. The Stage II FBRs are designed to "breed" more fuel than they consume.

Advantages of FBRs:

FBRs are designed with several safety measures and features which follow redundancy and diversity principles.

Fast Breeder Reactors are safe and efficient apart from the benefits from environmental considerations.

Economic viability of FBRs depends on successful operation of PFBR and subsequently successful commissioning and operation of FBRs in the country.

Electricity generated by FBR would be a source of green energy as the waste from the first stage nuclear programme is reprocessed and used as fuel in FBR.

The spent fuel from this reactor can be fed back into the reactor core several times, till the spent fuel contains only short lived fission products.

There is no need of large quantity of fuel materials for the annual external feed and thus eliminates the need for large capacity waste storage spaces with complex construction features. (Total 261 words)

Q.17. 'Climate Change' is a global problem. How India will be affected by climate change? How Himalayan and coastal states of India will be affected by climate change? (Answer in 250 words)

Important Points for Answer:

- *Climate Change*
- *Factors*
- *Impact on India*
- *On Himalayan States*
- *On Coastal States*

Answer: Climate change pertains to distribution of weather patterns when that change lasts for an extended period of time. It affects all countries and parts of the world as it is a global phenomenon.

Factors responsible for climate change may be natural or human. Natural factors include biotic processes, variations in solar radiation received by Earth, plate tectonics, and volcanic eruptions while human factors include pollution, use of certain types of gases, etc.

India is one of the 6th most vulnerable countries to climate change impacts. Extreme events will become more frequent or more severe due to climate change. The implications of a changing climate are particularly severe for India.

Heatwaves persisted breaking a record of 51 degrees Celsius in Rajasthan in May 2016. More than 1,000 people died of hyperthermia or dehydration. The persisting drought and heat waves affected more than 33 crore people, and were followed by an extreme monsoon season from June to October in eastern, western and central India. In 2016, India reported the highest number of deaths due to extreme weather (2,119 fatalities) and suffered losses of more than INR 1.4 trillion in property damage.

The climate change will affect Himalayan States due to melting of glaciers which will result into flood in rivers. Floods may create havoc in terms of loss to lives and property. Landslides also increase due to imbalanced water flow in rivers.

In the costal states, sea level rises due to effect of climate change and they run the risk of being submerged under water. Increased temperature adds to salinity of water at costal states. (Total 263 words)

Q.18. On December 2004, tsumani brought havoc on 14 countries including India. Discuss the factors responsible for occurrence of Tsunami and its effects on life and economy. In the light of guidelines of NDMA (2010) describe the mechanisms for preparedness to reduce the risk during such events.(Answer in 250 words)

Important Points for Answer:
- *Tsunami of December 2004*
- *Factors for Tsunami*
- *Effects of Tsunami*
- *NDMA mechanism*

Answer: On 26 December 2004 an earthquake of 9.1 magnitude occurred near Sumatra of Indonesia in the Indian Ocean. Due to its impact, tsunami waves struck Indian Ocean countries.

A tsunami is a large ocean wave that is caused by sudden motion on the ocean floor. This sudden motion could be an earthquake, a powerful volcanic eruption, or an underwater landslide. The impact of a large meteorite could also cause a tsunami. Tsunamis travel across the open ocean at great speeds and build into large deadly waves in the shallow water of a shoreline.

It killed 250,000 people across 14 countries including Indonesia, Sri Lanka, India, Maldives, Thailand, etc. Many people went missing. Bottlenecks created by tsunami in communication and infrastructure also hampered the disaster management measures. Supply of essential items were affected. Reconstruction cost created deficits in budgets of many countries.

The 2004 tsunami prompted NDMA to formulate Tsunami Risk Management Guidelines to outline inter-agency roles and responsibilities, tsunami risk preparedness, mitigation and response.

The Guidelines recommends practical and effective ways for awareness generation, capacity building, education, training and research & development for better tsunami risk management.

The Guidelines explore options for effective dissemination of tsunami alert and warning messages generated by INCOIS.

Structural Mitigation measuresgive a brief guidance on design and construction of new structures as well as strategies for protecting lifeline and priority structures from Tsunamis along the seafront.

Astrong mechanism has been recommended for effective emergency response by involving local police network, civil defence volunteers wherever available, home guards, State Disaster Response Forces and National Disaster Response Force. (Total 263 words)

Q.19. Mob violence is emerging as a serious law and order problem in India. By giving suitable examples, analyze the causes and consequences of such violence.(Answer in 250 words)

> **Important Points for Answer:**
> - *Mob violence*
> - *Incidens in India*
> - *Examples*
> - *Causes*
> - *Consequences*

Answer: Mob violence is when people resort to violent means against any individual, group or establishment for certain reason. It may be pre-meditated or may develop on the stop. All people involved in the mob violence may not know each other but they combine due to mob psychology.

In the first six months of 2017, 20 cow-terror attacks were reported. The attacks include mob lynching, attacks by vigilantes, murder and attempt to murder, harassment, assault and gang-rape. In two attacks, the victims were chained, stripped and beaten, while in two others, the victims were hanged.

In the Pratapgarh incident involved the regrettable death of Zafar Khan after an argument about open defecation. Four Dalit youth were flogged in Una by cow vigilantes.

Such mob violence have recently been happening due to various causes, religious, communal, political or social unrest. Differing in nature, these incidents are invariable cases of social fault-lines. They are issues of law and order which need to be tackled strongly.

Thousands of citizens' protest named 'Not in My Name' against the recent incidents of mob killings took place all over India in June 2017. Leaving those involved in mob violence will encourage others to escape law machinery. It will increase communal hatred. Such mobocracy has been taking place in India, over various reasons. Recent Patel violences in Gujarat for reservation demands have more or less replicated Gurjar demands of reservation.

There is dire need for the law machinery to take strong actions against such reported actions of mob violence. (Total 255 words)

Q.20. The scourge of terrorism is a grave challenge to national security. What solutions do you suggest to curb this growing menace? What are the major sources of terrorist funding? (Answer in 250 words)

> **Important Points for Answer:**
> - *Terrorism as a challenge*
> - *Suggestions*
> - *Funding of terrorists*

Answer: Terrorism has increased all over the world. India started facing terrorism problems since late 1980s, first in Punjab and then in Jammu and Kashmir. The same spreader throughout the country as the strategy of terrorist changed. The terrorism has become national security challenge to many countries, including India.

Suggestions:

Solution to terrorism requires a comprehensive approach by security agencies of the country. First of all, there requires greater coordination between all state police authorities so movement of any suspected terrorist activities can be curbed at the initial stage.

Any indication of radicalisation by youngsters should be strictly monitored and their activities should be strictly watched.

International coordination with friendly countries should be adopted to reduce the menace of terrorism.

Stricter punishment and fast track judicial settlement of cases related to terrorism should be provided for. Not only terrorists, but whoever aids or supports them should be punished severely.

Funding of terrorists:

Financing of terrorism happens through black money and cross border activities. Such transfer of money should be checked.

Any illegal activities in the country or at cross border also may be responsible for terrorist funding. Drug trade and narcotics sale are sometimes connected with terrorist funding. Such activities should be curbed.

Cooperation with other countries in counterterrorism and terrorist funding should be adopted for tracking terrorist activities.

Money laundering, cash debiting schemes, wire transfers by charitable trusts, cash handling of big amount, corporate layering, using of multiple accounts to collect funds, etc are some methods used for terrorism funding. (Total 250 words)

SOLVED PAPERS

PAPER–IV

Section–A

Q.1. Conflict of interest in the public sector arises when

(a) official duties,

(b) public interest, and

(c) personal interest

are taking priority one above the other.

How can this conflict in administration be resolved? Describe with an example. (150 Words, 10)

Answer: Conflict of interest in the public sector arises in case a personal interest comes in conflict of public interest while performing official duty. It can be to protect private personal interest or to promote the one.

For example, a bank manager while granting a loan in official duty faces conflict in case of an undeserving application by a relative. Likewise an administrator in a recruitment panel faces a candidate who is her personal friend. As individuals and member of society, officers face such challenges. The conflict of

Conflict of interest is not wrong in itself but it should be managed and exeçuted properly.

It can be excluded by following steps:

1. Declaring conflict of interest
2. Recusing from the case where there is conflict
3. Being objective, should always keep public interest above the personal interest.

In such cases, one should uphold integrity expected from a public servant and should work in promotion of public spirit. (Total 153 words)

Q.2. Examine the relevance of the following in the context of civil service: (150 Words, 10)

(a) Transparency

(b) Accountability

(c) Fairness and justice

(d) Courage of conviction

(e) Spirit of service

Answer: (a) Transparency: It implies openness of decision making and freedom of information to citizen. It is relevant for civil services as it permit accountability, good governance, public participation and careful utilisation of public funds.

(b) Accountability: It means answerability of civil servant for his decisionto public for his acts or omission.Accountability helps in curtailing corruption and increases public confidence.

(c) Fairness and justice: Fairness means impartial and just treatment or behaviour without favouritism or discrimination.Justice is the legal or philosophical theory by which fairness is administered. It means a civil servant should be fair and just in performing own duties.

(d) Courage of Conviction: Courage means taking decision fearlessly, strength in the face of pain or grief. While conviction is a firmly held belief or opinion. A civil servant should be able to courageously uphold his conviction which is based on rules and integrity.

(e) Spirit of Service: Devotion for public duty is the spirit of service. This is relevant for civil servant as they have to keep public interest above private interest. (Total 160 words)

Q.3. Young people with ethical conduct are not willing to come forward to join active politics. Suggest steps to motivate them to come forward. (150 Words, 10)

Answer: Whole India has 65% young population, representation under age 30, in politics near to 0%. Politics is considered gutter and no one went to enter it for cleaning, as there is always fear of getting dirty. Politics today is marred by corruption. Therefore young people with noble ideal, energy and passion who can play very good part in the politics should join politics and bring change.

Following can be steps to motivate them:

1. Parties may allot certain number of tickets to youth
2. Decreasing role of money in election and provide for state funding
3. Motivating and educating youth through various programmes like youth parliament.
4. Promoting debate and discussion for their role by giving examples of young successful politician.
5. Panchayats candidature can be limited to people up to 45 only. So young people enter politics at grassroots level.

Recently India has seen a number of young leaders entering politics like Jignesh Mewani, Hardik Patel, Alpesh Thakor and Kanahiya Kumar. (Total 162 words)

Q.4. (a) One of the tests of integrity is complete refusal to be compromised. Explain with reference to a real life example. (150 Words, 10)

Integrity is defined as the quality of being honest and having strong moral principles. It is consistent behaviour,without fear or favour, in transparent manner. Integrity requires a person to be bound by moral principles in all circumstances even at the cost of loss, post or promotion. Adverse situation is real test of integrity.

Not to bowdown under any political pressure, courage and conviction to stand by one's own decision, challenging powerful and influential people for their unethical decision—are attributes of a person of an integrity.

For example, Gandhiji suspended non-cooperation movement after Choura-Chouri incidence as non-violence was at core to his integrity.Similarly justice Manmohan Sinha set aside election of India Gandhi, the most influential person of the time, to upheld integrity without any fear.

Keeping promises even if it takes extra efforts, not cheating even when getting chance, being faithful in a relationship, telling true quality of product while selling—are examples of integrity.

(Total 161 words)

Q.4.(b) Corporate social responsibility makes companies more profitable and sustainable. Analyse. (150 Words, 10)

Corporate social responsibility (CSR) is a company's initiative remedied the environmental and social impact of its operation. It also denotes responsible way of making profit i.e., taking care of all the stakeholders involved in the process.

Corporates are part of society and they should work for the society. People and environment are important components to get profit inany business. Responsible work practice increases brand value and goodwill of the company. Trust and faith of people helps abusiness to flourish in long run.

Similarly, taking care of environment by not polluting it, is dividend for all employee, employer and society. For instance, keeping pollution at check reduces cost on health expenditure of employees.

For example, Tata is known for its sound ethical business practices. They work for society by providing schools, hospitals, charity, etc.,through CSR. This increases its brand and visibility. This makes company more profitable and sustainable. (Total 151 words)

Q.5. (a) "Great ambition is the passion of a great character. Those endowed with it may perform very good or very bad acts. All depends on the principles which direct them."

—Napoleon Bonaparte.

Stating examples mention the rulers (i) who have harmed society and country, (ii) who worked for the development of society and country. (150 Words, 10)

Answer: Passion and ambition are good attribute of personality, but the result depends on the principles and ethics that guide the character.

For example, Hitler was a man of great ambition and passion. But he harmed the society and the country as his attitude was not shaped by moral values. Killing millions Jews, getting involved in the 2nd World War, harmed humanity at large.

On the other hand, leaders like Abraham Lincoln also had passion and ambition. A poor peasant became the President of USA only because of his ambition. He worked for abolition of slavery, a malpractice in the society for many years.

A person driven by such ambition performs acts depending on his own understanding of good or bad. Chauvinistic and racial behaviour of leaders are motivated by their ambition and passion. So is the dedication of scientists, social workers and other leaders who work constantly for human values. Thus, value behind the passion is the most important factor to drive the person. (Total 164 words)

(b) "If a country is to be corruption free and become a nation of beautiful minds, I strongly feel there are three key societal members who can make a difference. They are father, the mother and the teacher." —A. P. J. Abdul Kalam. Analyse. (150 Words, 10)

Answer: Corruption is mainly based on moral value system of a society. If a person has strong ethics and moral conduct, he would not give or take bribe, nor would he be involved in any other type of corruption.

But these values and moral codes are imbibed by family and schools. In family, father and mother, through their teachings and behaviour, give foundational lessons of morality to the child which he carries through out his life. Gandhi had strong imprint of his father and mother on his character.

Another person that strongly influences a person's moral values is his teacher. Kautilya influenced Chandragupta to become a great leader. Teachers are role model for children on early days. Teachers, through teaching and preaching, develop though process and judgements in a person. This is responsible in his behaviour as a part of society.

Therefore, to make the society corruption free, the three individuals have great social responsibility. (Total 154 words)

Q.6. (a) How will you apply emotional intelligence in administrative practices? (150 Words, 10)

Answer: Emotional intelligence is the ability to identify and manage your own emotions and the emotions of others. Emotional intelligence is balance of head and heart. It gives authority to respond to the challenges of ones life and career in a positive manner.An emotionally intelligent administrator is able to handle a situation in balanced manner. He is not overtaken by favour or biased emotions. He tackles the situation in an objective manner.

While using emotional behaviour, he gives a soothing feeling to his superior and subordinates. Dealing with a conflict in peaceful and constructive manner requires emotional intelligence. He takes into account emotional ethics and uses interpersonal skills for the given situation. It gives capacity to perform in certain demanding and hostile environment, to manage own anger and remain focused and cooperative.

Similarly administrator uses his emotional intelligence to manage inter-personal relationship peer relationship, negotiation and motivation to get good result in work-environment. (Total 155 words)

(b) Strength, peace and security are considered to be the pillars of international relations. Elucidate. (150 Words, 10)

Answer: Today the world is full of international conflicts—China's assertion in South China Sea, Refugee crisis in Europe, Terrorism, Civil wars in Africa, etc. In the given situation, strength, peace and security has become more important values.

Economic, military and strategic strength of a country plays an important role in deciding its international stature. A strong country can manage and maintain international relations.

Peace among nations is important factor of international situation. Maintaining and keeping peace is prime function of United Nations. India's concept of 'Vasudhaiv Kutumbkam' i.e. the World Family concept is in line of maintaining peace.

Security of existence is assurance that a country will always seek in its international behaviour. While at risk, the country will increase its defence power, make alliances and seek to grow stronger.

Thus, any country, in its international relations, will always depend on its own strength, ideals of peace and perceived security. If any of these factors are lacking, it will change the country's behaviour. (Total 164 words)

Q.7. (a) The crisis of ethical values in modern times is traced to a narrow perception of the good life. Discuss. (150 Words, 10)

(b) Increased national wealth did not result in equitable distribution of its benefits. It has created only some "enclaves of modernity and prosperity for a small minority at the cost of the majority." Justify. (150 Words, 10)

Answer: Since the economic reforms of 1991, India has become better in economic terms. However, the increase in wealth has not been distributed equitably.

As per one report, the difference in the wealth share held by India's poorest 10 per cent and the richest 10 per cent is enormous.

The richest 10 per cent Indians holds 370 times the share of wealth that it's poorest hold.India's richest 10 per cent have been getting steadily richer since 2000, and now hold nearly t74% total wealth. Also, India's 1% super-rich have been getting richer even faster.

Thus, the increased national wealth has created enclave of modernity among 10-20% of Indians who have prospered at the cost of remaining 80-90% of Indians. Minority, Women, uneducated and underprivileged people have not been benefited by the economic progress. Many social and political programmes have not resulted into success due to corruption and lack of political will. This has resulting into social, economic, and political danger to the nation. (Total 166 words)

Q.8. (a) Discipline generally implies following the order and subordination. However, it may be counter-productive for the organisation. Discuss. (150 Words, 10)

Answer: Discipline means practice of obedience, observing regulation and code of conduct. Following the order of senior and giving absolute subordination has been termed as discipline.

Due to such subordination, sometimes creativity, innovation, dissenting opinion, counter views are not allowed in organisation. It fails to utilise the young talent and new ideas from juniors.

This has many times become counter productive due to single sided approach. It follows top down approach and does not inspire confidence in the junior office members.

Many MNCs do not follow such subordination and order following practices but encourage free discussion and dissenting views. In Indian government and companies, this is not followed which has resulted into policy paralysis and environment of official fear and apathy.

Many bureaucrats are given freedom of work to solve the problems of naxalism. Officers who are given discretion are performing well. Had the Patel were not given free hand by Nehru, India might not had been integrated. (Total 157 words)

(b) Without commonly shared and widely entrenched moral values and obligations, neither the law, nor democratic government, nor even the market economy will function properly.

What do you understand by this statement? Explain with illustration in the contemporary times. (150 Words, 10)

Answer: Moral values of people are basis of maintaining law and order in the society. If people are morally strong, they will not commit crimes. This will give basis for implementation and enactment of laws. Ram Rajya is not possible without saint like people. Frequent violation of law is due to lower ethical code followed by people.

Similarly, democratic government depends on its voter base. Unless voters have higher moral standards, government cannot form better policies. Issues of appeasement will not come to fore if voters believe in just society and government. Use of money and muscle power in today's politics is due to lower moral standards of voters.

Market economy depends on company and consumer. Unethical competition among companies will mislead consumers. If people take ethical values and business practice of a company seriously, no company will be able to cheat any customer. The basis of market economy, free market and buyer-seller relations depend on moral and ethical practices of both. (Total 161 words)

Section–B

Q.9. You are an honest and responsible civil servant. You often observe the following:

(a) There is a general perception that adhering to ethical conduct one may face difficulties to oneself and cause problems for the family, whereas unfair practices may help to reach the career goals.

(b) When the number of people adopting unfair means is large, a small minority having a penchant towards ethical means makes no difference.

(c) Sticking to ethical means is detrimental to the larger developmental goals

(d) While one may not involve oneself in large unethical practices, but giving and accepting small gifts makes the system more efficient.

Examine the above statements with their merits and demerits. (250 Words, 20)

Answer: (a) There is a general perception that adhering to ethical conduct one may face difficulties to oneself and cause problems for the family, whereas unfair practices may help to reach the career goals.

Merits (i) Difficulties are part and parcel of life. Even after compromising ethical value one faces many problems and there is always inner conflict of conscience.

Demerits (ii) It is true that remaining ethical is a challenge for personal and family comfort. Even career is put to stake like no promotion, frequent transfer, even falsely implicating criminal charges, etc.

(b) When the number of people adopting unfair means is large, a small minority having a penchant towards ethical means makes no difference.

Merits: Even small group of honest and ethical people can make a huge difference. Mills are covered by starting small steps. Gandhiji alone took the vow for "Satyagraha" and "non-violence"—which was later followed by thousands.

Demerit: As it is evident in today's environment that few honest people are not able to change the prevalent corruption, nepotism, power show-off, antipathy towards weaker section. Majority are unethical resulting unethical society.

(c) Sticking to ethical means is detrimental to the larger developmental goals

Merits: Development should not be seen only in economic terms but also on terms of equity, justice, sustainability, happiness, peace, etc. Sticking to ethical value helps in achieving long terms sustainable developments.

Demerits: While taking decision for development of the country sticking to all type of ethics like environmental ethics, concern for vulnerable and weak, social ethics—is difficult task.

(d) While one may not involve oneself in large unethical practices, but giving and accepting small gifts makes the system more efficient.

Merit: Some incentives for good works can be given for efficient working by way of gifts, which does not inculcate habit of corruption.

Demerits: Integrity requires not compromising with ethical value in any situation. Corruption, big or small, eroded moral value. This gives rise to greed and can have disastrous effect.

Q.10. You are aspiring to become an IAS officer and you have cleared various stages and now you have been selected for the personal interview. On the day of the interview, on the way to the venue you saw an accident where a mother and child who happen to be your relatives were badly injured. They needed immediate help.

What would you have done in such a situation? Justify your action. (250 Words, 20)

Answer: Accident of relative on day of interview is exactly stressing, but as a human being I have to manage the situation and handle the crisis as it is part and parcel of life.

I will take following stepsin this grim situation:

First of all, I will give them first aid and try to make them calm by psychologically supporting. Then I will call for ambulance to send them to hospital. I can also take them to the nearby hospital if I can arrange some vehicle to the spot. I may call my other relatives as I have to go for interview as well. I will inform the UPSC about being late so that I do not miss my interview. I will also use stronger intelligence to calm down myself. After arranging some person or relative, I will go to UPSC for interview and well place my position with all evidence. UPSE may consider my request and can reward me.

Reasons and justifications for the above steps are:

If I will not help the person in crisis, I may not become a good civil servant.

As Gandhiji has said that among all courts, court of conscience is supreme, no one can evade such court. Compassion, empathy care, love is basis of human life.

If I leave them on their situation, it can create crisis of conscience. I may appear to interview on time, but I will loose my mental peace. So I will handle the situation following middle path of Buddha.

(Total 251 words)

Q.11. You are the head of the Human Resources department of an organisation. One day one of the workers died on duty. His family was demanding compensation. However, the company denied compensation because it was revealed in investigation that he was drunk at the time of the accident. The workers of the company went to strike demanding compensation for the family of the deceased. The Chairman of the management board has asked for your recommendation.

What recommendation would you provide the management?

Discuss the merits and demerits of each of the recommendations. (250 Words, 20)

Answer: In the above case, worker has died during working hours of the organisation and family is demanding compensation. However, it is noticed that worker was drunk at the time of accident.

As HR executive, I would recommend that due investigation may be carried out about reason of death. There are facts in favour of and against the worker's family's right to get compensation. As he died on duty, his family is entitled to compensation. However, if the cause of death was his drunkenness, his family may not be entitled to get the compensation.

Therefore, a detailed inquiry report would be suitable. I would recommend the management to go as per rule.

Merits of my recommendations are that due procedure of law will be followed and worker's family will get compensation if they deserve it.

However, if the inquiry report reveals to the contrary, workers may continue with strike and family members may exert pressure on the management. It may result into loss of reputation and working hours.

But providing compensation, just due to pressure tactics will encourage them to continue such behaviour and management will be at loss.

If compensation is given to the worker against his entitlement, it will certainly help the poor family but will set a wrong precedence. There can be other ways to help the poor family.

At the same time, if worker is entitled to compensation, his family must be paid the same. Justice to the family of the deceased should be done as breadwinner has died.

If there was proportionate negligence, partial compensation may be paid. (Total 262 words)

Q.12. You are the manager of a spare parts company A and you have to negotiate a deal with the manager of a large manufacturing company B. The deal is highly competitive and sealing the deal is critical for your company. The deal is being worked out over a dinner. After dinner the manager of manufacturing company B offered to drop you to the hotel in his car. On the way to hotel he happens to hit motorcycle injuring the motorcyclist badly. You know the manager was driving fast and thus lost control. The law enforcement officer comes to investigate the issue and you are the sole eyewitness to it. Knowing the strict laws pertaining to road accidents you are aware that your honest account of the incident would lead to the prosecution of the manager and as a consequence the deal is likely to be jeopardised, which is of immense importance to your company.

What are the dilemmas you face? What will be your response to the situation? (250 Words, 20)

Answer: *Expected dilemmas and their analysis:*

1. Truthfulness vs. Dilution of facts
2. Justice to the victim and his family vs. Protection of the manager

Since deal is crucial for company, if I tell the truth about the accident it can jeopardise the deal. It will also put my career on stake. At the same time all the workers working in the organisation will get affected.

But diluting facts by telling lie will go against my personal value. I will be held accountable to my conscience. I may get the contact by compromising.

Justice to the family of the victims should also be done. Life of the person cannot be jeopardise due hasty act of any person. If I turn my eyes from this situation, it will be like participating in the crime.

But protection of manager will earn me trust of both companies and I may be promoted. I will certainly get the contract.

Following would be my response in the giving situation:

I will give account of the situation truthfully to the police.

Since life of an innocent has been endangered, it is my moral duty to help the victim and enforcement of law effectively. It will have deterrence in longer run. If Mr. B is left unpunished he can repeat it in future and do it with anyone else.

Though it can cause loss to the deal but compromising on conscience is bigger loss. Deal can be sealed due to economic reasons, not on the basis of personal relation. (Total 251 words)

Q.13. A building permitted for three floors, while being extended illegally to 6 floors by a builder, collapses. As a consequence, a number of innocent labourers including women and children died. These labourers are migrants of different places. The government immediately announced cash relief to the aggrieved families and arrested the builder.

Give reasons for such incidents taking place across the country. Suggest measures to prevent their occurrence. (250 Words, 20)

Answer: *Reason for such incidences:*

Greed of the builder: Consideration of money and profit are responsible for such type of illegal construction in the society.

Nexus between builders and Municipal Corporation officers and political class: Violation of construction rule as not possible without connivance of Municipal Corporation officers and political class. There are instances where builders bribe the officials and political class for such illegal construction.

Weak implementation of construction norms: Administrators are not able to enforce the norms by proper verification and inspection. This attitude of apathy is also responsible for sorry state of affairs.

Participation of general public: Even citizens are encouraging such builders by buying illegally constructed flats.

Culture of consumerism and deteriorating moral standard of society is also responsible for such type of incidence.

Use of spurious material, faulty design system is also responsible for this problem.

Measure to prevent such incidences:

Housing is in demand due to rapid urbanisation. People are buying illegal property as affordable housing is not available to middle class. Government should come up with affordable and sustainable housing in the cities.

Strict implementation of laws and monitoring of constructions by the municipal officers will discourage such illegal construction. Proper investigation should be done in such cases and all stake holders involved should be held accountable.

Public should also resist buying such houses as their quality is not good and safety is compromised.

Builders should get punishment through justice. It will act as deterrence. Moreover, compensation to victim should be given by builders.

Initiative such as RERA is a welcome step in curbing such construction. (Total 262 words)

Q.14. You are a Public Information Officer (PIO) in a government department. You are aware that the RTI Act 2005 envisages transparency and accountability in administration. The act has functioned as a check on the supposedly arbitrarily administrative behaviour and actions. However, as a PIO you have observed that there are citizens who filed RTI applications not for themselves but on behalf of such stakeholders who purportedly want to have access to information to further their own interests. At the same time there are these RTI activists who routinely file RTI applications and attempt to extort money from the decision makers. This type of RTI activism has affected the functioning of the administration adversely and also possibly jeopardises the genuineness of the applications which are essentially aimed at getting justice.

What measures would you suggest to separate genuine and non-genuine applications? Give merits and demerits of your suggestions. (250 Words, 20)

Answer: As a Public Information Officer, I do not have choice to reject any of the RTI applications on grounds of being genuine or otherwise, except on the grounds mentioned in the RTI Act 2005.

However, for suggesting measures in RTI Act, as amendment, so that the purpose of RTI is truly solved, I would suggest that:

Applicant of RTI should be required to disclose purpose of asking information.

An applicant, filing multiple RTI applications, should be discouraged by charging cumulatively higher fees.

Journalists and media organisations should be given separate window for filing RTI which are to be used for commercial purpose.

Commercial use of information should be allowed, but charges should be higher and time frame should be more.

Merits and demerits of these suggestions:

Suggestion: Asking reasons for filing such application

Merit: (a) It will give satisfaction about genuineness of the applicant.

Demerit: It will go against the spirit of current RTI as the Act does not provide for asking reason.

Suggestion: Increasing fees for filing RTI application

Merit: It will dater frivolous application

Demerit: Genuine case of poor and weak may be affected as they may not be able to file RTI at increased cost.

Suggestion: Keeping record of those filing frivolous petition:

Merit: Such applicant will be caught red-handed. It will also create deterrence to others.

Demerit: It can go against genuine applicants and process may become cumbersome.

Suggestion: Making RTI system available to commercial use:

*Merit:*It will help media to disseminate important information to public.

*Demerit:*It will encourage wealthy media houses to use government machinery for their purposes.

(Total 263 words)

(MAIN) **2018** | **Civil Services Exam.**

General Studies

SOLVED PAPERS

PAPER–I

Section–A

Time Allowed : Three Hours *Maximum Marks : 150*

Q.1. Safeguarding the Indian art heritage is the need of the moment. Comment. (10)

Important Points for Answer:
- *Write a brief sketch of Indian art heritage*
- *Highlight the importance of art heritage*
- *Enumerate the challenges and threats to art heritage*
- *Conclusion*

Answer: India has a diverse cultural traditions, traditional expressions, intangible cultural heritage comprising masterpieces which need institutional support and encouragement with a view to addressing areas critical for the survival and propagation of these forms of cultural heritage. The centralized scheme for concerted efforts in the direction of professionally enhancing awareness and interest in Intangible Cultural Heritage (ICH), safeguarding, promoting and propagating it systematically.

The Ministry of Culture has formulated a Scheme titled "Scheme for Safeguarding the Intangible Heritage and Diverse Cultural Traditions of India", with the objective of reinvigorating and revitalizing various institutions, groups, individuals, identified non-MOC institutions, non-government organisations, researchers and scholars so that they may engage in activities for strengthening, protecting, preserving and promoting the rich intangible cultural heritage of India.

The Scheme will cover all recognized domains of ICH such as oral traditions and expressions, including language as a vehicle of the intangible cultural heritage, Performing arts, Social practices, rituals and festive events, Knowledge and practices concerning nature and the universe, traditional craftsmanship etc.

Lok Sabha has passed The Ancient Monuments and Archaeological Sites and Remains (Amendment) Bill, 2017.This act provides for preservation of ancient and historical monuments and archaeological sites and remains of national importance. Adopt a Heritage: Apni Dharohar, Apni Pehchaan", is a collaborative effort between the Ministry of Tourism, Ministry of Culture and Archaeological Survey of India (ASI), and State/UTs Governments. The Project aims to develop synergy among all partners to effectively promote "responsible tourism".

Monument Mitras through the innovative concept of Vision Bidding, where the agency with best vision for the heritage site will be given an opportunity to associate pride with their CSR activities.

Q.2. Assess the importance of the accounts of the Chinese and Arab travellers in the reconstruction of the history of India. (10)

Important Points for Answer:

- *Introduce by placing the travel accounts in historical sources.*
- *Illustrate with examples usefulness of Chinese traveller's for constructing India history.*
- *Illustrate with examples usefulness travel accounts of Arabs for constructing Indian history*
- *Conclusion*

Answer: The Indian Sub-continent is one of the earliest civilisations in the World that made dream destination for the travellers and scholars. The oldest accounts of India which have come down to us from Foreign Travellers. But although India figures in the writings of Herodotus and Ctesias, these consist largely of incredible tales.

Fa-Hien was the first Chinese monk to travel to India in search of great Buddhist scriptures. He described his journey in his travelogue 'Record of Buddhist kingdoms' Hiuen Tsang came from China to India in search of Buddhist belief and practice. He visited India during the reign of Harshavardhana. His book is Si-yu-ki or the 'Records of Western World. He has been described as the "prince of pilgrims" and his accounts carry a lot of information on the political, social and religious set up of India. Hiuen Tsang visited Kashmir, Punjab and proceeded to Kapilavastu, Bodh-Gaya, Sarnath, and Kusinagara. He studied in the University of Nalanda of his accounts reflect ancient India.

Al-Masudi (Arab) An Arab traveller, He has given an extensive account of India in his work 'Muruj-ul-Zehab.' Shihabuddin Al-Umari (Arabian Traveller).He came from Damascus. He has given a vivid account of India in his book, 'Masalik albsar fimamalik al-amsar Al Beruni was an Islamic scholar who was "commissioned" by Mahmud of Ghazni to write his monumental commentary on Indian philosophy and culture Kitab f tahqiq ma li'l-hind.

Q.3. Throw light on the significance of the thoughts of Mahatma Gandhi in the present times. (10)

Important Points for Answer:

- *Introduce with brief sketch of Gandhi's personality (30-40 words)*
- *Relevance of Gandhi's thoughts in social, political and economic issues faced by mankind these times*
- *Conclusion*

Answer: Mohandas Karamchand Gandhi, gave a new dimension to Ahimsa [non-violence]- an eternal, natural and the highest human value, in theory and practice. As the best and true representative of Indian Culture in his own time, Gandhi was a peacemaker's mentor.

The ideas or philosophy of Mahatma Gandhi in his firm belief in "mutual-dependence of man's activities on one other" and "unity of human-life", which is an indivisible whole. In his own words: "The whole gamut of man's activities...constitutes an indivisible whole. You cannot divide life, social, economic, political and purely religious, into separate watertight compartments." Mahatma Gandhi believed that all human activities, essentially influencing each other, build ways for a life. In this regard, many philosophies also confirm the belief of the Mahatma. Intellectuals are well aware of interdependent development. This makes life more meaningful and effective; and helps in achieving goals such as Truth. Gandhi called upon people to come forward in such a manner. He also emphasized upon adoption of Ahimsa [non-violence], which is the eternal, natural and supreme human value. For Gandhi, non-violence is an active, pure and all-timely value. It is the best means to reach the Truth. In other words, only through Ahimsa can life be made meaningful. Gandhi had the firm opinion that except non-violence, there is no other means to reach a goal. Without Ahimsa, one cannot know the absolute Truth. In this regard Gandhi wrote the following in Young India: "Means are after all everything.

There is no wall of separation between the means and the end." Non-violence is the nucleus in Gandhi's ideas. In other words, his views revolved around Ahimsa. And as mentioned, it is the only means to achieve Truth, and to achieve Truth is the goal of one's life, or to get completeness of life. In this chain, the second point relates to Gandhi's actions. The actions he undertook on the basis of non-violence consistently gave new dimensions to his views; they made them firm and mature. Therefore, it is necessary to know the intentions at the root of his actions. Some people believed that most of the actions , taken by Gandhi were dedicated to the welfare of Indians. Indians were the centre of his actions in South Africa and India. To ascertain freedom of India and to accord justice to Indians was the prime objective of his non-violent actions. But this opinion is not true. The welfare of all human beings was at the root of his actions.

Gandhi's ideas according to the demand of time and circumstances. And, this can be perceived well through the series of events pertaining to three mass actions-the Non-Cooperation [1920], the Civil Disobedience [1930] and the Quit India [1942]-launched to make India free from the British Empire. In this regard Mahatma Gandhi himself has written in one of the issues of Harijan: "I am not at all concerned with appearing to be consistent. In my search after Truth I have discarded many ideas and learnt many new things. Old as I am in age, I have no feeling that I have ceased to grow inwardly or that my growth will stop at the dissolution of the flsh." It is clear that Gandhi's ideas, in spite of staying within the domain of non-violence, and even while adhering in search of Truth, are dynamic. They can be refied to suit the present circumstances.

Q.4. Why is Indian Regional Navigational Satellite System (IRNSS) needed? How does it help in navigation? (10)

Important Points for Answer:
- *Brief introduction on Indian Regional Navigational Satellite System (IRNSS)*
- *Objective of Indian Regional Navigational Satellite System (IRNSS)*
- *How does it help it navigation?*
- *Conclusion*

Answer: IRNSS, also termed as NAVIC (Navigation with Indian Costellation) is a constellation of 7 satellites Which envisages an autonomous regional navigation system that provides accurate real-time positioning and timing services. It covers India and an area extending about 1500 sq.km around India. IRNSS Comprises of 4 GSO and 3 GEO satellites.

Following figures shows the coverage of IRNSS and Countries having their own regional navigational Systems.

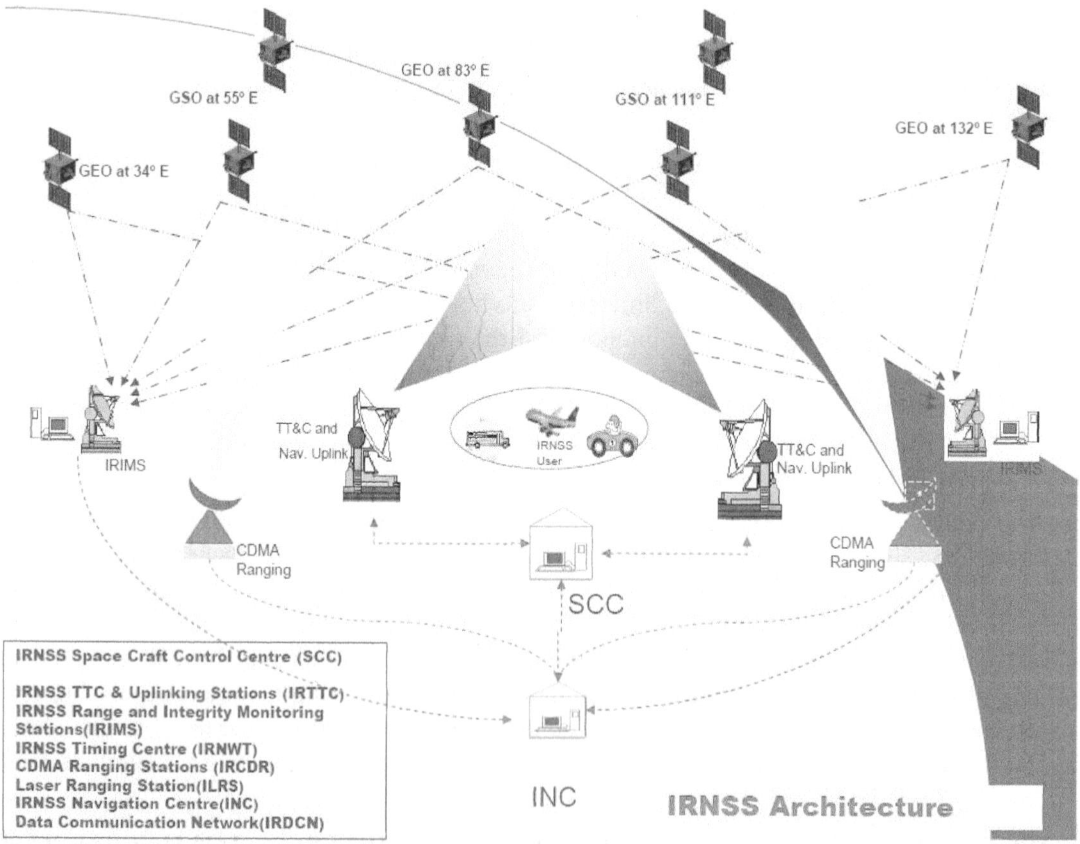

IRNSS provides 2 types of Services:
- Standard positioning service (SPS) - accurate more than 20 m for civilian use
- Restricted Service (RS) - Military use

The down of the 21st Century marked the need for a Regional NSS as it became necessary during hostile conditions (Kargil war 1999) i.e., Denial of Access to navigation by USA. Moreover, these are the probable reasons to instigate NAVIC:

- Self-reliance - To achieve self - reliance.
- Technological advancement - To venture into unknown arenas
- More secure and reliable communication. During hostile Conditions
- To Improve navigation
- To improve Credibility & form a part of elite group having Regional navigation satellite system.
- With improved accuracy than GPS, IRNSS will help in navigating fishermen & sailors by showing them shortest route where there is big concentration of this and prevent them from venturing into foreign waters.
- It will aid relief & rescue operations conducted during floods, earthquakes etc.
- Moreover, IRNSS will help in navigation in the following ways.
  (a) Disaster Management
  (b) Vehicle Tracking & fleet Management
  (c) Integration with Mobile phone
  (d) Precise Timing
  (e) Mapping & Geodetic Data Capture
  (f) Navigation for hikers & travelers
  (g) Visual & Voice Navigation
  (h) Terrestrial, Aerial & Marine Navigation
- With IRNSS in place, India in an elite group of nations possessing such a system will not only improve India's navigation, security. Self - reliance but-will also improve India's Credibility & Position in the International Arena.

Q.5. Why is India taking keen interest in the Arctic region? (10)

Important Points for Answer:
- *Introduction on importance of Arctic region.*
- *Importance of arctic region for India*
- *Conclusion*

Answer: Arctic Region, the enormous area around the North Pole spreading over 1/6th of the earth's landmass is increasingly being affected by external global forces – environmental, commercial & strategic & in turn is poised to play an increasingly greater role in shaping the course of world affairs.

India's engagement with Arctic region dates back to nearly a decades when it signed the treaty between Norway, USA Denmark, France, Italy, Japan, Netherland, Great Britain & Ireland called as 'Svalbard Treaty' in Feb 1920 in Paris.

Since then, India has been closely following developments in the Arctic region in the light of new opportunities & challenges emerging for itself & international community due to GW induced melting of Arctic's ice caps.

Today India's interest in the Arctic region are based on the following 4 pillars:

1. **Scientific** : With India's scientific base 'Himadri' set up in the Arctic Region in 2007, India is poised to carry out studies in disciplines like Glaciology, Atmospheric Science & Biological Sciences. Moreover, with a view to carry out comprehensive assessment of flora & fauna & their response to Anthropogenic activities.
2. **Environmental** : India initiated its Arctic Research Program with thrust on climate change in circumpolar north.

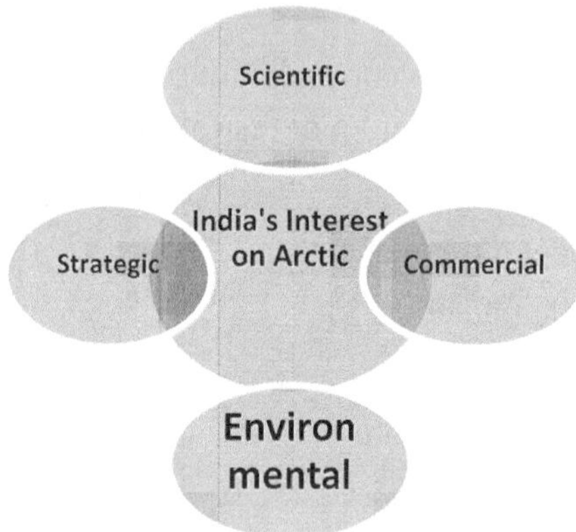

Following objectives are:

- To study the relation between Arctic climate & its effect on Indian monsoon & affecting ocean currents.
- To study sea ice using satellite data to estimate the effect on Global Warming.
- To study emission of GHG like Methane released due to thawing of permafrost regional.

3. **Commercial** : Arctic region is thought to account for 13% of undiscovered oil, 30% of undiscovered natural gas, 20% of undiscovered natural gas liquids. Hence, several nations are eyeing for dominance of resources.
4. **Strategic** : The melting of Arctic's ice opens up several new sea routs thereby reducing distance between Asian Poportion & northern Europe by 40% rather than transporting through Middle East. Countries like Russia, Canada, USA will, dominate over resources & sea routes which will dramatically change world affairs. With India receiving its Observer status to the Arctic council in 2013, & seminar held by Carnegie India between India & Finland, India is committed to contribute to deliberations of the council & to develop a safe, stable & secure Arctic.

Q.6. Define mantle plume and explain its role in plate tectonics. (10)

Important Points for Answer:
- *Introduction on mantle plume.*
- *Role of mantle plume in plate tectonics.*
- *Conclusion*

Answer: Hot spot volcanism is unique because it does not occur at the boundaries of Earth's tectonic plates, where all other volcanism occurs. Instead it occurs at abnormally hot centers known as mantle plumes. Mantle plumes are exceptionally hot areas fixed deep below the Earth's crust.

At least 122 hot spots have been active in the past 10 m.y. Several of them lie on mid-oceanic ridges or close to them. The most prominent are Iceland, Azores and Tristan da Cunha

Role of Mantle plumes:

1. On the movement of Plates

Mantle plumes are one of the mechanisms for the movement of plates. As the mantle plumes diverge beneath the plates they exert an extensional force. This extensional force causes the plates to be stretched and finally to be ruptured. The convection currents thus carry the plates with themselves. This was the way Africa got ruptured and its moving away in two different directions along the East African Rift Valley.

2. On the Continents

1. As the plume reaches the lithosphere, it spreads out laterally doming surficial zones of the Earth and moving them along in the directions of radial flow. This causes Epeirogenic movement.

The centre of the Afar triangle in Ethiopia is one site of plume that flowed upward and outward carrying the Arabian, African, and Somali plates and moved away from the centre of the triangle. They are also probably capable of causing surface uplift over areas in excess of 100kms across, both by the direct effects of heating of the lithosphere and by the associated thickening of the crust through the addition of enormous quantities of igneous material.

2. On the continents, mantle plumes have probably been responsible for generating voluminous and extensive accumulations of Basalt flows, such as those of the Karoo (South Africa) and the Deccan (India), many of which are located at passive margins and were thus originally close to sites of continental breakup.

3. On the continents the manifestation of Mantle plume is best seen in Cosgrove Volcanic chain in Australia.

4. Mantle plume location beneath Yellowstone national Park has been thinning North America for sometime, and is likely to thin the whole of surface causing it to open to spew the underlying volcano.

3. On the Oceans

On the oceans, mantle plumes create lines of large volcanoes (such as the Hawaiian chain) if the overlying plate is moving with respect to the plume. As the oceanic plate is moves over a hot spot, successive eruptions can produce a linear series of peaks or seamounts on the moving crustal plate. In such a series, the youngest peak is above the hot plume and the seamounts increase in age as the distance from the hot spot increases.

In this manner, inactive cones were linearly arranged (also showing direction of plate movement) but the end that is still over the hot spot continues to be active.

Q.7. What are the consequences of spreading of 'Dead Zones' on marine ecosystem? (10)

Important Points for Answer:
- *Introduction on Dead Zone.*
- *Consequences of spreading of 'Dead Zones' on marine ecosystem.*
- *Conclusion*

Answer: Dead Zone is an area in water body that contains little or no oxygen (or they are hypoxic) in bottom and near-bottom water. Mostly they occur naturally but it can be caused by excessive nutrient pollution from human activities coupled with other factors. They are well-known off western coasts of North and South America, off coast of Namibia and off west coast of India in Arabian Sea.

In recent times, warming of the atmosphere through climate change is predicted to lead expansion of 'dead zones' in the ocean.

In dead zone area most marine life either dies, or, if they are mobile such as fish, leave the area. Habitats that would normally be teeming with life become, essentially, **biological deserts**.

One of the largest dead zones forms in the Gulf of Mexico every spring. Nutrients such as nitrogen flow from North America's Corn Belt through streams and rivers before ending up in the Gulf.

The dead zones or Oxygen Minimum Zones (OMZ) in the Arabian Sea have been growing in size. It is the thickest and the most intense OMZ among the world's oceans and covers an area of around two million sq km.

Q.8. "Caste system is assuming new identities and associational forms. Hence, caste system cannot be eradicated in India." Comment. (10)

Important Points for Answer:
- *Introduce prevalence of caste in ancient and contemporary India*
- *Discuss causes for such a manifestation---Constitutional, Political, Social, Economical*
- *Conclude with drawbacks and measure needed to mitigate them*

Answer: The caste system, with its societal stratification and social restrictions, continues to have a major impact in the country. Belying popular perception, caste based inequality is prevalent in cities too along with villages in India.

The causes for caste -based inequalities in cities are numerous -

- Same caste marriages or endogamy- Despite spread in education and awareness, marriages are still based on caste identities. This perpetuates the caste hierarchies.

- Limited occupational mobility - Caste based occupations are being pursued generations after generations, which does not help in blurring the caste lines.
- Limited social mobility - Ingrained attitude with orthodoxy does not help either. Class mobility (socio-economic status) and social mobility (caste based) do have little synergies and caste identities continue to sway social discourse.
- Concentration of means of production and wealth- It has been observed that the wealth and job creation is still in hands of people from upper/dominant castes.
- Positive discrimination/reservation: This system too has, in some way, strengthened caste system.
- Lack of awareness among lower castes about their rights - little awareness about constitutional safeguards and legal provisions in the lower castes has resulted in the perpetual dis-empowerment of these sections.

Because of the same, many adverse consequences (of inequality) are visible in cities -

- Inequality in terms of access to schooling/education and health leads to perpetual poverty and dis-empowerment of the disadvantaged sections.
- Ghettoization /residential segregation specially of SCs/STs results in less social intercourse and thus, weakens social cohesion.
- Unequal access to basic amenities (water, sanitation) gives way to substandard life.
- Unequal income levels and wealth in longer term fuel social tension which if left unchecked, may threaten social and political stability of the country.
- Caste based politics specially in U.P and Bihar is also a consequence.

Thus, we should strive towards unshackling the caste barriers by favorable social ,political, legal and economic actions so that we move towards a more inclusive society devoid of social cleavages based on caste and inequalities.

Q.9. 'Despite implementation of various programmes for eradication of poverty by the government in India, poverty still exists'. Explain by giving reasons. (10)

Important Points for Answer:
- *Introduce and list the failure of some important poverty eradication programs since independence*
- *Highlight challenges of the face of poverty, its multiple-facets.*
- *Give suggestions for a future social change*

Answer: Poverty is the inability of people to live their lives as per their wishes and potential. Poverty is construed mainly in an economic dimension. But that is a limited approach. A broader approach is needed which considers poverty from economic, social and political dimensions to effectively tackle it. Behavioral economics has added another dimension to poverty which is mindset. Before we analyse what causes poverty, it is essential to understand that the reason for finding the cause is to tackle and resolve it to alleviate poverty. Hence, a cause which is broad is a better tool than a narrow approach.

Mindset is a cause because it is assumed that rational choices by people accompanied by their skills and hard work can make them overcome poverty. Accordingly, people are in poverty because they make irrational choices. They spend more instead of saving. They consume unwarranted and unnecessary goods instead of essential ones. They do not plan Long term but reap short term gains. They do not invest in productive and sustainable assets but temporary goods. This approach recommends government to focus on changing people's mindset and aid them in making right decisions. Such an approach is not appropriate because it has an inherent assumption that poor have low mental capacity. It is an indirect way of telling that rich are rich because they are smart and intelligent but poor are poor because of their low IQ. Moreover, such approach makes us concentrate entirely on the poor leaving the capitalists and rich out if the poverty debate.

A CSR initiative wouldn't have been if such approach is followed. Additionally, it moves us away from the other causes such as persisting inequality, the high risk environment of the poor where unexpected changes in weather or market put them in a poverty trap, the structural issues of poor education, health facilities etc. The structural approach is broader, it can be easily monitored and evaluated and it puts the responsibility on all stakeholders. Such a broad approach is needed, hence it's not mindset but the market which is the main cause.

Q.10. How the Indian concept of secularism different from the western model of secularism? Discuss. (10)

Important Points for Answer:

- *Define the concept of secularism and its origin*
- *Elaborate on the difference by briefing the context of Western and Indian society.*
- *Conclusion*

Answer: ***Secularism :***

The separation of religion and state is the foundation of secularism. It ensures religious groups don't interfere in affairs of state, and the state doesn't interfere in religious affairs.

Indian model is positive that is no complete separation of state from religion. State can interfare in religion for social reforms Restrictions on right to religion.

State deal with different religion with different faction within religion Society is deeply religious but polity is secular.

Financial and other help to religion by state Western concept is negative that is complete separation if state and religion.

French model: society is religious so complete separation is possible Prohibition of religion symbol on educational institutions.

Ban on burkha, tarban and skullcap - Jew etc French model is on freedom from religion.

American model: Compete freedom of religion of individual Religion neutrality is expected from government servant No help from state to religion Less regulation by state to religion.

Section–B

Time Allowed : Three Hours *Maximum Marks : 250*

Q.11. The Bhakti movement received a remarkable re-orientation with the advent of Sri Chaitanya Mahaprabhu. Discuss. (15)

Important Points for Answer:
- *Introduce by a brief sketch of Bhakti movement*
- *Chaitanya movement and its unique features*
- *Conclude briefly*

Answer: The greatest saint of the Bhakti movement was Shri Chaitanya, popularly known as Gouranga Mahaprabhu. He was born in 1486 A.D. at Navadweep in West Bengal. His childhood name was Nimai or Biswambhar Mishra .At the age of twenty two he came in contact with a saint named Ishwar Puri at Gaya who initiated him with hymns of Lord Krishna. In 1510, at the age of twenty four, he renounced the world and became a sanyasi. His name was changed from Nimai to Shri Chaitanya and went on pilgrimage to various places like Dwarka, Vrindavan and Mathura.

Chaitanya was an exponent of the Radha-Krishna cult .Chaitanya's teachings centred round 'love'–from intense human love to divine love. He opened the doors of divine love to all by chanting and singing the glories of Krishna in the form of Kirtans. Kirtan is not merely a religious song, but a feeling of ecstasy emanating from love and devotion, accompanied by singing and dancing of the highest spiritual order when one can feel the presence of Almighty. In fact, Chaitanya believed that by singing Kirtan alone one can realise God, because it transports the mind from the material world to the divine world.

Chaitanya was a champion of social liberation. He denounced caste system and stood for the universal brotherhood of man. Chaitanya died in 1533 in the premises of Jagannath temple at Puri while singing kirtan. His followers believed that Shri Chaitanya merged with Lord Jagannath whom he considered to be the embodiment of Krishna. Goswamis of Vrindavan were his prominent disciples who carried forward their master's philosophy. Chaitanya's teachings and message of love still remain a great source of spiritual inspiration to the people of eastern India in particular

Q.12. Discuss whether formation of new states in recent times is beneficial or not for the economy of India. (15)

Important Points for Answer:
- *Briefly write about re-organisation of states in India*
- *Illustrate with examples economic benefits of smaller state recently carved.*
- *Illustrate with examples economic drawbacks associated with smaller states*
- *Conclusion*

Answer: The formation of Chhattisgarh, Jharkhand and Uttarakhand after years of struggle against injustice and exploitation had nourished hopes of democracy, but these were belied because:

- Representatives of these regions colluded with national parties prioritising identity politics over the appeals and struggles for justice of its own people.
- Tribal, SCs AND STs have been victims of exploitation, discrimination, forceful evictions, denial of rights and land grabbing even after formation of autonomous states.
- The Forest rights act 2006,PESA act, 5TH schedule provisions, land reform acts, redistribution and decentralisation initiatives empowering Gram Sabha have been only partially implemented.
- Also the real empowerment comes from devolution of power to local bodies, which has not happened.
- The parties in parent state and the issues thereof still have a large bearing on domestic politics
- Often Tribe Advisory Council and Gram Sabhas are not in consonance over issues like resources
- There are vested interests in keeping the people illiterate, unemployed etc. as most of these regions are minerals rich and many big corporates eye these regions.
- Many welfare schemes not properly implemented due to distance and awareness reasons. Tribal are not aware of their Constitutional rights

Were objectives achieved?

- The states of Jharkhand and Chhattisgarh are mineral and resource regions. despite this both regions suffer from acute poverty, illiteracy, malnutrition and unemployment.
- This is because locals don't get due share in licensing, mining, royalty and profits
- Political instability, immoral defections(e.g. -in Uttarakhand),vested interests(e.g.-coal scam), horse-trading and repeated on-off President's rule(e.g.- in Jharkhand) prevents continuity and predictability in policies adversely affecting citizen welfare.
- Persistent LWE, thereafter CRPFs operation and then retaliation have left state citizenry in a crossfire and a constant spinoff

To create more decentralisation and deepening of democracy, the empowerment of local bodies is required which is not comprehensive. For example State Finance Commission is irregular. Mining rights and corruption of government officials have often clashed. Large displacement of people happens and land reforms are poor and so are all socio-economic parameters

Thus we need to take multiple measures to ensure grass-roots democracy, rights and entitlements for the poor in these regions if we want an assured and peaceful development of the region

Q.13. Why indentured labour was taken by the British from India to their colonies? Have they been able to preserve their cultural identity over there? (15)

Important Points for Answer:

- *Introduce Briefly about Indentured labour system in 19th century*
- *Underline the reasons for recruiting Indians as Indentured labourers by British*
- *Cultural synthesis of those indentured labourers who settled back and their form of protest*
- *Conclude briefly*

Answer: During British Era a new kind of slavery started in the early 19th century, in which Indians were exported to various parts of the world as Indentured Labour. Indenture Lit. Means a contract binding one party into the service of another for specified term.

Initially the Portuguese were dominating African slave trade.In 17th Century Company received a charter from the king of England for purposes of trade in slaves, the share of the king in the profits from slave trade was fixed at 25 per cent. From 1826 to 1830 more than 3 thousand Indian Laboures Were transported from India to Colonies.

Slavery abolition Act 1833 Abolished Slavery throughout the British Empire. After That Demand for Indian Indentured Laboures Increased Dramatically After the abolition of Slavery in 1834.They Were sent some times in large Numbers, to plantation Colonies Producing High Value crops such as Sugar & Tea in Africa & Caribbean .Many Indians agreed to become Indentured Laboures to Escape the widespread Poverty & Famine in 19th Century. Indentured Labour were recruited to work on Sugar, Cotton & Tea Plantation & Rail Construction projects in Colonies.

Q.14. "The ideal solution of depleting ground water resources in India is water harvesting system." How can it be made effective in urban areas? (15)

Important Points for Answer:
- *Brief introduction on depleting ground water resources in India*
- *Water harvesting as solution to depleting ground water resources in India*
- *Conclusion*

Answer: India with its 2.4% of its total landmass, had blessed with abundant groundwater reserves. But since the last decade, it is decreasing at an alarming rate. Ground water is the world's most extracted raw material supplying and sustaining a range of human activity. Yet, because it is invisible and its supply of ten taken for granted, it is often inadequately acknowledged in policy and debates about preservation of Groundwater reserves.

According to Advanced Centre for Water Resources Development & Management (ACWADAM) report, India is responsible for 25% of the global annual total of GW extracted that creates 60% vulnerability in GWR across the country. Hence, a major solution for the depletion of GWR is Rain water Harvesting technique.

Causes of Depletion of Ground Water Reserves:

(1) Ignorance

(2) Green Revolution Excessive Irrigation

(3) Over Exploitation

(4) Surface –Run off

(5) Excessive Use of Fertilizers

(6) Wastage Uncertain rainfall

(7) Pollution

Rain water harvesting is a technique or strategy for the collection of rainwater and storing it in the right way for future use. Various techniques can be used for RWH like Rooftop Rainwater Harvesting, Plunging Watershed to avoid surface run-offs. Recharge Pit, use of Abandon wells etc.

Rooftop rainwater harvesting is an effective measure in urban areas for recharging aquifers.

The water so conserved would infiltrate and percolate raising groundwater level and help in increasing soil moisture and ultimately address the issues of water scarcity in urban areas.

The following Ware some of the techniques which can increase the efficiency of Water Harvesting in urban areas :-

(1) Diversion of surface run-off or roof top rainwater stored in tanks through existing wells, borewells or by constructing new wells, shafts or spreading basins in catchment areas.

(2) Roof top rainwater harvesting system should be made mandatory in urban areas. Recently, NGT passed such an order for Delhi University schools & colleges.

(3) By amending buildings byelaws as undertaken by TN Govt.

(4) By spreading awareness generation system of incentives & prizes as undertaken by Paani Foundation & MH Govt.

(5) Listing of names of organization & people related to water wastage etc. With technologies in place, this situation esp. in urban areas calls for the urgent need for community based groundwater management & understanding the importance and maintenance of aquifers that hold & supply groundwater

Q.15. Defining blue revolution, explain the problems and strategies for pisciculture development in India. (15)

Important Points for Answer:

- *Brief introduction on blue revolution*
- *Problems of pisciculture development in India*
- *Strategies of pisciculture development in India*
- *Conclusion*

Answer: Blue Revolution or the Neel Kranti Mission was launched in 1960 with a view to enhance Fish Production and achieve economic prosperity of the country as well as contribute towards food and Nutritional security through full potential utilization of water resources for fisheries development in a sustainable manner ,keeping in view the bio-security & environment concerns.

India is the second largest producer of fishes in the world after china with 7517km long coastline, India has a huge potential in developing fisheries and eventually the economy.

Following are some of the objectives of the mission: (1) To fully tap the fish potential of the country both in the inland and marine sector and triple the production by 2020.

(2) To transform the sector as a modern industry with special focus on new technologies and processes.

(3) To ensure participation of fishers & fish farmers to increase productivity.

(4) To enhance food and nutritional security of the country.

Blue Revolution encompasses all the schemes that provides focused development & management of fiheries, covering inland fisheries, aqua culture, deep sea fishing ,pisciculture undertaken by NFDB(National Fisheries Development Board).

Though the vision and the objectives will enhance Fishiness development but there are certain issues for pisciculture development that needs to be addressed :

(1) Pollution of inland and coastal waters degrades the ecosystem hampering the quality and quantity of Fishes.

(2) Lack of cold storage and post- harvest facilities further degrades the pisiculture development.

(3) Luck of technology induction and technical know-how to maximize the production.

(4) Lack of financial credit assistance supplied by small land/pond holdings which acts as a hurdle for fisheries development.

(5) Improper or lack of value addition to the output that can scale up pisciculture.

(6) Lack of regulatory market facilities.

Following are some of the mitigation strategies to Enhance fisheries development.

(1) Protection of the coastal regions for abetment of pollution like CRZ.

(2) Stricter policies & norms to protect Coastal Costal fragile region.

(3) Setting up of basic infrastructure like cold storage facilities, availability of fish food etc.

(4) Creation of institutional structures like marketing Societies with fishermen.

(5) Improving skill development in piscuculture i.e., National Skill India Mission Should support Blue Revolution, Gradation, standardization and Branding of fish & fishery products.

(6) Creation of market info. System with application of ICT tools.

With such strategies in place, and its proper implementation & execution, India could be the world's largest producer in near future.

Q.16. What is the significance of Industrial Corridors in India? Identifying industrial corridors, explain their main characteristics. (15)

Important Points for Answer:
- *Brief introduction on industrial corridor in India*
- *Significance of Industrial Corridors in India*
- *Industrial corridors in India and their main characteristics.*
- *Conclusion*

Answer: An industrial corridor is basically a corridor comprising of multi-modal transport services that would pass through the states as main artery. An industrial corridor aims to create an area with a cluster of manufacturing or other industry. Such corridors are often created in areas that have preexisting infrastructure, such as ports, highways and railroads. These modalities are arranged such that an "arterial" modality, such as a highway or railroad, receives "feeder" roads or railways.

Significance of Industrial Corridors:

It is argued that benefits of industrial development should be reaped by all states and regions so as to avoid developmental divide between states.

(1) The establishment of NMIZ in a scattered manner along the industrial corridor across the length of the state would prevent distress migration and provide people with job opportunities close to their dwelling place.

(2) it will prevent concentration of industries in one particular location which exploited the environment beyond its carrying capacity and caused environmental degradation.

(3) As efficiency creeps in India's industrial production structure due to improved transportation system and health labour force, the production costs would come down

(4) The production of export surplus would generate employment opportunities and raise per capita incomes.

(5) Moreover, people would find job opportunities close to their homes and would not have to migrate to far-off places thereby preserving family as an institution. This will also increase social integration in the country.

(6) The spread effects of industrial corridors in socio-economic terms are many such as setting up of industrial townships, educational institutions, roads, railways, airports, hospitals that will generate employment and raise standard of living.

Characteristics:

(1) Industrial Corridors recognize the inter-dependence of various sectors of the economy and offer effective integration between industry and infrastructure leading to overall economic and social development. Industrial corridors constitute world class infrastructure.

(2) Industrial corridor provides opportunities for private sector investment.

(3) Decreased transportation and communications costs, improved delivery time and reduction in inventory cost.

Q.17. Mention core strategies for the transformation of aspirational districts in India and explain the nature of convergence, collaboration and competition for its success. (15)

Important Points for Answer:

- *Brief introduction on transformation of aspirational districts in India*
- *Core strategies for the transformation of aspirational districts in India*
- *Convergence, collaboration and competition for success of aspirational districts*
- *Conclusion*

Answer: Aspirational Districts Programme: The 'Transformation of Aspirational Districts' programme aims to quickly and effectively transform these districts. The broad contours of the programme are Convergence (of Central & State Schemes), Collaboration (of Central, State level

'Prabhari' Officers & District Collectors), and Competition among districts driven by a mass Movement. With States as the main drivers, this program will focus on the strength of each district, identify low-hanging fruits for immediate improvement, measure progress, and rank districts.

The Government is committed to raising the living standards of its citizens and ensuring inclusive growth for all – "Sabka Saath Sabka Vikas". To enable optimum utilization of their potential, this program focuses closely on improving people's ability to participate fully in the burgeoning economy. Health & Nutrition, Education, Agriculture & Water Resources, Financial Inclusion & Skill Development, and Basic Infrastructure are this programme's core areas of focus. After several rounds of consultations with various stakeholders, 49 key performance indicators have been chosen to measure progress of the districts. Districts are prodded and encouraged to fist catch-up with the best district within their state, and subsequently aspire to become one of the best in the country, by competing with, and learning from others in the spirit of competitive & cooperative federalism.

NITI Aayog in partnership with the Government of Andhra Pradesh has created a dashboard for monitoring the real-time progress of the districts. District Information Officers underwent training on March 23, 2018 on how to enter data to the dashboard and generate MIS (Management Information System) reports. On April 1, 2018 districts will start entering data. Beginning May 2018, districts will be ranked based on progress made ('delta ranking') on a real-time basis. The dashboard will be open to the public to monitor the progress of the aspirational districts.

Q.18. 'Women's movement in India has not addressed the issues of women of lower social strata.' Substantiate your view. (15)

Important Points for Answer:

- *Introduce issues raised by Women's movement in last decade.*
- *Identify problems unique to women among lower strata*
- *Identify reasons for not getting attention*
- *Give progressive measures for a social change*

Answer: Women's movement in India has come a long way since the humble efforts of Raja Ram Mohan Roy and Ishwar Chand Vidyasagar to fight for women's rights.

In their time, it was the upper social strata who were subjected to inhumane practices like Sati. However, the scenario seems to have changed today. Women of lower social strata either belonging to lower castes, minority religion or economically backward regions continue to face hardships.

Political sphere: Elite women with influence occupying offices in governments, panchayats and other bodies.

Economic sphere: Glass ceiling breaking in corporations like google, microsoft. But the wage gap remains prominent for semi-skilled and unskilled workers.

Social sphere: The worst forms of Patriarchy is more prominent in the lower social strata. Haryana with primarily agricultural economy had the poorest child sex ratio.

Education sphere: Access to both lower and higher education remains limited.

Women empowerment can happen when everyone works towards it—the government, society, families, and individuals.

The government programs targeted towards women empowerment have started to bear fruits. Beti Bachao Beti Padhao, Dhanlaxmi scheme and others have acted as catalysts to promote behavior and mindset changes.

The society should be forthcoming to support women. The story of Phogat Sisters tells us how women can bring accolades to the country. All started with a father, an individual questioning established norms.

Q.19. 'Globalisation is generally said to promote cultural homogenisation but due to this cultural specificities appear to be strengthened in the Indian society.' Elucidate.

Important Points for Answer:

- *Introduce how globalisation promotes homogenisation through causes and examples*
- *Identify unique cultural reactions called "Glocalistion" through current examples and give reasons.*
- *Conclusion*

Answer: Globalisation refers to the increases interconnected due to technological advancements leading to a shrinking of time and space and flattening of the world. Though thought of as an economic phenomena, it is now accepted to impact all spheres of life – political, social and cultural.

In its initial days, globalisation was equated with westernisation or americanisation which meant that the culture of the west was spreading across the globe. One could travel to new york and new delhi and find them to be similar in almost all spheres including culture. Thus globalisation was supposed to have a homogenizing tendency.

However, the relationship between globalisation and culture is a complex one. Globalisation has not been able to replace old existing cultures. Instead evidence suggests that globalisation has strengthened them and even modified them.

1. Indian cuisines traveling to the west. Indian food restaurants are now available all around the world. Indian curries and masalas have also become a part of our soft power diplomacy.

2. Ancient indian practices like yoga and ayurveda being adopted around the globe. People are now looking for the most authentic experience.

3. With the advent of ecommerce, global value chains and internet, local arts and crafts are also. Top hotels of the world are buying handwoven Indian designs sourced from traditional communities. Ikkat, block painting, etc designs are gaining popularity world over.

4. Traditional Indian forms of music and communities like the Manganiars are being studied in the Berkeley School of Music.

5. Contemporary cinema Bollywood has increased its fan following across the globe.

At the same time, local cultures are modifying western cultures. McDonalds serving a menu catering to Indian taste buds is a case in point. This phenomena has been termed as 'glocalisation'

From the above, it can be seen that the relationship between globalisation and culture is complex with each impacting the other. The above examples indeed prove that cultural specificities appear to be strengthened in the Indian society.

Q.20. 'Communalism arises either due to power struggle or relative deprivation.' Argue by giving suitable illustrations. (15)

> **Important Points for Answer:**
> - *Define the concept. Explain vulnerability of Indian society due to its diversity.*
> - *Give arguments in support or against*
> - *Suggest measures for its mitigation*

Answer: Communalism in the Indian context refers to the ideology which states that society is divided into different religious communities whose interests differ from, and at times oppose, each other. Historically, Indian society has been regarded as a melting pot of various religions that have been tolerant of each other. However, the British policy of divide and rule laid the foundations of communalism which the Indian state has found hard to tackle post-independence.

Communalism indeed arises due to power struggle and relative deprivation

Power struggle: Power struggle between political parties leading to vote bank politics with each trying to garner votes based on identity markers such as religion. Eg. Congress and BJP both trying to appease Muslims and in turn strengthening the Hindu Muslim divide. -Between majority and minority groups. Eg. Sikhs and Hindus.

Relative deprivation

Deprivation makes groups to fight for limited resources.

Case with Assamese and Non-Assamese. Deprivation of the native groups led to movements throughout the state.

Deprivation makes it easier to influence a group. Rather than self-introspect they blame others for their condition. It causes them to support anyone who can help them marginally move above their misery.

Vice President Ansari had pointed out the relative deprivation among Muslims to be the biggest causes of communal tension.

Long-Term Remedy for Communalism

1. There is a need to initiate the process of de-communalization of the people at all levels, say, by exposing communal assumptions, by explaining to them the socio-economic and political roots of communalism, and by letting them know that what the communalists project as problems are not the real problem and what they suggest as remedies are not the real remedies.
2. Communalism of state and of the political elite in power has to be checked because it leads to inaction against communal violence and covert or overt political and

ideological support to communalism by the state apparatuses, including the media under state control.

3. Communalization of civil society also needs to be checked because it leads to more communal roots and other forms of communal violence. It is here that intellectuals, political parties, and voluntary organizations can be the most effective.
4. The role of education, particularly value-oriented education, both in schools and colleges is important in preventing communal feelings.
5. The media can prove to be significant in preventing communal feelings. Communal press can be banned and legal action can be taken against communal writers.
6. The ideology that economic development, industrialization, the growth of capitalism and the growth of the working class would automatically weaken and ultimately eliminate communalism should not be overplayed.

SOLVED PAPERS

PAPER–II

Section–A

Time Allowed : Three Hours *Maximum Marks : 150*

Q.1. In the light of recent controversy regarding the use of Electronic Voting Machines (EVM), what are the challenges before the Election Commission of India to ensure the trustworthiness of elections in India?

> **Important Points for Answer:**
> - *Brief introduction of EVM and controversy surrounding it.*
> - *Express the challenges before the ElectionCommission to ensure the trustworthiness of elections in India.*
> - *Conclusion*

Answer: The Election Commission (EC) recently conducted a meeting with all major political parties. The objectives of this meeting are making the electoral process more transparent, inclusive and credible.

In this context, there were three major demands:

1. giving up on electronic voting machines (EVMs) and moving back to paper ballots
2. linking voter identification cards to Aadhaar
3. cap on election expenditure of political parties

Tussle with EVMs: Most of the parties flagged the issue of malfunctioning of electronic voting machines (EVMs). EVMs have typically been questioned by parties after losing elections. However, it is claimed that EVMs are tamper-proof. The provision of voter-verifiable paper audit trail (VVPAT) machines has further enhanced EVMs' credibility. Besides, a return to the ballot paper system would also not be advisable. As, it would come with huge environmental costs and logistical issues.

Demanding Aadhaar linkage: The demand for linking Aadhaar to voter ID cards is prompted by concerns about the existence of ghost voters. E.g. the Congress has complained about 6 million fake voters in the electoral rolls of Madhya Pradesh. It is true that Aadhaar would go a long way in eliminating these fake voters. But notably, Aadhaar itself is not a proof of citizenship. Moreover, there are privacy concerns related to Aadhaar. So mandating it as the final adjudicator for voting rights is questionable

Q.2. Whether National Commission for Scheduled Castes (NCSC) can enforce the implementation of constitutional reservation for the Scheduled Castes in the religious minority institutions? Examine.

Important Points for Answer:

- *Brief introduction about the National Commission for Scheduled Castes (NCSC) and Religious minority institutions.*
- *Constitutional provisions for safeguard of minority rights and powers of NCSC*
- *Conclusion*

Answer: SC Ruling That Minority Rights Cannot be Waived is a Boost for Minority Institutions The landmark judgment will have implications on the minority character case of Aligarh Muslim University pending in the Supreme Court as well as Jamia's case in the Delhi high court. In any democratic society, the constitutional impulse for giving some special rights to minorities stems not from the desire to create a 'pampered' or 'appeased' section of population but to give to them a sense of security and confidence.

The issue of minorities in a plural and diverse polity like India's evolves from the basic reality of tension and dialectics between the unit and the whole or the individual and society. Today, minority institutions are coming under threat with the BJP-led government changing longstanding official policy on, for example, the minority character of Aligarh Muslim University (AMU) and Jamia Millia Islamia. The erstwhile UPA government had gone in appeal to the Supreme Court against the Allahabad high court decision in Naresh Agrawal (2005) in which it denied AMU's minority character and struck down a few provisions of the 1981 amendment to the Aligarh Muslim University Act, 1920.

SC/ST students study in AMU

As per the data collected by the National Institutional Ranking framework (NIRF) in 2016-17, the total number of students studying in various undergraduate and postgraduate courses at AMU stood at 17,259. Of these, 3,180 students hail from 'socially challenged categories (SC, ST and OBC), whereas 14,011 are from 'economically backward classes'. Therefore, there are a sizeable number of both socially backward as well as economically backward class students studying in AMU, albeit lower, but in the whole scheme of things the university is playing a significant role in educating the underprivileged youth. The reservation policy, the law and the rationale behind exemption of minority educational institutions has passed the Supreme Court's test. We as a society must recognise those reasons and especially so in constitutional offices.

Q.3. Under what circumstances can the Financial Emergency be proclaimed by the President of India? What consequences follow when such a declaration remains in force?

Important Points for Answer:

- *Brief introduction on emergency*
- *Elaborate on circumstances under which financial emergency is proclaimed*
- *Consequences of financial emergency*
- *Conclusion*

Answer: Article 360 in The Constitution Of India 1949.

(1) If the President is satisfied that a situation has arisen whereby the financial stability or credit of India or of any part of the territory thereof is threatened, he may by a Proclamation make a declaration to that effect

(2) A Proclamation issued under clause (1)

(a) may be revoked or varied by a subsequent Proclamation;

(b) shall be laid before each House of Parliament;

(3) During the period any such Proclamation as is mentioned in clause (1) is in operation, the executive authority of the Union shall extend to the giving of directions to any State to observe such canons of financial propriety as may be specified in the directions, and to the giving of such other directions as the President may deem necessary and adequate for the purpose.

(4) Notwithstanding anything in this Constitution

(a) any such direction may include

(i) a provision requiring the reduction of salaries and allowances of all or any class of persons serving in connection with the affairs of a State;

(ii) a provision requiring all Money Bills or other Bills to which the provisions of Article 207 apply to be reserved for the consideration of the President after they are passed by the Legislature of the State;

Q.4. Why do you think the committees are considered to be useful for parliamentary work? Discuss, in this context, the role of the Estimates Committee.

Important Points for Answer:

- *Significance of Parliamentary Committees)*
- *Role of Estimates committee*
- *Challenges before Parliamentary Committees*
- *Conclusion*

Answer: The Parliament has to perform complex and varied kind of functions. A committee can be called a Parliamentary committee if it is appointed or elected by the house or nominated by the Speaker or the Chairman; it has a secretariat provided by the Lok Sabha/Rajya Sabha secretariat.

The various Standing Committees of the Parliament are mentioned below:

(1) Public Accounts Committee

(2) Estimate committee

(3) Comittee on public undertakings

Committee On Estimates: The Committee on Estimates, constituted for the first time in 1950, is a Parliamentary Committee consisting of 30 members, elected every year by the Lok Sabha from amongst its Members. The Chairperson of the Committee is appointed by the Speaker from amongst its members. A Minister cannot be elected as a member of the Committee and if a member after selection to the Committee is appointed a Minister, the member ceases to be a Member of the Committee from the date of such appointment.

Term of Office: The term of office of the Committee is one year.

Functions: The functions of the Committee on Estimates are:

(a) to report what economies, improvements in organisation, efficiency or administrative reform, consistent with the policy underlying the estimates may be effected;

(b) to suggest alternative policies in order to bring about efficiency and economy in administration;

(c) to examine whether the money is well laid out within the limits of the policy implied in the estimates; and

(d) to suggest the form in which the estimates shall be presented to Parliament. The Committee does not exercise its functions in relation to such Public Undertakings as are allotted to the Committee on Public Undertakings by the Rules of Procedure and Conduct of Business of Lok Sabha or by the Speaker.

Q.5. "The Comptroller and Auditor General (CAG) has a very vital role to play." Explain how this is reflected in the method and terms of his appointment as well as the range of powers he can exercise.

Important Points for Answer:
- *Significance of method and terms of appointment of CAG*
- *Powers of CAG and Constitutional vitality of the post*
- *Conclusion*

Answer: Chapter V under Part V of the Indian Constitution deals with the Comptroller and Auditor General of India (CAG). CAG is responsible for auditing the accounts of the Union and State governments and public sector organizations, and for maintaining the accounts of State governments. The reports of the CAG are taken into consideration by the Public Accounts Committees. CAG enjoys the same status as a judge of Supreme Court of India.

Article 149 : Duties and powers of the Comptroller and Auditor-General

The Comptroller and Auditor-General shall perform such duties and exercise such powers in relation to the accounts of the Union and of the States and of any other authority or body as may be prescribed by or under any law made by Parliament and, until provision in that behalf is so made, shall perform such duties and exercise such powers in relation to the accounts of the Union and of the States as were conferred on or exercisable by the Auditor-General of India immediately before the commencement of this Constitution in relation to the accounts of the Dominion of India and of the Provinces respectively.

Article 150: Form of accounts of the Union and of the States

The accounts of the Union and of the States shall be kept in such form as the President may, on the advice of the Comptroller and Auditor-General of India, prescribe.

Article 151: Audit reports

(1) The reports of the Comptroller and Auditor-General of India relating to the accounts of the Union shall be submitted to the President, who shall cause them to be laid before each House of Parliament.

(2) The reports of the Comptroller and Auditor-General of India relating to the accounts of a State shall be submitted to the Governor of the State, who shall cause them to be laid before the Legislature of the State.

Q.6. "Policy contradictions among various competing sectors and stakeholders have resulted in inadequate 'protection and prevention of degradation to environment." Comment with relevant illustrations.

> **Important Points for Answer:**
> - *Briefly introduce about policy paralysis*
> - *Discuss about degradation of environment*
> - *Discuss different examples and illustrations*
> - *Conclusion*

Answer: Growing challenges of pollution, water scarcity, global warming, population explosion, ozone depletion, icebergs melting, islands submerging, reduction in food production, increase in diseases etc. have resulted in a new concept called Sustainable development.

Economic development is improving the economy for benefit of humans by various means like increasing food production, infrastructure, industrial output, usage of natural resources etc.

If I am posted as District Collector, I will take following measures for sustainable development.

1. Will Encourage Organic Farming, agro-forestry, and production of Bio-fuels in villages like Gobar gas, ethanol from molasses and will work on ways and means of their usage for vehicles apart from house cooking etc.
2. Will work on collaborating with R&D institutions technologies like laying roads with degradable plastic instead of Coal tar etc.
3. Will work on aspects like recycling used water in Villages through an well integrated drainage system and are fed to agricultural farms or local ponds.
4. Will work with NGOs and Society in eradicating the practices like burning the debris of post-harvest of crops for reducing pollution and particulate matter.
5. Will encourage use of Bicycles even in towns and cities among citizens for improving health and reducing pollution, congestion etc. problems.

It is with active civil society cooperation sustainable development is possible and can be a great way for sustaining human race.

Q.7. Appropriate local community level healthcare intervention is a prerequisite to achieve 'Health for All' in India. Explain.

> **Important Points for Answer:**
> - *Introduction*
> - *Need for the policy*
> - *Government schemes in the health sector*
> - *Briefly explain measures to be taken*
> - *Conclusion*

Answer: Article 47 of Indian constitution says that it shall be the duty of the state to raise the level of nutrition and the standard of living and to improve public health. Health sector policy making in India is extremely challenging and have many obstacles. Despite the Government providing free care in public hospitals the burden of out of pocket expenditure remains quite high.

National Health Mission

The NHM sought to revitalize rural and urban health sectors by providing flexible finances to the State Governments. It comprises of 4 components namely,

- National Rural Health Mission,
- National Urban Health Mission,
- Tertiary Care Programs and
- Human Resources for Health and Medical education.

NHM brought together at National level the two departments of Health and Family welfare. Goevrnment initiative like Ayush, Telemedicine, IT, Involving Community etc.

Q.8. E-governance in not only about utilization of the power of new technology, but also much about critical importance of the 'use value' of information. Explain.

Important Points for Answer:
- *Advantages of new technology*
- *Utility of information*
- *Way forward*

Answer: Citizens contact government for various reasons such as trying to influence public policy, to addressing personal concerns that they have, conducting government transactions, and finding information on benefits and services that government offers. e-Governance is one such channel of public service delivery. E-governance is much more than a technological initiative but is made of a complex set of relationships between the stakeholder's commitment, structured developmental processes and adequate infrastructural resources.

Successful e-governance implementation is about four main components:

- Identification of needs of end-users,
- Business Process Modification, use of IT,
- Government intent.
- Deficiencies in any of these would result in e governance projects failing to achieve their objectives.

According to ARC, achieving the desired results would require full political backing, a determined and resolute approach by all organizations and departments of Government as well as active and constructive participation by the public. It would require providing institutional and physical infrastructure for taking e-Governance initiatives across our cultural and regional diversities and the creation of an environment that would encourage the adoption of ICT. Thus, apart from the technical requirement, success of e-Governance initiatives would depend on capacity building and creating awareness within government and outside it.

Q.9. "India's relations with Israel have, of late, acquired a depth and diversity, which cannot be rolled back." Discuss.

Important Points for Answer:
- *Introduce status of Indo-Israel relations presently and in the past*
- *Elaborate on traditional and new areas of cooperation*
- *Conclusion*

Answer: This is only the second visit by an Israeli prime minister after a gap of 15 years since Ariel Sharon in 2003. The visit is significant especially after India voted in the UN General Assembly last month against recognising Jerusalem as Israel's capital.

Issues: Agriculture and water, cyber security, Trade:$4bn (2016-17) healthcare and security oil and gas, Tourism Technology, Defence, Palestine India has been trying hard to balance its current relationship with Israel with its historical support to the Palestinian cause. This delicate balancing by New Delhi is very necessary and is in India's best interest. Any significant change from India's current stance seems improbable right now. The good thing is that Israel seems to understand India's position, which is a sign of maturity. This could lead to a healthy and strong relationship between these two major powers in the international system.

Q.10. A number of outside powers have entrenched themselves in Central Asia, which is a zone of interest to India. Discuss the implications, in this context, of India's joining the Ashgabat Agreement, 2018.

Important Points for Answer:
- *Introduce importance of central Asia for India*
- *Elaborate on outside powers and their interest in the area*
- *Discuss implications for India joining Ashgabat agreement*
- *Conclusion*

Answer: Ashgabat Agreement:

It is an international multimodal transport and transit corridor between Central Asia and the Persian Gulf, established in 2011. The Agreement was first signed by Uzbekistan, Turkmenistan, Iran, Oman and Qatar. While Qatar subsequently withdrew from the agreement in 2013, Kazakhstan and Pakistan joined the grouping in 2016.

The Ashgabat Agreement came into force in April 2016. Its objective is to enhance connectivity within the Eurasian region and synchronize it with other regional transport corridors, including the International North–South Transport Corridor (INSTC).

Significance of India's entry into Ashgabat:

India's joining of the Ashgabat Agreement makes a greater prospect for enlarging both the operational and practical scope of Chabahar to become a vital gateway and the shortest land route to Central Asia.

Connecting to Afghanistan via Chabahar has been essential for India and it has already sent shipments of wheat to Afghanistan through Chabahar port.

Its accession to the Ashgabat Agreement would enable India to utilise the existing transport and transit corridor to facilitate trade and commercial interactions with the Eurasian region.

In general, joining the Ashgabat Agreement would make it easier for India to reach out to Central Asia which houses strategic and high-value minerals including uranium, copper, titanium, iron ore, etc.

Kazakhstan alone wants to increase its non-oil exports by 50 per cent by 2025, without direct transport access India cannot procure the Central Asian riches needed for its manufacturing economy.

Section–B

Time Allowed : Three Hours *Maximum Marks : 250*

Q.11. Whether the Supreme Court Judgement (July 2018) can settle the political tussle between the Lt. Governor and elected government of Delhi? Examine.

Important Points for Answer:

- *Insight into the Supreme Court Judgement*
- *Analysis of the judgement*
- *Conclusion*

Answer: Supreme Court ends Delhi govt vs L-G power tussle: bA five-judge Bench of the Supreme Court unanimously held that the Lieutenant Governor (LG) of Delhi is bound by the "aid and advice" of the popularly-elected Arvind Kejriwal-led Aam Aadmi Party (AAP) government and both have to work harmoniously with each other. It noted that there is no room for anarchy or absolutism in a democracy.

Chief Justice of India (CJI) Dipak Misra, who wrote the opinion for himself, and Justices A.K. Sikri and A.M. Khanwilkar held that except for issues of public order, police and land, the Lieutenant Governor is bound by the "aid and advice of the Kejriwal government, which has the public mandate."

Every "trivial difference of opinion" between the LG and the NCT government cannot be referred to the President for a decision. The issues referred should be of substantive or national importance. In this regard, the CJI interpreted the phrase "any matter" in the proviso to Article 239AA(4) as not "every matter."

Elected representatives would be reduced to a cipher if 'any matter' in Article 239AA (4) was interpreted as every matter of governance, Justice Chandrachud agreed. "This Constitutional Court would be doing a disservice if an elected government is reduced to a mere form without substance," he wrote.

The CJI wrote that a reference to the President was only an exception and not the general rule. "In this context, even in case of differences of opinion, the LG and the NCT government should act with constitutional morality and trust for each other. The LG cannot act without applying his mind and refer everything to the President."

The NCT government needs only to inform the LG of its "well-deliberated" decisions. The government need not obtain his "concurrence" in every issue of day-to-day governance.

Q.12. How far do you agree with the view that tribunals curtail the jurisdiction of ordinary courts? In view of the above, discuss the constitutional validity and competency of the tribunals in India.

Important Points for Answer:
- *Introduction on Tribunals*
- *Constitutional validity and competency of Tribunals*
- *Conclusion*

Answer: Tribunals, one of the bodies of administrative adjudication in India, have witnessed much debate in the recent years. The tribunals were established with the object of providing a speedy, cheap and decentralised determination of disputes arising out of the various welfare legislations.

Another important reason for the new development was that while the courts were accustomed to dealing with cases primarily according to law, the exigencies of modern administration requires the adjudication of disputes not necessarily on the basis of technical questions of law, but also after considering the policy intentions and the public interest.

Besides, tribunals were also seen as bodies manned by experts who could professionally and fairly deal with the issues which though challengeable in courts of law, yet required technical expertise. The Railway Claims Tribunal, CESTAT ITAT, Labour Tribunals, the Companies Tribunal, various Compensation Tribunals, Revenue Courts of various States, etc., can be cited as examples of such tribunals.

However, increasing tribunalisation which refers to the perception of usurping of certain judicial powers from courts by tribunal, arises from the over interpretation of Article 50 of Indian constitution which deals with separation of judiciary from executive It points out the State shall take steps to separate the judiciary from the executive in the public services of the States.

Recently, the Department of Legal Affairs in the Law Ministry had recently proposed the idea for "possibility of merging the functions of tribunals with some other tribunals" to avoid "overlapping/ identical functions" being discharged by them.

However, not all tribunals are insulated to mainstream judiciary like Rent Control Tribunals, Motor Vehicles Tribunals, Labour Tribunals etc are part of the judiciary and are working better than the independent tribunals. Thus, despite so many concerns, tribunals have been pivotal and effective in addressing disputes in past.

Q.13. Indian and USA are two large democracies. Examine the basic tenets on which the two political systems are based.

Important Points for Answer:
- *Similarities between India and USA*
- *Core features that are similar*
- *Way forward*

Answer: Being the largest democratic countries in the world, both United States and India are based on federalism in their political structure. US became a Federal Republic State by promulgating its constitution in the year 1789; whereas India became a Socialist, Sovereign, Secular, Democratic Republic by formally launching its constitution only in the year 1950.

Similarities between US and India:-

1. Written constitution
2. Bill of Rights and Fundamental Rights
3. Supremacy of the Federal or Union Government
4. Division of Labor and Separation of Powers
5. Powers of Checks and Balances

Differences between the federalisms of US and India:

1. The Constitution of US is more rigid than the Indian Constitution
2. While US has the Presidential form of Government, India has the Parliamentary form of Government
3. Differences between the legislatures of US and India: In India, the lower house or the Lok Sabha is more powerful and its members are directly elected by the people and the members of the Upper house or Rajya Sabha are indirectly elected every two years.
4. Differences in the judicial system between US and India: While the US has an advanced judicial system, India has a rapidly developing judicial system. India has integrated judiciary with.

Supreme Court been given very wide powers, including appellate (Civil and criminal) jurisdiction. The Supreme Court of American has not been given such type of appellate jurisdiction.

1. India has single citizenship for Union and state while in USA there is dual citizenship- one Federal Citizenship- another State Citizenship.
2. In India Center has been residuary powers while in USA States have residuary powers.

Q.14. How is the Finance Commission of India constituted? What do you know about the terms of reference of the recently constituted Finance Commission? Discuss.

Important Points for Answer:
- *Constitution of the Finance Commission of India*
- *Terms of reference of the 15th Finance Commission*
- *Controversial terms in the reference*
- *Conclusion*

Answer: Article 280 provides for FC (a quasi-judicial body) constituted by the President. Finance Commission can make recommendations to the President

(i) Distribution of the taxes to be shared between C&S, allocation & respective shares

(ii) The principles which should govern the Grant-in-Aids by Centre to the states

(iii) The measures need to augment Consolidated Fund of the state

(iv) Any other matters referred to it by the President

The Union Government *with the approval President* of India has constituted 15th Finance Commission which will make recommendations for the five years commencing 1 April 2020 till 31 March 2025.

NK Singh, former bureaucrat and ex-Member of Parliament will be Chairman of 15th Finance Commission.

Terms of Reference:

The Commission will make recommendations on distribution of net proceeds of taxes between Centre and States, the principles which should govern grants-in-aid of revenues of States out of Consolidated Fund of India.

It will also suggest measures needed to augment Consolidated Fund of State to supplement resources of Panchayats and Municipalities in State on basis of recommendations made by Finance Commission of State.

It will also review current status of finance, debt levels, cash balances, deficit and fiscal discipline efforts of Centre and States and recommend fiscal consolidation roadmap for sound fiscal management. While making its recommendations, it will look at resources of Central Government and State Governments for five years commencing on 1st April 2020 on basis of levels of tax and non-tax revenues likely to be reached by 2024-25.

It is imperative for commission to examine implications of GST on finance of the Centre and states. It will look at impact of GST, including payment of compensation for possible loss of revenues for 5 years. It may also consider proposing measurable performance-based incentives for States, at appropriate level of government.

Q.15. Assess the importance of the Panchayat system in India as a part of local government. Apart from government grants, what sources the Panchayats can look out for financing developmental projects?

Important Points for Answer:

- *Introduce Panchayat System in India*
- *Discuss the importance of PRI's*
- *Sources of finance*
- *Measures to strengthen PRIs*
- *Conclusion*

Answer: The 73rd and 74th Amendments passed in 1993, which introduced panchayats and municipalities in the Constitution, reserve one-third of seats for women in these bodies. In some states the reservation in PRIs for women even extended to fifty percent. However, there are many stumbling blocks to the political empowerment of women. For example:

Despite several states extending 50% reservation to women, gender-based discrimination is evident from reports that the elected women representatives acted as mere figureheads, while the real power lied with men, more so in the case of illiterate women. In many parts of India, especially in northern states the husband performs the duties of the women pradhans and gram sabha members in lieu of the women themselves.

Non-cooperation of the male members that they primarily face on the basis of gender discrimination. In many cases when women heads were seen as too assertive or challenging the male-dominated authority, they were humiliated or even killed.

Often, the men of the village do not accord them the respect and regard that is their due. Due to lack of knowledge and information and in some cases illiteracy, very often they have to depend upon the second hand knowledge. Officials take advantage of their inexperience and poor education.

Women are scarcely elected from non-reserved seats. Effective devolution is so uneven and inadequate that oftentimes, even the ablest women are crippled for want of the rightful allocation of functions, finances and functionaries without which effective Panchayati Raj is rendered impossible.

Thus, it is important that rather than just superimposing the rights at the ground level, certain fundamental changes are brought in the socio-economic structures of the village as per the principles of equality and liberty enshrined as fundamental rights in our constitution.

Q.16. Multiplicity of various commissions for the vulnerable sections of the society leads to problems of overlapping jurisdiction and duplication of functions. Is it better to merge all commissions into an umbrella Human Rights Commission? Argue your case.

Important Points for Answer:
- *Safeguards for the vulnerable sections*
- *Advantages of a unified Human Rights Commission*
- *Cons of such a unified body*
- *How to improve present situation*
- *Conclusion*

Answer: The national commissions were formed with the objective to oversee the implementation of human rights and civil liberties. The exercise began in January 1978 with the establishment of a central Minorities Commission, followed by a joint Scheduled Castes and Scheduled Tribes Commission.

The Minorities Commission was eventually rechristened as the National Commission for Minorities (NCM) and placed under an Act of Parliament. National Commission for Women Act was passed and it was set up in January 1992, In quick succession, government decided to set up a National Human Rights Commission (NHRC).

In 2004 Two national commissions one for minority educational institutions and protection of child rights was setup. Union government has conferred constitutional status on the National Backward Classes Commission.

Concerns with the national commissions:

The composition and appointment mechanism for various national commissions widely differ. While the NHRC is headed by a former Chief Justice of India and has two members each from amongst judges and human rights experts, all appointed by a high level statutory committee.

The Chairman and members of the National Commission on Minorities and National Commission for Women are appointed by the government in its unrestricted discretion. While aspirants for the chair and membership of NCM should only be persons of eminence, ability and integrity, the NCW chair is simply to be one committed to the cause of women.

Major implication: The record of successive governments in adhering to the prescribed touchstones of national commissions is disappointing.

Under the noses of these supposedly autonomous national bodies, the situation of citizens' human rights and civil liberties has been moving from bad to worse. All these institutions are maintained with an exorbitant budget and put a hole on the state exchequer and ultimately an unwarranted burden on taxpayers.

Q.17. How far do you agree with the view that the focus on lack of availability of food as the main cause of hunger takes the attention away from ineffective human development policies in India?

Important Points for Answer:
- *Introduce the concept of hunger*
- *Discuss few illustrations*
- *Discuss briefly the ineffectiveness of development policies*
- *Suggest corrective measures*
- *Conclusion*

Answer: Few months back there young girls recently died of starvation in the heart of New Delhi. The death of these children follows a series of reports of alleged starvation deaths over the last six months, mostly from Jharkhand but also from other states such as Karnataka, Chhattisgarh and Uttar Pradesh.

In each of these cases, fact- finding reports and newspaper stories have documented failures of the system in reaching entitlements to the affected families.

Key provisions of NFSA:

The National Food Security Act (NFSA) includes provisions for subsidised grains from the PDS, school meals for school going children, maternity entitlements and supplementary nutrition for young children through anganwadi centres.

In this particular instance, the eldest girl should have been attending school (guaranteed under the Right of Children to Free and Compulsory Education Act) and getting a regular mid-day meal.

The other two children should have been getting supplementary nutrition from an anganwadi centre. A fact-finding report prepared by the Delhi Rozi Roti Adhikar Abhiyan revealed that while these services were available in the area, the girls and their parents did not have access to any of these.

This was presumably because it was more difficult for them to get enrolled as they were migrants and did not have the necessary documents. Even in all other cases of alleged starvation deaths reported so far there has been a documentation of denials of either NFSA entitlements or social security pensions (for the aged/single women) due to bureaucratic hurdles and/or resource constraints imposed by the state.

Way out:

The implementation mechanism for the existing schemes should be tightened. Other initiatives such as community kitchens in urban areas, diversified food baskets through the PDS particularly in tribal areas, provision of school meals during vacations and so on need to be replicated across the country.

Further, requirements such as mandatory Aadhaar authentication which in a number of these cases has been an underlying cause for exclusion should not be allowed.

A truly universal system of social security that pays special attention to reaching out to the most vulnerable communities needs to be put in place.

Q.18. The Citizen's Charter is an ideal instrument of organisational transparency and accountability, but it has its own limitations. Identify the limitations and suggest measures for greater effectiveness of the Citizen's Charters.

Important Points for Answer:

- *Introduce Citizen's Charter*
- *Elaborate on its features*
- *Discuss in detail its limitations*
- *Suggest corrective measures*
- *Conclusion*

Answer: Citizen's Charter is a document which represents a systematic effort to focus on the commitment of the Organization towards its Citizens in respects of Standard of Services, Information, Choice and Consultation, Non-discrimination and Accessibility, Grievance Redress, Courtesy and Value for Money.

This also includes expectations of the Organization from the Citizen for fulfilling the commitment of the Organization.

What are the components of Citizen Charter?

A good Citizen's Charter should have the following components:

1. Vision and Mission Statement of the Organization

2. Details of Business transacted by the Organization
3. Details of Citizens' or Clients'
4. Statement of services including standards, quality, time frame etc. provided to each Citizen/ Client group separately and how/ where to get the services
5. Details of Grievance Redress Mechanism and how to access it
6. Expectations from the Citizens' or Clients'
7. Additional commitments such as compensation in the event of failure of service delivery

What are the guidelines to be followed while developing a Citizen Charter?

DPARG lists out the guidelines for the effective Citizen Charter formulation as follows :

1. Setting up of a Task Force in the Organization to formulate the Citizen's Charter
2. Identification of all stakeholders in the Organization and major services provided by Organization;
3. Setting up of a Core Group in the Organization;
4. Consultation with Clients/ Stakeholders/ Staff (Primarily at cutting-edge level) and their representative associations;
5. Preparation of Draft Citizen's Charter;
6. Submission of draft Charter to Department of Administrative Reforms and Public Grievances;
7. Consideration of the Charter by Core Group;
8. Modification of Charter by the Ministry/ Department n the basis of suggestions/ observations by the Core Group;
9. Approval by Minister-in-charge;
10. Formal issue/ release of Charter and putting up on website;
11. Sending copies to People's Representatives and all stakeholders;
12. Appointment of a Nodal Officer to ensure effective implementation

Way forward:

The need for citizens and staff to be consulted at every stage of formulation of the Charter. The need for creation of database on consumer grievances and redress. The need for wider publicity of the Charter through print media, posters, banners, leaflets, handbills, brochures, local newspapers etc. and also through electronic media.

Q.19. What are the key areas of reform if the WTO has to survive in the present context of 'Trade War', especially keeping in mind the interest of India?

Important Points for Answer:

- *Problems in WTO structure*
- *Current problems and reasons behind trade wars Reforms for sustainability of WTO*

Answer: Bilateral agreements like TTIP, TPP etc. are weakening the multilateral arrangements that looked after the LDCs (Least Developed Countries).

IPRs being used to curtail access to medicines in poorer countries. WTO TRIPS gives waiver to LDCs with respect to patent protection of pharmaceutical products. This is being diluted/eroded in bilateral agreements. These agreements are being made outside WTO

What should be India's stance?

Till now, India is rigid in its demands of say agricultural subsidies, access to services etc. This rigidness has led to stalemate in WTO negotiations and hence developed world is moving towards bilateral/multilateral arrangements outside of WTO. Policy maker should adopt a more give and take attitude in trade matters without compromising on India's need for food security. The emergence of plurilateral agreements is a warning that the world will simply pass by ignoring India's interest.

How India can negotiate?

India needs to identify its trade interest areas and propose alternative negotiating templates. One such area is biopiracy, protection of traditional knowledge, and the link between the WTO's Trade-Related Aspects of Intellectual Property Rights agreement and the Convention on Biological Diversity. There have been several instances of biopiracy in the past, of Indian traditional knowledge, such as the patenting of the wound-healing properties of *haldi* (turmeric). Being among the 12 mega biodiversity-rich countries, India needs to bring this issue to the negotiating table in its own free trade agreements.

What is Generalised system of preferences (GSP) system and its impact on India?

Generalised system of preferences is a system of preferential treatment to developing and Least Developed Countries(LDCs) to boost their exports.

Although the exemption was made to help developing countries and LDCs to compete with developed countries in the international markets, the benefits have accrued mainly to richer developing countries like India and Brazil.

Recent negotiations of renewal of GSP for Indian gem and jewellery industry in the USA will boost the sector which is facing slowdown owing to low global demand in the international markets. Similar negotiations are also going with countries like Israel and Belgium.

Way forward

The sector is extremely important for the Indian economy as it is labour intensive and export oriented. Any system that increases the export of India will have a positive impact by providing employment, bringing in foreign exchange. This has a cascading effect in the economy. So, such steps are welcome and government of the day must engage in constructive negotiations with developed countries for such concessions.

Q.20. In what ways would the ongoing US-Iran Nuclear Pact Controversy affect the national interest of India? How should India respond to its situation?

Important Points for Answer:
- *Introduce Iran nuclear pact and recent controversy with Iran*
- *Elaborate on how India's national interest is affected by it*
- *Elaborate on response India should have*
- *Conclusion*

The United States has pulled out of the Iran nuclear deal. It is imperative at this juncture to look at the possible global implications and for India in particular.

About the deal :

It is officially called the Joint Comprehensive Plan of Action (JCPOA). It was signed between Iran and the P5, plus Germany and the EU in 2015.

Under the deal:

(i) most of Iran's enriched uranium was shipped out of the country

(ii) a heavy water facility was rendered inoperable

(iii) operational nuclear facilities were brought under international inspection

Implications for India

Energy: Until 2010-11, Iran was India's second-largest oil supplier after Saudi Arabia but it slipped in subsequent years as international sanctions hit Iran. It is now India's third-largest supplier after Iraq and Saudi Arabia but following the 2015 deal, the supplies rose considerably. India and Iran have strategic interests in keeping the relationship sustainable but it should be insulated from the impact of sanctions.

Chabahar port: Chabahar port is both a financial and a strategic investment for India. The engagement between India and Iran on Chabahar has gathered momentum. The work is expected to be completed soon. Possible American sanctions could hit infrastructure development in Chabahar. This could affect the pace of development and cause a delay. However, India may still have options if other signatories stick with the JCPOA

West Asia: Trump's move would mean US engaging with Iran's regional rivals Saudi Arabia and Israel. This could destabilise the region where over 8 million Indian migrants live and work. Military tensions in West Asia have forced India to evacuate its nationals in the past.

India-US relationship: In Trump's administration, the US has been hard on Pakistan. It has asked India to be more proactive in the Indo-Pacific, with an eye on China. However, India has been wary of committing too much on the Indo-Pacific strategy. The India-US-Japan-Australia Quad' is also in the nascent stage. Moreover, uncertainties exist over the relationship with Russia.

NSG: India is aspiring to join the Nuclear Suppliers Group (NSG). Given this, it has to make a clearer articulation of commitment to JCPOA. This will help with the Europeans, especially the French, who are backing India's NSG membership bid.

Way forward

India's goal of helping Afghanistan's reconstruction may be affected if Chabahar is slowed down. India may likely argue with its interlocutors in Washington. It could stress that access to Afghanistan is a shared objective of both countries.

The government should look at options like the rupee-rial trading mechanism. Opening of Iranian banks in India and Indian banks in Iran could be considered. This would facilitate movement of money and income between the two countries. It is a moment for India and Iran to plan for similar crises in future.

SOLVED PAPERS

PAPER–III

Section–A

Time Allowed : Three Hours *Maximum Marks : 150*

Q.1. "Access to affordable, reliable, sustainable and modern energy is the sine qua non to achieve Sustainable Development Goals (SDGs)".Comment on the progress made in India in this regard.

Important Points for Answer:
- *Introduce the importance of SDGs*
- *Explain means to achieve the goal.*
- *Express steps taken by India in this regard*
- *Way forward*

Answer: India's biggest challenge in energy sector is to square the circle between the government's commitment to provide universal access to affordable and reliable energy, on one hand, and the imperative to weaken the linkage between economic growth, energy demand and environmental degradation, on the other.

How to manage?

1. It can be tackled by establishing an integrated planning process.
2. It must factors in the implications of decisions concerning fossil fuels on renewables and vice-versa.
3. It must also enable the fulfilment of short-term objectives without compromising longer-term goals.
4. The short-term challenge is to correct the imbalances in the energy value chain, to minimise avoidable losses and to create a unified energy market.

For example, surplus generating power capacity, but approximately 40% of the country still faces power shortages and/or has no access to electricity.

There are leakages across the transmission and distribution chains.

The medium- to long-term challenge is to redesign and restructure the institutions of energy governance to enable and facilitate holistic energy planning and an integrated energy market.

As a first step in that direction, the government should consider legislating an omnibus 'Energy responsibility and Security act'. Cities are the reasons for surging energy demand and air pollution.

The government should devolve energy administration of cities to autonomous and constitutionally safeguarded 'city energy ombudsmen'.

These ombudsmen should be empowered to tackle issues related to energy efficiency, demand conservation, waste management, urban redesign and transportation, and to develop and implement focused, small-scale and distributed solutions.

The govt. would also have to invest in the supportive infrastructure (for example, grid system, charging network, etc), regulations (for example, standardised protocols), skills and innovation.

Given the long lead times involved in transiting from one energy system to another, it needs a 'bridge' fuel. Natural gas is that fuel. A Gujarat modelled state-wide pipeline grid must be available to the whole nation to have a smooth transition from fossil fuel to renewable energy. A detailed study on what will be required to shift from the incumbent fossil fuel energy system to a 'clean energy' system based on 'horizon' technologies would be a right step in realizing India's commitments.

Q.2. Comment on the important changes introduced in respect of the Long term Capital Gains Tax (LCGT) and Dividend Distribution Tax (DDT) in the Union Budget for 2018-2019.

Important Points for Answer:

- *Define both the concepts*
- *Discuss key highlights of Budget 2018*
- *Way forward*

Answer: Under the 7th Schedule of our Constitution, the Union is empowered to levy taxes on income other than agriculture- such as Corporation Tax, Personal Income Tax, Hotel Receipt Tax, Interest Tax, Fringe Benefit Tax, Capital Gains Tax (CGT), Dividend Distribution Tax (DDT)

Define in under the Indian taxation system,

1. Capital Gain Tax (CGT) is levied on any profit arising from sale of 'Capital Asset'. Depending on the length / duration of the ownership before selling of the asset, this tax is further divided into 1) Long term CGT and 2) Short term CGT.

2. Dividend Distribution Tax (DDT) is levied on the amount of profits paid by the company in the form of dividends to its shareholders.

Until now, if an investor sold his shares / (equity) Mutual Fund units after holding it for a period longer than 12 months then his profits were not subjected to Long term capital gains tax. Finance Minister observed that the profits made from such activities were over Rs.3.60 lakh crores per year. And majority of this profit was cornered by large corporates and high net worth individuals (HNI).

Dividend Distribution Tax (DDT) is levied on the dividend paid by the company to its shareholders. Two major changes were made here in Budget 2018-19

1. Previously Equity Mutual Fund distributing income to its investors, were not subject to DDT. Now they're subjected to 10% DDT.
2. MNCs and local unscrupulous companies would announce merger / amalgamations of their profit making subsidiary company with loss making subsidiary company, in order to reduce their DDT liabilities to promoters. To reduce the tax-avoidance through this loophole, Budget-2018 made certain technical changes in the computation of Dividend Distribution Tax (DDT).

A good taxation system should exhibit "progressivity" i.e. those with higher incomes should taxed at higher rates. However, the previous system exempted even rich persons' profits from LCGT, and helped companies / promoters to dodge the DDT. Budget-2018 has taken appreciative reforms to address these issues.

Q.3. What do you mean by Minimum Support Price (MSP)? How will MSP rescue the farmers from the low income trap? (Answer in 150 words)

Important Points for Answer:

- *Define MSP*
- *Briefly explain its importance*
- *Discuss the highlights of Budget 2018*
- *Conclusion*

Answer: MSP is the price at which the government offers to procure farmers' produce during the season. The farmers are free to sell their produce to government agencies or in the open market.

It is when market prices fall below the MSP that government agencies step in to buy the crop to protect the growers. It aims to safeguard the interest of the consumer by ensuring supplies at a reasonable price.

Mechanism of MSP:

The Cabinet Committee of Economic Affairs announces the MSP at the start of each sowing season, taking into account the recommendations of the Commission for Agricultural Costs and Prices (CACP).

The key considerations, while recommending the MSP for crops, are demand and supply, production cost, price trends in the domestic and international market and the likely implications of the price on consumers.

The CACP's recommendations are in the form of price policy reports every year, separately for five groups of commodities: kharif crops, rabi crops, sugarcane, raw jute and copra.

Way forward:

Farmers across the country have been facing problems of selling their produce at the minimum support price.

Problems like delay in the setting up of procurement centres, exploitation by commission agents defeat the purpose of MSP. Taking advantage of the complexities in the supply chain, middlemen appear to be causing disparities in the price.

Q.4. Examine the role of supermarkets in supply chain management of fruits, vegetables and food items. How do they eliminate number of intermediaries?

> **Important Points for Answer:**
> - *Introduction*
> - *Discuss the role of supermarkets*
> - *Briefly describe the elimination of intermediaries*
> - *Way ahead*

Answer: A supermarket is a self-service retail shop offering a wide variety of food and household products. Examples include Reliance Retail, Big Bazaar, ITC-Choupal fresh stores.

Under the state APMC acts, farmers can sell their produce at regulated APMC mandis only. To bring his produce to the mandi, a farmer has to bear the transportation cost, unloading cost. No guarantee that his produce will be purchased at the Mandi. Farmer is exploited through improper weighing, unnecessary deduction, excess commissions and delayed payments.

Supply Chain Management of super market

Supermarkets directly procure from the farmers near the urban areas. For the farmers living faraway from urban areas, the supermarkets usually tie up with "aggregators" (such as farmers' cooperatives and private logistics companies) to obtain the cereals, pulses, fresh fruits & vegetables.

This is not to say that supermarket SCM doesn't require Hamals, transporters, weighmen and graders but variety of agents, brokers and middlemen are eliminated. As a result, even if supermarket doesn't offer the farmer prices higher than Mandi, still his transportation & unloading costs are saved.

Supermarkets usually work on "low-margin-high-volume" business strategy; as a result the end-consumer may get the said items at a reasonable price. Thus, supermarkets' supply chain management (SCM) of fruits, vegetables and food items benefit both farmers and the consumers.

Conclusion:

Sustainable Development Goal (SDG) requires countries to halve per capita global food waste and reduce post-harvest losses along supply chains, by 2030. Elimination of excessive number of intermediaries in the agri-market is therefore need of the hour.

Q.5. Discuss the work of 'Bose-Einstein Statistics' done by Prof. Satyendra Nath Bose and show how it revolutionized the field of Physics.

> **Important Points for Answer:**
> - *Describe briefly the evolution of Bose-Einstein Statistics along with the specific contribution of S.N. Bose to the theory*
> - *Briefly describe the major applications of this theory in physics*
> - *Conclude with the promise the theory holds for future*

Answer: Satyendra Nath Bose predicted the fifth state of matter called Bose –Einstein Condensate, a state of matter in which atoms morphs into almost zombie like state or in a quantum form. It atoms are cooled to almost absolute zero temperature they move like a one wave-like formation. Fundamental components of ordinary matter are fermions and boson. Bosons unlike fermions prefer to occupy same state of level. Fermions obey Pauli's Exclusion Principle. These are never in exactly same state i.e. energy, momentum, spin etc. Bose –Einstein Statistics is the branch of quantum statistics applies to system of particles of zero or integral spin that do not obey Pauli's Exclusion Principle.

This work triggered an explosion in atomic physics research after development of laser cooling. This enabled to observe and study strange quantum properties. Also develop new insights into quantum mechanics. Now it is possible to develop Quantum Computers, quantum communication technologies based on qubits.

Q.6. What are the impediments in disposing the huge quantities of discarded solid wastes which are continuously being generated? How do we remove safely the toxic wastes that have been accumulating in our habitable environment?

Important Points for Answer:
- *Briefly introduce Solid waste.*
- *Discuss about the impediments in disposing the huge quantities of discarded solid wastes in India.*
- *List down the ways to remove safely the toxic wastes in our environment.*
- *Conclusion*

Answer: Rising population along with improving living standards is responsible for increased generation of solid waste. Safe disposal of the waste is must to prevent environmental damage, maintain health and hygiene. But it faces difficulties because of lack of awareness, lack of environment friendly attitude, proper collection, timely transportation to the dump yards, lack of and use of appropriate and advanced technology, peoples' opposition to existing and proposed dump yard sites, administrative apathy, lack of will power and corruption.

Solid waste is of different types like biodegradable, non-biodegradable, toxic, nontoxic, hazardous non-hazardous. Biodegradable waste is disposed by converting into compost or bio-fuel. Toxic waste which may contain e-waste, industrial waste etc. is disposed by using techniques like chemical treatment, landfills in specially built and sealed container, deep burial, autoclaving, microbial treatment, bioremediation, incineration etc. Reducing the waste generation during production or at source, making environment friendly products, recycling it and reusing are practical way.

Q.7. What is wetland? Explain the Ramsar concept of 'wise use' in the context of wetland conservation. Cite two examples of Ramsar sites from India.

Important Points for Answer:
- •*Briefly introduce wetlands*
- *Discuss about the Ramsar concept of wise use.*

Answer: Wetlands once considered as lands transitional between terrestrial and aquatic ecosystems where the water table is usually at or near the surface or the land is covered by shallow water are treated as distinct ecosystems with specific ecological characteristics, functions and values. Wetlands include flood plains, swamps, marshes, fishponds, tidal marshes natural and manmade wetlands. Wise Use concept of Ramsar Convention on Wetland, intergovernmental treaty signed in 1971 is the conservation and sustainable use of wetlands and all the services they provide, for the benefit of people and nature. They have immense biodiversity, are suitable habitats for endangered and rare species of birds and animals, endemic plants, insects besides sustaining migratory birds. In addition are essential, for the health, welfare and safety of people who live in or near them. Government of India launched National Wetland Conservation Programme (NWCP) in 1985/86. Some of the Ramsar Wetlands sites are Wular Lake, Chilika Lake, Bhitarkanika mangrove etc.

Q.8. Sikkim is the first 'Organic State' in India. What are the ecological and economical benefits of Organic State?

Important Points for Answer:
- *Introduce the concept of organic agriculture.*
- *Discuss the ecological and economical benefits of it.*
- *Conclusion.*

Answer: Sikkim became the first Organic State by implementing organic agricultural practices. Organic Farming or cultivation is environmentally sound practice. It avoids use of chemical fertilizers, pesticides, herbicides and other harmful toxic chemical widely used as part of modern agriculture to increase agriculture production. It also relies on use of organic manure or compost, naturally suitable and traditionally proven cycles of cropping patterns. Though it may lead to subsistence farming which may not suffice to cater the needs of increasing population, it is sustainable agriculture practice. It helps to preserve soil micro-flora thus maintain fertility, support water and soil conservation. In long term it may help to increase production also. It also helps to stop soil, water pollution and entry of harmful toxic chemicals in food chains and ecosystem i. e. bioaccumulation and biomagnifications thus promoting health and maintaining ecological balance. It will help in conserving biodiversity and overcoming adverse effects of global warming, climate change.

Q.9. The China Pakistan Economic Corridor (CPEC) is viewed as a cardinal subset of China's larger 'One Belt One Road' initiative. Give a brief description of CPEC and enumerate the reasons why India has distanced itself from the same.

Important Points for Answer:
- *Describe briefly CPEC.*
- *List the reasons India has distanced itself.*
- *Conclusion*

Answer: The previous Chinese investments in the continent of Africa as well as in India's neighbourhood in Sri Lanka and Myanmar have faced strong local backlash for several reasons.

Many of the projects have proved economically unviable, thus impeding the ability of recipient countries to service the loans. A debt to equity swap leaves them with the undesirable option of China owning strategic assets in their countries which can likely be used for military purposes.

The tempting loans come with many riders and the recipient countries have to source much of their material from China. Often, a Chinese state-owned enterprise leads the project and large numbers of labourers, including low-skilled ones, are imported from China itself. All kinds of charges, ranging from environmental degradation to labour exploitation, have been levelled against Chinese companies

Initial Response :

Pakistan hesitant to accept the tariffs for power produced by projects under CPEC. The refinery built by a Chinese state-owned company in Kyrgyzstan has found it difficult to source crude oil. Political and social discontent in the Central Asian country is already growing. Entire national election campaigns were held on an anti-China plank in countries like Zambia and Sri Lanka. For many of the BRI projects, even the Chinese admit will end up bleeding money

Measures India can take:

Infrastructure boost: A wait-and-watch strategy on the BRI does no harm for the moment but New Delhi should simultaneously step up its infrastructure building in India and the neighbourhood.

Partnership with Japan: It should look to pool its resources with the Japanese Partnership for Quality Infrastructure (PQI). Even if India and Japan cannot match the scale and ambitions of BRI, they will gradually begin to attract partners which will likely be alienated as the true costs and motives of Chinese investments begin to show

Q.10. Left Wing Extremism (LWE) is showing a downward trend, but still affects many parts of the country. Briefly explain the Government of India's approach to counter the challenges posed by LWE.

Important Points for Answer:
- *Define LWE*
- *Give details of the approach that GoI has adopted to deal with LWE*

Answer: Left Wing Extremism region is demarcated by the union government to notify the districts which are affected by left wing extremism.

It is spanning across 106 districts in 10 States, namely Bihar, Jharkhand, Andhra Pradesh, Maharashtra, Odisha, Telangana, West Bengal, Madhya Pradesh, Uttar Pradesh and Chhattisgarh.

Affected regions categorized into three parts:

1. **Severely affected -** Chhattisgarh, Jharkhand, Odisha and Bihar
2. **Partially affected -** West Bengal, Maharashtra and Andhra Pradesh
3. **Slightly affected -** Uttar Pradesh and Madhya Pradesh

Challenges for the government

The National Policy & Action Plan constituted by the MoHA had been introduced to reduce the concentration of Naxal affected districts.

All expenses incurred by the affected areas were covered under the Security Related Expenditure (SRE) Scheme.

This provides funds for projects related to development such as infrastructure, transportation, communication, bridges and schools.

Under which mobile towers, boarding schools and roads were installed in LWE affected areas.

Government also aims for a multi-pronged strategy which primarily includes development and security aspects of affected districts.

Section–B

Time Allowed : Three Hours *Maximum Marks : 250*

Q.11. How are the principles followed by NITI Aayog different from those followed by the erstwhile planning commission in India?

Important Points for Answer:
- *Introduction about NITI Aayog*
- *Limitations of Planning Commission as an institution*
- *Discuss the working of NITI Aayog*
- *Difference between the two.*
- *Conclusion*

Answer: The cabinet resolution similar to one that laid the foundation of PC in 1950 has led to the formation of National Institution for Transforming India (NITI) Aayog with the objective to evolve a shared vision of national developmental priorities, sectors and strategies.

It aims at developing the overall planning strategy with the "bottom up approach" compared with the "top down" approach followed by the PC.

The new think tank has a different structure than the PC in respect of the following:

1. The Aayog will have a Vice-Chairperson to be appointed by PM instead of the Deputy Chairperson.
2. The Aayog would have two levels of councils, governing councils of CM's of the states and LG's of UT's. It would also have a regional council for issue specific objectives.
3. The Aayog would also have experts from relevant institutions on a part time basis as compared to the eight full time members.
4. The Union ministers have been retained as the ex-officio members as were in the PC.
5. The Aayog would also have a CEO to be appointed for a fixed tenure in the rank of secretary.
6. The Aayog might have a separate secretariat as the need arises.

7. Subject experts, practitioners and others would also be nominated from time to time by the PM.

The need of the hour is to bring about a systemic change and not just a structural change. What is now required is a change in the culture of planning. The PC was conceived as a knowledge bank and think tank, which was supposed to act as a repository of the domain knowledge and specialised skills in different subject domains. But the focus shifted from functions like perspective planning, project policy analysis, program implementation to power centric functions like approval of schemes, resource outlay and the like.

This reflects the chronic malaise afflicting the planning commission. Hence it would sometimes become imperative to rebuild the institutions with fresh set of objectives and related support structure in place of re-structuring. But it is equally important that the Aayog learns from the practical experiences of the PC which has to a great extent been successful in carrying out its objectives in the past.

Q.12. How would the recent phenomena of protectionism and currency manipulations in world trade affect macroeconomic stability of India?

Important Points for Answer:

- *Introduce the concept of macroeconomic stability*
- *Elaborate on macroeconomic stability in India*
- *Discuss the dangers from protectionism and currency manipulation*
- *Way forward*

Answer: US under Trump is imposing tariff barriers on all major economies. US's decision to impose fresh tariffs on China follows his recent imposition of steep tariffs on steel and aluminium imports from Canada, European Union and Mexico on national security grounds.

Trade war:

A situation in which countries try to damage each other's trade, typically by the imposition of tariffs or quota restrictions.

Action taken by India:

India has notified higher tariffs on 29 items imported from United States (US).

This is was in retaliation against US announcement imposing tariffs on steel and aluminium items 25% and 10% respectively imported from all countries except Canada and Mexico in March 2018 to compensate from loss of revenue.

The 29 items includes agricultural products such as almonds, apples, chickpeas, lentils, and walnuts, and industrial inputs such as some grades of iron and steel products.

Implications:

Consumers in America and the rest of the world are likely to suffer as their respective governments make it costlier for them to access foreign goods and services.

As former Reserve Bank of India Governor Raghuram Rajan aptly put it, the ongoing trade war is a "lose-lose situation" for the warring parties. The only winners will be special interest groups and consumers in countries that do not engage in the tit-for-tat tariff war, but their winnings will come at the cost of global growth.

Conclusion:

This leads to eventually slower global economic growth. The World Bank has warned that the effect of the increased use of tariffs to regulate international trade could be similar to the significant drop in global trade after the financial crisis a decade ago. It is high time countries worldwide come together to promote the cause of free trade.

Q.13. Assess the role of National Horticulture Mission (NHM) in boosting the production, productivity and income of horticulture farms. How far has it succeeded in increasing the income of farmers?

Important Points for Answer:
- *Introduce horticulture*
- *Discuss about NHM*
- *State its advantages and suggestive measures*
- *Conclusion*

Answer: A National Horticulture Mission was launched in 2005-06 as a Centrally Sponsored Scheme to promote holistic growth of the horticulture sector through an area based regionally differentiated strategies. The scheme has been subsumed as a part of Mission for Integration Development of Horticulture (MIDH) during 2014-15.

What is National Horticulture Mission?

National Horticulture Mission is a government mission to support horticultural production in the country. NHM is a Centrally Sponsored Scheme in which Government of India contributes 85%, and 15% is met by the State Governments.

India ranks second in the global production of fruits and vegetables next to China. It was started in 2005-06 but now subsumed in MIDH.

Contribution in agricultural productivity:

Rise in horticulture, although grown in less area the production is higher than food grains. Horticulture is now 1/3rd of agriculture GDP.

Horticulture is the branch of agriculture that deals with the art, science, technology, and business of growing plants. It includes the cultivation of medicinal plants, fruits, vegetables, nuts, seeds, herbs, sprouts, mushrooms, algae, flowers, seaweeds and non-food crops such as grass and ornamental trees and plants. Floriculture and livestock has also seen rapid growth

Need to more transformation:

They require different marketing and processing support, which is different to the traditional agriculture. More vulnerable to price fluctuations than food grains.

Most of the farmers (more than 80%) engaged in production of these crops are small and marginal farmers with little support from traditional agricultural policies such as insurance, marketing infrastructure, support prices and subsidies.

Hence, our agricultural policies should be geared towards supporting and protecting these farmers.

Q.14. How has the emphasis on certain crops brought about changes in cropping patterns in recent past? Elaborate the emphasis on millets production and consumption.

Important Points for Answer:

- *Introduce the interrelation between MSP and market distortion*
- *Elaborate on dominance of wheat and rice)*
- *Discuss the importance of millets for India*
- *Strategy to bring balance*

Answer: Crop pattern refers to the proportion of area under different crops at a particular period of time. Factors affecting cropping pattern.

Geographical Factors:

1. Type of soil e.g. black soil in Deccan plateau is good for cotton
2. Type of climate – In the summers where temperature is high tropical crops like- Gaur, Bajara while in winter temperate crops like mustard, wheat is grown.
3. Type of rainfall e.g. In the dry regions where the rainfall is scanty and/uncertain, more dependence on rain fed crops like coarse cereals. Water logging areas cultivate rice.
4. Type of topography e.g. tea is grown on gentle slopes

Economic Factors:

1. Most important in determining the cropping pattern of the country
2. Price and Income Maximization: Price variations exert an important influence on acreage shifts. The variation in the inter-crop prices led to shifts in acreage as between the crops. The maintenance of a stable level of prices for a crop provides a better incentive to the producer to increase the output than what a very high level of price does, if there is no uncertainty of this level being maintained over a number of years.
3. Farm Size: There is a relationship between the farm size and the cropping pattern. The small farmers are first interested in producing food grain for their requirements. Small holder therefore devotes relatively small acreage to cash crops than large holders.
4. Insurance against Risk: The need to minimize the risk of crop failures explains diversification in a farm
5. Availability of irrigation: Irrigation: irrigation availability led to cultivation of rice in arid areas of Punjab and Haryana. Lack of irrigation in Bundelkhand region led to cultivation of coarse cereals more.
6. labour availability: major reason of tea plantations succeeding in Darjeeling and not in Himachal Pradesh was availability of labour from Up and Bihar and not in HP

7. Subsistence farming

Historical factors

1. Plantations introduced by British
2. Tenure – Under the crop sharing system, the landlord has a dominant voice in the choice of the cropping pattern and this helps in the adoption of income maximising crop adjustments.

Government Policies:

1. The legislative and administrative policies of the government may also affect the cropping pattern. Food Crops Acts, Land Use Acts, intensive schemes for paddy, for cotton and oilseeds, subsidies affect the cropping pattern.
2. MSP – farmers shifting to wheat, rice
3. Green Revolution – skewed cropping pattern in Northern India towards wheat and rice from coarse cereals and pulses

Social factors

1. Food habits also play a role – East and South India prefers rice as staple food while it is wheat in North India.

Millet

Millet is a common term to categorize small-seeded grasses that are often termed nutri-cereals or dryland-cereals. It includes sorghum, ragi, pearl millet, small millet, proso millet, foxtail millet, barnyard millet, kodo millet and other millets. They are adapted to harsh environment of the semi-arid tropics and require low or no purchased inputs, thus they are backbone for dry land agriculture.

Emphasis on millets production and consumption

Government has approved 2018 as National Year of Millets to boost production of the nutrient-rich millets and the sunrise agri-industry involved in it.

Observation of Year of Millets will help in promotion of production and consumption of millets. It will substantially contribute in fight against targeted hunger and mitigate effect of climate change in long run.

Popularizing millets will also benefit future generations of farmers as well as consumers. Millets are smart food and good for consumers, farmers and planet multiple and has untapped uses such as food, feed, biofuels and brewing.

Q.15. Why is there so much activity in the field of biotechnology in our country? How has this activity benefitted the field of biopharma?

Important Points for Answer:

- *Introduce with importance of biotechnology vis-à-vis India.*
- *Explain why and what activities have taken place in the field in our country.*
- *Illustrate with examples the benefits accrued to Biopharma sector by initiatives of government and private sector.*
- *Conclude with major issues and future potential for Biopharma sector in India*

Answer: Biotechnology industry includes biopharma, bio-services, bio-agri, bio-industrial and bio-informatics. Biotechnology industry in India is growing at greater rate as $1.1 billion biotechnology industry in 2005 became $7 billion in 2015. It may further grow to $100 billion by 2025.

India is one of the top biotechnology destinations. The reasons are large consumer base, growing demands for healthcare services, food and nutrition, huge domestic market with increasing disposable income etc. The government has adopted product patent regime and other initiatives leading to intense research and development activities. Ministry of Science and Technology has launched program to promote the production of biological drugs. Now the focus is on development of new vaccines, biotherapies, diagnostics and medical devices. India has become number one producer of Hepatitis B vaccine. We have potential to become major producer of transgenic rice, GM crops, GM vegetables. It may help to capture global market and turn research concept into workable products.

Activities benefitted the field of biopharma

The mission would attract an investment of Rs 1,500 crore from the central government over a period of five years. Half of the funding would be funded through a loan from World Bank.

The mission will be implemented by Biotechnology Industry Research Assistance Council (BIRAC), a public sector undertaking working under the Department of Biotechnology (DBT).

The mission will focus on key areas that would supplement country's technological and product development capabilities in the biopharmaceutical sector to enable the sector to become globally competitive over the next 10-15 years.

The significance of the mission lies in the fact that National Biotechnology Development Strategy 2015-2020 announced by the Department of Biotechnology (DBT) lays emphasis on making the country achieve USD 100 billion biotech industry by 2025.

The mission will concentrate on development of specific products such as vaccines, biotherapeutics, medical devices and diagnostics etc.

The mission will help in building and strengthening domain specific knowledge and management skills at the same time creating and enhancing technology transfer capabilities in public and private sector.

Q.16. With growing energy needs should India keep on expanding its nuclear energy programme? Discuss the facts and fears associated with nuclear energy.

Important Points for Answer:

- *Introduce by highlighting the conflict between energy needs and the need to enhance clean energy capacity*
- *Elaborate on the need, current usage and future potential of nuclear energy*
- *Highlight the various fears associated with nuclear energy*
- *Conclude with a balanced view of need for growth in nuclear energy but with precautionary measures*

Answer: India's energy demands are vast and growing. The fifth largest electricity producer in the World is facing shortage and significant section of population do not have access to electricity. Energy is key input for accelerating economic growth. GDP growth has to be accompanied by growth in consumption of primary energy including electricity.

Looking at environmental concerns we should focus on development and utilization of renewable sources of energy. Important factors of consideration while achieving the goal of energy security are high dependency, availability of technology, affordability, etc. But it can be achieved by increasing the share of nuclear energy which at present stood at just 3-4 %. It is one of the cleanest sources of energy, relevant for meeting short term and long term demands and having strategic implications also.

About 14 percentage of the total electricity produced is nuclear in the world. Few hundred reactors are used for it. India; no exception should continue and speed up with its three stage nuclear energy program. Fears in the minds of people are aggravated due to accidents like Chernobil and Fukusima. Possibility of failure, accident, sabotage, terrorist attacks, war may lead to challenging situation as leakage of or spreading of radioactive substances, energy, radiation may be beyond our control. It also generate huge radioactive waste, disposal of which may damage environment. India do have vast experience of running nuclear reactors without any significant accident or failure or compromising security factors. Technology never fails but human being may. If we take enough care there should not be any kind of fear regarding nuclear energy.

Q.17. How does biodiversity vary in India? How is the Biological Diversity Act,2002 helpful in conservation of flora and fauna?

Important Points for Answer:
- *Introduce with brief overview of India's biodiversity.*
- *Give an account of biodiversity in India.*
- *Discuss about how Biological Diversity Act, 2002 is helpful in conservation of flora and fauna in India.*
- *Conclusion*

Answer: The number variety and variability among the living organisms is called Biodiversity. India is one of the leading biodiversity rich countries in the world. It accounts for 7-8% of the species of the world with just 2.4 % of the land area. India's biodiversity includes over 90000 animal species and about 45000 plants species. Of these so many species are endemic. Large number of amphibians, reptiles and Indian plants are endemic. These are distributed in its ten bio-geographic regions. It occurs at three different levels, ecosystem, species and DNA.

India has three biodiversity hotspots. Western Ghats and North East are immensely biodiversity rich areas. A vast coast is also repository of variety of marine ecosystems. India enacted Biological Diversity Act 2002 in pursuant to United Nations Convention on Biological Diversity (CBD). Then Biodiversity Rules 2004 were notified. The purpose of the Act is to conserve biodiversity, sustainable use of its components and fair and equitable sharing of benefits arising out of utilization of genetic resources. This Act sets up statutory bodies like National Biodiversity Authority at

Central, State Biodiversity Boards at state and Biodiversity Management Committees at local level. It aims to respect and protect traditional knowledge of local communities, people participation. It also provided for sharing of benefits of knowledge and information related to use of biological resources with local people as they are conservers of it. The act enabled notification of heritage sites thus management and conservation of it. The National and State Biodiversity Fund is also helping is conservation and management.

Q.18. Describe various measures taken in India for Disaster Risk Reduction (DRR) before and after signing 'Sendai Framework for DRR (2015-2030)'. How is this framework different from 'Hyogo Framework for Action, 2005'?

Important Points for Answer:

- *Introduce the disaster situation in India.*
- *Discuss Measures taken in India for DRR before and after signing Sendai Framework for DRR.*
- *Difference between 'Hyogo Framework for Action and 'Sendai Framework for DRR*

Answer: An agreement was signed by UN members in UN 3rd world conference on disaster risk reduction to continue Hyogo framework for action (HFA) and it is called as the Sendai framework. The four priority areas of Sendai Framework are

1. Understanding Risk
2. Strengthening Risk Governance
3. Investing in disaster resilience
4. Improve capacities for disaster response as well as building back better after disasters.

The GOI took the following measures post sendai Framework in the area of disaster management.

As committed in the sendai conference, India successfully hosted the Asian ministerial conference on Disaster Reduction (AMCDRR) and adopted New Delhi declaration and our PM announced 10 point agenda on disaster risk reduction.

GOI issued a set of priority actions to all the state governments based on the goals, targets and priorities of sendai Framework 2015-2030.

The National disaster response force is strengthened and GOI approved in creating National disaster response reserve (NDRR) through a revolving fund of 250 cores.

The GOI making consistent efforts to promote regional co-operation by using the SAARC countries. SAAMDEx is an SAARC disaster management exercise done to seek international co-operation during disasters.

In order to increase the capacity building, the National institute of disaster management (NIDM) signed MoU between Jawaharlal Nehru University for financial assistance and academic co-operation and to establish a centre for excellence in disaster research and resilience building.

P.M. 10 Point Agenda

It ensure that all development projects airports, roads, canals, hospitals, schools, bridges are built to appropriate disaster resilient standards and contribute to the resilient of communities they seek to serve.

Work towards risk coverage for all – starting from poor households to small and medium enterprises to multinational corporations to nation states.

Encourage greater involvement and leadership of women in disaster risk management.

Invest in risk mapping globally for all hazards. Leverage technology to enhance, the efficiency of our disaster issues. Utilize the opportunities provided by social media and mobile Technologies. Build on local capacity and initiative.

It also ensure that the opportunity to learn form a disaster is not wasted. It brings about greater cohesion in international response to disasters. It also Develop a network of universities to work on disaster issues.

Q.19. Data security has assumed significant importance in the digitized world due to rising cyber-crimes. The Justice B. N. Srikrishna Committee Report addresses issues related to data security. What, in your view, are the strengths and weaknesses of the Report relating to protection of personal data in cyber space?

Important Points for Answer:
- *Introduction substantiating the given statement.*
- *Strengths of the reports.*
- *Weaknesses of the report*

Answer: There is a need to ensure growth of the digital economy while keeping personal data of citizens secure and protected. Even though the Information Technology Act contains certain provisions about data protection and handling, experts are of the opinion that India needs a fresh data protection law with the increased digitisation led by Aadhaar, the Goods and Service Tax and the push towards a digital economy. IT Act may also be inadequate to deal with the current requirements since it was drafted almost 17 years ago in 2000 and was amended last in 2008.

Draft Data Personal Data Protection Bill

- For data processors not present in India, the Act will apply to those carrying on business in India or other activities, such as profiling, which could cause privacy harms to data principals in India.
- The draft also provides for penalties for the data processor as well as compensation to the data principal to be imposed for violations of the data protection law.
- It has suggested a penalty of ₹15 crore, or 4% of the total worldwide turnover of any data collection/processing entity, for violating provisions.
- Failure to take prompt action on a data security breach can attract up to ₹5 crore or 2% of turnover in penalty.
- Personal data, the draft law states, may be processed on the basis of the consent of the data principal, given no later than at the commencement of the processing.

- The processing of sensitive personal data should be on the basis of explicit consent.
- The law will not have retrospective application and will come into force in a structured and phased manner.
- Processing that is ongoing after the coming into force of the law would be covered.
- Other personal data may be transferred outside the territory of India with some riders. However, at least one copy of the data will need to be stored in India.
- On right to be forgotten, the draft states that data principal will have the right to restrict or prevent continuing disclosure of personal data by a data processor.
- The committee has not treated data as property as the relationship between the individual and entities with whom the individual shares his personal data is one that is based on a fundamental expectation of trust.
- The draft law will go through the process of inter-ministerial discussions and the Cabinet as well as parliamentary approval.

Data Protection Authority

- The Justice Srikrishna committee has recommended the creation of a Data Protection Authority that will be in charge of ensuring that entities processing data do so in keeping with the law.
- The DPA, a sector agnostic body, will ensure that every entity that handles data is conscious of its obligations and that it will be held to account in case of failure to comply.
- The authority will be governed by a board consisting of six whole-time members and a chairperson appointed by the Union government on the recommendation of a selection committee.
- The selection committee shall consist of the Chief Justice of India or her nominee (who is a judge of the Supreme Court of India), the Cabinet Secretary, Government of India, and one expert of repute who has special knowledge of, and professional experience in, areas related to data protection, information technology, data management, data science, cyber and Internet laws and related subjects.
- The members of the DPA are to be individuals of integrity and ability with special knowledge of, and professional experience of not less than 10 years in, areas related to data protection, information technology, data management, data science, cyber and internet laws and related subjects.
- The DPA members will have a five-year term, subject to a suitable retirement age and their salaries will be prescribed by the Central government.
- Broadly, the DPA will have four departments and related functions: monitoring and enforcement; legal affairs, policy and standard setting; research and awareness; and inquiries, grievance handling and adjudication.
- The DPA will be stating codes of practice, conducting inquiries, and issuing warnings and injunctions.

Exemptions

- The expert committee has recommended that processing of data for certain interests such as security of the state, legal proceedings, research and journalistic purpose, may be exempt from certain obligations of the proposed data protection law.

- For the creation of a truly free and fair digital economy, it is vital to provide certain exemptions from obligations that will facilitate the unhindered flow of personal data in certain situations.
- These exemptions derive their necessity from either a state or societal interest.
- It, however, added that adequate security safeguards must be incorporated in the law to guard against potential misuse.
- The processing of personal data in the interests of the security of the state shall not be permitted unless it is authorised pursuant to a law and is in accordance with the procedure established by such law, made by Parliament and is necessary for, and proportionate to, such interests being achieved.
- It has been recommended in the report that the Central government should expeditiously bring in a law for the oversight of intelligence gathering activities.
- The research exemption has not been envisaged as a blanket one and only those obligations that are necessary to achieve the object of the research will be exempted by the Data Protection Authority (DPA).
- It further added that to strike a balance between freedom of expression and right to informational privacy, the data protection law would need to signal what the term 'journalistic purposes' signifies, and how ethical standards for such activities would need to be set.

Protecting the data of children

- The committee on data privacy has made specific mention of the need for separate and more stringent norms for protecting the data of children, recommending that companies be barred from certain types of data processing such as behavioural monitoring, tracking, targeted advertising and any other type of processing which is not in the best interest of the child.
- It is widely accepted that processing of personal data of children ought to be subject to greater protection than regular processing of data.
- The justification for such differential treatment arises from the recognition that children are unable to fully understand the consequences of their actions.

Q.20. India's proximity to two of the world's biggest illicit opium-growing states has enhanced her internal security concerns. Explain the linkages between drug trafficking and other illicit activities such as gunrunning, money laundering and human trafficking. What countermeasures should be taken to prevent the same?

Important Points for Answer:

- *Explain the given statement.*
- *Draw the linkage between drug trafficking and other illicit activities.*
- *Give countermeasures to prevent this.*

Answer: India is wedged between the world's two largest areas of illicit opium production, the Golden Crescent and the Golden Triangle. This proximity has traditionally been viewed as a source of vulnerability, since it has made India both a destination and a transit route for opiates produced in these regions.

This proximity has also enhanced India's concern of internal security as once the route for trafficking drugs are created they also act as the route for gunrunning, money laundering and human trafficking. These drug traffickers form cartels and enter into organized crime once they get familiar with the ways to bypass the authorities and security to traffic whatever gives them profit. India has 3 main routes for trafficking:

1. Eastern border: India has porous border with many neighbouring countries in the east like Nepal, Bangladesh and Myanmar. These countries are major illicit opium growing states or are part of the route to traffic them into India. We have seen large number of human trafficking from these states and also the gunrunning in the North-Eastern states to aid the naxalites and tribal people.

2. Western Border: Due to tough terrain and lack of proper fencing, border with Pakistan also acts as a route for trafficking of drugs, humans (mostly terrorists), guns and money to aid infiltrations and secessionists in Kashmir and other parts of India.

3. Sea Route: India has a vast coast and tough to secure moreover these route and traffickers create corruption and make the sea ports vulnerable for trafficking. Nexus between drug traffickers and custom officers on the ports help these organized criminals to let other things pass too. Even terrorist have used sea route as we have seen in 26/11 Mumbai case.

Money laundering also takes place with the help of these routes and Hawala transactions to pay for the trafficked items i.e. drugs, guns or humans. Sometime drug trafficking and other illicit activities act as barter system to pay for one with the other.

Countermeasures that can be taken are:

Coordination among various agencies needs to be improved. Information/intelligence gathering regarding trafficking, its analysis and dissemination capabilities need to be strengthened.

The issue of corruption among the border guarding forces as well as in other concerned agencies has to be dealt with in a pragmatic manner. Various domestic laws enacted for the control of trafficking should be implemented stringently and severe punishments should be accorded to drug stockists.

Agencies such as the SDOMD should be reinvigorated. Capacity building of personnel involved in prevention of trafficking in India and its neighbouring areas should be enhanced.

Above all greater cooperation with neighbours on matters of trafficking need to be forged. Borders need to be sealed properly as the issue has been raised time and again.

SOLVED PAPERS

PAPER–IV

Section–A

Time Allowed : Three Hours *Maximum Marks : 150*

Q.1 (a) State the three basic values, universal in nature, in the context of civil services and bring out their importance. (150 Words, 10 Marks)

Important Points for Answer:
- *Explain three important values briefly required in civil services.*

Answer: Following values are universal in nature and are important in the context of civil services as well.

- **Integrity:** This value is recommended for civil services as it governs the professional conduct of civil servants. This value will help a civil administrator uphold high personal and professional standards in all circumstances. If integrity of government decision making is compromised by public official's private interest, then that would be the biggest threat to the administration. Whereas a person with integrity has the ability to implement and achieve the larger goal of public welfare. Despite multiple transfers, Tukaram Mundhe, an IAS offier of Maharashtra cadre refused to succumb to political pressures. He is working with integrity and uprightness towards his duties and responsibilities.
- **Empathy:** A civil service officials needs to be empathetic towards the society he/she wishes to strive for. This value will definitely help an official to understand the society and their experiences. He/ she can use this understanding to guide himself/herself in policy making. An empathetic officer will be able to understand and predict the effects and responses of society towards a particular policy. So empathy or lack of it can make or break how good a policy is. A doctor-turned-IPS officer Dr Abhishek Pallava is providing medical consultation and services in a remote and backward region of Chhattisgarh affected by Maoist activities even while leading anti-Naxalite operations.
- **Transparency:** This value is fundamental element of good governance. If this value is being encouraged at every step of governance it will automatically generate accountability about administration. Whatever decisions taken or policy designed should be open for the public analysis. In the long run, this value is necessary and inevitable for the administration. Meghalaya is the first state in India to implement a law that makes social audit of government programmes and schemes a part of government practice. The main objective of the law is to promote transparency and continuous public vigilance to ensure accountability and efficiency.

(b) Distinguish between "Code of ethics" and "Code of conduct" with suitable examples. (150 Words, 10 Marks)

Important Points for Answer:
- *Explain Code of ethics and Code of conduct.*
- *Discuss key differences between them.*

Answer:
- Code of ethics govern broader choices, while codes of conduct govern specific actions of the employees; together these two concepts represent two common ways that administrative units use to self-regulate.
- Code of ethics refers to value statements. It behaves like the Constitution with general principles to guide the behavior; outlining a set of principles that affect decision-making. When faced with ethical dilemmas or debatable situations, what's articulated in the Code of ethics can help guide decision making. For example, if an organization is committed to protecting the environment and "being green", the Code of ethics will state that there is an expectation for any employee faced with a problem, to choose the most "green" solution.
- Code of ethics attempt to provide guidance about values and choices to influence decision making. Ethical standards generally are wide-ranging and non-specific, designed to provide a set of values or decision-making approaches that enable employees to make independent judgments about the most appropriate course of action.
- Code of conduct might list several specific norms or rules relevant to different areas of organizational operations, or industry, that employees need to obey. The Code of conduct outlines specific behaviours that are required or prohibited as a condition of ongoing employment. In 2014, The Indian Government based on consultations with the state governments, issued the All India Services (Conduct) Amendment Rules, 2014, stating, that every member of the service shall take decisions solely based on merit and in public interest and use public resources efficiently, effectively and economically.
- Code of conduct assert that some specific actions are appropriate, others inappropriate. Conduct standards generally require little judgment. Members of the organisation are supposed to follow them. Violation or non obedience will not be acceptable and incur penalty on them.

Q. 2 (a) What is meant by public interest? What are the principles and procedures to be followed by the civil servants in public interest? (150 Words, 10 Marks)

Important Points for Answer:
- *Define public interest.*
- *Explain it principles and procedures in perspective of civil services.*

Answer: Public interest is welfare of the society at large, whose recognition, promotion, and protection by government and its agencies is expected at every level of administration. It is an integral part of the discourse, law, regulation and governance of modern democracies. The people who make government decisions are supposed to act in the best interest of the public rather than for themselves, for political parties, or for private corporations. Public administrators at all levels of government are ethically bound to protect the public interest. Procedures to be followed by civil servants in public interest involves following steps:

- Carrying out functions fairly and impartially;
- Complying with the principles of procedural fairness/natural justice;
- Acting reasonably;
- Ensuring accountability and transparency;
- Exposing corrupt conduct or serious maladministration;
- Avoiding or properly managing private interests conflicting with official duties; and
- Acting apolitically in the performance of official functions.

(b) "The Right to Information Act is not all about citizens' empowerment alone, it essentially redefines the concept of accountability." Discuss. (150 Words, 10 Marks)

Important Points for Answer:
- *RTI Act significance to social accountability*

Answer:

- Right to Information Act, 2005 has made its impact felt in the functioning of government bodies and the larger governance discourse. A positive change has been observed in India in the last decade in the power equation between the citizens and those in power.
- The term accountability has two main elements; answerability- the need for justification of actions; and enforcement- the sanction that could be imposed if the action or justification of actions is found to be unsatisfactory. RTI act has strengthened the core values of democracy by making the administration directly responsible and accountable towards people. In times before RTI, the nature of accountability in the administration was indirectly responsible to people via parliament. It was more concerned about procedural issues. But RTI changed the nature of this accountability. Now it's more concerned about outcomes.
- Initially the scope of accountability was 'internal', but RTI has widened the scope of the accountability. The Right to Information Act is intended to promote accountability and transparency in government by making the process of government decision making more open.
- By entrenching a legal right to access information, citizens are equipped with a tool which will enable them to gain the information they need if they are to effectively engage in the development processes which are occurring around them.

Q. 3 (a) What is meant by conflict of interest? Illustrate with examples, the difference between the actual and potential conflicts of interest. (150 Words, 10 Marks)

Important Points for Answer:
- *Define conflict of interest.*
- *Highlights of differences between actual and potential conflict of interest.*

Answer: A conflict of interest arises when what is in a person's best interest is not in the best interest of another person or organization to which that individual owes loyalty. A conflict of interest can also exist when a person must answer to two different individuals or groups whose needs are at odds with each other. In this case, serving one individual or group will injure the other.

Actual conflict of interest

- A case of conflict of interest where a person has to presently decide between the conflicting interests (often personal v/s public).
- Cases where personal interests and public interests can clearly be identified and understood. It shows complete binary not only with respect to the means and ends of the decisions but also outcomes of the decisions when there are actual conflicts of interest.
- ICICI Bank and its CEO, Chanda Kochhar, were accused of actual conflict of interest, in allowing a loan to a corporate group which had dealings with her relatives.

Potential conflict of interest

- A case of conflict of interest where a person might have to decide in future between the conflicting interests.
- Here, personal interest and public interest may not be clearly defied and identified.
- Potential conflict of interest could be avoided while actual conflict of interest needs to be managed.
- E.g. resource allocation decision between two or more conflicting communities from one of which you are also part of it and your future generation may affect by the decision which will be taken by the current situation.
- Rahul Dravid was accused of potential conflict of interest when he was both- the mentor of an IPL cricket team as well as the coach of the under 19 Indian cricket team.

(b) "In looking for people to hire, you look for three qualities: integrity, intelligence and energy. And if they do not have the fist, the other two will kill you." - Warren Buffett what do you understand by this statement in the present-day scenario? Explain. (150 Words, 10 Marks)

Important Points for Answer:
- *As per Warren Buffet, understanding the importance of integrity.*

Answer:

- Integrity is about moral dimension and intelligence and energy are about competence and resources. If moral quality is missing in a person, then there are high chances that intelligence and energy of a person could be misused in a wrong direction. Integrity gives more idea about 'what a person will do?' and intelligence and energy gives more idea about 'how will he/she do it?'
- Intelligence can be acquired and especially in today's era, where knowledge is at our fingertips, it can be acquired without much difficulty. Whereas it is not at all clear how to acquire integrity when absent.

- These days, it has been observed that people who are intelligent and knowledgeable got involved into corrupt practices. Therefore it has become an inevitable value which needs to be inculcated in the society. Knowledge without integrity has potential to do harm to the public good.
- Pakistani nuclear scientist A Q Khan who stole nuclear secret and experts who launched cyber crimes could be the examples where lack of integrity caused irreparable damage to the societies.

Q. 4 (a) "In doing a good thing, everything is permitted which is not prohibited expressly or by clear implication." Examine the statement with suitable examples in the context of a public servant discharging his/her duties. (150 Words, 10 Marks)

Important Points for Answer:
- *Values of public servant.*
- *Explain the significance of discharging of his/her duties.*

Answer:

- A public servant working at the grassroot level has to face diverse challenges. No matter how meticulously laws and regulations have been framed, they cannot cover every aspect of public affairs. Hence, the idea of discretionary powers. If a public servant were to restrict himself/herself only to what has been stipulated, she will not be able to serve interests of the public. He/She has to take initiative and use her best judgment in deciding the course of action.
- Going beyond the 'call of duty' is what is expected of a good civil servant. It is in this regard that the quote guides us to spare no efforts in achieving the required good. In using our discretion and going beyond the call of duty, individuals should refrain from doing anything illegal. Illegality not only is constituted by what the letter of the law specifies, but also by what the spirit of the law indicates. If our actions pass neither explicitly not implicitly violate any law, then that is acceptable in public affairs.
- E.g.- Consider Armstrong Pame who facing a shortage of funds, crowd sourced the building of a road. This shows initiative on his part as well as dedication to public service.

(b) With regard to morality of actions, one view is that means are of paramount importance and the other view is that the ends justify the means. Which view do you think is more appropriate? Justify your answer. (150 Words, 10 Marks)

Important Points for Answer:
- *Key highlights of the Utilitarianism approach with examples*

Answer:

- Utilitarianism advocates that ends are more important than means. They hold that as long as maximum pleasure of maximum number of people is achieved, we do not need to worry about how it was achieved. In other words ends justify means.

- Deontologists on the other hand argue that it is the means that determine the morality of actions; and ends or consequences should not be focused while making a decision.
- One could argue that in almost all cases, means are as important as the ends. It would be erroneous to privilege one over other. However, there can be exceptional circumstances where one gets preference over another. For example- if fundamental rights are being violated then the overall action cannot be justified on the basis of consequence alone. In such cases, means need to be given utmost importance. In contrast, if there is only one means to achieve a desired end, then perhaps in such exceptional conditions ends can justify means.

Q. 5 (a) Suppose the Government of India is thinking of constructing a dam in a mountain valley bound by forests and inhabited by ethnic communities. What rational policy should it resort to in dealing with unforeseen contingencies? (150 Words, 10 Marks)

Important Points for Answer:
- *Define rational policy and associated contingencies*

Answer:

- Submergence of critically endangered flora and fauna;
- Submergence of habitat of ethnic communities;
- Cloud burst leading unprecedented rainfall;
- Landslides;
- Increasing presence of humans in protected areas.

Policies:

- Identification of critically endangered and endemic species.
- Plan to relocates and conserve these species in similar climate elsewhere.
- Proper rehabilitation and compensation to the ethnic communities that are likely to be displaced.
- Identifying natural drainage that can take care of unprecedented rainfall and removing any blockage to water flow, if any.
- Ensuring minimum human encroachment on the banks of water streams.
- Identifying areas which are likely to experience landslides with the help of experts in geology.
- Taking appropriate measures like planting trees or putting steel net on the area prone to landslides.
- Shielding protected areas from the interference of human beings that may arise with the start of construction of the dam.
- Compensating the loss of forest through forestation of the other areas.
- Installing flood warning system to people living downstream of the dam in case of unprecedented rainfall leading to opening of gates of the dam.
- Creating proper transport infrastructure like roads and public transport to take care of connectivity in case of calamity creating disaster like situation.
- Providing resources to local authorities to tackle disaster like situations.

(b) Explain the process of resolving ethical dilemmas in Public Administration. (150 Words, 10 Marks)

Important Points for Answer:
- *Discussing ethical dilemmas.*
- *Resolving procedure associated with this.*

Answer:

- Determine whether there is any ethical issue or dilemma or it is the case of the conflict of values, or interests, or capabilities, etc.
- Identifying key values and principles involved in this situation and what meanings and limitations are attached to these values that are competing with each other.
- Rank the values or ethical principles that are most relevant to the issue or dilemma.
- Provide reasons for prioritizing one value over the other.
- Explore all courses of action that can be taken to resolve ethical dilemmas.
- Develop an action plan that is consistent with the priorities set earlier and that are central to the dilemma.
- Involve stakeholders such as clients, subordinates, and superiors in prioritizing the values and then developing action plans.
- Implement the action plans by using most appropriate skills and competencies that are necessary to put the plan in the action.
- Develop competencies such as sensitive communication, skillful negotiation, and cultural competence and think of using these competencies to resolve ethical dilemmas.
- Reflect on the outcome of ethical decision making process employed so far. It should be done in terms of its impact on the stakeholders and organization as a whole.
- Develop a training plan to train people in the organization to be able to identify the ethical issues and dilemmas and to be able to acquire necessary knowledge and skills to resolve ethical dilemmas they face while working in the organization.
- Develop a plan for periodic review of the process employed in resolving ethical dilemmas.

Q.6. What do each of the following quotations mean to you in the present context? (a) "The true rule, in determining to embrace, or reject any thing, is not whether it has any evil in it; but whether it has more evil than good. There are few things, wholly evil or wholly good. Almost everything, especially of governmental policy, is an inseparable compound of the two; so that our best judgment of the preponderance between them is continually demanded." – Abraham Lincoln (150 Words, 10 Marks)

Important Points for Answer:
- *Discuss the statement coined by Sir Abraham Lincoln.*
- *Elucidate it importance in governance.*

Answer:

- In today's context when we witness opposition to some of the government policies, this quote appears very relevant to provide the basis for such opposition.
- It means every government policy will have some negative and unintended effects. For example use of CCTVs, installed for public safety and for public surveillance could lead to violation of right to privacy.
- However, we cannot completely do away with the policies only because they have some lacunae.
- This can be seen especially in the light of development vs. environment debate. This quote offers us a guideline to arrive at the decision whether a policy is good or bad. This requires evaluation of net effect of the policy on public life. By identifying negative effects we can take precautionary and preventive measures to minimize or eliminate the harmful effects of the policy being framed, if any.
- Although policy makers might not be able to come up with a policy that will be perfect all the time, they should take the help of experts wherever possible and inch ever closer to balancing the interests of all stakeholders.

(b) "Anger and intolerance are the enemies of correct understanding." –Mahatma Gandhi (150 Words, 10 Marks)

Important Points for Answer:
- *Discuss the anger and intolerance topics from the perspective of M.G. Gandhi.*

Answer:

- Understanding something demands us to realize the interconnection between what is familiar to us and what is unfamiliar to us.
- However sometimes we come across few things or aspects or dimensions of human life that seem completely different or alien to us.
- This either creates a sense of awe and wonder or a sense of repulsion and fear. If we run away from these different things or continue to oppose them just because they seem alien to our ways of life, we lose opportunity to understand how these things are related to us or something that is familiar to us.
- In today's context the reactions of conservative elements to issues such as decriminalization of same sex relations or lifting of ban on entry of women into a temple can be understood in this context. Instead of getting familiar with the new and different things people get angry at such different dimensions of human life and lose opportunity to develop a clear understanding of these new things.

(c) "Falsehood takes the place of truth when it results in unblemished common good." - Tirukkural (150 Words, 10 Marks)

Important Points for Answer:
- *Tirukkural statement on falsehood and its significance.*

Answer:

- This statement from Tirukkural helps us to resolve ethical dilemma in cases where we are supposed to determine whether to lie or to do harm to society.
- Truth generally is the ideal, but in rare circumstances where it conflicts with generating the common good, perhaps a slight compromise is permitted.
- In such a case, it can be argued that if resorting to falsehood creates beneficial effects, it acquires the status of the truth.
- In case of public administration, when unprecedented works or projects are being undertaken where nobody has prior knowledge or experience, in this case leaders, in order to inspire people might be economical with truth and make people believe that they together can overcome the challenges and make things happen. Over a period it becomes a truth and people start doing things with a confidence that was not seen earlier.

Section–B

Time Allowed : Three Hours *Maximum Marks : 250*

Q. 7 Rakesh is a responsible district level officer, who enjoys the trust of his higher officials. Knowing his honesty, the government entrusted him with the responsibility of identifying the beneficiaries under a health care scheme meant for senior citizens. The criteria to be a beneficiary are the following:

(a) 60 years of age or above.

(b) Belonging to a reserved community.

(c) Family income of less than 1 Lakh rupees per annum.

(d) Post-treatment prognosis is likely to be high to make a positive difference to the quality of life of the beneficiary.

One day, an old couple visited Rakesh's office with their application. They have been the residents of a village in his district since their birth. The old man is diagnosed with a rare condition that causes obstruction in the large intestine. As a consequence, he has severe abdominal pain frequently that prevents him from doing any physical labour. The couple has no children to support them. The expert surgeon whom they contacted is willing to do the surgery without charging any fee. However, the couple will have to bear the cost of incidental charges, such as medicines, hospitalization, etc., to the tune of rupees one lakh. The couple fulfils all the criteria except criterion 'b'. However, any financial aid would certainly make a significant difference in their quality of life. How should Rakesh respond to the situation? (250 words)

Answer:

- Rakesh should not identify the case of old man under this assigned health scheme because the old man does not belong to a reserved community. Allowing the old man to tap benefit from the health care scheme will defeat the larger purpose of social justice for reserved community because the old man is from economically poor background but not socially disempowered the way economically poor, old, and socially marginalized patients are for whom the scheme was initially framed.

- If we allot this health care assistance through this scheme to old man, it may set a precedence in which other economically vulnerable old patients will also create benefit from this scheme which will be difficult to deny if we allow one person to utilize same service. At this situation the socially, economically, marginalized geriatric population for whom this scheme is founded will not serve its actual purpose. Here one must understand that even though economical poverty is crucial reason for drudgery; it is not as multidimensional and as severe as economical poverty borne out of social and economic injustice.
- The right mode of action for the Rakesh should be to engage with the doctors, hospital who are going to undertake the surgery of old man free of cost to convince them to consider this particular case as medical philanthropy/medical corporate responsibility for not taking money for incidental charges or charge less.
- Rakesh can also introduce the old man to "Jana Aushadhi shops" which are generic drugs outlets where they can purchase same effective drug with affordable cost.
- Introduce the couple to the Rashtriya Bima Yojana , Atal Pension Yojana, and mobilize the discretionary fund from collector's office.
- Hospitalization of the old man by Rakesh could be achieved by developing initiatives like crowd funding, developing hospitalization fund through private donations.
- Rakesh can also talk with a number of hospitals , NGO, charity commissioner to develop 'medical assistance fund' for future cases of old patients who are economically vulnerable but do not belong to reserved community.

Long term response:

- Rakesh can also use innovative methods like networking and mobilizing various surgeons, medics, hospitals, private entities, drug sellers association, Jana Aushadhi centers to develop a mechanism where few hospitals and surgeons could be identified for the initiative of free of cost surgery or affordable cost surgery for at least 2 days a month.
- For longer policy decision Rakesh should brief this reoccurring phenomenon of old people from non-reserved community desperately needing health assistance to his seniors so that policy level decisions in the form of schemes, laws, and geriatric health policy should be framed at state level as well as national level.
- Talking with the seniors to keep them under the loop of this specific case.

Q.8. As a senior officer in the Ministry, you have access to important policy decisions and upcoming big announcements such as road construction projects before they are notified in the public domain. The Ministry is about to announce a mega road project for which the drawings are already in place. Sufficient care was taken by the planners to make use of the government land with minimum land acquisition from private parties. Compensation rate for private parties was also finalized as per government rules. Care was also taken to minimize deforestation. Once the project is announced, it is expected that there will be a huge spurt in real estate prices in and around that area.

Meanwhile, the minister concerned insists that you realign the road in such a way that it comes closer to his 20 acres farm house. He also suggests that he would facilitate purchase of a big plot of land in your wife's name at the prevailing rate which is very nominal, in and around the proposed mega road project. He also tries to convince you by saying that there is no harm in it as he is buying the land legally. He even promises to supplement your savings in case you do not have sufficient funds to buy the land. However, by the act of realignment, a lot of agricultural land has to be acquired, thereby causing considerable financial burden on the government, and also displacement of the farmers. As if this is not enough, it will involve cutting down of a large number of trees, denuding the area of its green cover. Faced with this situation, what will you do? Critically examine various conflicts of interest and explain what are your responsibilities as a public servant. (250 Words, 20 Marks)

Answer:

Conflicts of interest:

- Public gain vs. private gain
- Breach of public trust vs. maintaining level playing field
- Whistle blowing vs. intra departmental communication with minister to maintain integrity and uprightness of policy decisions
- Accountability towards people's welfare vs. accountability towards representative of the people
- Environment conservation vs. development
- Development vs. displacement

Appropriate Responses :

- I will not go to the media to open this information. It will disrupt the whole preparation of project and create biased and non-level playing field.
- To remain upright and firm on my stance supporting earlier blue print of the project.
- Reject the offer of land and monetary assistance for buying the land in my wife's name.
- If minister pushes this demand informally then ask him to make a demand in writing 'as a evidential reference' to show it to the authorities and media if too much pressure builds up from the minister's side.

Responsibilities as a public servant :

- Maintain unbiased, neutral behavior in decision making while planning and execution of such a crucial project.
- Maintain the importance and sanctity of information by not disclosing information other than official public forum.
- Hold the spirit of personal and public integrity alive by not succumbing to the pressure and temptation of lucrative offers by minister and not bowing down to the unjust, unethical pressure of minister for fulfillment of personal demands.
- Focus more on the larger public welfare and to maintain legitimacy of government decisions.
- Effective use of the public resources to protect environment.

Q. 9 It is a State where prohibition is in force. You are recently appointed as the Superintendent of Police of a district notorious for illicit distillation of liquor. The illicit liquor leads to many deaths, reported and unreported, and causes a major problem for the district authorities.

The approach till now had been to view it as a law and order problem and tackle it accordingly. Raids, arrests, police cases, criminal trials—all these had only limited impact. The problem remains as serious as ever. Your inspections show that the parts of the district where the distillation flourishes are economically, industrially and educationally backward. Agriculture is badly affected by poor irrigation facilities. Frequent clashes among communities gave boost to illicit distillation. No major initiatives had taken place in the past either from the government's side or from social organizations to improve the lot of the people.

Which new approach will you adopt to bring the problem under control? (250 Words, 20 Marks)

Answer:

- Crimes are by product of many aspects such as social, economic, educational etc.
- It is not just a law and order situation but larger systemic issue.

Adopted new approach

- First stop the illicit distillation and selling of liquor
- As per the governmental guidelines along with 'Excise department' possibility of legalisation of illegal distillation and illegal liquor sell can be explored. This can be mobilised as an effort to avoid production and consumption of spirit/methanol which can lead to more death and health related hazards than ethanol.
- This legalisation can also create 'legal-rational deterrence against the illegal distillation and selling of the liquor.
- Engage with the woman in this area to push or to form SHG, Mahila Bachat Gat and connect them with corporates through 'corporate social responsibility' to start their own productive livelihood activity and financial inclusion
- Create police assistance in the form of 'Police Mitra' to stop physical violence and exploitation of women by men.
- Boost the activity of beat policing, community policing to develop better public-police interactions.
- Engage with the youth in this area to develop them as 'zero police' which will work as the 'eyes and the ears of the police' to bridge the public and police gap and ensure public trust building activities.
- The Denotified tribes, Nomadic tribes. Scheduled Castes, Scheduled Tribes, and communities who are by generations involved in the business of illicit liquor production and being at the receiving end of the wrath of police administration should be given training and skill development in self enterprise development and agriculture allied services. Here police S.P can work as a catalyst to work for mobilizing skill training modules and resources from NGO, private players, etc. corporates, prisons department.

- To ensure sensitive and efficient policing system in the cases of communal conflicts.
- Involve schools, colleges, youth groups, religious leaders, public representatives to make awareness about the illicit distillation and hazards of consumption of illicit liquor.
- Involve de-addiction centres, agricultural colleges, district civil administration to bring out 'citizen services kiosk' to get appropriate information of job and self-enterprise options.
- As an SP, one must ensure effective police organization at the district level to ensure efficient response to the offences like domestic violence, dowry cases, caste atrocities etc. to avoid of atrocities generating out of selling and consumption of illicit liquor.
- Arrest and deliver 'Tadipar notices' to the habitual offenders from illicit liquor industry. This will lead to the breaking of 'skill- production nexus' of activity of the illicit liquor distillation activity.

Q.10 A big corporate house is engaged in manufacturing industrial chemicals on a large scale. It proposes to set up an additional unit. Many States rejected its proposal due to detrimental effect on the environment. But one State government acceded to the request and permitted the unit close to a city, brushing aside all opposition. The unit was set up 10 years ago and was in full swing till recently. The pollution caused by the industrial effluents was affecting the land, water and crops in the area. It was also causing serious health problems to human beings and animals. This gave rise to a series of agitations demanding the closure of the plant. In a recent agitation thousands of people took part, creating a law and order problem necessitating stern police action. Following the public outcry, the State government ordered the closure of the factory. The closure of the factory resulted in the unemployment of not only those workers who were engaged in the factory but also those who were working in the ancillary units. It also very badly affected those industries which depended on the chemicals manufactured by it. As a senior officer entrusted with the responsibility of handling this issue, how are you going to address it? (250 Words, 20 Marks)

Answer:

- The plant cannot be restarted, even if company is assuring changes in their manufacturing processes to ensure less pollution. It is difficult to convince people since; public image of the plant is in negative light.
- Carry out detailed project planning and evaluation operations in the area to understand how many and which social, economic sections of the society is well off and worsen off due to the plant's presence.
- Fix the onus of responsibility of the effluent pollution on the company involved in the excretion of effluent in the nearby surroundings.
- Investigation should be initiated against the officials who allowed the establishment of the plant in the state in spite of knowing that it was rejected by other states for its pollution. This may lead to further revelation of the nexus, if any in the malpractices and mal-administration within the industry and state government.

- Develop inclusive cluster of the various industries in the local region which will help the unemployed labour to develop skill and industry specific training which will generate their livelihood but won't be environmentally hazardous.
- Simultaneously carry out reskilling, training, and development program of labour who are now unemployed by the closing down of plant to get absorbed in other industries or start their own self enterprise to ensure their livelihood. MUDRA loan, Stand Up India etc. schemes can be used for this purpose.
- Carry out health assistance programs not only for humans but also for affected animals. Create the system of compensation for affected person through responsible industry.
- Ensure unemployment allowance to those labours who have lost their job since the plant have been closed down. This allowance should be recovered from company responsible for the pollution.
- Engage with other ancillary units, industrial companies, local communities to work towards detoxification and depolluting activities of the environment where land, water, and crops have been affected by industrial effluent.
- This could be achieved by conducting social impact assessment and environmental impact assessment.
- Working on redeveloping the natural organic texture, content, and healthy microbial flora and fauna in the local soil to mitigate the problems of the effluent already present in the soil. This is crucial for rebuilding agriculture and agriculture allied industries.
- Methods like 'Bio remediation' and 'Rhizo remediation', 'Phyto remediation' in the contaminated sites can play major role in reducing the pollution of water and land of the local contaminated area.
- Develop cottage, agricultural allied industry like packaging, dry logistics, processing to shift unemployed labour to the productive and gainful employment.

Q.11 Dr X is a leading medical practitioner in a city. He has set up a charitable trust through which he plans to establish a super-speciality hospital in the city to cater to the medical needs of all sections of the society. Incidentally, that part of the State had been neglected over the years. The proposed hospital would be a boon for the region. You are heading the tax investigation agency of that region. During an inspection of the doctor's clinic, your officers have found out some major irregularities. A few of them are substantial which had resulted in considerable withholding of tax that should be paid by him now. The doctor is cooperative. He undertakes to pay the tax immediately. However, there are certain other deficiencies in his tax compliance which are purely technical in nature. If these technical defaults are pursued by the agency, considerable time and energy of the doctor will be diverted to issues which are not so serious, urgent or even helpful to the tax collection process. Further, in all probability, it will hamper the prospects of the hospital coming up. There are two options before you:

1. Taking a broader view, ensure substantial tax compliance and ignore defaults that are merely technical in nature.

2. Pursue the matter strictly and proceed on all fronts, whether substantial or merely technical. As the head of the tax agency, which course of action will you opt and why? (250 words)

Answer:

Response:

- Pursue the matter strictly and proceed on all fronts whether substantial or merely technical, provided sufficient time should be given for the medical practitioner to clear tax compliance issues which are purely technical in nature.

Justification:

- We don't want the doctor's work towards the community to stop or to get affected if he pursues the purely technical issues of tax compliance.
- As far as major irregularities of tax compliance are concerned, the doctor has already undertaken to pay tax. This shows his cooperation and spirit of honesty towards his duty as a citizen for tax compliance.
- Although tax compliance of technical nature are not major irregularities but still they are crucial for maintaining overall procedure of tax compliance and cannot be ignored. Here 'window of opportunity' should be given to the doctor who seems to be cooperating with the taxation agency.
- After all, tax agency and doctor's efforts are towards providing public service to the large sections of the society. Taxation agency head, while following his statutory duty, should not lose sight of the larger public interest and welfare and should avoid compromising the human utility of institutional mechanisms like taxation and tax collection where rules, processes, and institutional mechanisms themselves become means. Treating them as ends in themselves is against larger humanitarian ethics as well as constitutional ethics.

Q.12. Edward Snowden, a computer expert and former CIA systems administrator, released confidential Government documents to the press about the existence of Government surveillance programmes. According to many legal experts and the US Government, his actions violated the Espionage Act of 1917, which identified the leak of State secrets as an act of treason. Yet, despite the fact that he broke the law, Snowden argued that he had a moral obligation to act. He gave a justification for his "whistle blowing" by stating that he had a duty "to inform the public as to that which is done in their name and that which is done against them."

According to Snowden, the Government's violation of privacy had to be exposed regardless of legality since more substantive issues of social action and public morality were involved here. Many agreed with Snowden, Few argued that he broke the law and compromised national security, for which he should be held accountable.

Do you agree that Snowden's actions were ethically justified even if legally prohibited? Why or why not ? Make an argument by weighing the competing values in this case. (250 Words, 20 Marks)

Answer:

Justification of Snowden's action :

- It was his moral obligation.

- Whistle blowing is not an act of treason and is not anti-national. In fact it is a patriotic act which is done to protect the rights and interests of the citizens of the nation.
- Snowden's action is giving importance to ethics rather than legality.
- Snowden's action was based on the sense of guarding public good. He violated secrecy agreement but maintained social contract of a democratic nation with its citizens.
- Common good approach.
- Rights approach.
- Legally culpable but law itself was unjust and unconstitutional.

Objections against Snowden's action :

- Broke the law – Espionage Act of 1917
- Compromised national security. It has created a question mark on the legitimacy of the government.
- Snowden's decision to whistle blow is taken based on the sense of self-righteousness where agency, decision of others are compromised. Maybe some people won't be comfortable with their information being tapped by government for the sake of national security but wouldn't want to put national interest in jeopardy by whistle blowing in public by Snowden.
- Selective choice of action by Snowden. According to him, data snooping of each and every citizen should be considered as immoral. Governments shall not justify their actions when it comes to data snooping of citizens from other countries.
- As a systems administrator Snowden had entered into a 'contract' with the American State. Therefore his action is considered as 'breach of contract'. His sudden action puts doubts over his professional ethics and integrity.
- Snowden did not access the internal mechanism and directly disclosed the information in the public domain. It can create an information asymmetry and amounts to unprofessional behaviour.

(MAIN) **2019** | **Civil Services Exam.**

General Studies

SOLVED PAPERS

PAPER–I

Section–A

Time Allowed : Three Hours *Maximum Marks : 250*

Q.1. Highlight the Central Asian and Greco-Bactrian elements in the Gandhara art. (Answer in 150 words) (10)

Important Points for Answer:

- *Introduction of the Gandhara art*
- *Discuss the Greco Bactrian and Roman elements.*
- *Explain the Central Asian Influence*
- *Conclusion*

Answer: Introduction of the Gandhara art:

The Gandhara region was settled in the northwestern part of the Indian Subcontinent. This region was continuously ruled by the Greeks, Kushanas, Shakas, Mauryas, Sungas for many centuries. The school of art which developed here around the beginning of the Christian era known as Graeco-Buddhist, Graeco-Roman or Indo Greek with the influences between Indian craftsmen and Greek-Roman and Central Asian counterparts.

The Gandhara School was influenced less by Greek than by Roman art because of the Greek kingdoms of Bactria and North West India had long vanished when this school emerged. This gave rise to a new form of art which had mind of Indian and hand of Roman.

Discuss the Greco Bactrian and Roman elements:

We must attribute this syncretistic school to the Greco-Bactrian heirs of Alexander and the trade with the West, encouraged by the rising prosperity of Rome.

As Buddhism spread, Buddhists came into contact with the Indo-Greeks who had settled in the north west of the subcontinent. The Greeks had an old tradition of representing their gods in human form. The Buddhist adopted this tradition as well, depicting the Buddha in an identical fashion.

The mother of the Buddha resembled the Athenian matron. Many early Gandhara Buddhas have Apollonian faces, their draperies (cloths) arranged in the style of a Roman toga (garment) and with very curly hair.

The Buddhas of Gandhara, though perhaps lacking in the spirituality of those of the Gupta period, are gentle, graceful and compassionate, while some of the plaques are vivid and energetic.

Explain the Central Asian Influence:

Invasions of the Bactrian Greeks and Saka-Pahilavas on India and its subsequent political contact with Central Asia under the Kushanas resulted in immense cultural intermingling between the two regions. These foreign groups gradually lost their foreign identity and many of them adopted Buddhism. Central Asian contacts brought a fresh wave in the art of sculpture making. Buddhist sculptures of the Gandhara School evolved as a result of the amalgamation of the Indian and the Greek styles.

The new devotional Buddhism demanded iconic worship, and figures of the Buddha and Bodhisattvas were produced in large numbers, as well as small votive plaques (Sacred objects) depicting scenes from the Buddha's life or Jataka stories.

The school continued after the great Kushanas, though with less prosperous times it produced few works in stone, but many in plaster or stucco.

Conclusion:

Therefore, Gandhara school of art has both Central Asian and Greco Bactrian elements. Its influence was felt far beyond the bounds of India, and can be traced even in China.

Q.2. The 1857 Uprising was the culmination of the recurrent big and small local rebellions that had occurred in the preceding hundred years of British rule. Elucidate. (Answer in 150 words) (10)

Important Points for Answer:

- *Introduction of the revolt of 1857*
- *Brief description about various local rebellions occurred between 1757-1857 period*
- *Conclusion*

Answer: The Revolt of 1857 was the most dramatic instance of India's struggle against foreign rule. But it was no sudden occurrence. From 1763 to 1856, there were more than 40 major rebellions apart from 100s of minor ones.

Recurring local rebellions that had occurred in the preceding hundred years of British rule:

The cumulative effect of British expansionist policies, economic exploitation and administrative innovations over 100 years (1757-1857) had adversely affected the position of all sections of

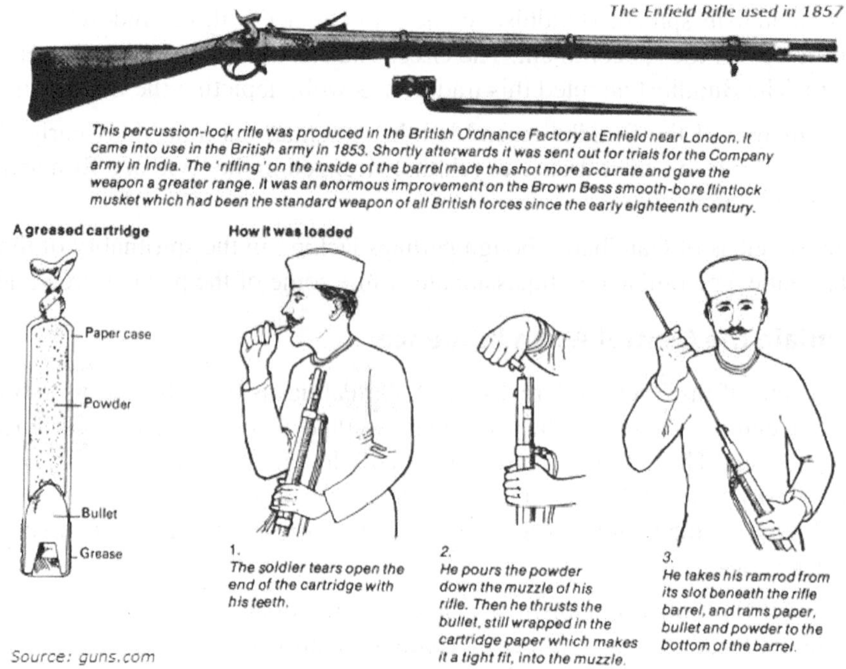

people like rulers of Indian states, sepoys, zamindars, peasants, traders, pundits, moulvies etc. The popular resistance took various forms like civil rebellions, tribal uprisings and soldier mutinies.

Civil rebellions:

The series of civil rebellions, which run like a thread through the first 100 years of British rule, were often led by deposed rajas and nawabs or their descendants, uprooted and impoverished zamindars, landlords and poligars and ex-retainers and officials of the conquered Indian states. The economic decline of the peasantry was reflected in 12 major and numerous minor famines from 1770 to 1857. These led to rebellions like,

- Sanyasi rebellion, made famous by Bankim Chandra Chatterjee in his novel Anand Math, lasted from 1763 to 1800.
- Chuar uprising which covered five districts of Bengal and Bihar from 1766 to 1772 and then, again, from 1795 to 1816.
- Rangpur and Dinajpur rebellion in 1783. Poligars of Tamil Nadu during the 1790.
- Raja of Vizianagram revolted in 1794. Orissa zamindars rebellion in 1804-17.
- Kittur uprising, led by Chinnava, 1824. Satara uprising, 1841 Tribal Revolts Bhil uprisings, 1818-31.
- The Kols of Chhotanagpur rebelled from 1820 to 1837.
- Santhal Uprisings - 1855

Sepoy Mutinies:

The resentment of the Indians had found expression in a number of mutinies and insurrections from time to time in different parts of the country; to mention only a few, the mutiny at Vellore in 1806, at Barrackpore in 1824, at Ferozepur in February 1842, closely followed by the mutiny of 7th Bengal Cavalry and 64th Regiment in 1849, 66th N.I. in 1850 and the 38th N. I. in 1852 etc.

Conclusion:

The 1857 uprising was the culmination of above rebellions. Therefore, the century after 1757 witnessed a number of popular mobilizations, revolts and mutinies against foreign rule and its attendant evils. The pinch of the loss of independence, foreign intrusion into local autonomy, introduction of administrative innovations, excessive land revenue demands dislocation of economy was felt in different regions of India at different points of time and as such caused disturbances mostly of a local nature. The simmering discontent burst out into a violent storm in 1857 which shook the British Empire in India to its very foundations.

Q.3. Examine the linkages between the nineteenth century's Indian Renaissance and the emergence of national identity. (Answer in 150 words) (10)

Important Points for Answer:

- *Introduction of the Indian Renaissance*
- *Describe the linkage between Indian Renaissance and national identity*
- *Conclusion*

Answer: A spirit of renaissance (rebirth) pervaded the whole country with the entry of the Europeans in 18th century. Indian intellectuals closely scrutinized the country's past and found that many beliefs and Practices were no longer of any use and needed to be discarded.

They also discovered that many aspects of India's cultural heritage were of intrinsic value to India's cultural awakening. The result was the birth of new ideas which called Indian Renaissance (Rebirth) and gave a national identity.

Linkages between 'Indian Renaissance' and national identity

In the 19th century educated-Indians began to examine afresh their religious beliefs and customs and their social practices in the light of new knowledge of Western science and philosophy which they had acquired.

The result was various religious and social reform movements in Hindu religion like the Brahmo Samaj, the Prarhana Samaj, the Arya Samaj, the Ramakrishna Mission, the Theosophical Society. Similar movements reformed Muslim, Sikh and Parsi societies also.

In the religious sphere the reform movements combated religious superstition, attacked idolatry, polytheism and hereditary priesthood. In the social sphere, these movements attacked the caste system, untouchability and other social and legal inequalities, these movements were progressive in character for they sought reorganization of society on democratic lines and on the basis of ideas of individual equality, social equality, reason, enlightenment and liberalism. This resulted in the birth of modern ideas like democracy, republicanism, constitutionalism thorough out the Indian sub-continent. Since many reform movements drew their inspiration from India's rich cultural heritage, these promoted pan Indian feelings and a sense of self-respect and spirit of patriotism and nationalism and finally national identity – India as a single political, cultural unit without divisions in the country.

Conclusion

In India, the Indian renaissance was mainly driven by socio-religious reform movements. Some religious reformers sought to revive the religions like Hinduism and Islam by reverting completely to the back ages. Some of these movements instead of looking forward they looked back and started glorifying their respective past religious history. This led to schism among the Hindu and Islamic revival groups and led to India's partition due to emergence Islam identity as an Islamic nation instead of India as single secular nation.

Q.4. Assess the impact of global warming on the coral life system with examples. (Answer in 150 words) (10)

Important Points for Answer:
- *Introduction of the Coral reefs harbour.*
- *Implications of the global warming on coral life system*
- *Measures taken towards protecting coral life system*

Answer: Coral reefs harbour the highest biodiversity of any ecosystem globally. Despite covering less than 0.1% of the ocean floor, reefs host more than 1/4th of all marine fish species, in addition to many other marine animals. So, Coral reefs are often called the "tropical rainforests of the sea" for their astounding richness of life. They directly support over 50 Crore people worldwide, mostly in poor countries. Additionally, reefs provide a wide variety of ecosystem services such as subsistence food, protection from flooding and sustaining the fishing and tourism industries. Their disappearance will therefore have economic, social and health consequences.

Impact of global warming on coral life system

They are among the most threatened ecosystems on Earth, largely due to unprecedented global warming and climate changes, combined with growing local pressures. Over the years, reefs around the world have suffered from mass coral bleaching events as a result of the increase in global surface temperature caused by anthropogenic greenhouse gas emissions.

When conditions such as the temperature change, corals expel the symbiotic algae living in their tissues, responsible for their colour. A spike of 1–2°C in ocean temperatures sustained over several weeks can lead to bleaching, turning corals white. If corals are bleached for prolonged periods, they eventually die. Coral bleaching events often lead to the death of large amounts of corals. According to UNESCO, the coral reefs in all 29 reef-containing World Heritage sites would cease to exist by the end of this century if we continue to emit greenhouse gases under a business-as-usual scenario.

Precautionary Steps

Limiting global average temperature to well below 2°C above pre-industrial levels and pursuing efforts to limit the temperature increase to 1.5°C, in line with the Paris Agreement on climate change, provides the only chance for the survival of coral reefs globally. If the agreement is fully implemented, we will likely see a decrease in atmospheric carbon concentrations.

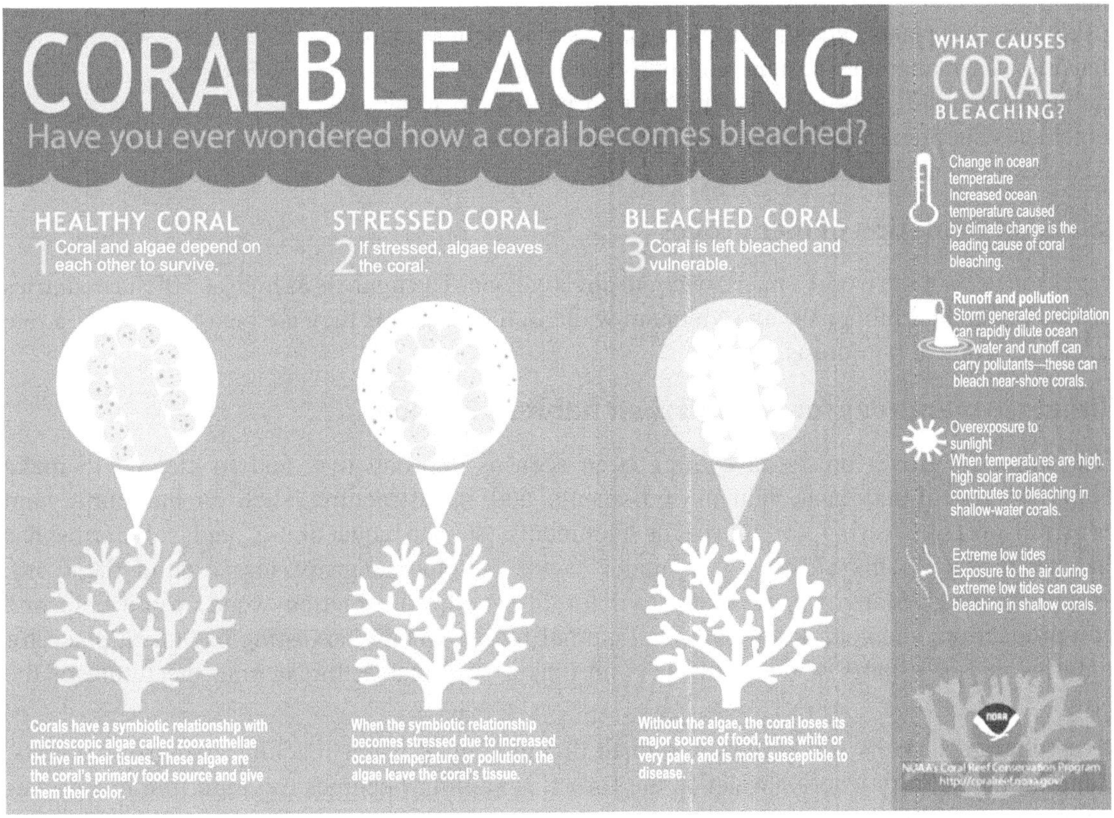

Reinforcing commitments to the Paris Agreement must be mirrored in all other global agreements such as the Sustainable Development Goals. There also needs to be a transformation of mainstream economic systems and a move towards circular economic practices. These are highlighted in SDG 8 (inclusive and sustainable economic growth) and SDG 12 (sustainable consumption and production patterns). Investments should also include support for research at the frontiers of biology, such as genetic selection of heat-resistant corals that can withstand rising global temperatures.

Q.5. Discuss the causes of depletion of mangroves and explain their importance in maintaining coastal ecology. (Answer in 150 words) (10)

Important Points for Answer:
• *Introduction of the mangroves plant*
• *Brief description about the causes of depletion of mangroves*
• *Discuss the role of maintaining the coastal ecology*

Answer: Introduction of the mangroves plant:

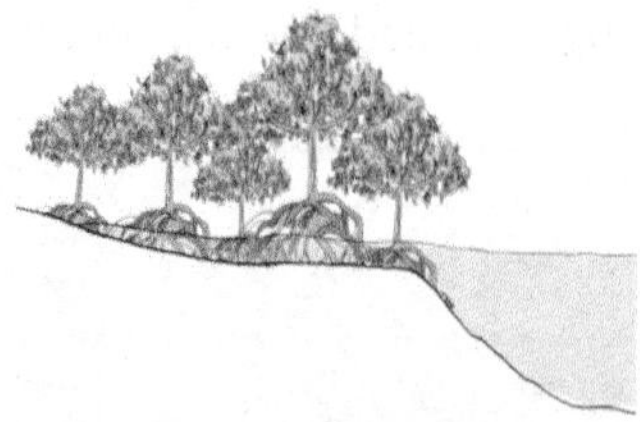

Mangroves are plants that survive high salinity, tidal regimes, strong wind velocity and muddy anaerobic soil – a combination of conditions hostile for other plants. Not all coastal areas are suitable for mangrove plantation as mangroves require an appropriate mix of saline and freshwater and soft substrate like mudflats to be able to grow and perpetuate. Such ecosystem plays a dominant role in sustaining the coastal ecological balance.

Causes of depletion of mangroves

More than 35% of the world's mangroves are already gone. The figure is as high as 50% in countries such as India, the Philippines, and Vietnam, while in the Americas they are being cleared at a rate faster than tropical rainforests.

Threats to mangrove forests and their habitats include:

Clearing: Mangrove forests have often been seen as unproductive, and so cleared to make room for agricultural land, human settlements and infrastructure (such as harbours), and industrial areas. Clearing for tourist developments, shrimp aquaculture, and salt farms has also taken place. This clearing is a major factor behind mangrove loss around the word. **Overharvesting:** Mangrove trees are used for firewood, construction wood, wood chip and pulp production, charcoal production, and animal fodder. While harvesting has taken place for centuries, in some parts of the world it is no longer sustainable, threatening the future of the forests.

River changes: Dams and irrigation reduce the amount of water reaching mangrove forests, changing the salinity level of water in the forest. If salinity becomes too high, the mangroves cannot survive. Freshwater diversions can also lead to mangroves drying out. In addition, increased erosion due to land deforestation can massively increase the amount of sediment in rivers. This can overcome the mangrove forest's filtering ability, leading to the forest destruction.

Overfishing: The ecological balance of food chains and mangrove fish communities can also be altered.

Destruction of coral reefs: Coral reefs provide the first barrier against currents and strong waves. When they are destroyed, the stronger than-normal waves and currents reaching the coast can undermine the fine sediment in which the mangroves grow. This can prevent seedlings from taking root and wash away nutrients essential for mangrove ecosystems.

Pollution: Fertilizers, pesticides, and other toxic man-made chemicals carried by river systems from sources upstream can kill animals living in mangrove forests, while oil pollution can smother mangrove roots and suffocate the trees.

Climate change: Mangrove forests require stable sea levels for long-term survival. They are therefore extremely sensitive to current rising sea levels caused by global warming and climate change.

Role of mangroves in maintaining coastal ecology:

The benefits of mangroves are many. They prevent coastal erosion. They serve as food webs and enhance the fishery production of nearby coastal water by exporting nutrients and detritus.

They provide habitats for wildlife ranging from migratory birds to estuarine crocodiles, tigers, etc. The filtering effect of mangrove forests protects vital coral reefs and sea grass beds from damaging siltation.

Mangrove wetlands and forests act as a shelter belt against cyclones. In Orissa a few years ago, villages surrounded by mangrove forests survived the fury of cyclones, unlike other villages. They provide nursery grounds for a number of commercially important fish, prawn, crabs and molluscs. Mangroves are a source of firewood, of wood products such as timber, poles and posts, and of non-wood produce such as fodder, honey, wax, tannin, and dye and plant materials for thatching.

Mangrove protection is to be perceived as one of the important components of Integrated Coastal Zone Management.

Q.6. Can the strategy of regional resource-based manufacturing help in promoting employment in India? (Answer in 150 words) (10)

Important Points for Answer:

- *Brief introduction about the current employment situation in India*
- *Define regional source based manufacturing*
- *Justify the regional source based manufacturing help in promoting employment*
- *Conclusion*

[N.B. Explanatory answers are brief in nature, so the aspirants can make is precise according to the world limit and requirement of the question]

Answer: Introduction about the current situation of Employment in India:

According to the recently released Periodic Labour Force Survey (PLFS) the unemployment rate in the country in 2018 was at 5.3% in rural India and 7.8% in urban India, resulting in overall unemployment rate of 6.1%. Its effect is highest in manufacturing sector and precisely automobile sector because of weak demand.

Will regional resource-based manufacturing help in promoting employment?

A thriving manufacturing nation, Malaysia was also in similar situation when recession hit in 1997. It led to severe job crisis when demand for FDI led export-oriented industries fell steeply. Then their government devised a mechanism to boost employment by reviving local Rubber Industry. It not only increased the employment locally but made Malaysia a leader in Rubber Production. Thus, regional resource-based manufacturing will promote Employment.

How does regional resource-based manufacturing help in promoting employment?

- **Availability of raw material:** Easy availability of resources near manufacturing area makes investment in the industrial setup more effective, which will create more job opportunities. Different types of resources promote different types of industries.

- Agro Based Industries: Obtain raw material from agriculture. Cotton textile, Jute textile, Sugar and vegetable oil are some examples.
- Mineral Based Industries: Iron and steel, aluminum and cement industries fall under this category.
- Pastoral Based Industries: Depend up on animals for their raw material. Leather tanning, dairy, Meat manufacturing, etc are some of the pastoral based industries.
- **Forest Based Industries**: Ayurvedic products related, Herbal medicine related, Paper manufacturing, etc are few examples.
- **Plantation Based Industries**: Depends on plantation of commercial crops at large scales. Thriving Cashew and rubber industries in Kerala, Palm oil manufacturing in Andhra Pradesh are few examples, Tea estates of Assam and Tamil Nadu are mass employment providers to local tribes.
- **Local Human Resource Pooling**: Since manufacturing is setup in vicinity of nearby habitations, it will promote.
- Reduce migration to Urban areas and create more employment opportunities locally.
- **Enriched Cooperative culture:** Since many cooperatives already are involved in utilizing local resources for their livelihood, an industrial setup will promote its scale and reach.
- **AMUL cooperative:** is the best example where a small milk cooperative turned into a giant.
- **Awarding GI**: GI tags to locally produced goods is also very remunerative to local manufacturers.
- GI tags to Banginapalle and Alphonso mangoes not only increased the revenue of farmers but also encouraged them to invest in food processing industries as well.
- **Increased R&D on locally available products:** Will increase investment on the manufacturing of locally available products.

Conclusion:

Many pundits say that Indian economy is not fast accelerating because of its neglect on manufacturing sector. To bridge this lacunae government is concentrating to promote manufacturing in India with schemes like Make in India and setting up Special Economic Zones, but to create many more job opportunities in this sector it should invest its energies in promoting local resource-based industries as well.

Q.7. Discuss the factors for localisation of agro-based food processing industries of North-West India. (Answer in 150 words) (10)

Important Points for Answer:

- *Introduction of the mangroves plant*
- *Highlights of the localization of agro-based food processing industries in the North-West Indian region*
- *Key factors for their localisation*
- *Conclusion*

Answer: Food processing is a large sector that covers activities such as agriculture, horticulture, plantation, animal husbandry and fisheries. Agro based food processing industry is defined as a set of techno-economic activities, applied to all the products, originating from agricultural farm, aqua cultural sources, livestock and forests. In the food processing various steps included such as farming, drying, fermentation, malting and other packaging techniques. Broadly it can be shown as: Farm inputs → Farming → Processing → Marketing → Logistics → Retail (Consumer).

Localisation of agro-based food processing industries North-West India

- North-West India covering Delhi, Northern Rajasthan, Haryana and Punjab, is a favourite destination for agrobased food processing industries.
- Prominent companies in food processing sector in North-Western states like Punjab are ITC, Amul, Pepsico, Nestle, Cargil , Walmart, Reliance.

Mains factors for their localization

Geographical location:

- Fertile soil for Agriculture. Hilly regions in Punjab are known for Horticulture.
- Surplus Water availability made the growth of crops and food processing possible. The plains of Indus and Ganga system in Haryana are favourable for crops like Wheat, Sugarcane.

Allied Industries

- Presence of high-tech manufacturing clusters like Ludhiana.

Transportation facilities

- National Highways and Railways provide good connectivity to all parts of the North west.

Economic Policies

- Ease of doing business in states like Punjab.
- Proposal for Mega food parks like in ludhiana, Phagwara and Fazilka under the Amritsar-Kolkata industrial corridor.
- "Recently, 150 renowned business houses, including ITC, Pepsi, Mahindra, Godrej, Cargill, Nerolac, Reliance, had invested Rs 7,000 crore in Punjab in the agro and food processing sector.

Conclusion

Agro based industries are so much beneficial for our country because it has less investment cost and give beneficial products. We use waste material as a substrate and that waste material give valuable product and also help in economy of the country.

Q.8. What makes the Indian society unique in sustaining its culture? Discuss. (Answer in 150 words) (10)

Important Points for Answer:

- *Introduction about Indian culture and its constituents*
- *Briefly discuss about the feature of Indian society towards contributing sustainability of its culture.*
- *Conclusion*

Answer: Introduction about Indian culture and its constituents:

Any society and every society is a continuation of the past, but a range of continuity is maintained even in the midst of change coming into the same society from time to time. This is how the identity of a society is maintained over a period of time.

Contemporary Indian society is changing rapidly with the emergence of Westernization such as modern means of transport and communication, Democratization, Urbanization, Industrialization, percolation of English Education etc. Yet Indian society has been more of a cultural entity rather than a structural entity. Which is evident from the remarkable resilience Indian society is showing, for example: When caste is sought to be dislodged from the religious domain (by the continuous reform movements), it enters into political process and caste consciousness comes back.

The join family norms instead of fading away in the face of urbanization and industrialization is still retained by adapting to the process of democratization and acceptance of dissent.

- In the face of scientific temper, religiosity and ritualism also increased and a substantial segment of the modern educated class shows latent and sometime overt acceptance of the religious phenomenon sometimes steeped in irrationality and superstition. Moreover, even the religious ideologies that emerged outside India such as Islam and Christianity too accept some of these attributes and become 'Indianized'. Interaction between Little tradition (followed by peasants and folk) and Great tradition (followed by elite few) helps in cultural continuity in the face of modernization, westernization etc. These interactions are clearly visible even to date, for example:
- A common sight in the Indian villages is Pooja for tractor – a product of modern technology.
- A sick person even after visiting doctor goes to pir, faqir to have Taveez (amulet).

Conclusion:

All these examples point to the fact that what is being continued is a transformed version of the past. Ustad Bismillah Khan playing Shehnai on the thresh hold Kashi Vishwanath temple immediately after performing Haj at Mecca is a pleasant sight to many. It tells us that there is something inherent in Indian civilization, which facilitates the cultural continuity.

Q.9. "Empowering women is the key to control population growth" Discuss. (Answer in 150 words) (10)

Important Points for Answer:
- *Introduction world population prospects*
- *Briefly discuss the measures to control population explosion*
- *Correlate women empowerment with controlling population*
- *Conclusion*

Answer: A recent U.N report—'World Population Prospects 2019' stated that, by 2027 India's population is projected to surpass China's population of 1.5 Billion. Which is quite worrying as even India is nearing the target of achieving TFR of 1.8, with present rate at 2.4 and nearly 23 states and U. Ts already attaining 2.1 our expected population size by 2027 is huge. It will not only impact the Economic growth of our country but also have a serious effect on our Climate because of the additional demand for available resources.

Measures to control population explosion

To reduce the population explosion of India successive governments have taken many measures like promoting family planning activities by providing better health facilities, making available contraceptives and pregnancy kits through ASHA workers, imparting sex education among youth among other measures. But with the prevailing regressive norms in society like patriarchy, Economic disparity and illiteracy, women are being placed at much disadvantaged position which is denting the overall family planning initiatives of the government. So Empowering Women is the most effective way to reduce fertility rates and achieve a sustainable population size that respects the limits of Earth's carrying capacity.

Correlate women empowerment with controlling population, it's including:

- Ensuring equal participation of girls and women in education and the work place;
- Giving women sovereignty over their bodies, including unrestricted access to modern contraception and abortion;
- Ending the practice of child- and forced marriage, which violate girls' rights to a healthy, fulfilling life;
- Granting women full equality under all laws and ending all policies that disadvantage women;
- Eliminating patriarchal attitudes and behaviours that cause women to suffer and that prevent them from accessing positions of power;
- Providing adequate parental leave and childcare opportunities that enable women to have the same unhindered career progression as their partners.

Conclusion

To reduce the population growth at any cost government is mulling to bring in Population Regulation Bill-2019 which calls for punitive action against people with more than two living children and making them devoid of all government services, which may impact the poorest and most marginalized sections of the population and worsen their impoverishment. But it is imperative on the government to recognize that this problem of Population growth is more rooted in culture and gender discrimination in family and society, so empowering women and making them have sovereignty over their mind and body is the best way forward curtail population growth.

Q.10. What are the challenges to our cultural practices in the name of secularism? (Answer in 150 words) (10)

Important Points for Answer:

- *Introduction about the idea of Indian Secularism*
- *Challenges faced by Indian model of secularism*
- *Conclusion*

Answer: The cultural practices could vary from love of the ethnic, fondness for classical music and dance, pursuit of literature, propagation of our traditional fine arts abroad, behavior in day to day events, like respect for elders, veneration for learning.

Defining Secularism

- There is no consensus across the globe regarding the definition of secularism.

French model

- The French model of secularism envisages a radical separation between politics and religion in the name of progress. This model of secularism cannot contribute to the diversity of society as long as it does not engage in an equal dialogue with different religions and cultures.

Communist model

- Communist philosophy disregards all religions. It may lead to creation of a dictatorship style or totalitarian state in which state disregard all positive aspects religions. In such system, consciously anti-religious ideology is propagated.

Threat to cultural practices if definition is seen through the prism of French and Communist Model

- In the both types of above secular definitions, even good cultural practices are threatened in societies where culture and religion are intermixed. Religion and cultural practices cannot be separated in societies like India. It may lead to fundamentalism as well.

Some challenges to our cultural practices in the name of secularism in the Indian Context:

- Thinking religion as an "obstacle to progress."
- Considering diversity as a threat to Unity of the country.
- De-emphasis of spirituality in public life.
- Considering good practices like Yoga, devotion to nature as God as non-secular practice and irrational.
- Making Science and Spiritualism are two worlds apart which cannot be intermixed.
- Strong belief that scientific progress takes place only by repudiating religious cultural practices. For example ISRO praying to Gods before launching a Scientific Mission is also considered a hindrance to scientific progress.

Dangers of these Models on Society as a whole

- It may advocate a sectarian attitude towards religion and do not encourage the process of dialogue and interdependence among faiths. Western-inspired secularism, as implemented by Mustafa Kemal Ataturk in Turkey or by Reza Shah in Iran is always cited as the source of political instability in the Middle East. Millions died in Chinese Cultural Revolution in the name of anti-Confucius crusade.

Indian Model of Secularism

- Therefore, India followed a unique form of secularism which suits Indian conditions. For the founding fathers of contemporary India secularism did not mean practicing irreligious atheism. Indian secularism advocates a form of neutrality and non-preferentialism in regard to different religions. Sarvapelli Radhakrishnan, an Indian philosopher-statesman described secularism in India as "an attitude of true humility" which respected "the conscience of all individuals." He considered Indian secularism "not irreligious and not narrowly religious, but deeply spiritual."

- Jawaharlal Nehru explained his view on secularism in 1961, in the following terms: "We talk about a secular state in India. It is perhaps not very easy even to find a good word in Hindi for "secular". Some people think it means something opposed to religion. That obviously is not correct.... It is a state which honors all faiths equally and gives them equal opportunities." In this context, religious minorities can best be protected by a democratic state that ensures religious tolerance.

Conclusion

Societies are not born secular. Instead, the societies that are practising varying degrees of secularism had to undergo transformation from traditional (religious/sacred) to secular. The process of secularization has played its part in this transformation. Therefore, the challenges to our cultural practices can be resolved not by abandoning the secularism, but to formulate it as a philosophy with spiritual values, rather than solely a policy of the state.

Q.11. Many voices had strengthened and enriched the nationalist movement during the Gandhian phase. Elaborate. (Answer in 250 words) (15)

Important Points for Answer:

- *Introduction about nationalist movement during Gandhian Phase*
- *Briefly discuss about various voices strengthened and enriched the nationalist movement*
- *Conclusion*

[N.B. Explanatory answers are brief in nature, so the aspirants can make is precise according to the world limit and requirement of the question]

Answer: The Indian national movement was an organized mass movement which sustained for nearly a century to attain India's Independence. It led to the formation of Indian National Congress in 1885, spearheaded many movements like Swadeshi, Non-Cooperation, Quit India and culminated with the Independence. During this long and arduous process, many independent voices arose parallel to the main stream nationalism led by INC and Gandhiji. These voices were some times in opposition to main stream Nationalism, but were always in confrontation with common enemy called British. But they did not weaken the national movement instead strengthened and enriched it.

Many voices: how they strengthened and enriched the nationalist movement?

Voices of Muslims:

Muslims under the support of Gandhiji rallied in the Khilafat movement, which used a pan-Islamic symbol to forge a pan-Indian Muslim unity, went a long way in producing unprecedented Hindu-Muslim rapport. Later it brought many Muslims into the nationalist movement and created awareness about the rights of Muslims. But later due to many reasons Muslims thought of having their own identity, so they supported in the growth of Muslim league. Though both Muslim league and INC were in Confrontation with many internal issues on how elections to be held, how constitution should be written etc., But they were always united in dream of freedom from British.

Voices of Non-Brahmans and Dalits:

There were movements which instead of seeking positional changes within the caste system, questioned the fundamentals of this social organization, the most notable of them being the non-Brahman movements in western and southern India and some of the more radical movements among the dalit groups. Despite there was rift among major leaders like Gandhiji and B.R. Ambedkar in the approach towards empowerment, both aimed at preserving the self-respect and dignity of life. This dimension of freedom struggle has left a great legacy in Indian history and its positive results are still fresh even after 70 years of Independence.

Voices of Business People:

After 1922 due to the deteriorating economic conditions all sections of the Indian business community were drawn more closely to the side of nationalism, the industrialists included. In 1927 the Indian capitalists, despite their differences and clash of interests, formed their own organisation, the FICCI.

The business groups favoured constitutionalism and "pressure group politics". The Indian business class expected economy to be developed along independent, self-reliant lines rather than as an appendage to the colonial state.

Voices of Workers:

The gradual industrialisation of India did not only bring the Indian capitalists into the foreground of public life, it also created an industrial working class.

The workers' attitudes to colonial state were shaped by their earlier experience with the authorities in the villages. There they encountered the landlord-state combination, while in the industrial centres they witnessed alliance of the Indian capitalists and viewed as an extension of that same alien imperialist culture. They formed trade unions and demanded for their rights. This enriched the nationalist movement as many leaders came to support them and demanded reforms for their welfare.

Voices of Women:

Generally, Women were restricted to home and were not allowed to appear in public. But their role in public life improved with the emergence of Gandhian phase. When the Non-cooperation movement started in 1921, Gandhi initially prescribed a limited role for women, i.e., that of boycott and swadeshi. But women claimed for themselves a greater active role. In November 1921 a demonstration of a thousand women greeted the Prince of Wales in Bombay. Gradually, women's active role in the public space became accepted in society. Women became conscious and actively participated in the political struggles, and also identified themselves in many ways with the emerging nation.

Voices of Revolutionaries:

At some point of time in the national movement youth felt that all the avenues of peaceful protest and political action were too mediocre and out of desperation they fell back upon individual heroic action and the cult of the bomb.They played a major role in arousing the mood of entire nation towards freedom struggle. Few such examples are: Bhagat Singh, Chandra Sekhar Azad, Surya Sen etc.

Voices of Socialists:

After success of Bolshevik revolution in Russia, many Indians were influenced by Socialism and its ideologies. **M.N Roy**, one such early socialist was the first proponent of constitution for India. Later Socialism and their voices became so popular that even INC adopted socialism as an ideology for developing its socio-economic policies in 1936 session. Many INC leaders like Jawahar lal Nehru, Subash Bose were deeply influenced by Socialism which also shaped India even after independence.

Conclusion

Thus, though the national movement based itself on a clear-cut anti-colonial ideology, it had the vision of a civil libertarian, democratic, secular and socially radical society. The Indian economy was to be developed along independent, self-reliant lines. It was this vision, combined with anti-colonial ideology and a pro-poor radical socioeconomic orientation that enabled the national movement to base itself on the politically awakened and acquired the character of a popular, people's movement.

Q.12. Assess the role of British imperial power in complicating the process of transfer of power during the 1940s. (Answer in 250 words) (15)

Important Points for Answer:
- *Introduction about British imperial power in India during 1940s.*
- *Describe the role of the British in complicating the process of transfer of power*
- *Conclusion*

[N.B. Explanatory answers are brief in nature, so the aspirants can make is precise according to the world limit and requirement of the question]

Answer: In 1939, the British Government without any reference to Indian public opinion declared India a belligerent state. This was strongly protested against by the INC and other parties and intensified the demand for purna swaraj (complete independence).

To allay the resulting discontent, the Viceroy (Lord Linlithgow), in January 1940, declared that "Dominion Status after the War". This did not satisfy Indians and continuous negotiations for transfer of power started. Finally, The Indian Independence Act, 1947 provided for the transfer of power on the basis of grant of Dominion Status to two successor states of India and Pakistan.

The role of the British in complicating the process of transfer of power:

From the August Offer 1940 to Mountbatten Plan of 3rd June 1947, the British authorties have complicated the plan of transfer of power to the successor Dominions of India and Pakistan. This led to the deteriorating communal situation and spread of violence created a near lawless situation in the country.

August Offer 1940

On August 8, 1940 (on the eve of "the Battle of Britain") came out a new declaration of policy, called "the August Offer" It is to give more control over administration to Indians. This declaration recognised at least the natural and inherent right of the people of the country to determine the form of their future constitution, and explicitly promised Dominion Status. However, the Congress rejected this offer, and Gandhiji even went so far as to declare that the declaration widended the gulf between nationalist India and the British rulers. The Muslim League went on to say that "the Partition of India was the only solution of the most difficult problem of India's future constitution." The stalemate continued while the war went on in all its fury.

Cripps Mission 1942

On March 11, 1942, Mr. Winston Churchill (the Prime Minister) announced that Sir Stafford Cripps mission. It gave a declaration that immediately upon the cessation of hostilities steps shall be taken to set up in India in the manne pescribed hereafter an elected body, charged with the task of framing a new Constitution for India along with many other provisions. Gandhiji called the Declaration "a post-dated cheque" to which some one added the words, 'on a failing banks.'

Quit India Movement 1942

After the failure of the Cripps Mission, there was a feeling of frustration among all sections of the people. Gandhiji gave a 'Do or Die' slogan. With this Quit India Movement started and thousands of people died in the struggle. The situation in India complicated further with communal tensions as well in the process. Gandhiji out of frustration urged the British in the Harijan that "Leave India in God's hands, or in modern parlance, to anarchy. Then all parties will fight one another Iike dogs, or will, when real responsibility faces them come, to a reasonable agreement."

Wavel Plan and Shimla conference, 1945

Lord Wavell who had succeeded Lord Linlithgow as Governor-General, now made an attempt to resolve the deadlock in India emerged out of a demand for a separate Muslim country. He arranged a conference to find a solution for the transfer of power but wound up the Conference by declaring a failure of the talks.

The Cabinet Mission Plan, 1946

The failure of the Simla Conference naturally added to the sense of frustration in the country. In March 1946, Prime Minister Attlee declared in the House of Commons, "We are very mindful of the rights of minorities and minorities should be able to live free from fear. On the other hand, we cannot allow a minority to place a veto on the advance of the majority". The Cabinet Mission reached Delhi on March 24, 1946, for deciding the principles and procedure relating to the constitutional issue and transfer of power. As the Congress and the League could not come to any agreement on the fundamental issue of the unity or partition of India, the Mission also could not find a possible solution.

Communal conflicts 1946

Communal tensions intensified and killings took place on the streets of Calcutta and in many other places.

Atlee Statement, February 20, 1947

The next step on the fateful road to India's destiny was the important announcement by the British prime Minister, Mr. Clement Attlee. He went on to make the momentous declaration: "The present state of uncertainty is fraught with danger and cannot be indefinitely prolonged. His Majesty's Government wish to make clear that it is their definite intention to take necessary steps to effect the transference of power to responsible Indian hands by June, 1948."

Mountbatten Plan 1947

He said in the plan that "His majesty's Government propose to introduce legislation during the current session for the transfer of power this year on a Dominion Status basis on one or two successor authorities according to decisions taken as a result of this announcement." The 3rd June Plan proposed to transfer power without the slightest delay.

The Indian Independence Act, 1947

The Plan 3rd June was accepted by all the political parties in the country. The Muslim League was jubilant because it had, got their 'homeland' though it was 'truncated and moth-eaten'. The Congress accepted the partition of the country because it was unavoidable under the circumstances of continuous communal conflicts.

Conclusion

Therefore, with the policy of 'Divide and Rule' the British imperial power has complicated the process of transfer of power during the 1940s.

Q.13. Explain how the foundations of the modern world were laid by the American and French Revolutions. (Answer in 250 words) (15)

Important Points for Answer:
- *Introduction about French revolution*
- *Highlights the contribution of American revolution and French revolution to modern world*
- *Conclusion*

Answer: Constitutionalism, Democracy, Republicanism, laissez-faire and social equalities, etc. are the bed rock for the Modern world. The American and French Revolution opened new chapters and marked a turning point in the history of humankind.

The contribution of American Revolution for foundation of the modern world

American Revolution made the American colonies free from colonial domination. It inspired many colonies to gain independence from European Colonial Powers in South America and Asia. Thus decolonization started. The first democratic government with a written constitution in the world became a reality. This promoted constitutionalism in the world.

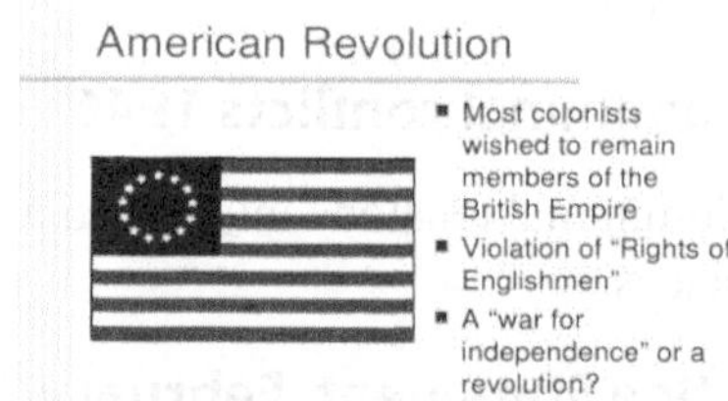

Democracy with separation of powers on the model suggested by French thinker Montesquieu was founded in USA and later in many countries. Republic of the U.S.A. was established. Thus Republicanism spread across the continents. The Bill of Rights ensured fundamental rights to the citizens of the U.S.A. This laid foundation for the Fundamental rights movement across the world.

It introduced new political, social and economic set up in the United States of America. In turn in the world with Laissez-faire (Open and liberal economy) and open society. Capitalism took strong roots in the world.

The contribution of the French Revolution for foundation of the modern world:

French Revolution influenced not only the French public but left an indelible impression on Europe and the entire world. French Revolution was against the Aristocracy and reactionary elements. Across the continents the struggle was ensued against the privileged sections of society and laid foundations for true Democracy.

It introduced for the first time the idea of republicanism based on "Liberty, Equality and Fraternity". These ideas had influenced all the continents of the Earth. The French Revolution rejected tyranny, divine right, conservatism, and feudal vestiges associated with rulers. This inspired many countries to get freedom from such tyranny in their own countries like in the case of South America, Europe and Asia. Republicanism spread across the continents.

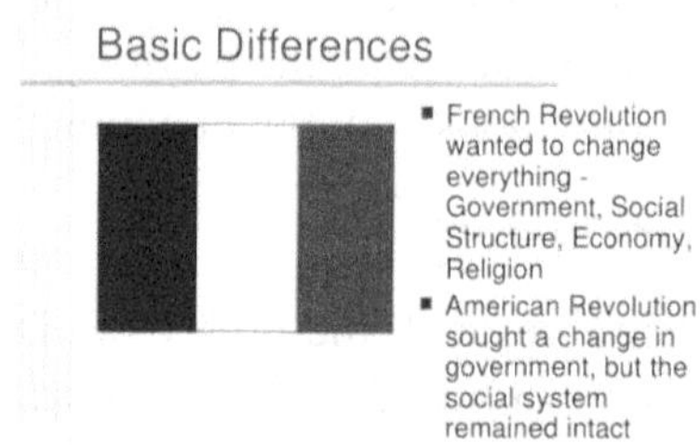

French Revolution played an important role in the Unification of Italy, Unification of Germany and laid foundation for modern Europe. It also led to labour movements for rights of the workers in England and Europe and caused the foundation of ideals like Marxism and Communism which have transformed the modern state in countries like Russia and China.

Conclusion

Therefore, American Revolution began the process of decolonization and laid foundation for a free and independent world while the French Revolution put an end to the age old absolute monarchy, feudal laws and social inequality. Thus, both laid the foundation of modern world.

Q.14. What is water stress? How and why does it differ regionally in India? (Answer in 250 words) (15)

Important Points for Answer:

- *Introduction about Water stress*
- *Highlights the factors due to water stress condition in India*
- *Conclusion*

Answer: Introduction:

Water stress is a situation when the demand for water exceeds the available amount during a certain period or when poor quality restricts its use. Water stress causes deterioration of fresh water resources in terms of quantity (aquifer over-exploitation, dry rivers, etc.) and quality (eutrophication, organic matter pollution, saline intrusion, etc.).

Water stress condition in India:

India is home to 17% of world's population but has only 4% of the world's freshwater resources, and about two lakh people die every year due to inadequate water, sanitation and hygiene. India is suffering a very significant water crisis with economic growth, livelihoods, human well-being, as well as ecological sustainability at stake.

How and why does it differ regionally in India?

Because of the varied geography and burgeoning population, water stress in India differs regionally which is quite evident from the recent happenings like when Maharashtra was reeling under severe floods because of excessive rains Chennai was suffering from acute shortage of water. This is both because of natural and man-made reasons.

Natural:

Because of its vastness and diverse geographical features, some areas get more rain while others don't. for example, Mawsynrum receives highest rainfall and Thar desert the lowest. Monsoons which account for 70% of county's annual rainfall has become inconsistent.

Manmade:

Cropping patterns in the Indian states reveals a frightening inefficiency and suboptimal planning that is causing most water related problems, including depletion of the ground water tables at an alarming rate. According to an ICRIER study, water guzzling crops like sugarcane and paddy are grown in states like Maharashtra, Uttar Pradesh (UP) and Punjab, using up lakhs of liters of irrigation water per hectare. Our international trade in agricultural commodities & industrial produce is contributing to large quantities of virtual water loss through the export of water-intensive crops.

Pollution and Discharge of industrial waste is severely affecting areas in and around river basins.

Unplanned urbanization is killing local bodies which came into picture recently during Chennai floods.

Rainfall wastage is causing sever water stress in rain fed areas and 70% of India is rain-fed for irrigation.

Poor sanitation results in water contamination and makes it unusable that leads to widespread diseases and wastage of public resources. Over exploitation of ground water resources are not only reducing the ground water table but also polluting the pristine underground aquifers.

Conclusion:

To tackle the complex water challenge facing India, it is imperative to take a holistic view of water, starting with the hydrological system, the interactions of this system with climate change on the one hand, and with human factors across agriculture, industrial, and energy production activity on the other. We urgently require a transition from this 'supplyand-supply-more water' provision to measures which lead towards improving water use efficiency, reducing leakages, recharging/restoring local waterbodies as well as applying for higher tariffs and ownership by various stakeholders. The setting up of new Jal Shakti Ministry by Union Government to tackle severe water crisis in India is a first step in right direction.

Q.15. How can the mountain ecosystem be restored from the negative impact of development initiatives and tourism? (Answer in 250 words) (15)

Important Points for Answer:

- *Introduction about importance of mountain ecosystem*
- *Highlights about the destruction of mountain ecosystem due to development initiatives and tourism*
- *Measures taken to restore the mountain ecosystem*
- *Way forward*

Answer: Mountain ecosystems include a wide range of small and big habitats, and are sensitive to disturbance by human activity. Developmental initiatives like mining, tourism and issues like climate change, crime and poverty all threaten the intricate balanced of life that mountains support.

Destruction of mountain ecosystem due to development initiatives and Tourism

Mountain landscapes are particularly fragile and susceptible to change and degradation. Landslides, avalanches, torrents and rock falls can alter the landscape unexpectedly.

- Tourism activities often involve the development and intense use of tracks, paths and sports slopes by vehicles, non-motorized transport and pedestrian traffic.
- Visitor presence is also usually concentrated in small areas, contributing to increased noise and waste.
- The negative environmental effects of poorly managed developmental initiatives and tourism can include vegetation clearing and soil erosion, removal of scarce habitat, altering of critical landscapes and water flows, water and air pollution, and wildlife relocation or behavioral changes.
- The introduction of exotic and invasive species and diseases can also have a significant negative impact on local plant and animal species.

Measures to restore the mountain ecosystem:

Developmental activities and Tourism can also generate positive impacts as it can serve as a supportive force for peace, foster pride in cultural traditions, help avoid urban relocation by creating local jobs.

Measures to restore the mountain ecosystem:

- Comply with all relevant environmental legislation and regulations.
- Usage of Indigenous or local knowledges and conservation practice.
- Use resources sparingly, reduce waste and recycle.
- Greater inclusion of community groups and grassroots organizations within policy making and execution.
- Showing Gender sensitivity in the mountain ecosystem management.
- Social learning and nature-based solutions with an emphasis on women, youth, indigenous and local communities.
- Raise awareness about conservation and the values of our mountains.
- Maintain mountains as clean, safe and healthy environments. Take all litter with you. Do not destroy the wildlife.
- Apply carrying capacity concept to all major tourist destinations;
- Implement and monitor tourism sector Standards and apply performance based incentives for States faring well on the standards.

Way forward:

- Assessment of nature & extent of Shifting Cultivation area, improved policy coherence & improved access to related programs/schemes are key recommendations to transform shifting cultivation.
- Strengthening of skill & entrepreneurship will require focus on identified priority sectors where mountains have advantage, investment in trainers, assessors and training centers in industry partnership.
- Having a Central Data Management Agency for Mountain areas like Himalayas to provide data with high fidelity scenario while addressing data sharing, access, authenticity and comparability issues will go a long way in addressing data related issues.
- Avoiding pressure on the ecosystem by adopting ecofriendly like promoting Regional resource based industries with local community participation.

Q.16. How is efficient and affordable urban mass transport key to the rapid economic development of India? (Answer in 250 words) (15)

Important Points for Answer:

- *Introduction about Urban Mass Transport System*
- *Highlights the scenarios of Urban Mass Transport System in India*
- *Conclusion*

Answer: Introduction about Urban Mass Transport System:

Urban Mass transportation is the movement of people within urban areas using group travel technologies such as buses and trains. The essential feature of mass transportation is that many people are carried in the same vehicle (e.g., buses) or collection of attached vehicles (trains). This makes it possible to move people in the same travel corridor with greater efficiency, which can lead to lower costs to carry each person or—because the costs are shared by many people—the opportunity to spend more money to provide better service, or both.

Highlights the scenarios of Urban Mass Transport System in India:

India is experiencing rapid urbanization and the trend is expected to continue in the future as well. Hence, the focus on providing sufficient and quality public transport in cities is as critical as improving the inter-city connectivity. Across nations, and through decades, economic development has been correlated to personal mobility. So, as India aspires to be the second largest economy in the world, behind China by 2050, we must prepare for a rapid increase in demand for urban mobility.

How is efficient and affordable urban mass transport key to the rapid economic development in India?

While the current use/adoption of Public Transport appears lower for India compared to a select few other countries, there is an emergent need to enhance the capabilities and services of public transport to not only improve the adoption at current volume of passenger trips but also for the future demand:

Help people access jobs easily

Good transport links can widen people's job-search area and help them find employment. It can also reduce commuting times and reduce the cost of living. Public transport is especially important for lower income groups, where 42 per cent lack access to a personal transport. High-skilled workers are more likely to travel across longer distances to work, especially if they are following good job opportunities.

Support innovation, productivity and economic growth in cities and the national economy.

Transport can encourage firms to locate near one another, bring them closer to their supply chain and share expertise. The increase in concentration (mainly referred to as 'agglomeration economies') improves firms' performance and increases productivity.

Help cities attract new firms.

Good transport networks can reduce costs and improve access to skilled labour. Almost 60 per cent of firms consider transport infrastructure as a major influence on their business location

Unlock new development sites for business and housing.

In order for new houses or businesses to be built, roads, bus services and rail must be in place to service them. Good Urban transport facilities help in growth of Satellite Cities, which will drive away the population and industrial density from cities core to outskirts.

Help shape greener and healthier places.

- Reducing the reliance on cars and promoting greener modes of transport (such as public transport or cycling) can relieve congestion and reduce carbon emissions.
- Good transport can also improve individuals' health and reduce healthcare costs.

As India traverses the cusp of urbanization and gains momentum with economic development, it is imperative that we steer our urban mobility architecture to be an asset and not a liability. Transforming urban mobility requires a clear articulation of goals, careful framing of policies, targeted investments, and rigorous implementation backed by enforcement.

Q.17. How do ocean currents and water masses differ in their impacts on marine life and coastal environment? Give suitable examples. (Answer in 250 words) (15)

Important Points for Answer:

- *Introduction about ocean currents and water masses*
- *Describes how ocean currents and water masses felt their impact on marine life and coastal environment with examples*
- *Conclusion*

Answer: Introduction about ocean currents and water masses:

Ocean currents:

The ocean currents of surface water of the oceans upto the depth of 100 meters are called surface ocean currents which involve only 10 percent of the total water mass of all the oceans.

Water Masses:

Water mass is a body of ocean water with a distinctive narrow range of temperature and salinity and a particular density resulting from these two parameters. Antarctic bottom water is an important water mass that forms on the Antarctic continental shelf as a cold.

Ocean currents and water masses felt their impact on marine life and coastal environment:

Ocean currents and Marine life with examples:

Ocean currents act as distributing agents of nutrients, oxygen and other elements necessary for the existence and survival of fishes. Warm ocean currents when met with cold currents provide a suitable environment for fish to breed. Examples are meeting points of Gulf stream and Labrador currents, Oyashio and Kuroshio. Ocean currents transport planktons from one area to the other area. These planktons are useful food for fishes.

Gulf Stream carries planktons from Mexican Gulf to the coasts of Newfoundland and north-western Europe. It may be pointed out that many significant fishing grounds have developed in these areas. Sometimes, a few ocean currents destroy planktons. For example, El Nino current destroys planktons off the Peruvian coasts and causes several diseases resulting into mass deaths of fishes.

Ocean currents and coastal environment with examples

Ocean currents while flowing along the coasts modify their weather conditions. The most effective impacts of ocean currents are seen on the temperature of affected coastal lands. The effects are both positive (beneficial) and negative (injurious) for flora and fauna.

Temperature (+ve)

- The warm currents, when they reach colder areas, do not allow their temperatures to fall rather they keep them relatively warmer in winter months.
- The temperatures of the coastal countries (e.g. the Great Britain, Norway, Sweden, Denmark. Netherlands etc.) are higher during winter than the average temperatures for their respective latitudes due to the effects of the north Atlantic warm current.

Temperature (-ve)

- The Gulf Stream, on the other hand, raises the temperature of Atlantic and Gulf coastal plains of the USA during summer months and causes and intensifies heat waves and thus becomes responsible for hazardous weather conditions. Sometimes, the temperature rises so rapidly that several people die of sun strokes. The coastal lands of the east and south-east USA are not benefitted from the warming effects of the Gulf Stream during winter because the winds are off shore i.e. winds blow from the mainland towards the Atlantic Ocean. *Precipitation.*
- The winds blowing over warm currents pick up moisture and help in increasing the amount of precipitation in the affected coastal areas.
- For example, the North Atlantic Drift and Kuroshio current bring in sufficient rainfall along the western coasts of Europe and eastern coasts of Japan respectively.

Water Masses (Oceans) and coastal environment and marine life:

Watermassesdohavephysicalparameterslike:temperature,salinity,depth,currents,waves,turbulence, turbidity. They play a crucial role in the dynamics of marine ecosystems and can be altered by human activities, especially in coastal areas.

The physical parameters of seawater are essential because they structure the water masses and determine the various habitats that provide the environmental conditions required for marine life. These conditions influence the production and the growth of plankton and fish species. The dispersion and dwelling of larvae for many benthic and pelagic species depend on hydrographical factors.

They also play an important role for the exchanges between the sea and the atmosphere and between the various layers of water. For instance, the weakening of the surface mixing process can induce a poor oxygenation of the seawater and sometimes lead to anoxic situations and a sudden mortality of some species. Changes in the physical parameters of seawater can then have an impact on the spawning, breeding and feeding areas of marine organisms.

Conclusion

So the ocean currents and their impact has been analysed in depth while the impact water masses we need to be studied more extensively. Future scientific studies must be carried out the impact of these two phenomenons.

Q.18. Do we have cultural pockets of small India all over the nation? Elaborate with examples. (Answer in 250 words) (15)

Important Points for Answer:

- *Brief introduction about the concept of nation*
- *Highlights the reasons behind the emerging the cultural pockets with examples*
- *Conclusion*

Answer: Culture is the common understanding, which is learnt and developed through social interaction with others in society. A common understanding within a group demarcates it from others and gives it an identity. But cultures are never finished products. They are always changing and evolving. So, Culture is that complex whole which includes knowledge, belief, art, morals, law, custom and any other capabilities and habits acquired by man as a member of society.

While some jatis, sects and communities have an individual ethos, they also have organic links with other elements of the population of the region, which develops a cultural personality over time. So that culture which developed over a region is cultural region or cultural pocket.

Highlights the reasons behind the emerging the cultural pockets:

The people in such a region may share ethnic origins, language, and cultural traits. More important are their shared historical experiences as well as ecology and environment. Powerful empires and dynasties directly or indirectly contributed to the shaping of cultural pockets. The great empires had central cultural zone, but in a diluted form their influence extended to distant peripheries also. The kingdoms accepting their suzerainty were left culturally undisturbed. So Cultural Pockets evolved over time (and in fact are still changing). Also, what we understand as regional cultures today are often the product of complex processes of intermixing of local traditions with ideas from other parts of the subcontinent.

Some examples:

- Development of Malayalam culture with the influence of Sanskrit in its language and Theater art during Cheras.

- Bengalis developed a cuisine centered around Fish. That even Bengali brahmins who were not allowed to eat non-vegetarian food, but the popularity of fish in the local diet made the Brahmanical authorities relax this prohibition for the Bengal Brahmanas. The Brihaddharma Purana, a thirteenth-century Sanskrit text from Bengal, permitted the local Brahmanas to eat certain varieties of fish.
- Miniature Painting culture spread in Mughal ruled areas. With the decline of the Mughal Empire, many painters moved out to the courts of the emerging regional states. As a result, Mughal artistic tastes influenced the regional courts of the Deccan and the Rajput courts of Rajasthan.

Conclusion:

The nationalist movement, while emphasizing the unity and integration of india, also appealed to ethnic, linguistic, and regional sentiments for mobilizing support. In the process regional cultural pockets received a new impetus for consolidation.

Q.19. What are the continued challenges for women in India against time and space? (Answer in 250 words) (15)

Important Points for Answer:
- *Introduction about the status of women in Indian Society*
- *Highlights the challenges for the women in India against time and space*
- *Highlights the various aspects of challenges*
- *Conclusion*

Answer: Introduction about the status of women in Indian Society:

There is a considerable ambiguity about the nature and status of women in Indian society. Some sacred texts give them an exalted status by saying "Gods live where women are worshipped." But there is another profile of women also sanctified by religious writings that she is fickle and fragile sop they should always be protected against all odds at all stages of her life. As time passed women role in society became submissive to men in relation to power.

Highlights the challenges for the women in India against time and space:

The challenges women face today are not of recent origin but continuing from ages. The problems women face even to date are interplay of historical, economic, social and political forces which are shaping and reshaping the gender equations.

The various aspects of challenges:

1. Constitutional Challenge: The Constitution which provides Equality to everyone and prohibits discrimination on the grounds of religion, race, caste, sex or place of birth, but it also guarantees freedom of religion. The right to freely profess, practice and propagate religion. This provision of religious freedom takes away much of the freedom and equality extended to women by the constitution. Because family and personal law is rooted in the religious codes, women do not have equal rights within the family or to property.

2. **Political Challenges**
   - **Less Political participation**: The passage of Women reservation bill which will confer 33% of seats to them in Loksabha seems to be a distant dream. Recognising the significance of roles of women in decision making process in the society is critical to strengthen women's agencies for building a progressive society with equality of opportunities among all citizens.
   - **Pati Panchayats:** Women sarpanchs accounted for 43 per cent of total gram panchayats (GPs) across the country. But their actual participation is very less as their husbands take over their roles in many villages.
3. **Socio – Cultural Challenges:**
   - **Gender Discrimination:** Women face discrimination right from the birth in the form of female feticide and infanticide.
   - **Patriarchy:** is forcing upon women less decision-making power and making all her energies are tied to husband's lineage.
   - **Temple Entry:** In many places women entry into temples is denied based on their menstrual rituals. In the recent example of Sabarimala even though Supreme Court allowed temple entry for women, some patriarchal tendencies in society are preventing it to happen.
   - **Dowry**: It is still an Impending cultural problem to date.
   - **Domestic Violence:** It has become part and parcel of women's life.
   - **Crime against Women:** Rape, Honor Killings and sexual harassment at work places are frequently happening against them.
4. **Education and Economic Challenges:**
   - **Low Literacy rates:** Though women literacy is sharply increasing, but there is a huge gap of 15% in its rate.
   - **Pay Gap:** According to Monster Salary Index (MSI) showed the overall gender pay gap in India was 20 percent. It found that the gap was narrower in the early years of experience. While men with 0–2 years of experience earned 7.8 percent higher median wages than women, in the experience group of 6–10 years of experience, the pay gap was 15.3 percent. The pay gap becomes wider at senior level positions as the men with 11 and more years of tenure earned 25 percent higher median wages than women.
   - **Land and Property Rights:** Even to date women are being denied the family property although with The Hindu Succession Act in place. And even if women get some property, they are unable to use it according to their wish.

Conclusion

This is why we should be optimistic and actively promote gender parity, and facilitate avenues for women to progress in their career and become independent of societal inhibitions.

Q.20. Are we losing our local identity for the global identity? Discuss. (Answer in 250 words) (15)

Important Points for Answer:
- *Introduction about the concept of global identity*
- *Introduction about the concept of local identity*
- *Linkage between each other*
- *Conclusion*

Answer: Every individual develops a complete image of his "self or identity" because of interactions within his social environment. While it was family, values and culture of a society which played a major role in forming one's environment in the past, now it is because of many facets of globalization like;

- **Modern Education** and percolation of English language in place of local languages.
- **Western Fashion Statements** and growing interest towards events like Miss Universe and Miss World.
- **Netflixization** and larger consumption of Western Creative Content.
- **Mcdonaldization** and growing likeliness for global cuisines like Chinese, Thai, Mexican etc.
- **Walmartization** and the loss of local Kirana shops and village fairs.
- **Westernization** of our festivals and rituals, for example changing rings during marriage and utilizing DJ as entertainer during village festivals.

But we are not losing our local identity entirely and this trend of leaning towards global environment is localized either by their promoters or receivers themselves, for example:
- Promoting Yoga, Ethics and values based on India's ancient knowledge in Educational institutions is a new phenomenon.
- Mix of Indian and western Dressing styles to form Indo western outfits.
- McDonald sells only vegetarian and chicken products in India and not its beef products.
- Even foreign streaming services like Netflix and Amazon Prime use Indian languages in producing new content.

Conclusion

Identity cannot be seen as an unchanging fixed entity that can either collapse or remain the same when faced with social change. Identity tends to Glocalise (Mixing of the global with the local), which is evident from the emerging food trends like Pizza – Dosa; glocalised FMCG products like Charcoal Tooth Pastes, Ayurvedic Soaps etc.; Using sophisticated western technologies to make Indian epics like Bahubali.

SOLVED PAPERS

PAPER–II

Time Allowed: Three Hours *Maximum Marks: 250*

Candidates should attempt ALL questions strictly in accordance with the instructions given under each question.

Q.1. Do you think that Constitution of India does not accept principle of strict separation of powers rather it is based on the principle of 'checks and balance'? Explain (Answer in 150 words) (10)

Important Points for Answer:
- *Introduction about separation of powers*
- *Brief note about strict separation of powers*
- *Separation of powers in Indian context*
- *Conclusion*

Answer: Introduction:

Legislature, executive and judiciary are the three organs of government. Together, they perform the functions of the government, maintain law and order and look after the welfare of the people. According to Constitution Separation of powers between them is part of the basic structure, so no law can be passed to abrogate to that extent.

Brief note about strict separation of powers:

The theory of Doctrine of Separation of Power was first propounded by Montesquieu, a French scholar in and 1747 published in his book 'Espirit des Louis' (The spirit of the laws). Montesquieu found that if the power is concentrated in a single person's hand or a group of people then it results in a tyrannical form of government. To avoid this situation with a view to checking the arbitrariness of the government he suggested that there should be clear-cut division of power between the three organs of the state i.e. Executive, Legislative and the Judiciary. It is followed in Presidential form of governments like USA and others.

Separation of powers in Indian context:

The Constitution of India ensures that they work in coordination with each other and maintain a balance among themselves. This is evident from its provisions like:

- India being parliamentary system, executive and the legislature are interdependent: the legislature controls the executive, and, in turn, is controlled by the executive.
- Judiciary strikes down the unconstitutional laws made by Legislature.
- Parliament can impeach judges of Supreme Court and High Courts of states for their incompetence and mala fides.
- Executive, the president, can exercise his veto powers over the bill passed by Legislature.

Conclusion:

In India, separation of functions is followed and not of powers and hence, the principle is not abided in its rigidity. In India, separation of functions is followed and not of powers and hence, the principle is not abided in its rigidity. Hence strict separation of powers is not followed but a system of checks and balances is embedded in Indian Constitution.

Q.2. "The Central Administrative Tribunal which was established for redressal of grievances and complaints by or against central government employees nowadays is exercising its powers as an independent judicial authority." Explain (Answer in 150 words) (10)

Important Points for Answer:

- *Introduction about Central Administrative Tribunal*
- *How does Central Administrative Tribunal works?*
- *Brief description about the Central Administrative Tribunal exercising its powers as an independent judicial authority*
- *Conclusion*

Answer: Introduction about Central Administrative Tribunal:

The Central Administrative Tribunal (CAT) was constituted in 1985 and the motivation behind setting it up was that officers and employees working in the Government would have an easier option to register their issues, including grievances and disputes, and will be able to seek redressal without having to run from one court of law to the other.

How does Central Administrative Tribunal works?

The CAT exercises original jurisdiction in relation to recruitment and all service matters of public servants covered by it. Its jurisdiction extends to the all-India services, the Central civil services, civil posts under the Centre and civilian employees of defense services. It is guided by the principles of natural justice. These principles keep the CAT flexible in approach.

Is CAT exercising its powers as an independent judicial authority?

In a recent case Uttarakhand HC issues contempt notice to CAT chairman for willful disobedience of its judgement. CAT also took strong objections to a recent verdict of Delhi High Court. It indicates that CAT is trying to ascertain its Individuality and trying to act as an independent judicial authority.

Conclusion:

Though CAT has original jurisdiction over grievances of service personnel, but the verdicts given by it are bound to be appealed at the higher levels of judiciary starting from High courts. So, CAT is part of the interdependent Indian Judiciary complex.

Q.3. What are the methods used by the farmers organisations to influence the policy makers in India and how effective are these methods? (Answer in 150 words) (10)

Important Points for Answer:
- *Introduction about farmers organizations and their contribution to India's GDP growth*
- *Methods used by the farmer's organizations and their effectiveness*
- *Way forward*

Answer: Half of India's population works on farms, but farming contributes only 15% to the country's GDP. Often farmers in India are burdened with high input costs and lower minimum income on the produce. Which is forcing them to come out and raise their voice and Farmers organizations like All India Kisan Sabha, Farmers wing of CPI, Kisan Morcha of BJP etc. are using different methods to make government hear about their grievances.

Methods used by the farmer's organizations and their effectiveness:

Petition to three organs of the government:

In many cases they make their grievances heard through Petitions to;

1. **Executive:** Submitting their grievances to either a central or state Minister or to the President.
2. **Legislature:** Passing their petitions as Private Members Bill. For Example, two farmer bills seeking 'freedom from indebtedness' and the 'right to guaranteed remunerative minimum support price (MSP)' were introduced in Lok Sabha in 2018 as private member bills by, member of parliament which were prepared by the All India Kisan Sangharsh Coordination Committee.
3. **Judiciary:** Farmers are making effective use of Public Interest Litigation (PIL) tool of courts to present their grievances. And this route turned out to be fruitful which is evident from recent court verdicts directing Central Government to look into unsolved Insurance claims, judicious use of water resources etc.

Way forward:

These protests are very effective in making policy makers hear them. Though farmers grievances are broad, the relief they get out of these protests is very short term in the nature of hike in MSP, Farm Loan Waivers or Insurance Coverage, which are no way a solution burgeoning threats Farmers face like Climate Change, Universalisation of crops, Water Stress, Failing Monsoons, Increasing Production cost and Low prices for their produce. To solve these issues there need to be a revolution in Farming sector.

Q.4. From the resolution of contentious issues regarding distribution of legislative powers by the courts, Principle of Federal Supremacy and Harmonious Construction have emerged Explain. (Answer in 150 words) (10)

Important Points for Answer:
- *Introduction*
- *Doctrine of Harmonious Construction*
- *Resolution of contentious issues regarding distribution of legislative powers by the courts:*
- *Conflict in Centre-State Relations over statutes:*
- *Conclusion*

Answer: The rule of federal supremacy is a technique to avoid absurdity, resolve conflict and ensure harmony between the Union and state laws. If this principle of union supremacy is excluded, it is not difficult to imagine its deleterious results.

Doctrine of Harmonious Construction:

When there is a conflict between two or more statues or two or more parts of a statute then the rule of harmonious construction needs to be adopted. The rule follows a very simple premise that every statute has a purpose and intent as per law and should be read as a whole. In the case in which it shall be impossible to harmonize both the provisions, the court's decision regarding the provision shall prevail.

Conflict in Centre-State Relations over statutes:

- In case of a conflict between the Central law and the state law on a subject enumerated in the Concurrent List, the central law prevails over the state law.
- During a National Emergency, The Parliament acquires the power to legislate with respect to matters in the State.
- Bills on certain matters enumerated in the State List can be introduced in the state legislature only with the previous sanction of the president.

Resolution of contentious issues regarding distribution of legislative powers by the courts:

As Supreme Court has the original jurisdiction to solve the dispute between center and state, it has come into play many a times. Few recent examples are:
- Kaveri Water Board Management.
- Contentious issues of law and order involving CBI between center and states are always solved by the courts.

Conclusion:

With the timely intervention of Courts and by following the principle of federal supremacy and harmonious construction, it is aiding in the successful functioning of the federal system, or else there will be every possibility of our two-tier political system being stultified by interference, strife, legal chaos and confusion caused by a host of conflicting laws, much to the bewilderment of the common citizen.

Q.5. What can France learn from the Indian Constitution's approach to secularism? (Answer in 150 words) (10)

Important Points for Answer:
- *Introduction*
- *Criticism for French concept of secularism*
- *Indian Concept of Secularism*
- *What can France learn from the Indian Constitution's approach to secularism?*
- *Conclusion*

Answer: French concept of secularism discourages religious involvement in government affairs, especially religious influence in the determination of state policies; it also forbids government involvement in religious affairs, and especially prohibits government influence in the determination of religion. However, it doesn't preclude a right to the free exercise of religion.

Criticism for French concept of secularism:

In early 20th-century France—a fairly homogenous, Christian nation—this was a straightforward attempt to protect government from the sway of the Catholic Church. But in modern France—a decidedly more heterogeneous and multi-religious society—this insistence on secularism is thorny. In the spirit of laïcité, France passed a law in 2004 banning religious symbols and clothing, like crosses, kippas, and headscarves, in public schools. This step instead of promoting equality, disintegrated Minorities from society.

Indian Concept of Secularism:

The Indian secularism is the positive concept giving equal respect to all religions or protecting all religions equally.

What can France learn from the Indian Constitution's approach to secularism?

1. **Article 15:** The State shall not discriminate against any citizen on the ground of religion. So, all religions are given importance and treated equally.
2. **Article 25:** All persons are equally entitled to freedom of conscience and the right to freely profess, practice and propagate any religion including Minorities.
3. **Article 30:** All minorities shall have the right to establish and administer educational institutions of their choice. It will better help in integrating the minorities in main stream society.

Conclusion:

As India was a multi -religious society from its inception, it had to adopt positive concept of Secularism to push all communities forward. As France which was earlier a homogeneous Christian society has become multi religious with development and migration should adopt the positive concept of secularism for betterment of all the communities in its society.

Q.6. Despite consistent experience of high growth, India still goes with the lowest indicators of human development. Examine the issues that make balanced and inclusive developed elusive. (Answer in 150 words) (10)

Important Points for Answer:
- *Introduction*
- *India stand in some key Development Indices*
- *Issues that make balanced and inclusive development elusive*

Answer: India is among the fastest growing countries in the world and has climbed up to 77th position in the Ease of Doing Business Index from 130 few years back, Its Growth rate though steady is more than many developing economies. But it is faring poorly on the human development front, ranked 130 in Human Development Index (HDI), which means that millions of Indians have less healthcare and education than in more advanced countries or even in Emerging Economies like the BRICS where India's rank is the lowest. Even among SAARC members, India's Human Development Index (HDI) rank is lower than Sri Lanka and Maldives and a little higher than Bhutan, Bangladesh, Pakistan, Afghanistan and Nepal.

Where does India stand in some key Development Indices?

1. Human Development Index (which calculates Life expectancy, Literacy, National income) – 130/189 countries.
2. Gender Development Index – 149/160 countries.
3. Multi-Dimensional Poverty Index – Nearly 20% of Indians are poor

Issues that make balanced and inclusive development elusive:

1. **Problems being faced by women:** Patriarchal society of India is draining efforts in the direction of women empowerment. India's maternal mortality ratio remains high 130/1lakh live births. Women's empowerment in terms of mean number of years of schooling is only 4.8 years compared to 8.2 years for males.

2. **Problems in achieving universal health care:** The public health expenditure is as low at 1.4 per cent of the GDP, with which it is difficult to achieve the goal towards universal healthcare. There is a huge disparity between urban and rural healthcare. Rural India is painfully short of doctors, nurses, medicines and hospitals. Low insurance penetration is making out of the pocket expenditure on medicines and health care a burden on poor.
3. **Poverty:** The number of poor in India has decreased no doubt, but there are 200 million people or 21.2 per cent living below poverty line defined as people with income below $1.90 per day.
4. **Less income distribution:** Decreasing employment rate is worrisome. Many overvalued people are applying for undervalued jobs.

5. **Hurdles in Universal Education:** Even with continued efforts, literacy rate is only 75%. Lack of toilets in schools, Rote Learning, dismal infrastructure is few issues plaguing the target of universal education.
6. **Lack of Justice:** India has not ratified UN conventions on torture, rights of migrant workers and their families, and protection against enforced disappearance. This is a serious lacuna for a country that otherwise has a commitment to democracy and the rule of law.

Conclusion:

With the growing realisation that development is a multidimensional achievement, the gains of economic reforms must help build capabilities and improve the health of all sections. Sustaining and improving the quality of life will depend on policies crafted to handle major emerging challenges such as urbanisation, the housing deficit, access to power, water, education and health care.

Q.7. There is a growing divergence in the relationship between poverty and hunger in India. The shrinking of social expenditure by the government is forcing the poor to spend more on non-food essential items squeezing their food-budget. – Elucidate. (Answer in 150 words) (10)

Important Points for Answer:
- *Introduction*
- *The shrinking of social expenditure by the government*
- *The shrinking of social expenditure by the government is forcing the poor to spend more on non-food essential items squeezing their food-budget*
- *Conclusion*

Answer: Earlier it was believed that wealth created with the economic development will solve the problem of hunger. But recent trends shows that it is contrary which is evident from the fact that, though India lifted 271 million people out of poverty in ten years (experiencing the fastest absolute reductions in poverty in the 2019 Multidimensional Poverty Index), India suffers from a level of hunger that is very serious(ranking 103/119 countries in Global Hunger Index).

The shrinking of social expenditure by the government

1. **Health:** As of now, the country spends 1.15 per cent of the GDP on health. Which is very less in comparison to many developed economies. Even though government launched new universal health care policy, Ayushman Bharat, Its benefits are reaching to all as Private hospitals and doctors were reluctant to get onto the AB programme, as they find it badly designed, not capturing their realities in terms of costs.
2. **Education:** The government has been reducing spending on education (budget estimates) — it dropped from one per cent of the country's income in the government's first Budget in 2014-15 to 0.62 per cent in 2017-18. The share of Sarva Shiksha Abhiyan, a national programme for universal elementary education, in the total allocation dropped to 29 per cent in 2017-18 from 31 per cent in 2016-17.
3. **Electricity:** The free fall of fuel prices and still existing excise duties on it make it much costly. With reduced expenditure by government on fuel subsidies. The cost of electricity is increasing.

The shrinking of social expenditure by the government is forcing the poor to spend more on non-food essential items squeezing their food-budget:

Because of shrinking social expenditure by the government (government spending on nutrition, public health, family welfare and relief on account of natural calamities has reduced significantly in the last four years.), makes the urban and rural poor dependent on private entities for non -food essential services like education, healthcare, transportation, fuel and lighting, which are likely to be more expensive.

The share of monthly expenditure devoted to these items has increased at such a pace that it has absorbed all the increase in real income over the past three decades. This has led to a "food budget squeeze", which led to the stagnance of real food expenditure over the last two decades.

Q.8. Implementation of Information and Communication Technology (ICT) based Projects/ Programmes usually suffers in terms of certain vital factors. Identify these factors, and suggest measures for their effective implementation (Answer in 150 words) (10)

Important Points for Answer:

- *Introduction of ICT and its usefulness*
- *Problems in Implementation*
- *Suggested measures*
- *Conclusion*

[N.B. Explanatory answers are brief in nature, so the aspirants can make is precise according to the world limit and requirement of the question]

Answer: India pushes hard towards a digital society, the government schemes aims to transform the entire ecosystem of public services through the use of Information and Communication Technologies. For this it launched an umbrella program called Digital India with the vision to transform India into a digitally empowered society and knowledge economy.

ICT and how useful it is:

Information and Communication Technologies (ICTs) have been making considerable impact on the society due to their universal application and appeal. Many businesses, urban and rural communities have seen the positive contribution of ICTs in several dimensions like increases in efficiencies, communications and information on anytime-anywhere basis. But still there are many issues plaguing its effective implementation.

Problems in Implementation

1. **Low digital infra penetration:** No universal broadband connectivity at 50 Mbps to every citizen. Internet connectivity to all Gram Panchayats still remains a distant dream. Investments in the Digital Communications Sector have slowed down.

2. **Less Digital knowledge:** While digital connectivity and literacy have increased over time, these have not adequately translated into digital knowledge of public affairs. ICT services are being given only in English or Hindi. Manpower for this New Age Skill is very less.

3. **Privacy Concerns:** We have already witenessed Privacy issues regarding misuse of Aadhaar details. Lack of manufacturing of Electronic Devices required for enabling ICT programs in India, is making ICT program implementation costly and also prone to data theft.Cyber crime is an impending threat which every country is facing today.

4. **Data Storage issues:** As data is new oil and with ICT comes the question of Data storage.

Solutions:

1.Digital Infrastructure as a Utility to Every Citizen:

- Availability of high speed internet as a core utility for delivery of services to citizens.
- Cradle to grave digital identity that is unique, lifelong, online and authenticable to every citizen.
- Mobile phone & bank account enabling citizen participation in digital & financial space.
- Easy access to a Common Service Centre.
- Shareable private space on a public cloud.
- Safe and secure cyber-space

2.Governance & Services on Demand:

- Seamlessly integrated services across departments or jurisdictions.
- Availability of services in real time from online & mobile platforms.
- All citizen entitlements to be portable and available on the cloud.
- Digitally transformed services for improving ease of doing business.
- Making financial transactions electronic & cashless.
- Leveraging Geospatial Information Systems (GIS) for decision support systems & development.

3.Digital Empowerment of Citizens:

- Universal digital literacy.
- Universally accessible digital resources.
- Availability of digital resources / services in Indian languages.
- Collaborative digital platforms for participative governance.
- Citizens not required to physically submit Govt. documents / certificates.

Establish a comprehensive data protection regime for digital communications that safeguards the privacy, autonomy and choice of individuals. Enforce accountability through appropriate institutional mechanisms to assure citizens of safe and Secure digital communications infrastructure and services.

Q.9. The time has come for India and Japan to build a strong contemporary relationship, one involving global and strategic partnership that will have a great significance for Asia and the world as a whole. Comment. (Answer in 150 words) (10)

Important Points for Answer:
- *Introduction*
- *Why India and Japan need a strong contemporary relation with global and strategic partnership?*
- *Key Areas of Cooperation*
- *Challenges ahead*

[N.B. Explanatory answers are brief in nature, so the aspirants can make is precise according to the world limit and requirement of the question]

Answer: India and Japan share a long history of tradition and culture with the spread of Buddhism there. This relation further strengthened in recent times when Japan's Suzuki Motor Corporation's historic investment in India in the early 1980s, which transformed the automobile sector, ties between the two countries have grown from strength to strength.

Why India and Japan need a strong contemporary relation with global and strategic partnership?

- India and Japan must endeavor to work together for a rules-based and inclusive world order that fosters trust and confidence by enhancing communication and connectivity to ensure rule of law, unimpeded trade and flow of people, technology and ideas for shared prosperity.
- This relation is a corner stone of India's Act East Policy through the India-Japan Act East for implementing projects for enhancing connectivity, sustainable forest and ecological management, disaster risk reduction and people-to people exchanges.

Key Areas of Cooperation:

1. **Economy:** Japan, which is the largest bilateral donor for India, has been extending bilateral loans and grant assistance since 1958. Japan has been allowed to invest in India's North-East, which has been a no-go area for other countries. The Shinkansen (Japanese bullet train) is being introduced in the busy Mumbai-Ahmedabad section in India.
2. **Defence:** India and Japan along with US have been taking part in the Malabar naval exercises which is strengthening our maritime naval relations. Deepen bilateral security and defence cooperation and institute Foreign and Defence Ministerial Dialogue (2+2).
3. **Guiding Demographic dividend:** Synergizing India's demographic dividend with Japan's capital and technology will realize the true potential of the India-Japan economic partnership for a prosperous future.
4. **Health:** To linking of Japan's Asia Health and Wellbeing Initiative (AHWIN) with India's healthcare initiatives such as Ayushman Bharat will be very beneficial for India's growing Health demand.
5. **Partnership for Global Action:** Growing collaboration for achieving the Sustainable Development Goals (SDGs). Strengthening environmental partnership in areas such as

pollution control, sustainable biodiversity management, chemical and waste management, climate change and waste water management.

Challenges ahead:

The bilateral trade between New Delhi and Tokyo in 2017-18 stood at a meagre $15.71 billion, whereas the Sino-Indian bilateral trade in 2017 stood at $84.44 billion in spite of the political tensions between India and China.

The two sides have also been unable to collaborate in the defense sector in spite of huge potential. Japan and India have no major conflict of interests and Tokyo's "Free and Open Indo-Pacific Vision" gels well with New Delhi's "Act-East Policy." This is proving ever truer as New Delhi and Tokyo inch closer to each other.

Q.10. Too little cash, too much politics, leaves UNESCO fighting for life. Discuss the statement in the light of US withdrawal and its accusation of the cultural body as being anti-Israel bias. (Answer in 150 words) (10)

Important Points for Answer:

- *Introduction*
- *Why US withdrew from UNESCO?*
- *Crisis at UNESCO*
- *How this affects the Organization?*
- *Conclusion*

Answer: Founded in 1946, UNESCO (United Nations Educational, Scientific and Cultural Organization) aims "to contribute to the building of peace, the eradication of poverty, sustainable development and intercultural dialogue" through the international circulation of ideas. Most famously, it protects cultural heritage around the world, from the Great Wall of China to Belgian beer culture, from the Stone Circles of Senegambia in Gambia to India's yoga tradition.

Why US withdrew from UNESCO?

The US left the organization in protest of UNESCO's anti-Israel bias, like Palestine, which has not been granted full membership to the United Nations, is a UNESCO member; The West Bank city of Hebron was recently named an official world heritage site in a UNESCO statement that also called Israeli occupation of the territory illegal. (Israel, another UNESCO member, argues that the ancient monuments in Hebron should be considered Jewish heritage.).

However, it would be a mistake to view the American decision primarily as a response to those resolutions. Instead, Washington's current exit from UNESCO integrates seamlessly into a longer historical trajectory of instrumental engagement with the organization.

Crisis at UNESCO:

1. **Stripping away of cash:** At the heart of this recent problem is a financing crisis since 2011, when UNESCO voted to admit Palestine as a full member state and Washington responded by halting payment of its annual dues. From then UNESCO is running on low budgets.
2. **Politics in UNESCO:** Japan, has threatened to withhold dues over the inclusion of the 1937 Nanjing Massacre in the body's "Memory of the World" programme. Russia and Ukraine have been at odds over Crimea, with Kiev accusing Moscow of trying to legitimize its annexation of the territory through UNESCO.

How this affects the Organization?

- Without U.S. money, UNESCO, which employs around 2,000 people worldwide, has been forced to cut programmes, freeze hiring and fill gaps with voluntary contributions.
- These politics and megre budgets will affect its already existing projects like UNESCO world heritage conservation and UNESCO MAN and Biosphere programmes.

Conclusion:

UNESCO was all about solidarity and creating a climate for peace between countries, but nations now use their dues to influence its programmes. So, countries should see UNESCO from that angle and not to influence other countries though political gestures.

Q.11. On what grounds a people's representative can be disqualified under the Representation of People Act, 1951? Also mention the remedies available to such person against his disqualification. (Answer in 250 words) (15)

Important Points for Answer:
- *Introduction*
- *Grounds behind people's representative can be disqualified under the representation of people act, 1951*
- *Remedies available to such person against his disqualification*
- *Conclusion*

Answer: The Representation of the People Act, 1951 provides for the conduct of election of the Houses of Parliament and to the House or Houses of the Legislature of each State. It also deals with the qualifications and disqualifications for membership of those Houses, the corrupt practices and other offences in connection with such elections.

Grounds behind people's representative can be disqualified under the representation of people act, 1951:

The reasons are as follows;

- He must not have been found guilty of certain election offences or corrupt practices in the elections.
- He must not have been convicted for any offence resulting in imprisonment for two or more years. But, the detention of a person under a preventive detention law is not a disqualification.

- He must not have failed to lodge an account of his election expenses within the time.
- He must not have any interest in government contracts, works or services.
- He must not be a director or managing agent nor hold an office of profit in a corporation in which the government has at least 25 per cent share.
- He must not have been dismissed from government service for corruption or disloyalty to the State.
- He must not have been convicted for promoting enmity between different groups or for the offence of bribery.
- He must not have been punished for preaching and practising social crimes such as untouchability, dowry and sati.

Remedies available to such person against his disqualification

Lily Thomas case (2013) had implied automatic disqualification once a person was convicted irrespective of whether he or she was acquitted by the top court. EC would then have the seat declared vacant and hold polls to fill it up. Before this there was a three-month period for a disqualified MP to appeal in court.

The offence of filing a false affidavit, doesn't account as a corrupt practice under RPA Act. So it will cause only 6 months of imprisonment and it doesn't result in disqualification of the candidate.

As a result, the safeguard provided in the RPA against convicted criminals acting as representatives does not operate effectively, due to the low numbers of convictions and the high levels of delay.

Conclusion:

On the question whether a member is subject to any of the above disqualifications, the president's decision is final. However, he should obtain the opinion of the election commission and act accordingly.

Q.12. "Parliament's power to amend the Constitution is a limited power and it cannot be enlarged into absolute power." In the light of this statement explain whether Parliament under Article 368 of the Constitution can destroy the Basic Structure of the Constitution by expanding its amending power? (Answer in 250 words) (15)

Important Points for Answer:
- *Introduction*
- *Defining basic structure of Indian Constitution*
- *Constitutional provisions for amending it*

Answer: Article 368 of the Constitution deals with the powers of Parliament to amend the Constitution and its procedure. It states that the Parliament may, in exercise of its constituent power, amend by way of addition, variation or repeal any provision of the Constitution in accordance with the procedure laid down for the purpose. However, the Parliament cannot amend those provisions which form the 'basic structure' of the Constitution. this was ruled by the Supreme Court in the *Kesavananda Bharati* case (1973).

Defining basic structure of Indian Constitution:

The basic structure doctrine is an Indian judicial principle that the Constitution of India has certain basic features that cannot be altered or destroyed through amendments by the parliament. Thus, it gives extra power to court to review and strike down any constitutional amendments and act enacted by the Parliament.

The Supreme Court is yet to define or clarify as to what constitutes the 'basic structure' of the Constitution. To from the various judgements, the following have emerged as 'basic features' of the Constitution or elements/components/ingredients of the 'basic structure' of the constitution:

1. Supremacy of the Constitution
2. Sovereign, democratic and republican nature of the Indian polity
3. Secular character of the Constitution
4. Separation of powers between the legislature, the executive and the judiciary
5. Federal character of the Constitution
6. Unity and integrity of the nation
7. Judicial Review
8. Free and Fair elections, etc.

Constitutional provisions for amending it:

Like any other written Constitution, the Constitution of India also provides for its amendment in order to adjust itself to the changing conditions and needs. However, the procedure laid down for its amendment is neither as easy as in Britain nor as difficult as in USA. In other words, the Indian Constitution is neither flexible nor rigid but a synthesis of both.

The checks the constitution placed for parliament to amend it:

1. **Special Majority:** The bill must be passed in each House by a special majority, that is, a majority (that is, more than 50 per cent) of the total membership of the House and a majority of two-thirds of the members of the House present and voting.
2. **No joint sitting:** Each House must pass the bill separately. In case of a disagreement between the two Houses, there is no provision for holding a joint sitting of the two Houses for the purpose of deliberation and passage of the bill.
3. **Ratification by half of the state legislatures:** If the bill seeks to amend the federal provisions of the Constitution, it must also be ratified by the legislatures of half of the states by a simple majority, that is, a majority of the members of the House present and voting.
4. **Judicial Review:** Courts can intervene and check whether it passes the test of 'not breaching the Basic structure of the constitution'.

Can article 368 of the constitution can destroy the Basic structure of the constitution by expanding its amending power?

This Act amended Article 368 and declared that there is no limitation on the constituent power of Parliament and no amendment can be questioned in any court on any ground including that of the contravention of any of the Fundamental Rights. Since the Constitution had conferred a limited amending power on the Parliament, the Parliament cannot under the exercise of that limited power enlarge that very power into an absolute power. Indeed, a limited amending power is one of the basic features of the Constitution and, therefore, the limitations on that power cannot be destroyed. In other words, Parliament cannot, under article 368, expand its amending power so as to acquire for itself the right to repeal or abrogate the Constitution or to destroy its basic features.

Q.13. "The reservation of seats for women in the institutions of local self-government has had a limited impact on the patriarchal character of the Indian Political Process." Comment (Answer in 250 words) (15)

Important Points for Answer:

- *Introduction*
- *Defining local self-government (LSG)*
- *Constraints women in LSG face while discharging their duties*
- *Conclusion*

Answer: After independence the participation of women in politics especially in the elected bodies was very low. It has been stated in various national and international forums that participation in decision-making bodies is very essential for women to improve their status in society. The 73rd and 74th constitutional amendments facilitated the large-scale participation of women in political institutions at the local and regional levels. These constitutional amendments made it mandatory for 33% members of decision-making bodies in local self-government (LSG) institutions to women.

What is LSG?

LSG is a local level government, which is constituted of and run with the active participation of the people of a locality, village or a group of villages in case of panchayat, and a ward in case of municipality or Municipal Corporation. In India LSG was prevalent from ancient times like sabha and samiti of vedic age or 'UR' of cholas. It got institutionalized and constitutionalized with the passage of 73rd and 74th amendment acts in 1991.

Women in LSG:

In all the LSG elections held after April 1993 reservation of seats for women has become mandatory. As a result, the participation of women has increased dramatically.

Constraints women in LSG face while discharging their duties

1. **Full time house wife part time Politician:** Their family members do not free them from their domestic chores. Elected women 'continued to perform all those duties that are expected of a full-time housewife' so the women are not capable of making their own deliberations and taking independent decisions. When a panchayat or municipal seat is

reserved for woman normally the wife or a family member of the sitting member gets the nomination. Lack of interest in politics prevents the women members from emerging as effective leaders. Often, after the completion of one term the reluctant women members lose the motivation to run for the second term.

2. **Lack of training:** Lack of training in interpreting the government rules, circulars and orders and lack of organizational acumen in keeping the members of the opposition faction and parties united and disciplined is another reason that keeps the women members dependent on the male leaders. Taking advantage of the situation the male members continue to control the real power in running the LSG bodies while keeping the women members marginalized.

3. **Male prejudice:** In the male dominated society and in the masculinized political field the women will get very little space to operate freely and develop their political selves. Female members of the local bodies are actually controlled by their husbands or fathers, or influential party leaders. Women elected members are not allowed to move freely as there is an overall fear of insecurity. There are instances of violence against the elected members in order to dishearten and threaten them.

Conclusion:

Through their active participation in the LSGs and in the development programmes the women will grow in social awareness and political consciousness and would turn out to be active agents of the democratic order and activists of a silent democratic revolution. The Faster this happens the more secure would be the future of Indian democracy.

Q.14. "The Attorney-General is the chief legal adviser and lawyer of the Government of India." Discuss. (Answer in 250 words) (15)

Important Points for Answer:
- *Introduction*
- *Appointment and Term*
- *Duties and Functions*
- *Rights and Limitations*

Answer: The Constitution (Article 76) has provided for the office of the Attorney General for India. He is the highest law officer in the country.

Appointment and Term

The Attorney General (AG) is appointed by the president. He must be a person who is qualified to be appointed a judge of the Supreme Court. He holds office during the pleasure of the president. This means that he may be removed by the president at any time. Conventionally, he resigns when the government (council of ministers) resigns or is replaced, as he is appointed on its advice. The remuneration of the AG is not fixed by the Constitution. He receives such remuneration as the president may determine.

Duties and Functions:

As the chief law officer of the Government of India, the duties of the AG include the following:

- To give advice to the Government of India upon such legal matters, which are referred to him by the president.
- To perform such other duties of a legal character that are assigned to him by the president.
- To discharge the functions conferred on him by the Constitution or any other law.

The president has assigned the following duties to the Attorney General:

- To appear on behalf of the Government of India in all cases in the Supreme Court in which the Government of India is concerned.
- To represent the Government of India in any reference made by the president to the Supreme Court under Article 143 of the Constitution.
- To appear (when required by the Government of India) in any high court in any case in which the Government of India is concerned.

Rights and Limitations:

- In the performance of his official duties, the Attorney General has the right of audience in all courts in the territory of India. Further, he has the right to speak and to take part in the proceedings of both the Houses of Parliament or their joint sitting and any committee of the Parliament of which he may be named a member, but without a right to vote.
- He enjoys all the privileges and immunities that are available to a member of Parliament.

Following limitations are placed on the Attorney General in order to avoid any complication and conflict of duty:

- He should not advise or hold a brief against the Government of India.
- He should not advise or hold a brief in cases in which he is called upon to advise or appear for the Government of India.
- He should not defend accused persons in criminal prosecutions without the permission of the Government of India.
- He should not accept appointment as a director in any company or corporation without the permission of the Government of India.
- However, the Attorney General is not a full-time counsel for the Government. He does not fall in the category of government servants.

Q.15. Individual Parliamentarian's role as the national law maker is on a decline, which in turn, has adversely impacted the quality of debates and their outcome. Discuss. (Answer in 250 words) (15)

Important Points for Answer:

- *Introduction*
- *Discuss the role of a Member of Parliament*
- *Reasons behind declining the legislative and deliberative roles of parliamentarian*
- *What has adversely impacted the quality of debates and their outcome?*

Answer: A Member of Parliament (MP) holds a very important position in a parliamentary democracy like India. With 543 MPs in the Lok Sabha (Lower House) representing more than 1.2 billion people, a Lok Sabha MP on an average represents more than 2.2 million people. A Rajya Sabha (Upper House) MP is the voice of his State in Parliament, and as such, has a very important role in our federal political system.

Role of a Member of Parliament:

1. **Legislative role of an MP:** The primary role of an MP is as a legislator. According to Article 111 of the Constitution of India, any Bill becomes an Act only if passed by both houses of Parliament and assented to by the President. Additionally, when a Bill is introduced in either House of Parliament, the MPs are supposed to debate on various provisions of the Bill, and propose amendments if they so wish.
2. **Deliberative role of an MP:** In the Indian constitutional scheme, the Executive (government) is accountable to the legislature. This principle of accountability is realized partly by elected representatives (MPs) asking questions to government ministers, including the Prime Minister, in Parliament through provisions like Question Hour and a Zero Hour during which written and oral questions can be asked by MPs.
3. **Developmental role of an MP:** Apart from his role in Parliament, an MP also has an important developmental role in his/her State or constituency.
4. **The MP can fulfill this role with the aid of the following provisions:** MPLADS – Under the Member of Parliament Local Area Development Scheme (MPLADS) every MP is allocated Rs.5 crore per year for initiating developmental works in his constituency.

In recent times the legislative and deliberative roles of parliamentarian are in decline because of the following reasons:

- Growing Unitary party system in parliament is crushing the individuality of a parliamentarian.
- Strengthening of Office of Whips is shrinking individual responsibility of a parliamentarian.
- Anti-defection law is restricting the voice of parliamentarians. Because of this in cases where even he doesn't align with party's decision he is forced to support it.
- Tenure long elections are also reducing the quality time of the parliamentarians in enriching their knowledge.
- The number of days, parliament in session has declined from 100 to 70 days. This is also hampering the time they require to take part in effective debate.
- The basic idea of holding debates and forming national consensus has given way to loud protests and settling of individual political scores.
- Collusion between MPs is also reducing the quality of Questions debated in parliament.
- Lack of proper opposition is also adding fuel to the improper discussions in parliament.

This has adversely impacted the quality of debates and their outcome:

- Many bills and budgets are being passed without even proper discussion.
- The quality of Question hour discussions have reduced drastically.

- The reduced productivity of the sessions is resulting in Monetary loss, wastage of time, and most importantly, delay in the decision-making on vital issues of public importance
- Number of private members bills introduced in parliament reduced drastically.
- Increase the number of working days to minimum 100, which was proposed by a private members bill 'Parliament (Enhancement of Productivity) Bill, 2017'.
- Opposition should be given more importance and their questions answered diligently.
- Anti – defection law be made applicable to only major issues.
- Frequent exchange of Best practices being followed in other parliaments world over with our parliamentarians.

Q.16. In the context of neo-liberal paradigm of development planning, multi-level planning is expected to make operations cost-effective and remove many implementation blockages. – Discuss. (Answer in 250 words) (15)

Important Points for Answer:
- *Introduction*
- *How operations become cost-effective and remove many implementation blockages?*
- *Conclusion*

Answer: The concept of multi-level regional planning may be defined as 'planning for a variety of regions which together form a system and subordinate systems'. Multi-level planning involves all hierarchies of administrative, geographical, political and regional levels in planning process. It involves active participation of the lower hierarchical levels in information generation, data collection, policy suggestion, plan implementation and monitoring of all developmental activities. The administrative level the multi-level planning in India are: (1) Centre, (2) States, (3) Districts, (4) Blocks, and (5) Villages.

Multi-level planning based on Geography includes:
- Hill Areas Development Programme (HADP),
- Western Ghats Development Programme (WGDP) and
- Border Area Development Programme (BADP).

How operations become cost-effective and remove many implementation blockages?

1. **Resources for Planning**
   - Planning process becomes practical and flexible.
   - Planned based on locally available resources and human resources.
   - The cost of using local resources far lower than the using centralized resources
   - Efficient utilization of resources
2. **Better Integration of components**
   - Integration with sub-regional units becomes easier and effective on the ground.

- Correct assessment of connectivity and infrastructure

3. **People participation**
   - Local participation in the development process.
4. **Inclusive development**
   - Effective percolation of benefits to people.
   - Bottom up approach gives better results compared to trickle-down effect.
   - Community services like education, health, local infrastructure is better managed as the ownership of people is well known.
   - Local issues are tackled effectively and progress is visible on the ground.

5.Improve transparency and reduces corruption

- It empowers the ordinary citizens and improves transparency and accountability.
- Corruption at all levels of hierarchy can be removed.
- Most of the resource leakages can be stopped and implementation blockages can be removed.

Conclusion

Before the Amendment of the Constitution in 1992 through 73rd and 74th amendment acts, the task of plan formulation was basically carried out by the Centre and the State governments. The other levels (district, block, and village) of the planning process came into the picture only at the implementation stage of planning. However, after 1992, the lower levels of planning have been given more powers in the formulation and implementation of their plans and financial provisions.

Q.17. The need for cooperation among various service sectors has been an inherent component of development discourse. Partnership bridges the gap among the sectors. It also sets in motion a culture of collaboration and team spirit. In the light of statements above examine India's development process. (Answer in 250 words) (15)

Important Points for Answer:
- *Introduction*
- *Service Sectors scenarios in India*
- *Highlights of the 12 champion service sectors*
- *Cooperation and coordination among them*

Answer: Development is the process in which someone or something grows or changes and becomes more advanced. India in its growth story took the help of Primary (Agri related) as well as secondary (manufacturing) sectors to achieve higher standards of development. But the latest entrant into this process after liberalization, the service sector, is boosting the economy into another league with its inherent quality of globalization and integrating world order.

Service Sectors:

The services sector is not only the dominant sector in India's GDP (it has contributed 54.17 per cent of India's Gross Value Added), but has also attracted significant foreign investment flows, contributed significantly to exports as well as provided large-scale employment. The services sector has contributed 57.12 % of India's Gross Value Added at current prices in H1 2018-19. India is a net services exporter of US$ 77.56 billion during 2017-18 employing 33% of India's population. India is a growing services powerhouse of the world as the world largest outsourcing destination for IT & IT enables services, a popular medical tourism spot, growing Infrastructure and Construction services market, an attractive destination for VFX, animation & post-production services and many more. Keeping this huge potential in mind government has identified 12 champion service sectors.

12 Champion service sectors:

Champion Services Sectors refers to the 12 identified sectors where the Government wants to give focused attention for promoting their development, and realizing their potential. These include:

1. Information Technology & Information Technology enabled Services (IT& ITeS),
2. Tourism and Hospitality Services,
3. Medical Value Travel,
4. Transport and Logistics Services,
5. Accounting and Finance Services,
6. Audio Visual Services,
7. Legal Services,
8. Communication Services,
9. Construction and Related Engineering Services,
10. Environmental Services,
11. Financial Services and
12. Education Services.

A dedicated fund of Rs. 5000 crores have been proposed to be established to support initiatives for sectoral Action Plans of the Champion Sectors.

Cooperation and coordination among them:

No particular sector can work in isolation. For example, Agricultural sector utilizes Electric Pump sets for irrigation, which is a product of manufacturing sector. And also, a car manufacturing company utilizes the services of Tertiary sector for better customer satisfaction (like integrating Maps in to driving and also self-driving technologies using ITES). This cooperation is enhancing their performance.

Q.18. Performance of welfare schemes that are implemented for vulnerable sections is not so effective due to absence of their awareness and active involvement at all stages of policy process. – Discuss (Answer in 250 words) (15)

Important Points for Answer:
- *Introduction*
- *Welfare Schemes for vulnerable sections*
- *Ineffectiveness in implementation*
- *Way ahead & Conclusion*

Answer: Vulnerable sections are those groups of people who are more likely to be attacked or harmed, either physically or emotionally in the environment they are living, which can be explained with few examples:

- An elderly parent who is unable to provide livelihood for the household no more.
- A disabled person who is considered as burden to family.
- A migrant who has no place to live.

Welfare Schemes for vulnerable sections:

- Schemes educating and imparting skills among ST's and SC's and other back ward classes of society.
- Effective implementation of 'prohibition of Manual Scavengers Employment' and providing better facilities for them.
- An integrated program for Empowering and improving the quality of life of Older People.
- Beti Bachao Beti padao scheme for saving girl child from societal inhibitions and educating them.
- Sabla scheme for empowering adult women.
- Rashtriya Bal SwasthyaKaryakram (RBSK) for overall development of Adult women including awareness about their health.
- Janani Suraksha Yojana (JSY) for safeguarding women while giving birth and after that.
- Insurance schemes like PM jan Jeevan Bima Yojana, Jeevan Jyothi bema yojana etc are being given to provide insurance coverage.

Ineffectiveness in implementation:

Though all these schemes are well intentioned and planned. They are falling flat when it's coming to implementation. Implementation hurdles are many fold, but they can be classified in to two categories:

Problem at government side:

- There are too many schemes to be monitored.
- There is unwillingness to accept poor performance, for fear of being questioned by Parliament or adverse press publicity.
- Capacity to do monitoring is limited, and often does not exist. Thus, there is neither will nor capability for the task.

- No proper channel to verify whether all the grievances are redressed.
- Improper functioning of Common Service Centers which will work as nodes for information dissemination at remote levels.

Problem at beneficiary side:

- Illiteracy.
- Lack of awareness about the schemes which are being implemented because of
- Very less digital knowledge, to skim through different websites to look into the schemes which would apply to them.
- Unable to distinguish between misinformation, makes beneficiaries vulnerable to fake news.
- Lack of instinct to Question when they are denied a service which is intended for them, makes them more vulnerable.

Way ahead:

Government is trying to make strenuous efforts to make their programs reach intended beneficiaries at various levels. On such great example being Implementation of Right to Information (RTI) in 2005, which provides people with all the required information.

Conclusion:

The challenge in implementation of government scheme would be to ensure that the information flow remains unhampered over time along with the plugging of leakages at the top level. While digital connectivity and literacy have increased over time, these have not adequately translated into digital knowledge of public affairs. So, it is important to educate the citizenry about the use of data on various schemes intended for them.

Q.19. The long-sustained image of India as a leader of the oppressed and marginalised nations has disappeared on account of its new found role in the emerging global order. Elaborate. (Answer in 250 words) (15)

Important Points for Answer:

- *Introduction*
- *New found role in the emerging global order*
- *Does it mean the long-sustained image of India as a leader of the oppressed and marginalised nations has disappeared?*
- *Highlights the role of India in world affairs*
- *Conclusion*

Answer: During cold war period, India was seen as a bright spot as a representative of the oppressed and marginalised nations who were suffering from colonialism and imperialism. But the change in world order post Societ-Union breakup and economic crisis in early 1990s have fundamentally changed the way India look at the world.

New found role in the emerging global order:

The economic diplomacy has taken front seat in dealing with the world. Reaping the benefits of economic liberalization towards economic growth and prosperity has become major focus of diplomacy after economic crisis in 1991. Economic prosperity was seen as a 'tide that lifts all boats. It is also seen as the key to India's attainment of great power status and recognition at the world stage.

USA: India started looking at big economic power houses like USA which was not so close ally during Cold war period. The nuclear deal of 2006 despite heated debates in India was made between USA and India.

USSR and Russia: India did show such closeness with Russia the successor of the erstwhile USSR as was shown during Cold War period.

Israel: India also moved so closely with Israel. This development was completely different from pre-1991 years.

UNSC: Looking for UNSC permanent seat by joining G4 group – India, Germany, Japan, Brazil, without any representation from the African continent.

Does it mean the long-sustained image of India as a leader of the oppressed and marginalised nations has disappeared?

The developments after 1991 have created an impression that India no longer willing to lead the poor nations of the Third World in a struggle against imperialism. India is no longer wishing to project its power merely within the conflicted confines of its own neighbourhood. India is pressing its suit on the world stage

Highlights the role of India in world affairs: India still accords priority to security issues and retains its nuclear weapons option. India stresses are Anti-terrorism, Inclusive Globalization, Nuclear Disarmament, Energy Security, Investing in Africa.

Conclusion:

On balance, given its unique socio-economic, security conditions of the time modern India is articulating and prioritizing its national interests while dealing with the world. But it also raises its voice over collective interests of the world which includes the issues of poor and marginalized countries as well.

Q.20. What introduces friction into the ties between India and the United States is that Washington is still unable to find for India a position in its global strategy, which would satisfy India's national self-esteem and ambitious. Explain with suitable examples. (Answer in 250 words) (15)

Important Points for Answer:
- *Introduction*
- *Highlights the friction areas between India and the United States*
- *The areas of cooperation between India and the United States*
- *Conclusion*

Answer: India's foreign policy is based on a strong sense of nationalism and feeling of historical, cultural, and strategic uniqueness. Indian leaders expect that the USA would recognize India's importance in the international order and confer on it an equality of status. Despite plenty of positive momentum, many sticky issues may affect the future progress in Indo-U.S. relations.

Highlights the friction areas between India and the United States:

1. Oil imports:

New Delhi has been forced to stop concessional oil imports from both Iran and Venezuela, and these heavy-handed American tactics have led to sharp rise in India's oil import bill. India's energy security requires a stable Middle East and New Delhi cannot be expected to downgrade its profile in the region.

2. Strategic importance of Iran:

The U.S. attempts to undercut India's strategic ties with Iran are going to pose serious challenges for Indian foreign policy.

3. Terrorism:

The common concerns of India and Iran about threat of jihadist terrorism emanating from Pakistani territory make Iran an important geopolitical partner of India.

4. GSP:

The GSP is a preferential trade program that gives developing countries like India easier access to the American market by reducing duties on their exports. India has been a huge beneficiary of the Generalized System of Preferences (GSP) program, but the USA administration is moving ahead to end it.

5. E-commerce:

Washington also wants India to relax e-commerce rules. Many rounds of talks on a comprehensive trade package have failed to yield any breakthrough.

6. UNSC Reforms:

USA's support for India's permanent member status is not turning into practical shape.

The areas of cooperation between India and the United States:

1. Military Cooperation:

The Logistics Exchange Memorandum of Agreement (LEMOA), which allows the Indian and American forces to use each other's facilities, was signed in 2016. The Communications

Compatibility and Security Agreement (COMCASA) was signed during the inaugural "two-plus-two" talks in 2018.

2. China Factor:

India and the U.S. seem determined to counter China's maritime expansion, which is seen as a threat to their trade routes in the Indian and Pacific Oceans.

3. Terrorism:

The USA has been more vocal for New Delhi's fight against terrorism. The present USA administration has also thrown its weight behind the International Monetary Fund (IMF) to reinforce the Financial Action Task Force (FATF) demands on Pakistan.

Conclusion:

Thus, the analysis of both co-operative and frictional areas shows that the Indo-U.S. ties have gathered momentum fuelled by strategic realities and political convergence. Understanding India's sensibilities and self-esteem will give USA a long-term perspective in dealing with India.

SOLVED PAPERS

PAPER–III

Time Allowed : 3 hours *Maximum Marks : 250*

Candidates should attempt ALL questions strictly in accordance with the instructions given under each question.

Q.1. Enumerate the indirect taxes which have been subsumed in the Goods and Services Tax (GST) in India. Also, Comment on the revenue implications of the GST introduced in India since July 2017. (Answer in 150 words) (10)

Important Points for Answer:

- *Introduction*
- *The Intended Mission of GST*
- *Revenue implications of the GST introduced in India since July 2017*
- *Conclusion*

Answer: The GST (Goods and Services tax) the biggest tax reform in India founded on the notion of "one nation, one market, one tax" was introduced in India on 1 July 2017. It replaced many indirect taxes being levied by the central and state governments. It has changed the taxation landscape is in India.

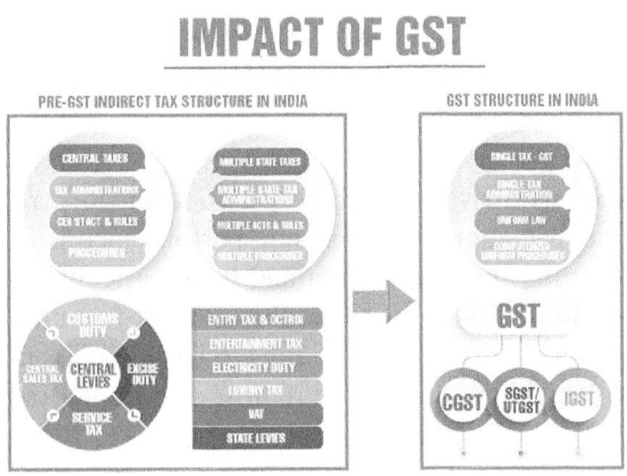

The Intended Mission of GST:

- To create 'one nation one tax'
- To ensure timely compliance
- To bring in transparency
- To improve ease of doing business for taxpayers
- Ultimately to reduce the tax burden for the common man

Revenue implications of the GST introduced in India since July 2017:

The assessee base:

- In the pre-GST period, traders had to comply with the rules and regulations of various tax departments and laws. Now, tax compliance has been easier for traders. This has augured well for the government as the revenue base has expanded exponentially. The assessee base under GST has increased by about 85 per cent in the past two years. On the eve of the GST rollout, the assessee number stood at around 65 lakh, which has gone up to 1.20 crore now.

Revenue collection:

- The government's revenue collection has also gone up. The average revenue collection per month in the eight months of 2017-18 was Rs 89,700 crore per month. This propelled the annual revenue collection by about 12 per cent. The monthly average revenue collection increased further in 2018-19 by about 10 per cent to Rs 97,100 crore.

Increase in buoyancy:

- In the first year (2017-2018) of implementation of GST, revenues grew by 11.9% and the buoyancy was 1.20. A buoyancy ratio over 1 shows progressiveness in the revenue growth and opens up the prospect of a rising tax-to-GDP ratio. This is a significant improvement over the pre-GST period when the buoyancy ratios for state value added tax (VAT) and central indirect taxes were less than 1.
- A further surge in GST revenue will happen once land and real estate is brought under the GST net. This will clean up the land market and the revenue gains will be more on the direct tax side as more transactions are reported under GST.

Conclusion:

Two years have passed since its arrival, and there's a widespread perception that GST revenue growth has not lived up to expectations. The revenue performance is especially creditable given the transitional difficulties during implementation and teething technical problems with the GST Network (GSTN). GST is still a work in progress. It is evident from the 35 meetings of the GST Council that has made 90 amendments in the GST rules. The council is now rolling out a new GST return filing system that will enable traders to file returns in a single format once a month instead of multiple formats.

Q.2. Do you agree with the view that steady GDP growth and low inflation have left the Indian economy in good shape? Give reasons in support of your arguments. (Answer in 150 words) (10)

Important Points for Answer:
- *Introduction*
- *Present Economic situation*
- *Measure taken to keep the economy again on track*
- *Conclusion*

Answer: The Indian economy has scored an average 7.5 per cent growth of GDP annually for last 5 years. Even though there are controversies about the exact numbers, most economists are agreed that the trend is upwards. For the past few years, the government has handled inflation better than ever in the past two decades. Good management of inflation has kept the Indian economy on track.

Present Economic situation:

Inflation

- Low inflation is often a good thing. But it may not always be a sign of health if it keeps falling. While a low inflation is good for consumers, it is also a sign of weak demand and thus takes away the pricing power of producers, discouraging fresh investments and job creation.
- In recent months, India's wholesale price index-based inflation came in at a 23-month low of 2.02%, and core inflation, at 31-month low of 0.8%, have raised concerns on whether the country has a low inflation problem now.

GDP:

- GDP growth sliding to a six-year low of 5 per cent in the June quarter, on a massive slowdown in consumption and private sector investments. The Reserve Bank of India also sharply cut its economic growth projection for this fiscal to 6.1 per cent from 6.9 per cent earlier, but expressed hope that the growth will recover in the second half of 2019-20.

Slowdown in various sectors:

- There is an acute slowdown in the manufacturing and agriculture sectors on the back of a slowdown in aggregate demand - both consumption and investment demand. Except for mining activity and power generation, all other productive sectors have slowed on a year-on-year basis.

Global scenario

- An escalation of trade tensions between USA-China, a hard or no-deal Brexit and increased volatility in global financial markets pose downside risks to the baseline growth path, it said.

Measure taken to keep the economy again on track:

Finance Minister has announced a number of steps to revive economic growth and shore up market confidence, including;

- Promises of upfront release of funds for recapitalisation of public sector banks (PSBs) and merger of PSBs

- A massive 10 percentage point cut in corporate taxes
- Rolling back recent tax hikes on foreign and domestic equity investors and several measures for industries.
- The government further liberalised foreign direct investment (FDI) rules in many sectors, in an effort to get economic growth back on track.
- The government allowed 100% foreign investment for coal mining, associated infrastructure and sales of fuel.

Conclusion:

Therefore, a moderate level of inflation that does not pinch the consumer and encourages business activity is usually considered good for the economy. As part of the Monetary Policy Framework, the government has mandated the RBI to keep retail inflation at 4%, within a band of 2 percentage points. The weight of structural factors has gone up in the slowdown and mere monetary stimulus may not work beyond a limit. Thus, once again structural reforms are necessary to keep the economy back on growth trajectory.

Q.3. How far is Integrated Farming System (IPS) helpful in sustaining agricultural production? (Answer in 150 words) (10)

Important Points for Answer:
- *Introduction*
- *How is sustainable agricultural production achieved though IFS?*
- *Way forward*

Answer: Integrated Farming System (IFS) is an interdependent and interlocking production systems based on crops, animals and related subsidiary elements in such a way that maximize the utilization of nutrients of each system and minimize the negative effect of these systems on environment. The interrelated, inter-dependent-interlocking nature of IFS involves the utilization of primary produce and secondary produce of one system, as basic input of the other system, thus making them mutually integrated as one whole unit.

How is sustainable agricultural production achieved though IFS?

The role of IFS in attaining sustainable agricultural production includes:
- Maximization of yield of Agriculture and provide steady and stable income.
- Rejuvenation of soil productivity and achieve agro ecological equilibrium.
- Control the growth of insects and weeds population through natural cropping system management and keep them at low level of intensity.
- Reducing the use of chemical fertilizer and other harmful agrochemicals and pesticides to provide pollution free produce.

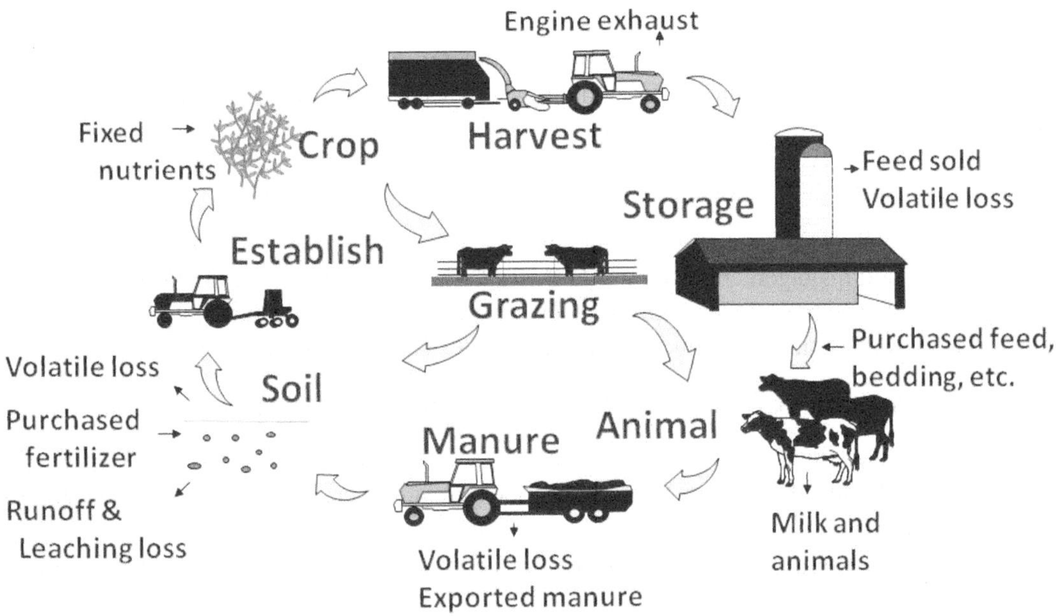

Illustration: Integrated Farming System model

- Increase in natural resource use efficiency by early recycling of nutrients.
- Mitigation of negative impact of agriculture or livestock on environment.
- Farming households with livestock would be able to better withstand distress caused due to extreme weather conditions and crop failures.

Way forward:

Agriculture industry contributes 17% of India's total GDP, out of which, the 27% comes from Animal Husbandry and overall, the dairy, poultry and aqua industries contribute 4.4% to the nation's GDP. These numbers signify the crucial role played by these sectors in our economy. In addition to it, rural economy was dependent on agriculture and its allied sectors such as poultry, dairy and others and IFS provides gainful employment to a large number of youngsters from rural areas.

Therefore, the Integrated Farming System (IFS) helpful in sustaining agricultural production.

Q.4. Elaborate the impact of National Watershed Project in increasing agricultural production from water-stressed areas. (Answer in 150 words) (10)

Important Points for Answer:
- *Introduction*
- *Impact on increasing agricultural production from water-stressed areas*
- *Impact of National Watershed Project*

Answer: Watershed management is the process of guiding and organizing the use of water and land and other resources in a watershed to provide desired goods and services without adversely affecting soil and water resources. Integrated watershed management program (IWMP) was implemented since 2009-10, for supporting watershed development in 28 States. From 2015-16 onwards, the IWMP is being implemented as the Watershed Component of Pradhan Mantri Krishi Sinchayi Yojana (PMKSY).

Neeranchal, World Bank aided National Watershed Project is designed to give technical support to Integrated watershed management program (IWMP). IWMP is aimed at helping farmers and public to harness natural resources to the optimum level, thereby increasing productivity and making farming and allied activities economically viable in water-stressed areas.

Impact on increasing agricultural production from water-stressed areas:

National Watershed Project aimed at ensuring access to irrigation to every farm (Har Khet Ko Pani) and efficient use of water (Per Drop More Crop). Neeranchal is primarily designed to address the following concerns:

- Bring about institutional changes in watershed and rainfed agricultural management practices in India.
- Build systems that ensure watershed programmes and rainfed irrigation management practices are better coordinated, and have quantifiable results.
- Devise strategies for the sustainability of improved watershed management practices for long time.
- Through technical assistance to improve incremental conservation outcomes and agricultural yields for communities in selected sites

Impact of National Watershed Project:

- Reduce surface runoff of rainwater
- Increase recharge of ground water and better availability of water in rainfed areas
- Increase rain fed agriculture productivity
- Aid in Animal husbandry there by increase in Dairy production.

Q.5. How was India benefitted from the contributions of Sir M. Visvesvaraya and Dr. M.S. Swaminathan in the fields of water engineering and agricultural science respectively? (Answer in 150 words) (10)

Important Points for Answer:

- *Introduction about the contribution*
- *How India benefitted from the contributions of Sir M.Visvesvaraya in the fields of water engineering?*
- *How India benefitted from the contributions of Dr. M. S. Swaminathan in the fields of agricultural science?*
- *Conclusion*

Answer: The contribution of Sir M. Visvesvaraya in the field of water engineering and Dr. M. S. Swaminathan in the area of agricultural science is commendable. Their contribution had a lasting impact on Indian society as a whole.

How India benefitted from the contributions of Sir M.Visvesvaraya in the fields of water engineering?

- Sir M. Visvesvaraya stands out as the pioneering Indian engineer. He began as a civil engineer in Bombay Presidency in 1884. But it was his engineering feat at Sukur in Sindh Province (then part of Bombay Presidency) in 1893-1895 that brought him fame.
  - He devised an ingenious method to filter the muddy and discoloured water of Indus by digging a well on riverbed and creating a tunnel below the river to bring drinking water for the city to the pumping station.
  - Later on, he specialized in irrigation, water supply and drainage works.
  - His notable projects include The Krishna Raja Sagara Lake and dam, which was built in 1924. At the time, it was the largest reservoir in India.
  - He was involved in Pune suburban water supply project.
  - He devised sluice gates at Lake Fife in Khadakvasala, Pune for which he took patent. This technology stopped the loss of excess water.
  - He also lent consultancy services to Nizam of Hyderabad after the great Musi floods of 1908. The two projects he advised the Nizam government was related to sewerage and reservoir of river Musi, a tributary of Krishna in 1909.

How India benefitted from the contributions of Dr. M. S. Swaminathan in the fields of agricultural science?

- He ushered in green revolution and laid a firm foundation for India's food security.
- Swaminathan has been called the "Father of Green Revolution in India" for his role in introducing and further developing high-yielding varieties of wheat in India.
- Swaminathan advocated to moving India to sustainable development, using environmentally sustainable agriculture, sustainable food security and the preservation of biodiversity, evergreen revolution.
- His vision and lucidity of expression have captivated more than a whole generation of agricultural scientists.

Conclusion:

Thus, their vision, foresight, intellectual capability and the abilities to connect the research findings with people of the country have earned them great respect across the spectrum.

Q.6. What is India's plan to have its own space station and how will it benefit our space programme? (Answer in 150 words) (10)

Important Points for Answer:
- *Introduction about space station*
- *India's plan to have its own space station*
- *How will it benefit our space programme?*

Answer: Space has been the new frontier of 21st Century. India has made remarkable progress in Space Technology and Planetary Exploration in the last two decade and took major strides in utilizing the operational space systems in various fronts of national development—commercial, strategic, societal and economic. In this direction India is mulling to have its own space station.

A space station, also known as an orbital station, is a spacecraft capable of supporting a human crew in orbit for an extended period of time that lacks major propulsion or landing systems. Stations must have docking ports to allow other spacecraft to dock to transfer crew and supplies. Space stations have most often been launched for scientific purposes, but military launches have also occurred.

India's plan to have its own space station:

- To have a separate space station in the space is the ambition of India. ISRO, first, will launch a small module for conducting microgravity experiments.
- According to Dr. Sivan, Chairman of the ISRO, the proposed space station is envisaged to weigh 20 tonnes and serve as a facility where astronauts can stay for 15-20 days. It would be placed in an orbit 400 km above earth.

Docking technology

- ISRO is about to conduct a Docking Experiment next year. The space agency has to master the complex docking technology as it is an essential building-block process for setting up the country's own space station and sending humans to that station. It involves latching of one satellite with another with the help on-board cameras and constant monitoring by the earth station.

Space station after Gaganyaan

- Indian Space Research Organisation (ISRO) will begin working on its space station following its first manned mission to space, called Gaganyaan (which means "space vehicle" in Sanskrit), in 2022—just in time to commemorate 75 years of the country's independence from Britain.
- Gaganyaan aims to send a crew of two to three people to space for a period of up to seven days. The spacecraft will be placed in low Earth orbit of 300-400 km (186-248 miles).
- The detailed project report on setting up a space station will be submitted to the government after the Gaganyaan mission. The time frame for launching space station is 5-7 years after Gaganyaan.

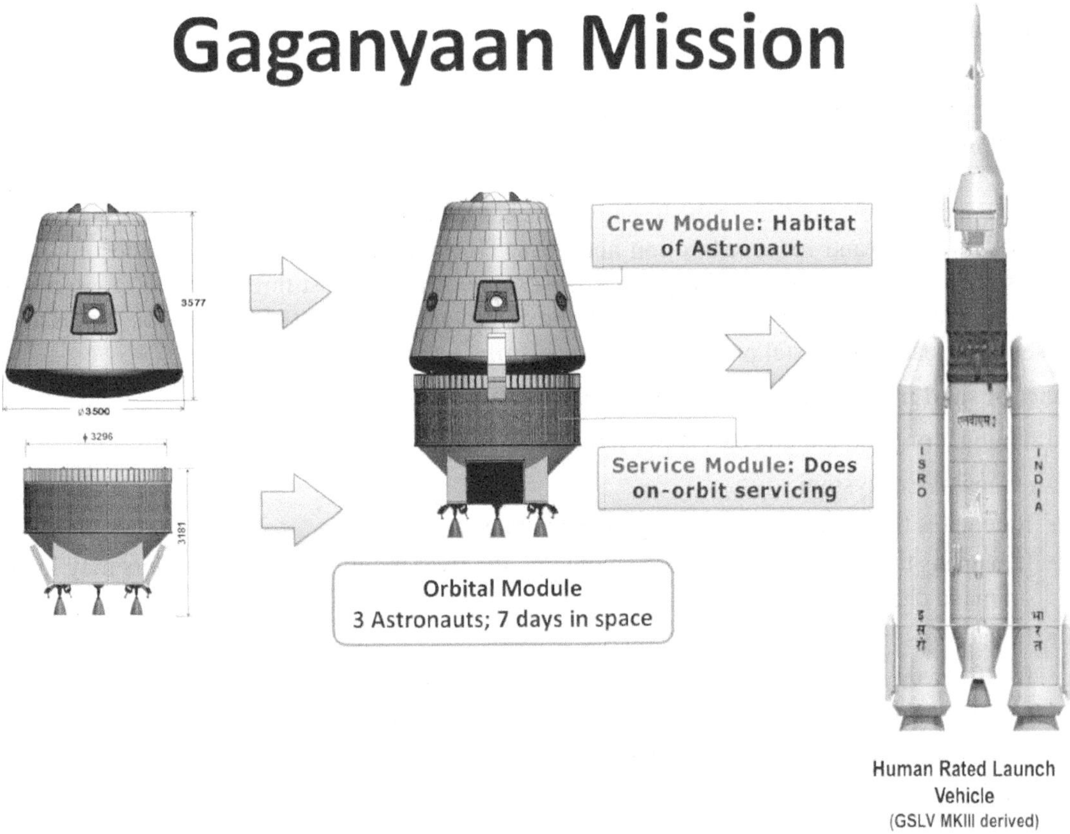

How will it benefit our space programme?

- It will inspire the young minds to take an interest in scientific fields.
- The space station will make it possible for Indians to have an ongoing presence in space.
- The laboratories present in space station allow to do research that could not be done anywhere else. This scientific research benefits whole mankind. Space research is even used in everyday life.
- Scientists also study what happens to the body when people live in microgravity for a long time.
- All of these lessons will be important for future space exploration.

Q.7. Coastal sand mining, whether legal or illegal, poses one of the biggest threats to our environment. Analyze the impact of sand mining along the Indian coasts, citing specific examples. (Answer in 150 words) (10)

Important Points for Answer:
- *Introduction*
- *Impact of sand mining along the Indian coasts, citing specific examples*
- *Conclusion*

Answer: For centuries, sand along the Indian coasts has been mined for use as aggregate in concrete, for heavy minerals, and for construction activities. However, recent unregulated and unmindful coastal sand mining, whether legal or illegal, poses one of the biggest threats to our environment. Sand mining in many localities has resulted in the complete destruction of beach ecosystems along with severe impacts to coastal protection and tourism.

Impact of sand mining along the Indian coasts, citing specific examples

Sand mining along the Indian coasts does have the following effects:

1. On Coastal Ecosystem
- It depletes the streambed and along coastal areas
- It deepens the rivers and estuaries and enlarge the river mouths and coastal inlets may lead to dramatic channel readjustments.
- It leads to soil erosion.
- It affects the water tables and may lead to saline-water intrusion from the nearby sea. Its effect is even more dangerous when sea level rises topographical disorder
- It causes severe ecological imbalance

2. *On People*
- Saline-water intrusion disturbs the drinking water and irrigation water system and affects the local people who are dependent on it.
- It leads to destruction of beaches and affects tourism further affects livelihood of people who are depending on it.
- It reduced protection from storms, tsunamis, and wave events and cause damage to coastal population

3. *Wildlife*
- Destruction of aquatic and riparian habitat.
- Native species in streams which are uniquely adapted to the habitat conditions are affected.
- Coastal barriers for cyclones and Tsunami like Mangroves may disappear.

4. *On Structures*
- It is also a threat to bridges and nearby structures and damage to land use patterns

5. Examples
- Sundarban Mangrove forests are being depleted.
- The live of Olive Ridly Turtles on the beaches of Odisha severely affected.
- Coastal ecosystem near Krishna-Godavari rivers badly affected

Conclusion:

In many cases, addressing the issue of sand mining requires addressing the local issues that allow it to persist. This includes poverty, corruption, and unregulated development.

Q.8. Vulnerability is an essential element for defining disaster impacts and its threat to people. How and in what ways can vulnerability to disasters be characterised? Discuss different types of vulnerability with reference to disasters. (Answer in 150 words) (10)

Important Points for Answer:
- *Introduction*
- *How and in what ways can vulnerability to disasters be characterized?*
- *Different types of vulnerability with reference to disasters*
- *Conclusion*

Answer: India, due to its, physiographic and climatic conditions is one of the most disaster prone areas of the world. Vulnerability to disasters of Chemical, Biological, Radiological and Nuclear (CBRN) origin also exists. In such circumstances, Vulnerability is an essential element for defining disaster impacts and its threat to people. Heightened vulnerabilities to disaster risks can be related to increasing population, urbanisation, industrialisation, development within high-risk zones, environmental degradation, and climate change.

How and in what ways can vulnerability to disasters be characterized?

According to United Nations (UN) International Strategy for Disaster Reduction (ISDR) Terminology on Disaster Risk Reduction, Vulnerability describes the characteristics and circumstances of a community, system or asset that make it susceptible to the damaging effects of a hazard. There are many aspects of vulnerability, arising from various physical, social, economic, and environmental factors. Examples may include:

1. Poor design and construction of buildings,
2. Inadequate protection of assets,
3. Lack of public information and awareness,
4. Limited official recognition of risks and preparedness measures, and
5. Disregard for wise environmental management.

Different types of vulnerability with reference to disasters.

There are four (4) main types of vulnerability:

1. Physical Vulnerability: It may be determined by aspects such as population density levels, remoteness of a settlement, the site, design and materials used for critical infrastructure and for housing.

Example: Wooden homes are less likely to collapse in an earthquake, but are more vulnerable to fire. Himalyan regions are more prone to earthquakes than any other place in India.

2. Social Vulnerability: It refers to the inability of people, organizations and societies to withstand adverse impacts to hazards due to characteristics inherent in social interactions, institutions and systems of cultural values.

Example: When flooding occurs some citizens, such as children, elderly and differently-able, may be unable to protect themselves or evacuate if necessary.

3. Economic Vulnerability: The level of vulnerability is highly dependent upon the economic status of individuals, communities and nations. The poor are usually more vulnerable to disasters because they lack the resources to build sturdy structures and put other engineering measures in place to protect themselves from being negatively impacted by disasters.

Example: Poorer families may live in squatter settlements because they cannot afford to live in safer (more expensive) areas.

4. Environmental Vulnerability: Natural resource depletion and resource degradation are key aspects of environmental vulnerability.

Example: Wetlands are sensitive to increasing salinity from sea water, and pollution from stormwater runoff containing agricultural chemicals, eroded soils, etc.

Conclusion:

In order to make India disaster resilient, achieve substantial disaster risk reduction, and significantly decrease the losses of life, livelihoods, and assets – economic, physical, social, cultural, and environmental, it is essential to maximize the ability to cope with disasters at all levels of administration as well as among communities. Therefore, characterizing the vulnerability of different regions plays is crucial role in defining disaster impacts and its threat to people.

Q.9. The banning of 'Uamaat-e-Islam' in Jammu and Kashmir brought into focus the role of over-ground workers (OGWs) in assisting terrorist organizations. Examine the role played by OGWs in assisting terrorists organizations in insurgency affected areas. Discuss measures to neutralize influence of OGWs. (Answer in 150 words) (10)

Important Points for Answer:
- *Introduction*
- *The role of over-ground workers (OGWs) in assisting terrorist organizations:*
- *Measures to neutralize influence of OGWs*

Answer: In 2019 February, the Home Ministry has banned for 5 years the Jammu and Kashmir-based group, Jamaat-i-Islami (JeI), as "an unlawful association" under Section 3 of the Unlawful Activities (Prevention) Act, 1967.

It was expected to rein in over-ground workers (OGWs) network of terrorist outfits, particularly Hizbul Mujahideen, and put brakes on extreme radicalization and recruitment of locals for terror related activities.

The role of over-ground workers (OGWs) in assisting terrorist organizations:

1. Propagating separatist and radical ideology

2. Funding the terrorists and their activities
3. Logistics support
4. Intelligence support
5. Ferrying of arms
6. Providing shelter
7. Mobilizing people for breaking law and order like stone pelting in Kashmir
8. Recruitment to the terror organizations and other giving human resources for other activities

Measures to neutralize influence of OGWs:

Twin policy of Security and Development strategies are required for neutralizing their influence.

Development strategies:

- Development as the first agenda to counter such anti-social elements
- Attract the people towards the Indian government though development
- Enable the people to participate in the democratic process of the state
- Reducing the feelings of alienation.

Security strategies:

- Train police personnel to provide efficient law and order conditions for development.
- Lawful Audit of the Non-profit organizations and their source of funding to Watch over terror funding.
- Increasing intelligence apparatus
- Enhanced surveillance over suspicious activities
- Community participation in the governance in removing the separatist propaganda.

Q.10. What is CyberDome Project? Explain how it can be useful in controlling internet crimes in India. (Answer in 150 words) (10)

Important Points for Answer:
- *Introduction about CyberDome Project*
- *Controlling internet crimes in India*
- *Conclusion*

Answer: In order to address the highly challenging and dynamic nature of cyber threats, Kerala police have established a Centre of Excellence called CyberDome. It is a technological research and development Centre of Kerala Police Department conceived as a Cyber Centre of excellence in cyber security as well as technology augmentation for effective policing.

It envisages as a high tech public-private partnership Centre of collaboration for different stakeholders in the domain of cyber security and handling of cyber crimes, in a proactive manner.

Controlling internet crimes in India:

- It prevents cyber crimes through the development of a cyber threat resilient ecosystem in the state.
- It defends against the growing threat of cyber attacks by synergizing with other departments and nodal agencies of the State.
- It makes a collective coordination among the Government departments and agencies, academia, research groups, non-profitable organizations, individual experts from the community, ethical hackers, private organizations, and other law enforcement agencies in the country, with an aim of providing a safe and secure cyber world for each and every citizen in the state.
- It linked up to many national and international cyber security collaborations as well as to the law enforcement agencies to fight against the borderless nature of the cyber crimes.
- Apart from the Government stakeholders, the Centre is also working hand in hand with industry fraternity in public-private partnership model for equipping the Kerala Police by adapting the latest technologies, in a rapidly changing environment.
- Cyberdome is thus operating an online office of technical experts, ethical hackers, and competent cyber security professionals, who assist the police in the area of cyber security, cyber crime investigation and domain knowledge updating.
- This online office is also holding a group of specially selected experts having professional competency, who can give assistance and suggestions to the police to tackle the various cyber policing issues, cropping up in the cyber world.

Conclusion:

Thus, CyberDome Project is to meet the long term security challenges in the digital arena of the modern world, by bridging the gap between the latest innovations in the cyber space and the skill set development of Kerala Police.

Q.11. It is argued that the strategy of inclusive growth is intended to meet the objectives of inclusiveness and sustainability together. Comment on this statement. (Answer in 250 words) (15)

Important Points for Answer:
- *Introduction*
- *Objectives of inclusiveness and sustainability*
- *Conclusion*

Answer: The rapid and sustained poverty reduction requires inclusive growth that allows people to contribute to economic growth as well as benefit from the economic growth. The strategy for inclusive growth should not just be a conventional strategy for growth to which some poverty reduction elements have been added. On the contrary, it is a strategy which aims at achieving a particular type of growth process which will meet the objectives of inclusiveness and sustainability.

Objectives of inclusiveness and sustainability

(a) **Inclusiveness:** In the short run, governments could use income distribution schemes (inclusiveness), but such schemes cannot be an answer in the long run without sustainable growth. Hence, rapid pace of growth is unquestionably necessary for substantial poverty reduction.

(b) **Sustainability:** But for this rapid growth to be sustainable in the long run, it should be broad-based across sectors, and inclusive of the large part of the country's labor force.

(c) **Inclusive growth:** Therefore, inclusive growth refers both to the pace and pattern of growth. The idea that both the pace and pattern of growth are critical for achieving a high, sustainable growth record, as well as poverty reduction. The inclusive growth approach takes a longer term perspective as the focus is on productive employment rather than on direct income redistribution, as a means of increasing incomes for excluded groups. Inclusive growth encompasses equity, equality of opportunity, and protection in market and employment transitions – is an essential ingredient of any successful growth strategy. The idea of equality of opportunity in terms of access to markets, resources, and unbiased regulatory environment for businesses and individuals.

The inclusive growth definition is in line with the absolute definition of traditional pro-poor growth, but differs from it in the following ways:

(i) Traditional absolute pro-poor growth can be the result of direct income redistribution schemes, but for growth to be inclusive, productivity must be improved and new opportunities for employment created; and

(ii) The pro-poor growth concept has traditionally focused on growth and poverty measures whereas the inclusive growth definition focuses on analysis of the sources of, and constraints to sustained, high growth and poverty reduction.

Conclusion

Sometimes a country that has grown rapidly over a decade may not see substantial reduction in poverty rates. Such growth which is not inclusive in nature is not sustainable in the long run. Therefore, for growth to be sustained in the long run, it must be broad-based across sectors. Thus, the policies for inclusive growth are an important component of most strategies for sustainable growth as well as cover all sections of society in the growth process.

Q.12. The public expenditure management is a challenge to the Government of India in the context of budget making during the post-liberalization period. Clarify it. (Answer in 250 words) (15)

Important Points for Answer:
- *Introduction*
- *Budget making and public expenditure management*
- *Challenge to the government of India in public expenditure management*
- *Conclusion*

Answer: After 1991 (Post-liberalization period), there is a realization on the role of institutional arrangements in influencing budget outcomes in the area of public expenditure management. The role of government has changes from a major participant in the economic growth process to facilitator to the growth process.

Budget making and public expenditure management:

- The following aspects must be taken into consideration while making budget with;
- Fiscal discipline – Maintaining the Fiscal Deficit less than 3% of the GDP.
- Strategic allocation of resources for income distribution Schemes like subsidies, DBT, etc.
- Operational efficiency – Reducing the leakages in the expenditure.
- The essential requirements for public expenditure management include
  - (a) Planning and budgeting
  - (b) Link between policy making and policy implementation
  - (c) Well-functioning accounting and financial management systems
  - (d) Performance-focus
  - (e) Appropriate links between budgeting and other systems of the Government.

Challenge to the government of India in public expenditure management:

- Indian society still needs subsidies on the food, fertilizer and energy.
- Indian economic growth is not fully growing at its potential. So, the revenue to the state is still at lower levels.
- In order to meet the expenditure, government is borrowing and causing high Debt/GDP ratio.
- More income goes for paying interest rates. Indian debt is 'stubbornly high'.
- Revenue deficit is still at higher levels.
- Global recession in 2008 led to suspension of FRBM Act and made it ineffective to control the fiscal deficit.
- Stress in banking sector is raising NPAs and may cause more pressure on public expenditure management in protecting the Banking sector.
- An Expenditure Management Commission (EMC) was also established to recommend major expenditure reforms that will enable the government to lower its fiscal deficit.

Conclusion:

The rapid and inclusive growth is the necessity of the hour. Only higher GDP growth with inclusiveness and sustainability will reduce the need of the subsidies and relieve the government from 'stubbornly high' debt.

Q.13. What are the reformative steps taken by the Government to make food grain distribution system more effective? (Answer in 250 words) (15)

Important Points for Answer:
- *Introduction*
- *Reformative steps taken by the government*
- *Conclusion*

Answer: A number of initiatives were taken to make foodgrain management more efficient and to ensure food security in the country.

Reformative steps taken by the government:

1. Consumer Level Reforms:

- **Automation of Fair Price Shops:** Use of Point of sale (PoS) at FPS.
- **Direct Benefit Transfer (Cash)**: "Cash Transfer of Food Subsidy Rules, 2015" were notified on August 21, 2015 under which food subsidy is directly credited to the account of the beneficiaries.
- **Aadhaar Seeding in PDS:** To weed out duplicate/in-eligible/bogus ration cards and to enable rightful targeting ration cards have been Aadhaar seeded.
- **Deletion of ration cards:** As an outcome of digitization of Ration Cards/beneficiary records, de-duplication due to Aadhaar seeding, transfer/migration/deaths, change in economic status of beneficiaries and during the run-up to and implementation of NFSA a total of 2.33 crore ration cards have been deleted/cancelled. Based on this the Government has been able to achieve Rightful Targeting of Food Subsidies.
- **Digital/Cashless/Less-cash Payments in PDS**: To promote the use of less-cash/digital payment mechanisms, the Department has issued detailed guidelines for use of AePS, UPI, USSD, Debit/Rupay Cards and e-Wallets on 7th December 2016. At present in 10 States/UTs a total of 50,117 FPSs are enabled for digital payments.

2. FCI Reforms

- **Silos: Use of modern technology in storage:** A road map for creation of 100 Lakh MT storage capacity in the form of Steel Silos by FCI and other agencies including State Governments on PPP mode for wheat and rice has been approved. Construction has been planned in 3 phases upto 2019-20.
- **Depot Online System:** To bring all operations of FCI Godowns online and to check leakages and automate operations at depot level, a "Depot Online" system was launched.
- **Supporting the Farmers:** FCI has initiated special efforts for procurement in the Eastern States of India, where there were frequent complaints of distress sale of paddy and procurement system was ineffective.

Conclusion:

These are some of the measures among others to create an effective food grain distribution system.

Q.14. Elaborate the policy taken by the Government of India to meet the challenges of the food processing sector. (Answer in 250 words) (15)

Important Points for Answer:
- *Introduction*
- *The key challenges identified in the food processing sector*
- *Initiatives taken by the Government*
- *Conclusion*

Answer: Aptly recognised as the 'sunrise industry', food processing sector provides vital linkages between the two pillars of our economy – manufacturing and agriculture. The Food Processing industry in India is undergoing a significant transformation. The Government has made commendable efforts to promote investment in the industry by way of channeling resources through various schemes as subsidies and grants.

The key challenges identified in the food processing sector:

- **Poor supply chain linkages**: India's agriculture market has a long and fragmented supply chain that results in high wastage and high costs, especially due to seasonality, perishability, and variability of produce.
- **Infrastructure bottlenecks**: The export related infrastructure for agri-produce is grossly inadequate, especially at sea ports and airports. More than 30 percent of the produce from the fields gets spoilt due to poor post-harvesting facilities and lack of adequate storage infrastructure.
- **Lack of skilled manpower**: The agricultural workforce is inadequately skilled across different levels of food processing.
- **Low adherence to quality standards:** India lacks basic standardization and certification infrastructure. Given the size of the food processing industry, there is a huge gap in the availability of laboratories, trained manpower, and certification agencies. The Indian government has taken some reformatory steps to strengthen the food processing industries.

Initiatives taken by the Government:

1. **Establishing Mega Food Parks:** Ministry of Food Processing Industries is focusing on boosting the food processing industry so that agriculture sector grows exponentially and become a major contributor to doubling the farmer's income and aid 'Make in India' initiative of the government.
2. **Creation/Expansion of Food Processing Preservation Capacities (CEFPPC)-** 134 projects have been approved under the scheme till December 2018.
3. **Creating integrated Cold Chain:** The Scheme of Integrated Cold Chain and Value Addition Infrastructure as one of the component of Pradhan Mantri Kisan Sampada Yojana with the objective of arresting post-harvest losses of horticulture & non-horticulture produce and providing remunerative price to farmers for their produce.

4. **Towards cleanliness:** Efforts towards cleanliness were undertaken under Swachhta Pakhwada. It was an organised Swachhta Awareness Programme and training camps for street vendors on food safety across. The awards are also conferred to cleanest Mega Food Parks and Cold Chains.
5. **Advances in Food Processing Technology:** Providing a strong platform through conferences and meetings for knowledge sharing and meaningful discussion among the industry, academia, researchers and farmers which would potentially take the food sector growth to a newer heights.

Conclusion:

These efforts have placed the food processing industry on a high growth trajectory. Along with these steps new steps like encouraging State Agricultural Universities to commence courses in food packaging, processing, bio-technology, information technology in agriculture and such allied fields will strengthen the industry in future.

Q.15. How is the Government of India protecting traditional knowledge of medicine from patenting by pharmaceutical companies? (Answer in 250 words) (15)

Important Points for Answer:
- *Introduction*
- *The measures to protect the traditional knowledge*
- *Establishing Traditional Knowledge Digital Library (TKDL)*
- *Preventing the grant of wrong patents:*
- *Conclusion*

[N.B. Explanatory answers are brief in nature, so the aspirants can make is precise according to the world limit and requirement of the question]

Answer: Over the years, Intellectual Property rights have been formulated as individual, monopolistic rights to protect the innovative, novel and utilitarian ideas of the human mind. Traditional Knowledge (TK) was thus undervalued.

India is a diverse country in all senses. It is counted among the 'megadiverse' countries due to its innumerable genetic resources (GRs) and associated Traditional Knowledge. With advancements in technology around the world, GRs and associated TK are vulnerable to bio- piracy and similar threats. With a view to protecting biodiversity and associated Traditional Knowledge, the government of India has taken various measures.

The measures to protect the traditional knowledge:

In the first step to stop multinational companies patenting traditional remedies from local plants and animals, the Indian government has effectively licensed lakhs of local treatments as "public property" free for anyone to use but no one to sell as a "brand".

The move comes after scientists noticed an alarming trend – the "bio-prospecting" of natural remedies by companies abroad. After trawling through the records of the global trademark offices, officials found thousands of patents had been issued for "medical plants and traditional systems". Some of the measures are highlighted below.

Establishing Traditional Knowledge Digital Library (TKDL):

- The Ministry of AYUSH had established Traditional Knowledge Digital Library (TKDL) in collaboration with Council for Scientific & Industrial Research (CSIR).
- As per the information provided by the CSIR, TKDL consisting of more than 2.90 lakh medicinal formulations of Ayurveda, Unani and Siddha which are available in the public domain, in five international languages namely English, Japanese, French, German and Spanish.
- To facilitate the protection of country's traditional knowledge, access of TKDL has been provided to International Patent offices (IPOs) under International Agreement.
- In addition, pre-grant opposition on patent applications along with prior evidences from TKDL are submitted on a regular basis.

Preventing the grant of wrong patents:

- TKDL has been successful in preventing the grant of wrong patents in many cases.
- For further facilitating the prevention of grant of wrong patents at International Patent Offices (IPOs), International Access Agreements on TKDL have been concluded with United States Patent & Trademark Office, European Patent Office, Canada Patent Office, Germany Patent Office, Japan Patent Office, United Kingdom Patent Office and others.
- Apart from bio-piracy, to prevent misappropriation of Yoga, Ministry of AYUSH through Sangeet Natak Akademi has filed nomination of Yoga at UNESCO to include Yoga in the representative list of the Intangible Cultural Heritage of Humanity.

The Biological Diversity Act, 2002:

- The Biological Diversity Act, 2002 also aims conservation of biological resources, sustainable use of its components and fair and equitable sharing of benefits arising out of the use of biological resources.
- Further, the Biological Diversity Act, 2002 requires every local body to constitute a Biodiversity Management Committee (BMC) within its area with the objective to prepare People's Biodiversity Register in consultation with local people.
- The Register shall contain comprehensive information on availability and knowledge of local biological resources, their medicinal use or any other traditional knowledge associated with them.

Nagoya Protocol:

The coming into force of the Nagoya Protocol has great benefits for the defence of indigenous people's rights over their resources, and strengthens India's already robust protective measures. India is signatory to the protocol.

Conclusion:

India's battle to protect its traditional treatments is rooted in the belief that the developing world's rich biodiversity is a potential treasure trove of starting material for new drugs and crops. This only protects the humanity both in India and across the Globe.

Q.16. How can biotechnology help to improve the living standards of farmers? (Answer in 250 words) (15)

Important Points for Answer:
- *Introduction*
- *Biotechnology and living standards of farmers*
- *Conclusion*

Answer: Biotechnology refers to the industrial use of micro-organism, living plant and animal cells to produce substances useful to the people. Biotechnology promises to bring important changes in plant as well as livestock production. In agriculture, it will affect all steps of the production chain, from agrochemical inputs and breeding to final food processing. Living standards of farmers can be improved with careful use of biotechnology.

Biotechnology and living standards of farmers

Both growing plants and rearing animals are two important tasks of a farmer. Biotechnology improves the standards of these two areas.

Plant breeding and Biotechnology:

Plant breeding has been enhanced considerably by in vitro development of improved varieties which are better adapted to a specific environment. The application of tissue culture has several advantages, including:

1. The rapid reproduction and multiplication of plants;
2. The production of healthy plants, free of viruses and pathogenic agents;
3. The rapid adaptation and selection of plants that are resistant to specific stress factors (for instance, salinity and acid soils);
4. The availability of seed material throughout the year (rather than seeds which are subject to the seasonal cycle);
5. The possibilities to produce species that are difficult to reproduce or that reproduce and grow slowly; and
6. Improved possibilities for the storage and transportation of genetic material.
7. Production of Biofertilizer
8. Production of Biopesticides

Animal rearing and Biotechnology:

Applications of biotechnology to animal production centre on four fields:

1. Reproduction, selection and breeding;
2. Animal health;
3. Feeding and nutrition; and
4. Growth and production.

Improving living standards of farmers:

Agricultural biotechnology can be used to improve the nutritional content of a variety of crops in an effort to meet the needs of an increasing population. Genetic engineering can produce crops with a higher concentration of vitamins.

Conclusion:

Potential of biotechnology should be integrated into farming to augment food production. Government needs to harness the potential of biotechnology through innovative initiatives like Biotech-Kisan. Technological intervention like this can help us achieve the goal of doubling farm income by 2022. Biotechnology should not be seen, learnt and practiced in isolation, but in tandem with other branches. Proper use of biotechnology tools is very vital. Scientists should strive to learn not only advanced technology but also to realise the right way to use them.

Q.17. Define the concept of carrying capacity of an ecosystem as relevant to an environment. Explain how understanding this concept is vital while planning for sustainable development of a region. (Answer in 250 words) (15)

Important Points for Answer:

- *Introduction*
- *The relation between carrying capacity and sustainable development*
- *Planning for sustainable development of a region*
- *Conclusion*

Answer: In ecological terms, the carrying capacity of an ecosystem is the size of the population or community that can be supported indefinitely upon the available resources and services of that ecosystem. The term of sustainable development was introduced by Brundtland Report for the World Commission on Environment and Development in 1987. Sustainable development is the development that meets the needs of the present without compromising the ability of future generations to meet their own needs.

The relation between carrying capacity and sustainable development:

The carrying capacity of an ecosystem is understood in terms of capital. In the context of sustainability, communities have several different types of capital that need to be considered– Natural, Human,

Social, and built capital. Together, these types of capital are referred to as community capital. However, these capital items are not long last forever.

Therefore, carrying capacity of an ecosystem should not be disturbed for sustainable development. Otherwise, future generations will face the dangers of the existential threats as the capitals required for life will diminish and disappear altogether.

Thus, all these types of capital need to be cared, nurtured and improved over time to live in harmonious relation with the ecosystem.

Planning for sustainable development of a region:

The following factors are very crucial for carrying out a plan for sustainable development:

1. The amount of resources available in the ecosystem
2. The size of the population or community
3. The amount of resources each individual within the community is consuming

Conclusion:

All these factors are dependent on the carrying capacity of the ecosystem of the region. A community that is degrading or destroying the ecosystem on which it depends is using up its community capital and is living unsustainably. Thus, understanding carrying capacity concept is vital while planning for sustainable development of a region.

Q.18. Disaster preparedness is the first step in any disaster management process. Explain how hazard zonation mapping will help disaster mitigation in the case of landslides. (Answer in 250 words) (15)

Important Points for Answer:

- *Introduction*
- *Disaster preparedness process:*
- *How Hazard zonation mapping help in disaster mitigation in the case of landslides?*
- *Hazard zonation maps have different uses with examples*
- *Conclusion*

Answer: Disaster preparedness is a continuous and integrated process resulting from a wide range of risk reduction activities. It requires the contributions of many different areas - ranging from training and logistics, to health care, recovery, livelihood to institutional development. It is the first step in any disaster management process.

Disaster preparedness process:

The comprehensive disaster preparedness for any type of disaster like earthquake, cyclone, landslide, etc. strategy includes:

- Hazard, risk and vulnerability assessments

- Preparedness plans
- Coordination
- Information management
- Early warning systems
- Resource mobilization
- Public education, training, Drills and simulations
- Community-Based disaster preparedness

How Hazard zonation mapping help in disaster mitigation in the case of land-slides?

Landslide hazard zone mapping involves a detailed assessment and analysis of the past occurrences of landslides in conditions of their location, size and incidence with respect to various geo-environmental factors that cause landslides and mass movements. Landslide hazard zonation map included a map separating the draw out varying degrees of predictable slope stability. The map has an inbuilt factor of forecasting and hence is of probabilistic nature.

Depending upon the methodology adopted and the comprehensiveness of the input data used, a landslide hazard zonation map is able to provide help concerning some or all the following individual factor maps:

- Landslide location
- Slope steepness
- Landuse/ landcover
- Geology or lithology
- Density of drainages
- Rainfall

Hazard zonation maps have different uses. Some of them are as follows:

- Preparation of development plans for cities, dams, roads, and other development works
- General purpose master plans and land use plans
- Discouraging new development in hazard prone areas
- Selection of best activity pattern based on risk zones
- Quick decision making in rescue and relief operations.

Conclusion:

Therefore, landslide hazard zonation mapping help in disaster mitigation in the case of landslides.

Q.19. Indian Government has recently strengthened the anti-terrorism laws by amending the Unlawful Activities (Prevention) Act (UAPA), 1967 and the NIA Act. Analyze the changes in the context of prevailing security environment while discussing the scope and reasons for opposing the UAPA by human rights organizations. (Answer in 250 words) (15)

Important Points for Answer:
- *Introduction*
- *Why the opposition by human rights organizations to the UAPA*
- *Changes in the context of prevailing security environment:*
- *Conclusion*

Answer: In order to strengthen the agencies to provide more security to the nation from the dreaded acts of terrorists, Indian government has recently strengthened the anti-terrorism laws by amending the unlawful activities (Prevention) act (UAPA), 1967.

Changes in the context of prevailing security environment:

The Unlawful Activities (Prevention) Amendment Bill, 2019 was introduced to amend the Unlawful Activities (Prevention) Act, 1967. The Act provides special procedures to deal with terrorist activities, among other things.

Who may commit terrorism: Under the Unlawful Activities (Prevention) Act, 1967, the central government may designate an organisation as a terrorist organisation if it:

(i) commits or participates in acts of terrorism,

(ii) prepares for terrorism,

(iii) promotes terrorism, or

(iv) is otherwise involved in terrorism.

The Bill additionally empowers the government to designate individuals as terrorists on the same grounds.

- Approval for seizure of property by NIA: Under Under the Unlawful Activities (Prevention) Act, 1967, an investigating officer is required to obtain the prior approval of the Director General of Police to seize properties that may be connected with terrorism. The Bill adds that if the investigation is conducted by an officer of the National Investigation Agency (NIA), the approval of the Director General of NIA would be required for seizure of such property.
- Investigation by NIA: Under the Act, investigation of cases may be conducted by officers of the rank of Deputy Superintendent or Assistant Commissioner of Police or above. The Bill additionally empowers the officers of the NIA, of the rank of Inspector or above, to investigate cases.
- Insertion to schedule of treaties: The Act defines terrorist acts to include acts committed within the scope of any of the treaties listed in a schedule to the Act. The Schedule lists nine treaties, including the Convention for the Suppression of Terrorist Bombings (1997), and the Convention against Taking of Hostages (1979). The Bill adds another treaty to the list. This is the International Convention for Suppression of Acts of Nuclear Terrorism (2005).

Why the opposition by human rights organizations to the UAPA:

- There is an opposition to the amendments based on some of the following dimensions.
- **Ambiguous rules:** The UAPA amendments empower the government to designate individuals as terrorists. But, the rules are ambiguous.
- **Impact on Fundamental rights**: It is alleged that Law allows a person to be called a terrorist without FIR, chargesheet or trial. Under the law, the police are allowed a time period of 180 days for investigation as opposed to 60 to 90 days under criminal law. It is a violation of fundamental rights under:
  (i) Article 21 - Right to Life and liberty
  (ii) Article 19 - Right to Free Speech and Expression
- **Not effective Measure:** Mere the amendments are not successful in controlling terrorism rather the government should strengthen the judicial system for timely implementation of rulings in terrorism-related cases to create fear in minds of terrorists.
- **Affects federal structure**: The provisions were against the federal structure of the country. The Act gives more power to the central government.
- **Stigma in society**: It affects the social life a person like family, job, etc. once an individual is designated as a terrorist.
- **Lack of faith on the intentions of the government**: It is alleged that the act may be used to target dedicated human rights activists and NGOs for mere expressing the opinions which are against the government of the day.

Conclusion:

Designating an individual as a terrorist raises serious constitutional questions and has the potential for misuse. The practice of designating individuals under anti-terrorism laws, prevalent in several countries, is seen as being necessary because banned groups tend to change their names and continue to operate. However, there must be a set of procedures for designating an individual a terrorist. Parliament must consider whether an individual can be called a 'terrorist' prior to conviction in a court of law.

Q.20. Cross-border movement of insurgents is only one of the several security challenges facing the policing of the border in North-East India. Examine the various challenges currently emanating across the India-Myanmar border. Also, discuss the steps to counter the challenges. (Answer in 250 words) (15)

Important Points for Answer:

- *Introduction*
- *Various challenges currently emanating across the India-Myanmar border*
- *The steps to counter the challenges*
- *Conclusion*

Answer: The India-Myanmar border has recently made the headlines after the Indian army made a surgical strike against insurgents at the border and the Myanmar Army reportedly conducted counter insurgency operations against Indian insurgents groups. But cross border movement of insurgents is only one of several security challenges facing the policing of the border.

Various challenges currently emanating across the India-Myanmar border:

- Proximity to one of the world's largest opium producing areas, the Golden triangle and resulting security challenge. This result in Drug trafficking, Human trafficking and Arms trafficking
- The India-Myanmar border has a unique arrangement in place called the Free Movement Regime (FMR). The FMR permits the tribes residing along the border to travel 16-km across the boundary without visa restrictions. This often paves way for illegal movement of migrants in to Indian territory.
- Cross border movement of insurgent groups like National Socialist Council of Nagaland – Khaplang (NSCN-K) and Meitei insurgent groups.
- Rohingya crisis in Myanmar's Rakhine state led to huge influx of illegal migrants.

The steps to counter the challenges:

- The exercise of National Register of Citizens process in states like Assam.
- Cooperation in Boundary management. Joint inspection of boundary pillars and construction of additional boundary pillars on the border as a means to avoid any confusion on this account.
- Intelligence-sharing among security agencies of India and Myanmar.
- India offered capacity-building programmes for Myanmar police, Narcotics, Wildlife Crime Control.
- Counter insurgency operation like Operation Sunrise

Conclusion:

The Indian government has been alive to the threats that emanate from a poorly guarded India–Myanmar international border. Given that poor security along the India–Myanmar border poses a challenge to India's security, it is imperative that India strengthens security of the border and redoubles its efforts to meaningfully engage Myanmar to effectively manage this border.

SOLVED PAPERS

PAPER–IV

Section–A

Time Allowed : 3 hours *Maximum Marks : 240*

Candidates should attempt ALL questions strictly in accordance with the instructions given under each question.

Q.1. (a) What are the basic principles of public life? Illustrate any three of these with suitable examples. (150 words) 10 (b) What do you understand by the term 'public servant'? Reflect on the expected role of public servant. (150 words) 10

(A)

Important Points for Answer:
- *Introduction about public life*
- *Basic principles of public life with examples*
- *Conclusion*

Answer: The basic principle during a democracy is that every one persons holding authority derive it from the people; in alternative words, all public functionaries are trustees of the individuals. With the enlargement of the role of state, public functionaries exercise extensive influence over the lives of individuals. The district relationship between the general public and also the officers needs that the authority entrusted to the officials be exercised within the best interest of the individuals or in 'public interest'. The Nolan Committee, that made public the subsequent seven principles of public life Selflessness, Integrity, objectiveness, answerability, Openness, Honesty, Leadership.

Basic principles of public life

- **Selflessness:** Selflessness is dezired quality in a public servent as he is opted to do work for welfare of the masses not for the individual good of himself. Selflessness leads to formation of policies and taking decision for the development and improvement of life of the peoples associated with him.

  For eg. Tukaram Omble of Maharashtra police tackled Kasab one of the terrorists of Mumbai attack so that he couldn't attack his fellow servicemen. Thus showing exemplary courage and the highest degree of selflessness by giving away his life for the cause of his nation.
- **Accountability:** Holders of public office are accountable to the public for their decisions and actions and must submit themselves to the scrutiny necessary to ensure this. Accountability leads to responsibility for the public servent to treat the mass like their own and must work for their holostic development.

For eg. Vikram Sarabhai accepted the failure of ISRO first mission without actually putting it on the mission head (APJ Abdul Kalam). Thus taking full accountability for the failure of his team.

- **Leadership:** Holders of public office should exhibit these principles in their own behaviour. They should actively promote and robustly support the principles and be willing to challenge poor behaviour wherever it occurs. Efficient leadership by a learned and trained public servent tends to formation of programs and decisions for the collective good of everyone.

  For eg. Lal Bahadur Shastri used to fast every Monday to save grains for poor people of the country and he gave a call for the nation to follow it. Thus exhibiting a true example of how leaders should lead from the front.

  Public servants are the real norisher of the masses and is thus they are considered to be the wellwisher by the peoples. A public servent must possess his duties honestly and effectively.

(B

Important Points for Answer:
- *Introduction about the term 'public servant'*
- *Describe the role of public servant*

Answer: Public servant are often delineate as a personal World Health Organization works for the state and whose main duty is related to the welfare of public and society. The duties embody providing service to the general public within the kind of protection, administration or maintainance.

Key features of a public servant

- **Selflessness:** The public servant is anticipated to stay welfare of public and society on top of his/her own.
- **Empathetic:** The public servant should be able to perceive the sentiments and emotions of public for making a most positive impact through his actions.
- **Moral integrity:** The public servant ought to hold high morals and moral beliefs whereas playing his role.

Expected role of Public servant

Official duties:

Administration: The public servant needs to give governance to the general public thus as to make sure that welfare of society is maintained.

Protection: The public servant is needed to guard rights of people and supply security to society from threats.

Services: The public servant additionally provides varied services to the society in making and maintaining holding like roads, cleanup infrastructure etc.

Moral duties:

- **Inspiration:** The public servant can be played as a role model who can inspire individuals in doing well for the society through their acts.
- **Mediation:** A public servant can act as a mediator to resolve disputes and fights in his own capacity. He must consider being a neutral entity.

Thus, employee as an edge isn't restricted to a specific job or duty instead it's a good go effort that ensures financial aid.

Q.2. (a) Effective utilization of public funds in crucial to meet development goals. Critically examine the reasons for under-utilization and misutilization of public funds and their implications. (150 words) 10

(b) "Non-performance of duty by a public servant is a form of corruption." Do you agree with this view? Justify your answer. (150 words) 10

(A)

Important Points for Answer:
- *Introduction*
- *Reasons behind under utilization and mis utilization of funds*
- *Implication of such conditions*
- *Conclusion*

Answer: Public funds are the funds created for the developmental activities to benefit the public directly. In India to welfare the masses public fund has been divided in a number of schemes and aspirational policies. In a developing country with such a huge population there is a number of complaints regarding the under or mis utilization of funds.

Reason for underutilization or misutilization of funds:

1. **Corruption:** Corruption at every level and the feeling of good for own leads to a narrow mindset of the authoroties, which indirectly affects fund distribution among levels of implementation.
2. **Regional difference:** Difference within society on basis of caste and region also create a sense of competation for the development of alltogether mass.
3. **Political difference:** Political rivary due to number of political parties. Due to such rivary one or many political party acts to be a bottleneck in the development aspirations of other party.
4. **Red tappism:** A number of attacks on workers and crushing of developmental activities are common in naxal affected areas. This hatered attitude towards government also tends to loss of money on development.
5. **Diversion:** A fund allocated for an activity is utlized for another activity. This create diversion in the funds and neglect of work for which the fund is allocated.

Implication of such conditions:

1. **No or Underdevelopment:** These kind of bottlenecks are responsible for lack or delay of developments. Due to such delay, it is the public which get affected the most.
2. **Rise of hate against government:** Such bottlenecks in development create anger for government and in turn make people naxalites or terrorist for their welfare.
3. **Rise of crimes:** As the people lack with development and opportunities, this indirectly increases crimes within society.
4. **Loss of confidence in governance:** Due to such lags in development processes, people also loose their confidence in governance which in turn will be harmful for ruling party in further elections.

Conclusion:

Political togetherness and Development of masses is the main motive of a democratic form of government. Government must work in removing bottlenecks and strengthening of system so that the aspirations of government and needs of people are fulfilled fully and on time.

(B)

Important Points for Answer:
- *Introduction*
- *Role of public servant*
- *Meaning of non performance*
- *Conclusion*

Answer: Transparency International regards corruption as abuse of power that erodes the material of society. It undermines people's trust within the social group, in its establishments and its leadership. A distrustful or apathetic public will then become one more hurdle to difficult corruption.

All civil servants are entrusted with public duty for the welfare of the lots. Negligence to the general public duty price lots by loss of their freedom, health, education, rights and even life typically, and hence, neglect of duty by a employee is additionally a variety of corruption. For example: A doctor not reaching hospital on time threatens the lifetime of the patients, a tutor not acting his duty not solely endangers the long run of kids however of society as an entire and a cops not doing what's mandated in riotous state of affairs results in loss of life.

Corruption amounts to breach of religion reposed by the general public in official and violation of the rights of people. It presents a roadblock to effective administration, law and order, failure to action of objectives of welfare policies and eventually guarantee of realisation of constitutional goals like social, economic and political justice.

Non-performance of duty by public servants for which they are morally, legally and constitutionally mandated to do is a form of corruption as the **Prevention to the Corruption Act** considers non-performance of public duty as an offence.

Therefore, it's essential for each official to perform their duty as mandated so as to uphold the constitutional values and become a vehicle for amendment within the lifetime of lots, so common public will get pleasure from what they're entitled to.

Q.3. (a) What is meant by the term ' constitutional morality"? How does one uphold constituitonal morality? (150 words) **10**

(b) What is meant by 'crisis of conscience'? How does it manifest itself in the public domain? (150 words) **10**

(A)

Important Points for Answer:
- *Defining constitutional morality*
- *How does one uphold constitutional morality?*

Answer: 'Constitutional morality' are often outlined as an ethical responsibility of a private to be trustworthy towards constitutional values and uphold them with utmost integrity, with none compromise.

How to uphold constitutional morality?

- **Criticise non-constitutional practices:** It is necessary to talk up against any actions, that you are feeling as bootleg or unethical beneath the constitution. By going against the convention and taking an ethical status, you act as a preserver of constitutional values.

  Example: As a employee you see that basic constitutional rights (Freedom, equality etc) are being desecrated and you opt to talk up, notwithstanding the implications.
- **Propagating the importance to public:** To solely our beliefs and actions for upholding constitutional values isn't enough. it's our duty to teach public relating to the importance to uphold these ideals. this can be fruitful for our democracy on the long-standing time.

  Example: Conducting programmes in faculties wherever youngsters are trained to instill constitutional values and follow them in their day to day life.

Way forward

It has been discovered that young officers are resigning from service and aim to uphold 'constitutional morality', that they assert is being desecrated. However the very fact is that 'constitutional morality' are often higher preserved by being a part of the system and initiating reforms instead of figuring out of the system.

Thus, we are able to conclude that upholding' constitutional ethicality' is so important a part of our official furthermore as moral duty and it wants combined efforts of all the sections of the society to create it potential.

(B)

Important Points for Answer:
- *Introduction*
- *How does it manifest in public domain?*
- *Conclusion*

Answer: Crisis of Conscience refers to the awkward situation when one's actions are contrary to one's beliefs and values. Sometimes, we are not able to act in the way that is in compliance to our value and principles. Either due to some external exegencies or material greed, we, sometimes, sideline our voice of conscience and act in a contrary way. This, if done for a material greed, degrades our human nature and suppresses our conscience. However, there are also circumstances when, due to some external reasons beyond our control, we are not able to act according to our beliefs. Such situations create a feeling of guilt and shame.

- It manifests within the method process by civil servants wherever the choice will impact an enormous variety of individuals. the matter arises after they are controlled below some ministerial influence to require immoral selections or implement unethical policies.
- It manifests within the tussle between ethics and also the law. For example, proscribing public movement in geographic region for upholding law and order raised things of crisis of conscience. Similarly, despite having a position as a 3rd gender, transgenders still face oppression, social process, lack of employment opportunities that forces them to resort to beggary, and this failure to determine to them lifetime of dignity may be a manifestation of the crisis of conscience publicly domain.

It is common to come back across such crises of conscience publicly domain wherever lives and selections overlap and are available face to face virtually anytime. The key to beat such crisis of conscience for employee is thru keeping all dimensions in mind, releasing himself from needs or pressures and staying calm and faithful public service system of rules and legal framework.

Q.4. (a) Explain the basic principles of citizens charter movement and bring out its importance. (150 words) 10

(b) There is a view that the Official Secrets Act is an obstacle to the implementation of Right to information Act. Do you agree with the view? Discuss. (150 words) 10

(A)

Important Points for Answer:
- *Introduction*
- *Principles of citizen charter*
- *Importance of citizen charter*

Answer: Citizen's Charter could be a document of voluntary commitments created by a government organization to the citizens/client teams in respect of the services/schemes being provided to them or to be provided to them.

Principles of Citizen Charter

- **Quality:** improving the quality of services
- **Choice:** for the users wherever possible
- **Standards:** specifying what to expect within a time frame
- **Value:** for taxpayers money
- **Accountability:** of the service provider (individual as well as organisation)
- **Transparency:** in rules, procedures, schemes and grievance redressal
- **Participative:** consult and involve

Importance

- It is helpful in making administration more transparent and accountable.
- It is citizen-centric in nature and makes the administration more citizen friendly.
- It promotes good governance
- It improves service delivery to the citizens.
- It provides a pathway for grievance redressal.

A Citizen Charter cannot be an end in itself, it is rather meant for an end a tool to ensure that citizens always remain at the utmost priority of any service delivery model.

(B)

Important Points for Answer:
- *Introduction about The Officials Secret Act*
- *Correlated RTI with the Officials Secret Act*

Answer: The Officials Secret Act (OSA) enacted by the British Government in 1923, to curb down its Enemy States, acts contrary to provisions of RTI. Not only is it anachronistic and lacks usage in a liberal, modern day democracy, it creates obstacles in the implementation of RTI, in the following ways:

- Colonial era act.
- Majorly used by government to withhold information from citizens by citing security concerns.
- Also used to cover up government impropriety.
- Used as a draconian weapon of threat against Journalists and activists to unearth governmental shortcomings.
- Used to silence specific investigations undertaken by citizens or civil society.
- May lead to wrongful suspicion of spying on citizens.

Right to Information Act 2005 mandates timely response to citizen requests for government information. Right to Information also empowers citizens to official inspect any Government work or to take the sample of material used in any work. It may be noticed that these two acts are at loggerheads. The aim of Right to Information act act is to empower voters and convey regarding transparency within the governance whereas the Official Secrets Act withholds information of sensitive nature in the interest of state security. It's going to be thought-about a tiny low worth for RTI instead of the obstacle to the implementation of RTI.

Q.5. (a) What do you understand by probity in governance? Based on your understanding of the term, suggest measures for ensuring probity in government. (150 words) 10

(b) "Emotional Intelligence is the ability to make your emotions work for you instead of against you." Do you agree with this view? Discuss. (150 words) 10

(A)

Important Points for Answer:
- *Introduction*
- *Measures to Ensure Probity in Government*

Answer: Probity in Governance may be a very important would like for execution the governance system and socio-economic development. It is outlined as adherence ethical and moral values like honesty. Integrity, rectitude, uprightness etc. It is the presence of procedural integrity with high standards of moral behaviour.

Probity in Governance in addition elucidates that rather than the quality administration values of performance, integrity and loyalty. It is vital for civil officers to adopt what is more as undertake ethical and integrity values, that has respect for human rights, morality publically life and compassion for the downtrodden and dedication to their welfare.

Measures to Ensure Probity in Government

Lack of probity in governance has become one in every of the most important menaces of society. To drill integrity and adherence to moral practices among them bound strides may be taken:

- A dedicated unit to administrate the violation of Code of ethics and Code of conduct by government officials be set up both at state and centre level.
- To ensure information can accessible to common public through websites.
- Require declaration of assets and liabilities of government employees verified by proper auditing.
- To establish an Independent Anti-Corruption Agency.
- Citizens Advisory Boards to incorporate ideas of common public in improving governance.

Important Points for Answer:
- *Introduction*
- *How Emotional Intelligence works?*
- *Conclusion*

(B)

Answer: Emotional Intelligence (EI) refers to the flexibility to know one's own emotions and people of others to control and manage them and utilize them to execute tasks. It is the premise of the social skills of directors that contribute to structure effectiveness. These set of skills are imperative to affect the challenges of administration like political interference, communication with people and conflict management.

E.I. works in your favour in the following manner:

- It helps in maintaining objectivity while dispensing work
- It leads to efficient and desired outcomes.
- Increases trust among colleagues.
- Reduces stress and any extreme outburst.
- Helps in understanding the state of mind of others.
- Prepares you to deal with unexpected circumstances.
- Emotional Intelligence might facilitate an official to be motivated and to inspire her/his subordinates to execute the given tasks with efficiency.
- Emotional Intelligence helps official in proscribing the overflowing of their emotions and keeping their temperament in restraint just in case of any unwarranted influences.
- Moreover, EI helps the Civil servant to possess associate degree empathic perspective towards the folk, particularly poor and vulnerable ones.

Thus, Emotional Intelligence helps in curbing the randomness and extremity of emotions. This more ends up in a positive perspective and stable performance instead of making any hindrance which can go against us.

Q.6 What do each of the following quotations mean to you?

(a) "An unexamined life is not worth living" - Socrates (150 words) 10

(b) "A man is but a product of his thoughts. What he thinks he becomes." - M.K. Gandhi. (150 words) 10

(c) "Where there is righteousness in the heart, there is beauty in the character. When there is beauty in the character, there is harmony in the home. When there is harmony in the home, there is order in the nation. When there is order in the nation, there is peace in the world." - A.P.J. Abdul Kalam. (150 words) 10

Important Points for Answer:
- *Narrate the quotes in ethical viewpoints.*

(A)

Answer: Life isn't price living if someone fails to hunt knowledge and information on the way to live an honest life. Both knowledge and wishdom can facilitate individuals recognize and understand life and notice price in it. Socrates, a thinker, educates individuals on the requirement to look at life and choose the way to board it. He developed the thought of unexamined life undeserving to measure, throughout his trial within the court.

Socrates claimed an honest life in his trial as a result of he served the voters in some ways. for instance, he discouraged individuals from following personal ambitions and inspired ethical perfection. In different words, a moral or ethical life is a good life and in order to lead a good life, it is important to examine one's life. In the process of examination of one's life one comes to know the good aspects and the bad aspects of their life. Without an examined life, a person is likely to gloss over their follies without attempting to reform themselves.

(B)

Gandhi's stress on reworking the religious configuration of personalities as being important for any social or political modification is clear in his quotation regarding however one's thoughts underscore one's actions.

The quotation explains that a person is delineated by the thought he chooses.

Thoughts is sensible or unhealthy, negative or positive. Since a person thinks sensible or unhealthy, he attracts sensible or unhealthy. Since a lot of Gandhi's philosophy has its basis in ethics or ethical rightness of associate degree action, Gandhi's quote is also seen as a caution or warning to refrain from wrong or unethical actions. The idea of all action is assumed or thinking. Gandhi emphasised upon suggests that over ends. In different words, victimization the proper suggests that is very important. To him, positive thoughts are just like the sensible seeds that once seeded within the mind can bear positive fruits. Therefore, it's necessary to drill positive thoughts.

(C)

The above quote highlights the importance of inculcating right values or ethical values. The quote more goes on to point out how with right values everything around as well as the family, the society conjointly the} nation as also the planet is set right. It is conjointly evident from the quote that inner transformation is additional vital than external reforms. A nation doesn't become orderly by a excess of laws, rules, and laws. The UNO has did not eliminate the scourge of violence and war from our world as a result of there's no order within the nation and therefore the reason for that's there is lack of harmony in the society and among the people. However, once every personalities begin to grasp the importance of morality to be inculcated right from the first days we will expect abundant of the strain and violence in personal life, home, and society to disappear.

SECTION–B

Q.7. You are heading the rescue operations in an area affected by severe natural calamity. Thousands of people are rendered homeless and deprived of food drinking water and other basic amenities. Rescue work has been disrupted by heavy rainfall and damage to supply routes. The local people are seething with .anger against the delayed limited rescue operations. When your team reaches the affected area, the members. One of your team members is even severely injured. Faced with this crisis, some team members plead with you to call off the operations fearing threats to their life.

In such trying circumstances, what will be your response? Examine the qualities of a public servant which will be required to manage the situation. (250 words) 20

Important Points for Answer:
- *Introduction*

Answer: My response in such a fervent atmosphere should be thoughtful, cogent and humane because there are various dilemmas involved. Leaving thousands unattended, when they are completely dependent on government help, would be an act of timidity and self preservation which is unbecoming of a public servant.

Morale upliftment: The primary response on behalf of me, because the head of the rescue mission, is to reorient the main focus of the cluster towards our real objectives. Since a number of them are requesting to decision off the mission I want to exhort them, with examples like—throughout the 2014 Floods in Jammu and Kashmir, once the NDRF team started rescue mission, they were pelted with stones, their boats were snached and one in every of them was injured however they didn't yield and went on to rescue quite 50000 people.

Initially, once spiritual leader was walk barefoot in riot hit areas of Noakhali, his path was strewn with items of glass and animal waste matter by the riot-affected people. Later, His unafraid courageousness and love for humanity created a miracle, once people themselves secure to not retaliate.

Here, the anger of individuals is misplaced because of the popular perception of presidency servants. Once, people witness renunciation, dedication and courageousness within the rescue work they're going to begin cooperating.

Secondly, I might attempt to persuade people by taking facilitate from those that are willing to get together, in such an exercise native leaders may facilitate.

Apart from this, I will be able to attempt to get cooperation from the government with regard to protection of my team members in order that they will not be hurt in serving to the people.

Qualities required to effectively manage such situation

- **Spirit of service:** Since the rescue team is vulnerable to physical and verbal attacks,only some higher cause can help an officer in composed and coordinated rescue work.
- **Leadership:** In such circumstances,finality of any decision lies completely on the wisdom of the leader. He/She also needs to lead the team from the front; displaying personal courage and conviction.
- **Empathy and Emotional Intelligence:** An officer needs to have empathy and emotional intelligence for understanding the behavior of disgruntled local people otherwise one may abort the relief mission or resort to use of force-which will only heighten their anger.
- **Power of persuasion:** People seething with anger are reactive and short-sighted, making them agree for something requires the power of persuasion.
- **Patience and Presence of mind:** A Public Servant can not afford to make spontaneous decisions in such situations. Any further course of action should be guided by considerate assessment and swift thinking.

Thus, we need to have a sensitivity of the situation and not blame people for their reactions. Empathy and support is the key to rescue people in problems.

Q.8. Honesty and uprightness are the hallmarks of a civil servant. Civil servants possessing these qualities are considered as the backbone of nay strong organization. In line of duty, they take various decisions, at times some become bonafide mistakes. As long as such decisions are not taken intentionally and do not benefit personally, the officer cannot be said to be guilty. Though such decisions may, at times, lead to unforeseen adverse consequences in the long-term.

In the recent past, a few instances have surfaced wherein civil servants have been implicated for bonafide mistakes. They have often been prosecuted and even imprisoned. These instances have greatly rattled the moral fibre of the civil servants.

How does this trend affect the functioning of the civil services? What measures can be taken to ensure that honest civil servants are not implicated for bonafide mistakes on their part? Justify your answer. (250 words) 20

Important Points for Answer:
- *Introduction*
- *Affect on the functioning of the civil services*
- *Measures to ensure that honest civil servants are not implicated for bonafide mistakes*
- *Justification*

Answer: The role of civil servants is to take decisions which have huge ramifications on the socio-economic growth of the country. However, instances of wrongful prosecution of honest officers deeply impact the morale of honest officers. It has multiple effects on the functioning of civil services in India:

Affect on the functioning of the civil services

- **Impact on decision-making of officers:** Officers will be averse to expressing their views. This may further aggravate red-tapism due to fear of departmental action for their incorrect decisions.
- **Hampers economic growth:** With increasing private sector participation in public services, fear of prosecution may restrict honest officers to take progressive, bold and courageous decisions across sectors. Delay in taking key decisions will lead to poor governance.
- **Tool to harass honest officers:** Corrupt political leaders and bureaucrats may harass honest officers through baseless complaints and investigations.
- **Impact on reputation of honest officers:** Prosecution of honest officers leads to mental agony and heavy financial loss besides being defamed in the society.

Measures to ensure that honest civil servants are not implicated for bonafide mistakes

- **Ensuring maximum transparency in administration:** The key policy making decisions should be made ensuring maximum clarity and openness about how decisions are taken.

- **Legislative actions:** As recommended by the **Hota Committee report,** amendment to Section 13(1)(d) of Prevention of Corruption Act , 1988, that deals with criminal misconduct by a public servant is a welcome step. It will protect honest civil servants from malicious prosecution and harassment.
- **Reducing politicization of bureaucracy:** The fear of transfers, denial of promotions, or being punished post retirement may impact decision making of officers. Ensuring fixed tenure to civil servants is a much needed step for systemic reforms in civil services.

Justification

- Since every decision taken may not prove to be correct in the long run, it is unjust to prosecute honest officers for genuine mistakes. Young and aspiring civil servants should preserve the key values of honesty, impartiality and fearlessness.
- Dynamic and honest officials, who are risk-takers for the greater good, must be encouraged, not restrained. No bureaucrat or public official should be fearful for a bona fide decision.
- Officers must stick to honesty and righteousness and ultimately there is victory of right over wrong.

Thus, the need of the hour for the civil servants is to follow the code of ethics along with code of conduct.

Q.9. As apparel manufacturing company having large number of women employees was losing sales due to various factors. The company hired a reputed marketing executive, who increased the volume of sales within a short span of time. However, some unconfirmed reports came up regarding his indulgence in sexual harassment at the work place.

After sometime, a woman employee lodged a formal complaint to the management against the marketing executive about sexually harassing her.

Faced with the company's indifference in not taking cognizance of her grievance, she lodged an FIR with the Police.

Realizing the sensitivity and gravity of the situation, the company called the woman employee to negotiate. In that she was offered a hefty sum of money to withdraw the complaint and the FIR and also give in writing that the marketing executive is not involved in the case. Identify the ethical issues involved in this case. What options are available to the woman employee? (250 words) **20**

Important Points for Answer:

- *Alleged sexual harassment at workplace by the marketing executive.*
- *Marketing executive important resource for the company as he increased sales in a short period of time.*
- *Company management's indifference in not taking cognizance of the woman's complaint.*
- *Company pressurizing the woman employee to withdraw the case.*

Answer: In this case the moral problems with molestation and also the truth of the unconfirmed reports on molestation are concerned. The two issues are interlinked. The third issue is that the issue of felony to suppress the reality.

There are unofficial reports regarding the promoting executive's action of molestation. Since, it's unofficial we tend to don't understand whether or not the marketing executive is truly guilty of molestation. A proper investigation is required to verify the accusation. Once the allegation is verified once correct investigation, we might be during a higher position to address the problem.

On the premise of investigation, if the marketing executive is involved, the law would take its own course. However, if the marketing executive is found not guilty, the whole case loses its advantage. However, within the gift case the girl will settle for the bribe and shut one's mouth, but this would not be an ethical solution. Moreover, it would encourage the accused. An ethical approach would expect her to resist the lure of cash and plow ahead with the investigating. Additionally, she will be able to conjointly create the company a celebration in collusion with the marketing executive for providing her bribe and conjointly for company's indifference to her complaints. Although this option is troublesome one with the likelihood that she might lose her job and may be concerned during future proceedings, this can be the foremost moral choice for her. The opposite choice is straightforward and profitable however unethical even on her half.

Q.10. In a modern democratic polity, there is the concept of political executive and permanent executive. Elected people's representatives form the political executive and bureaucracy forms the permanent executive. Ministers frame policy decisions and bureaucrats execute these.

In the initial decades after independence, relationship between the permanent executive and the political executive were characterized by mutual understanding, respect and co-operation, without encroaching upon each others domain.

However, in the subsequent decades, the situation has changed. There are instances of the political executive insisting upon the permanent executive to follow its agenda. Respect for and appreciation of upright bureaucrats has declined. There is an increasing tendency among the political executive to get involved in routine administrative matters such as transfers, postings etc. Under this scenario, there is a definitive trend towards 'politicization of bureaucracy'. The rising materialism and acquisitiveness in social life has also adversely impacted upon the ethical values of both the permanent executive and the political executive. What are the consequences of this 'Politicization of bureaucracy'? Discuss. (250 word) 20

Important Points for Answer:

- *Political neutrality and impartiality*
- *Integrity and probity*
- *Courage of conviction*
- *Following the code of conduct*
- *Legal responsibility*

Answer: Cooperation between elective representatives and bureaucrats is crucial for democratic governance of the country. However, because of 'politicization of bureaucracy', there's a deterioration within the functioning of the civil services.

Consequences of politicization of bureaucracy

- **Detrimental to moral fibre of bureaucrats:** Even honest civil servants with political leanings have compulsion to require biased choices in favour of one political group.
- **Dilemma in personal v/s professional life:** A bureaucrat indulged in material edges ought to compromise together with his conscience or inner voice simply to be in tune with outside reality, thereby worrying his mental peace and work ethics. The person loses self respect and trust of his family and children who inculcate such inadequate values from him.
- **Impact on governance system:** Lack of nonpartisanship in functioning of civil servants has direct impact on their choices in day to day administration either publically service delivery or implementing financial aid schemes.
- **Problems in chaotic situations:** Difficult circumstances like communal riots demands officers with strict political neutrality. Biased choices will result in loss of lives and property. Hence, a functionary should be in command of his choices in such things. Hence, a civil servant must be accountable for his decisions in such situations.
- **Policy paralysis:** Fear of political feud against non-cooperative officers within the sort of frequent transfers, delay in promotions, etc leads to red-tapism and culture of secrecy in their decision making.
- **Negative impact on civil society:** Civil servants occupying high positions within the government are role models for young aspiring Indians. Their impartial perspective is prejudicial to the social group ethics at large.

Therefore, a civil servant should be politically neutral. As a civil servant, one has the responsibility towards public and should adhere to constitutional principles keeping his conscience intact.

Also, a civil servant ought to be able to serve at any position at any time. worry of transfer shouldn't refrain a civil servant from his commitment towards public cause and bigger interest of society.

Q.11. In one of the districts of frontier state, narcotics menace has been rampant. This has resulted in money laundering, mushrooming of poppy farming, arms smuggling and near stalling of education. The system is on the verge of collapse. The situation has been further worsened by unconfirmed reports that local politicians as well as some senior police officers are providing surreptitious patronage to the drug mafia. At that point of time a woman police officer, known for her skills in handling such situations is appointed as Superintendent of Police to bring the situation to normalcy. If you are the same police officer, identify the various dimensions of the crisis. Based on your understanding, suggest measures to deal with the crisis. (250 words) 20

Important Points for Answer:
- *Introduction*
- *Various dimensions of the crisis*
- *Measures to deal with the crisis*

Answer: The situation within the aforesaid district looks intimidating, with the social and administrative system inching towards a complete collapse. Consequentially, the prevalence of such a situation should be resulting in wastage of human and social capital, rise in crime rates, and endangering the long run prospects of the district and its people.

The district is grappling with myriad problems which have various dimensions of the crisis can be summarised as below:

- **Legal dimension:** The activities like money laundering, poppy farming,arms smuggling,emanating from narcotics menace, are legally prohibited under respective laws.
- **Security dimension:** Border districts in India are susceptible to subversive groups trying to undermine democracy and authority of the State. Arms smuggling and money laundering provides financing their anti-social activities.
- **Social dimension:** A society ridden with such maladies can never focus on education, health, development, empowerment and welfare which are the key aims of a welfare state.
- **Economic dimension:** Involvement of people in such activities will lead to the emergence of a black economy eating away at the vitals of a state.
- **Political and administrative dimension:** Local political leaders and senior police officers are hand in glove with the drug mafia and are providing clandestine support to them- which raises the question of moral and ethical propriety.

Measures to deal with the crisis

- Since the problems have permeated through the social, political and administrative structures, my response, as a lady Superintendent of Police should be calculated, precise and swift, with long term implications in mind.
- Firstly, a thorough investigation must be conducted within the police establishment to identify the black sheep and they should be subjected to lawful punishment.
- Since my district lies in a frontier state; there is a possibility of involvement of transnational elements. For this, the police force must act in tandem with Border security personnel as a result of with rigorous patrolling and search operations native components are often isolated.

India's frontier districts need to remain economically prosperous, socially in harmony and free of illegal criminal networks because an afflicted district can have long-term adverse implications on the security, unity and integrity of India.

Q.12. In recent times, there has been an increasing concern in India to develop effective civil service ethics, codes of conduct, transparency measures, ethics and integrity systems and anti-corruption agencies. In view of this, there is a need being felt to focus on three specific

areas, which are directly relevant to the problems of internalizing integrity and ethics in the civil services. These are as follows:

1. **Anticipating specific threats to ethical standards and integrity in the civil services,**
2. **Strengthening the ethical competence of civil servants and**
3. **Developing administrative processes and practices which promote ethical values and integrity in civil services. Suggest institutional measures to address the above three isssues. (250 words)** **20**

Important Points for Answer:
- *Ethical integrity of civil servants.*
- *Probity in governance.*
- *Moral aptitude of civil servants.*
- *Accountability and responsibility.*
- *Transparency and citizen participation.*

Answer: In recent times, there is an increasing expectation from ordinary citizens, business leaders and and Civil Society for higher standards of moral behaviour and integrity within the Civil Services. To promote this, various methods like Code of Conduct, Citizen Charters, etc have been developed. However, the focus should also be on internalizing professional ethics and integrity in civil services to form it additional citizen-friendly.

Specific focus issues and measures to address them

- **Red-tapism:** Unnecessary administrative complexities to effective service delivery ought to be known and removed.
- **Culture of Secrecy:** Decisions created by civil servants and public officers ought to be made as clear and open as doable. Reasons should tend for official selections.
- **Biasedness and Partisan Attitude:** Implementation of conduct rules and code of ethics so as to make knowledgeable and non-partisan civil service hierarchy.
- **Elitism of civil servants:** Public orientation in Civil servants is crucial to extend public participation and improve public service delivery. Civil servants ought to tend correct coaching to confirm citizen-friendly behaviour.

Strengthening the ethical competence of civil servant

- **Training and performance appraisal:** This would incentivise the honest civil servants and create them role models for others to emulate
- **Reward and honours:** It will infuse competition within the civil services to perform higher and develop innovative solutions for public service.
- **Promotion of inclusive work culture:** Diluting strict hierarchy to extend the cooperation among public officers to increase the effectiveness of services.
- **Social and cultural competence:** This would facilitate the functionary to grasp the various Indian society and perform as per the high aspirations of the general public.

- **Promoting accountability:** Effective laws that need civil servants to administer reasons for his or her official choices. For eg. RTI act.
- **Reducing Corruption:** Punitive provision like Prevention of Corruption Act and Whistleblower Protection act, technological Interventions in the form of e-governance to remove discretion, promotion of Social Auditing etc to ensure accountability of the administrative work.
- **Human Resource management strategies:** Performance-based pay, Lateral Entry, Multi-Phase coaching can increase the potency and quality of public service delivery.
- **Internal and External Committees:** To ensure redressal of complaints and grievances of civil servants and public. This improves the work culture and aligns the behaviour of public servants to the required civil services values.
- **Code of Conduct Rules:** It ensures acceptable behaviour from public servants that ought to be unbiased and non-partisan.

Promotion of moral behaviour and integrity in civil servants, and revamping the general public administration is essential to confirm that the policies of welfare are enforced in true spirit. It would improve the responsiveness of public servants towards the common group. Also, trust would increase within the government setup. Larger social capital will successively facilitate within the promotion of moral governance.